INTERNATIONAL PUBLIC GOODS AND TRANSFER OF TECHNOLOGY UNDER A GLOBALIZED INTELLECTUAL PROPERTY REGIME

In this collection, distinguished economists, political scientists, and legal experts discuss the implications of the ever more globalized protection of intellectual property rights for the ability of countries to provide their citizens with such important public goods as basic research, education, public health, and sound environmental policies. Such items increasingly depend on the exercise of private rights over technical inputs and information goods, which could usher in a brave new world of accelerating technological innovation. However, higher and more harmonized levels of international intellectual property rights could also throw up high roadblocks in the path of follow-on innovation, competition, and the attainment of other social objectives. It is at best unclear who represents the public interest in negotiating forums dominated by powerful knowledge cartels. This is the first book to assess the public processes and inputs that an emerging transnational system of innovation will need to promote technical progress, economic growth, and welfare for all participants.

INTERNATIONAL PUBLIC GOODS AND TRANSFER OF TECHNOLOGY UNDER A GLOBALIZED INTELLECTUAL PROPERTY REGIME

Edited by

KEITH E. MASKUS
AND JEROME H. REICHMAN

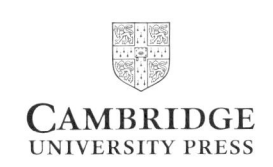

CAMBRIDGE
UNIVERSITY PRESS

CAMBRIDGE UNIVERSITY PRESS
Cambridge, New York, Melbourne, Madrid, Cape Town, Singapore, São Paulo

CAMBRIDGE UNIVERSITY PRESS
The Edinburgh Building, Cambridge CB2 2RU, UK
Published in the United States of America by Cambridge University Press, New York

www.cambridge.org
Information on this title: www.cambridge.org/9780521603027

© Keith E. Maskus and Jerome H. Reichman 2005

This book is in copyright. Subject to statutory exception
and to the provisions of relevant collective licensing agreements,
no reproduction of any part may take place without
the written permission of Cambridge University Press.

First published 2005

Printed in the United Kingdom at the University Press, Cambridge

A catalogue record for this book is available from the British Library

ISBN-13 978-0-521-84196-2 hardback
ISBN-10 0-521-84196-8 hardback
ISBN-13 978-0-521-60302-7 paperback
ISBN-10 0-521-60302-1 paperback

Cambridge University Press has no responsibility for
the persistence or accuracy of URLs for external or
third-party internet websites referred to in this book,
and does not guarantee that any content on such
websites is, or will remain, accurate or appropriate.

CONTENTS

List of contributors x
Preface xiii

PART I   **International Provision of Public Goods under a Globalized Intellectual Property Regime** 1

SECTION 1   THE CONCEPT OF PUBLIC GOODS IN THE EXPANDING KNOWLEDGE ECONOMY   1

1 The Globalization of Private Knowledge Goods and the Privatization of Global Public Goods   3
   Keith E. Maskus and Jerome H. Reichman

2 The Regulation of Public Goods   46
   Peter Drahos
   Comment: Norms, Institutions, and Cooperation   65
   Robert O. Keohane

3 Distributive Values and Institutional Design in the Provision of Global Public Goods   69
   Peter M. Gerhart

SECTION 2   PRESERVING THE CULTURAL AND SCIENTIFIC COMMONS   79

4 *Koyaanisqatsi* in Cyberspace: The Economics of an "Out-of-Balance" Regime of Private Property Rights in Data and Information   81
   Paul A. David

5 Linkages Between the Market Economy and the Scientific Commons   121
   Richard R. Nelson
   Comment I: Public Goods and Public Science   139
   Eric Maskin

6 Sustainable Access to Copyrighted Digital Information Works in Developing Countries 142
Ruth L. Okediji

7 Agricultural Research and Intellectual Property Rights 188
Robert E. Evenson
Comment II: Using Intellectual Property Rights to Preserve the Global Genetic Commons: The International Treaty on Plant Genetic Resources for Food and Agriculture 217
Laurence R. Helfer

PART II **Innovation and Technology Transfer in a Protectionist Environment** 225

SECTION 1 TECHNOLOGY TRANSFER UNDER INTERNATIONAL INTELLECTUAL PROPERTY STANDARDS 225

8 Can the TRIPS Agreement Foster Technology Transfer to Developing Countries? 227
Carlos M. Correa
Comment I: Technology Transfer on the International Agenda 257
Pedro Roffe

9 Patent Rights and International Technology Transfer Through Direct Investment and Licensing 265
Keith E. Maskus, Kamal Saggi, and Thitima Puttitanun
Comment II: TRIPS and Technology Transfer – Evidence from Patent Data 282
Samuel Kortum

10 Proprietary Rights and Collective Action: The Case of Biotechnology Research with Low Commercial Value 288
Arti K. Rai

SECTION 2 STIMULATING LOCAL INNOVATION 307

11 Do Stronger Patents Induce More Local Innovation? 309
Lee G. Branstetter

12 Markets for Technology, Intellectual Property Rights, and Development 321
Ashish Arora, Andrea Fosfuri, and Alfonso Gambardella

13 Using Liability Rules to Stimulate Local Innovation in Developing Countries: Application to Traditional Knowledge 337
Jerome H. Reichman and Tracy Lewis

14 Stimulating Agricultural Innovation 367
Michael Blakeney

CONTENTS

PART III **Sectoral Issues: Essential Medicines and Traditional Knowledge** 391

SECTION 1 DEVELOPING AND DISTRIBUTING ESSENTIAL MEDICINES 391

15 Managing the Hydra: The Herculean Task of Ensuring Access to Essential Medicines 393
Frederick M. Abbott

16 Theory and Implementation of Differential Pricing for Pharmaceuticals 425
Patricia M. Danzon and Adrian Towse

17 Increasing R&D Incentives for Neglected Diseases: Lessons from the Orphan Drug Act 457
Henry Grabowski
Comment: Access to Essential Medicines – Promoting Human Rights Over Free Trade and Intellectual Property Claims 481
Heinz Klug

SECTION 2 PROTECTING TRADITIONAL KNOWLEDGE 493

18 Legal and Economic Aspects of Traditional Knowledge 495
Graham Dutfield

19 Saving the Village: Conserving Jurisprudential Diversity in the International Protection of Traditional Knowledge 521
Antony Taubman

20 Legal Perspectives on Traditional Knowledge: The Case for Intellectual Property Protection 565
Thomas Cottier and Marion Panizzon
Comment: Traditional Knowledge, Folklore and the Case for Benign Neglect 595
David L. Lange

21 Protecting Cultural Industries to Promote Cultural Diversity: Dilemmas for International Policymaking Posed by the Recognition of Traditional Knowledge 599
Rosemary J. Coombe

PART IV **Reform and Regulation Issues** 615

SECTION 1 BALANCING PUBLIC AND PRIVATE INTERESTS IN THE GLOBAL INTELLECTUAL PROPERTY SYSTEM 615

22 Issues Posed by a World Patent System 617
John H. Barton

viii CONTENTS

23 Intellectual Property Arbitrage: How Foreign Rules Can Affect Domestic Protections   635
Pamela Samuelson

24 An Agenda for Radical Intellectual Property Reform   653
William Kingston
Comment: Whose Rules, Whose Needs? Balancing Public and Private Interests   662
Geoff Tansey

25 Diffusion and Distribution: The Impacts on Poor Countries of Technological Enforcement within the Biotechnology Sector   669
Timothy Swanson and Timo Goeschl

26 Equitable Sharing of Benefits from Biodiversity-Based Innovation: Some Reflections under the Shadow of a Neem Tree   695
Gustavo Ghidini

SECTION 2 THE ROLE OF COMPETITION LAW   707

27 The Critical Role of Competition Law in Preserving Public Goods in Conflict with Intellectual Property Rights   709
Josef Drexl

28 Expansionist Intellectual Property Protection and Reductionist Competition Rules: A TRIPS Perspective   726
Hanns Ullrich

29 Can Antitrust Policy Protect the Global Commons from the Excesses of IPRs?   758
Eleanor M. Fox
Comment I: Competition Law as a Means of Containing Intellectual Property Rights   770
Carsten Fink

30 "Minimal" Standards for Patent-Related Antitrust Law under TRIPS   774
Mark D. Janis
Comment II: Competitive Baselines for Intellectual Property Systems   793
Shubha Ghosh

SECTION 3 DISPUTE SETTLEMENT AT THE WTO AND INTELLECTUAL PROPERTY RIGHTS   815

31 WTO Dispute Settlement: Of Sovereign Interests, Private Rights, and Public Goods   817
Joost Pauwelyn

32 The Economics of International Trade Agreements and Dispute Settlement with Intellectual Property Rights   831
Eric W. Bond

33 Intellectual Property Rights and Dispute Settlement in the World Trade Organization   852
Wilfred J. Ethier

34 WTO Dispute Resolution and the Preservation of the Public Domain of Science under International Law   861
Graeme Dinwoodie and Rochelle Cooper Dreyfuss

35 Recognizing Public Goods in WTO Dispute Settlement: Who Participates? Who Decides? The Case of TRIPS and Pharmaceutical Patents Protection   884
Gregory Shaffer

Index   909

CONTRIBUTORS

Frederick M. Abbott is Edward Ball Eminent Scholar and Professor of International Law, Florida State University College of Law

Ashish Arora is Professor of Economics and Public Policy at the Heinz School of Public Policy, Carnegie Mellon University

John H. Barton is George E. Osborne Professor of Law Emeritus, Stanford University School of Law

Michael Blakeney is Herchel Smith Professor of Intellectual Property Law and Director, Queen Mary Intellectual Property Research Institute, University of London

Eric W. Bond is Professor of Economics, Vanderbilt University

Lee G. Branstetter is Associate Professor of Finance and Economics, Columbia University School of Business

Rosemary J. Coombe is Canada Research Chair in Law, Communication and Culture, York University

Carlos M. Correa is Director of the Center on Interdisciplinary Studies on Industrial Property and Economics, University of Buenos Aires, and Director of the South Center Project on Intellectual Property and Development, Geneva.

Thomas Cottier is Professor of Law and Director, World Trade Institute, University of Bern

Patricia M. Danzon is Professor of Economics at the Wharton School of Business, University of Pennsylvania

Paul A. David is Professor of Economics, Oxford University and Stanford University

Graeme Dinwoodie is Professor of Law & Norman and Edna Freehling Scholar, Director of the Program in Intellectual Property Law, Chicago-Kent College of Law

Peter Drahos is Head of RegNet, Research School of Social Sciences, Australian National University

Josef Drexl is Director, Max Planck Institute for Intellectual Property, Competition and Tax Law, Munich

Rochelle Cooper Dreyfuss is Pauline Newman Professor of Law, New York University School of Law

Graham Dutfield is Herchel Smith Senior Research Fellow, Queen Mary Intellectual Property Research Institute, University of London

Wilfred J. Ethier is Professor of Economics, University of Pennsylvania

Robert E. Evenson is Professor of Economics, Yale University

Carsten Fink is an Economist in the Geneva office of the World Bank

Andrea Fosfuri is Associate Professor of Management, Universidad Carlos III Madrid, and Research Affiliate, Centre for Economic Policy Research, London

Eleanor M. Fox is Walter J. Derenberg Professor of Trade Regulation, New York University School of Law

Alfonso Gambardella is Professor of Economics, Sant'Anna School of Advanced Studies, Pisa

Peter Gerhart is Professor of Law, Case Western Reserve University School of Law, Cleveland.

Gustavo Ghidini is Professor of Intellectual Property and Competition Law, Luiss Guido Carli University, Rome

Shubha Ghosh is Professor of Law, University of Buffalo School of Law, State University of New York

Timo Goeschl is Lecturer in Environmental and Resource Economics, University of Cambridge

Henry Grabowski is Professor of Economics, Duke University

Robert O. Keohane is Professor of International Affairs at the Woodrow Wilson School of Public and International Affairs, Princeton University

Laurence R. Helfer is Professor of Law, Vanderbilt University Law School

Mark D. Janis is Professor of Law and H. Blair & Joan V. White Intellectual Property Law Scholar, University of Iowa College of Law

William Kingston is Research Associate, School of Business Studies, Trinity College, Dublin

Heinz Klug is Associate Professor of Law, University of Wisconsin Law School

Samuel Kortum is Professor of Economics, University of Minnesota

David L. Lange is Professor of Law, Duke University School of Law

Tracy Lewis is Martin L. Black Professor of Economics, Fuqua School of Business, Duke University

Eric Maskin is A.O. Hirschman Professor of Social Science, Institute for Advanced Study, Princeton University

Keith E. Maskus is Stanford Calderwood Professor of Economics, University of Colorado at Boulder

Richard R. Nelson is George Blumenthal Professor of International and Public Affairs, Columbia University

Ruth L. Okediji is William L. Prosser Professor of Law, University of Minnesota College of Law

Marion Panizzon is Lecturer in Law, University of Zurich

Joost Pauwelyn is Associate Professor of Law, Duke Law School

Thitima Puttitanun is Assistant Professor of Economics, San Diego State University

Arti K. Rai is Professor of Law, Duke Law School

Jerome H. Reichman is Bunyan S. Womble Professor of Law, Duke Law School

Pedro Roffe is Director, Project on Intellectual Property Rights and Development, United Nations Conference on Trade and Development – International Center for Trade and Sustainable Development (UNCTAD – ICTSD)

Kamal Saggi is Professor of Economics, Southern Methodist University

Pamela Samuelson is Chancellor's Professor of Law and Information Management, University of California at Berkeley School of Law and Co-Director, Berkeley Center for Law and Technology

Timothy Swanson is Professor of Economics, University College, London

Gregory Shaffer is Professor of Law, University of Wisconsin Law School

Geoff Tansey is a Consultant to the Quaker United Nations Office, Geneva, who has also worked with the UK Department for International Development

Antony Taubman is Acting Director, Traditional Knowledge Division, World Intellectual Property Organization (WIPO) and Senior Lecturer, Faculty of Law, Australian National University

Adrian Towse is Director, Office of Health Economics, London

Hanns Ullrich is Professor of Law, European University Institute, Florence

PREFACE

In recent years the world has moved sharply toward successive strengthening – and harmonization – of intellectual property protection. There has emerged, at an unprecedented level, both a globalized regime of private rights in information and new foundations for a basic international system of innovation. This new system will have profound implications for the nature of such processes as innovation, technology transfer, market competition, and economic development. It also raises essential and sometimes disturbing questions about potential impacts on the ability of governments to provide critical public goods, both within and across countries. Such goods include public health, nutrition, education, environmental protection, cultural identity, and other elements of social importance that must rely increasingly on the exercise of private rights over technical inputs.

It is possible that the globalized intellectual property regime will improve markets for trading information internationally by encouraging invention and resolving inherent failures in technology transactions. It is also conceivable that the system will throw up high roadblocks in the path of follow-on innovation, competition, and the attainment of public goods. These questions are deep and complex and require sustained analysis.

The clear difficulties of this task constitute one of the main reasons that the editors of this volume decided to organize the Conference on International Public Goods and Transfer of Technology under a Globalized Intellectual Property Regime in April 2003 at Duke University.[1] This was a major attempt to subject the complex conceptual foundations of the changing worldwide intellectual property regime to systematic legal and economic analysis.

The conference brought together a distinguished group of economists, political scientists, and legal experts to assess the public processes and inputs they deemed likely to become indispensable in a transnational system of innovation that, while still dependent on territorial law, must aim to promote technical progress, economic growth and welfare for all participants. The

---

[1] Conference on International Public Goods and Transfer of Technology under a Globalized Intellectual Property Regime, held at Duke University School of Law, Durham, North Carolina on 24–26 April 2003. Oral presentations are available at: http://www.law.duke.edu/trips/webcast.html.

contributors were also urged to think broadly and to propose means to minimize the social costs and enhance the benefits that might ensue from the TRIPS Agreement and related standard-setting initiatives by deliberately taking into account the promotion of public goods.

Their responses constitute the contributions to this volume. They have been organized under four major rubrics. Part I is entitled "International Provision of Public Goods under a Globalized Intellectual Property Regime." In the first section of this part, framework papers and associated commentaries analyze the concept of public goods in the expanding knowledge economy. A second section turns directly to issues of preserving the public commons in the areas of science, access to information, and agricultural technologies.

Part II of the volume addresses the general theme of "Innovation and Technology Transfer in a Protectionist Environment." In the first section of this part, framework papers focus on obstacles to the transfer of technology under international intellectual property standards and the impacts of those standards on the means of information transfer. Additional analysis focuses on implications of stronger private rights in information for moving technology into the public domain. A second section is aimed at understanding how the new system might affect incentives for local innovation in developing countries and how the system might be improved for that purpose.

Part III, entitled "Sectoral Issues: Essential Medicines and Traditional Knowledge," first takes on the critical problem of ensuring that access to medicines is not worsened by the international intellectual property system via the exercise of patents and protection of clinical test data. Various contributors offer both positive and negative assessments of the potential for the new regime to improve innovation and distribution of medicines and to meet the needs of poor countries. The second task is to offer comprehensive analysis of basic problems of protecting traditional knowledge in the new environment of globalized intellectual property systems.

The volume turns last, in Part IV, to numerous contributions gathered under the general theme of "Reform and Regulation Issues." A first section deals with balancing public and private interests in the specific intellectual property regimes, including reforms of the global patent regime. A second section fully explores the role of competition law in a worldwide market for knowledge goods. A final set of papers, dealing with dispute settlement at the WTO and intellectual property rights, emphasizes the need for WTO panels to take public goods into account.

The editors of this volume wish to thank the Rockefeller Foundation, the John D. and Catherine T. MacArthur Foundation, the McGuire Center for International Studies at the University of Colorado, the Center for the Study of the Public Domain at Duke University, and the Center for the Public Domain for their generous support of the conference in April 2003. In organizing the conference and preparing this volume, the editors also received considerable assistance from a variety of people, including Jennifer Jenkins, Aaron Lang, Heather Ritch, Jeff Wasikowski, Debbie Upchurch, and, especially, Patricia Reichman. We are extremely grateful for their contributions, counsel, and hard work. We also thank Finola O'Sullivan, Jane O'Regan and Anna-Marie Lovett, and others at Cambridge University Press for their advice and patience as we edited the large and diverse set of chapters in this volume.

Finally, we wish to acknowledge the willingness of Cambridge University Press and Oxford University Press to work together on this project. Oxford University Press is the publisher of *Journal of International Economic Law*, whose editor, John Jackson, agreed to publish a selection of the chapters appearing in this volume in the June, 2004 issue (Volume 7, number 2). Early versions of the chapters published in that issue include Maskus and Reichman, "The Globalization of Private Knowledge Goods and the Privatization of Global Public Goods" (pages 279–320); Drahos, "The Regulation of Public Goods" (pages 321–340); Barton, "Issues Posed by a World Patent System" (pages 341–358); Branstetter, "Do Stronger Patents Induce More Local Innovation?" (pages 359–370); Cottier and Panizzon, "Legal Perspectives on Traditional Knowledge: The Case for Intellectual Property Protection" (pages 371–400); Ullrich, "Expansionist Intellectual Property Protection and Reductionist Competition Rules: A TRIPS Perspective" (pages 401–430); Dinwoodie and Cooper Dreyfuss, "WTO Dispute Resolution and the Preservation of the Public Domain of Science under International Law" (pages 431–448); Ethier, "Intellectual Property Rights and Dispute Settlement in the World Trade Organization" (pages 449–458); and Shaffer, "Recognizing Public Goods in WTO Dispute Settlement: Who Participates? Who Decides?" (pages 459–482). Revised and expanded versions of those contributions appear in this volume, and we are deeply grateful to both Presses for permitting us to circulate them as widely as possible.

KEITH E. MASKUS and JEROME H. REICHMAN

PART I

International provision of public goods under a globalized intellectual property regime

SECTION 1
The concept of public goods in the expanding knowledge economy

1

The globalization of private knowledge goods and the privatization of global public goods

KEITH E. MASKUS
JEROME H. REICHMAN*

Abstract
I. Introduction and conceptual framework
    A. International public goods and intellectual property rights
    B. Technology transfer after the TRIPS agreement
II. Re-regulating the global marketplace to protect knowledge as a private good
    A. Legal and organizational impediments to the creation and diffusion of knowledge goods
        1. Preserving temporary competitive advantages with international intellectual property standards
        2. Instability and loss of balance in developed intellectual property regimes
        3. Exporting a dysfunctional system to the rest of the world?
    B. Impact of intellectual property standards on the reserved welfare powers of WTO members
III. Balancing public and private interests in an emerging transnational system of innovation
    A. Developing countries as defenders of the competitive ethos
        1. A moratorium on stronger international intellectual property standards
        2. An institutional infrastructure for reconciling existing IPRs with national and regional systems of innovation
    B. Maintaining the supply of knowledge as a global public good
        1. Dynamic properties of knowledge as a global public good
        2. Nurturing a transnational system of innovation

---

* Keith Maskus is Professor in, and Chair of, the Department of Economics at the University of Colorado, Boulder, Colorado. J.H. Reichman is the Bunyan S. Womble Professor of Law at Duke University School of Law, Durham, North Carolina. This chapter is based on a paper presented at the Conference on International Public Goods and Transfer of Technology under a Globalized Intellectual Property Regime, held at Duke University School of Law on 4–6 April 2003.

ABSTRACT

Global trade and investment have become increasingly liberalized in recent decades. This liberalization has lately been accompanied by substantive new requirements for strong minimum standards of intellectual property (IP) protection, which moves the world economy toward harmonized private rights in knowledge goods. While this trend may have beneficial impacts in terms of innovation and technology diffusion, such impacts would not be evenly distributed across countries. Deep questions also arise about whether such globalization of rights to information will raise roadblocks to the national and international provision of such public goods as environmental protection, public health, education, and scientific advance. This chapter argues that the globalized IP regime will strongly affect prospects for technology transfer and competition in developing countries. In turn, these nations must determine how to implement such standards in a pro-competitive manner and how to foster innovation and competition in their own markets. Developing countries may need to take the lead in policy experimentation and IP innovation in order to offset overly protectionist tendencies in the rich countries and to maintain the supply of global public goods in an emerging transnational system of innovation.

I. Introduction and conceptual framework

Economists studying international trade remain optimistic about the ability of liberal trade policies and integration into the global economy to encourage growth and raise people in poor countries out of poverty. For example, in a recent speech at Duke University, the World Bank's former Chief Economist, Nicholas Stern, showed figures depicting a significant rise in per capita GDP across developing countries as a whole in recent years.[1] His point was that, despite other obstacles to growth, more open markets, improved governance, and increasing entrepreneurial activity were generating a positive impact in poor countries. Even Oxfam, an organization that has been highly critical of globalization, in a recent report recognized the role that open trade regimes have played in providing greater opportunities for the impoverished to benefit from extended markets.[2]

---

[1] Nicholas Stern, International Action for Fighting Poverty: An Historic Opportunity, Lecture given at Duke University (2 Sept. 2003). *See also* J.H. Reichman, Managing the Challenge of a Globalized Intellectual Property Regime, Paper presented to the Second Bellagio Meeting on Intellectual Property and Development, UNCTAD/ICTSD, 17–20 Sept. 2003 (discussing Stern's thesis); David Dollar & Aart Kraay, Trade, Growth, and Poverty, Development Research Group, The World Bank (2001) (unpublished manuscript, on file with authors).

[2] OXFAM, RIGGED RULES AND DOUBLE STANDARDS: TRADE, GLOBALISATION, AND THE FIGHT AGAINST POVERTY (2002).

In general, we share this confidence but argue that a considerable qualification needs to be made. Open trade and investment regimes work best to encourage development and structural transformation where markets for information and technology transfer are competitive in ways that permit innovation, learning, and diffusion to flourish. Put differently, for poor countries to take advantage of globalization opportunities, they need to absorb, implement, and even develop new technologies.

An inability to do so risks increasing fragmentation and divergence from the technology-driven world economy rather than growing integration and convergence. Indeed, one could have applied Stern's optimistic description to the centrally planned economies of Eastern Europe over the period 1950–1975. They had high rates of savings (even if forced) and capital accumulation, and were generating apparently high growth. However, these economies failed to establish effective innovation systems: they lacked skills, infrastructure, and the entrepreneurial culture that could encourage competition and learning, and they relied instead on protected and inefficient industrial behemoths. These establishments could not cope well with competitive pressures dependent upon economic liberalization, and their economies stagnated.

A different kind of technological roadblock may be facing developing countries in their efforts to integrate into the world economy. A central element in global policy is the ever-increasing levels of required protection for information, technology, and creative activity through exclusive intellectual property rights (IPRs). This trend is most evident in the Agreement on Trade-Related Aspects of Intellectual Property Rights (TRIPS Agreement), a component of the Agreement Establishing the World Trade Organization (WTO).[3] The TRIPS Agreement sets out a comprehensive set of minimum protection standards that Members must observe and enforce with respect to patents, copyrights, trademarks, geographical indications, confidential business information, industrial designs, and integrated circuit designs.[4] Even stronger rules are being widely established through bilateral and preferential trade agreements that the United States and the European Union have negotiated with developing countries.[5]

---

[3] Agreement on Trade-Related Aspects of Intellectual Property Rights, 15 Apr. 1994, Marrakesh Agreement Establishing the World Trade Organization, Annex 1C, LEGAL INSTRUMENTS – RESULTS OF THE URUGUAY ROUND vol. 31, 33 I.L.M. 81 (1994) [hereinafter TRIPS Agreement].

[4] See, e.g., J.H. Reichman, Universal Minimum Standards of Intellectual Property Protection under the TRIPS Component of the WTO Agreement, in INTELLECTUAL PROPERTY AND INTERNATIONAL TRADE: THE TRIPS AGREEMENT 21 (C.M. Correa & A. Yusuf eds., 1998); see generally JAYASHREE WATAL, INTELLECTUAL PROPERTY RIGHTS IN THE WTO AND DEVELOPING COUNTRIES (2001); CARLOS M. CORREA, INTELLECTUAL PROPERTY RIGHTS, THE WTO AND DEVELOPING COUNTRIES (2000).

[5] See, e.g., Peter Drahos, Developing Countries and International Intellectual Property Standard-Setting, 5 J. WORLD INTELL. PROP. 765 (2002); Keith E. Maskus, Strengthening Intellectual Property Rights in Lebanon, in CATCHING UP WITH THE COMPETITION: TRADE

Recent agreements reached at the World Intellectual Property Organization (WIPO) on the electronic transmission of works protected by copyrights or related rights[6] and ongoing negotiations at that organization on harmonization of patent rights[7] continue the drive to ratchet upward global protection regimes.

The evolving system of stronger private rights in new technologies could lead to global gains in innovation and additional market-mediated information transfers to developing countries.[8] Indeed, one can argue that the harmonization of IPRs provides developing countries with tools for technology-driven development that they would otherwise lack. By wisely managing these tools, developing countries may obtain additional foreign direct investment (FDI), more licensing of high-quality technologies, and more access to advanced knowledge goods.

We do not dispute the potential for such outcomes, although we believe that the scope for achieving them in different nations much depends on innovation policies and other complementary factors.[9] In this introductory chapter, however, we raise some fundamental concerns about the implications of the new regime for the ability of firms in developing countries to break into global – or even domestic – markets and compete effectively. It seems increasingly likely that stronger global IPRs could reduce the scope for such firms to acquire new, and even mature, technologies at manageable costs. The natural competitive disadvantages of follower countries may become reinforced by a proliferation of legal monopolies and related entry barriers that result from global minimum intellectual property (IP) standards. Such external restraints on competition could consign the poorest countries to a quasi-permanent status at the bottom of the technology and growth ladder.

We find it ironic that, as tariffs, quotas, and other formal barriers to trade are dismantled, there has been a strong push to re-regulate world technology markets. Although the ratcheting up of global IPRs could adversely affect the growth prospects of developing countries, these nations have so far exerted little

---

OPPORTUNITIES AND CHALLENGES FOR ARAB COUNTRIES 251–52 (B. Hoekman & J. Zarrouk eds., 2000).

[6] WIPO Copyright Treaty, adopted by the Diplomatic Conference on 20 Dec. 1996, WIPO Doc. CRNR/DC/94 (23 Dec. 1996); WIPO Performances and Phonograms Treaty, adopted by the Diplomatic Conference on 20 Dec. 1996, WIPO Doc. CRNR/DC/95 (23 Dec. 1996); *see generally* Pamela Samuelson, *The U.S. Digital Agenda at WIPO*, 37 VA. J. INT'L L. 369 (1997).

[7] WIPO, Standing Committee on the Law of Patents, Draft Substantive Patent Law Treaty, Ninth Session (Geneva, 12–16 May 2003), SCP/9/2, *available at* http://www.wipo.int/scp/en/documents/session_9/pdf/scp9_2.pdf (visited 5 Jan. 2004) [hereinafter Draft Patent Law Treaty]. *See also* John H. Barton, *Issues Posed by a World Patent System* [this volume].

[8] KEITH E. MASKUS, INTELLECTUAL PROPERTY RIGHTS IN THE GLOBAL ECONOMY 109–42 (Institute for International Economics 2000) [hereinafter MASKUS, IP RIGHTS].

[9] *Id.* at 199–232.

influence on standard-setting exercises. Indeed, the progressive re-regulation of world markets for knowledge goods is not driven by a broad consensus of economic agents in the developed world. Rather, pressures to elevate IP norms are exerted by powerful private interests whose lobbying activities hold sway in legislative and regulatory initiatives in rich countries and international forums.

These efforts are largely detached from the traditional goal of domestic IP systems to strike a balance between commercial profitability and public-interest concerns. To the extent that this imbalance makes it harder for entrepreneurs in developing countries to obtain inputs they need to compete in the production of knowledge goods, these countries could discover that the re-regulated global economy had in effect removed the rungs on which they could advance.[10]

As private interests take precedence over public concerns, moreover, we argue that the proliferation of exclusive rights could raise fundamental roadblocks for the national and global provision of numerous other public goods, including scientific research, education, health care, biodiversity, and environmental protection.[11] The architects of the new system evidently have paid little attention to these issues, believing that a clear specification of strong property rights could establish appropriate incentives for private development of modalities to advance these and other public activities. In our view, the greater likelihood is that the privatization of public-interest technologies could in many cases erect competitive barriers, raise transactions costs and produce significant anti-commons effects, which tend to reduce the supply of public goods related to innovation as such, and also to limit the capacity of single states to perform essential police and welfare functions not otherwise available from a decentralized international system of governance.[12]

In Part I of this chapter, we set out some basic principles and observations regarding the provision of global public goods (GPG) and how that provision is implicated by the increasingly internationalized system of IP protection. In Part II, we evaluate legal and organizational impediments to the creation and diffusion of knowledge goods in a re-regulated global economy. In particular, we point out that unbalanced IP regimes in developed countries may be triggering counterproductive results and the concomitant risk that efforts to lock in the temporary competitive advantages of powerful technology cartels may raise costs for the developing world.

---

[10] *See, e.g.,* Commission on Intellectual Property Rights (CIPR), Integrating Intellectual Property Rights and Development Policy 8–9, 11–27 (2002) [hereinafter CIPR].

[11] *See* below text accompanying nn. 100–27.

[12] In this article, we offer only an overview of essential concepts regarding global public goods and their interaction with IP protection. These issues are covered more extensively in other treatments. *See, e.g.,* Peter Drahos, *The Regulation of Public Goods* [this volume]. For an extensive discussion of the concepts and problems of provision and distribution of such goods, *see* PROVIDING GLOBAL PUBLIC GOODS: MANAGING GLOBALIZATION (Inge Kaul et al. eds., United Nations Development Program 2003) [hereinafter PROVIDING GPG].

In Part III, we consider the seemingly paradoxical possibility that, as developing countries experiment with their own IP regimes, and with associated regimes of competition law and innovation promotion, they might re-inject a needed global stimulus to dynamic competition. They could also contribute to the evolution of national and regional strategies to maintain the supply of other essential public goods that has been compromised by the crosscutting effects of efforts to privatize the creation and distribution of knowledge and information as such.

A. *International public goods and intellectual property rights*

Global public goods might usefully be defined as those goods (including policies and infrastructure) that are systematically underprovided by private market forces and for which such under-provision has important international externality effects.[13] The concept that a good is "public" stems from a combination of non-rivalry in consumption and nonexcludability in use.[14] An item is nonrival if its use by one actor does not restrict the ability of another actor to benefit from it as well. A good is nonexcludable to the extent that unauthorized parties ("free riders") cannot be prevented from using it. Classic examples include national defense, environmental protection, and investments in new technical information. Each of these endeavors generates results that are essentially nonrival and at least partially nonexcludable. In consequence, private markets would not provide them at all or would do so at deficient levels relative to those demanded by citizens. A role for government thus arises to resolve this market failure.

Those concerned about the efficient provision of public goods must address three fundamental issues.[15] First, what are the optimal levels of the various goods to be supported? The answer depends on the underlying demand for such goods, and it may be difficult to reveal the preferences of citizens accurately. Second, how are the desired goods to be provided? Note that public policies may provide goods directly through taxes, subsidies, and public production. Alternatively,

---

[13] An "externality effect" means that a failure to provide the public good imposes costs on third parties. For example, pollution arising in some countries may affect health status in others, or financial volatility in one nation may generate follow-on fragility elsewhere. In general, national policymakers are not likely to consider the well-being of foreign citizens in setting their own policies regarding public goods, which is why GPG require some form of global coordination. *See* PROVIDING GPG, above n. 12; Daniel G. Arce, *Leadership and the Aggregation of International Collective Action*, 53 OXFORD ECON. PAPERS 114 (2001).

[14] Economic analysis of public goods has a long standing in the literature. *See* Paul A. Samuelson, *The Pure Theory of Public Expenditure*, 36 REV. ECON. & STAT. 387 (1954); TODD SANDLER, COLLECTIVE ACTION: THEORY and APPLICATIONS (1992).

[15] *See* PROVIDING GPG, above n. 12, at 36–40.

policies may indirectly provide public goods through such regulations as competition policy, intellectual property rights, and price controls.

For example, IPRs provide a second-best resolution of the excludability – also called appropriability – problem inherent in developing knowledge goods, which could otherwise be distributed at the marginal cost of making copies.[16] To the extent that such rights elicit benefits from investment that exceed these social costs, they may be welfare enhancing over either market-driven solutions or pure public provision and distribution.

A third question for policymakers is to determine the best jurisdictional level for providing public goods. As a general rule, the more localized the need, the narrower should be the jurisdiction. Thus, police, public schools, and voting processes are typically seen as local obligations under United States law and practice. National defense, macroeconomic policy, and foreign policy are federal obligations.

How to organize the provision of GPG without adequate international mechanisms has become a difficult and pressing question in recent years. In practice, this function has been left largely to national or sub-national authorities. Because there are international spillover impacts, however, reliance on national provision likely fails to meet global needs efficiently or equitably. Approaches to providing GPG are required at the international level because national regimes generally disregard cross-border externalities and the resulting need for policy coordination.

Many critical public goods have become increasingly global in their effects and supply needs.[17] It is fair to say that, whereas analysis of the need for integrated systems has a long history, the actual organization, provision and distribution of GPG are at an early and critical stage. This situation is well illustrated by the emerging global system of IP protection. By long tradition, IPRs were constituted as a national policy prerogative, with relatively little attention paid to coordinating standards across countries. However, wide variations in national regulations can have significant international static and dynamic externalities.[18]

For example, recent economics literature points to several reasons why, acting on their own interests, countries would tend to protect new technology and product development at a level that is lower than would be globally optimal.[19] The main reason is that some of the gains from innovation accrue

---

[16] See MASKUS, IP RIGHTS, above n. 8, at 36–38.   [17] See PROVIDING GPG, above n. 12.
[18] Keith E. Maskus, *Regulatory Standards in the WTO: Comparing Intellectual Property Rights with Competition Policy, Environmental Protection, and Core Labor Standards*, 1 WORLD TRADE REV. 135 (2002).
[19] Philip McCalman, *National Patents, Innovation, and International Agreements*, 11 J. INT'L TRADE & DEV. 1 (2002); Gene M. Grossman & Edwin L.-C. Lai, International Protection of Intellectual Property (2002) (unpublished manuscript); Suzanne Scotchmer, The Political Economy of Intellectual Property Treaties (2002) (unpublished manuscript).

to consumers and users in other countries, a benefit that framers of IPRs would not take into account in setting domestic standards. Countries with limited innovation capacities would logically free ride on foreign R&D investments by offering only limited technology protection. Some means of international coordination, perhaps within the ambit of the WTO, thus arguably would move global standards closer to the optimum by elevating incentives to invest.

To be sustainable, however, this coordination should take into account the development and social needs of different economies. In principle, this objective calls for a mix of differential and flexible standards, along with compensatory side payments to induce free riders to adopt and enforce stronger IPRs.

To be sure, there is some flexibility permitted developing countries in implementing the TRIPS standards.[20] Yet, even the minimum TRIPS requirements may overly burden poor nations in some circumstances. Furthermore, to benefit from residual flexibilities requires a degree of legal and regulatory expertise that may exceed the capacity of many countries for the foreseeable future. While the WTO Agreement offers some scope for implicit side payments through greater market access in developed countries for exports from developing countries, progress in achieving such access has been uneven.[21] Thus, serious questions arise as to the sustainability of the attempt in TRIPS to resolve the international externality aspects of protecting new knowledge goods.

An additional criticism leveled at the emerging IPR system is that the agenda for increasing protection has been articulated and pushed by rich-country governments effectively representing the commercial interests of a limited set of industries that distribute knowledge goods. Even within some developed countries, the tendency to espouse a protectionist IP agenda seems more a reflection of policy capture than a reasoned attempt to balance domestic needs, and the long-term effects on real innovation have yet to be ascertained. At the global level, the virtual inability to date of public-minded interest groups to affect this agenda raises further questions about the sustainability of TRIPS and other elements of the system.[22]

If the initial impetus for a trade-related intellectual property initiative was to prevent wholesale duplication of high-tech products, the TRIPS Agreement went well beyond that objective. Whether it strikes an appropriate balance between the needs of developers, users, and public authorities on a global scale remains open to question. At least in the short run, it seems likely to shift the

---

[20] J.H. Reichman, *From Free Riders to Fair Followers: Global Competition under the TRIPS Agreement*, 29 N.Y.U. J. INT'L L. & POL. 11 (1997) [hereinafter Reichman, *Free Riders to Fair Followers*].

[21] *See, e.g.*, World Bank, Global Economic Prospects and the Developing Countries 2002, at 37–64 (2001).

[22] *See, e.g., id.* at 145–49; Carlos M. Correa, *Internationalization of the Patent System and New Technologies*, 20 WIS. INT'L L.J. 523, 544–50 (2002).

rules sharply in favor of IP developers,[23] while the potential for long-term gains for the poorest countries seems cloudy at best.[24]

We have suggested that the emerging international IP system bears characteristics of a GPG but that it seems flawed in execution and design. Moreover, this regime influences the ability of governments to provide other public goods. First, TRIPS constrains them from pursuing certain avenues for promoting imitation, innovation, and related social policies. Second, stronger private rights in information may raise roadblocks against deploying new technologies that could help improve the provision of environmental protection, health care, biological diversity, and basic scientific research. These topics are examined below in Part II.

B. *Technology transfer after the TRIPS agreement*[25]

The international flow of technological information and its successful integration into domestic production and management processes are central to the ability of firms in developing countries to compete in the global economy. Technological change is a principal source of sustained growth in living standards and is essential for the transformation and modernization of economic structures. In most instances, developing countries find it cheaper and faster to acquire foreign technologies than to develop them with domestic resources. Such technologies may "spill over" into wider improvements in productivity and follow-on innovation in the domestic economy.

International technology transfer (ITT) is a comprehensive term covering mechanisms for shifting information across borders and its effective diffusion into recipient economies. It refers to numerous complex processes, which range from innovation and international marketing of technology to its absorption and imitation. There are also many different channels through which technology may be transferred. One major conduit consists of trade in goods, especially capital goods and technological inputs. A second is foreign direct investment (FDI), which generally transfers technological information that is newer or more productive than that available from local firms. A third is technology licensing, which may occur either within firms or between unrelated firms. Licenses typically involve the purchase of production or distribution rights and the technical information and know-how required to exploit them.[26]

---

[23] Philip McCalman, *Reaping What You Sow: An Empirical Analysis of International Patent Harmonization*, 55 J. INT'L ECON. 161 (2001).
[24] MASKUS, IP RIGHTS, above n. 8; Pamela J. Smith, *How Do Foreign Patent Rights Affect U.S. Exports, Affiliate Sales, and Licenses?*, 55 J. INT'L ECON. 411 (2001).
[25] This section draws on Keith E. Maskus, Encouraging International Technology Transfer, draft report to UNCTAD/ICTSD (2003) [hereinafter Maskus, Encouraging International Technology].
[26] James R. Markusen & Keith E. Maskus, *General Equilibrium Approaches to the Multinational Firm: A Review of Theory and Evidence*, in HANDBOOK OF INTERNATIONAL TRADE 320

There are also important non-market channels of ITT. Perhaps most significant is the process of imitation through product inspection, reverse engineering, and trial and error. A related mechanism is triggered when technical and managerial personnel leave a firm and start a rival firm based on information learned in the original location. Still another means is to study information available from patent applications. Thus, patents provide both a direct source of technology transfer, through FDI and licensing, and an indirect source through legally regulated disclosures. Indeed, "trade in ideas" is a significant factor in world economic growth, and developing economies could gain considerably more access to foreign technologies as international firms take out patents in their locations.[27] Nevertheless, this benefit remains dependent on local abilities to learn from incoming technological information, and on the diffusion practices or strategies of technology-exporting firms.

Much knowledge appears to be transferred through the temporary migration of students, scientists, and managerial and technical personnel to universities, laboratories, and conferences located mainly in the developed economies. Finally, technical information may be available from the public domain, making it free for taking, or from a research commons accessible with certain restrictions.[28]

International markets for trading technologies are inherently subject to failure due to distortions attributable to concerns about appropriability, problems of valuing information by buyers and sellers, and market power, all strong justifications for public intervention at both the domestic and global levels. Technology developers are interested in reducing the costs and risks of making transfers, along with protecting their rights to profit from them. They argue that effective protection and policy supports for markets are necessary to increase the willingness of innovative firms to provide knowledge about their production processes to firms in developing countries. Technology importers are interested in acquiring knowledge and products at minimal cost. Some observers argue that this objective is best met by limiting the exclusive rights to exploit technology.[29]

(K. Choi & J. Harrigan eds., 2003); A. ARORA ET AL., MARKETS FOR TECHNOLOGY: THE ECONOMICS OF INNOVATION AND CORPORATE STRATEGY 115–42 (2001).

[27] Jonathan Eaton & Samuel Kortum, *Trade in Ideas: Patenting and Productivity in the OECD*, 40 J. INT'L ECON. 251 (1996).

[28] *See, e.g.*, J.H. Reichman & Paul Uhlir, *A Contractually Reconstructed Research Commons for Scientific Data in a Highly Protectionist Intellectual Property Environment*, 66 LAW & CONTEMP. PROBS. 315 (2003) [hereinafter *A Contractually Reconstructed Research Commons*]. *See generally* THE ROLE OF SCIENTIFIC AND TECHNICAL DATA AND INFORMATION IN THE PUBLIC DOMAIN (J.M. Esanu & Paul Uhlir eds., National Research Council 2003) [hereinafter ROLE OF SCIENTIFIC AND TECHNICAL DATA].

[29] Theory favoring IPRs may be found in I. Horstmann & J.R. Markusen, *Licensing versus Direct Investment: A Model of Internalization by the Multinational Enterprise*, 20 CAN. J.

While the close and complex relationships between intellectual property rights and ITT cannot be fully discussed here,[30] it is useful to consider some of the main impacts, both positive and negative, that stronger global IPRs may have on international information flows. First, the preponderance of econometric studies suggests that market-mediated flows of technology respond positively to the strengthening of patent laws across countries. This finding applies to international trade flows, especially in patent-sensitive industries and capital goods, as regards patents in middle-income and large developing countries.[31] However, trade flows to poor countries seem unresponsive to patent laws. Similarly, recent studies of patents and inward FDI find positive impacts on more advanced and larger developing countries, but not on poor and small countries.[32] Licensing volumes between U.S. firms and unrelated concerns in larger developing countries also expand with the rigor of local patent regimes.[33]

A reasonable interpretation of these findings is that there are threshold effects in market-based licensing. Economies with low incomes and limited technological capacity present neither attractive markets nor a competitive imitation threat. Because their intellectual property regimes are not particularly important in attracting ITT, it seems unlikely that the standards implemented in compliance with TRIPS will encourage additional technology transfer to the poorest countries. However, at higher incomes and technological capacities, IPRs become an important factor in this regard, even though they are only one of a list of variables that influence ITT. Other important factors include effective infrastructure, efficient governance, market size and growth, and proximity to suppliers and demanders.[34]

The literature also suggests that stronger patent rights may be expected to raise considerably the rents earned by international firms as patents become more valuable, with the result that firms in developing countries would pay

---

ECON. 464 (1987); A. Arora, *Contracting for Tacit Knowledge: The Provision of Technical Services in Technology Licensing Contracts*, 50 J. DEV. ECON. 233 (1996). For a critical view, see Carlos M. Correa, *Can the TRIPS Agreement Foster Technology Transfer to Developing Countries?* [this volume].

[30] *See, e.g.*, Keith E. Maskus, *The Role of Intellectual Property Rights in Encouraging Foreign Direct Investment and Technology Transfer*, 9 DUKE J. COMPAR. & INT'L L. 109 (1998); Kamal Saggi, International Technology Transfer: National Policies, International Negotiations, and Multilateral Disciplines, report to Commonwealth Secretariat (2003).

[31] *See* Smith, above n. 24; Keith E. Maskus & Mohan Penubarti, *How Trade-Related are Intellectual Property Rights?*, 39 J. INT'L ECON. 227 (1995).

[32] Smith, above n. 24; MASKUS, IP RIGHTS, above n. 8.

[33] Guifang Yang & Keith E. Maskus, *Intellectual Property Rights and Licensing: An Econometric Investigation*, 127 WELTWIRTSCHAFTLICHES ARCHIV 58 (2001); Michael Nicholson, Intellectual Property Rights and International Technology Transfer: The Impact of Industry Characteristics (2002) (unpublished manuscript, on file with U.S. Federal Trade Commission).

[34] Markusen & Maskus, above n. 26.

more for the average inward protected technology.[35] Expansion of breadth, scope, and length of patents would tend to amplify this result. Thus, there are countervailing impacts in middle-income countries: higher volumes of ITT but increased payments per unit of technology. Moreover, recipient countries are more likely to benefit where the supply of technologies is competitive and local firms are capable of adapting them effectively into production processes.[36]

While the evidence supports the claim that TRIPS standards could enhance ITT (at least into the larger and more advanced developing economies) through better performing technology markets, it should be weighed against national historic experience. Few now-developed economies underwent significant technological learning and industrial transformation without the benefit of weak intellectual property protection.[37] A good example is Japan, which from the 1950s through the 1980s pursued an industrial property regime that favored small-scale innovation, adaptation and diffusion, and the licensing of new technologies. Key features of this system included pre-grant disclosure, rapid opposition to patent grants, narrow patent claims, local reliance on utility models and advantages for licensing.[38] Another example is South Korea, which in the 1970s encouraged domestic firms to acquire and adapt mature technologies available on international markets for purposes of developing local innovation capacities.[39]

The extent to which the emerging global IP regime may be expected to enhance or impede ITT thus poses a complicated question. Answering it is made even harder because technology transfer across borders involves a mixture of private activities and public measures of encouragement (or discouragement). This mixture varies in cost and efficiency by sector, country, and over time, which suggests that globalized IP protection could have both complex and suboptimal effects unless accompanied by appropriate complementary policy approaches.[40]

The new system raises entry barriers for firms and competition in the poorest countries, while even the middle-income nations find their scope of action limited. Market distortions due to misuses of intellectual property rights

---

[35] McCalman, above n. 19; The World Bank, above n. 21, at 132–34.
[36] Maskus, Encouraging International Technology, above n. 25.
[37] Z. Khan, Intellectual Property and Economic Development: Lessons from American and European History, Commission on Intellectual Property Rights, Background Paper 1A (2002); N. Kumar, Intellectual Property Rights, Technology and Economic Development: Experiences of Asian Countries, Commission on Intellectual Property Rights, background paper 1B (2002).
[38] Janusz A. Ordover, *A Patent System for Both Diffusion and Exclusion*, 5 J. ECON. PERSP. 43 (1991).
[39] Linsu Kim, Technology Transfer and Intellectual Property Rights: Lessons from Korea's Experience, UNCTAD/ICTSD Working Paper (2002).
[40] MASKUS, IP RIGHTS, above n. 8, at 143–60.

may also be harder to detect or police in developing than in developed countries. Moreover, new or relatively untested forms of intellectual property protection that choke access to upstream information inputs – including scientific and technical data as such – could narrow access to the research commons and limit other transfer mechanisms, with incalculable long-term effects on ITT as it used to occur.[41]

In our view, governments in developing countries need to be pro-active in ensuring that the net effect of expanded IP protection is to enhance access to technology and to encourage its domestic adaptation and diffusion. Potential gains in dynamic competition are reason enough for this approach. An additional important factor is that tightened protection raises significant questions regarding the ability to access international technology and information to improve the provision of broader public goods. In the rest of this article we explore these issues in more detail.

II. Re-regulating the global marketplace to protect knowledge as a private good

One paradox of an increasingly global economy is that it ultimately requires collective action to further enhance the social benefits of free competition in an unruly marketplace that the General Agreement on Tariffs and Trade (GATT) and the Agreement Establishing the World Trade Organization (WTO) have progressively liberated from state-imposed barriers to trade.[42] Who should take responsibility for this regulatory task in the absence of any duly constituted global governance authority and how to identify measures that would actually promote global welfare without creating disguised barriers to trade remain daunting problems for a decentralized international system.[43]

---

[41] See, e.g., Rebecca S. Eisenberg, Bargaining over the Transfer of Proprietary Research Tools: Is this Market Failing or Emerging?, in EXPANDING THE BOUNDARIES OF INTELLECTUAL PROPERTY: INNOVATION POLICY FOR THE KNOWLEDGE SOCIETY 223 (Rochelle Dreyfuss et al. eds., 2001) [hereinafter EXPANDING THE BOUNDARIES OF IP]; Arti K. Rai, Proprietary Rights and Collective Action: The Case of Biotechnology Research with Low Commercial Value [this volume]; J.H. Reichman, Database Protection in a Global Economy, 2002 REVUE INTERNATIONALE DE DROIT ECONOMIQUE 455 (2002) [hereinafter Reichman, Database Protection]; J.H. Reichman & Pamela Samuelson, Intellectual Property Rights in Data ?, 50 VAND. L. REV. 51 (1997).

[42] Multilateral Agreements on Trade in Goods, 15 Apr. 1994, WTO Agreement, Annex 1A, 33 I.L.M. 1154 (1994) [hereinafter GATT 1994]; WTO Agreement, above n. 3.

[43] While the extent and degree of regulation that is needed remains controversial, even the most laissez-faire economists recognize problems attributed to market failures, market distortions, and other factors that decrease overall efficiency and welfare. See, e.g., MASKUS, IP RIGHTS, above nn. 8, 18. Others stress concerns about potential "races to the bottom" in regulatory standards. See, e.g., JOSEPH STIGLITZ, GLOBALIZATION AND ITS DISCONTENTS (2002).

Nowhere are these tensions more acute than in the knowledge goods sector of the world economy, a sector that is the most dynamic of all in terms of potential growth and yet partially resistant to any consensus-based economic analytical framework. Here, according to classical intellectual property theory, knowledge begins life as a public good available to all and as an input into the generation of additional knowledge. It subsequently becomes artificially scarce as states grant IPRs to stimulate investment in the production of private knowledge goods. The resulting tensions between the long-term benefits of these legal monopolies, which tend to elevate the level of competition over time,[44] and the social costs of restraining competition in the meanwhile[45] are recognized in Article XX(d) of the GATT itself.[46] This provision, which generally assigns responsibility for enacting IPRs to the WTO Members' domestic legislatures, admonishes them to observe a criterion of reasonable necessity and to avoid "disguised restriction[s] on international trade."[47]

A. Legal and organizational impediments to the creation and diffusion of knowledge goods

Drawing the lines between knowledge goods accessible to all and those subject to private property rights has always been a delicate, controversial, and economically uncertain task in even the most developed economies. Periods of relatively weak and relatively strong levels of protection have alternated over time, often at fairly short intervals, with little consensus in law or economics about the cumulative lessons to be learned. How to ensure that the social benefits of maximizing investment in current innovation are not offset by the social costs of deterring future innovation and impeding current competition is no clearer today than it was 50 years ago.[48] The question has become especially difficult to

---

[44] Lehman, *The Theory of Property Rights and the Protection of Intellectual and Industrial Property*, 16 INT'L REV. INDUS. PROP. & COPYRIGHT (IIC) 525 (1985); Edmund Kitch, *Nature and Function of the Patent System*, 30 J.L. & ECON. 265 (1977).

[45] Hanns Ullrich, *Expansionist Intellectual Property Protection and Reductionist Competition Rules: A TRIPS Perspective* [this volume].

[46] GATT 1994, above n. 42, art. XX(d).

[47] *Id.* This provision is, of course, subject to subsequent treaties, notably the TRIPS Agreement, which further limits states' rights. Nevertheless, the pro-competitive mandate of this provision, taken in the larger context of reserved powers under GATT art. XX generally, remains of cardinal importance to the meshing of private and public goods in further international regulation. *See* below text accompanying nn. 124–25.

[48] *See, e.g.*, JAMES BOYLE, SHAMANS, SOFTWARE AND SPLEENS: LAW AND THE CONSTRUCTION OF THE INFORMATION SOCIETY 25–46 (1996) [hereinafter BOYLE, SHAMANS, SOFTWARE & SPLEENS]; John H. Barton, *The Economics of TRIPS: International Trade in Information-Intensive Products*, 33 GEO. WASH. INT'L L. REV. 473 (2001); Roberto Mazzoleni & Richard R. Nelson, *Economic Theories About the Benefits and Costs of Patents*, 32 J. ECON. ISSUES 1031 (1998).

answer with regard to newer, cutting-edge technologies that obstinately refuse to behave like the traditional technologies of the industrial revolution.[49]

Today, moreover, the regulation of knowledge goods in national markets impinges on the provision of other public goods – health, education, scientific research, agriculture and the environment – in ways that were virtually unknown to previous generations. The centrality of innovation in dynamic developed economies has fostered a process of "enclosure" and privatization that increasingly threatens the provision of those other public goods that citizens take for granted and identify with the very exercise of state sovereignty.[50]

When these unresolved tensions between public and private interests in the production of knowledge goods are transferred from their territorial base in nation states to the nascent world market, they become far more acute. This follows because the stakes are much higher,[51] empirical evidence with which to assess the conflicting claims of high and low protectionists remains scarce, and nations have varying economic interests. The adverse effects of these uncertainties are then made worse by another paradox of the international trading system that one of us emphasized at the start of the Uruguay Round. Here we refer to the tendency of rich countries, that traditionally urged free competition on the rest of the world, to demand strong legal monopolies to protect private knowledge goods in international trade, and the tendency of poor countries to want unbridled competition with respect to these same knowledge goods, most of which are produced at great cost in the technology-exporting countries.[52]

1. Preserving temporary competitive advantages with international intellectual property standards

To understand why new distortions in the global market for knowledge goods seem to crop up faster than the old ones disappear, it is well to recognize that

---

[49] See, e.g., Arti K. Rai, *Fostering Cumulative Innovation in the Biopharmaceutical Industry: The Role of Patents and Antitrust*, 16 BERKELEY TECH. L.J. 813 (2001); James Boyle, *Enclosing the Genome: What the Squabbles over Genetic Patents Could Teach Us*, in PERSPECTIVES ON PROPERTIES OF THE HUMAN GENOME PROJECT 97 (F. Scott Kieff ed., 2003); J.H. Reichman, *Saving the Patent Law from Itself: Informal Reflections on Systemic Problems Afflicting Developed Intellectual Property Regimes*, in PERSPECTIVES ON PROPERTIES OF THE HUMAN GENOME PROJECT, above, at 289 [hereinafter Reichman, *Saving the Patent Law from Itself*].

[50] See, e.g., James Boyle, *The Second Enclosure Movement and the Construction of the Public Domain*, 66 LAW & CONTEMP. PROBS. 33 (2003) [hereinafter Boyle, *Second Enclosure Movement*].

[51] See, e.g., Joseph Stiglitz, *Knowledge as a Public Good*, in GLOBAL PUBLIC GOODS: INTERNATIONAL COOPERATION IN THE 21ST CENTURY (Inge Kaul et al. eds., 1999); Paul David, *The Political Economy of Public Science*, in THE REGULATION OF SCIENCE AND TECHNOLOGY 38 (Helen Lawton Smith ed., 2001).

[52] See, e.g., J. H. Reichman, *Intellectual Property in International Trade: Opportunities and Risks of a GATT Connection*, 22 VAND. J. TRANSNAT'L L. 747 (1989).

there is even less consensus among economists about how to regulate the global market for knowledge goods than exists in successful national markets, and that these uncertainties are aggravated by inequalities between rich and poor nations. The need to set standards *ex ante* – in order to reduce the public good character of facts, ideas, discoveries, and research results in favor of developing private knowledge goods – then compounds all the governance problems that beset transnational regulatory exercises in general.[53]

There is, for example, no expert body of legal and economic scholars charged with disinterested analysis of these issues, or with the collection of systematic inputs from all affected interests. The one agency entrusted with managing intellectual property rights at the international level – the World Intellectual Property Organization (WIPO) – has recently interpreted its legislative mandate as one of progressively elevating intellectual property rights throughout the world. Whether this strategy actually benefits innovation or the world's inhabitants seems to count for little in implementing this mandate.[54]

Even if this "democratic deficit" were overcome, differences of resources, institutional capabilities, and organization could still combine to create both a knowledge gap and a power gap at the regulatory center owing to the inexperience and ineffectiveness of the developing countries as a whole to manage their interests in this sector. Most of these states do not yet treat intellectual property as an integral part of national or regional systems of innovation. They are compliance oriented, not given to interagency review of the issues, but rather prone to leaving them to their intellectual property bureaus and to bartering concessions in this area for advantages in other areas, without any solid basis for calculating the true costs and benefits of these tradeoffs.[55]

Most developing countries lack access to impartial technical assistance, and must rely instead on assistance funded by sources whose interests are not necessarily in line with theirs.[56] They are also advised by nongovernmental organizations (NGOs), which have managed to produce an impressive array of

---

[53] *See, e.g.,* Paul David, Koyaanisqatsi *in Cyberspace: The Economics of an "Out-of-Balance" Regime of Private Property Rights in Data and Information,* [this volume]; Mark Lemley, Ex Ante versus Ex Post Justification for Intellectual Property, working paper (2003); Frederick Abbott, *The Future of IPRs in the Multilateral Trading System, in* TRADING IN KNOWLEDGE 36, 44 (C. Bellman et al. eds., 2003) (stressing indeterminacy in the economic analysis of TRIPS-related issues owing to lack of objective data).

[54] *See, e.g.,* Carlos Correa, *Formulating Effective Pro-development National Intellectual Property Policies, in* TRADING IN KNOWLEDGE, above n. 53, at 209, 214 (criticizing WIPO Secretariat for emphasizing "the benefits and largely ignoring the costs of IPR protection" and generally failing "to present the range of options available to developing countries"). *See generally* Sisule F. Musungu & Graham Dutfield, Multilateral Agreements and a TRIPS-plus World: The World Intellectual Property Organization (WIPO), Quaker U.N. Office, Geneva, TRIPS Issues papers No. 3 (2003).

[55] *See, e.g.,* Correa, above n. 54. For the situation prior to 1994, see J. WATAL, above n. 4.

[56] *See* Musungu & Dutfield, above n. 54; papers presented at UNCTAD/ICTSD Second Bellagio Conference, 17–20 Sept. 2003.

public-oriented outcomes in an increasing number of forums.[57] Yet, good as they sometimes are in tactical maneuvers on well-defined issues, such as public health, the NGOs' contribution cannot compensate for the general inability of the developing countries to integrate multilateral negotiations into broader national and regional innovation strategies.[58]

Those few developing countries that have built some capacity to participate in standard-setting exercises may run into coercive pressures from governments and corporations whose interests they challenge. Increasingly, such pressures are exerted in bilateral, unequal bargaining situations in which ever-higher IPRs are demanded without regard to the legal or political consequences of undermining the basic MFN principles of the GATT itself.[59] In effect, this regulatory gap at the center is left at the mercy of powerful state actors representing the interests of corporate clients at the international level. These clients, which may constitute a de facto "knowledge cartel,"[60] control the distribution of a disproportionately large share of existing technologies without necessarily being particularly innovative themselves. Their membership typically does not include the small- and medium-size entrepreneurs, who drive innovation in the United States, nor does it include the universities and public research institutes who depend on constant access to facts, data, discoveries, and the research results of others.

Because the members of this knowledge cartel depend on sales of existing innovation, they push their governments to regulate the global market in ways that lock in temporary competitive advantages without necessarily advancing the global public interest in innovation, competition, or the provision of complementary public goods. Indeed, representatives of the global public interest are unlikely to be seated at the table where hard-law negotiations take place.[61] Without a legitimizing governance process that adequately represents all stake-holders, the baseline need to support both public and private interests in the transnational market for knowledge goods thus risks being compromised in at least two ways.

First, there is a pronounced risk that a substantial component of the recently liberated global trade market will become re-regulated through IPRs to reflect dubious practices in developed markets for knowledge goods that may actually

---

[57] *See* Laurence R. Helfer, *Regime Shifting: The TRIPS Agreement and New Dynamics of International Intellectual Property Lawmaking*, 29 YALE J. INT'L L. 1 (2004).

[58] *Cf.* John Barton, *Integrating IPR Policies in Development Strategies*, *in* TRADING IN KNOWLEDGE, above n. 53, at 57, 60–64.

[59] *See* Frederick M. Abbott, *Trade Diplomacy, the Rule of Law and the Problem of Asymmetric Risks in TRIPS*, Quaker United Nation Office Occasional Paper 13 (Sept. 2003), *available at* http://www.geneva.quno.info/pdf/OP13 Abbottfindft rev_1.pdf (visited 1 May 2003); Drahos, above n. 5.

[60] "The difficulty of entry into markets dominated by multinational oligopolies is thus compounded by the international IP system." Barton, above n. 58, at 61. *See generally*, Hanns Ullrich, above n. 45.

[61] *See* Helfer, above n. 57 (distinguishing hard and soft law processes).

hamper both innovation and competition in the long run. Second, there is the further risk that an over-regulated market for knowledge goods could compromise the ability of nation states to supply other public goods that only they can provide in a decentralized world economy.

2. Instability and loss of balance in developed intellectual property regimes

The drive to stamp out free-riding practices thus tends to obscure serious problems engendered by the radical transformation of IP policies that has occurred in developed countries. This transformation constitutes a prolonged effort to strengthen the protection of investors in cutting-edge technologies, especially computer programs and biogenetically engineered products, which fit imperfectly within the classical patent and copyright paradigms.[62]

Under the classical IP system, as implemented in the United States through the mid-1960s, for example, the strong legal monopolies of the patent law protected only a narrow layer of discontinuous inventions that fell outside the technical trajectories guiding the day-to-day application of normal scientific discoveries.[63] Entrepreneurs constrained to innovate in a highly competitive economy looked to the liability rules of unfair competition law, especially trade secret law, to provide natural lead time in which to recoup their investments, and to the rules of trademark law to maintain a foothold in the market based on their reputations as producers of quality goods.[64] Because copyright law excluded industrial products in virtually every form,[65] their producers could not hope to avoid the rigors of competition by masquerading as authors of literary and artistic works. As for the rest, vigorously enforced antitrust laws, supplemented by a robust doctrine of patent misuse, rid the market of deleterious patent pools and other barriers to entry and, in the view of Professors Mowery and Rosenberg, by disciplining Bell Labs and IBM, paved the way for the technological leaps of the 1970s and 1980s.[66]

---

[62] *See generally* J.H. Reichman, *Legal Hybrids between the Patent and Copyright Paradigms*, 94 COLUM. L. REV. 2432 (1994); J.H. Reichman, *Charting the Collapse of the Patent-Copyright Dichotomy*, 13 CARDOZO ARTS & ENT. L.J. 475 (1995); *see also* JAMES BOYLE, SHAMANS, SOFTWARE, & SPLEENS, above n. 48, at 119–44; Pamela Samuelson et al., *A Manifesto Concerning the Legal Protection of Computer Programs*, 94 COLUM. L. REV. 2308 (1994).

[63] *See, e.g.*, Nelson and Merges, *On the Complex Economics of Patent Scope*, 90 COLUM. L. REV. 839 (1990).

[64] Samuelson & Scotchmer, *The Law and Economics of Reverse Engineering*, 111 YALE L.J. 157 (2003).

[65] Baker v. Selden, 101 U.S. 99 (1879); Sears, Roebuck & Co. v. Stiffel Co., 376 U.S. 225 (1964); Compco Corp. v. Day-Brite Lighting, Inc., 376 U.S. 234 (1964).

[66] David S. Mowery & Nathan Rosenberg, *The U.S. National Innovation System*, in NATIONAL INNOVATION SYSTEMS 29–75 (Richard R. Nelson ed., 1993).

This classical system of intellectual property protection obliged innovators to look to the public domain for the basic inputs of most technological development. They took the availability of vast amounts of government-generated or government-funded scientific data and technical information for granted; and they assumed that facts and data generated by non-confidential public research endeavors at universities and other nonprofit institutions would become public goods available to all.[67] Investors also assumed that sub-patentable innovations could be reverse-engineered by proper means that would endow competitors with improvements and lower cost modes of production. They further assumed that even patented inventions would enter the public domain at fairly short intervals and that it was not inordinately difficult to work around these inventions if the commercial payoffs justified the effort. However, basic underlying scientific discoveries would remain freely available.

If we now fast forward to a descriptive analysis of the current U.S. system, one could hardly imagine a starker contrast. The United States Court of Appeals for the Federal Circuit, entrusted by Congress to manage the patent system, has deliberately remolded that system to protect investment as such, rather than discontinuous technical achievements that elevate the level of competition. The patent system has accordingly degenerated to protecting incremental slivers of know-how applied to industry, including those very business methods that were formerly the building blocks of the free-enterprise economy.[68]

The copyright system, expanding in the same direction, now confers virtually perpetual protection on computer software and digital productions of all kinds, and it encourages creators to surround even their unprotectable technical ideas and components with untouchable electronic fences.[69] Once surrounded by these fences, even the underlying facts and data may be put off limits; while one-sided electronic adhesion contracts may override public interest exceptions favoring education and public research, and they may even prohibit reverse engineering by honest means.[70]

---

[67] Reichman & Uhlir, above n. 28 (citing authorities); *see also* Rebecca Eisenberg, *Proprietary Rights and the Norms of Science in Biotechnology Research*, in THE ECONOMICS OF SCIENCE AND INNOVATION 357 (The International Library of Critical Writings in Economics, 117:1) (P.E. Stephan & D.B. Audretsch eds., 2000) (originally published under the same title in 97 YALE L.J. 177 (1987)).

[68] State St. Bank & Trust Co. v. Signature Fin. Group, Inc., 149 F.3d 1368 (Fed. Cir. 1998); Reichman, *Saving the Patent Law from Itself*, above n. 49.

[69] Digital Millennium Copyright Act of 1998, 17 U.S.C. §§ 1201–1205 (2000) [hereinafter DMCA]; Pamela Samuelson, *Mapping the Digital Public Domain: Threats and Opportunities*, 66 LAW & CONTEMP. PROBS. 147 (2003).

[70] Bowers v. Baystate Techs., 320 F.3d 1317 (Fed. Cir. 2003); J.H. Reichman & Jonathan Franklin, *Privately Legislated Intellectual Property Rights: Reconciling Freedom of Contract with Public Good Uses of Information*, 147 U. PA. L. REV. 875 (1999); Nina Elkin-Koren, *A Public-Regarding Approach to Contracting Over Copyrights*, in EXPANDING THE BOUNDARIES OF IP, above n. 41, at 191; Jane C. Ginsburg, *U.S. Initiatives to Protect Works of Low Authorship*, in EXPANDING THE BOUNDARIES OF IP, above n. 41, at 55.

As hybrid IP regimes multiply to fill still other perceived gaps in the system, there are virtually no products sold on the general products market that do not come freighted with a bewildering and overlapping array of exclusive property rights that discourage follow-on applications of routine technical know-how.[71] Weak enforcement of antitrust laws then further reinforces the barriers to entry erected upon this thicket of rights, while the need to stimulate and coordinate investment in complex innovation projects justifies patent pools, concentrations of research efforts, and predatory practices formerly thought to constitute misuses of the patent monopoly.[72]

The end results of this process, which James Boyle has felicitously called the "Second Enclosure Movement,"[73] are not fully known, but the problems it is already causing for developed systems of innovation shed light on the larger problems facing the international economy. The availability of upstream data and scientific information from the public domain is shrinking at the very moment when advances in Internet technologies make it possible to link both centrally located and distributed data repositories as never before. A growing thicket of rights surrounds gene fragments, research tools, and other upstream inputs of scientific research, and the resulting transaction costs impede and delay research and development undertaken in both the public and private sectors.[74] Lost research and competitive opportunities appear to be mushrooming as exchanges of even government-funded research results become problematic.[75] As well-known economists point out, complex research and development projects at every level – whether public or private – will become increasingly impracticable if too many owners of too many rights have to be tithed along the way.[76]

---

[71] See J.H. Reichman, *Of Green Tulips and Legal Kudzu: Repackaging Rights in Subpatentable Innovation*, 53 VAND. L. REV. 1743 (2000) [hereinafter Reichman, *Green Tulips*].
[72] See, e.g., Ullrich, above n. 45.
[73] Boyle, *Second Enclosure Movement*, above n. 50. See generally Duke Symposium on Intellectual Property Rights and the Public Domain, 66 LAW & CONTEM. PROBS 1 (2003).
[74] See, e.g., Michael A. Heller & Rebecca S. Eisenberg, *Can Patents Deter Innovation? The Anticommons in Biomedical Research*, 280 SCIENCE 698 (1998); Rai, above n. 41; Rebecca S. Eisenberg, *Bargaining over the Transfer of Proprietary Research Tools*, in EXPANDING THE BOUNDARIES OF IP, above n. 41; see also Walter W. Powell, *Networks of Learning in Biotechnology: Opportunities and Constraints Associated with Relational Contracting in a Knowledge-Intensive Field*, in EXPANDING THE BOUNDARIES OF IP, above n. 41.
[75] See Reichman & Uhlir, above n. 28.
[76] See, e.g., Richard Nelson, *Linkages Between the Market Economy and the Scientific Commons* [this volume]; Paul A. David, A Tragedy of the Public Knowledge "Commons"? Global Science, Intellectual Property and the Digital Technology Boomerang, SIEPR Discussion Paper No. 00–02, Stanford Institute for Economic Policy Research (2000), *available at* http://siepr.stanford.edu/papers/pdf/00-02.html (last visited 8 Jan. 2004); Paul David & Michael Spence, *Towards Institutional Infrastructures for E-Science: The Scope of the Challenge*, OXFORD INTERNET INSTITUTE (14 Sept. 2002).

Meanwhile, the sharing norms of science and the principle of open access to data have begun to break down as universities commercialize publicly funded research products. New intellectual property rights in collections of data – adopted in the E.U. and pending adoption in the U.S.[77] – further undermine these norms by enabling scientists, universities, and entrepreneurs to retain control of data and technical information even after the publication of research results in articles or after public disclosure for purposes of filing patent applications on such results.[78]

These and other social disutilities cast light on the problems afflicting the international system and raise serious questions about its future prospects. They represent the unintended consequences of an excess of regulation and interference with market forces. In allowing large multinational firms to lock in temporary advantages,[79] the IP system could discourage innovation by those same small and medium-sized firms that depend on access to public domain inputs for developing applications of new technologies.

In this environment, economists fear that the ratcheting up of intellectual property standards will boomerang against the capacity to innovate in developed countries.[80] They ask whether the breakthrough inventions of the recent past would still be possible in a protectionist environment and in the presence of a shrinking public domain.[81] They make us question whether future innovation will flourish in a dynamic, transnational system of innovation liberated from excessive governmental regulation or flounder in a re-regulated, ever more anti-competitive market that increasingly resembles the top-down economies that trailed behind U.S. high-tech industries in the past.

3. Exporting a dysfunctional system to the rest of the world?

Logically, the shift to a high-protectionist agenda in the developed countries should spark a cautious and skeptical response from the rest of the world for a number of reasons. First, the TRIPS Agreement itself, coupled with the WIPO

---

[77] Directive 96/9/EC of the European Parliament and of the Council on the legal protection of databases, 1996 O.J. (L 77), at 20 (27 Mar. 1996) [hereinafter E.C. Database Directive]; H.R. 3261, 108th Cong. (1st Sess. 2003); *see generally* Reichman, *Database Protection*, above n. 41.

[78] *See, e.g.*, Reichman & Uhlir, above n. 28; Royal Society, Keeping Science Open: The Effects of Intellectual Property Policy on the Conduct of Science, Policy Doc. 02/03 (Apr. 2003) [hereinafter Royal Society Report].

[79] *See, e.g.*, PETER DRAHOS & JOHN BRAITHWAITE, INFORMATION FEUDALISM (2002); SUSAN K. SELL, POWER AND IDEAS: NORTH-SOUTH POLICIES OF INTELLECTUAL PROPERTY AND ANTITRUST (1998); SUSAN K. SELL, PRIVATE POWER, PUBLIC LAW: THE GLOBALIZATION OF INTELLECTUAL PROPERTY RIGHTS (2003).

[80] See David, above n. 76 and accompanying text. Professor David speaks explicitly of a "boomerang" effect. *Id.*

[81] *See* above nn. 73–76; Graeme B. Dinwoodie & Rochelle Cooper Dreyfuss, *WTO Dispute Settlement and the Preservation of the Public Domain of Science under International Law* [this volume].

Copyright Treaties of 1996,[82] foreshadowed a revolutionary transformation of the legal and economic infrastructures in developing countries, and they need a lengthy period of time in which to digest and adjust to these reforms. These countries can hardly absorb the unknown social costs of new intellectual property burdens when the real costs of the last round of legislative initiatives are still making themselves felt.[83] Yet, this reality has not attenuated the pressures for TRIPS-plus standards in both multilateral and bilateral forums.

A second reason for diffidence in developing countries is the scholarly debate that the high-protectionist agenda has generated in both the United States and Europe, and the corresponding fears that this agenda could harm investment and research-based innovation in the long run. If the critics prove right, then the last thing the developing countries should want to do is to emulate these policies.

Consider, for example, that the drive to further harmonize the international minimum standards of patent protection at WIPO[84] has occurred at the very time when the domestic standards of the United States and the operations of its patent system are under critical assault. That country's patent system has been subject to scathing criticism in numerous law journal articles,[85] in the scientific literature,[86] and even in magazines of general circulation.[87] New proposals to reform both the domestic and international patent systems appear frequently, and commissions to study or propose reform are operating on numerous fronts.[88] How, under such circumstances, could it be timely to harmonize

---

[82] *See* above nn. 3, 6.   [83] *See* CIPR, above n. 10, at 155–57.

[84] WIPO Draft Patent Treaty, above n. 7.

[85] *See, e.g.*, Arti K. Rai, *Engaging Facts and Policy: A Multi-Institutional Approach to Patent System Reform*, 103 COLUM. L. REV. 1035 (2003); Jay P. Kesan, The Private and Social Costs of the Patent System: Why Bad Patents Survive in the Market and How We Should Change, working paper (2004) (citing articles by Thomas, Leung, Quillen and Ogden, Baird and others); Jay P. Kesan, *Carrots and Sticks to Create a Better Patent System*, 17 BERKELEY TECH. L.J. 763 (2002); Robert Merges, *As Many as Six Impossible Patents before Breakfast: Property Rights for Business Concepts and Patent System Reform*, 14 BERKELEY TECH. L.J. 577 (1999); John Allison & Mark Lemley, *The Growing Complexity of the United States Patent System*, 82 BOSTON U. L. REV. 77 (2002).

[86] *See, e.g.*, Heller & Eisenberg, above n. 74; John K. Barton, *Reforming the Patent System*, 287 SCIENCE 1933 (2000); *see also* Eisenberg, *Bargaining over the Transfer of Proprietary Research Tools*, above n. 41; John P. Walsh et al., *Effects of Research Tool Patents and Licensing on Biomedical Innovation*, in PATENTS IN THE KNOWLEDGE-BASED ECONOMY 285–340 (W.M. Cohen & S.A. Merrill eds., National Research Council 2001).

[87] James Gleick, *Patently Absurd*, NEW YORK TIMES MAGAZINE, 12 Mar. 2000, at 44.

[88] *See, e.g.*, John K. Barton, above n. 86; Rai, above n. 85; Paul Edward Geller, *An International Patent Utopia?*, 25 E.I.P.R. 515 (2003). At the time of writing, both the Federal Trade Commission and the National Research Council were conducting studies of the U.S. patent system with a view to launching reform proposals. *See also* Mark A. Lemley, *Rational Ignorance at the Patent Office*, 95 NW. U. L. REV. 1 (2001) (finding that poor patent examination procedures save resources because few patents are actually litigated or licensed). Taken to their logical conclusion, Prof. Lemley's findings would ironically suggest that an efficient worldwide patent regime should revert to the

and elevate international standards of patent protection – even if that were demonstrably beneficial – when there is so little agreement in the U.S. itself on how to rectify a dysfunctional apparatus that often seems out of control?

Even in the courts themselves, which, in the United States, still operate at some degree of removal from lobbying and other political pressures, there are elements of change, uncertainty, and disarray that do not bode well for an international standard-setting exercise. In the past few years, for example, the U.S. federal courts have significantly changed the way patent claims are interpreted; narrowed the doctrine of equivalents in patent infringement actions; practically eliminated the research exemption under which universities had operated for 50 years or more; expanded patent protection of computer programs in ways that both the domestic and European authorities had previously opposed; and opened patent law to the protection of business methods in ways that have disrupted settled commercial activities.[89]

These events should make U.S. authorities cautious about surrendering the power to undertake adjustments in the future, and policymakers in the rest of the world should become wary of locking themselves into the untested results of ad hoc judicial tinkering in a single country.[90] It is therefore disconcerting to think of "harmonizing" the international patent system at such a time, when the risks of unintended harm to worldwide competition seem high, and when the only basis for a consensus on harmonization might be to squeeze out the remaining flexibilities in the TRIPS Agreement.

One can paint a similar picture with respect to copyright and related rights laws. Here, the developing countries, acting in concert with user interests in the developed countries, managed to ensure that the 1996 WIPO treaties governing works transmitted in digital media continued to allow certain privileged uses and exceptions permitted by prior law.[91] Notwithstanding this outcome at the

---

registration system previously used in France and Italy, and not the examination system derived from U.S. and German practice.

[89] Markman v. Westview Instruments, Inc., 52 F.3d 967 (Fed. Cir. 1995), *aff'd*, 917 U.S. 370 (1996); Festo Corp. v. Shoketsu Kinzoku Kogyo Kabushiki Co., 234 F.3d 558 (Fed. Cir. 2000), *vacated by* 122 S. Ct. 1831 (2002); Duke v. Madey, 307 F.3d 1351 (Fed. Cir. 2002); *In re* Alappat, 33 F.3d 1526 (1994); State St. Bank & Trust Co. v. Signature Fin. Group, Inc., 149 F.3d 1368 (Fed. Cir. 1998). *See generally* Gerald Sobel, *Competition Policy in Patent Cases and Antitrust, in* PERSPECTIVES ON PROPERTIES OF THE HUMAN GENOME PROJECT, above n. 49, at 23, 26–41 ("The Federal Circuit's transformation of the law").

[90] *Cf., e.g.*, Ruth L. Okediji, *Public Welfare and the Role of the WTO: Reconsidering the TRIPS Agreement*, 17 EMORY INT'L L. REV. 821, 822–25 (2003).

[91] *See, e.g.*, WIPO Copyright Treaty, above n. 6, arts. 8, 10; Agreed Statements Concerning the WIPO Copyright Treaty, Concerning Article 10, adopted by the Diplomatic Conference on 20 Dec. 1996, WIPO Doc. CRNR/DC/96 (23 Dec. 1996); Samuelson, above n. 6; Ruth Okediji, Development in the Information Age: Issues in the Regulation of Intellectual Property Rights, Computer Software and Electronic Commerce, UNCTAD/ICTSD (2003).

international level, the United States and the European Union both ignored these provisions and cut well back on permitted uses in their domestic implementation laws;[92] and they have been pressing developing countries for still higher standards of protection in bilateral negotiations.

Yet, these domestic initiatives to expand and strengthen copyright protection of works transmitted over digital telecommunications networks have generated popular resistance to copyright norms in the United States as well as strenuous academic concerns about free competition, free speech, privacy, and the need to ensure access to inputs for future creative works.[93] Further harmonization efforts in this climate thus amount to a gamble from which bad decisions and bad laws are far more likely to emerge than good laws that appropriately balance public and private interests.

There are still other risks of participating in further harmonization exercises that are even more sobering. First, certain new initiatives – such as the European database protection right[94] – could radically subvert the classical intellectual property tradition built around patents and copyrights, with unintended consequences that could elevate the costs of research and development across the entire knowledge economy. While pressures to adopt similar legislation in the United States mount, legal and economic analysis of database protection as a generator of anti-competitive effects and of potential obstacles to innovation also grow more refined and alarming.[95] Such premature initiatives could undermine sound economic development everywhere, and action in this regard at the international level would require great caution under the best of circumstances.[96]

In this climate, it is difficult to see that developing countries have anything to gain from new efforts to strengthen IP standards. As matters stand, these international standard-setting exercises are not being conducted either to

---

[92] DMCA, above n. 69; Directive 2001/29/EC of the European Parliament and of the Council on the harmonization of certain aspects of copyright and related rights in the information society, 2001 O.J. (L 167) 10 (22 May 2001); *see generally* JESSICA LITMAN, DIGITAL COPYRIGHT: PROTECTING INTELLECTUAL PROPERTY ON THE INTERNET (2001).

[93] *See, e.g.*, Yochai Benkler, *Through the Looking Glass: Alice and the Constitutional Foundations of the Public Domain*, 66 LAW & CONTEMP. PROBS. 173 (2003); Samuelson, above n. 69. *See generally* THE DIGITAL DILEMMA: INTELLECTUAL PROPERTY IN THE INFORMATION AGE (National Research Council 2000).

[94] E.C. Database Directive, above n. 77.

[95] *See, e.g.*, David, above n. 53; Royal Society Report, above n. 78. *See also* Jacqueline Lipton, *Balancing Private Rights and Public Policies: Reconceptualizing Property in Databases*, 18 BERKELEY TECH. L.J. 773 (2003).

[96] *See* Reichman, *Database Protection*, above n. 41 (proposing minimalist interim agreement to avoid wholesale duplication of noncopyrightable collections of data). Equally problematic as a candidate for "harmonization" is competition law, which still affords a potential range of checks and balances on legal monopolies and restrictive licensing agreements. *See* Ullrich, above n. 45; Eleanor Fox, *Can Antitrust Policy Protect the Global Commons from the Excesses of IPRs?* [this volume].

promote their interests or the global public interest. On the contrary, the developing countries play virtually no role in norm formation (partly due to their disorganized institutional apparatus),[97] and the global public interest is hardly represented at the negotiating tables in the developed countries themselves, much less in international forums where hard law is enacted.[98] From this perspective, even if the developing countries possessed more bargaining power than they do, they should remain wary of further harmonization exercises in the absence of effective strategies for preserving and enhancing the public good side of the equation. Until this gap in international lawmaking has been suitably addressed, such initiatives will continue to suffer from a basic design defect.

Any gains in efficiency of operations and lower transaction costs that greater harmonization might entail are likely to be offset by losses of sovereign power to control the single states' own innovation policies; by a shrinking public domain; by still higher costs of technological inputs and reverse engineering; and by growing thickets of rights that will make transfer of technology harder for those operating outside patent and IP pools (pools that could soon include major research universities as well as corporate holding companies). With every rise in international IP standards, moreover, there will likely be a corresponding loss of flexibility under the TRIPS Agreement and still greater risks deriving from the possible claims of nonviolatory acts of nullification that new standards may engender in the future.[99]

B. Impact of intellectual property standards on the reserved welfare powers of WTO members

An International Task Force on Global Public Goods was recently created at the initiative of France and Sweden to explore further the concept of GPG, to clarify the definition, and to propose concrete and operational recommendations to policymakers. In assessing how such goods could collectively be harnessed to reduce poverty and enhance welfare, this group has given priority to "peace and security; trade regimes; financial stability; control of communicable diseases; and sustainable management of the national commons."[100] A sixth item, "knowledge," is also included in the list for its "classical public good properties." However, the task force believes that this rubric requires a separate and particular treatment owing to its "cross-cutting" nature and to the ever-increasing role of knowledge as both a private and public good.[101]

---

[97] *See* below text accompanying nn. 153–57.   [98] *See generally* Helfer, above n. 57.
[99] *See* TRIPS Agreement, above n. 3, arts. 64.2, 64.3.
[100] *See* International Task Force on Global Public Goods, Report of the First Meeting, 25–26 Sept. 2003, *available at* http://www.gpgtaskforce.org/bazment.aspx (visited 21 Dec. 2003).
[101] *Id.*; *see* below text accompanying nn. 159–76.

As programs like this one emerge to focus attention on the role of GPG in advancing the welfare of developing countries, they increasingly encounter obstacles and problems stemming from the existence of patents and other IPRs held by universities, research institutes, and the private sector on fundamental research technologies.[102] These intellectual property rights may play a positive role, especially when they enable private investors to take publicly funded research results out of the laboratory and into the stream of commerce.[103] Increasingly, however, these rights have invaded the research commons itself and made it both costly and difficult to obtain cutting-edge technologies needed for public health, agriculture, environmental protection, and the provision of other public goods.[104]

Private capture of the global regulatory process for IP standard setting not only undermines the ability of governments in developing countries to devise and promote their own national systems of innovation. It also erodes national control over the provision of non-TRIPS public goods by other affected ministries that lack inputs into the intellectual property standard-setting exercises.

The risks of progressively entangling the WTO Members' police and welfare powers in the coils of IP treaties are aggravated by the poor organizational capacities of developing countries and their lack of expertise, which have so far impeded recourse to public-interest tools that the TRIPS Agreement still makes available.[105] They are further aggravated by the practice of excluding those who disagree with the knowledge cartel from key negotiating forums and from a disinclination to include those who speak for the public interest or the preservation of complementary public goods in "technical" standard-setting exercises.

The stakeholders excluded from the process of norm building in the field of IPRs have not quietly faded away, but have, on the contrary, worked through numerous NGOs to defend global public goods against further encroachment in parallel or alternative forums. This strategy of "regime shifting"[106] imitates that of the knowledge cartel, which in the 1990s shifted the regulation of IPRs from WIPO, whose secretariat at that time was overtly sympathetic to the goals

---

[102] Barton, above n. 58, at 61.
[103] See, e.g., Rebecca S. Eisenberg, *Public Research and Private Development: Patents and Technology Transfer in Government-Sponsored Research*, 82 VA. L. REV. 1663 (1996).
[104] See, e.g., Boyle, above n. 49; Correa, above n. 22, at 545–48; Robert E. Evenson, *Agricultural Research and Intellectual Property Rights* [this volume]; Arti K. Rai & Rebecca S. Eisenberg, *Bayh-Dole Reform and the Progress of Biomedicine*, 66 LAW & CONTEMP. PROBS. 289 (2003).
[105] For a major exception, see Decision of the South African Competition Commission concerning AIDS medicines, *available at* www.cptech.org/ip/health/sa/settlement12092003.pdf (visited 7 Feb. 2004). *See generally* J.H. REICHMAN WITH CATHERINE HASENZAHL, NON-VOLUNTARY LICENSING OF PATENTED INVENTIONS: THE LAW AND PRACTICE OF THE UNITED STATES (UNCTAD/ICTSD 2003) (discussing broad reliance on government use provisions in U.S. law).
[106] Helfer, above n. 57.

of developing countries, to the GATT (later to become the World Trade Organization), where market power was the prevailing influence.

As Professor Laurence Helfer shows, these parallel efforts to balance the private interests of intellectual property rights holders against larger public interest goals have been increasingly successful with respect to public health, biodiversity, plant genetic resources, human rights, and the protection of traditional knowledge and culture.[107] The most dramatic success came in the area of public health, where the NGOs' campaign for access to essential medicines culminated in the Ministerial Declaration on TRIPS and Public Health, and in the supplementary decision of 30 August 2003.[108] Also noteworthy from this perspective is the work of NGOs within United Nations human rights bodies, which "has led to the adoption of non-binding declarations and interpretive statements that emphasize the public's interest in access to new knowledge and innovations and assert that states must give primacy to human rights where the two sets of obligations conflict."[109]

Professor Helfer identifies at least four different goals that NGOs have striven to fulfill in these parallel regime-shifting initiatives. First, they seek to promote and maximize desired policy outcomes that differ from those of IP stakeholders, particularly where those policy outcomes "have been ignored or marginalized in other international regimes."[110] Second, they have created safety valves that help to relieve pressure for action at the WTO by

[107] "Increasingly broad and vocal consortiums of ... NGOs ... are challenging the 'moral, political and economic legitimacy' of TRIPS, focusing on provisions of the treaty that affect public health, human rights, biodiversity, and plant genetic resources." Helfer, above n. 57, at 3. *See, e.g.,* Convention on Biological Diversity, 5 June 1992, 31 I.L.M. 818, *available at* http://www.biodiv.org/convention/articles.asp (last accessed 28 July 2004); International Treaty on Plant Genetic Resources for Food and Agriculture (ITPGR), *opened for signature* 3 Nov. 2001 (not yet entered into force); Helfer, above n. 57, at 22–28, 32–34.

[108] WTO Doha Ministerial Conference, Declaration on the TRIPS Agreement and Public Health, WT/MIN(01)/DEC/W/2 (14 Nov. 2001), 41 I.L.M. 755 (2002) [hereinafter Doha Declaration on TRIPS and Public Health]; Decision of General Council of 30 Aug. 2003, Implementation of Paragraph 6 of the Doha Declaration on the TRIPS Agreement and Public Health, WT/L/540 (1 Sept. 2003), 43 I.L.M. 509 (2004). *See generally* Frederick M. Abbott, *The Doha Declaration on the TRIPS Agreement and Public Health: Lighting a Dark Corner at the WTO,* 5 JIEL 469 (2002); Duncan Matthews, *WTO Decision on Implementation of Paragraph 6 of the Doha Declaration on the TRIPS Agreement and Public Health: A Solution to the Access to Essential Medicines Problem?,* 7 JIEL 73 (2004).

[109] Helfer, above n. 57, at 38 (citing authorities); *see generally id.* at 37–43; Audrey R. Chapman, *The Human Rights Implications of Intellectual Property Protection,* 5 JIEL 861, 867 (2002) (stating that "from a human rights perspective, intellectual property protection is understood more as a social product with a social function, and not primarily as an economic relationship").

[110] Helfer, above n. 57, at 48. "By attending meetings, submitting information to expert and working groups and interacting with government officials ... in the biodiversity, PGR,

"consigning an issue area to a venue where consequential outcomes and meaningful rule development are unlikely to occur."[111] Third, regime shifting focuses efforts on generating norms that operate to check or counter the goals of the high protectionist coalitions and thereby provide governments "a 'safe space' in which to analyze and critique those aspects of TRIPS ... they find ... problematic."[112] Fourth, NGO activities seek to blend or integrate new hard and soft law rules into both WTO and WIPO processes as a means of focusing attention on other public goods besides innovation, and of enabling "developing countries to achieve outcomes not attainable" in any single negotiating forum.[113]

There are, of course, risks of overkill and unintended consequences inherent in these regime-shifting exercises. Putting human rights behind the drive for access to essential medicines clearly strengthened the claims of those dying from AIDS while governments debated the intricacies of patent law and the effects of reference pricing on the cost of medicines in developed countries.[114] It has done little to clarify the complex problems of funding risky research and development that lie at the heart of the patent system,[115] although new NGO initiatives that focus specifically on devising alternative research and development strategies may yield more promising results in the future.[116]

Similarly, while the drive for legal protection of traditional knowledge under some form of intellectual property right could give poor countries a bigger stake in the global market for knowledge goods,[117] it could further privatize resources – especially genetic resources – that were previously treated as agricultural public goods. It could also make innovation and creativity more difficult in the very countries that are the richest suppliers of traditional knowledge, especially if foreign firms that acquired these inputs subject to

---

public health, and human rights regimes, NGOs can shape debates over intellectual property protection in ways that are foreclosed to them within the trade regime." *Id.* at 48.

[111] *Id.* at 49. This may serve the interests of both developing and developed countries in different ways. *See id.* at 49–50.

[112] *Id.* at 58.

[113] *Id.* at 48–55. *Cf. also* Boyle, *Enclosing the Genome*, above n. 49 (stressing deeper moral and philosophical dimensions of this focus).

[114] *See, e.g.*, Patricia Danzon & Adrian Towse, *Theory and Implementation of Differential Pricing for Pharmaceuticals* [this volume].

[115] *See, e.g.*, Alan O. Sykes, *TRIPs, Pharmaceuticals, Developing Countries and the Doha "Solution,"* 3 CHI. J. INT'L L. 47 (2002).

[116] *See* Henry Grabowski, *Increasing R&D Incentives for Neglected Diseases: Lessons from the Orphan Drugs Act* [this volume]; James Love & Tim Hubbard, From TRIPS to RIPS: A Better Trade Framework to Support Innovation in Medical Technologies, presented at the workshop on economic issues related to access to HIV/AIDS care in developing countries, Agence Nationale de Recherches sur le Sida, Marseille, France (2003), *available at* http://www.cptech.org/ip/health/rndtf/trips2rips.pdf (visited 30 Jan. 2004).

[117] *See* Thomas Cottier & Marion Panizzon, *Legal Perspectives on Traditional Knowledge: The Case for Intellectual Property Protection* [this volume].

"benefit sharing" royalty agreements were under no effective ancillary obligations to share their technological know-how with the countries of origin.[118] Above all, legal protection of traditional knowledge could boomerang against developing countries as a group if they were tempted to trade it for a strong database protection treaty, as the European Union proposes.[119]

In any event, the burgeoning encroachment of international IPRs on the reserved welfare and police powers of states constitutes an anomaly in public international law that must be fixed before it cripples the WTO and fatally weakens the infrastructure that supports world trade. One should not view this as some minor irritant to be blamed on NGOs or recalcitrant developing countries. Telling poor people in rich countries that the TRIPS Agreement prevents domestic policymakers from regulating access to essential medicines will not long remain politically feasible. As matters stand, if nothing had been done to address the plight of millions dying of AIDS because of TRIPS patent rights, then the WTO would have contributed to the greatest health tragedy in history.[120]

Similar errors must be prevented in other critical areas. Until there are some agreed global governance mechanisms for food security, agriculture, education, public health, environmental protection, scientific research, and other public goods, states cannot be presumed to have surrendered sovereign police and welfare powers in the course of intellectual property standard-setting exercises at which their ministries of health, education, agriculture, and public welfare played little or no role.

Professor Robert Howse has suggested that WTO dispute-settlement panels in cases covered by the TRIPS Agreement could attenuate such conflicts by invoking article 8.1 of that Agreement.[121] This provision recognizes the power of states "in formulating or amending their laws and regulations, [to] adopt measures necessary to protect public health and nutrition, and to promote the public interest in sectors of vital importance to their socio-economic and technological development ... [if] consistent with the provisions of this

---

[118] *See, e.g.*, Gustavo Ghidini, *Equitable Sharing of Benefits from Biodiversity-Based Innovation* [this volume].

[119] That solution could limit the ability of researchers and entrepreneurs in developing countries to access scientific and technical data and information – the most important input into the knowledge-based economy – at the very moment when digitized network technologies could make such data available as never before. It could also elevate the costs of innovation everywhere while creating global barriers to entry in favor of a handful of firms that hold disproportionate market power in the supply of information as such. *See, e.g.*, Reichman & Uhlir, above n. 28; Reichman, *Database Protection*, above n. 41.

[120] *See* Frederick Abbott, *Managing the Hydra: The Herculean Task of Ensuring Access to Essential Medicines* [this volume].

[121] Robert Howse, *The Canadian Generic Medicines Panel: A Dangerous Precedent in Dangerous Times*, 3 J. WORLD INTELL. PROP. 493 (2002) (criticizing the decision in Canada – Patent Protection of Pharmaceutical Products (Generic Medicines), WT/DS114/R (WTO Dispute Settlement Panel 17 Mar. 2000)).

Agreement."[122] It could allow panels to interpret TRIPS provisions in the light of other relevant international laws, including "'soft law' sources, such as resolutions and authoritative reports and policy statements of relevant international forums."[123]

While endorsing this proposal, we think that respect for domestic authority over the provision of public goods outside the TRIPS framework must ultimately rest on a more solid foundation if the WTO's own infrastructure is to become stabilized over time. Here, perhaps, another lesson to be drawn resides, by analogy, in the express list of reserved state police and welfare powers set out in article XX of the General Agreement on Tariffs and Trade.

This provision subjects state power over intellectual property laws to a criterion of "reasonableness" when derogating from the pro-competitive mandate of the GATT.[124] It further subjects the exercise of reserved state powers generally to two additional criteria, set out in the accompanying *chapeau* clause, namely, that resulting measures shall not be applied in ways that "would constitute a means of arbitrary or unjustifiable discrimination between countries where the same conditions prevail" or in ways that constitute "a disguised restriction on international trade."[125] While the precise legal impact of these provisions on post-TRIPS state action remains to be clarified, we think they point the way to a broader principle. If the TRIPS Agreement is not to become a Trojan horse that enabled corporate distributors of private knowledge goods to disrupt the provision of global public goods, the continued exercise of WTO Members' police and welfare powers must be buttressed by an implied or express understanding that all international intellectual property standard-setting exercises presuppose a kind of de facto "article XX" limitation in reverse. States that agree to engage in such exercises cannot thereby be tacitly understood to waive or surrender these reserved powers.

On the contrary, and in conjunction with both the Preamble to the TRIPS Agreement itself[126] and article 8.1, it must be generally understood that the implementation of international IP standards is necessarily limited by criteria

---

[122] TRIPS Agreement, above n. 3, art. 8.1.
[123] *See* Howse, above n. 121, at 504. *Cf.* United States – Import Prohibition of Certain Shrimp and Shrimp Products, WT/DS/26, 69 ¶ 169 (WTO Appellate Body 12 Oct. 1998); *but see* European Communities – Measures Concerning Meat and Meat Products (Hormones), WT/DS/26, 48 ¶ 123 (WTO Appellate Body 13 Feb. 1998) (declining to evaluate impact of "precautionary principle" in international law). *See generally* JOOST PAULWELYN, CONFLICT OF NORMS IN INTERNATIONAL LAW: HOW WTO LAW RELATES TO OTHER RULES OF INTERNATIONAL LAW (Cambridge University Press 2003).
[124] *See* GATT 1994, above n. 42, art. XX(d).   [125] *See id.* art. XX.
[126] "Recognizing the underlying public policy objectives of national systems for the protection of intellectual property, including developmental and technological objectives." TRIPS Agreement, above n. 3, Preamble.

of reasonableness. These standards, as implemented, must not become disguised barriers to the exercise of those other police and welfare powers that are normally reserved to states.[127]

Where, in short, there is a conflict between private IPRs and the sovereign preservation of other public goods affecting, for example, competition, public health, sustainable agriculture, environmental protection, and the guarantees of human rights, WTO panels should respect the reserved powers of states unless they had expressly delegated their regulatory powers to some international authority or otherwise explicitly bargained them away. In the presence of any such conflict, moreover, WTO tribunals should place the burden of proof on states defending private claimants to show that their interpretation of the relevant international standards would meet these limiting criteria and would not unreasonably compromise the provision of public goods otherwise reserved to states.

III. Balancing public and private interests in an emerging transnational system of innovation

All countries could benefit from a functionally efficient transnational system of innovation if low barriers to entry enabled entrepreneurs anywhere to invest in the production and distribution of knowledge goods. The reduction of trade barriers, the broadening of global capital markets, and the relative harmonization of intellectual property standards could then channel the flow of investments to innovators wherever they were situated and enable them to access and utilize the technological inputs they needed, whether by purchase or license. These same investors could then export the resulting knowledge goods in the relative security that international minimum standards of IP law would protect their respective lead time advantages against free riding duplicators who contributed nothing to the collective costs of research and development (R&D).[128]

In such a system, public safeguards should also enable digital telecommunications networks to link the providers of scientific and technical inputs in an endless research commons.[129] Global incentives to innovate would then reward entrepreneurs who converted these inputs into value-adding, follow-on applications with unprecedented transnational payoffs.

---

[127] *Cf.* J. H. Reichman, *Securing Compliance with the TRIPS Agreement after* U.S. v. India, 1 JIEL 585, 594–97 (1998) (discussing mix of national autonomy and IPR agreements in Appellate Body's decision in India – Pharmaceutical Patents decision); Graeme B. Dinwoodie, *The Architecture of the International Intellectual Property System*, 77 CHI. KENT L. REV. 993, 1005–06 (2002); Okediji, above n. 90, at 870–72.
[128] *See, e.g.,* MASKUS, IP RIGHTS, above n. 8, at 192–94; Reichman, above n. 4.
[129] *See, e.g.,* Reichman & Uhlir, above n. 28, at 356–60; *see generally* LAURENCE LESSIG, THE FUTURE OF IDEAS: THE FATE OF THE COMMONS IN A CONNECTED WORLD (2002).

In practice, however, economic realities in the post-TRIPS environment may differ significantly from these potential outcomes.[130] Objective difficulties of accessing technical information generated abroad and of adapting it to local conditions still hamper the catch-up activities of firms in developing countries. International IP standards augment these difficulties by elevating the cost of inputs and by making the task of reverse engineering by honest means more costly and sometimes impossible. Additional obstacles arise when high prices charged for foreign technologies make locally produced goods uncompetitive, when foreign suppliers refuse to license needed technology at all, or when they impose unreasonable terms and conditions that restrict exports and otherwise create barriers to entry.[131]

We do not mean to overstate the case or to sound unduly pessimistic. The reform of the worldwide intellectual property system has undoubtedly improved the infrastructure supporting the exchange of knowledge goods, and researchers have begun empirically to evaluate the positive contribution to economic growth this makes possible.[132] The case of the Indian software industries, for example, shows just how fast small- and medium-sized industries in developing countries can catch up once the relevant technical know-how becomes embedded in an appropriate commercial environment.[133] Impressive technological gains have also occurred in many other countries, including Brazil, China, and South Africa.

The point is that, as a rudimentary transnational system of innovation begins to take shape, it consists of many different components at different levels of development whose intellectual property needs and interests vary considerably. If, indeed, one looks beyond the North–South conflict of interests that informed yesterday's debates about IP standards, one might better view the developing countries today as territorial economic arenas in which a proportionately larger collection of small- and medium-sized entrepreneurs operate without the benefits of basic research results available to their counterparts in developed countries.

---

[130] *See, e.g.*, CIPR, above n. 10, at 20–29; Drahos, above n. 5; Ullrich, above n. 45.
[131] *See, e.g.*, CIPR, above n. 10, at 24–26; Barton, above n. 58, at 60–64; Correa, above n. 29.
[132] *See* MASKUS, IP RIGHTS, above n. 8; ARORA ET AL., above n. 26.
[133] These industries benefited particularly from a previous brain drain and from the resulting return of know-how to the poorer country of origin. Moreover, much of the basic research results emanating from government-funded scientific and educational institutions in developed countries, particularly the United States, do become at least nominally available through digital telecommunications networks to scientists, innovators, and entrepreneurs even in the poorest and most remote countries. *See generally* Reichman & Uhlir, above n. 28, Part II (mapping the public domain for research results, and describing the legal infrastructure that supports it). Skills needed to adapt such results to the production of locally suitable knowledge goods are obtainable on the international labor market, and they seem likely to emerge on local labor markets as well in response to the heightened production of such goods.

While the technical expertise of such firms lags well behind that of similarly sized firms that drive innovation in, say, the United States, these are differences of degree, not kind. All such firms tend to have more in common with each other than they do with the large multinational companies that are often not very innovative at all, but mainly powerful distributors of innovation originating from smaller, more dynamic firms.

Like the biggest firms, small- and medium-sized entrepreneurs – wherever situated – need IPRs to appropriate the fruits of their investments at home and to facilitate sales, licensing, and direct investments abroad. They also need these rights to defend themselves from the predatory practices of the large multinationals.[134] However, these firms would logically oppose the drive for TRIPS plus levels of intellectual property protection that tended to expand and multiply exclusive rights, limit access to the research commons, and diminish the space for reverse engineering or other pro-competitive strategies built around value-adding applications of new technologies.[135]

A. Developing countries as defenders of the competitive ethos

Because a disproportionately large number of such entrepreneurs may be located in developing countries, governments in those nations could become the defenders and promoters of a transnational system of innovation in which properly balanced intellectual property rights were not ends in themselves, but rather the means of generating more scientific and technical inputs into a healthy competitive environment. To the extent that these governments represented the interests of both consumers and follow-on innovators, they would want to maintain the flows of publicly available scientific and technical information that traditionally fueled innovation in the United States; to preserve and strengthen the rights to reverse-engineer routine innovations by proper means; to foster the exchange of technical know-how between innovators at work on common technical trajectories; and to ensure that regulatory solutions to overcome market failure did not create barriers to entry or otherwise impoverish the public domain.[136]

To this end, the developing countries need to integrate the international IP standards codified during the Uruguay Round into their national and regional systems of innovation in ways that maximize the benefits and minimize the social costs. This difficult and financially burdensome task requires them to master and defend the flexibilities still residing in the TRIPS Agreement; to match those flexibilities with their respective, often widely different innovation assets and other comparative advantages; and to forge a pro-competitive

---

[134] *See, e.g.*, Herbert Hovenkamp et al., *Anticompetitive Settlements of Intellectual Property Disputes*, 87 MINN L. REV. 1719 (2003).
[135] *See, e.g.*, Correa, above n. 22, at 544–49.
[136] *See, e.g.*, UNCTAD, THE TRIPS AGREEMENT AND DEVELOPING COUNTRIES 15–28 (1996).

strategy with respect to the technologically more advanced countries, within the confines that the WTO Agreement makes legally possible.[137]

To succeed in this endeavor, there are at least three necessary, if not sufficient pre-conditions. First, developing countries as a group need to halt or opt out of new international intellectual property standard-setting exercises that would only complicate their task and narrow their options. Second, they will need to rationalize their decision-making and interagency governance structures so as to coordinate the activities of their intellectual property bureaus with policy decisions affecting the design of their national systems of innovation. Third, they will have to dedicate significant efforts and resources to conserving and promoting those public goods that are increasingly undersupplied in developed countries but that remain indispensable to rapid technological and overall social progress in developing countries.

1. A moratorium on stronger international intellectual property standards

Building an effective transnational system of innovation is a sobering task because the choice and disposition of optimal incentive structures have become increasingly uncertain in both theory and practice, especially as regards new technologies,[138] and because neither high-protectionist interests in developed countries nor low-protectionist interests in developing countries could be expected to advocate principles appropriately balancing the needs of innovators with those of followers.[139] From this perspective, further harmonization is not an improper goal, but rather a premature exercise under the new and uncertain conditions that attend the development of cutting-edge technologies generally and information-based technologies in particular.

Here the single most daunting problem is how to allocate public and private interests in such goods, given that their raw materials – information – necessarily perform a dual function as both outputs and inputs of a "cumulative and sequential" innovation process.[140] As matters stand, the complex nature and

---

[137] *See generally* Reichman, *From Free Riders to Fair Followers,* above n. 20.

[138] *Compare, e.g.*, Richard Epstein, *Steady the Course: Property Rights in Genetic Material*, in PERSPECTIVES ON PROPERTIES OF THE HUMAN GENOME PROJECT, above n. 49, at 153–93, *with* Rochelle Cooper Dreyfuss, *Varying the Course in Patenting Genetic Material: A Counter-Proposal to Richard Epstein's Steady Course*, in PERSPECTIVES ON PROPERTIES OF THE HUMAN GENOME PROJECT, above n. 49, at 195–208 *and* Reichman, *Saving the Patent Law from Itself,* above n. 49. *See generally* Dan L. Burk & Mark A. Lemley, *Policy Levers in Patent Law,* 89 VA. L. REV. 1575 (2003).

[139] *See esp.* Okediji, above n. 90, at 825–72 (discussing some theoretical implications of multilateral IP negotiations).

[140] *See, e.g.*, Niva Elkin-Korin, *A Public Regarding Approach to Contracting over Copyrights*, in EXPANDING THE BOUNDARIES OF IP, above n. 41, at 191, 195–98; Richard R. Nelson, *Intellectual Property Protection for Cumulative Systems Technology,* 94 COLUM. L. REV. 2674 (1994); Reichman & Franklin, above n. 70, at 884–99.

pace of cutting-edge innovation so outstrips the conventional assumptions of the patent and copyright paradigms handed down from the nineteenth century that disinterested economists and policymakers in the most technologically advanced countries lack both the experience and the evidence to draw these lines with confidence.

Contrary to the special interests' relentless propaganda, in other words, intellectual property law has not arrived at the end of history. On the contrary, the turmoil generated by the TRIPS Agreement and its aftermath, including the WIPO Copyright Treaties,[141] suggests that we stand at the threshold of an era in which unanswered questions about the role of IPRs in a networked information economy demand a lengthy period of "trial and error" experimentation, like that which ensued after the adoption of the Paris and Berne Conventions in the 1890s.

In order to validate empirically the loose claims made for and against different modes of protection, we will thus need a period of time in which states at different levels of development accommodate existing international standards to their own nascent or evolving systems of innovation.[142] This would yield a new body of "laboratory effects," to use Ladas's phrase, with which to compare and test different development strategies.[143] In the long run, the resulting empirical data could make it possible for states to trade further intellectual property concessions on a win-win basis, without coercion and with fewer risks that powerful interest groups had rigged the rules to lock in fleeting competitive advantages.

The time has come, in short, to take intellectual property off the international law-making agenda and to foster measures that better enabled developing countries to adapt to the challenges that prior rounds of harmonization had already bred.[144] Such a moratorium would then enable both high and low protectionist countries to test their respective strategies against actual results without fear that the market openings nominally available to developing country entrepreneurs would be foreclosed by premature, ill-advised, or unbalanced efforts to re-regulate that same marketplace at their expense.

A "time out" along these lines would make it possible, for example, to evaluate growing fears that overprotection of research results in developed countries will produce anti-commons effects and lost competitive opportunities likely to retard the pace of innovation over time. It would allow

---

[141] *See* above n. 6.

[142] *Accord*: John F. Duffy, *Harmony and Diversity in Global Patent Law*, 17 BERKELEY TECH. L.J. 685, 709–25 (2002); *see also* Boyle, above n. 49.

[143] STEPHEN P. LADAS, PATENTS, TRADEMARKS AND RELATED RIGHTS – NATIONAL AND INTERNATIONAL PROTECTION 9–16 (1975); *see also* Graeme B. Dinwoodie, *A New Copyright Order: Why National Courts Should Create Global Norms*, 149 U. PA. L. REV. 469, 514–15 (2000); Graeme B. Dinwoodie & Rochelle Cooper Dreyfuss, above n. 81.

[144] *Cf.* LADAS, above n. 143, at 15 (criticizing "trend toward viewing 'harmonization' as a good thing no matter what the problems are, as an end in itself" and stressing costs to single nations that may make it "simply undesirable or impracticable").

room for any countries so inclined to experiment with alternative forms of protecting investment, including proposals for more open-source initiatives[145] and for compensatory liability regimes that could reconstitute the shrinking semi-commons that historically mediated between exclusive intellectual property rights and the public domain.[146] It would allow time for the worldwide scientific community to reformulate its data exchange policies and to reconstruct contractually the public domain for scientific and technical information that has recently come under a privatizing assault.[147]

A moratorium on stronger international intellectual property standards would especially help developing countries shift their attention and limited resources away from compliance-driven initiatives[148] toward programs to potentiate their national and regional systems of innovation. It would, for example, give them time to adapt promising new initiatives to their own environments, such as programs to encourage the transfer of technology from universities and public research centers to the private sector, which have produced mixed results in the United States.[149] It would also give them breathing room in which to formulate competition laws and policies rooted in fairness, in concerns to lower barriers to entry, and in the need to ensure that market-induced transfers of technology were not thwarted by refusals to deal and unreasonable licensing terms or conditions.[150]

Efforts to institute such a moratorium could, however, run up against legitimate concerns in developed countries to prohibit free riding on investments in new technologies that enter the global marketplace. Developing countries that demand a moratorium on stronger intellectual property standards must therefore remain willing to oppose free-riding practices that undermine incentives to invest in new technologies everywhere.[151] A willingness to accommodate legitimate concerns about free riding could defuse potentially heated conflicts and remove controversial topics, such as database protection,

---

[145] *See, e.g.,* Yochai Benkler, *Coase's Penguin,* 112 YALE L. REV. 369 (2002); *see also* Creative Commons *available at* http://www.creativecommons.org.

[146] Reichman, *Green Tulips,* above n. 71; Jerome H. Reichman & Tracy Lewis, *Using Liability Rules to Stimulate Local Innovation in Developing Countries: Application to Traditional Knowledge* [this volume].

[147] *See* above nn. 28, 129 and accompanying text.

[148] *See, e.g.,* Peter Gerhart, *Distributive Values and Institutional Design in the Provision of Global Public Goods* [this volume]; *Beyond the Treaties: A Symposium on Compliance with International Intellectual Property Law,* 32 CASE W. RES. J. INT'L L. 357 (2000).

[149] *See* Rai & Eisenberg, above n. 104.

[150] *See, e.g.,* Ullrich, above n. 45; Correa, above n. 29.

[151] It was a failure to recognize a need to protect research and development investments in innovative technologies against unbridled free riding that led developed countries to demand adoption of the TRIPS Agreement within the WTO framework in the first place. *See, e.g.,* Gail E. Evans, *Intellectual Property as a Trade Issue: The Making of the Agreement on Trade Related Aspects of Intellectual Property,* 18 WORLD COMPETITION, L. & ECON. REV. 137 (1994). This mistake should not be repeated.

from a more ambitious standard-setting agenda.[152] It would also reinforce the credibility of a demand for a moratorium on further harmonization efforts by accompanying it with a "clean hands" doctrine that would reassure investors in all countries.

  2. An institutional infrastructure for reconciling existing IPRs with national and regional systems of innovation

The minimum international standards of intellectual property protection already mandated by the TRIPS Agreement are not uniform law, and WTO Members retain considerable flexibility in the ways those standards can be incorporated into their domestic legal systems.[153] The challenge for every developing country is to enact laws and implement policies that, while consistent with international minimum standards, also effectively promote national development priorities.[154] In so doing, single governments should also take into account the possibilities of cooperative actions or strategies that could reduce the overall social and economic costs of compliance with those obligations for any given region as a whole.

All developing countries should accordingly consider the feasibility of establishing a high-level, permanent working group on trade-related innovation policies, which could become the focal point for interagency review with respect to the integration into domestic law of existing and evolving international legal standards affecting innovation. These working groups or advisory councils would not duplicate the activities of national IP bureaus. They should instead play a supervisory role that requires inputs from those bureaus but that subjects policy-making decisions of importance to a suitable interagency review process concerned with national development strategy.[155]

---

[152] See, e.g., Reichman, *Database Protection*, above n. 41 (proposing interim international agreement against wholesale duplication).
[153] See UNCTAD, THE TRIPS AGREEMENT AND DEVELOPING COUNTRIES, above n. 136, at 32; World Bank, Global Economic Prospects and the Developing Countries 2002, above n. 22, at 140–44.
[154] See Reichman, *Free Riders to Fair Followers*, above n. 20. Mastering the legal and economic challenges of the standards mandated under the WTO Agreements further requires that countries should, in general, avoid adopting "off the rack" model laws that may codify or embody objectives different from those likely to accommodate their own needs. See generally J.H. Reichman, Ruth Okediji, and Jayasharee Watal, Draft UNDP Flagship Program on Innovation, Culture, Traditional Know-How and Bioresources, prepared for the Special Unit for Technical Cooperation Among Developing Countries (TCDC), Apr.–May 2000 [hereinafter Draft UNDP Program].
[155] This proposal was first put forward in Draft UNDP Program, above n. 154. The proposed interagency working groups could oversee the sustained training of cadres and updating of knowledge needed by governments to formulate policy options over time. They could also undertake the following additional endeavors:

Each regional or sub-regional group of developing countries should also consider the feasibility of establishing a similar working group for the purposes of coordinating positions on matters of common concern. These regional councils, once established, could benefit from the pooling of resources and expertise among their members to become centers for formulating regional standards concerning IPRs and for consensus building for future bilateral and multilateral negotiations bearing on innovation policies.

In putting forward these proposals, we make no assumptions that developing countries would think alike on the relevant issues or that members of any regional group will readily embrace a common position. The opposite is true. What experience demonstrates is that any coalition of developing country interests will be more effective than the absence of such a coalition.[156] Compromise positions staked out by regional groups can block the most egregious proposals emanating from special interest coalitions, and can sometimes even lead to universally valid intellectual property legislation of value to the developing countries.[157]

The organization of national and regional interagency working groups would reduce the dependence of developing countries on ad hoc support by foundations, NGOs, and *pro bono* legal counsel. The existence of such organizations would further ensure early detection of new protectionist initiatives, facilitate prompt reactions to them, and enable the formation of coalitions to resist them if undesirable or to modify and support them if desirable. It would also make it possible to appoint subcommittees that could follow ongoing initiatives at WIPO and the WTO, and support the work of permanent delegations and regional political caucuses at these and other intergovernmental organizations on a continuing basis.

Above all, the existence of national and regional working groups on trade-related innovation policies would enable developing countries to formulate broad-based strategies to resist pressures at the bilateral and multilateral levels for undesirable demands for protection. Collective action to resist such pressures seems more likely to succeed than leaving each state to fend for itself, in

---

Coordinate activities to enable consensus building at the national level;

Support the training and sensitization of law enforcement officials to ensure a cadre of skilled personnel in each developing country and to formulate regional enforcement standards based on national positions;

Coordinate inter-council activities with a view to identifying best practices and models for adaptation by other countries and to facilitating consensus building at the regional level;

Support the activities of national, regional and international nongovernmental organizations (NGOs), which identify with the mission of the advisory councils.

See id.

[156] See, e.g., Abbott, above n. 53, at 42–43; Okediji, above n. 90, at 842–61 (discussing role of coalitions in TRIPS negotiations).

[157] See, e.g., Samuelson, above n. 6.

which case there is simply no institutional infrastructure for promoting a systematic and coordinated response to what has become a systematic and coordinated drive to re-regulate the global economy.

B. Maintaining the supply of knowledge as a global public good

Critical to the future success of an emerging transnational system of innovation is its ability to ensure the production and adequate supply of needed public inputs known to have fueled the production of private knowledge goods in the technologically most advanced economies.[158] This topic is relatively new and extremely complex, and the need for collective international action has been inadequately studied.

1. Dynamic properties of knowledge as a global public good

In thinking about the uncertain properties of knowledge as a global public good, the intimate and complex relationship between knowledge and trade requires particular attention, especially in light of the TRIPS Agreement and related issues that were previously discussed. In principle, international trade law rooted in the GATT and the WTO Agreement should stimulate worldwide competition in the provision of goods and services generally, including knowledge goods. At the same time, qualitative leaps in knowledge as a product of aggregate investment in R&D also depend on private intellectual property rights, especially patents, which deliberately restrain trade in the short run in order to elevate the level of competition later on.[159]

In this process, knowledge plays at least a triple role. Existing knowledge fuels the production of additional knowledge as an input from any commons accessible to any given set of researchers or entrepreneurs. New knowledge emerges fresh from publicly supported research endeavors, often involving massive expenditures, whence it may enter a research commons, as typically occurred in the United States, or it may attract proprietary rights of either a public or private nature.[160] Finally, new knowledge may come to light from privately funded research and development initiatives, or from public-private

---

[158] See, e.g., Michael Callon, Is Science a Public Good ?, 19 SCI. & HUM. VALUES 395, 400 (1994); Nelson, above n. 76; David, above n. 53; Stiglitz, above n. 51.

[159] John H. Barton, The Economics of TRIPS: International Trade in Information Intensive Products, 33 GEO. WASH. INT'L REV. 473, 486–91 (2001) (stressing tradeoffs between short-term costs to consumers in higher prices and long term benefits through increased innovation).

[160] See E.C. Database Directive, above n. 77; Reichman & Uhlir, above n. 28, at 325–50. The tendency of intellectual property rights to make new knowledge artificially scarce in order to reward investors then impacts on the provision of other public goods, including free trade, the preservation of the natural commons or efforts to promote public health, in ways that, as previously discussed, may trigger resentment and public outcry around the world. See above text accompanying nn. 28, 129 & 152.

partnerships. In this form, it may or may not become available as an input for open research in the future, depending upon the modalities of intellectual property protection – including permanent rights in collections of data – that investors obtain under national and international law.

Further complicating any assessment of appropriate international action affecting the provision of knowledge as a global public good is the fact that its positive role in domestic systems of innovation, though palpable and universally recognized, is not well understood nor fully elaborated. Nor do the most successful systems of innovation demonstrate any common or universal set of practices in this respect that could readily be transcribed to the international level.

In the United States, for example, especially during the Cold War period, massive amounts of federal money were spent on producing data and research, usually through universities and other scientific institutes. Under traditional U.S. law, all government-generated data automatically entered the public domain, where this gave a huge fillip to both public and private research. Most publicly funded research results likewise became widely available under both the sharing ethos of science and "open access" policies that federal funding agencies imposed.[161]

Recently, however, funds for government-generated data have shrunk; and there is a growing tendency for government agencies to license such data from the private sector under increasingly restrictive conditions. Moreover, government-funded research results are increasingly transferred to the private sector under exclusive patent rights,[162] made possible by the Bayh-Dole Act of 1980.[163] New IPRs in digital transmissions and collections of data may further augment the privatization of government-funded research at the expense of the scientific community's sharing ethos and traditional open access policies.[164]

In the European Union, in contrast, government-generated data were traditionally subject to exclusive property rights, and some recent research suggests that this practice greatly hampered development in some sectors, such as weather-related innovation.[165] At the same time, government-funded research in the E.U. is increasingly likely to be transferred to the private sector through patents, while all collections of data – including publicly funded data – have become subject to powerful and potentially permanent exclusive property

---

[161] *See generally* Reichman & Uhlir, above n. 28, at 325–50.
[162] *See id.* at 366–71; Rai & Eisenberg, above n. 104.
[163] Pub. L. No. 96–517, 6(a), 94 Stat. 3015, 3019–28 (1980) (codified as amended at 35 U.S.C. §§ 200–12 (2000)).
[164] *See* Reichman & Uhlir, above n. 28, at 361–415.
[165] Peter Weiss, *Conflicting International Public Sector Information Policies and Their Effects on the Public Domain and the Economy*, in ROLE OF SCIENTIFIC AND TECHNICAL DATA, above n. 28, at 129–32.

rights under the E.C. Directive on Databases of 1996.[166] The impact of these measures on overall research and development in the E.U. remains to be seen, but the scientific community there has voiced growing concerns.[167]

Practices with respect to the provision of knowledge as a public good in developing countries are quite different and even harder to evaluate. Here there has always been a disproportionately large reliance on the public sector, with uneven but sometimes commendable results.[168] However, efforts to open up previously "command economies" to private enterprise in these countries have put new pressures on existing modes of producing knowledge goods in the public sector, and new modes of transferring knowledge from the public to the private sector are badly needed in any case. As the drive to stimulate investments in private research and development acquires momentum in more developing countries, careful thought will have to be given to preserving and enhancing a public sector research infrastructure that was formerly taken for granted.

This brief survey confirms that ensuring the provision of knowledge as an essential public good in an incipient transnational system of innovation would be extremely difficult to manage under the best of circumstances owing to the diversity of practices among existing systems and to the changes underway within these systems. This task is made still more difficult by relentless pressures to ratchet up international standards of intellectual property protection without regard to, and often at the expense of, traditional modes of generating knowledge as a public good.

This one-sided push for privatization requires a collective response aimed at preserving the roles of both knowledge and competition as international public goods. Calibrating this response, however, is difficult precisely because national experiences in technology-exporting countries are both diverse and changing, while the challenge and problems of protecting investment in cutting-edge technologies today makes reliance on even the most successful national solutions of the past problematic.

2. Nurturing a transnational system of innovation

This perplexity gives rise to a troubling conundrum. Without an organized, collective movement to promote and enhance the supply of knowledge as a public good, the transnational system of innovation taking root in the wake of

---

[166] *See* above n. 77.
[167] Paul A. David, Will Building "Good Fences" Really Make "Good Neighbors" in Science? Digital Technologies, Collaborative Research on the Internet and the EC's Push for the Protection of Intellectual Property, Stanford Institute for Econ. Pol'y Res., Discussion Paper No. 00-33 (2000), *available at* http://www-econ.stanford.edu/faculty/workp/swpo/005.html (last visited 1 Aug. 2004); *see also* Royal Society Report, above n. 78.
[168] *See, e.g.,* Helfer, above n. 57. *See also* Cottier & Panizzon, above n. 117.

the TRIPS Agreement could become suboptimal and skewed from the outset. Yet, without a lengthy period of experimentation in both developed and developing countries, policymakers lack the experience and data to confidently design the balance of public and private interests that should prevail in that same system. This conundrum in itself constitutes a valid justification for a moratorium on international intellectual property standard-setting exercises, and it underscores the need for national and regional experiments that could shed more light on how a transnational market for knowledge goods should ultimately be structured.

To the extent that developing countries could successfully ensure that their respective systems of innovation promoted healthy competition in knowledge goods while otherwise delivering an adequate supply of public goods, they could more readily and capably articulate these same interests in multilateral negotiations affecting the future shape of a transnational system of innovation. This experience would arm them with serious counter-proposals to avoid the excesses of intellectual property protection that some developed countries have embraced.

The long-term prospects for an emerging worldwide system of innovation ultimately depend on the level of investment it attracts, on the quantity and quality of innovation it stimulates, and on the degree of healthy competition it sustains. While intellectual property law will necessarily play a crucial role in attaining positive outcomes, such a system cannot fulfill its promise if it becomes prematurely shackled by the intellectual property policies and norms favored by any particular group of powerful companies or countries. On the contrary, the evidence shows that small- and medium-sized companies continue to generate the bulk of real technological advances,[169] and any regulatory scheme developed for this system must take their needs and interests into account.

Pro-competitive pressures generated from within the emerging transnational system of innovation could then reverberate upon highly protectionist national systems in developed countries. They could embolden, if not empower, coalitions of small- and medium-sized entrepreneurs there to seize the political initiative and recalibrate the balance of public and private interests in their domestic intellectual property regimes.[170]

It is well to remember that the law and economics disciplines still know relatively little about how an incipient transnational system of innovation should best be organized and regulated in the short and medium terms. Countries big and small, rich and poor, find themselves at the start of a new era, in which serious thought and bold experimental undertakings will be

---

[169] See most recently Josh Lerner, The New New Financial Thing: The Sources of Innovation Before and After "State Street," N.B.E.R. Working Paper No. W10223 (Jan. 2004).

[170] For illustrations of measures that might be taken in developed countries without violating the TRIPS Agreement, see Dinwoodie and Cooper Dreyfuss, above n. 81.

needed to identify the optimal mix of public and private goods in this broadened but largely uncharted domain. The one sure conclusion that follows from this analysis is that hardening past experience into possibly flawed international rules to regulate this emerging transnational system should be avoided. What is needed, instead, is a long period of experimentation under pro-competitive conditions that could yield instructive "laboratory effects" comparable to those that gradually led to the progressive development of international intellectual property law after the Berne and Paris Conventions – the "Great Conventions" – were established in the 1890s.

2

The regulation of public goods

PETER DRAHOS[*]

Abstract
Introduction
I.   Public goods and preferences
II. Distinguishing public goods
III. The regulation of public goods
     A. The regulation of artifacts
     B. The regulation of skill-embodied information
     C. The regulation of norm-dependent public goods: The private shaping of public goods
IV. Preferences, power, and the regulation of public goods
Conclusion

ABSTRACT

The chapter examines the complex ways in which public goods are regulated. The provision and distribution of public goods is deeply affected by the degree of excludability of those goods and the regulatory context of that excludability. Using a decentered conception of regulation, the chapter shows through various examples how state and non-state actors regulate each other's capacities to provide, access, and distribute public goods. The chapter includes a discussion of the regulation of knowledge by the rules of intellectual property.

Introduction

Public goods range from those that are constituted by norms (peace, order, and good government) to those physical goods that provide a collective benefit independently of any norms (forests and algae that consume carbon are two examples). Such goods are typically defined in terms of two qualities: non-rivalry

---

[*] Peter Drahos is Head of RegNet, Research School of Social Sciences, Australian National University.

in consumption and non-excludability.[1] Knowledge is perhaps the quintessential public good and there has long been a fundamental debate about how best to ensure its development and distribution.

Adam Smith observed that goods of general benefit to a society would have to be funded by means of a general contribution.[2] This potentially left a large range of goods to be provided through the public budgetary process. But after the recognition that most of the real economy operated in the messy world of impure public goods, attention began to focus on ways in which public goods could be provided through some form of exclusion, thereby allowing the market to play a much greater role in the provision of such goods.[3] By focusing on the excludability of a good, economic theory began to develop the idea that groups or clubs could capture the benefits of public goods that they had funded.[4] Intellectual property rights are essentially means of permitting exclusive use to knowledge in order to encourage its further development. The focus in economics continues to be on the basic issue of the role of government in allocating resources to the production of public goods. The discussion has expanded to include issues relating to the provision of international or global public goods (for example, protection of the ozone layer, the control of epidemics, increasing agricultural yields).[5] International public goods can be distinguished by the extent to which individual contributions affect the level at which the good is supplied.[6]

Theorizing about the provision of public goods has become a long story in economics. In contrast, this chapter in short fashion draws attention to some of the ways in which public goods are regulated. Public goods have specific regulatory contexts that affect their provision as well as their distribution and uptake. The benefits of some public goods (for example, cleaner air) flow automatically while the benefits of others (for example, technical knowledge) do not. One consequence of this is that even if the problem of provision is

---

[1] ROBERT COOTER & THOMAS ULEN, LAW AND ECONOMICS 42 (Addison-Wesley Longman 3d ed. 2000); RICHARD CORNES & TODD SANDLER, THE THEORY OF EXTERNALITIES: PUBLIC GOODS, AND CLUB GOODS 3 (Cambridge University Press 1986). Non-rivalry in consumption is used by Cornes and Sandler interchangeably with indivisibility of benefits.
[2] ADAM SMITH, AN INQUIRY INTO THE NATURE AND CAUSES OF THE WEALTH OF NATIONS, Book IV, ix. 52 (R.H. Campbell & A.S. Skinner eds., Clarendon Press 1976).
[3] See P.A. Samuelson, *Pure Theory of Public Expenditure and Taxation*, in PUBLIC ECONOMICS 108 (J. Margolis & H. Guitton eds., Macmillan 1969).
[4] CORNES & SANDLER, above n. 1, at 3.
[5] See, e.g., TODD SANDLER, GLOBAL CHALLENGES: AN APPROACH TO ENVIRONMENTAL, POLITICAL, AND ECONOMIC PROBLEMS (Cambridge University Press 1997); GLOBAL PUBLIC GOODS (Inge Kaul et al. eds., Oxford University Press 1999); Marco Ferroni, Reforming Foreign Aid: The Role of International Public Goods, OED Working Paper No. 4 (The World Bank 2000); THE WORLD BANK, WORLD DEVELOPMENT REPORT 2000/2001: ATTACKING POVERTY (Oxford University Press 2001).
[6] Todd Sandler, *Global and Regional Public Goods: A Prognosis for Collective Action*, 19 FISCAL STUD. 221, 224 (1998).

solved for a given public good, the problem of distribution may not be. Restricting access to a public good is sometimes a deliberate choice. Moreover, such restriction can be done by regulating the movement of private goods. The regulation of defense, we will see, provides examples of this. So do restrictions on use of goods embodying intellectual property. In short, the message of this chapter is that we gain a better understanding of public-good problems by locating them in their regulatory contexts.

A better understanding of those regulatory contexts rests on the adoption of a decentralized conception of regulation. This is not a claim that can be pursued here. The classical command and control conception of regulation pays insufficient attention to the complex causality of regulatory effects. Essentially, the decentralized approach sees regulation as involving a plurality of types of actors, a variety of legal and non-legal norms and the use of techniques beyond that of sovereign command by the state.[7] This decentralized understanding of regulation has become the dominant paradigm in regulatory scholarship, including the study of global regulation.[8]

Increasingly, the regulation of public goods takes place by means of global standards. When, for example, the Basel Committee on Banking Supervision issues guidelines on capital adequacy standards that are adopted by the world's banks, the stability that these and other guidelines bring to the world's financial system is a global public good. Similarly, it may be argued, albeit in a more controversial context, that a global system of intellectual property regulation encourages the international distribution of knowledge goods.

The regulatory processes that lead to the creation of international public goods may only minimally involve states. Private actors have been and remain profoundly important in the generation of standards that lead to public goods. The Plimsoll line, the line painted on the hulls of ships to show overloading, was an innovation that was globally spread by the private classification societies and underwriters of Lloyd's of London who were naturally interested in the safety of the ships they insured.[9] The rules developed by Lloyd's surveyors eventually became the foundation for the International Load Line Convention of 1930.

Generally, in the context of business regulation, states are both regulators and regulatees.[10] In the past, states have been regulated by non-state actors such as the British East India Company and financiers like the Rothschilds. Today, business organizations, such as the major accounting firms, and international organizations, such as the IMF and the WTO, in various ways regulate states.

---

[7] For an excellent overview of the decentralized understanding of regulation, *see* Julia Black, *Critical Reflections on Regulation*, 27 AUSTL. J. LEGAL PHIL. 1 (2002).

[8] For discussion of this approach in the context of global regulation, *see* William E. Scheuerman, *Reflexive Law and the Challenges of Globalization*, 9 J. POL. PHIL. 81 (2001).

[9] JOHN BRAITHWAITE & PETER DRAHOS, GLOBAL BUSINESS REGULATION 421–22 (Cambridge University Press 2001).

[10] *Id*. at 27.

States are also the objects and subjects of regulation when it comes to public goods. In various ways they regulate for the production of those goods, but also find that their capacity to regulate is affected by international organizations and that the capacity of their citizens to gain access to some public goods is regulated by other states or business organizations.

One advantage of discussing public goods from the perspective of regulation is that it enables the public goods issue to be more clearly linked to theories within the regulatory literature that move the problem of regulation beyond a simple market versus state contest. A public good is not a single good, but an effect with complex antecedents made up of a set of complementary goods (private and public) and different types of social actors. Theories recognizing that regulation is more than a two-actor play and making a virtue of regulatory innovation are more likely to provide strategies for dealing with problems relating to the supply and maintenance of public goods.[11] In relation to global public goods where there is no sovereign provider, but simply a lot of imperfect multilateral institutions, considerable innovation is needed.

The remainder of the chapter is structured in the following way. Section I contains a brief description of the standard definition of public goods and the problems that preferences pose for the production of public goods. Section II proposes some distinctions amongst public goods that influence their regulation. Using these distinctions, Section III provides some examples of the different ways in which public goods are regulated. Section IV outlines some ways in which the unequal distribution of power affects the regulation of public goods. A short conclusion then follows.

I. Public goods and preferences

The non-excludability of a good is a contingent matter. It is easier to exclude individuals from the use of a bike than it is from national defense. A combination of locks and the law do a tolerable job in the case of bikes. It is not logically impossible to exclude people from the benefits of national defense, but it is costly, both in economic and non-economic ways, to do so. Non-rivalry is an attribute that is true of some goods and not of others. It is not true of an apple, for example. Circumstances can affect whether a good is non-rivalrous in consumption. The breath of air that I take on my country walk does not for practical purposes diminish the supply available to you. It is a different matter, however, if we are trapped in a small dark space, as were the crew of the submarine Kursk, where the air supply cannot be renewed. With one class of goods, knowledge goods, non-rivalry in consumption would appear to be a necessary feature. My use of the multiplication table leaves it free for others to

---

[11] *See, e.g.,* IAN AYRES & JOHN BRAITHWAITE, RESPONSIVE REGULATION (Oxford University Press 1992).

use. Its use by me does not consume it, any more than my drawing of a rectangle on a piece of paper consumes the property of rectangularity.

In the case of purely private goods, efficiency is generally best met by market arrangements in which suppliers compete to meet consumer demands. Consumers have nothing to gain by hiding their preferences for goods. If they do so, they fail to obtain the benefit of the goods as well as failing to contribute to the possibility of further price competition. The matter is different for public goods. The costs of exclusion combined with its non-rivalrous nature make it possible for a potential consumer of the good to get its benefit without paying for it. A rational strategy for consumers is to hide their preference for the good because they will be able to free ride on its provision.

Problems of appropriation act to deter private suppliers of public goods. Public goods may also be supplied through individual voluntary acts or group cooperation. Self-interest is not the only motive that operates in individuals, but the fact that it is an important one sets limits on the extent to which voluntary arrangements can be relied upon to correct for market failure. Another response to undersupply of public goods by the market is to look to their provision by government. Government, itself a public good, allows for the creation of binding arrangements for the provision of other public goods. But here preferences also present problems. Mancur Olson's analysis of the logic of collective action provides one example.[12] Concentrated interests are more likely to organize to gain a legislative outcome than diffuse interests because concentrated interests face lower costs of organization and greater individual gains. Diffuse interests face the reverse problem.

The demand of concentrated interest groups for legislation will be affected by the relevant electoral structure. If money is important to re-election, the demands of those concentrated interests making generous donations to election campaigns are likely to be met. This logic explains why, for example, logging or mining interests can trump the preferences of citizens for higher levels of environmental public goods. The adverse impact of interest groups upon legislative output has, in the United States, led some to argue that courts ought to engage in robust judicial review of economic legislation in particular in order to lessen the effects of rent-seeking legislation.[13]

Self-interested preferences lie at the root of social dilemmas in which individuals have to choose between social cooperation and following their self-interest.[14] By following the latter they prevent the possibility of

---

[12] MANCUR OLSON, THE LOGIC OF COLLECTIVE ACTION (Harvard University Press 1965).
[13] *See* Cass R. Sunstein, *Interest Groups in American Public Law*, 38 STAN. L. REV. 29 (1985).
[14] The formal modelling of social dilemmas has become dominated by game theory. Different game forms such as Prisoner's Dilemma, Chicken game, Trust game and Leader game are used to explain the level of public goods to be found within a given

cooperation bringing about better gains for all. In the case of the public goods dilemma, individuals gain by not contributing to the production of a good from which, they reason, they will in any case get the benefits.

The commons dilemma has a similar sort of incentive structure, except that the individual now gains through taking from a common resource in an unrestrained way rather than contributing to its costs of production. The outcome is the destruction of a resource (fisheries, forest, water-supply) that all individuals would have been better off saving through cooperation. The intellectual commons also has difficult incentive problems. In contrast to the resource commons, where the gains come from taking, the gains to individuals using the intellectual commons come from acts of exclusion.[15] As the range and frequency of these acts increase, the intellectual commons ends up being underutilized. It is evident that intellectual property protection fundamentally affects incentives to exclude others from using knowledge, perhaps generating an anticommons problem.

Thus, although the incentive structure of these dilemmas is similar, they pose different regulatory challenges in terms of effectiveness and responsiveness. A standard solution to the problems of the physical commons is to grant private property rights. The intellectual commons requires a different solution since the problem lies in the exercise of property rights. In the case of the physical commons, when property rights are used as the regulatory strategy individuals gain something, whereas in the case of the intellectual commons a strategy based on restricting the right of exclusion involves individuals losing something.

Regulation based on taking something away from individuals is bound to run into considerable levels of resistance. In the case of intellectual property rights, for example, probably the first-best strategy is not to grant extensive rights in the first place. Regulation based on acts of taking (for example, compulsory licensing) is probably the second-best option in terms of effectiveness since individuals face the risk and uncertainty of losing gains.

---

context. For examples, *see* Sandler, above n. 6, at 221; Daniel G. Arce & Todd Sandler, *Transnational Public Goods: Strategies and Institutions*, 17 EUR. J. POL. ECON. 493 (2001); Scott Barrett, *International Cooperation for Sale*, 45 EUR. ECON. REV. 1835 (2001). Where game theory identifies an equilibrium that is sub-optimal in terms of the supply of a public good, new rules and institutions have to be designed. Scholars of regulation aim at an understanding of the effectiveness of norms, compliance issues, the relationship of legal norms to social practices, complementarities between different kinds of regulation and the techniques of regulation that are most likely to bring success.

[15] The tragedy of the intellectual commons is under-exploitation. *See* PETER DRAHOS, A PHILOSOPHY OF INTELLECTUAL PROPERTY 63 (Dartmouth Publishing Co. 1996). The problems of the intellectual commons have been developed in the theory of the anti-commons. *See* Michael A. Heller, *The Tragedy of the Anticommons: Property in the Transition from Marx to Markets*, 111 HARV. L. REV. 621 (1998); James M. Buchanan & Yong J. Yoon, *Symmetric Tragedies: Commons and Anticommons*, 43 J.L. & ECON. 1 (2000).

II. Distinguishing public goods

Public goods are pervasive and diverse phenomena. This is for the reason that Samuelson observes. Once one moves from the case of a pure private good, most processes and activities have some kind of consumption externality and therefore end up located in the public-good domain.[16] Everything from the humble algae floating in large numbers in the high seas to government has been identified as providing or being a public good. Aside from their pervasiveness, the "publicness" of public goods comes in degrees and is contingent on circumstances and characteristics. The degree to which the quality of non-excludability applies to a good is affected by social norms and technologies and this in turn affects where the good is at any point in time on the public goods continuum. Camera technology has raised the costs of excluding others from the use of personal image. Encryption technology has probably lowered the costs of making information excludable.

The contingent nature of public goods makes it hard to generalize about the most efficient mode of supply. Within the context of global and regional public goods, Todd Sandler has argued for a more differentiated treatment of public good problems, suggesting that the factors of differentiation are "the aggregation of the individual contributions to the public good, the number of essential participants, the range of spillovers, the pattern of benefits and costs among agents, the intertemporal character of the public good, the extent of uncertainty and the presence of a leader nation."[17]

Public goods can be classified in various ways. We have already seen that there is a distinction between pure and impure public goods and that they can be classified according to scope of effects – local, national, regional, global. It is also clear that some public goods exist independently of norms, others exist as norms and yet others are dependent for their existence on other public goods. The benefits that the humble algae provide in the form of the absorption of carbon or the benefits of the earth's atmosphere are not, in the first instance, dependent upon norms.

Constitutions are an example of public goods that are constituted by norms. They also illustrate that the production of some public goods is dependent upon the prior existence of other public goods. Constitutions enable the authoritative production of legal norms and they help bring legitimacy and stability to governments. The example of constitutions also shows that some public goods can be thought of as primary public goods, where primary means that it is rational for individuals to want more of that good rather than less. It is rational because the primary good is foundational to other goods (private

---

[16] See Samuelson, above n. 3, at 108. [17] Sandler, above n. 6, at 223.

and public) that individuals need in order to fulfill their specific goals and desires.[18]

Another distinction that matters for present purposes is between capability-independent public goods and capability-dependent public goods. The benefits that are provided by biological assets, such as algae, forests, and the ozone layer, flow automatically and are not dependent upon individuals possessing some further capability. This is not true of other classes of public goods. For example, the benefits of chemical formulae and engineering specifications do not flow automatically. Free riders wishing to make use of them have to have certain capabilities.

In the case of information there is an important distinction between codified information and uncodified information or knowledge (the two are used interchangeably in this chapter).[19] Codified information will be used here to mean information that has been externalized by means of some formal, symbolic system (for example in technical drawings, mathematical notation, in journals, paintings, patent specifications and so on). At the other end of the continuum there is uncodified information that may simply exist as information known by a single individual or as a social practice among a community.

Much traditional knowledge, for example, exists only as social practice. The example of traditional knowledge also illustrates that the distinction between codified and uncodified knowledge does not align with the distinction between secret and public information. The healing properties of turmeric, for example, have been widely known in India for centuries, but this knowledge exists largely in uncodified form.[20]

Related to the distinction between codified and uncodified information is the notion of embodiment.[21] In order to avoid a confusing overlap between codification and embodiment, we shall confine embodiment of information to two types of cases. Information can be embodied in a product or process (artifact-embodiment) or in the skill of a person (skill-embodiment).

Codified or uncodified knowledge links to artifact-embodiment or skill-embodiment in various ways. Codifed knowledge in the form of a technical drawing or a chemical formula may be embodied in a product such as a

---

[18] This sense of primary is taken from John Rawls' discussion of primary social goods. These goods overlap considerably with public goods. See JOHN RAWLS, A THEORY OF JUSTICE 92 (Oxford University Press 1973).

[19] For a comprehensive discussion of this distinction, see THOMAS A. MANDEVILLE, UNDERSTANDING NOVELTY: INFORMATION, TECHNOLOGICAL CHANGE AND THE PATENT SYSTEM 49–57 (Ablex Publishing Corp. 1996).

[20] Knowledge about the use of turmeric to heal is an example of a typical grandmother's remedy. See GRAHAM DUTFIELD, INTELLECTUAL PROPERTY RIGHTS, TRADE AND BIODIVERSITY 65 (Earthscan 2000).

[21] Mansfield, for example, observes that knowledge is embodied in methods of production, designs, products, and services. EDWIN MANSFIELD, THE ECONOMICS OF TECHNOLOGICAL CHANGE 3–4 (W. W. Norton & Co. 1968).

piece of furniture or a medicine. Uncodified knowledge may also be the subject of artifact-embodiment. Eccentric Englishmen who rebuild Roman weapons, such as the trebuchet, rediscover a lot of uncodified knowledge. Information that is embodied as a skill may be codified. For example, the skills of a worker may be studied and codified in software that is in turn used to drive a robotic product that models those skills.

The degree of codification of information and its type of embodiment affect the public-good qualities of information in important ways. Information that has been codified and is artifact-embodied may involve lower acquisition cost for potential users than other information. It is cheaper to copy a CD put out by a rock band than to go to their concert and record their performance. Not all codified and artifact-embodied information exhibits public-good qualities. For example, the small Australian firm CEA Technologies supplies radar equipment to the US Navy. Despite the high level of sophistication of its technology, CEA does not own a single patent.[22] The schematics that underpin its various radar and communications technologies are highly codified but kept secret. Competitors can reverse engineer the products to obtain the schematics, but this is costly and time-consuming. By the time competitors have achieved it, CEA has innovated, and competitors are left with yesterday's technology.

The degree of codification of information can also affect its quality of non-rivalry. Information is sometimes uncodified and embodied within an individual in a way that it is not separable from that individual (such as a special skill or talent). Potential users of information in this form are faced with a zero-sum game. A good example is the scramble for German scientific talent after World War II. Once it had dawned on the United States and the United Kingdom that the acquisition of German hardware was not enough to enable them to appropriate the technology, there followed a rush to grab key German scientists.[23] This was a zero-sum game, for once the United States acquired Werner von Braun and his team of rocket scientists, others lost them.

In summary, we have the following set of distinctions. Public goods may be norm-independent or norm-dependent and they may be capability-independent or capability-dependent. Some public goods are primary goods in that they are essential gateways to other kinds of public goods. In the case of information, its public-good qualities will be strongly affected by the degree of the codification of the information and its type of embodiment. Figure 1 schematically summarizes these distinctions as they relate to information. The

---

[22] Stated by the CEO of CEA Technologies in his presentation at the 2002 Defence Intellectual Property Conference, Canberra, Australia, 9 May 2002.
[23] For an account, *see* TOM BOWER, THE PAPERCLIP CONSPIRACY: THE BATTLE FOR THE SPOILS AND SECRETS OF NAZI GERMANY (Michael Joseph 1987).

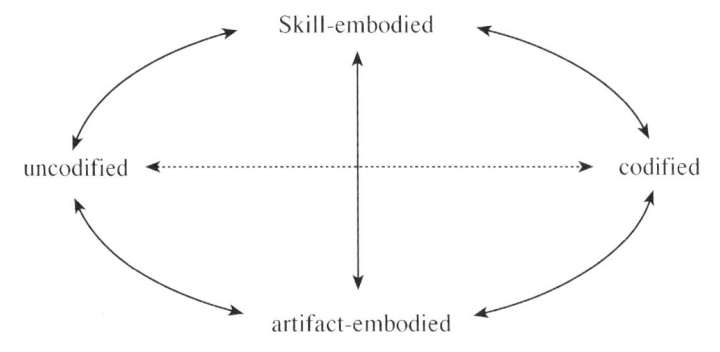

```
              Skill-embodied
                    ↑
     ↙        ↑           ↘
uncodified ←--------+--------→ codified
     ↖        ↓           ↙
                    ↓
             artifact-embodied
```

Figure 1

arrows indicate that, in some cases, by gaining access to information in one form it is possible to gain access to it or related information in other forms.[24]

III. The regulation of public goods

In this section, I discuss aspects of regulating public goods in their various forms, accounting for the interrelationships among them.

A. *The regulation of artifacts*

Defense used to be presented as the paradigmatic instance of the pure public good, but it has come to be seen as an impure public good.[25] Defense is an interesting example of a public good because it shows how states are not just regulators of public goods but, in turn, have their sovereign capacities to provide such goods regulated by other states. Defense is an example of a knowledge-intensive industry. In the case of the United States, investment in defense-related research is a dominant strategy – the country will continue to invest regardless of what other states do.[26] Knowledge, depending on what has been done about its excludability, can fall into the category of an impure or a pure public good. It follows that a state, such as the United States, which invests heavily in knowledge generation in the defense sector, faces potential free-riding problems.

---

[24] The extent to which one form of information can act as a gateway to others is set by regulation. Whether a manufacturer, for example, can use the artifact to gain access to the other three forms depends on the law of reverse engineering. *See* Pamela Samuelson & Suzanne Scotchmer, *The Law and Economics of Reverse Engineering*, 111 YALE L.J. 1575 (2002).

[25] CORNES & SANDLER, above n. 1, at 4.

[26] ETHAN BARNABY KAPSTEIN, THE POLITICAL ECONOMY OF NATIONAL SECURITY: A GLOBAL PERSPECTIVE 171 (McGraw-Hill 1992).

As it happens, this is a case where free riding does not deter investment, but it does make it rational for the United States to look at ways in which to regulate the acquisition of that knowledge by other nations. Over the years, one regulatory strategy that has been used targets the actual movement of the relevant technological product. A piece of defense technology is an example of artifact-embodiment. The artifact potentially presents a path to the codified information that is embodied in the technology, some of the uncodified knowledge (this may be deduced or learned through the process of reverse engineering) as well as the skills relevant to the making of the artifact. One way in which states with leading-edge technologies seek to restrict access to information about defense-sensitive technologies is to impose controls on the movement of the technologies.

In the United States, for example, the Bureau of Export Administration regulates the export of encryption technologies that have military uses.[27] An elaborate structure for controlling the movement of defense technologies was set up in 1949. Known as the Coordinating Committee (CoCom), its aim was to prevent U.S., Japanese, and Western European companies from selling militarily useful technology to Soviet bloc countries.[28] Under the Atoms for Peace Initiative, announced in 1953, the United States released large amounts of technical data and supplied materials related to the production of nuclear energy to states that agreed to controls to ensure that the materials would be used for peaceful purposes.[29]

Defense is an example of restrictions on the movement of products aimed at preventing others from gaining the benefit of a public good. But there are cases where restrictions on the movement of goods might form part of a regulatory strategy that aims at increasing the range of those who benefit from a public good. One illustration of this occurs in the pharmaceutical sector. The benefits of R&D that takes place in large multinational companies on diseases that affect developing country populations can be extended to those populations (or part of them) by preventing the cheap drugs that are supplied to those countries from being re-exported to high-priced markets that are also supplied by those companies.[30]

There are also examples where restrictions on access to a physical good defeat a broader policy goal of providing a public good. For example, the deposit of microorganisms under the Budapest Treaty on the International Recognition of the Deposit of Microorganisms for the Purposes of Patent Procedure has given rise to a system of International Depositary Authorities

---

[27] Matthew Crane, *U.S. Export Controls on Technology Transfers*, DUKE L. & TECH. REV. 30 (2001).

[28] One of the best studies of CoCom is STUART MACDONALD, TECHNOLOGY AND THE TYRANNY OF EXPORT CONTROLS: WHISPER WHO DARES (Macmillan 1990).

[29] BRAITHWAITE & DRAHOS, above n. 9, at 297.

[30] Keith E. Maskus, *Ensuring Access to Essential Medicines: Some Economic Considerations*, 20 WIS. INT'L L.J. 563, 569 (2002).

and detailed procedures that make gaining access to deposited microorganisms (and therefore information about them) difficult.

B. *The regulation of skill-embodied information*

The skills that are embodied in individuals are regulated in various ways. Firms do so by means of private law, such as contract. They do so because, as Arrow observed, it is the firm's workers that "carry the firm's information base."[31] The skill that a person has can be bought and sold in a market and is in this way a private good. But skills relate to public goods in various ways. Obviously the exercise of skill may lead to creation of new public goods. Some public goods, as we saw earlier, are capability-dependent, meaning they require skills for effective use. The rules of the road rely on citizens being able to read traffic signs. The concentration of scientists in least-developed countries tends to be very low, setting limits on the technical capability of these countries to make use of knowledge, even if it is delivered as a pure public good. Of more immediate value to these countries are subsidized private goods (such as medicines).

The regulation by states of skilled labor through immigration policies, education policies, employment law, and intellectual property law all play a key role in the acquisition by states of capabilities that allow them to generate new public goods or to access public goods provided by other states. Immigration policies, for example, can encourage flows of skilled workers around the globe. One feature of these flows is the brain drain from developing countries to developed countries, something that has been of concern to developing country governments for many decades.[32]

The brain-drain problem raises some important issues from the point of view of public goods. Clearly, developing country governments that invest in education will lose the social payoff of this investment if large numbers of skilled workers leave for better conditions in developed countries. The loss of skilled workers also impacts negatively on a country's capacity to absorb technology transfer since the presence of scientific and technical knowledge embodied in professional networks is key to successful technology transfer and further development.[33]

Trade secret law and employment law also have important effects on the diffusion of knowledge within an economy. The transfer of knowledge and technology within liberal market economies is heavily dependent upon the

---

[31] Kenneth J. Arrow, *in* MICHAEL PERELMAN, CLASS WARFARE IN THE INFORMATION AGE 59 (St. Martin's Press 1998).
[32] *See* the various UN resolutions cited in Jagdish Bhagwati, *The International Brain Drain and Taxation, in* THE BRAIN DRAIN AND TAXATION: THEORY AND EMPIRICAL ANALYSIS, II 3 (Jagdish Bhagwati ed., North-Holland Publishing Company 1976).
[33] Barry Bozeman, *Technology Transfer and Public Policy: A Review of Research and Theory*, 29 RES. POL'Y 627, 649 (2000).

movement of skilled labor.[34] The fluidity of this market is itself affected by rules that determine what information employees may use when they switch to another employer and under what conditions.

Public goods, as these examples show, cluster in important ways. Furthermore, they may or may not function as complementary goods. If, for example, the efficiency of or returns from one public good is improved by the presence of another, they can be said to be complementary.[35] The economic and social returns from intellectual property systems, for instance, are affected by other public goods, such as education. Strong intellectual property regimes that deliver the public good of knowledge through the market have their efficiency improved if they are complemented by labor markets that allow skilled workers to move among firms. Here, restrictions on the use of codified information are counterbalanced by regulation that allows for the movement of skill-embodied information.

Institutions can also be mismatched thereby leading to inefficiencies. Imposing higher standards of intellectual property protection on developing countries that suffer from severe shortages of skilled labor means that intellectual property rights are less likely to achieve their incentive effects and may simply worsen a developing country's terms of trade.

Markets are dependent upon a range of primary public goods that come in the form of rules and institutions (the rule of law, contract, property, banking, corporations, securities and stock exchanges). A flourishing capitalism equipped with such institutions allows entrepreneurs the freedom to act and to create the spontaneous ordering that is said to characterize markets. The regulation of public goods that serve as inputs into the exercise of skill by individuals also has important effects on these processes of spontaneous ordering. For example, over time societies have evolved different regulatory models for the intellectual commons (an information commons). An intellectual commons can be negative (open to individual appropriation) or positive (in the co-ownership or co-use of all and not open to appropriation) and inclusive (open to all) or exclusive (open to a select group).[36]

The relationship between the different types of commons and market processes of ordering are not especially well understood, but there is little doubt that there are important connections. Take, for example, computer gaming culture. When individuals purchase games, such as Blizzard Entertainment's Warcraft or Diablo, they are also given the use of a set of tools with which to construct new game scenarios. When the Warcraft game

---

[34] Peter A. Hall & David Soskice, *An Introduction to Varieties of Capitalism*, in VARIETIES OF CAPITALISM: THE INSTITUTIONAL FOUNDATIONS OF COMPARATIVE ADVANTAGE 31 (Peter A. Hall & David Soskice eds., Oxford University Press 2001).
[35] Peter Hall and David Soskice define institutional complementarities in this way. *See id.* at 17.
[36] *See* DRAHOS, above n. 15, at 57–60.

addict creates a hot new scenario it can be sent to other players, taken to gaming centers or uploaded onto battle.net, the company's free online game service.

Battle.net is an intellectual commons in which players try out the many different scenarios provided by other players or by Blizzard itself. Players are given the option of downloading the scenarios they use. Games of this kind have led to the formation of loyal user communities that become important resources for the firms that design the games in the first place. Sequels to Blizzard's games sell fast and in the millions of copies.

The strategy of using a commons to help build a community of users has been around for a while. Before it became the biggest patenter of software algorithms, IBM in the 1950s made its source code available to all programmers and encouraged them to share and modify the software that ran on its mainframes.[37]

Although a commons can be structured in different ways, typically it is linked to a narrative of joint enterprise. Individuals that share similar values and sensibilities are drawn in by the narrative and so begin a process of community formation. The commons and its accompanying narrative trigger a sequence that leads to the formation of social norms, a group and group identity. As gaming culture and the free software movement have shown, a commons and its narrative can initiate processes of ordering that see the skills and knowledge of individuals harnessed in exciting and economically significant new ways.

One of the interesting features of information economies is that, just as the role of intellectual commons in processes of production are being recognized, those commons are the subject of increasing formal regulation. The regulation is predominantly private in nature through facilitative forms of law, such as contract and intellectual property.[38] The effects of this are not easy to predict.[39] Some forms of commons and intellectual property rights can coexist and are in fact complementary. Blizzard Entertainment, for example, creates its common within a framework of intellectual property rights. In other cases intellectual property rights allow for command and control style interventions that disrupt commons-initiated processes of production that are based on an absence of intellectual property.[40]

---

[37] PETER DRAHOS & JOHN BRAITHWAITE, INFORMATION FEUDALISM 170 (Earthscan 2002).

[38] Facilitative forms of law on the classical view are seen as non-coercive, but thinkers associated with the American Realist movement developed a different view of facilitative regulation. For a discussion, see Robert B. Seidman, *Contract Law, the Free Market, and State Intervention: A Jurisprudential Perspective, in* STATE, SOCIETY AND CORPORATE POWER 17–39 (Marc R. Tool & Warren J. Samuels eds., Transaction Publishers 2d ed. 1989).

[39] On the causal and moral complexity of the relationship between intellectual property and the public domain, see William Van Caenegem, *The Public Domain: Scienta Nullius?*, 6 EUR. INTELL. PROP. REV. 234 (2002).

[40] See LAWRENCE LESSIG, THE FUTURE OF IDEAS 212–13 (Random House 2001).

C. The regulation of norm-dependent public goods: The private shaping of public goods

Some public goods, we noted earlier, exist as norms and yet others are dependent upon norms. Norms also matter to pre-existing public goods, such as biological assets in the form of forests, wildlife, and microorganisms. Here society faces the classical commons dilemma in which individuals continue to deplete these biological assets because to date various cost-internalization techniques based on taxes and property rights have not been found or implemented sufficiently well, and governments have not acted to subsidize the preservation of these public good assets at the levels that are needed.[41] The use of norms, especially legal norms, to erect exclusionary barriers to public goods can in certain cases, such as environmental assets, lead to efficiency gains. In other cases making a public good excludable leads to efficiency losses. The recent extension of the copyright term in the U.S. is a case in point.[42] Social norms, efficiency, and public goods line up in complex contingent ways.

The use of norms by government to change the character of existing public goods or to create new ones also faces a powerful critique in the economic analysis of group behavior that started with Olson's analysis (described in Section I) of the logic of collective action. Olson applied this logic to account for the different economic performances of nations.[43] There Olson spells out a number of implications of his theory, including the fact that countries by and large will not have enough organized groups to allow optimal bargaining to take place, that small groups retain disproportionate organizational power, and that such groups "reduce efficiency and aggregate income" within societies.[44]

Olson's analysis leads to the conclusion that many of the public goods that are supplied by government line up with private rather than public interest. The economic growth problems of societies, especially stable societies, stem not from an underproduction of public goods, but an overproduction. The solution lies in eliminating much of the law and regulation that relates to economic production.[45]

Whether or not Olson's theory is generalizable to explain differing economic growth rates of nations is not a question for this chapter to answer.[46]

---

[41] For a discussion, *see* Christopher D. Stone, *What to Do about Biodiversity: Property Rights, Public Goods, and the Earth's Biological Riches*, 68 S. CAL. L. REV. 577 (1995).

[42] For a discussion, see Wendy J. Gordon, *Authors, Publishers, and Public Goods: Trading Gold for Dross*, 36 LOY. L.A. L. REV. 159 (2002).

[43] OLSON, above n. 12.

[44] *Id.* at 47; *see also id.* at 74 for a list of implications.

[45] Olson would, however, keep antitrust law. *See* OLSON above n. 12, at 236.

[46] For a critical analysis, *see* HUGH STRETTON & LIONEL ORCHARD, PUBLIC GOODS, PUBLIC ENTERPRISE, PUBLIC CHOICE 68–71 (St. Martin's Press 1994).

However, it does describe quite well some processes of private organizational power that lead to the capture of rents. The business lobbying in the 1980s that eventually produced the signing of the Agreement on Trade-Related Aspects of Intellectual Property Rights (TRIPS) in 1994, as part of the package of agreements of the Uruguay Round of Multilateral Trade Negotiations is a good example of where Olson's theory has application.[47]

In the early 1980s the CEOs of Pfizer, IBM, and Du Pont, sitting on the President's Advisory Committee on Trade Negotiations, began a campaign that led to the formation of a lobbying organization (the Intellectual Property Committee) and the enrolment of European business in an international business coalition that ultimately persuaded the U.S. government and the European Community to make an international agreement on intellectual property their top priority.[48] By contrast, the users and consumers of intellectual property rights, which represented a broad and diffuse constituency, were not organizationally represented at these negotiations.

IV. Preferences, power, and the regulation of public goods

For those who believe that public goods are generally undersupplied there is, as we saw in Section I, a simple explanation in the form of the operation of self-interested preferences. In a world where self-interest is the dominant motive of citizens, game theory says that the dominant strategy of individual citizens will be not to contribute to public goods.

Self-interest is only one motive in the complex circle of motives that underpin the choices of individuals.[49] Theories that make it their sole focus tend to be weak on predictive power and look to their verification for the occasional matching case study. And as we suggested in the previous section, Olson's theory captures the TRIPS story. But Olson's theory does little to explain the rise of the hundreds of thousands of groups that make up international civil society because individuals acting voluntarily and rationally would, on his view of human motivation, never come together to create public goods for themselves, much less others.[50]

In order to explain such groups Olson's theory requires that there be some mechanism of coercion or some positive incentive for individuals to participate in the relevant group. So, if we cannot find, in the large civil society movements that fight for farmers' rights in the South, evidence of a mechanism

---

[47] Agreement on Trade-Related Aspects of Intellectual Property Rights, 15 Apr. 1994, Marrakesh Agreement Establishing the World Trade Organization, Annex 1C, LEGAL INSTRUMENTS – RESULT OF THE URUGUAY ROUND vol. 31, 33 I.L.M. 81 (1994).
[48] For a detailed account, see DRAHOS & BRAITHWAITE, above n. 37.
[49] For a discussion of this claim in the context of economic theory, see STRETTON & ORCHARD, above n. 46, chs. 1, 2.
[50] OLSON, above n. 12, at 19–20.

of coercion or promises of say, a Club Med holiday, we must conclude that the individuals in these movements are acting irrationally. By definition this makes their actions hard to understand or predict.

Another reason why public goods may be underprovided, which the focus on self-interested behavior tends to mask, lies in the role that power plays in shaping the provision and distribution of public goods. The encounters that took place between developed and developing countries over the setting of international intellectual property standards in the 1960s and 1980s illustrates this role. After World War II, many developing countries were faced with the demand for mass education and moved to provide this as a public good. One of the things they sought was a better deal from developed countries on access to textbooks in the form of a revision to the copyright standards contained in the Berne Convention. Ultimately, developing countries failed because Western publishers were able to persuade governments to block the deal that developing countries wanted.[51]

During the 1980s, the multilateral negotiations in the GATT over TRIPS were profoundly affected by the use of trade enforcement tools by the U.S. and to a lesser extent the E.C.[52] Developing countries that led the opposition to the U.S. agenda on intellectual property in the GATT were at the bilateral level systematically threatened with trade sanctions. The result of the multilateral negotiations was an agreement on intellectual property standards that required developing countries to apply the standard of excludability to knowledge goods much more extensively than they had in the past.[53] The effects of this regime shift on developing country economies will emerge over time.

More immediately, the globalization of standards of excludability will require developing countries to rethink the ways in which they regulate for provision of public goods in their respective countries. In India, for example, the regulation of pharmaceutical markets was based on an integrated strategy consisting of encouraging local production of bulk drugs by foreign firms, prohibiting the patenting of pharmaceutical products, limited patenting of pharmaceutical processes, price controls and encouraging cooperation between Indian firms and publicly funded laboratories.[54] The pharmaceuticals that arrived in the hands of Indian consumers thus were the products of a complex mix of pure and impure public goods and processes of private production and market competition.

---

[51] See DRAHOS & BRAITHWAITE, above n. 37, at 74–79.
[52] S.K. Sell, *Intellectual Property Protection and Antitrust in the Developing World: Crisis, Coercion, and Choice*, 49 INT'L ORG. 315 (1995).
[53] As Reichman points out, TRIPS standards will set "the level of competition for knowledge goods" in the global economy. See J.H. Reichman, *The TRIPS Agreement Comes of Age: Conflict or Cooperation with the Developing Countries?*, 32 CASE W. RES. J. INT'L L. 441, 442 (2000).
[54] Assad Omer, *Access to Medicines: Transfer of Technology and Capacity Building*, 20 WIS. INT'L L.J. 551, 559–60 (2002).

In the post-TRIPS environment, India's capacity to regulate for the provision of public goods has been circumscribed by patent standards that require the recognition of patents on pharmaceutical products. Under these conditions, all developing countries face a more restricted set of choices when it comes to public goods in the context of health care. They can hope that under tighter and more global standards of excludability markets will provide the public goods they need at a price they can afford. Alternatively, they will have to fund the research into pharmaceutical products as a pure public good.

Mechanisms of power and coercion are also relevant to understanding why it is that the regulation of public goods fails to respond to the demands of citizens for higher levels of some public goods. There is evidence that citizens want more public goods in the form of higher standards in areas such as food safety regulation, consumer protection, environmental protection, and nuclear safety.[55] There is also evidence that preferences for public goods are less price elastic and more other-regarding than preferences for private goods.[56]

One reason those preferences do not, at the global level, get translated into international public goods has to do with the nature of global regulatory standard-setting processes. Those processes are not based on the collection of individual preferences and global social choice. Instead they involve contests of principles between complex alliances of state and non-state actors with different mechanisms at their disposal.[57]

In environmental regulation, NGOs pursuing principles of regulation and sustainable development line up against business organizations interested in economic growth and deregulation. Moreover, some states, business organizations and multinational companies are able to draw on money and deploy mechanisms of economic coercion, such as trade sanctions, that are not available to other actors. One reason why big business is such an influential actor in areas ranging from food standards regulation to telecommunications is that it has the resources to send technical people to the thousands of standard-setting committees that end up defining the level of public goods in these areas.

Processes of regulatory globalization do sometimes result in the creation of public goods that many citizens would most probably support, but their emergence has little to do directly with those preferences.[58] The Montreal Protocol of 1987, which requires members to reduce their emission of ozone-depleting chemicals, is a global public good. Its creation was the product of a complex and fragile alliance of key U.S. multinational producers, such as Du Pont, environmental NGOs, the Reagan Administration, the Nordic countries,

---

[55] *See* the references cited in BRAITHWAITE & DRAHOS, above n. 9, at 609.
[56] Daphana Lewinsohn-Zamir, *Consumer Preferences, Citizen Preferences, and the Provision of Public Goods*, 108 YALE L.J. 377, 401 (1998).
[57] BRAITHWAITE & DRAHOS, above n. 9, at 7.
[58] Indirectly, the existence of such preferences helps to support and legitimate the work of public interest groups.

Switzerland, Canada, and the United Nations Environment Program.[59] It is a good example of how an entrepreneurship of global public goods is possible under conditions of globalization.

Conclusion

One way to understand the obstacles to the provision of public goods is by analyzing the way in which preferences and incentive structures operate. A lot can also be gained by looking at the factors that differentiate them as well as their regulatory context. Once we attend to this context, we can see that there is a range of issues that relates to both the provision and distribution of public goods. In the global regulatory context, states sometimes, in effect, have their sovereignty over the provision of public goods eroded. TRIPS and its effect on the provision of knowledge goods is a case in point. The provision of public goods may also fail if states do not have sufficient levels or kinds of primary goods that act as gateways to others. States may do much better in the provision of public goods if they match them in ways that produce complementarities. Mismatches produce a drop in efficiency.

Markets may deliver spontaneously some public goods (the free software movement), but this apparent spontaneity is itself an outcome of the regulation, both private and public, of other public goods, such as the commons. The regulation of public goods is full of surprises. Regulating the movement of private goods can inhibit, promote, or defeat the provision of a public good. Public goods are the subject of trades. In the case of nuclear regulation, one public good (technical data) was traded by the United States in order to set limits on the creation of national public goods (the use of nuclear technology for defense purposes by other states) in an attempt to achieve a global public good (non-proliferation). Mechanisms of power and coercion are fundamental to understanding the public goods that are and are not provided. Even where citizens reveal their preferences for public goods, the imperfect institutions on which they pin their hopes may fail to deliver them.

---

[59] BRAITHWAITE & DRAHOS, above n. 9, at 264–65.

COMMENTARY

Comment: Norms, institutions, and cooperation

ROBERT O. KEOHANE[*]

I am neither an economist nor an expert on intellectual property rights. Instead, I am a student of world politics. The responsibility for my being a commentator rests entirely with the editors of this volume!

What little I have to say relates mostly to Peter Drahos' very interesting chapter, since he refers to the "... imperfections of global institutions to regulate activity involving production of public goods."[1] Paul David's chapter alludes to certain problems that arise internationally – in competition between the United States and the European Union, and with respect to developing countries.[2] To that extent, my comments are relevant to his fascinating contribution as well.

1. Distinctive problems of the world political economy

In the background of both chapters is a set of problems having to do with politics at the global level, which are characterized by a lack of effective comprehensive government and a fragmentation of law. Five problems can be singled out as particularly important.

1 *Incentives* are not well-designed for efficiency. The issue of incentives is at the heart of this volume. Internationally, there are often incentives for actors to externalize the costs of their actions on those outside of their countries or economic unions. Actors also have incentives to free-ride on the accomplishments of others, unrestrained by government action.
2 *Institutions* at the global level are weak. Their rulings are often not authoritative in a meaningful, operational sense.
3 *Power* is distributed in a highly asymmetrical fashion. The United States, the European Union, and to a lesser extent large, rich states such as Japan have a great deal of influence in the World Trade Organization (WTO), in

---

[*] Robert O. Keohane is Professor of International Affairs at the Woodrow Wilson School of Public and International Affairs, Princeton University. Between 1996 and 2004, he was James B. Duke Professor of Political Science, Duke University.
[1] Peter Drahos, *The Regulation of Public Goods* [this volume].
[2] Paul David, Koyaanisqatsi *in Cyberspace: The Economics of an "Out-of-Balance" Regime of Private Property Rights in Data and Information* [this volume].

stipulation and implementation of the TRIPS agreement, and in domains not regulated by international institutions. Small, poor states have little influence: they are "policy-takers," rather than "policy-shapers." In his chapter, Paul David declares that "nothing presently compels" countries that are TRIPS signatories from not following the U.S. and European lead on intellectual property laws. From a positive political standpoint, he should have said: "Nothing but the likelihood that powerful states will otherwise employ threats and coercion" presently compels such conformity. The predictive implications of the two statements are different.

4 Much of the politics of intellectual property rights, like other international politics, revolves around *distributional issues* rather than around how to create more efficient arrangements. The salient questions are: "Who gets what, when, and how?" as Harold Lasswell entitled a book long ago.[3] To understand what is happening, one needs to examine the struggles among actors – state and nonstate – and not merely to take a bird's-eye view and, on that basis, prescribe optimal policies.

5 In the absence of authoritative government, it is difficult to arrive at solutions and avoid both bargaining deadlock and noncompliance with rules. From a game-theoretic perspective, there are always *multiple equilibria*, and often incentives of participants to hold out for better results than those on offer.[4]

When he was Secretary of State, George Schultz once observed that "nothing ever gets settled in this town." Agencies continue to fight even when they appear to have lost. This is even more true in world politics – since authoritative decisions that even appear to resolve problems are rare.

2. Strategic and institutional solutions

These problems are daunting. The classic domestic solutions of passing binding legislation are not available. But certain characteristic institutional responses, and strategies, have emerged. It is worthwhile to reflect on them.

First, as Peter Drahos points out, "... self-interest is only one motive in the complex circle of motives that underpin the choices of individuals."[5] *Norms of appropriateness* do emerge in world politics, as James March and Johan Olsen have pointed out.[6]

The more subtle point is that if certain norms emerge as dominant, even purely self-interested actors will have incentives to follow them. As in game theory, the

---

[3] HAROLD LASSWELL, POLITICS: WHO GETS WHAT, WHEN AND HOW? (Peter Smith Publishing 1990).
[4] *See, e.g.*, ROGER B. MYERSON, GAME THEORY: ANALYSIS OF CONFLICT (Harvard University Press 1991).
[5] Drahos, above n. 1.
[6] JAMES G. MARCH & JOHAN P. OLSEN, REDISCOVERING INSTITUTIONS: THE ORGANIZATIONAL BASIS OF POLITICS (Free Press 1989).

behavior of agents is affected not only by self-interest but also by their beliefs about others' beliefs. Indeed, interests are incomprehensible without an awareness of the beliefs that lie behind them. And even beliefs about beliefs can be as solid as any material interests. According to Searle, prestige, for instance, is a "social fact," like a dollar bill.[7] Although prestige is genuinely real, its importance does not lie in its material manifestation but in the beliefs people hold. Both money and prestige matter a great deal in politics, but only insofar as people hold beliefs about others' beliefs. Hence, even pure egoists will seek to mimic the behavior of principled altruists if there is a prevailing belief that behaving in this way is an essential signal that one is a trustworthy person worthy of respect.

Therefore, the inculcation of socially beneficial norms is one way to help overcome problems and achieve effective action in world politics.

Second, even if the pursuit of pure self-interest is acceptable, some bargaining and enforcement problems can be solved by getting institutional incentives right. The WTO is an illustration. States have incentives to abide by Appellate Body rulings to maintain their reputations – so that they can challenge other states' policies. And enforcement takes place horizontally – through monitoring by firms and states – rather than through a centralized policing process.

Third, institutions can help to overcome the problem of multiple equilibria by providing focal points for solutions. A prime example is the ruling of the European Court of Justice in the *Cassis de Dijon* (1979) case, in favor of "mutual recognition" as a practice in the European Community.[8] This ruling provided a focal point, selected from among many possible solutions to the harmonization problem.

Another way to overcome problems of multiple equilibria is for powerful, rich actors to choose their preferred outcome and provide side-payments to other states to join. This is what was done with respect to the international conventions and protocols on depletion of the ozone layer.[9] It was not done, toward the developing countries, with respect to gaining their cooperation on the Kyoto Protocol to deal with climate change.

Another, more indirect strategy is to manipulate the time horizons of decision-makers. It is a common strategy of courts, seeking to make constitutional law, to rule in a way that does not offend the power-holders now, but that constrains their successors. The European Court of Justice has used this strategy to enhance its authority. One commentator[10] writes:

> "Member states understood that the legal precedent established might create political costs in the future, and thus they were not fooled by

---

[7] JOHN SEARLE, THE CONSTRUCTION OF SOCIAL REALITY (Free Press 1995).
[8] Case 120/78, Rewe-Zentral A.G. v. Bundesmonopolverwaltung für Branntwein (Cassis de Dijon Case), 1979 E.C.R. 649, 3 C.M.L.R. 494 (1979).
[9] *See* RICHARD E. BENEDICK, OZONE DIPLOMACY: NEW DIRECTIONS IN SAFEGUARDING THE PLANET (Harvard University Press 1991).
[10] Karen Alter, *Who Are the "Masters of the Treaty?" European Governments and the European Court of Justice*, 52 INT'L ORG. 121, 143 (1998).

seemingly apolitical legalese or by the technical nature of law. But national governments were willing to trade off potential long-term costs so long as they could escape the political and financial costs of judicial decisions in the present."

3. Conclusions

Global institutions will remain imperfect – in the field of intellectual property rights as well as all other areas. Asymmetrical power, competing distributional interests, and weak institutionalization will make it hard to reach comprehensive agreements that enhance efficiency. But norms matter, and institutional incentives that promote effectiveness can sometimes be created. Furthermore, strategies that have worked in other areas may be promising in this one. I suggest at least considering strategies that create worthwhile focal points, offer judicious side-payments, or manipulate the time horizons of decision-makers.

3

Distributive values and institutional design in the provision of global public goods

PETER M. GERHART[*]

I. Introduction
II. Embedded distributive values
III. Distribution/policymaking at the international level
IV. A typology of distributional issues
V. A suggested approach

I. Introduction

Two interrelated issues are woven through the chapters in this volume. The first is the issue of institutional design: how should we structure the institutions that make international intellectual property law? To address this issue, we must ask such key questions as who should be invited to participate in the system; what norms, rewards, and ideals determine their incentives; what resources are they given; and what goals do they seek? The second issue relates directly to the goals of the international intellectual property system – in particular, we must decide what mix of efficiency and distributive goals we want the system to pursue. These two issues are interrelated because institutional design determines whether specified goals can be met; the output of any institutional process is very much related to the process itself.[1] We must therefore consider how we can design institutions to ensure a good match between institutional capabilities and institutional goals.

As many of the contributions to this volume suggest, distributive issues are embedded in decisions about the provision of public goods, including decisions about the provision of public knowledge goods on a global basis.[2]

---

[*] Peter Gerhart is Professor of Law, Case Western Reserve School of Law, Cleveland, Ohio.
[1] See generally NEIL K. KOMESAR, IMPERFECT ALTERNATIVES – CHOOSING INSTITUTIONS IN LAW, ECONOMICS, AND PUBLIC POLICY (1994). See also Peter Drahos, *The Regulation of Public Goods* [this volume].
[2] See, e.g., Keith E. Maskus & J.H. Reichman, *The Globalization of Private Knowledge Goods and the Privatization of Global Public Goods* [this volume]; Ruth Okediji, *Sustainable Access to Copyrighted Digital Information Works in Developing Countries* [this volume]; Carlos Correa, *Can the TRIPS Agreement Foster Technology Transfer to Developing Countries?* [this volume]; Frederick Abbott, *Managing the Hydra: The Herculean Task of Ensuring Access to Essential Medicines* [this volume].

The problem, in a nutshell, is this: because intellectual property systems use markets to allocate access to intellectual property, how might policymakers design intellectual property systems to ensure that those who lack the wherewithal to use the market have access to knowledge goods?

I want briefly to build on the particular examples of distributive issues that are raised in this volume by sharing some more general thoughts about distributive issues in the design of intellectual property systems and how those issues might be addressed. In particular, I will (1) explain the ways in which distributive issues are embedded in intellectual property policy (both nationally and internationally); (2) describe the difficulty that policymakers have in meeting both efficiency and distributive goals in the international sphere; (3) suggest a general typography of the distributional issues that are raised by the contributions to this volume, and (4) offer a suggested approach toward an institutional design that might deliver a better mix of both efficiency and distributional equity in the provision of global public goods.

II. Embedded distributive values

It may seem odd at first to talk about distributive values in the context of intellectual property; we are used to thinking of intellectual property as a system of incentives designed to correct the appropriability problem, and therefore, as an efficiency-enhancing system. A moment's reflection will clarify that view. While the central issue of intellectual property law is how to get the incentives right, once the need for appropriate incentives is identified, the distributive question asks who should pay for those incentives. That distributive question is separable from the issue of how much incentive we have to provide in order to get an efficient level of investment in inventive activity.

In fact, the general incentive issue separates into three questions. First, we must decide how much incentive to provide; second, we must separately determine whether we obtain that incentive from one group of users or another; and, finally, we must decide whether the overall package of incentive payments matches both our efficiency and our distributive goals.

Although we normally do not highlight this distributive question when we talk about national intellectual property systems, it always remains relevant. In national systems, our choice of public support for research and its relation to a patent property system depends not only on the nature of the inventive activity, but also on whether we want taxpayers or users (or both) to pay for the incentive.[3] We can choose publicly supported research when the benefits of the research are likely to be diffuse enough to justify asking taxpayers to fund it.

---

[3] In the United States, after the Bayh-Dole Act of 1980, 35 U.S.C. § 200 et seq. (2000), we have a mixed system in which the federal government funds much university research but allows the universities to patent research results. This is an explicit attempt to distribute some of the costs of the incentive to taxpayers and some to consumers.

Where the benefits are more focused, we can induce the research by granting property rights in the results; this distributes the cost of the research among those who benefit from it.

Similarly, access rights are often influenced by ability to pay. The exhaustion doctrine in copyright law gave us lending libraries, and thus supported the distributive goal of providing access to those who could not otherwise pay for copyrighted literary property. Moreover, national intellectual property systems have always been enacted against the backdrop of national systems of redistribution that shift the cost of access from poor users to the general community or even to rights owners.[4]

III. Distribution/policymaking at the international level

If, as I have suggested, distributional issues are inherent in the design of national intellectual property systems, then policymakers and analysts need to pay attention to the difference between policymaking at the national and international levels. In implementing national policy, we often create one set of institutional arrangements to achieve efficiency goals and another set of institutional arrangements to achieve distributive goals. Hence, we have a patent system for efficient incentives and a social protection system to make access available to the poor. Indeed, one hallmark of contemporary public policy at the national level is the way we segregate the domain of efficiency goals from the domain of distributive goals. For example, efficiency goals have come to fully dominate antitrust law,[5] while distributive goals that might have been incorporated into antitrust law have been relegated to policies of direct subsidization. This strategy yields certain advantages institutionally, while allowing each nation to choose the mix of efficiency and distributional values that matches its preferences and situation.

When we make policy in the international sphere, however, we encounter a different problem. We can begin consideration of institutional design and distributive goals in international institutions by recognizing one important

---

[4] Governments can achieve such redistribution through direct transfer payments, by harnessing governmental purchasing power to drive prices down, or by using price controls to guarantee access. Many industrialized countries, for example, impose price controls on patented prescription drugs. *See* Robert Weissman, *A Long, Strange TRIPS: The Pharmaceutical Industry Drive to Harmonize Global Intellectual Property Rules, and the Remaining WTO Legal Alternatives Available to Third World Countries*, 17 U. PA. J. INT'L ECON. L. 1069, 1074 (1996). Even in the United States, the federal government requires drug companies seeking Medicaid payments to provide rebates on Medicaid sale of some drugs (*see* 42 U.S.C. § 1396r-8 (2000)), and the United States Supreme Court recently upheld a Maine statute requiring even greater rebates (Pharm. Research & Mfgs. of Am. v. Walsh, 538 U.S. 644 (2003)).

[5] *See e.g.*, Mark Janis, *"Minimal" Standards for the Patent-Related Antitrust Law under TRIPS* [this volume]; Eleanor Fox, *Can Antitrust Policy Protect the Global Commons from the Excesses of IPRs?* [this volume].

facet of international policymaking – namely, that although we have developed strong international institutions for creating wealth, we have no sound institutional mechanism for determining how that wealth should be distributed.[6] Reaching distributive goals requires a strong sense of shared community values or a belief that distributional goals are important components of efficiency goals. Thus far, no real community of nations has developed, in part because the nation-state stands in its way and in part because international negotiations define success in parochial, rather than communitarian, terms. Moreover, the link between distributive goals and individual or national welfare is blurred by the prevailing ideology that a rising tide lifts all boats and by some uncertainty about how to make redistributive policies work.[7]

As a result, although institutions like the World Trade Organization (WTO) and World Intellectual Property Organization (WIPO) promote an efficient system of global trade and investment, we have found no way to tax those who benefit from the efficiency of the global system in order to support those who do not. The World Bank and the United Nations perform helpful functions in redistributing debt capital and channeling voluntary support, but they have not developed mechanisms of redistribution on the scale that is used by national governments.

One challenge we face with regard to the provision of global public goods, therefore, is to determine whether a system that promotes efficiency values but not distributive values is sustainable, and to consider whether welfare might be improved if we could achieve a better mix of efficiency values and distributive values. The issue of affordable medicine and global health policy elucidates the question, even if it does not show us a clear answer.[8]

It is not surprising, then, that so many of the contributors to this volume would highlight the forgotten issues of distributional equity when they appraise the international intellectual property system, and why they would recommend institutional arrangements to address those issues. Proposals for a

---

[6] Joel P. Trachtman, *Legal Aspects of a Poverty Agenda at the WTO: Trade Law and "Global Apartheid,"* 6 JIEL 3 (2003).

[7] *See, e.g.,* WILLIAM EASTERLY, THE ELUSIVE QUEST FOR GROWTH (2002). For many, of course, redistribution policy plays no role in international economic matters. For example, the so-called Washington Consensus – that mix of policy advice that provides the outline of policy prescriptions for developing countries – is heavily weighted toward efficiency concerns, with scant attention paid to distributive issues, either within countries or between countries. *See generally,* THE POLITICAL ECONOMY OF POLICY REFORM (John Williamson ed., Institute for International Economics 1994). Similarly, the prevailing globalization ideology that growth will come to countries that follow liberal economic policies leaves little room for redistributive policies. *See generally,* DANI RODRIK, THE NEW GLOBAL ECONOMY AND DEVELOPING COUNTRIES: MAKING OPENNESS WORK (Overseas Development Council 1999).

[8] *See, e.g.,* Abbott, above n. 2; *see also* Patricia M. Danzon & Adrian Towse, *Theory and Implementation of Differential Pricing for Pharmaceuticals* [this volume]; Gregory Shaffer, *Recognizing Public Goods in WTO Dispute Settlement: Who Participates? Who Decides?* [this volume].

Global Fund for Medicines and for mandatory transfer of technology to poor countries are but two ways of embodying the redistributive ideal by making sure that the international intellectual property system accommodates those who cannot afford access to knowledge goods that are the foundation for human welfare. How should we understand these distributional issues, and how might we design institutions that reach our distributive ideals?

IV. A typology of distributional issues

We see at least three types of distributive issues within this volume, each involving its own issue of institutional design. The first distributive issue is how the gains from exchange are to be divided. When negotiators reach a bargain, we can expect that they will maximize the gains from exchange, but by what measure do we assess how these gains are distributed between them? Because the WTO operates by allowing countries to exchange wealth-creating opportunities,[9] and because the TRIPS Agreement is the product of such an exchange,[10] one should ask whether the gains from any deal that formulates international intellectual property law are distributed fairly.

Several contributors to this volume have suggested that the exchanges that gave rise to the TRIPS Agreement may have been negatively affected by institutional design problems, so that we have reason to doubt that the gains from the exchange were divided evenly.[11] We can briefly summarize the range of problems that analysts have specified. Gains may be unevenly divided because parties have different levels of knowledge about intellectual property rights and their impact; certain parties may have received less and given more than they would have if they had been fully informed. If so, the antidote is to design international mechanisms for redressing the imbalance of knowledge, either through the kind of capacity-building mechanisms that exist now or through structural limitations on the ability of one party to reap disproportionate benefits from a deal.

Gains may also be unevenly divided because bargains are weighted by wealth, or because they are affected by threats of punishing retaliation if suitable agreements are not reached.[12] If so, the antidote is to encourage

---

[9] See, e.g., Joost Pauwelyn, *WTO Dispute Settlement: Of Sovereign Interests, Private Rights, and Public Goods* [this volume].

[10] Agreement on Trade-Related Aspects of Intellectual Property Rights, 15 Apr. 1994, Marrakesh Agreement Establishing the World Trade Organization, Annex 1C, LEGAL INSTRUMENTS – RESULTS OF THE URUGUAY ROUND vol. 31, 33 I.L.M. 81 (1994) [hereinafter TRIPS Agreement].

[11] See e.g., Abbott, above n. 2; Correa, above n. 2; Shaffer, above n. 8; see also Timothy Swanson & Timo Goeschl, *Diffusion and Distribution: The Impacts on Poor Countries of Technological Enforcement within the Biotechnology Sector* [this volume].

[12] See, e.g., Robert Keohane, *Comment: Norms, Institutions and Cooperation* [this volume]. See generally SUSAN K. SELL, PRIVATE POWER, PUBLIC LAW: THE GLOBALIZATION OF INTELLECTUAL PROPERTY RIGHTS (2003).

coalition building among the poor and powerless countries, and to find ways to limit unilateral threats of retaliation that distort the subject matter of the bargaining. That is occurring now with respect to attempts to limit the TRIPS-plus agenda of the United States, albeit with only marginal success. Some disproportion of benefits is inherent in a system where the benefits depend on unpredictable future events, but this element of randomness can be counteracted by building flexibility into the system so that the Members can adjust the bargain to take into account the poverty of some Members, in the light of unforeseen or unforeseeable circumstances. Indeed, that is a common interpretation of the impact of the Doha Declaration on the TRIPS obligations.[13] The call by Professors Maskus and Reichman in this volume for a moratorium on new heightened intellectual property harmonization is an attempt to prevent the TRIPS flexibilities that support equity from becoming rigidities that promote rigor mortis.[14]

Even aside from particular bargaining problems in the international sphere, the relation between institutional design and the distribution of gains from exchange is also implicated in the choice between property rules and liability rules, although the focus here is on the distribution of gains between individual right-holders and right-users. Property rules give a property owner the right to exclude others from using his property unless the use falls within a recognized exception or defense. Because property rules are generally well defined and are therefore easy to enforce, they allow a property owner to enjoy most of the value of his property, while leaving its user only enough value to ensure that he or she will forego the next best alternative. Classical liability rules, by contrast, make the protection of property rights insecure and expensive because they depend on litigation to define the scope of the rights, and because liability rules leave the scope of access rights relatively undefined. Liability rules advantage the user and, therefore, allow him to extract some of the value of the right that would, under a property regime, go to the rights holder.

The choice between property rules and liability rules as institutional mechanisms for rewarding investment may therefore turn on how we want the returns on investments to be distributed between the right-owners and right-users. We would favor property rules whenever we believe that most of the reward should go to the original investor, and we would use liability rules when we think that the actor who uses the product of investment – especially to improve it – should share in that value.[15]

---

[13] WTO Doha Ministerial Conference, Declaration on the TRIPS Agreement and Public Health, WT/MIN(01)/DEC/W/2 (14 Nov. 2001) [hereinafter Doha Declaration on TRIPS and Public Health]; *see* Peter M. Gerhart, *Slow Transformations: The WTO as a Distributive Organization*, 17 AM. U. L. REV. 1045 (2002).
[14] *See* Maskus & Reichman, above n. 2, at III.A.1.
[15] *Cf.* J.H. Reichman & Tracy Lewis, *Using Liability Rules to Stimulate Local Innovation in Developing Countries: Application to Traditional Knowledge* [this volume].

A second but related type of distributive issue found in these pages is how we divide the cost of providing public goods. Once we have determined that we need a lighthouse, how do we determine who pays for it? Do we distribute the cost among taxpayers or among users, and, if we distribute the cost among users, do we charge different fees for commercial vessels and pleasure boaters? In other words, how do we establish institutions to help us assess benefits and distribute costs to match those benefits?

This is an exceedingly difficult question to address. Because individual actors will try to minimize costs to themselves, while free-riding on costs paid by others, it is difficult to ask the actors themselves to determine both the optimal amount of investment in global public goods and how the costs of those goods should be allocated. Yet, that is precisely what we ask countries to do when they negotiate through organizations like the WTO. Sound institutional design is, therefore, essential if we are to ensure that global investment in public goods becomes optimal and that the cost of those goods is distributed in some form that fairly matches costs with benefits.

Here, Robert Keohane helps us by suggesting several approaches that minimize the pitfalls.[16] Negotiators should be asked to first address the question of which norms or general principles the distributive decisions will be made under. Will negotiations, in other words, be conducted under the constraint that poor countries gain at least as much as wealthy countries, and how will that constraint be enforced? Will negotiations build in transfer payments or enforceable technology transfer rights as a way of achieving equity? Although individual negotiators will no doubt argue for norms that they think will benefit them when applied, debate over norms can generate reasoned discussion and consensus. Moreover, because the discussion of general allocation principles is one step removed from their application, it allows the negotiators to accept and justify the negotiation results based on neutral principles, which may make the outcomes more politically palatable.

When politically feasible, the negotiating process could be further strengthened by allowing a disinterested tribunal to review particular agreements in light of the norms that the parties have adopted to govern the negotiation. In national systems, judges wielding common law or statutory adjudicatory power oversee the system of consensual exchanges by overturning exchanges that are unconscionable or that are reached through duress, fraud or mistake. Parties bargain with these constraints in mind, which reinforces the norms of fairness that naturally arise in the bargaining context. A healthy international system that respected distributive values could provide for similar judicial review of international agreements to determine whether they meet norms of fairness in the division of rewards. Although this approach would have to be exercised gingerly, with due respect for the doctrine of *pacta sunt servanda* and

---

[16] *See* Keohane, above n. 12.

the need to preserve the stability of mutual cooperation, the approach could curb opportunistic behavior by powerful countries and would reinforce norms leading to the fair distribution of the gains from cooperation.

The process of defining the appropriate level of investment in public goods and of allocating its cost would also be advanced if bargaining norms included respect for local conditions, with a view to achieving an appropriate match between costs and benefits within each country or groups of countries. Moreover, policymakers should build into the lawmaking process a degree of flexibility in the face of changing circumstances. Finally, side payments to facilitate cooperation and to deal with special situations can be effective,[17] so long as they are not extorted through strategic exploitation of negotiating positions.

The final type of distributive question is the most difficult of all: how do we accommodate the needs of the poor within a market system? The issue arises because a market system is an institutional framework within which we allocate decision-making power over property by giving one vote to each dollar. How then can such a system accommodate the needs of those who have few votes? This question becomes especially significant in the area of intellectual property because, after invention has occurred, the problem is always too little money and never too little supply.[18]

V. A suggested approach

Because policymakers confront a world with no institutional mechanism for making transfer payments between countries, we have relied on several forms of crypto-redistribution to build redistributive values into the global system. Capacity building, a subject of several contributions to this volume, depends on the kind of unilateral payments that are redistributive in nature. Similarly, if it were ever given real effect, the stipulation in Article 66.2 of the TRIPS Agreement that Members of the WTO should subsidize their own companies to support the transfer of technology to poorer countries[19] could serve as an ingenious model for harnessing national self-interest in the pursuit of distributive goals.[20] Moreover, when countries decide not to use dispute resolution to press for expansive rights under the TRIPS Agreement, we can understand their forbearance – based, as it is, on the poverty of those who need access to medicines – as a kind of redistributive act.

---

[17] *Id.*
[18] Paul A. David has recognized this in his chapter, entitled Koyaanisqatsi *in Cyberspace: The Economics of an "Out-of-Balance" Regime of Private Property Rights in Data and Information* [this volume]. He relies on the insight of Amartya Sen, that we must distinguish between famines that are caused by too little food and famines that are caused by too little money to afford an adequate distribution of food. AMARTYA SEN, DEVELOPMENT AS FREEDOM 160 (Anchor Books/Doubleday 1999).
[19] TRIPS Agreement, above n. 10, art 66.2.   [20] *See* Correa, above n. 2.

In light of these crypto-redistribution measures, perhaps it is not too futuristic to suggest that the community of nations should expand on these examples and consider more direct distributive mechanisms. John Barton's recommendation for a global patent system[21] helps us to illustrate one way to think about this problem. He ingeniously shows the many ways in which a global patent system would increase efficiencies and global wealth. The search for more efficient systems is not the only issue that must be addressed, however.

Because we can separate the issue of *how* we get a more efficient system from the issue of *who* enjoys the wealth that is generated by those efficiencies, we need not, and should not, assume that the wealth generated by a more efficient system simply inures to the benefit of the inventive community. It is an open question whether the wealth that is created by a more efficient system should benefit only the inventive community (which we would want if we thought that this would give us a more allocatively efficient level of investment in inventive activity) or the user community (which we could accomplish by simultaneously modifying some other aspect of the level of protection, say the length of protection or the scope of fair use rights).[22] Barton himself recognizes that we can separate the issue of how we get a more efficient system from the issue of who benefits from that system by suggesting that some of the revenue from global patent applications could be used to support the aspirations of inventors from impoverished countries.

Our imagination need not be limited to the distribution of revenue that is generated by patent applications, however; on the contrary, we could use the global patent itself to work toward a redistributive result. We could enact a tax on the holders of global patents (say, on sales of patented products) and use the proceeds to subsidize access to essential medicines or other essential products in order to provide a better balance between incentives and access. By taxing those who gain from globalization in order to advance the welfare of those who do not, international institutions could help achieve both efficiency and distributive justice.

It may be that globalization will continue to flourish if it is supported only by international institutions that create wealth, and not by institutions that redistribute wealth. We cannot, however, be assured of that, for market systems have always benefited from, and flourished with, systems of social protection. We might find that globalization would flourish more if we could take advantage of opportunities to tax those who benefit from the process in order to support those who do not.

---

[21] John H. Barton, *Issues Posed by a World Patent System* [this volume].
[22] *Cf.* Okediji, above n. 2; Graeme Dinwoodie and Rochelle Cooper Dreyfuss, *WTO Dispute Resolution and the Preservation of the Public Domain of Science under International Law* [this volume].

PART I

International provision of public goods under a globalized intellectual property regime

SECTION 2
Preserving the cultural and scientific commons

4

Koyaanisqatsi in cyberspace: The economics of an "out-of-balance" regime of private property rights in data and information

PAUL A. DAVID[*]

Abstract
I. The argument
II. Knowledge, information economics and the "three P's"
III. Intellectual property rights protections in economic theory and history
IV. Forces behind the recent policy push for a stronger global IPR regime
V. ICTs, "weightless" goods and services, and databases in the new economy
VI. The E.U.'s *sui generis* property right in databases and its implications
VII. Reconsidering the traditional economic rationale for copyright protection
VIII. Modest proposals: IPR policies to preserve the public knowledge commons
IX. Conclusion

ABSTRACT

Koyaanisqatsi is a Hopi Indian word that translates into English as "life out of balance," "crazy life," "life in turmoil," all meanings consistent with indicating "a way of life which calls for another way of living." While not wishing to suggest either that the international regime of intellectual property rights protection of scientific and technical data and information is "crazy" or that it is "in turmoil," this chapter argues that the persisting drift of institutional change towards a stronger, more extensive and globally harmonized system of protection has dangerously altered the balance between private rights and the public domain. In this regard, we have embarked upon "a way of life which calls for another way of living."

High access charges imposed by holders of monopoly rights in intellectual property have overall consequences for the conduct of science that are particularly damaging to programs of exploratory research, which are recognized to be

---

[*] Paul A. David is Professor of Economics, Stanford University and All Souls College, The University of Oxford.

critical for the sustained growth of knowledge-driven economies. The urgency of working towards a restoration of proper balance between private property rights and the public domain in data and information arises from considerations beyond the need to protect the public knowledge commons, upon which the vitality of open science depends. Policymakers who seek to configure the institutional infrastructure to better accommodate emerging commercial opportunities of the information-intensive "new economy" – in the developed and developing countries alike – therefore have a common interest in reducing the impediments to the future commercial exploitation of peer-to-peer networking technologies that are likely to be posed by ever-more stringent enforcement of intellectual property rights.

I. The argument

Koyaanisqatsi is a Hopi Indian word. It translates as "life out of balance," "crazy life," "life in turmoil," "life disintegrating," all meanings consistent with indicating "a way of life which calls for another way of living." For those who have already encountered this word as the title of the powerful 1983 documentary film and heard the ominous chanting of "Koyaanisqatsi" over the score, its resonance may seem rather too doom-laden for the context in which I am invoking it on this occasion.[1] In truth, I do not mean to suggest either that the international regime of intellectual property rights (IPRs) for protecting scientific and technical data and information is "crazy" or that it is "in turmoil." But, I will argue that the persisting drift of institutional change towards a stronger, more extensive and globally harmonized system of intellectual property (IP) protections during the past two decades has dangerously altered the balance between private rights and the public domain in data and information. In this regard we have embarked upon "a way of life which calls for another way of living."

To put the argument more concretely and specifically, I share the view of some observers that the emergent conjunction of statutory protections for technical systems of "self-help" for copyright holders and *sui generis* legal

---

[1] *See* Wikipedia, The Free Encyclopedia (text available under the terms of the GNU Free Documentation License), *at* http://www.wikipedia.org/wiki/Koyaanisqatsi (last modified 16 Feb. 2003). The film consists mostly of slow-motion and time-lapse footage, starting with a cave painting, progressing to footage of various natural environmental phenomena such as waves and cloud formations, and then to footage of man-made events, including traffic formations, bombings, and desolate urban landscapes; it invites comparison between various natural and technological phenomena, by following slow-motion images of crashing waves with those of clouds billowing around a mountainside, and an aerial shot of a cityscape with a closeup of a computer chip. At the film's end, an extended sequence of a booster rocket slowly disintegrating as it falls to earth culminates with the presentation of a number of generally dour Hopi prophecies, warning against human disruption of the natural order in efforts to exploit it: "If we dig precious things from the land, we will invite disaster."

protection of property rights in databases does threaten the "disintegration" of a cornerstone of the historical regime of copyright.[2] I refer to the precept that whereas ideas, facts and their modes of expression "naturally" belong in the public domain, granting private parties *temporary* possession of exclusive rights to exploit these may serve important, socially beneficial purposes. Instead, in the increasingly "out-of-balance" regime towards which we seem to be headed, the premise is that "information goods" that can be fixed in digital form are "intellectual assets" and should be treated symmetrically with all other forms of private property. That is, they should be subject to *perpetual* private ownership under the protection of copyright and copyright-like statutes, and technical means of enforcing those rights.

These developments carry worrisome implications for the long-run vitality of scientific and technological research and all the societal benefits deriving therefrom. The advancement of knowledge is a cumulative process, in which new findings are disclosed rapidly and widely so that they may be discarded if unreliable, or confirmed and brought into fruitful conjunction with other bodies of reliable data and information.[3] "Open science" institutions provide an alternative to the intellectual property approach to dealing with difficult problems that arise in the production and distribution of information under competitive market conditions. Although not a perfect solution to those problems, and one that requires public patronage of research agents who are enjoined to quickly disclose and freely share information about their methods and findings, "open science" depends upon a specific non-market reward system to solve a number of resource allocation problems arising from the characteristics of information as an economic good. The collegiate reputational reward systems conventionally associated with open science practice do create conflicts been the ostensible norms of "cooperation," on the one hand, and on the other, the incentives for non-cooperative rivalrous behavior on the part of individuals and research units that are drawn into racing to establish "priority." Despite those sources of inefficiency in the allocation of research resources, open science is properly regarded as uniquely well suited to the goal of maximizing the rate of growth of the stock of reliable knowledge.[4]

---

[2] In particular, *see* J.H. Reichman & Paul F. Uhlir, *A Contractually Reconstructed Research Commons for Scientific Data in a Highly Protectionist Intellectual Property Environment*, 68 LAW & CONTEMP. PROBS. 317 (2003).

[3] *See, e.g.*, Suzanne Scotchmer, *Standing on the Shoulders of Giants: Cumulative Research and the Patent Law*, 5 J. ECON. PERSP. 29 (1991).

[4] For further development of these points, which are not treated extensively in this essay, *see* Paul A. David, *The Economic Logic of "Open Science" and the Balance between Private Property Rights and the Public Domain in Scientific Data and Information: A Primer*, in THE ROLE OF SCIENTIFIC AND TECHNICAL DATA AND INFORMATION IN THE PUBLIC DOMAIN: PROCEEDINGS OF A SYMPOSIUM 19–34 (J.M. Esanu & P.F. Uhlir eds., National Academies Press 2003).

High access charges imposed by holders of monopoly rights in Intellectual Property (IP) have important consequences for the conduct of science. These are particularly damaging to exploratory research programs that are critical for the sustained growth of knowledge-driven economies. Lack of restraint in privatizing the public domain in data and information has effects similar to those of non-cooperative behaviors among researchers, especially in regard to the sharing of access to raw data-streams and information, and the systematic under-provision of the documentation and annotation required to create reliably accurate and up-to-date public database resources. Both can significantly degrade the effectiveness of the research system as a whole.

Considered at the macro-level, open science and commercially oriented R&D based upon proprietary information constitute complementary sub-systems.[5] The public policy challenge that now needs to be faced is to keep the two sub-systems in proper balance. This requires not only adequate public funding of "open science" research, but also deliberate action to halt, and in some areas reverse, the excessive incursions of claims to private property rights over material that would otherwise remain in the public domain of scientific data and information.

Yet, today there are many writers in the business press, academic economists, lawyers and policy makers who see the matter quite differently.[6] The central association of information technologies and information goods with the New Economy has suggested that the world is now leaving behind the epoch of material capitalism and entering that of "Intellectual Capitalism." Accordingly, on this view, assuring the continued vitality of the market system requires new institutional and technical innovations to protect IPRs from the potentially disruptive effects of the rapid advance of digital information technologies and computer-mediated telecommunications.

Much of the justification for that view, and hence for the sanguine and in some quarters enthusiastic view of recent trends in the elaboration and extension of IP protections, rests on little evidence and inadequately careful economic analysis. There are a number of respects in which the new technological environment is compounding the drawbacks of using legal monopolies to solve the problems that the "public goods" features of information pose for competitive markets. The urgency of working towards restoring proper balance between private property rights and the public domain arises from considerations beyond the need to protect the public knowledge commons upon which open science depends. Economists lately have come around to the view that the "public goods problems" heightened by the dramatically falling costs of reproducing and distributing digital information may also have become more manageable under market

---

[5] *Id.*
[6] For notable exceptions, *see* John H. Barton, Preserving the Global Scientific and Technological Commons, Stanford University Law School (manuscript 2003); James Boyle, *The Second Enclosure Movement and the Construction of the Public Domain*, 66 LAW & CONTEMP. PROBS. 33 (2003).

competition without recourse to copyright and copyright-like protections. Protections for producers of "the first copy" from "unfair dealing" constitutes an alternative approach to copyright, and one that is more directly responsive to the economic issues of unfair competition that have beset publishers from the era of Gutenberg onwards. On that reading, policymakers who seek to configure the institutional infrastructure to better accommodate emerging commercial opportunities of the information-intensive "new economy" may have a common interest in reducing the impediments – posed by ever-more stringent enforcement of IPRs – to the future commercial exploitation of networking technologies.

The following sections of this chapter adumbrate and elaborate on this argument. They begin with the economics of information and take notice of the existence of alternative solutions to the problems of appropriating value in the case of commodities that have the properties of public goods.

II. Knowledge, information economics and the "three P's"

Knowledge may be viewed as a commodity. But, it is not a commonplace commodity. Nor is information, which we may distinguish from the cognitive human capabilities subsumed under the label of "knowledge." Some, but not all, forms of knowledge can be codified as information, rendering it more readily transmitted, classified and stored. Even so, information, like knowledge, remains highly differentiated and has no obvious natural units of measurement. It can have utility as a pure consumption good or as a capital good, and often as both. It is unusual in that, as a pure capital good yielding a stream of material benefits when combined with other kinds of assets, information and knowledge possess intrinsic economic values. Such is the case, for example, with regard to information about the operation of a cost-saving manufacturing process or the design of a product with better quality attributes.

A yet-more remarkable property is information's extreme *indivisibility*, coupled with its durability: once a bit of knowledge has been obtained, there is no value to acquiring it a second time. There is no societal need to repeat the same discovery or invention, because a piece of information can be used again and again without exhausting it. Even more important is that knowledge differs from ordinary "private" commodities in being what economists refer to as a *non-rival* good: it can be possessed and enjoyed jointly by all who care to make use of it.[7]

This insight is not new. Consider the following passage in a letter written in 1813 to Isaac McPherson, a Baltimore inventor, by Thomas Jefferson:[8]

---

[7] This observation forms the point of departure of the classic analysis of the economics of R&D due to Kenneth Arrow, *Economic Welfare and the Allocation of Resources for Invention*, in THE RATE AND DIRECTION OF INVENTIVE ACTIVITY: ECONOMIC AND SOCIAL FACTORS (Richard R. Nelson ed., Princeton University Press 1962).

[8] THE LIFE AND SELECTED WRITINGS OF THOMAS JEFFERSON (MODERN LIBRARY EDITIONS) 629–630 (A. Koch & W. Peden eds., 1972).

"If nature has made any one thing less susceptible than all others of exclusive property, it is the action of the thinking power called an idea, which an individual may exclusively possess as long as he keeps it to himself; but the moment it is divulged, it forces itself into the possession of every one, and the receiver cannot dispossess himself of it. Its peculiar character, too, is that no one possesses the less, because every other possesses the whole of it. He who receives an idea from me, receives instruction himself without lessening mine; as he who lights his taper at mine, receives light without darkening me. That ideas should freely spread from one to another over the globe, for the moral and mutual instruction of man, and improvement of his condition, seems to have been peculiarly and benevolently designed by nature, when she made them, like fire, expansible over all space, without lessening their density in any point, and like the air in which we breathe, move, and have our physical being, incapable of confinement or exclusive appropriation."

It seems clear that Jefferson grasped the essential point that the cost of transmitting useful knowledge in codified form is negligible in comparison to the costs of creating it; and saw that were it not for society's need to encourage the pursuit of ideas by rendering such pursuits economically viable, such information should be distributed freely.[9]

Non-rival possession, low marginal cost of reproduction and distribution which makes it difficult to exclude others from access, and substantial fixed costs of original production, are the three properties familiarly associated with the definition of a "public good." As is well known, when these characteristics are present competitive markets – in which price tends to be driven down to the costs of supplying the marginal unit of the commodity – in general perform quite badly. Competitive producers' revenues will not even cover their full costs of production, much less appropriate the use value of the goods to the public. Indeed, the attempt to make the beneficiaries pay for value received would so reduce demand as to result in an inefficiently low level of consumption.

In the literature of public finance economics, three principal alternative allocative mechanisms are proposed as solutions to "the public goods problem."[10] One is that society should provide independent producers with subsidies financed by general taxation and require that the goods be made available to the public freely or at a nominal charge. A second mechanism would have the state levying general taxes to finance its direct participation in production and

---

[9] This does not mean that knowledge of all kinds can be transferred at low marginal costs. Uncodified knowledge, which in many instances resists codification and remains "tacit," is more difficult to transmit between agents, except through personal demonstrations. On the implications of tacitness in regard to science and technology policies, and the economics of codification of knowledge, *see, e.g.*, R. Cowan et al., *The Explicit Economics of Codification and Tacit Knowledge*, 9 INDUS. & CORP. CHANGE 211 (2000).

[10] *See, e.g.*, Todd Sandler, *Assessing the Optimal Provision of Public Goods*, in PROVIDING GLOBAL PUBLIC GOODS: MANAGING GLOBALIZATION 131(I. Kaul et al. eds., 2002).

distribution and contracting where necessary with private agents to carry out this work. Here, again, the objective is to supply the good at nominal prices. The third solution is to create a publicly regulated private monopoly, which would be able to charge consumers prices that will secure a "normal" rate of profit. This does not guarantee that consumers will be lined up to purchase the goods and services in question. In other words, the legal right to exclude other producers from the market for a product does not, in and of itself, create a profitable monopoly.

While the elements of non-excludabilty and "non-rivalry" qualify information as a "public good" for purposes of economic policy analysis, ideas and information remain distinguished in two respects from the mass of conventional public goods, such as traffic lights, flood control systems, and airport beacons and radar landing beams. The first difference is that the attributes of the commodity – i.e., typically, the complete contents of the information itself – are not known beforehand. Indeed, they are not known automatically to all the interested parties even when the new knowledge becomes available in codified form. This *asymmetry in the distribution of information* greatly complicates the process of arranging contracts for the production and use of new knowledge.[11]

The second differentiating feature is *the cumulative and interactive nature of knowledge*. The stock of scientific and technological knowledge grows by incremental additions, each advance building upon and sometimes altering the significance of previous findings in complicated and often unpredictable ways.[12]

The importance of these differentiating features notwithstanding, it is useful to notice a striking correspondence between the three solutions for the standard public goods problem – subsidies, direct production, and regulated monopoly – and the three main institutional arrangements that may be deployed to address the so-called "appropriability problem" to which the public goods characteristics of information gives rise. In order to encourage the provision of scientific and technological knowledge, modern states typically deploy several of these. I have referred on previous occasions to the three principal institutional devices as "the three P's": public *P*atronage, *P*rocurement by State agencies through contracting arrangements, and the legal exclusive ownership of (intellectual) *P*roperty.[13] Each of these mechanisms exhibits special deficiencies

---

[11] A model explaining this problem in the international context is found in Ignatius Horstmann & James R. Markusen, *Licensing versus Direct Investment: A Model of Internalization by the Multinational Enterprise*, 20 CAN. J. ECON. 464 (1987).

[12] Thomas Jefferson remarked upon this too: "The fact is, that one new idea leads to another, that to a third, and so on through a course of time until someone, with whom no one of these ideas was original, combines all together, and produces what is justly called a new invention." THE LIFE AND SELECTED WRITINGS OF THOMAS JEFFERSON, above n. 8, at 686.

[13] *See, e.g.*, P.A. David, *Intellectual Property Institutions and the Panda's Thumb: Patents, Copyrights, and Trade Secrets in Economic Theory and History*, in GLOBAL DIMENSIONS OF INTELLECTUAL PROPERTY RIGHTS IN SCIENCE AND TECHNOLOGY 226 et seq.

as well as specific virtues in its effects upon resource allocation; none offers a perfect solution to the appropriability problem. We focus here on intellectual property rights, and examine their virtues and deficiencies in the case of the copyright system, which is less often discussed than patents.[14]

The term patronage stands for the system of awarding publicly financed prizes, research grants, and other subsidies to private individuals and organizations engaged in intellectual discovery and invention, in exchange for full public disclosure of their creative achievements. It characterizes the pursuit of open scientific inquiry, and is the dominant institutional and social mode of organization associated in the Western democratic societies with the conduct of academic science.

Procurement is associated with governmental contracting for intellectual work, the products of which it will control and devote to public purposes. Whether or not the information thereby produced will be laid open for public use is a secondary issue, albeit an important matter for public policy. Sensitive defense-related research usually is conducted under government auspices in secure, closed laboratories, whereas much public contract R&D and the scientific work of governmentally managed laboratories is undertaken with the intention of wide dissemination of the findings.

The third arrangement is for society to grant private producers of new knowledge exclusive property rights to the use of their creations, which thereby establishes conditions for the existence of markets in these forms of intellectual property and enables the originators to collect (differential) fees for the use of their work by others. Here, under the Property rubric, are found the specific legal contrivances of the patent and copyright, and, somewhat more problematically, the trade secret.

III. Intellectual property rights protections in economic theory and history

The creation and assignment of intellectual property rights convey a monopoly right to the beneficial economic exploitation of an idea (in the case of patent rights) or of a particular expression of an idea (in the case of copyright) in return for the disclosure of the idea or its expression.[15] This device allows the organization of market exchanges of exploitation rights, which, by assigning pecuniary value to commercially exploitable ideas, creates economic incentives

---

(M. Wallerstein et al. eds., National Academy Press 1993). On the connection between patronage institutions and the conduct of "open science," *see, e.g.*, P.A. David, *Common Agency Contracting and the Emergence of "Open Science" Institutions*, 88 AM. ECON. REV. 15 (1998).

[14] *See, e.g.*, Stanley M. Besen & Leo J. Raskind, *An Introduction to the Law and Economics of Intellectual Property*, 5 J. ECON. PERSP. 3 (1991).

[15] *Id.*

for people to go on creating new ones, as well as finding new applications for old ones.[16] By allocating these rights to those who are prepared to pay the most for them, the workings of IP markets also tend to prevent ideas from remaining in the exclusive (secret) possession of discoverers and inventors who might be uninterested in seeing their creations used.

Thus, a potential economic problem addressed by a system of IPRs is the threat that unfair competition, particularly the misappropriation of the benefits of someone else's investment and effort, may destroy the provision of information goods as a commercially viable activity. The nub of the problem here is that the cost of making a particular information good available to a second, third, or thousandth user is not significantly greater than that of making it available to the first one. Since the Gutenberg revolution, the same technical advances that have lowered the costs of reproducing "encoded" material (text, images, and sounds) also have permitted "pirates" to appropriate the contents of the first copy without bearing the expense of its development. Unchecked, this form of unfair competition could render unprofitable the initial investment.

Producers of ideas, texts, images, music, and other creative works are subject to economic constraints, even when they do not invariably respond to different market incentives. If they had no rights enabling them to derive income from the publication of their works, they might create less and possibly be compelled to spend their time doing something entirely different but more lucrative. Thus, there is an important economic rationale for establishing IPRs.

To summarize, the property solution, which creates rights to the fruits of intellectual creations, possesses a number of definite virtues. These may be quickly adumbrated for the case of patents:[17]

- The patent provides a solution to the economic problem of the intellectual creator. By increasing the expected private returns from innovation, it acts as an incentive mechanism to private investment in knowledge production.
- Patents facilitate the market test of new inventions because they allow disclosure of the related information while (in principle) protecting against imitation.
- Patents create transferable rights and, therefore, can help structure complex transactions that also concern unpatented knowledge.
- Patents are a means to signal and evaluate the future value of the technological effort of the companies that own them. This is particularly useful in the cases of new or young companies for which other classes of "intangibles" cannot be used for proper evaluation.

---

[16] For example, ASHISH ARORA ET AL., MARKETS FOR TECHNOLOGY: THE ECONOMICS OF INNOVATION AND CORPORATE STRATEGY (MIT Press 2001), describes such markets fully in the context of international transactions in technology.

[17] For more discussion, *see* Robert Merges & Richard R. Nelson, *On the Complex Economics of Patent Scope*, 90 COLUM. L. REV. 839 (1990).

- This way of providing market incentives for certain kinds of creative effort leaves the valuation of the intellectual production to be determined *ex post*, by the willingness of users to pay. It thereby avoids having society try to place a value on the creative work *ex ante* – as would be required under alternative incentive schemes, such as offering prizes or awarding individual procurement contracts for specified works.

However, establishing a monopoly right to exploit that first copy, alas, turns out not to be a perfect solution. The monopolist will raise the price of every copy above the negligible costs of its reproduction, and, as a result, there will be some potential users of the information good who will be excluded from enjoying it. The latter represents a waste of resources, referred to by economists as the deadweight burden of monopoly: some people's desires will remain unsatisfied even though they could have been fulfilled at virtually no additional cost.

This is but one of the things that are likely to go awry in the case of patent protection. Other "vices" of patents include the following. First, both the "first to invent" and "first to file" bases for awarding patents create incentives for duplicative "races" that result in socially excessive R&D expenditures.[18] Similarly, patents may be sought and used strategically as tools to raise rivals' costs by confronting them with the threat of infringement suits. A corresponding catalogue of "virtues" and "vices" for copyright is given in the Text Box that follows.

Thus, the subject of IP policies has proved troublesome for the economics profession, as it presents numerous situations in which the effort to limit unfair competition and provide adequate "market incentives" for innovation demonstrably may result in a socially inefficient resource allocation. Human institutions, however, rarely are perfect. From both the viewpoints of legal theory and economic analysis, there is much to be said for regarding patent and copyright institutions as remarkably ingenious social contrivances, whereby protection of the discoverer's or inventor's exclusive right to exploit new knowledge commercially is exchanged for the disclosure of information that creates a public good. Further, the public good may be drawn upon to produce additional discoveries and inventions.[19] All of this is managed by leaving the economic

---

[18] Such problems are discussed in Roberto Mazzoleni & Richard R. Nelson, *Economic Theories about the Benefits and Costs of Patents*, 32 J. ECON. ISSUES 1031 (1998).

[19] For the legal and economic interpretations, respectively, *see, e.g.*, Rebecca Eisenberg, *Patents and the Progress of Science: Exclusive Rights and Experimental Use*, 56 U. CHI. L. REV. 1017 (1989); P. Dasgupta & P.A. David, *Information Disclosure and the Economics of Science and Technology*, in ARROW AND THE ASCENT OF MODERN ECONOMIC THEORY 519 (G. Feiwel ed., New York University Press 1987); P. Dasgupta & P.A. David, *Toward a New Economics of Science*, 23 RES. POL'Y 487 (1994); Paul A. David, *The Evolution of Intellectual Property Institutions*, in SYSTEMS TRANSFORMATIONS: EASTERN AND WESTERN ASSESSMENTS: PROCEEDINGS OF THE TENTH CONGRESS OF THE INTERNATIONAL ECONOMICS ASSOCIATION (A. Aganbegyan et al. eds., 1994).

value of the right to be determined by the workings of the market, which thereby removes it from the realm of political discretion.

Economic Virtues and Vices of Copyright Protection

Analytical justification: Copyright protection addresses the problem of high fixed (first copy) cost and low marginal cost. In conventional applications where text and images were embodied in physical media, registration secured disclosure of original expressive works.

Virtues:

- Incentives for creative productions;
- Reward for derivative innovation benefits;
- "Versioning" permits price discrimination based on urgency of demand for information;

Vices:

- "Deadweight" burden of monopoly, heavy for "minority taste" users;
- "Super-inefficiencies" when applied to network goods (especially compatibility standards, interface standards);
- Impediments to cumulative innovation, unless mitigated by "fair use" exclusions;
- Inhibits development of modular system innovation (e.g., software system design).

It must be recognized that the actual provisions of the laws affecting IPRs may not fully honor this social bargain. For example, in practice the disclosure provisions often prove insufficient to overcome the incentives that patentees usually have to withhold some pertinent information, either for their private use or as a basis to extract additional rents for the transfer of complementary know-how.[20]

Delays in the release of information add to the academic research community's concerns over the way that the workings of the patent system restrict access to new scientific and technological findings. U.S. patent law follows the principle that priority in invention, rather than being first to file a patent application, is what matters. It therefore allows applicants a one-year grace period after publication. But most foreign systems award patents on a "first to file" basis, which means that even American researchers are induced to delay publication until they have prepared patent applications to secure rights in

---

[20] *See, e.g.*, Carlos Correa, *Can the TRIPS Agreement Foster Technology Transfer to Developing Countries?* [this volume].

other countries. Since the passage of the 1980 Bayh-Dole Act, which authorized universities in the United States to seek patents on innovations arising from federally funded research projects, there has been more-or-less continuous modification of institutional rules toward lengthening the permissible duration of delays placed on the publication of research findings for purposes of allowing the filing of patent applications.[21]

From the standpoint of academic researchers, the greatest deficiency of the statutory disclosure requirements is that they may be met by divulging little scientific or technical data. The patent itself is of only limited interest and serves mainly as a notice that the patentees may be willing to supply more useful information, for some fee. Moreover, researchers' ability to make use of the divulged information is not assured until the end of the patent life because it excludes others from making and using it. That the use of an invention for purposes of research, and hence in generating further discoveries and innovations, ought not be proscribed was long taken for granted in the United States. On this premise, researchers were allowed to defend themselves from infringement suits on grounds of experimental use – so long as the infringer was able to show that no commercial benefit was derived thereby.[22] However, the United States Court of Appeals for the Federal Circuit has recently overruled these assumptions.[23]

---

[21] The effects of the Bayh-Dole legislation (35 U.S.C. §§ 200–211 (2000)) on university patenting activity are reviewed in THE SOURCES OF INDUSTRIAL LEADERSHIP (D.C. Mowery & R.R. Nelson eds., Cambridge University Press 1999); David C. Mowery et al., *Growth of Patenting and Licensing by U.S. Universities: An Assessment of the Effects of the Bayh-Dole Act of 1980*, 30 RES. POL'Y 99 (2001); Wesley Cohen et al., University-Industry Research Centers in the United States, Report to the Ford Foundation (Carnegie Mellon University 1994) (reporting findings from a survey of U.S. university-industry research centers on the distribution of permitted restraints on publication to allow for the filing of patent applications); *see also* DAVID C. MOWERY & RICHARD R. NELSON, IVORY TOWER AND INDUSTRIAL INNOVATION: UNIVERSITY-INDUSTRY TECHNOLOGY TRANSFER BEFORE AND AFTER THE BAYH-DOLE ACT IN THE UNITED STATES (Stanford University Press 2004). The significance of these delays and other restrictions is discussed in Paul A. David, *Difficulties in Assessing the Performance of Research and Development Programs*, in AAAS SCIENCE AND TECHNOLOGY POLICY YEARBOOK 1994, at 293 (A.H. Teich et al. eds., American Association for the Advancement of Science 1994).

[22] Kenneth W. Dam, Intellectual Property and the Academic Enterprise, John M. Olin Law & Economics Working Paper No. 68, at 7–8 (University of Chicago 1999), points out that because the case law has tended to reject the "experimental use" defense against infringement suits whenever the researcher might profit, this exception to patent protection is less likely to prove beneficial for academic researchers in fields like biomedical sciences, where even publicly-funded "basic" research may yield short-term economic payoffs. Given the case law precedents in the United States, the drive on the part of university administrators to exploit patent rights under the provisions of the Bayh-Dole Act may thus be seen as contributing indirectly as well as directly to creating more formidable barriers to the ability of academic researchers to rapidly access new research tools and results.

[23] Madey v. Duke Univ., 307 F.3d 1351 (Fed. Cir. 2002), *cert. denied*, 539 U.S. 958 (2003).

The same situation does not arise with conventional copyright, which protects the published form in which ideas have been expressed. Only that which is fully disclosed can qualify the author for legal protection against infringers. Because it is difficult to establish that unauthorized copies were made of a text that had not been made public, authors seeking legal protection for their work have every incentive to hasten its disclosure. Moreover, in recognition of the cultural and scientific benefits of expository and critical writings, and of further research based upon published information and data – not to mention the interests of authors in having such usage made on the basis of accurate representations of their work – statutory exceptions traditionally are provided to permit fair-use of copyrighted material. Largely for these reasons, this form of IP protection historically did not raise serious objections on the grounds of impeding rapid access to new scientific or technological data and information. However, the situation has changed.

IV. Forces behind the recent policy push for a stronger global IPR regime

The economic prominence of intellectual property, and concerns to strengthen the legal protections afforded patents, copyrights and trademarks, have been growing in recent years. The value of IP is increasing as a share of average total firm value, the number of patent applications is growing at double-digit rates in the major patent offices, and licensing and cross-licensing are being employed with greater frequency than ever, particularly in high-technology industries.

The greater intensity of innovation, characteristic of the knowledge-based economy, and the increase in the propensity to patent, are the main factors of this quantitative evolution.[24] In 1998, 147,000 U.S. utility patents were granted, an increase of 32 percent compared to 1997. Over the past 10 years, both patent applications and patent grants have increased at a rate of about six percent per annum, compared to about one percent per annum in the preceding forty years.

There is a qualitative aspect to the growth of patenting as well. Patents are being registered on new types of objects, such as software, genetic creations and devices for electronic trade over the Internet, and by new actors (universities and public-sector researchers). This general trend is also reflected in the increase in exclusivity rights over instruments, research materials and databases. While all of this may be seen as contributing to a dramatic expansion of "the knowledge market,"[25] the proliferation of exclusive rights on whole areas of intellectual creation equally represents an unprecedentedly large incursion upon the public domain of scientific and technical data and information.

---

[24] *See* Samuel Kortum & Joshua Lerner, *Stronger Protection or Technological Revolution: What Is Behind the Recent Surge in Patenting?*, 48 CARNEGIE-ROCHESTER CONF. SERIES ON PUB. POL'Y 247 (1998).

[25] *See* A. ARORA ET AL., above n. 16.

Many factors explain this trend. A first factor is simply that patents are becoming an intangible asset of increasing importance, both for signaling the value of new or small companies and for assisting firms involved in innovation-based competition. A second factor is the increasing value of the strategic use of patents as bargaining chips, for the strengthening of national and regional legal systems of intellectual property makes the expected benefits of amassing portfolios of legal rights outweigh their costs.[26]

The third factor deals with changes in patenting policy in the United States and Europe. Today, pro-patenting policies of patent offices mean that patentability criteria have gradually been eased and extended to new subject matter areas. Many research results became patentable, as a result of both court and patent office decisions. The increasing ability to patent fundamental knowledge, research tools and databases is part and parcel of a broader movement towards strengthening IPRs.

Other important factors include powerful commitments to basic research by private firms in certain sectors and changes in the behavior of universities and public institutes to become more oriented towards exploiting intellectual property as a means of capturing revenue[27] and promoting economic development in their regions.[28] This sea-change has also seen the privatization of some of the activities of governmental agencies, which became major players in the contractual research market.[29]

These trends do not necessarily lead to an excess of knowledge privatization. In many cases the establishment of IPRs strengthens private incentives, allows the commitment of substantial private resources, and thereby improves the conditions of commercialization of inventions. Moreover, the introduction of private rights does not totally prevent the diffusion of knowledge, even if it does limit it. Finally, a large proportion of private knowledge is disseminated outside the market system, either within consortia or by means of networks of trading and sharing of knowledge, the foundation of the unintentional spillovers discussed by several authors.[30]

---

[26] *See* Bronwyn H. Hall & Rosemarie Ham Ziedonis, *The Patent Paradox Revisited: An Empirical Study of Patenting in the U.S. Semiconductor Industry, 1979–1995*, 32 RAND J. ECON. 101 (2001), for the defensive use of patent portfolios in an industry that prior to the 1980s had been characterized by low propensity to patent.

[27] *See* R. Henderson et al., *Universities as a Source of Commercial Technology: A Detailed Analysis of University Patenting, 1965–1988*, 80 REV. ECON. & STAT. 119 (1998).

[28] Irwin Feller, *Federal and State Government Roles in Science and Technology*, 11 ECON. DEV. Q. 283 (1997).

[29] *See* Adam Jaffe & Joshua Lerner, *Reinventing Public R&D: Patent Policy and the Commercialization of National Laboratory Technologies*, 32 RAND J. ECON. 167 (2001).

[30] *See, e.g.*, ERIC VON HIPPEL, THE SOURCES OF INNOVATION (Oxford University Press 1988); Paul A. David, *The Political Economy of Public Science*, in THE REGULATION OF SCIENCE AND TECHNOLOGY (Helen Lawton-Smith ed., 2001).

Nevertheless, there is reason for concern when all these developments show a general shift from one view to another of the role of IPRs. By tradition, IPRs are considered as one of the incentive structures society employs to elicit innovative effort. They co-exist with other incentive structures, each of which has costs and benefits as well as a degree of complementarity. The new view is that IPRs are the only means to commercialize the intangible capital represented by knowledge and should therefore be the basis for markets in knowledge exchange.

The restructuring of the legal regimes relating to patents and copyrights, and the adjustments of behavior to the new incentives it creates, are likely to affect the organization and conduct of scientific research and publishing. Indeed, these impacts are bound to figure among the more prominent unexpected consequences of the same digital infrastructure technologies that were created by publicly sponsored scientists and engineers. Unfortunately, at least some of these repercussions now appear to be detrimental to the long-term vitality of the practice of open science in the world's academic research communities.[31] Such an untoward effect does not follow from the technology itself. It comes, instead, from failing to maintain a healthy balance between the domain of publicly supported knowledge production and exchanges and the sphere of private, proprietary R&D and profitable businesses based upon information goods.

One source of difficulty in preserving such balance is immediately apparent. An attractive short-run strategy of business development entails utilizing enhanced information processing and telecommunications in conjunction with the assertion of private property rights over publicly provided data and information products. Rather than having to produce wholly new content for distribution, an obvious first line of enterprise is to make use of what comes freely and most readily to hand.

One can expect this approach to continue, and with it the commercial exploitation of larger and larger portions of the body of codified scientific knowledge and observational data that has been built up under public patronage and maintained as a common, readily accessible research resource. Sometimes the commercialization of public databases makes good economic sense because private firms may have technical or marketing capabilities that would add value for a variety of end users, whereas existing government agencies might lack that competence. Such was shown to be the case in regard to the distribution and packaging by commercial weather information services of data gathered by the U.S. National Oceanic and Atmospheric Administration.[32]

---

[31] Reichman & Uhlir, above n. 2. *See also* Arti K. Rai, *Proprietary Rights and Collective Action: The Case of Biotechnology Research with Low Commercial Value* [this volume].

[32] For material underlying this and the following discussion, see NATIONAL RESEARCH COUNCIL, BITS OF POWER: ISSUES IN GLOBAL ACCESS TO SCIENTIFIC DATA 116–124 (National Academy of Sciences 1997).

However, the possibility of seriously adverse consequences elsewhere in the national research system, from ill-designed policies and programs to promote proprietary exploitation of public knowledge resources, also needs to be recognized. Consider what ensued from the Reagan Administration's sponsorship of the Land-Remote Sensing Commercialization Act (1984), under which a monopoly on Landsat images was awarded in 1985 to the Earth Observation Satellite (EOSAT) Company, a joint venture of Hughes and RCA. The price of Landsat images immediately rose tenfold, from $400 per image to $4000.[33] This permitted EOSAT to attract profitable business from commercial customers and the federal government, although virtually none from academic and independent researchers. Indeed, the impact of the privatization of Landsat operations upon basic research being conducted by university groups around the world was devastating, as they suddenly went from being "data rich" into a condition not of actual "data poverty" so much as one of data "non-entitlement."[34]

The EOSAT Company secured its monopoly position in the market for satellite images by virtue of being given physical control over the source of (Landsat) images. A similarly damaging outcome for academic researchers could follow from the exercise of the market power that a commercial provider of a scientific database might gain under intellectual property protection, especially under a legal regime that granted indefinitely renewable copyright-like protection to the database contents, whether or not the database was otherwise copyrightable.[35]

The recent extension of copyright to software has itself permitted a breach of the disclosure principle that parallels the one already noted in regard to patents. Under American copyright law (in order to qualify to pursue infringers for damages), it is sufficient to register only some sample extracts of a computer program's text, rather than the entire body of code.[36] Moreover, there is no requirement to disclose the underlying source code; copyright registration can be obtained on the basis of a disclosure of just the machine language instructions. While this practice surely can be seen to violate the principle that no burden of undue experimentation should be placed upon second comers, the latter requirement holds only in the case of patent law. It never was

---

[33] Id.
[34] The introduction here of the term "non-entitlement" is a deliberate allusion to Amartya Sen's observation that people starved in the Indian famine of 1918 not because the harvest was inadequate to feed them, but because the rise in grain prices had deprived them of "entitlement" to the food that actually was available. See AMARTYA SEN, POVERTY AND FAMINE: AN ESSAY ON ENTITLEMENT AND DEPRIVATION (1981).
[35] It will be seen (from the discussion below) that such also may be the import of the European Commission's Directive on the Legal Protection of Databases, 96/9/EC, 1996 (L 77) 20.
[36] 17 U.S.C. §§ 101, 102(a) (2000) (as interpreted by Copyright office regulations).

contemplated that one might be able to register a text for full copyright protection without practically disclosing its contents to interested readers.

A further, more generally disconcerting set of developments may prove destructive to the effectiveness of traditional fair-use exemptions for research (and educational) purposes – even where such provisions continue to be made. This threat has emerged only recently in the form of digital technologies that limit "on line" copying of electronic information. Advanced encryption systems now underpin many computing and communications security services, and permit a wide variety of security objectives to be achieved, along with assurance of message authentication and data integrity, as well as privacy and confidentiality goals. There are other techniques for marking and monitoring the use of distributed digital information, such as water marking, which attaches a signal to digital data that can be detected or extracted later to document assertions about its provenance, authenticity, or ownership; and fingerprinting, which embeds a mark in each copy that uniquely identifies the authorized recipient.

Self-help or copyright-management systems that make use of encryption or prevent unauthorized copying allow copyright holders to enforce their legal claim to capture economic value from users of the protected material, and also enable selective access to elements of content that makes it more feasible for the vendor to engage in price discrimination. Marking and monitoring techniques, in contrast, do not allow direct enforcement of copyrights, but can be used to deter unauthorized copying and distribution of information by facilitating tracking of errant data to the original recipients who were responsible for its improper use.

These advances in digital technology enhance economic efficiency insofar as they reduce the costs of enforcing a statutory property right and thereby secure whatever societal benefits copyright legislation is designed to promote. Yet, in the currently prevailing enthusiasm for stronger IP protection, the American drafters of the 1998 Digital Millennium Copyright Act included a provision that prohibits the circumvention of "any technological measure that effectively controls access" to a copyrighted work, and outlawed the manufacture, importation or public distribution of any technology primarily produced for the purpose of such circumvention.[37] The problem posed by this statutory reinforcement for applications of novel self-help technologies is simply that it may render impossible the fair-use of copyrighted material by researchers and educators, leaving the provision of information access for such purposes to the discretion of copyright holders.

---

[37] For discussion of the policy issues raised by self-help systems, Digital Millennium Copyright Act (1998), 17 U.S.C. § 1201 *et seq.* (2000), see Kenneth Dam, *Who Says Who Can Access What? The Policy Crisis over Cryptography in the Information Age*, SCI. TECH. & L. (New York Academy of Sciences 1998).

This, however, is not the only serious assault upon the traditional means of permitting publicly supported open science communities to pursue their work untrammelled by the protections afforded to copyright owners. As attractive as the prospect of more powerful self-help technologies may appear to be in curtailing "digital piracy," such remedies would create a threat to the achievement of a reasonable regime for the allocation of scientific and technological information goods while providing protection for private investments in information goods. One way in which it is feasible to approximate the efficient workings of a system of discriminatory pricing for data and information is to allow educators, scholars and researchers to invoke fair-use exemptions from the requirements for licensing material that is copyrighted or otherwise legally protected by statute. In effect, this approach would set differentially lower prices for the use of information goods in producing and distributing knowledge – indeed, prices that would approximate the negligible marginal costs of digital reproduction and transmission.

So far I have considered only the most straightforward and obvious of the potentially adverse consequences of turning over parts of the public knowledge domain to information monopolists. The staking out of property rights to scientific knowledge has potentially serious and subtler implications for the circulation of information and its use in research. These may be grouped, for the sake of convenience, under the general heading of transaction costs increases. Firstly, it is possible that IP-related transaction costs may increase so much that the result can be the blockage of knowledge exploitation and accumulation. Policy makers and academics alike have focused especially on the tragedy of the anticommons in biotechnology and microprocessors, the potentially deleterious effect of strong IP protection for databases on academic science, and the extension of patentability to new subjects such as computer programs and more recently business methods.[38]

Secondly, efforts and costs devoted to sorting out conflicting and overlapping claims to IPRs will increase, as will uncertainty about the nature and

---

[38] On these points, *see*, respectively, Michael A. Heller & Rebecca S. Eisenberg, *Can Patents Deter Innovation? The Anticommons in Biomedical Research*, 280 SCIENCE 698 (1998); B.H. Hall & R.H. Ziedonis, above n. 26; Paul A. David, The Digital Technology Boomerang: New Intellectual Property Rights Threaten Global "Open Science," Stanford University Department of Economics Working Paper No. 00016 (2000); Pamela Samuelson, *Intellectual Property in the Digital Economy: Why the Anti-Circumvention Regulations Need to be Revised*, 14 BERKELEY TECH. L.J., 519 (1999); J.H. Reichman & Pamela Samuelson, *Intellectual Property Rights in Data?*, 50 VAND. L. REV. 51 (1997); J.H. Reichman, *Database Protection in a Global Economy*, 2002 REVUE INTERNATIONALE DE DROIT ECONOMIQUE 455 (2002); Pamela Samuelson et al., *A Manifesto Concerning the Legal Protection of Computer Programs*, 94 COLUM. L. REV. 2308 (1994); Iain Cockburn, Issues in Business Method Patents, NBER Working Paper (Boston University 2001).

extent of legal liability in using knowledge inputs. Again policy makers and academics are concerned with the increase of litigation costs, including indirect costs, which may distort the innovative behavior of small companies.[39] As put well by John Barton,[40] there is a problem when "the number of intellectual property lawyers is growing faster than the amount of research." Trends in Europe show that this is no longer a purely American problem.

V. ICTs, "weightless" goods and services, and databases in the new economy

The twentieth century witnessed a transition to knowledge-driven productivity gains and economic growth in the industrially advanced economies, a process that spread further to the late-comers to industrialization. All economic activity is knowledge-based in the sense that the state of the arts in production, the conventions of commerce, and the norms of consumption all entail possession of information and cognitive skills. In the knowledge-driven economy, by contrast, the continuous search for new, reliable knowledge and the generation and absorbing of new information are centrally responsible for structural change and material progress. Efficiency gains now depend on sustained capacity for identifying and solving problems.

Accordingly, an increasing share of society's domestic resources comes to be devoted to activities of the latter sort, which form and recombine heterogeneous intangible knowledge-assets to generate further knowledge-assets. Recent decades have seen a significant acceleration in the pace of this historical transition. This developmental surge has been associated with the dramatic advances in information and communication technologies (ICT), especially the progress of digital computing and its convergence with telecommunications. The cluster of innovations – integrated circuits on silicon wafer, digital switches, electro-optical networks, and computer operating systems and applications – that has made possible the Internet can be conceptualized as a new and potent general purpose technology (GPT). This is a tool set that may be utilized in many ways, including combining with, transforming, and thereby enhancing the productivity and profitability of other, pre-existing technologies and organizational modes. The digital GPT cluster is not displacing "the old economy" but instead manifesting its potential for renewal.

A central feature common to the diverse processes of economic renewal presently underway is their intensified dependence upon the generation, capture, processing, transmission, storage and retrieval of information. The spectacularly declining costs of performing those activities promotes this intensification and

---

[39] See, e.g., Joshua Lerner, *Patenting in the Shadow of Competitors*, 38 J.L. & ECON 463 (1995).
[40] John Barton, *Reforming the Patent System*, 287 SCIENCE 1933, (2000).

induces the search for still newer uses toward which accumulating bodies of information can be put in order to form the capabilities referred to as knowledge. These processes include the capacity to find – or impose – order (information) in the myriad streams of data that now can be captured and subjected to systematic analysis. These reasons have made distributed databases and the tools to work with them increasingly prominent on the landscape of the digitally "renewed economy." The knowledge-driven society relies more heavily upon, and finds new and more productive uses for, the mundane entities that we call databases. These objects exemplify the enhanced role and social value that information assets of all sorts are coming to acquire in the modern, digital economy.

Of course, scientific and scholarly inquiry has long created collections of objects and observations as a means of preserving materials that could form the basis of later study and provide the necessary support for the collective memory that allows the cumulative advancement of knowledge. In former times, scientific databases were comparatively small and feasible for individuals and small groups of researchers to compile, annotate and maintain by labor-intensive methods. They often were published as typeset tables or simple, on-line documents. Recently, however, the size and complexity of scientific databases has grown enormously, and the potentialities of exploiting that data also have mounted. The necessary activities are absorbing increasing resources from publicly funded research programs in science and engineering, and there has been a commensurate expansion of the pressure upon researchers to find ways of extracting revenues from these "assets," so as to defray the costs of creating and maintaining them. In some degree, that pressure reflects the perception that the commercial database business can be lucrative.

The development of on-line databases has been proliferating in the world of business as well. Yet, the rapid growth of the commercial database industry in the United States during the 1990s, summarized by the statistics in the following Table, might present something of a puzzle to those who regard the necessity of stronger IP protection in the "new economy environment" to be a self-evident proposition. The 1991 decision of the U.S. Supreme Court (in the case of *Feist Publications v. Rural Telephone Service Co.*) removed the remaining legitimacy of the argument that the producer of a database was entitled to the protections of copyright law on the basis of the sheer "sweat of the brow" effort invested in the activity of compilation, regardless of whether such investment had involved a significantly original, creative achievement.[41] Despite this finding, the number of databases has increased sharply.

---

[41] Feist Publications v. Rural Tel. Serv. Co., 499 U.S. 340 (1991). The practical importance of the "sweat of the brow" argument for the legal protection of database investors in the United States has tended to be exaggerated. Legal opinion divided on the question, but, as Maurer and Scotchmer, have noted, courts in New York and California – the two main jurisdictions where copyright litigation traditionally occurred – did not accept this argument for extending copyright to databases. Both before and following the 1991

Performance of U.S. database industry post Feist v. Rural Telephone (1991)

Performance indicators	1991	1997	% change
Number of databases	7,637	10,338	35%
Number of files within databases (billions)	4.0	11.2	180%
Number of online searches (millions)	44.4	88.1	98%
Private sector's share in number of databases	*	70%	78%

*The private sector's share in 1977 was 22%.
Source: http://www.databasedata.org/hr1858/legalprt/hegalprt.html.

Both before and following the *Feist* ruling, copyright applied to the original selection, co-ordination, and arrangement of data within a database. Industry proponents of *sui generis* legislative protection voiced alarm that comprehensive electronically stored databases, being works of especially "low authorship" and containing material that was in the public domain, would not meet the standard set by copyright law. They argued that there was a compelling need to modify existing IP institutions to protect incentives for productive investments in this form of information asset from being undermined by "electronic piracy" in the new technological environment.

The scope of limitations established by the lost "sweat of the brow" protection for database producers could not be readily perceived by observers who were not steeped in the intricacies of the U.S. courts' treatment of copyright infringement claims. Nor was it evident to inexpert participants in the debates over the significance of the *Feist* ruling that most of the databases of substantial commercial valuable (i.e., those really worth pirating) contained many linked fields, and the selection and arrangement of data in these are sufficiently complex tasks to constitute some minimal level of creativity on the part of the author. U.S. copyright law clearly prevents the wholesale copying of such (non-trivial) database structures, and thus affords their publishers significant protection even in the post-*Feist* era. These points were still less discernable to spectators in Europe, among them the members of the European Commission's High-Level Expert Group who, at just that point in time, were considering policies to promote the development of "the Information Society."[42]

>   *Feist* ruling, copyright applied to the original selection, co-ordination, and arrangement of data within a database; many defendants therefore have been found liable for copyright infringement since 1991. See Stephen M. Maurer & Suzanne Scotchmer, *Database Protection: Is It Broken and Should We Fix It?* 284 SCIENCE 1129 (1999).

[42] The background of the EC Directive is discussed in P.A. David, *A Tragedy of the Public Knowledge "Commons"? – Global Science, Intellectual Property and the Digital Technology Boomerang*, RES. POL'Y (Special Issue on IPR Protections' Impact on Scientific Research)

Yet, had they looked more closely at the prevailing business practices, the High-Level Group would have discovered that a wide variety of other appropriation devices was available and was being successfully deployed by U.S. database businesses.[43] In the case of the so-called "full text" databases, which often consist entirely of copyrighted documents, the contents do not lose their protected status by virtue of having been incorporated into a database. Another appropriation device available under existing law is the use of copyrighted enhancements: databases frequently are sold in a package along with advanced software. Because software is copyrightable (and in some instances patentable), would-be database copiers must either try to market a different version of the material, which is likely to be less useful to users, or make their own investment in developing search tools to package with the copied contents.

Furthermore, U.S. technical database firms availed themselves of a variety of self-help protections against free-riding. Custom and semi-custom databases prepared for a small number of users provide virtually automatic protection against third parties. More generally, contracts between the owners of such databases and their customers that limit the latter's right to use or disclose the contents to third parties are enforceable as trade secrets, even where the underlying information and data cannot qualify for statutory protection.

Where information was distributed to larger numbers of customers, the industry availed itself of the use of shrinkwrap and clickwrap licenses,[44] search-only and password protected websites, and the frequent updating of contents, editing and enhancements of search facilities – all of which are especially valuable to researchers in rapidly changing branches of science. Besides these means, Stephen Maurer's survey of industry practice found that "a significant number of products are sold without any protection at all, sometimes for comparatively high prices."[45] The explanation is that large vendors can afford to circulate catalogues that enable them to reach a small number of customers who are prepared to pay high prices for comparatively obscure titles, whereas the smaller would-be copiers cannot afford the expense of trying to bring their wares to the attention of those same purchasers.

Thus, there was little if any substance to the rationale made by the E.C.'s High-Level Expert Group in their 1992 draft Directive, which called upon the Member States of the E.U. to implement statutory protections for intellectual

---

(P.A. David & B.H. Hall eds., forthcoming), *available at* http:siepr.stanford.edu/wpapers/index.html.

[43] *See* Stephen M. Maurer, Raw Knowledge: Protecting Technical Databases for Science and Industry, Report Prepared for NRC Workshop on Promoting Access to Scientific and Technical Data for the Public Interest, at 19 (1999).

[44] *See, e.g.,* J.H. Reichman & Jonathan A. Franklin, *Privately Legislated Intellectual Property Rights: Reconciling Freedom of Contract with Public Good Uses of Information*, 147 U. PA. L. REV. 875 (1999).

[45] Maurer, above n. 43, at 21.

property in the form of databases. Their argument was that such protection was needed to "level the playing field" so that European database creators could compete on less disadvantageous terms with their American counterparts.

VI. The E.U.'s *sui generis* property right in databases and its implications

A new and unexpected direct threat to the academic research enterprise in science and engineering thus emerged in mid-1990s as a result of the extension of *sui generis* copyright protection to databases, even to those containing non-copyrightable material. This institutional innovation crystallized in the European Union Directive on the Legal Protection of Databases.[46] It enjoined member states to create a new, broadly comprehensive type of intellectual property. These rights were free from a number of the important and long-standing limitations and exceptions traditionally provided by copyright law in order to safeguard access to information used in socially beneficial, knowledge-creating activities, such as research and teaching. The E.U. Directive applies equally to non-electronic and electronic databases, even though it originated as a strategic industrial policy response to the commercial development of on-line (electronic) databases in America.

Further, as a device to secure international acceptance of the new approach initiated by this Directive, reciprocity provisions were included. The latter in effect threatened the commercial creators of databases who were nationals of foreign states outside the E.U. with retaliatory infringement of copyright material in their products, unless their respective governments became signatories to a World Intellectual Property Organization (WIPO) draft convention on databases. This convention had been framed to embody the essential provisions of the protection established under the E.U. Directive.[47]

---

[46] *See* above n. 35.
[47] The 1996 draft was entitled: "Basic Proposal for the Substantive Provisions of the Treaty on Intellectual Property in Respect of Databases ... ," WIPO Doc. CRNR/DC (30 Aug. 1996) [hereinafter E.C. Directives on Databases]. It has been pointed out that in this regard, as well as in others, the E.U. Directive called for a departure from the principle of administering commercial laws on a national treatment basis, under which a country's domestic laws (whether for intellectual property protection, or unfair business practices) should treat foreign nationals like the country's own citizens. The principle of national treatment is embodied in Article 3 of the TRIPS Agreement, as well as more generally in the Paris Convention (20 Mar. 1883, *as revised at* Stockholm on 14 July 1967, 828 U.N.T.S. 305) (on patents and trademark protection) and the Berne Convention (9 Sept. 1886, *as revised at* Paris on 24 July 1971, 1161 U.N.T.S. 3) (on copyright protection). Objections to this departure were recorded in the testimony of the General Counsel of the U.S. Department of Commerce (Andrew J. Pincus), in the 106th Congress House Hearings on H.R. 1858, *Consumer and Investor Access to Information Act of 1999, Hearing on H.R. 1858 Before the House Subcomm. on Telecomm., Trade, and Consumer Prot.*, 106th Cong. § F (1999).

The European Commission's strategy set in motion an Administration-initiated legislative response in the U.S. Congress, which has led to two competing draft statutes being actively debated to this point in time. The response began in May 1996 with the introduction, at the behest of the U.S. Patent and Trademark Office, of House Bill H.R. 3531, short-titled the "Database Investment and Intellectual Property Antipiracy Act of 1996."[48] This first and ill-considered rush to legislate soon encountered opposition from the U.S. academic research community and non-commercial publishers of scientific information.[49] Although the Bill was not enacted, the legislative genie was let out of the bottle, and two further pieces of unsuccessful legislation have been proposed. The first was "The Collections of Information Antipiracy Act," H.R. 345, which was introduced in January 1999 and represents a reincarnation of the pernicious approach taken in the original legislative proposal. A second bill, "The Consumer and Investors Access to Information Act," H.R. 1858, was introduced in May 1999 and contained provisions protecting access to database information that are more responsive to the objections raised against H.R. 3531. This bill failed to gain support in the Senate, but its proponents have promised to try again.

A rapid review of the main features of the E.C.'s Database Directive of 1996 highlights the following problematic points:[50]

- The Directive's *sui generis* approach departs from the long established principles of intellectual property law by removing the distinction between protection of expression and protection of facts and ideas, a distinction that is central in U.S. copyright law and was embodied in the TRIPS agreement.
- Compilers of databases in the E.U. now are able to assert ownership and demand payment for licensing the use of content already in the public domain, including material that otherwise could not be copyright-protected. In complying with the Directive, member states do not provide any specific incentives for the generation of new database content, as distinguished from new compilations. Nor can it be thought that copyrights in databases are being granted as part of a social bargain, in exchange for the public disclosure of material that hitherto was not revealed.
- A second distinction, fundamental in copyright law, between original expressive matter and pre-existing expressive matter, has been discarded

---

[48] Database Investment and Intellectual Property Antipiracy Act of 1996, H.R. 3531, 104th Cong. (1996).
[49] NATIONAL RESEARCH COUNCIL, above n. 32; NATIONAL RESEARCH COUNCIL, A QUESTION OF BALANCE: PRIVATE RIGHTS AND THE PUBLIC INTEREST IN SCIENTIFIC AND TECHNICAL DATABASES (National Academy of Sciences Press 1999); J.H. Reichman & Paul Uhlir, *Database Protection at the Crossroads: Recent Developments and Their Impact on Science and Technology*, 14 BERKELEY TECH. L.J. 793 (1999).
[50] The following draws upon the documented legal analysis in NATIONAL RESEARCH COUNCIL, above n. 32, at 148–153.

by language of the Directive. The latter fails to attach any legal significance to the difference between expressive matter that already exists (arguably in the public domain) and matter that is original and newly disclosed. Domestic laws and national courts that reaffirm this omission in effect allow a database maker to qualify for renewal of the 15-year term of exclusive rights over the database as a whole, simply by making a significant investment in updates, additions, revisions.[51]

- Strict limitations upon re-use of database contents are imposed by the Directive, requiring third-party regeneration or payment for licenses to extract such material. This would inhibit integration and recombination of existing scientific database contents with new material to provide more useful, specialized research resources.
- But regardless of whether or not it is possible in theory to regenerate the raw contents of a database from publicly available sources, under the terms of the Directive, investors in database production can always deny third parties the right to use pre-existing data in value-added applications, even when the third parties are willing to pay royalties on licenses for such use. It would therefore be possible for an initial database producer simply to block subsequent creation of new, special-purpose databases, which reproduced parts of existing compilations, wherever the regeneration of such data *de novo* was infeasible or costly. Examples include compiling years of remote-sensing satellite observations, assembling data-tracks from high energy particle collision detectors, or developing multi-year bibliographic compilations of scientific publications and citations thereto.
- Where a database maker also held the exclusive rights to license previously copyright-protected publications, it would be entirely proper under the terms of the Directive to refuse third parties licenses in that material, while incorporating it within a database protected under the terms of the E.C. Directive. The Directive excludes conditions for compulsory licensing and fails to provide remedies for abuse of the legal protections newly accorded to database investors. Thus, it opens the door for the construction of indefinitely renewable monopolies in scientific data, whether or not that data may be technically regenerated.

---

[51] *See* E.C. Directive on Databases, above n. 35, arts. 7(1) (providing an initial 15-year term from the date of completion); 7(2) (extending protection for an additional 15 years if the database "is made available to the public in whatever manner" before the initial term expires); 7(3) (allowing 15-year renewals for "[a]ny substantial change, evaluated qualitatively or quantitatively, to the contents of a database ... from the accumulation of successive additions, deletions or alterations, which ... result in ... a substantial new investment."). Under U.S. copyright law, only the additions and revisions themselves – which would be considered as "derivative work" from the prior original expressive matter – would be entitled to fresh legal protection. *See* 17 U.S.C. §§ 101, 103, 106(2) (2000).

- The Directive abandons the principle of fair use for research, as distinct from extraction and use of data for purposes of illustration in teaching or research. How "illustrative use" is to be interpreted remains ill defined, pending some infringement litigation that would provide opportunity for a court ruling in the matter. But the current consensus among IP scholars is that "illustration" falls far short of the normal scope of research use of copyrighted material.[52]

The absence of fair-use exclusions for research (and research training) creates the prospect of a two-way squeeze on publicly funded research programs, as the costs of obtaining commercially supplied data are likely to rise. The ten-fold rise in the unit prices of remote-sensing satellite images that immediately followed the privatization of Landsat satellite operations in 1985, and its withering effects upon university-based research projects, may be recalled in this connection.[53] Continuing pressures for cuts in government budgets and the priority that is accorded to applications-oriented research over exploratory science are likely to encourage derogation to commercial database generators of the function of compiling, updating and publishing databases. One risk that arises is the threat to data quality in separating database creation and maintenance from the scientific expertise of the research community that creates and uses the data. Another is the resulting squeeze on public research resources, as already restrictive appropriations would have to be spent on purchasing data and database licenses.

The benefits to society of enabling private appropriation of the economic value of databases (and similar areas in other research fields, such as new genetic diagnostic kits or drug therapies) depend on changes in the probability of valuable discoveries in both the near term and the long run. The rights granted by the E.C.'s Database Directive restructure the "information space" so as to readily extract licensing fees from users. This should have the predictable effect of restraining searches without much expectation of quickly finding something with high applications value. In other words, the probabilities of unexpected discoveries would be further reduced by the economically restricted utilization of the facility. Targeted searches may be affordable, but wholesale extraction of database contents to permit exploratory search activities is especially likely to be curtailed.

The adverse influences of the consequent lost discoveries are likely to ripple outwards. The development of new and more powerful search devices and techniques of pattern recognition, statistical analysis, and the like are discoveries that would be made collectively more likely through the exploratory use of data by a larger number of researchers. Therefore, some cost of extracting economic rents will likely come in the form of smaller research benefits in the

---

[52] *See, e.g.*, Reichman & Uhlir, above n. 49; Reichman & Samuelson, above n. 38.
[53] *See* discussion above in text accompanying nn. 33–35.

future. Consider also the possibly deleterious effect of setting up a model of IP exploitation of databases upon the construction of some new, presently unimagined information tools that would require the assembly (and licensing) of myriad information components from many diverse sources.

A concrete illustration of the creative power of collaborations built to exploit enhanced digital technologies is provided by the vast, multi-dimensional "information space" that has been built up over many years by the research community coordinated today by the European Bioinformatics Institute (EBI). This "virtual library" is a dynamic collective research tool rather than a simple repository of information. The ordinary conceptualization of "a database" is too static, and, in a sense too pre-structured, to comprehend the potential for discoveries that has been created by this collective construct. Yet, as the EBI's Director has testified, this information space began to be formed long before the research communities involved gave any consideration to intellectual property restrictions on the use of the information contents that were being linked for subsequent retrieval and analysis. The implication was clear that it would be far more difficult in today's environment to create this particular research tool.[54]

VII. Reconsidering the traditional economic rationale for copyright protection

The advent of technologies that greatly reduced both the fixed and variable costs of reproduction and transmission of information elicited strong defensive reactions from business publishing interests. It was said that unrestricted use of plain paper photocopiers in the hands of readers threatened the profitability of conventional publishers. However, careful economic analysis has shown that such is not necessarily the case. Under the traditional analysis of the social efficiency of copyright law, it was held that stringent protection against unauthorized copying could generate social as well as private losses from underutilization of the intellectual asset. Yet, this is not true in cases where the cost to consumers of obtaining an unauthorized copy is greater than they would be charged by a copyright holder who had a strict, enforceable monopoly. That is, strengthening copyright protection could enhance social welfare even without stimulating the production of new works of authorship, so long as lax restraints on copying reduced the demand for authorized copies ("originals") greatly in relation to total consumption of the work in question.[55]

---

[54] See Statement by Graham Cameron, in IPR Aspects of Internet Collaborations, Strata Programme Working Group Report, EUR 19456 (European Commission, Directorate General Research April 2001).

[55] See I.E. Novos & M. Waldman, The Effects of Increased Copyright Protection: An Analytical Approach, 92 J. POL. ECON. 236 (1984); W.R. Johnson, The Economics of Copying, 93 J. POL. ECON. 158 (1985), for these two argument, respectively.

However, those arguments rested crucially on the supposition that the private cost to the consumer of copying an authorized original was greater than the copyright monopolists' marginal costs. However, this assumption has in many situations been invalidated by advances in copying technologies.[56] The complementarity in production between authorized "originals" and low-cost copies could mean (under conditions in which the demand for copies of such works was sufficiently price elastic) that a more permissive law regarding copying – by allowing utilization of highly efficient copying technology – actually could increase the effective demand for originals as well.

Furthermore, the most profitable way for business to exploit the potential monopoly power conveyed by legal protections for intellectual property is not always that of trying to extract the maximum consumer surplus from each individual user. Even traditional "content owners" of information goods such as books, video-recordings, CDs, and software programs may be able to reap greater profits by allowing sharing (the *free* copying for use) of information goods among certain groups of consumers. The candidate groups would be those whose members were closely integrated socially and whose collective willingness to pay exceeded the sum of their individual revealed demands for the commodity in question.[57]

This represents an important qualification of the widely asserted claim that digitally assisted, low marginal cost reproduction encourages "piracy" that must be injurious to copyright holders, and therefore warrants introduction of stronger protections against all unauthorized copying. In the context of the present discussion, it is especially appropriate to point out that spatially distributed scientific and engineering research *networks* are paradigmatic of the self-selected producer groupings whose information goods requirements might be more profitably met by publishers and vendors who permitted or facilitated free (intra-group) sharing.[58]

The key condition for arguments of this sort is that allowing customers to bundle themselves into such consumer units permits increased aggregate sales, so long as the groups are "natural clubs" (for example, families and scientific research teams) that organized themselves for some other purpose than spreading the fixed costs of acquiring access to the copyable information product.

---

[56] S.J. Liebowitz, *Copying and Indirect Appropriability: Photocopying of Journals*, 93 J. POL. ECON. 945 (1985).

[57] For further discussion, see P.A. David, A Tragedy of the Public Knowledge "Commons"?, Oxford IP Research Centre Working Paper 19 et seq. (2000) (referring to Yannis Bakos et al., Shared Information Goods, University of Chicago Law and Economics Working Paper No. 67 (2d. Series) (Feb. 1999), and forerunners in this vein).

[58] Moreover, in "the knowledge society" – where collaborative generation of new ideas and practices is expected to characterize a larger and larger segment of business activity – the scientific research network, conceived of as a form of "competence based club," may become a paradigm for an economically much larger part of the market for information-goods that are research inputs.

But, in actuality, the restrictions on group membership could be dispensed with in technological circumstances that restricted the ease of producing copies. Where the latter were embedded in a physical medium, such as a printed book, publishers could benefit from the formation of club-like organizations that aggregated individual consumer demands into effective "bundles." The English book trade thus came eventually to take a tolerant, and even appreciative, view of the local commercial circulating libraries that arose during the eighteenth century to cater to the growth of demand for popular literature.[59]

In fact, the experience of commercial circulating libraries conforms to economic models demonstrating that lax restraints on copying (or free sharing) could be compatible with profitable publishing. More recent and more intricate theoretical arguments have raised more profound challenges to the traditional rationale for copyright protection in the digital information age. In a pioneering and mathematically elegant analysis, Boldrin and Levine show that, even in the absence of restrictions on the copying of a new information good, competitive markets can support a socially efficient equilibrium in the production and consumption of information assets.[60]

The underlying idea is that, although unrestricted copying eventually will drive the price of the marginal copy to zero, it does not happen rapidly. Even if new technology has made copying rapid and essentially costless at the margin, the authors point out that consumption use may degrade the reproduction rate and the supply of copies cannot instantly undergo infinite expansion. Hence, the possessor of a first copy, or the original instance of the intellectual or cultural work, has an asset that can command a positive price under competitive conditions. Its price reflects the present value of the future flow of marginal utilities that subsequent copies will yield to impatient consumers. Thus, the notion that free-riding on the part of consumers would leave the producer of the first copy with nothing for her efforts is unjustifed, because the process takes time and there is a value to reading the best seller, or viewing the latest DNA sequence, sooner rather than later.

Still more recently, this line of analysis has been taken a very significant step farther by Quah.[61] The ability of competitive equilibrium prices to support the socially efficient dynamic allocation, which maximizes the present value of the future stream of consumers' utilities, survives the complete removal of all the restrictions that copyright law (and analogous *sui generis* legal protections

---

[59] *See* Richard Roehl & Hal R. Varian, *Circulating Libraries and Video Rental Stores*, 6(5) FIRST MONDAY (2000), *available at* www.firstmonday.dk/issues/issue6_5/roehl/index.html#r8.
[60] Michele Boldrin & David K. Levine, *The Case Against Intellectual Property*, 92 AM. ECON. REV. 209 (2002); Michele Boldrin & David K. Levine, Perfectly Competitive Innovation, Federal Reserve Bank of Minneapolis Staff Report No. 303 (Mar. 2002).
[61] Danny Quah, 24/7 Competitive Innovation, LSE Working Paper (Apr. 2002), *available at* http://econ.lse.ac.uk/staff/quah.

for works of "low authorship") allows possessors of "the first copy" to impose upon licensed users. Whereas in the Boldrin-Levine model the terms of the weakened license permit purchasers to make copies only for future consumption purposes, Quah's analysis shows that the first copy can command a positive value even when those copies can be sold in competition with those supplied by the original producer of the information good, so long as the rate at which copies can be generated remains bounded from above.[62]

Commercial database firms in the United States appear to understand at least one facet of the economic reality that is reflected in these theoretical propositions. Copyright or other legal protections was not necessary for them to run profitable businesses, in part because they could charge a premium to customers who wanted access to early updates of the contents and wished to put the information they extracted into other, equally unprotected databases.[63] To be sure, these results do not go so far as to say that the competitive market valuation of the "first copy" always would be sufficiently large to cause every possible information asset to be created. The cost of the creative effort may be too large, but we do not ask competitive markets for conventional commodities to provide them even when the cost of doing so exceeds what consumers would be willing to pay.

In light of these deepening doubts about the old rationale for legal monopolies in readily copied and widely shared information goods, the current rush to tighten the copyright regime and encourage strict enforcement of "anti-piracy" provisions of all kinds may come to be perceived as a serious mistake. This is so not only because it will turn out to have been unnecessary for the socially efficient production and distribution of an increasingly important class of commodities in the New Economy, or because it will have consequences that were injurious to the conduct of open science. In addition, policy makers are likely to suffer more obloquy if it becomes evident that their enthusiasm for entrenching the old IP institutions was antithetical to the development and exploitation of profitable new business opportunities.

Among some leading innovators concerned with the future trajectory of e-commerce, there is growing recognition that the conventional regime of proprietary controls over the use of information by industry may hinder exploitation of new profit opportunities being created by digital, networked technology. In Internet-based media industries, peer-to-peer (P2P) services

---

[62] The quickening rate of copying that Quah's analysis, *id.*, contemplates is alluded to by the reference to "24/7-time" – the continuous, "round the clock every day of the week" pace at which the Internet permits economic activity to run. At the limit, where copying becomes infinitely rapid, Quah finds that the intuition of the traditional economic argument that competitive markets will fail is regained. The first copy (asset price) and the price of the marginal consumption flow both go to zero.

[63] As noted earlier, U.S. database firms also provide a variety of complementary services, including efficient and rapid search algorithms, which also contribute to the profitability of their operations in the absence of intellectual property protection for the database contents.

have emerged, featuring shared storage, shared information and shared processing. The new P2P applications devolve significant autonomy and control to independent nodes in the network ; they capitalize on under-utilized network-connected computing resources at the edge of the network ; and they operate as transparent end-to-end services across an Internet of uneven and temporary connections. One vision of the future sees the greater effectiveness of this comparatively unstructured and self-organized mode of producing and delivering new information to individual users as the basis for new and competitive commercial services. These services will challenge the incumbency of traditional business forms in information-intensive production and distribution activities.

Not surprisingly, therefore, spokespersons for P2P business applications have been worried by the threat that proprietary standards strategies on the part of platform vendors would create barriers to collaborative computing in the same way that scientists engaged in distributed Internet projects worry about IP-created barriers to the flow of information, and the diminishing future prospects for easy voyages of exploration in "information space." Here is Esther Dyson's formulation of the threat to P2P, and a possible means of avoiding it:

> "The growth of P2P services will be retarded if this world fragments into warring proprietary platforms, forcing users to make unpalatable choices and killing synergistic network effects. Some existing proposed standards fit naturally into P2P models, including simple object access protocol (SOAP) and universal discovery description and integration (UDDI).... At some point it will make sense to have at least *de facto* standards for common P2P elements. Standards bodies [which under ANSI rules preclude adoption of proprietary specifications that are not freely licensed] provide a place for industry participants to gather, compare notes, identify shared challenges and find common ground."[64]

At the 2001 World Economic Forum meeting in Davos, Switerzland, Richard Li, executive Chairman of Pacific Century CyberWorks, is reported to have voiced essentially the same worries, according to news accounts. "His biggest concern about the development of broadband technology was the conservatism of many content providers who were determined to retain copyright protection and unwilling to consider creative new business models."[65] Significantly enough, the emerging P2P approach to network-based computing and computer-mediated telecommunications services, and the demonstrated capacity of that non-hierarchical form of machine organization to mobilize distributed intelligence for the rapid solution of new problems, has

---

[64] *Release 1.0*, 10(2) ESTHER DYSON'S MONTHLY REPORT 8 (22 Nov. 2000), *available at* http://release1.edventure.com.
[65] *Industry Leaders See a New Era in the Tech Revolution*, INTERNATIONAL HERALD TRIBUNE, 30 Jan. 2001, at 1.

strong elements of homomorphism with the historical functioning of "invisible colleges" in the open science domain.[66]

What has changed is the qualitative effects of the technological capacity to link "distributed intelligent resources" in a host of differentiated sub-communities at negligible cost and thus provide rapid capabilities of searching the "information spaces" thereby created. What hitherto had been the peculiar organizational facility for discovery and invention that scholarly inquiry afforded practitioners of open science may become a much more widely relevant mode of generating innovative information goods.

The transformation that appears to be bringing the world of P2P network-based commerce and the world of "invisible colleges" of academic inquiry into closer alignment is intriguing and potentially promising for the future synergetic interactions between those two spheres of human endeavor. It stands in much greater need of concerted public policy support than the present impetus being given to the negotiation of university–industry collaborative research agreements with IP provisions acceding to the monopoly-protecting strategies familiar to conventional R&D-intensive businesses.

My point in drawing attention to the parallels between the organization of open-science communities and the information-intensive strategies emerging in the domain of cyber-commerce is simply this: policymakers in both the industrially advanced countries and in other regions who are echoing their views may be making a serious error in pressing university and public-institute research groups to secure and manage proprietary rights to the use of new knowledge. However fashionable this current policy trend may be at present, those subscribing to it may be trying to ride the wave of the past at the expense of building the wave of the future. In actuality, if such efforts to create wealth from knowledge through IPRs succeeded, the result might be to have rendered more difficult their economies' eventual development of novel kinds of computer-network intensive service organizations and the other new lines of e-business.

Rather than seeing open science communities as asserting claims that stand in the way of the exploration and exploitation of profitable business opportunities built on exclusive ownership and control of digital content, their characteristic mode of disclosure and data-sharing might well be regarded as a precursor and paradigm of future "New Economy" activities that will fully exploit the potentialities opened by the Internet. To put this thought in proper historical perspective, the ethos and mode of organization that have been associated historically with publicly supported scientific work

---

[66] See P.A. David, *Communication Norms and the Collective Cognitive Performance of "Invisible Colleges,"* in CREATION AND TRANSFER OF KNOWLEDGE: INSTITUTIONS AND INCENTIVES 115 (G.B. Navaretti et al. eds., Physical Verlag 1997); P.A. David et al., *The Research Network and the "New Economics of Science,"* in THE ORGANIZATION OF INNOVATIVE ACTIVITIES IN EUROPE 303 (A. Gambardella & F. Malerba eds., Cambridge University Press 1999).

groups (at least since the seventeenth century) now could be coming into its own as the basis for new forms of *commercial* activity feasible in the Digital Age. This certainly is what some observers of the open source software movement now suggest.[67] What policymaking for economic development in the twenty-first century ought to consider carefully, therefore, is how to avoid promoting an entrenchment of durable IP regimes that could fatally obstruct that evolution.

VIII. Modest proposals: IPR policies to preserve the public knowledge commons

What sort of intellectual property arrangements will be best suited to the socially efficient exploitation of the production and consumption possibilities emerging in the "weightless economy," and to the construction of the "digital information spaces" in which globally collaborative programs of discovery and invention are likely to flourish? The policy position on copyright and copyright-like protections of intellectual property that I advocate here is meliorist, rather than radical.[68]

In truth, I am attracted by the elegance of the controversial idea of creating a positive right to fair use of legally protected information and research tools for educational and research purposes. There are indications that international institutions may see a link here between intellectual property and human rights.[69]

---

[67] *See, e.g.*, P.A. David (Principal Investigator), The Organization and Viability of Open Source Software: A Proposal to the National Science Foundation, Stanford Institute for Economic Policy Research Paper (22 Jan. 2001), *available at* http://siepr.stanford.edu/programs/opensoftware-David/NSF-CISE/Open Four Final.htm. *See also* J.-M. Dalle et al., Advancing Economic Research on the Free and Open Source Software Mode of Production, SEPR. Discussion paper no. 04–03 (December 2004, *available at* http://siepr.stanford.edu/papers/pdf/04–03.html.

[68] *See, e.g.*, P.A. David, A Tragedy of the Public Knowledge "Commons"? Global Science, Intellectual Property and the Digital Technology Boomerang, Stanford University Department of Economics Working Paper 00–16 (Oct. 2000), *available at* http://www-econ.stanford.edu/faculty/wpapers/index.html; P.A. David, The Consequences for Internet-Mediated Research Collaborations of Broadening IPR Protections, *in* IPR Aspects of Internet Collaborations, above n. 54, *available at* http://europa.eu.int/comm/research/area/ipr_en.html.

[69] The joint panel discussion organized by WIPO and the Office of United Nations High Commission for Human Rights, to commemorate the 50th anniversary of the Universal Declaration of Human Rights, addressed issues such as biodiversity, the production of traditional (ethnic) knowledge and innovation, the right to culture, health, non-discrimination, and scientific freedom. *See* WIPO, Intellectual Property and Human Rights, WIPO Publication No. 762 (1998). Another possible straw in the wind is to be seen in Article 10 of the European Convention on Human Rights, which prescribes the right to freedom of speech as protecting not only the positive right to expression, but the right to receive information. Universal Declaration of Human Rights G.A. Res. 217A (III), U.N. GAOR, UN Doc A/810, at 71 (1948).

However, the involvement of human rights courts in intellectual property law is likely to be a distant and incremental evolution, if it happens at all. It therefore seems expedient to attend to less far-reaching means of improving the present state of affairs.

Developed and developing economies alike have a shared interest in halting and, if possible, reversing the trend toward the further strengthening and extension of IPRs to every conceivable form of information. My convictions in this regard have crystallized as a response to the prospective implications of the European Union's database legislation, the proposals for similar *sui generis* protections that surfaced in the U.S. Congress, and the likelihood that the European Commission soon will follow the United States in introducing new criminal law sanctions to reinforce the effectiveness of digital "self help" technologies, such as watermarking and encryption. These institutional changes appear to me as last-ditch efforts to entrench an approach to IPRs that is being rendered increasingly obsolete by the technological developments driving "the New Economy." Yet, worse than exemplifying ingenious adaptations to preserve the workability of an old legal regime, the continuation of this trend may seriously curtail the benefits developed and developing societies alike are able to derive from vastly expanded access to scientific, technological and cultural knowledge.

When considering the available courses of action to counter threats to the pursuit of knowledge arising from recent expansions of intellectual property protections, distinctions of two kinds help to simplify the discussion. First, there is an obvious difference between the altered terms and the scope of statutory IP protections, on the one hand, and legislative steps designed to reinforce the use of "self help" technologies that enable copyright owners to control the dissemination of digital content, on the other. A second distinction has to be drawn between the situation of countries where legislative innovations affecting intellectual property may be under consideration, and those in which such statutes already are *faits accomplis*. The questions of practical interest concern implementation and enforcement.

For most nations the appropriate recommendations in regard to both the technological and the legal measures that would restrict access to digital data used for research and training would seem to follow Nancy Reagan's admonition to youths who are offered the opportunity to experiment with addictive drugs: "Just say 'No' !" This option remains open to all countries that are signatories to the TRIPS Agreement and also to those who have not yet joined the WTO. To date, there is no international convention in force for the legal protection of databases, and the articles of the TRIPS Agreement do not pertain to database protection *per se*. Thus, unless a case were successfully made for interpreting the *sui generis* protections for databases created by the E.C. Directive of March 11, 1996 as somehow being covered under copyright, nothing in the TRIPS agreements would oblige other nations to follow the (misdirected) leaders in this regard. Such an interpretation, moreover, would be utterly tendentious in view of the numerous respects in which the terms of the E.C. Database Directive deviate from the principles embraced by national and international copyright law.

Much the same general position may be advanced in regard to the possible products of the legislative drive to provide legal reinforcement for technological measures of self help on the part of copyright owners. As has been noted previously, the U.S. Digital Millennium Copyright Act includes language making it illegal to furnish means of circumventing "any technological measure that effectively controls access" to a copyrighted work. As dubious and in some respects as counterproductive as these sections of the law have been found to be by both legal and technical experts,[70] it remains conceivable that an effort will be made to press other countries into following suit. However the issue in this case is not one of legal principle, but instead belongs to the wider and unresolved debate about the feasibility and desirability of uniform international standards of *enforcement* of intellectual property rights.

Nothing presently compels countries that have signed TRIPS to arrive at uniformity in the degree of enforcement of their IP laws. It is true that the international conventions and laws governing patents, trademarks, copyrights, trade secrets, industrial designs, semiconductor mask works, and still other protections must be "effectively implemented and enforced" by each of the nations belonging to the WTO. Nevertheless, the term "effectively" remains subject to considerable variations in interpretation.[71] In addition, the Agreement explicitly recognizes several bases for exemptions from the provisions made for protection of the rights of owners of intellectual property, including appeal to fair use or public interest.[72] Inasmuch as national

---

[70] On the question of "counterproductive" effects, Dam, above n. 37, notes the testimony by cryptography experts to the effect that the wording of the 1998 DMCA (17 U.S.C. § 1201) would make it illegal even to devise and distribute algorithms used in testing encryption systems by trying to defeat them and, more generally, would greatly impede research aimed at making such devices cheap and faster to apply. This point nicely recapitulates the larger theme that what the would-be protectors of technological innovation frequently fail to grasp is that information is an input in the process of generating new knowledge.

[71] *See* J.H. Reichman, *Securing Compliance with the TRIPS Agreement After U.S. v. India*, 4 J. INT'L. ECON. L. 585 (1998); J.H. Reichman, *Enforcing the Enforcement Procedures of the TRIPS Agreement*, 37 VA. J. INT'L L. 335 (1997) on the interpretation of the enforcement articles included in Part III of the TRIPS Agreement; *and* the survey of implementation issues in Louise Keely, Pathway from Poverty? Intellectual Property and Developing Countries, Centre for Economic Performance Special Report (Apr. 2000).

[72] *See* Agreement on Trade-Related Aspects of Intellectual Property Rights, 15 Apr. 1994, Marrakesh Agreement Establishing the World Trade Organization, Annex 1C, LEGAL INSTRUMENTS – RESULTS OF THE URUGUAY ROUND vol. 31, 33 I.L.M. 81 arts. 13, 17, 24, 27.2, 30, 37 (1994). *See also id.* arts. 31 (compulsory licenses), 8.1 (measures to prevent abuse), 40 (control of anti-competitive practices).

governments retain the right to create a haven for "fair use" of protected intellectual property in the public interest, their ability to effectively exercise that right would be impeded by requiring that they prevent their own nationals from circumventing unilaterally imposed access blocking technologies.

The foregoing remarks obviously apply to the situation in which the developing economies find themselves with respect to IPRs that would have seriously inhibited worthy public interest activities, had not the latter gained statutory exemptions under the laws' provisos for fair use. It remains an interesting question as to whether the sphere of applicability extends still farther. Could this analysis also encompass retroactive remedial legislative actions on the part of the economically advanced member states of the E.U. that have not yet implemented the E.C. Directive on the Legal Protection of Databases in their national laws? Whereas some countries, such as the United Kingdom, were quick to implement the Directive without entering any exceptions or liberalizing interpretations, other European states, such as the Netherlands, Greece, Ireland, Italy, Portugal, and Spain, have not rushed to comply with its terms. This has opened a window for attempts to modify the Directive's force by suitable interpretations in the way it is implemented. But, rather than leaving it to individual members to undertake to ameliorate the harm that a literal acceptance and enforcement of the Directive might do to the scientific research community in Europe, it would be far more satisfactory for the E.C. to now propose a harmonized set of fair use exemptions as a minimal remedial step.

That solution, however, is unlikely to emerge spontaneously. A considerable amount of political pressure would have to be brought to bear upon the Commission, perhaps from a coalition formed among the smaller member states that have yet to implement the Directive. Yet, in view of the politically fragmented condition of Europe's basic science research communities, the prospects of an effective coalition emerging would remain rather remote unless it were energized by business corporations, similar to those in the United States, who have lobbied actively against counterpart database legislation. The political economy, therefore, is likely to turn not upon the implications for science and technology in Europe, but instead upon whether there exists a significant section of European industry that comes to perceive the Directive as harmful to their economic fortunes.

The important principle to be established is simple: whatever legal rights that societies construct regarding "intellectual property," whether under international patent and copyright regimes or by *sui generis* protections, the licensing terms available to "owners" should never be allowed to create inefficient artificial impediments to the intensive utilization of the contents of virtual archives and information tools. As I have suggested, this principle may be just as important for the future of new commercial ventures based upon computer-mediated telecommunications as it is for the fundamental research organized by non-profit institutions. It should be widely recognized that such a principle is not necessarily detrimental to profitable enterprise in information-goods markets.

In the view of most economists, the "first best" allocation system in situations where goods are produced with high fixed costs but far lower marginal costs, is to apply what is known as the "Ramsey pricing" rule. This fits the case of information products, such as scientific publication and data, where the first-copy costs are very great in relationship to the negligible unit costs of copies. Ramsey pricing in essence amounts to price discrimination between users with inelastic demand and users for whom demand is extremely price-sensitive. The former class of buyers will bear high prices without curtailing the quantity purchased, and hence not suffer great reductions in consumption utility, whereas the low prices offered to those in the second category will spare them the burden of damaging cutbacks in use.

The case might then be made for treating scholars and public sector, university-based researchers as having highly elastic information and data demands. Such a characterization would follow from considering that this category of knowledge-workers is employed on projects that have fixed budget allocations from public (or non-profit) entities, organizations that are expected to promote the interests of society at large. Given the strong complementarity between their data and information requirements, on the one hand, and the other resources they use in their research, on the other, raising the real prices of the former inputs would sharply reduce the quantity of useful work that such projects can accomplish so long as their budgets remain fixed. Obviously, there is no workable economic or political mechanism that would serve to "index" the nominal value of public research budgets on the prices of commercially provided data. Even were such mechanisms to be found, the commitment to implement them on the part of the rich societies would likely result in pricing the use of scientific information and data beyond the reach of many poorer societies.

The general thrust of the policy advocated here is thus quite simple. Statutes that would establish legal ownership rights for compilers of scientific and technological databases also should include provisions mandating compulsory licensing of scientific database contents at marginal costs (of data extraction and distribution) to accredited individuals and research institutions. The implication is that the fixed costs should be covered by lump-sum subscription charges, which would be waived in the case of researchers engaged in constructing and maintaining these databases under the auspices of publicly supported projects.

A fully consistent, yet bolder, recommendation would have the same provisions apply more broadly. They could be extended to all the users of such data and information resources who agreed to distribute the data they generated on the same basis as that on which they had been able to access the data used in creating them. Such universal application of the so-called "Copyleft" principle in the GNU General Public License leaves open the possibility to commercial ventures of licensing and direct marketing of ancillary and complementary goods and services.[73] By such means firms might recoup the fixed costs of their contribution to the "information infrastructures" they would make in participation with publicly sponsored researchers.

Further and still more far-reaching reforms affecting patents on research tools would follow from this approach. The first would institute a public policy of "patent buy-outs," under which public tax revenues would be used to purchase the rights to this class of inventions, and place them in the public domain.[74] A possible device to prevent confiscation of valuable patents at arbitrarily low compensation or awards of inappropriately high "prizes" to patentees would take the following provision. Such inventions would be made legally subject to compulsory licensing at a reasonable royalty rate, and the (regulated) rights to the revenue stream would then be publicly auctioned, with the government standing ready to acquire the rights for the public domain by default if a pre-announced "reservation price" was not attained by a private purchaser.

There are circumstances where significant patent protection might be warranted by the high fixed costs that public regulatory policies impose upon the private developers of innovative commodities that are readily reverse-engineered and cheaply copied. An example is the extensive field-testing requirements for pharmaceutical products and medical devices. However, these represent the exception rather than the rule, and the end products themselves typically do not have the essential public-goods properties associated with information-goods and information-tools. Rather, it is the product safety-testing information regarding new pharmaceuticals and other complex and potentially dangerous products that actually constitute the public goods. Yet, it should be pointed out that a convincing economic case has still to be made for using legally constructed monopolies to solve the resulting appropriability problem, rather than, say, public procurement contracts for safety testing.[75]

---

[73] David McGowan, *The Legal Implications of Open Source Software*, 2001 ILL. L. REV. 241 (2001); Yochai Benkler, *Coase's Penguin, or Linux and the Nature of the Firm*, 112 YALE L.J. 369 (2002).

[74] Michael Kremer, *Patent Buyouts: A Mechanism for Encouraging Innovation*, 113 Q.J. ECON., 1137 (1998).

[75] Purely fiscal arguments would have to show the existence of socially more productive alternative uses of the claims on resources used (or withheld by their owners) as a consequence of the state's reliance on general tax revenues to provide product- and process-safety information upon which to base its regulatory decisions. It might be noticed that there already is a specific (and hidden) form of state subsidization of private investment in field trials of drugs and medical devices. In the UK, for example, the hospital and clinical facilities of the National Health Service are placed at the disposal of researchers who conduct those trials on behalf of the commercial developers of the innovations.

IX. Conclusion

The American poet Robert Frost's ode to individualism celebrates the stone fences that distinguish the rural landscape of upland New England: "good fences make good neighbors." Perhaps it is so, where the resource involved is land, onto which the livestock from neighboring farms otherwise may wander to graze and thereby destroy the provender of the animals already pastured there. But is it so, too, when one scientist pores over the data gathered by another? Simple consideration of the public-goods nature of information tells us that such is not the case.

Information is not like forage, depleted by use for consumption. Data sets are not subject to being over-grazed but, instead, are likely to be enriched and rendered more accurate, and more fully documented the more that researchers are allowed to comb through them. It is by means of wide and complete disclosure, and the skeptical efforts to replicate novel research findings, that scientific communities collectively build bodies of reliable knowledge. Thus, there is good reason for hesitating to embrace private property rights as a universal resource-allocation mechanism.

In the realm of knowledge, information and scientific data, an overly literal application of the metaphor of property, emphasizing the desirability of socially enforced rights to exclude trespassers, may lead towards perverse economic policies in scientific and technological research. By its very nature, the alternative to proprietary research – the pursuit of open science – requires patronage from external sources of grant and contract funding, or from those who are personally engaged, and often from both.

The central problems facing researchers in the developing countries are rooted in a lack of adequate material resources to pursue their work in the effective, open mode of cooperation with scientists throughout the world. Thus, it is tempting for them to think of embracing proprietary research as the solution to the income constraints under which they presently labor. The same thought will occur naturally to those who wish to help these less advantaged colleagues. After all, this course of "self help" in meeting the rising costs of modern scientific research demonstrably has proved attractive to the administrators of many far better endowed universities and public institutes in the industrially advanced regions and also to individual researchers who see in it a means of advancing both their work and their standard of living.

In the developed countries, this course has provided at best only a small margin of incremental research support, averaging 8–10 percent among research universities in the United States. Yet, in some fields, and particularly in the life sciences, where the share of funding from industrial sources approaches 25 percent at the leading institutions, the commercialization movement is perceptibly encroaching upon the culture of academic research and challenging the ethos of collaborative, open science. Consequently, we must worry that applying the same "remedy" to mend the economic disabilities of open science in the developing countries would have more profound transforming effects, and might in the end result in further isolating researchers there from the remaining sources of cooperative exchange with publicly supported colleagues and institutions elsewhere. In the private property rights system we have a readily prescribed and potentially potent "cure" for the condition of impoverished open science. Unfortunately, it is one in which the patients die. We really do need to think of something better.

5

Linkages between the market economy and the scientific commons

RICHARD R. NELSON[*]

I. Introduction
II. Practice and understanding evolve together
III. The provision of public science
IV. The need to preserve the scientific commons
   A. The role of patent law
   B. Universities and the scientific commons

I. Introduction

Modern capitalism has been a powerful driver of technological advance.[1] Analysis of that process has emphasized the business firms and entrepreneurs that develop and introduce new products and processes.[2] However, it is also widely recognized that the power of market-driven invention and innovation often is dependent on the strength of the science base from which they draw. This science base largely is the product of publicly funded research, and the knowledge it creates is generally open and available for potential innovators to use.[3] That is, the innovative and dynamic components of the capitalist engine depend extensively on a publicly supported scientific commons.

In this chapter, I argue that the scientific commons is becoming privatized. While this privatization has been limited to date, there are real dangers that unless

---

[*] Richard R. Nelson is George Blumenthal Professor of International and Public Affairs, Columbia University.
[1] This paper draws extensively from Richard R. Nelson, *The Market Economy, and the Scientific Commons*, 33 RES. POL'Y 455 (2004).
[2] *See, in particular,* JOSEPH SCHUMPETER, CAPITALISM, SOCIALISM AND DEMOCRACY (Harper & Row 1942); Paul M. Romer, *Endogenous Technological Change*, 98 J. POL. ECON. S71 (1990).
[3] RICHARD R. NELSON, NATIONAL INNOVATION SYSTEMS (Oxford University Press 1993), analyzes public research and impacts on markets. *See also* DAVID MOWERY & RICHARD R. NELSON, THE SOURCES OF INDUSTRIAL LEADERSHIP (Cambridge University Press 1999); Paul David, Koyaanisqatsi *in Cyberspace: The Economics of an "Out-of-Balance" Regime of Private Property Rights in Data and Information* [this volume].

arrested soon, important portions of future scientific knowledge will fall outside the public domain. This outcome could be harmful for both the future progress of science and for commercial technological progress. The erosion of the scientific commons will be difficult to contain, much less roll back. In this essay, I wish to raise basic concerns and to suggest a promising strategy for containing the damage.

Before making this case, I need to clear some intellectual underbrush. As discussed later in the chapter, a number of influential philosophers and sociologists of science have put forth a theory about the generation of knowledge that until recently has served well to protect the scientific commons. Today, this theory is inadequate, largely because it does not sufficiently recognize the nature of the modern scientific enterprise, nor does it characterize well how society gains from it. Indeed, this theory does not explain why privatization and markets are encroaching on the commons and the problems that emerge from that trend. I therefore examine the shortcomings of the theory, first in broad form and later in more critical terms.

A central postulate of the traditional theory is that, outside of industry, the work of scientists should be – and is – motivated by the search for basic knowledge and understanding, and that the practical payoffs that may come from successful research are largely unpredictable. Vannevar Bush[4] is one among many proponents of public support of science who put forth this theme. He argued that it would be a mistake to take perceived prospects of commercial success as a guide to where scientific funds should be allocated. The reason that scientific research often has practical payoffs is serendipity, the chances of which are greatest when researchers are free to attack what they see as the most challenging scientific problems in the way they think most promising. To re-orient the system toward science with the evident potential for commercial applications would make it much less beneficial over the long run.[5]

The theory rests on the complementary idea that decisions regarding what questions to explore, and evaluation of the performance of scientists and research programs, should rest primarily with scientists working in the field. For either the government or the market to intervene extensively into the allocation of scientific research resources would destroy its productivity. In the terms used by one philosopher, society should appreciate and protect "The Republic of Science".[6]

The third belief or ideal is that the results of scientific research should be published and otherwise laid open for all to use and evaluate. As Robert Merton argued, the spirit of science is "communitarian" regarding access to the knowledge and techniques it creates.[7] All scientists are free to test the validity of their

---

[4] See VANNEVAR BUSH, SCIENCE, THE ENDLESS FRONTIER (National Science Foundation 1945).
[5] Cf. id.   [6] Michael Polanyi, The Republic of Science, 1 MINERVA 54 (1967).
[7] ROBERT MERTON, THE SOCIOLOGY OF SCIENCE: THEORETICAL AND EMPIRICAL INVESTIGATIONS (University of Chicago Press 1973).

colleagues' results and to build on them in their own research. Because the results of scientific research are placed in the public domain for testing and further development, the bulk of scientific knowledge accepted by the community is reliable.[8] Scientific knowledge itself is cumulative. These are basic reasons why the scientific enterprise has been highly effective as an engine of discovery. And economists often have argued that keeping science open is the most effective policy for enabling the public to draw practical benefits from it.

I argue here that the part of the theory stressing the value of open science is in danger of being denied. A major reason is that originally this ideal seemed a natural consequence of the first two parts of the theory: that the practical payoffs from scientific research largely arrive through serendipity and that the allocation of scientific resources should be guided by the informed judgments of scientists regarding the most important problems to work on. Keeping scientific findings in the public domain and sustaining public funding of research based on peer review would therefore be an important part of an incentive and control system for fostering productive science.[9]

However, the first basic premise of the theory never has been fully true. Indeed, in this era of biotechnology, it is clear that both the funders and the researchers consider well the possible practical payoffs from what they are doing. Further, the second premise never has been fully consistent with the research funding decisions of the major sponsors. But if, in fact, much of scientific research is consciously aimed at problems with solutions of major and broadly predictable payoffs, what is the case against harnessing market incentives to the performance of research and to the use of research results? Put differently, why should the privatization of research results be considered a concern?

My argument is that eroding the scientific commons poses dangers for the advancement of both science and technology. I will develop this argument as follows.

Section II is concerned with how technological advance draws from science. I will argue primarily that science is valuable as an input to technological change these days because most scientific research is in fields that are oriented to providing knowledge of use in particular areas. These are the scientific fields that Donald Stokes[10] located in "Pasteur's Quadrant", where the research aims for deep understanding, but the field itself is oriented towards achieving practical objectives. Examples include improving health, achieving better understanding of the properties of materials, and developing a powerful theory

---

[8] This reliability has been emphasized by JOHN ZIMAN, RELIABLE KNOWLEDGE (Cambridge University Press 1976).
[9] For a discussion along these lines, see P. Dasgupta & Paul David, *Towards a New Economics of Science*, 23 RES. POL'Y 487 (1994).
[10] DONALD STOKES, PASTEUR'S QUADRANT: BASIC SCIENCE AND TECHNOLOGICAL INNOVATION (Brookings Institution Press 1996).

of computing. At the same time, there typically remains considerable uncertainty about how to make effective use of new knowledge. There are great advantages, therefore, to society in leaving open new scientific knowledge to all competent parties who want to work from it.

Section III begins with a brief review of the ideological and political debates that occurred after World War II and have shaped present thinking about public policy towards science. It also contrasts that rhetoric with the science support system that actually emerged. The fact that a substantial share of government research funding comes from agencies with relatively clear applied missions explains both why such a large fraction of overall research lies in Pasteur's Quadrant and how government is able to link research funding to national objectives without engaging in detailed control of research. For example, one of the reasons why cell biology now is such a dynamic field is the belief that improving basic understanding might develop solutions for cancer or enable us to understand better how receptors work.

Still, the advances in understanding emanating from scientific work seldom lead immediately to the solution of practical problems. Rather, they provide the knowledge and tools to address them more effectively. For this reason, the findings of basic science set the stage for follow-on applications work. I propose, therefore, that for society to gain maximal benefit from its support of basic science, there must be open access to scientific research results. Open access permits many potential inventors to work with new knowledge. Privatizing knowledge with exclusive commercial rights permits access only to those offered permission by the rights owner.

Section IV discusses the current situation and dangers in more detail. The argument then turns to a number of measures that bear some promise to resolve these problems.

II. Practice and understanding evolve together

It is almost universally appreciated that the power of modern technological innovation depends greatly on its ability to draw from science. However, the nature of the linkages between science and technology is poorly understood in general. Understanding them correctly is necessary for having an effective discussion about appropriate public policy towards science. Thus, this section discusses what scholars of technological advance believe about these issues.

Technologies involve both a body of practice, manifest in the artifacts and techniques that are produced and used, and a body of understanding that supports, surrounds, and rationalizes the former. Traditionally, an important part of the body of understanding supporting practice generally is grounded in the empirical experience of inventors and users regarding what works, mistakes made, reliable problem solving methods, and the like. In recent years, however, nearly all powerful technologies have had strong connections with particular fields of science.[11] These connections, of course, are central in the discussion of this essay.

There is a widespread belief that modern fields of technology are, in effect, applied science, in the sense that given a strong base of scientific knowledge, in most cases the development of new technology is relatively routine, once the practical target is specified. Indeed, Schumpeter argued that by the mid-twentieth century, this approach was dominant, and the kind of competition among firms that had over the prior century made capitalism such a powerful engine of progress no longer was necessary.[12] With strong science, technological advance could be planned, in his view. Yet, careful studies of how technological advance actually proceeds in the modern era clearly show that the invention process cannot be planned in any detail, and competition remains an essential part of it.[13]

Virtually all empirically oriented scholarly accounts of how technology progresses have highlighted that the process is evolutionary in the following senses.[14] First, at any time there generally are a wide variety of efforts going on to improve prevailing technology or to supplant it with something radically better. These efforts generally compete with each other, and the winners and losers in this competition are determined largely through market performance after the investments are made. Second, today's efforts to improve technologies are informed considerably by the successes and failures of earlier projects. While there are occasional major leaps that radically transform best practice, for the most part technological advance is cumulative.[15] Scholars of technological advance also have stressed that the advanced technologies of a given era almost always are the result of the work of many inventors and developers. Technological advance is a collective, cultural, and evolutionary process.

The claim that technological advance is evolutionary does not deny the powerful body of understanding and technique used to guide the efforts of those

---

[11] See Alvin Klevorick et al., *Sources and Significance of Inter-industry Differences in Technological Opportunities*, 24 RES. POL'Y 185 (1995).

[12] SCHUMPETER, above n. 2.

[13] See, e.g., Nathan Rosenberg, *Uncertainty and Technological Change*, in THE MOSAIC OF ECONOMIC GROWTH (R. Landau et al. eds., Stanford University Press 1996); RICHARD R. NELSON & SIDNEY WINTER, AN EVOLUTIONARY THEORY OF ECONOMIC CHANGE (Cambridge University Press 1982).

[14] See e.g., G. BASALLA, THE EVOLUTION OF TECHNOLOGY (Cambridge University Press 1988); E. CONSTANT, THE ORIGINS OF THE TURBOJET REVOLUTION (Johns Hopkins University Press 1980); JOEL MOKYR, THE LEVER OF RICHES (Oxford University Press 1990); NELSON & WINTER, above n. 13; H. PETROSKI, THE EVOLUTION OF USEFUL THINGS (Alfred Knopf 1992); W. VINCENTI, WHAT ENGINEERS KNOW AND HOW THEY KNOW IT (Johns Hopkins University Press 1990); JOHN ZIMAN, TECHNOLOGICAL INNOVATION AS AN EVOLUTIONARY PROCESS (Cambridge University Press 2000); Giovanni Dosi, *Sources, Procedures, and Microeconomic Effects of Innovation*, 26 J. ECON. LITERATURE 1120 (1988).

[15] Rosenberg, above n. 13.

who seek to advance it, at least in modern times. A strong body of scientific understanding enlarges the area within which an inventor has vision and can make informed judgments regarding what particular paths are promising as solutions. Also, science and engineering provide powerful means of experimenting and testing new ideas and designs without going to full-scale operational versions. Thus, strong science enables the process of designing and inventing to become more productive and powerful than it would be otherwise. Put differently, while strong science does not solve practical problems, it increases the advantages to society of having many competent actors striving to improve the art.

The connections between the "body of practice" aspect of a technology and the "body of understanding" part need to be understood in this context. Virtually all modern technologies are supported by a strong body of science or scientific understanding that illuminates how techniques work, provides insight into the factors that constrain performance, and offers clues about promising pathways. Nonetheless, much applied technological practice remains only partially understood. Medical scientists still lack good understanding of just why and how certain effective pharmaceuticals do their work, and theories about that can change from time to time.[16]

Technological practice and understanding tend to co-evolve, with each leading the other at different times. Thus, the germ theory of disease developed by Pasteur and Koch, by pointing clearly to a certain kind of cause, led to successful efforts to get certain diseases (now known to be caused by external living agents) under control.[17] Maxwell's theory of electromagnetism led to inventions by Hertz and Marconi, culminating in radio. On the other hand, the discovery by Shockley and his team at Bell Laboratories that a semiconducting device they had built as an amplifier worked in a way different from that predicted led him to understand that there was something incomplete about the theory in physics regarding the electrical characteristics of semiconductors. This realization in turn led to his theoretical work and a Nobel Prize. Rosenberg has argued that a number of the more challenging puzzles faced by science have been made visible by new technologies and the need to explain why they work.[18]

Much of the development of modern science should be understood as the result of institutionalized responses to these challenges and opportunities. Specialized fields of applied science or engineering often developed out of the experience of more generally trained scientists working on the problems of a particular industry. Thus, the field of metallurgy came into existence as chemists worked on problems of quality control in the steel industry.[19] Similarly,

---

[16] On changes in medical theories, *see* ROY PORTER, THE GREATEST BENEFIT TO MANKIND (W.W. Norton 1997).
[17] *Id.*   [18] Rosenberg, above n. 13.
[19] Nathan Rosenberg, *Technological Change in Chemicals*, *in* CHEMICALS AND LONG RUN ECONOMIC GROWTH: INSIGHTS FROM THE CHEMICAL INDUSTRY (A. Arora et al. eds., John Wiley & Sons 1998).

chemical engineering developed as a field of research as chemical-products industries grew. The physics of mechanical forces long had been useful for civil engineers designing buildings and bridges. But with the new physics of electricity and magnetism, a whole new set of science-based industries was launched. As complex electrical "systems" came into place, the new field of electrical engineering grew up. Later on, the invention of the modern computer would spawn the field of computer science. Stronger knowledge in chemistry and biology led to the development of a collection of specialized fields involved in agricultural research. Such fields as pathology, immunology, and cardiology emerged for teaching and research at medical schools.

All of these fields of science are in "Pasteur's Quadrant." Research often probes for deep understanding, but broad programs of endeavor are dedicated explicitly to solving particular kinds of practical problems and advancing practical technology. In the United States, Western Europe, and Japan, these applied sciences account for the lion's share of the resources going into the support of science.

Several scholars have stressed that science is a system of knowledge.[20] The test that guides whether new reported findings or theories are accepted into the body of accepted knowledge is: "Are they valid? Are they true?" Popper and his followers have argued that there can be no firm positive answer to that question.[21] The ability of results or implications to stand up under attempts at refutation or exploration may be the best humans can do. From this philosophical perspective, the quest in science is for understanding in its own right.

On the other hand, as Vincenti and others who have reflected on the similarities and differences between technological and scientific knowledge have argued, the central test for technological knowledge is: "Is it useful?"[22] Technological knowledge is part of a cultural system that is concerned with achieving practical ends, rather than knowledge for its own sake.

By far the greatest share of modern scientific research, including that done at universities, is in fields where practical applications are foundations of the definition of a field. And, not surprisingly, these are the fields on which efforts to advance technology mostly draw. Two recent surveys have asked industrial R&D executives to identify the fields of academic research that contributed most to their successes.[23] The fields they listed were exactly those discussed above.

---

[20] KARL POPPER, THE LOGIC OF SCIENTIFIC DISCOVERY (Basic Books 1989); D. Campbell, *Evolutionary Epistemology*, in THE PHILOSOPHY OF KARL POPPER (P. Schelpp ed., Open Court Publishing Company 1974); ZIMAN, above n. 8, and other scholars develop this view.

[21] *See* POPPER, above n. 20.   [22] VINCENTI, above n. 14.

[23] *See* Alvin Klevorick et al., above n. 11; Wesley Cohen et al., Protecting Their Intellectual Assets: Appropriability Conditions and Why US Manufacturing Firms Patent (or Not), National Bureau of Economic Research Working Paper No. w7522 (2000).

The more recent of these studies also asked about the kind of research output that was most valuable to industry, and the most important pathways through which industry gained access.[24] In distinction from much of the current policy discussion, prototype technologies were not rated an important output of academic research for most industries, though biotechnology was an exception. Rather, general research results and research techniques were rated as useful much more often than prototypes, even in biotechnology. In a related vein, in most industries the respondents reported that the most frequent use of university research results was in solving problems in particular projects rather than in triggering the initiation of new projects.

In most industries the most important channel through which people in industry learned of and gained access to results of public research was through publications and open conferences. Put another way, industry currently gets most of its benefit from academic science through open channels. In their narrower but more detailed study of the pathways through which research results of the MIT departments of mechanical and electrical engineering get to industry, Agrawall and Henderson reach a similar conclusion.[25]

I want to stress again that in all fields of technology that have been studied in any detail, including those where the background science is very strong, technological advance remains an evolutionary process. Strong science makes that process more powerful but does not reduce the importance of having multiple paths explored by a number of different researchers. From this perspective, the fact that the bulk of scientific knowledge is open, and available through open channels, is extremely important. This situation supports the efforts of a significant number of individuals and firms who possess the scientific knowledge they need in order to compete in this technological evolution.

III. The provision of public science

Successes in World War II in government support for R&D in weapons development and medical technologies commanded considerable public attention.[26] In both the United States and the United Kingdom, the discussion about the appropriate postwar role of public science was structured by an implicitly Schumpeterian recognition of the central role of companies with their own R&D capabilities. Emphasis was placed on the system of public science, performed in universities and public laboratories, that was strongly complementary to the separate corporate R&D system and would raise the productivity of innovation overall.

---

[24] Cohen et al., above n. 23.
[25] A. Agrawall & R. Henderson, *Putting Patents in Context: Exploring Knowledge Transfer at MIT*, 48 MGMT. SCI. 41 (2002).
[26] *See* BUSH, above n. 4.

The system of public support of science and R&D that emerged in these countries in the 1950s involved elements of both government control over scientific resource allocation, as advocated by Bernal,[27] and Polanyi's "Republic of Science"[28] that preferred broad public funding but would leave direction of that funding into specific projects in the hands of scientists and peer review. In both countries the mission-oriented agencies became the primary government supporters of basic research. Thus, in the United States, the Department of Defense has funded basic work in computers, materials science, and electrical engineering. The Atomic Energy Commission (later the Department of Energy) has supported high-energy physics. The National Institutes of Health became the primary funders of university research in the biomedical sciences. In contrast, the National Science Foundation, the only significant research funding agency without a specific mission beyond the general support of science, has been a small player relative to the mission-oriented agencies. Overall, the bulk of research done in the United States, funded by government and undertaken in universities and public laboratories, is in fields falling within Pasteur's Quadrant.

In these research areas, scientists themselves generally decide and manage the details of the work. Nevertheless, the allocation of public funding across fields is strongly influenced by political processes and the judgments of public officials. Further, the motivations scientists have in performing research are influenced, at least indirectly, by perceptions of social or technological needs that guide sciences in Pasteur's Quadrant.

Because most basic research is in Pasteur's Quadrant, science has contributed much to technological advance and supports confidence in the ability of the scientific community to steer its efforts in socially productive directions. But it also implies that the lines between basic science and applied science are blurred and cannot be sharply drawn. It raises the question of where the publicly supported "Republic of Science" should end and the market should begin. Indeed, scholars such as Bush provided little in the way of coherent argument about where the one stopped and the other began.[29] Despite its obvious importance, this question has aroused little analytical interest outside of economics.

Economists analyze the appropriate scope of government activity in science and technology with theoretical concepts of externalities and public goods. Externalities are benefits and costs of private economic activity that accrue to those other than the direct decision makers. For example, economists have emphasized the "spillovers" from industrial R&D, which are information and technical capacities created by a firm's efforts to create better products and

---

[27] J.D. BERNAL, THE SOCIAL FUNCTIONS OF SCIENCE (Routledge & Kegan Paul 1939).
[28] Polanyi, above n. 6. This view was espoused as well by BUSH, above n. 4.
[29] BUSH, above n. 4.

processes that it cannot fully capture. These spillovers benefit other firms, including competitors. In general, theories of the externalities from R&D have not been arguments to support or expand the domain of public science, but rather arguments that industrial research in some circumstances should be encouraged by tax advantages or subsidies to reduce private costs.

The concept of public goods is of more direct relevance to the appropriate domain of public science. The most salient aspect is that a public good is "non-rivalrous in use," meaning that it can be used by all at the same time without eroding the quantity or quality for any one user.[30]

Knowledge is a premier example of a non-rivalrous good in this sense. There is no "tragedy of the commons" for a pure public good like knowledge.[31] To deny access to knowledge, or to ration it, can result in extensive costs with little social benefit. For example, if access to certain bodies of scientific knowledge or techniques were withheld from capable researchers, the latter might be prevented from developing productive improvements or ascertaining wider uses. Also, it was widely presumed that the results of basic scientific research were too remote from applications to be patentable. Thus, public support of basic science was necessary. This broad perspective on basic research of course fits well the theory about science prominent at that time, that was discussed earlier.

In recent decades, two key developments challenged this view of basic science in the United States. First, the courts ruled that at least some of the results of basic research could be patented.[32] Second, Congress passed the Bayh-Dole act of 1980, which strongly encouraged universities to take out patents on their research results, arguing, without much support, that it would facilitate firms to make practical use of the results under a license.[33] The first of these developments significantly enhanced the incentives of private firms to engage in basic research where the results could be patented and to license their patents to other firms. The second has greatly changed the way universities provide access to their research findings. In consequence, important areas of science are now far more subject to market decisions than in the past. Significant amounts of scientific understanding and technique now are private property rather than part of the commons.[34]

A common response is that there is little to be concerned about in this trend. The belief is widespread that, if markets can and will support research, it is

---

[30] *See* Peter Drahos, *The Regulation of Public Goods* [this volume].
[31] On the tragedy of the commons, *see* JOSEPH E. STIGLITZ, ECONOMICS OF THE PUBLIC SECTOR (W.W. Norton 3d ed. 2000).
[32] Diamond v. Chakrabarty, 447 U.S. 303 (1980).
[33] For a detailed discussion, *see* Rebecca Eisenberg, *Public Research and Private Investment: Patents and Technology Transfer in Government Sponsored Research*, 82 VA. L. REV. 1663 (1996).
[34] *See* NATIONAL RESEARCH COUNCIL, INTELLECTUAL PROPERTY RIGHTS AND RESEARCH TOOLS IN MOLECULAR BIOLOGY (National Academy Press 1997).

self-evidently an efficient solution and therefore beneficial. From this point of view, the main argument for government support of basic research – that there are substantial long-run benefits to society, and private enterprises have little incentive to undertake it, because of difficulties in establishing exclusive property rights and long time lags and uncertainties involved in commercializing results – is undermined. Rather, it is argued, if these impediments to market organization of research are reduced, let the market take over.

But this argument ignores the fact that an open scientific commons has been integral to scientific progress. I know of no field of basic science where knowledge has increased dramatically that has not been structured as a "Republic of Science". A careful history of important scientific controversies, such as the foundation of the genetic code and whether the expansion of the universe is decelerating or accelerating, shows the centrality of public science, wherein all participants have access to much the same facts and the debates are open. One cannot come away from reading Judson's history of the development of molecular biology without respecting the powerful role of open science in the progress of knowledge.[35] Similarly, Porter's history of medical knowledge and practice details many cases in which progress was made through a system of free replication or refutation of the arguments and findings of others.[36]

The arguments that open science is critical for the advancement of basic knowledge, and that open science facilitates technological progress, are mutually reinforcing. Keeping the body of scientific knowledge largely open for all to use, in efforts to advance both science and technology, is extremely important, a claim that is not sufficiently recognized in current policy discussions.

I conclude this section by briefly setting out three possible responses to the encroachment of private ownership into what had been the domain of public science. The first is to cede the contested turf and embrace the idea that basic research findings can be patented. After all, royalties earned through university patenting and private licensing solutions can diminish the need for public funding of certain fields of science. The second is for public science and private rights to coexist and compete. This is essentially the policy that developed regarding research on the human genome. The argument is that public supported research, with open access to its results, provides beneficial competition to private efforts.[37] A third approach is to try to roll back market forces, seeing them not only as likely undesirable but also as something occurring under a given set of policies, which can be changed. Upstream patenting of ownership claims to basic science, such as the genetic code, by publicly funded universities and private companies poses dangers for the knowledge commons. Thus, perhaps patent law and practice and the Bayh-Dole Act need to be revised.

---

[35] HORACE JUDSON, THE EIGHTH DAY OF CREATION (Cold Spring Harbor Press 1996).
[36] PORTER, above n. 16.
[37] For a discussion see Rebecca Eisenberg & Richard R. Nelson, *Public versus Proprietary Science: A Useful Tension?*, DAEDALUS 89 (Spring 2002).

My position on this fundamental question is a combination of the second and third positions. I believe it important to preserve as much of the scientific commons as possible, though doing so will not be easy.

IV. The need to preserve the scientific commons

Scholars have identified at least two kinds of situations where the presence of patents on basic scientific results can hinder research.[38] One of these is blockage of access to aspects of the knowledge and techniques used broadly to further advance a field. This sometimes is referred to as privatization of research tools.[39] The second relates to situations where advancement towards a useful product or technique may involve transgressing on several patents held by different parties.[40]

These potential obstacles to progress were the subject of a major recent study.[41] That study did not find evidence of major problems stemming from the need to assemble large numbers of permissions or licenses in order to engage in research. On the other hand, the survey did identify a number of instances where the holder of a patent on an important input or a pathway did not widely license and, in some cases, worked to keep a monopoly on use rights. In some of these cases, the patented finding had been achieved through research at least partially funded by the government. Such outcomes are not beneficial from society's standpoint, for patent policy presumably aims to maximize the gains from publicly funded research.

In my view, what we know is sufficiently disturbing to call for consideration of policies that can limit the scope of the patenting problem. Two broad policy arenas bear on this issue. One is intellectual property rights law and another is the approach of universities and public laboratories to protecting their research findings, along with government policy regarding the university research it funds. I discuss next what is needed to preserve an appropriately wide area of public scientific knowledge.

A. The role of patent law

The advent of patents on genetic codes and materials raises basic questions of whether scientific facts or natural phenomena should be patentable.

---

[38] For a general discussion, see Robert Merges & Richard R. Nelson, *The Complex Economics of Patent Scope*, 90 COLUM. L. REV. 839 (1990).
[39] See NATIONAL RESEARCH COUNCIL, above n. 34.
[40] Michael Heller & Rebecca Eisenberg, *Can Patents Deter Innovation? The Anticommons in Biomedical Research*, 280 SCIENCE 698 (1998).
[41] John Walsh et al., *Research, Patenting, and Licensing in Biomedical Innovation, in* PATENTS IN THE KNOWLEDGE-BASED ECONOMY (Wesley Cohen & Steven Merrill eds., National Academy of Sciences 2003).

By tradition, the subject matter of patents has been man-made inventions, with discoveries of nature not subject to protection. However, the lines between natural substances and principles and man-made counterparts are blurry. Nearly a century ago, a landmark patent law case was concerned with whether purified adrenalin, which had been achieved by a new process, warranted a product patent, or simply a patent on the process. The proponents of a product patent argued that adrenalin was not pure in its natural state.[42] The decision was that a product patent could be issued, setting a precedent that has held for years. Recent patents on purified proteins and isolated genes and receptors emphasize something that inventors have developed or modified from its natural state.

A recent article considers the implications of a patent granted on a monoclonal antibody that binds to a particular antigen on stem cells and is capable of recognizing those cells and supporting processes for isolating them.[43] Both antigens and antibodies are natural substances, but antibodies cloned by a particular process have been judged not to be natural. The particular method for identifying the antigen clearly was patentable. However, the patent claimed rights to "other antibodies" that can recognize and pick out that antigen, in effect establishing ownership of the antigen. The authors argue, correctly in my view, that this inclusion made the patent unreasonably broad and that it should have been scaled back by the patent office and the courts. Nevertheless, one can see the unclear lines between natural and artificial substances. The patentee could argue that the "invention" was a patentable method of recognizing a particular antigen and the particular antibody used was just an exemplar. The patent in question was licensed exclusively to a particular company and, in turn, later used effectively to close down another firm that had achieved a process capable of isolating stem cells using a method judged to infringe.

The problem of deciding the patentability of a research tool, the future use of which is largely in further research, seems inevitable for activities in Pasteur's Quadrant. In this illustration, the original work was done by an oncologist at Johns Hopkins University. The research was both fundamental and aimed at developing understandings and techniques that would be useful in dealing with cancer.

This complex issue arises in scientific fields concerned with advancing understandings of technologies, such as computer science and aeronautical engineering. For example, research done at Stanford during the 1920s aimed to develop good engineering principles for the design of aircraft propellers.[44] The results were not patented and were disclosed openly to the general aviation

---

[42] Parke-Davis & Co. v. H.K. Mulford & Co., 189 F. 95, 103 (C.C.S.D.N.Y. 1911), *aff'd in part and rev'd in part*, 196 F. 496 (2d Cir. 1912).
[43] Avital Bar-Shalom & Robert Cook-Degan, *Patents and Innovation in Cancer Therapeutics: Lessons from CellPro*, 80 MILLBANK Q. 637 (2002).
[44] VINCENTI, above n. 14.

design community. However, had they so desired, the researchers probably could have posed their results in terms of patentable processes useful in propeller design. Further, a significant share of research in computer science is concerned with developing concepts and principles that help improve design. Until recently, little of this work seems to have been patented, but portions of it surely could be.

I am not optimistic that the problem of broad patents on research outputs and tools can be resolved through patent law. One may suggest several policy changes to the patent office and the courts, but the innate problem of blurriness between fundamental and practical research will remain.

First, more care should be taken not to grant patents on discoveries that largely are of natural phenomena. This could be achieved by requiring applicants to make a strong showing that the subject matter is "artificial" and by limiting the scope of the patent to those artificial elements. Despite its blurriness, the dividing line has been let slip too far toward protecting natural substances, and leaning hard in the other direction is warranted. In the case of purified natural substances, there should be a greater tendency to limit the patent to the process and not permit protection of the purified product itself.

Second, it is important to establish a relatively strict interpretation of the meaning of "utility" in patent applications. This issue is particularly important for patents that claim the research result in question can be used to achieve some related useful result, making a case for usefulness once removed. The problem is that the direct utility then is as an input to research, the kind of generic technology that should be kept open and in the public domain. A stricter interpretation would require compelling demonstration of significant progress towards a particular practical solution, especially if combined with the suggestion below about restricting patent scope.

Third, as regards patent scope, there is a strong tendency for applicants to claim practice far wider than they actually have achieved.[45] The case above of a claim covering "all antibodies" that identify a particular substance is a case in point. While there are obvious advantages to the patentee of being able to control a wide range of possible substitute technologies, there are significant benefits to society as a whole of disallowing broad blocking of potential competition. Convincing the patent office and the courts of the high economic costs of excessively broad patents is a top priority in preserving the commons.

The important objective is to prevent patents from blocking broad participation in research in a field. One way to advance this goal would be to establish an explicit research exemption, analogous to the fair use exemptions in copyright law, in patent law.[46] Indeed, there is a long history of statements by judges to the

---

[45] Merges & Nelson, above n. 38.
[46] *See* Maureen A. O'Rourke, *Toward a Doctrine of Fair Use in Patent Law*, 100 COLUM. L. REV. 1177 (2000). On fair use in copyright law, *see* Ruth Okediji, *Sustainable Access to Copyrighted Digital Information Works in Developing Countries* [this volume].

effect that use of patented technologies in pure research is not an infringement.[47] Universities have relied on this interpretation to justify their freedom of research.

A recent Appellate Court ruling has changed the situation.[48] In deciding an infringement suit against Duke University, the Court argued that doing basic or applied research was part of the central business of a university and that the institution gained funding and prestige from its research. Thus, it was reasonable under the law for a patent holder to require that a university researcher take out a license before using patented materials. While the Supreme Court may overrule this decision, it is unlikely. Therefore, it now appears that exemption for use in basic research will come into place only if there is new legislation.

An interesting proposal for a research exemption was put forth by Cooper-Dreyfuss,[49] and I present a slightly amended version here. Under the proposal, a university or non-profit research organization would be immune from prosecution for using patented materials in research if two conditions were satisfied. First is that those materials were not available on reasonable terms (this is my amendment), and second is that the institution agreed not to patent anything that came out of the research. I would amend the second condition to permit patenting but under terms that would allow use on a nonexclusive, royalty free basis. There could be some difficulty in determining whether the patented materials were available at "reasonable" terms, but in many cases they may not be available at all. It might also be hard to determine whether a patent emanated from a particular research project. But these problems do not seem unusually difficult compared with other matters that are often litigated. Moreover, under such law, it is unlikely that there would be much litigation.

The advantage of such a proposal is that it would afford open access to research results for university researchers while preventing those researchers from adding further to the problem of inappropriate patents in science. Ironically, the principal obstacle to achieving this policy is, in my view, the universities themselves, because of their growing dependence on licensing revenues.

B. Universities and the scientific commons

The policies of universities will be critical in determining whether or not the vast bulk of the results of future scientific research will be placed in the

---

[47] See, e.g., Whittemore v. Cutter 29 F. Cas. 1120, 1121 (C.C.D. Mass. 1813) (No. 17,600); Dugan v. Lear Avia, Inc., 55 F. Supp. 223, 229 (S.D.N.Y. 1944), aff'd, 156 F.2d 29 (2d Cir. 1946); Poppenhusen v. Falke, 19 F. Cas. 1048, 1049 (C.C.S.D.N.Y. 1861) (No. 11,279).

[48] Madey v. Duke Univ., 307 F.3d 1351 (Fed. Cir. 2002), cert. denied, 539 U.S. 958 (2003).

[49] Rochelle Cooper-Dreyfuss, Varying the Course in Patenting Genetic Material: A Counter-Proposal to Richard Epstein's Steady Course, in PERSPECTIVES ON PROPERTIES OF THE HUMAN GENOME PROJECT 195, 204–208 (F. Scott Keiff, ed., Academic Press 2003). See also Graeme Dinwoodie and Rochelle Cooper Dreyfuss, WTO Dispute Resolution and the Preservation of the Public Domain of Science under International Law [this volume].

commons. Universities almost certainly will continue to do the great majority of basic science. If they have policies of laying their research results largely open, most science will continue to be in the public domain. However, today universities do not generally support the idea of a scientific commons, except in terms of their own rights to undertake research. In the Bayh-Dole era, universities have become a major part of the problem, avidly defending their rights to patent their research results and license as they choose.[50]

This position represents a major shift from the universities' traditional support of open science. Prior university practice was consistent with research programs designed to contribute to economic development.[51] For example, university research played a major role in the development of agricultural technology. The hybrid seed revolution, which made possible the dramatic increases in productivity in corns and other grains, stemmed from work on basic concepts and techniques at experimental stations. These basic techniques were made public knowledge. Universities also made available on generous terms the seeds they developed, while research on plant nutrition and plant diseases and pests helped companies identify and design effective fertilizers and insecticides. Very little of this university research was patented.

American engineering schools have a long tradition of doing research to help industry, as exemplified by Stanford's role in developing principles of propeller design. Several universities played key roles in developing early electronic computers. There was some patenting of devices that came out of university engineering research, but also a commitment to advance basic engineering understanding as common property. Finally, U.S. medical schools long have been contributors to technical advance in medicine and the enhanced ability of doctors to deal with human illness. Prior to the 1980s, there was little patenting, and many medical schools had an articulated policy of dedicating research results to the public commons.

The change in attitudes emerged as a result of several developments.[52] First, during the 1970s and 1980s, there was a broad ideological change in the United States toward a belief that patents were almost always necessary to stimulate invention. Second, the rise of molecular biology and the development of the principal techniques of biotechnology made university biomedical research a central locus of work leading to new pharmaceuticals and research techniques. Third, as noted, several key court decisions made many of these developments

---

[50] *See* Jerry G. Thursby et al., *Objectives, Characteristics and Outcomes of University Licensing: A Survey of Major U.S. Universities*, 26 J. TECH. TRANSFER 59 (2001).

[51] For detailed discussions of the following claims, *see* Nathan Rosenberg & Richard R. Nelson, *American Universities and Technical Progress in Industry*, 23 RES. POL'Y 323 (1994); *See also* DAVID MOWERY & NATHAN ROSENBERG, TECHNOLOGY AND THE PURSUIT OF ECONOMIC GROWTH (Cambridge University Press 1989).

[52] *See* David Mowery et al., *The Growth of Patenting and Licensing by American Universities*, 30 RES. POL'Y 99 (2001).

patentable. The possibility of earning substantial income from university research attracted university officials and scientists. For example, the patenting of the Cohen-Boyer gene splicing process, and the flow of substantial revenues to the two universities that held the rights, provided a strong indication of the potential for licensing university inventions.[53] This patent was granted prior to the passage of the Bayh-Dole Act. For its part, the Act legitimated university patenting.

In my view, there is nothing wrong per se with universities patenting what they can from their research output. In some cases, patenting may facilitate technology transfer, though in many cases the university more likely is simply earning money from what it used to make available for free. The worrisome cases are those in which universities license exclusively or narrowly a research result that is potentially of wide use. Also problematic are situations in which universities limit rights to improve their research outcomes to a few companies in circumstances where there still is so much uncertainty regarding how best to proceed that participation by a number of companies is efficient. These forms of university research outputs should be placed in the commons.

I also believe there is nothing particularly wrong if access to certain parts of the commons requires a modest fee. It would be beneficial for universities to recognize that if they patent basic research results, they have an obligation to license them to all who wish to use them at reasonable fees.[54] However, a policy of open licensing of certain research results is not likely to be adopted voluntarily by universities because it would not be seen as maximizing expected revenues from intellectual property.

In consequence, the key policy is to reform the Bayh-Dole Act. The objective here is not to eliminate university patenting, but to establish a presumption that university research results, patented or not, should generally be made openly available at very low transaction costs and reasonable fees. This policy would not foreclose exclusive licensing in those circumstances where it is necessary to gain effective technology transfer. Rather, it would establish the presumption that such cases are the exception rather than the rule. It is important for legislation to recognize that university research results are most effectively disseminated to users if placed in the public domain and that exclusive or restricted licensing may deter widespread use at considerable economic and social cost. Thus, exclusive licensing should require an explicit rationale.[55]

---

[53] Kenneth S. Dueker, *Biobusiness on Campus: Commercialization of University-Developed Biomedical Technologies*, 52 FOOD & DRUG L.J. 453 (1997).

[54] Similarly, with respect to patented "research tools" created by industry research, my concern is less with open use at a fee, but with decisions not to make the tools widely available.

[55] *See, e.g.*, Arti Rai & Rebecca Eisenberg, *Bayh-Dole Reform and the Progress of Biomedicine*, 66 LAW & CONTEMP. PROBS. 289 (2003) (making a similar argument for amending the Bayh-Dole Act). *See also* J.H. Reichman & Paul Uhlir, *A Contractually Reconstructed*

Such reforms would strengthen the hand of those who believe that universities should be contributing to the scientific and technological commons. Currently, such university researchers and administrators seem to be defying both the law and internal interests. It also would provide legitimacy to government funding agencies to press for licensing with broad access. The recent tussle between the National Institutes of Health and the University of Wisconsin regarding stem cell patents illustrates the potential value of an amended Bayh-Dole Act.[56] In that case the University originally intended to establish a profitable exclusive license for a firm. The NIH, in effect, indicated that unless the university licensed widely and liberally, it would consider the institution's licensing policies when evaluating future research proposals. The university then acceded to the licensing policies advocated by NIH.

The Cell-Pro case mentioned earlier, as analyzed by Bar-Shalom and Cook-Deegan, might have gone differently had the open-licensing amendment been in place.[57] It is likely that the NIH recognized early the value of allowing more than one company to work with the new technique for identifying stem cells, and of having widespread research use allowed, and therefore would have balked at the exclusive license that was given had it had standing to do so. Later the NIH was asked to open use of the patented technique, under the "march-in" provisions of Bayh-Dole, but did not do so because the way the legislation is written makes such a step exceptional. The reform language proposed here would have placed NIH in a far stronger position to accede to the request to open up.

Many university administrators and researchers certainly would resist the proposed amendment on the grounds that it would diminish their ability to maximize financial returns from their patent portfolio. The principal support for university patenting with freedom to license as they wish comes from universities themselves and is based on their perception of their own financial interests. However, the case for exclusive licensing on grounds that it facilitates technology transfer no longer is credible. Thus, the case that the current policy is against the public interest should carry the day if made vigorously. It is also important that if universities were constrained to offer open licensing except in rare circumstances, their resistance to a research exemption of the sort proposed by Cooper-Dreyfuss would be dampened.

Research Commons for Scientific Data in a Highly Protectionist Intellectual Property Environment, 66 LAW & CONTEMP. PROBS. 315 (2003).

[56] Press Release, National Institute of Health, National Institutes of Health and WiCell Research Institute, Inc., Sign Stem Cell Research Agreement (5 Sept. 2001), *available at* http://www.nih.gov/news/pr/sep2001/od-05.htm (last visited 21 July 2004).

[57] *See* above n. 43, and accompanying text.

COMMENTARY I

Comment: Public goods and public science

ERIC MASKIN*

A major theme in Paul David's contribution to this volume[1] is that the recent strengthening of intellectual property rights (IPRs) in the United States and elsewhere is a worrying development. I certainly agree that the development is cause for concern, but perhaps some elaboration will help clarify just why it is so disturbing.

Let us focus on the *supply* side, that is, on the promotion of innovation, which, after all, is the primary justification for creating IPRs in the first place. Of course, strengthening property rights also affects consumers on the *demand* side. But if the rate of invention diminishes after a strengthening of IPRs, which I will argue[2] is quite plausible, then the overall outcome is unambiguously negative, because these monopoly rights will drive up prices for the goods deriving from innovation.

As David observes, there are two major effects on innovation from making IPRs stronger. The *direct* effect is to encourage more invention. If I am going to be rewarded with a longer or broader patent whenever I discover something, I will have correspondingly more incentive to try to make such a discovery. However, the *indirect* effect is to *deter* innovation. If the property right you have to your invention is strengthened, you will then have more monopoly power over me if I try to use your invention to make one of my own. In other words, it will now be more expensive for me to innovate, and so I have less incentive to do it.

Because these two forces tug in opposite directions, the net result may not be clear. I will suggest, however, that as two features of innovation grow more prominent, the latter effect becomes increasingly likely to dominate. The first feature, especially evident in the software, computer, and semiconductor industries, is the *sequential* nature of innovation, the idea that each new

---

* Eric Maskin is Albert O. Hirschman Professor, School of Social Science, Institute for Advanced Study, Princeton.
[1] *See* Paul David, Koyaanisqatsi *in Cyberspace: The Economics of an "Out-of-Balance" Regime of Private Property Rights in Data and Information* [this volume].
[2] The argument is developed in detail in James Bessen & Eric Maskin, Sequential Innovation, Patents, and Imitation, MIT Department of Economics Working Paper No. 00–01 (Jan. 2000) (*revised* 2002).

invention builds in an essential way on its predecessor.[3] The second is that innovation is also *complementary*, meaning that typically different inventors take significantly different research lines to the same end, so that the overall probability that the end is reached grows when the number of potential inventors increases.[4]

I will not attempt here to establish the claim that these two features have become increasingly characteristic of many modern industries, especially those industries mentioned above – although it is backed by a considerable body of evidence. But if accepted, it implies that intellectual property rights – in particular, patents – should be made *weaker* not stronger. Roughly, the argument goes as follows. If patents are weakened, then my direct incentive to innovate will be attenuated. However, if innovation is sequential, then, assuming that I *do* discover something, the next invention down the line may have to build on my discovery. Indeed, I may try to build on it myself. Moreover, if innovation is also complementary then you, as a different inventor, will enhance the likelihood of the next discovery being made if you try to build on my invention too. A weaker patent regime will make it easier for you to do that. Furthermore, if the next invention is, in fact, attained, this will work to my benefit too, either because I discover it myself or because I can build on your discovery.

Thus, if sequentiality and complementarity are important enough, the incentive to innovate will be improved by weakening patent protection and damaged by strengthening it. This, I believe, is an important reason why Paul David's apprehensions about current trends in intellectual property could well be justified.

Let me turn to Peter Drahos' paper. Toward the end, Drahos notes that, despite evidence that people would like more global public goods, remarkably few such goods are actually produced. The question is why. He suggests that the answer may lie in the lack of international agreements on public-good provision – rather than treaties, we see clashes of will between parochial interests.[5]

I think that the disease may be even worse than Drahos' diagnosis indicates. Even if we could overcome current squabbling and reach global agreements, we would still face the problem that these cannot be externally enforced but only

---

[3] *See* Suzanne Scotchmer, *Standing on the Shoulders of Giants: Cumulative Research and the Patent Law*, 5 J. ECON. PERSP. 29 (1991); Michele Boldrin & David K. Levine, Perfectly Competitive Innovation, Federal Reserve Bank of Minneapolis, Research Department Staff Report No. 303 (2002).

[4] Michael Gort & Steven Klepper, *Time Paths in the Diffusion of Product Innovations*, 92 ECON. J. 630 (1982) (showing that the rate of innovation in many industries is correlated with firm entry, which supports the notion that complementarity plays a significant role in invention).

[5] Peter Drahos, *The Regulation of Public Good* [this volume]. On the nature of international public goods, *see* GLOBAL PUBLIC GOODS: INTERNATIONAL COOPERATION IN THE 21ST CENTURY (Inge Kaul et al. eds., Oxford University Press 1999).

self-enforced. That is, the agreements would work only to the extent that no signatory could profit by reneging.

The Anti-Ballistic Missile treaty is a case in point. That agreement was effective and adhered to for many years – not because the United States or the Soviet Union (later Russia) would have been hauled before some judge had one of them violated the terms, but only because neither side had the incentive to pull out unilaterally. Once withdrawal was perceived as advantageous by the Bush administration, the treaty's death was immediate.

The same problem is likely to plague any other international agreement for public goods. A treaty may be cleverly drawn up so that all nations gain from it initially and therefore sign on. But as soon as the calculus changes for even one major participant, the agreement is doomed.

6

Sustainable access to copyrighted digital information works in developing countries

RUTH L. OKEDIJI*

I. Introduction
II. The normative equation of the international copyright system: Creativity and access
    A. Defining access
    B. The access landscape in international copyright relations
III. The new copyright environment
    A. TRIPS and its progeny: Incorporation, coordination and interpretation of international copyright rules
    B. From Stockholm to Paris
        1. The move from coordination to institutions
        2. Consolidating the organizational framework
        3. Legitimacy, sequential revision and accommodation strategies
IV. The Berne Appendix as market failure
    A. Structure of the Berne Appendix
    B. Critical observations
V. Rethinking the access problem
    A. Creative access
    B. A network of access mechanisms: The global rules
        1. Jurisdiction of the three-step test under the TRIPS Agreement
        2. The idea/expression dichotomy
        3. The Berne Appendix and the WCT
VI. The useful art(s) of progress: Social welfare in an international perspective
    A. Rescuing access from digital bondage
    B. Specific proposals
        1. An international fair use doctrine
        2. Increasing the accountability of international intellectual property institutions and decreasing the pressure to participate in new developments

---

* Ruth L. Okediji is William L. Prosser Professor of Law, University of Minnesota Law School, Minneapolis, MN. I would like to thank Jerome Reichman and Keith Maskus for comments on earlier drafts of this contribution. Mary Rumsey and Tomas Feldman provided valuable and dedicated research assistance, for which I am also very grateful.

3. Berne, TRIPS and side deals: Contending with strategic negotiations
4. Developing a proportional approach to access
5. Developing doctrines to address violations of copyright's underlying public policy
6. Limiting the use of soft law

VII. Conclusion

I. Introduction

Intellectual property rights are an important part of the regulatory environment necessary to promote and support economic growth in the digital age. Recent gains in productivity growth in leading developed countries are strongly related to investments in information technology and correlate with the extent to which such technology, or technology-driven goods and services, are diffused throughout the economy.[1] Attaining adequate levels of technology investment and diffusion requires a policy framework that prioritizes research, enhances competitiveness and facilitates the flow of knowledge among firms. Granting property rights in the fruits of innovative and creative endeavor has long been the policy tool of choice to accomplish these objectives.[2] Incessant demands by the information industry and other proprietors of creative works for stronger global protection have been rationalized as a condition for maintaining adequate levels of innovation, competition and cross-border investment.

---

[1] *See* OECD, THE NEW ECONOMY: BEYOND THE HYPE (2001); OECD, MEASURING THE INFORMATION ECONOMY (2002); OECD, ICT AND ECONOMIC GROWTH: EVIDENCE FROM OECD COUNTRIES, INDUSTRIES AND FIRMS (2003); OECD, SEIZING THE BENEFITS OF ICT IN A DIGITAL ECONOMY (2003). These reports are *available at* www.oecd.org.

[2] The dominance of property rules as the preferred mode for compensating creators has recently been challenged by proponents of new types of liability rules. Professor Reichman has been the leading voice in favor of liability rules as a superior system for addressing problems associated with market failures inherent in a property rule regime, particularly with respect to small-scale innovative activity. *See, e.g.*, J.H. Reichman & Tracy Lewis, *Using Liability Rules to Stimulate Local Innovation in Developing Countries: Application to Traditional Knowledge* [this volume]; J.H. Reichman, *Of Green Tulips and Legal Kudzu: Repackaging Rights in Subpatentable Innovation*, 53 VAND. L. REV. 1743 (2000) (favoring liability rules for innovation that fails legal standards for protection under patent or copyright regimes); J.H. Reichman & Pamela Samuelson, *Intellectual Property Rights in Data?*, 50 VAND. L. REV. 51, 148 (1997) ("[a] built-in automatic license is ideally suited to weak regimes seeking no more than a minimalist, pro-competitive cure for chronically insufficient lead time. Experience demonstrates, moreover, that innovators and borrowers within a given sector will bargain around liability rules, if the law itself clearly establishes a baseline obligation."); J.H. Reichman, *Legal Hybrids Between the Patent and Copyright Paradigm*, 94 COLUM. L. REV. 2432 (1994).

The emphasis on information technology as a major contributor to economic growth further consolidated industry influence over intellectual property policy, and provided a gloss for the pervasive pattern of rent-seeking that has characterized contemporary innovation policy in the developed countries. The concerted efforts of the knowledge industries were largely responsible for the extraordinary conclusion of the Agreement on Trade-Related Aspects of Intellectual Property Rights (TRIPS Agreement),[3] which established a global baseline to usher the developing world into a worldwide system of heightened protection for intellectual property. The TRIPS Agreement was followed rapidly by other multilateral and bilateral agreements, each with new levels of protection for intellectual goods and for the technologies that control the terms of access and use by consumers.[4]

What has been conspicuously absent in the considerable mobilization of political resources to secure "maximum-strength" global protection of intellectual property rights is an attendant commitment to establish access to intellectual goods as an integral component of the international innovation and competition framework. Extensive legalized control of digital content through technological measures has significantly heightened the costs (and risks) of using knowledge goods,[5] and it establishes a presumption against the role of copyright law in facilitating access to creative expression except by licensing. Together with the deployment of private law terms to complement copyright's basic bundle of privileges,[6] the current regulatory environment for information works tends to reinforce a growing global awareness of an inalienable and impermeable right of ownership in digital works.

Yet, there are well-known positive welfare gains when property rights are constructed in a way that promotes efficient bargaining, either by providing

---

[3] Agreement on Trade-Related Aspects of Intellectual Property Rights, 15 Apr. 1994, Marrakesh Agreement Establishing the World Trade Organization, Annex 1C, LEGAL INSTRUMENTS – RESULTS OF THE URUGUAY ROUND vol. 31, 33 I.L.M. 81 (1994) [hereinafter TRIPS Agreement].

[4] *See, e.g.*, World Intellectual Property Organization (WIPO) Copyright Treaty, 20 Dec. 1996, S. Treaty Doc. No. 105–17, 36 I.L.M. 65 [hereinafter WCT]; WIPO Performances and Phonograms Treaty, 20 Dec. 1996, 36 I.L.M. 76 [hereinafter WPPT]; Australia-United States Free Trade Agreement, ch. 17, Intellectual Property Rights, art. 17(4) (DMCA anticircumvention provisions), *at* http://www.dfat.gov.au/trade/negotiations/us_fta/final-text/chapter_17.html; FTAA – Free Trade Area of the Americas, Draft Agreement, art. XX, Intellectual Property Provisions, *available at* http://www.ftaa-alca.org/FTAADraft03/Chapter XX_e.asp.

[5] *See* 17 U.S.C. § 1201(a)(3)(B) (2000) (outlining when a "technological measure" "effectively controls access to a work"). *See also* Laura N. Gasaway, *The New Access Right and Its Impact on Libraries and Library Users*, 10 J. INTELL. PROP. L. 269 (2003).

[6] *See, e.g.*, Lowry's Reports, Inc. v. Legg Mason, Inc., 186 F. Supp. 2d 592 (D. Md. 2002) (finding a contractual right to restrict use of contents); *see also* J.H. Reichman & Jonathan A. Franklin, *Privately Legislated Intellectual Property Rights: Reconciling Freedom of Contract with Public Good Uses of Information*, 147 U. PA. L. REV. 875 (1999).

default rules that owners and would-be users can leverage,[7] or by limiting the scope or permissible exercise of property rights in situations where there is likely to be market failure or other market distortions. Nationally defined limitations and exceptions to intellectual property rights, as well as competition policy, have served coordinately to ensure that the exercise of owners' rights does not trammel the more fundamental interests of advancing the public welfare in the regulation of public goods.[8]

In this chapter, I address existing doctrines and possible means afforded by the international copyright system to secure sustainable access to copyrighted digital works within the framework of national economic development policies. Today's skewed emphasis on greater levels of protection effectively converts the social welfare gains from access into additional rent or "supernormal" profits for copyright owners, most of whom reside outside of the developing world. The welfare effects of such profits even in developed countries have become a highly contested issue.[9] The point, however, is that while economic rents *may* encourage additional future creativity, the precise amount of this creative surplus is uncertain. What seems more certain is that welfare

---

[7] *Cf.* Ian Ayres & Eric Talley, *Solomonic Bargaining: Dividing a Legal Entitlement to Facilitate Cosean Trade*, 104 YALE L.J. 1027 (1995).

[8] *Cf.* Peter Drahos, *The Regulation of Public Goods* [this volume].

[9] This issue was argued intensely during the constitutional challenge to the U.S. Copyright Term Extension Act. *See* Eldred v. Ashcroft, 537 U.S. 186, 212, fn.18 (2003) (" . . . copyright law celebrates the profit motive, recognizing that the incentive to profit from the exploitation of copyrights will redound to the public benefit by resulting in the proliferation of knowledge . . . The profit motive is the engine that ensures the progress of science. Rewarding authors for their creative labor and 'promot[ing] . . . Progress' are thus complementary; . . . copyright law serves public ends by providing individuals with an incentive to pursue private ones.") (internal citations omitted). *See also*, William M. Landes & Richard A. Posner, *Indefinitely Renewable Copyright*, 70 U. CHI. L. REV. 471, 489–90 (2003) (arguing that copyright expiration doesn't necessarily promote efficient exploitation of the public domain). Landes and Posner also argue that due to "discounting to present value, incentives to create intellectual property are not materially affected by cutting off intellectual-property rights after many years. . . ." *Id.* at 475; Deirdre K. Mulligan & Jason M. Schultz, *Neglecting the National Memory: How Copyright Term Extensions Compromise the Development of Digital Archives*, 4 J. APP. PRAC. & PROCESS 451(2002) (stating that "[d]espite the supposed incentives copyright offers to authors and publishers, today much of our cultural heritage lies fallow, withheld from the public domain by bloated copyright terms, and removed from the stream of commerce because copyright holders reap little profit from them. The truth is that by the time even pre-CTEA copyright terms expire, few books, movies, or musical works are being published for profit. Most copyright owners let their works fall out of print, which means that they languish in literary limbo."). In other contexts, commentators have suggested that enhancing the reward for innovative activity by, for example, expanding the scope of protection, encourages further innovation. *See e.g.*, Louis Kaplow, *The Patent-Antitrust Intersection: A Reappraisal*, 97 HARV. L. REV. 1813, 1823–24 (1984) (patents); Peter S. Menell, *An Analysis of the Scope of Copyright Protection for Application Programs*, 41 STAN. L. REV. 1045, 1059 (1989) (software).

gains from all forms of access will improve static welfare. Broader access will also have a positive effect on dynamic welfare by encouraging additional creativity at lower cost.

An international system that preserves a balance between proprietary interests and the broadest possible availability of public goods is of considerable importance to both developed and developing countries.[10] However, the combined economic and technological obstacles that developing countries must overcome compel a rigorous examination of how to maximize access to public goods within the framework of existing treaties, particularly given the technologically enhanced capacity of rights owners to control access to digital content. The international system must incorporate the principle of access, and its supporting mechanisms, as a core component of the global innovation and competition regime.[11]

My interest in integrating access as an essential principle of the international copyright system is hardly radical. The international system has traditionally recognized the residual power of states to prescribe means of access to protected works under specified conditions. However, new institutional, economic and technological developments increasingly disable efforts to protect copyright policy interests other than those that are firmly aligned with the economic prerogatives of owners of intellectual goods.

Part II provides a definition of access, and a brief discussion of the means through which it has been addressed both in the national (using the example of the United States) and international contexts. In Part III, I examine the relationship between the TRIPS Agreement, which establishes the global framework for copyright protection, on the one hand, and the World Intellectual Property Organization (WIPO) treaties, which deal specifically with digital age protection, on the other.[12] These treaties set the framework for the new copyright environment. The analysis is directed at defining the current scope of negotiated access to digital and non-digital works. Part III also traces the development of the institutional framework that governs international copyright relations, and how the demands of developing countries ironically resulted in the establishment of an administrative apparatus that many commentators now view as hostile to development interests.

---

[10] The TRIPS Agreement, above n. 3, art. 7, expresses the need for this balance. *See also* Laurence R. Helfer, *Regime Shifting: The TRIPS Agreement and New Dynamics of International Intellectual Property Lawmaking*, 29 YALE J. INT'L L. 1, 5 (2004) (noting the importance of balancing intellectual property protection and access to public health goods); Sol Picciotto, *Private Rights vs. Public Interests in the TRIPS Agreement*, 97 AM. SOC'Y INT'L L. PROC. 167, 168 (2003) (criticizing WIPO actions that "neglect the important balance between private rights and the public interest in the definition of IPRs"); James Thuo Gathii, *Rights, Patents, Markets and the Global AIDS Pandemic*, 14 FLA. J. INT'L L. 261, 324 (2002).

[11] *Cf.* Keith E. Maskus & Jerome H. Reichman, *The Globalization of Private Knowledge Goods and the Privatization of Global Public Goods* [this volume].

[12] *See* TRIPS Agreement, above n. 3; WCT, above n. 4; WPPT, above n. 4.

In Part IV, I evaluate the intricate scheme of the Appendix to the Berne Convention for the Protection of Literary and Artistic Works,[13] which is the dominant and only explicit access regime currently existing in international copyright relations. In Part V, I analyze and outline the access problem, focusing on the various ways in which access has been legally constructed in the international system. I am skeptical of the dominant presumption that digital networks will unduly skew the copyright balance against owners of protected works in the absence of digital controls in the developing world. I conclude that the WIPO Internet treaties are premature for many developing countries, and certainly for all of the least-developed countries. In Part VI, I offer suggestions and strategies for the development of global access norms that should enhance benefits to all countries by situating access tools as a central part of international copyright law and policy.

II. The normative equation of the international copyright system: Creativity and access

Historically, national copyright norms determined the boundaries of the international copyright system. This nation-centered international copyright system served to determine the minimum standards of protection, but at the same time reserved to member states the right to impose appropriate limitations and exceptions. In the course of modern international relations, however, the role of the state in setting domestic copyright policy has been transformed by the ascendant role of private stakeholders in the development of copyright laws.[14] Other developments have fundamentally transformed the copyright lawmaking process: international rules increasingly occupy the domestic copyright policy space; a variety of new international institutions have become engaged with intellectual property issues; digital technologies defy territorial boundaries and effect barriers around content; and private ordering exemplified by the Uniform Domain Name Dispute Resolution system is fast becoming an acceptable model for dealing with disputes in the multi-jurisdictional space of the Internet.[15] In sum, the international system has become a major source of *domestic* copyright norms, which has destabilized and, in some instances,

---

[13] Berne Convention for the Protection of Literary and Artistic Works, 9 Sept. 1886, *completed at* Paris on 4 May 1896, *revised at* Berlin on 13 Nov. 1908, *completed at* Berne on 20 Mar. 1914, *revised at* Rome on 2 June 1928, *at* Brussels on 26 June 1948, *at* Stockholm on 14 July 1967, and *at* Paris on 24 July 1971, 1161 U.N.T.S. 3, S. Treaty Doc. No. 99–27 (1986) [hereinafter Berne Convention].

[14] *See* JESSICA LITMAN, DIGITAL COPYRIGHT: PROTECTING INTELLECTUAL PROPERTY ON THE INTERNET, 23, 135–63 (Prometheus Books 2001).

[15] *See* Graeme Dinwoodie, *The New International Intellectual Property Law System: New Actors, New Institutions, New Sources*, 98 ASIL PROC. (2004) [hereinafter Dinwoodie, *The New International Intellectual Property Law System*].

inverted the traditional sphere of sovereign prerogative with far-reaching consequences for the normative principles that potentiate access to content.

A. Defining access

Access is a multi-layered term that encompasses the unencumbered right to utilize a creative work (uncompensated creative access); privately negotiated terms of use between owners and users (negotiated access); qualified opportunities to utilize certain types of works through compulsory licensing (mandatory compensated access); as well as the opportunity to purchase and own the physical embodiment of the protected content (bulk compensated access). These various forms of access operate independently or, under some circumstances, in tandem to provide stable opportunities for society to benefit from creative works.

Copyright law facilitates access to protected creative works by two principal means. First, it promotes access through a range of doctrinal tools that limit the scope of copyrightable subject matter.[16] Second, within the scope of legitimate subject matter, copyright law provides access through complex rules, such as compulsory licensing of particular categories of works,[17] specific exceptions,[18] as well as general limitations imposed by omnibus provisions designed to, among other things, promote important social objectives that may also involve creative use of a work.[19] Copyright laws in most industrialized countries reflect some combination of these various limitations and exceptions to the exclusive rights granted to copyright owners.

Ideally, the range and design of access "routes" (or principles) available to users in any given country is closely related to the welfare vision that drives the copyright bargain between authors and the public. For example, what kind of works does the government want consumers to have more access to – literary, artistic, or musical? What uses are being prioritized – educational, private or public uses? Are there cultural and legal interests that have to be accommodated, such as privacy or free speech? Other factors that affect the design of access principles include the nature of the copyrighted subject-matter (e.g., software), which may occasion customized access rules. The structure of the relevant industry also affects the design. For example, within the music industry in the United States, a combination of private negotiations, compulsory licensing, and the right to fair use operates to facilitate access to musical works.

---

[16] The most prominent of these is the idea/expression dichotomy, which is now an international principle embodied in the TRIPS Agreement, above n. 3, art. 9(2).

[17] For example, compulsory licensing for making mechanical recordings of protected musical works, and for performance of musical works in jukeboxes, certain cable transmissions, and public broadcasting. *See* 17 U.S.C.A. §§ 111, 115, 116, 118 (2000). For an overview of the complex scheme of music copyrights, *see* Lydia Pallas Loren, *Untangling the Web of Music Copyrights*, 53 Case W. Res. L. Rev. 673 (2003).

[18] *See, e.g.*, 17 U.S.C. §§ 102(b), 108–22 (2000).

[19] *See, e.g.*, 17 U.S.C. § 107 (2000) (fair use provision).

The point is that the design and operation of access principles should be uniquely suited to the public interest goals that are fundamental to a society at any given point in its development.

B. *The access landscape in international copyright relations*

In developed countries, the debate over access to digital content has focused largely on how recent legislative and judicial developments threaten limits on copyright protection that have traditionally facilitated *uncompensated* and unencumbered access to creative works. For example, legislation that added twenty years to the internationally required minimum term of life plus fifty years[20] proved extremely controversial in the United States,[21] as was legislation implementing the World Intellectual Property Organization Copyright Treaty's (WCT)[22] anti-circumvention and anti-trafficking provisions.[23] With respect to developing countries, however, concerns about access to protected works are primarily focused on bulk access as opposed to creative access. The central issue is how to provide copyrighted works to consumers at reasonable prices and on terms that do not erode downstream creativity.

In this context, bulk access for educational purposes is particularly important. In the digital age, moreover, the distinction between bulk and creative access is largely attenuated: one-sided, standardized contractual agreements define purchasers as "licensees" and not "owners," and thus restrict the scope of what consumers can do with digital works even in private spaces. Legal protection for technological controls that monitor or otherwise determine how consumers utilize digital goods further eviscerates notions of "ownership" and any rights traditionally associated with possessing a hard copy of a creative work. If worldwide implementation of the WCT follows the United States and European models, the distinction between bulk and creative access for digital works could disappear entirely, since copyright owners will be empowered technologically to control all forms of access in the digital environment.

In many countries, access for some uses, such as private use or use associated with freedom of speech, is designed to be uncompensated. Generally, however, the market resolves most issues of access through private bargains (negotiated

---

[20] Sonny Bono Copyright Term Extension Act, Pub. L. No. 105–298, § 102, 112 STAT. 2827, 2827–28 (1998) (codified at 17 U.S.C. §§ 301–304 (2000)).

[21] The legislation was challenged in court but was ultimately upheld as a constitutional exercise of Congress's regulatory power over copyright law. *See Eldred v. Ashcroft*, 537 U.S. at 187.

[22] *See* Digital Millenium Copyright Act, Pub. L. No. 105–304, 112 STAT. 2860, (1998) [hereinafter DMCA]; WCT, above n. 4.

[23] The DMCA's anti-circumvention provisions are codified at 17 U.S.C. § 1201 (2000); the anti-trafficking provision is codified at 17 U.S.C. § 1201(a)(2) (2000). For criticism of the DMCA, *see, e.g.*, Glynn S. Lunney, Jr., *The Death of Copyright: Digital Technology, Private Copying, and the Millennium Copyright Act*, 87 VA. L. REV. 813 (2001).

access) between owners and users. Other forms of access can be viewed as efforts to address various forms of market failure.[24] In the absence of market failure, negotiations over access rights will be influenced by the baselines established through legal rules concerning the property owner's entitlements. Because access rules, operating as limitations and exceptions, are directed at advancing the larger public interest underlying the copyright grant, they should properly be understood as Pigouvian taxes; that is, an exercise of state power to regulate intellectual property rights for the social good. One would expect, then, well-defined property rights to support such bargaining.

In practice, however, limitations and exceptions to copyright protection, when construed as rights for the *public*,[25] are (perhaps inherently) not sufficiently defined to reduce uncertainty in the marketplace for users. Limitations and exceptions associated with uncompensated access typically offer no risk-proof information to consumers, *ex-ante*, as to the permissible range of uses. Instead of providing users with leverage to negotiate access on terms that are reasonable, the high transaction costs associated with determining the precise scope of limitations and exceptions in copyright law nullify much of the prospective bargaining advantage that consumers (including those in developing countries) might otherwise employ in negotiating both bulk (compensated) access and creative (uncompensated) access to protected works.

Uncertainty is inherently a part of the design of limitations and exceptions, whether in domestic legislation or in international treaties. Even where, as in the case of digital goods, uncertainty with respect to the freedom to use a protected work is diminished by the proliferation of "rights management" tools,[26] legislation that protects these tools has favored owners over consumers.

---

[24] *See, e.g.*, Harper & Row Publishers, Inc. v. Nation Enter., 471 U.S. 539, 566 n.9 (1985) (citing with approval economists who believe "... fair use exception should come into play only in those situations in which the market fails."). *See also* Wendy J. Gordon, *Fair Use as Market Failure: A Structural and Economic Analysis of the Betamax Case and its Predecessors*, 82 COLUM. L. REV. 1600 (1982). Recent judicial opinions in the United States have highlighted the role of the market as the dominant means for obtaining access to copyrighted works. *See, e.g.*, Am. Geophysical Union v. Texaco, Inc. 60 F.3d 913, 930 (2d Cir. 1994), *cert. dismissed*, 516 U.S. 1005 (1995) ("Though the publishers still have not established a conventional market for the direct sale and distribution of individual articles, they have created ... a workable market for institutional users to obtain licenses for the right to produce their own copies of individual articles. . . . [T]he Copyright Act explicitly provides that copyright holders have the 'exclusive rights' to 'reproduce' and 'distribute copies' of their works ... and since there currently exists a viable market for licensing these rights for individual journal articles, it is appropriate that potential licensing revenues for photocopying be considered in a fair use analysis.").

[25] *See* Julie E. Cohen, *Lochner in Cyberspace*, 97 MICH. L. REV. 462, 476, 566–67 (1998).

[26] U.S. Patent and Trademark Office, Technological Protection Systems for Digitized Copyrighted Works: A Report to Congress, 4–10 (2003), *available at* http://www.uspto.gov/web/offices/dcom/olia/teachreport.pdf (describing methods of digital rights management).

With one important exception, the Appendix to the Berne Convention for the Protection of Literary and Artistic Works,[27] the international copyright system has historically deferred to national legislation for determination of the appropriate welfare calculus through the specific construction of access mechanisms in domestic markets. This approach was consistent, of course, with the minimum levels of coordination among national copyright standards prior to the conclusion of the TRIPS Agreement. As a result of the integration of intellectual property into the international trade regime, the traditional equilibrium of the welfare concept in intellectual property has been upended by the paradoxical tendency to equate the greatest opportunities for enhancing welfare with the strongest levels of protection.[28] Consequently, not only has the TRIPS Agreement intruded into the domestic prerogatives of World Trade Organization (WTO) Members for developing welfare criteria,[29] but the incipient jurisprudence of the WTO's dispute settlement process has yet to reflect a commitment to access to protected works as a cognizable component of the global copyright system.[30]

This institutional restraint that characterizes the WTO dispute settlement panels may reflect an attempt at neutrality in the face of current national debates over the appropriate scope of copyright protection in the digital age. In industrialized countries, the access mechanisms of copyright law face multiple challenges. The unbridled extension of copyright law through the agency of para-copyright regimes to enhance protection for digital works,[31] unremitting efforts to extend protection to previously uncopyrightable subject matter,[32] and judicial decisions that constrain existing limitations to copyright[33] all have serious implications for a balanced national copyright system.

---

[27] *See* Berne Convention, above n. 13, Appendix [hereinafter Berne Appendix].
[28] *See* Ruth Gana Okediji, *Copyright and Public Welfare in Global Perspective*, 7 IND. J. GLOBAL LEGAL STUD. 117 (1999) [hereinafter Okediji, *Copyright and Public Welfare*]. However, this trend ignores the classical thrust of GATT rules against government intervention in the marketplace and ignores the extent to which IPRs are themselves artificial products of such intervention. *See* Maskus & Reichman, above n. 11.
[29] *See* Ruth L. Okediji, *Public Welfare and the Role of the WTO: Reconsidering the TRIPS Agreement*, 17 EMORY INT.'L L. REV. 819 (2003) [hereinafter Okediji, *Public Welfare*]; Carlos M. Correa, *Managing the Provision of Knowledge: The Design of Intellectual Property Laws*, *in* PROVIDING GLOBAL PUBLIC GOODS: MANAGING GLOBALIZATION 410 (Inge Kaul et al. eds., 2003).
[30] *See* Okediji, *Public Welfare*, above n. 29. [31] DMCA, above n. 22.
[32] *See, e.g.*, Database and Collections of Information Misappropriation Act of 2003, H.R. 3261, 108th Cong. (2003), *available at* http://thomas.loc.gov; http://frwebgate.access.gpo.gov/cgi-bin/getdoc.cgi?dbname=108_cong_bills&docid=f:h3261ih.txt.pdf (proposing copyright-like/misappropriation protection to certain types of databases); TRIPS Agreement, above n. 3, art. 10.1 (mandating copyright protection of computer programs).
[33] *See, e.g.*, Am. Geophysical Union v. Texaco, Inc., 60 F.3d 913 (2d Cir.), *cert. dismissed*, 516 U.S. 1005 (1995); Princeton Univ. Press v. Michigan Document Servs., 99 F.3d 1381 (6th Cir. 1996), *cert. denied*, 520 U.S. 1156 (1997).

In this new environment of copyright lawmaking, the obligation to secure necessary access mechanisms to effect copyright's core mission of enhancing domestic welfare can no longer remain the primary province of the state. The international system should assume responsibility for expanding access principles as a positive feature of copyright treaties, both to counterbalance the development of new exclusive rights, and to facilitate greater levels of access under existing treaties. As harmonization constrains and, in some cases, prohibits the exercise of residual power by single members of copyright treaties, access must become an integral part of the normative equation of international copyright law.

III. The new copyright environment

Just as an expanded notion of property during the industrial era sought principally to reconcile new forms of economic organization with industrial technologies, copyright protection for digital content similarly recognizes an unprecedented level of economic power for owners of protected works. The conclusion of the TRIPS Agreement was an indispensable first step in the larger vision of transforming copyright law for the "new" economy.[34] Shortly thereafter, two treaties that address the needs of copyright owners in the digital environment were negotiated within the auspices of the World Intellectual Property Organization (WIPO). The WCT and the WIPO Performances and Phonograms Treaty[35] (WPPT) entered into force in 2002. Both treaties set forth, in ontological fashion, "the need to introduce new international rules to address new questions raised by technological developments" in light of the profound "impact of the development and convergence of information and communication technologies" on the creation and use of creative expression.[36] To date, 46 countries have ratified the WCT[37] and 43 countries have joined the WPPT.[38] Of these ratifications, many are from developing and a few from least-developed countries.

---

[34] *See* Peter Drahos, *BITs and BIPs*, 4 J. WORLD INTELL. PROP. L. 791, 791–92 (2001) (suggesting that the TRIPS negotiations were conditioned on an explicit understanding that a multilateral bargain would end bilateral and unilateral pressure on developing countries with respect to strengthening of intellectual property rights).
[35] *See* WCT, above n. 4; WPPT, above n. 4.
[36] *See* WCT, above n. 4, Preamble, paras. 2, 3; WPPT, above n. 4, Preamble, paras. 2, 3.
[37] WIPO Copyright Treaty, 36 I.L.M. 65, S. Treaty Doc. No. 105–17, at 1 (1997) (Status as of 15 July 2004), *available at* http://www.wipo.int/treaties/en/documents/pdf/s-wct.pdf.
[38] WIPO Performances and Phonograms Treaty, 36 I.L.M. 76, S. Treaty Doc. No. 105–17, at 18 (1997)(Status on 15 July 2004); *available at* http://www.wipo.int/treaties/en/documents/pdf/s-wppt.pdf.

A. TRIPS and its progeny: Incorporation, coordination and interpretation of international copyright rules

The WIPO Internet treaties are special agreements adopted within the ambit of article 20 of the Berne Convention.[39] In its current form, article 20 provides that members of the Berne Convention may enter into other agreements concerning copyright law, but only if such "special agreements" grant to authors rights that are greater than the rights provided by the Berne Convention, or the agreements do not contain provisions that are "contrary" to the Berne Convention. As to member countries with pre-existing bilateral agreements, article 20 recognizes the Berne-legitimacy of such agreements only to the extent that the two conditions (*i.e.*, more extensive treatment of authors' rights and no inconsistency with Berne) are satisfied. Bilateral agreements deemed inconsistent with the Berne Convention thus have no point of attachment with the Convention; such agreements are precluded entirely from the possibility of affecting the integrity of the Berne Convention obligations through a "later in time" hierarchy of international agreements. To fully understand why access mechanisms have been difficult to emphasize in the international copyright context, one must understand the structure of the premier copyright treaty, the Berne Convention, and its long-standing, single-minded focus on maximum protection for authors' rights.

At their initial stages, multilateral accords generally attempt to establish a modest set of agreed principles – a set of "minimum" standards likely to be acceptable to a sufficiently large number of states,[40] or at the least a strong core of such states. With respect to the first iteration of the Berne Convention, the Berne Act,[41] minimum standards thus naturally had to correlate to a significant

---

[39] *See* WCT, above n. 4, art. 1(1); Berne Convention, above n. 13, art. 20.

[40] *See, e.g.*, ILO Convention (No. 147) Concerning Minimum Standards in Merchant Ships (29 Oct. 1976); Paul Crampton & Milos Barutciski, *Trade Distorting Private Restraints: A Practical Agenda for Future Action*, 6 SW. J. L. & TRADE AM. 3, 56 (1999) (advocating multilateral agreement on minimum standards in area of competition law as a "modest attempt at achieving progress"); Robert L. McGeorge, *The Pollution Haven Problem in International Law: Can the International Community Harmonize Liberal Trade, Environmental and Economic Development Policies?*, 12 WIS. INT'L L. J. 277, 354–55 (1994) (referring to minimum standards in multilateral environmental treaties); David R. Downes, *New Diplomacy for the Biodiversity Trade: Biodiversity, Biotechnology, and Intellectual Property in the Convention on Biological Diversity*, 4 TOURO J. TRANSNAT'L L. 1, 29 (1993) (urging multinational development of minimum standards for control of genetic resources and biodiversity).

[41] The original Berne Convention was signed on 9 September 1886 in Berne, Switzerland, 12 MARTENS NOUVEAU RECUEIL (ser. 12) 173. The subsequent revisions and amendments are as follows: Additional Act and Declaration of Paris, *done on* 4 May 1896, 24 MARTENS NOUVEAU RECUEIL (ser. 12) 758; Act of Berlin Revision *done on* 13 Nov. 1908, 1 L.N.T.S. 243; Additional Protocol of Berne, *done on* 20 Mar. 1914, 1 L.N.T.S. 243; Rome Revision, *done on* 2 June 1928, 123 L.N.T.S. 217; Brussels Revision, *done on* 26 June 1948, 331

degree with existing national practices, as well as common practices in the extensive network of bilateral copyright agreements.[42] Many bilateral copyright agreements in existence at the time were associated with broader treaties dealing generally with commerce among European states.[43] Consequently, the original minimum standards of the Berne Act drew heavily from three sources: national norms and practices of the negotiating states, common elements of existing bilateral copyright agreements, and principles of bilateral commercial treaties.[44] In this context, the classic conception of "minimum standards" was pragmatically instrumental. It recognized existing normative criteria for the protection of creative works, incorporated prevailing legal structures affecting the negotiating parties, and coordinated the various obligations in a clear effort to secure a multilateral compromise.

In this initial exercise of copyright multilateralism, it was critically important to accord sufficient weight to national realitie – economic, political and cultural – of the negotiating states. As a result, the formulation of article 20 of the Berne Act was entirely consistent with the minimum standards established. Those states that provided stronger protection than the minimum standards could continue to pursue bilateral relations reflecting these higher standards; but those states that objected to stronger levels of protection were locked into the negotiated minimum standards. To the extent that these negotiated standards were derived substantially from existing practice, the minimum standards of the Berne Act were appreciably consistent with the overriding principle of deference to national prerogative. Importantly, the real possibility of an exit from the Agreement, and the absence of formal and effective sanctions for breaches of the negotiated obligations, imposed a discipline on the early Berne Convention negotiations to pursue true substantive minima in the multilateral context.[45]

Having addressed existing obligations of member states in article 20, the negotiations then dealt with the prospect of future copyright agreements under article 15. Article 15 of the Berne Act recognized the sovereign right of member states to continue to pursue "special agreements" relating to copyright

U.N.T.S. 217; Stockholm Revision, *done on* 14 July 1967, 828 U.N.T.S. 221; Paris Revision, *done on* 24 July 1971, 1161 U.N.T.S. 3.

[42] *See* SAM RICKETSON, THE BERNE CONVENTION FOR THE PROTECTION OF LITERARY AND ARTISTIC WORKS: 1886–1986, at 35–36 (Kluwer 1987).

[43] *Id. See also*, Ruth Okediji, *Back to Bilateralism? Pendulum Shifts in International Intellectual Property Protection*, 1 U. OTTAWA J. L. & TECH. 125 (2004) [hereinafter Okediji, *Back to Bilateralism*].

[44] Notably, the eminent principles of national treatment and the most favored nation clause. *See* RICKETSON, above n. 42; Okediji, *Back to Bilateralism*, above n. 43.

[45] Another way to understand the nature of these minimum standards is to consider the game theoretic notion of a "core," which represents the bargaining range of a game. *See* Okediji, *Public Welfare*, above n. 29, at 850–851 (discussing the core of the TRIPS Agreement).

protection, but again limited this right to agreements that either granted greater protection to authors, or that "embody other stipulations not contrary to the present Convention."[46]

The design of articles 15 and 20 of the Berne Act yielded three distinct results. First, from its genesis, the Berne Convention was clearly intended to constitute the preeminent and primary source of international copyright obligations. Article 15 ensured that future copyright agreements would recognize the Convention as the touchstone of international copyright law, and it prohibited any deviations from the accepted principles reflected therein. Article 20 effectively set into motion a path-dependency that would serve, ultimately, to complement and reinforce the foundation established by the Berne Convention.

Second, path-dependency was guaranteed to consolidate the gains of future negotiating rounds, since the only way to avoid the reach of Berne obligations was to exit the treaty entirely. Third, articles 15 and 20 taken together meant that no other international copyright agreement different in substance, form or orientation[47] could successfully compete with the Berne Convention, for the reason that membership in the Berne Convention consisted of the most economically powerful states in the international economy as of 1886 and well into the mid-twentieth century.[48] During the Berlin Revisions of the Berne Convention in 1908, articles 15 and 20 were integrated into current article 20.

The mechanism of imposing constraints on special agreements was an early reflection of the commitment to modify the Convention only to provide stronger rights for authors. In the context in which it was negotiated, article

---

[46] RICKETSON, above n. 42, at 683.

[47] The United States declined membership in the Berne Convention even after it became a world power; however, it initiated the negotiation of another, less exacting, international agreement for copyright protection, the Universal Copyright Convention (UCC). Universal Copyright Convention, 6 Sept. 1952, Geneva, 6 U.S.T. 2731, T.I.A.S. No. 3324, 216 U.N.T.S. 132, *revised* 24 July 1971, Paris, 25 U.S.T. 1341, T.I.A.S. No. 7868 [hereinafter UCC]. The United States participated in the Berlin Conference with observer status, as it had done from the inception of the Convention.

[48] Shared interests that facilitate coalitions can be a function of common positions of power in the international arena, as illustrated by developed countries during the TRIPS negotiations. The compromise made intra-coalitionally among the developed countries reflects the equal interests of these countries and the inability of one country to make a unilateral decision about the TRIPS outcome. *See* Arthur A. Stein, *Coordination and Collaboration: Regimes in an Anarchic World*, 36 INT'L ORG. 299, 301 (1982) (identifying constrained interaction as a basic metric for the existence of international regimes); Gunner Sjostedt, *Negotiating the Uruguay Round of the General Agreement on Tariffs and Trade*, *in* INTERNATIONAL MULTILATERAL NEGOTIATION 44, 69 (I. William Zartman, ed., 1994) (noting the "leadership problem" stemming from the lack of U.S. hegemony during the Uruguay Round negotiations because power relationships among the leading countries had become more symmetrical).

20 was a logical extension of the baseline negotiated for multilateral copyright protection. Shifting political alignments among European states, coupled with the extensive network of bilateral treaties,[49] would have been constant threats to the security of the multilateral accord. Imposing constraints on the prospective agreements of Member States and limiting the effect of extant agreements affirmed the preeminence of the Convention's normative ethos favoring strong authorial protection. Article 20 thus established the foundation for the one-way ratchet characteristic of modern intellectual property lawmaking by ensuring that any incentives for states to bargain around the Convention would benefit authors. Where such bargains did take place, they could eventually influence multilateral revisions that would strengthen the minimum provisions of the Convention.

Reflecting on the structure of the Berne Convention, one must concede that the TRIPS Agreement was not the initial source of the current tendency in copyright law to heighten protection and limit access to creative works, either by extending authorial prerogatives or delimiting access mechanisms. From its inception, article 20 of the Berne Convention has given latitude for the argument that exceptions and limitations somehow detract from copyright law's (and thus the Convention's) fundamental purpose.

B. From Stockholm to Paris

An important pause in the one-way evolution of the Berne Convention occurred during the negotiations of the Stockholm Revision of 1967,[50] which confronted the large number of newly independent countries that had become part of the international community of states. By sheer volume alone, the possibility that these states would not join the Convention posed a threat to its stability and credibility. This threat was particularly palpable in view of the keenly felt absence of United States membership.[51] The preservation of the Berne Convention's self-image as the dominant multilateral copyright agreement was an important factor in considering changes that would encourage newly independent countries to become members.

The failure of the Stockholm Revision is well known. The Revision resulted in a "compromise" text, the Protocol, to address developing countries'

---

[49] RICKETSON, above n. 42, at 26–38 (1987) (describing the origins, extent and nature of bilateral copyright agreements).
[50] *See* Salah Basalamah, *Compulsory Licensing for Translation: An Instrument of Development?*, 40 IDEA 503, 507–509 (2000); Dorothy M. Schrader, *Analysis of the Protocol Regarding Developing Countries*, 17 BULL. COPYRIGHT SOC'Y 166, 182–83 (1969–70); Howard D. Sacks, *Crisis in International Copyright, The Protocol Regarding Developing Countries*, J. BUS. L. 26 (Jan.-Apr. 1969). The Stockholm Protocol Regarding Developing Countries appears at 828 U.N.T.S. 223, 281.
[51] *See* above n. 47, and accompanying text.

interests, but it proved ultimately unsuccessful as a model for international cooperation.[52] As concluded, the Stockholm Protocol allowed any developing country to adopt as many as five reservations to the Berne Convention. Each reservation would remain in effect for a ten-year period, unless the developing country did not consider itself to be in a position to withdraw the reservation. The first reservation gave developing countries the option of substituting a period of life plus 25 years, instead of life plus 50 years, as the minimum term of protection. Two reservations allowed the issuance of compulsory licenses for translations into national, official or regional languages if the author of the work failed to authorize such a translation within three years of first publication, and so long as national legislation provided for payment of just compensation. The fourth reservation limited the exclusive right to broadcast to broadcasts made for profit. Finally, the fifth reservation allowed compulsory licenses for "teaching, study, and research in all fields of education," with compensation rates for such use correlating with standards for payments made to national authors. In other words, it was a national treatment rule for payment of royalties pursuant to a compulsory license issued for the public purposes identified. This fifth reservation was, unsurprisingly, the most controversial of those set out in the Stockholm Protocol.[53]

Only three countries ratified the Stockholm Protocol in full.[54] More significantly, nine major countries positively signaled their rejection of the Revision,[55] and twenty-six countries acted affirmatively only with respect to the administrative provisions contained in articles 22–26 of the Stockholm Act.[56] The practical effect of this splinter was that the substantive provisions of the Stockholm Act are the only Berne Convention revisions that never became part of the international copyright framework.

But here I want to examine more deeply why the Berne Convention was not significantly imperiled by the Stockholm debacle. Indeed, the fundamental commitment to strong authorial control over copyrighted works was not at

---

[52] There is a wealth of literature on the Stockholm process and its ultimate failure. *See, e.g.*, Irwin A. Olian, *International Copyright and the Needs of Developing Countries: The Awakening at Stockholm and Paris*, 7 CORNELL INT'L L. J. 81 (1974); Nora Maija Tocups, *The Development of Special Provisions in International Copyright Law for the Benefit of Developing Countries*, 29 J. COPYRIGHT SOC'Y 402 (1982); Barbara A. Ringer, *The Role of the United States in International Copyright–Past, Present, and Future*, 56 GEO. L. J. 1050 (1968).

[53] Schrader, above n. 50, at 187 (noting that "the question of remuneration figured ... prominently in the controversy regarding the Protocol as a whole and this reservation in particular.").

[54] These were Senegal, Pakistan and Romania.

[55] These were Canada, Denmark, Finland, West Germany (Federal Republic), Israel, Spain, Sweden, Switzerland, and the United Kingdom.

[56] *See* Records of the Diplomatic Conference for the 5–24 July 1971 Paris Revision of the Berne Convention, 34 (1974).

all modified by the threats of exit or by the existence of the Universal Copyright Convention[57] (UCC), which offered weaker multilateral protection and which resonated far better with the interests of developing countries. The initial interest in having developing countries choose the Berne Convention over the UCC made it curious that the *developed* countries were not more concerned about the failure of Stockholm. Several factors merit consideration to explain the apparent imperviousness of the Berne Convention's cardinal emphasis on strong authors' rights, and the ostensible detachment of the developed countries from the demands of developing countries.

1. The move from coordination to institutions

The artificial distinction between "substantive" provisions and "administrative" provisions of the Berne Convention is a powerful testament to the ways in which process supplies unique, intractable and invisible sources of power in the multilateral context.[58] The development of a formalized institutional structure for international copyright law started at the Stockholm Conference, after more than eighty years of informal administration. This shift from "soft" coordination to "hard" institutional form has been largely ignored by scholars and commentators, and understandably so. The Stockholm Revision is considered principally in light of the confrontation between the developed and developing countries, and the ensuing tension between their competing demands. This confrontation overshadowed the entire revision process and obscured the far weightier transformation of the structure of the Berne Convention.

In particular, the Stockholm Revision established an Executive Committee[59] and an Assembly[60] to govern the Union and to facilitate implementation of the goals of the Convention. The Stockholm Revision also resulted in the establishment of WIPO, with the aim of consolidating the administration of the various intellectual property agreements previously under the jurisdiction of BIRPI.[61] The new institutional framework secured the progressive evolution of the Convention. Importantly, article 21 of the Stockholm Revision defined the Assembly as those countries of the Union bound by articles 22 to 26 (the

---

[57] *See* above n. 47.
[58] *See* Richard H. Steinberg, *In the Shadow of Law or Power? Consensus-Based Bargaining and Outcomes in the GATT/WTO*, 56 INT'L ORG. 339 (2002); Ruth L. Okediji, *Rules of Power in an Age of Law: Process Opportunism and TRIPS Dispute Settlement*, in HANDBOOK OF INTERNATIONAL TRADE: ECONOMIC AND LEGAL ANALYSIS OF LAWS AND INSTITUTIONS (E. Kwan Choi & J. Hartigan eds., 2004) [hereinafter Okediji, *Rules of Power*].
[59] *See* Stockholm Revision, above n. 41, art. 23.   [60] *See id.*, art. 22.
[61] BIRPI, the United International Bureaux for the Protection of Intellectual Property (in French, Bureaux Internationaux Réunis pour la Protection de la Propriété), resulted from the merger of the two secretariats created by the Paris Convention for the Protection of Industrial Property, 20 Mar. 1883, 13 U.S.T. 2, 828 U.N.T.S. 107, and the Berne Convention. BIRPI was the predecessor to WIPO.

administrative provisions) of the resulting Stockholm Act.[62] A country of the Union that still adhered to the lower standards of an earlier revision of the Berne Convention, could thus still accede to the administrative provisions in the Stockholm Act,[63] and thus participate in future revisions.

Once the mechanism to ensure repeated revisions was established, a member country could safely ignore the substantive provisions of the Stockholm Act without weakening its sovereign commitment to the multilateral agenda for strong authorial protection. Indeed, the ability of countries to independently ratify the administrative provisions had the perverse effect of simultaneously bolstering the Berne Convention and casting the Stockholm Act as an aberration in the Convention's history. The administrative provisions established a strong institutional apparatus to perpetuate the Berne Convention, but successfully abandoned the concessions offered to poor countries to address their development needs and priorities. In sum, the de-linking of the administrative and substantive provisions in the Stockholm Act effected a strategic isolation of the Stockholm Protocol's substantive provisions.

As I mentioned earlier, of the various components of the Stockholm Act, 26 countries ratified these administrative provisions, which established the dominant organizational framework (WIPO) responsible for international intellectual property regulation today. With the administrative provisions uncoupled from the Protocol and its substantive provisions, it was possible for the administrative section to enter into force as a binding legal instrument even if the other parts of the Act were unsuccessful. To reinforce this strategic ploy, *a la carte* ratification of, or accession to, the Stockholm Act was defined by the line between substantive and administrative provisions: countries had either to accept articles 1–21 *and* the Protocol as a bloc, or reject these substantive provisions as a bloc. There could be no uncoupling of the Protocol from the other substantive provisions.

Once the requisite number of ratifications was obtained, the administrative provisions of the Stockholm Act came into force in 1970. It was the only part of the Stockholm Act that survived the impasse between developed and developing countries. It was also the only part of the Stockholm Act necessary to ensure that, despite the demands of developing countries, the elaboration of stronger copyright norms would become an ongoing process at the multilateral level.

2. Consolidating the organizational framework

To confirm the enduring commitment of the Berne Convention to ever-increasing levels of protection, article 27(1) of the Stockholm Act hardened

---

[62] *See* Stockholm Revision, above n. 41, art. 21.
[63] This is, in effect, what happened when countries ratified the administrative provisions but not the Stockholm Revision itself. Those countries were bound only by the revisions they had signed earlier.

the earlier language of the Brussels Act[64] by making it mandatory to submit the Convention for periodic revision "with a view to the introduction of amendments designed to improve the system of the Union."[65] The establishment of a governing body and an institutional framework to administer the Berne Union logically supplied a forum where this mandatory revision could occur.

The shift from soft coordination to hard institutional organization, from permissive to mandatory revisions upwards, and the introduction of a facial distinction between process and substance actually strengthened the high protectionist ethos of the Berne Convention at a time when it purportedly faced its most serious challenge. It is as though the demands for modifying the Berne Convention simply calcified its protective posture and occasioned a discrete channeling of power to the ostensibly mechanical rules of administrative bureaucracy.

3. Legitimacy, sequential revision and accommodation strategies

The relatively short period of time between the Stockholm Act of 1967 and the Paris Conference of 1971 was an essential feature in consolidating the covert gains for developed countries from the Stockholm Act, while also seeking ways to address the extant challenge of incorporating developing countries into the system.[66] The pertinent question at this juncture was why developing countries did not simply invoke the threat of exit,[67] particularly when the existence of the UCC appeared to offer an alternative.

For all legal purposes, most developing countries were already members of the Berne Convention. This curious situation was the result of the formalistic interpretation of the Berne Convention, combined with a view of international law formulated by the International Office of BIRPI prior to the Stockholm Revision. Many developing countries whose colonial masters had been members of the Berne Convention were considered subject to the Convention under a default rule of continuity, unless the newly independent states affirmatively denounced it.[68] Even in the face of a denunciation, however, continuity was deemed the de facto rule for the period between the date of independence and the date of the denunciation.[69] In sum, any act – affirmative or otherwise – of the newly independent states placed them within the Convention even if just for a brief period of time,[70] at least until denunciation (if made) took effect.

---

[64] *See* Berne Convention, above n. 13.   [65] *Id.*, art. 27(1).
[66] A bare four years elapsed between the Stockholm and Paris Revisions. Prior to the Stockholm Revision, the last Revision conference had taken place in 1948 (Brussels Act), and there has not been another Revision since the Paris Revision in 1971.
[67] Only one country, Upper Volta, denounced the Berne Convention after Stockholm. *See* Upper Volta, Denunciation of the Berne Convention for the Protection of Literary and Artistic Works, 5 COPYRIGHT 235 (1969).
[68] RICKETSON, above n. 42, at 797–807.   [69] *Id.*
[70] Interestingly, in some instances of accession by a developing country, the BIRPI office implicitly treated the Convention as having lapsed between the period of independence

Further, the UCC contained a so-called safety clause, which sanctioned countries that left the Berne Convention.[71] This inter-regime cooperation meant that no competitive alternatives to Berne were realistically possible. At the same time, the tightening of the international copyright administration, combined with the absence of enforcement prospects in the international system, had negative implications for copyright protection. In effect, developing countries could still sign the agreements without expecting severe pressures for effective compliance.

The danger posed by this state of affairs to the effectiveness of the Berne Convention,[72] and the political necessity to respond to the Stockholm impasse, provided a strategic opportunity for the newly formed institutional organs of the Berne Union. The availability of a mechanism and structure within which to address the situation tended inherently to legitimize the nascent institutional structure of the Berne Union and gave it instant credibility with its constituents, particularly the developing countries, as well as the broader international community.

A Joint Study Group comprising the Permanent Committee for the Berne Convention and the Intergovernmental Copyright Committee for the UCC was soon established. The mandate of the Committee was focused on the needs of developing countries "while respecting the rights of authors," and on problems arising from the existence of two multilateral copyright agreements. The recommendation issued by the Committee formed the basis of the Paris Revisions with respect to developing countries, as well as for revisions of the UCC. Most notably, the recommendation called for a revision of the Stockholm Protocol and suggested that the Protocol should be separated from the Act itself.

---

and accession. *Id.* at 800–801. This led to an inequitable approach to the legal treatment of developing countries, in which a country that denounced the Convention could be considered bound until such denunciation, whereas a country that acceded to the Convention was deemed to have had a break in the application of the Convention in the period before such accession. It is also notable that, as colonialism became less palatable internationally, some colonial powers began to exclude their colonies from revisions of the Berne Convention that they ratified. It follows that, at independence, many former colonies were subject to earlier Acts of the Convention than the one in force in the European colonial power. RICKETSON, above n. 42, at 805–806. *See also* Ruth L. Okediji, *The International Relations of Intellectual Property: Narratives of Developing Country Participation in the Global Intellectual Property System*, 7 SINGAPORE J. INT.'L COMP. L. 315, 335–36 (2003).

[71] *See* UCC, above n. 47, art. XVII (Geneva Conference). During the Stockholm Revision Conference, a revision of the safety clause to except developing countries had been one of the items for study. *See* Revision of the Berne Convention, Records of the Paris Conference 34 (1971); *see also* Records of the Conference for the Revision of the Universal Copyright Convention, UNESCO 261 (1973).

[72] *See generally* Ndene Ndiaye, *The Berne Convention and Developing Countries*, 11 COLUM-VLA J.L. & ARTS 47 (1986).

This particular recommendation was ultimately reflected in the Paris Act, with an adoption of an Appendix for developing countries as an external instrument.

IV. The Berne Appendix as market failure

Like the Stockholm Protocol, the Berne Appendix establishes a system of compulsory licenses. Unlike the Stockholm Protocol, the Berne Appendix is extremely complex and inordinately driven by procedural conditions that must be satisfied before such licenses may be issued.[73] Even so, the Appendix grants a reversionary interest to the copyright owner by empowering the owner to terminate licenses granted to nationals of the developing country.[74] The Appendix also contains limitations on parallel imports of works produced under a compulsory license and requires just compensation at internationally cognizable standards.[75]

A. *Structure of the Berne Appendix*

The Berne Appendix compounded the problems that developing countries already faced in gaining access to foreign creative works by its labyrinthine process, complex conditions, and onerous terms. As a formal matter, one could argue that it is a legal instrument recognized by the international community. Substantively, however, the Appendix has not been successful in expanding either bulk or negotiated access to protected works. Like the Doha compromise on access to essential medicines,[76] the Berne Appendix requires a developing

---

[73] *See* Appendix to the Berne Convention, above n. 27, arts. V, V*bis*.

[74] If the owner makes the relevant translations/copies available in the country, that will terminate the national licensee's rights. The compulsory licensee selling the translations or copies can continue to sell only copies already printed. *Id*. art. II(6).

[75] *Id*. art. IV(4)-(5) (parallel imports); art. IV(6) (just compensation). Art. IV(4)(a) provides: "No license granted under article II or article III shall extend to the export of copies, and any such license shall be valid only for publication of the translation or of the reproduction, as the case may be, in the territory of the country in which it has been applied for. (b) For the purposes of sub-paragraph (a), the notion of export shall include the sending of copies from any territory to the country which, in respect of that territory, has made a declaration under article I(5)." The General Report covering the Appendix addresses the possibility of overcoming the restrictions on parallel imports where the developing country has no printing or reproduction facilities, but these exceptions are not reflected in the explicit terms of the Appendix.

[76] WTO Doha Ministerial Conference, Declaration on the TRIPS Agreement and Public Health, WT/MIN(01)/DEC/W/2 (14 Nov. 2001), 41 I.L.M. 755 (2002) [hereinafter Doha Declaration on TRIPS and Public Health]; Decision of General Council of 30 Aug. 2003, Implementation of paragraph 6 of the Doha Declaration on the TRIPS Agreement and Public Health, WT/L/540 (1 Sept. 2003), 43 I.L.M. 509 (2004). Only one country, Malawi, has notified UNICEF of its intent to take advantage of the provisions in Paragraph 7 of the Doha Declaration. *See* Hanne Bak Pedersen, *Access to ARV's: Procurement, Logistics, Infrastructure* (Dec. 2003), *available at* http://www.who.int/medicines/. A full discussion of the Doha compromise is beyond the scope of this chapter. But similar to the structure of

country to self-identify by notifying the appropriate institutional organization (in this case the Director General of WIPO) of its intention to avail itself of the Appendix.[77] Under article II, a developing country must wait at least three years after first publication before utilizing the compulsory license mechanism for translations, and it can do so only if the right owner has not exercised the translation right with respect to the language at issue.[78]

The three-year waiting period can be shortened in two circumstances. First, the period may be shortened to one year in cases where the language into which a work is to be translated is not in general use in one or more developed countries.[79] Second, the three-year period may be shortened with the *unanimous* consent of the developed member countries of the Berne Union in which the language that is the subject of the translation license is in general use, unless the language is English, French, or Spanish.[80] In essence, compulsory licenses for translations of English, French or Spanish works cannot be issued in less than three years from the date of first publication.[81] It is worth pointing out (the obvious) that these three languages are spoken in the vast majority of the colonial territories in Africa, Asia and the Americas.

The practical effect of the three-year ban is that the *only* means of access for most developing countries, during this time frame, to works first published in these languages is the copyright owner. For literary works used for educational purposes, particularly those in the technical and scientific fields, this provision also means that developing countries that decide to issue the compulsory license would be doing so for works that are likely to be outdated.

In addition to the three-year ban, the Appendix added a grace period of six months *after* a citizen of a developing country had filed for a compulsory license for the copyright owner to exercise the translation right.[82] If, within the six-month

the Doha compromise, the Berne Appendix declaration is a condition to legitimate use of the limitations contained therein. As of 2003, 10 countries had exercised the compulsory license provisions of the Berne Convention for teaching and translation. These are Algeria, Bahrain, Bangladesh, Cuba, Jordan, Korea, Kazakhstan, Mongolia, Philippines and Singapore. Thailand has exercised an option for compulsory licenses only for translations for the purposes of teaching, scholarship and research. *See* Sothi Rachagan, Copyright in Education – Reclaiming the Public Domain, presentation at Transatlantic Consumer Dialogue, Workshop on Global Access to Essential Learning Tools (New York, 5 Apr. 2004). *See also* Daniel J. Gervais, *The Internationalization of Intellectual Property: New Challenges from the Very Old and the Very New*, 12 FORDHAM INTELL. PROP. MEDIA & ENT. L.J. 929, 942, fn. 70 (2002) (stating that only eight of these countries had made the declaration pursuant to article I of the Appendix).

[77] Berne Appendix, above n. 27, art. II.   [78] *Id.* art. II(2)(a).
[79] *Id.* art. II(3)(a).   [80] *Id.* art. II(3)(b).
[81] *Id.* art. II(2)(a). The developing country must also ensure that its national legislation requires compulsory licensees to make a correct translation of the work. *Id.* art. IV(6)(b).
[82] *Id.* art. II 4(a). Note that for licenses that may be issued one year from publication (*i.e.*, for works to be translated into a language not in general use), the grace period is nine months from the date of application for the compulsory license.

period, the copyright owner exercises the translation right, the compulsory license cannot be issued. The six-month period thus offers an opportunity for the copyright owner to preclude issuance of the compulsory license, notwithstanding any investments already made by the citizen in the developing country.

Such a risk, given the socioeconomic conditions in most developing countries, is simply untenable. The risk is heightened by a provision that mandates termination of the compulsory license if at anytime (even after the end of the three-year waiting period), the copyright owner exercises the translation right and offers the publication for sale at a price "reasonably related to that normally charged in the country for comparable works."[83] Like the Doha compromise, these conditions render the cost of exercising a compulsory license for translation so high as to be economically unfeasible.[84]

Finally, article II licenses apply only to teaching, scholarship and research.[85] However, in developed countries, uncompensated access mechanisms exist for scholarship and research purposes, particularly if undertaken in a non-commercial context.[86] Imposing a compensatory regime for such uses in *developing* countries is unjustifiably burdensome and, more importantly, there is no legal basis for it under the Berne Convention. It is hardly plausible that the Berne Convention, which grants countries the discretion to define limitations for the reproduction right, could be interpreted to support the denial of such discretion to developing countries whose political, economic and cultural priorities arguably provide more substantial justifications for robust access rights. It is even less credible to suggest that the Appendix could be interpreted to take away from developing countries a right granted by the Convention to all countries, namely, the exercise of sovereign discretion to interfere with the market for copyrighted works to secure public interest objectives.

The Berne Appendix and the Doha compromise have uncannily similar structures, with a few differences, for the issuance of compulsory licenses to limit the author's exclusive reproduction right.[87] Article III licenses can only be obtained to reproduce and publish for use in connection with systematic instructional activities, and they may be issued after a five-year period from the date of first publication.[88] For works of natural and physical sciences, the period is shortened to three years.[89] For works of fiction, poetry, drama, music, and art, the waiting period is seven years.[90] A license to reproduce a translated work cannot be issued where the translation was not made by the copyright owner or under his authorization, or where the translation is not in a language in general use in the country in which the reproduction license is applied for.[91]

---

[83] *Id*. art. II(6).
[84] *Cf*. Carlos Correa, *TRIPS and Access to Drugs: Towards a Solution for Countries without Manufacturing Capacity?*, 17 EMORY INT'L L. REV. 389 (2003).
[85] *See* Berne Appendix, above n. 27, art. II(5).   [86] 17 U.S.C. § 107 (2000).
[87] *See id*. art. III.   [88] *Id*. art. III(3).   [89] *Id*. art. III(3)(i).
[90] *Id*. art. III(3)(ii).   [91] *Id*. art. III(5)(i)–(ii).

These provisions create an artificial distinction between the translation right and the reproduction right, and make it difficult for publishers in a developing country to utilize the compulsory license provisions for both rights simultaneously. Since the language in general use in most developing countries is the *lingua franca* of their colonial powers (predominantly French and English), the market for translated works in languages not in general use is quite small. Furthermore, works published pursuant to a validly issued *reproduction license* cannot subsequently be translated without additional authorization, subject to additional requirements. This means that each license regime leads to a market division where the economies of scale are such that a developing country citizen is unlikely to have sufficient incentive to apply for an article II translation license, even absent the risks, discussed above, associated with such a venture.

In many respects, the Berne Appendix anticipated all the complexities built into the Doha compromise on access to patented medicines,[92] as well as some of the conditions on compulsory licensing of patents in general that were embodied in the TRIPS Agreement.[93] For example, neither a translation nor a reproduction license may be granted under the Appendix unless the applicant demonstrates that she has requested and been denied authorization to translate or reproduce the work by the right owner, or shows that despite due diligence, the right owner could not be located.[94] The Appendix also requires that the applicant inform any "national or international information center" at the same time as the request is made to the copyright owner.[95] Like the Doha compromise, moreover, the Berne Appendix requires that works made pursuant to a compulsory license bear distinguishing marks[96] and, except in the case of a government license, prohibits the exports of works made under any compulsory license.[97] In all cases, just compensation, not necessarily consistent with local market rates, must be paid.[98]

---

[92] *See* above n. 76.   [93] TRIPS Agreement, above n. 3, art. 31.
[94] Berne Appendix, above n. 27, art. IV(1).
[95] *Id.* This provision enables national copyright offices in developed countries, for example, to locate the copyright owner, or more realistically, to send the copyright owner's contact information to the developing country applicant. If the owner cannot be found, the applicant must send, in prescribed form, copies of the application for the compulsory license to the publisher whose name is on the work, and to any national or international information center notified by the country in which the publisher is believed to have its principal place of business, or to the WIPO Director General. *Id.* art. IV(2).
[96] *See id.*, above n. 27, art. IV(3) (requiring the name of the author on all copies, and specifying that the title, and, in the case of translations, the title in its original language, also must be on all copies); *Id.*, art. IV(5) (requiring that all published copies bear a notice in the "appropriate language" stating that the copies are available for distribution only in the territory where the license applies). *Cf.* Doha Declaration on TRIPS and Public Health, above, n. 76; Decision of General Council of 30 Aug. 2003, above n. 76.
[97] Berne Appendix, above n. 27, art. IV(a)(c).
[98] *See id.* art. IV(6)(a)(i) (using a benchmark of freely negotiated agreements between citizens of the relevant two countries, i.e., the licensee's country and the owner's country).

The combined effect of article IV (1) and (2) is to create a "due process" system for a copyright owner whose work may become the subject of a compulsory license. The Berne Appendix, in essence, imposes a significant tax on the opportunity for access. The system treats uncompensated access as incompatible with copyright's core mission. Through the numerous obligations imposed on an applicant to exert significant effort to locate and contact the copyright owner, the Appendix even provides a de facto subsidy to the *copyright owner* by policing her copyright.

B. *Critical observations*

The Berne Appendix cannot offer the sole point of access for developing countries. As an initial matter, the article II translation license clearly should not apply to uses such as research or scholarship when conducted privately. The article II and article III licenses should also be construed very narrowly when applied to educational or other public interest uses.

For example, compulsory licenses outside the framework of the Appendix can and should also be used by developing countries to address problems with bulk access when the country determines that a rights holder has abused its market power. This prospect is external to the Berne Appendix, as it addresses undersupply of the market for general public purposes, rather than the limited instances (reproduction and translation) that the Appendix explicitly references for its terms. Mandatory compensated access on these grounds is not based on the "compromise" of an international agreement, but on the sovereign power of the state to regulate markets in the general public interest to ensure a competitive balance.

The international patent system acknowledges this reserved power of a state to issue a compulsory license to deal with market abuses.[99] A leading commentator on the Paris Convention has indicated that under this provision, member states are free to provide compulsory licenses or other legislative measures compelling access where the public interest so demands or justifies.[100] Examples of abuses that might result from the exercise of the patent grant include refusals to license on reasonable terms, undersupply of the

---

[99] *See* Paris Convention for the Protection of Industrial Property, above n. 61, art. 5(A) ("Each country of the Union shall have the right to take legislative measures providing for the grant of compulsory licenses to prevent the abuses which might result from the exercise of exclusive rights conferred by the patent, for example, failure to work."); TRIPS Agreement, above n. 3, art. 31; *see also* J.H. REICHMAN WITH CATHERINE HASENZAHL, NON-VOLUNTARY LICENSING OF PATENTED INVENTIONS: HISTORICAL PERSPECTIVE, LEGAL FRAMEWORK UNDER TRIPS, AND AN OVERVIEW OF THE PRACTICE IN CANADA AND THE UNITED STATES (UNCTAD/ICTSD 2002).

[100] *See* G.H.C. BODENHAUSEN, GUIDE TO THE APPLICATION OF THE PARIS CONVENTION FOR THE PROTECTION OF INDUSTRIAL PROPERTY 67–71 (1968).

market, or unreasonable pricing.[101] This framework is equally applicable to the copyright system.[102]

When it comes to matters affecting the public interest, most developed countries do not generally distinguish between copyright and patents because both regimes are designed to function similarly, by giving incentives to innovate for the advancement of public welfare. In the United States, for example, a growing number of cases have recognized the doctrine of "copyright misuse,"[103] taken directly from the patent context.[104] Patent misuse is directed at a patentee's efforts to affect the market for a patented product in a manner not contemplated by the patent grant, thus distorting the market dynamics for the patented product.[105] The growing copyright misuse doctrine in the United States is also concerned with anticompetitive uses of the copyright grant. More broadly, however, for both patent and copyright laws, uses that undermine the public policy objectives of the system are subject to redress through the misuse doctrine.[106] Public policy grounds for recognizing misuse are even more pronounced in the copyright context, with some courts explicitly confirming copyright misuse as a doctrine that extends beyond the antitrust arena.[107]

The TRIPS Agreement also explicitly recognizes the right of Members to adopt "measures ... needed to prevent the abuse of intellectual property

---

[101] *Id.* at 71. [102] *Cf.* TRIPS Agreement, above n. 3, arts. 2.1, 8.2, 40.1.

[103] *See generally* Brett Frischmann & Dan Moylan, *The Evolving Common Law Doctrine of Copyright Misuse: A Unified Theory and Its Application to Software*, 15 BERKELEY TECH. L.J. 865 (2000).

[104] *See, e.g.*, Lasercomb Am., Inc. v. Reynolds, 911 F. 2d 970 (1990); Practice Mgmt. Info. Corp. v. Am. Med. Ass'n, 121 F.3d 516 (9th Cir. 1997); Alcatel USA, Inc. v. DGI Tech., Inc., 166 F.3d 772, 793 (5th Cir. 1999).

[105] *See* Windsurfing Int'l, Inc. v. AMF, Inc., 782 F.2d 995, 1001 (Fed. Cir. 1986) ("The doctrine of patent misuse is an affirmative defense to a suit for patent infringement ... and requires that the alleged infringer show that the patentee has impermissibly broadened the 'physical or temporal scope' of the patent grant with anticompetitive effect." (citations omitted)).

[106] *See* Troy Paredes, Comment, *Copyright Misuse and Tying: Will Courts Stop Misusing Misuse?*, 9 HIGH TECH. L.J. 271, 277 (1994). An example of a public policy goal of copyright is the uncompensated use of work in the public domain. *See* F.E.L. Publ'ns, Ltd. v. Catholic Bishop, 214 U.S.P.Q. (BNA) 409, 413 fn 9 (7th Cir. 1982) (stating, in dicta, that "it is copyright misuse to exact a fee for the use of a musical work which is already in the public domain").

[107] *See* Assessment Technologies v. Wiredata, Inc., 350 F. 3d 640 (2003) ("The argument for applying copyright misuse beyond the bounds of antitrust, ... is that for a copyright owner to use an infringement suit to obtain property protection ... that copyright law clearly does not confer, hoping to force a settlement or even achieve an outright victory over an opponent that may lack the resources or the legal sophistication to resist effectively, is an abuse of process.") *See also* Mark A. Lemley, *Beyond Preemption: The Law and Policy of Intellectual Property Licensing*, 87 CAL. L. REV. 111, 152 (1999); Frischmann & Moylan, above n. 103.

rights ... or the resort to practices which unreasonably restrain trade ...."[108] Article 40 of the Agreement also speaks to the right of Members to address anticompetitive practices arising from the exercise of intellectual property rights.[109] The combined weight of these practices and provisions affords powerful ammunition to developing countries to negotiate bulk access to creative works and to preserve the domestic policy space necessary to implement access mechanisms in domestic legislation. Certainly, in the pre-TRIPS era, member states of the Paris Convention were free to define what constitutes an abuse of the patent grant. Nothing in TRIPS or other international agreements appears to take away this right.[110]

V. Rethinking the access problem

The bulk of the developing countries have never made the necessary declaration pursuant to article I of the Berne Appendix. Yet, despite almost three decades of inactivity, the Appendix was incorporated both into the TRIPS Agreement and the WCT.[111] In theory, these steps were meant to suggest that the provisions of the Appendix provide a means for developing countries to access digital informational works.[112] Given the failure of the Appendix in the print environment to engender market-based bulk access for developing countries, however, its potential – not to mention its relevance – for the digital environment becomes highly questionable. Consequently, developing countries should seriously consider resort to compulsory licensing outside the framework of the Appendix to address bulk access for public interest goals.

In the next section, I evaluate creative access mechanisms, their relationship to the Appendix, and the utility of the Appendix to address access concerns, with particular attention to digital works.

A. Creative access

In the digital environment, creative access is equally (and will eventually become more) important for developing countries than bulk access. Creative access mechanisms will determine how users can exploit content, as well as the terms on which they are able to obtain copies of the work. In general, existing creative

---

[108] TRIPS Agreement, above n. 3, art. 8.2.
[109] Id. art. 40. See also Hanns Ullrich, *Expansionist Intellectual Property Protection and Reductionist Competition Rules: A TRIPS Perspective* [this volume]; Joseph Drexl, *The Critical Role of Competition Law in Preserving Public Goods in Conflict with Intellectual Property Rights* [this volume]; Mark D. Janis, *"Minimal" Standards for the Patent-Related Antitrust Law Under TRIPS* [this volume].
[110] See BODENHAUSEN, above n. 100, at 71.
[111] See WCT, above n. 4, art. 1(4); TRIPS Agreement, above n. 33, art. 9.1.
[112] But see the limitation to print works for reproduction licenses. Berne Appendix, above n. 27, art. IV(7)(a).

access mechanisms were designed to deal primarily with exploitation. The Berne Appendix was not intended for the digital world and, by its terms, does not apply to works other than those published in print and analogous forms. Nevertheless, since exploitation of content represents an important aspect of knowledge diffusion, the existing legal framework for creative access deserves some attention.

The Berne Convention recognizes in general terms the possibility of limitations on protected works and, in some cases, it allows outright exclusion of certain categories of works. Other than the reproduction right, member states retain sovereign discretion in formulating national doctrines to serve access goals related to each of the rights granted. The language of the Convention, however, is merely permissive in many of these clauses; member states may choose whether and under what circumstances a particular limitation will be imposed.[113]

All previous conditions for access were incorporated into the TRIPS Agreement, but with the added constraint of a limiting principle to guide the exercise of sovereign discretion in formulating national access doctrines.[114] Article 9(2) of the Berne Convention already stated that the reproduction of literary and artistic works may be permitted: (1) "in certain special cases"; (2) provided that such reproduction does not "conflict with a normal exploitation of the work" and (3) "does not unreasonably prejudice the legitimate interests of the author."[115] The TRIPS Agreement extended this three-step test to all the Berne Convention rights, and not just the reproduction right,[116] thus "filling the gap" and eliminating the discretion (mentioned above) implicit in the Berne Convention's silence on limitations to the other rights. As I have argued elsewhere, this rider threatens creative access mechanisms, such as the fair use doctrine in the U.S., the open-ended test of which is arguably inconsistent with the strictures of the three-step test ordained in article 13.[117] Any limitations or exceptions provided by national legislation to any of the rights provided by Berne or TRIPS must satisfy this test.

Prior to the TRIPS Agreement, there was no mechanism to determine the precise meaning or scope of the three-step test, set out in article 9(2) of the Berne Convention, nor any means to enforce alleged violations of it. Consequently, Berne member countries frequently enacted limitations and

---

[113] *See, e.g.*, Berne Convention, above n. 13, arts. 2*bis*, 7(2)(6), 10, 10*bis*, 13(1).
[114] *See* TRIPS Agreement, above n. 3, art. 13.   [115] Berne Convention, above n. 13, art. 9(2).
[116] This provision covers all the mandatory rights under the Berne Convention, other than the moral rights codified in article 6*bis*, which are specifically excluded from TRIPS. *See* TRIPS Agreement, above n. 3, art. 9.1. For analysis of the Berne three-step test, see Jane C. Ginsburg, *Toward Supranational Copyright Law? The WTO Panel Decision and the "Three Step Test" for Copyright Exceptions*, Revue Int'l du Droit d'Auteur 3 (Jan. 2001); Ruth Okediji, *Toward an International Fair Use Standard*, 39 Colum. J. Transnat'l L. 75 (2000) (analyzing the relationship between TRIPS article 13 and the U.S. fair use doctrine) [hereinafter Okediji, *International Fair Use*]; Okediji, *Copyright and Public Welfare*, above n. 28, 911–13 (brief discussion of the *U.S. – Section 110(5)* dispute).
[117] *See* Okediji, *International Fair Use*, above n. 116.

exceptions to the reproduction right considering only domestic interests and priorities. The WTO Panel decision in *United States – Section 110(5) of the U.S. Copyright Act*[118] changed this landscape considerably.

Although TRIPS article 13 does not state the three-step test in precisely the same wording as article 9(2) of the Berne Convention,[119] the Panel viewed the structure and import of both provisions as substantially similar. The Panel determined that the first criterion of the three-step test, a "special case," does not refer to any special policy as such.[120] In other words, the purpose for a limitation or exception to copyright is irrelevant in determining whether the first condition is satisfied.[121] The Panel concluded that the first condition requires that exceptions and limitations imposed by national laws on any copyright rights should be clearly and narrowly defined.[122]

As to the second condition, the Panel held that "normal exploitation" includes all actual and *potential* uses of the work.[123] Conflict with normal exploitation arises where exempted uses compete in the market with the copyrighted work and deprive the owner of measurable economic profit.[124] With respect to the third condition, the Panel held that since any restriction to a copyright owner's rights prejudices the owner, the only issue for determination is when such prejudice becomes unreasonable.[125] To determine unreasonableness in the dispute before it, the Panel focused on fact-specific evidence as to the loss sustained by the copyright owners due to the contested exceptions in U.S. law.[126]

The conditions in the three-step test are cumulative; each condition must be satisfied before a limitation or exception is considered legitimate under TRIPS article 13. The burden of proving satisfaction of these conditions rests with the country whose law is under challenge. The Panel's interpretation of the three-step test, while commendable in some respects, clearly adopts a narrow perspective on the range of flexibility that enables a member to limit

---

[118] *See* WTO Panel Report on United States – Section 110(5) of the U.S. Copyright Act, WT/DS160/R (15 June 2000) [hereinafter WTO Panel Report].

[119] Article 13 of the TRIPS Agreement states: "Members shall confine limitations or exceptions to exclusive rights to certain special cases which do not conflict with a normal exploitation of the work and do not unreasonably prejudice the legitimate interests of the right holder." Some scholars contend that the use of the word "confine" in the TRIPS Agreement suggests that article 13 is a constraint on article 9(2) of the Berne Convention. *See, e.g.*, Paul Edward Geller, *International Copyright: An Introduction*, in INTERNATIONAL COPYRIGHT LAW AND PRACTICE § 5[5][b][ii] (Paul Edward Geller & Melville B. Nimmer eds., 1998); DANIEL GERVAIS, THE TRIPS AGREEMENT: A DRAFTING HISTORY AND ANALYSIS, 45–46, 89–90 (1998).

[120] WTO Panel Report, above n. 118, at 33, para. 6.105.

[121] The Panel did note, however, that a special public policy purpose could be useful in assessing the legitimate scope of the limitation. *Id.* at 34.

[122] *Id.* at para. 6.112.   [123] *Id.* at 48, para. 6.180.   [124] *Id.*

[125] *Id.* at para. 6.226.   [126] *Id.* at para. 6.238.

rights covered by international copyright law and to provide exceptions to the unauthorized exercise of those rights domestically.[127]

The expanded iteration of the three-step test, subsequently extended to article 10(2) of the WCT in 1996, carries the same constraint on sovereign discretion into the digital environment, notwithstanding the Agreed Statement which suggests otherwise.[128] This result is certainly the case where the rights at issue in the digital environment are rights mandated by the Berne Convention or the TRIPS Agreement. The effect of article 20 of the Berne Convention is to limit the possibility of lesser protection even in agreements that ostensibly regulate non-traditional copyright interests. So long as there is an effect on mandated copyright rights, there is a logical argument that limitations granted by member countries must be consistent with the three-step test, at least with respect to the reproduction right. For developing countries that have ratified the WCT, this argument becomes particularly strong, since the cumulative effect of Berne, TRIPS and the WCT weighs heavily against the unfettered exercise of sovereign discretion.

An initial concern with the Agreed Statement is the uncertainty about its legal status and its effect on the requirements of article 10 of the WCT, which restates the three-step test. Member states may attempt to rely on it to justify or expand limitations on, or exceptions to, the use of digital information works. For countries that choose to view the Agreed Statement as an interpretation of article 10 (and, by inference, of TRIPS article 13 as well), or as a reflection of legislative (negotiators') intent, any new limitations or exceptions must still satisfy the three-step test. If TRIPS jurisprudence on the scope of this test wields precedential influence on member states, or if the WIPO treaties are eventually incorporated into the TRIPS Agreement, as some developed countries have proposed,[129] the best case scenario is that existing limitations and exceptions in national laws would be "grandfathered" with respect to the digital environment.

---

[127] *See* Okediji, *International Fair Use*, above n. 116; Okediji, *Copyright and Public Welfare*, above n. 28.

[128] The Agreed Statement concerning article 10 provides: "It is understood that the provisions of article 10 permit Contracting Parties to carry forward and appropriately extend into the digital environment limitations and exceptions in their national laws which have been considered acceptable under the Berne Convention. Similarly, these provisions should be understood to permit Contracting Parties to devise new exceptions and limitations that are appropriate in the digital network environment. It is also understood that article 10(2) neither reduces nor extends the scope of applicability of the limitations and exceptions permitted by the Berne Convention." *See* Diplomatic Conference on Certain Copyright and Neighboring Rights Questions: Agreed Statements Concerning the WIPO Copyright Treaty, WIPO Doc. CRNR/DC/96, *adopted* 20 Dec. 1996.

[129] *See* Carlos Correa, *Review of the Trips Agreement: Fostering the Transfer of Technology to Developing Countries*, *available at* http://www.twnside.org.sg/title/foster.htm (noting Japan's expressed interest in "higher protection of intellectual property rights which has been achieved in other treaties or conventions in other fora appropriately" and characterizing this as "an obvious reference to the WIPO internet treaties").

Countries may also choose to ignore the Agreed Statement entirely, as the United States has done under the DMCA.[130]

In sum, given the difficulty of evading TRIPS jurisprudence and the uncertain legal status of the Agreed Statement, the dynamic benefits of digital technology for facilitating development goals[131] are likely to become surplus gains for copyright owners in the global digital environment. Positive legal rules are thus necessary to address both the dynamic or allocative efficiency concerns and the distributive or diffusion goals of member states.[132]

B. A network of access mechanisms: The global rules

An exhaustive analysis of the various exceptions and limitations contained in the Berne Convention is not the goal of this section. I will simply identify access mechanisms central to copyright law generally, and examine in brief the relationship between the Appendix and the WCT.[133]

1. Jurisdiction of the three-step test under the TRIPS Agreement

Access mechanisms can evolve in several ways. First, they can be constructed by national governments for works which are not subject to mandatory copyright protection under the Berne Convention. For example, the Berne Convention leaves it entirely up to member states whether to extend copyright protection to unfixed works;[134] to official texts of a legislative, administrative and legal nature, and the official translation of such texts;[135] the extent of protection for works of applied art and industrial designs;[136] political speeches and speeches delivered in the course of legal proceedings.[137] Member states also have complete discretion to determine the conditions for the reproduction by broadcast of public lectures and addresses;[138] the conditions for broadcasting and public communication of literary and artistic works by wire or other

---

[130] See Julie Cohen, *United States Implementation of the WIPO Copyright Treaty: Will Fair Use Survive?*, 21 EUR. INTELL. PROP. REV. 236 (1999) [hereinafter Cohen, *Will Fair Use Survive?*].

[131] See generally Ruth L. Okediji, *Development in the Information Age: Issues in the Regulation of Intellectual Property Rights, Computer Software, and E-Commerce*, UNCTAD-ICTSD Intellectual Property Rights & Sustainable Development Series Discussion Paper (Dec. 2003), available at http://www.iprsonline.org/unctadictsd/docs/Okediji_ECommerce.Dec03.pdf [hereinafter Okediji, *Development in the Information Age*].

[132] See, e.g., Peter Gerhart, *Distributive Values and Institutional Design in the Provision of Global Public Goods* [this volume].

[133] The extent to which the three-step test introduced in TRIPS Agreement, above n. 3, art. 13, could restrict previously unrestricted exceptions in the Berne Convention remains unclear.

[134] See Berne Convention, above n. 13, art. 2(2).   [135] *Id.* art. 2(4).   [136] *Id.* art. 2(7).

[137] *Id.* art. 2*bis*(1).   [138] *Id.* art. 2*bis*(2).

means;[139] and to permit reproduction of certain works for information purposes and for the purpose of reporting on current events.[140]

Importantly, countries have discretion to permit some use of protected works for teaching purposes.[141] Sovereign discretion over conditions under which works could be reproduced for teaching purposes has always been a national prerogative under the Berne Convention.[142] Unlike the other provisions, however, article 10(2), which deals with reproduction for teaching purposes, links national discretion to "fair practice." One leading commentator extends this link to the three-step test of article 9(2).[143] However, for provisions in which regulation is left solely to the discretion of the national governments, there is a strong case that the three-step test does not apply to limit the range of access mechanisms that may be imposed by states.

Even if the three-step test were ultimately extended to all rights under the TRIPS Agreement, that should not affect the outcome described above. Article 13 of the TRIPS Agreement is explicitly limited by reference to the Berne Convention's substantive principles. Where the Berne Convention itself imposed no obligations on member states, the three-step test of TRIPS should not extend to constrain national discretion. In essence, the test should be limited only to those *rights* guaranteed by the Berne Convention. Where sovereign states have the discretion to withhold a right, but choose nevertheless to grant it, the three-step test should not be a legitimate screen for the appropriateness of any limitations on such a right. Voluntarily proffered rights remain, however, still subject to the national treatment and most-favored-nation obligations.[144]

2. The idea/expression dichotomy

The subject matter of copyright protection is original expression. Article 2(1) of the Berne Convention defines the scope of copyrightable subject matter as literary and artistic works "whatever the mode or form of [their] expression."[145] However, domestic rules that excluded ideas from the scope of protection considerably attenuated the sweep of this provision,[146] and this idea/expression dichotomy, so elemental to copyright law, has now found express reference in the TRIPS Agreement.[147] Consequently, the mandatory exclusion of ideas from global copyright principles should be more powerfully associated with the preservation of the public domain.

---

[139] *Id.* art. 11*bis.* However, this discretion is limited by a duty to pay equitable compensation if compulsory licensing is imposed. *Id.* art. 11*bis*(2).
[140] *Id.* art. 10*bis.*
[141] *Id.* art. 10(2). However, the permitted use is said to be "by way of illustration in publications, broadcasts or sound or visual recordings for teaching ...." *Id.*
[142] *See* RICKETSON, above n. 42, at 494.   [143] *Id.* at 498.
[144] TRIPS Agreement above n. 3, arts. 3–4.   [145] Berne Convention, above n. 13, art. 2(1).
[146] *See, e.g.,* 17 U.S.C. § 102(b) (2000).   [147] *See* TRIPS Agreement, above n. 3, art. 9(2).

Simply put, the public domain is a jurisdictional "place" where unprotected subject matter resides.[148] Tributaries to the public domain include the idea/expression dichotomy, expiration of the copyright term, donated works, and the like.[149] The internationalization of the idea/expression dichotomy suggests that the jurisprudence of this vital principle can be considered part of the policy of international copyright law with practical effect in institutions such as WIPO.

In the United States, for example, application of the idea/expression dichotomy[150] has resulted in a number of judicial and administrative practices that exclude certain categories of works from protection. These include the *scenes a faire* doctrine, which excludes from protection "incidents, characters, or settings which are as a practical matter indispensable, or at least standard, in the treatment of a given topic";[151] and the so-called merger doctrine,[152] which precludes protection for works in which the idea and expression are inseparable, or where only a limited number of ways exist to express the idea.[153] More generally, the idea/expression doctrine is associated with the exclusion of short phrases,[154] blank forms, and "mere listings of ingredients as in recipes, formulas, compounds or prescriptions"[155] from copyright protection. In the international context, WIPO publications and technical assistance programs to developing countries could begin to emphasize these exceptions.

The idea/expression dichotomy constitutes a robust access rule, and its inclusion in the global copyright framework is a positive development. For all practical purposes, however, the application of this doctrine is fairly complex. The relative lack of sophistication of the judiciary in developing countries generally, and in the intellectual property area especially, renders the idea/expression dichotomy less viable at the moment as a tool for sustainable access.

---

[148] *See* David Lange, *Reimagining the Public Domain*, 66 LAW & CONTEMP. PROBS. 463 (2003).

[149] *See* Pamela Samuelson, *Mapping the Digital Public Domain: Threats and Opportunities*, 66 LAW & CONTEMP. PROBS. 147 (2003); *see also* Jessica Litman, *The Public Domain*, 39 EMORY L.J. 965 (1990).

[150] The idea/expression dichotomy, often attributed to the U.S. Supreme Court case, Baker v. Selden, 101 U.S. 99 (1879), considerably antedates that case and represents one of the oldest limiting doctrines in American copyright law. *See also* Copyright Circular 31, Ideas, Methods, or Systems, *available at* http://www.copyright.gov/circs/circ31.pdf. ("Copyright protection, therefore, is not available for: ideas or procedures for doing, making, or building things; scientific or technical methods or discoveries; business operations or procedures; mathematical principles; formulas, algorithms; or any other concept, process, or method of operation.").

[151] *See* A.A. Hoehling v. Universal City Studios, Inc., 618 F.2d 972 (2d Cir. 1980).

[152] BERNARD C. DIETZ, COPYRIGHT REGISTRATION PRACTICE § 28:16 (2d ed. 2003).

[153] *See* Morrissey v. Proctor & Gamble Co., 379 F. 2d 675 (1st Cir. 1967).

[154] *See* U.S. Copyright Office Circular 34, Names, Titles, Short Phrases not Copyrightable, *available at* http://www.copyright.gov/circs/circ34.pdf.

[155] *See* U.S. Copyright Office, Factsheet FL 122, Recipes, *available at* http://www.copyright.gov/fls/fl122.pdf.

At best, the application of the doctrine generally produces gains at the margins in terms of access. Even then, the granularity involved in analyzing allegations of infringement under the related doctrines of *scenes a faire* and merger will prove too costly for most developing countries.

Nonetheless, it is important to note that these doctrines could benefit the more advanced developing countries. In particular, they suggest that, with respect to scientific texts or fact-intensive educational materials, the range of copyright protection is relatively limited. Consequently, the reproduction right available for such works is said to be "thin," and could often be circumvented by downstream producers in developing countries by avoiding exact replication of the works. This would be akin to the current ability of users to extract unprotectable facts or data from compilations.[156] Translations of purely factual material, new arrangements of unprotectable information or other derivations of such works will not violate the reproduction right as currently understood.[157]

3. The Berne Appendix and the WCT

In the digital context, pre-existing legal opportunities for access may be completely denied by the use of anticircumvention technology that prevents access to digital works.[158] While article 11 of the WCT does not require protection against circumvention of digital controls beyond the scope that copyright law itself would permit, and the exercise of such protection is formally subject to limitations and exceptions,[159] the United States implementation of this provision in the DMCA effectively curtailed traditional copyright access principles in the digital environment.[160] Furthermore, a misuse defense has not so far proved successful against claims of DMCA violations.[161] Attempts by the United States to export this model to other jurisdictions have

---

[156] *See* Feist Publ'ns v. Rural Tel. Serv. Co., 499 U.S. 340 (1991).

[157] *See* TRIPS Agreement, above n. 3, arts 9.2, 10.2.

[158] WCT, above n. 4, art. 11 (stating that Members "shall provide adequate legal protection and effective legal remedies against the circumvention of effective technological measures that are used by authors in connection with the exercise of their rights under this Treaty or the Berne Convention and that restrict acts, in respect of their works, which are not authorized by authors concerned *or permitted by law*.") (emphasis added).

[159] *See id.* art. 10 (excepting "acts ... permitted by law").

[160] *See* Pamela Samuelson, *Why the Anticircumvention Provisions Should Be Revised*, 14 BERKELEY TECH. L.J. 519 (1999); Cohen, *Will Fair Use Survive?*, above n. 130. *See also* Jane C. Ginsburg, *Copyright Legislation for the Digital Millenium*, 23 COLUM.-VLA J.L. & ARTS 137 (1999); LITMAN, above n. 14.

[161] *See, e.g.*, Lexmark Int'l, Inc. v. Static Control Components, Inc., 253 F. Supp. 2d 943, 946 (E.D. Ky. 2003); *see also* Daniel C. Higgs, Lexmark Int'l, Inc. v. Static Control Components, Inc. & Chamberlain Group, Inc. v. Skylink Technologies, Inc.: *The DMCA and Durable Goods Aftermarkets*, 19 BERKELEY TECH. L.J. 5, 82 (2004) (stating that the copyright misuse defense "will usually fail in DMCA cases").

been a notable part of the bilateralism that has dominated international intellectual property regulation in the post-TRIPS era.[162]

The incorporation of the Berne Appendix into the WCT implies that the compulsory licensing scheme set out in the Appendix remains available to developing countries as an access mechanism in the digital environment.[163] It is important to note, however, that in the context of bilateral or regional trade agreements, the right – meaningful or not – to invoke the Appendix may be curtailed.[164] In any event, the Appendix is clearly a document of the print age: concepts such as publication, distribution and reproduction mean something entirely different in the digital environment.[165]

It is hard to imagine that the Appendix could become successful as an access tool for digital information works, if only because its framework needs significant reorientation for the different ways that digitization has altered traditional understanding of core copyright terms. However, the relevance of the Appendix for the digital environment also deserves a closer look from another perspective. In theory, the Appendix provides a means of access to qualifying countries to issue compulsory licenses for the reproduction of protected digital works for translation and teaching purposes. However, the right to reproduce ("utilize") works for teaching purposes is already a substantive part of the Berne Convention scheme under article 10.[166]

---

[162] See Okediji, *Back to Bilateralism*, above n. 43; Drahos, above n. 34. *See also* U.S.-Australia Free Trade Agreement, art. 17.4(7) (containing the DMCA anti-circumvention provisions), *available at* http://www.dfat.gov.au/trade/negotiations/us_fta/text/17_IP.pdf; Declan McCullagh, CNET News.com, US Exports DMCA in Trade Treaty, *at* http://news.zdnet.co.uk/business/0,39020645,2137659,00.htm; U.S.-Chile Free Trade Agreement, 6 June 2003, 42 I.L.M. 1026 (2003).

[163] The inclusion of the Appendix with articles 1–21 of the Berne Convention is pro forma for any copyright agreement within the Berne scheme. Since Stockholm, it has not been permissible to de-link the Appendix from the other Berne provisions.

[164] *See, e.g.*, North American Free Trade Agreement, art. 1705(6): "No Party may grant translation and reproduction licenses permitted under the Appendix to the Berne Convention where legitimate needs in that Party's territory for copies or translations of the work could be met by the right holder's voluntary actions but for the obstacles created by the Party's measures." North American Free Trade Agreement, 17 Dec. 1992, U.S.-Can.-Mex., 32 I.L.M. 612 (1993) (entered into force 1 Jan. 1994) [hereinafter NAFTA]. *See also generally* Sharan Leslie Goolsby, *Protection of Intellectual Property Rights under NAFTA*, 4 NAFTA L. & Bus. Rev. Am. 5 (1998).

[165] Laura N. Gasaway, *Values Conflict in the Digital Environment: Librarians Versus Copyright Holders*, 24 Colum.-VLA J.L. & Arts 115, 118 (2000) (noting differences between print copyright holders and digital copyright holders, and concluding that "[i]t is evident, however, that something has changed due to the growing presence of digital distribution technology ....").

[166] *See* Berne Convention, above n. 13, art. 10(2). *See also* Raquel Xalabarder, *Copyright and Digital Distance Education: The Use of Pre-Existing Works in Distance Education Through the Internet*, 26 Colum. VLA J.L. & Arts 101, 108 (2003).

From the negotiation history of the current article 10, countries may regulate how protected works are used for teaching purposes in the full panoply of formal educational institutions.[167] Article 10 does not exclude distance education, which is an important benefit of digital technology for development goals. Indeed, distance education was the primary target of this article. This means that institutions in developing countries may utilize computer networks for distance education without resort to any specialized regime, such as the United States has developed under the TEACH Act,[168] nor be concerned about the difficulty of the Appendix.

The combined effect of articles 10 and 11*bis* gives developing countries appreciable space to capture benefits from digital works for educational purposes. This does not necessarily render the Appendix superfluous. It does suggest that there are multiple avenues to access for educational purposes currently available under the global copyright system. The high transaction costs imposed by the Appendix can and should be avoided when reliance on article 10 and other complementary provisions of the Berne Convention can address the particular needs. Alternatives to the Appendix permit greater flexibility and involve domestic institutions directly, with no obligations to engage in costly and time-consuming negotiations.

One final point should be noted. It is baffling that educational concerns in developed countries enjoy the benefit of a relatively simple set of principles and a presumption in favor of discretion and access, while developing countries were steered on the path of a highly technical and limited access mechanism in the form of the Berne Appendix. The fact is that developed countries hardly rely at all on the limitations and exceptions in the Berne Convention to deal with educational needs. Public education in most developed countries is highly subsidized by the government, and the classic market-based transaction for access is clearly inapplicable in the controlled market that exists for the demand and supply of educational works. Heavy subsidization by the government means book purchases and educational licenses are generally not cumbersome impediments to access to content, although the TEACH Act has changed this situation with respect to digital distance education. The point is that, in the provision of public goods, particularly education, reliance on the Appendix should be a last resort – it should be invoked only where government uses of existing limitations have been exhausted. As a side note, nothing in the Berne Agreement itself addresses parallel importation, but the Appendix limits this

---

[167] General public education or adult literacy campaigns appear to be excluded from the ambit of article 10. *See* RICKETSON, above n. 42, at 498.

[168] *See* Technology, Education and Copyright Harmonization Act, Pub. L. No. 107–273, § 13301, 116 Stat. 1910 (2002) (codified at 17 U.S.C. §§ 110(2), 112(f)) [hereinafter TEACH Act]. The TEACH Act has been criticized for its complexity. *See, e.g.*, Kristine H. Hutchinson, Note, *The Teach Act: Copyright Law and Online Education*, 78 N.Y.U. L. REV. 2204 (2003).

option of access to creative works. Not utilizing the Appendix in this regard, and relying instead on other limitations, opens up the prospect of regional sources of materials to supplement the domestic market.

As with education, it is astounding that compulsory licenses in areas such as musical works or broadcasts in developed countries are part of the substantive positive law system of these countries, subject to few formalities or restrictions.[169] In contrast, the compulsory licensing system of the Appendix, purportedly intended to benefit the public interest in developing countries, is weighed down with conditions, riders and other provisos that impose obstacles to access that are greater than the main text of the Berne Convention itself.

VI. The useful art(s) of progress: Social welfare in an international perspective

The ubiquitousness of networks and the efforts of copyright owners to capture increased value from the different ways creative expression may be used and disseminated over digital networks have been the subject of intense public and academic discourse. There has been an impassioned debate about whether and how the traditional copyright vectors are necessary or sustainable in the digital environment. In this section, I focus principally on the particular conditions that directly bear upon access to protected works by users in developing countries. I argue for positive access mechanisms to be part of the global copyright system, for changes to the structure of the Berne Convention, and for greater attention to the administrative provisions that ultimately shape the direction of the global copyright system.

A. Rescuing access from digital bondage

As many copyright scholars have tirelessly argued, and judicial decisions have affirmed,[170] the copyright regime was not designed solely or even primarily as an instrument for private aggrandizement, nor are the theoretical foundations of copyright law premised on norms of absolute control.[171] In many respects,

---

[169] See Loren, above n. 17.
[170] See, e.g., Mazer v. Stein, 347 U.S. 201, 219 (1954) ("The economic philosophy behind the clause empowering Congress to grant copyrights and patents is the conviction that encouragement of individual effort by personal gain is the best way to advance the public welfare through the talents of authors and inventors in science and useful arts."); for scholarly arguments, see, e.g., Pamela Samuelson, *Copyright and Freedom of Expression in Historical Perspective*, 10 J. INTELL. PROP. L. 319, 238 (2003) ("During the modern era, the utilitarian rationale for copyright predominated: the goal of copyright law was to provide enough rights to provide adequate incentives to induce creators to innovate – but not more than this.").
[171] See Lunney, above n. 23.

the legal response to challenges of the digital age appears to have displaced the primacy of the creative element as a cornerstone of copyright protection.[172] This phenomenon is particularly evident in the DMCA,[173] which protects both traditional and non-traditional copyright interests. It is also evident in the controversial attempts, in the United States, to imitate the E.U.'s proprietary model of protection for producers of databases.[174]

The complex dynamic between the development of national and international intellectual property policy[175] has yielded an intricate web of proprietary rights formalized through a variety of mechanisms, without attention to the preservation of access as a core principle of copyright regulation. Taken together, these strategies seek to radically redefine the goals of copyright law, as well as the agency through which copyright policy is developed and implemented. While this trend has negatively affected the public interest vision that animated copyright law in the past, the inescapably global nature of digital works and the laws that protect them mean that the development strategies and goals of many poor countries also face new legal hurdles. The failure of the global copyright system to articulate positive and robust access doctrines is particularly striking with respect to digital information works that, in theory, should represent an immediate and important opportunity for developing countries to invest in the social infrastructure pertinent to development goals.[176]

Although interest group politics increasingly determine the legislative agenda for fashioning intellectual property rules both in national and international fora,[177] digitization still makes it possible to de-link copyright from any particular cultural or political hegemonic force, as content owners increasingly

---

[172] Harmonization of copyright norms has also exerted pressure on countries that traditionally demand relatively higher standards of creativity. See, e.g., Gerhard Schricker, "Farewell to the Level of Creativity" in German Copyright Law?, 26 INT. REV. IND. PROP. & COPYRIGHT L. 41 (1995) (discussing the effect of copyright harmonization on Germany's level of creativity requirement).

[173] See DMCA, above n. 22.

[174] See Database and Collections of Information Misappropriation Act of 2003, above n. 32.

[175] For discussion of this dynamic, see generally Graeme B. Dinwoodie, The Development and Incorporation of International Norms in the Formation of Copyright Law, 62 OHIO ST. L.J. 733 (2001); Graeme B. Dinwoodie, The Integration of Domestic and International Intellectual Property Lawmaking, 24 COLUM.-VLA J.L. & ARTS 307 (2000). See also Ruth Okediji, TRIPS Dispute Settlement and the Sources of (International) Copyright Law, 49 J. COPYRIGHT SOC'Y 585 (2001) (expressing skepticism that the WTO dispute settlement process will serve as a source of substantive international copyright law); Ruth Okediji, A Cartography of TRIPS Dispute Settlement and the Future of Intellectual Property Policy (2001) (unpublished manuscript on file with author) (examining the dynamic between the WTO dispute settlement process and sovereign prerogative over domestic intellectual property policy) [hereinafter Okediji, Cartography].

[176] See generally Okediji, Development in the Information Age, above n. 131.

[177] Okediji, Cartography, above n. 175.

secure control over access and use of digital works available to a global audience via computer networks. But the abiding reality of the digital divide suggests that the legal mechanisms, including treaties such as the WCT, are premature for most developing countries. Empirical evidence indicates that Internet penetration rates remain substantially low in most developing countries, as compared to developed countries.[178] Indeed, according to one of my own recent studies, developing and least-developed countries that have ratified the WIPO Internet treaties have some of the lowest Internet penetration rates in the developing world.[179]

For developing countries, then, the capacity to infringe is significantly limited by the lack of computers to access online content. Moreover, infrastructural and regulatory constraints affecting the telecommunication system in many developing countries undercut the operation of Moore's law[180] in most of these countries. While statistics do not tell the entire story, particularly in the area of Internet usage and availability, a number of studies and surveys indicate clearly the substantial gap in physical access to the online environment that exists between developed and developing countries.[181] The figures vary widely, but the reality of a digital divide nonetheless persists, with obvious implications for the risks to many developing countries of prematurely adopting a regime such as the WCT, without adopting explicit access safeguards at the same time.

The digital divide serves as a "natural" limitation on both creative and bulk access to digital information works in developing countries. This fact alone should alleviate concerns about unauthorized bulk copying in developing countries, because the technological resources usually do not permit access at

---

[178] *But see* Carsten Fink & Charles J. Kenny, *W(h)ither the Digital Divide?*, 5(6) INFO 1, 17 (Jan. 2003), *available at* http://www.developmentgateway.org/download/181562/W_h_ither_ DD_Jan_.pdf (suggesting that rates of Internet users per capita grew twice as fast in developing countries than in developed countries). For my purposes, however, the absolute gap is the real problem, since it is this measure that affects the capacity to access copyrighted works by the bulk of the population. The absolute per-capita gap is critical in copyright terms because access to digital works involves a convergence of various aspects of the digital divide, *viz.*, the gap in physical access; the gap in ability (measured by factors such as literacy rates and skills); gaps in actual use; and gaps in the capacity to circumvent technological devices that protect digital content. *See* Okediji, *Development in the Information Age*, above n. 131 (discussing the different components of the digital divide).

[179] *See id.*

[180] Moore's law states that the number of transistors on a chip doubles every 18 to 24 months. This would result in an expected $10 billion cost reduction in the first half-century of the computer age. The result is simply that costs to consumers are very low and will continue to decrease. *See* Gordon Moore, *Cramming More Components Onto Integrated Circuits*, 38 ELECTRONICS 114 (1965).

[181] However, a recent report suggests that the digital divide is not as significant in relative terms, due to the ability of countries to "leapfrog" technologies that represent evolutionary periods in digital development in the developed countries. *See* Fink & Kenny, above n. 178, at 15–24.

levels that would obviate the economic incentive of a copyright owner.[182] On the policy and legislative fronts, the digital divide compels the conclusion that developing countries can ill-afford to implement the WCT in the high-protectionist way that the United States and some E.U. countries have done. Developing countries should maximize the flexibilities inherent in TRIPS as well as the WCT, and they need to maintain them in bilateral and regional trade agreements.[183]

In addition to infrastructure and poverty, literacy rates in many of these countries also reflect another dimension of the access conundrum. As of 1996, when the WIPO Internet treaties were concluded, Burkina Faso, which ratified both treaties, had a reported illiteracy rate[184] of 90 percent and an average of one book per 70 citizens in the country.[185] Chile, also a developing country that ratified the treaties had, as of 1996, an illiteracy rate of about 10 percent and an average of seven books per 10 citizens.[186] Not a single developing or least-developed country that has ratified the Internet treaties can boast of an Internet penetration rate of more than 50 percent, and most do not have a literacy rate greater than 60 percent, or the availability of at least one book per citizen.[187] Under these abject circumstances, bulk and creative access is an indispensable part of building capacity in developing countries for their social, economic and political progress in the digital age.

B. Specific proposals

The right of access has been relegated to the margins of international copyright law. The development of legal rules facilitating access has been treated primarily as an issue reserved to states. In theory, this approach seems rational because the public welfare equilibrium varies from country to country, and the design of access principles will, in part, respond to the character of the public interest as defined nationally.

However, several important factors militate against relying on the freedom of developing countries to fashion appropriate access rules in domestic legislation in a post-TRIPS environment. First, it is well-known that a slew of bilateral and regional trade agreements seeks to impose on developing countries even greater levels of intellectual property protection, by requiring accession to the

---

[182] *Cf.* Trotter Hardy, *Property (and Copyright) in Cyberspace*, 1996 U. CHI. LEGAL F. 217, 220–28 (1996).
[183] *Cf.* Maskus & Reichman, above n. 11.
[184] Like Internet usage rates, illiteracy rates are difficult to measure. Countries define literacy differently, resulting in significant variations in the statistics.
[185] VLADIMIR F. WERTSMAN, THE LIBRARIAN'S COMPANION 16 (2nd) (1996).
[186] *Id.* at 20.
[187] *Id.* For adult literacy rates, *see* WORLD BANK, BUILDING INSTITUTIONS FOR MARKETS: WORLD DEVELOPMENT REPORT (2002).

WCT and WPPT and, in some cases, prescribing the precise manner of implementation of a digital copyright regime.[188] Second, as I have described in this chapter, the scope of limitations and exceptions in international copyright law has not been given adequate attention by scholars and commentators. Consequently, the jurisprudence of "access" in international copyright is largely undefined.

Only recently (and predominantly in the case of pharmaceuticals) has there been a movement in the international arena to determine the scope of limits on proprietary knowledge goods. Much of the activity has focused on ways to redress market abuse by rights owners through applications of competition policy or, more controversially, to consider parallel importation and compulsory licensing as mechanisms to ensure adequate supply of public goods in the market. As I have discussed, these strategies are equally available in the copyright context, particularly to address concerns about bulk access to protected works. As I also noted, however, in the digital context, these para-copyright access strategies may be less viable, given the level of power legally vested in rights owners to control access to and use of digital content. Moreover, where technological capacity limits access to digital content, resort to competition policy, for example, is unlikely to solve the need for access, and parallel importation becomes less useful. Consequently, there is a need for feasible avenues to address bulk and creative access to both print and digital materials in developing countries.

Leaving the design of access principles to domestic policy also obscures the fact that the international domain becomes the final source of validation for any domestic exceptions and limitations. In a harmonized global regime, domestic actions must be considered compliant with international agreements. Limitations and exceptions should thus be woven into the normative fabric of the international copyright system, which is now, for all intents and purposes, the dominant source of domestic copyright law.

1. An international fair use doctrine

In an earlier article, I argued for the development of an international fair use doctrine, both to preserve the scope of the doctrine in United States copyright jurisprudence and to insert public welfare concerns more explicitly into the jurisdictional space of the institutions responsible for administering the global copyright system.[189] Such a doctrine would stand apart from existing limitations and exceptions as an omnibus provision to promote access as well as other civil/democratic virtues. As proposed, the doctrine would not become subject to the Berne or TRIPS three-step test.[190]

---

[188] See above n. 162.   [189] Okediji, *Public Welfare*, above n. 29.   [190] Id.

2. Increasing the accountability of international intellectual property institutions and decreasing the pressure to participate in new developments

In addition to an international fair use doctrine, serious attention must be paid to the structure of copyright treaties and to the processes of negotiating new standards.[191] Professors Reichman and Maskus have argued, for example, for a moratorium on intellectual property lawmaking at the global level in order to allow a period of necessary experimentation with the system established by the TRIPS Agreement.[192] There is some concern, however, that the practical consequence of such a moratorium would be to drive intellectual property lawmaking into a kind of "black market" where rules are made "under the table," with no transparency or accountability.[193]

I argue that these black markets already exist in the form of bilateral agreements that require TRIPS-plus obligations; side-deals made possible through soft-law mechanisms that exert pressure on developing countries to intensify the pace of ratifying post-TRIPS intellectual property treaties;[194] and negotiated settlement under the WTO Dispute Settlement Understanding[195] process, which facilitates side-payments from developing countries that lack both the resources and expertise to contest the demands of developed countries,[196] while allowing rich countries to pay for violations rather than amend their domestic laws.[197]

3. Berne, TRIPS and side deals: Contending with strategic negotiations

I propose a moderate approach in which any moratorium would be linked to structural revisions of article 20 of the Berne Convention. In its current form, article 20 provides a legitimate basis for states to advance the agenda of unabated expansion of intellectual property rights, because it impedes the possibility of bargaining around the Berne Convention. The prospective reach of article 20 will continue to hinder efforts to legislate positive access

---

[191] Increasing attention has been directed to standard setting and to monitoring WIPO's role *vis a vis* developing country interests. *See* Sisule F. Musungu & Graham Dutfield, Multilateral Agreements and a TRIPS-Plus World: The World Intellectual Property Organisation (2003), *available at* http://www.geneva.quno.info/pdf/WIPO(A4)final 0304.pdf.

[192] *See* Maskus & Reichman, above n. 11.

[193] *See* Dinwoodie, *The New International Intellectual Property Law System*, above n. 15.

[194] Ruth L. Okediji, *The Institutions of Intellectual Property: New Trends in an Old Debate*, 98th ASIL Proc. (forthcoming 2004).

[195] Understanding on Rules and Procedures Governing the Settlement of Disputes, Marrakesh Agreement Establishing the World Trade Organization, Annex 2, 1869 U.N.T.S. 401, 33 I.L.M. 1226 (1994).

[196] Okediji, *Rules of Power*, above n. 58; Steinberg, above n. 58.

[197] Ginsburg, above n. 116. *See also* Joost Pauwelyn, *WTO Dispute Settlement: Of Sovereign Interests, Private Rights and Public Goods* [this volume].

mechanisms in subsequent agreements, while the enforcement mechanism of the TRIPS system could deter developing countries from experimenting with limitations and exceptions in their domestic laws.

The idea of establishing substantive maxima for copyright protection (in effect, another kind of moratorium) is appealing when considering the expansion of access mechanisms. Positive access mechanisms – or construing the negotiated agreement as a minimum *and* a maximum bargain – would mean that states are prohibited from negotiating higher standards than those imposed through the multilateral bargaining process. Such a principle would have the opposite effect of the current article 20 of the Berne Convention, namely, that states are prevented from negotiating prospective agreements that would be inconsistent with the legislated access mechanism provisions.

A recent decision by the United States Supreme Court noted a similar constraint on Congress, namely, that Congress cannot create a right that gives protection beyond the boundaries imposed by the Constitution.[198] Negotiated as a positive obligation to protect access, however, a prohibition against agreements that subvert or eliminate mechanisms for access would be less likely to offend notions of sovereignty. This proposal benefits from the argument that bilateralism undermines the multilateral scheme. While bilateral agreements may admit higher standards in the short term, extensive networks of bilateral agreements as we have them today may also import into the multilateral framework competing rivalries that may make consensus beyond the margins impossible, as states hold out for better deals outside of the WTO environment.

4. Developing a proportional approach to access

Development viability and economic growth are strongly correlated with education, R&D investment, innovation,[199] as well as stable institutions.[200] The limited availability of print materials in developing countries, both for

---

[198] *See* Dastar v. Twentieth Century Fox, 539 U.S. 23, 37 (2003) (noting that Congress cannot create a series of perpetual copyrights, and interpreting the Trademark Law to prevent such a result). *See also* Eldred v. Ashcroft, 537 U.S. 186 (2003).

[199] These are areas that industrialized countries also must watch carefully. *See* John Harwood, *Competitive Edge of U.S. is at Stake in the R&D Arena*, WALL ST. J. EUR., 17 Mar. 2004, at A2. *See also generally* OECD, ICT AND ECONOMIC GROWTH: EVIDENCE FROM OECD COUNTRIES, INDUSTRIES AND FIRMS (2003); OECD, SEIZING THE BENEFITS OF ICT IN A DIGITAL ECONOMY (2003), above n. 1.

[200] *See* Adelle Blackett, *Global Governance, Legal Pluralism and the Decentered State: A Labor Law Critique of Codes of Corporate Conduct*, 8 IND. J. GLOBAL LEGAL STUD. 401, 441 (2001) (stating that, at the 1999 World Economic Forum in Davos, "world economic and political elites...acknowledged the importance of stable institutions to accompany economic growth"). *See also* Douglass North, *Economic Performance Through Time*, 84 AMERICAN ECON. REV. 359 (1994); Tade O. Okediji, *The Efficacy of Institutions and Economic Growth: A Review Article*, Working Paper (2004).

public distribution and for educational purposes, poses a significant impediment to development. In particular, building capacity by enhancing the skills base of citizens in developing countries requires a robust market for literary and artistic works.

The Berne Appendix certainly needs reform if it is at all to be useful in expanding the market for print works. The advent of digital technology offers an opportunity for alleviating the harsh conditions imposed by the Berne Convention on developing countries. Unlike the case of patented medicines, most developing countries do have the capacity to reproduce copyrighted literary and artistic works. As digital information works become more dominant in developed countries, print works should become more readily accessible in developing countries, which will face considerable barriers to the diffusion of information technology for some time to come.

Limitations on access to digital informational works, whether under the WCT or as a consequence of poor infrastructure, can and should be offset by a proportional increase in access to print works. There are a variety of ways this goal could be accomplished, including eliminating the ban on inter-country exports of works produced under a compulsory license; eliminating the waiting period entirely; and eliminating the distinction between reproduction and translation licenses in order to improve economies of scale.

However the Berne Appendix is reformed, what seems clear at this point is that the lean markets for print works should not be compounded by restrictions – legal or otherwise – on access to digital works. Access in one sphere should be weighed against access in the other. The objective should be to enhance total access, while remaining sensitive to the interests of copyright owners. Proportional access between print and digital works is one way of balancing the competing welfare interests at stake.

5. Developing doctrines to address violations of copyright's underlying public policy

The ability to control digital works very easily translates into an owner's *de facto* expansion of the copyright power in a manner not contemplated by copyright policy. While such abuse of digital power may run afoul of competition laws, the recent experience of developed countries suggests that rights owners are enabled to exclude, constrain or otherwise limit the use of, or access to, digital works in a manner that violates the public policy goals of copyright law. The copyright misuse doctrine is increasingly an important tool to address such behavior in the United States. Although it currently remains unclear just how far courts will be willing to extend the doctrine, developing countries are well advised to consider and develop normative principles that determine the appropriate scope of the copyright owners' interests, and strategies of ownership/control that preserve the copyright balance between creativity and access.

6. Limiting the use of soft law

Finally, the increasing uses of soft law instruments, such as nonbinding recommendations or resolutions of WIPO committees,[201] must be balanced by limitations on the interpretative reach of TRIPS provisions. These soft law instruments are already difficult to assess from a transparency standpoint, and yet they exert important influence on copyright law, sometimes as much as the treaty provisions. Hard law more easily adverts the possibility of bargaining around the minimum standards by introducing maximum standards through positive law that may facilitate competitive negotiation over the boundaries of owners' rights, and could allow the introduction of access norms as part of the copyright metric. Institutional cooperation between standard-setting bodies, such as WIPO and the WTO,[202] must also be carefully scrutinized to prevent a monopoly over the policy space for countries to develop such limitations and exceptions.

VII. Conclusion

An important component of the economic gains associated with the digital age are intellectual property laws, which provide incentives to invest in innovation and creative activity. The salient justification for exclusive rights in the fruits of creative activity is that strong protection facilitates widespread dissemination of new technology by encouraging disclosure.[203] Rights granted by the patent

---

[201] *See, e.g.*, Standing Committee on the Law of Trademarks, Industrial Designs and Geographical Indications, Provisions on the Protection of Well-Known Marks, Joint Resolution Concerning Provisions on the Protection of Well-Known Marks, WIPO Doc. A/34/13, at 3 (4 Aug. 1999); CBD resolutions on biodiversity and the environment, *available at* http://www.biodiv.org/doc/meetings/bs/bswg-06/information/bswg-06-inf-04-en.pdf. *See also* WIPO-UNESCO African Regional Consultation on the Protection of Expressions of Folklore resolutions, *available at* http://www.wipo.int/documents/en/meetings/1999/folklore/pdf/wuaf_99_1.pdf.

[202] Agreement Between the World Intellectual Property Organization and the World Trade Organization (22 Dec. 1995), *available at* http://www.wto.org/english/tratop_e/trips_e/wtowip_e.htm.

[203] *See, e.g.*, Harper & Row Publishers, Inc. v. Nation Enter., 471 U.S. 539, 558 (1985). "By establishing a marketable right to the use of one's expression, copyright supplies the economic incentive to create and disseminate ideas .... The immediate effect of our copyright law is to secure a fair return for an 'author's' creative labor. But the ultimate aim is, by this incentive, to stimulate [the creation of useful works] for the general public good." *Id.* (citing Twentieth Century Music Corp. v. Aiken, 422 U.S. 151, 156 (1975)). *See also* Robert A. Kreiss, *Accessibility and Commercialization in Copyright Theory*, 43 UCLA L. Rev. 1, 4–5 (1995); TRIPS Agreement, above n. 3, art. 7 ("The protection and enforcement of intellectual property rights should contribute to the promotion of technological innovation and to the transfer and dissemination of technology ....").

and copyright systems are a well-established (though by no means the only or necessarily most effective) means to ensure the ability of firms to appropriate sufficient returns on their investment. The related trends of globalization and harmonization brought about a measure of cohesion in the international system for protecting creative expression, justified predominantly on utilitarian principles that pay homage to a strong commodification ethos. The promise of the digital age, despite its accompanying challenges, portends increased welfare gains from greater productivity, efficiency gains and reductions in transaction costs, as well as unparalleled access to information and creative works.

Each wave of technological and legislative change has been accompanied by great promise and large pitfalls. Sustainable access to creative works – both old and new – remains the cornerstone of a vibrant and literate society. An important objective of promoting and securing high levels of access to creative works is to enhance the capacity to absorb, utilize, adapt or otherwise benefit from the supply of creative works. This capacity is an important component of economic growth and development because, among other things, it is a necessary condition for ensuring a dynamic and sustainable innovation environment. Consequently, literacy and educational levels are significant factors in the calculus of how much and what type of access to copyrighted works is needed to promote economic development.

A central purpose of copyright law is to enhance the environment for national productivity by stimulating optimal levels of creative activity. Despite ongoing efforts to resist the formal ways that the public has been written out of the international copyright scheme, it is still the case that between technological controls, legal rules and the international economic framework, access to digital works is treated as a privilege rather than as an integral part of the sustainability of creative endeavor in the digital age. Positive access rules must be incorporated into the global system. The processes of standard-setting should be carefully monitored to preserve the national policy space for countries to implement meaningful limitations and exceptions. The digital environment for creative information works must be constructed to ensure that access-enhancing doctrines, and access itself, remain a cornerstone of copyright policy for the digital economy.

7

Agricultural research and intellectual property rights

ROBERT E. EVENSON*

1. Introduction
2. Science links, IPRs and public-private investments in research for inventions used in agriculture
    2.1 The agricultural mechanization revolution
    2.2 The agricultural chemical revolution
    2.3 The crop genetic improvement (Green) revolution
    2.4 The livestock industrialization revolution
    2.5 The Gene Revolution
3. The Green Revolution and the SPIA study
4. The Gene Revolution: Regulatory and IPR issues
5. Innovation-imitation capacity in developing countries
6. The future of agricultural research
7. Needed reforms

1. Introduction

The agricultural sector can be crudely characterized as having experienced five technological revolutions.[1] These revolutions differed in terms of timing. The origin of each revolution was in developed market economies, and each was diffused to developing economies at different rates depending on economic, soil and climate conditions and on the capacity of developing countries to innovate and imitate. Each revolution differed in the degree to which it was "science-linked" or "science-enabled." Each revolution varied in terms of the role of the public sector in the conduct of research and development (R&D). Finally, each revolution differed in terms of the degree to which intellectual

---

* Robert E. Evenson is Professor of Economics, Yale University.
[1] V.W. RUTTAN, TECHNOLOGY, GROWTH AND DEVELOPMENT: AN INDUCED INNOVATION PERSPECTIVE (Oxford University Press 2001) discusses several of the revolutions in his major work. The revolutions are also discussed in W.E. HUFFMAN & Robert E. EVENSON, SCIENCE FOR AGRICULTURE: A LONG TERM PERSPECTIVE (Iowa State University Press 1993).

property rights (IPRs) facilitated the origin of inventions and the diffusion of innovations.

The five revolutions in chronological order of innovation timing are agricultural mechanization, agricultural chemicals, crop genetic improvements (the Green Revolution), livestock industrialization, and recombinant DNA (rDNA; the Gene Revolution). In this chapter, I describe them and analyze the ability of countries to innovate and absorb agricultural technologies. Thus, in Section 2, I discuss the degree of science linkage and the role of IPRs in each revolution. In Sections 3 and 4, I describe the Green Revolution and the Gene Revolution, respectively, in more detail. In Section 5, I develop innovation and imitation (In-Im) capacity indexes for four groups of developing countries and describe the process of diffusion of technologies from originating countries (chiefly in the OECD market economies) to developing countries.

The chief conclusions of the analysis in Section 5 are that developing countries are diverse in terms of In-Im capacity and that this diversity is the dominant feature of the diffusion of agricultural technology.[2] A further conclusion is that the adoption and diffusion of technologies in the Green Revolution, livestock industrialization, and the Gene Revolution produced a reversal in relative price trends based on production costs. Figure 1 illustrates this finding in terms of the ratio of the index of prices received by farmers to the prices of all goods in the U.S. economy for the years from 1775 to 2000.[3] This figure shows that farm prices rose relative to all prices in the U.S. economy until World War I. This effectively meant that the costs of producing agricultural products were rising relative to the costs of producing all goods in the economy during this age of rapid industrial development in the U.S. economy.[4] It was also a period of slow progress in crop genetic improvement (CGI) and animal genetic improvement.[5]

After World War I, this situation changed, because CGI plant-breeding programs, including hybrid corn projects, began to produce productivity increases in the form of modern or higher-yielding varieties.[6] Price ratios were affected by World War II and by a price spike associated with the OPEC oil price rise in the early 1970s. But the post-World War II period has been characterized by falling farm product prices. These price declines have been of

---

[2] See Section 5 for a specific definition of In-Im classes.
[3] Bureau of Labor Statistics (BLS), National Income and Product Accounts (BA Services NA714_13) and (BLS Series NA714_18) for 1971–98. Other series from Historical Statistics of the United States: Colonial Times to 1970.
[4] See D.C. NORTH, GROWTH AND WELFARE IN THE AMERICAN PAST: A NEW ECONOMIC HISTORY (Prentice-Hall 2d ed. 1974).
[5] HUFFMAN & EVENSON, above n. 1, ch. 6 (discussing this evolution).
[6] See id.; Z. Griliches, Hybrid Corn: An Exploration in the Economics of Technical Change, 25 ECONOMETRICA 501 (1957) [hereinafter Griliches, Economics of Technical Change]; Z. Griliches, Research Costs and Social Returns: Hybrid Corn and Related Innovations, 66 J. POL. ECON. 419 (1958) [hereinafter Griliches, Research Costs].

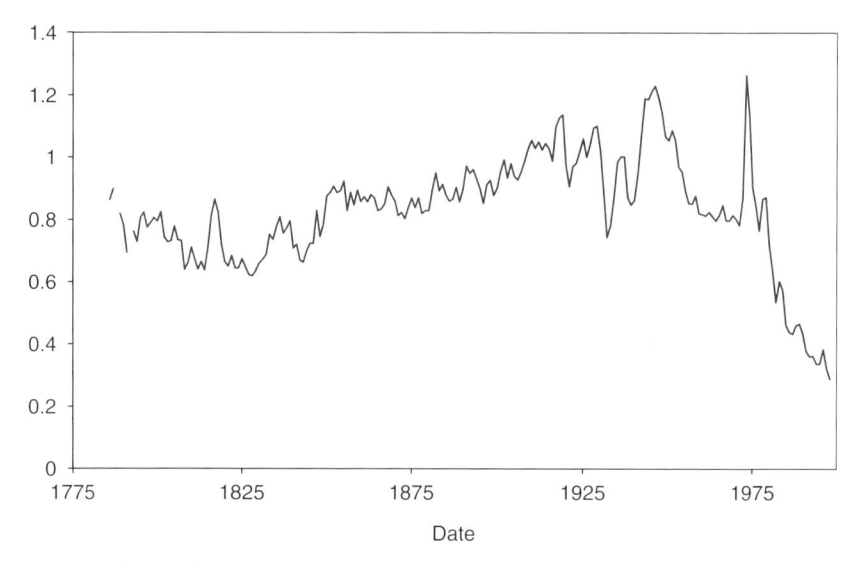

Figure 1: Index of Farm Prices / Index of All Prices

major magnitude and have been global in nature. The real price of farm products (crops and livestock) in 2003 was roughly 40 percent of the 1950 level.[7] Empirical studies effectively show that the agricultural sector has had Total Factor Productivity (TFP) growth rates roughly one percent higher than TFP growth rates for the rest of the economy over the past 50 years in all OECD economies.[8] These productivity differentials have been even greater for most developing countries.[9]

2. Science links, IPRs and public-private investments in research for inventions used in agriculture

It is of interest to compare the sources and characteristics of the five agricultural technological revolutions. Intellectual property rights have played a variety of roles, while governments have been involved to various degrees in all of them. Indeed, the interplay between public provision and private development has been central in technological progress.

---

[7] Refer to Figure 1.
[8] Total factor productivity (TFP) indexes measure real cost reduction (RCR) per unit of output at constant factor prices. For a discussion of these issues, see D.W. Jorgenson & F.M. Gollop, *Productivity Growth in U.S. Agriculture: A Postwar Perspective*, in PRODUCTIVITY, vol. 1, POSTWAR U.S. ECONOMIC GROWTH 389 (D.W. Jorgenson ed., MIT Press 1995); D.W. JORGENSON ET AL., PRODUCTIVITY AND U.S. ECONOMIC GROWTH (MIT Press 1987).
[9] CROP VARIETY IMPROVEMENT AND ITS EFFECT ON PRODUCTIVITY: THE IMPACT OF INTERNATIONAL RESEARCH (Robert E. Evenson & D. Gollin eds., CABI Publishing 2002) [hereinafter CROP VARIETY IMPROVEMENT].

2.1 The agricultural mechanization revolution

Science played a relatively small role in the mechanization revolution. Mechanical aptitude was more important than the understanding of engineering principles in the invention of mowers, reapers, cultivators and threshers in the nineteenth century.[10] As increasingly complex machines, tractors and combine harvesters were developed in the late nineteenth and early twentieth centuries, engineering skills became more important.[11]

Intellectual property rights were quite important in the mechanization revolution as numerous machines were patented.[12] By the latter part of the nineteenth century, thousands of patents were granted for plows, cultivators, mowers, sprayers, and the like. The development of steam power and, later, the row crop tractor depended on IPRs as reflected in patent data.[13] However, the public sector played a minor role in the mechanization revolution, concentrating on the development of such specialized machines as the tomato harvester and the blueberry harvester and related testing methods for soil compaction, machine safety, and the like.

2.2 The agricultural chemical revolution

The scientific fields of chemistry and applied chemical engineering developed roughly in parallel with chemical invention. Some chemical invention could be said to be science-enabled, but much of it was "empirical." Developments in fertilizer technology, especially the Haber process for producing ammonia using hydrocarbons, were of great importance.[14] The price of nitrogen fertilizer declined and later contributed to the induced innovation process in the Green Revolution. The development of herbicides and insecticides was also important in lowering the cost of farm production.[15]

As with mechanization, the agricultural chemical revolution was driven by private-sector firms undertaking R&D and utilizing IPRs. The public sector

---

[10] HUFFMAN & EVENSON, above n. 1, ch. 5.
[11] For a discussion of agricultural invention, see *id.*
[12] *Id.* chs. 1, 5; D.J. de Solla Price, *Is Technology Historically Independent of Science? A Study in Statistical Historiography*, 6 TECH. & CULTURE 553 (1965); A.P. USHER, HISTORY OF MECHANICAL INVENTIONS (Harvard University Press 1954).
[13] Robert E. Evenson, *Inventions Intended for Use in Agriculture and Related Industries: International Comparisons*, 73 AM. J. AGRIC. ECON. 887 (1991) (discussing agricultural inventions).
[14] R. Landau & N. Rosenberg, *Successful Commercialization in the Chemical Process Industries*, in TECHNOLOGY AND THE WEALTH OF NATIONS 73 (N. Rosenberg et al. eds., Stanford University Press 1992).
[15] Robert E. Evenson, *Technical Change in U.S. Agriculture*, in GOVERNMENT AND TECHNICAL CHANGE: A CROSS INDUSTRY ANALYSIS (R.R. Nelson ed., Pergamon Press 1984); B. Achilladelis et al., *A Study of Innovation in the Pesticide Industry: Analysis of the Innovation Record of an Industrial Sector*, 16 RES. POL'Y 175 (1987).

was a minor player in this phase of technical change, and its role was largely confined to testing and evaluating products and advising farmers on effective agronomic practices.[16]

2.3 The crop genetic improvement (Green) revolution

The crop genetic improvement revolution stands in sharp contrast to the mechanization and agricultural chemical revolutions in that it was driven by public-sector Agricultural Experiment Station (AES) programs. The AES "model" was developed in the mid nineteenth century and continues to serve the agricultural sector well.[17] The AES programs devoted to CGI were not well developed in the United States or other developed countries until the late nineteenth and early twentieth centuries. One of the earliest advances in plant breeding was the development of hybrid corn varieties (and later hybrid sorghum, millet, and rice varieties).

A prominent economist first documented this development and illustrated the diffusion process.[18] Griliches' work showed that the private sector eventually came to dominate the hybrid crop seed sector, but not because of IPRs. Rather, hybridization methods produce a one-generation "heterosis" effect that cannot be replicated in farmer-saved seed (as is the case for other crops).[19] This entails the use of "inbred lines" (many of which actually have been developed in AES CGI programs) and the ultimate crossing of these lines into hybrids.

In fact, IPRs for CGI programs were not available in the United States until the Plant Patent Act in 1930.[20] This provided a weak form of protection for asexually reproduced plants.[21] In 1960, the Plant Variety Protection (PVP) Act[22] extended "Breeders' Rights" protection to sexually reproduced plants.[23]

---

[16] See HUFFMAN & EVENSON, above n. 1. See also L. ROGIN, THE INTRODUCTION OF FARM MACHINERY IN ITS RELATION TO THE PRODUCTIVITY OF LABOR IN THE AGRICULTURE OF THE UNITED STATES DURING THE NINETEENTH CENTURY, University of California Publications in Economics, vol. 9 (University of California Press 1931).

[17] G. Grantham, *The Shifting Locus of Agricultural Innovation in Nineteenth Century Europe: The Case of the Agricultural Experiment Stations*, 3 RES. ECON. HIST. 191 (1984).

[18] Griliches, *Economics of Technical Change*, above n. 6 (relating diffusion to economic variables).

[19] See Griliches, *Economics of Technical Change*, above n. 6; Griliches, *Research Costs*, above n. 6; see also HUFFMAN & EVENSON, above n. 1.

[20] Plant Patent Act of 1930, Pub. L. No. 71-245, 46 Stat. 376 (1930).

[21] W. Lesser, *Patenting Seeds in the United States of America: What to Expect*, 9 INDUS. PROP. 360 (1986).

[22] Plant Variety Protection Act, Pub. L. 91-577, 84 Stat. 1542 (1970).

[23] J.M. Strachan, *Plant Variety Protection in USA*, in INTELLECTUAL PROPERTY RIGHTS IN AGRICULTURAL BIOTECHNOLOGY ch. 5 (F.H. Erbisch & K.M. Maredia eds., CABI Publishing 2d ed. 2004).

The PVP Act was modeled on rights extended by the International Union for the Protection of New Varieties of Plants (commonly known by its French acronym, UPOV). The UPOV Act was amended most recently in 1991.[24] This form of protection is generally considered to be the preferred "*sui generis*" method required in the Agreement on Trade-Related Aspects of Intellectual Property Rights (TRIPS), a component of the Agreement Establishing the World Trade Organization (WTO), as discussed further below.[25]

For its part, the Green Revolution was an extension of AES CGI programs to developing countries and is described in more detail in Section 3.

2.4 The livestock industrialization revolution

The livestock industrialization (LI) revolution is partly based on animal genetic improvement (AGI) inventions, partly on animal pharmaceutical inventions, and partly on institutional inventions and developments, particularly those associated with the development of retailing supermarkets for food products and with "fast food" restaurants.[26]

At the beginning of the twentieth century, most livestock products, milk, meat and eggs were produced on family farms as was most feed for livestock. By the end of the twentieth century, livestock production was almost completely industrialized. Poultry production was undertaken in confined broiler-layer systems. Pork and dairy production was also industrialized in large units, and large beef-feed lots located in favorable feeding locations replaced the older systems of production. Most livestock production now takes place in specialized units (i.e., most feed is purchased), and the bulk of output is now contracted in a form of vertical integration of producers, processors and retailers.[27]

Within this system, major gains in animal breeding have taken place and the cost of most livestock products has fallen. Animal health products, such as vaccines and antibiotics, have been important to maintain these industrial

---

[24] International Convention for the Protection of New Varieties of Plants, 2 Dec. 1961, 33 U.S.T. 2703, 815 U.N.T.S. 89, *as revised at* Geneva on 10 Nov. 1972, on 23 Oct. 1978 and on 19 Mar. 1991.

[25] The TRIPS Agreement permits the exclusion from patentability of "plants and animals, other than microorganisms, and essentially biological processes for the production of plants and animals, other than non-biological and microbiological processes. However, members shall provide for the protection of plant varieties either by patents or by an effective *sui generis* system or by combination thereof." Agreement on Trade-Related Aspects of Intellectual Property Rights, 15 Apr. 1994, Marrakesh Agreement Establishing the World Trade Organization, Annex 1C, LEGAL INSTRUMENTS – RESULTS OF THE URUGUAY ROUND vol. 31, 33 I.L.M. 81 (1994) [hereinafter TRIPS Agreement], art. 27.3.

[26] D. Hu et al., *The Emergence of Supermarkets with Chinese Characteristics: Challenges and Opportunities for China's Agricultural Development*, 22 DEV. POL'Y REV. 557 (2004).

[27] A.L. Katchova & M.J. Miranda, *Two-Step Environmental Estimation of Farm Characteristics Affecting Marketing Contract Decisions*, 86 AM. J. AGRIC. ECON. 88 (2004).

systems. These products have relied on IPR protection for their development and marketing.[28]

The public sector has played only a modest role in the LI revolution. Some animal pharmaceutical products have been developed in the AES system, and many "best practices" advances have been made as well.[29] Most U.S. veterinarians are trained in these AES-related systems. But the major technological developments continue to be the product of private-firm R&D programs.

This system of industrialization is now being extended to developing countries and is transforming livestock production in these countries.[30]

2.5 The Gene Revolution

The Gene Revolution, or the conscious introduction of living organisms to imbue plants with particular useful features, has been characterized by two major features. It has been "science-enabled" to a large extent and has also been led by the private sector.[31] In consequence, it has been dependent on IPRs. Because of the complexity involved, I defer discussion of the associated IPRs and industrial development for the gene revolution to Section 4 of this chapter.

As these various technological eras have taken place, the balance between public support and private R&D has changed. For developed countries, most early inventions for agricultural use were produced by farmers and industrialization in the United States. However, the land grant university system, established in 1862, created a demand for agricultural science and led to the establishment of the State Agricultural Experiment Station System (SAES) in 1878.[32] By the early part of the twentieth century, the balance of research expenditures was two-thirds public, but by the end of the twentieth century the balance was one-third public.[33]

3. The Green Revolution and the SPIA study

The development of modern or high-yielding crop varieties (MVs) for developing countries began in concerted fashion in the late 1950s.[34] In the mid-1960s, scientists developed MVs of rice and wheat that were subsequently released to farmers in Latin America and Asia. The success of these MVs was characterized as a "Green Revolution."[35] Early rice and wheat MVs were

---

[28] Robert E. Evenson & D. Johnson, *Introduction: Invention Input-Output Analysis*, 9 ECON. SYS. RES. 149 (1997).
[29] HUFFMAN & EVENSON, above n. 1, ch. 5.   [30] Hu et al., above n. 26.
[31] Robert E. Evenson, *Agricultural Biotechnology*, in TECHNOLOGICAL INNOVATION AND ECONOMIC PERFORMANCE 367 (B. Steil et al. eds., Princeton University Press 2002).
[32] HUFFMAN & EVENSON, above n. 1, at ch. 1.   [33] *Id.* ch. 4.
[34] Y. HAYAMI & V.W. RUTTAN, AGRICULTURAL DEVELOPMENT: AN INTERNATIONAL PERSPECTIVE (Johns Hopkins University Press 1985).
[35] CROP VARIETY IMPROVEMENT, above n. 9.

rapidly adopted in tropical and sub-tropical regions with good irrigation systems or reliable rainfall. These MVs were associated with the first two International Agricultural Research Centers (IARCs): the International Center for Wheat and Maize Improvement (CIMMYT) in Mexico and the International Rice Research Institute (IRRI) in the Philippines. There are now 16 such centers that operate under the auspices of the Consultative Group for International Agricultural Research (CGIAR).[36] These centers currently support about 8,500 scientists and scientific staff, and the annual budget of the CGIAR is currently around $340 million.

A recent study initiated by the Special Project on Impact Assessment (SPIA) of the CGIAR's Technical Advisory Committee has compiled the most extensive data yet assembled on the breeding, release, and diffusion of modern varieties.[37] The SPIA study allows for a detailed analysis of the impact of international research for eleven major food crops, by region and country, for the period 1960–2000.

The early successes in breeding rice and wheat MVs reflected the advanced state of research on those crops in the late 1950s. Researchers at IRRI and CIMMYT had free access to rich stocks of genetic resources and drew on extensive breeding experience in developed countries. For both crops, breeders incorporated dwarfing genes that allowed the development of shorter, stiff-strawed varieties. These varieties devoted much of their energy to producing grain and relatively little to producing straw or leaf material. They also responded better to fertilizer than traditional varieties.[38]

For other crops, however, breeding work aimed at the developing world could not rely on prior work in developed countries. In cassava or tropical beans, for example, there was essentially no research or elite germplasm available in the 1960s.[39] As a result, the development of MVs was slower for these crops. But over the following decades, international research led to the development of improved varieties in many crops. The SPIA study documents that by 2000, there were more than 8,000 MVs released in the 11 crops studied, as depicted in Figure 2. These MVs were released by more than 400 public breeding programs and seed boards in over 100 countries. Contrary to some

---

[36] V.W. RUTTAN, AGRICULTURAL RESEARCH POLICY (University of Minneapolis Press 1983).
[37] See Robert E. Evenson & D. Gollin, Assessing the Impact of the Green Revolution, 1960–2000, 300 SCIENCE 758 (2003); CROP VARIETY IMPROVEMENT, above n. 9.
[38] RUTTAN, above n. 36.
[39] N.L. Johnson et al., The Impact of CIAT's Genetic Improvement Research on Beans, in CROP VARIETY IMPROVEMENT, above n. 9, at 257; N.L. Johnson et al., The Impact of IARC Genetic Improvement Programmes on Cassava, in CROP VARIETY IMPROVEMENT, above n. 9, at 337.

Annual MV Release

Latin America

Asia

Middle East-North Africa

Sub-Saharan Africa

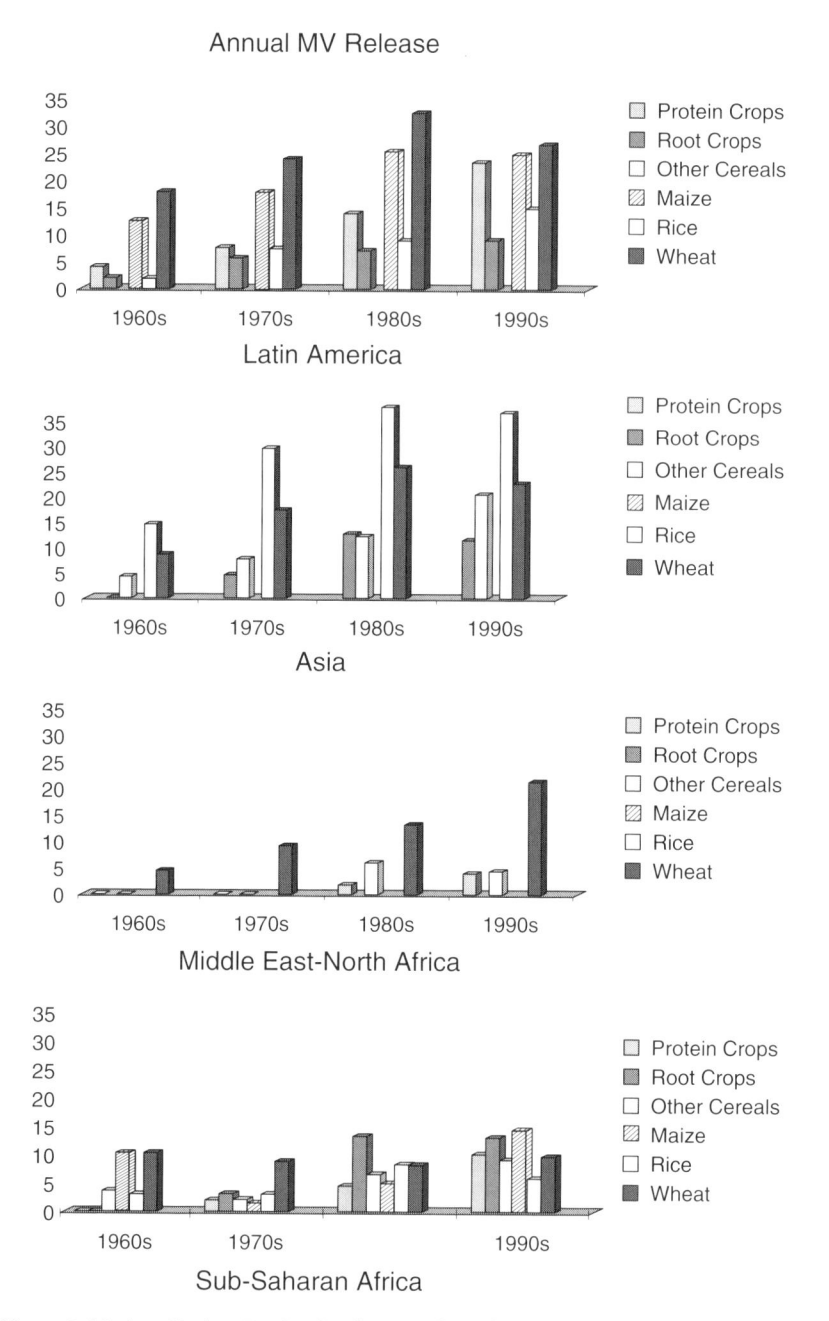

Figure 2: Modern Variety Production by Decade and Region

views of the Green Revolution,[40] the annual rate of MV releases has actually increased since the 1960s. There are, however, a number of important disparities in the development of MVs, especially by agro-ecological zone (AEZ). For sorghum, millet, and barley – crops grown primarily under semi-arid and dryland conditions – few modern varieties were bred until the 1980s. The same was true for the major pulses and for root crops, especially cassava. Regional disparities were also important. Even for maize and rice, few varieties were available until the 1980s for the Middle East/North Africa and for Sub-Saharan African countries.[41]

For most crops in most regions, modern variety adoption occurred soon after modern varieties were released, as shown in Figure 3. There are, however, important differences across crops and regions in the date at which significant adoption of MVs first occurred and in the subsequent growth rates of adoption.[42] For example, although significant numbers of MVs were released in Sub-Saharan Africa in the 1960s and 1970s, there was little adoption of new varieties by farmers, except for wheat.[43] The data suggest that in the 1960s and 1970s, national and international programs may have sought to "short-cut" the varietal improvement process in Sub-Saharan Africa by introducing unsuitable varieties from Asia and Latin America, rather than engaging in the time-consuming work of identifying locally adapted germplasm and using it as the basis for breeding new varieties.[44] This pattern remained until the 1980s, when more suitable varieties finally became available based on research targeted specifically to African conditions.

More generally, diffusion patterns reflect the importance of location-specific breeding. For most crops, researchers sought first to develop a productive "plant type" (for example, a high-yielding semi-dwarf) for each major AEZ to serve as a platform for local adaptation, and then subsequently bred for location-relevant traits, such as resistance to diseases, pests, and abiotic stresses.[45] This second-stage research proved extremely important. For India, the SPIA study

---

[40] D. Dalrymple, Development and Spread of High Yielding Rice Varieties in Developing Countries (Bureau for Science and Technology, Agency for International Development 1986); D. Dalrymple, Development and Spread of High Yielding Wheat Varieties in Developing Countries (Bureau for Science and Technology, Agency for International Development 1986).
[41] Robert E. Evenson, The Green Revolution in Developing Countries: An Economist's Assessment, Bureau of Economic Studies Occasional Paper No. 19 (Macalester College 2002).
[42] Griliches, *Economics of Technical Change*, above n. 6, showed that the methods for hybridizing corn varieties constituted the "invention of a method of invention" and that location-specific breeding programs were required to connect this method into varieties available to farmers.
[43] See Evenson, above n. 41.   [44] Id.
[45] MODERN RICE TECHNOLOGY AND INCOME DISTRIBUTION IN ASIA (C.C. David & K. Otsuka eds., Lynne Rienner Publishers 1993).

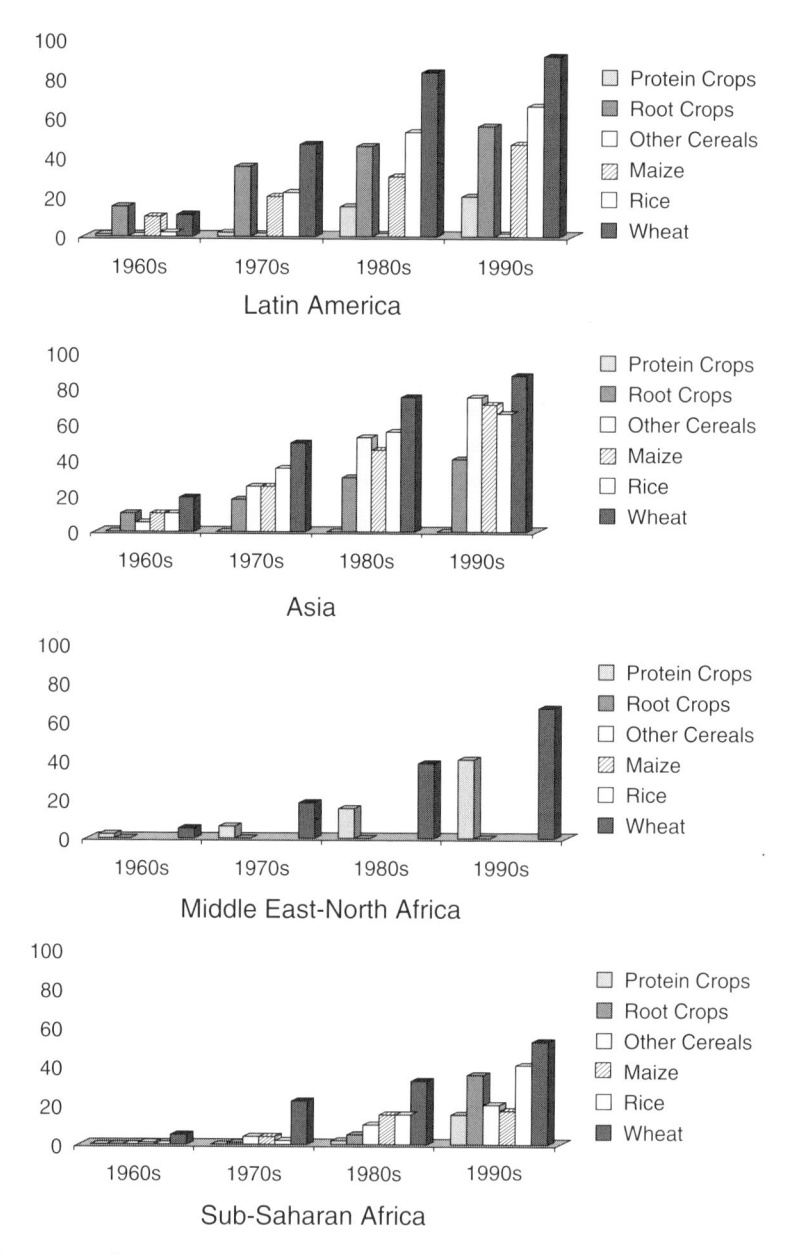

Figure 3: Modern Variety Diffusion by Decade and Region.

suggests that the first generation of improved rice varieties (the basic semi-dwarf plant type) would have been planted on only 35 percent or so of irrigated and rain-fed rice land. The subsequent generations of MVs increased adoption rates to more than 80 percent, with large ensuing benefits for both producers and consumers.

For most of the modern varieties in the SPIA study, complete or near-complete plant genealogies could be constructed. The study analyzed these genealogies to look for two types of international contributions to varietal improvement. Direct contributions were defined as varieties developed in international institutions and then released by national programs without further crossing. Indirect contributions were defined to include varieties that were crossed in programs run by National Agricultural Research Services (NARS) but which had parents or ancestors bred in IARCs.

The evidence on such contributions points to several striking results. First, there have been large IARC indirect contributions. More than 35 percent of MVs released and adopted were based on crosses made in these international centers.[46] Fifteen percent of NARS-crossed MVs had an IARC-crossed parent, and an additional seven percent had another IARC-crossed ancestor. It is important to note that these parental materials were exchanged with no intellectual-property restrictions. Varieties with IARC ancestry were also more widely planted than other varieties.

Second, the international flows of NARS-crossed MVs have been low. For rice, where such data were available, only six percent of MVs originated when one national program released a variety that was crossed by an NARS in another developing country. By contrast, most IARC-crossed MVs were released in several countries.

Third, the contributions of developed countries have been negligible. Less than one percent of MVs included in their genealogies any crosses made in public or private sector plant breeding programs in developed nations.[47] Fourth, the contributions of the private sector were also small. Private-sector work was limited to "hybrid" varieties of maize, sorghum, and millet. Private breeding programs for these crops were developed only after "platform" varieties were developed in IARC and NARS programs. It should be noted that genetically engineered MVs appeared only after 1996 and have been planted in only three or four developing countries.

A fifth conclusion is that IARC research has complemented NARS breeding programs. By providing improved germplasm for NARS breeding projects, international breeding efforts increased the productivity of those national programs. Because of this IARC-NARS complementarity, the existence of the

---

[46] *See* Evenson, above n. 41.
[47] As with hybrid corn varieties, the location specificity of varieties limits their transfer from one AEZ to another. D. Gollin & M. Smale, *Valuing Genetic Diversity: Crop Plants and Agroecosystems*, *in* BIODIVERSITY IN AGROECOSYSTEMS 237 (Wanda W. Collins & Calvin O. Qualset ed., CRC Press 1998).

international centers actually stimulated national investment in NARS research.[48] This germplasm effect was not impeded by IPRs or other regulatory restrictions.

Table 1 provides data on the production impacts of MVs over the past 40 years.[49] Not all of the production growth from 1961–2000 was due to MVs, and this table shows how production growth can be disaggregated into increases in area planted and increases in yields. Yield growth in turn can be decomposed into the contributions of MVs and the contributions of all other inputs (e.g., fertilizer, irrigation, mechanization, and labor).

One striking feature of the data in Table 1 is that the gains from MVs were larger in the 1980s and 1990s than in the preceding two decades, despite popular perceptions that the Green Revolution was effectively over by this time.[50] Overall, the productivity data suggest that the Green Revolution is best understood not as a one-time jump in production, occurring in the late 1960s, but rather as a long-term increase in the trend growth rate of productivity. This was because successive generations of MVs were developed, each contributing gains over previous generations.

Table 1 shows that in the early Green Revolution period (1961–1980), MVs contributed significantly to growth in Asia and Latin America, but relatively little in other areas. For all developing countries, MVs accounted for 21 percent of the growth in yields and about 17 percent of production growth. Area expansion accounted for about 20 percent of the increases in production, and the rest came from intensification of input use.

The late Green Revolution period (1981–2000) differed from the early period in several important respects. In part because prices to farmers were declining, production growth was slower in all regions except Sub-Saharan Africa. The area under food crop cultivation remained flat overall, with declines in Latin America offsetting the continued expansion of agricultural lands in Sub-Saharan Africa and the Middle East–North Africa region. Yield growth accounted for almost all of the increases in food production in developing countries (86 percent). Furthermore, the MV contribution to yield growth was higher in the late Green Revolution period than in the early Green Revolution period, accounting for almost 50 percent of yield growth and 40 percent of production growth for all developing countries. This indicates that in the late Green Revolution period, production gains were more dependent on MVs than in the early period, and that MV contributions were greater in the late period.

---

[48] The elasticity of NARS MV production with respect to NARS breeding resource was estimated to be .65. The complementary effect of IARC breeding materials was .35. *See* CROP VARIETY IMPROVEMENT, above n. 9.

[49] Robert E. Evenson & D. Gollin, above n. 37.

[50] *See* ANDERSON ET AL., RICE SCIENCE AND DEVELOPMENT POLITICS: RESEARCH STRATEGIES AND IRRI'S TECHNOLOGIES CONFRONT ASIAN DIVERSITY (1950–1980) (Clarendon Press 1991).

Table 1: *Growth rates of food production, area, yield, and yield components, by region and period*

	Early Green Revolution 1961–80	Late Green Revolution 1981–2000
Latin America		
Production	3.083	1.631
Area	1.473	−0.512
Yield	1.587	2.154
MV Contributions to Yield	0.463	0.772
Other Input/Ha	1.124	1.382
Asia		
Production	3.649	2.107
Area	0.513	0.020
Yield	3.120	2.087
MV Contributions to Yield	0.682	0.968
Other Input/Ha	2.439	1.119
Middle East–North Africa		
Production	2.529	2.121
Area	0.953	0.607
Yield	1.561	1.505
MV Contributions to Yield	0.173	0.783
Other Input/Ha	1.389	0.722
Sub-Saharan Africa		
Production	1.697	3.189
Area	0.524	2.818
Yield	1.166	0.361
MV Contributions to Yield	0.097	0.471
Other Input/Ha	1.069	−0.110
All Developing Countries		
Production	3.200	2.192
Area	0.683	0.386
Yield	2.502	1.805
MV Contributions to Yield	0.523	0.857
Other Input/Ha	1.979	0.948

Notes: Data on food crop production and area harvested are taken from FAOSTAT data, revised 2003 (http://apps.fao.org/page/collections?subset=agriculture) on total cereals, total roots and tubers, and total pulses. Asia consists of "Developing Asia" less the countries of the "Near East in Asia." Africa consists of "Developing Africa" less the countries of the "Near East in Africa" and the countries of "North-West Africa." The Middle East-North Africa consists of "Near East in Africa," "Near East in Asia," and "North-West Africa." Latin America includes Latin America and the Caribbean. Crop production is aggregated for each region using area weights from 1981. Estimates of production increases due to MVs are from Evanson & Gollin, above n. 37. Growth rates of other inputs are taken as a residual. Growth rates are compound and are computed by regressing time series data on a constant and trend variable. The totals for "All Developing Countries" are derived by weighting the regional figures by 1981 area shares.

Although input use intensified in the late Green Revolution period, productivity gains from MVs allowed food production to increase dramatically with only modest increases in the area planted to food crops and with relatively slow growth in the use of such inputs as fertilizer and irrigation.

Behavior of the Sub-Saharan African region was unusual in both periods. Yield growth made only minor contributions to production growth in both periods, and the MV contributions to yield growth were also low, although considerably higher in the more recent period. Production growth was based almost entirely on extending the area under cultivation. In short, this region achieved a very partial and incomplete Green Revolution, with a number of countries realizing virtually no MV contributions to food production growth.[51]

The limited scope of the Green Revolution in Sub-Saharan Africa was in part due to the mix of crops grown in the region (where root crops and tropical maize are dominant food crops) and in part due to the agro-ecological complexities of the region and associated difficulties in producing suitable MVs. Table 1 shows that such yield growth as was realized in Sub-Saharan Africa was almost entirely contributed by MVs, with little contribution from fertilizers and other inputs.

Why did Sub-Saharan Africa get so little growth from varietal improvement until the 1990s? The inherited state of knowledge and the pre-existing stocks of improved germplasm were important factors in differential regional performance. Clearly, institutional and political failure also mattered.[52] But Figures 2 and 3 and the underlying data suggest that some of Sub-Saharan Africa's low growth reflected the lack of usable modern variety technology until the 1980s and 1990s. Recent evidence is more promising, however. Varietal improvement appears finally to be making an impact in Sub-Saharan Africa in rice, maize, cassava, and other crops.

More generally, the differences in productivity impacts across regions reflect dramatic underlying disparities in the availability and impact of suitable MVs across different agro-ecological zones.[53] The largest initial impacts (in wheat and rice) were in irrigated areas and in rain-fed lowlands with food-water control. But outside of these environments, varietal improvement was slower and more limited. This was not for lack of effort, for IRRI and CIMMYT, along with many national programs, sought to adapt rice, wheat, and maize MVs to "marginal" environments. And newer IARCs, such as the International Center for Agriculture in the Dry Areas (ICARDA), the International Center for Research in the Semi-Arid Tropics (ICRISAT), the

---

[51] *See* Evenson & Gollin, above n. 49.
[52] It also appears that high transaction costs in fertilizer markets limited fertilizer use on modern varieties in Sub-Saharan Africa. A.F.D. AVILA & Robert E. EVENSON, TOTAL FACTOR PRODUCTIVITY GROWTH IN AGRICULTURE: THE ROLE OF TECHNOLOGICAL CAPITAL (forthcoming 2005), utilizes a Technology Capital concept to make this point.
[53] CROP VARIETY IMPROVEMENT, above n. 9, ch. 2.

International Institute for Tropical Agriculture (IITA), and others, were specifically developed to provide research of use to marginal environments. But this research took time to pay dividends, and the diffusion of MVs into less favorable agroecologies was slow.

4. The Gene Revolution: Regulatory and IPR issues

The term biotechnology was first introduced by Ereky in 1919 to describe fermentation technologies.[54] The term molecular biology was introduced in 1938 to describe science below the cellular level.[55] In its modern usage biotechnology refers to technologies that use living organisms to make medical products, plants and animals. The terms "genetic engineering" and "recombinant DNA" (rDNA) describe these technologies.

According to Ruttan there were four major advances necessary to modern biotechnology.[56] First was the 1938 identification of DNA as the carrier of genetic information by Delbruck of Cal-Tech. Second was the 1953 discovery by Watson and Crick of the double helix structure of DNA. Third was the 1973 demonstration of a method for stably inserting DNA from foreign organisms into a host genome by Cohen and Boyer of Stanford (the recombinant DNA technique). Finally, there was the 1975 invention of hybridoma (fusion) technology by Kohler and Milstein.

These developments in fundamental knowledge anticipated the usefulness of techniques based on this science. The first stage in biotech industry development took the form of university-industry collaborative complexes. In 1976, Genentech was formed to commercialize recombinant DNA techniques. Stanford University acquired the Cohen-Boyer patent rights (not granted until 1980 for a product patent and 1984 for a process patent), and Genentech provided a grant to Boyer for laboratory access.[57]

By the early 1980s, university–industry contracts were becoming important, though they have receded since as industry groups have matured.[58] Among the early contracts were the 1982 Monsanto-Washington University (St. Louis) and the DuPont–Harvard contracts. Monsanto became a dominant player in the plant biotechnology field and, by the late 1980s, was spending significant sums on R&D (more than 100 million dollars per year, a sum greater than all crop research for Sub-Saharan Africa).[59]

---

[54] See RUTTAN, above n. 1, at 369.
[55] W. Weaver, The "Natural Sciences" Rockefeller Foundation Annual Report 203–221 (1938).
[56] RUTTAN, above n. 1.
[57] Id. at 378; M. KENNEY, BIOTECHNOLOGY: THE UNIVERSITY-INDUSTRIAL COMPLEX 156–179 (Yale University Press 1986).
[58] See Evenson, above n. 31.   [59] Id.

As new firms began to develop products, new regulatory structures were required. Thus, as new products were developed, IPRs, especially patent rights, expanded in parallel. As regards regulations, the Agricultural Plant Health Inspection Service (APHIS) regulated field trials. The Environmental Protection Agency (EPA) regulated pest control in plants. And the Food and Drug Agency (FDA) developed regulations for food safety.[60]

Turning to IPRs, the *Chakrabarty-Diamond* case in 1980 opened up the scope for patenting living materials.[61] The 1985 *Hibberd* decision opened the system to living plants.[62] The 1987 *Allen* decision expanded protection to non-human animals.[63]

The second phase in plant biotechnology development was the "Life Science" company. This entailed the acquisitions of seed firms (DeKalb, Pioneer, and Holden) by agricultural biotechnology firms (Monsanto, DuPont, and Novartis [Aventis]). These Life Science firms were intended to provide the biotech firms with access to the experience of the seed industry and to more conventional breeding techniques.[64]

The Life Science firm concept has now fallen victim to an exceptional degree of consumer resistance and political group hostility to genetically modified organisms (GMOs) or GM foods. This hostility has slowed developments in regulatory regimes and produced bans on imports of GM foods to Europe (as of 1998) and labeling and traceability (L&T) regulations in Europe as well (as of 2000). Advocates of stiffer regulatory regimes (including effective bans on GM food sales) have pushed the "precautionary principle" as a guideline for regulation.[65] The regulatory battles are currently at a standstill, and WTO rules associated with the Sanitary and Phytosanitary Agreement (SPS) and the Technical Barriers to Trade Agreement (TBT) are being brought into the debate.

It might be argued that the agricultural biotech Life Science firms became victims of their own marketing blunders. Had they understood the nature of

---

[60] R.L. Paarlberg et al., *Regulation of GM Crops: Shaping an International Regime*, in THE REGULATION OF AGRICULTURAL BIOTECHNOLOGY 1 (Robert E. Evenson & V. Santaniello eds., CABI Publishing 2004).

[61] U.S. Supreme Court decision in *Diamond v. Chakrabarty*, 447 US 303 (1980), held that "anything under the sun," apart from human beings, could be patented. Following this decision, the general approach that patent officers have taken is that gene sequences are inventions when they have been isolated and purified.

[62] Since the *Hibberd* decision of the Patent Office Board of Appeals and Interferences, the scheme with which only one claim covering one plant variety is permitted in each application has been in decline, and the normal patent system has opened up to applications that covered plant varieties. *In re* Hibberd, 227 USPQ (BNA) 443 (1985).

[63] *Ex parte* Allen, 2 USPQ2d 1425 (Bd. Pat. App. & Inter. 1987). The first animal patent was granted to Harvard University for the Onco Mouse. A moratorium on animal patenting was imposed for several years.

[64] *See* Evenson, above n. 31.   [65] *See* Paarlberg et al., above n. 60.

food consumers, as do firms in the food industry, they would have supported voluntary labeling (now they are likely to have mandatory labeling) and encouraged the emergence of premiums for GM-free products, along the lines of the organic food industry.

Two additional IPR issues have emerged from the Convention on Biodiversity (CBD).[66] The CBD was supported by developing countries because it called for the recognition of "farmers' rights" associated with farmer selected "landraces" or farmers' varieties. The basic materials used by conventional plant breeders are landraces and mutants in the cultivated species and closely related non-cultivated species [weedy relatives]. All biological materials can be sources for recombinant DNA methods. Developing countries consider themselves rich in these resources and hence support CBD rights.[67] However, the need for potential payment for these rights places under threat the exchange of genetic resources, which was at the heart of the Green Revolution, until a means of recognizing these rights can be found.

The Food and Agriculture Organization (FAO) has taken responsibility for maintaining the system of free exchange of genetic resources between research programs. The International Undertaking on Plant Genetic Resources is the mechanism by which this is being done.[68]

A second CBD issue emerged from the 2000 Cartagena Biosafety Protocol (CBP).[69] The CBP permits blocking of imports or requiring of labels on a "precautionary" basis without firm scientific evidence of risk. It is currently blocking transboundary movements of living GMOs.[70] The CBP assumes

---

[66] Convention on Biological Diversity, 5 June 1992, 31 I.L.M. 818, *available at* http://www.biodiv.org/convention/articles.asp (last accessed 28 July 2004). *See* W. Lesser, *Intellectual Property Rights under the Convention on Biological Diversity*, *in* AGRICULTURE AND INTELLECTUAL PROPERTY RIGHTS: ECONOMIC, INSTITUTIONAL AND IMPLEMENTATION ISSUES IN BIOTECHNOLOGY 35 (V. Santaniello, et al. eds., CABI Publishing 2000) (discussing the implication of the CBD).

[67] For evidence that developed countries created valuable landraces, see D. Gollin, *Valuing Farmers' Rights*, *in* AGRICULTURAL VALUES OF PLANT GENETIC RESOURCES 217 (Robert E. Evenson et al. eds., CABI Publishing 1998).

[68] *See* Laurence R. Helfer, *Using Intellectual Property Rights to Preserve the Global Genetic Commons: The International Treaty on Plant Genetic Resources for Food and Agriculture* [this volume]; *see also* D. Alker & F. Heidhues, *Farmers' Rights and Intellectual Property Rights – Reconciling Conflicting Concepts*, *in* ECONOMIC AND SOCIAL ISSUES IN AGRICULTURAL BIOTECHNOLOGY 62 (Robert E. Evenson et al. eds., CABI Publishing 2002) (discussing FAO's role in this).

[69] Cartagena Protocol on Biosafety to the Convention on Biological Diversity, 29 Jan. 2000, 39 I.L.M. 1027 (2000), *available at* http://www.biodiv.org/biosafety/protocol.asp (last accessed 28 July 2004); *See* M. Blakeney, *International Proposals to Regulate Intellectual Property Rights in Plant Genetic Resources*, *in* THE REGULATION OF AGRICULTURAL BIOTECHNOLOGY 35 (Robert E. Evenson & V. Santaniello eds., CABI Publishing 2004).

[70] *Id.*; *see* Paarlberg et al., above n. 60.

that many developing countries lack biosafety protections. The evident conflict between the CBP and the SPS agreement is now under negotiation.[71]

The Codex Alimentarius of the FAO is also involved in regulation. The Codex establishes food standards and codes of hygiene. The 1995 SPS Agreement gives responsibility to the Codex for maintaining food safety standards.[72]

Lurking in the background are features of the TRIPS Agreement permitting the exclusion of "plants and animals" from patentability under Article 27.3 (b) if an effective *sui generis* system is implemented for protecting plant varieties. However, plant breeders' rights systems are weak and not well supported by courts.[73] In effect, this situation may offer little or no IPRs for plants and animals. But the unstated part of Article 27.3 (b) is that patent protection is to be provided to biotechnology products and processes that are not living multicellular plants and non-human animals. This includes patents on biotechnology methods and techniques as well as on specific "genes" (e.g. the *Bt* gene).

The impact of these patent rights is illustrated in the case of "Golden Rice," wherein a Swiss research center achieved enhanced production of Beta-Carotene in rice plants.[74] This trait has the potential to reduce the health consequences of Vitamin A deficiency, a major health problem in developing countries. After developing the plant, the Swiss researchers found that they might be liable for possible infringement of several process or technique patents. There is some uncertainty as to whether the use of the scientific techniques for research purposes constituted infringement or whether the marketing of products enabled by the technique constituted infringement. But this case illustrates the complex nature of IPRs in the Gene Revolution.

---

[71] The WTO is under pressure from a number of European states to adjust its own rules to accommodate the more precautionary approach. D. Heumilluer & T. Josling, *Trade Restrictions on Genetically Engineered Foods: The Application of the TBT Agreement*, in THE REGULATION OF AGRICULTURAL BIOTECHNOLOGY, above n. 69.

[72] The Codex is an intergovernmental body established in 1962, responsible for managing a joint FAO/WHO Food Standards Programme. So far the Codex has developed more than 200 food standards for commodities and more than 40 codes of hygiene and technological practice. The Codex has a nearly universal membership of 163 member states. Prior to 1995, the Codex was neither a powerful nor a prominent instrument of global governance, since its standards had no force in international law. All this changed when the new SPS Agreement entered into force on January 1, 1995. In an appendix to the SPS Agreement (Annex A), the Codex is given responsibility for maintaining the international standards relevant to food safety that should be recognized by the WTO.

[73] Robert E. Evenson, *Intellectual Property Rights and Asian Agriculture*, 1 ASIAN J. AGRIC. & DEV. 23 (2004).

[74] Blakeney, above n. 69.

5. Innovation-imitation capacity in developing countries

Many discussions of developing countries and technological change utilize a simple North-South distinction.[75] But this distinction masks the large degree of diversity of innovation-imitation competence or capacity among developing countries.

To illustrate this diversity, consider Figure 4 where four In-Im capacity classes are defined using six objective indicators.[76] For a given period, a country can be placed into a unique In-Im class based on these indicators. The imitation indicators include literacy and agricultural extension. The innovation indicators include agricultural research programs (almost entirely public until recent years), R&D in manufacturing firms, foreign direct investment and IPRs. Based on these indicators, countries were placed into classes I to IV for each of three periods, 1961–1976, 1971–1986 and 1981–1996. Thus, for example, a country ranked 112 was placed in category I for the first two periods and then category 2 in the final period. The 90 developing countries in these classes are shown in Figure 5.

Consider the countries ranked 111. These countries have remained in the lowest In-Im class for all three periods and are basically "failed states." They do not have the capacity to enforce laws and regulations. Some cannot even deliver the mail. They have not realized Green Revolution technology and have no Gene Revolution capacity.

The 112 countries began to develop In-Im capacity in period 3. None, however, has achieved productivity-driven industrial growth. A few have achieved Green Revolution gains, but these are very marginal. The 274 million people in the twenty-one 111 and 112 countries have realized little or no growth in per capita income (see Table 2). They remain almost completely excluded from the development process.

The 222, 223 and 233 countries have innovative capacity in agriculture. Most have plant breeding programs and all have realized some Green Revolution gains. Few of these countries have Gene Revolution capabilities, though Kenya has a program. This collection of 30 countries in groups 222, 223 and 233, with a population of 651 million people, exhibits an important feature of developing country diversity. Specifically, these countries have scored some success in public-sector innovation through plant breeding (a partial Green Revolution), but none can be described as having imitation success. That is,

---

[75] See J. Bhagwati, *U.S. Trade Policy: The Infatuation with Free Trade Areas*, in THE DANGEROUS DRIFT TO PREFERENTIAL TRADE AGREEMENTS (J. Bhagwati & A. Krueger eds., AEI Press 1995).

[76] These classes are taken from Robert E. Evenson, *Agricultural Production and Productivity in Developing Countries*, in THE STATE OF FOOD AND AGRICULTURE 2000: LESSONS FROM THE PAST 50 YEARS 243 (Food and Agriculture Organization of the United Nations 2000).

Figure 4: In/Im Capital Indicators for Developing Countries.

INDICATORS	In/Im-I	In/Im-II	In/Im-III	In/Im-IV
Adult male literacy	Less than 50%	More than 50%	More than 50%	More than 65%
Agricultural research investment/Agr VA	Less than 1%	1% to 2%	More than 2%	More than 2%
Agricultural extension/Agr VA	Less than 1%	1% to 2%	1% to 2%	More than 2%
Foreign direct investment/GDP	Little or none	Less than 2%	More than 2%	More than 2%
R&D in manufacturing firms/value added	None	None	Less than 3%	More than 3%
Intellectual property rights	None	None	Weak	Moderate

Source: Evenson, 2000

Figure 5: Country In/Im Classifications 1961–76, 1971–86, 1981–1996.*

111	112	222	223	233	333	334	344	444
Afghanistan	Angola	Burkina Faso	Bangladesh	Dominican Republic	Cuba	Algeria	Chile	Argentina
Zaire (Congo)	Benin	Cote d'Ivoire	Botswana	Ghana	Indonesia	Bolivia	China	Brazil
Congo /Brazzaville	Burundi	Guatemala	Cameroon	Kenya	Iran	Ecuador	Colombia	Costa Rica
Ethiopia	Cambodia	Lao DPR	Korea (DPR)	Nigeria	Iraq	Egypt	Malaysia	South Africa
Somalia	Chad	Liberia	Madagascar	Paraguay	Jordan	El Salvador	Mexico	
	Gabon	Malawi	Mali	Peru	Libya	Honduras	Morocco	
	Gambia	Sudan	Mongolia	Senegal	Mauritius	India	Thailand	
	Guinea	Togo	Namibia	Sierra Leone	Oman	Jamaica		
	Guinea Bissau	Uganda	Nicaragua	Sri Lanka	Pakistan	Saudi Arabia		
	Haiti		Tanzania	Vietnam	Panama	Tunisia		
	Mauritania			Zambia	Philippines	Turkey		
	Mozambique				Syria	Uruguay		
	Nepal				Trinidad-Tobago	Zimbabwe		
	Niger				United Arab Emirates			
	Rwanda				Venezuela			
	Yemen							

* This figure only includes countries with a population of more than one million in 1998.

Table 2: Economic Indicators by In/Im Class

Country Code	Total Population 1998 (Million)	Annual Growth Rate 1978–1998 (%)	Annual Growth Rate 1962–1992 (%)	GDP Per Capita PPP 1999 (US$)	Rural Population Density People per Km² of Arable Land 1999	Irrigated Land % of Crop Land 1979–1981	Irrigated Land % of Crop Land 1997–1999	Fertilizer Consumption 100 Grams per Hectare of Arable Land 1979–1981	Fertilizer Consumption 1997–1999	Cereal Yield Kg per Hectare 1978–1981	Cereal Yield Kg per Hectare 1998–2000	Agricultural Productivity Agricultural Value Added per Worker 1995 $ 1979–1981	Agricultural Productivity 1998–2000	Competitive Industrial Performance Index 1985	Competitive Industrial Performance Index 1998
111	142.2	2.81	2.30	707	486.9	9.6	9.8	25.1	12.7	907.9	844.4	248.7	263.9		
112	131.7	2.78	−0.76	1256	503.9	8.8	12.9	61.2	115.0	940.1	1157.3	274.2	284.2	0.001	0.006
Group I	273.8	2.79	0.77	981	495.4	9.2	11.4	43.1	63.8	924.0	1000.8	261.4	274.1	0.001	0.006
222	107.8	2.66	0.32	1302	309.2	5.2	4.9	149.1	264.0	1038.2	1167.2	834.1	877.9	0.008	0.017
223	231.8	2.27	1.12	2797	842.6	17.4	35.4	755.1	936.4	1808.2	2384.0	325.2	424.2	0.008	0.009
233	311.2	2.46	1.37	1817	550.4	11.5	25.3	277.7	1091.4	1612.4	2242.2	619.9	821.3	0.012	0.013
Group II	650.8	2.46	0.94	1972	567.3	11.4	21.8	393.9	763.6	1486.0	1931.1	593.0	707.1	0.010	0.010
333	586.3	2.48	2.61	3383	468.1	33.2	37.8	637.2	1230.4	1954.4	2766.8	1055.2	1432.1	0.026	0.076
334	1221.8	2.09	2.31	2814	444.3	25.2	34.6	494.4	1168.5	1476.7	2504.1	457.1	632.6	0.036	0.054
Group III	1808.1	2.28	2.46	3098	456.2	29.2	36.2	565.8	1199.1	1715.5	2635.4	756.1	1032.3	0.030	0.070
344	1516.8	1.40	3.93	4181	616.6	40.2	36.5	1329.1	2642.6	2860.9	4485.8	444.1	688.6	0.031	0.133
444	205.8	1.75	2.38	7991	67.0	3.9	4.9	794.9	1097.4	1635.4	2818.8	2963.4	5403.8	0.135	0.147
Group IV	1722.6	1.57	3.15	6085	341.8	22.0	20.7	1062.0	1870.0	2248.2	3652.3	1703.8	3046.2	0.090	0.140

Source: UNIDO Scoreboard database

they essentially have not experienced productivity-driven growth in industrial employment. All are ranked very low on the UNIDO competitiveness indicator in Table 2.[77] This is an anomaly in that many early development modelers actually expected the modernization of industry to "transform" traditional agriculture.[78] This industry-driven transformation did not happen. Note that many of these countries are members of WTO but basically do not have functioning IPR systems. Some have IPR laws but lack mechanisms for enforcement of these laws.[79]

The 1.8 billion people living in the 28 countries in classes 333 and 334 have reached the stage of industrial competitiveness or near competitiveness. They have made the requisite investments in In-Im capacity that can support economic growth in the four-percent range, which is high by global standards. Many actually realize this growth as shown in Table 2. Those not realizing this growth are engaged in civil conflict or suffer from macroeconomic mismanagement.[80] For the largest country in the group, India, growth has been limited by a prior unwillingness to achieve openness.[81]

The 11.7 billion people in the 11 countries in the 344 and 444 classes have invested in the capacity to achieve high economic growth (up to eight percent per capita). As with the 333–334 group, countries not realizing this growth typically suffer from macroeconomic mismanagement, as exemplified by Argentina.[82]

6. The future of agricultural research

Future directions in research differ for developed and developing countries. For developed countries, Gene Revolution (rDNA) techniques will dominate. Gene Revolution products will be produced predominantly in the private sector. The Life Science form of industrial organizations is currently under stress because earnings have fallen short of expectations, and investors in some of the large chemical-pharmaceutical companies argue that the agricultural part of the business should be established as a separate business.[83] One of the

---

[77] This index is explained in UNIDO, Ranking of Economies by the Competitive Industrial Performance Index, 1985 and 1998, Industrial Development Report 2002/2003: Competing through Innovation and Learning 43 (2003).
[78] This was the perspective of the dual economy models. See G.S. TOLLEY & V. THOMAS, THE ECONOMICS OF UBANIZATION AND URBAN POLICIES IN DEVELOPING COUNTRIES (The World Bank 1987).
[79] Juan Carlos Ginarte & Walter G. Park, Determinants of Patent Rights: A Cross-National Study, 26 RES. POL'Y 283 (1997) (ranking economies by enforcement regimes).
[80] See AVILA & EVENSON, above n. 52.   [81] India did engage in reforms in 1991.
[82] The Asian Tiger economies, Hong Kong, Singapore, Taiwan, and South Korea, are no longer considered developing countries in this classification. A number of former Soviet Union Republics have reverted to developing country status, but they are not considered here as well.
[83] See Evenson, above n. 31.

challenges that industrial firms face is to achieve more effective management of licensing IPR-protected techniques.

The expansion of IPRs to cover genetic inventions effectively means that such items are on a par with mechanical-electrical, chemical and pharmaceutical inventions. Public-sector experiment station research will produce some new products and a few new processes. But private biotech firms will be leaders in the production of new products. Thus, the public-sector AES programs will have roles similar to those for mechanical and chemical inventions.

There is little doubt among scientists that the direction of molecular biology science is moving toward supporting biotechnology product invention. The potential for this science-driven (enabled) technology is greatest for the health-pharmaceutical sector, but it is also great for plants and animals.[84] As new plant products are developed, there is considerable scope for bio-energy sources, including bio-fuels. For example, a large part of the corn crop is already being converted to ethanol, and the scope for oil crops is also high. New health products are likely to be produced from crops and animals.

Public sector AES programs will play important roles in the Gene Revolution. The first is to conduct "pre-breeding" studies to identify promising genetic resources (primarily genes) and to refine methods and techniques. Genomic studies and proteomic studies will be undertaken by both public and private programs, but public programs will dominate.[85]

The second role of the public sector will be to inform the regulatory process and to provide policy advice to regulatory bodies. This task will encompass food safety issues and environmental issues. Public-sector university-based research on food safety and environmental issues has more credence than does the R&D of private agricultural biotech firms, and this research is important to the development of accepted regulations.

The situation for developing countries is more complex because the capacity to imitate and innovate is so diverse. Many developing countries lack the private-sector capacity to imitate or copy Gene Revolution products. Many lack IPRs to support imitation or adaptive invention. Interestingly, the capacity to innovate in agriculture is actually more broadly diffused than is the capacity to imitate. This may be seen in Table 2 where the 222–223–233 countries had a Green Revolution but have not reached industrial competitiveness.

The agricultural research future for the countries that had not developed a level-3 capacity by 1961 (55 countries with a population of 975 million) is based on an expansion of the Green Revolution, i.e., on the continued production of generations of MVs and on the extension of MVs to more marginal areas. These gains will primarily be produced by public sector IARC-NARS

---

[84] Id.
[85] See A. Naseem & J.F. Oehmke, *Should the Public Sector Conduct Genomics R&D?*, in THE REGULATION OF AGRICULTURAL BIOTECHNOLOGY, above n. 69.

programs. Private multinational firms are simply not interested in these countries.[86] Some of these countries have realized imitation gains driven by extension programs. Average farm productivity levels in some countries have increased from 60 to 70 percent of the frontier to 70 to 80 percent of the frontier, but this source of productivity has almost been exhausted.[87] Further gains will require moving the frontier forward.

The Gene Revolution actually has promise for Group I and II countries because recombinant DNA techniques are suited to developing host plant traits, such as insect resistance, disease resistance, and drought tolerance, and this science is congruent with the platform–traits strategy of the Green Revolution. But unless the IARCs become more aggressive in producing Gene Revolution products and acquiring IPRs to distribute them in germplasm form, the Gene Revolution remains years away for these countries.

The countries with In-Im level-3 status as of around 1961 are in a different position because they have the capacity to achieve rapid economic growth. This is both because they have realized Green Revolution gains in agriculture and because many have realized industrial competitiveness improvements. Not all have realized "miracle" growth due to military conflicts and macroeconomic mismanagement problems. However, most of these countries are capable of running modern IPR systems, though some are reluctant to do so.

Some of these countries have acquired Im-In capacity through welcoming direct foreign investment, but some of the more xenophobic countries have acquired capacity through inward-looking domestic policies. For example, India paid a price in the form of the "Hindu rate of growth" until the economic reform of the early 1990s produced "Hindu plus" growth in the past several years.[88]

For agricultural research, the Green Revolution will continue to be the central driver of productivity gains for most of the Group III and IV economies. These economies are mechanizing, and marketing systems are changing. Many of these economies are benefiting from importing mechanical and chemical inventions produced abroad.

The traditional IARC-NARS Green Revolution system has been slow to acquire Gene Revolution capacity. The IARCs provided aggressive leadership in the Green Revolution. They are not doing so in the Gene Revolution, in part

---

[86] None of these countries has significant Foreign Direct Investment. *See* United Nations Conference on Trade and Development, World Investment Report 2002 (UNCTAD 2002).

[87] Production frontier measurement has been pioneered by G.E. Battese & T.J. Coelli, *A Model for Technical Inefficiency Effects in a Stochastic Frontier Production Function for Panel Data*, 20 EMPIRICAL ECON. 325 (1995).

[88] India reported ten percent real growth in the first quarter of 2004.

because the CGIAR support system is experiencing declining support and some donors oppose the Gene Revolution.[89]

But several Group III and IV country programs are aggressively building Gene Revolution capacity.[90] This capacity will put them in a position to produce and import Gene Revolution products in the next 20 years. Several countries are already importing the "Genes for Rent" products available in the market (e.g. *Bt* cotton and Glyphosate Tolerant soybeans).

The development of more coherent regulatory rules and practices will influence the possible gains for the Gene Revolution. So will the development of more efficient IPR licensing arrangements. We will probably see some market development for GM-free food markets (especially where the raw material cost share is low, as in margarine), and this will alleviate some of the consumer resistance issues. However, in developing countries there will be long time lags in the diffusion of Gene Revolution products, with the rate of diffusion depending on In-Im capacity.

7. Needed reforms

The diversity between developed and developing countries is important. Group I developing countries lack the institutions to meet anything but the most minimal regulatory conditions. Group II countries do not presently have institutional settings to meet WTO-TRIPS or CBD and related obligations. They could develop them in 20 years or so, but most of these countries still conclude that they can succeed with minimal institutional development. They also imagine that they do not need substantive investments to imitate and acquire technical capability from more developed countries.[91] Unfortunately, this view is misguided. These nations are far from being competitive in industrial production and do not have efficient service sectors. Their only dynamic sector is typically the agricultural sector.

In principle, the WTO-TRIPS requirements should (unless completely avoided) move them in the direction of becoming competitive. These countries do not presently have rDNA or genetic engineering capacity beyond minimal levels, and it will be some time before they acquire it. However, the IARCs could deliver Gene Revolution products to Group II countries if they were more aggressive in bargaining for IPRs on their behalf. Many rDNA products can be

---

[89] Robert E. Evenson, GMOs: Prospects for Increased Crop Productivity in Developing Countries, *presented at* Institute of Food and Agricultural Sciences (IFAS), The Role of GMOs in Trade Disputes (San Antonio Oct. 2003) (discussing reasons for limited IARC activity).

[90] J. Komen et al., *Managing Proprietary Technology in Agricultural Research*, *in* ECONOMIC AND SOCIAL ISSUES IN AGRICULTURAL BIOTECHNOLOGY 193 (Robert E. Evenson et al. eds., CABI Publishing 2002).

[91] Few developing countries emphasize building R&D capacity in industry.

delivered in plants and breeding lines that can then go into conventional breeding programs. An IARC (or some international foundation), for example, could purchase rights to drought-tolerant IPR-protected products and distribute breeding lines to a specified set of NARS programs.

For Group III developing countries, the situation is different. These countries have the institutional capacity to meet international regulatory standards. At present, they do not have the political interests to do so. Most see IPRs as dominated by obligations to pay for foreign inventions that should, in some sense, be "spill-in" gains and available for "free-riding." Almost all of those countries downplay or neglect the potential benefits from stimulating domestic inventions.

Most Group III countries have benefited from foreign direct investment, and they could probably be more demanding of multinational firms by requiring that more R&D programs be located in their countries.[92] These countries may be under the illusion that they can meet WTO-TRIPS conditions easily and build weak breeders' rights programs. But they may not appreciate the full implications of patent protection for biotechnology processes and products outside the "plants and non-human animals" issues in Article 27.3(b). They will also have to address CBD provisions.

Group III countries will continue to be served by Green Revolution gains from public sector IARC-NARS programs. As with Group II, IARCs (or other agencies) could negotiate for IP-protected biotechnology rights for these countries. But suppliers may be reluctant to provide them, especially to countries such as India. Even so, India (which is about to move to Group IV) has the skills and institutions to negotiate on its own. Countries interested in Gene Revolution access in the next 20 years will have to develop the biosafety institutions and the market institutions to support such access.

Group IV developing countries are candidates for using IPRs, biosafety and environmental regulations to their own best advantage. They have the skills, the markets, and the industrial competitiveness (after many years of investment) to realize rapid growth. The implicit penalties from foreign technology suppliers' "withholding access to latest technology" are sufficiently high that this group of countries should have little interest in playing the piracy game. In effect, Group IV countries should actually buy the WIPO-WTO package in pretty much the same form as do the OECD countries.

Finally, for developed countries, many issues must be addressed before the Gene Revolution and WTO issues are resolved. The broad scale "marketing blunders" by the agricultural biotechnology firms in the 1950s have cost the industry dearly. The consumer resentment associated with the battle against labeling likely will result in mandatory labeling and traceability rules. High transaction costs are associated with L&T regulations in the European Union.

---

[92] Many multinational firms do conduct R&D in a number of locations.

The political hostility associated with "Frankenfoods" will be with us for some time, despite the fact that so far there is no evidence of food safety problems. The TRIPS part of WTO is probably not going to be a serious issue among the OECD countries. But the SPS and TBT issues will continue to be unresolved for some time.

COMMENTARY II

Using intellectual property rights to preserve the global genetic commons: The International Treaty on Plant Genetic Resources for Food and Agriculture

LAURENCE R. HELFER[*]

Over the last twenty years, national governments, patent owners, farmers, plant breeders, researchers, and a diverse array of non-governmental organizations (NGOs) have engaged in a vigorous debate over how to conserve and utilize the world's plant genetic diversity. On one side of this debate are advocates of a pure global commons regime, which would allow researchers, breeders, and farmers free and unfettered access to all plant genetic resources (PGRs), including those held in international seed banks, in national collections, and *in situ* on public lands. On the other side are advocates of a private property approach, which seeks to encourage plant-related innovations in agriculture and biotechnology by allowing isolated and modified genetic resources to be owned by patentees and commercial plant breeders. A critical issue in this ongoing controversy concerns the role of intellectual property rights (IPRs), and, in particular, where to draw a boundary between plant genetic materials that must remain in the public domain and those that can be privatized.

Debates over where to fix this boundary date back to the "seed wars" of the early 1980s,[1] during which governments in developing countries pressured the Commission on Genetic Resources for Food and Agriculture (CGRFA) to staunch the flow of PGRs from centers of biodiversity in the developing world to plant breeding industries in industrialized nations.[2] These governments argued that commercial plant breeders were using PGRs to develop new proprietary plant varieties without compensating the countries

---

[*] Laurence R. Helfer is Professor of Law, Vanderbilt University Law School, Nashville, TN.
[1] Jack Kloppenburg, Jr. & Daniel Lee Kleinman, *Seed Wars: Common Heritage, Private Property, and Political Strategy*, 95 SOCIALIST REV. 6 (1987).
[2] *See* JOHN BRAITHWAITE & PETER DRAHOS, GLOBAL BUSINESS REGULATION 405 (2000); MICHEL PETIT ET AL., WHY GOVERNMENTS CAN'T MAKE POLICY: THE CASE OF PLANT GENETIC RESOURCES IN THE INTERNATIONAL ARENA 7 (2002).

that had provided the raw materials for their innovations.[3] In response, the CGRFA adopted a declaration known as the International Undertaking on Plant Genetic Resources ("the Undertaking"),[4] which stated that *all* PGRs – naturally occurring plants, plant materials held in genetic storage banks, and cultivated plant varieties – were part of the "heritage of mankind and consequently should be available without restriction" for scientific research, plant breeding, and conservation.[5] Relying on the Undertaking's open access principle, international gene banks acquired extensive collections of seeds and began to freely grant access to seed samples for research, breeding and training, but barred recipients from claiming IPRs in the materials distributed.[6]

Although the Undertaking was merely a non-binding statement of principles, it was opposed by the United States and some European governments, who argued that the document conflicted not only with a multilateral treaty – the International Union for the Protection of New Varieties of Plants[7] – but

---

[3] *See* Neil D. Hamilton, *Who Owns Dinner: Evolving Legal Mechanisms for Ownership of Plant Genetic Resources*, 28 TULSA L.J. 587, 600–01 (1993). Such uncompensated uses are sometimes referred to as "biopiracy," a term that has been loosely used to refer to any act by which a commercial entity seeks to obtain intellectual property rights over biological resources that are seen as "belonging" to developing states or indigenous communities. *See* CEAS Consultants (Wye) Ltd., Centre for European Agricultural Studies, Final Report for Directorate General Trade, European Commission, Study on the Relationship Between the Agreement on TRIPS and Biodiversity Related Issues 78 (2000).

[4] International Undertaking on Plant Genetic Resources, Report of the Conference of the United Nations Food and Agriculture Organization (FAO), 22d Sess., U.N. Doc. C/83/REP (1983).

[5] *Id.* art. 1. *See id.* art. 5 (stating that governments and institutions adhering to the Undertaking will make samples of PGRs available "free of charge, on the basis of mutual exchange or on mutually agreed terms").

[6] *See* Agreement Between [name of Centre] and the Food and Agriculture Organization of the United Nations (FAO) Placing Collections of Plant Germplasm under the Auspices of FAO, art. 3(a) (1994), *reprinted in* Booklet of CGIAR Centre Policy Instruments, GUIDELINES AND STATEMENTS ON GENETIC RESOURCES, BIOTECHNOLOGY AND INTELLECTUAL PROPERTY RIGHTS 2, 3 (Sept. 2001) (setting forth common texts of agreements between individual CGIAR members and FAO, stating that genetic materials are held "in trust for the benefit of the international community").

A large percentage of the world's total *ex situ* PGRs are held by the International Agricultural Research Centres of the Consultative Group on International Agricultural Research (CGIAR). *See* CGIAR Research: Genebanks and Plant Genetic Resources, http://www.cgiar.org/impact/genebanksdatabases.html (visited 1 Aug. 2004) (noting that CGIAR centers "together maintain over 700,000 samples of crop, forage and agroforestry genetic resources in the public domain").

[7] The International Union for the Protection of New Varieties of Plants ("UPOV") was adopted by several European states in 1961 to recognize and protect *sui generis* intellectual property rights for commercial plant breeders. The acronym UPOV comes from the French, *Union Internationale pour la Protection des Obtentions Végétales*. The treaty, which has been expanded through the adoption of new Acts in 1972, 1978 and 1991, requires states to grant breeders certain exclusive rights to exploit the new plant varieties they create. For an overview of the UPOV's provisions, see Laurence R. Helfer, Intellectual

also with their national patent laws, which grant intellectual property rights in isolated and purified genes.[8] This opposition led to a revision of the Undertaking that attempted (with limited success) to reconcile the common heritage principle with plant breeders' rights.[9]

Faced with growing uncertainty over the regulation and ownership of PGRs, developing countries and NGOs hoping to defend the global commons sought to develop legally binding rules to delineate a clear boundary between public and proprietary genetic resources. The result was seven years of contentious negotiations hosted by the UN Food and Agriculture Organization, which ultimately led to the creation of a new framework agreement: the International Treaty on Plant Genetic Resources for Food and Agriculture (the "PGR Treaty").[10] The PGR Treaty was finalized in November 2001, the same month in which the WTO launched its new round of multilateral trade talks in Doha. The treaty entered into force on 29 June 2004. As of that date, it had been ratified by fifty-five nations and signed by an additional fifty nations. Most of the states parties are developing countries and members of the European Union. The United States has signed but not yet ratified the treaty.[11]

The most noteworthy feature of the PGR Treaty is the novel institutional mechanism it creates to facilitate the exchange of seeds and plant materials for research, breeding, and training. Specifically, the treaty establishes a new "multilateral system" to which member states and their nationals will be granted "facilitated access."[12] The multilateral system is a form of "limited common property"[13] composed of 64 food and feed crops, which account for

---

Property Rights in Plant Varieties: An Overview with Options for National Governments, FAO Legal Papers Online #31, at 12–18 (July 2002), *available at* http://www.fao.org/Legal/prs-ol/paper-e.htm.

[8] *See* DAN LESKIEN & MICHAEL FLINTER, INTELLECTUAL PROPERTY RIGHTS AND PLANT GENETIC RESOURCES: OPTIONS FOR A *SUI GENERIS* SYSTEM 34 (Issues in Genetic Resources, No. 6, at 8) (International Plant Genetics Resources Institute 1997) (reviewing national laws).

[9] *See* Agreed Interpretation of the International Undertaking, Res. 4/89 adopted by FAO Conf. 25th Sess. (11–20 Nov. 1989) ¶ 1 (asserting that plant breeders' rights were "not incompatible" with the common heritage principle).

[10] International Treaty on Plant Genetic Resources for Food and Agriculture, *opened for signature* 3 Nov. 2001, official text *available at* http://www.fao.org/ag/cgrfa/IU.htm [hereinafter PGR Treaty]. *See* Mohamed Ali Mekouar, A Global Instrument on Agrobiodiversity: The International Treaty on Plant Genetic Resources for Food and Agriculture, FAO Legal Papers Online #24, at 3 (Jan. 2002), *available at* http://www.fao.org/Legal/prs-ol/paper-e.htm (stating that the PGR Treaty was "the result of a laborious and lengthy, hard-fought seven-year negotiating process").

[11] *See* International Treaty on Plant Genetic Resources for Food and Agriculture: Participants, *available at* http://www.fao.org/Legal/TREATIES/033s-e.htm (last visited 15 July 2004).

[12] PGR Treaty, above n. 10, arts. 10–13.

[13] Carol M. Rose, *The Several Futures of Property: Of Cyberspace and Folk Tales, Emission Trades and Ecosystems*, 83 MINN. L. REV. 129, 132 (1998) (defining "limited common

the bulk of human nutrition.[14] In exchange for access to this communal seed treasury held in government and international seed banks, private parties that incorporate materials from the multilateral system into commercial products must pay a percentage of their profits to a trust account,[15] which will be used to promote benefit-sharing and conservation of PGRs, particularly with regard to farmers in developing countries.[16]

The new PGR Treaty is thus the first binding international agreement to expressly recognize the public domain status of certain genetic materials, and to create a concrete, mandatory funding mechanism to preserve the global genetic commons. These are important points of departure from the Convention on Biological Diversity (CBD), which recognizes states' sovereign right to control the PGRs within their borders and to regulate their use through national access laws and bilateral contracts with seed and pharmaceutical companies.[17]

Although states reached consensus on the broad architecture of the new seed treaty, they strongly disagreed about the details. The drafters understood that tension exists between a principle of open access to genetic resources and the grant of proprietary rights in such resources. Specifically, they saw that the treaty's success hinged on allowing private parties to commercialize follow-on innovations based on the raw genetic materials acquired from the multilateral system. Only through such commercialization would sufficient revenue be generated to fund the treaty's benefit-sharing and conservation goals. However, the multilateral system itself would be threatened if large parts of the seed treasury could be privatized through the grant of IPRs.

The core of the debate focused on whether to bar patenting of isolated and purified genes extracted from seeds placed in the common seed pool. In the final round of negotiations, governments adopted article 12.3(d), which states that access to the multilateral system will only be provided on the condition that:

---

property" as "property held as commons amongst the members of a group, but exclusively vis-à-vis the outside world").

[14] PGR Treaty, above n. 10, Annex I (listing 35 food and 29 feed crops).

[15] Payments are mandatory when the commercialized product has limits on its availability for use in further research and breeding, and voluntary when the product is freely available for such purposes.

[16] Different types of benefit sharing mechanisms are provided for under the PGR Treaty. These include the exchange of information, access to and transfer of technology, capacity building, and the sharing of benefits arising from commercialization. See Philippe Cullet, The International Treaty on Plant Genetic Resources for Food and Agriculture, IELRC Briefing Paper No. 2003–2, at 4, available at http://www.ielrc.org/content/f0302.htm.

[17] Convention on Biological Diversity (CBD), 5 June 1992, UNEP/Bio.Div./N7-INC5/4, 31 I.L.M. 818 (1993). The CBD was opened for signature in May 1992 and entered into force in December 1993. As of December 2002, 187 states had ratified the Convention. See Parties to the Convention on Biological Diversity, available at http://www.biodiv.org/world/parties.asp.

> Recipients shall *not* claim any intellectual property or other rights that limit the facilitated access to [PGRs], or their genetic parts or components, in the form received from the multilateral system.[18]

A brief explanation of the final stages of the treaty's negotiating history is essential to deciphering this rather cryptic text.

The two distinct clauses at the end of the article – "their genetic parts or components" and "in the form received from the multilateral system" – were included as separate bracketed text going into the final round of negotiations. Developing states and NGOs that opposed patent protection sought to retain the first clause and delete the second, whereas the United States wanted the first deleted and the second retained. As a compromise, the delegates voted to retain *both* clauses after defeating a proposal by the United States to delete article 12.3(d) from the treaty altogether.[19]

The critical issue for interpreting article 12.3(d) is just how far a seed's genetic blueprint must be modified so that the resulting genetic material is no longer "in the form" received from the multilateral system. Most observers agree that a new plant variety or extracted genes as incorporated into such a variety would be sufficiently distinct to qualify for IPR protection. A more contentious question is whether merely isolating and extracting a gene from a seed, without more, constitutes a sufficient alteration of genetic material. Some NGOs active in the treaty's negotiation have argued that the IPR ban extends even to DNA fragments isolated from their natural state.[20] But this approach conflicts with the position of the United States, the E.U., Canada, and Australia, who addressed the article's textual ambiguity by entering on the official record interpretive statements that nothing in the treaty conflicts with IPRs recognized under national laws and international intellectual property agreements, such as the TRIPS Agreement.[21]

One way to help resolve these conflicting constructions would be for the PGR Treaty's Governing Body, the new intergovernmental entity charged with implementing the treaty and monitoring compliance by member states, to collaborate with officials negotiating in the WTO's Doha Round. The issues the Governing Body will face when it begins operations (likely in late 2004) represent considerable challenges. Highlighted below are three of the many difficult tasks this new institution will confront.

---

[18] PGR Treaty, above n. 10, art. 12.3(d) (emphasis added). This same ban must be included in standardized Material Transfer Agreements that all private parties seeking to access the multilateral system must execute. *Id.* art. 12.4.
[19] For a discussion of the negotiating history, see Helfer, above n. 7, at 51.
[20] Some NGOs have gone even further, arguing against both the patenting of isolated genes and the commercialization of genetic resources generally. *See* GRAIN, The International Treaty on Plant Genetic Resources: A Challenge for Asia 5, 7 (Feb. 2002).
[21] *See* Verbatim Record, Food and Agriculture Organization Conference, 31st sess., 4th Plenary Meeting, 3 Nov. 2001, C 2001/PV/4.

First, it must draft "material transfer agreements."[22] Those who receive PGRs from the multilateral system must sign contracts that specify the permissible uses of the plant materials. But the terms of these contracts have yet to be negotiated, including such key issues as: (1) the scope of IPR protection in derivative products; (2) which acts of commercialization trigger an obligation to contribute to the treaty's trust account, and in what amount; and (3) the procedures to be adopted for tracking compliance.

To aid the Governing Body in this drafting work, the Commission on Genetic Resources has convened a panel of experts to recommend terms to be included in a standard material transfer agreement.[23] This is a formidable task, but these experts need not reinvent the wheel; they should build upon the work of other advisory bodies, such as the World Intellectual Property Organization's (WIPO) Intergovernmental Committee on Intellectual Property and Genetic Resources, Traditional Knowledge and Folklore, which has spent the last two years studying the IPR provisions of material transfer agreements.[24]

---

[22] Material Transfer Agreements (MTAs), sometimes referred to as biodiversity prospecting contracts, are agreements between national governments or indigenous peoples that own or control access to genetic resources and a commercial entity that seeks access to those resources. See Helfer, above n. 7, at 10. They "consist of enforceable agreements between the provider and recipient of the transferred genetic materials which create specific rights and obligations for each party." Intergovernmental Committee on Intellectual Property and Genetic Resources, Traditional Knowledge and Folklore, Second Session (10–14 Dec. 2001), Operational Principles for Intellectual Property Clauses of Contractual Agreements Concerning Access to Genetic Resources and Benefit-Sharing, WIPO/GRTKF/IC/2/3 ¶ 4 (10 Sept. 2001).

[23] First Meeting of the Commission on Genetic Resources for Food and Agriculture acting as Interim Committee of the ITPGR, CGRFA-MIC-1/02/REP, Annex D (9–11 Oct. 2002) (setting forth terms of reference for the expert group on the terms of the standard material transfer agreement). Issues the expert group will consider include: (1) "what should be the level, form and manner of payments in line with commercial practice;" (2) "what constitutes commercialisation;" (3) what constitutes incorporation of material accessed from the Multilateral System; and (4) "by what means will the MTA ensure the application of Article 12.3."

The difficult negotiating issues that the expert's group will face were foreshadowed by the Commission's negotiation of a draft interim Material Transfer Agreement to be used by International Agricultural Research Centers pending the entry in force of the new treaty. The draft agreement essentially mirrors the text of article 12.3(d) without resolving its ambiguities. See Ninth Regular Session of the Commission on Genetic Resources for Food and Agriculture, CGRFA-9/02/REP Appendix E, (14–18 Oct. 2002).

[24] For a detailed review of the IGC's work and supporting documents, see http://www.wipo.org/globalissues/index.html. See also Operational Principles for Intellectual Property Clauses of Contractual Agreements Concerning Access to Genetic Resources and Benefit-Sharing, WIPO/GRTKF/IC/2/3 (10 Sept. 2001).

The Conference of the Parties to the Convention on Biological Diversity has also recently considered the elements to be included in Material Transfer Agreements. See

Second, the Governing Body must decide whether to expand the multilateral system. As stated earlier, the PGR treaty covers only a selection of the world's food and feed crops. Other crops were excluded from the treaty at the urging of biodiversity-rich states, who hoped to reap unilateral gains through bioprospecting contracts and national access laws. But the treaty's crop list is not static, and the Governing Body can propose amendments to expand the list. Whether member states will agree to such an expansion may depend on whether the treaty's funding mechanisms generate tangible financial benefits for those developing states with the most to lose from relinquishing their claim to sovereignty over genetic resources.[25]

Third, the Governing Body must consider the incentives for private parties to enter the multilateral system. At present, the treaty covers only PGRs in international seed banks and PGRs controlled by governments. But it also encourages private parties and non-profit institutions (such as plant breeders, universities, and botanical gardens) to contribute their own seed collections to the system.[26] If private parties fail to contribute, the Governing Body may consider denying them access to the communal seed treasury.[27]

Bonn Guidelines on Access to Genetic Resources and Fair and Equitable Sharing of the Benefits Arising Out of their Utilization, Decision VI/24 on Access and Benefit-sharing as Related to Genetic Resources, Appendix I: Suggested Elements for Material Transfer Agreements, *in* Decisions Adopted by the Conference of the Parties to the Convention on Biological Diversity at its Sixth Meeting (7–19 Apr. 2002), *available at* http.www.biodiv.org/decisions/default.asp?lg=0&m=cop-06.

[25] For a pessimistic assessment of the financial benefits the treaty will generate, see Robert J. L. Lettington, The International Undertaking on Plant Genetic Resources in the Context of TRIPS and the CBD, International Center for Trade and Sustainable Development, Bridges: Between Trade and Development, Year 5, No. 6, at 11–13 (July-Aug. 2001) ("These provisions are extremely unlikely to generate substantial funds, the seed industry is simply not that profitable a business in global terms, and the likely royalty rate that industry will accept is going to be low, probably substantially less than one percent of sales.").

[26] Three basic categories of plant genetic resources for food and agriculture (PGRFA) are covered by the multilateral system. The first includes material held under the management and control of the states party to the PGR Treaty. This would include national collections and *in situ* resources found on public property. It is also likely to be understood so as to include *in situ* plant genetic resources found on private land in states that vest the rights to genetic resources in the state rather than in the landowner. The second category is the *ex situ* collections of the Consultative Group on International Agricultural Research (CGIAR) and other international institutions that agree to submit their collections to the authority of the Governing Body, an arrangement similar to that which is currently in force between FAO and twelve CGIAR centers. The final category is other private collections whose owners are to be encouraged to submit them to the authority of the Governing Body. *See id.* at 11–12.

[27] PGR Treaty, above n. 10, art. 11.

Each of these three open issues is likely to prove contentious. It remains to be seen whether governments have the will to cooperate – both within the institutional framework of the PGR Treaty and with other intergovernmental bodies – to preserve the global genetic commons and the plant genetic diversity on which the world has come to depend.

PART II

Innovation and technology transfer in a protectionist environment

SECTION 1
Technology transfer under international intellectual property standards

8

Can the TRIPS Agreement foster technology transfer to developing countries?

CARLOS M. CORREA*

Introduction
I.   Transfer of technology and IPRs
II. Technology transfer in the TRIPS agreement
     A. Objectives and principles
     B. Control of anti-competitive practices in contractual licenses
     C. Disclosure of patent information
     D. Compulsory licenses
         1. Lack of or insufficient working
         2. Refusal to deal
     E. Compulsory licenses as vehicles for technology transfer
III. Transfer of technology to least developed countries (LDCs)
IV. Conclusions

Introduction

Since the 1970s, developing countries have expressed in various international fora their preoccupation about access to foreign technologies as a means of enhancing their technological capabilities[1] and of narrowing the deep North-South gap in development levels. In response, developed countries argued during the Uruguay Round negotiations that strengthening and expanding the protection of intellectual property rights (IPRs) was a key condition to promote increased flows of technology transfer to developing countries. This argument has been repeatedly articulated by TRIPS enthusiasts and the industries that most benefit from the international rules set forth in the TRIPS Agreement.[2]

---

* Carlos M. Correa is Director of the Center on Interdisciplinary Studies on Industrial Property and Economics, University of Buenos Aires, Argentina, and Director of the South Center Project on Intellectual Property and Development, Geneva, Switzerland.
[1] The pre-TRIPS proposal to adopt an International Code of Conduct on Transfer of Technology clearly illustrated this concern. See S. PATEL ET AL., INTERNATIONAL TECHNOLOGY TRANSFER: THE ORIGINS AND AFTERMATH OF THE UNITED NATIONS NEGOTIATIONS ON A DRAFT CODE OF CONDUCT (Kluwer Law International 2000).
[2] Agreement on Trade-Related Aspects of Intellectual Property Rights, 15 Apr. 1994, Marrakesh Agreement Establishing the World Trade Organization, Annex 1C, LEGAL

Developing countries, however, have become increasingly skeptical about the existence of a virtuous relationship between IPRs and technology transfer. This skepticism underpins the request by these countries to establish a Working Group on Trade and Technology Transfer in the WTO, as agreed upon by the Doha Ministerial Conference, in November 2001.[3]

A number of studies have been conducted to assess the impact of IPRs on technology transfer.[4] However, the available evidence is limited and ambiguous, as is the case with regard to studies of the implications of IPR regimes on the flows of foreign direct investment. Some countries with "weak" IPR protection schemes, such as South Korea, Taiwan, Brazil, had been among the major technology borrowers in the pre-TRIPS era. The reverse situation can also be found. Countries (including many African countries) with standards of protection comparable to those in force in developed countries have recorded a poor or insignificant performance as technology importers. The simple explanation is, of course, that IPRs are but one of many factors – and arguably not the most important factor – that affect cross borders flows of technology.[5]

This chapter briefly considers, first, the relationship between IPRs and technology transfer,[6] and second, it explores different aspects of the TRIPS Agreement that are relevant to technology transfer. Although there are many aspects of domestic IP laws still subject to national discretion that may influence the extent of technology transfer and the power of third parties to gain access to foreign technologies,[7] this chapter focuses on the international rules contained in that Agreement.

INSTRUMENTS – RESULTS OF THE URUGUAY ROUND vol. 31, 33 I.L.M. 81 (1994) [hereinafter TRIPS Agreement].

[3] WT / MINCO1 / DEC / W / 2 (14 NOV. 2001).

[4] *See, esp.* KEITH MASKUS, INTELLECTUAL PROPERTY RIGHTS IN THE GLOBAL ECONOMY (Institute for International Economics 2000); *see also* Keith E. Maskus & Jerome H. Reichman, *The Globalization of Private Knowledge Goods and the Privatization of Global Public Goods* [this volume].

[5] A few studies that attempt to assess the weight of IPRs (in general) on transfer of technology decisions indicate that they generally are of medium importance. Thus, an OECD survey on international technology licensing named limited or unsatisfactory protection of industrial property rights as one of the three main problems and disincentives associated with licensing in less developed countries (rank 3, cited by 75 percent of respondents) after foreign exchange controls and government regulations on transfer of technology agreements. OECD, INTERNATIONAL LICENSING: SURVEY RESULTS (1987). Another OECD study of the computer software industry found that the lack of legal protection was considered by firms to be of "medium importance" (20–38% of respondents). OECD, THE INTERNATIONALIZATION OF SOFTWARE AND COMPUTER SERIVCES (1989). These perceptions may have changed, however, since the 1990s, as IPRs became a more important concern for many firms.

[6] Although other forms of transfer are not excluded, this chapter focuses on the transfer of technology by means of licensing and other contractual arrangements between unrelated firms.

[7] Such as the breadth of patent claims and the inventive step standard used to examine patent applications. However, residual domestic discretion in these matters may be substantially reduced if the current negotiations at WIPO concerning the harmonization of substantive

I. Transfer of technology and IPRs

Process improvements are common in firms working with mature technologies that mainly compete on a price basis. In areas where competition relies on product differentiation, product improvement is crucial. In most developing countries, however, R&D at the firm level is very limited. Technological change is substantially limited to "minor" or "incremental" innovations leading to process or product improvements.

The transfer of foreign technology, in the form of capital goods, turn-key plants, licenses and technical assistance, has constituted an important source of innovation for developing countries. Technology transfer has been, and will continue to be, one of the main mechanisms through which developing countries may advance their industrialization processes.[8] In fact, the flows of foreign technologies explain to a great extent the dynamics of the national innovation systems at different stages of industrialization.[9]

Based on Schumpeter's lucid insights, the evolutionary theory of innovation has shown that scientific inputs play a growing role in the innovative process,[10] and that a significant part of innovation originates from learning by doing, including tacit and non-tacit components. Crucial to this theory is the concept that knowledge is "localized" at the level of particular firms, and that it evolves and is accumulated as the firms gain experience in its application and improve upon it.[11] The evolutionary theory also indicates that technological change

---

patent laws were to succeed. *See, e.g.,* C. Correa & S. Musungu, The WIPO Patent Agenda: The Risks for Developing Countries, South Center TRADE Working Paper No. 12 (2002).

[8] *See generally* S. RADOSEVIC, INTERNATIONAL TECHNOLOGY TRANSFER AND CATCH-UP IN ECONOMIC DEVELOPMENT (Edward Elgar Pub. 1999); THE ECONOMICS OF TECHNOLOGY TRANSFER (Sanjaya Lall ed., Elgar Reference Collection 2002).

[9] *See, e.g.,* L. Kim & K. Dahlman, *Technology Policy for Industrialization: An Integrative Framework and Korea's Experience,* 21 RES. POL'Y 437 (1992). A "national innovation system" may be defined as the set of institutions whose interactions determine the innovative performance of national firms. *See, e.g.,* NATIONAL INNOVATION SYSTEMS (R. Nelson ed., Oxford University Press 1993).

[10] *See* J. SCHUMPETER, THE THEORY OF ECONOMIC DEVELOPMENT (Harvard University Press 1934); J. SCHUMPETER, CAPITALISM, SOCIALISM AND DEMOCRACY (5th ed., George Allen & Unwin Publ. Ltd. 1943). However, a clear distinction must be made between the role of technology, on the one hand, and of scientific knowledge, on the other. Innovation depends on the actual capacity to understand and implement technologies for production. Science may certainly constitute a source for innovation, but technical capacity and investment are required to transform scientific outputs into commercially viable products and processes. Access to science cannot be equated to access to technology, even if it is often a first step on the path to modern forms of innovation.

[11] The *cumulative* nature of innovative capacity implies the possibility of different paths in the learning process, and it predicts major obstacles for closing the technology gap merely "by leaps," as the "leapfrogging theory" had erroneously suggested. *See, e.g.,* C. Pérez & L. Soete, *Catching up in Technology: Entry Barriers and Windows of Opportunity, in* TECHNICAL CHANGE AND ECONOMIC THEORY (G. Dosi et al. eds., Pinter 1988).

follows certain "trajectories" within a given "technological paradigm," and it recognizes the relationship existing between technology and investment. The process of technology learning is far from automatic; it requires a careful and deliberate resource allocation. Innovation is related to investment both in capital goods and in intangibles (e.g. research and development, software) in differing combinations that depend on the type of technology employed.[12]

These observations have significant implications for the process of technology transfer to developing countries.[13] Technology is not just information that can be easily communicated (as Solow postulated),[14] but its transfer requires a capacity to learn and investment to incorporate it into the firm's production system. Not surprisingly, developed-country firms account for the bulk of international transfer of technology. Relatively advanced firms in South Korea, Taiwan, and other newly industrialized countries have been able to benefit more from that mechanism than firms in poorer countries.[15]

In addition to factors that limit access to technology on the demand side, firms that possess technology often have little incentive to transfer it to developing countries. First, the globalization of the economy and the extensive liberalization of markets in developing countries allow technology owners to directly export innovative products without resorting to foreign direct investments or licensing. Second, innovative firms are particularly reluctant to transfer technology that may help a potential licensee to become a competitor in the global market,[16] or when they perceive a risk of "leakage" leading to imitation. Third, for a licensing out operation to be attractive, the recipient's market and expected profit should at least compensate the licensor for his transaction costs and risks. While some companies license out their technologies either to enrich themselves at the expense of the competition or to put

---

[12] See, e.g., RICHARD NELSON & SIDNEY WINTER, AN EVOLUTIONARY THEORY OF ECONOMIC CHANGE (The Belknap Press of Harvard University Press 1982); G. DOSI, TECHNICAL CHANGE AND INDUSTRIAL TRANSFORMATION (MacMillan 1984); C. Freeman & C. Perez, The Diffusion of Technical Innovations and Changes of Techno-Economic Paradigm, Paper Presented at Conference on Innovation Diffusion, Venice (1986).

[13] See, e.g., Charles Cooper, Relevance of Innovation Studies to Developing Countries, in TECHNOLOGY AND INNOVATION IN THE INTERNATIONAL ECONOMY 1 (Charles Cooper ed., Edward Edgard United Nations University Press 1994).

[14] In the 1950s, Solow assumed technology to be easily accessible to everyone. See Robert Solow, Technical Change and the Aggregate Production Function, 39 REV. ECON. & STAT. 312 (1957); Robert Solow, Growth Theory and After, 78 AM. ECON. REV. 307 (1988). Under Solow's assumption, all countries might share the same pool of technology and, hence, should have the same opportunities to grow.

[15] See, e.g., UNCTAD, FOSTERING TECHNOLOGICAL DYNAMISM: EVOLUTION OF THOUGHT ON TECHNOLOGICAL DEVELOPMENT PROCESSES AND COMPETITIVENESS: A REVIEW OF THE LITERATURE (1996).

[16] See, e.g., C. Correa, Trends in Technology Transfer – Implications for Developing Countries, 21 SCI. & PUB. POL'Y 369 (1994).

potentially competing licensees in a strategically disadvantageous position (so long as the license keeps them from developing their own technologies), others more opportunistically seek income from non-strategic technological assets.[17]

Does the availability of effective IPR protection provide foreign companies an added incentive to transfer their protected technologies to developing countries? Where cutting-edge and easy to imitate technologies are at stake, such as in the case of biotechnology-based products, and where "tacit," non-codified knowledge is an essential component of the technology package, transfer is more likely to take place if it is bundled with patents and other IPRs. If protection of such rights and of trade secrets in the potential borrowing country is weak, owners are unlikely to enter into transfer of technology contracts. The lack or insufficient protection of IPRs may actually discourage technology transfer in such circumstances. But the appropriability problem must not be overstated: fairly simple and robust contracts can accomplish, in the absence of specific IP protection, an efficient transfer of know-how.[18]

The availability (and enforceability) of IPRs will, by no means, create a sufficient incentive for the transfer of technology to occur. As explained below, moreover, strong IP protection can sometimes make access to technology more problematic, rather than facilitating it. In fact, once the patent monopoly is relaxed, "competition drastically changes the incentives for an incumbent to license its technology to potential entrants. In particular, when there are multiple technology holders, not only do they compete in the product market, but they also compete in the market for technology."[19]

To the extent that an IP right-holder can control the use of his technology, he can decide when, where and how to use it and, particularly, whether to transfer it or not to foreign subsidiaries or unaffiliated companies. IPRs give the right-holders the power (not absolute, however, as discussed below) to choose the ways in which technology can be utilized, if at all, in those countries where protection has been obtained. In some cases, increased IP protection may lead foreign firms to close down manufacturing facilities in developing countries, so long as they can safely export protected products from other sites.[20] The experience of the pharmaceutical industries in some Latin American countries after product patent protection was introduced for medicines suggests that this effect is real and not mere speculation.[21]

---

[17] *See, e.g.*, Patrick Sullivan, *Key Terms and Strategic Positioning, in* TECHNOLOGY LICENSING: CORPORATE STRATEGIES FOR MAXIMIZING VALUE 17–23 (John Wiley & Sons 1996).

[18] *See, e.g.*, ASHISH ARORA ET AL., MARKETS FOR TECHNOLOGY: THE ECONOMICS OF INNOVATION AND CORPORATE STRATEGY 93 (MIT Press 2001).

[19] *Id.* at 195.

[20] *See, e.g.*, Sanjaya Lall, Indicators of the Relative Importance of IPRs in Developing Countries, ICTSD/UNCTAD Issue Paper No. 3, at 8 (2001).

[21] *See, e.g.*, Carlos Correa, *Reforming the Intellectual Property Rights System in Latin America*, 23 THE WORLD ECON. 851 (2000).

IPRs also allow right holders to charge royalties higher than those they would have obtained in the absence of protection. High royalties can make technology unaffordable for local firms, or reduce the resources available for local R&D. In addition, since royalty levels increase the costs of production, borrowing firms may find it more difficult to compete, particularly in an open, globalized market. High levels of IP protection can also deepen negotiating imbalances and lead to the imposition of abusive practices that restrain competition.[22]

II. Technology transfer in the TRIPS agreement

Several provisions of the TRIPS Agreement (e.g., articles 7, 8.2, 40 and 66.1) specifically refer to technology transfer.[23] Other aspects regulated by the Agreement (disclosure, compulsory licenses) may also have implications for the transfer of technology.[24]

A. *Objectives and principles*

The negotiation of the TRIPS Agreement confronted two diverging approaches with regard to the role of IPRs. The primary objective of the proponents of the Agreement was to secure the rights of intellectual property owners to exploit, at their own discretion, their protected assets. They emphasized the *protection* of intellectual property rights as such, and not their effective exploitation by the title holders themselves or by third parties.

In contrast, developing countries were concerned about the relationship between IPRs and access to, and transfer of, technology. Their representatives approached these negotiations with a clear understanding of their weakness in the generation of new science and technology. At the time the negotiations took place, only a very small fraction of world expenditure on R&D was accounted for by those countries. The situation is not too different today, as shown in Table 1. Ten developed countries account for 84 percent of global resources spent on R&D annually, control 94 percent of the technological output in terms of patents taken out in the United States, and receive 91 percent of global cross-border royalties and technology license fees.

The developing countries' concerns about the implications of stronger IPRs for transfer of technology received some, but limited attention during the Uruguay Round negotiations. Overall, the TRIPS Agreement reflects the

---

[22] An abundant literature has dealt with restrictive practices in licensing agreements. *See, e.g.,* ALAN GUTTERMAN, INNOVATION AND COMPETITION POLICY: A COMPARATIVE STUDY OF REGULATION OF PATENT LICENSING AND COLLABORATIVE RESEARCH & DEVELOPMENT IN THE UNITED STATES AND THE EUROPEAN COMMUNITY 217–326 (Kluwer Law International 1997).
[23] *See* TRIPS Agreement, above n. 2, arts. 7, 8.2, 40, 66.1.
[24] *See id.* arts. 29, 31.

Table 1: *Major source countries of technologies in the world (2000)*[25]

Country	R&D Expenditure		US Patents taken, 1977–2000		Technology fees received (1997)	
	$ billion	% of total	'000	% of total	$ billion	% of total
USA	212.8	40.8	1337	57	33.8	42.2
Japan	90.1	17.3	429.4	18	6.9	8.6
Germany	42	8.0	173.8	7	11.9	14.9
France	28.1	5.4	68.2	3	2.2	2.7
UK	22.6	4.3	67.4	3	5.8	7.2
Italy	12.1	2.3	29	1	1.6	2.0
Canada	11.4	2.2	48.4	2	1.3	1.6
Netherlands	7.5	1.4	22	1	6.2	7.7
Sweden	7.1	1.4	22.9	1	0.4	0.5
Switzerland	4.8	0.9	31	1	2.8	3.5
Subtotal 10	438.5	84.0	2229.1	94	72.9	91.0
World	522	100.0	2364.9	100	80.1	100.0

high-protectionist paradigm advocated by the United States and other developed countries. Thus, the Preamble to the Agreement does not contain any reference to transfer of technology. The negotiating parties expressed "the need to promote effective and adequate protection of intellectual property rights" but not to promote its transfer.[26] The consideration of "underlying public policy objectives" including "developmental and technological objectives," can be read to relate only to "the national systems for the protection of intellectual property" and not more generally to innovation systems.[27]

---

[25] *Reproduced from* Nagesh Kumar, Intellectual Property Rights, Technology and Economic Development: Experiences of Asian Countries, Study prepared for the Commission on Intellectual Property Rights (CIPR) (2002).

[26] TRIPS Agreement, above n. 2, Preamble, para. 1. However, they did take pains to ensure that "measures and procedures to enforce intellectual property rights do not themselves become barriers to legitimate trade." *Id.*

[27] *Id.*, para. 5. However, the tradition in the U.S. is to incorporate users' rights, and the appropriate level of competition into the calculus of "underlying policy objectives of national [IP] systems," by a balancing of public and private interests. Hence, even this paragraph could elicit an interpretation unfavorable to developing countries. *Cf.* Maskus & Reichman, above n. 4 (stressing need for WTO panels to balance goals of TRIPS against pro-competitive goals of GATT and to consider the critical role of public goods in incipient transnational system of innovation).

However, article 7 of the Agreement did more explicitly reflect some of the developing countries' concerns about this matter:

> The protection and enforcement of intellectual property rights should contribute to the promotion of technological innovation and to *the transfer and dissemination of technology*, to the mutual advantage of producers and users of technological knowledge and in a manner conducive to social and economic welfare, and to the balance of rights and obligations.[28]

Because article 7 states that IPRs "*should*" contribute to the promotion of technological innovation and to the transfer and dissemination of technology, some observers have read "should" to mean that article 7 is a mere hortary provision. However, it rather seems to indicate that IPRs do not necessarily promote innovation and the dissemination and transfer of technology, but that they should do so. Members must accordingly implement their obligations under the Agreement in a way that effectively contributes to those objectives.

Moreover, even if article 7 is not viewed as an operative provision, it does provide guidance to WTO panels and the Appellate Body. The interpretation of the Agreement's provisions must be made in accordance with customary rules of public international law.[29] Article 31 of the Vienna Convention on the Law of Treaties[30] – deemed by GATT/WTO jurisprudence as a codification of such rules[31] – explicitly requires consideration of the "purpose" of the treaty. If the Agreement itself contains a definition of its purpose, as article 7 provides, panels and the Appellate Body cannot ignore it in interpreting other provisions of the Agreement.

The panel report in *Canada – Patent Protection for Pharmaceutical Products* (relating to the so-called "Bolar" exception) was particularly important in clarifying the weight to be given to the "Objectives" (article 7) (as well as the "Principles" contained in article 8) when interpreting the Agreement's other provisions. The panel stated that

> Obviously, the exact scope of article 30's authority will depend on the specific meaning given to its limiting conditions. The words of those conditions must be examined with particular care on this point. Both the goals and the limitations stated in articles 7 and 8.1 must obviously be

---

[28] TRIPS Agreement, above n. 2, art. 7.
[29] *See* Marrakesh Agreement Establishing the World Trade Organization, 15 Apr. 1994, Annex 2, Understanding on Rules and Procedures Governing the Settlement of Disputes [hereinafter DSU], 33 I.L.M. 1126, art. 3.2.
[30] Vienna Convention on the Law of Treaties, *entered into force* 27 Jan. 1980, 1155 U.N.T.S. 331, 8 I.L.M 679 (1969).
[31] *See, e.g.*, Daya Shanker, *The Vienna Convention on the Law of Treaties, the Dispute Settlement System of the WTO and the Doha Declaration on the TRIPS Agreement*, 36 J. WORLD TRADE 721 (2002).

borne in mind when doing so as well as those of other provisions of the TRIPS Agreement which indicate its object and purposes.[32]

Of course, the "purpose" of the Agreement may be understood differently depending on particular philosophical or ideological positions,[33] but article 7 nonetheless establishes a rule that cannot be substituted by the personal opinions of panels or the Appellate Body. The *Canadian Pharmaceutical Products* panel report is questionable in this regard. The panel there elaborated its own conception of the "policy" underpinning the domestic patent laws, focusing entirely on the interests and expectations of patent owners.[34] The panel thus overlooked the fact that the dissemination and transfer of knowledge are public policy objectives as important as the promotion of innovation itself.[35]

Understandably, developing countries have attached considerable interpretive importance to article 7 (as well as to article 8), as indicated in the Doha Declaration on the TRIPS Agreement and Public Health,[36] which these countries actively promoted. Paragraph 5(a) of this Declaration states that

> In applying the customary rules of interpretation of public international law, each provision of the TRIPS Agreement shall be read in the light of the object and purpose of the Agreement as expressed, in particular, in its objectives and principles.[37]

Article 8.2 is also an important provision for the discussion of transfer of technology in the context of the TRIPS Agreement. It recognizes the need to adopt "appropriate measures" to prevent "the resort to practices which adversely affect the international transfer of technology." There is a caveat, however, that limits the reach of possible State measures: they must be "consistent with the provisions" of the Agreement.[38]

Although article 8.2 addresses the right of Members to adopt legislation aimed at correcting certain practices of IPRs owners, it is not limited to the

---

[32] *See* Canada – Patent Protection for Pharmaceutical Products, WT/DS114/R ¶ 7.26 (WTO Dispute Settlement Panel 2000).
[33] Although article 31 of the Vienna Convention essentially mandates a literal interpretation, it does not exclude teleological elements. It is difficult, in fact, to think of judgments that are absolutely neutral in terms of policy objectives.
[34] "The normal practice of exploitation by patent owners, as with owners of any other intellectual property right, is to exclude all forms of competition that could detract significantly from the economic returns anticipated from a patent's grant of market exclusivity... Patent laws establish a carefully defined period of market exclusivity as an inducement to innovation, and the policy of those laws cannot be achieved unless patent owners are permitted to take effective advantage of that inducement once it has been defined." Canada – Patent Protection for Pharmaceutical Products, above n. 32, ¶ 7.55.
[35] *See, e.g.*, P. WELFENS ET AL., GLOBALIZATION, ECONOMIC GROWTH AND INNOVATION DYNAMICS 138 (Springer 1999). *See also* Maskus & Reichman, above n. 4.
[36] *See* WTO, Doc. WT/MIN(01)/DEC/W/2 (14 Nov. 2001).
[37] *Id.* para. 5(a).   [38] TRIPS Agreement, above n. 2, art. 8.2.

control of restrictive practices in voluntary licensing agreements, as stipulated in article 40.[39] For instance, unreasonably high royalties may deter the transfer of technology and – as many developing countries did in the past under "transfer of technology" laws[40] – Members may establish policies to deal with technology pricing and other aspects of transfer of technology transactions.[41] Nevertheless, the extent to which such policies, if adopted, may be successful remains unclear, given that technology owners, in principle, enjoy under IPRs the right to refuse to transfer their technologies.[42]

B. *Control of anti-competitive practices in contractual licenses*

Section 8 of the TRIPS Agreement contains a set of rules aimed at the "control of anti-competitive practices" in voluntary licenses.[43] These rules may be regarded as one of the few concrete applications in the Agreement of the general principle set out in article 8.2.[44]

The text of article 40.1 recognizes that some licensing practices pertaining to intellectual property rights that restrain competition "may have adverse effects on trade and impede the transfer and dissemination of technology."[45] As drafted, this principle is wider in scope than article 8.2 in the sense that it includes "dissemination" in addition to technology transfer. In contrast, article 40.1 is worded more restrictively to the extent that the practices considered are only those that "impede" such a transfer or dissemination (and not necessarily those which "adversely affect" them).[46]

Article 40.2 is an unusual provision in the context of the TRIPS Agreement. Unlike most other provisions in the Agreement, it does not contain specific

---

[39] *Id.* art. 40.
[40] *See, e.g.*, Carlos Correa, *Innovation and Technology Transfer in Latin America: A Review of Recent Trends and Policies*, 10 INT'L J. TECH. MGMT. 815.
[41] Questions may arise as to the threat posed by possible "non-violation" complaints in the case of measures regulating certain aspects of licensing agreements. However, the admissibility of such complaints in the context of TRIPS is still under debate. There are solid reasons to consider that they should not be admitted.
[42] *See* the discussion on "refusal to deal" below.
[43] TRIPS Agreement, above n. 2, Section 8: Control of Anticompetitive Practices in Contractual Licenses, is implemented in a single article, *viz.*, art. 40, which interfaces with art. 8. For an analysis of this section, see Pedro Roffe, *Control of Anticompetitive Practices in Contractual Licenses Under the TRIPS Agreement*, in INTELLECTUAL PROPERTY AND INTERNATIONAL TRADE: THE TRIPS AGREEMENT (Kluwer Law International 1998); Hans Ullrich, *Expansionist Intellectual Property Protection and Reductionist Competition Rules: A TRIPS Perspective* [this volume].
[44] TRIPS Agreement, above n. 2, art. 8.2. *See also id.* art. 31(k) relating to compulsory licensing to remedy anti-competitive practices (another application of this principle).
[45] *See id.* art. 40.1.
[46] *Compare id.* art. 40.1 (" ... may impede the transfer and dissemination of technology") *with id.* art. 8.2 (" ... practices which unreasonably restrain trade or adversely affect the international transfer of technology").

obligations to regulate restrictive practices as such. Instead, while expressly allowing Members to adopt measures to control or prevent such practices, it takes pains to establish *limits* to national action in this field.[47] The assessment of restrictive practices must be made *case-by-case*. In order to be actionable, such practices should

(1) constitute an "abuse" of intellectual property rights; and
(2) have an "adverse effect on competition in the relevant market."[48]

Article 40.2 thus adopts a "rule of reason" approach to assess anti-competitive effects, and thereby settles a debate that divided developed and developing countries during the long and unsuccessful negotiations of the proposed International Code of Conduct on Transfer of Technology under UNCTAD auspices.[49] During those negotiations, developing countries sought the adoption of a broader test, based on the assessment of restrictive practices as they adversely affected development and not merely competition. This rejection by developed countries of such a test was one of the main reasons for the collapse of the International Code negotiations in 1985.[50]

Although the TRIPS Agreement is a binding international instrument (whereas the Code of Conduct was conceived as a voluntary instrument), article 40.2 of the TRIPS Agreement falls short of the Code's objectives in many respects. The Agreement merely allows national legislation to adopt measures to control restrictive practices, under certain conditions, but (with the exception of a few examples considered below) it does not contain internationally agreed rules on the specific practices that may be deemed anti-competitive. The proposed Code also included substantive chapters on the obligations and responsibilities of parties engaged in technology transfer transactions, and it imposed duties concerning international cooperation and the settlement of disputes. The TRIPS Agreement is mute on these issues.

Article 40.2 provides a few *examples* of practices that may be deemed restrictive.[51] They include:

---

[47] *Id.* art. 40.2. Another provision of this nature is contained in article 53.2 of the Agreement, which limits Members' ability to enact certain types of enforcement rules.

[48] *Id.* art. 40.2.

[49] *See* UNCTAD Doc. TD/COT TOT/47 (1985). The Code of Conduct was developed and promoted by the United Nations Conference on Trade and Development (UNCTAD).

[50] The tests adopted in article 40.2 imply that the existence of adverse effects on development stemming from restrictive licensing practices may not be a sufficient ground to condemn a practice if it does not equally affect competition in the "relevant market."

[51] Previous drafts of the Agreement included a significantly longer list, in which restrictions on research and on use of personnel, price fixing, exclusive sales or representation agreements, tying agreements, export restrictions and other practices were mentioned. *See* the Chairman's draft text of 22 November 1990, which was discussed at the Montreal Mid-Term Review of December 1990. *See also* the list of practices as negotiated by the U.N. Conference on a Code of Conduct on Transfer of Technology, UNCTAD TD/COT TOT/47 (1985).

- exclusive grant back provisions, i.e., those that oblige the licensee to transfer the improvements made on the licensed technology exclusively to the licensor;
- obligations imposed on the licensee not to challenge the validity of licensed rights;
- coercive package licensing, i.e., the obligation for the licensee to acquire from the licensor other technologies or inputs he does not need or desire.[52]

Finally, article 40.3 establishes a consultation system applicable to cases where a Member (Member A) considers that a national or domiciliary of another Member (Member B) is undertaking practices in violation of the former's laws and regulations concerning anti-competitive practices. In this situation, Member A may request consultations with Member B and the latter "shall accord full and sympathetic consideration to, and shall afford adequate opportunity" for such consultations.[53] In addition, Member B is obliged to cooperate "through the supply of publicly available non-confidential information of relevance to the matter in question and of other information available to the Member, subject to domestic law and to the conclusion of mutually satisfactory agreements concerning the safeguarding of its confidentiality by the requesting Member."[54]

Consultations may also be requested by a Member whose nationals or domiciliaries are subject to proceedings in another Member concerning alleged violations of the latter's legislation on anti-competitive practices. In this case, the requesting Member "shall be granted an opportunity for consultations" with the other Member under the same conditions as in the case presented above.[55]

In both situations, the resulting consultations will be without prejudice to any action under the relevant national law and "to the full freedom of an ultimate decision of either Member."[56] There are no records about the actual use of this consultation system. It does not seem to have afforded any assistance to developing countries in dealing with restrictive practices in transfer of technology transactions.

C. Disclosure of patent information

According to article 29.1 of the TRIPS Agreement, Members shall require disclosure of the invention "in a manner sufficiently clear and complete for the invention to be carried out by a person skilled in the art." Members *may* also require the applicant "to indicate the best mode for carrying out the invention known to the inventor at the filing date or, where priority is claimed,

---

[52] TRIPS Agreement, above n. 2, art. 40.2.
[53] *Id.* art. 40.3.   [54] *Id.*   [55] *Id.* art. 40.4.   [56] *Id.* art. 40.3.

at the priority date of the application."[57] It has been argued that the disclosure of inventions mandated by article 29.1 constitutes a mode of transfer of technology within the TRIPS Agreement,[58] but there are several problems with this argument.

First, although full disclosure of the invention is a basic principle of patent law and remains one of the traditional justifications for the granting of exclusivity to the inventor,[59] patent specifications generally convey the minimum information required to get the patent granted. Skilled patent agents would normally avoid including information that may help competitors to invent around or rapidly implement the invention, once the patent has expired. In addition, when several embodiments of an invention are claimed, often the applicant omits information allowing the reproduction of all such embodiments by a third party.[60]

Second, until the patent expires, a party interested in using the protected technology in countries where the patent has been granted will always need a license from the patent owner. In other words, disclosure makes the invention known but not immediately accessible for exploitation without permission.

Third, in some cases, such as where inventions pertain to microorganisms, access to the relevant knowledge only becomes possible through access to the biological material itself. Such access may be made available to third parties with the publication of the patent application (as provided under European law),[61] but it is allowed for experimental purposes only, and not for commercial use.

Fourth, patent specifications are difficult to implement for technicians in developing countries without experience in a particular technical field, especially because such specifications seldom include the actual know-how (which usually is not available at the time the application is filed) necessary for executing the invention.[62] As mentioned above, technological capacity is cumulative and, hence, catching up based on patent documentation alone is unlikely.

---

[57] *Id.* art. 29.1.
[58] For an analysis of this issue, *see* Lynn Mytelka, Creating Opportunities for Learning and Innovation Through Trade and Technology Transfer, Presentation to the Working Group on Trade and Technology Transfer, Geneva (16 Apr. 2002). *See also* J.H. Reichman, *The TRIPS Component of the GATT's Uruguay Round: Competitive Prospects for Intellectual Property Owners in an Integrated World Market*, 4 FORDHAM INTELL. PROP. MEDIA & ENT. L.J. 187 (1993).
[59] *See, e.g.*, EDITH PENROSE, THE ECONOMICS OF THE INTERNATIONAL PATENT SYSTEM 31 (Johns Hopkins Press 1951).
[60] Some patent offices, such as the European Patent Office, accept that the disclosure need not include specific instructions as to how all possible variants within the claim definition can be obtained. *See, e.g.*, T. COOK ET AL., PHARMACEUTICALS BIOTECHNOLOGY & THE LAW 80 (Stockton Press 1991).
[61] In the United States, access to a deposited sample is possible after granting of the patent.
[62] This is why it was earlier suggested that the description of the invention should be sufficiently detailed as to teach the invention to a local expert. *See, e.g.*, UNCTAD, THE TRIPS AGREEMENT AND DEVELOPING COUNTRIES 33 (1996).

Finally, most patents are never industrially executed and, in many cases, developing a product or process based on a patented idea requires significant experimental and development work. Moreover, meeting the patentability requirements does not ensure the marketability and commercial success of any invention. Only 37 percent of U.S patents are renewed 11.5 years after they issue, while at any given time 95 percent of existing patents are unlicensed and over 97 percent generate no royalties.[63]

In sum, the informative effects of patent grants cannot be deemed a substitute for transfer of technology mechanisms through which companies in developing countries actually gain access to proven and commercially viable technologies.

D. Compulsory licenses

1. Lack of or insufficient working

The obligation to work a patent – understood as the local manufacture of the patented product or use of the patented process – was first established in the United Kingdom and incorporated into many national laws during the nineteenth and twentieth centuries.[64] During the twentieth century, however, most industrialized countries relaxed or eliminated such an obligation in order to facilitate the transborder activities of transnational corporations in increasingly globalized markets. Many scholars and developing country authorities, however, continue to regard such an obligation as an essential element to balance the patent system, precisely because it may create opportunities for the transfer of technology.[65]

Not surprisingly, the admissibility of the local working obligation was one of the most controversial issues in the course of the TRIPS negotiations. The difficulties encountered in attempting to reach an agreement are evidenced by the language of the compromise contained in article 27.1. It states that "patent rights shall be enjoyable without discrimination ... whether products are imported or locally produced."[66] According to one interpretation, this clause would ban working obligations that require industrial execution of the invention

---

[63] *See, e.g.*, Samson Vermont, *The Economics of Patent Litigation, in* FROM IDEAS TO ASSETS 332 (John Wiley & Sons 2002).

[64] For a comprehensive study of compulsory licensing in North American law and practice, *see* J.H. REICHMAN WITH CATHERINE HASENZAHL, NON-VOLUNTARY LICENSING OF PATENTED INVENTIONS, PART I – HISTORICAL PERSPECTIVE, LEGAL FRAMEWORK UNDER TRIPS AND AN OVERVIEW OF THE PRACTICE IN CANADA AND THE UNITED STATES (UNCTAD/ICTSD Sept. 2002) [hereinafter HISTORICAL PERSPECTIVE]; PART II – THE CANADIAN EXPERIENCE (UNCTAD/ICTSD Oct. 2002) [hereinafter THE CANADIAN EXPERIENCE]; PART III – THE LAW AND PRACTICE OF THE UNITED STATES (UNCTAD/ICTSD forthcoming 2004) [hereinafter LAW AND PRACTICE OF THE UNITED STATES] (draft version available at www.ictsd.org).

[65] *See, e.g.*, M. Halewood, *Regulating Patent Holders: Local Working Requirements and Compulsory Licences at International Law*, 35 OSGOODE HALL L.J. 243 (1997).

[66] TRIPS Agreement, above n. 2, art. 27.1.

in the granting country, and any residual duty to work could be satisfied through importation.⁶⁷ Nevertheless, as discussed below, article 27.1 may be interpreted as allowing working obligations, in line with article 5A of the Paris Convention.⁶⁸

The national laws of numerous WTO Members have adopted and continue to maintain local working obligations.⁶⁹ The Uruguay Round records also reveal that during the negotiations several developing countries defended the right to impose working requirements.⁷⁰ The negotiating history of the TRIPS Agreement does not support the hypothesis that those countries withdrew their

---

⁶⁷ *See, e.g.*, JAYASHREE WATAL, INTELLECTUAL PROPERTY RIGHTS IN THE WTO AND DEVELOPING COUNTRIES 318 (Kluwer Law International 2001); NUNO PIRES DE CARVALHO, THE TRIPS REGIME OF PATENT RIGHTS 162 (Kluwer Law International 2000).

⁶⁸ *See* Paris Convention for the Protection of Industrial Property, as last revised at Stockholm on 14 July 1967, 828 U.N.T.S. 305, art. 5A. Article 5A(2) of this treaty provides as follows:

> Each country of the Union shall have the right to take legislative measures providing for the grant of compulsory licenses to prevent the abuses which might result from the exercise of the exclusive rights conferred by the patent, for example, failure to work.

This provision was incorporated into the TRIPS Agreement of 1994. *See* TRIPS Agreement, above n. 2, art. 2.1.

⁶⁹ A review of comparative law made by Oxfam found working obligations in the patent laws and regulations of Indonesia and Cuba; Ghana, Ireland, South Africa, Sudan and Zimbabwe (based on former United Kingdom laws); Greece and Lesotho (compulsory licensing linked to local working); Turkey, Spain and Portugal (certificate of working required); Sweden, Norway, Finland and Iceland (local working tied to reciprocity); India; Israel; Zaire; Thailand; Pakistan; Liberia. *See* Oxfam, Local Working Requirements and the TRIPS Agreement: Using Patent Law as a Means of Ensuring Affordable Access to Essential Medicines, A Case Study from the U.S.-Brazil Dispute (draft) (2001), *available at* http://www.field.org.uk/papers/pdf/twrta.pdf. *See also* UK Patents Act 1977, ch. 37 (as amended by the Copyright, Designs and Patents Act 1988), § 48(3), and Denmark Consolidated Patents Act, § 45(1); Halewood, above n. 65.

⁷⁰ *See, e.g.*, Negotiating Group on Trade-Related Aspects of Intellectual Property Rights, Including Trade in Counterfeit Goods, *Meeting of Negotiating Group of 2, 4 and 5 April 1990*, Note by the Secretariat, MTN.GNG/NG11/20 para. 34 (24 Apr. 1990); Negotiating Group on Trade-Related Aspects of Intellectual Property Rights, Including Trade in Counterfeit Goods, *Existence, Scope and Form of Generally Internationally Accepted and Applied Standards/Norms for the Protection of Intellectual Property*, Note Prepared by the International Bureau of WIPO, MTN.GNG/NG11/W/24 2 (5 May 1988); Negotiating Group on Trade-Related Aspects of Intellectual Property Rights, Including Trade in Counterfeit Goods, *Meeting of Negotiating Group of 11, 12 and 14 December 1989*, Note by the Secretariat, MTN.GNG/NG11/17 para. 41 (23 Jan. 1990); Negotiating Group on Trade-Related Aspects of Intellectual Property Rights, Including Trade in Counterfeit Goods, *Meeting of Negotiating Group of 11–12 May 1989*, Note by the Secretariat, MTN.GNG/NG11/12 para. 5 (13 June 1989); *id.* para. 36; Negotiating Group on Trade-Related Aspects of Intellectual Property Rights, Including Trade in Counterfeit Goods, *Meeting of Negotiating Group of 30 October – 2 November 1989*, Note by the Secretariat, MTN.GNG/NG11/16 para. 24 (4 Dec. 1989); Negotiating Group on Trade-Related Aspects of Intellectual Property Rights, Including Trade in Counterfeit Goods, *Meeting*

position on local working when they accepted the ambiguous text adopted in article 27.1 of the Agreement. Nor does the language allowing members to regulate abuses exclude local working, which remains the quintessential abuse under article 5A of the Paris Convention.[71]

The United States initiated a case against Brazil under WTO rules arguing that article 68 of the Brazilian patent law was inconsistent with the TRIPS Agreement. That provision authorizes the government to grant a compulsory license if the patent owner fails to work the subject matter of the patent in Brazil.[72] A critical issue in addressing the validity of working obligations is whether article 27.1 – the non-discrimination clause in the patent section of TRIPS – also governs article 31, which sets out the conditions for the granting of compulsory licenses.[73] Developing countries contend that article 27.1 should not be read in a way that restricts the use of compulsory licenses, for instance, on the grounds of non-working. They have argued in this regard that:

> As regards the relationship of the provisions related to compulsory licenses with articles 27.1 and 28 of TRIPS, we believe that both set of provisions address different matters and circumstances. In no way do articles 27.1 and 28 limit the right of Members to issue compulsory licenses.[74]

In *Canada – Patent Protection for Pharmaceutical Products*, the WTO panel held as "an acknowledged fact" that articles 30 (exceptions) and 31 (compulsory licenses) of the TRIPS Agreement were subject to the non-discrimination clause in article 27.1 of the Agreement.[75] However, the factual and legal bases for this finding are unconvincing.[76] It would seem more logical to limit certain exceptions

---

of Negotiating Group of 12–14 July 1989, Note by the Secretariat, MTN.GNG/NG11/14 para. 75, 83 (12 Sept. 1989).

[71] *See* TRIPS Agreement, above n. 2, arts. 8.2, 40; Paris Convention, above n. 68, art. 5A (*quoted* above n. 68); REICHMAN WITH HASENZAHL, HISTORICAL PERSPECTIVE, above n. 64, at 10.

[72] Article 68 (1) of the Brazilian Industrial Property Code (Law No. 9.279) reads as follows:

> The following may also be ground for compulsory licensing:
> (1) failure to work the subject matter of a patent on the territory of Brazil, failure to manufacture or incomplete manufacture of the product or failure to completely use a patented process, except for failure to work due to lack of economic viability, in which case importing shall be admitted; or
> (2) marketing that does not satisfy the needs of the market.

[73] *See* TRIPS Agreement, above n. 2, arts. 27.1, 31.

[74] African Group, Barbados, Bolivia, Brazil, Cuba, Dominican Republic, Ecuador, Honduras, India, Indonesia, Jamaica, Pakistan, Philippines, Peru, Sri Lanka, Thailand, and Venezuela, TRIPS and Public Health IP/C/W/296 (June 29, 2001), at 8.

[75] Canada – Patent Protection for Pharmaceutical Products, above n. 32, ¶ 7.91.

[76] For a critical analysis of the panel's willingness to push the non-discrimination clause this far, see Graeme B. Dinwoodie & Rochelle Cooper Dreyfuss, *WTO Dispute Resolution and the Preservation of the Public Domain of Science Under International Law* [this volume].

to certain fields of technology, rather than being forced to apply them to fields where such measures were not required.

In addition, the "patent rights" referred to in article 27.1 are defined in article 28.1, which only requires the granting of *negative* rights with regard to the exploitation of the invention, that is, the right to prevent third parties from using (without authorization) the patented invention. Therefore, a sound interpretation of article 27.1 (based on the rules of the Vienna Convention), read in conjunction with article 28.1, would suggest that the products mentioned in article 27.1 were *infringing* products, not the products of the patent owner itself, since patents only confer exclusionary rights in relation to the former. In other words, article 27.1 forbids discrimination between *infringing* imported and *infringing* locally-made products, but it does not rule out the establishment of differential obligations with regard to non-infringing imported and locally-made products (i.e., products made or imported by the patent owner or with his/her consent).

The non-discrimination clause of article 27.1 may apply, for instance, to a case in which the rights enjoyed by patent owners who import legitimate products are different (substantially or procedurally) from the rights of patent owners who domestically manufacture them. For instance, Section 337 of the U.S. Tariff Act was found inconsistent with the GATT in *United States–Section 337 of the Tariff Act of 1930*,[77] since it accorded less favorable treatment to imported products challenged as infringing U.S. patents than the treatment accorded to similarly challenged products of United States origin.[78]

2. Refusal to deal

Compulsory licenses granted on the ground of "refusal to deal" may also constitute a mechanism for the transfer of technology. Although article 31(b) of the TRIPS Agreement only refers to the refusal of a voluntary license as a precondition for granting compulsory licenses,[79] such a refusal can be deemed an *autonomous* ground for the granting of a compulsory license. The Agreement, as explicitly recognized in paragraph 5(b) of the Doha Declaration on the TRIPS Agreement and Public Health, does not limit the grounds that Members may determine for the granting of compulsory licenses,[80] with a sole exception for the case of semiconductor technology.[81]

---

[77] *See* WTO Doc. L/6439-365-345 (7 Nov. 1989).
[78] *See, e.g.*, M. Haedicke, *U.S. Imports, TRIPS and Section 337 of the Tariff Act of 1930*, 31 INT'L REV. INDUS. PROP. & COPYRIGHT. L. (IIC) 771, 774 (2000).
[79] TRIPS Agreement, above n. 2, art. 31(b).
[80] WTO, Declaration on the TRIPS Agreement and Public Health, WT/MIN(01)/DEC/W/2 ¶ 5(b) (Doha, 14 Nov. 2001).
[81] TRIPS Agreement, above n. 2, art. 31(c).

A refusal to deal as a ground for granting a compulsory license is well-established in some national laws.[82] In the United Kingdom and in other countries that have followed its legislative model, a refusal to deal may lead to the grant of a compulsory license when an export market is not being supplied, when the working of any other patented invention that makes a substantial contribution is prevented or hindered, or the establishment or development of commercial or industrial activities in the country is unfairly prejudiced.[83]

In Australia, a compulsory license for "refusal to deal" may be granted unless the patentee can prove that it would equally refuse to license in a competitive situation.[84] Questions have also been raised in the United States about whether the refusal to deal may be anti-competitive when it allows a patentee to block follow-on research, particularly if the initial patent was overly broad.[85]

Compulsory licenses within the framework of competition law have been granted in Europe on the grounds of refusal to deal. The application of the doctrine of access to an essential facility was considered in some of these cases. This doctrine has mainly dealt with access to vertically integrated natural monopolies, but it has also been applied in other contexts.[86]

Thus, a decision by Belgian courts in 1995 imposed a compulsory license on two copyright collecting societies, in favor of two cable distributors who had been refused the right to transmit by cable in Belgium the German Cable SATI. Refusing the authorization for a reasonable remuneration was deemed to be abusive.[87] More significant was the decision of the European Court of Justice

---

[82] *See, e.g.*, Patent Law of the People's Republic of China, Section § 51 (1992); German Patent Law (Text of 16 Dec. 1980, as last amended by the Laws of 16 July and 6 Aug., 1996) § 24(1); Austrian Patent Law (Federal Law of 1970, as last amended by the Law of 23 May 1984, amending the Patent Law and the Law Introducing Patent Treaties) § 36(2); Ireland's Patents Act 1992 § 70(2) (27 Feb. 1992). For Israel, see Michael Cohn, *Compulsory Licensing in Israel Under Pharmaceutical Patents – A Political Issue?*, 27 PATENT WORLD 22 (1990). In Canada, a compulsory license can be granted under the Patent Act in cases of refusal to license; a showing of anticompetitive effects is not necessary to establish this "abuse." *See, e.g.*, N. Gallini & M. Trebilcock, *Intellectual Property Rights and Competition Policy: A Framework for the Analysis of Economic and Legal Issues*, in THE ECONOMICS OF INTELLECTUAL PROPERTY, VOLUME IV: COMPETITION AND INTERNATIONAL TRADE 30 (E. Towse & R. Holzhauer eds., Elgar Reference Collection 2002).

[83] UK Patent Act (as revised in 1977) § 48.3.d.

[84] *See* Michael O'Bryan, *Refusal to License Intellectual Property under the Australian Trade Practices Act*, 42 PATENT WORLD 10 (1992).

[85] *See* Donald McFetridge, *Intellectual Property, Technology Diffusion, and Growth in the Canadian Economy*, in COMPETITION POLICY AND INTELLECTUAL PROPERTY RIGHTS IN THE KNOWLEDGE-BASED ECONOMY 91 (Robert Anderson & Nancy Gallini eds., University of Calgary Press 1998).

[86] *See, e.g.*, I. RAHNASTO, INTELLECTUAL PROPERTY RIGHTS, EXTERNAL EFFECTS, AND ANTI-TRUST LAW 144 (Oxford University Press 2003).

[87] David Lantham, *Should Competition Law Be Used to Compel the Grant of Licenses of Intellectual Property Rights?*, 180 REVUE INTERNATIONALE DE LA CONCURRENCE 24, 25 (1996).

(ECJ) of 6 April 1995 in *Magill*.[88] In its judgment, the Court confirmed that Radio Telefis Eireann (RTE) and Independent Television Publications Limited (ITP), who were the only sources of basic information about program scheduling that was indispensable raw material for compiling a weekly television guide, could not rely on national copyright provisions to refuse to provide that information to third parties. Such a refusal, the Court held, in this case constituted the exercise of an intellectual property right beyond its specific subject matter and, thus, an abuse of a dominant position under article 86 of the Treaty of Rome.

The court argued that RTE and ITP held a dominant position, because they were the only source in Ireland of the basic information necessary to produce weekly television programming guides and were thus in a position to reserve for themselves the secondary market for weekly television guides by excluding all competition from that market. The Court considered that whilst refusal to grant a license in exercising an intellectual property right is not of itself an abuse of a dominant position, it may become an abuse where special circumstances exist. Such circumstances included the lack of an actual or potential substitute for a weekly television guide, the existence of a specific, constant and regular demand for such a guide, and the fact that the refusal to grant a license to Magill to produce such a guide prevented the appearance of a new product on the market, which RTE and ITP did not offer.[89]

In the *Magill* case, the broadcasters' abusive conduct prevented the emergence of a "new" product on the market. Subsequent cases (*Tiercé Ladbroke*,[90] *Oscar Bronner*,[91] IMS[92]) indicated that preventing the emergence of a new product was not a *sine qua non* condition for the application of the doctrine of access to an essential facility under article 82 of the EC Treaty. What really mattered was whether the IP holder, by refusing to license, was preventing access to an essential facility.[93]

At the same time, case law has established that a refusal to deal does not of itself constitute an abuse of a dominant position. Such abuse will only be found in the presence of other factors, such as, for example, where a denial to supply

---

[88] Cases C-241/91P & C-242/91P, 1995 E.C.R. I-743.
[89] *See, e.g.*, David Lartham & Svenja Geissmar, *Should Competition Law Be Used to Compel the Grant By Owners of Intellectual Property Rights of Licenses in Respect of Their Creations?*, 178 Revue Internationale de la Concurrence 7, 9 (1995).
[90] Case T-504/93, Tiercé Ladbroke v. Commission, 1997 E.C.R. II-923, [1997] 5 C.M.L.R. 309 (1997).
[91] Case C-7/97, Oscar Bronner GmbH & Co. KG v. Mediaprint Zeitungs- und Zeitschriftenverlag GmbH & Co. KG and Other, 1998 E.C.R. I-7817, [1999] 4 C.M.L.R. 112.
[92] Interim Order of Commission, 3 July 2001, 2002 O.J. (L59) 18, [202] 4 C.M.L.R. 58.
[93] In Intel v. Via Technologies (Cases A3/2002/1380 & A3/2002/1381, [2002] E.W.C.A. Civ. 1905 (20 Dec. 2002), the English Court of Appeal also ruled that it was possible to defend a patent infringement claim by contending that the enforcement of the patent would enable the holder of the patent to act in breach of articles 81 or 82 of the EC Treaty. F. Fine, AT-IP Report, Electronic Newsletter of the Intellectual Property Committee (2003).

would put the competitor out of business or eliminate competition in a related market. In *Volvo v. Veng*[94] and *Renault*,[95] the ECJ demonstrated reluctance to interfere with intellectual property rights where refusals to deal were primarily motivated by the interest in preventing competitors from imitating protected subject matter.

In the United States, the patent law, as amended in 1988, provides that "no patent owner otherwise entitled to relief for infringement ... of a patent shall be denied relief or deemed guilty of a misuse or illegal extension of the patent right by reason of his having ... refused to license or use any rights to the patent ...."[96] This amendment protects a patentee from a counterclaim of misuse; in applying it, courts have held that a patentee cannot be held liable for unilaterally refusing to sell or license a patented invention.[97] Alleged monopolists' refusals to deal and conditional refusals to deal with respect to exclusive intellectual property rights continue, however, to be the subject of litigation and debate in the United States.[98]

In *Image Technical Services, Inc. v. Eastman Kodak Co*,[99] the Ninth Circuit Court of Appeals examined the extent to which a dominant patentee can alter its behaviour to restrict access to protected products. The court recognized the conflict between antitrust and IP doctrine and concluded that patentees are not immune from antitrust liability. Although it held that "... a monopolist's desire to exclude others from its protected work is a presumptively valid business justification for any immediate harm to consumers," the court found that the presumption in favor of IP rights was undermined by Kodak's conduct and that Kodak had acted in an illegal, anticompetitive manner.[100]

However, the United States Court of Appeals for the Federal Circuit (which has sole appellate jurisdiction over disputes involving alleged patent infringement) disagreed with the Ninth Circuit's interpretation in a case whose facts were nearly identical to those of *Kodak*.[101] The Federal Circuit in reviewing the protection conferred by the Patent Act, emphasized the right to refuse to license a patent, and rejected the argument that a refusal to sell or grant a license to a lawful patent can give rise to antitrust liability. It added that "a patent may confer the right to exclude competition altogether in more than one antitrust market."[102] The court found only three exceptions to this

---

[94] Case 238/87, 1988 E.C.R. 6211, [1989] 4 C.M.L.R. 122, C.M.R. 14498.
[95] Case 53/87, Maxicar v. Renault, 1988 E.C.R. 6039, [1990] 4 C.M.L.R. 265.
[96] 35 U.S.C. § 271(d)(4) (2000) (added to § 271 by Pub. L. No. 100–703, § 201 (1988)).
[97] John Taladay & James Carlin Jr., *Compulsory Licensing of Intellectual Property Under the Competition Laws of the United States and European Community*, 10 GEORGE MASON L. REV. 443, 445 (2002).
[98] *See, e.g.*, J. Gleklen & J. MacKie-Mason, THE ANTITRUST SOURCE, July 2002, *available at* http://www.abanet.org/antitrust/source/july.html.
[99] 125 F.3d 1195 (9th Cir. 1997).
[100] *See, e.g.*, Taladay & Carlin, above n. 97, at 446.
[101] CSU, L.L.C. v. Xerox Corp., 203 F.3d 1322 (Fed. Cir. 2000). [102] *Id.* at 1327.

principle: illegal tying, fraud on the Patent and Trademark Office, or sham litigation. In all other circumstances "the patent holder may enforce the statutory right to exclude others from making, using, or selling the claimed invention free from liability under the antitrust laws."[103]

The Federal Circuit explicitly rejected the "rebuttable presumption" adopted by the Ninth Circuit in *Kodak*, determining that subjective motivation for refusing to license is irrelevant to the three identified exceptions.[104] The *Kodak* and *Xerox* contradictory decisions leave considerable uncertainty about the validity of a refusal to deal in the patent field and, not surprisingly, indicate that the Federal Circuit is generally inclined to protect the patent owner's right to refuse a license except in the very narrow circumstances referred to.

In sum, while experience with refusals to deal as a ground for compulsory licenses in Europe and the United States is limited, it nonetheless indicates that the use of this modality is possible, and that it may sometimes provide a basis for obtaining access to patented technology. Of course, developing countries need not adopt the standards applied in these countries, since they have full freedom to define the grounds for granting of compulsory licenses.[105] Such countries may adapt the "access to essential facilities" doctrine so as to include cases in which patent protection impedes competition, particularly in key specific areas, such as medicines.

E. *Compulsory licenses as vehicles for technology transfer*

If, as argued, developing countries are legally able to impose compulsory licenses for non-working or refusal to deal, could such licenses constitute an important vehicle for the transfer of technology to these countries? While technically competent companies (such as pharmaceutical generic firms in India) might rely on such licenses to obtain the right to commercialize products that they could otherwise reverse-engineer, less technically endowed firms are unlikely to benefit from a mechanism that does not ensure access to required know-how and technical assistance, which may be essential for the absorption and putting into operation of the relevant technology. Patent specifications, as previously explained, generally include minimal information, and are an insufficient basis for manufacture. Moreover, production know-how is generally developed after the application was filed. Compulsory licenses only permit use of a patent, but do not oblige the patentee to transfer the technological package developed to execute the invention. There have been some antitrust cases in the United States, however, where a transfer of know-how was required as part of a compulsory license or a settlement decree.

---

[103] *Id.* [104] Taladay & Carlin, above n. 97, at 448–449.
[105] It is important to note that bilateral trade agreements that include intellectual property matters (such as the USA-Jordan, USA-Singapore, USA-Chile agreements) can limit such a freedom and restrict the right to adopt different grounds for compulsory licenses.

For instance, on July 6, 1994, the U.S Federal Trade Commission (FTC) required Dow Chemical to license to a potential entrant intangible dicyclomine assets, including "all formulations, patents, trade secrets, technology, know-how, specifications, designs, drawings, processes, quality control data, research materials, technical information, management information systems, software, the Drug Master File, and all information relating to the United States Food and Drug Administration Approvals" that are not part of the acquired company's physical facilities or other tangible assets.[106] In *FTC v. Xerox Corporation*, a consent decree was issued according to which the patent and know-how barriers to competition developed by Xerox were eliminated by requiring Xerox to license some of its patents free of royalty, and the rest at low royalties, and to offer all of its office copier know-how royalty-free to U.S. patent licensees.[107]

There are, however, certain factors that may discourage the use of compulsory licenses as a means of acquiring technology not available from the market on reasonable terms and conditions. First, a compulsory license may be revoked when the circumstances that led to its granting have ceased to exist and are unlikely to recur.[108] If, for example, such a license was granted to remedy a situation of abusive prices, it may be revoked when prices are normalized, a possibility that the patent owner controls. Paradoxically, the more efficient a compulsory licensee becomes in remedying an anti-competitive situation, the higher the risk of losing the license he has obtained. The precarious nature of a compulsory license could thus discourage the incentive to request any such license, since potential licensees may lack sufficient time to recover their investments. Although the legitimate interests of the compulsory licensee should be considered before revocation of the license is decided,[109] it remains highly uncertain how this safeguard will be applied.[110]

Second, given the likely stiff opposition by patent holders to the granting of compulsory licenses, many domestic companies may prefer to negotiate a voluntary agreement or to look for other options, rather than to confront patent holders (often actively backed by their governments). The costs of litigation may be substantial, and the ensuing uncertainty about the validity of the compulsory license or the compensation to be paid may also reduce interest in requesting it.

Third, compulsory licenses must be *non-exclusive*; this means that the patent owner can continue to exploit the invention and directly compete with the

---

[106] See 59 Fed. Reg. 34625–01 (6 July 1994).
[107] Federal Trade Commission v. Xerox Corporation, 86 F.T.C. 364 (1975). See also REICHMAN WITH HASENZAHL, LAW AND PRACTICE OF THE UNITED STATES, above n. 64 (discussing use of compulsory licenses in mergers and acquisitions as well as consent decrees).
[108] TRIPS Agreement, above n. 2, art. 31(g).   [109] See id.
[110] In some cases, government use of the patented invention may provide a viable alternative. See, e.g., REICHMAN WITH HASENZAHL, LAW AND PRACTICE OF THE UNITED STATES, above n. 64 (discussing extensive reliance on this instrument in the U.S.).

compulsory licensee, leveraging the advantages conferred by technical knowledge and the prestige of brand names. The patent owner also retains the right to grant any voluntary licenses he wishes. In practice, the market share that compulsory licensees obtain may be small and even insignificant, on account of the reputation and dominant presence of the patent owner in that same market.[111]

Finally, once a compulsory license is granted, the licensee becomes bound to pay a royalty, to be determined in accordance with "the economic value" of the license.[112] In the United States, such licenses have been granted against a royalty generally determined on the basis of the "willing-buyer, willing-seller" formulation in government use cases.[113] Although in these cases royalties have ranged from four to sixteen percent (and rarely exceed ten percent),[114] royalty rates tend to be modest in most cases involving anti-competitive considerations.[115] For instance, in the case of the Ciba-Geigy and Sandoz merger (1997), the FTC specified that the royalties for the non-exclusive Cytokine licenses (which involved gene therapy), and the Anderson gene therapy patent, could be no greater than three percent of the net sales price.[116]

Compulsory licenses were granted in Canada for patented pharmaceutical products during the 1970s and 1980s against payment of a standard royalty rate of 4 per cent.[117] In the United Kingdom, royalty rates charged for "licenses of right" granted pursuant to the 1977 revision of the UK Patent Act were reportedly higher than those indicated for the United States and Canada. The royalties paid varied from about 23 percent to 31 percent, while most of the reported royalty rates ranged from 25 percent to 28 percent on the licensee's selling price.[118]

To sum up, the availability of compulsory licenses (as currently regulated under the TRIPS Agreement) will not automatically solve the problems of

---

[111] See, e.g., J. Watal, *Pharmaceutical Patents, Prices and Welfare Losses: A Simulation Study of Policy Options for India Under the WTO TRIPS Agreement*, 23 WORLD ECON. 733 (2000).
[112] TRIPS Agreement, above n. 2, art. 31(h).
[113] See, e.g., REICHMAN WITH HASENZAHL, LAW AND PRACTICE OF THE UNITED STATES, above n. 64, ch. V (discussing government use at length).
[114] Id.; See also R. McGrath, *The Unauthorized Use of Patents by the United States Government or its Contractors*, 18 AM. INTELL. PROP. L. ASS'N Q.J. 349, 349–359 (1991).
[115] See REICHMAN WITH HASENZAHL, LAW AND PRACTICE OF THE UNITED STATES, above n. 64, chapter II (discussing intersection of intellectual property and antitrust laws). See also Sol Goldstein, *A Study of Compulsory Licensing*, LICENSING EXECUTIVE SOCIETY 124 (1977).
[116] See Press Release, FTC Accord in Ciba Geigy/Sandoz Merger to Prevent Slowdown in Gene Therapy Development & Preserve Competition in Corn Herbicides, Flea-control Markets (7 Dec. 1996), *available at* http://www.ftc.gov/opa/1996/12/ciba.htm. As mentioned above, there have also been some cases of compulsory licenses conferred in the United States on a royalty-free basis, in antitrust cases. The Supreme Court has not vetted this practice.
[117] See, e.g., REICHMAN WITH HASENZAHL, THE CANADIAN EXPERIENCE, above n. 64.
[118] See, e.g., David Cohen, *Applications for Licences of Right in the United Kingdom*, 20 PATENT WORLD 28 (1990).

access to technology in developing countries. It is certainly advisable that such countries fully utilize the room for maneuver left by the TRIPS Agreement in this area, especially to obtain the rights to use protected technologies not otherwise available on reasonable terms whenever there exists technical capacity to do so. They will also need the capacity to resist legal actions by patent holders and political pressures by their governments. The threat of compulsory licenses may also be useful, *inter alia*, to challenge the dominant position of patent holders[119] and eventually to obtain price reductions.[120]

Compulsory licenses may increase both static and dynamic efficiency as well. As the evolutionary theory of innovation has shown, routine productive activities and cumulative learning at the plant level are important sources of innovation.[121] The use of a patented process or the manufacturing of a patented product under a compulsory license can lead to follow-on innovations or new innovative concepts in the relevant technical field. Hence, while improving allocative efficiency, compulsory licenses may also have a positive effect on the future flows of innovations and dynamic efficiency.

However, the usefulness of compulsory licenses as effective mechanisms for technology transfer and learning will be limited where the technical and entrepreneurial capabilities of potential recipients are weak, or where States are more vulnerable to political pressures. From this angle, compulsory licenses may be less effective where they are needed the most to foster technological development.[122]

III. Transfer of technology to least developed countries (LDCs)

The TRIPS Agreement requires the adoption by developed countries of measures for promoting and encouraging technology transfer, but this obligation is limited to the benefit of least-developed countries.[123] Article 66.2 states:

> Developed country Members shall provide incentives to enterprises and institutions in their territories for the purpose of promoting and

---

[119] *See, e.g.,* GUTTERMAN, above n. 22, at 69.

[120] As illustrated by the case of Brazil, where the government was able to obtain, in 2001, a price reduction of up to 70 percent for AIDS drugs Nelfinavir and Efavirenz from Roche and Merck, respectively. *See* Commission on Intellectual Property Rights, Report: Integrating Intellectual Property Rights and Development Policy 43 (2002). The United States obtained a similarly drastic reduction in the price of stockpiled Cipro during the recent Anthrax scare by threatening to impose a compulsory license for government use. *See* REICHMAN WITH HASENZAHL, LAW AND PRACTICE OF THE UNITED STATES, above n. 64, ch. V.

[121] *See, e.g.,* Cooper, above n. 13, at 8.

[122] For instance, paragraph 6 of the Doha Declaration on the TRIPS Agreement and Public Health, above n. 80, addresses the problem of use of compulsory licenses in countries lacking or with insufficient manufacturing capacity in pharmaceuticals.

[123] *See* TRIPS Agreement, above n. 2, art. 66.2. Measures to be taken under this provision are often called "home country measures."

encouraging technology transfer to least-developed country Members in order to enable them to create a sound and viable technological base.[124]

LDCs have repeatedly noted at the Council for TRIPS that little or no action has been taken by developed countries to specifically implement their obligations under article 66.2. In response to this concern, paragraph 11.2 of the Implementation Decision adopted by the WTO Ministerial Conference at the start of the Doha Round of Multilateral Trade Negotiations in 2001 stated the following:

> Reaffirming that the provisions of article 66.2 of the TRIPS Agreement are mandatory, it is agreed that the TRIPS Council shall put in place a mechanism for ensuring the monitoring and full implementation of the obligations in question. To this end, developed-country members shall submit prior to the end of 2002 detailed reports on the functioning in practice of the incentives provided to their enterprises for the transfer of technology in pursuance of their commitments under article 66.2. These submissions shall be subject to a review in the TRIPS Council and information shall be updated by Members annually.[125]

Similarly, paragraph 7 of the Doha Declaration on the TRIPS Agreement and Public Health, reaffirmed

> ... the commitment of developed-country Members to provide incentives to their enterprises and institutions to promote and encourage technology transfer to least-developed country Members pursuant to article 66.2.[126]

In the light of the texts adopted at the Doha Ministerial Conference, there is no doubt that article 66.2 establishes an *obligation* on developed countries. Although this provision leaves great leeway to developed countries to determine what kind of incentives to apply, it does positively require the establishment of some system of encouragement for the transfer of technology to LDCs. This interpretation has been confirmed by the Decision of the Council for TRIPS of 19 February 2003, which having regard, *inter alia*, to the instructions of the Ministerial Conference to the Council for TRIPS contained in paragraph 11.2 of the Decision on Implementation-Related Issues and Concerns,[127] and "with a view to putting in place a mechanism for ensuring the monitoring and full implementation of the obligations in article 66.2," established that

> Developed country Members shall submit annually reports on actions taken or planned in pursuance of their commitments under article 66.2. To this end, they shall provide new detailed reports every third year and, in the intervening years, provide updates to their most recent reports. These

---

[124] *Id.* [125] WT/MIN (01)/17 (20 Nov. 2001).
[126] Doha Declaration on TRIPS and Public Health, above n. 80, ¶ 7.
[127] WT/MIN (01)/17 (20 Nov. 2001).

reports shall be submitted prior to the last Council meeting scheduled for the year in question.[128]

Based on this information, which shall be reviewed by the Council at its end-of-year meeting annually, the Council shall "discuss the effectiveness of the incentives provided in promoting and encouraging technology transfer to least-developed country Members in order to enable them to create a sound and viable technological base."[129] The reports "shall, provide, *inter alia*, the following information:

(a) an overview of the incentives regime put in place to fulfil the obligations of article 66.2, including any specific legislative, policy and regulatory framework;
(b) identification of the type of incentive and the government agency or other entity making it available;
(c) eligible enterprises and other institutions in the territory of the Member providing the incentives; and
(d) any information available on the functioning in practice of these incentives.[130]

An interesting interpretive question is whether article 66.2 may be complied with on the basis of programs (as maintained by several development aid agencies) mainly aimed at providing technical assistance that substantially involves the transfer of readily accessible, generally mature technologies already available from the public domain. The object of the TRIPS Agreement is the protection of IPRs. It does not deal with public-domain technologies. Hence, the only logical interpretation seems to be that the obligation under article 66.2 will be satisfied if developed countries adopt incentives that encourage the transfer of technologies subject to IPRs, and not merely unprotected technologies. Nevertheless, LDCs may benefit from transfers of non-proprietary technologies, such as knowledge provided by consultants, machinery

---

[128] WTO Doc. IP/C/28 (20 Feb. 2003).   [129] *Id.* ¶ 2.
[130] *Id.* ¶ 3(d). Such information could include:

–statistical and/or other information on the use of incentives in question by the eligible enterprises and institutions;
–the type of technology that has been transferred by these enterprises and institutions and the terms on which it has been transferred;
–the mode of technology transfer;
–least-developed countries to which these enterprises and institutions have transferred technology and the extent to which the incentives are specific to least-developed countries; and
–any additional information available that would help assess the effects of the measures in promoting and encouraging technology transfer to least-developed country Members in order to enable them to create a sound and viable technological base.

manufacturers and other suppliers. In fact, in an early industrialization phase licensing of technology may play a secondary role as a technology source, compared to suppliers of equipment and materials and clients.[131]

Another important question is whether the obligation under article 66.2 would be deemed satisfied by the establishment of certain incentives, even if they do not lead to an effective transfer of technology to LDCs. The Doha Implementation Decision, as well the Decision of the Council for TRIPS, require the submission of reports on "the functioning in practice" of the incentives provided to their enterprises, which suggest that the effectiveness of the measures adopted is to be considered in assessing compliance. In fact, article 66.2 provides for a standard ("enabling LDCs to create a sound and viable technological base") against which compliance must be judged.[132]

It remains to be seen whether the reaffirmation by the Doha Ministerial Conference of the obligations under article 66.2 will have any practical impact on developed countries' actions in this area, and on the building up of technological capacity in LDCs. Achieving this goal requires time, technical competencies and investment, not to mention managerial capacity, in order to create or strengthen the capacity to absorb foreign technologies and put them into efficient operation. It also requires incentives that effectively induce companies in developed countries to transfer their IPR-related technologies, although no assessment has been made about the nature and magnitude of the incentives necessary to that end.

Developed countries may provide different types of incentives to comply with this obligation. For instance, tax breaks or other subsidies may be offered to companies that supply technology to LDCs. However, under the Agreement on Subsidies and Countervailing Measures, subsidies contingent upon the export of goods are prohibited.[133] Therefore, only subsidies for the transfer of technology in an *intangible* form may be acceptable. It would be important, in this regard, that the outcome of negotiations under article XV of GATS, relating to subsidies,[134] do not foreclose the possibility of using subsidies to encourage the transfer of technology to LDCs and other developing countries.

---

[131] As illustrated by the case of South Korea, where only a third of needed technical information was obtained through licensing. *See, e.g.,* H. Pack, *The Cost of Technology Licensing and the Transfer of Technology,* 19 INT'L J. TECH. MGMT. 77, 80 (2000).

[132] TRIPS Agreement, above n. 2, art. 66.2.

[133] Agreement on Subsidies and Countervailing Measures, 15 Apr. 1994, Marrakesh Agreement Establishing the World Trade Organization, Annex 1A, LEGAL INSTRUMENTS – RESULTS OF THE URUGUAY ROUND, 33 I.L.M. 1143 ¶ 3 (1994).

[134] General Agreement on Trade in Services (GATS), 15 Apr. 1994, Marrakesh Agreement Establishing the World Trade Organization, Annex 1B, LEGAL INSTRUMENTS – RESULTS OF THE URUGUAY ROUND, 1869 U.N.T.S. 183, 33 I.L.M. 1167 art. XV (1994).

IV. Conclusions

The TRIPS Agreement was essentially conceived as a means of strengthening the control by rights holders over intellectual creations and technologies, and not with the objective of increasing the transfer and use of technology globally. The transfer of technology was not, in fact, a concern of TRIPS proponents, and the possible effects of the new protectionist standards on such transfer were never seriously considered during the negotiations or thereafter.

Technology is traded as a commodity, in a notoriously imperfect market, particularly in the case of frontier technologies.[135] The transfer of technology requires a willingness of technology owners to part with it and the capacity (technical, financial, etc) of the recipient to put it into commercial operation. National or international law cannot guarantee that these conditions will be met. No legal tool, even if skillfully designed, can provide a real solution to the problem of transfer of technology. But government intervention may provide incentives to promote such transfers, empower would-be recipients in developing countries to obtain authorization to use foreign companies' IPRs (when such use is unreasonably refused), and to correct abusive practices in licensing agreements.

The implementation of the TRIPS Agreement is likely to affect transfers of technology in an uneven way. It may, on the one hand, create the conditions necessary for such a transfer to take place, to the extent that technology owners may become more confident and willing to part with their knowledge if effective protection against imitation in the importing country is available. But strong IPRs may, on the other hand, impair the capacity of potential recipients in developing countries to gain access to, and pay for, needed technologies. IPR owners enjoy, in principle, the legal power to decide whether to exploit products and processes in such countries and how to do so (via direct exports, foreign direct investment or licensing). The TRIPS Agreement has but increased that power.

Stronger IPRs will make the "catching up" processes in developing countries more difficult, because imitation via reverse engineering will be excluded on a wider scale, while the costs of obtaining licenses are likely to increase, if they are obtainable at all. This is regrettable from a development perspective, but it was not an unexpected consequence for the proponents of the Agreement, led by a transnational coalition of powerful corporations from the United States, Europe and Japan.[136]

The room available within the TRIPS Agreement to foster technology transfers to developing countries is quite small. The problems of *access* to technology seem today more fundamental than those relating to the *conditions* under which

---

[135] *See, e.g.,* G. Helleiner, *The Role of Multinational Corporations in the Less Developed Countries' Trade in Technology*, 3 WORLD DEV. 161 (1975); Pack, above n. 131, at 80.

[136] *See, e.g.,* S.K. SELL, PRIVATE POWER, PUBLIC LAW: THE GLOBALIZATION OF INTELLECTUAL PROPERTY RIGHTS 97 (Cambridge University Press 2003).

the actual transfer may take place.[137] Future work in this area may include the development of disciplines, at the national or international level, to promote access to technology in cases of refusal to deal and non-working, and to regulate restrictive practices in licensing contracts. The issue of access to the results of publicly funded R&D may also be considered, with an aim to prevent restrictions on its transfer to developing countries, especially for research purposes.[138]

It also seems necessary, as suggested by a number of developing countries, to identify ways to take "full advantage of the flexibility" inherent in the TRIMS Agreement,[139] GATS[140] and other WTO Agreements, and to relax the restrictions that certain provisions in WTO agreements may impose on the transfer and dissemination of technology, "with a view to making the necessary amendments for facilitating and ensuring the transfer of technology on fair and advantageous terms and in line with the special and differential treatment provisions."[141]

This exercise, if successful, may reduce or eliminate some potential normative obstacles to the transfer of technology. However, it would not provide the incentives needed for the technology owners to do so, nor necessarily increase developing countries' legal capacity to gain access to required technologies.

---

[137] In contrast to the situation prevailing in the 1970s and 1980s (when the International Code of Conduct on Transfer of Technology was negotiated) where access to relatively mature technologies was greater, and it permitted developing countries to advance (often in the context of protected markets) their industrialization processes. *See, e.g.*, C. Correa, *Emerging Trends: New Patterns of Technology Transfer*, in THE INTERNATIONAL TRANSFER OF TECHNOLOGY: THE ORIGINS AND AFTERMATH OF THE UNITED NATIONS NEGOTIATIONS ON A DRAFT CODE OF CONDUCT (Kluwer Law International 2000).

[138] Such as the substantial local manufacturing requirement established by U.S. law (35 U.S.C. § 209 (2000)), with regard to patented research results under the Bayh-Dole Act of 1980. 35 U.S.C. §§ 200–212 (2000). *See also* John Barton, *Integrating IPRs Policies in Development Strategies*, in TRADING IN KNOWLEDGE 57 (C. Bellman et al. eds., 2003) (proposing international treaty to preserve scientific commons); J.H. Reichman & P.F. Uhlir, *A Contractually Reconstructed Research Commons for Scientific Data in a Highly Protectionist Intellectual Property Environment*, 66 LAW & CONTEMP. PROBS. 315 (2003).

[139] Trade-Related Investment Measures, 15 Apr. 1994, Marrakesh Agreement Establishing the World Trade Organization, Annex 1A, LEGAL INSTRUMENTS – RESULTS OF THE URUGUAY ROUND, 33 I.L.M. 1144 (1994). The TRIMS Agreement does not prevent Members from establishing performance requirements relating to technology transfer. *See, e.g.*, CARLOS CORREA & NAGESH KUMAR, INTERNATIONAL RULES FOR FOREIGN INVESTMENT: TRADE-RELATED INVESTMENT MEASURES (TRIMS) AND DEVELOPING COUNTRIES (ZED Books & Academic Foundation 2003).

[140] *See* GATS, above n. 134.

[141] *See* the communication from Bangladesh, Cuba, Dominican Republic, Egypt, Honduras, India, Indonesia, Jamaica, Kenya, Mauritius, Pakistan, Sri Lanka, Tanzania, Uganda, and Zimbabwe to the WTO Working Group on Trade and Transfer of Technology, WT/WGTT/W/2 paras. 4, 6 (15 Apr. 2002).

In sum, the issues affecting the transfer of technology to developing countries are unlikely to be resolved within the limited contours of the TRIPS Agreement and other WTO disciplines. Expanded use of the flexibilities allowed by such rules is an important component of any future strategy, but a set of complementary measures and innovative schemes will be necessary in order to reduce the dramatic North-South asymmetry in technological capacities and to attain the development objectives that the international community endorsed at the Johannesburg Summit on Sustainable Development.[142]

---

[142] UNITED NATIONS, THE ROAD FROM JOHANNESBURG: WORLD SUMMIT ON SUSTAINABLE DEVELOPMENT: WHAT WAS ACHIEVED AND THE WAY FORWARD (2003), *available at* http://www.un.org/esa/sustdev/media/Brochure.pdf.

COMMENTARY I

Comment: Technology transfer on the international agenda

PEDRO ROFFE*

Introduction

The controversial and divisive debate on transfer of technology, which acquired importance on the international economic agenda with the launching of the unsuccessful negotiations concerning a Draft Code of Conduct in the 1970s, remains a subject of continuing multilateral negotiations. The main agenda of the 1970s[1] was to close the technological gap between developed and developing countries and to secure "equal opportunities for all countries" and "special treatment for the developing countries."[2] At the center of the debate was the interface between intellectual property rights (IPRs) and transfer of technology. Important contributions to this discussion have been made in this volume. This comment offers some general obervations about the nature of the debate and its evolution, and about the principal contributions to this chapter.

I. Technology transfer on the international agenda

Since the 1970s, perceptions of the problems attending the transfer of technology have changed. At first, much of the debate focused on technology transfer *per se* and, in particular, on the terms and conditions of technology transactions. Technology was generally assumed to be like any other product, and its transfer resembled the typical transaction between a seller and a buyer. The *tacit* elements of the transfer and the fact that local learning of new skills may have been necessary to complete the transaction were not given much consideration. Such information problems were not taken into account because firms were assumed to operate with full knowledge of the market for inputs,

---

* Pedro Roffe is the Director of the UNCTAD-ICTSD Project on Intellectual Property Rights and Development. The views expressed in this note are his own.
[1] *See* INTERNATIONAL TRANSFER OF TECHNOLOGY: THE ORIGINS AND AFTERMATH OF THE UNITED NATIONS NEGOTIATIONS ON A DRAFT CODE OF CONDUCT (S. Patel et al. eds., Kluwer Law International 2001) [hereinafter INTERNATIONAL TRANSFER OF TECHNOLOGY].
[2] Preamble, Draft International Code of Conduct on Transfer of Technology. *See* INTERNATIONAL TRANSFER OF TECHNOLOGY, above n. 1, Annex II.

including technology. Firms were also presumed to behave rationally when acquiring technologies, selecting only those that were appropriate to local conditions. Thus, any problems with technology transfer were cast largely in terms of the mechanisms of, and conditions for, technology transfer and the obstacles resulting from the exercise of monopoly power in the international market. Accordingly, policy prescriptions focused on measures designed to facilitate easier access to foreign technology and to eliminate defects in the international market for technology.

Our understanding of the process of technology transfer has since undergone significant changes. Technology is no longer considered to be like any other product that can be bought and sold in the market without consideration of the need for capacity-building in recipient countries and the tacit elements that make for effective transactions. The globalization of markets in conjunction with rapid advances in technology, especially biotechnology and information and communications technology, has changed the dynamics of comparative advantage, as well as perceptions of the process of technology transfer.[3]

One new factor has been the upgrading of technological capabilities in countries such as the Republic of Korea, Singapore, and Taiwan (China). This phenomenon taught us that, in building technological dynamism, what matters most is not the transfer of technology as such but rather what happens to the technology once it has been transferred. It requires us to pay greater attention to the processes of technology adaptation and domestic technological mastery than to the nature of commercial transactions as such. Furthermore, the process of transferring technology turns out to be much more complex than it appeared in the past; it involves not only a commercial transaction of a product, such as a machine, but also the transfer of the knowledge and skills needed to operate the machine, as well as other important elements of the transfer process, including intellectual property rights and investment.[4]

With technology rapidly advancing, intangible investments now dominate the production and investment patterns of most dynamic enterprises. The knowledge component of the output of manufacturing goods is estimated to have risen from 20 percent in the 1950s to 70 percent in 1995.[5] As the Secretary-General of the United Nations Conference on Trade and Development (UNCTAD) observed, "the knowledge factor appears to be the most important element in the shaping of the new international economic order, as it alters radically the state of overall equilibrium created by the century-old industrial world and the associated comparative advantage that

---

[3] See UNCTAD, FOSTERING TECHNOLOGICAL DYNAMISM: EVOLUTION OF THOUGHT ON TECHNOLOGICAL DEVELOPMENT PROCESS AND COMPETITIVENESS: A REVIEW OF LITERATURE, U.N. Sales No. E.95.II.D.21 (1996).
[4] See P. Roffe & T. Tesfachew, *The Unfinished Agenda*, in INTERNATIONAL TRANSFER OF TECHNOLOGY, above n. 1, at 381.
[5] See T.A. STEWART, INTELLECTUAL CAPITAL (Nicholas Bradley 1997).

it has enjoyed."[6] The critical role of knowledge in economic development, the relative competitiveness of enterprises in different countries, and the emergence of what has been characterized as a *learning economy* is now widely recognized.[7] At the normative level, this recognition has been reflected in, among other things, the special attention paid to the protection of intellectual property rights and of foreign investment in international negotiations.

The failure of the Code of Conduct negotiations, which were launched in the mid-1970s and continued until the mid-1980s, did not, however, lessen the concerns about impediments to the transfer of technology that were under discussion. On the contrary, these issues have remained a recurrent theme in multilateral deliberations. In the context of multilateral environmental agreements (MEAs), for example, the issue of transferring environmentally sound technologies has been a regular feature of agreements negotiated since the Rio de Janeiro Earth Summit in 1992. The transfer of such technologies to developing countries is often presented as an essential condition for successful realization of the aims of these MEAs.

At the policy level, as observed above, much of the analysis formerly focused on the imperfections of the technology transfer process and on the role played by transnational corporations. Emphasis was placed on defensive measures to remedy defects in the international market for technology.[8] Today, by contrast, defensive measures are less in vogue because market imperfections are better addressed by improving competitiveness and the contestability of markets than by directly intervening to influence the conditions on which the transfer of technology takes place. Transfer of technology from abroad remains important – not as a substitute but rather as a stimulus to domestic technological dynamism.

However, international efforts to deal with the issue of technology transfer continue to focus on the acquisition of technology and, as illustrated by the TRIPS Agreement, such efforts normally take the form of general, exhortatory statements.[9] The broad objective of the TRIPS Agreement is to have the *protection and enforcement of intellectual property rights* contribute *to the*

---

[6] R. Ricupero, *Trade and Technology: Issues at Stake for Developing Countries*, in UNCTAD, TECHNOLOGY, TRADE POLICY AND THE URUGUAY ROUND, U.N. Doc. UNCTAD/ITP/23 (1990).

[7] *See* WORLD BANK, KNOWLEDGE FOR DEVELOPMENT, WORLD DEVELOPMENT REPORT 1998/1999 (Oxford University Press 1999).

[8] *See* C. Correa, *Emerging Trends: New Patterns of Technology Transfer* and A. Omer, *An Overview of Legislative Changes*, in INTERNATIONAL TECHNOLOGY TRANSFER, above n. 1.

[9] *See e.g.*, Agreement on Trade-Related Aspects of Intellectual Property Rights, 15 Apr. 1994, Marrakesh Agreement Establishing the World Trade Organization, Annex 1C, LEGAL INSTRUMENTS – RESULTS OF THE URUGUAY ROUND, vol. 31, 33 I.L.M. 81 (1994) [hereinafter TRIPS Agreement], art. 66.2 ("Developed country Members shall provide incentives to enterprises and institutions in their territories for the purpose of promoting and encouraging technology transfer to least-developed country Members in order to enable them to create a sound and viable technological base.").

transfer and dissemination of technology.[10] It also stipulates that developed countries shall provide incentives to their enterprises and institutions to promote and encourage technology transfer to the Least-Developed Countries (LDCs).[11]

As in the past, the responsibility for facilitating the transfer of technology falls on the home government of transnational firms. However, there are obvious limitations to this approach: transnational firms generally do not develop industrial technologies with the needs of host country firms or markets in mind. This reality, of course, does not mean that home countries cannot design policies and incentives to improve the transfer of technology to developing countries. Indeed, with this objective in mind, a number of them have instituted policies, such as investment insurance programs for firms that invest abroad.[12]

It is also essential to note that coherent structures and policies in receiving countries are prerequisites to the enhancement of domestic capacities and, consequently, to the assimilation and dissemination of foreign technology. In this respect, the domestic intellectual property regime is one among many factors that cannot be seen in isolation from other policies, particularly those affecting the operation of national innovation systems.[13] Each country's national innovation system is comprised of suppliers, customers, R&D institutions, universities, technological institutes and bridging institutions, such as sectoral and innovation centers, industry associations, institutions involved in education and training, and financial institutions geared to financing new initiatives. The level of sophistication and effectiveness of national innovation systems, however, differs among countries. A key property of any given system is that the nature of its component parts is less important than the ways in which they interact and perform as a dynamic whole.[14]

II. IPRs and transfer of technology

The evidence produced so far concerning the claimed links between stronger IPRs, greater investment flows, and enhanced R&D and technology transfers remains inconclusive. The relationship between levels of IPR protection and the volume

---

[10] *Id.* art. 7. [11] *See* above n. 9.
[12] *See* UNCTAD, FOREIGN DIRECT INVESTMENT AND DEVELOPMENT, U.N. Doc. UNCTAD/ITE/IIT/10 (vol. I), U.N. Sales No. E.98II.D.15 (1999); UNCTAD, WORLD INVESTMENT REPORT, U.N. Doc. UNCTAD/WIR/2003, U.N. Sales No. E.03.II.D.8. (2003).
[13] The general goal of national innovation systems is to enhance a country's stock of technical knowledge and know-how, which occurs both through acquisition and learning of foreign technology and the development of institutions and technical capabilities at home.
[14] *See* UNCTAD, INVESTMENT AND INNOVATION POLICY REVIEW: ETHIOPIA, U.N. Doc. UNCTAD/ITE/IPC/Misc.4, U.N. Sales No. GE.02 – 500021 (2002).

and quality of inward flows of technology is complex, and is likely to involve many factors whose relative importance will vary widely from one country to another.[15]

Theoretically, it seems logical to assume that IPR availability constitutes a prerequisite for the international transfer of certain new technologies – especially those that can be easily copied. One would expect companies to be reluctant to lose control of technologies that often cost large sums to develop to countries where domestic firms could copy and produce knowledge goods that would compete with those made by the innovators. Accordingly, the only way to encourage companies to transfer proprietary technologies is to offer IPR protection that is strong enough to allow them to charge prices that reflect the costs of innovation, or alternatively, to encourage them to commit to direct foreign investment (FDI) or to joint ventures in which they maintain more control over their technologies.[16]

Much uncertainty nonetheless remains regarding the effects of IPRs on technology transfers to developing countries. These effects probably depend on the level of development of a receiving country, the specific technological fields involved, the behavior and absorptive capacity of single local firms and the general macroeconomic environment of the host country. In other words, a one-size-fits-all approach is ill-conceived. Simply strengthening and enforcing IPRs is not a recipe for increased local innovation, technology transfer and FDI. The recently published report of the Commission on Intellectual Property Rights concluded that

> in most low income countries, with a weak scientific and technological infrastructure, IP protection at the levels mandated by TRIPS is not a significant determinant of growth. On the contrary, rapid growth is more often associated with weaker IP protection. In technologically advanced developing countries, there is some evidence that IP protection becomes important at a stage of development, but that stage is not until a country is well into the category of upper middle income developing countries.[17]

III. The contributions to this volume

The chapters in this volume by Carlos Correa,[18] Arti Rai,[19] and Keith Maskus, Kamal Saggi, and Thitima Puttitanun[20] complement each other and provide

---

[15] UNCTAD, THE TRIPS AGREEMENT AND DEVELOPING COUNTRIES, U.N. Doc. UNCTAD/ITE/1, U.N. Sales No. E.96.II.D.10 (1997).
[16] Intellectual Property Rights: Implications for Development, UNCTAD-ICTSD Policy Discussion Paper (Aug. 2003).
[17] Integrating Intellectual Property Rights and Development Policy, Report of the Commission on Intellectual Property (Sept. 2002).
[18] Carlos Correa, *Can the TRIPS Agreement Foster Technology Transfer to Developing Countries?* [this volume].
[19] Arti Rai, *Proprietary Rights and Collective Action: The Case of Biotechnology Research with Low Commercial Value* [this volume].
[20] Keith Maskus et al., *Patent Rights and International Technology Transfer Through Direct Investment and Licensing* [this volume].

new insights into the longstanding debate about the transfer of technology to developing countries and the specific interface between IPRs and transfer of technology. Their contributions fall in different categories. Maskus, Saggi and Puttitanun look at the impact of IP protection on FDI and licensing as two main channels of transfer of technology. Arti Rai focuses on publicly funded research as a potential source of opportunities for developing countries. Carlos Correa deals with the TRIPS Agreement and its potential impact on impediments to the transfer of technology.

Maskus and co-authors reconfirm the results of other recent studies showing that the impact of IPRs on transfer of technology to developing countries depends on the level of economic and technological development in specific receiving countries.[21] Moreover, their paper goes beyond earlier work, for example, in its emphasis on the issues of costs of imitation and the fixed costs of technology transfer. This approach introduces new elements into the analysis. Often, the higher levels of skill, technological learning and investment required to develop even imitating capabilities are ignored in assessing the implications of intellectual property regimes for technology transfer. But, as highlighted in their paper, they can be important determining factors in decisions of owners of proprietary technology.

What remains unclear, however, are the implications of these findings for investment and technology policies of recipient countries. For example, is it always the case that a recipient firm needs to undertake some R&D on its own in order for technology transfer to succeed? The experiences of South East Asian countries suggest otherwise. Also, if, as rightly pointed out, imitation and reverse engineering involve costs and high levels of skills, then why should transnational corporations worry about transferring technology to low-technology economies even in the absence of strong IPR protection?

Arti Rai's paper brings a new dimension to the debate: it concerns how collective rights are to be managed and how developing countries might benefit from publicly funded research. She underscores the role played in some countries by universities in obtaining patents, e.g., in the biomedical arena, and she discusses their new commercialization policies. One important conclusion is that, to serve developing countries' needs, public sector institutions need to consider intellectual property issues carefully.

Rai's paper raises key questions that call for further inquiries about how to realize the potential benefits of publicly funded research for transfers of technology to developing countries. She alludes to some solutions, such as clearing houses or IPR banks. Some work was done on this topic in the past, but only with limited operational results. The issues raised in her paper are no

---

[21] *See* L. Kim, Technology Transfer and Intellectual Property Rights: Lessons from Korea's Experience, UNCTAD-ICTSD Issue Paper (2002); S. Lall, Indicators of the Relative Importance of IPRs in Developing Countries, UNCTAD-ICTSD Issue Paper (2001).

doubt connected with Maskus and his co-authors' concerns about the costs involved in adaptation, imitation and absorption.

Finally, Correa's paper looks at the same issues from a normative perspective. It deals comprehensively with the TRIPS Agreement and its relationship to transfers of technology. He analyzes the Agreement in terms of its objectives and principles, its provisions on anti-competitive practices, its provisions regarding the disclosure of patent information, its compulsory licensing mechanism, and its special rules for LDCs. He contributes an original view of how TRIPS can stimulate or hinder the transfer of technology to developing countries.

Correa's point of departure is that the TRIPS Agreement focuses primarily on protection and only marginally on the transfer of technology. Although his paper is consistent with Maskus et al.'s discussion of the relative impact of intellectual property protection on foreign direct investment and licensing, Correa remains less confident about the positive impact of intellectual property on transfer of technology to developing countries.

Correa's discussion of LDCs raises important questions. He emphasizes the mandatory nature of article 66.2 of the TRIPS Agreement and elaborates on the measures that developed countries should adopt. However, his emphasis on IPR-related measures requires some additional comments.

The negotiating history of article 66.2 sheds little light on problems of implementation.[22] The incorporation of the provision into the Agreement was a last minute attempt by developing countries to rebalance the final deal. Developed countries were not keen on such a change and succeeded in limiting its scope to the LDCs only.

A suggestion that the incentives required by article 66.2 should be limited to IPR-related measures could be too narrow an approach and of little practical use to LDCs. IPR-related measures are more domestic in nature and could be characterized as steps that a host country could adopt to attract, facilitate and modulate the transfer of technology. Home countries of international firms would have a limited role in this respect. However, considering the various channels of technology transfer, one could identify a number of other incentives – not necessarily IPR-related – that home countries could adopt to encourage transfer of technology to developing countries. Certainly, the TRIPS Agreement is an intellectual property instrument, but Article 66.2 is expressly concerned with creating *a sound and viable technological base* in host countries.

Moreover, the system established by the Council for TRIPS to monitor the implementation of article 66.2 does not restrict its scope to IPRs. It refers,

---

[22] *See* UNCTAD-ICTSD, Resource Book on TRIPS and Development (Cambridge University Press 2005).

among other things, to incentives related to any *mode of technology transfer* without other qualifications.[23]

In brief, the three papers make excellent contributions to a long and unfinished debate about the transfer of technology to developing countries. They enhance our understanding of the issues and aid in the continuing search for solutions.

---

[23] Decision by the Council for TRIPS of February 2003, WTO Doc. IP/C/28.

9

Patent rights and international technology transfer through direct investment and licensing

KEITH E. MASKUS

KAMAL SAGGI

THITIMA PUTTITANUN[*]

1. Introduction
2. Economics of access to foreign technology
   2.1 Recipient country characteristics
   2.2 Firm characteristics
   2.3 Intellectual property rights and technology transfer
3. A model of the choice between investment and licensing
4. Evidence supporting the hypothesis
5. Policy conclusions

1. Introduction

A central concern among policymakers is to understand how the shift toward stronger protection of intellectual property rights (IPRs) may affect access of developing countries to advanced proprietary technologies from firms in developed countries.[1] Developing countries, including least-developed countries, place considerable hope in the power of foreign technology to improve the productivity and growth performances of their economies. Indeed, a key plank of the Doha Declaration calls on developed countries to find means of encouraging technology transfer to the least-developed nations, as specified in Article 66.2 of the Agreement on Trade-Related Aspects of Intellectual Property Rights at the World Trade Organization.[2]

---

[*] Keith E. Maskus is Professor of Economics and Department Chair, University of Colorado at Boulder. Kamal Saggi is Professor of Economics, Southern Methodist University. Thitima Puttitanun is Assistant Professor of Economics, San Diego State University.

[1] For a comprehensive discussion, see Keith E. Maskus, Encouraging International Technology Transfer, International Centre for Trade and Sustainable Development, Issue Paper No. 7 (2004).

[2] Agreement on Trade-Related Aspects of Intellectual Property Rights, 15 Apr. 1994, Marrakesh Agreement Establishing the World Trade Organization, Annex 1C, LEGAL

The extent to which international technology flows would increase as a result of strengthening IPRs depends importantly on the state of access to technological information. Such access is determined by a variety of factors.[3] Impediments may come from many sources in the recipient country, including weak domestic absorption capacities, poor infrastructure, restrictions on inward technology, trade, and investment flows, and inadequate regulatory systems. In this context, strengthening intellectual property (IP) protection could play a positive and important role in mitigating the costs such factors raise for investors and thereby expanding technology flows.[4] It should be evident from this brief description, however, that simply strengthening IPRs alone cannot suffice to improve access significantly. Rather, the intellectual property regime needs to be buttressed by appropriate infrastructure, governance, and competition systems in order to be effective.

One should note, however, that patents can block technology transfers under certain circumstances.[5] Firms may choose to withhold technological information from particular countries for competitive reasons, a strategy that is facilitated by globalized IPRs. The specter of anticompetitive deployment of patents and patent pools in order to discourage local firms from learning technologies through imitation and reverse engineering surely looms large in the context of weak competition enforcement in most developing economies.[6] Thus, as ever in the area of IPRs, there is a balancing act to pursue in linking policy on technology protection to the needs of economic development.

Our aim in this chapter is to make two contributions to this question. First, we provide an extensive discussion of the economic literature on this subject in order to bring out important themes for policymakers. Second, we add to the literature by positing a simple model in which a multinational firm can choose between transferring a technology abroad through either foreign direct investment (FDI) or licensing. The decision is affected in two ways by a tightening of patent protection. On the one hand, by raising the costs of imitation on the part of local firms, this policy change makes the firm more likely to engage in both forms of transfer. On the other hand, by reducing the relative fixed costs of reaching and enforcing licensing contracts, stronger protection should shift incentives toward

INSTRUMENTS – RESULTS OF THE URUGUAY ROUND vol. 31, 33 I.L.M. 81 (1994) [hereinafter TRIPS Agreement], art. 66.2.

[3] Maskus, above n. 1. *See also* Kamal Saggi, International Technology Transfer: National Policies, International Negotiations, and Multilateral Disciplines, Report for Commonwealth Secretariat (2003).
[4] KEITH E. MASKUS, INTELLECTUAL PROPERTY RIGHTS IN THE GLOBAL ECONOMY (Institute for International Economics 2000).
[5] Maskus, above n. 1. *See also* Integrating Intellectual Property Rights and Development Policy, Report of the Commission on Intellectual Property Rights (2002).
[6] *See* Eleanor Fox, *Can Antitrust Policy Protect the Global Commons from the Excesses of IPRs?* [this volume]; Carlos M. Correa, *Can the TRIPS Agreement Foster Technology Transfer to Developing Countries?* [this volume].

that form of transfer and away from FDI. However, we identify a subtle interaction between these two impacts that implies a different response, depending on whether the firm resides in a low-innovation or a high-innovation sector. We also test this model with U.S. contract data and find good support for it.

2. Economics of access to foreign technology

We provide an overview of the central literature from economics on the relationship between intellectual property protection and access of enterprises in technological follower nations to foreign proprietary technology. This is a complex question that can only be highlighted here.[7]

A central point is that successful technology transfer is generally costly and complex. A complete transfer that takes place through formal channels involves the shift of codified knowledge (blueprints, formulas, management techniques, customer lists), tacit knowledge (know-how, information gained from experience), and contractual obligations (payments, territorial restrictions, conditions on use, profit-sharing, tax liabilities). These formal channels include FDI, licensing, joint ventures, and various mixed forms. The costs of making such transfers vary among channels, as do the subsequent costs of production and performance monitoring.[8] Indeed, these costs are often at the heart of decisions made among these modes.

Technologies are also transferred through informal channels.[9] Most evidently, much technological information flows across borders through international trade in advanced inputs, reverse engineering of technology embodied in goods and services, and replication of production processes in published patents.[10] It is clear that much information spills across borders through such uncompensated channels, with a positive impact on local productivity.[11]

---

[7] Keith E. Maskus, *The Role of Intellectual Property Rights in Encouraging Foreign Direct Investment and Technology Transfer*, 32 DUKE J. COMP. & INT'L L. 471 (1998), provides an extensive discussion. *See also* Organization for Economic Cooperation and Development (OECD), The Impact of Trade-Related Intellectual Property Rights on Trade and Foreign Direct Investment in Developing Countries, Doc. TD/TC/WP(2002)42/FINAL (2003).

[8] *See* DAVID J. TEECE, THE MULTINATIONAL CORPORATION AND THE RESOURCE COST OF INTERNATIONAL TECHNOLOGY TRANSFER (Ballinger Press 1986). *See also* Saggi, above n. 3.

[9] Maskus, above n. 1.

[10] *See* Wolfgang Keller, *Geographic Localization of International Technology Diffusion*, 92 AM. ECON. REV. 120 (2002); Jonathan Eaton & Samuel Kortum, *Technology, Geography, and Trade*, 70 ECONOMETRICA 1741 (2002).

[11] David Coe et al., *North-South R&D Spillovers*, 107 ECON. J. 134 (1997); Eaton & Kortum, above n. 10; Jonathan Eaton & Samuel Kortum, *Trade in Ideas: Patenting and Productivity in the OECD*, 40 J. INT'L ECON. 251 (1996); Keller, above n. 10. Richard E. Baldwin et al., Multinationals, Endogenous Growth and Technological Spillovers: Theory and Evidence, Centre for Economic Policy Research, Working Paper No. 2155 (1999), provide such results in different analytical frameworks.

Indeed, this productivity enhancement may be due at least as much to efforts of local firms to make improvements upon technologies from abroad.

Although copying of books, videos, and CDs receives most of the attention regarding conflicts over IP protection, imitating most products is not straightforward.[12] Empirical evidence indicates that imitation is a costly activity for a wide range of high-technology goods, such as chemicals, drugs, electronics, and machinery. One study found that the costs of imitation average 65 percent of the costs of innovation (and very few products are below 20 percent).[13] However, these estimates are outdated, and in such areas as pharmaceuticals and biotechnology, imitation costs have declined relative to original innovation.[14]

The likelihood that firms in a particular country will have access to, and successfully absorb, technological information through either informal or formal channels, depends on characteristics of the country in which they are located, capacities of the firms themselves, and the nature of the technologies in question.[15]

2.1 Recipient country characteristics

The recipient nation's ability to attract and absorb technology depends on a wide variety of factors. Most obviously, the size and expected growth of an economy's market acts as a major incentive for inward licensing and FDI.[16] Besides this demand-side factor, large economies provide scope for plant-level scale economies, distribution economies, and agglomeration advantages.

The impacts of openness to trade and investment are more subtle. Liberal economies have greater access to imported goods and capital, with embodied technologies that may be learned and diffused through the economy. However, FDI, at least of a horizontal nature, is attracted by restraints on trade in order to benefit from protected markets.[17] Vertical FDI seems more attracted to open economies because such investment is generally designed to produce exports.[18] There is not much evidence available on the relationship between openness and licensing.

---

[12] *See* Robert E. Evenson & Larry E. Westphal, *Technological Change and Technology Policy*, in HANDBOOK OF DEVELOPMENT ECONOMICS vol. 3A, at 2209 (Jere Behrman & T.N. Srinivasan ed., North Holland 1995).

[13] *See* Edwin Mansfield et al., *Imitation Costs and Patents: An Empirical Study*, 91 ECON. J. 907 (1981).

[14] MASKUS, above n. 4, offers a critical discussion.   [15] Maskus, above n. 7.

[16] *See* David Wheeler & Ashoka Mody, *International Investment Location Decisions: The Case of U.S. Firms*, 33 J. INT'L ECON. 57 (1992); David L. Carr et al., *Estimating the Knowledge-Capital Model of the Multinational Enterprise*, 91 AM. ECON. REV. 693 (2001); Guifang Yang & Keith E. Maskus, *Intellectual Property Rights and Licensing: An Econometric Investigation*, 137 WELTWIRTSCHAFTLICHES ARCHIV 58 (2001).

[17] JAMES R. MARKUSEN, MULTINATIONAL FIRMS AND THE THEORY OF INTERNATIONAL TRADE (MIT Press 2002); David L. Carr et al., above n. 16.

[18] MARKUSEN, above n. 17.

Labor skills are a central element in attracting technology, in terms of both the nature of goods traded and of capital and technology imported. Evidence suggests that direct investment generally seeks locations with an abundance of skilled and semi-skilled workers rather than economies in which low wages reflect lagging productivity.[19] A significant skill basis is important for absorbing know-how successfully and for deploying a work force that effectively complements modern technologies. While labor-intensive sectors are more likely to seek low-wage locations, even these cost advantages are attenuated by low productivity, high absenteeism, and the like.[20]

Numerous studies demonstrate that adequate physical and telecommunications infrastructure and a significant supply of producer and financial services are positive determinants of inward FDI and technology contracts.[21] Political and economic stability are important also, as is a transparent governance structure. In this context, an important task for encouraging technology transfer is the development of local capacity for providing public and private services and for efficient public administration.

The role of geographic distance in limiting trade flows and FDI is well-established. Because of this factor, the ability of countries that are remote from major markets to achieve technological spillovers through trade and investment is severely limited.[22] Perhaps equally important is the technological distance at which a country is located from the information frontier. Countries are more likely to absorb technology and learn from it when they are engaging in innovation themselves. In this regard, policies regarding education, capital accumulation, R&D incentives, integration of research done in universities and public laboratories with private-sector commercialization, and other aspects of the innovation system can be significant.[23]

An important reason that some degree of domestic innovation capacity is critical is that imitation, learning, and innovation are themselves dynamic and cumulative processes, in which information is incrementally improved and diffused through competition.[24] In this context, the design of appropriate incentives for competition and small-scale innovation, in addition to

---

[19] See S. Lael Brainard, *An Empirical Assessment of the Proximity-Concentration Tradeoff Between Multinational Sales and Trade*, 87 AM. ECON. REV. 520 (1997); Carr et al., above n. 16.
[20] MARKUSEN, above n. 17.
[21] See, e.g., David L. Carr et al., *Competition for Multinational Investment in Developing Countries: Human Capital, Infrastructure, and Market Size*, in CHALLENGES TO GLOBALIZATION 383 (Robert E. Baldwin & L. Alan Winters eds., University of Chicago Press 2004); Wheeler & Mody, above n. 16.
[22] See Keller, above n. 10; Eaton & Kortum, above n. 10. [23] MASKUS, above n. 4.
[24] See Suzanne Scotchmer, *Standing on the Shoulders of Giants: Cumulative Research and the Patent Law*, 5 J. ECON. PERSP. 29 (1991); Keith E. Maskus & Christine R. McDaniel, *Impacts of the Japanese Patent System on Productivity Growth*, 11 JAPAN & WORLD ECON. 557 (1999); Jerome H. Reichman, *From Free Riders to Fair Followers: Global Competition Under the TRIPS Agreement*, 29 N.Y.U. J. INT'L L. & POL. 11 (1993).

successful absorption of foreign technology, is particularly important for developing countries.

2.2 Firm characteristics

Evidence suggests that for technology transfer to succeed, the recipient firm may need to undertake some R&D on its own.[25] The essential reason is that without an understanding of the research and experimentation process the transactions costs in acquiring and deploying the technology may be high and uncertain, making effective absorption infeasible. More directly, firms undertaking R&D presumably are better positioned to engage in effective reverse engineering and imitative production. Technology management is also a complex activity that improves with experience.[26]

2.3 Intellectual property rights and technology transfer

To provide focus for what would otherwise be an overly broad discussion, we emphasize theory and empirical evidence in the economics literature about the relationship between intellectual property protection in developing countries and flows of technology through FDI and licensing.

The theoretical literature has often investigated the effect of IP enforcement on technology transfer and FDI in endogenous growth models, where technology flows from developed countries (labeled "North") to developing countries (labeled "South").[27] These papers are linked through their use of the quality-ladders model or the love-of-variety model of dynamic technical change.[28] In a model with exogenous rates of Northern innovation, Helpman showed that a decline in the amount of effort devoted to imitation by firms in developing countries would limit technology flows to the South.[29] By associating a

---

[25] See Saggi, above n. 3.
[26] See Manjula Luthria & Keith E. Maskus, *Protecting Industrial Inventions, Authors' Rights, and Traditional Knowledge: Relevance, Lessons, and Unresolved Issues*, in EAST ASIA INTEGRATES: A TRADE POLICY AGENDA FOR SHARED GROWTH 95–114 (Kathie Krumm & Homi Kharas eds., Oxford University Press 2004).
[27] Other approaches also exist. For example, in a strategic partial equilibrium model, Sharmila Vishwasrao, *Intellectual Property Rights and the Mode of Technology Transfer*, 44 J. DEV. ECON. 381 (1994), argued that the lack of adequate enforcement of technology transfer agreements may encourage FDI relative to licensing. In her screening model, depending on the type of licensee, licensing may or may not lead to imitation. The trade-off between FDI and licensing is that FDI avoids the risk of imitation at the expense of higher production costs.
[28] These models were developed extensively by GENE GROSSMAN & ELHANAN HELPMAN, INNOVATION AND GROWTH IN THE GLOBAL ECONOMY (M.I.T. Press, 1991).
[29] Elhanan Helpman, *Innovation, Imitation, and Intellectual Property Rights*, 61 ECONOMETRICA 1247 (1993).

reduction in imitation with stronger IPRs, Helpman provided the first detailed welfare analysis of patent enforcement in developing countries. In his model, a strengthening of intellectual property protection was not in the interest of such countries and could, in the long run, reduce global innovation and thereby restrict global welfare.[30] Edwin Lai extended Helpman's model to allow for FDI and argued that both FDI and innovation would be encouraged if the South were to strengthen its IPRs.[31] The common weakness of both models is that stronger patent enforcement is modeled as an exogenous decline in the rate of imitation by firms in developing countries.

Guifang Yang and Keith Maskus studied the effects of Southern IP enforcement on both the rate of innovation in the North and the extent of technology licensing undertaken by Northern firms.[32] A key assumption in their model is that strengthened patent rights would increase the licensor's share of profits and reduce the costs of enforcing licensing contracts, thereby making licensing more attractive. Thus, in their model, both innovation and licensing would rise as patent protection in the South became stronger.

Amy Glass and Kamal Saggi analyzed the implications of Southern IP protection in a comprehensive product-cycle model of trade and FDI.[33] In their model, Southern imitation targets both multinational firms producing in the South and purely Northern firms producing in the North. They treated stronger patents as an increase in imitation cost stemming, say, from stricter uniqueness requirements. They found that FDI actually would fall with a strengthening of Southern IP protection. This result arises because an increase in the cost of imitation would diminish FDI by reducing the supply of Southern labor available for producing in Northern affiliates.

It is clear from this discussion that the theoretical literature does not give an unambiguous prediction regarding the effects of stronger Southern IP protection on the extent of technology transfer through FDI and licensing. Empirical evidence provides some insights, but because much of it exists at the aggregate level and relies on survey evidence, it should be treated cautiously. Surveys of U.S. multinational firms found that such firms are more willing to invest in countries with stronger IPRs.[34] These studies also suggested that IPRs are

---

[30] *Id.*
[31] Edwin Lai, *International Intellectual Property Rights Protection and Rate of Product Innovation*, 55 J. Dev. Econ. 133 (1998).
[32] Guifang Yang & Keith E. Maskus, above n. 16.
[33] Amy J. Glass & Kamal Saggi, *Intellectual Property Rights and Foreign Direct Investment*, 56 J. Int'l Econ. 387 (2002).
[34] For evidence, see Jong-Wha Lee & Edwin Mansfield, *Intellectual Property Protection and U.S. Foreign Direct Investment*, 78 Rev. Econ. & Stat. (1996); Edwin Mansfield, Intellectual Property Protection, Foreign Direct Investment, and Technology Transfer, International Finance Corporation, Discussion Paper 19 (1994). *But see* Paul J. Heald, *Misreading a Canonical Work: An Analysis of Mansfield's 1994 study*, 10 J. Intell. Prop. L 309 (2003), for a criticism of the Mansfield study. Heald points out that aggregative

important for location decisions in FDI, though the importance varies with type of investment. A further result was that perceived weakness of IP protection was significantly and negatively related to investment decisions across countries, suggesting that countries that strengthen their patent regimes could attract additional FDI inflows.[35]

A more complete treatment of FDI requires recognizing that Northern firms have options over how to transact technology through the market. For example, FDI could increase with IP enforcement, but this policy could more readily encourage licensing by lowering the risk of opportunism in market transactions.[36] Studies that ignore the possibility of licensing (or joint ventures) are likely to overstate the effect of IPRs on inward FDI.

Therefore, a more subtle analysis may be needed. Increased IP enforcement by a developing nation may indeed make it a more attractive location for production. However, the technologies transferred for that purpose might flow through licensing rather than FDI, so that the net effect on FDI is ambiguous. Later in this chapter, we develop a simple model that focuses on the effect of IPRs on the choice between licensing and FDI.

Using data for 1982 on U.S. exports and sales of overseas affiliates of U.S. firms, one study attempted to identify the cross-country determinants of both exports and sales of multinational affiliates of U.S. firms.[37] The most interesting finding was that U.S. firms export higher-than-expected volumes to their affiliates in countries that have weak IP regimes. The author suggested that this result may reflect attempts by U.S. firms to limit technology leakage to their rivals abroad by confining production within the United States. This interpretation fits well with a central theme of this chapter: multinational firms adjust their portfolio of strategies to react optimally to various policies and market conditions they face in host countries.

Empirical evidence indicates that the level of IP protection in a country may affect the composition of FDI in two different ways.[38] First, in industries for which IPRs are crucial (pharmaceuticals, for example), firms may refrain from investing in countries with weak patent protection. Second, regardless of the industry in question, multinational enterprises are less likely to set up manufacturing and R&D facilities in countries with weak IP regimes, and more likely to set up sales and marketing ventures because the latter run no risk of

economic surveys of Mansfield's type are misleading because they ignore important specifics of national patent regimes.

[35] Mansfield, above n. 34.
[36] Yang & Maskus, above n. 32; Pamela J. Smith, *How Do Foreign Patent Rights Affect U.S. Exports, Affiliate Sales, and Licenses?*, 55 J. INT'L ECON. 411 (2001).
[37] *See* Michael J. Ferrantino, *The Effect of Intellectual Property Rights on International Trade and Investment*, 129 WELTWIRTSCHAFTLICHES ARCHIV 300 (1993).
[38] *See* Lee & Mansfield, above n. 34; Beata Smarzynska-Javorcik, *Composition of Foreign Direct Investment and Protection of Intellectual Property Rights: Evidence from Transition Economies*, 48 EUR. ECON. REV. 36 (2004).

technology leakage. This finding is consistent with results in a careful econometric study that distinguishes between incentives for a multinational enterprise to transfer technology abroad within a firm and those for independent licensing outside the firm.[39] In countries where local imitation capacity is significant, multinational firms are more likely to shift from FDI to licensing as intellectual property rights are made more secure.

These studies present useful findings, but are unable to address perhaps the most central question of all. Does a country's IP regime affect its economic growth through enhancing inward technology flows? Although there are several theoretical analyses of this question, empirical studies are scarce. One such study used cross-country data on patent protection, trade regime, and economic fundamentals.[40] The authors found that IP protection, as measured by the degree of patent strength, is an important determinant of economic growth. Somewhat more interestingly, they found that a strengthening of patent rights is more conducive for growth when it is accompanied by a liberal trade policy.

A possible interpretation of this finding is that, by increasing foreign competition, trade liberalization not only curtails monopoly power granted by patents but also ensures that such monopoly power is obtained only if the innovation is truly global.[41] If firms in other countries can export freely to the domestic market and have better products or technologies, a domestic patent cannot provide strong monopoly power. Furthermore, trade liberalization itself can improve productivity.[42] Thus, the results suggest that IP enforcement matters over and above trade orientation, and that they may have mutually reinforcing effects.

3. A model of the choice between investment and licensing

As discussed in the preceding section, a firm wishing to transfer proprietary technological knowledge through formal channels may choose between FDI and licensing.[43] These are complicated processes, and the choice depends on numerous factors relating to the absorptive capacity of the recipient nation,

---

[39] See Smith, above n. 36.
[40] See David M. Gould & William C. Gruben, *The Role of Intellectual Property Rights in Economic Growth*, 48 J. DEV. ECON. 323 (1996).
[41] See MASKUS, above n. 4.
[42] See James R. Tybout & Daniel Westbrook, *Trade Liberalization and the Structure of Production in Mexican Manufacturing Industries*, 39 J. INT'L ECON. 53 (1995), using data from Mexican manufacturing firms and finding that trade liberalization is associated with higher rates of productivity growth.
[43] In this model, we ignore the possibility of joint ventures, which may be considered a hybrid of the ownership forms and transfers in FDI (full ownership and an internal transfer) and licensing (no claim on ownership and an external transfer).

market size and growth, the threat of imitation, and the legal protection of technology.[44] The choice depends as well on the nature of the technology to be transferred and the relative costs of transferring it through the different channels. In this section we provide a model demonstrating that the impact of a strengthening of technology protection, for example through stronger patents, on the transfer mode depends on the innovativeness of the industry in question.[45]

Specifically, if more rigorous patents significantly reduce the threat of local imitation while also lowering the relative cost of licensing, they would favor transfer through FDI for a lower-technology process or product and through licensing for a higher-technology activity. This insight is distinctive from, and more general than, the standard view in the economics literature that stronger IP protection would favor licensing over FDI.[46]

Consider a single multinational firm owning a technology that may be transferred to a recipient location through either FDI (the formation of a fully owned subsidiary) or arm's-length licensing with an unaffiliated firm. Both options incur a fixed transfer cost of the following form:

$$F^j = P^j + C^j(k) \tag{1}$$

where $j = L, F$ denotes licensing or FDI. Fixed costs are comprised of two distinctive components. First are production-related costs, denoted P, such as investment in equipment, altering production lines, and establishing distribution channels. While these differ between FDI and licensing contracts, they are independent of the strength of intellectual property rights, indexed by k. The second component is costs of contractual elements in transferring knowledge, denoted C. These include such costs as finding legal representation, developing mutually agreeable contract parameters, and enforcing the contract.[47]

We make the reasonable assumption that total fixed costs are higher for FDI than for licensing. The idea is that FDI is a long-term commitment to a location, and this requires more investment in understanding legal and cultural systems and in establishing production and distribution facilities.[48] In contrast, the foreign firm would not absorb these costs in a licensing contract. Thus, we posit that $F^F > F^L$.

It is reasonable to suppose that the costs of achieving acceptable and enforceable contracts decline with the strength of patent rights for both FDI and licensing deals. Thus, we assume that $\frac{dC^j(k)}{dk} < 0$ for $j = F, L$, where an increase in k indicates a more rigorous patent regime. However, it is also

---

[44] See MASKUS, above n. 1 and above n. 7.
[45] A related framework is put forward by Michael Nicholson, Intellectual Property Rights and International Technology Transfer: The Impact of Industry Characteristics (2002) (manuscript, Federal Trade Commission).
[46] Maskus, above n. 7, describes this conventional view in detail.
[47] See TEECE, above n. 8.   [48] See MARKUSEN, above n. 17.

plausible that the rate at which these contractual costs decline with k is faster for licensing contracts:

$$\left|\frac{dC^F(k)}{dk}\right| < \left|\frac{dC^L(k)}{dk}\right| \tag{2}$$

This condition assumes that a strengthening of intellectual property rights lowers contractual licensing costs more than it lowers contractual FDI costs. The justification is that licensing involves developing contracts with unknown parties and transferring technology to an agent external to the licensor firm. In an environment with relatively weak patent rights, it is presumably more difficult to prevent defection of this agent from the licensing contract.[49] Such defection is less likely under FDI contracts, which are internal to the multinational firm.

The multinational firm faces two risks in exploiting its technological advantage. The first is that a rival firm could invent a newer technology that renders its knowledge asset worthless. We assume that a large pool of potential innovators exists in the global market, and their innovation incentives are unaffected by changes in the patent regime of the recipient country. The probability of successful innovation is assumed to follow a Poisson process with arrival parameter i that by assumption is independent of k.[50]

The second risk is that the technology will be imitated by a local firm in the recipient country. We make the strong assumption that imitation is equally likely whether the technology is transferred through FDI or licensing. The notion here is that imitation requires reverse engineering by an unaffiliated local firm, which can only inspect the product itself whether produced by a subsidiary or licensee. Successful imitation also destroys the value of the proprietary knowledge asset. We assume that imitation also follows a Poisson process, with arrival parameter $m(k)$, where $\frac{dm}{dk} < 0$. That is, stronger patent rights reduce the rate of imitation.

Consider the decision made by the multinational firm between FDI and licensing. The multinational chooses one of the two modes at some initial date, taking account of the fact that the instantaneous flow profit from FDI is likely to be higher than that from licensing because the latter contract requires sharing the profits with the licensee.[51] Thus, we assume that $\pi^F > \pi^L$, where these parameters indicate current-period (instantaneous) profits. However, firms are interested in maximizing the lifetime discounted value of their assets,

---

[49] Yang & Maskus, above n. 32, discuss this factor.
[50] This assumption of a Poisson-distributed arrival rate is common in the theoretical literature, as exemplified by Lai, above n. 31; Glass & Saggi, above n. 33; and Yang & Maskus, above n. 32.
[51] There is considerable evidence that rent sharing is central to licensing contracts. See FAROK J. CONTRACTOR, LICENSING IN INTERNATIONAL STRATEGY: A GUIDE FOR PLANNING AND NEGOTIATIONS (Quorum Books 1985); Yang & Maskus, above n. 32.

so we must compare these values over time. Permit r to be the discount rate that firms use to compute the present values of future profits. Applying standard techniques from this literature, we may compute the discounted present value of a firm engaging in FDI as[52]

$$V^F = \frac{\pi^F}{i + m(k) + r} - F^F(k) \tag{3}$$

Similarly, lifetime firm value under licensing is

$$V^L = \frac{\pi^L}{i + m(k) + r} - F^L(k) \tag{4}$$

The firm would choose to engage in FDI if $V^F > V^L$. We can analyze this choice by working with the condition for indifference between FDI and licensing:

$$V^F - V^L = 0 \Leftrightarrow \frac{\pi^F}{i + m(k) + r} - F^F(k) = \frac{\pi^L}{i + m(k) + r} - F^L(k)$$

This equation may be written as

$$\Delta\pi = (i + m(k) + r)\Delta F(k) = (m(k) + r)\Delta F(k) + i\Delta F(k) \tag{5}$$

where $\Delta\pi = \pi^F - \pi^L > 0$ and $\Delta F(k) = F^F(k) - F^L(k) > 0$.

Equation (5) is a straight line with intercept $(m(k) + r)\Delta F(k)$ and slope $\Delta F(k)$. It is drawn in Figure 1 as line FL_0. In Figure 1 we choose label $Z(k)$ for $\Delta\pi$. Above this FL line, the firm value from FDI is higher than that from licensing and firms prefer FDI (region F). Below the line, firms prefer licensing (region L). The intuition underlying the positive slope of line FL_0 is that as the risk of becoming obsolete due to new innovation increases (that is, the rate of innovation i goes up), the expected period of time during which a firm earns profits from its technology diminishes. Thus, the firm must earn higher instantaneous profits from FDI to make it indifferent to licensing because of the higher fixed cost associated with FDI.

Now consider the primary question of interest. How does a strengthening of patent rights alter the decision between FDI and licensing? Suppose that the recipient country increases k (i.e., the strength of IPRs). This has two direct effects in our model. First, the cost of imitation increases, and the rate of imitation $m(k)$ would decline. Second, the fixed costs of both FDI and licensing would decline, though the reduction would be greater for licensing, and the relative cost of undertaking FDI accordingly would rise:

$$\frac{d\Delta F}{dk} = \frac{dC^F}{dk} - \frac{dC^L}{dk} > 0. \tag{6}$$

---

[52] See Helpman, above n. 29; Glass & Saggi, above n. 33; and Yang & Maskus, above n. 32, for examples.

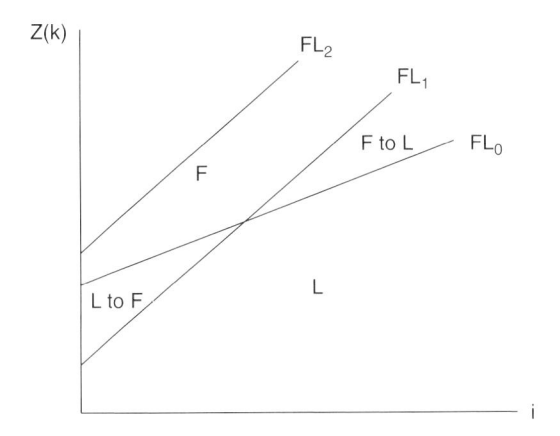

Figure 1. The impact of patents on FDI and licensing with variable innovation

We thus have two cases to consider. In case 1, let the relative decline in contracting costs be dominated by the reduction in imitation threat:

$$\frac{d((m+r)\Delta F)}{dk} = \frac{dm}{dk}\Delta F + (m+r)\frac{d\Delta F}{dk} < 0 \qquad (7)$$

In this case, the indifference line between FDI and licensing would both shift downward (from equation (7)) and become steeper in slope (from equation (6)), as shown in Figure 1 by the line labeled FL_1. In consequence, the new line would lie below the old line for low rates of innovation and above it for high rates of innovation. The implication is the following. *A strengthening of patent protection makes the firm more likely to undertake FDI and less likely to undertake licensing when the global rate of innovation is low. However, when the rate of innovation is high, a tightening of patent rights encourages licensing and discourages FDI.*

Case 2 permits the reduction in change in relative contracting costs to dominate:

$$\frac{d((m+r)\Delta F)}{dk} > 0.$$

In this case a strengthening of IPR both shifts up the indifference line and makes it steeper, as shown in Figure 1 by the line labeled FL_2. As a result, the new line always lies above the old line, and the area favoring licensing over FDI becomes unambiguously larger. Thus, we have the following prediction. *When a stronger patent regime reduces the risk of imitation moderately but has a marked impact on relative fixed costs of contracting under licensing and FDI, the firm is more likely to engage in licensing no matter what the global rate of innovation may be.* This case is close to the standard conception in the literature that, as intellectual property protection improves, firms become more willing to sell their technologies externally to unrelated enterprises.

To summarize, there is a central tradeoff in this model between the change in relative contracting costs and the threat of imitation. In countries where the rate of imitation is quite sensitive to a strengthening of patent rights, but that tightening reduces moderately the fixed costs of licensing relative to FDI, the impact on whether technology arrives through FDI or licensing depends on the rate of global innovation. Taking the rate of innovation to vary across industries, in this case a stronger IP regime favors FDI in sectors with low rates of innovation and licensing in sectors with high rates of innovation. In countries where the rate of imitation is not very sensitive to stronger patents, such a policy change would encourage licensing.

4. Evidence supporting the hypothesis

Widely accepted economic theory claims that when a country's IPRs are strengthened, it should experience increasing flows of both FDI and licensing, but there should be a tendency for licensing to rise faster than FDI (that is, for a substitution into arm's-length contracting and joint ventures).[53] Our model suggests that the latter relationship may depend also on the innovativeness of the industries involved and the relative impact of patents on imitation costs and fixed costs of technology transfer.

Testing this model requires a simultaneous equations framework in which firms are permitted to choose between FDI and licensing (and exporting as a default option), depending on both industry R&D characteristics and recipient country characteristics. We discuss the approach and results of a recent study of this subject that is directly relevant to the hypothesis.[54] In this study, the author employed a detailed data set from the United States Bureau of Economic Analysis (BEA) that contains the number (or "counts") of U.S. firms engaged in FDI or licensing in 1995 and exporting in the year 1994. The data exist at the level of 3-digit BEA codes, providing information on 135 industries operating in 62 countries. Industries cover agriculture, primary goods, manufactures, and services. Thus, the dependent variable in the analysis is the count of such contracts of each kind, by industry and country.

---

[53] *See* Ignatius Horstmann & James R. Markusen, *Strategic Investments and the Development of Multinationals*, 28 INT'L ECON. REV. 109 (1987); Maskus, above n. 7.

[54] For a complete description of the analysis, see Thitima Puttitanun, Essays on Intellectual Property Rights, Innovation, and Technology Transfer (2003) (unpublished dissertation, University of Colorado at Boulder). *See also* Michael Nicholson, Intellectual Property and Internalization: An Empirical Investigation (2002) (manuscript, Federal Trade Commission), who performed a related econometric analysis with similar results.

Several independent variables were included in the analysis. Real GDP in the recipient country was used as a measure of market size, which has a strong effect on all inward commercial flows. A second variable was distance in kilometers from each country's national capital to Washington DC, as a measure of transport costs and monitoring difficulties in FDI contracts. A third variable was a measure of the effective (productivity-adjusted) wage rate in manufacturing for each country. Also included was an index of economic freedom, which was taken to be an (inverse) proxy for the fixed costs of investing. Finally, the strength of patent rights in each recipient country was measured by the Ginarte-Park index for 1990.[55] The index ranges from zero to five, with higher values indicating stronger protection.

Because many of the count observations are zero (especially in licensing), the analysis required use of a special regression approach called the multinomial logit model. This estimation was performed for all industries and for industries broken down into high R&D sectors and low R&D sectors. For this purpose, R&D expenditures were taken to include all costs related to the development of new products and services. High-technology sectors were taken to be those with ratios of R&D to sales in excess of three percent, while low-technology sectors were those with ratios below three percent.[56]

Table 1 summarizes regression results for the coefficients on the patent index.[57] The econometric approach standardizes the implicit coefficients on exports (the default mode of technology transfer) to zero. Thus, the coefficients in the FDI and licensing equations reflect impacts of IPRs on these channels of transfer compared to exporting. It may be seen that both coefficients are positive and significantly different from zero at the 95% level of confidence

Table 1. *Estimated coefficients and marginal impacts of patents on probabilities of entry modes*

	Model coefficients		Marginal impacts	
	FDI	License	FDI	License
All industries	0.383*	0.215*	0.0837	0.0007
Low R&D	0.440*	0.219*	0.0991	−0.0042
High R&D	0.315*	0.195*	0.0568	0.0112

*indicates significantly different from zero at 95% confidence level.

---

[55] See Juan Carlos Ginarte & Walter G. Park, *Determinants of Patent Rights: A Cross-National Study*, 26 RES. POL'Y 283 (1997), for details on this index.
[56] Nicholson, above n. 54, collected this data and provided the breakdown into high-technology and low-technology sectors.
[57] Remaining results are available in Puttitanun, above n. 54.

for all three industry groups. Taking all industries together, the coefficient of 0.383 on FDI indicates that a one-unit increase in the patent index tends to raise the probability of a firm engaging in FDI rather than exporting by a factor of 1.47 (= exp(0.383)). The same increase in the patent index would raise the odds of licensing relative to exporting by a factor of 1.24. Interestingly, both the FDI and licensing coefficients in the low-R&D sectors are higher than average, while those in the high-R&D sectors are lower than average.

That our model is consistent with the data may be seen in the last pair of columns, in which we report the marginal effects of an increase in the patent index on entry decisions, computed at the mean values of all independent variables. Thus, over all sectors a rise in patent protection increases the probability of FDI by 8.37 percent, but only barely increases the probability of licensing. There is a sharp distinction in this regard between low-R&D sectors and high-R&D sectors. In the former group, a rise in patent protection raises the probability of FDI by 9.9 percent and actually *reduces* the likelihood of a licensing contract. This finding suggests that, in sectors with low innovation rates (assuming that low R&D ratios correlate with low rates of product introduction), a strengthening of patents shifts incentives at the margin toward investment and away from licensing, as suggested by the model. In contrast, in sectors with high innovation rates, there is a greater tendency to enter into licensing contracts and a reduced tendency to employ FDI, compared to the average.

This result points out the importance of the relative impacts of intellectual property protection on fixed costs and imitation costs. Specifically, the result is consistent with case 1 in our model, in which the reduction in fixed contracting costs of licensing relative to FDI was small in comparison with the reduction in imitation threat from local rivals. In this context, multinational firms in low-technology sectors seem especially willing to transfer technology through FDI in comparison with licensing as patent rights are strengthened in developing countries.

5. Policy conclusions

A major concern about the global trading system is whether the evolving intellectual property system will enhance or hinder the transfer of technology through private markets. Indeed, the WTO has established a Working Group on Trade and Technology Transfer to study precisely such issues.[58] While that work program is aimed at finding means of encouraging cross-border knowledge flows, it must be informed by evidence about the relationships between such flows and IPRs.

---

[58] *See* Saggi, above n. 3.

In this chapter we have reviewed basic economic theory and evidence about the determinants of technology flows through FDI and licensing, particularly as these are affected by patent rights or other forms of technology protection. We did so in order to bring out certain subtleties about both the aggregate impacts of IPRs and the substitution effects between transferring information to foreign subsidiaries (FDI) and to unrelated firms through arm's-length technology sales (licensing).

Regarding the aggregate effects, in theory a strengthening of patent rights in developing countries could reduce or expand access to foreign technologies. The former problem would arise essentially because of enhanced market power on the part of technology developers, who could choose not to offer certain technologies or to raise access fees. It would be exacerbated by the higher cost of imitation in recipient countries. However, stronger IPRs may be expected also to reduce the costs of reaching and enforcing contracts, while raising the returns to FDI and licensing, thereby expanding the aggregate flows of technology. While the empirical evidence on this issue remains somewhat murky, the preponderance of results from econometric studies suggests the impact could be large and positive in developing economies with the ability to absorb technology.[59] In this regard, developing countries may wish to focus resources on improving their absorptive capacities through improved governance, strengthened education programs, targeted technology inducements, and competition policies.

Turning to substitution effects, standard economic theory argues that as a country's IP regime is strengthened, multinational enterprises would choose to shift away from FDI and toward licensing at the margin. Again, there is evidence to support this claim.[60] However, we have put forward a simple model focusing on the relative impact of IPRs on reducing contracting costs in FDI and licensing. We find that the standard prediction holds only in sectors with rapid innovation rates, which presumably are higher-technology industries. In lower-technology industries, it is more likely that stronger patents would induce firms to shift toward greater use of FDI and lesser use of licensing. To the extent that lower-income developing countries hope to attract FDI in such sectors, which presumably are more important in the medium term as a means of exploiting comparative advantage in international trade, strengthened IPRs would have this additional benefit.

We conclude by noting that our analysis should not be taken to imply that all developing countries will experience rising FDI and licensing as a result of TRIPS, nor that any particular country's economic well-being will be improved. However, the insights offered here should be of use to policymakers in fashioning their overall responses to the new intellectual property requirements.

---

[59] See MASKUS, above n. 4, for a review, and Smith, above n. 36, for a recent comprehensive analysis.

[60] *See* Smith, above n. 36.

COMMENTARY II

Comment: TRIPS and technology transfer – Evidence from patent data

SAMUEL KORTUM[*]

1. Introduction

Will developing countries win or lose from a regime of stronger intellectual property protection? Answering this question will ultimately require a quantitative analysis. The three chapters in this section, while not quantitative, do a good job of laying out the potential effects on developing countries, both positive and negative, of this new regime.

Carlos Correa argues that stronger intellectual property rights (IPRs) in developing countries will diminish the transfer of existing technology to them.[1] One means of such transfer of knowledge is through active imitative activity in developing countries, exactly the type of activity that stronger IPRs are designed to halt. As a student of Robert Evenson, I learned that a critical step on the road to development is to become a good imitator.[2]

While Carlos Correa is concerned about getting *existing* technology to developing countries, Arti Rai worries about the potential negative effects of stronger IPRs on the creation of *new* technology for developing countries.[3] Her point is that in a regime of strong IPRs (even if only in developed countries), upstream patents may raise the transactions cost of doing research for developing-country problems. Rai illustrates these problems nicely with examples and case studies.

Keith Maskus, Kamal Saggi, and Thitima Puttitanun point out that developing countries could actually gain by providing stronger IPRs.[4] The mechanism is that tighter protection makes it more likely that technology owners will be willing to transfer technology knowing that they will be able to appropriate some of the benefits. These authors go on to model the choice between licensing

---

[*] Samuel Kortum is Professor of Economics, University of Minnesota.
[1] Carlos M. Correa, *Can the TRIPS Agreement Foster Technology Transfer to Developing Countries?* [this volume].
[2] *See* Robert E. Evenson, *Agricultural Research and Intellectual Property Rights* [this volume].
[3] Arti K. Rai, *Proprietary Rights and Collective Action: The case of Biotechnology Research with Low Commercial Value* [this volume].
[4] Keith E. Maskus et al., *Patent Rights and International Technology Transfer through Direct Investment and Licensing* [this volume].

and foreign direct investment (FDI), examining how this choice is influenced by the strength of IPRs.

After reading these chapters, one feels better informed, but still far from having an answer to the question about the net gain (or loss) to developing countries of stronger intellectual property protection. In the analysis that follows, I want to focus on the consequences of developing countries' themselves strengthening IPRs, as required of them by the TRIPS Agreement.[5] Furthermore I want to pursue an easier question: *Have patent seekers responded to the expectation that developing countries will provide stronger protection?* If they have not, then we should be able to put tighter bounds on the gains and losses, and, hence, the net effect of strengthening IPRs in developing countries.

2. Evidence in Patent Data

It is natural to look at patent data to detect a response to the strengthening of property rights in developing countries. Do we see a jump in the demand for patent protection in these countries? One could argue that it is too early to tell since much of the promised strengthening of patent protection is not yet in place. But, because patents are options on future returns,[6] those seeking patents will be forward-looking. If inventors now anticipate much stronger patent protection in developing countries as those nations come into compliance with their obligations under TRIPS, they should already be much more likely to seek protection there.

2a. Hypotheses

If stronger patents in developing countries matter, we should observe an influx of inventors seeking patent protection in developing countries. Past research[7] has established that inventors from anywhere are more likely to seek patents (designated by P) in rich countries (as measured by GDP per capita, y) and in large countries (as measured by total GDP, Y). I represent this relationship, linear in logarithms, as:

$$\ln P = B_0 + B_1 \ln Y + B_2 \ln y. \qquad (1)$$

An overall rise in patenting (proportional across countries) would show up as an increase in the constant term, B_0. A move toward seeking protection in

---

[5] Agreement on Trade-Related Aspects of Intellectual Property Rights, 15 Apr. 1994, Marrakesh Agreement Establishing the World Trade Organization, Annex 1C, LEGAL INSTRUMENTS – RESULTS OF THE URUGUAY ROUND vol. 31, 33 I.L.M. 81 (1994) [hereinafter TRIPS Agreement].
[6] This point is made and analyzed by Ariel Pakes, *Patents as Options: Some Estimates of the Value of Holding European Patent Stocks*, 54 ECONOMETRICA 766 (1986).
[7] *See* Jonathan Eaton & Samuel Kortum, *Trade in Ideas: Patenting and Productivity in the OECD*, 40 J. INT'L ECON. 251 (1996), and the earlier work cited there.

developing countries should show up as rise in the constant term, together with a decline in the slope, B_2, of patenting with respect to per capita GDP. I will look for evidence in patent data of this decline in B_2.

2b. The Data

The World Intellectual Property Organization (WIPO) publishes data annually on patent applications and patent grants by reporting country.[8] The most recent year available covers patent applications filed and patents granted in 2001. For comparisons over time, I combined the 2001 data with patent statistics for 1991 and 1996. Fifty-three countries reported data on both applications and grants in each of these three years. I merged the patent data with measures of GDP and GDP per capita, measured in internationally comparable prices.[9] Due to missing data on GDP, I had to drop two countries, bringing the total number in the sample to 51.

2c. A Statistical Mirage

I begin with the figures on patent applications. For this analysis, patent applications have the advantage of being dated in the year when patent protection is sought and are thus not distorted by backlogs at the national patent offices.[10] Furthermore, my past research with Jonathan Eaton using patent applications in the late 1980s and early 1990s showed that these data behave in a predictable way with respect to economic variables.[11]

Performing a regression analysis (separately for each of the years, 1991, 1996, and 2001) based on equation (1) yielded the following coefficients (with standard errors in parentheses):

1991: $\ln A_{91} = -18.577 + .774 \ln Y_{91} + .840 \ln y_{91}$ $R^2 = .705$
      (2.602)   (.120)   (.211)

1996: $\ln A_{96} = -8.086 + .489 \ln Y_{96} + .587 \ln y_{96}$ $R^2 = .334$
      (3.786)   (.173)   (.303)

2001: $\ln A_{01} = 2.042 + .290 \ln Y_{01} + .184 \ln y_{01}$ $R^2 = .126$
      (3.535)   (.160)   (.269)

---

[8] World Intellectual Property Organization, *Industrial Property Statistics*, available at http://www.wipo.int/ipstats/en/index.html (last visited 16 July 2004).
[9] These data are available in THE WORLD BANK, WORLD DEVELOPMENT INDICATORS (Oxford University Press 2003).
[10] See Zvi Griliches, *Patent Statistics as Economic Indicators: A Survey*, 28 J. ECON. LIT. 1661 (1990).
[11] Eaton & Kortum, above n. 7; Jonathan Eaton & Samuel Kortum, *International Technology Diffusion: Theory and Measurement*, 40 INT'L ECON. REV. 537 (1999).

Notice that the fit of the equation is very good in 1991 and falls dramatically over time. More to the point of my hypothesis, the constant term rises and the coefficient on per capita GDP drops substantially over time, which indicates that inventors have become much more likely to seek protection in developing countries. Could this result be an early indication of a rush to protect intellectual property in developing countries? The short answer is, "No".

Further investigation revealed a huge problem in interpreting patent applications data from WIPO in recent years. By 2001, WIPO counts of patent applications had little to do with the intentions of patent seekers to obtain protection in any particular country. Rather, they reflected the fact that it had become very inexpensive to retain the option to seek protection in over 100 countries. When this option is retained by an applicant, WIPO counts it as a patent application in each of these countries.

How did this situation evolve? Over the past decade, the Patent Cooperation Treaty (PCT) system has become the primary means of seeking patent protection internationally. The PCT system allows an inventor to file a single international patent application, that can be used to pursue patent protection in any PCT member state. The system has grown increasingly popular over time along three dimensions. First, more inventors are filing international applications. In 1991 there were just 22,247 international patent applications, in 1996 there were 47,291, and by 2001, that number had grown to 103,947.[12] Second, the number of PCT member states has grown as well. There were 87 members at the end of 1996 and 115 at the end of 2001. Third, international patent applicants increasingly choose the option to have their application apply to all PCT member states. In 1996, 45.2% of applications chose that option, while 77.0% did so in 2001.[13] The fee structure has changed, so that once an applicant chooses the option of applying for protection in at least six countries, there is no additional fee in keeping the option for all 115 countries.[14]

These changes in the workings of the PCT interact with the way in which WIPO counts patent applications. If an inventor files an international application and chooses to retain the option to seek protection in all countries, then WIPO counts this international application as a patent application in each PCT member country. Yet, as WIPO acknowledges: "Such applicants extend the effects of their international applications to as many States as might later be of interest to them, deferring the decision as to which States they wish to proceed in."[15] Since most patent applications now follow the PCT route, the effect on application counts by WIPO is substantial. The resulting counts of applications bear little relationship to the ultimate intentions of the inventors seeking patent protection.

[12] WIPO, above n. 8.
[13] WIPO, *Yearly Review of the PCT* (various issues), *available at* http://www.wipo.int (as "PCT Annual Statistics").
[14] *Id.* [15] *Id.*

Further analysis of the data on patent applications lends support to this view. Amazingly, by 2001 most countries, without regard to their level of development, were receiving the same order of magnitude of patent applications as reported by WIPO. There are seven exceptions, i.e., countries that received orders of magnitude fewer applications than the rest: Zambia, Pakistan, Egypt, Guatemala, Botswana, Malta, and Hong Kong. These were exactly the seven countries in the dataset that had not joined the PCT as of late 2001 (Zambia joined on November 15, 2001).

Another issue that distorts the WIPO patent applications data is the way in which applications are counted when protection is sought via the European Patent Office.[16] For African countries, a similar distortion arises when patent protection is sought via the African Regional Industrial Property Organization (ARIPO).

2d. What is Really Happening?

Since the data on patent applications from WIPO are problematic, I next turned to figures on patent grants.[17] Inspection of these data in 1991, 1996, and 2001 indicated no jump in patents granted in developing countries, with the single big exception of China. To examine the issue in more detail, I performed a regression analysis based on equation (1). I look for evidence that patent grants have risen more in developing countries, which should show up as a flatter slope of patent grants with respect to GDP per capita. Below are results from regressions run separately for each year.

1991: $\ln G_{91} = -20.827 + .786 \ln Y_{91} + .923 \ln y_{91} \quad R^2 = .850$
$\quad\quad\quad\quad (1.766) \quad\quad (.081) \quad\quad\quad (.144)$

1996: $\ln G_{96} = -18.769 + .695 \ln Y_{96} + .946 \ln y_{96} \quad R^2 = .762$
$\quad\quad\quad\quad (2.240) \quad\quad (.103) \quad\quad\quad (.179)$

2001: $\ln G_{01} = -20.936 + .783 \ln Y_{01} + .909 \ln y_{01} \quad R^2 = .803$
$\quad\quad\quad\quad (2.140) \quad\quad (.097) \quad\quad\quad (.163)$

These results indicate that the number of patents granted has remained a very stable function of GDP and GDP per capita. There is little evidence in the data of changing regression coefficients.

To examine this issue more formally, I pooled all the data and ran a single regression. I then tested for equality (across years) of the slopes with respect to GDP per capita (in doing so I allowed the intercept to shift, but imposed a single slope with respect to GDP).[18] In the results I could not reject, at any

---

[16] This issue is discussed at length in Jonathan Eaton et al., *International Patenting and the European Patent Office: A Quantitative Assessment*, in PATENTS, INNOVATION AND ECONOMIC PERFORMANCE (OECD Conference Proceedings, 2004).

[17] These figures were also taken from WIPO, above n. 8.

[18] WILLIAM GREENE, ECONOMETRIC ANALYSIS, ch. 7 (Prentice Hall 2002), describes how to impose restrictions on regression equations and how to test those restrictions.

standard level of statistical significance, the hypothesis that the slope with respect to GDP per capita remained constant over time. Thus, in statistical terms, the relationship between patent grants and development has been stable for some time.

3. Conclusion

In this comment, I have dodged the question of whether developing countries win or lose by providing stronger IPRs.[19] I attempt to answer a simpler question instead. *Have patent seekers responded to the expectation that developing countries will provide stronger protection?* If the answer is no, then it becomes more difficult to argue that the stakes are so large for the question of net losses or gains.

In looking at data on patent applications, it appears that there has been a huge rush to obtain patent protection in developing countries. That result turned out, however, to be a statistical mirage. By 2001, the patent applications data published by WIPO are essentially meaningless for inferring the intentions of patent seekers.

Data on patent grants, on the other hand, paint a clear picture. There is no evidence of a shift in patent granting behavior across countries over the decade from 1991–2001. A simple regression equation does amazingly well at predicting patents granted in a country in 1991 based on the granting country's GDP and GDP per capita. With the same coefficients, it does nearly as well in 1996 and in 2001. Furthermore the number of patents granted in most developing countries remains miniscule. Therefore, my answer to the question in italics is, "No".

There are limits to the interpretation of these results. First, I did see a big jump in patents granted in some rapidly growing low and middle-income countries, including China, Turkey, Brazil, Korea, and Portugal. Perhaps the debate about net benefits is really about the costs and benefits to developing countries of providing stronger protection. Second, for administrative reasons, patent grants may respond after a time lag to the increased demand for patent protection. One might be able to address this issue by examining the backlog of patents pending in developing countries.

---

[19] *See also* Lee G. Bransteter, *Do Stronger Patents Induce More Local Innovation?* [this volume].

10

Proprietary rights and collective action: The case of biotechnology research with low commercial value

ARTI K. RAI[*]

I. The impact of upstream proprietary rights
    A. Increases in upstream proprietary rights
    B. Do upstream proprietary rights impede follow-on research?
II. The prospect of collective action
III. Public-sector efforts at collective action
IV. Limitations of public-sector collective action
    A. The role of the private sector
    B. Obstacles unrelated to intellectual property
V. Conclusion

In areas of cumulative research, such as biotechnology, broad patents on fundamental research tools have the potential to create impediments to follow-on research and development (R&D).[1] Impediments to R&D may also be created by a possible "anticommons" or "thicket" of upstream rights.[2] Whether such impediments actually arise in any given case is of course an empirical question. From an empirical standpoint, the net impact of recent

---

[*] Arti K. Rai is Professor of Law, Duke University School of Law. I thank Yochai Benkler, Wes Cohen, Amy Kapczynksi and participants in the April 2003 Duke symposium on International Public Goods for very helpful comments. Alan Bennett, Lita Nelsen, and Anthony So are also due thanks for providing valuable information. Any mistakes or omissions are mine alone.

[1] See, e.g., Arti K. Rai, *Fostering Cumulative Innovation in the Biopharmaceutical Industry: The Role of Patents and Antitrust*, 16 BERKELEY TECH. L.J. 813 (2001); see also Robert P. Merges & Richard R. Nelson, *On the Complex Economics of Patent Scope*, 90 COLUM. L. REV. 839 (1990) (discussing general problem of broad rights on pioneer inventions).

[2] Michael Heller & Rebecca Eisenberg, *Can Patents Deter Innovation? The Anticommons in Biomedical Research*, 280 SCIENCE 698 (1998). It is important to note that both problems (a broad patent as well as a proliferation of patents) can arise simultaneously. See Merges & Nelson, above n. 1, at 894 (discussing historical examples of this situation in semiconductor and aircraft industries). This counter intuitive result can occur because the patent system permits subsequent improvers to stake patent claims within the scope of an initial inventor's broad claim. Additionally, as discussed further below, assertions of tangible property rights over research tools that are difficult to replicate independently further increase upstream complexity.

increases in upstream biotechnology rights is far from clear.[3] It is fair to say, however, that one standard market solution to greater rights intensity – the reduction of transaction costs through formal or informal pooling and exchange of rights[4] – has not emerged. Rather, in the commercial arena, significant transaction costs and licensing fees have simply become part of the cost of doing business. Although these costs have probably reduced profits, foreseeable sales revenues have generally been sufficiently high at least for ongoing projects, that the profit incentive has not been eliminated.[5]

In contrast, when follow-on research is conducted in the university context,[6] or by non-profit institutions that target the developing world,[7] foreseeable payoffs are either highly uncertain or are clearly small. In these contexts, large transaction and licensing costs may pose a more pressing problem. On the other hand, at least in the context of low-margin research, there is reason to be optimistic that the "standard" solution of collective rights management may actually emerge. When the follow-on research in question is of demonstrably low commercial value, there is no reason for upstream rights holders to fear that they are foregoing large downstream rents. Thus, even though conditions in the biotechnology sector may, as a general matter, work against collective action, low-margin research may be an exception. Non-profit institutions, such as universities that are highly sensitive to reputational pressures, should be the easiest players to enlist in developing collective approaches. Fortunately, in both agricultural and health-related biotechnology, non-profit institutions own a significant percentage of patents.[8]

---

[3] *Compare* Heller & Eisenberg, above n. 2, *and* Arti K. Rai & Rebecca S. Eisenberg, *Bayh-Dole Reform and the Progress of Biomedicine*, 66 LAW & CONTEMP. PROBS. 289 (2003) (discussing possible problems for follow-on research) *with* John Walsh et al., *The Patenting and Licensing of Research Tools and Biomedical Innovation*, *in* PATENTS IN THE KNOWLEDGE-BASED ECONOMY 285 (National Academies Press 2003) (finding that upstream rights do not generally stop product development but expressing caution about certain types of patents). *See also* Iain Cockburn, *The Changing Structure of the Pharmaceutical Industry*, 23 HEALTH AFF. 10 (2004) (discussing advantages and disadvantages of upstream rights).

[4] *See, e.g.*, Robert Merges, *Contracting into Liability Rules: Intellectual Property Rights and Collective Rights Organizations*, 84 CAL. L. REV. 1293 (1996).

[5] The study by Walsh, Arora, and Cohen, which concluded that R&D projects went forward despite significant increases in licensing and transaction costs, focused on the commercial sector. The authors conducted interviews with scientists, intellectual property managers, and business people from 25 different firms (10 pharmaceutical firms and 15 biotechnology firms). In contrast, they conducted interviews with personnel from only 6 universities. Walsh et al., above n. 3, at 292.

[6] Eric Campbell et al., *Data Withholding in Academic Genetics: Data from a National Survey*, 287 JAMA 473 (2002) (survey of academic geneticists).

[7] *See* below, nn. 38–44 and accompanying text.

[8] *See* below, nn. 64–66 and accompanying text.

In fact, low-margin research is the area of biotechnology in which we have seen the most significant movement towards collective rights management. In the area of agricultural biotechnology research for developing countries, a 22-university consortium, the Public Sector Intellectual Property Resource for Agriculture, has been established to address impediments posed by upstream rights. Considerable efforts are also being made to achieve collective action in the areas of health-related biotechnology for developing countries. Moreover, although universities and other non-profit institutions are probably the most likely participants in successful collective action initiatives, it may be possible to involve the private sector.

This chapter proceeds in four parts. Part I gives a brief history of recent rights expansion in upstream biotechnology. It argues that, while large firms that conduct research in biopharmaceuticals or in agricultural biotechnology may be able to expend the considerable sums of money necessary to circumvent obstacles posed by proprietary rights, it would be irrational for researchers working on projects of uncertain or low commercial value to expend such resources. This Part also gives evidence of situations in which upstream complexity appears to have impeded research of uncertain or low commercial value. Part II discusses the likelihood of collective action, particularly public-sector collective action, to reduce impediments to research of uncertain or low commercial value. It argues that collective action in the area of low-margin research has significant prospects for success. Part III describes efforts by the public sector to secure collective rights management for humanitarian purposes in the area of agricultural biotechnology. It also examines the feasibility of similar efforts currently under way in the area of low-margin biomedical research. Part IV concludes by discussing the extent to which the private sector might need to be involved as well as other limitations on public-sector collective action.

I. The impact of upstream proprietary rights

A. Increases in upstream proprietary rights

In the area of biotechnology research, both biomedical and agricultural, the last two decades have been characterized by a significant increase in the number of upstream proprietary rights.[9] In the biomedical area, the increase in upstream numbers is perhaps best demonstrated through the patent statistics of research universities.[10] While U.S. universities received only 264 patents in 1979, they had

---

[9] The number of proprietary rights in biotechnology as a whole has also increased. The Biotechnology Industry Organization reports that the number of biotechnology patents issued grew from 2,000 in 1985 to over 13,000 in 2000. Data *available at* www.bio.org/er/statistics.asp.

[10] Universities tend to conduct a significant amount of basic biomedical research. In contrast, according to one study, only 14% of private-sector pharmaceutical R&D in the 1990s was devoted to basic research. TRENDS IN FEDERAL SUPPORT OF RESEARCH AND GRADUATE EDUCATION 80 (Stephen Merrill, ed., 2001).

received 3,764 patents by 2000.[11] About half of recent university patents appear to be in the biomedical arena.[12] The number of plant biotechnology patents granted by the U.S. Patent and Trademark Office has also increased substantially in the past two decades.[13] Additionally, according to patent mapping done by Geoffrey Graff and his colleagues, these patents appear to cover virtually all of the basic technologies necessary to conduct research in agricultural biotechnology.[14]

Whether claim scope has increased is less clear. Indeed, given the apparent hostility of at least some members of the Court of Appeals for the Federal Circuit to broad biotechnology patent claims,[15] such claims may be suspect. Nonetheless, some patents with controversially broad claims have issued in recent years. For example, in June 2002, Harvard, MIT, and the Whitehead Institute received a patent on federally-funded research involving the NF-kB cell signaling pathway.[16] The patent claims all drugs that work by inhibiting the pathway. Because the NF-kB pathway is a fundamental pathway involved in diseases ranging from cancer and osteoporosis to atherosclerosis and rheumatoid arthritis, the patent may cover drug treatments for all of those diseases. Indeed, the exclusive licensee of the NF-kB patent, Ariad Pharmaceuticals, is suing, or threatening to sue, dozens of companies with drug products that inhibit the pathway.[17] Another recent example of broad claiming is the University of Wisconsin's patent on primate embryonic stem cells. The 1998 patent claims all such stem cells, no matter how they are derived. The patent makes these claims even though, at the time of the patent application,

---

[11] Assocation of University Technology Managers, FY 2001 Survey Summary, *available at* wwww.autm.net/indexie.html (last visited 28 June 2004).

[12] Arti K. Rai & Rebecca S. Eisenberg, *Bayh-Dole Reform and the Progress of Biomedicine*, 91 AM. SCIENTIST 52, 54 (2003) (citing data from Bhaven N. Sampat, Georgia Institute of Technology). *See also* D.C. Mowery et al., *The Growth of Patenting and Licensing by U.S. Universities: An Assessment of the Effects of the Bayh-Dole Act of 1980*, 30 RES. POL'Y 99, 117 (2001) (noting that leading patents at the University of California, Stanford, and Columbia "are concentrated in the biomedical arena.").

[13] Geoffrey D. Graff et al., *The Public-Private Structure of Intellectual Property Ownership in Agricultural Biotechnology*, 21 NATURE BIOTECHNOLOGY 989, 990 (2003).

[14] *Id.* at 991–95 (discussing patents on range of enabling technologies and trait technologies).

[15] *See, e.g.*, Univ. of Rochester v. G.D. Searle & Co., 358 F.3d 916 (Fed. Cir. 2004), *reh'g denied*, 375 F.3d 1303 (2004); Enzo Biochem, Inc. v. Gen-Probe, Inc., 285 F.3d 1013 (Fed. Cir. 2002), *on reh'g*, 323 F.3d 956 (2002); Regents of the Univ. of Cal. v. Eli Lilly, 119 F.3d 1559 (Fed. Cir. 1997). However, because all of these opinions are authored by a single judge and have been controversial both within the Federal Circuit and in the larger patent community, their long term viability is not clear.

[16] Nuclear Factors Associated with Transcriptional Regulation, U.S. Patent No. 6,410,516 (issued 25 June 2002).

[17] Sharon Begley & Laura Johannes, *Ariad Alleges Eli Lilly Drugs Infringe on Biomolecule Patent*, WALL ST. J., 28 June 2002, at C1; *see also* www.ariad.com/about/about/_nfkb.html (last updated 10 Mar. 2004).

researchers had succeeded in deriving the cells from rhesus monkeys and macaques only.[18]

Even when a research tool is not patented, universities and private firms may leverage their physical control over the tangible tool (particularly a tangible tool that cannot easily be replicated) into a percentage of the profits from subsequent commercial products. If the recipient of the tool is a commercial entity, the research tool owner may seek a reach-through royalty. If the tool recipient is a university, the research tool owner may seek a reach-through license to any subsequent intellectual property. An NIH working group study, conducted in the late 1990s, concluded that material transfer agreements ("MTAs") for the transfer of tools often contained reach-through terms.[19]

B. Do upstream proprietary rights impede follow-on research?

At least in theory, increased proprietary activity has the potential to impede subsequent research.[20] Patent licensing entails not only supra-competitive pricing but also possible transaction cost problems associated with imperfect information, disparate assessments of value, and strategic behavior. Where a broad patent covers a research tool that would, from a social welfare standpoint, be best developed through widespread licensing, the combination of transaction costs and high licensing fees may impede this socially desirable result.[21] In the case of multiple upstream patents (whether broad or narrow), transaction costs and licensing fees associated with securing freedom to operate may be particularly problematic.[22] A market optimist might counter such theorizing by noting that rights owners motivated to make a profit are likely to reduce transaction costs by forming collective rights institutions that allow relatively free exchange of rights. With respect to licensing fees, rational, profit-maximizing rights owners are also likely to price-discriminate in favor of resource-poor researchers.

For better or for worse, the issue of actual impact is very difficult to resolve in theory. Unfortunately, empirical evidence on the actual impact of upstream biotechnology rights also fails to yield a definitive conclusion. But it does suggest that neither the market optimists nor the market pessimists are entirely

---

[18] James A. Thomson, Primate Embryonic Stem Cells, U.S. Patent No. 5,843,780 (issued 1 Dec. 1998). To be sure, broad claiming on fundamental research is not entirely a new phenomenon. The Cohen-Boyer patent applications, which were filed in the late 1970s, broadly claimed one of the fundamental techniques of modern molecular biology – transforming a bacterial host with foreign DNA. The Cohen-Boyer patent was, however, licensed nonexclusively at a reasonable royalty.

[19] See generally National Institute of Health, Working Group Report on Research Tools, available at http://www.nih.gov/news/rsearchtools/index.htm.

[20] Merges and Nelson, above n. 1; Heller and Eisenberg, above n. 2; Michele Boldrin & David Levine, The Case Against Intellectual Property, 92 AM. ECON. REV. 209 (2002).

[21] Rai, above n. 1, at 833–34.   [22] Heller & Eisenberg, above n. 2.

correct. On the one hand, ongoing commercial projects do not appear to have been stopped by the inability to resolve concerns about upstream rights. On the other hand, there is evidence of delayed, redirected, or diminished research in areas where significant upstream proprietary positions exist.[23]

For present purposes, perhaps the most notable empirical result is the dog that did not bark: commercial patent pools and similar transaction cost-reducing institutions have not emerged. Rather, industry actors that produce end products, such as pharmaceutical companies, have put information in the public domain for the specific purpose of thwarting the proprietary designs of upstream firms.[24] To some extent, firms have also avoided transaction costs by simply ignoring research tool patents and hoping that if their infringement is detected, such detection occurs after the six-year statute of limitations has run out.[25] Finally, and perhaps most commonly, downstream firms have simply endured licensing and transaction costs that run into the millions of dollars as a necessary evil.[26] Though such costs may delay research (and may of course also represent dollars diverted away from additional research), they do not generally stop ongoing projects.

In contrast, in university contexts, where the immediately foreseeable payoff – commercial or academic – from research may not be high, researchers are unlikely to be willing or able to incur high transaction costs in order to gain access to upstream research. Such costs appear to have been mounting, as academic researchers increasingly receive research tools under restrictive MTAs. According to the 1999 report of an NIH working group on research tools, even MTAs that merely transfer tools from one academic researcher to

---

[23] Walsh et al., above n. 3 at 314 (one-third of respondents reported that proprietary rights caused delays); *id*. at 303 (4 of 25 industry respondents reported that they had redirected research based on upstream patent rights); *id*. at 310–14 (diminished research in the area of patented targets).

[24] *See generally* Robert Merges, *A New Dynamism in the Public Domain*, 71 U. CHI. L. REV. 183 (2004) (discussing "property-preempting initiatives" by pharmaceutical firms). One of these initiatives, the Single Nucleotide Polymorphism ("SNP") Consortium, an effort by pharmaceutical companies to put certain types of genomic information into the public domain, could be considered collective action of a sort. But efforts like the SNP Consortium, which aim to eliminate property rights, are quite different from property rights management. Downstream firms have also benefited from vigorous publicly funded efforts to undermine upstream rights. *See* Rai & Eisenberg, above n. 3, at 303–10 (discussing numerous activities undertaken by the National Institutes of Health in conjunction with academic scientists).

[25] Walsh et al., above n. 3, at 327.

[26] Industry participants report that, for any given project, they normally have to consider a large number of patents. Although they can reduce this number to a more manageable size, such reduction typically occurs in several rounds and often takes many months. *Id*. at 316. After these transaction costs have been incurred, a number of patents have to be licensed. In total, transaction and licensing costs can run into the millions of dollars. *Id*. at 315. Moreover, to the extent litigation is required, litigation costs often run into the millions of dollars.

another can contain reach-through claims; requirements to delay publication pending a determination of intellectual property rights; and prohibitions on transfer of the tools to other research institutions.[27]

In a 2000 survey conducted by Eric Campbell and his colleagues, 47 percent of academic geneticists who had, within the previous three years, made requests for additional data or materials relating to research published by other academics reported that they were ultimately unable to secure access to such data or materials.[28] This figure represents a substantial increase over the 34 percent figure reported in a prior survey conducted by the same authors in the mid 1990s. The authors' multivariate regression analysis of the later results indicates that, among both geneticists and other life scientists, involvement in commercial activities was a strong predictive factor for denying a request.[29] Moreover, when respondents who acknowledged denying requests for data or materials were asked to give reasons for denial, the primary reason they gave was the effort associated with such transfer.[30] Although this effort may include financial costs associated with physical transfer,[31] it probably also includes costs associated with difficulties in concluding complex negotiations over MTAs. Indeed, the survey authors specifically point to the complexity and restrictiveness of MTAs as creating impediments to sharing.[32]

As a consequence of these withholding behaviors, 28 percent of the respondents to the Campbell survey reported that they were unable to confirm published research results and 21 percent abandoned a promising line of research. One might reasonably hypothesize that those research projects that did not go forward because of access denials had uncertain commercial or academic payoffs, at least as compared to ongoing industry research.

With respect to patented materials to which they do not need physical access, there is evidence that academics reduce licensing and transaction costs by simply ignoring the patents.[33] Thus far, this "self-help" approach has

---

[27] *See* NIH, above n. 19, at 10.   [28] Campbell et al., above n. 6.
[29] *Id.* at 477. The multivariate regression coded for sex, location of training, number of publications, industry research support, engagement in commercial activities, involvement in human subjects research, geneticist or non-geneticist, and volume of requests. The only factor that was more strongly associated with access denial than engagement in commercial activities was "volume of requests received." Perhaps not surprisingly, those who received a large number of requests were more likely to have denied one than those who received a small number. *Id.*
[30] *Id.* at 478. Of course, self-reporting of reasons may be subject to bias. University scientists may be reluctant to admit that they are academically or commercially competitive.
[31] For some biomaterials, for example, the financial cost of physical transfer can be quite high. *See, e.g., Share and Share Alike*, 420 NATURE 602 (2002) (noting that the cost of duplicating the cDNAs described in a scientist's paper was more than $10,000). On the other hand, the authors did code financial costs separately from effort. Among reasons given, financial costs came in fourth. Campbell et al, above n. 6, at 478.
[32] Campbell et al., above n. 6, at 479 (noting that "it may be that material transfer agreements have become so complex and so demanding that they inhibit sharing.").
[33] Walsh et al., above n. 3, at 324–26.

enjoyed some success. Patentees have tended not to sue academics for their infringing uses, either because they are not aware of such uses or because (as market optimists would predict) refraining from such suits constitutes an informal regime of price discrimination in favor of cash-strapped researchers with whom patentees would like to maintain good relations.[34] This situation may be unstable, however. As universities are increasingly seen, particularly by the courts, as ordinary commercial players from whom damages can be extracted,[35] barriers to suit may diminish.

In the context of patented genetic diagnostic tests, for example, various industry players have already threatened to sue researchers, with the result, well-documented in empirical research by Jon Merz and Mildred Cho among others, that many academic diagnostic labs have stopped performing such testing.[36] Although the issue of diagnostic testing is complicated by the reality that it constitutes both research and a commercial service provided to patients, the impasse in this area suggests that, in the future, price discrimination may not work as a mechanism for mediating the tension between the supra-competitive pricing allowed by proprietary rights and the limited budgets of most academic labs.

Similarly, in the context of research that is demonstrably of low commercial value, there is some evidence that upstream proprietary rights have impeded downstream research. Consider the case of research into a malaria vaccine. The global disease burden associated with malaria is very significant, on the order of over one million deaths a year.[37] The social value of a malaria vaccine would therefore be quite high. Nonetheless, because the primary market for such a vaccine would be in the developing world, such research is of low commercial value. Moreover, the Malaria Vaccine Institute ("MVI"), the major philanthropic organization that is supporting research into a malaria vaccine, argues that upstream patent rights are an important factor in chilling vaccine R&D. Specifically, according to a patent analysis commissioned by the MVI, the patent landscape surrounding just one antigen likely to be relevant to any vaccine that is ultimately developed is quite complex. As many as 34 different groups of patents describe and claim the antigen, MSP-1, or the production and delivery thereof.[38]

In the area of agricultural biotechnology, commentators have pointed to multiple research projects of low commercial value that have been significantly delayed, or have not gone forward at all, because of upstream patent rights.

---

[34] *See id.*
[35] *See* Madey v. Duke University, 307 F.3d 1351 (Fed. Cir. 2002), *cert. denied*, 539 U.S. 958 (2003) (holding that there is no research exemption for universities, and emphasizing that universities nowadays engage in aggressive licensing and commercialization activities).
[36] Jon Merz et al., *Diagnostic Testing Fails the Test*, 415 NATURE 577 (2002).
[37] The World Health Organization estimates annual death from malaria at 1.1 million. *See* www.who.int/tdr/diseases/malaria/diseaseinfo.htm (last visited 14 Aug. 2004).
[38] MVI Patent Analysis (on file with author).

Specifically, restricted access to patented technologies has been identified as a significant barrier to development of subsistence crops relevant to the developing world.[39] A prominent example of upstream patent rights that have hindered creation of transgenic crops suited for subsistence farmers in developing countries are patents on two fundamental "enabling" technologies for inserting foreign genes into crops. The first of these patents, issued to Cornell University in July 1990, is licensed exclusively to Dupont.[40] The second of these patents, issued to Washington University in April 2000, is licensed exclusively to Ciba-Geigy (now Syngenta).[41]

The private-sector licensees of these patents have conducted – and have sublicensed others to conduct – transgenic crop research relevant to the developed world. More generally, through a strategic combination of research, licensing, and merger activity, large agricultural biotechnology companies have assembled the intellectual property necessary to produce new crops of interest to the developed world.[42] These companies have not, however, thus far shown interest in innovative research relevant to the developing world. The presence of proprietary rights has also hindered public-sector efforts at humanitarian research.[43] Similarly, private-sector proprietary positions have hindered public-sector efforts at conventional plant breeding directed to the needs of the developing world.[44]

Thus, in the context of research of uncertain or low commercial value, there is reason to be concerned about upstream proprietary rights. One question that might reasonably be asked, however, is whether collective action to reduce at least transaction costs – and perhaps even actual licensing costs – is likely to be more successful in the context of uncertain or low-margin research than it has been in the context of high-margin research. The next Part considers the conditions under which we are most likely to see collective rights management that reduces licensing and transaction costs.

---

[39] Atkinson et al., *Intellectual Property Rights: Public Sector Collaboration for Agricultural IP Management*, 301 SCIENCE 174 (2003); G. Conway & G. Toenniessen, *Feeding the World in the Twenty-first Century*, 402 NATURE C55 (1999).

[40] General Biolistic-Mediated Transformation of Cells, U.S. Patent No. 4,945,050 (issued 31 July 1990); *see also* Graff et al., above n. 13, at 992 (noting exclusive licensing to Dupont for most fields of use).

[41] General Agrobacterium-Mediated Transformation of Dicots, U.S. Patent No. 6,051,757 (issued 18 Apr. 2000); *see also* Graff et al., above n. 13, at 992 (noting exclusive license to Syngenta).

[42] Atkinson et al., above n. 39, at 174.

[43] *Id*. The presence of upstream patents has hindered not only low-value humanitarian R&D but also R&D in relatively low-value specialty crop areas, such as peanuts, broccoli, lettuce and tomatoes, in which the agrobiotech industry does not have a strong commercial interest.

[44] Jonathan Knight, *A Dying Breed*, 421 NATURE 568, 569 (2003).

II. The prospect of collective action

As institutional economists have frequently noted, securing collective action can be very difficult, particularly if the collective action requires sacrificing short-term gain.[45] Success is most likely when the parties involved have shared values and interests; their numbers are relatively small; and they engage in repeated, readily observable interactions.[46] Given such preconditions, norms of behavior can develop and departures from these norms can be sanctioned through mechanisms such as shaming or exclusion. Absent such preconditions, there is a tendency to defect and attempt to maximize one's individual gain at the expense of the collective. Moreover, where the collective action involves pooling proprietary rights in some fashion, there generally needs to be some agreement on the value of the individual proprietary rights.[47]

The institutional economists' assumption that only relatively small, close-knit groups can produce successful collective action has recently been challenged by growth in open-source software and other Internet-based cooperative projects. Participants in the development of open-source software are often relative strangers to each other. Nonetheless, they agree to work on software projects for which they will secure neither monetary reimbursement nor the usual sort of exclusive proprietary rights.[48] More generally, the transaction-cost lowering effect of the Internet has allowed the emergence of a new production mode, in which large numbers of relative strangers volunteer to work together on collective projects.[49] Because the informational inputs of large numbers of individuals can be readily evaluated and integrated, such reward mechanisms as prestige or reputation, which previously worked only in smaller groups, can be extended more broadly. Such open-source or commons-based

---

[45] The classic statement is MANCUR OLSON, THE LOGIC OF COLLECTIVE ACTION: PUBLIC GOODS AND THE THEORY OF GROUPS (Harvard University Press 1971). See also RICHARD CORNES & TODD SANDLER, THE THEORY OF EXTERNALITIES, PUBLIC GOODS, AND CLUB GOODS (Cambridge University Press 2d ed. 1996).

[46] See, e.g., ROBERT ELLICKSON, ORDER WITHOUT LAW: HOW NEIGHBORS SETTLE DISPUTES 3 (1991); ELINOR OSTROM, GOVERNING THE COMMONS 88–89 (1990).

[47] See Robert Merges, *Contracting Into Liability Rules: Intellectual Property Rights and Collective Rights Organizations*, 84 CAL. L. REV. 1293, 1345, 1353 (1996) (noting this point in the context of both informal and formal patent pools).

[48] Depending on the type of open-source software development involved, the participants may either renounce intellectual property rights in their software contributions or they may retain such rights but license them freely subject to the condition that those who use, or improve, the software make it available on the same terms. For a collection of licenses approved by the Open Source Institute, see www.opensource.org/licenses/index.php (visited 28 June 2003).

[49] Yochai Benkler, *Coase's Penguin, or Linux, and the Nature of the Firm*, 112 YALE L.J. 369 (2002). *Cf.* Lior Strahilevitz, *Social Norms from Close-Knit Groups to Loose-Knit Groups*, 70 U. CHI. L. REV. 357 (2003) (discussing situations in which relative strangers interact cooperatively).

production requires, however, not only low transaction costs but also low capital costs. In other words, volunteers must not be forced to invest resources other than time. In the area of "wet lab" biotechnology research, by contrast, large investments of capital are generally necessary.[50]

Barriers to collective action are likely to be particularly high when wet-lab research has high commercial value. In this context, the players involved – small biotechnology companies, large agribusiness and pharmaceutical companies, not to mention universities and federal funding agencies – have asymmetric motivations and interests. While firms that make profits from end-product patents might be able to reach agreement on licensing basic inventions widely on a low or no-royalty basis, small firms (and universities for that matter) that focus exclusively on upstream research might believe in licensing more selectively at a higher royalty.[51] The bargaining difficulties created by asymmetric interests are only exacerbated when parties hold asymmetric rights – that is, one party holds a broad foundational patent while other parties have narrower improvement patents. Compound these tactical asymmetries with informational deficits regarding valuation, and it is hardly surprising that we have not seen much movement towards collective rights management.

With respect to research of uncertain commercial value, the prospects for collective action should be higher. As an initial matter, for at least some of this research, the central players – primarily universities and other non-profit institutions – are more homogeneous. In addition, by definition, the likelihood of gain from strategic behavior is lower than in the context of high-margin research. Indeed, we have seen some evidence of collective self-restraint on the part of universities. For example, in the context of the Human Genome Project, academic scientists, working with the National Institutes of Health ("NIH"), achieved an approximation of university-level collective action by appealing to traditional scientific norms of open access: once the genome scientists had agreed not to seek proprietary rights in raw human genome sequence data, these scientists also managed to convince their respective institutions to go along with their agreement (the so-called "Bermuda principles").[52]

It is important to emphasize, however, that the collective action in this case was instigated by a tightly knit group of influential scientists who adhered to communal views of science; was backed by the institutional weight of the

---

[50] For a discussion of the ways in which the open-source model does and does not apply to biomedical research, see Arti K. Rai, "Open and Collaborative" Research: A New Model for Biomedicine, in INTELLECTUAL PROPERTY RIGHTS IN FRONTIER INDUSTRIES: SOFTWARE AND BIOTECHNOLOGY (Robert Hahn, ed., Joint Center on Regulatory Studies, AEI-Brookings) (forthcoming 2005).

[51] Arti K. Rai, Regulating Scientific Research: Intellectual Property Rights and the Norms of Science, 94 NW U. L. REV. 77 (1999), at 133 (making this point).

[52] Eliot Marshall, Genome Researchers Take the Pledge: Data Sharing, 272 SCIENCE 477 (1996).

National Institutes of Health ("NIH"); and was, to some extent, foisted on the scientists' respective universities. Without these preconditions, collective action at the university level may be difficult to achieve. The available empirical evidence indicates that, unlike the scientists who worked on the Human Genome Project, university technology-transfer officers are often evaluated on the basis of, and motivated in significant part by, the desire to increase licensing revenue.[53] Perhaps not surprisingly, then, agreements to secure collective action not led by scientists have been less than successful.

Consider the case of the Uniform Biological Materials Transfer Agreement ("UBMTA"). In this voluntary agreement, reached in 1995 between university technology-transfer officers from more than 100 institutions, the officers committed themselves to making unpatented biological materials freely available within the academic sector for research purposes. Compliance with this standard-form MTA does not appear to have been uniform. As noted earlier, an NIH working group found that, at least in the late 1990s, many transfers of research tools between universities contained onerous restrictions. Indeed, the Campbell survey discussed above found that geneticists requesting biological materials are particularly likely to be denied access.[54]

In the case of transfer of research tools between universities, however, we are dealing in most cases with research of uncertain rather than demonstrably low value. By definition, this uncertainty means that some of the materials may ultimately yield some profit. Failure to include proprietary restrictions in an MTA means the loss of these potential profits. As a consequence, university technology-transfer officers ("TTOs"), who are highly averse to losing revenue opportunities, may be reluctant to approve free distribution. Risk-aversion may be particular high for university technology-transfer officers who are less sophisticated, are under pressure to increase licensing revenues, or have unrealistic expectations of profitability.[55]

Because of the distinction between research of uncertain and low value, the less-than-complete success of the UBMTA does not necessarily bode ill for efforts at university collective action in the humanitarian context. While universities and technology transfer officers may be uncomfortable about foregoing an uncertain, but potentially large, revenue stream, they should be less concerned about relinquishing monetary gains from licensing directed towards

---

[53] Jerry Thursby et al., *Objectives, Characteristics and Outcomes of University Licensing: A Survey of Major U.S. Universities*, 26 J. TECH. TRANSFER 59 (2001) (over 70% of 62 technology transfer offices surveyed reported that their primary goal was licensing revenues).

[54] Campbell et al., above n. 6, at 478.

[55] Although university technology licensing operations are generally not profitable, a few universities, such as Columbia and the University of California system, have garnered considerable revenue from such licensing. The example of these universities may be enticing to less profitable offices.

developing-country research. In the latter case, the value of the revenue stream foregone is quite modest. The possibility of significant reputational benefit at modest financial cost should also make collective action enticing for universities and other non-profit institutions.

III. Public-sector efforts at collective action

Given this backdrop, it is not surprising that public-sector institutions have launched significant efforts to manage proprietary rights in a manner that benefits the developing world. Roger N. Beachy, president of the Donald Danforth Plant Science Center in St. Louis, Missouri, recently authored an editorial in *Science* noting that, at his Center, all research and licensing agreements alert parties that the Center will preserve the availability of intellectual property rights for meeting the needs of developing countries.[56] Beachy argues that the experience of the Danforth Center over the past three years has been that private-sector companies have been willing to accept such restrictions on licensing. He urges all academic and non-profit research institutions to include such terms in their licensing agreements. As he points out, "[a]lthough there may be a modest financial cost of taking such a position, the potential benefits in terms of regaining public trust, and ultimately of deploying technologies where they may be needed most, far outweigh the financial or opportunity costs."[57]

Indeed, 21 non-profit institutions with heavy research agendas in agriculture, as well as the U.S. Department of Agriculture, have now joined together to heed Dr. Beachy's call. They have publicly committed themselves to articulating "best practices" that include the possibility of systematically retaining rights so as to allow public-sector researchers freedom to operate in the context of research oriented towards the developing world.[58] The collective institutional framework within which these best practices will be articulated is the newly established Public-Sector Intellectual Property Resource for Agriculture ("PIPRA").[59]

PIPRA will also be responsible for studying the possibility of pooling complementary technologies held by the public sector and making these technology "packages" available at a low royalty for agricultural research applications in the public sector and in developing countries.[60] Finally, PIPRA will assist in developing a collective public-sector IP asset database that will supplement existing efforts

---

[56] Roger Beachy, *IP Policies and Serving the Public*, 299 SCIENCE 473 (2003).
[57] *Id.* at 473.
[58] *See* www.pipra.org/activities.php; *see also* Atkinson et al., above n. 39, at 175 (statement by Presidents of 14 of these 22 institutions).
[59] Some individual universities have already undertaken humanitarian licensing in particular contexts. For example, U.S. Patent No. 5,859,339 (issued 12 Jan. 1999), granted to Regents of the University of California for a gene that enhances resistance to Xanthomonas, is now being made available to developing countries at zero royalty. Fischer et al., *Collaborations in Rice*, 290 SCIENCE 279 (2000).
[60] www.pipra.org/activities.php.

to inform researchers about freedom to operate without facing proprietary obstacles. In other words, PIPRA will assist researchers in determining the countries in which key patents are held and to whom the patents have been licensed.[61]

Proliferating proprietary rights have impeded developing country-oriented research not only into transgenic crops but also into new techniques of conventional breeding.[62] One recent collective effort to address this problem involves a consortium of researchers at twelve institutions that is making publicly available molecular biology techniques that will assist in conventional breeding of wheat. The primary technique is "marker assisted selection" or MAS. While conventional breeding has traditionally relied on visible traits to select improved varieties – a procedure that often requires waiting many generations – MAS looks for markers that are inherited along with the desired trait. The MAS process thus allows plants that carry the trait to be picked out quickly. The consortium website contains research protocols and marker sequences that researchers all over the world can freely access and use.[63]

Even without the participation of private-sector patentees, collective action by universities and other non-profit institutions has the potential to be quite effective. In the area of agricultural technologies, the public sector owns 24 percent of plant biotechnology patents granted in the United States between 1982 and 2001. Many of these patents cover fundamental research tools that are essential for future research.[64] Although some publicly owned patents – such as methods for gene transfer – have unfortunately already been licensed exclusively to the private sector, licensing of enabling technologies on which the public sector is currently working, such as selectable markers, could be done under the best practices articulated by PIPRA. Even with respect to patents that have already been licensed exclusively, public-sector ownership could conceivably assist renegotiation.[65]

At a minimum, useful collective efforts towards promoting freedom to operate could result from making transparent the countries in which key patents have been filed as well as the licensing status of technologies owned by the public sector. In promoting freedom to operate, one significant advantage organizations such as PIPRA will presumably have over existing patent mapping efforts (for example, those conducted by the Center for the Application of Molecular Biology to International Agriculture) is that PIPRA members will know the licensing status of the patents they hold. PIPRA members may also be able to determine more readily than third party organizations the range of countries in which their licensees have filed patent applications.

---

[61] Id. [62] Knight, above n. 44. [63] Id.
[64] See generally Graff et al., above n. 13, at 992–94 (discussing enabling technologies and trait technologies patented by the public sector).
[65] For example, in 2001, Yale University, the owner of a patent on the anti-AIDS drug d4T, and Bristol-Myers Squibb, its exclusive licensee, agreed to refrain from enforcing their patent rights in South Africa.

In the biomedical arena, the public-sector presence is also quite significant. In the genomics area, for example, 42 percent of patents are owned by either universities, non-profit research institutes, or the U.S. government.[66] Some efforts at public-sector collective action for humanitarian purposes are also beginning to take shape. For example, the London-based Centre for the Management of Intellectual Property in Health Research and Development ("MIHR"), an organization set up in 2002 to improve access to health products in developing countries, has drafted a best-practices handbook on intellectual property management.[67] Some of these best practices relate to licensing schemes that universities can use to ensure that their technology transfer benefits developing countries. For example, Lita Nelsen, head of the MIT Office of Technology Transfer and MIHR advisor, suggests that universities might prohibit licensees from filing developing-country patents on research tools that can be used without further development.[68]

Of course, whether efforts such as those being initiated by PIPRA and MIHR will ultimately be successful is not certain. Even purely prospective approaches, such as securing widespread university adoption of a collective approach to humanitarian licensing, may prove difficult. Although the revenue potential in research directed towards developing countries is modest, many difficult questions regarding the specifics of how humanitarian licensing should be done remain unresolved.[69]

For example, eliminating barriers to research relevant to developing country diseases might require more than a prohibition on the filing of patents in developing countries. To the extent that the capacity to do research on diseases that affect developing countries exists primarily in developed countries, an effective humanitarian use license may have to include a provision allowing such research in developed countries as well. A newly formed coalition of student groups, the Universities Allied for Essential Medicines, has proposed an interesting model, the Open Access License ("OAL"), which could be extended to allow research in developed as well as developing countries. Under the OAL, universities would specifically preserve access for entities that wanted to use the licensed material to do research on diseases that primarily affect developing countries.[70] Although the

---

[66] Stephen McCormack & Robert Cook-Deegan, DNA Patent Database (slide presentation on file with author).
[67] MIHR Handbook of Best Practices for Management of Intellectual Property in Health Research and Development [hereinafter MIHR Handbook], *available at* www.mihr.org.
[68] *Id.* at 75–77.
[69] Communication from Stephen Hansen, American Association for the Advancement of Science (AAAS) (11 Aug. 2004). AAAS has brought together various groups interested in humanitarian licensing and is aiming to accelerate drafting of model agricultural and biomedical humanitarian use licenses.
[70] OAL Draft (on file with author).

OAL is currently restricted to research materials that are used in the manufacture of end-product drugs,[71] the model could be extended to all research tools.

Under a direct application of the OAL approach, licensees would also be required to grant back any improvement patents, so that these patents would also be available for open use in research on neglected diseases. Given the ease with which improvement patents can be obtained, particularly in the area of biotechnology,[72] a grant back might be very important for ensuring a robust public domain in research tools. However, private-sector licensees might be quite reluctant to sign on to a grant-back approach, particularly for research tools.[73]

The success of one initiative in the AIDS vaccine arena, the International AIDS Vaccine Initiative ("IAVI"), indicates that some type of collective action might be possible. IAVI funds research and development on AIDS vaccine candidates for the developing world. Specifically, IAVI focuses on HIV-1 subtypes C and A, which are the major subtypes of HIV-1 prevalent in sub-Saharan Africa, India, and China. In contrast, HIV-1 subtype B, on which most vaccine research to date has focused, is prevalent in North America and Europe. Organizations that receive such funding (including, to date, Oxford University, the Imperial College of Science and Technology, and the Aaron Diamond AIDS Research Center) must agree, as a condition of such funding, to make any vaccine that is developed available at a "reasonable price" in the developing world.[74] Reasonable price includes actual costs of production, as well as a profit margin, but does not include R&D costs. To the extent that a given organization does not succeed in developing and manufacturing a vaccine, it must give IAVI royalty-free rights to practice any patent it has in the area of vaccine research.[75] That public-sector organizations would agree to relinquish control over patent rights relevant to the developing world suggests that collective management of university rights in a manner helpful to the developing world may be realistic.[76]

---

[71] With respect to patents on, and related proprietary information concerning end-product drugs, the OAL Draft also preserves open access for entities that want to manufacture the drug for use in developing countries.
[72] See, e.g., In re Deuel, 51 F.3d 1552 (Fed. Cir. 1995) (setting a low nonobviousness threshold for obtaining a biotechnology patent).
[73] See MIHR Handbook, above n. 67, at 76 (suggestion by Lita Nelsen that licensees might be unwilling to give universities power over improvement patents, particularly "if the university's invention, at the time it was licensed, is still far from a product.")
[74] The definition of reasonable price is based on a number of criteria, including the income level of the developing country. Developing countries are those that meet World Bank criteria for lower and middle income countries. IAVI currently has agreements with six Vaccine Development Partnerships and intends to be in Phase III trials on one candidate vaccine by 2004.
[75] See IAVI Industrial Collaboration Agreement (on file with author).
[76] Of course, in the IAVI context, the agreement to relinquish control over patent rights was necessary in order to secure research funding. Tying university research funding to successful collective action might be a particularly effective mechanism for encouraging

IV. Limitations of public-sector collective action

Even if successful, voluntary collective action by public-sector institutions to address the needs of developing countries has limitations. One obvious limitation is that such institutions own only a portion of the relevant intellectual property. Even in the area of agricultural biotechnology, which has long been dominated by public-sector research, only about one-quarter of patents are held by public institutions. In addition, critical public-sector patents – such as the technology for inserting new genes into plants – are effectively owned by private enterprises because they have been licensed exclusively with no reservation of rights. Hence, the role of the private sector merits discussion.

A. The role of the private sector

Where research and development confronts proprietary rights held by private-sector institutions, addressing the obstacles posed by such rights may be more difficult. Nonetheless, the public sector may be able to catalyze collective action across the public-private divide. Consider, for example, the case of transgenic B-carotene-enhanced rice (so-called "Golden Rice"). Golden Rice, which could alleviate vitamin-A deficiency suffered by as many as 400 million individuals in the developing world, was created by Ingo Potrykus and his colleagues at the publicly-funded Swiss Federal Institute of Technology in Zurich. But producing this rice for the developing world involved overcoming the barriers posed by more than 70 patented or proprietary methods and materials belonging to 32 different companies. After substantial effort by the public sector, including significant personal negotiation by Potrykus himself, agreements were reached that allowed public-sector scientists to proceed with research to develop lines of Golden Rice without paying licensing fees. In particular, Potrykus and his public-sector allies were able to persuade a number of major companies, including Monsanto, Syngenta, and Bayer, to donate their proprietary technologies for production of B-carotene-enhanced rice in the developing world.[77]

With respect to research focused on developing-country diseases, IAVI has had some success in enlisting the private sector on the same terms as the public sector. Currently, it has three private collaborators. More generally, the development of therapies to treat developing-country diseases will likely be assisted by

---

such action. At least in the U.S., however, the ability of the National Institutes of Health and other funding agencies to issue a credible threat in this regard is severely hampered by the existing technology transfer regime, principally the Bayh-Dole Act of 1980. *See generally* Rai & Eisenberg, above n. 3.

[77] Monsanto has also put its rice genome into the public domain, so as to allow the public International Rice Genome Sequencing Project (IRGSP) to finish the task more quickly and at lower cost.

access to small-molecule chemical libraries.[78] These libraries are generally held as trade secrets by pharmaceutical companies. If pharmaceutical companies could be assured that use of their libraries would be restricted to developing-country diseases, they might be willing to donate their libraries for research on those diseases. Even where public-sector action does not catalyze *donation* of private proprietary technologies for the developing world, it might help to produce intellectual property clearinghouses where rights to such technology would be available at relatively low cost.[79]

B. *Obstacles unrelated to intellectual property*

Another important set of objections to reliance on voluntary collective action derives from the reality that intellectual property rights represent only a part of the problem in terms of generating R&D oriented towards the developing world. Perhaps most obviously, once upstream intellectual property hurdles are overcome, public-sector funding will be necessary to pay for the large capital and labor costs of research and development.[80] These R&D costs are likely to be particularly high in the area of biomedical research.

For example, although IAVI has cash reserves of approximately $250 million, this is only about half of the sum the organization says it needs to execute its plans.[81] In contrast, in the year 2000, the pharmaceutical company Merck devoted $2.4 billion to developing an AIDS vaccine for the developed world.[82] Nonetheless, even if upstream proprietary rights represent only a small portion of the problem with respect to producing biotechnological products for the developing world, collective action can work to ensure that such rights do not pose an obstacle.

---

[78] Small-molecule drugs, which can usually be taken orally, work to "knock out" molecules (so-called "targets") that are implicated in the onset or progression of a given disease.

[79] Geoffrey Graff & David Zilberman, *An Intellectual Property Clearinghouse for Agricultural Biotechnology*, 19 NATURE BIOTECHNOLOGY 1179 (2001).

[80] In many cases, the technical difficulty of the task is also considerable. For example, in the case of a potential AIDS vaccine for the developed world, efforts have been ongoing since the late 1980s. Yet, the candidate vaccines have yielded little in the way of clinical success. Developers of products for developing countries, particularly in the biomedical arena, may also face considerable hurdles in terms of getting regulatory approval. For example, approval for conducting phase III efficacy trials in the developing world can be difficult to obtain.

[81] Laurie Garrett, *Back To Basics: AIDS at 20*, NEWSDAY, 5 June 2001. As various commentators have noted, public-sector funding could operate as either a "push" or "pull" mechanism. Under a push mechanism, such as that employed by IAVI, the public sector funds the research directly. Under a pull mechanism, the public sector might guarantee a paying market for a particular vaccine or therapy. For more analysis, see Henry Grabowski, *Increasing R&D Incentives for Neglected Diseases: Lessons from the Orphan Drug Act* [this volume].

[82] Garrett, above n. 81.

V. Conclusion

Private-sector collective action that facilitates free rights exchange is often proposed as an efficient solution to difficulties created by increasing proprietary complexity in the research arena. This chapter has argued that, at least in the area of biotechnology, we have not seen such activity, and we should not be surprised by its absence. What we should expect, and what has in fact arisen, is public-sector collective action in research areas of low commercial value. Although such public-sector collective action has many limitations, it is a valuable first step towards generating research that addresses the health problems and food security needs of developing countries.

PART II

Innovation and technology transfer in a protectionist environment

SECTION 2
Stimulating local innovation

11

Do stronger patents induce more local innovation?

LEE G. BRANSTETTER[*]

Abstract
Introduction
I.   Patents and innovation: Historical evidence
II. The Japanese experience
III. Patents and technology transfer
Summary

ABSTRACT

One of the central arguments advanced by proponents of stronger intellectual property rights (IPRs) systems is that strengthening such systems induces higher levels of innovation by domestic firms. This article reviews several empirical studies undertaken by economists to assess the validity of this claim. Most studies fail to find evidence of a strong positive response by domestic innovators that could be reasonably ascribed to the effects of stronger IPRs. The benefits of stronger IPRs – to the extent that they exist at all – are more likely to come instead from an acceleration in the domestic deployment of advanced technology by the affiliates of foreign firms.

Introduction

Many contributors to this volume have noted the global trend towards strengthened intellectual property rights.[1] Since strengthening its own patent

---

[*] Lee G. Branstetter is Associate Professor of Finance and Economics at the School of Business, Columbia University.
[1] *See* Keith E. Maskus & Jerome H. Reichman, *The Globalization of Private Knowledge Goods and the Privatization of Global Public Goods* [this volume]; Richard R. Nelson, *Linkages Between the Market Economy and the Scientific Commons* [this volume]; Carlos M. Correa, *Can the Trips Agreement Foster Technology Transfer to Developing Countries?* [this volume].

system in the 1980s, through the establishment of the Federal Circuit Court of Appeals and through broadening the definition of what is patentable, the United States has been active in attempting to convince other nations to adopt stronger intellectual property rights (IPRs), and America's long campaign has achieved considerable success.[2] Over the course of the 1980s and early 1990s, several nations were persuaded to enter into bilateral agreements with the United States. These agreements involved unilateral strengthening of the trading partners' intellectual property (IP) systems.[3] Eventually, the United States was successful in its bid to incorporate the Agreement on Trade-Related Intellectual Property Rights (TRIPS) into the charter of the World Trade Organization (WTO).[4]

This trend towards stronger IPRs has been controversial, to say the least. It has been extensively criticized by many in the developing world, on several grounds, including the possibility that providing more monopoly power to multinational corporate incumbent patent holders will lead to "rent extraction" from poor developing countries.[5] Advocates of stronger IPRs, primarily located in rich countries, counter that stronger protection in developing countries will induce a higher level of innovation in those countries and a higher level of technology transfer from developed countries.[6]

---

[2] Nancy Gallini, *The Economics of Patents: Lessons from Recent U.S. Patent Reform*, 16 J ECON. PERSP. 131 (2002), is an excellent essay providing a comprehensive review of the recent theoretical literature on changing patent policy in the United States and the lessons that can be drawn for the economic analysis of patent protection; A. Jaffe, *The U.S. Patent System in Transition: Policy Innovation and the Innovation Process*, 29 RES. POL'Y 531 (2000), provides another overview of the debate concerning the impact of changes in U.S. patent policy on domestic innovation.

[3] This diplomatic effort is chronicled in some detail in MICHAEL RYAN, KNOWLEDGE DIPLOMACY: GLOBAL COMPETITION AND THE POLITICS OF INTELLECTUAL PROPERTY (Brookings Institution Press 1998); E. UPHOFF, INTELLECTUAL PROPERTY AND U.S. RELATIONS WITH INDONESIA, MALAYSIA, SINGAPORE, AND THAILAND (Cornell Southeast Asia Program 1990). See also SUSAN K. SELL, PRIVATE POWER, PUBLIC LAW: THE GLOBALIZATION OF INTELLECTUAL PROPERTY RIGHTS (Cambridge University Press 2003).

[4] Agreement on Trade-Related Aspects of Intellectual Property Rights, 15 Apr. 1994, Marrakesh Agreement Establishing the World Trade Organization, Annex 1C, LEGAL INSTRUMENTS – RESULTS OF THE URUGUAY ROUND, vol. 31, 33 I.L.M. 81 (1994).

[5] See M. Stillwell & C. Monagle, Review of the TRIPS Agreement under Article 71.1, South Centre Occasional Paper 15 (Dec. 2000), at www.southcentre.org/publications; Correa, above n. 1. On rent transfers, see The World Bank, Intellectual Property: Balancing Incentives with Competitive Access, Global Economic Prospects and the Developing Countries 2002, at 129. See also Philip McCalman, *Reaping What You Sow: An Empirical Analysis of International Patent Harmonization*, 55 J. INT'L ECON. 161 (2001).

[6] See ROBERT M. SHERWOOD, INTELLECTUAL PROPERTY AND ECONOMIC DEVELOPMENT (Westview Press 1990); KEITH E. MASKUS, INTELLECTUAL PROPERTY RIGHTS IN THE GLOBAL ECONOMY (Institute for International Economics 2000).

I. Patents and innovation: Historical evidence

Because the full provisions of the TRIPS Agreement will not be implemented in all countries for some time, a full accounting of its impact on either "local innovation" abroad or international technology transfer remains as a task for the future. However, history provides us with a number of patent reform episodes, which constitute "quasi-natural experiments" in patent policy, from which we can make some inferences concerning the impact of stronger patents on local innovation. The empirical literature on this topic remains subject to further development, but some interesting findings have already emerged. Space and time constraints prevent me from doing justice to every significant contribution to this emerging literature. I will, therefore, concentrate on a handful of papers, with apologies to the excellent articles and hardworking scholars that my circumscribed review will unfortunately omit.

In studying the impact of patent reform on "local innovation," one can either study a particular policy change in great depth, or attempt to examine the average impact of a number of reform episodes. An interesting example of the latter approach is the recent contribution of Joshua Lerner,[7] who examined the impact of nearly every significant patent reform episode over the last 150 years in a large number of countries. Lerner found in this history that strengthening local patent laws typically did not increase domestic patent applications, but did lead to statistically and economically significant increases in patenting by foreigners in the reforming country. These findings were robust to attempts to control for the endogeneity of patent reform.[8] On average, it seems, stronger local patent laws have not stimulated local innovation.[9]

How should we interpret these findings? The recent work on "cumulative innovation" within the theoretical literature on patent design has demonstrated that excessively broad patent rights can actually retard the pace of innovation.[10] This happens because initial patent holders are able to block the necessary "follow-on" research in a technology field, and this foregone innovation could have increased quality and lowered product prices to the

---

[7] Joshua Lerner, Patent Protection and Innovation over 150 Years, National Bureau of Economic Research Working Paper No. 8977 (2002).
[8] That reform may be endogenous means that it arises from political and economic pressures rather than being a solely exogenous event. Because multiple endogenous events may be jointly caused by other factors, econometric analysis must control for such factors. See Lerner, above n. 7, for details.
[9] On the other hand, Lerner's findings are consistent with the view that stronger IPRs lead to greater deployment by foreigners of new technology developed abroad. This is an idea to which I will return at the end of this essay.
[10] See J. Bessen & E. Maskin, Sequential Innovation, Patents, and Imitation, MIT Department of Economics Working Paper No. 00–01 (2000). This paper and much other recent work is influenced by the model presented in J. Green & S. Scotchmer, *On the Division of Profits between Sequential Innovators*, 26 RAND J. ECON. 20–33 (2001).

point where a new class of inventions becomes widely used.[11] Lerner views his own results through the lens of this recent theoretical work.[12] Two other authors recently provided both a theoretical model and empirical evidence on the pace of innovation in U.S. information technology industries.[13] They found that innovation costs in this sector were increased by some forms of technology protection, which they submitted as evidence in favor of the cumulative innovation view.

International economists have suggested another reason why changes in local patent regimes might have a limited effect on innovation by domestic entities. If many or most domestic innovating agents also sell their innovative products on global markets, as well as in the domestic market, then IPR regimes abroad may matter even more than IPR regimes at home. This is likely to be particularly true for countries in which the internal market is a relatively small fraction of the global market for technology-intensive commodities. If the IPR regime in the larger "foreign" market is already strong, strengthening the local regime may have a marginal impact on local agents' incentives to invest.[14]

II. The Japanese experience

A number of recent econometric case studies of particular patent reforms reached broadly the same conclusion as Lerner, namely, that strengthening local patent rights did not seem to lead to increases in innovative input or output.[15] I will discuss in detail two of these recent studies, which I know well

---

[11] A number of important papers have developed the "cumulative innovation" view, including, but not limited to, Robert Merges & Richard Nelson, *On the Complex Economics of Patent Scope*, 90 COLUM. L. REV. 839 (1990); Suzanne Scotchmer, *Standing on the Shoulders of Giants: Cumulative Research and the Patent Law*, 5 J. ECON. PERSP. 29 (1991); Green & Scotchmer, above n. 10; T. O'Donoghue et al., *Patent Breadth, Patent Life, and the Pace of Technological Progress*, 7 J. ECON. & MGMT. STRATEGY 1 (1998).

[12] Lerner, above n. 7.   [13] Bessen & Maskin, above n. 10.

[14] *See* G.M. Grossman & E. L.-C. Lai, International Protection of Intellectual Property, NBER Working Paper No. 8704 (2002).

[15] Other econometric case studies with an international focus include F. M. Scherer & S. Weisburst, *Economic Effects of Strengthening Pharmaceutical Patent Protection in Italy*, 26 INT'L REV. INDUS. PROP. & COPYRIGHT L. 1009 (1996); A. Kawaura & Sumner La Croix, *Japan's Shift from Process to Product Patents in the Pharmaceutical Industry: An Event Study of the Impact on Japanese Firms*, 33 ECON. INQUIRY 88 (1995); Sumner La Croix & A. Kawaura, *Product Patent Reform and Its Impact on Korea's Pharmaceutical Industry*, 10 INT'L ECON. J. 109 (1996). Among these, only Kawaura & La Croix, 1995, found evidence that innovative output was enhanced by stronger patent protection, and only in the context of a single industry. Another, and influential, paper examined the impact of changing U.S. patent laws and practices on patenting in the semiconductor industry; *see* Bronwyn Hall & R. Ziedonis, *The Patent Paradox Revisited: An Empirical Study of Patenting in the U.S. Semiconductor industry, 1979–1995*, 32 RAND J. ECON. 101 (2001).

(because I am one of the authors). In the first, Sakakibara and I examined in detail the impact of Japan's 1988 patent reforms on the innovative activity of Japanese firms.[16] While these reforms were complicated, they had the effect of broadening the potential scope of Japanese patent protection. In a follow-on study, Yoshiaki Nakamura and I examined some measures of Japanese innovative activity through 1999, thereby extending the focus through the "second wave" of Japanese patent reforms in the mid-1990s.[17]

A major feature of this second wave of patent reform was a change in administration of the patent system: bowing to U.S. pressure, Japan shifted from a pre-grant opposition system to a post-grant opposition system.[18] The mid-to-late 1990s also witnessed an increase in intellectual property litigation and the advent of large damage awards in patent infringement lawsuits, which demonstrated a change in the attitude of Japanese courts towards the rights of incumbent patent holders.[19]

Unlike many developing countries undergoing patent reforms in the 1980s and 1990s, Japan had a large number of domestically based, R&D-performing industrial enterprises that operated at or close to the global technology frontier in the years prior to patent reform.[20] Thus, scholars can observe, at the firm level, measures of inventive input (e.g., R&D expenditures or employment of scientific personnel) and output (e.g., patent applications) prior to, during, and after patent reform. If ever there were a context in which patent reform could be expected to have measurable effects on R&D inputs and outputs, Japan in the late 1980s would appear to be it.

This strong prior belief notwithstanding, Mariko Sakakibara and I found no evidence of an increase in either R&D input or output that could plausibly be ascribed to the effects of the patent reforms of the late 1980s.[21] Japan's general economic downturn in the 1990s forced many firms to reduce R&D spending

---

[16] See Mariko Sakakibara & Lee G. Branstetter, *Do Stronger Patents Induce More Innovation? Evidence from the 1988 Japanese Patent Reforms*, 32 RAND J. ECON. 77 (2001).

[17] See Lee G. Branstetter & Yoshiaki Nakamura, *Is Japanese Innovative Capacity in Decline?*, in STRUCTURAL IMPEDIMENTS TO GROWTH IN JAPAN (M. Blomstrom et al. eds., University of Chicago Press & NBER 2003)

[18] Branstetter & Nakamura, above n. 17; Keith E. Maskus & Christine R. McDaniel, *Impacts of the Japanese Patent System on Productivity Growth*, 11 JAPAN & WORLD ECON. 557 (1999).

[19] It was not until 1998 that the Japanese Supreme Court formally adopted a doctrine of equivalents. However, time-series evidence from IP litigation in Japan suggests that a shift to "pro-patent" legal practice was underway prior to that formal adoption. See Sakakibara & Branstetter, above n. 16.

[20] See C. FRED BERGSTEN & MARCUS NOLAND, RECONCILABLE DIFFERENCES? UNITED STATES–JAPAN ECONOMIC CONFLICT (Institute for International Economics 1993).

[21] See Sakakibara & Branstetter, above n. 16. These patent reforms of the 1980s were preceded by a significant patent change in the 1970s – the introduction of product patents for pharmaceuticals. The available evidence suggests that this patent change may have stimulated innovation in the Japanese pharmaceutical industry. Kawaura & La Croix,

and patenting activity, possibly swamping the impact of Japan's second wave of patent reforms. Nevertheless, controlling for the downturn in R&D spending at the firm level, Yoshiaki Nakamura and I were unable to find any evidence of an upturn in innovative performance following these reforms.[22] In fact, the trends in the 1990s tended to confirm the findings in the earlier article. If anything, R&D productivity grew, in relative terms, more slowly in the mid-to-late 1990s than in earlier years. Recent accounts in the Japanese language business press have increasingly pointed to the poor productivity of Japanese R&D spending as an impediment to the performance of the overall economy.[23]

Why did the patent reforms of the 1980s and 1990s fail to stimulate local innovation in Japan? In our later paper we provide several explanations, many of which potentially generalize to other countries.[24] First, and perhaps most obviously, R&D input has a cyclical component. In order for firms to invest in R&D, they need to expect that a growing market for their new or improved goods will allow them to recoup their investment. In the absence of this growth, stronger IPRs are an insufficient incentive to invest.

Second, even in the absence of broad or strongly enforced IPRs, it is possible for firms to appropriate some of the returns to investments in research.[25] The shortcomings of the pre-1988 patent system did not stop some Japanese firms from reaching (and even advancing) the technology frontier in their industries. However, the R&D strategies of these firms relied on other means of appropriation: the use of complementary manufacturing facilities and distribution channels, the development of globally recognized brand names, bringing innovations to the market quickly, and relying on secrecy rather than patents.[26]

---

above n. 15, offer one analysis of this change. However, this is not a general result because the introduction of product patents for pharmaceuticals in Korea and Italy in the 1980s yielded no such positive result, as found respectively in La Croix & Kawaura, above n. 15, and Scherer & Weisburst, above n. 15. Neither did the extension of Japanese pharmaceutical firms' patent clocks under a feature of the 1988 patent reform have any measurable positive impact; see Sakakibara & Branstetter, above n. 16.

[22] Branstetter & Nakamura, above n. 17.
[23] An English language summary of interviews with leading Japanese R&D policymakers and practitioners that conveys this pessimistic view is provided by D. Normile, *Japan Asks Why More Yen Don't Yield More Products*, 296 SCIENCE 1230 (2002). For a more balanced analysis by a leading Japanese scholar that nevertheless echoes some of these criticisms, see A. GOTO, INNOVATION AND THE JAPANESE ECONOMY (Iwanami Press 2000 (publication in Japanese)). For a collection of articles by Japanese economists exploring recent trends in intellectual property rights in Japan, see A. GOTO & S. NAGAOKA, INTELLECTUAL PROPERTY RIGHTS AND INNOVATION (University of Tokyo Press 2003 (publication in Japanese)).
[24] Branstetter & Nakamura, above n. 17. I hasten to emphasize that these points are somewhat speculative, based largely on conversations with Japanese practitioners. They have not yet been validated by statistical analysis.
[25] See MASKUS, above n. 6.   [26] Branstetter & Nakamura, above n. 17.

Reflecting this environment, industrial R&D expenditure was more highly concentrated in large industrial enterprises in Japan than was the case in the United States in the years prior to reform. Furthermore, the nature of Japanese R&D spending differed from that of U.S. firms. Corporate R&D expenditure tended to be more applied rather than basic, more focused on process rather than product innovation, and more closely related to the technologies embodied in the firms' current product portfolio rather than focused on fundamental technological advances.[27]

As Japanese manufacturing wages rose and the Japanese yen appreciated over the course of the 1980s, the strategy of appropriating returns to R&D investment through the possession of complementary manufacturing capabilities became less viable. Japanese manufacturers were "squeezed from below" by the expanding capabilities of lower-cost manufacturers in Taiwan, South Korea, and, increasingly, China. In fact, at the time of Japan's patent reform, many industrial companies were refocusing their R&D efforts on more basic research and intensifying activity with regard to product innovation.[28] A move toward stronger IPRs was arguably complementary to this shift in strategy and may have been a necessary condition for its success. However, if it was a necessary condition, it was far from sufficient.

Contemporary press accounts, interviews with Japanese R&D managers, and the econometric results of Branstetter and Nakamura all suggest that it has been difficult for Japanese firms, which had achieved a comparative advantage in a certain style of research, to successfully shift away from that style.[29] Aggressive attempts to pool engineering talent in central R&D labs pursuing more basic research have largely failed to generate the anticipated breakthroughs in proprietary technology.[30]

In the United States, the pursuit of more basic industrial research that is closely linked to recent breakthroughs in academic science relies heavily on the availability of large numbers of scientists and engineers with advanced degrees

---

[27] See Edwin Mansfield, *Industrial R&D in Japan and the United States: A Comparative Study*, 78 AM. ECON. REV. – PAPERS & PROC. 223 (1988), for an empirical analysis of the differences in private sector R&D in Japan and the United States.

[28] This "convergence" in U.S. and Japanese R&D investment is documented in W. Cohen et al., *Spillovers, Patents, and the Incentives to Innovate in Japan and the United States*, 31 RES. POL'Y 1349 (1998). A. Goto, *Introduction* to INNOVATION IN JAPAN (A. Goto & H. Odagiri eds., Clarendon University Press 1997), discusses its implications.

[29] Branstetter & Nakamura, above n. 17.

[30] Indeed, Japanese corporate R&D managers' criticisms of the shortcomings of their central R&D labs echo the criticisms made of large U.S. corporate R&D labs in the 1980s and early 1990s. For a review of the latter and a consideration of the consequences of their downsizing in the 1990s, see R. ROSENBLOOM & W. SPENCER, ENGINES OF INNOVATION: U.S. INDUSTRIAL RESEARCH AT THE END OF AN ERA (Harvard University Press 1996).

obtained at America's world-class universities.[31] Traditionally, a much smaller fraction of Japan's R&D workforce has gone through the complete process of Ph.D.-level academic training.[32] Science-based corporate R&D in the U.S. may also rely on a more developed tradition of research interaction between the private sector and university-based researchers. In addition, small high-technology start-ups have played an increasingly important role in U.S. corporate R&D – both as independent innovators and as partners in research collaborations with more established firms.[33] Some scholars would attribute some of the apparent recent rise in U.S. innovative productivity to this changing distribution of R&D effort across different organizational forms.[34]

The notion, stressed by Arora and his co-authors, that stronger IPRs may facilitate the development of "markets for technology," in which firms are able to specialize in the production of prototypes and product concepts and trade these ideas with other firms, is a useful one.[35] The idea that there are gains to specialization and trade is one of the oldest ideas in economics. The growth of these "markets for technology" could, in principle, raise the innovative output generated by a given level of R&D effort. As noted above, we may be seeing this in the contemporary United States.

However, the central point that I wish to stress here is that markets for technology require many institutional factors to support their existence. Strong IPRs are only one of these factors. In addition to strengthening its patent system, the Japanese government has taken significant steps to encourage university-industry research interaction. It has also increased the scale of doctoral-level training in the sciences and engineering. The Japanese government has also sought to remove legal and institutional barriers to the kind of high-technology entrepreneurship and startup activity that has long been

---

[31] For evidence of the strong and growing linkage between academic science and industrial R&D in the United States, see Nathan Rosenberg & Richard R. Nelson, *American Universities and Technical Advance in Industry*, 23 RES. POL'Y 323 (1994); F. Narin, et al., *The Increasing Linkage between U.S. Technology and Public Science*, 26 RES. POL'Y 317 (1997); Lee G. Branstetter, Is Academic Science Driving a Surge in Industrial Innovation?: Evidence from Patent Citations, Columbia Business School Working Paper (2003).

[32] For evidence of the gap between Japan and the United States in terms of large numbers of scientists and engineers with advanced degrees, see Daniel Okimoto & Gary Saxonhouse, *Technology and the Future of the Economy*, in THE POLITICAL ECONOMY OF JAPAN, VOLUME ONE: THE DOMESTIC TRANSFORMATION (K. Yamamura & Y. Yasuba eds., Stanford University Press 1987).

[33] See, among others, D. Robinson & T. Stuart, Financial Contracting in Biotech Strategic Alliances, Columbia Business School Working Paper (2002).

[34] See Samuel Kortum & Joshua Lerner, *What Is Behind the Recent Surge in Patenting?*, 28 RES. POL'Y 1 (1999).

[35] See A. Arora et al., *Markets for Technology, Intellectual Property Rights and Development* [this volume]; see also A. ARORA ET AL., MARKETS FOR TECHNOLOGY (MIT Press 2001).

visible in the United States.³⁶ However, these changes have yet to generate an obvious payoff, as our research would indicate. The long-term nature of these investments and institutional changes means that the economic returns – if they ever materialize – could remain years, if not decades, down the road.

Note that the problems with patent reform described in the preceding paragraphs differ somewhat from the problems with patent reform that scholars working in the "cumulative innovation" literature have stressed.³⁷ These two sets of problems are certainly not mutually exclusive, and both may be in part responsible for the lack of measurable progress in Japan in terms of the ability of patent reforms to increase innovative input or output.

However, it is worth noting that conversations with Japanese practitioners did not emphasize the role of excessively strong property rights by initial inventors as a barrier to progress. Rather, these conversations pointed to the difficulties and lags involved in changing the organizational structure of Japanese corporate R&D and the academic training of the Japanese R&D workforce in a way that maximizes the ability of firms to exploit the opportunities created by the new legal framework.³⁸

Viewed in this context, Lerner's results are perhaps less surprising. If it takes time, even in a context like Japan's, for firms to take advantage of stronger and broader IPRs by restructuring their R&D activities, then we could scarcely expect to discern rapid changes in poorer developing countries that remain much farther from the technological frontier. To invoke the language of international economics, firms in the United States and some Western European countries have a comparative advantage in the sort of research that is enabled by strong IPRs.³⁹ Elsewhere, one can change the laws relatively quickly, but it may take time for institutions and practices to shift in a way that fully exploits the opportunities created by the new legal framework.

III. Patents and technology transfer

If notions of cumulative innovation and (slowly) shifting comparative advantage in R&D limit the impact we would expect to see of stronger IPRs on local innovation, at least in the short to medium run, this still leaves open the possibility that such reforms could speed the diffusion of new innovations from outside

---

[36] For a review of some Japanese policy initiatives in this area, see Joshua Lerner et al., New Business Investment Company: October 1997, Harvard Business School Case No. N9–299–025 (1999).
[37] Bessen & Maskin, above n. 10.
[38] See Branstetter & Nakamura, above n. 17; Lerner et al., above n. 36.
[39] This comparative advantage may be seen in the fact that firms in the United States and Western Europe own far more patents abroad than do firms from other countries. See McCalman, above n. 5.

the country.[40] The idea is that, when dealing with high-technology multinational firms, developing countries should heed the following slogan: build it (strong IPRs) and they will come.[41] In principle, this idea could be valid for even the poorer countries that are unlikely to have a comparative advantage in innovative activity even in the long run. A number of researchers have attempted to assess the extent to which stronger IPRs induce additional technology transfer, using both theory and empirical analysis. Again, space constraints preclude a comprehensive review of the prior literature on this topic.[42] I will simply note here that data problems have been an important constraint to research progress, but the received literature points to a positive relationship between patent strength and technology transfer.[43]

With two additional authors I have also worked on this issue.[44] My coauthors and I were fortunate to have data at a considerably more disaggregated level than has generally been available to prior researchers. In our study, we use firm-level data concerning thousands of U.S. multinational firms' technology licensing activities with their foreign affiliates and unaffiliated firms.[45] Because we were able to observe the same multinational enterprises operating in both countries that changed their IP regimes and in similar countries that did not, we could take a "differences-in-differences" approach to the estimation of the impact of IP reform on technology transfer and related multinational activity.[46]

---

[40] See Kamal Saggi, Encouraging Technology Transfer to Developing Countries: Role of the WTO, Report to the Commonwealth Secretariat (2003).

[41] See SHERWOOD, above n. 6.

[42] MASKUS, above n. 6, provides an invaluable book-length study of IPRs issues in the context of international economic theory and policy. Significant empirical studies that have been published since that book include McCalman, above n. 5, and P. J. Smith, *How Do Foreign Patent Rights Affect U.S. Exports, Affiliate Sales, and Licenses?*, 55 J. INT'L ECON. 411 (2001). Important theoretical analyses include, but are not limited to, Elhanan Helpman, *Innovation, Imitation, and Intellectual Property Rights*, 61 ECONOMETRICA 1247 (1993); Edwin L.-C. Lai, *International Intellectual Property Rights Protection and the Rate of Producer Innovation*, 55 J. DEV. ECON. 133 (1998); James R. Markusen, *Contracts, Intellectual Property Rights, and Multinational Investment in Developing Countries*, 53 J. INT'L ECON. 187 (2001); Amy Glass & Kamal Saggi, *Intellectual Property Rights and Foreign Direct Investment*, 56 J. INT'L ECON. 387 (2002).

[43] Among the most significant recent empirical contributions are Guifang Yang & Keith E. Maskus, *Intellectual Property Rights and Licensing: An Econometric Investigation*, 137 WELTWIRTSCHAFTLICHES ARCHIV 58 (2001); Keith E. Maskus et al., *Patent Rights and International Technology Transfer through Direct Investment and Licensing* [this volume].

[44] See Lee G. Branstetter et al., Do Stronger Intellectual Property Rights Induce More Technology Transfer? Evidence from U.S. Multinationals, Columbia Business School, Working Paper (2003).

[45] See id. This working paper is available from the author upon request.

[46] Unlike some others in this literature, we use the term "technology transfer" to refer to transfers of technology from a multinational parent to its affiliates as well as to independent entities. We are seeking to measure "deployment" of new technology in a reforming

To summarize our results, we found evidence of both increased rent extraction and increased deployment of new technology following episodes of patent strengthening.[47] The volume of technology licensing payments remitted to U.S.-based multinationals from their own affiliates increased after IP reform. Where U.S.-based multinational firms had no affiliates in the reforming country, we found evidence of an increase in licensing to third parties. Of course, recorded licensing revenues could increase because of an increase in the quantity of technology employed, the price charged for use of a given technology, or both.

However, there was auxiliary evidence strongly consistent with the notion that a component of the increase in licensing revenues represented real deployment of new technology following IP reform. First, patterns in the data on international patenting supported this interpretation. After a strengthening of the intellectual property regime, both the level and the growth rate of foreign patenting in reforming countries increased. A legal change with no effective enforcement would conceivably be followed by no change in foreign patenting. A legal change that led to increased rent extraction might induce a short-lived "surge" of patenting, as firms sought protection over already deployed technologies, but this "surge" would presumably be short-lived. On the other hand, if the legal change led to deployment of new technologies, there would be an increase in both the level and the growth rate of patenting. This latter pattern is what we found in the data.[48]

Second, data on affiliate R&D spending also supported the view that stronger IPRs lead to an increase in deployment of new technology by U.S. multinationals. The commonly held view among practitioners is that affiliate R&D spending functions primarily as a complement, rather than a substitute, to the R&D of the parent, and that, in particular, a large component of R&D spending is focused on the adaptation of the parents' technology to the local environment.[49] We find that affiliate R&D spending tended to increase with technology licensing revenues after IP reform. This is consistent with the view that new technology was being deployed and that this deployment required an investment by the affiliate in modifying it for the local market.

What we have been unable to do so far is a net welfare calculation in which we subtract the costs of increased rent extraction from the benefits of increased technology installation. All we can say at this point is that the data seem to suggest that the latter effect is present and quantitatively significant.[50]

---

country, whether that deployment comes through technology licensing to third parties or to a firm's own affiliates.

[47] Branstetter et al., above n. 44.   [48] *Id.*

[49] *See* Saggi, above n. 40; Keith E. Maskus, *The Role of Intellectual Property Rights in Encouraging Foreign Direct Investment and Technology Transfer*, 9 DUKE J. COMP. & INT'L L. 109 (1998). *See also* W. Kuemmerle, *The Drivers of Foreign Direct Investment into Research and Development: An Empirical Investigation*, 30 J. INT'L BUS. STUD. 1 (1999).

[50] Branstetter et al., above n. 44.

Summary

To restate the results of empirical work to date, there is relatively little evidence that stronger IPRs stimulate local innovation, at least in the short to medium run. This does not prove that these positive effects do not exist, but a number of reasonably well-structured research projects conducted by competent scholars have generally failed to find them in most contexts.[51] The robust effects we have detected seem to point to an alternative source of gains from patent reform: more rapid deployment of technology generated in the world's research centers. However, recent studies also point to evidence of potential welfare losses in developing countries that strengthen their IP regimes.[52] An important agenda for future research is to determine the relative strengths of these positive and negative effects, and to see how the net impact depends on the nature of the reform and the state of development of the reforming country.

---

[51] The study by Kawaura & La Croix, above n. 15, seems to be an exception to the general rule.
[52] *See* McCalman, above n. 5.

12

Markets for technology, intellectual property rights, and development

ASHISH ARORA

ANDREA FOSFURI

ALFONSO GAMBARDELLA[*]

Abstract
1 Introduction
2 Markets for technology
   2.1 A tentative definition
   2.2 Empirical evidence
3 Patents and markets for technology
4 Markets for technology and international technology transfer
5 Policy implications for developing countries
6 Conclusion

ABSTRACT

We argue that stricter enforcement of intellectual property rights can, under some conditions, enhance the international diffusion of technology by fostering markets for technology. Developing economies should be prepared to exploit the opportunities opened up by the presence of such markets, which can significantly expand prospects for inward technology transfer.

1 Introduction

For centuries, the creation of markets has been one of the main drivers of economic development.[1] There is one activity, however, in which the

---

[*] Ashish Arora is Professor of Economics and Public Policy at the Heinz School of Public Policy, Carnegie Mellon University. Andrea Fosfuri is Associate Professor of Management, Universidad Carlos III, Madrid, and Research Affiliate, Centre for Economic Policy Research, London. Alfonso Gambardella is Professor of Economics, Sant'Anna School of Advanced Studies, Pisa.

[1] *See* N. ROSENBERG & L. BIRDZELL, HOW THE WEST GREW RICH (Basic Books 1986).

formation of markets has not evolved as smoothly as in others. Technologies have normally been embodied in goods, services and people, and markets for technologies that are not embodied in those elements have developed less commonly. This is epitomized by the Schumpeterian legacy,[2] which suggests that research and development (R&D) investment is most often the business of relatively large firms that integrate the search for innovation with their production and marketing assets. However, over the past ten to fifteen years, there has been a rapid growth in a variety of arrangements for the international exchange of technologies or technological services, ranging from R&D joint ventures and partnerships to licensing and cross-licensing agreements, through to contract R&D.[3] Along with this trend, specialized technology suppliers have emerged in many industries.

This chapter draws upon a decade-long research program on the nature and functioning of markets for technology – markets for intermediate technological inputs – and their implications for business and public policy.[4] In this essay we simply focus on the role of intellectual property rights (IPRs), most notably patents, in fostering the rise of markets for technology and the consequences for international technology transfer and development. Specifically, we shall argue here that the existence of markets for technology requires a change in the traditional view about IPRs as managing a tradeoff between *ex ante* incentives to innovate and *ex post* restriction to knowledge diffusion.[5] Instead, IPRs can, under some conditions, enhance the international diffusion of technology by fostering markets for technology.[6] Developing economies should be prepared to exploit the opportunities opened up by the presence of such markets, which can significantly expand prospects for inward technology transfer.

We begin in Section 2 with a tentative definition of markets for technology and by summarizing the empirical evidence on the size and importance of these markets. In Section 3 we go on to place into context the role of patents in the support of international technology markets. The discussion turns in Section 4 to how these markets induce greater flows of technology across borders. In

---

[2] J.A. SCHUMPETER, CAPITALISM, SOCIALISM AND DEMOCRACY (Harper & Row 1942).
[3] *See* A. ARORA ET AL., MARKETS FOR TECHNOLOGY: ECONOMICS OF INNOVATION AND CORPORATE STRATEGY (MIT Press 2001).
[4] *Id.*
[5] *See* K.J. Arrow, *Economic Welfare and the Allocation of Resources for Innovation*, in THE RATE AND DIRECTION OF INVENTIVE ACTIVITY 602 (R.R. Nelson ed., Princeton University Press 1962); W.D. NORDHAUS, INVENTION, GROWTH AND WELFARE: A THEORETICAL TREATMENT OF TECHNOLOGICAL CHANGE (MIT Press 1969).
[6] This point has also been emphasized by others, including J.W. Lee & E. Mansfield, *Intellectual Property Protection and U.S. Foreign Direct Investment*, 78 REV. ECON. & STAT. 181 (1996); A. Arora, *Contracting for Tacit Knowledge: The Provision of Technical Services in Technology Licensing Contracts*, 50 J. DEV. ECON. 233 (1996); G. Yang & K.E. Maskus, *Intellectual Property Rights, Licensing, and Innovation*, 53 J. INT'L ECON. 169, but is most extensively developed by ARORA ET AL., above n. 3.

Section 5 we offer policy recommendations for developing countries, while a final section contains brief concluding remarks.

2 Markets for technology

In this chapter we use the term "market" in a broad sense. In the conventional – and narrower – conception, market transactions are arm's-length, anonymous, and typically involve an exchange of a good for money.[7] Many, if not most, transactions for technology would fail one or the other criterion. Often they involve quite detailed contracts and may be embedded in technological alliances of some sort.[8] Thus, we shall often paint with a broad brush, contrasting conventional market transactions with processes for technology exchange inside a firm. To be sure, there are numerous hybrid forms of exchange that characterize market transactions in technology and that fall between the extremes discussed here.[9] We do not dispute the existence of such forms but focus on this basic distinction in order to sharpen the exposition.

2.1 A tentative definition

Technology comes in different forms and no general definition will fit all circumstances. For instance, technology can take the form of "intellectual property" (patents) or intangibles (e.g. a software program, or a design), be embodied in a product (e.g. a prototype or a device such as a computer chip designed to perform certain operations), or comprise technical services.[10] We will not attempt to define technology, treating it instead as an imprecise term for useful knowledge rooted in engineering and scientific disciplines.

Technology usually also draws from practical experience in production. In turn, this complexity means that technology transactions can take different forms, from pure licensing of well defined intellectual property to complicated collaborative agreements that may include the further development of the technology. Figure 1 summarizes our definition of the market for technology in the form of a simple typology, along with canonical examples for each case.

As Figure 1 shows, our definition of the market for technology is close to the one proposed by the U.S. Department of Justice in its Antitrust Guidelines for the Licensing of Intellectual Property.[11] That agency defines markets for technology as markets for "... intellectual property that is licensed and its close substitutes – that is the technologies or goods that are close enough

---

[7] O. WILLIAMSON, THE MECHANISMS OF GOVERNANCE (Oxford University Press 1996).
[8] See ARORA ET AL., above n. 3.   [9] See WILLIAMSON, above n. 7.
[10] See A. Arora, *Licensing Tacit Knowledge: Intellectual Property Rights and the Market for Know-how*, 4 ECON. INNOVATION & NEW TECH. 41 (1995).
[11] United States Dep't of Justice & Fed. Trade Comm'n, Antitrust Guidelines for the Licensing of Intellectual Property (6 Apr. 1995).

Figure 1: A simple typology of markets for technology

	Existing Technology	Future Technology or component for future
Horizontal Market / Transactions with actual or potential rivals	Union Carbide licensing Uniopol polyethylene technology to Huntsman Chemicals	Sun licensing Java to IBM; R&D joint ventures between rivals
Vertical Market / Licensing to non-rivals	Licensing of IP Core in Semiconductors	R&D joint ventures; Affymax licensing combinatoric technology to pharmaceutical firm.

substitutes significantly to constrain the exercise of market power with respect to the intellectual property that is licensed."[12] Our definition in Figure 1 also encompasses what the Department of Justice calls "markets for innovation," which are seen as markets for "future" technologies. These include arrangements in which the parties agree to conduct activities, jointly or independently, leading to future developments of technologies that will be exchanged (or jointly owned) among them. This is typically the market for contract R&D and the various types of technological alliances and joint ventures.[13]

2.2 Empirical evidence

How large and important are markets for technology today? To date, no systematic assessment of this phenomenon exists even for developed countries, let alone for technology trade between developing and developed countries. In order to provide some rough estimates, we used a commercial database compiled by the Securities Data Company (SDC).[14] The SDC database covers about 52,000 joint ventures, alliances, licenses, R&D funding, R&D collaborations, and other similar deals worldwide. The database reports the name of the companies involved, their ultimate parent companies, the main Standard Industrial Classification (SIC) code of the partner companies and their parents, the SIC code of the alliance, the date when the deal was announced, and a description of the deal.

We collected information on all transactions involving licensing or joint R&D. We read through the description of every transaction to ensure that

---

[12] *Id.* at 6.
[13] We shall ignore some relevant forms of technology exchange, such as mergers and acquisitions driven by the need to absorb external technology and the movement of people from one firm to another. Neither omission denies the importance of these forms.
[14] Securities Data Co., The SDC Joint Venture/Strategic Alliances Database (1998).

each deal related to a technology transaction, which could involve the licensing of new products, process technologies, new designs, or collaboration in the development of the technology. Table 1 shows the total number and value (in parentheses) of such transactions by sector between 1985 and 1997. The value of a transaction is calculated here as the sum of licensing and royalty payments and equity investments and R&D funding provided in return for licensing rights.

This table shows that there have been over 15,000 transactions in technology with a total value of over $320 billion, implying an average of nearly 1,150 transactions worth $25 billion per year. Since it is likely that we are undercounting transactions both early (when SDC data collection was presumably not as systematic) and late in the sample period, this figure is probably a lower bound. Indeed, if we confine ourselves to the sample of transactions from the 1990s, the average annual value increases to about $36 billion. To put these numbers in perspective, note that the value of total technology transactions is about nine percent of total non-defense R&D spending in the developed countries.[15] Moreover, there is likely a U.S. bias in these data, which miss some transactions involving only non-U.S. firms (in particular, between European and Japanese firms) and transactions with firms in developing countries.[16]

Table 1 also suggests that markets for technology are most developed in electronics and electronic components, business services, and chemicals. In an earlier analysis we reported some qualitative accounts of the dynamics of the semiconductor business.[17] That analysis also suggested that these are active fields in terms of technology transfers through various arrangements among independent companies. Business services include software, which likely accounts for a large share of the value of technology deals covered in this sector. Indeed, software is another industry in which such deals have developed significantly in recent years.[18] Finally, in the chemical industry, transactions in technology have been common for many years, including both the licensing of chemical-process technologies, compounds and especially pharmaceuticals, and the large number of technology transactions that characterize the modern biotechnology industry.[19]

3 Patents and markets for technology

The standard economic analysis of patents has focused on the tradeoff between the *ex ante* incentives to innovate and the *ex post* advantages of innovation diffusion.[20] As a result, attention has focused on the major policy questions related to the optimum length (and later, length and breadth) of the

---

[15] ARORA ET AL., above n. 3.   [16] *See* Securities Data Co., above n. 14.
[17] ARORA ET AL., above n. 3.   [18] *Id.*
[19] For an in-depth analysis of these industry case studies, *see id.* ch. 3.
[20] *See*, among others, Arrow, above n. 5 and NORDHAUS, above n. 5.

Table 1: The market for technology: Number and value (millions of 1995 dollars) of technology transactions, 1985–97, by sector

	1985–89	1990	1991	1992	1993	1994	1995	1996	1997	Total Number (Total Value)
SIC28	439	310	461	395	486	596	351	208	222	3496
	(5809)	(4102)	(6101)	(5227)	(6431)	(7887)	(4645)	(2753)	(2938)	(45893)
SIC35	129	115	210	188	195	192	164	63	69	1360
	(6280)	(5599)	(10224)	(9153)	(9493)	(9347)	(7984)	(3067)	(3359)	(64506)
SIC36	234	190	310	316	366	415	326	135	151	2479
	(10971)	(8908)	(14534)	(14816)	(17160)	(19457)	(15284)	(6329)	(7080)	(114539)
SIC73	143	207	360	334	363	610	770	405	424	3689
	(1740)	(2518)	(4380)	(4063)	(4416)	(7421)	(9368)	(4927)	(5158)	(43991)
SIC87	11	9	45	253	156	73	34	22	17	707
	(171)	(140)	(701)	(3939)	(2429)	(1137)	(529)	(343)	(265)	(9654)
All	174	209	468	523	560	540	545	289	293	3858
Others	(2781)	(2901)	(5471)	(6373)	(6549)	(6354)	(6658)	(3342)	(3156)	(43585)
Total	1130	1040	1854	2009	2126	2426	2190	1122	1176	15073
	(27753)	(24169)	(41410)	(43571)	(46479)	(51604)	(44469)	(20761)	(21956)	(322172)

Note: SIC28 = Chemicals; SIC35 = Industrial Machinery & Equipment; SIC36 = Electronic & Other Electric Equipment; SIC73 = Business Services; SIC87 = Engineering and Management Services.
Source: Authors' computations based on SDC data files. Values are estimated by weighting the number of transactions in technologies reported by SDC by the average value of the technology transactions for the sector computed from available information in the SDC database. See the text for details.

temporary monopoly to be granted.[21] But an important and much overlooked benefit of patents is their role in underpinning markets for technology by improving the efficiency of knowledge flows and facilitating the rise of specialized technology suppliers.[22] Patents can do so in several ways. First, the direct costs of knowledge transfer are lowered when the knowledge is codified and systematically organized. Strong patent protection provides incentives to codify and organize new knowledge in ways that are meaningful and useful to others. This is particularly important when innovation systematically originates in firms that will not develop and utilize the knowledge themselves.[23] Unfortunately, direct evidence for this impact is obviously difficult to find.

Second, successful technology transfer, especially to developing countries, requires substantial amounts of know-how, which is costly to transfer. The transfer costs are high in part because contracts for know-how are inefficient, and this difficulty is thought to favor direct investment by multinational corporations (MNCs) over licensing.[24] However, patents can help improve the efficiency of licensing contracts.

The available evidence on this claim is mixed. One of the present authors showed that efficient contracts for the exchange of technology can be written by exploiting the complementarity between know-how and any other technology input, most notably patents, that the licensor can use as a "hostage."[25] The same author used a sample of 144 technology-licensing agreements signed by Indian firms to test the empirical relevance of patents.[26] He employed the provision of three technical services – training, quality control, and help with setting up an R&D unit – as empirical proxies for the transfer of know-how. He found that the probability of technical services being provided was higher when the contract also included a patent license or a turnkey construction contract.

Analyzing data on international technology-licensing contracts of Japanese firms, another author found that Japanese firms report significantly more international contracts than domestic ones, and that weak patent regimes increase the probability that the Japanese firms would transfer technology to an affiliate (such as a subsidiary), instead of to an unaffiliated firm.[27] Similarly, U.S. firms are more likely to export or directly manufacture rather than license

---

[21] See N. Gallini, *The Economics of Patents: Lessons from Recent U.S. Patent Reform*, 16 J. ECON. PERSP. 131 (2002).
[22] ARORA, ET AL., above n. 3.
[23] See A. Arora & A. Gambardella, *The Changing Technology of Technical Change: General and Abstract Knowledge and the Division of Innovative Labour*, 23 RES. POL'Y 523 (1994).
[24] See, among others, W. Ethier, *The Multinational Firm*, 101 Q.J. ECON. 805 (1986); A. Fosfuri, *Patent Protection, Imitation and the Mode of Technology Transfer*, 18 INT'L J. INDUS. ORG. 1129 (2000).
[25] Arora, above n. 10, at 41. [26] A. Arora, above n. 6, at 233.
[27] S. Nagaoka, Impact of Intellectual Property Rights on International Licensing: Evidence from Licensing Contracts of Japanese Industry (2002) (unpublished manuscript, Hitotsubashi University, Tokyo).

technology in countries with weak patent regimes.[28] A study using data on export by French firms of technology services (which include not only licensing royalties, but also provision of technical assistance, engineering and R&D services) to 19 countries discovered that such exports are greater to countries with stronger patents, although this impact is stronger for higher-income destination countries.[29] Another study examined the effect of improved IPRs regimes on licensing by U.S. MNCs and reported a strong positive relationship.[30] Finally, a study using data from a survey of R&D labs in U.S. manufacturing finds that effective patent protection is associated with an increase in the percentage of R&D carried out with the intent of earning licensing revenues.[31]

In contrast, a number of other studies cast doubts on the link between IPR regimes and the extent or form of international technology transfer. One investigation using German data found only a very weak relationship.[32] Another reported a higher response of direct investment than licensing to changes in the level of IPRs protection.[33] One of the current authors similarly did not find that patent protection significantly affects the extent or composition of technology flow (whether as joint venture, direct investment or licensing) in the chemical sector.[34]

Thus, the available evidence in this regard is mixed. Moreover, the clearest evidence in this context was provided in a recent study.[35] Using detailed data on the technology royalty payments received by U.S. firms, and controlling for unobserved country, industry and firm fixed effects, that investigation found no evidence of an increase of technology licensing to unaffiliated parties for countries that strengthened patent protection, often in response to U.S. pressure.

---

[28] P.J. Smith, *How Do Foreign Patent Rights Affect U.S. Exports, Affiliate Sales, and Licenses?*, 55 J. INT'L ECON. 411 (2001).

[29] E. Bascavusoglu & M.P. Zuniga, Foreign Patent Rights, Technology and Disembodied Knowledge Transfer Cross Borders: An Empirical Application (2002) (unpublished manuscript, University of Paris I).

[30] G. Yang & K.E. Maskus, *Intellectual Property Rights and Licensing: An Econometric Investigation*, 137 WELTWIRTSCHAFTLICHES ARCHIV 58 (2001). Note that these various articles consider technology transfer in various forms, which is an important issue for a number of reasons.

[31] A. Arora & M. Ceccagnoli, Profiting from Licensing: The Role of Patent Protection and Commercialization Capabilities (unpublished manuscript, INSEAD & Carnegie Mellon University).

[32] C. Fink, *Intellectual Property Rights and U.S. and German International Transactions in Manufacturing Industries*, 9 DUKE J. COMP. & INT'L L. 163 (1997).

[33] T. Puttitanun, Intellectual Property Rights and Multinational Firms' Modes of Entry (2003) (unpublished manuscript, San Diego State University).

[34] A. Fosfuri, *Determinants of International Activity: Evidence from the Chemical Processing Industry*, 33 RES. POL'Y (2004).

[35] L.G. Branstetter et al., Do Stronger Intellectual Property Rights Increase International Technology Transfer? Empirical Evidence from U.S. Firm-Level Panel Data, World Bank Working Paper No. 3305 (2004).

It did, however, find that stronger patent protection enhanced technology flow to affiliated parties.[36]

The third potential contribution of patents to encouraging technology transfer is indirect. Patents can help specialized technology suppliers earn returns to their services, and thus facilitate a market for technology. Some authors argue that patents are likely to have a greater value for small firms and independent technology suppliers as compared to large established corporations.[37] Whereas the latter have several means to protect their innovations, including their manufacturing and commercialization assets, the former can only appropriate the rents from their innovation by leveraging the protection that patents provide.[38]

In a more recent paper, a model was developed based on an incomplete-contracting approach, in which stronger IPRs enhance the viability of specialized firms by reducing buyer opportunism.[39] The authors provided several examples of the role that patents play in the specialty chemical industry, specifically from such firms as Lonza or SupraChem, which specialize in the design and production of optically pure or "chiral" compounds used as inputs by the pharmaceutical industry. These firms must typically expend considerable effort in developing new molecules (or processes for developing new molecules) for their customers, the large pharmaceutical firms. This upfront cost, analogous to the cost of transferring tacit knowledge, makes the firm vulnerable to holdup by the customer. Ownership of patents covering the design of their input products provides these firms with some security if future trades with the customer firms do not come through, a possibility that the financial disclosure documents of chiral suppliers explicitly note.[40] Since

---

[36] *Id. See also* Lee G. Branstetter, *Do Stronger Patents Induce More Local Innovation?* [this volume].

[37] R. Merges, Property Rights, Transactions, and the Value of Intangible Assets (1998) (unpublished manuscript, Boalt School of Law, U.C. Berkeley); Arora & Gambardella, above n. 23, at 523.

[38] In some cases, policies designed in the naïve hope of encouraging small inventors have encouraged the abuse of the patent system. In the United States, for instance, there have been well-known cases where patents filed in the 1950s were ultimately issued more than twenty years later. Such patents (sometimes referred to as "submarine" patents because they are not visible for long periods after they are filed) have surprised many established firms. Also, some research suggests that smaller firms may be deterred from patenting in areas where better-financed rivals have patented; *see, e.g.*, J. Lerner, *Patenting in the Shadow of Competition*, 38 J.L. & ECON. 463 (1995).

[39] A. Arora & R. Merges, *Specialized Supply Firms, Property Rights and Firm Boundaries*, 13 INDUS. & CORP. CHANGE 451 (2003).

[40] *See, e.g.*, Press Release, Alkermes, Update on Collaborations: Undisclosed Compound (22 Apr. 2000), *available at* www.alkermes.com/news (emphasis added): "Alkermes today announced the mutual termination of a collaboration with [a division of Johnson and Johnson] for the development of a sustained release formulation of a ... product candidate for the treatment of hormone-mediated disorders. The identity of the product candidate has never been disclosed by the parties. *With the termination of the collaboration, Alkermes regains rights licensed to PRI for the development and marketing of sustained release*

stronger and better defined patents improve the efficiency of technology transactions and are, *ceteris paribus*, more valuable to small, specialized firms, they become a necessary condition for a well-functioning vertical division of innovative labor.

This view is supported by other research. For instance, it has been demonstrated that although patents play only a marginal role in encouraging R&D by semiconductor firms, they are of great importance for specialized semiconductor design firms, most of whom rely upon licensing their technology and providing associated technical and design services.[41]

Competition among upstream suppliers can be important for the form and extent of technology transfer. For instance, there is evidence that the rate of licensing of large, established firms increases with the number of potential technology suppliers. Similarly, it appears that leading chemical firms are more likely to license their technology instead of investing directly in sectors where other sources of technology are present.[42]

Of course, stronger patent protection entails a number of costs as well. For instance, where know-how is not needed for successful diffusion, patents may merely serve to increase the price that developing countries have to pay. A highly salient example of this situation arises in pharmaceuticals. Firms in a number of developing countries have the capability to reverse engineer a drug developed elsewhere, thereby making it available at a much lower price.[43] Indeed, in some cases, they can even develop more cost-effective processes for large-scale production. Strong patent protection in such cases mostly entails redistribution from poor to rich countries, with little in the way of offsetting efficiency gains.[44] Patent protection also requires significant administrative expertise and expenditures for

---

formulations of this class of compounds. Alkermes first announced the collaboration in December 1996. The objective of the collaboration was to apply the ProLease drug delivery system to a ... proprietary compound being developed for the treatment of hormone-mediated disorders. A ProLease formulation of the proprietary compound completed a human clinical trial in 1997 and demonstrated sustained release for the intended duration of time. [The partner] has discontinued further development of this compound."

[41] B. H. Hall & R. Ziedonis, *The Patent Paradox Revisited: Determinants of Patenting in the US Semiconductor Industry, 1980–1994*, 32 RAND J. ECON. 101 (2001).

[42] A. Fosfuri, *The Licensing Dilemma*, in PROCEEDINGS OF THE SIXTY-THIRD ANNUAL MEETING OF THE ACADEMY OF MANAGEMENT (CD-ROM), ISSN 1543–8643 (D.H. Nagao ed., 2003); A. Arora & A. Fosfuri, *Wholly Owned Subsidiary versus Technology Licensing in the Worldwide Chemical Industry*, 31 J. INT'L BUS. STUD. 555 (2000).

[43] A well known case is that of an Indian drug manufacturer, Cipla, which, in February 2001, offered to supply a triple-therapy AIDS drug cocktail for $350 per year to *Médecins sans Frontières* (Doctors Without Borders), a nonprofit medical group. Another Indian drug producer, Hetero Drugs Ltd., was reported to offer the same cocktail for $347 per year. Many observers felt that both drugs violated patents on the original drugs.

[44] P. McCalman, *Reaping What You Sow: An Empirical Analysis of International Patent Harmonization*, 55 J. INT'L ECON. 161 (2001).

institutional support and may waste important resources in potential legal disputes.[45]

4 Markets for technology and international technology transfer

We have argued that an important and frequently overlooked role of patents is in encouraging a market for technology. This raises the question of the role of such markets in international technology transfer. Technology markets are a precondition for the existence of specialized technology suppliers operating in vertical markets. Specialized suppliers can also act as a mechanism for knowledge transfer that resembles technological spillovers across firms, a subject that has attracted a great deal of attention from economists.[46]

Here, we focus our attention on the geographical dimension of these spillovers. The chemical processing industry provides an ideal example showing that the development of an upstream industry of specialized technology suppliers improves access, lowers investment costs, and reduces barriers to entry in the downstream industry, with beneficial effects on the aggregate investment in the latter.[47] Beginning in the 1930s and continuing into the 1960s, the modern chemical industry in the developed countries (henceforth "first world") grew rapidly. This stimulated the growth of firms that specialized in the design and engineering of the chemical processes, the so-called specialized engineering firms or SEFs. In the 1970s, and especially in the 1980s, as a modern chemical industry emerged in the developing countries (henceforth DCs), the industry benefited from the presence of the SEFs, which turned to sell their technologies to the chemical producers in DCs as well. Simply put, the growth of the chemical industry in the first world created an upstream sector, which later spurred the growth of the chemical industry in the developing countries. The important point is that the DCs benefited from the fact that the (fixed) cost of creating the SEF industry had already been incurred in the first world.[48]

Figure 2 summarizes the effects that we want to highlight here. First, the growth of the first-world market for a given chemical process encourages the rise of engineering firms specialized in the design of chemical plants for that process. This is the classic effect of the size of the market on the vertical division of labor in an industry.[49] When markets grow, there are activities that are more

---

[45] M. Finger & P. Schuler, Implementation of Uruguay Round Commitments: The Development Challenge, World Bank Working Paper No. 2215 (1999).
[46] *See*, among others, A. Jaffe, *Technological Opportunity and Spillovers of R&D: Evidence from Firms' Patents, Profits and Market Value*, 76 AM. ECON. REV. 984 (1986); D.T. Coe & E. Helpman, *International R&D Spillovers*, 39 EUR. ECON. REV. 859 (1995).
[47] A. Arora et al., *Specialized Technology Suppliers, International Spillovers and Investment: Evidence from the Chemical Industry*, 65 J. DEV. ECON. 31 (2001).
[48] *Id.*
[49] G. Stigler, *The Division of Labor is Limited by the Extent of the Market*, 59 J. POL. ECON. 185 (1951).

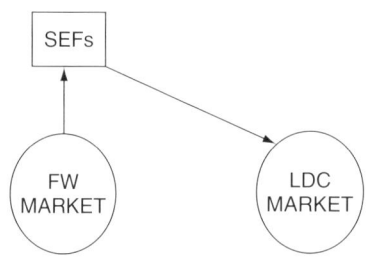

Figure 2: The Transmission of Growth Impulses through Specialized Engineering Firms

effectively performed by specialist companies (suppliers). The latter can serve a larger market than that of the individual downstream firms, thereby expanding their activities. In turn, by purchasing the input from the more efficient suppliers, the downstream industries benefit from the fact that they acquire the input at lower costs than if the individual companies had to produce it by themselves.

The second effect is that the SEFs in the first world alter the size of the developing country market. To understand this effect, suppose that first-world SEFs could not supply the DCs. Then, apart from relying on multinational corporations, DC firms would have to provide the engineering services themselves or rely on any domestic SEFs that might exist. In either case, DC firms would face high costs.[50] As a result, there would be fewer investments in chemical plants. Given the high transportation costs for many chemical products, this would imply slower growth of chemical supplies and of industrial activity more generally. The essential point is that the cost of setting up a chemical plant by a company from a developing country would be smaller in the presence of SEFs. In turn, more investments by these firms would take place than if there were no first-world SEFs acting as vectors of the process technologies.

In our book[51] we provide quantitative estimates of the importance of a division of labor in the chemical industry, using data on 139 leading chemical technologies. Our empirical analysis shows that investments in chemical plants in the DCs are greater the larger the number of technology suppliers (SEFs) that operate in the first world. Moreover, the effect of the SEFs is greater for chemical firms from the developing countries than for the MNCs investing in DCs. This factor arises because the latter firms have greater internal technological capabilities. Hence, for them, the presence of the SEFs is relatively less important.[52]

---

[50] See Arora et al., above n. 47.   [51] See ARORA ET AL., above n. 3.
[52] See Arora et al., above n. 47.

To get a sense of the order of magnitude of the impact that an upstream sector of technology suppliers has on the total investment of the downstream market, we estimated the effect of one additional SEF in a typical process market on the expected total dollar value of investment in the DCs in the same market.[53] We found that an additional SEF would increase investment by about $3 million per year per country. For all 38 DCs in our sample, the increase in investment in a typical process was approximately $114 million over the ten-year period 1980–1990. Most markets already had more than five SEFs, and thus the effect of an additional SEF was small. However, simple simulation analysis from our estimations showed that the effect of having one extra SEF in a market where one or fewer existed was sizable.

Of course, SEFs are not the only source of technology, and many large chemical firms also transfer technology overseas.[54] However, chemical producers have to trade off the gains from selling technology against the loss in actual or potential revenues from having more competition in selling the downstream products. Furthermore, the SEFs provide technologies with few strings attached and sell their technologies and expertise to all customers. The presence of SEFs could also force chemical firms to license more aggressively.[55]

5 Policy implications for developing countries

The previous section has argued that the presence of well-functioning markets for technology might be extremely beneficial for DCs. Since it is natural that these markets are far more likely to arise in large and technologically and economically advanced regions, the DCs need not focus on developing technology markets. Instead, they can focus on developing institutions that will enable their firms to participate more effectively in them.

The example of the Western European chemical industry in the years after World War II is a case in point.[56] The disruption due to the war and the rise of the petrochemical industry in the United States ought to have provided the U.S. chemical industry with a decisive advantage over its European rivals, whose expertise lay in coal-based processes. Yet, in a period of a few years, the German, British and French chemical industries had largely switched from coal to petroleum and natural gas as basic inputs. The availability of U.S.-developed refining and chemical engineering expertise made this switch possible. Further, the SEFs

---

[53] See ARORA ET AL., above n. 3. [54] See Fosfuri, above n. 34, for evidence.
[55] A. Arora & A. Fosfuri, *Licensing the Market for Technology*, 52 J. ECON. BEHAV. & ORG. 277 (2003).
[56] See A. Arora & A. Gambardella, *Evolution of Industry Structure in the Chemical Industry*, in CHEMICALS AND LONG TERM ECONOMIC GROWTH 379 (A. Arora et al. eds., John Wiley & Sons 1998).

played an important role in integrating and supplying technology to European customers. In the 1960s, the SEFs played a similar role in Japan.[57] Japanese industrial policy, which tended to restrict access to the Japanese market for foreign firms, was far more receptive to foreign technology imports. Indeed, the policy focus in this context was in creating the ability to absorb and adapt foreign technology.

Research and development expenditures and patenting are concentrated in the wealthier countries. In particular, the United States and Western Europe have a head start in terms of basic research and developing "generic" technologies, such as semiconductors and genetics. Their advantage lies not only in being the first movers, but also in the broader industrial base over which they can apply these findings. These advantages are less salient when technologies and products need to be adapted for local uses and needs. If one accepts that companies or industries located "near" users have an advantage when it comes to communicating with their markets and acquiring the relevant information for adapting the technologies, firms in other parts of the world could exploit this fact to reduce the U.S. and European advantages. Thus, even if the production of more basic technologies is concentrated, other regions can access these technologies and exploit their own proximity to users or their comparative advantage in developing complementary technologies, as long as markets for technology work well.[58]

In this regard, a key policy question for DCs is how to take advantage of the growth in technology trade worldwide. In sectors where markets for technology are established and technology can be traded effectively, countries or regions should specialize according to comparative advantages rather than attempt comprehensive programs of indigenous technology development. This proposition does not imply that countries should cease to invest in research and development. Rather, it implies that they should be more selective in terms of the sectors and types of activities on which they focus, at least in the short-to-medium run. Moreover, policies aimed at monitoring international

---

[57] *Id.*

[58] The experience of Reliance Petroleum is relevant. Reliance Petroleum is part of a large Indian conglomerate, the Reliance Group, that originated in the textile industry, then integrated backwards into intermediates (purified terephthalic acid for polyesters), and finally into the production of basic feedstock and refining. Reliance engaged Bechtel and several other very large contractors and successfully built the world's largest "grassroots" refinery, accounting for 25% of India's refining capacity, and downstream plants, in Gujarat, India. This facility came six months ahead of schedule and under budget. Clearly, although Reliance had invested in chemical engineering capabilities, more critical to its commercial success was the ability to identify and manage sources of technology. The Reliance experience suggests that much technology can be acquired through the marketplace by firms that have the appropriate, in-house managerial skills. *See* ARORA ET AL., above n. 3, at 307.

technological developments are important, as are institutions for enhancing the efficiency of contracts and reducing search costs.[59]

What about IP policy? If specialized technology suppliers are nurtured in developed countries, then it is the IPRs in those nations that are most relevant. The recent calls for harmonization and standardization of protection of IPRs across the globe is, therefore, not justified on this ground.[60] Indeed, it is unlikely that the strengthening or weakening of IPRs by individual DCs will have a noticeable effect on the global markets for technology (although a coordinated move might produce a sizable impact). However, since stronger IP protection can also improve the efficiency of technology transactions, it is also likely that stronger and better defined IPRs will improve the ability of DCs to benefit from technologies generated elsewhere, although as we have noted, the available evidence is mixed.[61]

These recommendations are not new, and developing countries may resist such an international division of labor in technology production and adaptation. The reasons may range from national pride to the control of strategic technologies. Whether or not such attitudes are justified, policymakers should recognize that well-functioning markets for technology increase the opportunity cost of sustaining them. Simply put, if others have already paid the fixed cost of developing technology, and competition among sellers implies that the price of the technology is related to the marginal cost of technology transfer, a strategy of developing the technology in-house and incurring the fixed cost all over again is likely to be inefficient. There is little point in national policies aimed at "reinventing the wheel," except possibly where such reinvention is a part of the process of building "absorptive capacity" or as a part of a long-run strategy to develop international technological leadership.

It is also important to recognize that, in a dynamic setting, countries specializing in technology adaptation need not give up the possibility of becoming technology producers, at least in some specific areas. For example, by starting with a policy of developing technologies complementary to those originated abroad, local firms and industries may gradually understand the nature of basic technology as well, possibly becoming producers of some key technologies.[62] The Indian software industry, for instance, started as a low-end

---

[59] See B. Hoekman et al., Transfer of Technology to Developing Countries: Unilateral and Multilateral Policy Options, World Bank Policy Research Paper No. 3332 (2004).

[60] See McCalman, above n. 44.

[61] K.E. Maskus, Encouraging International Technology Transfer, Paper for UNCTAD/ICTSD Project on Intellectual Property Rights and Sustainable Development (Dec. 2003), available at http://www.iprsonline.org/unctadictsd/docs/Maskus_TOT_December03.pdf. See also text accompanying nn. 20–45 above.

[62] See N. Rosenberg & E. Steinmueller, Why Are Americans Such Poor Imitators?, 78 AM. ECON. REV. PAPERS & PROC. 229 (1988); N. Rosenberg, The Role of the Private Sector in Facilitating the Acquisition of Technology in Developing Countries: A New Look at Technology Transfer (unpublished manuscript, Stanford University, 2001).

supplier of software components to major software companies, especially those in the United States.[63] There are signs that this strategy may gradually induce at least some of these companies to engage in more complex product development activities. A similar argument can be made for Irish software companies, which seem to have improved their ability to produce new software products in some niches of the market. In short, the pattern of specialization is not immutable over time. With luck and hard work, the advantages of specialization in lower-end technological activities (adaptation) could become the springboard for moving up the value chain. Learning through systematic interactions with users and the technology producers of more advanced countries may be critical for this process to occur.

6 Conclusion

We have documented the growing importance of markets for technology in the last fifteen years. Well-functioning markets for technology can help stimulate investment and growth in DCs by making available at relatively low prices technologies developed in the first world. DCs should focus on efficiently exploiting the opportunities opened up by these markets rather than trying to nurture their own specialized technology suppliers. In the presence of markets for technology, IPRs might play the additional role of improving the efficiency of contracts for the exchange of technology and technological services. DCs should therefore structure their IPRs policies with the objective of achieving the greatest benefits from existing markets for technology.

---

[63] A. Arora et al., *The Indian Software Services Industry: Structure and Prospects*, 30 Res. Pol'y 1267 (2001).

13

Using liablity rules to stimulate local innovation in developing countries: Application to traditional knowledge

JEROME H. REICHMAN
TRACY LEWIS[*]

I. Introduction and historical background
   A. Critique of the standard proposals
   B. Historical and comparative roots of a proposed compensatory liability regime
II. Designing a compensatory liability regime
   A. A simple model
      1. Descriptive analysis
      2. General observations
   B. Application of liability rules to the protection of traditional knowledge
      1. Understanding the problem: Traditional knowledge is know-how
      2. Solving the problem: A TK model of compensatory liability
   C. Further observations
         a. Administrative burdens
         b. The international dimension
III. Conclusion

When economists speak of an underlying legal structure that imposes an "absolute permission" requirement on access to, and use of, knowledge goods protected by intellectual property rights (IPRs), they typically have in mind the domestic patent and copyright laws. Under these and related intellectual property regimes,

---

[*] Jerome H. Reichman is the Bunyan S. Womble Professor of Law, Duke University School of Law; Tracy Lewis is the Martin L. Black Professor of Economics, Fuqua School of Business, Duke University, Durham, North Carolina. The authors wish to thank Graham Dutfield for his extremely helpful suggestions.

one cannot normally make use of a protected invention or creative work of authorship for specified purposes and for limited periods of time without prior authorization of the rights holder, typically in the form of a license.

When economists speak of liability rules, in contrast, they envision an underlying legal structure that permits third parties to undertake certain actions without prior permission, provided that they compensate injured parties for all or part of the costs they inflict. While typical examples are found in tort laws regulating the abatement of nuisances,[1] liability rules also abound in the realm of intellectual property law, where, however, their function has largely been overlooked or mischaracterized by legal and economic scholars.[2] In this context, liability rules conjure up a regime built on a "take and pay" principle. Under such a regime, second comers can access and use the protected subject matter for specified purposes without permission, but they must compensate the first comer for these uses in one manner or another.

This chapter discusses new forms of liability rules that might profitably be used to stimulate local innovation in developing countries. Our thesis is that a properly designed liability rule to protect small-scale innovation in developing countries would overcome investors' fears of market failure with fewer social costs than would accrue either under a regime of unbridled copying or under a regime of hybrid exclusive property rights, such as those embodied in laws that protect utility models, industrial designs, plant varieties, or miscellaneous other subject matters in developed countries.[3] We also show how this regime could solve many of the problems that proposals to protect traditional knowledge currently pose.

I. Introduction and historical background

Qualified experts have long agreed that most developing countries would benefit from one or more special intellectual property regimes to protect small-scale innovation, particularly utility model or "petty patent" laws.[4] This advice follows from the more limited technical capacities of producers

---

[1] *See, e.g.,* Guido Calabresi & A. Douglas Melamed, *Property Rules, Liability Rules, and Inalienability: One View of the Cathedral*, 85 HARV. L. REV. 1089, 1092 (1972).

[2] Some notable exceptions include: R.D. Blair & T.F. Cotter, *An Economic Analysis of Damage Rules in Intellectual Property Law*, 39 WM. & MARY L. REV. 1585 (1998); J.O. Lanjouw & J. Lerner, *Tilting the Table? The Predatory Use of Preliminary Injunctions*, 44 J.L. & ECON. 573 (2001); Robert P. Merges, *Contracting into Liability Rules: Intellectual Property Rights and Collective Rights Organizations*, 84 CAL. L. REV. 1293 (1996), and M. Schankerman & Suzanne Scotchmer, *Damages and Injunctions in Protecting Intellectual Property*, 32 RAND J. ECON. 199 (2001).

[3] *See generally* J.H. Reichman, *Legal Hybrids Between the Patent and Copyright Paradigms*, 94 COLUM. L. REV. 2432, 2453–2503 (1994) [hereinafter *Legal Hybrids*].

[4] *See, e.g.,* COMMISSION ON INTELLECTUAL PROPERTY RIGHTS, INTEGRATING INTELLECTUAL PROPERTY RIGHTS AND DEVELOPMENT POLICY 121 (2002) [hereinafter CIPR] (stating that, as compared with "the normal patent system, utility models or

in most of these countries, which are better suited to applications of inventions made elsewhere to local conditions than to developing bigger scale inventions from scratch, especially when the latter depend on basic research for which there is usually no adequate infrastructure.[5]

The Japanese experience empirically supports this approach. For decades, Japanese industries specialized in adapting or improving inventions developed elsewhere for further application. As we know, they were so successful that they often drove the original inventors out of the market for not keeping up fast enough with the pace of improvements. To the extent that intellectual property played a role in this transformative process, it was the Japanese utility model law that often carried the weight.[6] This law (unlike its German prototype) quickly broke its ties to industrial design as such and became a general-purpose petty patent law covering small-scale innovations generally (more or less as occurred in Italy).[7] Among other perceived benefits, this law enabled Japanese industries to surround foreign inventions with a bevy of lesser rights and thereby to induce their patent owners to enter into cross-licensing arrangements with improvers. Today, however, the utility model law of Japan is much less important because of major Japanese investments in basic research and the correspondingly enhanced role of patented technology there.[8]

Foreign experts thus find it logical to advise developing countries to emulate the Japanese example and to enact utility model laws to promote investment in small-scale innovation.[9] Moreover, for a variety of reasons not exclusively governed by

petty patent systems typically require a lower level of inventive step, provide a shorter period of protection, and in not being subject to any substantive examination prior to grant, are cheaper to obtain").

[5] Id. at 121 (stressing focus of small and medium size enterprises "on relatively small incremental improvements to existing products rather than the development of completely new products").

[6] See, e.g., Shoji Matsui, The Transfer of Technology to Developing Countries: Some Proposals to Solve Current Problems, 59 J. PAT. OFF. SOC'Y 612 (1977); Chen Ruifang, The Utility Model System and Its Benefits for China – Some Deliberations Based on German and Japanese Legislation, 14 INT'L REV. INDUS. PROP. & COPYRIGHT L. [I.I.C.] 493 (1983); Robert E. Evenson, Survey of Empirical Studies, in STRENGTHENING PROTECTION OF INTELLECTUAL PROPERTY IN DEVELOPING COUNTRIES – A SURVEY OF THE LITERATURE 33, 41–42 (Wolfgang. E. Siebeck ed., World Bank 1990)

[7] For details, see Legal Hybrids, above n. 3, at 2455–59. See generally Mark D. Janis, Second Tier Patent Protection, 40 HARV. INT'L L.J. 151 (1999).

[8] See KEITH E. MASKUS, INTELLECTUAL PROPERTY RIGHTS IN THE GLOBAL ECONOMY 143–48 (Institute for International Economics 2000) (stressing Japan's shift from an emphasis on learning and diffusion toward protecting underlying inventions through patents). See also Keith E. Maskus & Christine McDaniel, Impacts of the Japanese Patent System on Productivity Growth, 11 JAPAN AND THE WORLD ECONOMY 557–74 (1999).

[9] See above nn. 4, 6 & 8. See also Hanns Ullrich, GATT: Industrial Property Protection, Fair Trade and Development, in GATT OR WIPO – NEW WAYS IN THE INTERNATIONAL PROTECTION OF INTELLECTUAL PROPERTY 127, 153–55 (F.-K. Beier & G. Schricker eds., John Wiley & Sons 1989); Rudolf Krasser, Developments in Utility Model Law, 26 I.I.C. 950 (1995).

the drive for harmonization, the European Union also seems likely to adopt a federal utility model law in the near future,[10] which could engender some additional benefits from the transnational harmonization of intellectual property laws.

A. Critique of the standard proposals

As we see it, however, this well meaning advice to developing countries is based on the assumption that their only alternatives are either full patent protection of virtually all forms of technical innovation, as in the U.S.,[11] or a mixed patent-utility model regime, as in Italy, Germany, Japan, and prospectively, in the E.U. as a whole.[12] If this were true, then most developing countries would clearly benefit more from the latter option than the former.

The problems with *sui generis* intellectual property regimes, such as utility model laws and design protection laws, are legion,[13] however, and they can be summarized as a cumulative tendency to generate excessive social costs that outweigh the likely social benefits (which is what we mean by "over-protection").[14] These detriments include:

---

[10] *See* Green Paper on Utility Model Laws, Document COM (95) 370 final of 10 July 1995; Draft Utility Model Directive, Council Directive 97/0356 (COD), COM (1999) Official Journal of European Communities; Krasser, above n. 9.

[11] While this is currently the standard U.S. position, this country has begun to deviate from it by enacting *sui generis* laws to protect plant varieties, integrated circuit designs, and boat hull designs. *See Legal Hybrids*, above n. 3, 2465–71, 2478–80; Janis, above n. 7; *see also* J.H. Reichman, *Charting the Collapse of the Patent-Copyright Dichotomy*, 13 CARDOZO ARTS & ENT. L.J. 475, 504–06 (1995) [hereinafter, *Collapse of the Patent-Copyright Dichotomy*].

[12] *See* above n. 10. One recent source that does not make this assumption is CIPR, above n. 4, at 121 (noting and citing Prof. Reichman's proposal for a "compensatory liability regime").

Under either option, it is usually further assumed that any *sui generis* regime adopted to protect small-scale innovation would be supplemented by other *sui generis* regimes like those enacted in developed countries. Some of these regimes are already mandatory under international law. *See, e.g.,* Agreement on Trade-Related Aspects of Intellectual Property Rights, 15 Apr. 1994, Marrakesh Agreement Establishing the World Trade Organization [hereinafter WTO Agreement], Annex 1C, LEGAL INSTRUMENTS – RESULTS OF THE URUGUAY ROUND vol. 31, 33 I.L.M. 81 (1994) [hereinafter TRIPS Agreement], arts. 25–26 (obligations to protect industrial designs); *id.,* arts. 35–37 (obligations to protect integrated circuit designs); *id.,* art. 27.3(b) (obligation to protect plant varieties in the absence of plant patent protection); *id.,* art. 39.3 (ambiguous obligation to protect undisclosed clinical test data pertaining to pharmaceutical or agricultural chemical products).

[13] *See, e.g.,* Janis, above n. 7; J.H. Reichman, *Design Protection and the New Technologies: The United States Experience in a Transnational Perspective*, 1991 INDUS. PROP. & LE PROPRIÉTÉ INDUSTRIELLE (Pt. 1) (May 1991), 257–74 (Pt. 2) (June 1991).

[14] *Accord* Janis, above n. 7; *cf.* Calabresi & Melamed above n. 1, at 1107–08 (noting risk of under- or over-compensation from use of property rights without sound basis for *ex ante* valuation). *See generally* J.H. Reichman, *Of Green Tulips and Legal Kudzu: Repackaging Rights in Subpatentable Innovation*, 53 VAND. L. REV. 1753 (2000) [hereinafter *Green Tulips*].

- Overextended or hybrid exclusive rights disrupt the sharing of technical know-how that powers most scientific and technical progress, especially through spillovers that come from reverse engineering;[15]
- They thus block or slow the natural progression of follow-on applications by enabling the exclusive right holder to deny them or to hold out against their use,[16] and because third parties will not readily disclose such applications in licensing transactions affecting small-scale innovation;[17]
- These same exclusive rights impoverish the public domain by denying access to the routine innovation of other creative engineers, who would otherwise be free to reverse engineer by honest means;[18]
- They require elaborate negotiations and other transaction costs which, in relation to the caliber of the innovation at stake, are seldom worthwhile even if they could succeed;[19]
- They potentially generate lots of litigation whose costs are disproportionately large in relation to the social value of the innovation at issue;
- They breed high duplication costs because routine engineers must work around routine innovation that was previously available from the public domain or through reverse engineering from a semicommons, so the progressive elaboration of the common technical trajectory is either aborted or retarded;[20]
- The natural "open source" character of routine innovation operating under traditional trade secret laws is thereby destroyed;[21]
- Overextended or hybrid regimes reward investors with exclusive rights for investing in forms of innovation that market-force competition might require them to make anyway, just to stay competitive.

We contend that these problems are best avoided by a change in direction away from exclusive property right protection back toward a resurrection of liability rules like those underlying classical trade secret protection.[22] The

---

[15] *See most recently* J.H. Reichman, *Saving the Patent Law from Itself*, *in* PERSPECTIVES ON PROPERTIES OF THE HUMAN GENOME PROJECT 289, 291–95 (F. Scott Kief ed., 2003) [hereinafter *Saving the Patent Law*]. *See generally* Pamela Samuelson & Susan Scotchmer, *The Law and Economics of Reverse Engineering*, 111 YALE L.J. 1575 (2002).

[16] *See Green Tulips*, above n. 14; *see generally* Mark A. Lemley, *The Economics of Improvement in Intellectual Property Law*, 75 TEX. L. REV. 989 (1997).

[17] *See Green Tulips*, above n. 14, at 1767–71.   [18] *See Saving the Patent Law*, above n. 15.

[19] Difficulties of administration and enforcement may help to explain why entrepreneurs in many developing countries have lately made little use of utility model laws even where enacted. *See* CIPR, above n. 4, at 121.

[20] *See Saving the Patent Law*, above n. 15.   [21] *See id.*

[22] Despite certain "property-like" qualities implicit in the possibility of an injunction to deter improper appropriation of trade secrets, "liability for the appropriation of a trade secret rests on a breach of confidence or other wrongful conduct in acquiring, using, or disclosing secret information," and not on an exclusive rights rationale. RESTATEMENT (THIRD) OF UNFAIR COMPETITION §§ 39, 40 (1993). *See further* below n. 28 and accompanying text.

better solution is to modify and modernize such rules by adapting them to protect commercially valuable applications of know-how to industry in developing countries, with a view to enhancing their overall competitiveness in the incipient transnational system of innovation.[23]

B. Historical and comparative roots of a proposed compensatory liability regime

Historically, a robust regime of intellectual property rights rooted in actual or legal secrecy always mediated between patentable inventions and free competition.[24] These rules apply especially to routine innovation that cannot meet the nonobviousness requirement of domestic or international patent laws.[25]

Classical trade secret law reinforces the competitive ethos by ensuring that any second comer can reverse engineer any innovator's novel but unpatented application of know-how to industry by proper means.[26] But if improper means are used, the second comer must either pay compensation or suffer a delay in entering the market equivalent to the originator's lead-time advantages that were wrongfully curtailed.[27] This regime thus provides investors with natural lead time in which to recuperate investments and establish their trademarks, but it gives them no power to prevent follow-on applications by any third party who spends the time and money to reverse engineer by proper means. "In this respect, trade secret law behaves like a liability rule (or

---

[23] *Cf.* Keith E. Maskus & Jerome H. Reichman, *The Globalization of Private Knowledge Goods and the Privatization of Global Public Goods* [this volume], Pt. III ("Balancing Public and Private Interests in an Emerging Transnational System of Innovation"); J.H. Reichman, *From Free Riders to Fair Followers: Global Competition under the TRIPS Agreement*, 29 N.Y.U. J. INT'L L. & POL. 11, 26–85 (1996).

[24] This segment is based on *Saving the Patent Law*, above n. 15.

[25] 35 U.S.C. 103 (2000); TRIPS Agreement, above n. 12, arts. 27.1 (codifying nonobviousness standard of eligibility in patent law), 39 (codifying obligation to protect trade secrets within framework of international unfair competition law).

[26] Know-how consists of information about how to organize a certain production in the most efficient and competitively advantageous manner. *See* STEPHEN P. LADAS, PATENTS, TRADEMARKS AND RELATED RIGHTS: NATIONAL AND INTERNATIONAL PROTECTION § 867, at 1617 (1975). The term is not limited to an isolated technique or formula, but rather encompasses the entire industrial process from choice of raw materials to modalities of distribution, "a manufacturing art." FRANÇOIS MAGNIN, KNOW-HOW ET PROPRIETE INDUSTRIELLE 114 (1974). *See generally* WILLIAM KINGSTON, DIRECT PROTECTION OF INNOVATION 21–33 (Kluwer 1987).

[27] *See* above n. 22. As information, know-how may be kept under actual secrecy or under legal secrecy, but its commercial value normally depends on the degree of secrecy that surrounds it. However, secret know-how remains vulnerable to reverse engineering by honest means, so that in today's innovation-based markets, first comers obtain only lead-time advantages and any power conferred by their trademarks. *See, e.g.,* Samuelson & Scotchmer, above n. 15.

quasi-liability rule), with the added wrinkle that the rate or value of the entitlement is determined by the market and not by government intervention."[28]

In a recent article, Professor Reichman observed that the routine engineers working on common technical trajectories under the aegis of trade secret protection form a natural "open source" community that operates under a de facto sharing ethos.[29] The members of this community depend on the reciprocal insights and contributions they derive from the semicommons in which their shared body of technical knowledge resides and on their inability to remove these cumulative contributions from that semicommons.[30]

Because most innovation consists of cumulative and sequential applications of know-how to industry by routine engineers at work on common technical trajectories, free market economies in the nineteenth century depended primarily on the liability rules of unfair competition law (in which trade secret laws reside[31]) and only tangentially on the exclusive rights of patent law, which protected a relatively circumscribed set of nonobvious inventions beyond the reach of these same routine engineers.[32] However, this classical, pro-competitive system of industrial property law broke down rapidly in recent years because secrecy as a trigger for liability protection became increasingly scarce or irrelevant.

Beginning with industrial design in the late nineteenth century and continuing with software and biogenetic engineering in the late twentieth century, the routine engineer's applications of commercially valuable know-how to industry were increasingly embodied on or near the face of products distributed in the open market. Any second comer could duplicate them without need of incurring the time and costs of reverse engineering.[33] These conditions,

---

[28] *Legal Hybrids*, above n. 3, at 2440 fn. 29. "Nevertheless, the consent of the owner is not a prerequisite . . . ; the objectively determined value that allows a second comer to extinguish this entitlement is the (variable) cost of reverse engineering by proper means," unless the second comer voluntarily acquires the innovator's lead time in lieu of actually incurring these costs. *Id. Cf.* John C. Stedman, *Trade Secrets*, 23 Ohio St. L.J. 4, 21 (1967) (coining the term "disappearing rights").

[29] *See Saving the Patent Law*, above n. 15, at 294.

[30] *Id.* at 293–95. ("The progressive development of know-how is thus a community project that benefits from the countless small-scale contributions to the prior art by individuals who draw from the public domain to make improvements, and who thereby enrich the public domain by generating new information that others in the technical community may exploit to their own advantage.").

[31] *See* TRIPS Agreement, above n. 12, art. 39.1 (collocating international protection of trade secrets within article 10bis of the Paris Convention for the Protection of Industrial Property, 20 Mar. 1883 *as last revised at* Stockholm, 14 July 1967, 21 U.S.T. 1583, 828 U.N.T.S. 305 [hereinafter Paris Convention], which governs unfair competition law).

[32] *Cf.* Edmund W. Kitch, *The Nature and Function of the Patent System*, 20 J.L. & Econ. 265 (1977).

[33] *See* J.H. Reichman, *Computer Programs as Applied Scientific Know-How*, 42 Vand. L. Rev. 639, 656–69 (1989). *See also* Pamela Samuelson et al., *A Manifesto Concerning the Legal Protection of Computer Programs*, 94 Colum. L. Rev. 2208, 2332–65 (1994).

elsewhere encapsulated in the phrase "incremental innovation bearing know-how on its face,"[34] produced a chronic shortage of natural lead time and mounting fears of market failure and suboptimal investment in research and development owing to the rapid and widespread duplication of innovative products.[35]

The uncritical response of domestic and international rule makers has been to fill this perceived gap in intellectual property law with an expansion of exclusive property rights to address the risk of market failure.[36] Two strategies are combined. In one, patent eligibility standards are broadened and lowered to cover investment in routine innovation, and copyright protection is expanded beyond literary and artistic works in the historical and ordinary sense to encompass computer software and other applications of know-how to industry. The second strategy is to multiply hybrid regimes of exclusive property rights, which inevitably mutate into patent-like regimes that seek to suppress unauthorized follow-on applications.[37] These trends have been further intensified by the ability of investors to commercialize disembodied information as such in the digital online environment, without embodying it in physical artifacts, and by their successful lobbying campaign to reinforce electronic and contractual fencing mechanisms[38] through powerful new exclusive rights sounding in copyright and database protection laws.[39]

---

[34] See *Legal Hybrids*, above n. 3, at 2511.

[35] "Would-be investors in applications of know-how to industry understand that their contributions can be instantly duplicated without the second-comer having to defray the costs of reverse engineering ('zero lead time' problems)." *Saving the Patent Law*, above n. 15, at 295. *But see* M. Boldrin & D. Levine, *The Case Against Intellectual Property*, 92 AM. ECON. REV. 209 (2003), who assert that even the smallest lead time advantage may be sufficient to afford innovators sufficient compensation in the absence of patent or copyright protection.

[36] The deliberate nature of this legislative transformation, brought about by special interest lobbying, was clear to qualified observers. *See, e.g.,* JOSEPH JEHL, LE COMMERCE INTERNATIONALE DE LA TECHOLOGIE – APPROCHE JURIDIQUE 79, 110 (1985), who found:

[T]he protection of know-how tends to approach that conferred on patents.... Firms are trying to win recognition of an exclusive right in their know-how that is of the same nature as a patent. Their efforts aim in effect to obtain a right to be exercised against third parties, in general. One can therefore declare that the protection of know-how completes and imitates that of patents.

Id. at 110 (trans). *See also* WILLIAM KINGSTON, above n. 26, at 21–33 (deploring overextension of patents and advocating a suitable form of direct protection for merely incremental innovation).

[37] *See generally Green Tulips*, above n. 14, and *Legal Hybrids*, above n. 3; *see also Collapse of the Patent-Copyright Dichotomy*, above n. 11.

[38] *See, e.g.,* J.H. Reichman & Jonathan A. Franklin, *Privately Legislated Intellectual Property Rights: Reconciling Freedom of Contract with Public Good Uses of Information*, 147 U. PA. L. REV. 875 (1999).

[39] *See, e.g.,* Pamela Samuelson, *Mapping the Digital Public Domain: Threats and Opportunities*, 66 LAW & CONTEMP. PROBS. 148 (2003); J.H. Reichman, *Database*

In effect, a mindless proliferation of exclusive property rights has thus shrunk the vast semicommons previously governed by pro-competitive liability rules and converted "the collective knowledge available to the technical community as a whole into artificial private preserves, which have to be negotiated and combined to support investment in research and development."[40] In previous articles, Professor Reichman discussed the high social costs of these trends and the risk that, by making inputs into future innovation too costly and difficult to obtain, these ad hoc solutions could ultimately destabilize the national systems of innovation that rely on them to excess.[41] He argued, instead, that a more enlightened approach was to formulate a rational set of liability rules, not rooted in actual or legal secrecy, that could restore the historical buffer zone between exclusive intellectual property rights and free competition. To avoid the problems of over-protection identified above, without incurring the problems of under-protection likely to arise if small-scale innovators were left totally vulnerable to free-riding duplicators, the solution is to modify and modernize older forms of liability rules by adapting them to protect commercially valuable embodiments of know-how under present-day circumstances.

His proposal for a "compensatory liability regime," elaborated in two earlier articles[42] and further illustrated in this chapter, aims to accomplish this task. In our view, all countries – including technically advanced developed countries – could benefit from a compensatory liability regime that would broadly protect investment in subpatentable applications of know-how to industry.[43] Our

---

Protection in a Global Economy, 2002 REVUE INTERNATIONALE DE DROIT ECONOMIQUE 455 (2002); J.H. Reichman and Paul F. Uhlir, *A Contractually Reconstructed Research Commons for Scientific Data in a Highly Protectionist Intellectual Property Environment*, 66 LAW & CONTEMP. PROBS. 315, 361–415 (2003).

[40] *Saving the Patent Law*, above n. 15, at 296–97 (stressing emergence of anti-commons effects). See generally Michael A. Heller & Rebecca S. Eisenberg, *Can Patents Deter Innovation? The Anti-Commons in Biomedical Research*, 280 SCIENCE 698 (1998); James Boyle, *The Second Enclosure Movement and the Construction of the Public Domain*, 66 LAW & CONTEMP. PROBS. 33 (2003).

[41] *Saving the Patent Law*, above n. 15 at 299 (stressing the extent to which proliferating exclusive rights "disrupt the natural sharing mechanisms that benefit routine engineers, impede follow-on innovation, foster thickets of rights and other barriers to entry that slow the pace of innovation, and generally impoverish the public domain on whose inputs future innovators depend").

[42] See *Green Tulips*, above n. 15, and *Legal Hybrids*, above n. 3, at 2511–56 ("Portable Trade Secrets").

[43] By "subpatentable" innovation, we mean innovation that fails to meet the nonobviousness standard of eligibility for protection under the domestic patent laws currently in force, which differ from country to country. These innovations typically consist of applications of know-how and skilled efforts to industry. Here we have particularly in mind those types of small-scale innovations that are currently covered by *sui generis* exclusive rights in developed countries, and that create all the problems identified earlier. *See* above nn. 3, 11–22 and accompanying text.

main reason for contributing this chapter, however, is to argue that developing countries eager to stimulate local innovation might particularly find such a regime well suited to the technical capabilities of their small and medium sized entrepreneurs. These countries also occupy the best position to implement and experiment with liability rules in their domestic laws.[44]

Despite the logical appeal of liability rules for managing subpatentable innovation, many specialists advising developing countries have never seriously considered this option, and some dismiss it out of hand as misguided, speculative proposals.[45] We concede that few countries have enacted such laws, although there are more working examples of liability regimes than one might suppose.[46] However, one reason that developing countries have not sufficiently explored this option is precisely because their technical legal advisors either do not understand the purpose and economics of liability rules at all, and do not want to overcome their ignorance, or because special interest lobbies fear them and advise against them, or both. One way or another, fear and ignorance (plus critical attacks by some academics)[47] have until recently kept them off the agenda of most developing countries.

---

[44] *Cf.* CIPR, above n. 4, at 121 (noting need to test such proposals in developing countries).

[45] *See most recently* letter from Sybille E. Schalter, Max Planck Institute, Munich to Tinu Joshi, Development Commissioner, Ministry of Textiles, New Delhi, India, 8 July 2003 (on file with authors).

[46] *See, e.g.*, Italian Copyright Law No. 633 of 22 Apr. 1941, *as amended*, art. 99 (protecting technical drawings and engineering project designs under a liability regime); United Kingdom's Copyright, Designs and Patents Act 1988, ch. 48 §§ 213–64 (unregistered designs) (subsequently overridden by E.U. Design Regulation); United States Copyright Law, 17 U.S.C. § 115 et seq. (2000) (converting exclusive reproduction right in musical works to liability regime for mechanically recorded songs). The United States Semiconductor Chip Protection Act of 1984, 17 U.S.C. §§ 908(a) (2000) contains a de facto liability rule for unregistered mask works, which terminates if application for registration is not made within two years of first commercial exploitation. A similar principle was incorporated into the E.U.'s Design Regulation of 21 October 2002 implementing Council Regulation (EC) No 6/2002 of 12 December 2001 on Community Designs.

Recent research suggests that the regime implementing government use of patented inventions in the United States under 28 U.S.C. §1498 (2000) manifests many of the characteristics of a compensatory liability regime. *See* J.H. REICHMAN WITH CATHERINE HASENZAHL, NONVOLUNTARY LICENSING OF PATENTED INVENTIONS: THE LAW AND PRACTICE OF THE UNITED STATES, UNCTAD/ICTSD (2003) (draft version *available at* http://www.ictsd.org). Anecdotal evidence suggests that the use of compulsory licenses for dependent patents (blocking patents) in Italian law mimics the functions of a compensatory liability regime; further investigation is under way.

[47] *See, e.g.*, Robert P. Merges, *Of Property Rules, Coase, and Intellectual Property*, 94 COLUM. L. REV. 2655 (1994); Dennis S. Karjala, *Misappropriation as a Third Intellectual Property Paradigm*, 94 COLUM L. REV. 2594 (1994); Jane C. Ginsburg, *Four Reasons and a Paradox: The Manifest Superiority of Copyright over Sui Generis Protection of Computer Software*, 94 COLUM L. REV. 2559 (1994). *See also* Richard A. Epstein, *Steady the Course: Property*

Nevertheless, economic interest in the use of liability rules as a tool for managing intellectual property is growing,[48] and their potential benefits for developing countries have begun to attract official interest. The Commission on Intellectual Property Rights, for example, expressed interest in this approach, while recognizing that the administrative and enforcement aspects of such a system "need to be tested to assess its practicality in developing countries."[49] Younger scholars in different countries are writing doctoral dissertations on applications of compensatory liability principles to current intellectual property problems.[50] The prospect of some type of intellectual property protection for traditional knowledge has elicited keen academic interest in these proposals[51] and has led the World Intellectual Property Organization (WIPO) to include this scheme in recent proposals for future action.[52] As a result, it has become possible to focus serious high-level attention on liability rules for the first time, which is one of the purposes of this chapter, and which will make the case for them more robust.

Our own collaboration on this chapter is a case in point, because, so far as we know, it represents the first collaboration between an economist and an intellectual property scholar on proposals for liability rules to stimulate investment in innovation. Indeed, we ultimately intend to push the case for liability rules well beyond the protection of small-scale innovation and to propose a regime that could operate side by side with the patent law, as an alternative

---

Rights in Genetic Material, in PERSPECTIVES ON PROPERTIES OF THE HUMAN GENOME, above n. 15, at 153–94 (defending "all or nothing" approach).

[48] Virtually all of the serious economic investigations of liability rules to this point have focused on their application to nuisance law. Included among these are two path-breaking analyses, IAN AYRES, OPTIONAL LAW: REAL OPTIONS IN THE STRUCTURE OF LEGAL ENTITLEMENTS (forthcoming 2005); Ian Ayres & Eric Talley, *Solomonic Bargaining: Dividing a Legal Entitlement to Facilitate Cosean Trade*, 104 YALE L.J. 1027 (1995). These studies, even though the problems they address are most readily interpreted as applying to nuisance law reactions, are quite closely related to the approach we adopt here in our treatment of liability rules for innovation. *Cf.* also Samuelson & Scotchmer above n. 15, whose study of *Reverse Engineering* illuminates this field.

[49] CIPR, above n. 4, at 121.

[50] *See, e.g.*, Daehwan Koo, *Alternative Proposals and Effective Protection of Computer Programs*, 2 BUFF. INTELL. PROP. L.J. 49 (2003). At least three other dissertations that focus on compensatory liability rules are known to be underway in the U.S., U.K., and Belgium at the time of writing.

[51] *See, e.g.*, Thomas Cottier & Marion Panizzon, *Legal Perspectives on Traditional Knowledge: The Case for Intellectual Property Protection* [this volume]; Graham Dutfield, *Legal and Economic Aspects of Traditional Knowledge* [this volume]; Antony Taubman, *Saving the Village: Conserving Jurisprudential Diversity in the International Protection of Traditional Knowledge* [this volume]. *See also* Tom Dedeurwaerdere, Governance of Biodiversity as a Global Public Good: Bioprospection, Intellectual Property Rights and Traditional Knowledge (Research Unit on Biodiversity of the Centre for Philosophy of Law, Catholic University of Lovain-la-Neuve, Belgium, 5 February 2004).

[52] *See* WIPO Intergovernmental Committee on Intellectual Property and Genetic Resources, Traditional Knowledge and Folklore, Seventh Session, Geneva, WIPO/GRKTF/IC/7 (20 Apr. 2005).

regime to protect investment as such, but on different and socially less costly principles. That study will appear later.[53]

For present purposes, we can say that our study of liability rules in general so far supports the view that, insofar as most experts agree that developing countries should adopt some special intellectual property regime to promote investment in small-scale innovation, a modified liability rule (or compensatory liability regime, hereafter, CLR) would promote the interests of those countries better and at lower social costs than would a utility model law. In short, we think developing countries should experiment with a CLR in lieu of a utility model law and test the results.

If we are wrong, little harm would be done, because we are confident that a CLR will solve the problem of market failure at least as well as a utility model law. But if we are right, the payoffs from a CLR could be significant. Developing countries might then find themselves equipped with a new, user-friendly, intellectual property regime that would be tailor-made to their interests, in the sense that it would not block improvements or shrink the public domain, which is not true of utility model laws, design laws or other *sui generis* exclusive property rights. Moreover, because the U.S. and E.U. keep pressing these countries for stronger intellectual property protection, successful experimentation with a CLR could enable developing countries to respond to protectionist pressures in ways that did not impede their own needs to catch up and to access scientific and technical data and information generated elsewhere.[54]

In what follows, we shall first discuss the design of liability rules and how they can be implemented within existing institutions. We then briefly show how such a regime could stimulate investment in small-scale innovation within the reach of local producers operating in developing countries but without blocking improvements or access to shared know-how available from the public domain. Finally, we discuss additional benefits that a compensatory liability regime could deliver if applied to the thorny new problem of protecting traditional knowledge, and we provide a detailed model of such a regime.

II. Designing a compensatory liability regime

Quite simply, a liability rule is an option for one to use another party's innovation under specified conditions.[55] Ideally, the conditions for use should specify (1) how the innovation may be employed; (2) the period for which it may

---

[53] Tracy Lewis & J.H. Reichman, *Alternatives to Patents: Law and Economics of a Multipurpose Liability Rule*, paper presented to Ecoinformation Lecture Series (Duke University School of Law, Apr. 2004).

[54] *Cf.* Reichman, *Database Protection in a Global Economy*, above n. 39; J.H. Reichman & Pamela Samuelson, *Intellectual Property Rights in Data?*, 50 VAND. L. REV. 51, 145–51 (1997) (proposing liability rule approach to database protection).

[55] *Cf.* AYRES, OPTIONAL LAW, above n. 48.

be employed; (3) the monetary or in kind payment the innovator should receive as compensation (or at least a method for determining it); and (4) provisions for revising the terms of use upon mutual agreement of the innovator and user.[56]

In a previous article, Professor Reichman proposed a simple model, known as the Green Tulip Model, of a compensatory liability regime for subpatentable innovation.[57] In what follows, we first briefly summarize the key elements of that model and elaborate some general observations concerning its potential significance. We then proceed to discuss the special problems surrounding the protection of traditional knowledge, and we propose a new model ("The TK Model") specifically to resolve those problems.

A. A simple model

Under the simple model, a qualifying innovator obtains three distinct rights. These include a right to prevent wholesale duplication, a right to compensation from value-adding improvers, and a right to make use of a second comer's value-adding improvements for purposes of making further improvements of his or her own.

1. Descriptive analysis

The first entitlement given to qualifying innovators under a compensatory liability regime (CLR) is a right to prevent second comers from competing on the same market segment for a specified period of years with a product that constitutes a wholesale duplication of the innovator's initial product. This right applies even if the second comer clearly identifies the source of origin to avoid deceiving or confusing consumers.[58]

One can characterize this right either as a liability rule based on conduct, i.e., as a form of misappropriation to be lodged within the ambit of unfair competition law,[59] or as a limited power to exclude ("quasi-property right"). What matters is less the characterization than the fact that, under existing Anglo-American law, at least, subpatentable innovators obtain no such right[60] unless

---

[56] We provide details in our work-in-progress, above n. 53.
[57] See generally Green Tulips, above n. 14.
[58] See generally id. at 1787–91. It thus falls outside the ambit of existing unfair competition law in the U.S, see RESTATEMENT (THIRD) OF UNFAIR COMPETITION, above n. 22, §§ 38–40, and international law, see Paris Convention, above n. 31, art. 10bis. For a weaker version of this right, see below text accompanying nn. 124–25.
[59] Cf. Wendy J. Gordon, On Owning Information: Intellectual Property and the Restitutionary Impulse, 78 VA. L. REV. 149 (1992); Karjala, above n. 47. See also Rochelle C. Dreyfuss, Information Products: A Challenge to Intellectual Property Theory, 20 N.Y.U. J. INT'L L. & POL. 897 (1988).
[60] See above n. 58; C. Owen Paepke, An Economic Interpretation of the Misappropriation Doctrine: Common Law Protection for Investments in Innovation, 2 HIGH TECH. L.J. 55 (1987). Continental European law increasingly provides some vague prescriptions against

they qualify for one of the hybrid IPRs that produce the cumulative anti-competitive effects previously identified.

The second right available from a compensatory liability regime entitles qualifying innovators to reasonable compensation, for a specified period of time, from second comers who base value-adding improvements on the formers' novel technical contributions.[61] Implicit in this entitlement is the inability of qualifying innovators to prevent second comers from using or "borrowing" the protected technical contribution for purposes of making, producing and selling improved products, so long as the latter remain willing to pay the requisite compensation. In short, the second comer's absolute right to borrow for purposes of value-adding improvements is complemented by an absolute duty to pay reasonable compensation for this privilege.

The compensation to be paid is best understood as a contribution to the first comer's costs of research, development and marketing,[62] which avoids the free-rider problem inherent in knowledge goods.[63] The valuation problem is rendered manageable by two simplifying assumptions. One, suggested by Professor Lemley, is that an improver may usefully be understood to have made either a small, medium, or large improvement on the originator's own technical contribution,[64] which conversely implies that he took either a large, medium, or small quantum of the originator's protected subject matter. The second facilitating assumption is that, precisely because we are dealing with subpatentable innovation to begin with, the technical contributions at issue are generally small in scale and heavily conditioned by prior art in the public domain.[65] For this and other reasons, including decades of experience with valuing patented inventions taken for government use under section 1498 of the United States Code (which operates as a de facto liability regime),[66] the range of royalties available under the simple model could be relatively modest.[67] We are also comforted by the thought that arguing about a couple of percentage points in royalties, ideally before a mediator or an arbitrator, is

---

"parasitical copying." See ANSELM KAMPERMAN SANDERS, UNFAIR COMPETITION LAW: THE PROTECTION OF INTELLECTUAL AND INDUSTRIAL CREATIVITY 24–78 (1997).

[61] See *Green Tulips*, above n. 14, at 1778–81.   [62] See *Legal Hybrids*, above n. 3, at 2533–39.
[63] See, e.g., Wendy J. Gordon, *Asymmetric Market Failure and the Prisoner's Dilemma in Intellectual Property*, 17 U. DAYTON L. REV. 853, 854–59 (1992) (discussing conditions for market failure).
[64] See Lemley, above n. 16.
[65] See *Green Tulips*, above n. 14, at 1783–86 (affirming that "the single source of greatest value added to any small-scale innovation is always the public domain") (quote at 1785).
[66] See Reichman with Hasenzahl, above n. 46.
[67] See *Green Tulips*, above n. 14, at 1784 (suggesting a normal range of three to nine percent, while expressing willingness to consider "a range with more bite" if empirically justifiable). For an economic analysis of the valuation problem, *see* Lewis & Reichman, above n. 53 (work-in-progress).

socially preferable to litigating costly actions for infringement, at least where only subpatentable innovation is at stake.

The third distinct right that a compensatory liability regime confers on qualifying originators entitles them to make use of the second comers' own technical improvements, under specified conditions, for purposes of further improving the very products that initially qualified them for protection. However, the first comer must not himself become a wholesale duplicator of the improved product; and he must be willing to pay the second comer a reasonable compensation for his value-adding use of the latter's technical contribution during a specified period of time. In effect, this third right functions as a built-in grant-back clause, roughly analogous to the dependent licenses (or "anti-blocking" licenses) available in most foreign jurisdictions for patentable improvements to patented products.[68]

There are numerous other features of the simple model for a CLR that we omit here for reasons of space.[69] At this point, readers would understandably appreciate a concrete illustration, like that which accompanied the Green Tulip Model.[70] Rather than repeating that example here, however, we have provided – later in this study – another concrete illustration based on a hypothetical application of traditional knowledge to medicinal products in a hypothetical developing country.[71] Readers should feel free to consult that illustration at any time.

2. General observations

For reasons of space, we have deferred a detailed economic analysis of the compensatory liability concept to a later article.[72] Here we stress the pro-competitive nature of such a regime, which further distinguishes it from most other hybrid intellectual property rights. Under the latter regimes, which typically confer patent-like exclusive rights, second comers cannot make unauthorized improvements unless they are certain that they fall beyond the scope of protection that each regime affords.[73] Because, moreover, the technological know-how at issue is small in scale by definition,[74] second comers may feel disinclined to reveal it in the kind of upfront negotiations that might clarify these scope of protection problems, lest the first comer beat them to the punch, given the second comer's lack of either technical or legal leverage.[75] For

---

[68] *See* TRIPS Agreement, above n. 12, art. 31(l) (authorizing such licenses). For the unhappy situation in the U.S., where no such mandatory licenses are available, see Lemley, above n. 16.
[69] *See Green Tulips*, above n. 14, at 1781–96; *Legal Hybrids*, above n. 3, at 2529–56.
[70] *See Green Tulips*, above n. 14, at 1756–76.
[71] *See* below text accompanying nn. 116–28.   [72] *See* above n. 53.
[73] *See Green Tulips*, above n. 14. For an excellent analysis of the kind of problems this determination engenders, *see generally* Lemley, above n. 16.
[74] This smallness of scale is implicit in its characterization as "subpatentable." *See* above n. 43 and accompanying text.
[75] *See Green Tulips*, above n. 14, at 1766–71.

this and other reasons, we confidently predict that second comers would more actively and willingly pursue value-adding improvements under a CLR than under existing hybrid regimes that confer patent-like protection.

By the same token, a CLR avoids the consequences of market failure that might occur if small-scale innovators were otherwise left vulnerable to unbridled competition.[76] In such a raw state of affairs, where the first comer obtains nothing from improvers, both logic and experience predict some risk that the former may even disappear from the market and take their technical skills with them.[77] Yet, the first comer may in fact have made the qualitatively greater technical contribution to the larger community, and his inability to return to the fray if second comers free ride on his R&D costs may in itself constitute a major social cost that remains hidden from view.

From this perspective, the compensatory liability regime may usefully be understood as creating a kind of technology pool,[78] but one that advances, rather than undermines, the public interest. We defer a discussion of this concept to a later article. Nevertheless, we emphasize here that, by ensuring reciprocal access to small-scale applications of technical know-how to industry in return for relatively modest contributions to R&D costs, the CLR tends to restore or recreate the fruitful semicommons that previously depended upon reverse engineering and natural lead time in a climate of actual or legal secrecy.[79]

Enactment of a compensatory liability regime would also intrinsically reinforce efforts by local courts and administrators in developing countries to maintain a relatively high standard of nonobviousness in their domestic patent laws, consistent with the flexibility that the TRIPS Agreement still allows.[80] This premise follows from the availability of an alternative or second tier regime that would protect investment in innovation as such,[81] which should attenuate pressures to use the patent system as a roving unfair competition law to protect "slivers of innovation."[82] Over time, the mere existence of a compensatory liability regime should thus serve to flush lots of small-scale borderline innovation out

---

[76] See id. at 1763–66.
[77] This occurred, for example, in the case of spreadsheets, where the pioneer, Visicalc, eventually left the market after the superior redesign embodied in Lotus 1–2–3.
[78] Cf. Robert P. Merges, *Institutions for Intellectual Property Transactions: The Case of Patent Pools*, in EXPANDING THE BOUNDARIES OF INTELLECTUAL PROPERTY 123 (Rochelle Cooper Dreyfus et al. eds., Oxford University Press 2001).
[79] See above nn. 31–35 and accompanying text.
[80] As most recently recommended by CIPR, above n. 4, at 116 (urging developing countries "to explore whether a different higher standard [of nonobviousness] is more desirable" than "the currently prevalent low standard" in developed countries).
[81] Cf. KINGSTON, above n. 26.
[82] *Saving the Patent Law*, above n. 15, at 296 (criticizing use of lowered nonobviousness standards "to rescue commercially valuable slivers of innovation that had nowhere else to go").

of the local patent system[83] and into its more pro-competitive embrace, while offering otherwise productive innovators (including those operating within a university context) a legislative alternative to the patenting of research results.

Finally, the compensatory liability regime is designed to be neutral with respect to existing international standards of intellectual property protection. No such standards directly apply to liability rules, other than those governing trade secret laws and broader unfair competition norms.[84] While the TRIPS Agreement requires members to adopt the nonobviousness standard of patent law,[85] there is as yet no uniformity about this standard. Any state adopting a compensatory liability regime would still have to respect international rules of nonobviousness with regard to patents. This holds true for utility models in European Union law as it would for a compensatory liability regime in a developing country, and it would work out about the same, bearing in mind that national treatment will be required in virtually all cases.[86]

If developing countries were foolish enough to acquiesce in ongoing efforts to harmonize the nonobviousness standard of patent law and thus to further relinquish sovereignty in this regard,[87] then the compensatory liability regime, like utility model regimes, would continue to apply to subpatentable innovation, although more innovation might then be covered by patents. We would prefer to see the opposite. We would expect the existence of compensatory liability rules to drive the nonobviousness standard upwards, which would be better for worldwide innovation and competition.[88] In any event, the international rule of national treatment would almost always apply because of a recent WTO Appellate Body decision to this effect.[89] Anyone operating under a compensatory liability regime at home would remain free to apply for patents or *sui generis* exclusive rights abroad, and anyone operating under patents or a *sui generis* right abroad would remain free to seek compensatory liability protection in countries that afford it.[90]

---

[83] *Cf.* CIPR, above n. 4, at 116 (stating that the "objective of any standard should be to ensure that routine increments to knowledge, involving minimal creative effort, should not generally be patentable").
[84] *See* TRIPS Agreement, above n. 12., arts. 2.1 (incorporating Paris Convention, art. 10bis), 39.
[85] *See id.* art. 27.1.
[86] *See* United States – Section 211 Omnibus Appropriations Act of 1998, Appellate Body Report, WT/DS176/AB/R (2 Jan. 2002), *available at* http://www.wto.org/english/tratop_e/appellate_body_e.htm
[87] *See* Maskus & Reichman, above n. 23, at III.A(1).
[88] *See e.g.*, John H. Barton, *Issues Posed by a World Patent System* [this volume].
[89] *See* above n. 86.
[90] However, conflicts might theoretically arise with norms governing design protection and integrated circuit designs under the TRIPS Agreement, and with marketing rights to patented pharmaceuticals that sometimes apply, all of which we ignore here. For present purposes, we also ignore priority rights in designs and utility models under the Paris Convention. *Green Tulips*, above n. 14, at 1761–91.

B. Application of liability rules to the protection of traditional knowledge

We believe that the simple model (or Green Tulip Model), summarized at the outset of this chapter and previously illustrated by Professor Reichman, adequately describes how a compensatory liability regime might serve generally to stimulate investment in small-scale innovation in the developing countries. That model was partly premised on the need to protect novel plant varieties under international intellectual property law.[91] It was intended to demonstrate the superiority of liability rules over the patent-like hybrid regime that developed countries seek to impose on the developing world.[92]

In this section, we elaborate a comparable model to illustrate the potential application of compensatory liability rules to the protection of traditional knowledge ("the TK Model"). This topic has elicited favorable attention from both academic and political circles,[93] probably because it bridges the gap between the prevalent view in developed countries that traditional knowledge belongs in the public domain and the aspirations of many developing country governments for a strong exclusive property right in traditional knowledge.[94] A compensatory liability regime would effect a compromise between these two positions.[95] In particular, it would temporarily remove eligible traditional knowledge from the limbo of a true public domain and relocate it to a semicommons, from which it could freely be accessed and used

---

[91] *See* TRIPS Agreement, above n. 12, art. 27.3(b)(requiring WTO members to protect plant varieties either by patents "or by an effective *sui generis* system or by any combination thereof"). *See further* Michael Blakeney, *Stimulating Agricultural Innovation* [this volume]; Robert E. Evenson, *Agricultural Research and Intellectual Property Rights* [this volume].

[92] International Convention for the Protection of New Varieties of Plants, 2 Dec. 1961, 33 U.S.T. 2703, 815 U.N.T.S. 89, *as amended* 23 Oct. 1978, 33 U.S.T. 2703, 1861 U.N.T.S. 281 [hereinafter UPOV I], *as amended* 19 Mar. 1991, *available at* http://www.upov.int/en/publications/conventions/1991/pdf/act1991.pdf [hereinafter UPOV II].

[93] *See, e.g.*, Cottier & Panizzon, above n. 51; Dutfield, above n. 51; Taubman, above n. 51.

[94] The legal anthropologist, Rosemary Coombe, astutely observes that the construct of a public domain is itself a product of the observers' own social and cultural mores. *See* Rosemary Coombe, *Protecting Cultural Industries to Promote Cultural Diversity: Dilemmas for International Policymaking Posed by the Recognition of Traditional Knowledge* [this volume]; *see also* Taubman, above n. 51; Cottier & Panizzon, above n. 51 (recommending use of some traditional IPR, but not necessarily an exclusive property right, and welcoming attention to a compensatory liability regime).

[95] In reality, customary perceptions, practices and norms concerning TK vary widely. While the CLR fits between the two extremes, one can find communities in the world whose IP-related norms fall all along the continuum from very exclusive rights in some (but not all) useful knowledge, to no property rights at all in knowledge that may well have commercial value to others. *See, e.g.*, Russel L. Barsh, *Indigenous Knowledge and Biodiversity*, in Cultural and Spiritual Values of Biodiversity (Darrell A. Posey, ed., UNEP & Intermediate Technology Pubs.1999), at 73–76.

for specified purposes, in return for the payment of compensatory royalties for a specified period of time.[96]

Nevertheless, we recognize that the movement to include traditional knowledge within the worldwide intellectual property system raises certain unique problems that liability rules cannot resolve. Foremost among these is the perception that traditional knowledge necessarily partakes of the life and mores of indigenous peoples, which even the most carefully crafted intellectual property regime could disrupt.[97]

We agree that policymakers must take this very real concern into account. Even so, there is a growing demand from within native populations and their governments for the protection of traditional knowledge against unauthorized appropriations that cannot be ignored, especially in light of obligations arising under the Convention on Biological Diversity (CBD).[98] The advent of major academic institutes devoted to the scientific study and commercial application of ancient remedies in India and China, for example, point the way to the future and underscore the need for an appropriate form of intellectual property protection for those who develop and harbor traditional knowledge and who consent to participate in such an exercise.[99]

By the same token, a compensatory liability regime can do little to help any indigenous groups who are determined to keep their traditional knowledge secret or who, for one reason or another, prefer to opt out of an emerging worldwide scheme of intellectual property protection. In such cases, the most that international law can provide is some legal framework to reinforce the principles of prior informed consent and equitable sharing of benefits set out in the CBD, which, as Professor Correa points out, logically translate into measures to protect holders of traditional knowledge against specified forms of misappropriation.[100] In what follows, we accordingly assume that the holders

---

[96] Experts versed in international IP lore will doubtless recognize the imprint of a *domain publique payant* (paying public domain) on this model. *See, e.g.*, Taubman, above n. 51. However, there is more to it than that. While it is true that a CLR is far less radical and unfamiliar at the margins than critics pretend, as Professor Taubman points out, the model we propose is also far less familiar than a knowledge of existing liability rules might lead one to suppose.

[97] *See, e.g.*, Coombe, above n. 94; Taubman, above n. 51; *see also* David Lange, *Comment: Traditional Knowledge, Folklore and the Case for Benign Neglect* [this volume]; Paul J. Heald, *The Rhetoric of Biopiracy*, 11 Cardozo J. Int'l & Comp. L. 519 (2003) (expressing skepticism about the use of IPRs to protect traditional knowledge).

[98] Convention on Biological Diversity (CBD), 5 June 1992, 31 I.L.M. 818, *available at* http://www.biodiv.org/convention/articles.asp (last accessed 28 July 2004), art. 8(j). *See, e.g.*, Cottier & Panizzon, above n. 51; Dutfield, above n. 51; Blakeney, above n. 91.

[99] *See especially* Cottier & Panizzon, above n. 51. *See also* the work of Anil Gupta and his Honeybee Network, *discussed in* G. Dutfield, Intellectual Property, Biogenetic Resources and Traditional Knowledge (Earthscan Pubs. 2004), at 180–82.

[100] See CBD, above n. 98, arts. 1, 2, 8(j); C.M. Correa, Traditional Knowledge and Intellectual Property: Issues and Options Surrounding the Protection of Traditional

of traditional knowledge in question have voluntarily made it available in order to obtain the benefits of a compensatory liability regime.[101]

1. Understanding the problem: Traditional knowledge is know-how

While recognizing the need to keep traditional knowledge within a broader cultural matrix, we deem it equally important to avoid mystifying or unduly complicating the topic by supposing that traditional knowledge represents something truly new and unique in the intellectual property firmament, for which the "wheel" of protection must be reinvented from scratch. The proper point of departure is to collocate the problem of stimulating investment in commercial applications of traditional knowledge within the larger quest for appropriate means to promote investment in small-scale innovation generally, while taking into account the changed conditions that govern technological progress at the start of the twenty-first century.

From this perspective, traditional knowledge represents the oldest form of "cumulative and sequential innovation" known to man.[102] If this traditional lore has become commercially valuable today, it is because applications of know-how to industry generally represent one of the most valuable forms of commoditized information in today's knowledge-based economy.[103]

There are differences of degree, of course, but not of classificatory nature, between those who cultivate small-scale innovations by traditional means, primarily relying on instinct and trial-and-error, and those who use modern technical or scientific means to apply know-how to industry in the form of computer programs, industrial designs, or even many biogenetically engineered products. Traditional knowledge is more intuitive, not bound by formal technical paradigms, and, guided by instinct, it often takes place by slow accretions of experience over long periods of time. Like present-day applications of know-how to industry, however, it proceeds mostly by trial and

---

Knowledge, Quaker United Nations Office Discussion Paper 18 (2001); see also Dutfield, above n. 51. Protection against misappropriation can, however, conflict to some degree with the common law tradition that allows reverse engineering of trade secrets by proper means. How to reconcile this potential conflict is beyond the scope of this chapter.

[101] Moreover, rights in TK are usually accompanied by duties; so that even when knowledge is made available to the wider public for specified uses, tribal specialists may still retain obligations to spirits, to the elders or the community as a whole, in order to ensure that such knowledge is not misused. *See, e.g.*, Darrell A. Posey, *Selling Grandma: Commodification of the Sacred Through Intellectual Property Rights, in* CLAIMING THE STONES/NAMING THE BONES: CULTURAL PROPERTY AND THE NEGOTIATION OF NATIONAL AND ETHNIC IDENTITY (E. Barkan & R. Bush, eds., Getty Pubs., 2002), at 205–06.

[102] *See, e.g.*, Richard Nelson, *Intellectual Property Protection for Cumulative Systems*, 94 COLUM. L. REV. 2678 (1994); *see also* Richard Nelson, *Linkages Between the Market Economy and the Scientific Commons* [this volume].

[103] *See generally Legal Hybrids*, above n. 3, at 2504–29; *see also* J. JEHL (quoted above n. 36); KINGSTON, above n. 26. For a definition of know-how, see above n. 26.

error.[104] More to the point, the moment that either a traditional innovator (or his assignees) or a modern innovator decides to evaluate the prospects for an industrial application of their know-how, they both face a common risk of market failure if second comers can merely duplicate the end result without contributing to old or new costs of research and development.

It may be that a local craftsman adapts a traditional design to leather goods or tableware. It may be that a local shaman provides the larger community with a treatment for fever or kidney stones derived from native plants and materials. It may be that a local entrepreneur adapts a foreign water pump to suit his peculiar environmental needs, in which case he has generated some "new" technical know-how. What matters is not so much the technical degree of "novelty" that characterizes their respective contributions. From an economic perspective, what matters is that these outward-looking, commercially-minded practitioners should be able to appropriate the fruits of their creative efforts, skills, and collective or individual investments, and to establish reputational credentials. They should not have to fear being driven out of the market by free-riding second comers who duplicate their products without making any corresponding contributions of their own, who sell below the first comers' marginal costs and, in the worst case, appropriate reputational credit for the work of others.[105]

As the classical intellectual property system viewed it, all know-how pertained to technical communities, not to individuals. It belonged collectively to those "routine engineers" (in the patent sense) who depend on the reciprocal insights and contributions that the relevant technical community derives from the public domain, or more accurately, from the research semicommons that houses the results of reverse engineering by proper means.[106] The legal protection of know-how – at least in common-law countries – is thus organized around liability rules that discourage certain forms of conduct harmful to the community as a whole. It does not allow innovators to remove contributions to the knowledge semicommons by means of exclusive property rights.[107] As Steven Ladas phrased it in 1975, "know-how deserves protection only insofar as it is in consonance with the unhampered utilization of knowledge essential to the principle of free competition."[108]

2. Solving the problem: A TK model of compensatory liability

Consistent with the general tenor of this chapter, we believe that present-day applications of traditional knowledge to industry could benefit most from a

---

[104] See LADAS, above n. 26; see also MAGNIN, above n. 26. But see Heald, above n. 97 (differentiating problem of incentives for new innovation from that of equitable rewards for past contributions).
[105] On the last point, cf. Coombe, above n. 94.
[106] See Saving the Patent Law, above n. 15 at 293–95.
[107] See above nn. 25–35 and accompanying text.   [108] LADAS, above n. 26.

modified liability rule or what we have called a "compensatory liability regime." This regime can provide the benefit sharing outcomes desired by those who champion the rights of indigenous peoples[109] without impoverishing the public domain and without hindering follow-on innovation or otherwise creating barriers to entry.

Because traditional know-how has, by definition, usually existed for long periods of time, we must adapt the CLR concept to certain factual anomalies in order to achieve specific policy outcomes. Here we identify three distinct stages in which traditional knowledge might attract some degree of protection, and we differentiate the modalities of protection accordingly. Traditional knowledge first encounters national and international legal systems in the raw form in which its indigenous providers keep it, whether in absolute or relative secrecy, or perhaps in some geographically defined public domain.[110] The second stage of relevant consideration turns on the extent to which that knowledge is to be made available for nonprofit public research. The third stage, and the one that normally attracts the most attention, arises when either the indigenous providers or some external entrepreneur attempts to reap the benefits from commercial application of the knowledge in question.

So long as providers prefer to keep their traditional know-how in its raw or inchoate state, there is little room for formal intellectual property protection. As previously observed, any claim for compensation here arises either from an improper violation of the relative secrecy in which the know-how was held or of the social and religious constraints upon its use that the relevant community imposes,[111] and it is rooted in a theory of unjust enrichment. The Convention on Biodiversity provides some legal foundation to support such a claim in the international context; local legislation sounding in unjust enrichment may explicitly regulate these unauthorized uses; and there is a pattern of customary practice forming to support such claims against foreign entrepreneurs.[112]

When, instead, the appropriate indigenous providers signal their willingness to make traditional know-how available for commercial exploitation, then it becomes feasible to remove it even from a true public domain and temporarily transfer it to a semicommons, where it can attract protection under a compensatory liability regime along the lines discussed earlier in this chapter.[113] Under such a regime, the indigenous providers should possess a clear entitlement

---

[109] See, e.g., Cottier & Panizzon, above n. 51; Dutfield, above n. 51.
[110] See, e.g., Taubman, above n. 51; Coombe, above n. 94. [111] See Coombe, above n. 94.
[112] See, e.g., Taubman, above n. 51; Correa, above n. 101; Dutfield, above n. 51.
[113] This move in effect converts the status of the knowledge in question from that of a true public domain to a paying public domain, or semicommons. *Accord* Taubman, above n. 51. We beg all the thorny questions that may complicate the process of identifying the "appropriate indigenous providers" for purposes of triggering intellectual property protection, *cf.* Coombe, above n. 94, although we are encouraged by successful efforts in this regard, for example, in Australia and New Zealand case law. *See further* Taubman, above n. 51.

to prevent wholesale duplication of their compiled information and to reasonable compensation for all follow-on commercial applications of their traditional knowledge during a specified period of time.

One could argue that the duration of protection should be longer than we envision for present-day subpatentable innovation generally, in view of the equitable or "justice" goals that underlie the scheme[114] and of the typically slow accretion of traditional knowledge over time. By the same token, the royalty rates could be somewhat higher than those we envision for small-scale technical innovators generally, for much the same reasons.[115] However, no entrepreneur who invested in any commercial application of the traditional knowledge in question could prevent other entrepreneurs from investing in follow-on, value-adding applications of that same knowledge, and all investors would owe compensatory tithes to the indigenous originators, or, where applicable, to other entrepreneurs whose improvements had been borrowed as inputs for further follow-on applications.

Consider, for example, the following scenario. A certain tribe (T) in Ruritania holds traditional knowledge about, let us say, the bark and leaves of the "kew tree,"[116] which they have long used successfully to soothe and cure skin burns. The tribe's authorized representatives,[117] having been apprised of the government's efforts to protect traditional knowledge and to stimulate investment in local innovation, decide to make its knowledge available[118] under a compensatory liability regime. In this connection, we further assume that Ruritania will fiscalize the costs of clinical trials for all medicinal products based on T's traditional knowledge as a public good.

Assuming that T's burn remedy as derived from the kew tree had been properly registered under the local CLR, no one else (subject to Ruritania's territorial jurisdiction, at least) can duplicate this remedy for commercial purposes for a specified period of time, let us say, for a twenty-year period specifically provided for qualifying traditional knowledge. However, the research exemption incorporated into Ruritania's CLR should authorize access to and use of T's remedy for purposes of nonprofit public research.

---

[114] *Cf.* Cottier & Panizzon, above n. 51.
[115] *See* above nn. 62–67 and accompanying text. Use of some of the valuation techniques applied to government use of patents under current U.S. law might prove relevant here. *See* REICHMAN WITH HASENZAHL, above n. 46.
[116] Any resemblance between this kew tree and real world flora is purely coincidental.
[117] *See* above n. 113.
[118] We skim over the form of "making available" in some kind of registration system, possibly a database, in the knowledge that WIPO and others have studied these aspects in detail. *See, e.g.,* Cottier & Panizzon, above n. 51; Peter Drahos, *Indigenous Knowledge, Intellectual Property and Biopiracy: Is a Global Bio-Collecting Society the Answer?*, 2000 EUR. INTELL. PROP. L. REV. 245 (2000).

Shortly thereafter, local Firm A considers investing its own technical knowledge and skills to combine ingredients derived from kew tree bark and leaves with other ingredients known to its researchers, with a view to producing an improved treatment for burns. Observe that, if T possessed a patent or patent-like exclusive rights in its traditional knowledge, it could block A's follow-on application,[119] while Firm A might fear to disclose its own business plan or its formula, lest T go into partnership with others willing to pay more.

Instead, under the applicable CLR, Firm A knows that it can "borrow" T's knowledge of using kew tree bark and leaves to cure burns for purposes of deriving an improved product, subject to a duty to pay T compensatory royalties falling within a specified statutory range for a specified period of time. T's total earnings will then depend on the sums it receives from direct treatment by its shamans (or by other authorized practitioners) of burn patients[120] and on the royalties it receives from the sales of A's kew-tree based unguent. For present purposes, we assume that revenues from the latter source are relatively high in relation to the former, although the opposite could just as well occur.

Meanwhile, the owners of pharmaceutical Firm B (a locally owned subsidiary of a large foreign company incorporated in Ruritania) have observed Firm A's successful marketing of its kew-tree derived burn unguent with keen interest. Indeed, Firm B's executives authorized considerable R&D expenditures to identify the specific ingredients in the kew bark and leaves that produce healing effects; and they endowed the local university's chemistry department with a grant to help their own researchers to synthesize the active ingredients.[121] With this task accomplished, Firm B's researchers then proceeded to combine these ingredients with other ingredients it had already been using in existing products, to develop a new product for the rapid healing of surgical wounds.[122]

Because neither T nor Firm A holds patents or patent-like exclusive rights on the pre-existing remedies, they cannot prevent Firm B from developing its

---

[119] Unless the second comer's follow-on improvement itself acquired a patent or patent-like entitlement and the relevant legislation contained an anti-blocking provision, such as a compulsory license for dependent patents. *Cf.* TRIPS Agreement, above n. 12, art. 31(l). We ignore this possibility for present purposes.

[120] To the extent that the TK takes the form of a physical application, rather than the use of a product, royalties would also depend on a blanket license to be paid by medical practitioners for use of the TK, rather than on a case-by-case basis, which would be unwieldy and counterproductive to monitor. Needless to say, we are familiar with such blanket licenses – and with the collection societies needed to administer them – from copyright and related rights laws.

[121] *Cf.* Arti K. Rai & Rebecca S. Eisenberg, *Bayh-Dole Reform and the Progress of Biomedicine*, 66 LAW & CONTEM. PROBS. 289 (2003).

[122] In our minds, at least, the surgical wound treatment represents a different market segment from that on which Firm A's burn unguent is distributed.

value-adding surgical wound product.[123] By the same token, Firm B need not prematurely disclose its synthetic processing technology nor its business strategy to T or Firm A in order to obtain licenses, in which case fear of opportunistic behavior might have aborted the whole project. Instead, Firm B understands that it remains free to borrow both A's more refined burn cure know-how and T's original TK for purposes of developing its own follow-on product without obtaining permission. By the same token, Firm B also knows that it must pay compensatory liability royalties to both T and A for specified periods of time, in addition to recouping its own considerable costs of R&D. Firm B's business plan must accordingly factor these liabilities into its accounts from the start if it is to reap a profit in the end.

Let us now assume that Firm B's surgical wound cure scores a resounding success with medical practitioners. In that event, both T and Firm A may experience lottery effects that could greatly exceed any returns they might otherwise have obtained under an exclusive property rights regime. Firm A could also stand in a better position to develop additional products of its own than would be the case if exclusive rights blocked the trail of improvements. For example, Firm A could eventually borrow back Firm B's synthetic improvements to develop an improved, value-adding surgical wound treatment of its own, in return for compensatory royalties payable to both B and T.

We note in passing that the protection against wholesale duplication of a covered product, which is a salient feature of the CLR regime,[124] need not be coterminous in time with the protection against follow-on applications. For example, after a specified period, say, ten years, other Firms C might be allowed to produce competing versions of both A's burn cure and B's surgical wound treatment even for head-to-head competition in the same market segment.[125] In that event, generic producers C need not negotiate up-front licenses with T, B, or A. But C's prices must reflect the compensatory royalties they owe to T, B, and A for the remainder of the respective protection periods (which could themselves vary in length). Moreover, the applicable royalty rates might be higher for posterior generic reproduction than those applicable in cases where the second comers were actually generating value-adding improvements.

---

[123] If A held a patent and B held an improvement patent, we would have the blocking situation depicted above n. 119. If A held a patent and B held only a compensatory liability right, we would have a tricky situation analogous to the case in which one European producer owned a biotech patent that threatened to block another European's use of a plant breeder's right. It is instructive to note that, in such a case, the E.U.'s Directive on Biotechnology clearly envisions a compulsory license to unblock the use of the plant breeder's right. See E.U. Directive 98/44/EC (6 July 1998), art. 12, *available at* http://europa.eu.int/eur-lex/pri/en/oj/dat/1998/l_213/l_21319980730en 00130021.pdf (last visited 1 Aug. 2004).

[124] *See* above n. 58 and accompanying text.

[125] We assume this option would reflect a policy decision concerning public interest limitations to be imposed on even the already limited rights under a compensatory liability regime.

C. Further observations

The TK model of a compensatory liability regime outlined above represents a new and dynamic form of a "paying public domain," adapted to commercial applications of traditional knowledge. However, the relocation of traditional knowledge it envisions from an inchoate public-domain status to a legally defined semicommons should be temporary, not perpetual, and it should not last too long. In other words, we are seeking to define and legally identify specific beginning and ending points in time during which the collocation of traditional knowledge in a paying semicommons could likely yield greater social benefits than costs.[126]

In all cases, use of the protected traditional knowledge for nonprofit or public research purposes should be preserved either by law or by appropriate contractual templates.[127] This availability for public research further attenuates the social costs of temporarily relocating traditional knowledge to a paying semicommons. Nevertheless, if the public research results lead to qualifying new commercial applications, they should likewise become subject to the compensatory liability regime, with benefits to be shared with the indigenous providers.[128]

a. Administrative burdens Some observers have objected that a CLR might impose heavy administrative burdens on developing countries, and that they could not cope with the resulting volume of litigation. It is also said that the delay caused by administrative and judicial deficiencies would necessitate a very lengthy period of protection.[129] These well-meaning criticisms betray a misunderstanding of the differences between a liability rule and a regime of exclusive property rights.

Under our proposed liability rule, no injunction can issue to prevent unauthorized follow-on applications (although one could issue for slavish imitation during a specified period). Because there is normally no risk of an injunction, and the second comer remains legally entitled to borrow the originator's technical contributions for follow-on purposes, the need to involve the courts' judicial and administrative apparatus remains minimal. At bottom, the parties

---

[126] Some additional provisions may become necessary to protect databases housing specific collections of information or data concerning traditional knowledge against wholesale appropriation. See Reichman, *Database Protection in a Global Economy*, above n. 39.
[127] Cf. Reichman & Uhlir, above n. 39, at 425–60.
[128] If public research results lead to patentable applications, appropriate legislation should, of course, also ensure that benefits are shared with indigenous providers. See, e.g., Cottier & Panizzon, above n. 51.
[129] See Letter from Sybelle Schlatter, above n. 45.

have an accounting transaction, which presents problems of collection and verification, but this should not normally entail a judicial process.[130]

Developing countries that enact utility model laws could face greater judicial and administrative burdens than under a CLR (or at worst an equivalent burden). Moreover, the relevant burdens imposed by TRIPS-mandated intellectual property standards generally would greatly outweigh the burdens of implementing a compensatory liability regime, and only the poorest "least-developed countries" can avoid some of those burdens until 2016.[131]

As previously observed, a collection agency is needed to properly implement a compensatory liability regime. Some applications of traditional know-how, such as medical treatments (not products), would have to be regulated by blanket licenses that authorized a specific sector or group of practitioners to make use of specific applications under a negotiated payment schedule, because payments could not otherwise be recouped from patients one by one. This task is no more difficult for a collection agency to organize than the blanket licenses used for public performances of music or for the photocopying of periodicals in the United States.

We acknowledge that crafting modalities for the distribution of royalties among deserving indigenous providers poses well-known difficulties for which we offer no new solutions. We stress, nonetheless, that the collection of royalties under the automatic licenses of a compensatory liability regime raises separate and distinctly different issues from those of distribution. Until and unless such royalties are collected under enabling local legislation, there is nothing to distribute. Any problems of distribution thereafter should not impede early collection of royalties, which can be held in trust for the appropriate beneficiaries however these are to be determined. Care must be taken to keep transaction costs low – in the manner of the Harry Fox licenses in the United States[132] – lest administrators siphon off the benefits at the expense of indigenous providers.

b. The international dimension Developing countries that proceeded to enact compensatory liability regimes in their domestic laws would likely have to operate without formal international recognition of such regimes for an unknown period of time. Moreover, they would probably have to grant national treatment under such laws to all WTO nationals seeking their

---

[130] In the United States, where there is a liability regime within the copyright law for musical works reproduced on sound recordings, a private collection society (the Harry Fox Agency) manages some 200,000 voluntary licenses a year. *See* M. WILLIAM KRASILOVSKY & SIDNEY SHEMEL, THIS BUSINESS OF MUSIC 237–38 (Billboard Books 7th ed., 1995); Lydia P. Loren, *Untangling the Web of Music Copyrights*, 53 CASE W. RES. L. REV. 673 (2003).

[131] *See* WTO Doha Ministerial Conference, Declaration on the TRIPS Agreement and Public Health, WT/MIN(01)/DEC/W/2 (14 Nov. 2001) [hereinafter Doha Declaration on TRIPS and Public Health].

[132] *See* above n. 130.

protection, at least according to the WTO Appellate Body's path breaking decision on national treatment under both the Paris Convention and the TRIPS Agreement.[133] Members would not be entitled to demand for their citizens that foreign countries reciprocally provide similar CLR protection abroad, absent some treaty obligation to this effect.

This legal reality constitutes less of a handicap than one might suppose, however, in part because both the Paris Convention and the TRIPS Agreement will allow innovators operating in countries that adopt CLR regimes to claim patent and utility model rights abroad, where available, in all other WTO Members, without regard to reciprocity.[134] The fact that a national of Ruritania obtained only compensatory liability rights at home would thus not bar him from filing for utility model protection in other developing or developed countries. Nor would it prevent him from obtaining full patent protection in Occitania, if that country were foolish enough to protect small-scale innovation in its domestic patent law (as most developed countries increasingly tend to do).

In sum, while states that wish to protect applications of traditional knowledge under domestic regimes of compensatory liability cannot impose such regimes on foreign countries, neither can foreign countries prevent interested states from adopting such regimes. The first task is, therefore, for developing countries willing to experiment with such regimes to get underway and to share their experiences with other interested countries, ideally through the good offices of WIPO's Intergovernmental Committee on Traditional Knowledge, which is charged with elaborating proposals for international action. A period of experimentation would prove beneficial to all concerned with this issue, while the existence of such regimes in the domestic laws of some developing countries would further support demands for the recognition of rights in traditional knowledge at the international level.

To some extent, developing countries can use these domestic regimes and the growing demand for international recognition of rights in traditional knowledge as bargaining chips within the larger framework of "Bargaining Around the TRIPS Agreement."[135] However, care must be taken to avoid bad bargains. For example, any deal that required developing countries to recognize the European Union's perpetual exclusive property right in noncopyrightable databases would impose far greater social costs on developing countries

---

[133] See above n. 86.
[134] See above n. 86; Paris Convention, above n. 31, arts. 1(3) (definition of industrial property), 2(1) (national treatment), 4bis (independence of patents); TRIPS Agreement, above n. 12, arts. 2.1 (incorporating Paris Convention's substantive rules, now said to include national treatment), 3.1 (national treatment under TRIPS).
[135] See generally David Lange & J.H. Reichman, Bargaining Around the TRIPS Agreement: The Case for Public-Private Initiatives to Facilitate Worldwide Intellectual Property Transactions, 9 DUKE J. COMP. & INT'L L. 11 (1998).

than any benefits that a TK protection regime could possibly yield. By the same token, a compensatory liability regime for applications of know-how to industry could itself be adapted to provide a workable alternative model for database protection that might benefit all participating countries.[136]

III. Conclusion

This chapter has argued the case for the use of compensatory liability principles to stimulate small-scale or subpatentable innovation in developing countries. While we contend that all countries could benefit from laws embodying these principles,[137] developing countries in particular would find them more beneficial than the hybrid regimes of exclusive property rights – such as utility model laws, design protection laws, plant variety laws, and the like – that traditional legal scholarship usually endorses. A compensatory liability regime solves the problem of market failure arising from applications of know-how to industry under present-day conditions without the high social costs that hybrid regimes of exclusive property rights are known to generate. In particular, it encourages follow-on applications without creating barriers to entry and without impoverishing either the research commons or the public domain, as occurs under the hybrid regimes that developed countries have adopted.

To the extent that developing countries opt to experiment with compensatory liability regimes, they would find them beneficial in at least three important ways. First, it could give them an important tool with which to stimulate investment in small-scale innovation falling within the technical capabilities of local producers. Second, it could help to solve thorny problems surrounding the drive to bring owners of traditional knowledge into the realm of intellectual property protection without unduly disrupting their community ties and without removing this controversial subject matter from a semicommons accessible to all. Such a regime would, in short, help to preserve the natural open-source character of community-generated know-how, both new and old.

Third, successful experience with the use of liability rules in this one area could empower developing countries to adopt similar solutions to resolve other hard problems on the frontier of the worldwide intellectual property system, such as growing demands for the legal protection of noncopyrightable cultural artifacts, of noncopyrightable collections of data, and of confidential test data resulting from the clinical trials of new pharmaceutical products.[138] While these topics lie beyond the scope of this chapter, we are confident that

---

[136] *See, e.g.*, Reichman, *Database Protection in a Global Economy*, above n. 39; Reichman & Samuelson, above n. 53, at 145–51.
[137] A searching economic analysis of the superiority of liability rules over exclusive rights in these and other cases has been deferred to a later article. *See* above n. 53.
[138] *Cf.* TRIPS Agreement, above n. 12, art. 39.3.

compensatory liability principles would help to resolve the very thorny problems they currently pose for the international IP community.

Finally, looking down the road, we believe that compensatory liability principles could eventually constitute the basis for a bold new strategy to provide second-tier protection of medium and even large-scale innovation in developed countries, an alternative to the patent system that would directly protect investment as such without requiring nonobviousness and without blocking follow-on applications. This more advanced use of liability rules goes well beyond the protection of subpatentable innovation, discussed here, and represents a new theoretical point of departure for a future study.[139] Ideally, it would supplement the patent system and avoid the many distortions that currently arise when this system is applied to protect investment rather than truly nonobvious inventions. However, that topic lies beyond the scope of this chapter and will be discussed in a separate work in progress.

---

[139] *See* Tracy Lewis & J.H. Reichman, above n. 53 (work-in-progress).

14

Stimulating agricultural innovation

MICHAEL BLAKENEY*

Introduction
I. Historical background
   A. The road to UPOV
      1. Plant variety protection under the Paris Convention
      2. The Paris Conferences on special protection of 1957 and 1961
      3. Additional Act of 1972
      4. The Revision of 1978
      5. The Revision of 1991
   B. The TRIPS Agreement 1994
II. Implementing the differential treatment of patentable inventions and plant varieties
   A. Distinguishing the subject matters of protection
      1. The European experience
      2. Overlapping protection in the United States
   B. What is a plant variety for purposes of article 27.3(b) of the TRIPS Agreement?
   C. Technical issues concerning the *sui generis* protection of plant varieties
III. The Treaty on Plant Genetic Resources
IV. Farmers' Rights
V. Access to PGRFA and the Doha negotiating agenda

Introduction

This chapter provides an interest analysis of the initiation and elaboration of the industrial property laws that govern plant breeding. It surveys the historical origins of plant variety protection laws and the emergence of patenting as an important modality for the protection of agricultural innovation. It concludes

---

* Michael Blakeney is Herchel Smith Professor of Intellectual Property Law and Director, Queen Mary Intellectual Property Research Institute, Queen Mary College, University of London.

with an examination of the impact of these developments upon the international agricultural research environment.

I. Historical background

The first legislative proposal for the protection of agricultural innovations was the Papal States Edict of 3 September 1833 concerning the declarations of ownership of new inventions and discoveries in the fields of the technological arts and agriculture.[1] This general measure was never implemented. The inclusion of agriculture in this instrument could not be attributed to the incentivization of innovations in plant breeding, as it anticipated, by two decades, the 1865 publication of the experiments of Mendel on the principles of heredity and, by almost seventy years, the rediscovery of his work by Correns, von Teschermak and de Vries in 1900.[2]

Similarly, the inclusion of agriculture within the ambit of the 1883 Paris Convention for the Protection of Industrial Property[3] could not easily be reconciled with any incentive thesis. Article 1(3) of that Convention had declared that

> Industrial property shall be included within the broadest sense and shall apply not only to industry and commerce proper, but likewise to agricultural and extractive industries and to all manufactured or natural products, for example, wines, grain, tobacco leaf, fruit, cattle, minerals, mineral waters, beer, flowers and flour.[4]

Given the state of technology in 1883, the inclusion of these agricultural subjects within the concept of "industrial property" covered by the Paris Convention was probably related to the protection of trade marks and indications of source. The importance of the latter was reflected in the Second Conference of Revision of the Paris Convention, held at Madrid in 1890–91, which proposed a special agreement for the repression of false indications of origin.[5]

The possibility of including the subject of plant variety protection within the Paris Convention was addressed, for the first time, in 1955 by a meeting of

---

[1] B. Laclavière, *La Protection des Droits des Obtenteurs sur les Nouvelles Espèces ou Variétés des Plantes et la Convention de Paris du 2 Décembre 1961 pour la Protection des Obtentions Végétales* No.168, BULLETIN TECHNIQUE D'INFORMATION DES INGÉNIEURS DES SERVICES AGRICOLES (Apr. 1962), *cited in* A. Heitz, The History of the UPOV Convention and the Rationale for Plant Breeders' Rights, Paper delivered at UPOV Seminar on the Nature of and Rationale for the Protection of Plant Varieties under the UPOV Convention (Buenos Aires, 26–27 Nov. 1991).

[2] *See* R.W. ALLARD OF PRINCIPLES, PLANT BREEDING 7 et seq. (John Wiley & Sons 1960).

[3] Paris Convention for the Protection of Industrial Property, 20 Mar. 1883, *as revised at* Stockholm, 14 July 1967, 21 U.S.T. 1538, T.I.A.J. No. 6903, 828 U.N.T.S. 305 [hereinafter Paris Convention].

[4] Paris Convention, above n. 3, art 1(3) (as it appeared in the 1883 text).

[5] Madrid Arrangement for the Repression of False or Deceptive Indications of Source on Goods.

experts that had been convened to prepare the agenda for the Lisbon Revision Conference of the Paris Union, scheduled for 1958. The committee of experts concluded that it was premature to include this subject within the Paris Convention, and attempts to raise the matter in the resultant Lisbon Conference by the International Association for the Protection of Industrial Property (AIPPI), the International Chamber of Commerce (ICC), and the United Nations Food and Agricultural Organization (FAO), were unsuccessful.

The first national proposal that foreshadowed the protection of agricultural innovations under patent law was the introduction, in the United States Congress of 1906, of a "Bill to amend the laws of patents in the interest of the originators of horticultural products."[6] This bill was unsuccessful, as were similar bills introduced in 1907, 1908 and 1910. It was not until the Townsend-Parnell Act of 1930, the "Plant Patent Act," that agricultural innovations were recognized by Congress. This statute endures as sections 161–164 of the current United States patent law.[7]

Although part of the U.S. Patents Code, the Plant Patent Act created a *sui generis* system of protection for agricultural innovations that anticipated a number of the features of the International Convention for the Protection of New Varieties of Plants (UPOV).[8] For example, section 161 of the Plant Patent Act confined protection to asexually reproduced plants, because of the view that sexually reproduced varieties lacked stability.[9] The section also excluded tuber-propagated plants principally because of a concern that this would lead to monopolies in basic foodstuffs, such as potatoes.[10] Applicants for plant patents were accordingly required to asexually reproduce the plant in relation to which protection was sought, in order to demonstrate the stability of the characteristics that were claimed.

Section 161 also required that eligible new varieties should be "distinct." The statute did not define this requirement, although the Senate Committee Report accompanying the Act stated that "in order for a new variety to be distinct it must have characteristics clearly distinguishable from those of existing

---

[6] A Bill to Amend the Laws of the United States Relating to Patents in the Interest of the Originators of Horticultural Products, H.R. 18851, 59th Cong. (1906), *quoted in* Arguments Before the House Comm. on Patents on H.R. 18851, To Amend the Laws of the United States Relating to Patents in the Interest of the Originators of Horticultural Products, 59th Cong. 3–18 (1906).

[7] 35 U.S.C. §§ 161–164 (2000).

[8] International Convention for the Protection of New Varieties of Plants (UPOV), 2 Dec. 1961, *as revised* in 1972 and International Convention for the Protection of New Varieties of Plants, 23 Oct. 1978 [hereinafter UPOV 1978]. A further important revision occurred in 1991. See below n. 20 et. seq.

[9] 35 U.S.C. § 161 (2000). See S.B. Williams, *Intellectual Property Aspects of Plant Variety Genetic Engineering: View of an American Lawyer, in* UPOV, GENETIC ENGINEERING AND PLANT BREEDING 23 (1983).

[10] S. REP. NO. 71–315 (1930).

varieties" and that it was not necessary for the new variety to constitute "a variety of a new species."[11]

Legislation similar to the U.S. Plant Patent Act was adopted in Cuba (1937), South Africa (1952), and the Republic of Korea (1973), in an endeavour by those countries to align their patent systems with that of the United States.[12] The U.S. Act was further emulated in the draft Seeds and Seedlings Law, which was submitted to the German Parliament in 1930, the year in which the U.S. Act was adopted.[13] The German legislation provided protection to plant breeders for new varieties that were distinguishable from existing varieties in characteristics that were inheritable or transferable by vegetative propagation. The UPOV Convention's later concern with "essentially derived varieties"[14] was anticipated by the German Law's denial of protection to a variety obtained by a mere selection without important or substantial improvement of an existing protected variety.[15] The Law also authorized the registration of protected varieties as trade marks. However, this draft Law was never adopted by the German Parliament.

A. The road to UPOV

In Europe, the first formal suggestion for a *sui generis* type of protection for plant varieties occurred in the Congrès pomologique de France of 1911. A French Decree of 5 December 1922 introduced a Register for Newly-bred Plants,[16] and a similar system of seed certification was established by the Netherlands in 1932.

The first national statute that clearly anticipated the UPOV Convention was the Czech Law of 1921 on the Originality of Types, Seeds and Seedlings and the Testing of Horticultural Types.[17] It provided that registration of plant seed types entitled the registrant to place its material in commerce under a registered indication. The horticulturalist or producer who produced the original material obtained the exclusive right to make use of a registered trade mark covering the type.

A more obvious precursor to the UPOV Convention was the German Law of 27 June 1953, on the Protection of Varieties and the Seeds of Cultivated Plants. Article 1 of this statute stated that the purpose of protection was to promote the creation of useful (*wetvoll*) new varieties of cultivated plants. An exception was provided for non-food plants and varieties intended for export. A precondition for protection was that a variety should be "individualized" and stable. This anticipated the UPOV requirements of distinctiveness and stability. The registered owner of a protected variety had the exclusive right to produce

---

[11] Id., cited in J. Rossman, *The Preparation and Prosecution of Plant Patent Applications*, 17 J. PAT. OFF. SOC'Y 632 (1935).
[12] See Heitz, above n. 1, at 23. [13] *GRUR* 244 [1930]. [14] UPOV 1978, above n. 8, art. 5.
[15] Law on the Protection of Varieties and the Seeds of Cultivated Plants (1953).
[16] *PI* 28–29 (1923). [17] *PI* 70–71 (1922).

and sell seed of the variety. The Law also permitted the use of a protected variety for the creation of new varieties.

Also anticipating UPOV was the requirement that anyone who marketed seed of the protected variety was obliged to use the registered designation for the variety. As with UPOV, where under the German Law the variety designation was a registered trade mark, the trade mark proprietor could not object to the use of the designation where such use was compulsory.

Attempts had been made with varying degrees of success in a number of European jurisdictions to obtain patents covering plant varieties. In Germany, there were a number of decisions of the Beschwedesenat in 1934 and 1936 that approved the acceptance of applications for patents on tobacco and lupin seed, and in relation to the "seed of a small-seeded garden pea." However, these applications were withdrawn because of concerns about compromising agricultural policy that had been expressed by the Reichsnärstand.[18] In France, a patent had been secured on a rose variety in 1949, by a celebrated Rose breeder, Roger Meilland.[19] He then pursued successful patent applications in Belgium and Italy, but failed in an application in Switzerland. There were no applications in any of these countries outside the field of ornamental plants.

As with other categories of intellectual property, a key role in the inclusion of agricultural innovations within the international regulatory regime was played by industry associations. Mention has been made of the Congrès pomologique de France, held in 1911, which had called for special protection of plant varieties. The International Union of the Horticultural Profession also considered the matter at its Congresses in Luxemburg (1911), London (1912) and Ghent (1913). The International Institute of Agriculture in its 1927 Congress had stated that the protection of a denomination was insufficient and that a way had to be found to require "any grower who engaged in reproduction of those breeds for the purposes of sale to pay a royalty to the producer."[20]

The International Federation of Breeders of Staple Crops had, in its 1931 conference, expressed the hope that the legal status of new varieties should be assimilated to that of industrial inventions. Discussions concerning the creation of a new organization to agitate for the promulgation of an international legal regime for the protection of plant varieties occurred at the meetings of the International Breeders' Congress at Leeuwarden in 1936 and the 1937 Conference of the International Organization of Agricultural Industries, also held in the Netherlands. The direct result of these discussions was the foundation in Amsterdam, on November 17, 1938, of the International Association of Plant

---

[18] See Heitz, above n. 1, at 27.
[19] See B. Laclavière, The French Law on the Protection of New Plant Varieties, 10 INDUS. PROP. 44 (1971).
[20] UPOV, The History of Plant Variety Protection, in THE FIRST TWENTY-FIVE YEARS OF THE INTERNATIONAL CONVENTION OF THE PROTECTION OF NEW VARIETIES OF PLANTS 80 (UPOV 1987).

Breeders for the Protection of Plant Varieties (ASSINSEL). The first ASSINSEL Congress, held in Paris on 8–9 July 1939, adopted a three-point resolution:

(1) To accept internationally the filing of trademarks and appellations as a means of protection (pending introduction of a patent);
(2) To adopt the principle of a licence, to be drawn up by ASSINSEL for the purposes of multiplication and sale; and
(3) To accept internationally the definition of the word "original" [as] seed produced, offered or sold by the breeder of the variety or under his control by his licensees or successors in title.

The Second World War interrupted these developments. At its Semmering Congress in June, 1956, a resolution of ASSINSEL called for an international conference to promulgate an international system for the protection of plant varieties. The French Government had been approached by ASSINSEL, because it had indicated a favourable attitude.[21] Invitations were issued to 12 Western European countries[22] to attend a diplomatic conference in Paris, from 7 to 11 May 1957. The notes of invitation to the conference referred to the conclusions that had been reached at the 1954 Conference on the Development of Seed Production and Trade, held in Stockholm, that there should be an international agreement favourable to the protection of new plant varieties.

1. Plant variety protection under the Paris Convention

Meanwhile, the German delegation to the London Congress of the International Association for the Protection of Industrial Property (AIPPI) in 1932, which was led by Franz and Freda Wuesthoff, had proposed that patent rights should be established for plants manifesting entirely new characteristics, and that a lesser right, in the nature of a new denomination, should be provided for lesser creations. Other delegations opposed this initiative, particularly the British, which fought the extension of patenting to plants because of the damage that might be done to the patent system if protection became over-broad.[23]

The matter was taken up again in 1939, when it was decided to address the issue in the 1940 Congress of the AIPPI. However, with the interruption of war, the subject was not taken up again in any serious way by AIPPI, until its 1952 Congress in Vienna, when a variety of proposals were advanced. The Wuesthoffs renewed their proposal for a hybrid system of protection that would depend on the level of inventiveness. The delegations from Luxemburg, the Netherlands, Switzerland and the United Kingdom proposed a specific protection system. The Congress unanimously adopted the following text:

---

[21] Id. at 82.
[22] I.e., Austria, Belgium, Denmark, Finland, Federal Republic of Germany, Italy, the Netherlands, Norway, Spain, Sweden, Switzerland and the UK.
[23] See UPOV, above n. 20, at 78.

The Congress expresses the view that, in order to achieve effective protection for new plant varieties, the legislation of the countries of the [Paris] Union must:

1. Provide, in so far as it is not yet granted, for patent or equivalent protection for plants that possess important new properties, with a view to their exploitation, provided that their propagation is assured;
2. Place on an equal footing an invention's suitability for use in agriculture, forestry, market gardening and other comparable fields, and an invention's suitability for use in industry as provided in the patent laws of many countries.[24]

Another text was submitted to the subsequent AIPPI Congress at Brussels, which met in 1954. It declared that

The Congress expresses the wish that, in the legislation of each country of the Union:

1. Inventions relating to the plant kingdom be assimilated, with respect to their legal protection, to industrial inventions, in accordance with Article 1(3) of the text of the Paris Convention for the Protection of Industrial Property;
2. For plants that possess definable new characteristics, in so far as their faithful reproducibility is assured, there be provision for protection, where it is not yet granted, by the patent law, amended where appropriate, or by any other legislative or regulatory measure.

The various delegations adopted separate negotiating positions, and the final resolution of the Congress expressed the wish that "in the legislation of each of the countries of the Union, inventions relating to the plant kingdom be assimilated, with respect to legal protection, to industrial inventions and that plant varieties be also protected."[25] In practice, however, AIPPI was unable to interest the contemporaneous Paris Revision conferences to adopt plant variety protection as a subject for discussion.

2. The Paris Conferences on special protection of 1957 and 1961

On 22 February 1957, the French Government issued invitations to twelve Western European countries[26] to attend a Diplomatic Conference in Paris, to be held from 7 to 11 May 1957, to consider establishing an international regime for the protection of plant varieties. Participation was limited by the French to those states who were known to share its own concerns on this subject. Thus, the United States was not invited because it had "confined itself to plant patents for vegetatively reproduced varieties, with at best only a minor part to play as foods."[27]

---

[24] *Id.* [25] *Id.* at 80.
[26] *I.e.*, Austria, Belgium, Denmark, Finland, Federal Republic of Germany, Italy, the Netherlands, Norway, Spain, Sweden, Switzerland and the UK.
[27] *See* UPOV, above n. 20, at 82.

The conclusions of the 1957 Conference were set out in its Final Act, adopted on 11 May 1957. This instrument recognized the legitimacy of breeders' rights and established, as the preconditions for protection, that a variety had to be distinct from pre-existing varieties and sufficiently homogenous and stable in its essential characteristics. It defined the rights of the breeder and acknowledged the principle of the independence of protection in each country. It proposed that these principles be enshrined in an international convention and that a Drafting Committee and a Committee of Experts be established.

Following three meetings of the Drafting Committee and two meetings of Committees of Experts, the second session of the Conference was held in Paris from 21 November to 2 December, 1961. An International Convention for the Protection of New Varieties of Plants (UPOV) was presented for the Consideration of the Conference. An important question debated there was whether the UPOV Convention would be compatible with the Paris Convention. The debate on that subject produced the inclusion of article 2(1), which stated that "each Member of the [UPOV] Union may recognize the right of the breeder...by the grant of a special title of protection or a patent. Nevertheless, a Member State of the Union, whose national law admits of protection under both these forms, may only provide one of them for one and the same genus or species."

Article 4(1) applied the draft UPOV Convention to "all botanical genera and species," but it was envisaged that the Convention would have a gradual introduction. A list of thirteen genera was annexed to the Convention: wheat, barley, oats or rice, maize, potato, peas, beans, Lucerne, red clover, ryegrass, lettuce, apples, roses or carnations. Article 4(3) required each Member State on entry into force of the Convention to apply it to at least five genera from this list and, within eight years, to all the listed genera.

The UPOV Convention was signed on 2 December 1961 by the representatives of Belgium, France, the Federal Republic of Germany, Italy and the Netherlands. On 26 November 1962, the signatures of Denmark and the United Kingdom were added, followed by Switzerland on 30 November 1962. The Convention entered into force on 10 August 1968, following its ratification by the Netherlands, the Federal Republic of Germany and the United Kingdom. Denmark deposited its instrument of ratification on 6 September 1968 and France on 3 September 1971. Sweden deposited an instrument of accession on 17 November 1971.

3. Additional Act of 1972

Article 27 of the 1961 UPOV Convention provided for its periodic review, with the first revision scheduled for 1972. A Diplomatic Conference for this purpose was held on 7–10 November 1972. The primary objective of this Conference was to arrange the financial contribution rates of member states. The Additional Act for this purpose was signed by Belgium, Denmark, France, Federal Republic of Germany, Italy, Netherlands, Sweden, Switzerland and the U.K. The Additional

Act entered into force on 11 February 1977, after which it also obtained the accession of South Africa (7 October 1977) Israel (12 November 1979) and Spain (18 April 1980). Thus, within the first nineteen years of its life, the UPOV Convention had attracted the accession of only twelve states.

One reason for the reluctance of states to adopt the Convention was the stringency of its provisions, in particular the obligation of states to select either patent or UPOV-style protection for plant varieties. Work on a revision had begun as early as 1973, and in October 1974, the UPOV Council set up a Commission of Experts for the Interpretation and Revision of the Convention. Six sessions of this Commission were held between February 1975 and September 1977, and in December 1977, the Council called for a Diplomatic Conference to be held on 9–23 October 1978.

4. The Revision of 1978

In an endeavour to broaden the membership of the Convention, invitations were widely circulated, to permit non-member states to participate as observers. In the end, some 27 non-member states attended, including the U.S. and a number of developing countries. One result was an amendment of article 2 of the Convention to permit the accession of countries like the United States, which had laws allowing the double protection of varieties under patent and *sui generis* laws.[28]

The list of genera, annexed to the 1961 Convention was removed. This list had contained mainly species from temperate climates. Under the new article 4, Member States agreed to apply the Convention to at least five genera or species, rising to 24 genera or species within eight years. Additionally a grace period was introduced to permit the marketing of varieties twelve months prior to an application for plant variety protection being made. The revised Convention attracted the ratification of the United States on 12 November 1980.[29]

5. The Revision of 1991

A further broadening of the UPOV Convention occurred with the 1991 Revision.[30] The 1991 Act requires states to protect at least fifteen plant genera or species upon becoming members of the Act, and to extend protection to all

---

[28] *See* N. Byrne, Commentary on the Substantive Law of the 1991 UPOV Convention for the Protection of Plant Varieties, at 13 fn. 20. (CCLS 1991).

[29] *See* http://www.upov.org/en/publications/conventions/1978/act1978.htm (last visited 1 Aug. 2004). The United States became a party to the 1978 UPOV in 1981 by Executive Agreement. *See* H.R. Rep. No. 103–699, at 9 (1994).

[30] Act of 1991, International Convention for the Protection of New Varieties of Plants (official English transl.) (1991) [hereinafter UPOV II], *at* http://www.upov.org/en/publications/conventions/1991/act1991.htm (last visited 1 Aug. 2004). The United States signed the treaty in October 1991, but did not submit the treaty to the Senate for ratification until late 1995. Convention for the Protection of Plants, S. Exec. Rep. No. 105–15, at 1 (1998). The United States deposited its instrument of ratification on 22 January 1999, and it became

plant varieties within ten years.[31] In response to demands from breeders in industrialized counties, the 1991 Act required signatory states to make dual protection mandatory. The 1978 text merely permitted states to grant dual protection if they so desired. Through the definition of a "breeder" in article 1(c) as including a "person who bred, or discovered and developed, a variety," the 1991 Act makes explicit the requirement that even discovered varieties should be protected.[32]

The 1991 Act recognizes the right of breeders to use protected varieties to create new varieties. However, this exception is itself restricted to such new varieties as are not "essentially derived" from protected varieties.[33] The drafters added this restriction to prevent second generation breeders from making merely cosmetic changes to existing varieties in order to claim protection for a new variety. The concept of essential derivation has proved highly controversial in practice, however. Breeders have been unable to agree on a definition of the minimum genetic distance required for second generation varieties to be treated as not essentially derived from an earlier variety and thus outside of the first breeder's control.[34]

From the perspective of farmers, probably the most contentious aspect of the 1991 Act is the limitation of the farmers' privilege to save seed for propagating the product of the harvest they obtained by planting a protected variety "on their own holdings," [and] "within reasonable limits and subject to the safeguarding of the legitimate interests of the breeder."[35] Unlike the 1978 Act, the 1991 version of the farmers' privilege does not authorize farmers to sell or exchange seeds with other farmers for propagating purposes. This has been criticized as inconsistent with the practices of farmers in many developing nations, where seeds are exchanged for purposes of crop and variety rotation.[36] According to one authority, the "reasonable limits" referred to in article 15(2) requires states to restrict the acreage, quantity of seed and species subject to the farmers' privilege, while the requirement to safeguard breeders' "legitimate interests" requires farmers to pay some form of remuneration to the breeder for their privileged acts.[37]

---

effective on 22 February 1999. *See* Press Release No. 35, UPOV, Ratification by the United States of America of the 1991 Act of the International Convention for the Protection of New Varieties of Plants, at 1 (Jan. 22, 1999), *at* http://www.upov.org/en/news/pressroom/35.htm (last visited 1 Aug. 2004).

[31] UPOV II, above n. 30, art 3(2).   [32] UPOV II, above n. 30, art. 1(c).
[33] UPOV II, above n. 30, arts. 14(5), 15.
[34] *See* L. Helfer, Legal Study on Intellectual Property Rights in Plant Genetic Resources, FAO Legal Paper ¶ 1.1.1.4 (FAO 2001).
[35] UPOV II, above n. 30, art. 15(2).
[36] D. Leskien & M. Flitner, *Intellectual Property Rights and Plant Genetic Resources: Options for a Sui Generis System*, ISSUES IN GENETIC RESOURCES NO. 6, June 1997, at 60.
[37] ASSINSEL, Development of New Plant Varieties and Protection of Intellectual Property, Statement approved by the CSTA Board of Directors as a CSTA Position Document, No.A.99.47 (21 July 1999), *available at* cdnseed.org/press/A.99.47IP.htm.

A number of developing countries have resisted adopting the 1991 Act as the standard for plant variety protection laws. The foreign ministers of Organization for African Unity issued a statement at a January 1999 meeting calling for a moratorium on IPR protection for plant varieties until an Africa-wide system had been developed that granted greater recognition to the cultivation practices of indigenous communities.[38] This option is not open to those 90 or more countries that have entered into free trade agreements with the United States, since it insists that signatories adopt the 1991 version of UPOV.[39]

B. The TRIPS Agreement 1994

Probably the most notorious requirement of the TRIPS Agreement is that in article 27.3(b), which requires that Members "shall provide for the protection of plant varieties either by patents or by an effective *sui generis* system or by any combination thereof."[40] Article 8 of the Agreement, in enunciating the principles which are to animate it, provides that "consistent with the provisions of the Agreement, signatories may "adopt measures necessary to protect public health and nutrition, and to promote the public interest in sectors of vital importance to their socio-economic and technological development."[41] It would not be too difficult to construct an argument that the obligation to protect plant varieties might be inconsistent with a given nation's need for food security. However, the opening words of article 8 suggest that, in case of a conflict between these provisions, the obligations within the Agreement, such as article 27.3(b), are paramount.

The TRIPS Agreement does not prescribe any particular form of protection for plant variety innovations. It could have prescribed the UPOV Convention as the legislative norm, as it did with the Berne Convention for copyrights and the Paris Convention for industrial property.[42] Thus, Members have the option of enacting UPOV-like protection, of including plant varieties within their patent laws, of combining both forms of protection, or of combining UPOV-like protection with biodiversity conservation legislation.

II. Implementing the differential treatment of patentable inventions and plant varieties

Intellectual property law traditionally attempts to draw a distinction between inventions and discoveries, with the latter considered unprotectable.

---

[38] See Helfer, above n. 14, ¶ 2.2.3.
[39] See P. Drahos, *BITS and BIPS: Bilateralism in Intellectual Property*, 4 J. WORLD INTELL. PROP. 791 (2001).
[40] Agreement on Trade-Related Aspects of Intellectual Property Rights, 15 Apr. 1994, Marrakesh Agreement Establishing the World Trade Organization, Annex 1C, LEGAL INSTRUMENTS – RESULTS OF THE URUGUAY ROUND vol. 31, 33 I.L.M. 81 (1994) [hereinafter TRIPS Agreement], art. 27.3(b).
[41] *Id.* art. 8.   [42] *See id.* arts 2(1), 9(1).

Additionally, IP courts distinguish between the discovery of non-patentable material that exists in nature and patentable inventions. The general approach that patent offices have taken, following the U.S. Supreme Court's decision in *Diamond v. Chakrabarty*,[43] which held that "anything under the sun" apart from human beings could be patented, is that gene-sequences are to be treated as inventions when they have been isolated and purified. A number of patent offices in developed countries have permitted the patenting also of partial DNA sequences and Expressed Sequence Tags (ESTs).

Of course, it remains open to a court or a legislature to rule or provide that genetic material is not patentable, even in its isolated or purified form, because it is a mere discovery. Indeed, nothing in the TRIPS Agreement obliges countries to deem the isolation of genetic materials to be inventions. A number of developing countries exclude the patentability of genetic materials, for example, Mexico, or of materials existing in nature.[44]

In Europe, the Directive on the Legal Protection of Biotechnological Inventions specifically provides, in article 3.2, that "Biological material which is isolated from its natural environment or produced by means of a technical process may be the subject of an invention even if it previously occurred in nature."[45] However, article 53(b) of the European Patent Convention (EPC) excludes plant varieties, as well as "essentially biological processes," from the scope of patentable subject matter. This raises, in the first instance, the definitional distinction between plants and plant varieties.

A. *Distinguishing the subject matters of protection*

The 1991 UPOV Convention defines "plant variety" in terms of a plant grouping within a single biological taxon of the lowest known rank.[46] Such grouping can be:

- defined by the expression of characteristics (such as shape, height, colour and habit) resulting from a given genotype or combination of genotypes;
- distinguished from any other plant grouping by the expression of at least one of the said characteristics; and
- considered as a unit with regard to its suitability from being propagated unchanged.[47]

---

[43] 447 U.S. 303 (1980).   [44] Argentina, Brazil and the Andean Group Decision 486.
[45] 98/44/EC, 1998 O.J. (L 213) 13 (6 July 1998), art 3.2 [hereinafter European Biotechnology Directive].
[46] UPOV II, above n. 30, art. 2.   [47] *Id.*

1. The European experience

The first consideration of the distinction between plant and plant variety by the Technical Board of Appeal of the European Patent Office (EPO) occurred in 1984, in the *Ciba/Geigy* determination.[48] This concerned a plant which had been treated with a chemical compound to give it a degree of protection from the toxic side-effects of certain herbicides. The Examination Division had refused the patent application on the basis of article 53(c). This decision was reversed by the Technical Board of Appeal, which, applying the definition of plant variety in the UPOV Convention, stated that article 53(c) "prohibits only the patenting of plants or their propagating material in the genetically fixed form of the plant variety ... Plant varieties in this sense are all cultivated varieties, clones, lines, strains and hybrids."[49] In this case, the claims covered merely the application of a chemical treatment and not plant varieties as such.

This approach was applied by the Technical Board of Appeal in the *Lubrizol (Hybrid Plants)* case,[50] where the Board held that "the term 'plant varieties' means a multiplicity of plants which are largely the same in their characteristics (i.e. homogeneity) and remain the same within specific tolerances after every propagation or every propagation cycle (i.e. 'stability')."[51] The Board then ruled that as the hybrids at issue were not stable, they did not fall within the excluded category of plant varieties.

The European Biotechnology Directive permits the patentability of inventions concerning plants where "the technical feasibility is not confined to a particular plant ... variety."[52] Patent claims can therefore be made in respect of plant groupings, or as stated in Recital 31 to the Directive,

> Whereas a plant grouping which is characterized by a particular gene (and not its whole genome) is not covered by the protection of new varieties and is not excluded from patentability even if it comprises new varieties of plants.

This qualification was addressed by the Technical Board of Appeal in the *Novartis/Transgenic Plant* case.[53] The application concerned a patent containing claims to transgenic plants comprising, in their genomes, specific foreign genes, the expression of which resulted in the production of antipathologically active substances, and to methods of preparing such plants. The EPO had denied registration, supported by the Technical Board of Appeal, on the ground that art. 53(b) denied the patentability of an invention that could embrace plant varieties.

---

[48] Case T-49/83, [1984] O.J. E.P.O. 112.
[49] *Id.* at 114–15.   [50] Case T-320/87, [1990] O.J. E.P.O. 71.   [51] *Id.* at 79.
[52] Directive on the Legal Protection of Biotechnological Inventions, above n. 45, art. 4(1), para. 2.
[53] [2000] O.J. EPO 511.

In its decision of 20 December 1999, the Enlarged Board of Appeal indicated that it would favour the application because, in substance, it did not involve an application for a plant variety. This determination contains some useful guidance on the legal definition of plant varieties. The Enlarged Board of Appeal noted that the definitions of plant variety in the UPOV Convention and the E.C. Regulation on Community Plant Variety Rights refer to "the entire constitution of a plant or a set of genetic information," whereas a plant defined by a single recombinant DNA sequence "is not an individual plant grouping to which an entire constitution can be attributed." It observed that the claimed transgenic plants in the application before it were defined by certain characteristics that allowed the plants to inhibit the growth of plant pathogens. No claim was made for anything resembling a plant variety. The tribunal noted that, in the case of a plant variety right, an applicant had to develop a plant group, fulfilling in particular the requirements of homogeneity and stability, whereas in the case of a typical genetic engineering invention, a tool was provided whereby a desired property could be bestowed on plants by inserting a gene into the genome of a specific plant. The Enlarged Board observed that the development of specific varieties was not necessarily the objective of inventors involved in genetic engineering.

An interesting question raised by this case is the continuing role of plant variety protection in the modern world of genetic engineering. To what extent will a *sui generis* system for the protection of plant varieties secure the rights of plant breeders in the face of innovations in patent law? To what extent ought plant variety rights to be harmonized with patent rights? Given the developments in modern biotechnology, Farmers' Rights must be viewed both in the context of patents as well as in the light of plant variety protection.

2. Overlapping protection in the United States

The United States has never excluded biological material, including plant varieties, from the scope of patentable subject matter. Plant varieties can be protected in the United States under a system of plant patents, or under a system of utility patents or under the Plant Variety Protection Act (PVPA).[54] The Plant Patent Act[55] makes available patent protection to new varieties of asexually reproduced plants. Under this scheme a plant variety must be novel and distinct and the patentable invention, discovery or reproduction of the plant variety must not be obvious.

One of the disadvantages of the scheme is that only one claim, covering the plant variety, is permitted in each application. In practice, this scheme has been in decline since the *Hibberd* decision of the Patent Office Board of Appeals and

---

[54] Plant Variety Protection Act 7 U.S.C. §§ 2321–2583 (2000) [hereinafter PVPA].
[55] *See* above n. 7.

Interferences opened up the normal patent system to applications that covered plant varieties.[56] Following the opening of the patent system by the *Hibberd* decision, it became possible for an applicant for a patent to protect plant varieties and breeding under the U.S. Patents Act, provided they are demonstrably the fruits of human ingenuity.[57] This also has the advantage to the applicant that there is no farmer's privilege and only a limited experimental use exception.

The PVPA deals with plants that are produced sexually, by means of seeds. Varieties are protectable if they are new, distinct, uniform and stable.[58] In its 1994 amended form, this statute is consistent with the 1991 version of UPOV.

B. What is a plant variety for purposes of article 27.3(b) of the TRIPS Agreement?

As noted above, a crucial issue in the establishment of a *sui generis* regime would be the definition of the protected subject matter. Article 27.3(b) of the TRIPS Agreement requires the protection of "plant varieties," but it does not provide (as in the case of inventions) a definition of this term. Therefore, national laws have ample room to determine what is to be deemed a plant "variety" for the purposes of protection.

There have been lengthy discussions about the concept of "plant variety," particularly within the framework of UPOV. The scientific notion does not necessarily coincide with the legal concept. The law may require certain characteristics for a *protected* variety that may not be essential for a scientific definition.

Patent protection was not originally considered a particularly effective mode of protecting plant varieties. Prior to the development of modern biotechnology, the breeding of a new variety could be said to entail an inventive step, and such innovations as were made were likely to be deemed obvious rather than inventive.

However, with the extension of patent protection to recombinant methods for producing transgenic plants and the resulting products, patents have begun to assume an increasing significance in plant variety protection. The broader ambit of patent rights is a particular advantage of this form of intellectual property protection, because it covers plants, seeds and enabling technologies. Plant variety rights are highly specific to the variety, and their scope is limited by reference to the physical (propagating) material itself, combined with the description of the variety given in the documentary grant of the rights.

---

[56] 227 U.S.P.Q. 443 (1985).   [57] 35 U.S.C. §§ 100–103 (2000).
[58] PVPA, 7 U.S.C. §§ 2321–2583 (2000).

C. Technical issues concerning the sui generis protection of plant varieties

The principal technical issues concerning the implementation of effective *sui generis* protection of plant varieties under article 27.3(b) of the TRIPS Agreement[59] are: (a) what is meant by "effective"? and (b) what *sui generis* options are open to Members? Because article 27.3(b) provides no guidance on the question of what is meant by "effective," the debate in the TRIPS Council has focused on which *sui generis* systems satisfy the obligation. One interpretation is that "effective" refers to the enforceability of the plant variety protection rights granted by the relevant legislation.

Since the TRIPS provision makes no reference to the UPOV Convention, there is some leeway in domestic law for the formulation of *sui generis* systems.[60] Furthermore, key elements for the shaping of *sui generis* systems are either unclear or not defined. For example, there are several ways to define the term plant variety. When breeders seek protection under the traditional plant breeders' rights (PBR) system, plant varieties must meet the criteria that require them to be distinct, uniform and stable (DUS).[61] It has been suggested that "uniformity" and "stability" could be replaced by a criterion of "identifiability," which would allow the inclusion of plant populations that are more heterogenous, and thus take into account the interests of local communities.[62] The scope of protection could be limited to cover only the reproductive parts of plants, or it could be extended to include also harvested plant materials.

The TRIPS Agreement does not prohibit the development of additional protection systems. Nor does it prohibit the protection of additional subject matter to safeguard local knowledge systems or informal innovations, as well as to prevent their illegal appropriation.[63]

The original formulation and promulgation of the TRIPS Agreement had occurred largely without significant inputs from developing countries. Their principal negotiating position during the Uruguay Round had been to question the relevance of intellectual property for the General Agreement on Tariffs and Trade (GATT), particularly as the World Intellectual Property Organization (WIPO) had already been established as the United Nations' specialized agency for these matters. The failure of developing countries to address much of the substance of TRIPS during the Uruguay Round of Multilateral Trade

---

[59] *See above* nn. 40–41 and accompanying text.
[60] *See, e.g., Various Systems for Sui Generis Rights Systems*, 36 BIOTECH. & DEV. MONITOR 3 (1998), *available at* http://www.biotech-monitor.nl/new/index.php?link=publications.
[61] *See, e.g.,* UPOV II, above n. 30, art. 6(1).
[62] A. Seiler, *Sui Generis Systems: Obligations and Options for Developing Countries*, 34 BIOTECH. & DEV. MONITOR 2 (1998).
[63] *See, e.g.,* Thomas Cottier & Marion Panizzon, *Legal Perspectives on Traditional Knowledge: The Case for Intellectual Property Protection* [this volume].

Negotiations was sought to be remedied by their active participation in the review procedure. The various regional groupings of developing countries held meetings to agree upon a common negotiating position both for the TRIPS review and also for the review of the Convention on Biological Diversity (CBD).[64]

A communication to the WTO from Kenya, on behalf of the African Group, to assist in the preparations for the 1999 Ministerial Conference, pointed out that as the deadline for implementation of the developing countries' obligations under the TRIPS Agreement was January 2000, the scheduled review would precede actual implementation of those obligations. Developing countries would accordingly lack sufficient experience with the operation of the Agreement to conduct impact assessment studies of its implications.[65]

Furthermore, the communication pointed out that the review would preempt the outcome of deliberations in other related fora, such as CBD, UPOV, the FAO, International Undertaking on Plant Genetic Resources, and the development of an Organization of African Unity model law on Community Rights and Control of Access to Biological Resources. It proposed that an additional five years be allowed prior to the review of article 27.3(b).

The African Group further proposed that "after the sentence on plant variety protection in article 27.3(b), a footnote should be inserted stating that any *sui generis* law for plant variety protection can provide for:

(i) the protection of the innovations of indigenous and local farming communities in developing countries, consistent with the Convention on Biological Diversity and the International Undertaking on Plant Genetic Resources;
(ii) the continuation of the traditional farming practices, including the right to save, exchange and save seeds, and sell their harvest; and
(iii) preventing anti-competitive rights or practices which will threaten food sovereignty of people in developing countries, as is permitted by article 31 of the TRIPS Agreement."[66]

On 25 July 1999, a federation of Indigenous Peoples groups issued a statement for the purposes of the TRIPS review. The statement commences with the observation that "Humankind is part of Mother Nature, we have created nothing and so we can in no way claim to be owners of what does not belong to us. But time and again, western legal property regimes have been imposed on us, contradicting our own cosmologies and values."[67] It expresses concern that article 27.3(b) "will further denigrate and undermine our rights to our cultural and intellectual heritage, our plant, animal, and even human genetic

---

[64] Convention on Biological Diversity, 5 June 1992, 1995 U.K.T.S. No. 51 (Cmnd. 2915), 31 I.L.M. 818 [hereinafter CBD].
[65] WTO Doc. WT/GC/W/302 (6 Aug. 1999).   [66] *Id.*
[67] *Indigenous Raise Debate in Geneva*, GRAIN, 5 Nov. 1999, *available at* http://www.grain.org/bio-ipr/.

resources and discriminate against our indigenous ways of thinking and behaving."[68]

The same statement drew a distinction between private proprietorial rights and "indigenous knowledge and cultural heritage [which] are collectively and accretionally evolved through generations... The inherent conflict between these two knowledge systems and the manner in which they are protected and used will cause further disintegration of our communal values and practices."[69] The statement pleaded for a legislative structure that "builds upon the indigenous methods and customary laws protecting knowledge and heritage and biological resources" and that prevents the appropriation of traditional knowledge and integrates "the principle and practice of prior informed consent, of indigenous peoples as communities or as collectivities."[70] This statement was picked up by a submission of Cuba, Honduras, Paraguay and Venezuela to the TRIPS Council,[71] which affirmed that these countries "consider it fair to recognise the specific contribution of indigenous and tribal peoples and local communities to the cultural diversity and social and ecological harmony of mankind."

Responding to these developing country initiatives, the United States has urged that an effective *sui generis* system should clearly identify: (a) the subject matter of protection; (b) any limitations to the rights which will be granted under such a system; and (c) the legal remedies available to rights holders.[72] In relation to a *sui generis* system for the protection of plant varieties, the U.S. submission contended that all plant varieties should be covered, with the objective of encouraging the development of new varieties from the widest possible range of genera and species.[73] This submission also recommended confining the system of protection only to breeders or others specifically entitled through contract law or succession. The U.S. submission was unsympathetic to the claims of indigenous people for the protection of oral knowledge and practices, because of the inaccessibility of this information beyond the relevant indigenous community.[74]

Following the failure of the Seattle Ministerial Conference of the WTO, agitation for the inclusion of traditional knowledge within the international intellectual property regime shifted to WIPO. In a note, dated 14 September 2000, the Permanent Mission of the Dominican Republic to the United Nations in Geneva submitted two documents on behalf of the Group of Countries of Latin America and the Caribbean (GRULAC) as part of the ongoing debate in the WIPO General Assembly about "Matters Concerning Intellectual Property and Genetic Resources, Traditional Knowledge and

---

[68] *Id.*   [69] *Id.*   [70] *Id.*
[71] WTO General Council, Proposal on the Protection of the Intellectual Property Rights Relating to the Traditional Knowledge of Local and Indigenous Communities, WT/GC/W/362 (12 Oct. 1999).
[72] WTO, Review of the Provisions of Article 27.3(b): Further Views of the United States of America, WTO Doc. IP/C/W/209 (20 Sept. 2000).
[73] *Id.* at 2–3.   [74] *Id.* at 5.

Folklore."⁷⁵ The central thrust of these documents was a request for the creation of a Standing Committee on access to the genetic resources and traditional knowledge of local and indigenous communities. "The work of that Standing Committee would have to be directed towards defining internationally recognized practical methods of securing adequate protection for the intellectual property rights in traditional knowledge."⁷⁶

In order to explore the future application of intellectual property to the use and exploitation of genetic resources and biodiversity and also to traditional knowledge, it was suggested that the Standing Committee could clarify: (a) the notions of public domain and private domain; (b) the appropriateness and feasibility of recognizing rights in traditional works and knowledge currently in the public domain, and investigating machinery to limit and control certain kinds of unauthorized exploitation; (c) recognition of collective rights; (d) model provisions and model contracts with which to control the use and exploitation of genetic and biological resources, and machinery for the equitable distribution of profits in the event of a patentable product or process being developed from a given resource embodying the principles of prior informed consent and equitable distribution of profits in connection with the use, development and commercial exploitation of the material transferred and the inventions and technology resulting from it; and (e) the protection of undisclosed traditional knowledge.⁷⁷

At the WIPO General Assembly, the Member States agreed to the establishment of an Intergovernmental Committee on Intellectual Property and Genetic Resources, Traditional Knowledge and Folklore. Three interrelated themes were identified to inform the deliberations of the Committee. Specifically, they were charged to examine intellectual property issues that arise in the context of (i) access to genetic resources and benefit sharing; (ii) protection of traditional knowledge, whether or not associated with those resources; and (iii) the protection of expressions of folklore.⁷⁸

At the first session of the Intergovernmental Committee on Intellectual Property and Genetic Resources, Traditional Knowledge and Folklore ("IGC") held in Geneva from 30 April to 3 May 2001, the Member States determined the agenda of items on which work should proceed and prioritized certain tasks for the Committee. Principal among these was "the development of 'guide contractual practices,' guidelines, and model intellectual property clauses for contractual agreements on access to genetic resources and benefit-sharing."⁷⁹ Subsequent sessions have resulted in the formulation of "Operational

---

⁷⁵ WIPO Doc. WO/GA/26/9.   ⁷⁶ *Id*. Annex I § VII.   ⁷⁷ *Id*. Annex I, at 9–10.
⁷⁸ *See* WIPO, Matters Concerning Intellectual Property Genetic Resources Traditional Knowledge and Folklore, Doc. No. WO/GA/26/6 (25 Aug. 2000).
⁷⁹ *See* WIPO Doc. WIPO/GRTKF/IC/2/3 ¶ 1 (10 Sept. 2001). *See also* Cottier & Panizzon, above n. 63.

Principles for Intellectual Property Clauses of Contractual Agreements Concerning Access to Genetic Resources and Benefit-Sharing," a tool kit for the formulation of bioprospecting contracts, and the preparation of technical guides for patent offices concerning the protection of traditional knowledge in their search activities.[80]

III. The Treaty on Plant Genetic Resources

The TRIPS Agreement is primarily concerned with Members' obligations to establish a legal infrastructure to solidify the privatization of intellectual property rights on a transnational scale. Article 27.3(b) permits the extension of those private rights to genetic resources. The TRIPS Agreement is seen by some to be in tension with the Convention on Biological Diversity, which is concerned with conserving the "global genetic commons" for humankind.[81] The Conference of the Parties (COP) to the CBD has reported that the value and benefit of genetic materials in the global biosphere may be realized and shared through intellectual property rights.[82] The COP Secretariat has also noted the importance in the relationship between trade and biological diversity of the interrelationship between the TRIPS Agreement and the CBD.[83] The COP Panel of Experts on Access and Benefit Sharing concluded that IPRs were a significant influence upon benefit-sharing,[84] but consensus has not been achieved within the COP on whether this influence is positive or negative.

A significant recent development, which will have an important impact upon the negotiation of access to plant genetic resources, was the promulgation in November 2001 of the Treaty on Plant Genetic Resources.[85] This Treaty was the enactment in a binding form of the International Undertaking on

---

[80] Id.
[81] See, e.g., CBD, above n. 64, art. 2. See also F. MCCONNELL, THE BIODIVERSITY CONVENTION. A NEGOTIATING HISTORY (Kluwer 1996); L. Glowka et al., A Guide to the Convention on Biological Diversity (IUCN 1994).
[82] Conference of Parties, Convention on Biological Diversity, The impact of intellectual property rights systems on the conservation and sustainable use of biological diversity and on the equitable sharing of benefits from its use, ENEP/CBD/COP/3/22 (22 Sept. 1996).
[83] Conference of Parties, Convention on Biological Diversity, The Convention on Biological Diversity and the Agreement on Trade Related Intellectual Property Rights: Relationships and Synergies, UNEP/CBD/COP/3/23 (5 Oct. 1996).
[84] Conference of Parties, Convention on Biological Diversity, Report of panel of experts on access and benefit sharing, UNEP/CBD/COP/5/8 (2 Nov. 1999).
[85] International Treaty on Plant Genetic Resources for Food and Agriculture, opened for signature 3 Nov. 2001, official text available at http://www.fao.org/ag/cgrfa/IU.htm [hereinafter PGR Treaty]. See also Laurence Helfer, Using Intellectual Property Rights to Preserve the Global Genetic Commons: The International Treaty on Plant Genetic Resources for Food and Agriculture [this volume].

Plant Genetic Resources, which had been adopted by the 1983 Conference of the FAO.[86]

The International Undertaking had originally been predicated on the principle that plant genetic resources for food and agriculture (PGRFA) should be freely exchanged as a "heritage of mankind" and should be preserved through international conservation efforts. In subsequent years, the principle of free exchange was gradually narrowed by the impact of intellectual property rights upon agriculture. In November 1989, the 25th Session of the FAO Conference adopted two resolutions providing an "agreed interpretation" that plant breeders' rights were not incompatible with the Undertaking. The acknowledgment of compatibility for plant variety rights obviously benefited industrialized countries, which were active in seed production. In exchange for this concession, developing countries won endorsement of the concept of "farmers' rights."[87]

Subsequent negotiations on the text of the International Undertaking sought to reconcile the proposition that PGFRA were the common heritage of mankind with the sovereignty of states over their plant genetic resources. The Treaty on Plant Genetic Resources represents an attempt to resolve this tension in a formal instrument.

The objectives of the Treaty as stated in article 1 are "the conservation and sustainable use of plant genetic resources for food and agriculture and the fair and equitable sharing of the benefits arising out of their use, in harmony with the Convention on Biological Diversity, for sustainable agriculture and food security."[88]

Article 4 of the Treaty requires signatories "where appropriate" to "promote an integrated approach to the exploration, conservation and sustainable use of plant genetic resources for food and agriculture." Article 10.2 contains the agreement of the Contracting Parties to "establish a multilateral system, which is efficient, effective and transparent, both to facilitate access to [PGFRA] and to share, in a fair and equitable way, the benefits arising from the utilization of these resources, on a complementary and mutually reinforcing basis."[89] Facilitated access to PGFRA is to be provided in accordance with the conditions prescribed in article 12.3. Paragraph (d) of this provision declares that the recipients "shall not claim any intellectual property or other rights that limit the facilitated access" to PGFRA, or their "genetic parts or components," in the form received from the Multilateral System.[90] However, this clause does not prevent private parties from

---

[86] International Undertaking on Plant Genetic Resources for Food and Agriculture [hereinafter FAO International Undertaking].

[87] Farmers' Rights is generally understood as referring to the recognition of the contribution which traditional farmers have made to the development of new crop types through conserving of plant genetic resources and transmitting them to seed companies, plant breeders and research institutions. *See* below nn. 94–99 and accompanying text.

[88] Treaty on Plant Genetic Resources, above n. 85, art. 1.

[89] *Id*. arts. 4, 10.2   [90] *Id*. art. 12.3

claiming intellectual property rights in relation to germplasm that is modified by the recipient.[91]

Article 13.1 recognizes that benefits accruing from facilitated access to PGFRA shall be shared fairly and equitably. Article 13.2 envisages that the sharing of benefits should include the exchange of technical information, access to technology, capacity building and the sharing of monetary benefits from commercialization.[92]

Article 28 provides that the Treaty enters into force, ninety days after accession by forty countries. Until that date, the International Undertaking will remain operative.[93]

IV. Farmers' Rights

Article 9 of the International Treaty on Plant Genetic Resources for Food and Agriculture implements the proposal, first developed under the International Undertaking, that called for legal recognition of farmers' rights. The policy behind this recognition is stated in article 9.1, namely that

> The Contracting Parties recognize the enormous contribution that the local and indigenous communities and farmers of all regions of the world, particularly those in the centres of origin and crop diversity, have made and will continue to make for the conservation and development of plant genetic resources which constitute the basis of food and agriculture production throughout the world.[94]

Article 9.2 envisages that "the responsibility for realizing Farmers' Rights, as they relate to Plant Genetic Resources for Food and Agriculture, rests with national governments" and that national legislation should include measures relating to:

(i) protection of traditional knowledge relevant to plant genetic resources for food and agriculture;
(ii) the right to equitably participate in sharing benefits arising from the utilization of plant genetic resources for food and agriculture;
(iii) the right to participate in making decisions, at the national level, on matters related to the conservation and sustainable use of plant genetic resources for food and agriculture.[95]

Finally, article 9.3 provides that this article shall not be interpreted "to limit any rights that farmers have to save, use, exchange and sell farm-saved seed/propagating material."[96]

---

[91] *See also* Helfer, above n. 85 (discussing controversial nature of, and latent ambiguities in, this provision).
[92] Treaty on Plant Genetic Resources, above n. 85, arts 13.1, 13.2.
[93] *Id.* art. 28.   [94] *Id.* art. 9.1.   [95] *Id.* art 9.2.   [96] *Id.* art 9.3.

An assumption of article 9.1 is that the landraces used by traditional farmers are a dynamic genetic reservoir for the development of new varieties and for the transmission of desirable genetic traits. The traditional knowledge of local and indigenous communities is similarly perceived. While the goal of remunerating these groups for their past contributions to the development of plant genetic resources for food and agriculture production elicits little argument, the nature, quantum and distribution of this remuneration remains controversial.

Inevitably, any calculation of the equitable share that traditional farmers and indigenous communities might enjoy under a farmers' rights or traditional knowledge regime will be arbitrary. However the intellectual property system is no stranger to arbitrary calculations, for example, the twenty year length of a patent term that is intended to provide an opportunity for the compensation of all inventors, whatever the area of technology.[97] Similarly, the 25 years of exclusivity that the UPOV Convention provides for new varieties of trees and vines, takes no account of variations in R&D costs between the different varieties.[98]

The principal ways in which plant genetic resources are translated into food and agriculture production is through plant breeding and plant patenting. Standing at the heart of a farmers' rights regime is the concept of the equitable sharing of benefits with farmers for their contribution to innovations in plant breeding and plant patenting. It is estimated that about 6.5 percent of all genetic research undertaken in agriculture is focused upon germplasm derived from wild species and landraces.[99]

Article 9.2 obliges the Contracting Parties to the Plant Genetic Resources Treaty "to take measures," subject to their national legislation to protect and promote farmers' rights. The content of these rights is defined in the balance of that provision and embraces the protection of traditional knowledge, equitable benefit sharing and the right to participate in decision making. The Treaty leaves open the legal context within which farmers' rights are to be enacted.[100]

National legislation on farmers' rights tends to combine one of the versions of UPOV with some of the access principles set out in the CBD. The African Model Legislation for the Protection of the Rights of Local Communities, Farmers and Breeders, and for the Regulation of Access to Biological Resources, which was adopted by the OAU Heads of States Summit at Ouagadougou in June 1998, adopts a *sui generis* regime based on UPOV 1991.[101]

---

[97] TRIPS Agreement, above n. 40, art 33.   [98] UPOV II, above n. 30, art.13.
[99] See R. McNeely, *Biodiversity and Agricultural Development: The Crucial Institutional Issues*, in Tradeoffs or Synergies? Agricultural Intensification, Economic Development and the Environment 399 (D.R. Lee & C.B. Barrett eds., CABI 2001).
[100] Treaty on Plant Genetic Resources, above n. 85, art. 9.2.
[101] Draft African Model Legislation for the Protection of the Rights of Local Communities, Farmers and Breeders and for the Regulation of Access to Biological Resources of the Organization of African Unity (OAU), as contained in Annex III of document OAU/AEC/TD/MIN/7(iii); UPOV II, above n. 30.

However, most national statutes prefer access legislation combined with UPOV 1978.[102]

V. Access to PGRFA and the Doha negotiating agenda

In the same month that the International Treaty on Plant Genetic Resources for Food and Agriculture was concluded, the WTO Ministerial Meeting in Doha issued a Ministerial Declaration that set out the negotiating agenda for the next round of the multilateral trade negotiations within the WTO framework.[103] Article 19 of the Declaration instructed the Council for TRIPS, in pursuing its work program, "to examine, *inter ali*a, the relationship between the TRIPS Agreement and the Convention on Biological Diversity, the protection of traditional knowledge and folklore, and other relevant new developments" raised by Members pursuant to a general review of the TRIPS Agreement.[104]

Pursuant to this direction, the TRIPS Council has commissioned a number of studies on access to PGFRA in the context of the development objectives of the TRIPS Agreement. At the same time, the World Intellectual Property Organization has established an Intergovernmental Committee to consider the access issue in the light of case studies it has undertaken on the utilization of traditional knowledge in the exploitation of intellectual property rights.

The primary significance of bringing the access issue within the purview of the TRIPS Agreement is that this Agreement has been implemented by most countries, including the United States. Any access rules developed under TRIPS will thus be globally enforceable.

Paragraph 31 of the Ministerial Declaration calls for negotiations limited to "the relationship between existing WTO rules and specific trade obligations set out in multilateral environmental agreements," while preserving the rights of WTO members that are not parties to the treaty in question.[105] In his report for FAO on plant genetic resources, Professor Laurence Helfer has suggested that taken together, the foregoing provisions suggest that the Doha Round of trade negotiations "has opened a window of opportunity for states seeking to balance the protection of plant breeders' rights against other societal objectives."[106] Thus, it is posited, for example that the TRIPS Agreement could be amended to require countries to oblige every applicant seeking a patent or protection of a new plant variety to disclose the origin of plant genetic material upon which the invention or variety is based, or to demonstrate that the material was acquired with the prior informed consent of the country or community of origin.

---

[102] Examples of this approach include the Andean Community's Common System on Access to Genetic Resources (1996); Costa Rica Biodiversity Law (1998); India Community Intellectual Property Rights Act (1999); and Seeds and Plant Varieties Act (1975).
[103] WTO Ministerial Declaration. WT/MIN(01)/DEC/W/1 (14 Nov. 2001).
[104] *Id.* art. 19. [105] *Id.* art. 31. [106] Helfer, above n. 34.

PART III

Sectoral issues: Essential medicines and traditional knowledge

SECTION 1
Developing and distributing essential medicines

15

Managing the Hydra: The herculean task of ensuring access to essential medicines

FREDERICK M. ABBOTT[*]

I. The concept of essential medicines
II. Public goods, private markets and public finance
    A. Public goods and private markets
    B. Pandemics and public finance
    C. The political dimension
        1. The question of leadership
        2. At the national level
            a. Developed country side
            b. Developing country side
        3. At the multilateral level
    D. Socio-cultural factors and political responses
III. Regulatory obstacles and responses
    A. Regulatory streamlining
    B. Intersection of regulatory review and patents
    C. Rights in data and solutions
IV. Intellectual property related obstacles and responses
    A. Patents as obstacles
    B. Solutions to the problems posed by patents
        1. Compulsory licensing and government use
        2. Paragraph 7 and Least-Developed Countries
        3. Parallel trade and differential pricing
        4. Disciplining ancillary IPRs
V. Bulk procurement and related mechanisms
VI. Local production, transfer of technology, and the public sector
VII. Research and development
    A. The general R&D problem
    B. Drugs for neglected diseases
VIII. The emergence of competitors
IX. Conclusions – The hydra without Hercules

---

[*] Edward Ball Eminent Scholar Professor of International Law, Florida State University College of Law.

> It is one thing to describe the Augean stables - another thing to clean them
>
> Myres S. McDougal

I. The concept of essential medicines

The task of ensuring access to essential medicines presents a complex and embedded set of problems that will remain a persistent feature of the international governance landscape for the foreseeable future. According to the definition provided by the World Health Organization (WHO):

> Essential medicines are those that satisfy the priority health care needs of the population. They are selected with due regard to public health relevance, evidence on efficacy and safety, and comparative cost-effectiveness. Essential medicines are intended to be available within the context of functioning health systems at all times in adequate amounts, in the appropriate dosage forms, with assured quality and adequate information, and at a price the individual and the community can afford.[1]

The WHO's recommended list of essential medicines has been developed with a view to aiding procurement authorities in determining the supplies needed to treat local populations. The price of medicines is a significant factor in determining what should be included on the list since there is small utility in recommending expensive therapies that are not affordable. As the WHO observes:

> In developing countries, newer combination antimalarial medicines may be 30–200 times more expensive than chloroquine; medicines to treat multi-drug resistant tuberculosis may cost 20–30 times more than the usual DOTS treatment; and treatment of HIV/AIDS with anti-retroviral medicines may cost between $400–2500 per year.
>
> Most medicines budgets in developing countries are below $30 per person per year, with 38 countries having less than $2 per person per year.[2]

Nonetheless, the most recent WHO Essential Medicines list includes a significant number of antiretroviral medicines (ARVs) that are under patent.[3] These drugs may not be affordable for many HIV-positive individuals, even

---

[1] Introduction to World Health Organization's (WHO) 12th Model List of Essential Medicines, *available at* http://www.who.int/medicines.

[2] The Selection of Essential Medicines, WHO Policy Perspectives on Medicines No. 4 (June 2002), *available at* http://www.who.int/medicines.

[3] The following antiretroviral (ARVs) medicines are included on the 12th Model List: Nucleoside reverse transcriptase inhibitors (1) Abacavir (ABC) (2) Didanosine (ddI) (3) Lamivudine (3TC) (4) Stavudine (d4T) (5) Zidovudine (ZDV or AZT); Non-nucleoside reverse transcriptase inhibitors (1) Efavirenz (EFV or EFZ) (2) Nevirapine (NVP); Protease inhibitors (1) Indinavir (IDV) (2) Ritonavir (3) Lopinavir + Ritonavir (LPV/r) (4) Nelfinavir saquinavir (SQV) (NFV). The Model List is revised periodically.

taking into account recent price declines, unless public health budgets in developing countries are supplemented by international assistance.

The world community is presently confronted with tremendous public health challenges due to HIV/AIDS, malaria and tuberculosis. Yet, populations around the world, and especially in developing and least-developed countries, face heavy public health burdens from many sources, including other infectious diseases, diarrheal diseases, cancer, diabetes, heart and circulatory disease, and other conditions.[4] While HIV/AIDS is the most immediate problem, it is not enough to address only this scourge.

Although there has been considerable public debate concerning the effect of patents on access to medicines, ensuring adequate supplies involves an extensive regulatory framework encompassing a multiplicity of factors. These include:

- Research and Development
- Safety and Efficacy (including Liability)
- Manufacturing Systems and Controls (Good Manufacturing Practices)
- Intellectual Property
- Procurement, Distribution and Dispensing
- Health Care Personnel and Infrastructure
- Financing

Each of these elements in the essential medicines supply chain can and does act as a roadblock. Yet, each element is present for a reason. It is not helpful to supply inexpensive medicines if they are not safe and effective, or if they are prescribed to treat the wrong condition.

II. Public goods, private markets and public finance

The supply of essential medicines is a "public goods" problem in the sense that the private market does not adequately address it. Health care systems throughout the world require an array of low-cost medicines – some under patent by originators, some not - for distribution through public hospitals and clinics. But the provision of health care services is not limited to the public sector, even in the lowest-income countries.

---

[4] *See* Annex Table 3 of the World Health Organization, World Health Report 2002. In Africa, HIV/AIDS is the number one killer, with malaria, diarrheal disease and respiratory infections also major killers. Yet, cancer, cardiovascular disease and non-infectious respiratory disease are also major causes of premature death. In South-East Asia, cancer, cardiovascular disease and diabetes are major causes of premature death, along with HIV/AIDS, diarrheal diseases, TB and measles. Cardiovascular disease and cancer are major killers throughout the Americas. Many of the disease burdens disproportionately affect children.

A. Public goods and private markets

If the concept of "public goods" is limited to goods and services supplied by governments and non-governmental organizations (NGOs), then the problem of providing access to essential medicines might be described as a mixed public goods-private market problem. Consumers of health care services from private doctors and pharmacists require low-cost medicines just as consumers using public providers.

B. Pandemics and public finance

Even if the private market might be adapted in the general case to address the demand for essential medicines, pandemic scale public health problems, such as HIV/AIDS are beyond the capacity of market mechanisms. Pandemic scale public health problems overwhelm the financial capacity of developing countries, and they require international cooperation and a multilateral financial response.

The establishment of the Global Fund, and the more recent adoption by the United States of legislation to substantially increase funding of efforts to treat the HIV/AIDS pandemic, are steps in the right direction. Nevertheless, even assuming that the United States fulfills its recent promises, the budgeted amounts fall far short of that needed for a comprehensive response.

C. The political dimension

At the heart of the essential medicines problem is the lack of political will to address it. Whether the question is one of increasing public funding or adapting private market mechanisms to better accommodate the needs of individuals in differing economic circumstances, change cannot take place without the support of decision-makers in control of national governments and multilateral institutions.

1. The question of leadership

Within each nation, the public health budget competes with other governmental interests for priority. This reality prevails not only in countries that lack resources, but also in countries where there are substantial resources that are not directed toward the goals of disease prevention and treatment.

The problem of delivering treatment for the HIV/AIDS pandemic, while perhaps atypical among global public health problems, helps illustrate the political difficulties in ensuring access. Because the need to address HIV/AIDS is so apparent, the failure of political leadership to act calls attention to the difficulties affecting less striking problems.

2. At the national level

It is useful to compare and contrast leadership issues in the very different contexts of developed and developing countries.

a. Developed country side   Using the United States to illustrate the developed country side, the government provides massive medicines research funding through its National Institutes of Health (NIH), the bulk of which is directed to addressing disease problems in the United States.[5] Since many diseases, including HIV/AIDS, affect both the U.S. and developing countries, the NIH funding does indeed create "potential" public goods that are useful to developing countries. Yet, the medicines that result from NIH-funded research are patented (directly or indirectly) by pharmaceutical enterprises, and the pricing practices of these enterprises determine the level of access to them in developing countries.[6]

The U.S. Congress in early 2003 approved legislation authorizing a substantial increase in funds for treatment of HIV/AIDS in selected developing countries.[7] This may reflect a turning point in the formation of political will on the developed country side, but at least until now, budget allocations have been far too low to meaningfully address HIV/AIDS, let alone the other public health problems affecting developing countries.

The U.S. faces budgeting and resource constraints. Although these constraints may differ in scale from those affecting developing countries, they are nevertheless real. A decision to allocate a significant portion of the U.S. budget to aid for developing-country public health problems requires the support of local constituencies that are in a position to make competing resource demands.

Critical decisions concerning public health policy outside the United States are typically relegated to executive agencies concerned with commercial affairs,

---

[5] "The NIH, of course, is the focal point for American health research, spending about $28 billion a year pursuing basic research into cancer, heart disease, diabetes, AIDS and other life-threatening diseases. Most of the U.S. advances in health in the past 30 years have come from the agency that Dr. Zerhouni now heads." Moderator: Tammy Lytle, National Press Club President, Biomedical Challenges, National Press Club Luncheon with Dr. Elias Zerhouni, Director, National Institutes of Health (6 Mar. 2003). The Director of NIH, Dr. Elias Zerhouni, was recently quoted as follows:

> There's no doubt that NIH has been a terrific federal investment. It has been at the basis, if you will, of most of the discoveries made in the past 50 years that have advanced our health. Of over 100 Nobel prizes, half of all the American Nobel prizes have been trained or funded, developed with NIH's help. *Id.*

[6] *See* below discussion of NIH policies.
[7] Amy Goldstein & Dan Morgan, *Bush Signs $15 Billion AIDS Bill; Funding Questioned*, WASH. POST, 28 May 2003, at A2.

rather than health. External medicines policy has been determined principally by the U.S. Trade Representative (USTR), who has consistently represented the interests of the U.S. research-based pharmaceutical sector.[8] There has been little practical consideration given to the question of access to medicines in developing countries. There is a minimal voting constituency with an interest in external patents policy. The only counterbalance to a strictly commercially-oriented external policy is provided by NGOs. This contrasts with growing interest among U.S. consumers in domestic medicines patent policy, particularly as it affects pricing and access.

The problems arising from the ability of the external commercial trade apparatus to exercise control over medicines policy is becoming increasingly serious, because the United States has decided to override the flexibilities built into the TRIPS Agreement by negotiating high patent protection terms in bilateral and regional agreements.[9] This forum-shifting policy threatens to undermine progress that developing countries may otherwise make in obtaining lower-priced access to medicines through use of those flexibilities.

Secretary of State Colin Powell recently has begun to take a more visible role on HIV/AIDS questions, particularly with respect to Africa.[10] This is a positive

---

[8] The USTR is responsible for negotiating U.S. trade agreements, and as such is responsible for the drafting of provisions concerning protection of intellectual property rights (IPRs), data protection and related regulatory issues. The principal U.S. industry lobbying group for the domestic R&D based pharmaceutical industry is PhRMA (the Pharmaceutical Research and Manufacturers of America), see http://www.phrma.org. The President of PhRMA, Allen Holmer, is a former senior USTR official. PhRMA submits an annual Special 301 report to USTR setting out its objective on protection of IPRs (posted *id.*). USTR positions at the WTO on medicines issues typically restate positions developed and published by PhRMA, and USTR has recently advised developing country delegates in TRIPS negotiations that they should deal directly with the pharmaceutical industry to satisfy their concerns. *See, e.g., U.S. Wants Resolution to TRIPS, Public Health Debate Before Cancun*, INSIDE U.S. TRADE, 4 Apr. 2003.

[9] *See* Peter Drahos, Developing Countries and International Intellectual Property Standard-Setting, CIPR Background Paper (2002) (published in 5 J. WORLD INTELL. PROP. 765 (Sept. 2002)).

[10] For example, a recent article reports the following news:

> Powell, in a round of interviews on postwar Iraq, has been mentioning the issue frequently, saying that Bush will push even harder to advance the AIDS initiative.
>
> "Why? Because it's the biggest killer on the face of the earth, more so than any army, any regional instability, or anything anybody can imagine a weapon of mass destruction can do," Powell told US News & World Report. "The greatest weapon of mass destruction today on the face of the earth is the HIV virus, and it is a destroyer of people, families, nations, societies, and hopes in the poorest parts of the world. And it is spreading."

John Donnelly, *Bush to Seek Action on $15b AIDS Plan*, BOSTON GLOBE, 29 Apr. 2003, at A8.

development on the political side in the sense that it should facilitate additional financial support for treatment. However, the extent to which the State Department will broadly support access to medicines for developing countries remains an open question. The State Department was very active in the campaign the U.S. waged against South Africa over implementation of the Medicines Amendment Act,[11] and it has been an ardent supporter of pharmaceutical industry interests.

As regards financial support, the United States has done more than Europe to support access to medicines in developing countries, so it is not a matter of singling out the former. The European Commission is nearly as aggressive as USTR in representing the interests of the E.U. pharmaceutical sector,[12] and one of the reasons it can act in a somewhat more balanced way in multilateral forums is that it knows the U.S. will do some of its work for it. Since the European Commission and the E.U. member states are tough in their dealings with pharmaceutical companies at home (demanding strong price controls and other concessions), there is perhaps an even starker contrast between domestic and foreign policy in the E.U. than in the United States.

b. Developing country side The need for and importance of political leadership is perhaps even more apparent when viewing the developing countries. To take HIV/AIDS as an example once again, only a few developing country governments have made treatment a national priority, such as Botswana, Brazil, Thailand and Uganda.[13] Others, such as China, India, Russia and

---

[11] *See, e.g.*, Letter of Barbara Larkin, Assistant Secretary, Legislative Affairs, U.S. Dep't of State (5 June 1999) (enclosing Report on U.S. Government Efforts to Negotiate the Repeal, Termination or Withdrawal of Article 15(C) of the South African Medicines and Related Substances Act of 1965), *quoted in* Frederick M. Abbott, *The TRIPS-Legality of Measures Taken to Address Public Health Crises: Responding to USTR-State-Industry Positions that Undermine the WTO*, *in* THE POLITICAL ECONOMY OF INTERNATIONAL TRADE: ESSAYS IN HONOR OF ROBERT E. HUDEC 311, fn. 20 (Daniel L.M. Kennedy & James D. Southwick eds. Cambridge University Press 2002).

[12] The European Commission, for example, joined the United States in aggressively threatening South Africa for its adoption of the Medicines and Related Substances Control Amendments Act, Act 90 of 1997.

[13] The extent of success of these national programs differs, and depends on the level of financial resources available to address the problems. Brazil is a high income developing country that has instituted a program of universal access to public treatment for HIV/AIDS, and it has engaged in tough bargaining with the pharmaceutical industry over medicines prices (including the threat of compulsory licensing). Uganda has expressed strong political commitment to solutions, but is far more constrained by its budget. *See, e.g.*, Tina Rosenberg, *Look at Brazil*, N.Y. TIMES MAGAZINE, 28 Jan. 2001, at 26; Geoff Dyer & Amy Kazmin, *Thai Agency will Begin Production of Drug for AIDS*, FIN. TIMES, 17 Oct. 2002, at 12; *Lessons from Uganda's AIDS Success Story*, DAILY NEWS (HARARE), 26 Feb. 2003; Sudarsan Raghavan, *Botswana Wages Struggle Against AIDS*, KNIGHT RIDDER/TRIB. BUS. NEWS, 8 July 2003.

South Africa, have not made comparable commitments, even though the budgets of these countries would allow them to do considerably more.[14]

Each national political situation is different, and there is no question that for many countries dealing with HIV/AIDS, treatment will constitute a major financial burden. Even so, the difficulties of establishing a treatment program hardly excuse failing to do whatever lies within the government's means.

Consider the case of South Africa. Although its President at some stage questioned the link between HIV and AIDS, the absence of a meaningful treatment program until now resulted from additional factors. There has been skepticism about the efficacy of ARV treatment among the top echelon of the ruling political party (ANC). The HIV/AIDS problem predominantly affects the black population, and the white minority population (which owns the vast preponderance of productive assets) placed little pressure on the government to address it, at least until it appeared that corporate earnings might be affected. The government initially viewed ARV treatment largely in terms of the ongoing costs of medicines, without factoring in the impact on the economy if treatment were not provided. The local Pharmaceutical Manufacturers Association (PMA) fights with the government over any steps taken to promote low-cost access, and uses its financial resources to hire the country's small pool of specialist lawyers.

The government is meanwhile attempting to pull off one of the most difficult economic and social transitions attempted in modern history. It seeks to empower a majority population that was systematically excluded from property ownership, wealth accumulation and higher education, while at the same time providing an environment that will encourage the privileged minority to remain. The human catastrophe in Zimbabwe is a continuing reminder of what might happen if the government gets it wrong.[15]

None of the complexities of South African politics excuses the government's failure to implement an adequate HIV/AIDS treatment program, but they do illustrate the roadblocks that must be overcome. In the first instance, however, it will be difficult to overcome these and other obstacles if governments do not view public health as a priority.

---

[14] The failure of China, India, Russia and South Africa so far to implement effective treatment programs is well chronicled. *See, e.g.,* Geoff Dyer, *CIA Warns of New Frontiers in AIDS Epidemic: US Intelligence Predicts Russia, China and India Will Head a New Wave of Nations Falling Victim to HIV Infection,* FIN. TIMES, 4 Oct. 2002, at 10; *Number of HIV Carriers Hit 850,000 in China,* XINHUA ECON. NEWS SERVICE, 12 Apr. 2002, LEXIS; Sam Vaknin, *Europe's New Plague,* UNITED PRESS INT'L, 3 Dec. 2002; Shefalee Vasudev with Suman K. Chakrabarti, Nidhi Taparia Rathi & Amarnath K. Menon, *AIDS: The Mess,* INDIA TODAY, 9 Dec. 2002, at 42.

[15] Observations concerning South Africa are based on the author's experiences in that country and conversations with persons in and outside the government.

3. At the multilateral level

Many multilateral institutions, as well as regional institutions, are responsible for addressing some aspect of the essential medicines problem. These include the World Health Organization (WHO), other parts of the United Nations system (including UNAIDS, the Global Fund, the UN High Commissioner for Human Rights, the United Nations Development Program (UNDP), the United Nations Conference on Trade and Development (UNCTAD) and the World Intellectual Property Organization (WIPO), the International Monetary Fund (IMF), World Bank and World Trade Organization (WTO). Taking as a starting point that multilateral institutions have not as yet provided an adequate response to the demand for essential medicines, a few of the problems affecting the multilateral governance structure may be considered.

Multilateral institutions have different priorities, and not infrequently they work at cross purposes. The mandate of the WHO is to promote access to medicines,[16] and it pursues this objective by providing advice to developing countries regarding ways in which medicines can be obtained at lower prices. They also provide TRIPS-consistent legal advice regarding ways to overcome the obstacles posed by patent protection, including government use licensing and parallel importation.[17] The mandate of WIPO is to promote intellectual property protection.[18] WIPO representatives routinely encourage developing countries to adopt and maintain strict standards of IP protection and to avoid implementing or using the flexibilities recognized in the TRIPS Agreement. Two directly conflicting sets of advice can be given by WHO and WIPO to patent authorities and to trade and public health officials at the same meeting.[19] Given the divergent

---

[16] *See e.g.*, Constitution of the World Health Organization, arts. 1, 2, *at* http://www.who.int.

[17] *See, e.g., TRIPS, Globalization and Access to Essential Pharmaceuticals*, WHO Policy Perspectives on Medicines No. 3. (Mar. 2001).

[18] *See* Convention Establishing the World Intellectual Property Organization, 14 July 1967 (as amended on 28 Sept. 1979), 21 U.S.T. 1749, 828 U.N.T.S. 3, art. 3, providing:

> The objectives of the Organization are:
>
> (i) to promote the protection of intellectual property throughout the world through cooperation among States and, where appropriate, in collaboration with any other international organization.

[19] The author represented WHO at the first WIPO-WTO joint workshop for least-developed countries on the implementation of the TRIPS Agreement, held in Tanzania, 22–25 April 2002. After the author presented the special flexibilities on patents incorporated into paragraph 7 of the Doha Declaration on the TRIPS Agreement and Public Health (WT/MIN(01)/DEC/2 (14 Nov. 2001) [hereinafter Doha Declaration], the WIPO representative (Ms. Karen Lee) told the attendees that WIPO had been advised by friends in the pharmaceutical industry that they would cure AIDS within the next few years but only if strong patent protection was maintained, so the least-developed countries should not do anything that might weaken the protection afforded by patents.

perspectives of the various multilateral institutions, it perhaps is not surprising that their activities in respect of public health and medicines are not coordinated.

Multilateral institutions operate on instructions from national governments and have limited "independence." Although some secretariats, for example, the International Bureau at WIPO, play a significant role in policy formulation and execution, for the most part it is difficult for the secretariats to act without a clear mandate from national delegations. To the extent that the more economically and politically powerful delegations exercise significant control over the policies of the multilateral institutions, the latters' independence is further constrained. Part of this control emanates from the fact that powerful countries provide the preponderance of budgetary support for operations.

National governments appear substantially more susceptible to industry capture in their external relations dealings than in domestic affairs. In the United States, for example, the Office of the U.S. Trade Representative (USTR) appears to act almost exclusively at the behest of producer interests. This bias is particularly glaring in respect to the pharmaceutical sector and medicines issues where, in recent negotiations, the USTR has encouraged foreign governments to deal directly with the U.S. pharmaceutical industry to provide it an adequate level of comfort.[20] For the European Union as well, the disjunction between the way the pharmaceutical sector is treated as a matter of intra-Union regulation and the way it is promoted abroad is remarkable. At the intra-Union level the industry is heavily regulated, stringent price controls are imposed, and competition proceedings are initiated. Yet, as regards developing countries, the E.U. supports high levels of protection and open market access for its pharmaceutical sector.

The economics-driven institutions, such as the International Monetary Fund (IMF) and WTO, carry more influence with national governments than "softer" institutions, such as WHO. The WTO, in particular, develops its rules on the basis of bargaining over trade concessions. The pharmaceutical industry in countries belonging to the Organization for Economic Cooperation and Development (OECD) may obtain higher standards of patent protection (as it did in the Uruguay Round) in exchange for the grant of increased market access for textiles. From the standpoint of world public health, this is a very questionable means for establishing policy.

The United States has in recent years pursued policies with respect to the protection of its pharmaceutical sector that threaten to further weaken the multilateral governance framework. In particular, it has negotiated and concluded bilateral and regional free trade agreements that use the standards of the

---

[20] See *U.S. Wants Resolution*, above n. 8 (referring to Geneva press conference of U.S. Deputy Trade Representative Peter Allgeier referencing efforts "to foster a dialogue between companies and governments so that they both feel more comfortable"). *See also Pharmaceutical Companies Close to New Joint Position on TRIPS*, INSIDE U.S. TRADE, 11 July 2003.

WTO/TRIPS Agreement as a baseline for protective IP rules, but tighten those rules with so-called "TRIPS-Plus" restrictions. The demands made by the United States in bilateral FTA negotiations go well beyond increased protection of patents, to impact directly on the ways in which countries operate their public health systems.[21]

D. Socio-cultural factors and political responses

Political inattention to essential medicines problems does not arise in a vacuum. Political leaders respond to constituent demands, and constituents are motivated by their social interests. The people affected by the lack of access to essential medicines are the poor, and particularly the poor living in developing countries. A sufficiently influential part of international society does not yet place a value on redressing imbalances between enfranchised and disenfranchised peoples so as to generate demands on the political leadership for action. Absent a change in this value equation, it is doubtful that pressures on political leadership will emerge.

Notwithstanding this bleak reality, opportunities arise precisely because political leaders remain in power by satisfying their constituencies, including voters (in democratic states), financial backers and/or, in some cases, the military. Voting constituencies may be persuaded by effective communicators with access to media. Financial supporters respond to success and failure in securing profits. Military leadership may be influenced by budget allocation and security concerns.

Multilateral institutions, such as the WHO and World Bank, may provide a focal point for developing and disseminating effective, authoritative communication that will influence public voting constituencies. The financial sector will be influenced by allocation of larger budgets, whether for R&D or procurement. Medicines producers may be stimulated by the promise of access to new markets. The opening up of competition may offend the monopolist, but it will encourage those outside its control.

If one is pessimistic concerning the prospects for social value reorientation, a plausible alternative is to seek to redefine the self-interest of the enfranchised part of the global population in terms of redressing gross imbalances; that is Alexis de Tocqueville's "principle of self-interest rightly understood" as applied

---

[21] *See* Frederick M. Abbott, The Doha Declaration on the TRIPS Agreement and Public Health and the Contradictory Trend in Bilateral and Regional Free Trade Agreements, QUNO Occasional Paper 14 (Apr. 2004), *available at* http://www.quno.org; *and* Peter Drahos et al., The FTA and the PBS, Submission to the Australian Senate Select Committee on the U.S.–Australia Free Trade Agreement (2004). *See also* various requests to USTR from U.S. PhRMA in its 2003 Special 301 submission on regulatory concerns, *at* http://www.phrma.org and http://ustr.gov.

to public health.[22] Pointing to a threat to developed country public order based on developing country chaos would appear to be one avenue of persuasion. Yet, the self-interest of developed country individuals in developing country public health is less directly apparent than interests in military defense, and it is not clear that the public in developed countries is prepared to draw the self-interest connection.

The political dimension of the problem of providing access to essential medicines is not amenable to a neat formulaic solution. Designing and implementing solutions requires that political leaders give this a high priority. As noted at the outset, the problem of access is complex, embedded and will be persistent over time.

III. Regulatory obstacles and responses

The current international regulatory framework for medicines is characterized by segregated national and/or regional approval and registration authorities. This creates basic inefficiencies that delay the introduction of medicines into developed and developing country markets. Complex regulatory systems provide an extraordinary opportunity for legal "gaming" in the developed countries.[23] These gaming opportunities are magnified in the developing countries where regulatory systems are less well developed and transparent.

A. Regulatory streamlining

The proper focus of medicines regulatory systems must be to assure the quality, safety and efficacy of medicines, and not to act as a supplement to patent protection. Until recently, most countries have required that their public

---

[22] De Tocqueville observed:

> The Americans, on the other hand, are fond of explaining almost all the actions of their lives by the principle of self-interest rightly understood; they show with complacency how an enlightened regard for themselves constantly prompts them to assist one another and inclines them willingly to sacrifice a portion of their time and property to the welfare of the state. In this respect I think they frequently fail to do themselves justice, for in the United States as well as elsewhere people are sometimes seen to give way to those disinterested and spontaneous impulses that are natural to man; but the Americans seldom admit that they yield to emotions of this kind; they are more anxious to do honor to their philosophy than to themselves.
> ALEXIS DE TOCQUEVILLE, DEMOCRACY IN AMERICA, bk. II, ch. 8
>
> (From the Henry Reeve Translation, revised and corrected, 1839).

[23] See U.S. Federal Trade Commission, Generic Drug Entry Prior to Patent Expiration: An FTC Study (2002), http://www.ftc.gov/os/2002/07/genericdrugstudy.pdf [hereinafter FTC Orange Book Study].

health regulatory authorities approve each medicine placed into circulation, in some cases relying on decisions by foreign regulatory authorities. This situation imposes substantial burdens on registration authorities and creates inefficiencies that operate to the detriment of developing countries.

The WHO has initiated a program of prequalifying medicines with respect to quality, safety and efficacy, which includes certifying good manufacturing practices (GMP) of facilities producing them.[24] By relying on this WHO prequalification system, developing country regulators can avoid duplicating key medicines regulatory functions. However, the WHO prequalification program – while applauded by public health specialists for its role in accelerating access to HIV/AIDS treatments – has had difficulty obtaining the funding necessary to continue or expand its operation. While the program has drawn its regulators and inspectors from recognized European medicines authorities, the United States has so far indicated that only U.S. FDA approvals may be relied on in connection with the procurement of HIV/AIDS medicines with federal funds.[25]

Any consolidation of regulatory authority at the multilateral level creates a risk of capture by enterprises based in countries that exert a high degree of authority on those institutions. The WHO is not immune from this phenomenon.

B. Intersection of regulatory review and patents

The United States has in place a complex legislative and regulatory system allowing for the review of generic medicines during the patent term of the originator.[26] The so-called "Bolar" exception[27] was coupled with patent term extension.[28] The patent term extension covers the period during which the originator medicine was subject to regulatory review (subject to limitations), and the Bolar exception provides a counterbalance to the extended term by allowing generic producers to enter the market at the end of the term (in theory at least) without also being subject to a regulatory review delay.

---

[24] See website of the WHO Prequalification Project, http://mednet3.who.int/prequal/default.htm.
[25] See Jill Wechsler, *The not-approved-here syndrome: public health officials want to know: why is the United States opposed to the use of cheap generic AIDS drugs?*, PHARM. EXEC. (1 May 2004) (Lexis/Nexis); U.S. Department of Health and Human Services Food and Drug Administration Center for Drug Evaluation and Research (CDER) Guidance for Industry Fixed Dose Combination and Co-Packaged Drug Products for Treatment of HIV (May 2004), CCH Research Network, Guideline, FD&C-ARD ¶ Ñ41,499a.
[26] For a description, see FTC Orange Book Study, above n. 23.
[27] 35 USC § 271(e) (2000) (effectively reversing the decision of the Court of Appeals for the Federal Circuit rejecting a common law regulatory use exception argued as an experimental use defense). See Roche v. Bolar, 733 F.2d 858 (Fed. Cir. 1984).
[28] 35 USC §156 (2000) (extension of patent term).

For developing countries that are required to comply with the patent provisions of the TRIPS Agreement, the adoption of a regulatory review exception is a necessary feature of domestic patent law, which would reduce the harmful effect of monopolies. Whether or not patent term extension is appropriate for the United States, where consumers may be able to afford expensive patented medicines, it is inappropriate for developing countries. These latter countries are not in a position to fund Pharma activities embedded in patented medicines, which include advertising and administrative costs.

Pharma research funds are not spent in developing countries. Neither is a significant portion of Pharma research devoted to diseases of special relevance to developing countries. Indeed, while the benefits of Pharma research in terms of new medicines flow to consumers in developing countries, the cost of such medicines should be kept within their budget capacities.

C. Rights in data and solutions

Rights asserted in data compiled for regulatory purposes are not encompassed within conventional notions of intellectual property,[29] yet they have become one of the main instruments for preventing market entry by generic producers. Perhaps the most significant recent trend in the behavior of Pharma towards developing countries involves the assertion of regulatory data protection claims. At the multilateral level, these claims are based on Article 39.3 of the TRIPS Agreement, which restricts the disclosure of certain data by regulatory authorities and authorizes the originators of "new chemical entities" (NCEs) in the pharmaceutical field to prevent "unfair commercial use" of data regarding those NCEs submitted for regulatory purposes.[30]

The establishment of a multilateral regulatory approval authority under auspices of the WHO might serve to limit the possibility of asserting claims based on unfair commercial use of data submitted for regulatory purposes. If developing country governments allow medicines to be placed on the market by virtue of WHO approval process, there would hardly appear a basis for claiming that the governments or enterprises within their territories took unfair advantage of the relevant data.

---

[29] In 1996, however, the E.U. adopted a hybrid exclusive property right in noncopyrightable collections of data, which deviated from traditional IP concepts. *See, e.g.,* J. H. Reichman, *Database Protection in a Global Economy*, 2002 REVUE INTERNATIONALE DE DROIT ECONOMIQUE 455–504.

[30] Agreement on Trade-Related Aspects of Intellectual Property Rights, 15 Apr. 1994, Marrakesh Agreement Establishing the World Trade Organization, Annex 1c, LEGAL INSTRUMENTS – RESULTS OF THE URUGUAY ROUND Vol. 31, 33 I.L.M. 81 (1994) [hereinafter TRIPS Agreement], art 39.3. *See also* Carlos M. Correa, Protection of Data Submitted for the Registration of Pharmaceuticals: Implementing the Standards of the Trips Agreement (South Centre & World Health Organization 2001).

Public procurement authorities in developing countries are often the purchasers and distributors of medicines for use in public hospitals and clinics, and new medicines that are registered for purchase by such procurement authorities should not be deemed subject to "commercial use." The TRIPS Agreement does not require that registration authorities provide protection against the use of regulatory data for medicines that are procured for use in public health systems.

In other circumstances, the question of whether specific regulatory data may fall within the "unfair commercial use" provision of article 39.3 will depend on the facts. It would appear a rather stretched interpretation of "use" that mere reliance on the granting of registration in a foreign jurisdiction could constitute "use" of data, since there is no access to the data required.[31]

One reason for the shift by Pharma to assertion of claims based on rights in regulatory data is to cover the many situations in which local patents were not obtained on medicines. Without such claims, the introduction of generics could not be blocked under domestic patent law if the regulator's product was unpatented or unpatentable.

The United States has negotiated provisions in free trade agreements specifically designed to block reliance on data submitted for foreign regulatory approvals.[32] The effects of these provisions will vary with individual cases. Marketing approval is typically granted well before expiration of a patent term, so that if the originator of the data is a patent holder in the foreign market, there may be limited effect in extending the patent term. However, if the originator of the data does not hold a patent in the foreign market, then an approval-blocking mechanism in that foreign market will effectively act as a patent for the duration of the blocking term.

---

[31] *See, e.g.,* Correa above n. 30 (tracing legislative history of TRIPS Agreement, above n. 30, art. 39.3 to show that so broad an interpretation was not agreed to by the negotiations).

[32] The U.S.-Singapore FTA provides:

> Article 16.81:
>
> . . .
>
> 2. If a Party provides a means of granting approval to market products specified in paragraph 1 on the basis of the grant of an approval for marketing of the same or similar product in another country, the Party shall defer the date of any such approval to third parties not having the consent of the party providing the information in the other country for a period of at least five years from the date of approval for a pharmaceutical product and ten years from the date of approval for an agricultural chemical product in the Party or in the other country, whichever is later. (available at http://www.ustr.gov)

IV. Intellectual property related obstacles and responses

Patents are in essence financial instruments that permit investors to earn comparatively high returns from the assumption of investment risk. Patent holder behavior can be explained as an effort to maximize the benefits from a financial instrument.[33] All of this is consistent with the observable behavior of the research-based pharmaceutical industry. We may be able to tinker with the patent system so as to improve its responsiveness to the problems of the poor, but this tinkering will not provide a comprehensive solution. The patent is a market-based instrument, and an industry dependent on that instrument cannot be expected to provide solutions to essential medicines problems that are non-market based.

A. *Patents as obstacles*

Patents provide their holders with rights to prevent others from making, using, selling, offering for sale and importing protected products. By preventing the entry onto the market of equivalent products, patents prevent the emergence of competition based on the reduction of production costs while encouraging the innovation that may lead to new competitive products.[34] Although many factors affect the extent to which people have access to essential medicines, it is obvious that each step in lowering the price would enable more people to enter the treatment market.

Patents are complex and non-transparent instruments that have generated extraordinary opportunities for using legal measures to improperly impede the introduction of competitive generic products. Patents are often granted for claims that do not truly satisfy the criteria of patentability,[35] in many countries without substantive examination, and in many (if not all) countries with inadequate

---

[33] Jean Pierre Garnier, the CEO of GlaxoSmithKline, has observed that he is not the head of a charitable institution, and the company he heads should not be expected to behave like one. Sarah Boseley, *Jean Pierre Garnier, Head of Glaxo*, Special AIDS Report, THE GUARDIAN, 18 Feb. 2002, http://www.guardian.co.uk/aids. In his book recounting the sequencing of the human genome, John Sulston remarks at his surprise at discovering the "venality" of the market. JOHN SULSTON & GEORGINA FERRY, THE COMMON THREAD: A STORY OF SCIENCE, POLITICS, ETHICS AND THE HUMAN GENOME (2002). The head of a major World Bank health program recently observed to me that pharmaceutical patent holder behavior is very predictable, and should be accepted for what it is.

[34] See, e.g., Lee Branstetter, *Do Stronger Patents Induce More Local Innovation?* [this volume]

[35] In the United States, where patents are subject to relatively rigorous examination and very few patent claims reach the trial phase, about 30–35% of patents brought to trial are found invalid or unenforceable. Kimberly A. Moore, *Judges, Juries, and Patent Cases – An Empirical Peek Inside the Black Box*, 99 MICH. L. REV. 365, 392 (2002).

examination.[36] Very few patent offices have the expertise necessary to examine complex patent applications in the field of medicines, and those that have such capacity often are overburdened by the large number of applications received.

In the United States, invalid patents were routinely abused to prevent the introduction of generic medicines by listing the products at issue in the Food and Drug Administration's Orange Book.[37] Efforts to curtail these practices formed the basis of recent amendments to U.S. regulations governing the registration of generic medicines.[38] The U.S. is a heavily regulated market in which generic producers have substantial stakes in early entry to the market, and where NGOs monitor the pharmaceutical sector. Similar oversight is often weak or lacking in developing countries, where there is substantially less likelihood that abusive patent practices will be effectively controlled.

Medicines are often protected by multiple patents, and patent searching systems are not designed to identify medicines by their corresponding patents.[39] This creates a situation of legal insecurity for those contemplating the manufacture or procurement of new medicines.

Lawyers in developing countries with training to operate effectively in the patent environment are typically retained by established pharmaceutical enterprises. They do not have an incentive to challenge the validity of patents within their own legal systems.

Legal proceedings to challenge the validity of patents are costly and time-consuming. There are few individuals or enterprises with the incentives necessary to challenge the validity of patents, particularly when this entails confronting patent holders with substantial financial resources. (An incentive might, for example, be provided by a generic producer's prospect of securing a long-term government procurement contract.)

The patenting pattern in sub-Saharan Africa shows a high density of patents on critical ARVs in countries with the capacity to produce medicines and

---

[36] South Africa, for example, grants patents without substantive examination. The patent office of the African Regional Intellectual Property Office (ARIPO), as of 2001 had four patent examiners (presentation by ARIPO representative at Workshop on TRIPS and the Implementation of Its Safeguard in Relation to Pharmaceuticals in the WHO African Region, Harare, Zimbabwe, Aug. 2001).

[37] *See* U.S. Federal Trade Commission, above n. 23. This study found that patents had been grossly abused at the Food and Drug Administration to prevent the entry of generic drugs onto the U.S. market. A principal violator company has been the subject of consent injunction and has paid substantial fines. The U.S. market is subject to relative close monitoring by competition authorities and public interest groups. Yet potential competitive abuse of patents in foreign markets is not within the scope of U.S. antitrust law (absent a direct and substantial impact on the U.S. market), and equivalent capacities for monitoring and enforcement would be the exception in developing Members of the WTO.

[38] Food and Drug Administration Order, 68 Fed. Reg. 36676 (18 June 2003). Technical amendments, 69 Fed. Reg. 11309 (10 Mar. 2004).

[39] *See* Drug Patents under the Spotlight, Médecins Sans Frontières Report (22 May 2003), *available at* http://www.accessmed-msf.org.

comparatively high income. In South Africa, there are approximately twenty patents covering fourteen ARVs and fixed dose combinations.[40] In Zimbabwe, there are eleven patents covering seven ARVs and fixed dose combinations. In Kenya and Uganda there are eleven and ten patents, respectively, on seven and six ARVs and fixed dose combinations.[41]

The introduction of generic ARVs into the South African market has been substantially inhibited by patents. The U.S. and European Union, and their pharmaceutical enterprises, used strong-arm tactics to prevent the implementation of legislation intended to facilitate lower prices for patented medicines, and in doing so distorted the policies of the South African government.[42] Although that government has not been a model of good practices in addressing HIV/AIDS, the clock cannot be turned back to see whether those practices might have been different had the government not been so aggressively attacked. The few South African corporations that have provided ARVs to their workers have paid high patent holder/originator prices, limiting the scope of the programs.[43] NGOs and regional procurement authorities in South Africa continue to be inhibited in purchasing from generic producers in India.[44]

Moreover, despite public statements to the contrary, the research-based pharmaceutical companies are still asserting very strong pressure on South Africa to prevent it from obtaining lower-priced access to medicines. The 2003 Special 301 submission by U.S. PhMRA to USTR accused the South African government of a number of offenses against intellectual property interests.[45]

There is an increasing tendency on the part of the U.S. and E.U. trade negotiators to demand "patent term extension" based on the period during which medicines were under regulatory review as a part of bilateral and regional trade agreements.[46] From the standpoint of developing countries, this represents nothing more than a demand for increased rent payments (i.e., higher medicines prices) with little in the way of countervailing benefits.

---

[40] *Id.*   [41] *Id.*
[42] For some details concerning the abusive character of the litigation brought by the PMA against the government of South Africa, see Frederick M. Abbott, WTO TRIPS Agreement and Its Implications for Access to Medicines in Developing Countries, United Kingdom Commission on Intellectual Property Rights Study Paper 2a (Feb. 2002).
[43] Henri E. Cauvin, *Mining Company to Offer H.I.V. Drugs to Employees*, NY TIMES, 7 Aug. 2002; Claire Bisseker, *AIDS in the workplace – Anglo, De Beers Take Risky Lead in Free Treatment*, FIN. MAIL (South Africa) (16 Aug. 2002).
[44] *See, e.g.*, MÉDECINS SANS FRONTIÈRES/WORLD HEALTH ORGANIZATION, SURMOUNTING CHALLENGES: PROCUREMENT OF ANTIRETROVIRAL MEDICINES IN LOW- AND MIDDLE-INCOME COUNTRIES, § 4.8 (2003).
[45] *See* PhRMA Special 301 submission, above n. 21.
[46] *See* U.S.-Singapore, art. 16.8(4)(a) and U.S.-Chile FTA, art 17.10(2)(a), available at http://www.ustr.gov; each contain a provision extending the term of the patent if its granting is subject to "unreasonable" delay.

B. Solutions to the problems posed by patents

For developing countries seeking improved access to essential medicines, implementation of policies and legislation that would facilitate resort to compulsory and government use licensing provides the principal counterbalance to the adverse impact of patent monopolies.[47] Other strategies to consider include the use of waivers introduced by the Doha Declaration on TRIPS and Public Health, parallel trade, and differential pricing, all of which are briefly discussed below.

1. Compulsory licensing and government use

Compulsory licensing and government use serve several functions:

- They provide a favorable background for all price and licensing negotiations with patent holders;
- They serve as critical bargaining levers in specific negotiations (such as the U.S. Department of Health negotiations with Bayer concerning the price of Cipro and the Brazilian Health Ministry negotiations with Roche concerning the price of Viracept);
- They allow the realization of production by persons other than the patent holder.

The patent law of every country permits the government to use the patent for public purposes.[48] Even if a government use provision is not expressly written

---

[47] The author has addressed this subject in detail in Frederick M. Abbott, *Compulsory Licensing for Public Health Needs: The TRIPS Agenda at the WTO after the Doha Declaration on Public Health*, Quaker United Nations Office Occasional Paper 9 (Feb. 2002), *available at* http://www.quno.org, and in Abbot, above n. 42.

[48] The author is not aware of any patent law that prohibits the government from using patents, though the conditions under which such use is permitted vary. Brazil, South Africa, Switzerland, the United Kingdom and United States provide useful illustrations of the government use theme. For Brazil, see especially Presidential Decree No. 3,201 of 6 October 1999 implementing Article 71 of Law No. 9,279 of 14 May 1996. For South Africa, see Patents Act No. 57 of 1978 (as amended through 1997), which provides:

> 4. A patent shall in all respects have the like effect against the State as it has against a person: Provided that a Minister of State may use an invention for public purposes on such conditions as may be agreed upon with the patentee, or in default of agreement on such conditions as are determined by the commissioner on application by or on behalf of such Minister and after hearing the patentee.

The Swiss Federal Law for Patents on Inventions (of 25 June 1954, as last amended on 24 March 1995) provides:

> B. Expropriation of the Patent
> Art. 32. – (1) If public interest so requires, the Federal Council may wholly or partially expropriate the patent.

into the patent legislation, all governments reserve the right to take property for public purposes, and patents are no special exception to this general principle.[49]

No country facilitates government use of patents better than the United States. Under U.S. patent law, the government and its contractors are free to use any patent without notice to the patent holder, and the patent holder is precluded from obtaining an injunction against such use.[50] The patent holder

> (2) The former owner of an expropriated patent shall be entitled to full compensation which, in case of dispute, shall be fixed by the Federal Court; the provisions of Chapter II of the Federal Law of June 20, 1930, on expropriation shall apply by analogy.

For the United Kingdom, see Patents Act 1977 (as last amended by the Copyright, Designs and Patents Act 1988), arts. 55–59, including "Special provisions as to Crown use during emergency," providing *inter alia*:

> 59.–(1) During any period of emergency within the meaning of this section the powers exercisable in relation to an invention by a government department or a person authorised by a government department under section 55 above shall include power to use the invention for any purpose which appears to the department necessary or expedient –
>
> ...
>
> (b) for the maintenance of supplies and services essential to the life of the community;
>
> (c) for securing a sufficiency of supplies and services essential to the well-being of the community;

For the United States, see below nn. 50–51 and accompanying text.

[49] For an examination of compulsory licensing grounded in public interest or government use provisions, with particular reference to North American law and practice, see generally J.H. REICHMAN WITH CATHERINE HASENZAHL, NONVOLUNTARY LICENSING OF PATENTED INVENTIONS, PART I, HISTORICAL PERSPECTIVE, LEGAL FRAMEWORK UNDER TRIPS AND AN OVERVIEW OF THE PRACTICE IN CANADA AND THE UNITED STATES OF AMERICA (UNCTAD/ICTSD 2002); PART II – THE CANADIAN EXPERIENCE (UNCTAD/ICTSD 2002); PART III – THE LAW AND PRACTICE OF THE UNITED STATES (UNCTAD/ICTSD, Draft 2003) [hereinafter LAW AND PRACTICE OF THE UNITED STATES].

[50] U.S. legislation regulating the Court of Claims, 28 U.S.C. § 1498 (2000) provides:

> (a) Whenever an invention described in and covered by a patent of the United States is used or manufactured by or for the United States without license of the owner thereof or lawful right to use or manufacture the same, the owner's remedy shall be by action against the United States in the United States Court of Federal Claims for the recovery of his reasonable and entire compensation for such use and manufacture.
>
> ...
>
> For the purposes of this section, the use or manufacture of an invention described in and covered by a patent of the United States by a contractor, a subcontractor, or any person, firm, or corporation for the Government and with the authorization or consent of the Government, shall be construed as use or manufacture for the United States.

is given the right to obtain compensation in a proceeding before the Federal Court of Claims. The U.S. essentially uses a liability rule; the government is allowed to use the patent without precondition and for any purpose, but is liable to the patent holder to pay compensation.[51] The United Kingdom and Switzerland each grant the government sweeping authority to use patents.[52]

In the public procurement context, government use licensing provides a good solution to addressing patent monopolies. Patent laws typically subject government use licensing to substantially fewer procedural obstacles than for private compulsory licensing. Often the matter is handled by a decision of the Minister responsible for maintaining the patent register. There is no reason, however, why such authority cannot equally well be delegated to the Health Minister and, through that Minister, to the procurement authority.[53]

Compulsory and government use licensing can be used for importing medicines that are on-patent in the importing country and obtained lawfully outside the country, such as from a country that has not yet introduced pharmaceutical product patent protection. After January 1, 2005, when all developing countries are required to implement pharmaceutical product patent protection, the supply of new generic medicines will contract, and imported generic medicines will be more difficult to secure.

Negotiations at the WTO concerning Paragraph 6 of the Doha Ministerial Declaration on the TRIPS Agreement and Public Health[54] addressed the situation arising in 2005, in which countries needing to import medicines under compulsory (including government use) licenses may be unable to find sources of off-patent medicines.[55] On August 30, 2003, the General

---

[51] For details, see REICHMAN WITH HASENZAHL, LAW AND PRACTICE OF THE UNITED STATES, above n. 49, ch. V ("Government Use").

[52] *See* above n. 48.

[53] In the United States, for example, the "administrative and departmental agencies [that] also possess specific statutory authorization to make use of patented inventions ... include[e] ... the Department of Health and Human Services, the Department of the Interior, the Department of Defense, the Department of Energy, the Department of State, the National Aeronautical and Space Administration ("NASA"), and the Environmental Protection Agency." REICHMAN WITH HASENZAHL, LAW AND PRACTICE OF THE UNITED STATES, above n. 49, ch. V.

[54] WTO Fourth Ministerial Conference (Doha), Declaration on the TRIPS Agreement and Public Health, WT/MIN(O1)/DEC/2, (14 Nov. 2001). Paragraph 6 recognized the problem that countries with insufficient or no manufacturing capacity in the pharmaceutical sector have in making effective use of compulsory licensing, and directed the TRIPS Council to recommend an expeditious solution.

[55] *See* Frederick M. Abbott, *Compulsory Licensing for Public Health Needs: The TRIPS Agenda at the WTO after the Doha Declaration on Public Health*, Quaker United Nations Office, Occasional Paper 9, (Feb. 2002), *available at* http://www.quno.org; Abbott, above n. 42. *See also* Frederick M. Abbott, Negotiations in the WTO TRIPS Council Pursuant to Paragraph 6 of the Ministerial Declaration on the TRIPS Agreement and Public Health, World Bank Seminar (3 Feb. 2003), *available at* http://worldbank.org (B-Span archives).

Council of the WTO adopted the Decision on Implementation of Paragraph 6 of the Doha Declaration on the TRIPS Agreement and Public Health ("the Decision").[56] Adoption of the Decision was preceded by the reading of a Chairperson's Statement that expressed certain "shared understandings" of the Members regarding the way it would be interpreted and implemented. The Decision establishes a mechanism under which the restriction of Article 31(f) will be waived for an exporting Member when it is requested by an eligible importing Member to supply products under compulsory license issued in the exporting country, and it provides a waiver of Article 31(h) (remuneration) for the importing country when remuneration is paid in the exporting country.[57]

---

[56] Decision on Implementation of Paragraph 6 of the Doha Declaration on the TRIPS Agreement and Public Health IP/C/W/405 (30 Aug. 2003) [hereinafter Decision].

[57] *See* Frederick M. Abbott, *The WTO Medicines Decision: The Political Economy of World Pharmaceutical Trade and the Protection of Public Health*, 99 A. J. I. L. (forthcoming 2005); Carlos Correa, Implementation of the WTO General Council Decision on Paragraph 6 of the Doha Declaration on the TRIPS Agreement and Public Health (WHO 2004) [hereinafter Correa 2004]; Paul Vandoren & Jean Charles Van Eeckhaute, *The WTO Decision on Paragraph 6 of the Doha Declaration on the TRIPS Agreement and Public Health*, 6 J. WORLD INTELL. PROP. 779 (2003).

Paragraph 1 of the Decision defines "pharmaceutical product" broadly, and does not limit application of the solution to specific disease conditions. The definition expressly covers active pharmaceutical ingredients (APIs) and diagnostic "kits." The definition is sufficiently broad to encompass vaccines. It requires Members other than least developed Members (which are automatically included) to submit a notification of their intention to use the system in whole or in part, which notification may be modified at any time. This notification establishes the Member as an "eligible importing Member," and several developed Members have opted out of the system in whole or in a limited way.

Paragraph 2 of the Decision establishes conditions for use of the waiver. The importing Member must notify the TRIPS Council of its needs, and (except for Least-Developed Members), must indicate that it has determined that it has insufficient or no manufacturing capacity for the product(s) in question. The latter determination is made in accordance with an Annex to the Decision. When there is a patent in the importing Member, it must indicate that it has issued, or intends to issue, a compulsory license (except for Least-Developed Members that elect not to enforce patents pursuant to Paragraph 7 of the Doha Declaration). The exporting Member must notify the TRIPS Council of the terms of the export license it issues, including the destination, quantities to be supplied and the duration of the license. The products supplied under the license must be identified by special packaging and/or colouring/shaping. Before quantities are shipped, the licensee must post on a publicly accessible website the destination and means it has used to identify the products as supplied under the system.

Paragraph 3 provides for a waiver of the remuneration requirement for the importing country, and Paragraph 4 requires importing Members to implement measures proportionate to their means to prevent diversion of products imported under the system. Paragraph 6 provides an additional waiver of Article 31(f) for regional trading arrangements in Africa (i.e., more than half of which were Least-Developed countries when the Decision was adopted). This waiver allows a Member to export to countries

The obstacles to use of compulsory and government use licensing to redress any imbalance created by patent monopolies should not be minimized. While the threat of compulsory licensing may be easy enough to use as a bargaining lever in negotiations, the realization of production involves reverse engineering of the subject medicine, regulatory review, and achieving production in quantity and under good manufacturing practices. Accomplishing these steps may take one to three years.[58]

2. Paragraph 7 and Least-Developed Countries

WTO Ministers agreed, in paragraph 7 of the Doha Declaration on TRIPS and Public Health,[59] that Least-Developed Members should not be obligated to implement or apply TRIPS provisions regarding pharmaceutical product patents or regulatory data protection until January 1, 2016. Just as importantly, they also agreed that Least-Developed Members already allowing for such protection did not need to "enforce" such rules until that later date.[60] The

---

throughout the region under a single compulsory license, although it does not expressly waive the requirement for licenses to be issued by importing countries of the region. The main benefit of the waiver may be to allow the import of APIs, formulation into finished products, and export throughout the African region.

Paragraph 11 provides that the waiver will remain effective for each Member until an amendment has come into effect to replace it there, and that Members will commence negotiations for an amendment to be based, where appropriate, on the waiver. Although the Decision stated that the negotiations would have a view to completion within six months following the end of 2003, in June 2004 the TRIPS Council extended that tentative completion date until the end of March 2005.

The Chairperson's Statement indicates, *inter alia*, that Members will act in good faith in using the Decision, providing:

> "First, Members recognize that the system that will be established by the Decision should be used in good faith to protect public health and, without prejudice to paragraph 6 of the Decision, not be an instrument to pursue industrial or commercial policy objectives."

[58] D.G. Shah, speaking on behalf of the Indian generic manufacturing industry, has suggested that the lead time between initiating a compulsory licensing request in India and making available commercial quantities of the product may be three to four years. D.G. Shah, Presentation at meeting sponsored by Norweigian Ministry of Foreign Affairs and Quaker United Nations Office – Geneva, Utstein Kloster (20–23 July 2002). Eloan Dos Santos Pinhero, Director of the Brazilian public pharmaceutical enterprise, Far Manguinhos, has indicated that an ARV can be taken from the reverse engineering phase through to commercial production in one year. Presentation at The Crisis of Neglected Diseases International Conference (MSF-DNDi) (Mar. 2002).

[59] *See* Declaration on TRIPS and Public Health, above n. 54, para. 7.

[60] *Id.*, which provides in relevant part:

> We also agree that the least-developed country Members will not be obliged, with respect to pharmaceutical products, to implement or apply Sections 5

TRIPS Council adopted a decision confirming this flexibility,[61] and the WTO General Council added a waiver of Least-Developed Members' obligations regarding so-called "exclusive marketing rights," which might otherwise have been used as a substitute for patent protection to block production, importation and sales of medicines.[62]

The reason the right to "disapply" existing patents is important is that most of the Least-Developed Countries already have legislation authorizing pharmaceutical patent protection, largely as the by-product of the colonial administration of their legal systems. The authority to disapply patents is already being used by public procurement authorities in these countries to import generic versions of medicines that are on-patent in their countries.

3. Parallel trade and differential pricing

The TRIPS Agreement, as confirmed by paragraph 5(d) of the Doha Declaration,[63] allows each WTO Member to adopt a rule of international exhaustion of IPRs, and thus to permit parallel importation of medicines. This provision allows each country to seek the lowest priced, lawfully marketed medicine on the world market, which has an obvious benefit in terms of access to lower-priced medicines.

Historically, prices of medicines have varied widely throughout the developed and developing countries, and there have been significant opportunities to exploit pricing benefits through parallel trade.[64] For a long time, it was not uncommon for the prices of medicines to be higher in Africa than in

> and 7 of Part II of the TRIPS Agreement or to enforce rights provided for under these Sections until 1 January 2016, without prejudice to the right of least-developed country Members to seek other extensions of the transition periods as provided for in Article 66.1 of the TRIPS Agreement. We instruct the Council for TRIPS to take the necessary action to give effect to this pursuant to Article 66.1 of the TRIPS Agreement.

[61] Decision of the Council for TRIPS of 27 June 2002, IP/C/25, WTO Doc. No. 02–3664, *available at* http:/www.wto.org.

[62] WTO General Council, Least-Developed Country Members – Obligations Under Article 70.9 of the TRIPS Agreement with Respect to Pharmaceutical Products, WTO Doc. WT/L/478 (8 July 2002).

[63] *See* TRIPS Agreement, above n. 30, art. 6; Declaration on Trips and Public Health, above n. 54, para. 5(d), which provides:

> The effect of the provisions in the TRIPS Agreement that are relevant to the exhaustion of intellectual property rights is to leave each Member free to establish its own regime for such exhaustion without challenge, subject to the MFN and national treatment provisions of Articles 3 and 4.

[64] There is little hard data on the extent of parallel trade in medicines, although it is understood to be a common phenomenon in the intra-EU context. While saying that

Europe,[65] although wide public attention to this situation may have ameliorated this practice. While it is tempting to suppose that parallel trade opportunities exist because of price controls and related regulatory measures, evidence for this has been lacking.[66] Nonetheless, the heavily regulated nature of the pharmaceutical trade places constraints on the extent to which parallel trade opportunities can be readily exploited.[67]

Parallel trade remains an important mechanism for promoting price competition, but it is unlikely to provide the same level of pricing relief as could be obtained by compulsory licensing. In most cases, parallel traded medicines will have been placed on the market by the patent holder, and patent holder prices are likely to be higher than those that would be charged by a compulsory licensee. Still, it is important that this mechanism should be preserved and considered in strategic planning.

An argument can be made that differential pricing favors developing countries because it allows OECD-based Pharma companies to maintain high prices in OECD markets.[68] In essence, the OECD consumers subsidize advertising costs and R&D for developing country purchasers. Differential pricing and markets open to parallel trade are not mutually exclusive. Pharma companies may contract with purchasers in differentially-priced markets to prevent re-exports. In addition, the OECD countries already for the most part block parallel imports of medicines, which renders concerns over such practices in OECD markets illusory.

While differential (or "equity") pricing may be unavoidable as a near-term solution to the pharmaceutical needs of developing countries, such practices

---

there have been opportunities to exploit parallel trade, the author does not suggest that there have in fact been significant amounts of world parallel trade in medicines.

[65] This phenomenon was first called to the author's attention following a presentation at the Pre-UNCTAD X Seminar on the Role of Competition Policy for Development in Globalizing World Markets, Panel on Competition, IPRs and Transfer of Technology (Geneva, 14–15 June 1999). The author had recalled the pharmaceutical industry assertion that parallel trade would restrict access to inexpensive medicines in Africa. He was advised by several delegates that they waited for their travel to Geneva to buy medicines since they were more expensive in Africa, and was asked where the inexpensive medicines in Africa might be obtained. This anecdotal report was confirmed by several studies. *See, e.g.,* F.M. Scherer & Jayashree Watal, Post-Trips Options for Access to Patented Medicines in Developing Countries, WHO Commission on Macroeconomics and Health Working Paper No. WG4:1 (June 2001).

[66] *See id.*

[67] *See also* Patricia M. Danzon and Adrian Towse, *Theory and Implementation of Differential Pricing for Pharmaceuticals* [this volume].

[68] *See, e.g.,* John H. Barton, *Differentiated Pricing of Patented Products*, July 2001 WHO Commission on Macroeconomics and Health, CMH Working Paper Series, Paper No. WG4:2. *See also* Keith E. Maskus, Parallel Imports in Pharmaceuticals: Implications for Competition and Prices in Developing Countries, Final Report to the World Intellectual Property Organization (Apr. 2001).

present risks of long-term cartelization of the global medicines market. If the major OECD-based producers can sell at low prices in developing markets, they may be able to prevent the successful emergence of alternative low-cost producers. For this reason, it is important that those responsible for differential pricing arrangements recognize and address the importance of promoting generic competition. This might be accomplished through use of the compulsory licensing mechanism. Among developing countries, more work can be done to develop compulsory licensing arrangements that can be used to promote competition while providing remuneration to originators commensurate with public health and development realities.

4. Disciplining ancillary IPRs

Trademarks and copyrights play an ancillary role to patents as obstacles to access. The basic function of the trademark is to distinguish the origin of goods, and this function serves a legitimate public purpose. Ancillary uses of trademarks to block parallel imports, to restrict generic substitution and to prevent the functional coloring of equivalent medicines are against the public interest.

Copyright holders have asserted rights to prevent the re-use of information in doctor and patient leaflets accompanying medicines, including information in translations. Since copyright law does not protect facts or data, including scientific content, these claims are an abuse of copyright.

V. Bulk procurement and related mechanisms

Medicines producers may be able to reduce their per-unit costs by producing larger quantities of supply under longer term arrangements. Originator/patent holders on ARVs have argued that their ability and willingness to supply at low prices is dependent on the volume of purchase orders that can be used as the basis to scale up their production.[69] Individual medicines procurers may have difficulty negotiating best prices because of the absence of bargaining power or of transparency in negotiations with private sellers. Acquisition-by-acquisition negotiations on price and terms are time-consuming and a drain on personnel. Sellers and buyers of essential medicines may each benefit from bulk procurement arrangements that combine the purchasing power of governments and/or private medicines procurers with the scaling up of supply capacity.

While bulk procurement arrangements seem likely to reduce the prices of essential medicines, one should not view this option and that of generic production as mutually exclusive. The best way to assure low prices is by stimulating competition among generic producers. Pressure from these producers, largely in India, has effectively brought down prices of ARVs, and make large-scale treatment programs feasible. The World Bank is encouraging

---

[69] *See* Garnier, above n. 33.

generic production by adoption of policies that focus on purchases – including bulk purchasing – from the lowest priced lawful producer.[70]

The heart of the essential medicines problem is determining how to provide low-cost medicines that are safe and effective. Given limited financial resources, the price of medicines operates as a primary constraint on providing access. One feature of any system for providing essential medicines to developing countries is that they must be made available at or near their marginal cost of production in a competitive market. Developing country populations cannot afford to defray the costs of R&D undertaken in the OECD countries, and they certainly can not afford to pay the expenses associated with advertising and marketing.

VI. Local production, transfer of technology, and the public sector

The supply of low-cost essential medicines may be improved by the establishment of production facilities in various regions throughout the world.[71] "Local production" provides the infrastructure for enabling countries to make effective use of compulsory licensing. It provides an incentive for governments to procure medicines by channeling public funds to local enterprises, which augments local training and employment opportunities. Once a local pharmaceutical industry becomes established, it is likely to generate positive spin-offs, such as increased attention to local research and development funding for new medicines and related technologies.

Local production efforts should be designed to achieve appropriate efficiencies and economies of scale. In this respect, there is considerable promise for regional arrangements in which facilities and related infrastructure can be allocated in a way that provides benefits to all countries in a region. Meanwhile, countries in immediate need of complex medicines cannot delay their acquisition of imports simply because local production facilities can be built in the future.

Countries with populations requiring long-term large quantity supply of medicines, such as antiretrovirals, should become capable of producing locally. Otherwise, these countries will find themselves in an economically and politically vulnerable position.

In a perfect world, the most efficient and low-cost way to produce medicines for global consumption might be organized around a few very large-scale facilities located in only a few countries. This perfect world does not exist for any product, and there are sound political economy reasons why it does not exist for medicines.

Developing countries are increasingly cooperating with a view toward assisting each other in developing and implementing sustainable production programs. This kind of cooperation is vital.

---

[70] *See* BATTLING HIV/AIDS: A DECISION MAKER'S GUIDE TO THE PROCUREMENT OF MEDICINES AND RELATED SUPPLIES (Yolanda Tayler ed., World Bank 2004).

[71] *See, e.g.*, work program of Initiative for Pharmaceutical Technology Transfer (IPTT) (on file with author).

Public supply of sophisticated medicines has been accomplished successfully in Brazil and Thailand, and they provide models worthy of study. For the most part, however, the failure of the market to adequately provide essential medicines has not been offset by success in the public sector. There are obstacles here as well. The public sector is potentially burdened by its comparative inability to provide individual incentives, by inefficiency and cronyism.

Public sector supply of essential medicines is a demonstrably viable alternative to the private market. At the very least, the public sector should serve to fill gaps where the market fails. Whether the public sector might serve as the primary source of essential medicines supply is open to debate.

VII. Research and development

The crux of the debate concerning the use of flexibilities in the TRIPS Agreement, such as compulsory and government use licensing, to secure lower priced access to medicines has centered on the implications for R&D in the developed countries. There is no difference of opinion regarding the importance of R&D. The need for new medicines to treat and cure disease is unquestioned. From the standpoint of access to essential medicines, the question becomes "who will pay for the R&D, and how ?"

A. The general R&D problem

In a study prepared by this author for the British Commission on IPRs, an attempt was made to identify the contribution to Pharma R&D attributable to rents collected from the sale of patented medicines in developing countries. The informal estimates in that report suggested that such contribution was only marginally significant: namely, if developing countries gave no patent protection to pharmaceuticals at all, it would generate an aggregate loss of about one to one and a half billion dollars out of a total of $35 billion R&D funds spent annually by U.S. PhRMA companies in the United States and abroad (not to mention the billions spent annually by non-U.S.-based Pharma companies outside the United States).[72] Fully 90 percent of revenues of U.S. PhRMA companies in 2001 came from sales in the United States, Canada, Western Europe and Japan, while 0.3 percent came from sales in Africa.[73]

A recent report by the World Bank indicates that, in 2002, developed countries accounted for more than 95 percent of the $270 billion of the world's leading twenty country pharmaceutical markets, and that developing countries that might benefit from importing under compulsory licenses for medicines would

---

[72] Abbott, above n. 42. Recent data released by U.S. PhRMA indicates that its membership (which includes European and Japanese division spending in the U.S.) had an estimated worldwide R&D expense of $32.051 billion in 2002. PhRMA, Pharmaceutical Industry Profile, app., tbl. 1 (2003), at http://phrma.org.
[73] PhRMA 2003 Profile, above n. 74, app., tbl. 9.

probably account for less than one or two percent of global pharmaceutical sales.[74] According to U.S. PhRMA's most recent member company data, in 2001 its members spent 0.1 percent of their worldwide R&D dollars in Africa.[75]

The foregoing figures are approximations, and Pharma has begun assembling data to suggest that its future sales in developing countries (such as China) will account for a greater share of its R&D-supporting revenues.[76] Yet, even assuming that the developing country contribution to Pharma R&D will grow, everyone can agree at the outset that Least-Developed Countries for the foreseeable future will play no material role in contributing to Pharma R&D. Patent rents from these countries are essentially irrelevant to Pharma and to potential pharmaceutical innovation.

Do the developed countries rely on patent rents from middle and higher income developing countries to fund R&D? It seems unlikely, but more empirical research on this question would be useful. The tentative conclusion against such reliance is strongly reinforced by considering the role of public R&D funding in the United States.

The R&D budget of the National Institutes of Health for 2003 was $28 billion.[77] However this figure may be interpreted, this budget clearly swamps contributions from developing countries to U.S. R&D efforts. Moreover, NIH research funding is converted to Pharma patents without any significant royalty payments being returned to the public treasury.[78]

When discussing access to essential medicines, including ARVs, there is little reason to believe that developing countries would so take advantage of Pharma patents as to cause a material impact in the developed world. If so, what explains the aggressiveness with which the right to secure and protect patents in developing countries is defended? One possible explanation is that Pharma worries that developing country exporters will successfully build their

---

[74] Carsten Fink, Implementing the Doha Mandate on TRIPS and Public Health, World Bank Trade Note 5 (29 May 2003).
[75] PhRMA 2003 Profile, above n. 74, app., tbl. 4.
[76] Harvey Bale, PowerPoint Presentation at NYU Law School (Feb. 2003).
[77] *See* above n. 5.
[78] The U.S. Government Accounting Office data regarding the development, and the private versus public returns, on Taxol is astonishing. According to the GAO:

> "NIH's total Taxol-related spending [is] $484 million through 2002. BMS's sales of Taxol totaled over $9 billion from 1993 through 2002. BMS agreed to pay NIH royalties at a rate equal to 0.5 percent of worldwide sales of Taxol as part of a 1996 agreement to license three NIH Taxol-related inventions developed during the CRADA. Royalty payments to NIH have totaled $ 35 million." General Accounting Office Reports & Testimony, GAO-03–829, IAC (SM) Newsletter Database (TM) No. 7, vol. 2003, IAC-ACC-NO: 104886946 (LEXIS) (4 June 2003)

businesses on the basis of Pharma R&D and penetrate the higher income developed country markets.

In fact, pharmaceutical producers in India are increasingly penetrating the U.S. market,[79] and Chinese producers will undoubtedly follow. To enter the U.S. market, a Chinese or Indian producer either needs a license for a patented medicine or the capability to supply a medicine that is already off-patent. The presence or absence of patent protection in the Chinese or Indian markets may affect the overall profitability of the Chinese or Indian pharmaceutical industries, but the latter do not appear to lack the capital necessary to build facilities to penetrate the U.S. market. In short, while there may be some correlation between patent protection in the Indian, Chinese and U.S. markets, the one thing seems to have only a modest correlation with the other.

Will Pharma increasingly rely on sales of patented medicines in China (or India) for its own R&D and long-term survival? Perhaps, but imposing higher prices on consumers throughout the developing world due to concerns about access to the Chinese market is a poor way to protect Pharma's interests. These may be better protected directly in a political dialogue between the U.S. and China.

The National Institutes of Health are using public funds to create public goods in the form of R&D on new medicines. An assumption has been made that low-cost private patenting or licensing by Pharma of the relevant research results is the best way to reap the benefits from those public goods. It is worthwhile to consider whether the public good might in fact be increased in the United States and abroad by a broader pattern of licensing that brought multiple producers of medicines into the market and thereby provided low-cost access to medicines in the United States and in developing countries. Similar arrangements might be pursued by the E.U., Japan and Switzerland.

B. *Drugs for neglected diseases*

There is a specific market failure in the case of R&D on diseases of relevance primarily for developing countries, such as sleeping sickness, leishmaniasis, and Chagas disease. The market failure occurs because those afflicted by these diseases do not constitute a profitable private market for new treatments. Private R&D is not therefore directed to developing treatments.

This problem is being addressed in a concrete way by the Drugs for Neglected Diseases Initiative (DNDI),[80] a collaborative effort formed as an outgrowth of the Drugs for Neglected Diseases Working Group organized

---

[79] Author's discussions with D.G. Shah, representing the Indian generic pharmaceutical sector.
[80] Details available at http://www.accessmed-msf.org/dndi.asp.

by Doctors Without Borders. Other initiatives are also addressing this problem set.

There are other areas in which the private market, organized around patents, will not provide solutions to critical medicines issues. For example, when the U.S. determined that there was a pressing need for vaccines and treatments to be used to counter bio-terror threats, it immediately announced the availability of government subsidies for such efforts.

William Nordhaus wrote insightfully about the patent-subsidy tradeoff.[81] While he concluded that, in the general economic case, patents may be the more efficient means of generating innovation, this did not mean that public subsidies should not also play an important role in innovation. "Prizes" or fixed financial rewards for innovation are another alternative to patents.

When the goal of R&D is well defined, the inefficiencies associated with subsidies may well be minimized. A specific disease requiring a treatment or cure is a known objective. It is well to bear in mind that the United States has provided an enormous level of public subsidy to R&D on medicines.

VIII. The emergence of competitors

China is likely to emerge as a top-flight innovator and low-cost medicines supplier over the course of this decade. It has a strong technology base, the capital to build state of the art production facilities, and a traditional cultural interest in medicines and health. India is already accelerating competitive penetration of the OECD markets.

As China and India begin to challenge Pharma dominance of these markets, allegations of "unfair trade practices" are likely to be heard, and there most likely will be efforts to impose regulatory restrictions designed to protect Pharma.[82] At the same time, as Chinese and Indian enterprises cross the innovation curve and become net generators of new medicines, these countries may logically develop heightened interest in enforcing patents. They may also become interested in price discrimination, so as to make high margin sales in the OECD and lower margin sales in the developing world (including their own markets).

Interest in fostering lower-priced access to medicines should not be confused with idealizing or romanticizing the generic producer. With rare exception, pharmaceutical enterprises will seek to maximize their profits. Competitive markets are the best mechanism for encouraging lower prices, and generic production is necessary to achieving that end.

---

[81] WILLIAM D. NORDHAUS, INVENTION, GROWTH AND WELFARE (1969).
[82] An offsetting factor will be the interest of PhRMA in selling into the Chinese and Indian markets.

IX. Conclusions – The hydra without Hercules

Facilitating access to essential medicines requires political commitment and a plan of action. At present, most efforts are focused on urgent and immediate problems, such as addressing treatment for HIV/AIDS. These short-term priorities entail promoting additional funding for the procurement of medicines, encouraging generic production, impeding efforts to further cartelize the global pharmaceuticals market, and promoting R&D on drugs for neglected diseases. The press of these urgent needs makes focus on longer term and more comprehensive solutions to essential medicines issues difficult.

The mythical Hydra was a many-headed beast with a remarkable regenerative capacity. The public health situation in developing countries shares these characteristics. The problem is multi-faceted, and addressing one aspect often reveals new challenges. Even Hercules was unable to slay the Hydra single handedly. He required the help of an assistant. Hercules did, however, provide strong leadership and commitment. Political leadership and commitment is likewise needed to address the problem of access to essential medicines, and it is not yet clear from where such leadership and commitment will emerge.

16

Theory and implementation of differential pricing for pharmaceuticals

PATRICIA M. DANZON

ADRIAN TOWSE*

Abstract
1. Introduction
2. The cost structure of research-based pharmaceuticals and the economic role of patents
3. Efficient payment for R&D: Ramsey pricing
    3.1 Ramsey price differentials vs. profit-maximizing differentials
    3.2 Regulation versus competition
    3.3 Welfare conclusions on price discrimination
    3.4 Differential pricing does not imply cost-shifting
4. Actual vs. optimal price differentials and the breakdown of market separation: Parallel trade and external referencing
    4.1 The breakdown of market separation: Parallel importation and external referencing
    4.2 Cross-national price differentials
    4.3 Price differentials within the U.S.
5. Policies to maintain separate markets and price differentials
    5.1 Defining patents based on national boundaries, including the right to bar parallel trade
    5.2 Higher-income countries forego regulation based on foreign prices
    5.3 Implementing differential pricing through confidential rebates
    5.4 Structured discounts and a global tiered pricing structure
6. Compulsory licensing and the use of generics: Doha and beyond
7. Conclusions

---

* Patricia M. Danzon, PhD, is Professor of Economics at the Wharton School, University of Pennsylvania. Adrian Towse, MA and MA Phil, is Director of the Office of Health Economics, London.

ABSTRACT

This chapter argues that differential pricing can reconcile patents, which are essential incentives for innovation, with affordability of on-patent drugs in developing countries. The theory of Ramsey pricing provides a rigorous basis for differential pricing, based on cross-national differences in price elasticities, as an efficient way to pay for the global joint costs of pharmaceutical R&D. Such differential pricing would also be consistent with standard norms of equity, assuming that demand elasticities are inversely related to income.

To achieve appropriate and sustainable price differences does not require a regulatory system to establish and enforce differentials. Rather, equitable differentials could emerge as a result of market forces if appropriate institutional structures were in place. In particular, achieving such differentials will require either that higher-income countries forego trying to "import" low drug prices from low-income countries, through parallel trade and external referencing, or that such practices become less feasible. The most promising approach that would prevent both parallel trade and external referencing is for purchasers on behalf of developing countries to negotiate contracts with drug manufacturers that include confidential rebates. With confidential rebates, final transactions prices to purchasers can differ across markets while manufacturers sell to distributors at uniform prices, thus eliminating opportunities for parallel trade and external referencing.

The option of compulsory licensing of patented products to generic manufacturers may be important if generics truly have lower production costs or originators charge prices above marginal cost, despite market separation. However, given the risks inherent in compulsory licensing, it seems best to first try the approach of strengthening market separation to enable originator firms to maintain differential pricing. With assured market separation, originators may offer prices comparable to the prices that a local generic firm would charge, which would eliminate the need for compulsory licensing.

Differential pricing could go a long way to improve the access of developing countries to drugs that have markets in high-income economies. However, other subsidy mechanisms will be needed to promote research and development of drugs that have no high-income market.

1. Introduction[1]

At the center of the international debate over improving developing countries' (DCs) access to medicines is the role of patents.[2] In this chapter, we argue that

---

[1] This chapter is drawn from, and extends, an article the authors published as *Differential Pricing for Pharmaceuticals: Reconciling Access, R&D and Patents*, 3 INT'L J. HEALTH CARE FIN. & ECON. 183 (2003).

differential pricing makes it possible to reconcile patents, which are necessary for innovation, with affordability of drugs for DCs, at least for drugs with a market in affluent countries.[3] Under a well-designed differential pricing system, prices in affluent countries (and, to a lesser extent, middle-income countries) would exceed the marginal cost of production and distribution in these countries by enough, in aggregate, to cover the joint costs of research and development (R&D), while prices in DCs would cover only their marginal cost. Antibiotics and HIV-AIDS drugs exemplify medicines that serve both high-income and DC markets, for which differential pricing could simultaneously yield affordable prices to low-income countries while preserving incentives for R&D.[4]

For drugs to treat diseases found only in DCs, there is no affluent country market to cover the costs of R&D. But the prices that DC patients can afford to pay are insufficient to create incentives for innovators to invest in R&D. Thus some external subsidy – either a demand-side subsidy to patients or a supply-side subsidy to innovator firms – is necessary to create incentives to develop treatments for DC-only diseases.[5] Patents are necessary but will not suffice: having the legal authority to charge high prices is of no value if patients or governments cannot pay them. Various subsidy options have been proposed for funding R&D on DC drugs, but these are not discussed here.[6] The focus of this chapter is on the use of differential pricing for drugs that serve both high-income and DC markets.

The structure of the chapter is as follows. Section 2 reviews the importance of joint costs in the cost structure of the research-based pharmaceutical industry. Section 3 outlines the theory of Ramsey pricing, and it compares

---

[2] Developing countries are defined in this paper as least-developed countries (LDCs) and lower-income to middle-income economies. Thus, the definition excludes such high-income markets as Singapore, Hong Kong, and South Korea. Regarding the debate over patents and access, see other chapters in this volume. *See also* J. Watal, *Pharmaceutical Patents, Prices and Welfare Losses: Policy Options for India under the WTO TRIPS Agreement*, 23 WORLD ECON. 733 (2000).

[3] DCs have two primary needs for medicines. The first is access to medicines that target diseases that are prevalent in both high-income and low-income countries, which access requires affordable prices and distribution systems and health care infrastructure to assure effective use. Differential pricing can contribute to making these drugs affordable. The second need is for the development of new medicines to treat diseases that are prevalent in DCs but not in high-income countries. For a review of related issues, see World Health Organization, Commission on Macroeconomics and Health, Working Group 4, *available at* http://www.who.int/macrohealth/en/.

[4] Even with prices at marginal cost in DCs, the neediest patients may require subsidies for chronic medicines and for those with high production costs. In these cases, differential pricing can still be an important part of, but not the whole, solution.

[5] Michael Kremer, *Creating Markets for New Vaccines: Part II: Design Issues*, in INNOVATION POLICY AND THE ECONOMY 73 (Adam B. Jaffe et al. eds., MIT Press 2001); Michael Kremer, *Pharmaceuticals and the Developing World*, 16 J. ECON. PERSP. 67 (2002); H. Kettler & A. Towse, Public Private Partnerships for Research and Development: Medicines and Vaccines for Diseases of Poverty (Office of Health Economics Report (2002)).

[6] *See id.*

these Ramsey-optimal price differentials to the price differentials that in theory emerge in monopolistically competitive markets with entry. Section 4 examines the determinants of actual price differences within the US and across nations, reviews the effects of parallel trade and external referencing, and discusses the cost-shifting argument against differential pricing. Sections 5 and 6, respectively, discuss implementation of differential pricing and compulsory licensing. Section 7 concludes.

2. The cost structure of research-based pharmaceuticals and the economic role of patents

The research-based pharmaceutical industry in the U.S. spends 15.6 percent of its global sales on R&D, compared to 3.9 percent for US industry overall excluding drugs and medicines.[7] This sales-based measure understates R&D expense as a percentage of the total costs of developing and producing new drugs, because it omits the "opportunity" or capital cost of funds over the 8–12 years required for drug discovery and development.[8] Adding in this cost of funds, R&D accounts for roughly 30 percent of the total cost of developing, producing and marketing new drugs, with all costs measured as discounted present value at the time of product launch.[9] Firms will only invest in R&D if they anticipate that revenues will be sufficient to cover all these costs. A major challenge of pharmaceutical policy is to establish market and regulatory institutions that create incentives for an appropriate level of R&D and a pricing system to ensure patient access while recouping investment costs.

Appropriate pricing of drugs must be viewed in an international context because pharmaceuticals are potentially global products and R&D is a global expense. In other words, once the costs of drug discovery and development have been incurred for one country, serving other countries requires no additional R&D expense, unless they require different formulations, additional clinical trials and so on. Because R&D is largely a global joint cost, it cannot be causally allocated to specific countries.[10] The key policy questions are: What

---

[7] PHRMA (PHARMACEUTICAL RESEARCH AND MANUFACTURERS OF AMERICA), INDUSTRY PROFILE (2001).
[8] The opportunity cost is the highest alternative return that the company could have realized on the funds invested. See J.A. DiMasi et al., *The Cost of Innovation in the Pharmaceutical Industry*, 10 J. HEALTH ECON. 107 (1991); J.A. DiMasi et al., *The Price of Innovation: New Estimates of Drug Development Costs*, 22 J. HEALTH ECON. 151 (2003).
[9] P.M. Danzon, *Price Discrimination for Pharmaceuticals: Welfare Effects in the US and the EU*, 4 INT'L J. ECON. BUS. 301 (1997).
[10] To the extent that one country has significantly different regulatory requirements, these country-specific costs are not part of the joint costs. For example, if the US FDA requires additional testing or documentation, or Japan requires additional trials, compared to most other regulatory systems, these incremental, country-specific costs should be borne fully by the relevant country.

price differentials would lead to an appropriate allocation of this joint cost across users of pharmaceuticals globally, and how can market and regulatory institutions be designed to implement such price differentials?

Industrialized countries use patents as the basic mechanism to enable inventors to recoup R&D costs in all industries, including pharmaceuticals.[11] If there were no patents, "copy" products could enter freely and competition would force prices down to just cover the marginal costs of production and distribution incurred by copy products. But prices that cover marginal costs will not cover global joint costs of R&D of innovator firms. Hence free generic entry that results in marginal-cost pricing is incompatible with sustained incentives for R&D. The economic purpose of patents is, therefore, to bar entry of copy products for the term of the patent and to provide the innovator firm with a temporary opportunity to price above marginal cost and thereby recoup R&D expense. This policy is designed to preserve incentives for future R&D.

Economic theory views patent protection as a "second best" way to pay for R&D. In a "first best" or fully efficient outcome, all consumers whose marginal benefit exceeds marginal cost should use the product. However, because patents permit pricing above marginal cost, some consumers may forego the product even though their marginal benefit exceeds the marginal cost. But with large fixed costs of R&D, the first best solution is impossible because marginal cost pricing to consumers would generate inadequate revenue to sustain innovation unless the government subsidized R&D. However, raising the necessary taxes for such subsidies would undermine efficiency and possibly equity in other sectors of the economy, and allocating subsidies ex ante in a way that creates efficient incentives and avoids waste would be difficult, if not impossible. Thus, a patent system is generally viewed as the best practical approach to funding R&D in industrialized countries.

The requirement that all countries adopt standard 20 year product patents, as a condition of membership in the World Trade Organization (WTO), has encountered serious opposition by and on behalf of developing countries.[12] The assumption is that patent-holders would charge prices significantly above marginal cost and above the prices currently charged for copy products, making drugs even less affordable and leading to inadequate patient treatment. Some have argued for ex post government purchase of a patent or of licensing rights.[13]

---

[11] F.M. SCHERER & D. ROSS, INDUSTRIAL MARKET STRUCTURE AND ECONOMIC PERFORMANCE 621 (Houghton Mifflin Company 3d ed. 1990); J. TIROLE, THE THEORY OF INDUSTRIAL ORGANIZATION (MIT Press 1988).

[12] Hannah E. Kettler & Chris Collins, *Balancing Health Needs and Drug Research Incentives*, COOPERATION S.J., available at http://www.eldis.org/static/DOC11608.htm (last accessed on 10 June 2004). *See also* Watal, above n. 2.

[13] *See* M. Kremer, A Mechanism for Encouraging Innovation, Harvard University, Development Discussion Paper No. 533 (1996). Similarly, other authors propose such a scheme for drugs for DCs, with developed countries funding the purchase of licensing

Although patents may in theory enable originator firms to charge prices above marginal cost, the profit-maximizing price for a patent holder depends on many factors. Among these are the availability of substitute products, consumers' insurance coverage and willingness and ability to pay, the information and incentives of prescribing physicians and dispensing pharmacists, and market power of intermediaries, such as insurers or government procurers. Theory suggests that a patent-holder may rationally set prices near marginal cost in low-income markets if demand is highly price-elastic, provided that these low prices cannot spillover to other, potentially higher-priced markets in the same country or other countries.[14]

Some argue that this will not happen. For example, Lanjouw argues that patents will substantially increase drug prices in India.[15] However, this outcome would occur in part because of the potential for Indian prices to be increased through external referencing by high-income countries, and because she expects the extension of medical insurance (to cover some or all of the 70 percent of the currently uninsured population) to increase prices. The implicit assumption is that insurance is passive, making consumers less price sensitive but with no active interventions by insurers to control costs. We argue below that evidence from the United States and other countries indicates that powerful third-party payers can obtain lower prices than out-of-pocket purchasers.[16] We also discuss policies necessary to prevent price-spillovers and options to enable governments

---

rights. This would address the problem of lack of purchasing power as well as allocative efficiency. *See* M. Ganslandt et al., *Developing and Distributing Essential Medicines to Poor Countries: The DEFEND Proposal*, 24 WORLD ECON. 79 (2001). Lanjouw proposes a variant whereby companies can opt to either have patent rights in rich countries or in poor countries but not in both. However, this idea would not reduce the need to price above marginal cost in the rich markets and if, as we argue, prices in poor countries will be set close to marginal cost, then it would have no substantive effect on static efficiency. *See* J.O. Lanjouw, *A Patent Policy for Global Diseases: US and International Legal Issues*, 16 HARV. J.L. & TECH. 86 (2002). Unlike the Ganslandt et al. proposal, the Lanjouw proposal would not enhance incentives to develop drugs for predominantly DC diseases.

[14] *See* § 3.1 below. *See also* P. LAYARD & A. WALTERS, MICRO-ECONOMIC THEORY (McGraw-Hill 1978).

[15] *See* J.O. Lanjouw, Introduction of Pharmaceutical Product Patents in India: "Heartless exploitation of the poor and suffering?," NBER Working Paper Series No 6366 (1998). Watal and Fink also consider the case of India and model price increases following patent introduction, using assumptions about demand elasticity. However, the critical issue is the likely demand elasticity of third party payers purchasing for the currently uninsured, not the demand elasticity of those who are currently buying drugs. *See also* J. Watal, above n. 2; C. Fink, *Patent Protection, Transnational Corporations, and Market Structure: A Simulation Study of the Indian Pharmaceutical Industry*, 1 J. INDUS. COMPETITION & TRADE 101 (2001).

[16] It may be argued that third-party payers in DCs have less bargaining power than those in high-income countries, but there is no intrinsic reason why this should be the case. The key is an ability to deliver increased volume in exchange for price discounts, which effectively makes demand more elastic. This is discussed further below in § 4.3.

and other purchasers in DCs to bargain effectively on behalf of their populations to achieve the lowest possible price. We consider first, however, why economic theory finds that differential pricing can be efficient and why in practice it can be better delivered through market mechanisms, rather than regulation.

3. Efficient payment for R&D: Ramsey pricing

We present basic economic theory that specifies necessary conditions for (second best) efficiency in drug utilization and drug development.[17] These conditions are, first, that price P is at least equal to marginal cost MC in each market or country and, second, that prices exceed MC by enough, in aggregate over all markets, to cover the joint costs of R&D, including a normal, risk-adjusted rate of return on capital (F):

$$MB_j \geq P_j \geq MC_j, \text{ and} \tag{1}$$

$$\Sigma(P_j - MC_j) \geq F \tag{2}$$

The first equation is necessary for efficiency in Σ resource allocation and distribution, stating that marginal benefit in the jth market must at least equal the marginal cost of production in that market. In standard markets, prices paid by consumers are a lower bound on their perceived marginal benefit. In the case of health services, willingness to pay may include social insurance and possibly other subsidy payments, which reflect the willingness of higher-income taxpayers or countries to subsidize consumption for lower-income populations. The second equation is both a break-even condition for the firm and a necessary condition for efficient investment in R&D. These necessary conditions for efficiency in drug consumption, production and innovation do not imply or require that prices should be the same for all consumers.

The key policy question is: What pricing structure across markets would satisfy these two conditions and yield the greatest social welfare for consumers?

Ramsey optimal pricing (ROP) is the set of price differentials that yield the highest possible social welfare, subject to assuring a specified target profit level for the producer, usually a normal, risk-adjusted return on capital.[18] The ROP solution is that prices should differ across markets in inverse relation to their demand elasticities. In the case of a single product, the condition for the optimal markup of price over marginal cost for submarket j is:[19]

---

[17] J. TIROLE, THE THEORY OF INDUSTRIAL ORGANIZATION 133 (MIT Press 1988).
[18] See F.P. Ramsey, *A Contribution to the Theory of Taxation*, 37 ECON. J. 47 (1927); W.J. Baumol & D.F. Bradford, *Optimal Departures From Marginal Cost Pricing*, 60 AM. ECON. REV. 265 (1970).
[19] With multiple products and nonzero cross-price elasticities, optimal price mark-ups should take into account these cross-elasticity effects; with multiple firms, strategic

$$M_j = D/E_j \qquad (3)$$

where E_j is the own elasticity of demand in market j. Thus M_j, which is the mark-up of price over marginal cost in market j, should be proportional to the demand elasticity E_j. The proportionality term D is defined by the normal profit (or other) constraint. Thus if marginal cost is the same in all markets, ROP requires that prices differ depending only on demand elasticities. If marginal cost differs across markets, these conditions apply to mark-ups over market-specific marginal cost.

The intuitive explanation for ROP is simple. Recall that the ideal would be to charge all consumers their marginal cost, but this is not practical because pricing at marginal cost would not cover R&D. The Ramsey solution minimizes the welfare loss caused by departing from this ideal. More price-sensitive users should be charged a smaller mark-up over marginal cost than less price-sensitive users, because the price-sensitive users would reduce their consumption by proportionately more, if faced with the same prices.

Charging lower prices to more price-sensitive users is also consistent with equity, assuming that lower-income consumers have more elastic demand, on average. This assumption seems intuitively plausible and consistent with rough data that show a strong positive relationship across nations between per capita income and per capita spending on pharmaceuticals and health care.[20] Moreover, utilization of high-priced drugs is extremely limited in low-income countries. In part this reflects different medical needs, with primary need in DCs for drugs to treat infectious diseases, many of which are off-patent and available at low prices. The chronic diseases of more affluent countries, such as hypertension, depression, cancer and the like, do impose a heavy disease burden on lower-income countries. However, their use of rich-country drugs to treat these diseases is extremely limited, which implies much more elastic demand than in higher income countries. For example, one study found that prices for a US-market basket of drugs were on average similar in Mexico and

---

interactions by firms should also be taken into account. *See* R.R. Braeutigam, *Socially Optimal Pricing with Rivalry and Economies of Scale*, 15 RAND J. ECON. 127 (1984); *see also* J.-J. LAFFONT & J. TIROLE, A THEORY OF INCENTIVES IN PROCUREMENT AND REGULATION (MIT Press 1993); J.E. Prieger, *Ramsey Pricing and Competition: The Consequences of Myopic Regulation*, 10 J. REG. ECON. 307 (1996); Danzon, above n. 9.

[20] P. Musgrove et al., *Basic Patterns in National Health Expenditure*, 80 BULL. WORLD HEALTH ORG. 134 (2002); P.M. Danzon & M.F. Furukawa, *Prices and Availability of Pharmaceuticals: Evidence From Nine Countries*, HEALTH AFFAIRS, 29 Oct. 2003, at http://www.healthaffairs.org/WebExclusives/Danzon_Web_Excl_102903.htm (last accessed 29 Oct. 2003). We discuss below the anomaly of low income consumers within a country often paying out-of-pocket prices that are higher than those obtained by better off but insured consumers.

Chile to European prices, but utilization rates were much lower in Mexico and Chile, presumably reflecting their more elastic demand.[21]

3.1 Ramsey price differentials vs. profit-maximizing differentials

One common objection to ROP is that it proposes price differentials similar to those charged by a price discriminating monopolist (PDM). The monopolist's profit-maximizing mark-up in market j is:

$$M_j = 1/E_j \tag{4}$$

Comparing the price markups in equations (3) and (4), the *relative* markups across markets are the same under PDM as under ROP, but the *absolute* prices may differ due to the profit constraint factor, D (which is unity for the monopolist). Ramsey prices are derived to yield a specific rate of return for the firm, such as a normal competitive return on capital. By contrast, the unconstrained pure monopolist may realize more than a normal rate of return.

However in a monopolistically competitive market, that is, a market with unrestricted entry and exit of firms offering competing but differentiated products, competitive entry reduces *expected* profits to normal levels in the long run. The pharmaceutical industry is plausibly characterized as monopolistically competitive, given the ease of new entry by biotech firms and entry across therapeutic classes by established firms.[22] Under monopolistic competition, entry occurs until excess expected profits are eliminated for the marginal firm and the marginal product in each firm's portfolio of products. Ex post, of course, actual realized profits of a given firm may be above or below normal levels.

Given the scientific and market risks faced by the pharmaceutical industry, it is not surprising that expectations in pharmaceuticals are not always accurate. In a pair of studies, Grabowski and Vernon conclude that on average, new chemical entities (NCEs) launched in the 1980s and 1990s earned at most modest excess returns on average, but that 70 percent of new products generated insufficient global revenues to cover the average cost of R&D.[23] Some firms have been very successful, many new firms have been formed while others have

---

[21] *See* Danzon & Furukawa, above n. 20. Standard economic theory implies a negative relationship between per-capita income and the (uncompensated) price elasticity if the income elasticity of demand is positive and greater than unity, as illustrated in P.R.G. LAYARD & A.A. WALTERS, MICRO-ECONOMIC THEORY 138–41 (McGraw Hill 1978). This is a reasonable assumption as empirical evidence suggests that health care is income elastic. *See* Musgrove et al., above n. 20.

[22] *See* 2003–2004 PhRMA Annual Report, *at* http://www.phrma.org/publications/publications//2003-11-20.870.pdf.

[23] H.G. Grabowski & J.M. Vernon, *A New Look at the Returns and Risks to Pharmaceutical R&D*, 36 MGMT. SCI. 804 (1990); H.G. Grabowski & J.M. Vernon, *Returns on Research and Development for 1990s New Drug Introductions*, 20 PHARMACOECONOMICS 11 (2002).

exited through merger or other means, and average profitability has varied over time. Moreover, there is strong evidence that dynamic entry in response to *expected* profits occurs long before those profits are actually realized. The pace of entry of successive entrants to new therapeutic classes has accelerated, such that follower products now can enter within a year of the first drug in a new class.[24]

This similarity between the welfare-maximizing (ROP) and profit-maximizing pricing structures is not surprising and is fortuitous. It means that firms, pursuing their own self-interest, will attempt to set price differentials across markets that are second-best efficient and also meet standard norms of equity, assuming low-income consumers have more elastic demand. Entry should assure that, on average, profits are bid down to normal levels and price markups over marginal cost approximate ROP levels. In practice, price differentials between and within countries may differ from ROP levels, due to spillovers across markets, regulation and other factors discussed below.

Efficient ROP differentials should reflect consumers' "true" demand elasticities. It may be objected that, in practice, actual observed elasticities are reduced by private and social insurance, imperfect information and imperfect decisions of prescribing physicians. In theory, given certain assumptions, insured demand should reflect underlying consumer preferences, but in practice distortions exist in both private markets and public insurance decision-making.[25] Moreover, consumers may be imperfectly informed about the value of alternative drugs, and prescribing physicians may not search for low-priced alternative drugs. Given these common distortions in health-care markets, observed pharmaceutical demand elasticities may diverge from the "true" elasticities based on underlying preferences, including assistance programs. However, market and political forces should operate to reduce most discrepancies between "true" and observed elasticities, since such discrepancies would generally reduce consumer welfare. We discuss below important caveats to this conclusion.

Other observers have extended the case for Ramsey pricing of pharmaceuticals, arguing that optimal prices in poor countries may be below marginal cost.[26] This result follows from distributional objectives, specifically that in the absence of distribution through a global income tax, the price mechanism should be used to achieve socially desirable distribution outcomes in addition to efficient resource allocation. However, there are practical problems to implementing such a regime in a normal commercial environment. In

---

[24] *See* 2003–2004 PhRMA Annual Report, above n. 22.
[25] M.V. Pauly, *Taxation, Health Insurance, and Market Failure in the Medical Economy*, 24 J. ECON. LIT. 629 (1986).
[26] W. Jack & J.O. Lanjouw, Financing Pharmaceutical Innovation: How Much Should Poor Countries Contribute? Centre for Global Development, Working Paper No. 28 (2003).

particular, if companies are to recover costs including normal profit overall, they would have to charge prices above ROP levels in other countries. But this would not increase revenues if ROP prices are already at profit-maximizing levels. Moreover, if pharmaceutical markets in developed countries are roughly monopolistically competitive, as we suggest, then market forces would prevent companies from charging prices above "standard" ROP prices.

One solution, as these authors suggest in part, is for a purchaser acting on behalf of the developed world to buy at ROP and make the products available at zero or close to zero price to the poor populations of developing countries.[27] This would require a subsidy from sources external to pharmaceuticals, funded through tax revenues or charitable contributions in rich countries. It would reduce prices charged to the poor in DCs but would not affect the prices paid to manufacturers in these markets, which would remain at ROP levels. Financing a subsidy to DC prices through a broad-based tax in rich countries is both more practical and arguably more equitable than attempting to raise the revenue through higher prices paid by consumers of drugs in rich countries, who are disproportionately the sick and elderly.

3.2 Regulation versus competition

The ROP concept has been applied to the regulation of utilities.[28] However, while the pharmaceutical industry resembles utilities in having large joint costs and low marginal costs, these industries differ in important ways. The rationale for regulating utilities was that they were usually natural monopolies. By contrast, any market power enjoyed by owners of individual drugs derives primarily from the intentional grant of patents in order to permit pricing above marginal cost. Competition from therapeutic substitutes makes pure monopoly rare and temporary. Competition can be encouraged by the design of insurance arrangements, including co-payments for consumers and negotiation of volume-price offsets through formularies and similar mechanisms. Thus the monopoly rationale for regulation does not apply in the case of pharmaceuticals, which is closer to the model of monopolistic competition.

Traditional utility pricing formulae generally explicitly recognized the need to provide a reasonable return on capital. Because the utility's production capacity was country-specific, local users could not free ride: if they did not pay for capacity costs, their future access to services would obviously be at risk.[29] By contrast, the global nature of the joint costs of pharmaceutical R&D creates the incentive and opportunity for regulators in each country to free

---

[27] Id.
[28] Baumol & Bradford, above n. 18; *see also* J. LAFFONT & J. TIROLE, above n. 19.
[29] As these utilities expand across national boundaries, allocating joint costs across countries may become more problematic, and problems may arise similar to those already

ride, paying only country-specific marginal cost and leaving others to pay the joint costs. Moreover, the long lag between initiating R&D and bringing products to market means that even if current low prices do reduce R&D and hence the future supply of new drugs, it will be hard to attribute future lack of innovation to specific current policies or politicians.

Regulating prices based on costs is another regulatory approach to price setting. Since costs are passed through to prices, this approach distorts incentives for cost-minimization in any industry, as is well known.[30] If applied to the pharmaceutical industry, cost-based regulation would likely be imprecise and downward biased because full costs are unobservable and optimal allocation rules may be unknown or politically unacceptable. First, the full cost of an R&D project includes investments made over 10–15 years, which are hard to track, plus the time cost of money, which is not captured in accounting statements. Second, the full cost of developing a new drug includes the costs of the many failures or "dry holes" during the drug discovery and development process.[31] Third, the degree of jointness of R&D and production costs is hard to measure and, even if known, the appropriate sharing rule for joint costs between, say, Italians and Americans depends on demand conditions in their respective countries. Thus, in the case of pharmaceuticals, accounting costs do not provide an accurate measure of full economic costs or an appropriate benchmark for setting differential prices. If regulators based prices on allowable costs defined as costs that are clearly attributable to a specific product in a specific country, cost-based regulation would lead to prices that are inadequate to cover total costs.

The airline industry offers an example of differential pricing that works reasonably well without regulation in an industry characterized by large joint costs and monopolistic competitive market conditions. Since airline deregulation in the US, price differentials have increased while average price levels have fallen significantly.[32] Each airline may have some local monopoly power, but competition between incumbents, reinforced by entry of new airlines, constrains profits to achieve roughly normal levels on average.

---

experienced by pharmaceuticals. For an analysis of cross border trends in utilities, see International Labour Organisation, Challenges and Opportunities Facing Public Utilities, Tripartite Meeting on Challenges and Opportunities Facing Public Utilities, Report No. TMCOPU/2003 (International Labour Office 2003).

[30] H. Averch & L. Johnson, *Behavior of the Firm Under Regulatory Constraint*, 52 AM. ECON. REV. 1052 (1962).

[31] *See* DiMasi et al (2003), above n. 8.

[32] Adam D. Thierer, 20th Anniversary of Airline Deregulation: Cause for Celebration, Not Re-Regulation, The Heritage Foundation, Backgrounder #1173 (22 Apr. 1998), *available at* http://www.heritage.org/Research/Regulation/BG1173.cfm.

3.3 Welfare conclusions on price discrimination

A considerable literature has examined the welfare effects of price-discriminating monopoly relative to a single-price monopoly. Most of these models focus exclusively on static efficiency (to achieve the most efficient utilization of existing products), and ignore the dynamic effects on R&D.[33] In the static efficiency context, a necessary condition for price discrimination to increase social welfare is that output should become greater with differential pricing across markets than with a uniform price in all markets.[34] In the case of pharmaceuticals, it seems highly likely that this condition is met. If firms were to charge a single price globally, the manufacturer's choice of that price would be dominated by conditions in the United States.[35] Many consumers in low-income and middle-income countries would reduce consumption or drop out of the market entirely because they could not afford uniform price.

Conversely, consumption by low-income and middle-income consumers would increase considerably under price discrimination, at least for drugs with modest costs of production. For example, one author simulated worldwide pharmaceutical prices, revenues and number of consumers served under the extremes of price discrimination between each national market (i.e. one price per country) and a single global price.[36] He concluded that price discrimination increases access by a factor of roughly 4–7 times over uniform pricing. Access on this model can only be further increased by governments or other agencies financing the purchase of pharmaceuticals on behalf of low-income countries.

A further interesting feature of this model is that, comparing two countries with the same average GDP per capita, the country in which wealth is most concentrated would face a higher price under price discrimination because in such markets companies would rationally price for the rich market rather than the numerically larger (in terms of people) lower income market. Thus price discrimination *within* as well as *between* countries could significantly increase affordability and utilization by low-income populations, particularly in countries with a highly skewed income distribution. The efficiency case for price discrimination is even stronger in models that consider both dynamic

---

[33] Hal R. Varian, *Price Discrimination and Social Welfare*, 75 AM. ECON. REV. 870 (1985); See also D.A. Malueg & M. Schwartz, *Parallel Imports, Demand Dispersion, and International Price Discrimination*, 37 J. INT'L ECON. 167 (1994).
[34] See above n. 33.
[35] The profit maximizing global price would be based on the weighted-average elasticity of demand, where weights are each country's share of sales (see equation 5 below.) Since the United States accounts for almost 50 percent of global pharmaceutical sales, the single global price would approximate the optimal U.S. price.
[36] J. Dumoulin, *Global Pricing Strategies for Innovative Essential Drugs*, 3 INT'L J. BIOTECH. 338 (2001).

and static efficiency[37] and where demand dispersion between countries is great.[38]

3.4 Differential pricing does not imply cost-shifting

A common objection to differential pricing is that it implies "cost shifting" from low-price markets to high-price markets.[39] This argument either ignores the jointness of costs or mistakenly assumes that joint costs should be allocated equally to all users. As long as markets are separate, a firm would rationally set the price in each market based on conditions in that market, independent of prices in other markets. If low-price users cover at least their marginal costs and make some contributions to the joint costs of R&D, prices in high-price countries can be *lower* than they would have to be in the absence of such contributions.

If price differences were unsustainable, due to parallel trade and external referencing,[40] then manufacturers would tend to charge a single price that is between the differentiated prices that would have been offered. Under such uniform pricing, consumers with relatively inelastic demand may have somewhat lower prices due to associating with consumers with more elastic demand. Although the high-income, inelastic users may try to justify this as "eliminating cost-shifting," it could more appropriately be called "free riding" by the high-income, price-inelastic consumers on the low-income, price-elastic consumers.

4. Actual vs. optimal price differentials and the breakdown of market separation: Parallel trade and external referencing

Opposition to the differential pricing approach is based in part on the observation that actual price differences within countries and between countries do not appear to approximate likely ROP levels, given income differentials.[41] In fact, these observations show that the current system is not well designed to achieve appropriate price differentials. The status quo provides no evidence on how the approach might work if appropriate reforms were adopted.

4.1 The breakdown of market separation: Parallel importation and external referencing

The breakdown of market separation and hence of manufacturers' ability to maintain price differentials is probably the single most important obstacle to

---

[37] *See* J.A. Hausman & J.K. MacKie-Mason, *Price Discrimination and Patent Policy*, 19 RAND J. ECON. 253 (1988).
[38] *See* Malueg & Schwartz, above n. 33.
[39] Press Release, Leon Brittan, Speech on Pharmaceutical Pricing (European Commission 2 Dec. 1992).
[40] These terms are defined in the following section.
[41] F.M. Scherer & Jayashree Watal, *Post-TRIPS Options for Access to Patented Medicines in Developing Nations*, 5 J. INT'L ECON. L. 913 (2002).

lower prices in low-income countries. The primary factors are two policies favored by some middle and higher-income countries: importation (hereafter parallel trade) and external referencing.[42]

Parallel trade occurs when an intermediary exports an originator product from one country to another to profit from the price differentials set by the manufacturer. Parallel trade violates traditional patent rules, whereby the patent holder could bar unauthorized importation of its product. These traditional patent rules were preserved in the North American Free Trade Association (NAFTA).[43] However, the European Union authorizes parallel trade within the E.U., adopting the view that the originator firm exhausts its patent rights with respect to parallel trade once it places the product on the market anywhere in the E.U.[44]

The United States has enacted legislation to permit re-importation of drugs, but so far these provisions have not been implemented, due to quality concerns and doubts about whether cost savings would be passed on to consumers.[45] However, personal imports from Canada are sufficiently large to be attracting responses by manufacturers, and political pressure for legalizing importation into the United States from other developed countries is growing.

Parallel trade is often erroneously defended using the standard economic arguments for free trade, but these do not apply. Lower prices in countries that parallel export pharmaceuticals usually result from aggressive price regulation, lack of patent protection, or lower per capita income, factors that lead the originator firm to grant lower prices.[46] None of these factors creates an efficiency gain from trade. In fact, parallel trade can increase social costs, due to costs of transportation, re-labeling and quality control, and can reduce the

---

[42] Although high-income countries so far do not formally permit parallel imports from or referencing to poor countries, informal referencing does occur, and some importing has occurred, although it is illegal. *See, e.g.*, G. Dyer, *Netherlands Acts on Re-sold AIDS Drugs*, FINANCIAL TIMES, 22 Oct. 2002, at 8.

[43] North American Free Trade Agreement, 17 Dec. 1992 ch. 17, art. 1709, 32 I.L.M. 605 (1993).

[44] Treaty Establishing The European Community, ch. 2, 1997 O.J. (C 340) 3; Parallel Imports of Proprietary Medicines, European Commission Communication (19 Jan. 2004), *available at* http://europa.eu.int/comm/internal_market/goods/docs/medicines/2004–01-comm_en.pdf.

[45] Press Release, U.S. Senator Judd Gregg, Gregg Introduces Bill to Allow for Safe Importation of Prescription Drugs from Canada (2 June 2004), *available at* http://gregg.senate.gov/press/press060204.htm. H.R. 2427: The Pharmaceutical Market Access Act of 2003, Congressional Budget Office Cost Estimate, *available at* http://www.cbo.gov/showdoc.cfm?index=4852&sequence=0.

[46] Lower labor cost is only a small fraction of total production costs, hence is unlikely to account for significant price differences. The legal liability system in the United States may also contribute to higher prices there, at least for some drugs. See R. Manning, *Products Liability and Prescription Drug Prices in Canada and the United States*, 40 J.L. & ECON. 203 (1997).

welfare gains from differential pricing.[47] Most of the savings usually accrue to the intermediaries, not to the consumers or payers in the importing country who continue to pay the higher price.[48]

The second policy that erodes separate markets and promotes price spillovers is external referencing, which occurs when governments or other purchasers use low foreign drug prices as a benchmark for regulating their domestic prices. Such external referencing is used formally by the Netherlands, Canada, Greece and Italy, among others, and used informally by many other countries.[49] External referencing is equivalent to fully importing a lower foreign price. The risk that low prices granted in low-income countries would lead high-income countries to demand similarly low prices is probably an important obstacle to lower prices in the former nations.

Faced with price leakages due to external referencing and parallel trade, a firm's rational response is to attempt to set a single international price or narrow band of prices. Consistent with this prediction, companies frequently now attempt to obtain a uniform launch price throughout the EU, and launch may be delayed or precluded in countries that do not meet this target price.[50] Formally, if two markets L and H were linked, the profit-maximizing strategy would be to charge a single price P in both markets, with markup M, based on the weighted average of the demand elasticities in the two markets, with weights that reflect relative shares of total volume Q:[51]

$$M = 1/(E_H\ w_H + E_L\ w_L) \qquad (5)$$

where $w_L = q_L/Q$ and $w_H = q_H/Q$

Thus, if the low-income market were small and price-elastic, relative to the high-income market, the single price would be dominated by conditions in the high-income market. This single price could far exceed the price that would

---

[47] The UK and the Netherlands attempt to "claw back" the profit that accrues to the pharmacy when it dispenses a cheaper parallel import rather than brand. P. Danzon & J. Ketcham, Reference Pricing of Pharmaceuticals for Medicare: Evidence from Germany, the Netherlands and New Zealand, NBER Working Paper w10007 (Oct. 2003).

[48] See Malueg & Schwartz, above n. 33 (finding that mixed systems (in which blocks of countries with similar income levels permit parallel trade) yield greater benefits than either uniform pricing in all markets or complete discrimination (i.e. a different price in each country), provided that there were no "holes" in the groups.) They argue that the E.U. should put its member states into sub-groups banded by income and only permit parallel trade within each subgroup.

[49] President Clinton's 1994 Health Security Act proposed to limit U.S. prices to the lowest price in 22 countries. Health Security Act, H.R. 3600, 103d Cong. (1994).

[50] For evidence in lags with which products are launched, see P.M. Danzon et al., The Impact of Price Regulation on the Launch Delay of New Drugs: Evidence from Twenty Five Countries in the 1990s, The Wharton School Working Paper (2003).

[51] See Hausman & MacKie-Mason, above n. 37, at 256.

have been charged in the low-income market, had markets been separate, as determined by equation (4).

This elimination of price differentials is inefficient and inequitable. Consumers in low-income countries face inappropriately high prices and forego medicines, even though they might be willing to pay prices sufficient to cover their marginal cost. High-income countries might appear to benefit in the short run from trying to import low prices. But in the long run these countries are also likely to lose as the breakdown of differential pricing leads to lower revenues, less R&D and hence fewer new medicines.[52]

4.2 Cross-national price differentials

Cross-national price differentials appear to deviate significantly from what might be expected based on income as a proxy for price sensitivity. Some high-income countries have relatively low prices, while some low-income countries face high prices relative to their income level. For example, looking at a sample of list prices for 20 drugs in 14 countries in 1998, one author found a correlation between average price and per capita income of only around 0.5, with significant dispersion in this correlation across drugs.[53] Some prices in relatively poor countries were higher than U.S. prices. Another study found that for 15 AIDS antiretroviral drugs in 18 countries for the period 1995–1999 the average price was 85 percent of the U.S. list price, and 20 percent of these prices were above the U.S. level.[54] The authors found that per capita income did help to explain price differences, but the link weakened over the period as companies began offering discounts that were unrelated to average income. In a study of 249 molecules in nine countries, still other authors found that average price differentials for high-income countries were roughly commensurate with income differentials, but the two middle-income countries, Mexico and Chile, faced prices far out of line with their lower per capita income.[55]

Several factors contribute to the weak relationship between per capita income and prices. First, government purchasers or regulators in some high-income countries use their monopsony power to reduce prices to relatively low levels, using external referencing, internal reference pricing and other controls. Second, the threat of external price spillovers makes manufacturers reluctant to grant low prices to low-income countries for fear that these would undermine potentially higher prices in other countries.

---

[52] John Vernon, Price Regulation, Capital Market Imperfections and Strategic R&D Investment Behavior in the Pharmaceutical Industry: Consequences for Innovation (2003) (Applied Economics PhD Dissertation, University of Pennsylvania).
[53] K.E. Maskus, Parallel Imports in Pharmaceuticals: Implications for Competition and Prices in Developing Countries, Final Report to World Intellectual Property Organization (2001).
[54] F.M. Scherer & J. Watal, above n. 41. [55] Danzon & Furukawa, above n. 20.

Third, the tendency for prices in low-income countries to be inappropriately high, relative to their average per capita income, may reflect manufacturers' response to the internal price spillovers between high-income and low-income market segments within those countries mentioned earlier. The highly unequal distribution of income in some countries, and the lack of programs to provide subsidized medicines to poorer people, means that a small, high-income subgroup dominates potential pharmaceutical sales, leading to prices that are geared to that subgroup but are unaffordable for other subgroups.[56]

The ideal solution in such cases is to separate the submarkets within the country, for example, by establishing a program that serves the low-income subgroup only, with discounted prices that are not available to the higher-income subgroup. Although many developing countries in principle make drugs available at no or low charge to low-income patients through public hospitals and clinics, in practice many poor people purchase drugs in the private sector because public clinics are not geographically convenient, often require long waits, or simply do not have the drugs.[57]

4.3 Price differentials within the U.S.

In the United States, actual price differentials between market segments for on-patent drugs are reasonably consistent with inverse demand elasticities.[58] Health plans either manage their own pharmacy benefits or contract with pharmacy benefit managers (PBMs). These PBMs use tiered formularies to define lists of generic, preferred brand and non-preferred brand drugs, with significant co-payment differentials between the tiers. With incentives for consumers and sometimes physicians to use drugs on the preferred list, PBMs can shift market share to preferred drugs from non-preferred drugs, effectively increasing the demand elasticity facing pharmaceutical companies. Companies give larger discounts the greater is the PBM's ability to shift market share to drugs on the preferred tier. PBMs use similar strategies to negotiate discounts on dispensing fees charged by pharmacists.

By contrast, patients who have unmanaged drug coverage or no drug insurance get neither manufacturer discounts nor discounted pharmacy dispensing fees. They have no price-sensitive intermediary that can shift market share towards firms that offer lower prices.[59] Although in theory physicians might play this role, in practice physicians' prescribing decisions appear to be relatively price-insensitive. This U.S. experience suggests the value of having

---

[56] The results are equivalent to the situation when only one price can be charged as between a high-income and low-income countries. *See* Hausman & MacKie-Mason, above n. 37.
[57] Macroeconomics and Health: Investing in Health for Economic Development, Commission on Macroeconomics and Health, Report to World Health Organization (20 Dec. 2001).
[58] This is explained in more detail in Danzon, above n. 9, at 301.   [59] *Id.*

an intermediary that can influence demand and hence can bargain with manufacturers on behalf of consumers.

A major political obstacle to acceptance of differential pricing on behalf of DCs is the view that prices in the United States are too high for the uninsured and low-income populations.[60] This is, however, fundamentally an insurance problem that will be addressed for seniors by the new Medicare Drug Benefit, which should enable them to benefit from negotiated discounts on drug prices and dispensing fees similar to the discounts enjoyed by others with PBM-managed benefits.[61] Trying to address the perceived problem of high prices in the United States through parallel imports or external referencing to lower prices in other countries may not benefit that country in the long run because of the negative dynamic effects on R&D and the supply of new drugs. The short-run response is likely to be a reduced willingness of drug companies to offer lower prices in other countries, including lower-income countries, for fear that these discounts may be "imported" into the U.S. through referencing or parallel trade. This will exacerbate the existing tendency for lags in launch or non-launch of new drugs in countries with relatively low prices.[62]

Competitive discounting in the United States has been constrained since 1991 by the Medicaid "best price" provision, which requires manufacturers of branded products to give the public Medicaid program the largest discount that they give to any private customer.[63] But Medicaid demand is relatively price-inelastic because beneficiaries have low or zero co-payments and most states do not use formularies to shift demand to lower-priced drugs, at least until recently.[64] The effect of linking Medicaid's relatively price-inelastic market to the more price-elastic private market has been to reduce discounts that manufacturers are willing to grant to private buyers, as suggested by equation (5) above.[65] Thus, in

---

[60] Press Release, Uninsured Consumers Pay Too High a Price For Prescription Drugs in Washington, DC Area and Across the U.S., U.S. Public Interest Research Group News Room (15 July 2003), *available at* http://uspirg.org/uspirgnewsroom.asp?id2=10393&id3=USPIRGnewsroom& (last visited 4 June 2004).

[61] The Medicare Prescription Drug, Improvement, and Modernization Act of 2003, Pub L. No. 108–173, 117 Stat. 2066, *available at* http://thomas.loc.gov/cgi-bin/query/D?c108:4:./temp/~c108qPjAVJ. For analysis of the law, see the Kaiser Foundation *at* www.kff.org.

[62] *See* Danzon et al., above n. 50.

[63] Omnibus Budget Reconciliation Act of 1990, Pub. L. 101–508, 104 Stat. 1388 [hereinafter 1990 OBRA].

[64] Under the 1990 OBRA, Medicaid agreed to adopt open formularies in return for the best price discount provisions, that is, to give up the potential for state Medicaid buyers to use formularies to increase price elasticity in exchange for exploiting the discounts obtained by private sector purchasers. Some states no longer adhere to this. For example, Florida recently required companies to give larger discounts (or assure cost savings through other means) as a condition of having their drugs listed on the Florida Medicaid formulary.

[65] For evidence, see Congressional Budget Office (CBO), How the Medicaid Rebate on Prescription Drugs Affects Pricing in The Pharmaceutical Industry (Jan. 1996), *available at* http://www.cbo.gov/showdoc.cfm?index=4750&sequence=0.

the United States, leakages between markets tend to erode discounts in the more price-elastic markets, an effect that is consistent with the international price data reviewed above.

5. Policies to maintain separate markets and price differentials

A sustainable, broad-based differential pricing structure will only be possible if higher-income countries accept the responsibility to pay higher prices, foregoing the temptation to try to obtain the lower prices granted to low-income countries, and if middle-income countries recognize that it may be appropriate for them to pay prices that provide a return on R&D for at least part of their populations. We discuss next specific policies and recent initiatives that could help sustain price differentials. We then review the pros and cons of confidential negotiation; procurement processes and the associated publishing of price information; and proposals for transparent published discount structures.

5.1 Defining patents based on national boundaries, including the right to bar parallel trade

The simplest way to stop parallel trade is to define patents to include the right for a patent holder in each country to bar unauthorized imports of products that are under patent protection, that is, no doctrine of international exhaustion. This is consistent with traditional law on patent rights in the United States and in the countries comprising the E.U. with respect to non-member states. The economic efficiency case for national boundaries for patents is strongest for industries, such as pharmaceuticals, that incur significant global, joint R&D expense that is optimally recouped by differential pricing.

The World Trade Organization's Agreement on Trade Related Aspects of Intellectual Property Rights (TRIPS) has a provision permitting individual countries to choose their own policies on international exhaustion.[66] It is, therefore, possible for high-income countries to prohibit parallel trade and many do. It is, however, also possible for countries receiving low prices to ban parallel exports, thus protecting themselves from losing the benefit of these low prices.[67] It may be difficult for a low-income country to police a parallel-export ban, but there are strong incentives to do so. However, even if these measures

---

[66] Marrakesh Agreement Establishing the World Trade Organization [WTO Agreement], Annex 1C, Agreement on Trade-Related Aspects of Intellectual Property Rights, 15 April 1994, 33 I.L.M. 81 (1994) [TRIPS Agreement], art. 6.

[67] See Maskus, above n. 53. WTO laws prohibit export quotas, which may affect restrictions on parallel exportation. Patent holders could, however, design licensing agreements and purchasing contracts in such a way that their products were only legally available for sale in the domestic market, providing national competition regulations did not prohibit companies from including such restrictive clauses.

were to stop parallel trade, they would not prevent spillovers due to the external referencing of prices.

5.2 *Higher-income countries forego regulation based on foreign prices*

Any institutional framework to preserve differential pricing will only work if higher-income countries forego the temptation to reduce their prices by referencing lower prices in low-income countries. The U.K. Government recently committed itself not to benchmark or reference prices in developing countries.[68] We are not aware of similar commitments by other higher-income countries. However, even if governments of the G-8 countries committed not to reference DC prices, the risk would remain that other middle-income governments or advocates of lower prices in high-income countries would reference low DC prices if these were observable. If so, making these prices unobservable may be the best approach to achieving the lowest possible prices for DCs.

5.3 *Implementing differential pricing through confidential rebates*

Both parallel trade and external referencing can be addressed by manufacturers and purchasers in low-income countries or market segments using confidential rebates as part of their procurement arrangements. Such rebates should imply that the low prices granted to one purchaser are unobservable to others and cannot be copied. If discounts to low-income countries or market segments were given as confidential rebates paid directly to the ultimate purchaser, while wholesalers were supplied at a common price (or act as distribution agents who do not own the product), the opportunity for other purchasers to demand similar rebates would be eliminated. It also would eliminate the opportunity for wholesalers or other parallel traders to purchase the product at the low price intended for low-income countries and export it to higher-price countries, and would prevent leakages of products between market segments within countries.

Confidential discounts are the chief means by which U.S. managed-care purchasers get lower prices.[69] Discounts are targeted to payers that can move market share and, therefore, have elastic demand. Other, less-elastic purchasers cannot demand similar discounts because the price concessions are not known. In the case of low-income countries, discounts could also be negotiated and linked to specific volume of use. By making rebates payable *ex post* depending on volume of use (or by having a fixed-volume contract), the difficulties of

---

[68] *See* C. Short (Secretary of State for International Development), U.K. Working Group on Increasing Access to Essential Medicines in the Developing World, Policy Recommendations and Strategy Report to the Prime Minister (28 Nov. 2002).
[69] Danzon, above n. 9.

determining elasticities *ex ante*, due to bluffing and other bargaining strategies, would be reduced.

A second argument for keeping prices confidential is that it encourages competition, whereas publishing bid prices can promote tacit collusion between suppliers.[70] This occurs both because companies may seek only to beat the published price rather than to quote their lowest possible price[71] and because companies may send tacit signals to one another in the pattern of their bid prices.

The main argument for price disclosure is that transparency increases public accountability, enabling the public to see if buyers are doing a good job, and reduces the chance of collusion between procurement bodies and bidding companies. In the case of pharmaceuticals, there is also significant public pressure for companies to be seen to offer discounted prices to DCs. These disclosure objectives can, however, be achieved by audit by an approved third party, without incurring either the adverse spillover effects that result when prices are publicly observable or the risk of tacit collusion.

Implicit in these arguments for transparency is the assumption that DCs lack bargaining power, hence public scrutiny is required to see if companies have taken advantage of this. But if a small DC truly had very elastic demand, then it would be in the seller's self-interest to charge a price close to marginal cost, since this would be the profit-maximizing price if volume is highly responsive to price. If companies seek to charge high prices, they will lose business as low-income buyers look for other products, or, in the case of a single-source product, switch to other health priorities where their limited resources can be used more cost-effectively. The small size and low income of some DCs should not *per se* affect their ability to bargain for low prices unless manufacturers face significant fixed costs of operating in these countries (which is an unavoidable component of country-specific marginal cost) or there is significant risk of price spillovers to larger countries with less elastic demand.

It may, however, be useful for governments or other third-party procurers to bargain on behalf of low-income populations in DCs, analogous to the role played by PBMs in the US. If such procurement agents could negotiate confidential discounts and shift volume towards suppliers who gave the lowest prices while maintaining quality, the system should assure that small DCs

---

[70] In the case of a cartel, public disclosure makes it easier for participants to monitor each other's prices and hence to detect and sanction a company that undercuts the cartel price. *See* G.A. Stigler, *A Theory of Oligopoly*, 72 J. POL ECON. 44 (1964); F.M. Scherer, *How US Antitrust Can Go Astray: The Brand Name Prescription Drug Litigation*, 4 INT'L J. ECON. BUS. 239 (1997).

[71] In contrast, there is often price disclosure for context-specific public projects, such as buildings, where information on the winning price bid has limited spillover effects as it is a one-off purchase.

achieve the lowest feasible prices. In countries with a significant middle-income or high-income market segment, such procurement should be confined to the low-income population, in order to avoid pooling the less elastic high-income consumers with the more price-elastic low-income consumers. Procurement for low-income populations already exists for vaccines and some drugs, through UNICEF and public purchases by individual governments.[72] The supply prices of individual vaccine manufacturers to UNICEF are generally confidential.[73]

The Global Fund to Fight AIDS, Tuberculosis and Malaria is becoming a major purchaser of drugs for the treatment of HIV/AIDS, tuberculosis (TB) and malaria, buying multi-source, off-patent drugs as well as newer products, some of which may be on-patent.[74] Procurement is the responsibility of local recipients, but they must follow the procurement policies the Global Fund has developed, including using international procurement agencies when local skills are lacking. On price, the Global Fund requires three principles.[75] First is the use of competitive purchasing to get the lowest price, subject to meeting licensing and quality requirements. Second is that recipients must meet the stipulations of national law, albeit encouraging such laws to exploit the flexibilities in the international agreements, e.g., TRIPS and the Doha declaration. Third is the disclosure of prices paid by recipients, on principle, to provide transparency and accountability.

Sharing information on the prices paid is intended to increase purchasers' bargaining power by increasing their information about companies' willingness to supply. It also assures public accountability, assuming these posted prices are in fact the final transaction prices. However, if prices granted to DCs are observable, similar prices may be demanded by middle-income countries or by advocates for lower drug prices in high-income countries. Such referencing may make companies reluctant to offer low prices to Global Fund recipient countries if these prices are observable to all. In the case of the Global Fund, the clear focus on three diseases and on a defined list of countries may reflect a general recognition that prices offered to the Fund will not be available to other purchasers and that referencing is inappropriate. However, if this turns out not to be the case, then the Global Fund should review its policy on open publication of the prices it obtains in competitive tenders and consider

---

[72] Kremer, *Pharmaceuticals and the Developing World*, above n. 5.
[73] Personal communication from Steve Jarrett, UNICEF, to Patricia Danzon.
[74] The Fund expects that the first two rounds of grants will lead within 5 years to a six-fold increase in the numbers of patients in Sub-Saharan Africa receiving anti-retroviral drugs and a two-fold increase in the numbers in other DCs being treated, giving a total of 790,000 recipients. The numbers of additional patients receiving tuberculosis and malaria treatments should become even higher. *See* The Global Fund, Our Track Record, *at* http://www.theglobalfund.org/en/about/record/.
[75] Global Fund for AIDS, Tuberculosis and Malaria, Report of the Third Board Meeting, Item 10: Report of the Task Force on Procurement and Supply Management (2002), *available at* www.globalfundatm.org/publicdoc/Third%20Board%20Meeting.pdf.

whether a more limited publication available only to beneficiary countries could achieve its objectives without promoting spillovers.

It could be argued that if most high-income countries abstained from parallel trade and external referencing, then price confidentiality to DCs would not be necessary. In fact, several companies have publicly announced differential pricing policies for HIV/AIDS drugs for defined groups of low-income countries.[76] Such voluntary publishing of prices may be a response to political pressure for transparency, but it also suggests a lack of practical concern over spillover effects. However, these company policies do not disclose prices for other countries or for products to treat other diseases.[77] How this issue will evolve is in part an empirical question. If significant spillovers were to occur, companies may respond by withdrawing their publicly announced discounted prices. As noted earlier, independent audits can provide public reassurance without compromising low prices for DCs.

5.4 Structured discounts and a global tiered pricing structure

Some proponents of differential pricing have argued for regulatory frameworks within which companies would engage voluntarily in efficient differentiation. A recent example of this approach came from the E.U. Commission.[78] Others have argued that such an approach would lead to, or should lead to,[79] a published schedule of discounts, perhaps in the name of one or more international bodies, with discounts related to GDP per capita levels and to disease burden. We consider the E.U. proposal and the issues involved in moving to a more formal published schedule.

The European Commission Council Regulation is intended to create a voluntary global tiered pricing system for the prevention, diagnosis and treatment of HIV/AIDS, tuberculosis, malaria and related diseases for 76 of the poorest developing countries, including China, India and South Africa, and to prevent diversion of these products to other markets by ensuring that effective safeguards are in place and by expressly prohibiting re-importation of both on-patent and generic products.[80] To qualify, companies are asked to commit to supply medicines at a discount of 75 percent off the average "ex-factory" price

---

[76] MÉDECINS SANS FRONTIÈRES, UNTANGLING THE WEB OF PRICE REDUCTIONS: A PRICING GUIDE FOR THE PURCHASE OF ARVs FOR DEVELOPING COUNTRIES (3d ed. 2002).

[77] Wholesale price data can be purchased from IMS Health; however these data omit off-invoice discounts. See www.IMSHealth.com.

[78] See European Commission, Proposal for a Council Regulation to Avoid Trade Diversion into the European Union of Certain Key Medicines, COM(02)592 (30 Oct. 2002); Press Release, European Commission, Access to Medicines, IP/03/748 (26 May 2003), available at http://europa.eu.int/comm/trade/csc/med.htm.

[79] MÉDECINS SANS FRONTIÈRES, above n. 76.

[80] See European Commission, above n. 78.

in OECD countries[81] or at production cost plus 15 percent.[82] This proposal[83] was in line with a similar proposal from a U.K. Government Working Party.[84]

Médecins Sans Frontières (MSF) has argued strongly for a uniform preferential pricing system that would not leave discretion with companies. However, there are strong arguments against such a proposal. First, even if the aim were confined to achieving prices close to marginal production cost for drugs to treat HIV/AIDS, Malaria, and TB in the poorest countries, no single, simple percentage discount would achieve this, since production costs and relevant country-specific fixed costs differ. More generally, there is no simple formula to translate the multiple criteria for discounts, notably GDP per capita and disease burden, into a discount table specifying fixed discounts for specific countries that are appropriate across many diseases. Moreover, average per capita income for the entire population is less relevant than per capita income of the poorest groups, on whose behalf the government or some international agency would purchase. In countries with a sizeable middle class, confining discounts to the poorest groups may be necessary to encourage companies to give them the lowest feasible prices. In practice, many policymakers are reluctant to price discriminate within countries, on both political and practical grounds. For example, the U.K. Working Party rejects such differentiation within DCs on the grounds that costs would exceed benefits.[85]

Second, reaching agreement on a specific structured discount table by an international body seems unlikely, given the implications for those countries

---

[81] How the OECD prices would be calculated is not defined (e.g. sales weighted, GDP weighted or unweighted). Price information on the OECD discount option must be disclosed to the Commission in the application. Companies would be required to supply an annual sales report for each product to the Commission on a confidential basis. The implication is that prices offered would remain confidential.

[82] Under the production cost-plus option, company data would remain confidential; an independent auditor agreed by the manufacturer and the Commission would be required to certify that the price exceeds production cost by the allowed margin.

[83] These rates, together with the list of target countries and diseases, are included in Annexes to the Regulation. This makes them easier to amend and so to change the scope of the proposal.

[84] Following the 2001 G8 Summit, the U.K. Government set up a working group to establish "an international framework that would facilitate voluntary, widespread, sustainable and predictable differential pricing as the operational norm." *See* Short, above n. 68. The scope proposed was 49 DCs and all Sub-Saharan Africa (i.e. 63 countries in total), focusing initially on drugs to treat HIV/AIDS (including opportunistic infections), TB and malaria. There was no formula, but prices should be close to the cost of manufacture (undefined). Independent audit would be used where needed to ensure confidentiality whilst establishing whether a product met such criteria. The Working Group recommended systematic global monitoring by WHO (with methodology and improved databases) to determine whether differential pricing was significantly improving country access.

[85] C. Short, above n. 68.

and subgroups that would not get the lowest prices. The E.U. regulation proposes 75 percent discounts for the poorest 76 countries; the U.K. proposal applies similar discounts to 63 countries. Focusing on the poorest countries may reflect a view that other countries are able to look after themselves.[86] However, it likely also reflects the increasing difficulty of specifying appropriate discount percentages and classifying countries as one goes beyond the most essential drugs for the poorest countries.

By contrast, a system of confidential, negotiated rebates would be fully flexible and hence could be extended to the full range of drugs and countries that should benefit from some degree of discounts. This is extremely important, given the large and growing disease burden in DCs of non-infectious, chronic diseases, for which effective medicines exist but are unaffordable to the poor in these countries.

Third, as noted above, published discounts could freeze prices and undermine competition,[87] particularly in drug classes with few competitors. There is a risk that published prices become norms that preclude access to larger discounts. Alternatively, if such published prices become a starting point, from which buyers negotiate discounts through competitive bidding and possibly compulsory licensing, then need for published prices becomes doubtful.

Fourth, defining the benchmark price would be difficult and, as noted earlier, the EU regulation does not include a definition of price. Moreover, once the benchmark has been defined, the discount schedule effectively would link prices in different markets, implying a modified version of equation (5).[88] If prices in high-income countries were the benchmark from which discounts for low and middle-income countries were calculated, these high-income country prices may be affected by the linkages to other markets. For example, a discount structure intended to reduce prices in middle-income countries (by proposing fixed percentage discounts off high-income country prices) could lead to *higher* prices in some developed markets if the middle-income markets are large and relatively inelastic. Specifically, it may be profitable for companies to raise prices in a higher-income country (above the optimal level for that market) because application of the discount formula would result in a higher price in a large, middle-income country market where demand is inelastic. Such effects would be similar to the U.S. experience, where the requirement to give "best" private price to Medicaid led to smaller discounts for private buyers.[89]

Fifth, companies could refuse to offer these discounts to some or all of the listed countries. The only effective sanction would be bad publicity. Moreover, companies may resist such regulated, transparent discounts, even though they might be willing to offer similar discounts in confidential negotiations, both

---

[86] *Id.*; European Commission, above n. 78.   [87] For discussion, see above § 5.3.
[88] The prices in the two markets are not the same but are linked by a fixed discount percentage.
[89] CBO, above n. 65.

because of the risk of spillovers of these low prices and, more generally, because they might see scheduled discounts as a first step towards a comprehensive system of international price regulation. Such an approach would be highly inefficient given the competitive nature of the pharmaceutical industry.

As an alternative to scheduled discounts off benchmark prices, both the E.U. and U.K. governments propose regulating discounts as a mark-up over audited costs. This approach would avoid the pitfalls of linking prices across markets by a rigid discount schedule, but would have other problems common to all cost-based approaches. It might be manageable in the case of drugs for HIV/AIDS, TB and malaria for a defined list of least-developed countries. But if applied to a broader list of drugs and countries, including some that should appropriately contribute to R&D, cost-based pricing would raise major economic, accounting and political issues, some of which were mentioned earlier.

First, cost-plus pricing proposals leave unspecified whether marginal cost should include contributions towards production capacity for drugs where supplying the needs of DCs would require construction of additional production capacity. This problem is most acute for anti-retrovirals, for which existing capacity is inadequate to meet DC needs, and for vaccines and other new drugs that may be developed for DCs.[90] A related issue is whether marginal cost can include country-specific fixed costs.

Second, defining prices in terms of costs is widely recognized to be an inefficient approach to regulation in any industry, because cost plus pricing rules reduce incentives to keep costs down.[91] Third, in the case of countries from which some recovery of R&D is appropriate, the measurement and allocation of R&D costs pose additional problems. Product-specific accounting data would not reflect the cost of R&D failures, or the cumulative cost of R&D investments, plus the time cost of money, over the 10–15 year lag between drug discovery and product approval. There is no agreed mechanism for allocating the joint costs among countries.

Moreover, companies may be reluctant to disclose costs for competitive reasons and because they may be used in pricing formulas in developed markets. The fundamental problem is that, as discussed earlier, it is not generally appropriate to price a pharmaceutical in a particular market by reference to the cost of supplying that particular product to that market, even if this cost could be measured.[92]

In conclusion, negotiated, confidential price discounts are likely to provide the most efficient approach to achieving appropriate price differences.

---

[90] Manufacture of Antiretrovirals in Developing Countries and Challenges for the Future, Report by the Secretariat of World Health Organization Executive Board, EB114/15 (29 Apr. 2004).
[91] H. Averch & L. Johnson, *Behavior of the Firm Under Regulatory Constraint*, 52 AM. ECON. REV. 1052 (1962).
[92] *See* above § 3 on Ramsey pricing.

However, this approach would work best if bargaining were conducted by either an international or national procurement agency that can make price and volume commitments. Given the widespread skepticism about relying on private contracts, auditing could ensure that some details are subject to scrutiny without compromising the confidentiality of final prices. We note that companies and the Global Fund are making price information public and that the U.K. Working Party is proposing price monitoring by the WHO.[93] Our view is that these policies may need to be revisited if the price information is used by middle-income and high-income countries to demand lower prices for drugs.

It may be that, in this context, with disclosure confined to three diseases and a defined group of low-income countries, the risks of price leakage into other markets are outweighed by the benefits of increased bargaining power of DCs and their agents. However, attempts to generalize discount structures, as proposed by MSF, moving beyond a narrow number of diseases and countries, are likely to be counterproductive and to increase the prices paid by DCs for drugs.

6. Compulsory licensing and the use of generics: Doha and beyond

The TRIPS agreement introduced a minimum standard of 20-year patent protection for pharmaceuticals in all WTO countries with transitional arrangements for DCs. In particular, least-developed countries were exempt until 2006, and this exemption was extended to 2016 by the Doha Declaration.[94] IP protection was not backdated but applied prospectively, with a requirement to set up a mailbox from 1995, so that when patent protection was introduced, all products registered since 1995 could receive protection.[95]

Under Article 31 of the TRIPS agreement, compulsory licensing (which requires the patent holder to grant a production license to another entity, usually a local generic company) was permitted, albeit with requirements for negotiations with the patent holder and for royalties to be paid on "reasonable commercial terms." In "national emergencies" governments could dispense with the need to negotiate. However, compulsory licenses could only be issued "predominantly for the supply of the domestic market".[96]

Following widespread protests, the TRIPS agreement was revisited at the Doha Ministerial meeting in 2001.[97] A national emergency was said to include "public health crises including those relating to HIV/AIDS, tuberculosis, malaria and other epidemics."[98] It was also agreed to tackle the issue of restricting compulsory licensing to domestic use in order to enable countries with no domestic industry to import compulsory licensed products.

---

[93] Short, above n. 68.
[94] World Trade Organization, Declaration on the TRIPS Agreement and Public Health, WTO Doc. WT/MIN (01)/DEC//2 (14 Nov. 2001).
[95] TRIPS Agreement, above n. 66, arts. 70.8, 70.9.   [96] *Id.* art. 31(f).
[97] *See* WTO, above n. 94.   [98] *See id.* para. 1.

However, subsequent discussions to resolve this issue broke down at the end of 2002 over the permissible scope of licensing. The United States wanted to confine compulsory licensing to a defined number of DCs and to a limited number of diseases, including HIV/AIDS, TB, malaria and other epidemics. This was not acceptable to the other countries. Negotiations began again in 2003 and an agreement was reached in August 2003.[99]

Under the agreement, any WTO member with insufficient manufacturing capacity could in principle issue a compulsory license to import any pharmaceutical product. The product would be clearly identified through specific labeling or marking, and information posted on the WTO website. The exporting country would also notify the WTO. The importing country would take "reasonable measures" to prevent re-exportation. The use is not restricted to national health emergencies, although some countries indicated that they would only use it in those circumstances, and others indicated that they would not import at all under this provision. In a supplementary statement the WTO General Council Chairperson placed on record the "shared understandings" that the system would "not be an instrument to pursue industrial or commercial policy objectives," i.e. exporting countries would not use this agreement to advance the commercial interests of their generic industries.[100]

The case for compulsory licensing is strongest if compulsory licensees have a real production cost advantage over originator firms for a given product quality. However, since labor is a relatively small part of production cost and many multinational firms have plants in low-wage countries, it is not obvious that local firms would have a significant cost advantage. Any country-specific fixed costs of operating in a market must be incurred by generic companies also. Originator firms may incur higher costs of providing medical information, monitoring of adverse reactions, and other safety issues. However, if these services were valued at cost by the purchasing country, they would not imply a difference in quality-adjusted cost.[101] If the originator firm charged a price above marginal cost due to market power, the generic licensee would face the same incentives, unless there were multiple competitors.[102] Thus, to the extent

---

[99] WTO, Implementation of paragraph 6 of the Doha Declaration on the TRIPS Agreement and Public Health, WTO General Council Decision No. WT/L/540 (30 Aug. 2003), *available at* http://www.wto.org/english/tratop_e/trips_e/implem_para6_e.htm#asterisk.

[100] World Trade Organization, General Council Chairperson's Statement, Excerpt from the minutes of the General Council Meeting of 30 Aug. 2003, WTO Doc. WT/GC/M/82, para. 29 (13 Nov. 2003).

[101] It may also be that innovator companies value the data on the use of their product for product support in other markets, in which case they may not regard it as a cost to be recovered in local prices.

[102] Consistent with this idea, a sole generic producer in a market typically "shadow prices" just below the originator price. For more on shadow pricing, see H.G. Grabowski & J.M. Vernon, *Brand Loyalty, Entry and Price Competition in Pharmaceuticals After the 1984 Drug Act*, 35 J.L. & ECON. 331 (1992).

that originator firms do charge higher prices than would potential compulsory licensees, this may simply reflect the risk of price spillovers to other markets that is a concern for multinational R&D-based companies but not for generic manufacturers.[103] The appropriate solution is to reduce the risk of price spillovers, as described above, rather than to permit compulsory licensing.

However, if after the elimination of price spillover risks compulsory licensees still would have lower, quality-constant prices than originators, due to lower costs, there would be a case for permitting compulsory licensing of one or more local generic companies and permitting exports to countries that have no local generic producers. The compulsory licensing process should be done by competitive tender, with commitments to assure that the licensees in fact charge the lowest feasible price. This approach assumes that the benefits to consumers in the DCs from access to lower-price medicines would be large, and that the revenue loss and hence adverse effect on R&D incentives of originator firms would be small, because the latter firms' prices would have approximated marginal cost. It is important to note that having only one generic producer probably would not result in a significantly lower price than the originator's, unless the generic price is forced down by competitive tendering.[104] Any single supplier – generic or originator – would choose the profit-maximizing price. If demand conditions result in a price significantly above marginal cost, this would be true for the generic as for the originator.

Compulsory licensing may also be helpful in circumstances where low-income patients lack a third-party procurement agent to bargain on their behalf. In such cases, the availability of competing products made under compulsory licenses would exert competitive pressure on the originator firm's prices. Where governments or international agencies act as procurement agents, the potential threat to buy from generic companies via the use of compulsory licensing may be less relevant, particularly in therapeutic classes where multiple therapeutic substitutes provide competitive pressures. As discussed above, companies would have a commercial incentive to price close to marginal cost in these circumstances.[105]

The risk of permitting compulsory licensing is that this approach may expand to cover a broad range of countries seeking to use that tool to avoid

---

[103] Price spillovers are not a special concern for generic manufacturers, including those with international operations, assuming that they incur minimal investments in R&D. In any case, in such markets as the United States, Germany and the U.K., generic prices are determined by local competition, not by prices in other countries.

[104] For evidence on effects of number of generic competitors on prices, see P.M. Danzon & L. Chao, *Does Regulation Drive Out Competition in the Pharmaceutical Industry?*, 43 J.L. & ECON. 311 (2000).

[105] We note that the prices of some originator HIV/AIDS drugs as listed on the MSF website are below the prices offered by generic companies. This may reflect the impact of multiple generic competitors and also the particular global public concern about HIV/AIDS, but it may also reflect a lower manufacturing cost base and a recognition that target countries cannot afford to pay higher prices.

contributing above marginal cost to pay for R&D. Many middle-income and even high-income countries face health needs for their populations that exceed available budgets, especially as new drugs offer new treatment possibilities.[106] It is a fact of life in every country that "needs" are infinite but budgets are finite. Thus, many countries could make a hardship case for compulsory licensing of a wide range of drugs. In the absence of clear criteria to define which drugs and countries (or populations) should be eligible, the compulsory licensing approach is at risk of undermining the function of patents over broad markets and therapeutic categories. This approach may seem to offer cheap drugs to needy people in the short run, but at the risk of undermining incentives to develop new drugs in the longer run.

A second, often implicit rationale for compulsory licensing is industrial policy, since such licensing may transfer revenues that might have accrued to a multinational company to local firms. If there is an implicit infant-industry or local-production rationale for compulsory licensing, this argument should be made explicit and evaluated on its merits.

7. Conclusions

Differential pricing would go a long way towards making drugs that are developed for high-income countries available and affordable in DCs, while preserving incentives for R&D. Differential pricing based on Ramsey-pricing principles would be consistent with the criterion of economic efficiency. It would also adhere to standard norms of equity, assuming that demand elasticities are inversely related to income.

We have argued that appropriate price differentials could be achieved without a heavy regulatory structure, because manufacturers would have incentives to charge lower prices in countries with more elastic demand, if certain important impediments were removed. Unfortunately, current price differentials are not optimal, for several reasons. Manufacturers are reluctant to grant low prices in low-income countries because they can spill over to higher-income countries through parallel trade and external referencing. Further, pricing in some DCs is dominated by the demands of small, affluent populations, resulting in prices that are unaffordable to the majority of poorer people.

To achieve appropriate and sustainable price differences would require either that middle-income and higher-income countries forego these practices of trying to "import" low prices or that such practices become less feasible. The most promising approach would be for payers and companies to negotiate contracts that include confidential rebates. With confidential rebates, final transactions prices to purchasers can differ across markets without significant

---

[106] World Health Organisation, The World Health Report 2000: Health Systems – Improving Performance (WHO 2000).

differences in manufacturer prices to distributors, which eliminates opportunities for parallel trade and external referencing. As long as higher-income countries attempt to bargain for lower prices that are offered to poor countries, companies rationally would remain unwilling to make such offers. This problem severely undermines the ability of these countries to achieve access to existing drugs and creates hostility to patents. However, patents need not – and probably would not – entail high price-cost mark-ups in poor countries if companies could be confident that low prices granted them would not leak to high-income economies. Similar differential pricing may also be necessary within low-income countries, with confidential rebates to those purchasers that serve the poor.

Differential pricing alone cannot solve the problem of creating incentives for R&D to develop drugs for diseases that are confined to DCs. Differential pricing also would not fully resolve the problems of affordability for existing drugs if these have high marginal production or distribution costs or intermediary margins that make retail prices significantly higher than manufacturer prices. Chronic medications, especially those that are costly to produce, such as anti-retrovirals, may be unaffordable for the neediest populations even at prices close to marginal cost. In such contexts, differential pricing can reduce but not eliminate the affordability problem.

It is important that the option of compulsory licensing be available for use if generic firms have lower production costs than originators or if governments or other agencies cannot procure drugs on behalf of low-income populations. However, given the risks inherent in compulsory licensing, it seems best in practice first to try the approach of strengthening market separation and enable originator firms to maintain differential pricing. In these circumstances, originators may be expected to offer prices comparable to the prices that a local generic firm would charge, which would eliminate the need for compulsory licensing.

17

Increasing R&D incentives for neglected diseases: Lessons from the Orphan Drug Act

HENRY GRABOWSKI[*]

1. Introduction
2. Economics of the pharmaceutical R&D process
    2a. Costs and risks
    2b. R&D returns
    2c. The critical significance of patents in pharmaceuticals
3. The Orphan Drug Act of 1983
    3a. Push and pull incentive programs
    3b. Characteristics of the Orphan Drug Act
    3c. Orphan drug designation and approvals
    3d. Costs of orphan drugs
    3e. Revenues from marketed orphan drugs
    3f. Health benefits of orphan drugs
    3g. The ODA and new drugs for the neglected diseases of poor countries
4. An amended Orphan Drug Act for neglected diseases
    4a. Transferable patent exclusivity rights
    4b. Transferable priority review rights
    4c. Purchase guarantees
5. Summary and conclusions

1. Introduction

A number of studies point to the fact that new medicines have been a key factor underlying the substantial gains in longevity and quality of life realized by individuals over the last half century.[1] A recent survey by David Cutler and Mark McClellan analyzed the degree of medical progress in a number of major

---

[*] Henry Grabowski is Professor of Economics, Duke University.
[1] *See, e.g.*, David M. Cutler & Mark McClellan, *Is Technological Change in Medicine Worth It?*, 20 HEALTH AFF. 11 (2001); Frank R. Lichtenberg, *Are the Benefits of Newer Drugs Worth Their Cost? Evidence from the 1996 MEPS*, 20 HEALTH AFF. 241 (2001); MEASURING THE PRICES OF MEDICAL TREATMENTS (Jack E. Triplett ed., Brookings Institution Press 1999).

diseases.² They found pharmaceutical innovations have provided significant net benefits to patients across a wide spectrum of conditions, such as heart disease, cancer, and depression. These are diseases that are common to both developed and developing countries (i.e. "global diseases"). However, a review of the existing literature indicates relatively fewer R&D investment programs and medical advances devoted to diseases that are specific to and concentrated in developing countries.³ This would include infectious and tropical diseases, such as malaria, tuberculosis and leprosy, which afflict millions of individuals.

The basic challenge to stimulating more research and development on new medicines for these neglected diseases is how to overcome the barriers posed by the low income and ability to pay for health care that exists in developing countries.⁴ Insufficient revenues on the demand side of the market are combined with high fixed costs of R&D on the supply side. From a policy perspective, one needs to design government interventions that will alter the economic incentives that prevail in this situation.

The U.S. Orphan Drug Act of 1983 provides an instructive model in this case.⁵ Under this Act, the U.S. Congress created a set of incentives designed to encourage R&D investment on rare illnesses. This Act covers illnesses or conditions in the United States with a prevalence of less than 200,000 patients. Firms that develop drugs for rare conditions are eligible for a 50 percent tax credit on their clinical development expenses. Other incentives include development grants, counseling and guidance from the Food and Drug Administration (FDA), and a guaranteed seven-year market exclusivity period. This Act has led to an impressive increase in the number of new drugs for rare illnesses over the past two decades, with significant therapeutic benefits for patients.

The success of the U.S. Orphan Drug Act provides some insightful lessons for the R&D investment problem in the case of diseases endemic to developing countries. These diseases have been variously categorized as "diseases of poverty" or "neglected diseases."⁶ In this chapter we shall use the term neglected diseases. From an economic perspective, diseases such as malaria or tuberculosis are also orphan diseases, even though they afflict millions of individuals. As in the case of orphan drugs for rare illnesses, the expected returns from

---

² Cutler & McClellan, above n. 1.
³ Bernard Pecol et al., *Access to Essential Drugs in Poor Countries: A Lost Battle?*, 281 J. AM. MED. ASS'N 361; WHO, Investing in Health Research and Development: Report of the Ad Hoc Committee on Health Research Relating to Future Intervention Options (Geneva, 1996).
⁴ World Health Organization, Report of the Commission on Macroeconomics and Health (Geneva, 2002).
⁵ Orphan Drug Act, Pub. L. No. 97–414, 96 Stat. 2049 (1983), *codified at* 21 U.S.C.,§§ 360aa–360dd (2000).
⁶ *See* WHO, above n. 4; Jean O. Lanjouw, A Patent Policy Proposal for Global Diseases, Brookings Policy Brief (June 2001); Michael Kremer, *Pharmaceuticals and the Developing World*, 16 J. ECON. PERSP. 67 (2002).

investing in treatments for these diseases are too small to cover the high fixed cost of pharmaceutical R&D. One strategy for policymakers is to enhance the U.S. Orphan Drug Act and its international counterparts to change this situation.

In this chapter, I investigate the feasibility of developing an orphan drug-type program oriented to the neglected diseases of developing countries. In the next section, I review recent economic studies of the pharmaceutical R&D process and analyze the factors that contribute to the large costs of developing new medicines. Then I turn to an analysis of the Orphan Drug Act and how it altered the incentives for R&D investment in the case of drugs for rare diseases. The third section focuses on how various push and pull strategies could be employed to increase the R&D investment in neglected diseases. The final section provides a summary and conclusions.

2. Economics of the pharmaceutical R&D process

Competition in the research-based segment of the pharmaceutical industry is centered on the discovery and development of medicines that satisfy an unmet medical need or improve upon existing therapies. Pharmaceutical research and development is a complex, costly, risky, and time-consuming process. Over the past decade, several economic studies have been undertaken of the pharmaceutical R&D process.[7] These studies consider the probability of success, the cost and time to develop a new medicine, and the economic returns to drug R&D. They highlight the large technical and commercial risks associated with the pharmaceutical R&D process and the tremendous variability in the economic returns of new drug introduction.

2a. Costs and risks

The most obvious risk in drug development is that, despite a long and costly development process, most new drug candidates will not reach the market. Failure can result from toxicity, carcinogenicity, manufacturing difficulties, inconvenient dosing characteristics, inadequate efficacy, economic and competitive factors, and various other problems. Typically, a fraction of one percent of the compounds that are synthesized and examined in pre-clinical studies make it into human testing.[8] Of these, only about twenty percent of the compounds entering clinical trials survive the development and FDA approval

---

[7] Joe DiMasi et al., *The Price of Innovation: New Estimates of Drug Development Costs*, 22 J. HEALTH ECON. 151 (2003); F.M. Scherer, *The Link Between Gross Profitability and Pharmaceutical R&D Spendings*, 20 HEALTH AFF. 216 (2001); Henry Grabowski et al., *Returns on Research and Development for 1990s New Drug Introductions*, 20 PHARMACOECON. 11 (2002).

[8] Pharmaceutical Research and Manufacturers of America, Pharmaceutical Industry Profile 2003, at 3 (PhRMA 2003).

process.[9] The prospect of a long and uncertain development period for a new drug is another source of risk in the drug development process. Recent new drug approvals have averaged nine years from the beginning of clinical trials to final FDA approval. The discovery and pre-clinical periods can add another three to five years to this process.[10]

In a recent study, several co-authors and I examined the representative costs for new drugs whose mean introduction date was in the late 1990s.[11] Our average cost estimate incorporates the expenditures for drug candidates that fail in the R&D process, since these costs must be recouped from the revenues of successful drug candidates. We found that it required over $400 million in out of pocket expenditures (in 2000 dollars) to discover and develop the average U.S. new drug introduction.[12] If one also takes account of capital costs utilizing a risk-adjusted cost of capital appropriate for the pharmaceutical industry, capitalized R&D costs per new drug introduction are double the out of pocket costs.

R&D costs were shown to have increased at an annual rate of 7.4 percent above general inflation when compared to the costs for new drug introductions of the 1980s.[13] A major factor accounting for this growth in costs is the size and number of clinical trials, which increased significantly in the 1990s compared to earlier periods. Other important factors include the growing complexity of trials (i.e., more procedures per patient), an increased focus on chronic diseases, and greater costs to recruit and maintain patients for these trials.[14]

2b. R&D returns

In another study, two colleagues and I examined the distribution of returns for 1990–94 new drug introductions.[15] A key finding was that the sales and returns of new drugs exhibit tremendous variability. In particular, we found that a small number of drugs provide a disproportionate share of overall revenues. The search for these exceptional compounds, which generally involve significant therapeutic advances over established therapies, is a key driver of R&D competition in pharmaceuticals.

The worldwide life cycle of sales profiles for the top few deciles and the mean and median drugs are presented in Figure 1.[16] This distribution of returns in pharmaceuticals is highly skewed. We found that only three of ten new drugs cover the R&D costs incurred by the mean new drug (including the costs of failed compounds and discovery costs necessary to generate new product leads). Hence, the R&D process is like a lottery in which most drug

---

[9] Joe DiMasi et al., above n. 7, at 165.   [10] Id.   [11] Id.
[12] See id. at 161–67. There is considerable variability around this estimated value depending on whether the new compound is for an acute or chronic illness, the particular class of diseases it addresses, its degree of innovativeness, and several other relevant factors.
[13] Id.   [14] Id.   [15] Grabowski et al., above n. 7.   [16] Id.

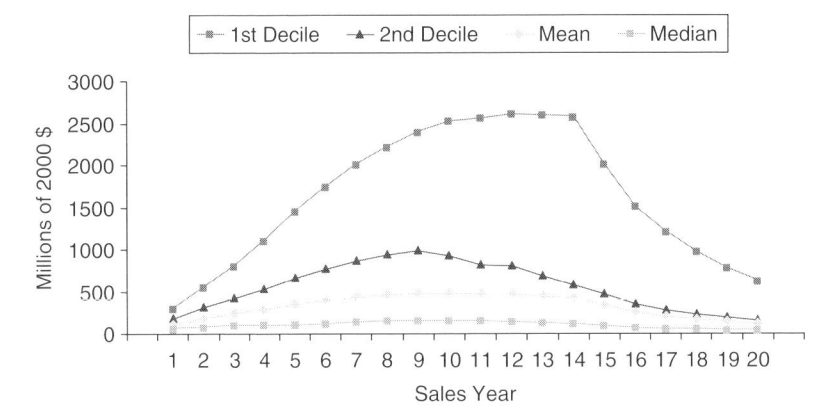

Figure 1. Worldwide Sales Profiles of 1990–94 New Chemical Entities

candidates taken into testing fail, a small number are marketed commercially and achieve modest financial returns, and a few drugs succeed in generating very large returns to the innovating firm.[17]

The highly skewed outcomes observed in Figure 1 reflect both the dynamic nature of the R&D process and the large scientific, regulatory and commercial risks that surround the process. Long time lags, the need to obtain regulatory approval from the FDA, and new drug introductions of competitors compound the various scientific and technical risks. These factors help explain the great variability in market sales and profitability that has been observed in every time cohort that we have examined since the 1970s.[18] Even the largest pharmaceutical firms, with extensive pipelines of new drug candidates, exhibit great variability in the number of approvals and sales from their R&D investment in a given period.[19]

Vernon and I have performed two studies on the factors that influence the size of a company's total R&D expenditures.[20] The two primary factors that we found to be economically significant determinants of R&D expenditures in these studies were a firm's expected returns and its internally generated funds. We found that roughly 25 percent of each million-dollar change in cash flow

---

[17] F.M. Scherer has shown that many industrial R&D activities are characterized by skewed outcome distributions. This is especially the case for venture capital investments. See F.M. SCHERER, NEW PERSPECTIVES ON ECONOMIC GROWTH AND TECHNOLOGICAL INNOVATION 71–80 (Brookings Institution Press 1999).

[18] Grabowski et al., above n. 7, at 23–28.

[19] See Henry Grabowski & John Vernon, *The Distribution of Sales Revenues from Pharmaceutical Innovation*, 18 PHARMACOECON. 21 (2000).

[20] Henry Grabowski & John Vernon, *The Determinants of R&D Expenditures in the Pharmaceutical Industry*, in DRUGS AND HEALTH (R. Helms ed., AEI 1981); Henry Grabowski & John Vernon, *The Determinants of Pharmaceutical Research and Development Expenditures*, 10 J. EVOLUTIONARY ECON. 201 (2000).

was directed toward increased R&D expenditures.[21] The cash flows from successful new products are therefore important in funding R&D for future new product innovations.

2c. The critical significance of patents in pharmaceuticals

Patents have been found to be critically important to pharmaceutical firms in appropriating the benefits from drug innovation.[22] The reason for this follows directly from the characteristics of the pharmaceutical innovation process. As discussed above, it takes several hundred million dollars to discover, develop, and gain regulatory approval for a new medicine. Absent patent protection, or some equivalent market barrier, imitators could free-ride on the innovator's FDA approval and duplicate the compound for a small fraction of the originator's costs. In essence, imitation costs in pharmaceuticals are extremely low relative to the innovator's costs of discovering and developing a new compound. Some form of market exclusivity or market barrier to easy imitation has been essential in this industry to allow pioneers to appropriate enough of the benefits from new drug innovation to cover their large R&D costs and earn a risk-adjusted return on their overall portfolio of R&D programs.

The importance of patents to pharmaceutical innovation has been demonstrated in several studies by economists.[23] By contrast, these studies found that many other research-intensive industries, such as computers and semiconductors, placed greater stress on factors like lead time and efficiencies in the production of new products accruing to first movers.[24] This reflects the fact that R&D costs and

---

[21] In a recent paper, Scherer also has focused on the relationship between pharmaceutical industry profits and R&D outlays. He found a high degree of correlation between the deviations in trends from these series, suggesting that R&D outlays are affected significantly by changes in profitability. He also found that the growth rates on gross margins were substantially lower than the growth rates for R&D outlays, leading to the possibility that growth rates for R&D could lessen in the future. F.M. Scherer, *The Link Between Gross Profitability and Pharmaceutical R&D Spendings*, 20 HEALTH AFF. 216 (2001).

[22] See Richard D. Levin et al., *Appropriating the Returns from Industrial Research and Development*, 3 BROOKINGS PAPERS ON ECON. ACTIVITY 783 (1987).

[23] Edwin Mansfield, *Patents and Innovation: An Empirical Study*, 32 MGMT. SCI. 173 (1986). Edwin Mansfield surveyed the chief research officers of 100 U.S. corporations and found that 60 percent of the innovations commercialized in 1981–1983 by the pharmaceutical firms would not have been developed without patent protection. His findings are consistent with more recent studies. See Levin et al., above n. 22; Wes Cohen et al., Appropriability Conditions and Why Firms Patent and Why They Do Not in the American Manufacturing Sector, Carnegie-Mellon University Working Paper (1997).

[24] In the Levin study, only 3 of 130 industries studied had a higher score than drugs (6.5 out of 7) on the importance of product patents. Conversely, computers and semiconductors had scores of 3.4 and 4.5 respectively on the importance of patents. See the comparative analysis of their computer file containing industry aggregates presented in F.M. SCHERER, INDUSTRY STRUCTURE, STRATEGY AND PUBLIC POLICY 361–362 (Harper Collins 1996).

investment periods are larger than average in pharmaceuticals while imitation costs are lower than in other high-technology industries.

The importance of patent protection in pharmaceuticals is further supported by comparing innovative performance of the pharmaceutical industries in countries with and without strong patent protection. In another study, I found that strong systems of patent protection exist in all countries with strong innovative industries in pharmaceuticals.[25] This is a major finding from analyzing the distribution of important new global drug introductions categorized by the nationality of the originating firms for the period 1970 to 1985. Similarly, longitudinal studies on the growth of R&D expenditures and foreign direct investment in Canada and Japan associated with changes in their patent systems for pharmaceuticals support the significance of intellectual property rights as incentives for innovation.[26]

3. The Orphan Drug Act of 1983

In this section I review the nature of the Orphan Drug Act (ODA) of 1983 and its impacts on drug development.

3a. Push and pull incentive programs

Given the economics of new drug development, strategies for stimulating R&D on orphan drugs and neglected diseases must work either to lower the costs of development ("push programs"), enhance the expected revenues after market launch ("pull programs"), or utilize a combination of both approaches. In the push category, prominent strategies include R&D cost sharing or subsidy programs, which can be accomplished through tax credits, research grants, and related economic incentives. Another potentially powerful push incentive involves programs designed to accelerate drug development and approval by the FDA and other regulatory bodies.

Pull programs work to increase the size of the benefits to innovators after market launch. Three types of pull programs are important. The first is

---

[25] Henry Grabowski, *Innovation and International Competitiveness in Pharmaceuticals*, in EVOLVING TECHNOLOGY AND MARKET STRUCTURE 167 (Arnold Heertje & Mark Perlman eds., University of Michigan Press 1990). *See also* Robert E. Evenson & Sunil Kanwar, Does Intellectual Property Protection Spur Technological Change?, Yale Economics Growth Center Discussion Paper No. 831 (2001).

[26] B. Pazderka, *Implications of Recent Changes in Pharmaceutical Patent Legislation in Canada*, in OECD, DIRECTORATE FOR SCIENCE TECHNOLOGY AND INDUSTRY, ECONOMIC ASPECTS OF BIOTECHNOLOGIES RELATED TO HUMAN HEALTH – PART II: BIOTECHNOLOGY, MEDICAL INNOVATION AND THE ECONOMY: THE KEY RELATIONSHIPS 159 (1998); Ian Neary, *Japanese Industrial Policy and the Pharmaceutical Industry*, in INDUSTRIAL POLICY AND THE PHARMACEUTICAL INDUSTRY 12 (Adrian Toswe ed., OHE 1995).

guaranteed market exclusivity for undertaking the costs and risks of developing a new medicine. This can be important in the case of medical compounds that have no or little patent protection remaining. It is also relevant to situations where the compound's patent protection is subject to uncertainty. The second pull mechanism is a guaranteed purchase agreement. This is relevant where there are no established markets for new medicines or where the resources to pay for these medicines are far below the cost of developing and producing them. This case is particularly relevant to the problem of drug research for diseases in developing economies, as discussed in the next section.

Another kind of pull program would grant firms a transferable right for developing a socially desirable but unprofitable medicine. For example, the firm could obtain the right to additional exclusivity on a drug compound of its choice in the U.S. market for undertaking development of a drug for diseases of poverty. Under the Food and Drug Administration Modernization Act (FDAMA) of 1997,[27] U.S. firms can obtain six months of added market exclusivity on approved medicines in exchange for doing additional clinical investigations to gain FDA approval for pediatric indications. The idea of a transferable or floating exclusivity right is a logical extension of this concept. Alternatively, the right could be structured around priority regulatory review status on a new drug application of the firm's choice. These concepts are explored later in this chapter.

3b. Characteristics of the Orphan Drug Act

In the case of the 1983 ODA, the incentives involve both push and pull elements.[28] First, the law established a 50-percent tax credit on clinical trials for orphan drug indications undertaken in the United States. Second, this was combined with a clinical research grants program, administered by the FDA, which focused on early clinical development (Phase I and II) and involved grants of between $150,000 and $300,000. A third important cost incentive involved providing FDA advice and counseling to sponsors on the characteristics of orphan-drug protocols. As discussed below, many orphan drugs have received priority review and fast-track development status, and FDA approval has been granted based on fewer total clinical subjects than for the average new drug introduction.

The ODA also includes one important pull incentive, which is a guaranteed seven-year market exclusivity period.[29] The FDA has characterized this as the most sought-after incentive. While this exclusivity runs concurrently with the regular patent term, it was a critical factor to many biotechnology drugs. Many of the original biotechnology compounds were natural substances that were not eligible

---

[27] Food and Drug Modernization Act of 1997, Pub. L. 105–115, 111 Stat. 2296 (1997) [hereinafter FDAMA].
[28] Sheila R. Schulman et al., *Implementation of the Orphan Drug Act: 1983–1992*, 47 FOOD & DRUG L.J. 363 (1992).
[29] *Id.*

for patents on the molecule itself. Several of these drugs also were targeted to diseases of low prevalence. Given the uncertainty that surrounded biotechnology patents during this period, the seven-year exclusivity period was an important market incentive to many biopharmaceutical firms.[30] This period of exclusivity was also important in the case of some older chemical entities that were found to be useful for orphan drug indications. In this regard, the first approved therapy for AIDS in 1987, Zovirax (AZT), was a compound that had previously been investigated as a cancer therapy in the 1960s. It received orphan drug status as well as a use patent.[31]

Orphan drug legislation was also enacted in Japan in 1993 and the European Union in 1999. These laws incorporate many of the push and pull incentives incorporated into the United States law.[32] Since the ODA has been in effect much longer than the corresponding acts in Japan and Europe, the focus of my analysis in this paper will be on the U.S. case.

3c. Orphan drug designation and approvals

The FDA concludes that the "ODA has been very successful – more than 200 drugs and biological products for rare diseases have been brought to market since 1983. In contrast, the decade prior to 1983 saw fewer than ten such products come to the market."[33] While a simple pre-ODA and post-ODA time series analysis does not prove causation, the more than tenfold increase in the rate of orphan drug approvals since 1983 is indicative that the Act has indeed been a powerful stimulus to increased R&D investment on rare illnesses.

As of May 2003, the FDA had granted 1,238 orphan drug designations to drug firms and organizations developing medicines for rare illnesses.[34] Furthermore, 238 of these orphan-designated drugs have received marketing approval.[35] Figure 2 shows the annual number of orphan drug approvals for the period 1983–2002.[36] Almost half (46 percent) of all orphan drug approvals were for new drug molecular entities or new biopharmaceuticals. The data in Figure 2 also imply that a large number of previously approved drugs received approval for orphan drug indications. There has been a tendency for the number of orphan drug approvals to decline in the last three years. This decline mirrors a similar decrease in new approved drug applications for pharmaceuticals since 2000. However the number of new orphan drug designations has remained relatively stable.

---

[30] Sheila R. Schulman & Michael Manocchia, *The U.S. Orphan Drug Programme 1983–1995*, 12 PHARMACOECONOMICS 313 (1997).
[31] Willis Emmons & Ashok Nimgade, Burroughs Wellcome and AZT, Case 9–792–004, Harvard Business School (1991).
[32] For a discussion of the specific features of each country's law, see Hannah E. Kettler, *Narrowing the Gap Between Provision and Need for Medicines in Developing Countries* (Office of Health Economics 2000).
[33] www.fda.gov/orphan/history.htm.
[34] www.fda.gov/orphan/designat/allap.rtf.   [35] *Id.*   [36] *See id.*

Figure 2. Orphan Drug Approvals, 1983–2002

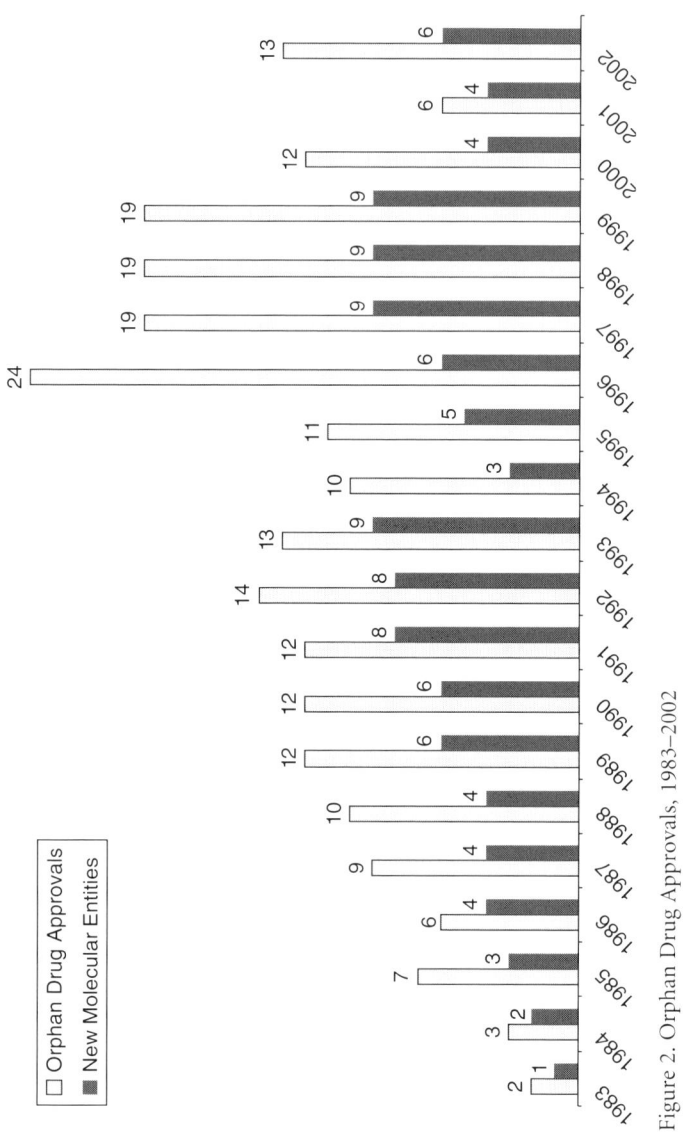

3d. Costs of orphan drugs

A 1993 study of the pharmaceutical industry by the Office of Technology Assessment (OTA) noted that the economics of orphan drug development and approvals may be different from that applicable to other new drug candidates. "These products (orphan drugs) may have a different cost structure from other New Chemical Entities (NCEs), not only because of the tax credit but also because they may involve smaller and shorter clinical trials than other drugs."[37] Available data sources for the number of subjects enrolled in trials and subsequent market sales suggest that the R&D cost structure for orphan drugs is indeed different from that of other NCE introductions.

In addition to protocol assistance from the FDA, many orphan drugs are also eligible for other FDA programs instituted in the 1980s and 1990s.[38] These include priority review, accelerated approval, and fast-track status. Under priority review, the FDA goal is to review new drug and biologics applications in six months or less. Priority review is reserved for new drugs that provide a significant improvement in safety or effectiveness. Most orphan drugs qualify for priority review. Accelerated approval was instituted in 1992 to speed the approval of new treatments for serious or life-threatening diseases. It allows approval to be granted at the earliest phase of development at which safety and efficacy can be reasonably established. This is often done on the basis of a single Phase II trial involving hundreds rather than thousands of patients.

The FDA's fast-track program was established under the FDAMA.[39] It consolidated and expanded the FDA's expedited development and accelerated approval regulations to allow for fast-track designation for drugs with the potential to address unmet medical needs for serious or life-threatening conditions. Fast-track development programs can take advantage of accelerated approval based on surrogate end points, rolling submissions of applications for marketing approval and priority review. A study by Tufts University's Center for the Study of Drug Development found that three years after the program was initiated, half of the 65 fast-track designated products in their analysis also had orphan designations.[40]

An analysis of orphan drug designations in the early 1990s found that nearly half of all orphan drugs up to that time were concentrated in three broad

---

[37] *See, e.g.,* OFFICE OF TECHNOLOGY ASSESSMENT, PHARMACEUTICAL R&D: COSTS, RISKS, AND REWARDS 71 (U.S. Gov't Printing Office 1993).

[38] Sheila R. Schulman & Jeffrey Brown, *The Food and Drug Administration's Early Access and Fast-Track Approval Initiatives: How Have They Worked?*, 50 FOOD & DRUG L.J. 503 (1995); Christopher Paul Milne, *Fast Track Designation Under the Food and Drug Modernization Act: The Industry Experience*, 35 DRUG INFO. J. 71 (2001).

[39] *See* FDAMA, above n. 27.

[40] FDA's Fast Track Program Results in 62% Approval Rate After First 3 Years, Tufts Center for the Study of Drug Development Impact Report vol. 3, No. 1 (Jan./Feb. 2001).

therapeutic areas – cancer, AIDS and genetic diseases.[41] These are generally life-threatening diseases of high unmet medical needs. To the extent that orphan drugs continue to be directed to therapeutic areas with these characteristics, they would become eligible for the FDA's accelerated approval and priority review and fast-track programs. Even if orphan drugs are not formally enrolled in these programs, those compounds that address high unmet medical needs could expect to undergo an accelerated development process, given that the FDA is charged with facilitating orphan drug approvals under ODA. Moreover, because orphan drugs are targeted to rare diseases and illnesses, it may be infeasible to enroll large numbers of patients in clinical trials in most instances.

Janice Reichert has examined the total number of subjects enrolled in trials for 12 new biopharmaceuticals that received FDA approval in the period 1994 to 2000.[42] The sample included seven orphan designated entities. She found that biopharmaceuticals as a group have a significantly lower number of clinical subjects than new drug entities. However, the biopharmaceuticals approved for orphan designated indications had a much smaller number of subjects than the non-orphans. In particular, the mean number of subjects for the seven orphan designated compounds was 576. The average non-orphan biopharmaceutical in her sample had three times as many participants in the trials.

Some data assembled from 1999 FDA marketing approval letters by T. Balasubramaniam are also consistent with the view that the total number of subjects for orphan drug approvals is much smaller than the average for all drugs. In particular, he found that the seven orphan drug marketing approvals in 1999 had a mean sample of 588 patients, with a range of between 152 and 1281 total patients.[43] This compares with an average of more than 5,000 subjects for the typical new drug introduction in the late 1990s.[44]

---

[41] Schulman et al., above n. 28.
[42] Janice M. Reichert, *Clinical Development of Therapeutic Medicines: A Biopharmaceutical Versus Pharmaceutical Product Comparison*, 35 DRUG INFO. J. 337 (2001).
[43] James Love, What Do U.S. IRS Tax Returns Tell Us About R&D Investment?, Consumer Project on Technology Presentation (16 Jan. 2003) (citing data and analysis provided by T. Balasubramaniam), *available at* www.cptech.org. Love also concludes that orphan drug costs are much lower based on aggregate IRS Form 8820 filings for the orphan drug tax credit. While these data are also supportive of OTA's hypothesis, it is important to note they understate firm R&D expenditures on a number of grounds. First, an analysis of FDA data for orphan compounds indicates that many firms file for orphan drug designation within a year before receiving marketing approvals. This would make most or all of their clinical expenditures ineligible for the credit. In addition, more than half of the orphan drug marketing approvals are for drugs already approved for non-market indications. Supplemental drug approvals would be expected to have significantly lower costs than those of new drug introductions. Finally, foreign clinical trials are not eligible for the credit unless they receive an exception based on insufficient subjects in the United States.
[44] Data collected by Parexel for a large number of molecular entities approved in the period 1998 to 2000 found that the mean number of patients per new drug approval (NDA) was over 5,000. *See* PAREXEL, PHARMACEUTICAL R&D STATISTICAL SOURCEBOOK (2001).

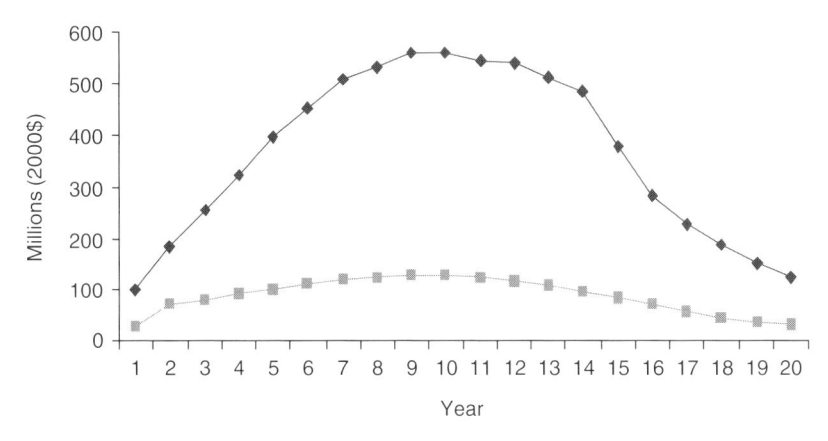

Figure 3. Average Sales of 1990–94 Orphan vs. Non-Orphan New Drug Introductions

3e. *Revenues from marketed orphan drugs*

In Figure 3, I have plotted sales life cycle profiles for new orphan and non-orphan drug introductions in the 1990–1994 cohort.[45] As one can see from this figure, the sales peak for the average orphan drug is in the neighborhood of $100 million compared with $500 million for the mean, non-orphan new drug introduction. While this is a large difference, it is important to keep in mind that sales of the average pharmaceutical are strongly influenced by a few high-volume compounds. In fact, the distribution of sales for orphan drugs is even more skewed than is that for non-orphan compounds.

Figure 4 shows the distribution of tenth-year sales for 1990–94 new orphan drug introductions.[46] There were 27 new orphan drugs launched in this period. The top quintile earned over $500 million in its tenth year on the market (which corresponds to the peak year for most orphan drugs). By contrast, the median quintile had tenth-year sales of only $29.5 million, and most of the drugs in the lower two quintiles had tenth-year sales of less than $10 million. Clearly, there is tremendous heterogeneity in the sales of orphan drugs. Most of these compounds have modest sales, but there are a few "wealthy orphans." The latter consist of some very expensive biopharmaceuticals that have revenues comparable to the pharmaceutical and biological products in the top-selling decile.[47]

The sales data in Figures 3 and 4 are strongly supportive of the conjecture of the Office of Technology Assessment that the R&D cost structure of orphan drugs is very different in nature from that of other drugs.[48] Even allowing for the possibility of a 50-percent tax credit, the sales of most orphan drugs would not support large-scale clinical trials involving several thousand patients, which

---

[45] Grabowski et al., above n. 7. [46] *Id.*
[47] *See* Grabowski & Vernon, above n. 19, at 25.
[48] *See* OFFICE OF TECHNOLOGY ASSESSMENT, above n. 37.

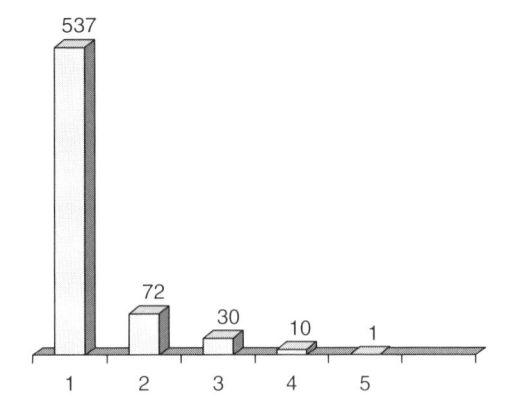

Figure 4. Distribution of 1990–94 Drug Sales by Quintiles

can cost hundreds of millions of dollars for the typical new drug approval. Based on available information on orphan-product sales and the number of subjects listed in the available new drug application (NDA) approval letters, it is reasonable to conclude that the representative orphan drug has R&D costs that are significantly lower than non-orphan compounds.

Clearly, FDA actions and programs under the ODA have been a major factor in the rapid growth in the number of drugs targeted to diseases of low prevalence. The application of the R&D tax credit has also significantly reduced the net costs for many orphan compounds, especially those of smaller biopharmaceutical firms. Finally, the exclusivity provision has also been critical for many compounds with expired or weaker patent protection.

3f. Health benefits of orphan drugs

In a recent paper, two authors investigated the health benefits to individuals suffering from rare illnesses in both the pre-ODA and the post-ODA periods.[49] For this purpose, they employed data on disease prevalence, prescription drug consumption, and longevity by three-digit ICD-9 disease codes in 1979 and 1998.[50] The measure of longevity used in their analysis is the percentage of individuals dying young, defined as dying before age 55.

---

[49] Frank R. Lichtenberg & Joel Waldfogel, Does Misery Love Company? Evidence from Pharmaceutical Markets Before and After the Orphan Drug Act, National Bureau of Economic Research Working Paper 9750 (June 2003).

[50] ICD-9 disease codes are a standard method to classify medical conditions for mortality data in death certificates. The related ICD-9-CMs are used to code morbidity data in inpatient and outpatient medical records. For more information, see the National Center for Health Statistics, The International Classification of Diseases, Ninth Revision (1996), available at www.cdc.gov/NCHS/icd9.htm.

Table 1 *FDA Approved Orphan Drugs for Neglected Diseases*

Disease	Drug	Sponsor	Designation Date	Approval Date
Malaria	Halofentrine	SKB	Nov. 1991	July 1992
	MefloquineHCL	HL Roche	April 1988	May 1989
Leishmaniasis	Liposomal AmpothericinB	Fujisawa	Dec. 1996	Aug. 1997
Meningitis	Cytarabine lipsomal	DepoTech	June 1993	April 1999
	Liposomal AmpotericinB	Fujisawa	Dec. 1996	Aug. 1997
Tuberculosis	Aminosalicylic Acid	Jacobus Pharm Co	Feb. 1992	June 1994
	Rifampin	HMR	Dec. 1985	May 1989
	R, I, P	HMR	Dec. 1985	May 1994
	Rifapentine	HRM	June 1995	June 1998
Trypanosoma	Eflornithine HCL	HMR	April 1986	Nov. 1990
Leprosy	Clofazimine	Novartis	June 1984	Dec. 1986
	Thalidomide	Celgene	Jul 1995	July 1998

Source: FDA, Office of Orphan Products Development, website (http://www.fda.gov/orphan), 1 July 2003; Kettler (2000), above n. 32, pp. 44–45

The analysts found that the percentage of individuals dying young from relatively rare illnesses (conditions existing for diseases at the 25th prevalence percentile) fell from 22 percent in 1979 to 16 percent in 1998, or six full percentage points.[51] By contrast, the percentage of individuals dying young from more common disease conditions (i.e., those in the 75th prevalence percentile) had fallen only two percentage points, from 13 to 11 percent over the same period. Moreover, the greatest percentage decline in individuals dying young occurred for disease categories in which there were greater availability and consumption of orphan drugs. This indicates that the availability of novel therapies for rare diseases had a statistically significant effect on the longevity of people suffering from these conditions.

That analysis provides evidence that the aggregate health effects of ODA for individuals suffering from rare diseases have been positive. Their analysis is

[51] Lichtenberg & Waldfogel, above n. 49.

also consistent with the fact that a large number of new molecular entities in the orphan drug category have been given priority ratings by the FDA (indicating they are significant advances over available therapies.)[52] Clearly, the Orphan Drug Act has been successful in encouraging many new therapies for rare diseases and illnesses that have provided significant health benefits to patients in terms of both quality of life and longevity.

3g. The ODA and new drugs for the neglected diseases of poor countries

There have been relatively few drugs developed under the ODA for tropical diseases and other neglected diseases of poor countries. As of July 2003, there were only twelve orphan drug approvals in the United States targeted specifically at tropical diseases, as shown in Table 1.[53] This group represents approximately five percent of the 238 market approvals for orphan designated indications. Moreover, most of these drugs are for conditions that either have some market in the developed countries or in the travelers' market (tuberculosis, malaria and meningitis) or have other approved indications with a market in developed economies.

Diseases that predominately affect poor countries are technically eligible for all the incentives of the ODA, given their low prevalence in the United States. However, there is a lack of market pull incentives in poor countries corresponding to the prevailing insurance reimbursement available in developed economies. In the case of the U.S. health system, most orphan drugs, once they receive FDA approval, are reimbursed by insurance companies as well as by the Medicare and Medicaid programs.[54]

The primary barrier to R&D investment in neglected diseases of poor countries is the low ability to pay in developing countries.[55] Many of these countries devote as little as $2 per capita per year to health care, reflecting their low GDP per capita.[56] Furthermore, there has been a reluctance of developed countries to

---

[52] See, e.g., CDER Report to the Nation for the years 2000 to 2003, at www.fda.gov/cder/reports. For earlier years, the March edition of *Pharmacy Times* gives a list of all new molecular entities' approvals for the prior year with their FDA ratings.

[53] AIDS-related drugs are excluded from this table. The sources for Table 1 are FDA, Office of Orphan Products Development, website: http://www.fda/gov/orphan (last visited 1 July 2003), and H. Kettler, above n. 32, at 44–45.

[54] Even in the case of very expensive orphan medicines, such as Ceredase for Gaucher's Disease, which can cost more than $100,000 per year for the initial treatment, this drug was covered by Medicare, Medicaid and private insurance companies. In addition, Genzyme provided the drug free to approximately five percent of patients without insurance. See Genzyme Corporation: Strategic Challenges with Ceredase, Harvard Business School Case 9–793–120 (17 May 1994). See also Christopher-Paul Milne, *Orphan Products – Pain Relief for Clinical Development Headaches*, Nature Biotechnology, 20 Aug. 2002, at 780.

[55] See Kremer, above n. 6; Lanjouw, above n. 6.   [56] See WHO, above n. 4.

come to their aid for health care, at least until recently. The ability-to-pay barrier is compounded by other barriers, including the lack of patent protection in many developing countries as well as an inadequate medical and political infrastructure to insure efficient and timely delivery of prescription drugs.[57]

Some drugs targeted to neglected diseases have been developed under the philanthropic programs of major pharmaceutical firms. The most notable of these programs is Merck's donation of the drug Mectizan (ivermectin) for river blindness. Merck has provided medical infrastructure support as well as free medicines for the treatment of this disease since 1987. More than 200 million individuals in 33 countries have been treated for river blindness under Merck's program.[58] Other important current initiatives include Glaxo SmithKline's drug albendazole for filariasis, and the anti-trachoma program of Pfizer and Novartis' multi-drug regimen for leprosy.[59] While drug-donation programs have made a strong contribution to eradicating the health threats for many significant diseases of poor countries, the problems are too broad in scope and R&D development costs are too large in scale to rely primarily on philanthropic donations from a handful of private firms and their non-governmental organization (NGO) partners.

A number of public-private partnerships (PPPs) also have emerged in recent years that target the development of new vaccines and medicines for diseases, such as malaria, tuberculosis (TB), and AIDS, that have a high burden in developing countries.[60] Under these arrangements, non-profit foundations and organizations plan to support many R&D projects at different stages of the development process. They also seek out both public and private institutions as research partners, using a variety of novel contractual relationships. Many of these agreements specify explicit price and volume requirements. For example the International AIDS Vaccine Initiative (IAVI) has provided research grants to support development of an AIDS vaccine targeted to African strains of the disease. The participating firms retain international patent rights to the technology, but must agree to supply any approved vaccines to the public sector in developing countries at reasonable prices and

---

[57] Keith E. Maskus, *Ensuring Access to Essential Medicines: Some Economic Considerations*, 20 WIS. INT'L L.J., 563 (2002).
[58] Private correspondence with Jeff Kempecos and Jeff Sturchio at Merck (on file with the author).
[59] Discussions with James Russo, Executive Director of the Partnership for Quality Medical Donations, *available at* www.pmq.org. *See also* Peter Wehrwein, Pharmacophilanthropy, Harvard University (1993), *available at* http://www.hsph.harvard.edu/review/summer_pharmaco.shtml.
[60] For an economic analysis of these public-private partnerships, see Hannah Kettler & Adrian Towse, Public Private Partnerships for Research and Development: Medicines and Vaccines for Diseases of Poverty, Office of Health Economics Report (Dec. 2002).

in sufficient quantities.[61] Similarly, the Global Alliance for TB Development has recently reached a licensing agreement with Chiron for the development of a new TB drug for which no royalties would be earned on sales in less-developed countries.[62]

At the present time, there is much experimentation with intellectual property rights and contractual terms. It is too soon to evaluate the success or feasibility of the basic financial model of the various partnership programs. Even if these highly targeted programs ultimately prove to be successful, it is still desirable that government bodies also consider a broad-based program of decentralized market incentives for developing treatments of neglected diseases. This task will be important for disease targets that are not part of the targeted donation programs of large multinational firms or the emerging partnerships described above. Furthermore, the targeted PPPs have an ambitious set of goals and may fall short of their funding plans. In any case, targeted PPP programs are likely to benefit from some complementary push and pull side incentives when they enter the later and more expensive part of the development distribution stage.

4. An amended Orphan Drug Act for neglected diseases

As discussed earlier, most of the cost-saving provisions of the ODA already apply to R&D investment for neglected diseases. While the R&D tax credit is specifically designed to cover domestic clinical trials, a firm can obtain the credit for foreign trials if the number of available subjects is too limited in the United States.[63] Neglected diseases would also be eligible for clinical research grant programs and priority reviews at the FDA.

It would help enhance these cost-side incentives if a list of designated diseases of high unmet needs in poor countries would automatically qualify for these tax credits and priority review without requiring firms to apply for such coverage. Because grants currently cover only clinical development trials, it would also be beneficial to earmark some grant funds specifically for basic research on these diseases to involve participation of university researchers and smaller biopharmaceutical firms in the discovery phase. This change would be particularly desirable given recent advances in biotechnology genomics and the understanding of the molecular basis of pathogenesis, which has enhanced the

---

[61] While agreements are tailored to each party, all define reasonable price based on income level of the country and other relevent factors. *See* www.iavi.org/pdf/ipagreements.pdf.

[62] *See* www.tballiance.org; Aimee Dingswell, *Chiron: Parsing the TB Universe*, BioCentury, 4 Feb. 2002.

[63] *See* Chris Milne et al., Orphan Drug Laws in Europe and the U.S.: Incentives for the Research and Development of Medicines for the Diseases of Poverty, WHO Commission on Macroeconomics and Health Working Paper No. WG 2:9, at 6 (2002), *available at* http://www.cmhealth.org/docs/wg2_paper9.pdf.

scientific opportunities for developing significant new vaccines and therapies for many infectious and tropical diseases.[64]

The basic challenge at the present time, however, is to add a significant market-pull incentive for neglected diseases, which can be combined with the R&D cost incentives that are, for the most part, already in place. Again, a key barrier causing low levels of R&D investment in the neglected diseases of poor countries is the lack of sufficient market revenues to undertake the high fixed costs of R&D. The existing R&D cost incentives in the ODA are not sufficient where markets for new drugs are so limited that even subsidized R&D costs cannot be covered.

This new incentive program needs to balance several objectives. First, the market-pull incentive must be large enough to overcome the barrier raised by insufficient market revenues. Second, the medicines should be distributed in poor countries at a price that is consistent with broad access. Third, the programs should be structured in such a manner that they receive support from important constituent groups and funding from policymakers. I next examine three policy options in this regard: transferable patent exclusivity, transferable priority review rights, and purchase funds or guarantees.[65]

4a. Transferable patent exclusivity rights

One idea that has been proposed by Kettler and others is a roaming or transferable patent exclusivity right.[66] Specifically, companies would be allowed to extend the patent life of a product of their choice for a pre-specified amount of time in high-income markets in exchange for developing and obtaining market approval for a neglected disease in poor countries. The process could work as follows. First, a list of qualifying disease categories would be prepared by a group of experts under the auspices of an international body, such as the WHO or World Bank. This group also would approve applications from companies for special neglected disease designations and possibly also set a price guideline that would facilitate access. When the product is approved by a public-health regulatory body and begins distribution in developing-country markets, the firm would receive the transfer exclusivity rights in the participating developed-country's market.

The program could incorporate a fixed extension period like the six-month exclusivity extension for pediatric indications under FDAMA. This would be the simplest case to administer from a bureaucratic standpoint. It also would

---

[64] See, e.g., MICROBIAL THREATS TO HEALTH: EMERGENCE, DETECTION, AND RESPONSE 184 (Mark S. Smolinski et al. eds., National Academies Press 2002) (discussing these new technologies); see also World Health Organization, World Health (2002), available at www.who.int/genomics.
[65] For a further discussion of how a modified orphan drug program might affect the R&D effort for specific diseases, see Milne et al., above n. 63.
[66] See Kettler, above n. 32.

send clear signals to firms on how much benefit they might expect from participation. Alternatively, firms could engage in negotiations on the number of extra months of exclusivity with a government regulatory agency, such as the U.S. Department of Health and Human Services, on a case-by-case basis at the time that the firm receives approval for their R&D program on a neglected disease.

Under the negotiated exclusivity scenario, the length of the extensions in the United States and other countries could be a function of the expected R&D costs and extra returns as well as the expected social value of a new medicine for the designated disease. However, this scenario would open a complex regulatory negotiation process in which all of the key variables would be subject to a high level of uncertainty. This would be especially the case for products at early stages of the R&D processes. Nevertheless, if authorities waited until a drug were successfully developed and much of this uncertainty had been reduced, issues of credibility would arise for the innovating firms. Once the drug was developed, government regulators would have a strong incentive to minimize the added exclusivity time in order to keep the costs of the program low. For these reasons, time period fixed up front, with a possible market cap on additional earnings, would appear to be a more feasible approach than a negotiated exclusivity approach.

Using the experience with the pediatrics exclusivity program as a guide, transferable exclusivity would likely become a powerful incentive program for increased R&D investment on diseases of poverty.[67] A major disadvantage with this proposal, however, is that the cost burden would be borne by consumers and payers of the drug granted the extended exclusivity. Given current concerns about escalating health care and prescription drug expenditures in the United States and other sponsoring countries, the proposal would likely face stiff opposition from insurance payers and patient groups. Indeed, recent proposed legislation on prescription drugs in the United States actually has moved in a different direction. In the Medicare Prescription Drug Improvement and Modernization Act of 2003, Congress has included various provisions to facilitate generic competition, and there are a number of federal and state legislators now pushing for drug importation as a cost containment measure.[68] Hence, the prospects for legislative passage of a proposal increasing the market exclusivity of existing patented drugs, even for such a worthy cause as more R&D for neglected diseases, would not appear to be great at the present time.

---

[67] According to PhRMA, in the four years from 1997 to 2001, pharmaceutical companies had launched 400 pediatric studies for about 200 drugs that were eligible for the six-month exclusivity. PhRMA, Pharmaceutical Industry Profile 2002, at 17 (PhRMA 2002).

[68] Medicare Prescription Drug Improvement and Modernization Act, Pl. 108–173 (2003). *See* Wendy Schacht & John Thomas, The Hatch Waxman Act: Proposed Legislation Affecting Pharmaceutical Prices, Congressional Research Services Issue Brief for Congress, IB10105 (5 Jan. 2004). For a discussion of the drug importation provision proposed by the House in July 2003, see Would Prescription Drug Importation Reduce U.S. Drug Spending?, Congressional Budget Office Economic and Budget Issue Brief (29 Apr. 2004). *See also* Ceci Connolly, *Drug Reimportation Plan Saves City $2.5 Million*, WASH. POST, 15 July 2004, at A03.

4b. Transferable priority review rights

An alternative to the transferable exclusivity proposal would be a transferable right of priority review by the regulatory authorities. If a firm had the option to elect priority review for one of its products designated for standard review by the FDA, this could also be a powerful incentive to undertake an R&D investment program on diseases affecting poor countries. Currently, the average time to review a non-priority new drug application by the FDA is 18 months. On the other hand, priority drugs take an average of around six months. Using the findings from my analysis of returns on pharmaceutical R&D for drugs introduced between 1990 and 1994, a reduction of one year in FDA review time would be worth approximately $300 million in increased present value for the average product in the top decile of compounds and more than $100 million for a product in the second decile.[69]

A potential problem with transferable priority review rights is that they could slow down the approval of other drugs in the United States, which are addressed to equally deserving or even more pressing needs. Like all government agencies, the FDA operates under budgeting and manpower constraints. The program should be configured to avoid such adverse consequences. In particular, the transferable priority review drugs could be put in a new review category and allocated resources from a separate budget funded by general revenues or new user fees.

The overall costs to society to fund a program of transferable priority review rights in exchange for firms developing new therapies for neglected diseases are likely to be much smaller than a transferable exclusivity rights program. Moreover, priority review rights are likely to be more valuable to smaller biotech firms that have no established products, but expect to launch new medicines in the near future. Finally, a government incentive program where the costs basically would be incurred to get drugs on the market sooner in both developed and developing countries is likely to be more acceptable politically than an incentive program that delayed patent expiration and generic entry for leading drug products.

4c. Purchase guarantees

Another pull mechanism that has been discussed extensively in the recent literature is the establishment of funds to purchase a pre-specified amount of new vaccine or drug that meets a given therapeutic profile for a neglected disease.[70] The idea is to overcome the ability-to-pay barrier to R&D investment

---

[69] Grabowski et al., above n. 7.
[70] See, e.g., Michael Kremer & Jeffrey Sachs, *A Cure for Indifference*, THE FINANCIAL TIMES, 5 May 1999, at 14.

by committing in advance to a level of market purchases that would allow a reasonable return on expected R&D outlays to firms that successfully developed new products. Products that exceed the established profile in terms of efficacy could be given a bonus payment. Compared to extended exclusivity or transferable priority review rights, purchase funds are a more novel approach without any real precedent in providing incentives for pharmaceutical R&D funding.

The purchase fund policy option has been elaborated in most detailed form by Michael Kremer in the context of the development of vaccines for the diseases of malaria, tuberculosis and HIV-AIDS.[71] Under this proposal, a sizeable fund, on the order of $250 to $500 million or more, would be established to purchase the new vaccines. Candidate vaccines would need to be approved by a regulatory agency, such as the FDA. They would be distributed at a low, affordable cost in eligible countries. Distribution would, however, be subject to a modest co-payment to insure that vaccines met a market test in terms of acceptability. In this way, the access issue would be addressed. Intellectual property rights would also be protected since the commitment would be to purchase only from original producers and licensees. Government purchasers in the developing countries would also have incentives to adhere to intellectual property rights in order to receive the highly subsidized price that came with participation in the program.

While purchase funds have a number of attractive features on economic grounds, there are also some basic problems that would need to be overcome. Foremost is the issue of credibility. As discussed earlier, pharmaceutical R&D typically spans a period of ten years or so. It can take another decade or more for firms to recoup the R&D costs and earn a competitive rate of return on this investment. Given the long time spans, firms would be concerned that the funding agencies either would renege or be unable to deliver on their commitments once a drug was successfully developed and approved. The leaders and priorities of governments and donor groups are subject to substantial changes over a 20-year period. Given that future government politicians and purchasers would have a strong incentive to try to obtain medicines as cheaply as possible once they became available, a creditable long-term purchase commitment is absolutely essential for this incentive program to work. Kremer has presented some ideas and options for enhancing credibility in the context of vaccine purchases for AIDS and malaria.[72]

Kremer, using information from industry analysts, estimates that a $250 to $500 million real annual market would be required to motivate substantial research for new vaccines in these disease areas.[73] In fact, this number seems

---

[71] Michael Kremer, *Creating Markets for New Vaccines – Part I: Rationale*, and *Part II: Design Issues, in* INNOVATION POLICY AND THE ECONOMY (Adam B. Jaffe et al. eds., 2001).
[72] *Id.*   [73] *See* Kremer, above n. 6, at 85.

low unless R&D costs can also be kept below average for the industry through use of orphan-drug tax credits, fast-track approval, and other means discussed above. At the same time, the high social value that would be associated with a vaccine against AIDS, malaria, or TB implies that a purchase fund of considerably larger size would still be an extremely cost-effective investment if it resulted in an effective vaccine against these diseases.

In the United States, Senators Frist and Kerry and Representatives Palosi and Dunn have advocated a tax credit on the sales of vaccines for AIDS, tuberculosis, and malaria to non-profit and international organizations serving developing countries.[74] Each dollar of sales would be matched by a dollar of tax credit. This would be a market-pull mechanism corresponding in spirit to the purchase fund concept. A similar measure was endorsed by the Clinton Administration in its fiscal year 2001 budget, but was not passed by Congress.[75]

The purchase fund approach would seem best suited, at least initially, to high profile diseases, such as AIDS, malaria and TB, with the largest disease burden in developing countries. These are diseases for which policymakers in developed countries and international donor organizations may be able to raise substantial earmarked funds. If so, purchase funds could be a natural complement to an expanded orphan drug program along the lines discussed. For example, an amended ODA that includes a transferable right of priority review would be a significant pull incentive applicable to all neglected diseases. Purchase funds then could be an option for certain diseases of high visibility and burden. Since pull programs do not become effective until a firm actually meets the requirements set out for the neglected disease, successful enterprises could choose between a purchase fund and transferable priority review if both options were available. Alternatively, policymakers could stipulate that certain high profile diseases with large purchase funds would not be eligible for transferable rights of priority review, but the diseases without designated purchase funds would have such option rights.

5. Summary and conclusions

The U.S. Orphan Drug Act has been a great success in encouraging the development of new drugs for rare diseases. Unfortunately, while new medicines for the neglected diseases of poverty are technically eligible for the incentives embodied in the Act, less than five percent of the orphan drug marketing approvals have been for such indications. The basic problem is insufficient expected revenues associated with the low ability to pay for health care in poor countries, coupled with the high fixed costs of R&D. In developed countries, orphan drugs are typically covered under national and employer

---

[74] The Vaccines for the New Millennium Act, HR 1504, 107th Cong. (2001).
[75] *See* Kremer, above n. 6, at 85.

health insurance plans, so this barrier has been surmounted in many cases, given the other incentives incorporated in the Orphan Drug Act: tax credits and grants, FDA accelerated review programs, and market exclusivity.

The focus of this chapter is to suggest means for extending the Orphan Drug Act to include a strong market-pull mechanism applicable to neglected diseases in poor countries. Prior authors have focused on transferable or roaming exclusivity rights and purchase funds as incentive mechanisms. In this chapter, the concept of a transferable right of priority review was developed as an alternative to transferable exclusivity rights. Transferable rights of priority review have advantages as a decentralized market incentive mechanism. In particular, they are likely to be more cost-effective and acceptable politically compared to transferable exclusivity incentive programs. Furthermore, they could be designed to complement government and private donor purchase funds targeted to specific conditions with high disease burdens, such as malaria and tuberculosis.

COMMENTARY

Comment: Access to essential medicines – Promoting human rights over free trade and intellectual property claims

HEINZ KLUG*

1. Introduction

Over the past five years, there has been an intense international debate, negotiations at the World Trade Organization (WTO) and a variety of political and legal struggles in various jurisdictions over access to affordable medicines in developing countries. Until recently, the debate focused on the ability of the existing medical infrastructure to address the HIV/AIDS pandemic; but more recently the focus has shifted to questioning whether the heightened patent protection of the TRIPS Agreement[1] allows countries sufficient flexibility to deal with domestic health crises.[2] This question has been increasingly driven by the impact of the global HIV/AIDS pandemic and the threat it poses to economic and political stability, particularly in Africa,[3] and it has motivated two new WTO agreements – at Doha and just before Cancun – aimed at providing flexibility under the terms of the TRIPS Agreement.[4] Most recently, the World

---

* Heinz Klug is a Professor of the University of Wisconsin Law School.
[1] Agreement on Trade-Related Aspects of Intellectual Property Rights, 15 Apr. 1994, Marrakesh Agreement Establishing the World Trade Organization, Annex 1C, LEGAL INSTRUMENTS – RESULTS OF THE URUGUAY ROUND vol. 31, 33 I.L.M. 81 (1994) [hereinafter TRIPS Agreement].
[2] Carlos Correa, *Implementing the TRIPS Agreement in the Patents Field – Options for Developing Countries*, 1 J. WORLD INTELL. PROP. 75 (1998); C. CORREA, INTELLECTUAL PROPERTY RIGHTS, THE WTO AND DEVELOPING COUNTRIES: THE TRIPS AGREEMENT AND POLICY OPTIONS (Zed Books 2000). *See also* Frederick Abbott, *Managing the Hydra: The Herculean Task of Ensuring Access to Essential Medicines* [this volume].
[3] A. De Waal, *Why the HIV/AIDS Pandemic is a Structural Threat to Africa's Governance and Economic Development*, 27 FLETCHER F. OF WORLD AFF. 6 (2003).
[4] WTO Doha Ministerial Declaration on the TRIPS Agreement and Public Health, WT/MIN(01)/DEC/2 (14 Nov. 2001) [hereinafter Declaration on TRIPS and Public Health]; WTO Council for TRIPS, Implementation of Paragraph 6 of the Doha Declaration on the TRIPS Agreement and Public Health, IP/C/W/405 (30 Aug. 2003) [hereinafter WTO, Implementation of Paragraph 6].

Health Organization (WHO), which has been at the forefront of these negotiations, declared that the "failure to deliver AIDS drugs to impoverished people is so grave that it has become a global health emergency."[5] With thousands of people dying each day, the question of access to affordable medicines can no longer be treated as a predominately intellectual property or trade-related issue. Rather, it requires the assertion of a human rights perspective to facilitate access to public goods, particularly when dealing with rights to the knowledge required to produce medicines that combat life-threatening diseases.[6]

Placing public health – in this case the global HIV/AIDS pandemic – at the center of this debate exposes the inherent tensions between the law and policies affecting free trade, intellectual property rights, development, and public health. Instead of debating whether the protection of intellectual property rights (IPRs) will eventually lead to increased innovation and foreign investment in developing countries,[7] or whether current drug prices are justified by the need for future research and development,[8] issues which presuppose a hierarchy of values dominated by free trade and IPRs, advocates of a human rights approach insist on the primacy of public health concerns. This position is supported by an approach to interpreting international agreements that takes the broad goals of the post-World War II United Nations system, particularly the emphasis on human rights reflected in the Universal Declaration,[9] as guiding principles. While this approach does not resolve the real policy debates over economic development, trade and the protection of intellectual property, it does raise questions about the relative importance of the so-called "soft law" set out in the preambles and general principles clauses of relevant treaties as opposed to the so-called "hard law" of specific treaty provisions that purport to

---

[5] Press Release, WHO, World Health Organization Says Failure to Deliver AIDS Medicines is a Global Health Emergency: Global AIDS Treatment Emergency Requires Urgent Response – No More Business as Usual (2003), available at http://www.who.int/mediacentre/releases/2003/pr67/en/print.html (visited 26 Sept. 2003).

[6] See I. Kaul & R.U. Mendoza, Advancing the Concept of Public Goods, in PROVIDING GLOBAL PUBLIC GOODS: MANAGING GLOBALIZATION 78, 84 (Inge Kaul et al. eds., Oxford 2003).

[7] Robert Sherwood, A Larger Context for Considering Pharmaceutical Patents in Developing Countries, 15 WORLD BULL. 76 (Jan.-Dec. 1999) (Institute of International Legal Studies, University of Philippines Law Center).

[8] H.E. Bale, Patent Protection and Pharmaceutical Innovation, 29 N.Y.U. J. INT'L L. & POL. 95 (1997); International Federation of Pharmaceutical Manufacturers Associations (IFPMA), TRIPS, Pharmaceuticals and Developing Countries: Implications for Health Care Access, Drug Quality and Drug Development (2000), available at http://www.ifpma.org/admin/MediaServer.jser?@_ID=431&@_MODE=GLB%20(2000). See also Henry Grabowski, Increasing R&D Incentives for Neglected Diseases: Lessons from the Orphan Drug Act [this volume].

[9] Universal Declaration of Human Rights, G.A. Res. 217A (III), U.N. GAOR, UN Doc A/810, at 71 (10 Dec. 1948).

guarantee free trade and protect the rights of property claimants against attempts by national governments to address pressing social needs.[10]

International law, however, provides no institutional mechanism for resolving these tensions. Instead, this failure in global governance leaves each negotiating or interest community to rely upon its own expertise and assumptions about subject matter and priority to define the parameters of its debate and feasible outcomes. Trade negotiators and their allied professionals, including some economists and trade lawyers, balance and barter concessions – greater IP protection for increased access to agricultural and textile markets[11] – while IP lawyers and other economists focus on increasing the likelihood of innovation and foreign investment.[12] While each arena is guided by its own constituting principles, the range of fora provides opportunities for powerful interests to shape the terrain upon which the rules governing particular issues, such as intellectual property, are formed.[13] However, the emergence of non-government organizations (NGOs) operating within the global system as observers and activists is providing a counter-weight to organized business, particularly in the context of the HIV/AIDS pandemic; NGOs have been campaigning and vocally raising concerns about the impact that policies tailored to suit organized business might have on the health of marginalized populations.[14] Furthermore, so long as the ministries of trade, industry and commerce were the only national authorities conducting the negotiations – whether at the WTO or World Intellectual Property Organization (WIPO) – the relationship between the exploding HIV/AIDS pandemic, access to essential medicines and the developing global trade regime remained in the background.

An effective human rights approach must not, however, be limited to the mere counter-assertion of rights – especially if it takes the form of a simple recitation of the long list of United Nations resolutions or other formal commitments to improving health in general, or even statements and resolutions specifically designed to address the HIV/AIDS pandemic. Rather, it should begin by defining the legal and institutional terrain on which multiple claims, norms and strategic interventions accumulate, with a view to either facilitating or hindering attempts to make public health the first level of concern. Such an approach must also recognize the ways in which different

---

[10] *See generally*, Laurence R. Helfer, *Regime Shifting: The TRIPS Agreement and New Dynamics of International Intellectual Property Lawmaking*, 29 YALE J. IN'L L. 1 (2004).
[11] JAYASHREE WATAL, INTELLECTUAL PROPERTY RIGHTS IN THE WTO AND DEVELOPING COUNTRIES (Kluwer Law International 2001).
[12] INTELLECTUAL PROPERTY RIGHTS IN EMERGING MARKETS (Clarisa Long ed., AEI Press 2000).
[13] Peter Drahos & John Braithwaite, INFORMATION FEUDALISM: WHO OWNS THE KNOWLEDGE ECONOMY? (New Press 2002). *See also* SUSAN SELL, PRIVATE POWER, PUBLIC LAW: THE GLOBALIZATION OF INTELLECTUAL PROPERTY RIGHTS (Cambridge University Press 2003).
[14] *See, e.g.*, Helfer, above n. 10; Abbott, above n. 2.

fora have provided alternative loci for competing normative and strategic interventions. These have ranged from the international to the domestic; from WIPO and the WTO to WHO, UNAIDS and the United Nations Conference on Trade and Development (UNCTAD); and from national trade offices to domestic courts. These fora have been used by all sides: those attempting to protect intellectual property, those working to facilitate the transfer of technology, and those trying to ensure affordable access to essential medicines. Although there have been formal links between some of these fora – with UNCTAD and WHO being invited to attend TRIPS Council meetings on the subject – and even more intensive informal interactions involving negotiators, drug companies, experts and NGOs, so long as these have remained within the rubric of trade negotiations and intellectual property rights, the legal framework has remained dominated by the prerogatives of the WTO agreements.

Focusing on the different sources of law governing human rights, trade, and intellectual property rights, I will argue that, in the debate over access to medicines, there is a need to view the relationship between them in terms of the broader normative goals of the international legal order, rather than simply treating them as bases for contending claims.[15] To do this, it is important to understand the recent and socially-constructed nature of the system of intellectual property rights guaranteed by the TRIPS Agreement and to recognize the implications of characterizing the rules as more or less flexible, or as subject to determination under a particular international or national regime. While much of the excellent academic work on this issue has focused on the construction of the TRIPS Agreement, its implementation, interpretation, or even the growing opposition to it, little attention has been paid to the legal assumptions and implications of the different sources and forms of rights and obligations being deployed by the different participants. Finally, I will focus primarily on the implications of choosing particular legal tools or approaches and the impact these choices have on the question of access to medicines and public health more generally.

2. Public health and access to medicines

Until recently, public health has been understood only in terms of measures that are necessary to prevent large-scale epidemics. This preventive approach is evident in the development of the idea of primary health care which "is a blend of essential health services, personal responsibility for one's own health and health-promoting action taken by the community."[16] The most effective means for achieving these goals have been the provision of clean water, good sanitation and more recently, widespread vaccination. While these remain the most

---

[15] *Cf.* JOOST PAUWELYN, CONFLICT OF NORMS IN PUBLIC INTERNATIONAL LAW: HOW WTO LAW RELATES TO OTHER RULES OF INTERNATIONAL LAW 158–236 (2003).
[16] World Health Organization (WHO), Concepts of Health Development, WHO 50TH (1998), *at* www.who.int/archives/who50/en/concepts.htm.

cost effective and broadly applicable ways to protect public health, the revolution in pharmaceuticals during the twentieth century has blurred the line between treatment and prevention. In the context of the HIV/AIDS pandemic, where prevention on its own has proven extremely difficult, the most effective approach seems to lie in the combination of preventive education, treatment, and the lowering of individuals' viral loads. Effective prevention must include treatment and today, particularly in developing countries, this requires access to affordable medicines, which are now understood to be integral to the achievement of public health goals.

At the beginning of the twentieth century, "aspirin was the only widely available modern medicine,"[17] but by the 1970s modern pharmaceuticals existed for nearly every major illness known to medical science. The problem was clearly one of access. According to Dr. Michael Scholtz, WHO's Executive Director of Health Technology and Pharmaceuticals, "one third of the world's population still lacks access to essential drugs while in the poorest parts of Africa and Asia, over fifty percent of the population do not have regular access to the most vital essential drugs."[18] It was in response to this situation that the idea of identifying a list of essential medicines arose and led to the launch of the WHO's essential medicines program in 1977. The program produced model lists of essential drugs that national governments use to make their own local lists; these lists make the task of providing prescribed medications more manageable by limiting the thousands of available medicines to approximately 200 essential ones.

By the turn of the century, over 160 countries had adopted essential drug lists and clinical treatment guidelines based on the WHO's model lists and selection criteria, which effectively doubled access to essential medicines. The criteria laid out for compiling these lists reflect a synergetic amalgam of public health and human rights concerns, with an emphasis on equal access and medical effectiveness. Drugs chosen for an essential medicines list must "satisfy the health needs of the majority of the population; be available at all times in adequate amounts and appropriate dosage forms; and be available at a price that individuals and the community can afford."[19] When it comes to choosing between different available drugs there are five key criteria: relative efficacy, safety, quality, price and availability. Reliance on these criteria has led to an emphasis on off-patent or generic drugs, which

---

[17] Dr. M. Scholtz, International Trade Agreements and Public Health: WHO's Role, Paper Presented at the Conference on Increasing Access to Essential Drugs in a Globalized Economy, at 1 (Amsterdam, 25–26 Nov. 1999), *available at* http://www.who.int/medicines/docs/WTO_Public_Health_Amsterdam_MS.html.
[18] *Id.*
[19] World Health Organization, WHO 50th: Concepts of Health Development (1998), *at* www.who.int/archives/who50/en/concepts.htm (last visited 3 Oct. 2003).

still comprise more than 90 percent of the medicines included on the model list.[20]

While the price of pharmaceuticals varies significantly between different markets,[21] the cost of most patented medicines remains beyond the reach of the bulk of the population in developing countries. This reality is starkly evident in the case of HIV/AIDS, where the emergence of drug regimes to manage the disease in the mid-1980s created a bifurcated epidemic. Opening the Thirteenth International AIDS Conference in Durban, South African High Court Judge Edwin Cameron claimed to embody "the injustice of AIDS in Africa because, on a continent in which 290 million Africans survive on less than one US dollar a day, I can afford medication costs of about $400 per month."[22] Accusing manufacturers of imposing prices that made drugs "unaffordably expensive," Cameron argued that the international patent and trade regime prevents the production and marketing of affordable drugs, despite earlier experience in India, Thailand and Brazil, that demonstrates the feasibility of producing key drugs at costs within reach of the developing world.[23]

Still today, despite a dramatic drop in the price of antiretrovirals, victims of the HIV/AIDS pandemic may be divided into those for whom contraction of HIV remains a death sentence and those for whom the disease is a chronic illness they are able to manage. The disparity in access to antiretrovirals that creates this divide is heightened by the lack of generic alternatives, which has fueled the demand for access to medicines in general and generic drugs in particular. Using affordability as one of the relevant criteria, the essential drug program promoted the use of generic drugs, a strategy which allowed the program to both limit costs and reduce conflict with the global patent-based pharmaceutical industry, which opposes generic substitution (particularly for products originating from countries that did not recognize the companies product patents). The inclusion of twelve antiretrovirals on the WHO's model essential medicines list in 2002[24] brought this tension to the fore and

---

[20] World Health Organization, The Use of Essential Drugs, Ninth Report of the WHO Expert Committee (including the Tenth Model List of Essential Drugs), Technical Report Series, No. 895 (2000).

[21] See, e.g., P. Danzon & A. Towse, *Theory and Implementation of Differential Pricing for Pharmaceuticals* [this volume].

[22] Justice Edwin Cameron, First Jonathan Mann Memorial Lecture: The Deafening Silence of AIDS, XIIIth International AIDS Conference, Durban, South Africa, 9–14 July 2000, *available at* http://www.tac.org.za/newsletter/2000/ns000717.txt

[23] *Id.*

[24] WHO, Department of Essential Medicines, Updating and Disseminating the WHO Model List of Essential Drugs: The Way Forward, draft (22 June 2001), *available at* http://www.who.int/medicines/organization/par/edl/orgedldev.html. See also WHO, Essential Drugs and Medicines Policy Department, WHO Medicines Strategy: 2000–2003, WHO Policy Perspectives on Medicines, No. 1 (Dec. 2000). Geneva.

made it clear that the program's primary reliance on generics for the effective delivery of affordable drugs was no longer tenable.

Research-oriented pharmaceutical manufacturers are involved in a relatively risky business, in which an average of only one "commercially viable drug emerges from every 4,000 to 10,000 compounds screened in a development process that may involve ten years of testing and clinical trials for efficacy and safety."[25] Compounding the high costs of development, however, are the relatively low costs of product imitation – through reverse engineering – and production, which creates what economists refer to as the appropriability problem. Patent law, which aims to reward innovation by providing a limited monopoly to the patent holder, provides intellectual property-intensive industries, such as the pharmaceutical industry, with one means of attaining profitability. But the fruits of medical innovation raise questions that go beyond profitability. As the WHO points out, medicines are "not simply just another commodity," but rather a public good.[26]

Access to essential drugs, from this perspective, becomes a critical part of the fundamental human right to health.[27] While WHO accepts that "patent protection stimulates development of needed new drugs," it argues that "countries must ensure a balance between the interests of the patent holders and the needs of society."[28] Advocating that "generic competition should begin promptly upon patent expiration" and that "preferential pricing is necessary for lower-income countries and should be actively pursued,"[29] WHO also argues that because the research and development priorities of the pharmaceutical industry do not necessarily respond to the needs of the bulk of the world's population, there should be public involvement to "ensure development of new drugs for certain priority health problems."[30] Thus, although WHO does not reject the idea of pharmaceutical patents, its position seems to question the unbridled power of private decision-making in the research effort and to claim some level of exception to the rights of patent holders for essential drugs. This prioritization of health over specific property rights becomes the key to a human rights approach.

---

[25] M. RYAN, KNOWLEDGE DIPLOMACY: GLOBAL COMPETITION AND THE POLITICS OF INTELLECTUAL PROPERTY 5 (Brookings Institution 1998). *See also* Grabowski, above n 8.
[26] Dr. G.H. Brundtland (Director-General of the WHO), International Trade Agreements and Public Health: WHO's Role, presented by video at the Conference on Increasing Access to Essential Drugs in a Globalized Economy (Amsterdam, 25–26 Nov. 1999), at 1, *available at* http://www.who.int/medicines/docs/WTO_Public_Health_Amsterdam_GHB.html.
[27] *See* Jonathan Mann et al., *Health and Human Rights, in* HEALTH AND HUMAN RIGHTS 7 (J. Mann et al. eds., Routledge 1999). *See also* Rebecca Cook, *Gender, Health and Human Rights, in* HEALTH AND HUMAN RIGHTS 262 (J. Mann et al. eds., Routledge 1999).
[28] Scholtz, above n. 17, at 3. [29] *Id.* [30] *Id.*

3. Towards a legal regime that promotes public health

Since the Second World War, it may have been assumed that public health issues, particularly those with transnational effects, would be coordinated by WHO as the relevant body within the United Nations system. The WHO constitution empowered the organization's governing body, the World Health Assembly, to adopt conventions as well as other international legal instruments, including binding regulations.[31] In practice, however, WHO has, until very recently relied more on the adoption of standards, principles and models supplemented by the body's annual reports and occasional declarations such as the Alma-Ata Declaration, which called upon countries and international organizations to adopt a system of primary health care.[32] When it came to the regulation of pharmaceuticals, the essential medicines program exemplified WHO's choice of standards rather than rules. Any binding legal rules controlling the availability of medicines remained rooted in two independent legal processes within national jurisdictions, one regulatory and the other based on the laws of the market, including the relevant intellectual property rules of each country.

Despite a long history of the international regulation of drugs,[33] the availability of any particular medicine still depends on its registration by the health authorities or other agencies empowered to decide which products meet the required standards of safety and effectiveness. Even after registration, access to these drugs depends on their affordability in the market and, for the vast majority of patients in the developing world, on whether the state is able to make the drug available through the public health system. In this latter case, states have mostly relied on the availability of generic substitutes or used their relative market power to bargain for sustainable public sector prices. Despite the state's formal status as sovereign power, many developing countries, particularly in Africa, in the era of structural adjustment and neoliberal fiscal constraints, have lost the capacity to keep their public hospital dispensaries well stocked. The implementation of national essential drugs programs that rely to a large extent on the model lists produced by WHO had provided one mechanism for governments to mange the supply, use and cost of pharmaceuticals.

By the 1990s, however, initiatives affecting health care, particularly within individual nations, seemed to have shifted away from reliance on WHO standards and towards incorporation of decisions made by a range of other

---

[31] D. FIDLER, INTERNATIONAL LAW AND PUBLIC HEALTH: MATERIALS ON AND ANALYSIS OF GLOBAL HEALTH JURISPRUDENCE 118 (Transnational Publishers 2000).

[32] WHO & UNICEF, Declaration of Alma-Ata, Report of the International Conference on Primary Health Care (1978).

[33] J. BRAITHWAITE & P. DRAHOS, GLOBAL BUSINESS REGULATION 360–98 (Cambridge University Press 2000).

international bodies, including the World Bank and the WTO.³⁴ Fueled by the debate over access to medicines in the context of the HIV/AIDS pandemic, the question of the relationship between health and trade policies began to complicate the WTO's trade agenda in the late 1990s. The adoption of the TRIPS Agreement as part of the world trade regime in 1994 fundamentally changed the global legal environment for the production and supply of medicines.³⁵

Despite these and other successes, the pharmaceutical industry's goal of having intellectual property rights enforced through the international trade regime continued to face strong opposition, especially from developing and newly industrialized countries.³⁶ Launching the Doha Round of Multilateral Trade Negotiations in November 2001 was made possible only after Members agreed to adopt the Doha Declaration on the TRIPS Agreement and Public Health.³⁷ Despite concerted opposition from multinational pharmaceutical corporations and a group of developed countries led by the United States, Switzerland and Japan, the 140 trade ministers gathered in Doha, Qatar, agreed that the TRIPS Agreement "does not and should not prevent Members from taking measures to protect public health ... [and] that the Agreement can and should be interpreted and implemented in a manner supportive of WTO Members' rights to protect public health and, in particular, to promote access to medicines for all."³⁸

At first blush, this seemed to be a major negotiating success for the developing world. Not only was this interpretation extended to all aspects of public health, not just pharmaceuticals, but it also emphasized the need to interpret the WTO agreements in more holistic ways. In essence, it accepted that an interpretation reducing barriers to free trade is not automatically the sole or correct understanding of the relevant agreements.

Despite opposition by the United States and Canada to any broad public health exception, their own threats to override Bayers' Cipro patent – in response

---

³⁴ G. WALT, HEALTH POLICY: AN INTRODUCTION TO PROCESS AND POWER (University of the Witwatersrand Press 1994); G. Walt, *Globalization of International Health*, 351 LANCET 434 (7 Feb. 1998).

³⁵ *See, e.g.*, Abbott, above n. 2. At the GATT Ministerial Meeting in 1982, intellectual property rights were discussed in the context of international trade relations for the first time. This was an early indication of the impact of a group of United States corporate leaders who, in the late 1970s, had "devised a strategy to improve intellectual property protection internationally until American standards became the international norm, especially in developing countries." RYAN, above n. 28, at 68. *See also* THE PHARMACEUTICAL CORPORATE PRESENCE IN DEVELOPING COUNTRIES 198 (L.A. Travis & O.P. Williams eds., University of Notre Dame Press 1993).

³⁶ *See* Abbott, above n. 2. *See also* Ruth Gana, *Prospects For Developing Countries Under the TRIPS Agreement*, 29 VAND. J. TRANSNAT'L L. 735 (1996); M. Adelman & S. Baldia, *Prospects and Limits of the Patent Provision in the TRIPS Agreement: The Case of India*, 29 VAND. J. TRANSNAT'L L. 507 (1996).

³⁷ Declaration on TRIPS and Public Health, above n. 4.   ³⁸ *Id.* para. 4.

to the mailed Anthrax attacks[39] – weakened their official claims that the strong protection of patents was the most effective means of securing access to required medicines. The Doha Declaration specifically recognizes the right of a Member to grant compulsory licenses, to determine what constitutes a national emergency or other circumstance of extreme urgency, and to establish its own regime for the exhaustion of intellectual property rights.[40] It also encourages developed countries to promote technology transfer to the least-developed countries, and it extends the initial transition period, with respect to pharmaceutical products, until 1 January 2016.[41] The understanding of the TRIPS Agreement reached in Doha constituted a major shift in the rhetoric about the protection of intellectual property rights; yet, given the realities of pharmaceutical production and distribution, little progress has been made towards actually ensuring access to urgently needed HIV/AIDS related medications.[42]

Despite acknowledging that many countries have "insufficient or no manufacturing capacities in the pharmaceutical sector" and thus cannot make effective use of compulsory licensing,[43] the declaration failed to accept the developing countries' claim that they have the right to grant compulsory licenses to producers in countries with greater manufacturing capacity in order to gain access to medicines. Instead, the declaration instructed the TRIPS Council to find a solution and to report to the WTO General Council by the end of 2002. Without the capacity to produce under compulsory licenses or to import generic equivalents of necessary medications, the problem of access for the millions infected with or suffering from life-threatening diseases in developing countries remained unresolved.

It took the TRIPS Council twenty-one more months to finally reach agreement in late August 2003 on the problem of access to medicines for countries that lack manufacturing capacity.[44] Heralded at first as the solution to the problem of lack of capacity, the pre-Cancun agreement has since been criticized as being unworkable for placing so many prerequisites on its implementation.[45] Before it can benefit from the decision, a country must prove that it

---

[39] *See* Paul Blustein, *Drug Patents Dispute Poses Trade Threat; Generics Fight Could Derail WTO Accord*, WASH. POST, 26 Oct. 2001, Sec. F, at E1. *See also*, Kavaljit Singh, Anthrax, Drug Transnationals and TRIPS: Profits Before Public Health, Z Magazine (December 2001), 39–42.

[40] Declaration on TRIPS and Public Health, above n. 4, para. 5.

[41] *Id.* para. 7.   [42] *See, e.g.*, Abbott, above, n. 2.

[43] Declaration on TRIPS and Public Health, above n. 4, para. 6.

[44] WTO, Implementation of Paragraph 6, above n. 4.

[45] *See* Carlos M. Correa, Implementation of the WTO General Council Decision on Paragraph 6 of the Doha Declaration on the TRIPS Agreement and Public Health (Draft, December 2003). *See also*, Carlos M. Correa, Implications of the Doha Declaration on the TRIPS Agreement and Public Health, Health Economics and Drugs, EDM Series No. 12, WHO/EDM/PAR/2002.3 (WHO June 2002).

lacks production capacity and access to affordable medicines, and that it has an existing health emergency. While the Canadian government has taken steps to change Canadian law to make the export of medicines produced under these compulsory licenses possible, the international brand-name pharmaceutical industry has begun to raise questions about whether the NAFTA Agreement precludes Canada from supplying these medicines. Even the Canadian government itself seems to be limiting its proposals to drugs designed to address HIV/AIDS, malaria and Tuberculosis, a restriction rejected by the developing countries and the pre-Cancun agreement.[46]

Once again, it seems that the question of access to essential medicines is being displaced by an assertion of prior legal commitments. The uncompromising principle of *pacta sunt servanda* is used to elevate notions of unrestricted trade above the health needs of millions of people around the world. While all participants in the debate deny any intention to restrict access or even to indirectly create such an effect,[47] it seems hard to deny that the failure to resolve the issue of compulsory licensing, since it was first raised by the international pharmaceutical industry in its 1997 case against the South African law implementing an essential drugs program, has in fact frustrated attempts to broaden access.

Even if it is accepted that the TRIPS Agreement was initially unsuited to accommodating the complexities of a global health emergency such as HIV/AIDS, it is hardly unreasonable to suggest that, in light of both new understanding of the magnitude of the pandemic and the emergence of effective medicines to address it, the principle of adapting to changed circumstances – or *rebus sic stantibus* – should have been applied to interpretations of the Agreement in order to facilitate attempts to address this exploding crisis. At the least, such an approach would justify the assertion of an article 30 exception under the TRIPS Agreement.[48] Instead, there has been a constant emphasis on the rather unique protection of private rights contained in the TRIPS Agreement and a denial of the legal effect of the so-called soft-law exceptions and principles of interpretation, which are also part of international trade law and essential to realizing public health goals.

4. Conclusion

After twenty years, the HIV/AIDS pandemic has finally been recognized as a global health crisis, yet the debates over access to public goods that are essential

---

[46] *See*, Press Release, 28 Apr. 2004, Canada Proceeds with Bill C-9 on Cheaper Medicines Exports: NGOs Say Initiative is Important, and Urge Other Countries to Avoid the Flaws in the Canadian Model, *available at* www.aidslaw.ca/Media/press-release/e-press-apr2804.pdf.
[47] International Intellectual Property Institute, Patent Protection and Access to HIV/AIDS Pharmaceuticals in Sub-Saharan Africa, Report prepared for WIPO (2000).
[48] *See* TRIPS Agreement, above n. 1, art. 30.

to defeating this scourge continue to be shaped less by concerns about public health than by principles of unrestricted trade and intellectual property rights protection. Within the legal field, the claims of the international patent-based pharmaceutical corporations are framed as rights to property, while the claims of NGOs and developing country governments seeking access to affordable medicines are characterized as legal exceptions to free trade or as the soft law principles contained in general preambular statements. These formal legal distinctions, based upon the interpretation of international agreements created in a context of asymmetrical power, are now relied upon to delay and avoid recognizing the urgent needs of those whose lives and futures are at stake.

Asserting a human rights perspective, from which the health impact of any particular interpretation is seen as an equally legitimate consideration in evaluating the validity of any particular legal option, could dissolve the stifling distinction between so-called hard law obligations and soft law principles or commitments. Introducing such a perspective might facilitate access to medicines by encouraging private investors to reconcile the need for compulsory licenses or other exemptions with their own investment calculus, including investments in generic production. It could also provide developing countries with a means to justify decisions to privilege policies securing access to medicines over concerns about their international trade commitments or threats from patent holders. Instead of relying on thin strands of legal flexibility, NGOs, international organizations, countries and governments attempting to address the global HIV/AIDS pandemic should promote a human rights-based interpretation that places public health ahead of economic claims.

PART III

Sectoral issues: Essential medicines and traditional knowledge

SECTION 2
Protecting traditional knowledge

18

Legal and economic aspects of traditional knowledge

GRAHAM DUTFIELD*

Introduction
I. The nature of traditional knowledge
   A. Broader and narrower definitions
   B. Negative definitions
   C. The question of ownership
II. The economic value of traditional knowledge
III. Legal measures to protect traditional knowledge
   A. Defensive protection measures
      1. Disclosure of origin proposals
      2. Compiling databases of traditional knowledge to serve as prior art
      3. A misappropriation regime
   B. Positive protection measures
      1. *Sui generis* IP regimes
      2. Database rights
      3. Global biocollecting society
      4. Compensatory liability regime
IV. Strategic considerations

Introduction

Traditional knowledge (TK) and its relationship to the formal IPR system has emerged as a mainstream issue in international negotiations on the conservation of biological diversity, international trade, and intellectual property rights. In the past few years, high-level discussions on the subject have been taking place at the World Trade Organization (WTO), the Conference of the Parties to the Convention on Biological Diversity (CBD), and at the World Intellectual

---

* Graham Dutfield is Herchel Smith Senior Research Fellow, Queen Mary Intellectual Property Research Institute, University of London. This article draws on work commissioned for the UNCTAD-ICTSD Capacity Building Project on TRIPS and Development.

Property Organization (WIPO), which has established an Intergovernmental Committee on Intellectual Property and Genetic Resources, Traditional Knowledge and Folklore (IGC). Several developing country governments in these forums have adopted the view that TK needs to be protected legally, and they have criticised the formal IPR system in its present form for not only failing to provide adequate protection for TK, but also for legitimising its misappropriation.[1]

Solutions to the protection of traditional knowledge under intellectual property law may be sought in the form of "positive protection" or "defensive protection." Positive protection refers to the acquisition by the TK holders themselves of an IPR, such as a patent or an alternative right provided by a *sui generis* system. Defensive protection refers to provisions adopted in the law or by the regulatory authorities to prevent IPR claims to knowledge, to cultural expression, or to a given product being granted to unauthorised persons or organisations. The distinction is somewhat artificial in actual practice, but is nonetheless useful conceptually, and is adopted in this chapter.

I. The nature of traditional knowledge

It is rather surprising that this issue has achieved so much prominence. For one thing, some of the governments most engaged in finding solutions have a poor record in extending secure land rights to indigenous peoples and in preventing violations of their basic rights. For another, there seems to be little consensus about what "traditional knowledge" actually means. In fact, this term is understood, misunderstood and applied in a variety of ways, some of which are based on assumptions that conflict with those held by other advocates and commentators. These assumptions pertain to the following areas:

- The identity and nature of TK holding societies
- The relationship between TK and other forms of knowledge
- The extent to which TK can (or cannot) be new and innovative
- Property rights in TK holding societies
- Authorship in traditional societies
- TK and folklore in relation to the public domain

A. Broader and narrower definitions

Despite these different views, the term "traditional knowledge" most commonly refers to knowledge associated with the environment rather than knowledge related to, for example, artworks, handicrafts and other cultural works

---

[1] See generally Thomas Cottier & Marion Panizzon, *Legal Perspectives on Traditional Knowledge: The Case for Intellectual Property Protection* [this volume].

and expressions (which are usually assimilated to folklore). According to one expert, traditional knowledge (or what she calls "traditional environmental knowledge") is

> a body of knowledge built by a group of people through generations living in close contact with nature. It includes a system of classification, a set of empirical observations about the local environment, and a system of self-management that governs resource use.[2]

One may validly respond to this definitional question in a very inclusive way or take a much more restrictive view of what a TK-holding society should look like. Starting with the inclusive view, one could reasonably argue that the existence of TK is not limited to certain types of society but, on the contrary, may be found in all societies no matter how modern they might appear to be and how *un*traditional much of the knowledge in circulation within them is. This is not to suggest that TK is easy to find in every society. Rather, the urbanisation and westernisation processes that have transformed many of the world's societies are unlikely to have resulted in the complete eradication of TK even in those countries that have experienced these phenomena the most comprehensively.

Many observers nonetheless prefer to apply the term more narrowly to knowledge held by tribal populations that live outside the cultural mainstream of the country in which these peoples are situated and whose material cultures are assumed to have changed relatively little over centuries or even millennia. When used this way, the term "traditional knowledge" refers primarily to the knowledge of indigenous and tribal peoples, as defined under the International Labour Organization Convention 169 Concerning Indigenous and Tribal Peoples in Independent Countries.[3] According to this Convention, "tribal peoples" refers to those

> whose social, cultural and economic conditions distinguish them from other sections of the national community, and whose status is regulated wholly or partially by their own customs or traditions or by special laws or regulations.[4]

"Indigenous peoples" refers to those peoples

> who are regarded as indigenous on account of their descent from the populations which inhabited the country, or a geographical region to which the country belongs, at the time of conquest or colonization or the establishment of present state boundaries and who, irrespective of their

---

[2] M. Johnson, *Research On Traditional Environmental Knowledge: Its Development and its Role*, in LORE: CAPTURING TRADITIONAL ENVIRONMENTAL KNOWLEDGE 3, 3–4 (M. Johnson ed., IDRC 1992).
[3] International Labour Conference, Convention 169 Concerning Indigenous and Tribal Peoples in Independent Countries, 27 June 1989, 72 ILO OFF.BULL. 59, 28 I.L.M. 1382.
[4] *Id.* art. 1.1(a).

legal status, retain some or all of their own social, economic, cultural and political institutions.[5]

Because it is so common to characterise TK holders as being members of such societies, the term "indigenous knowledge" is sometimes used instead of, interchangeably with, or as a sub-set of, traditional knowledge.

However, and to make matters still more complicated, the term "indigenous knowledge" is also used by others – often academics – in a slightly different way to express the localised nature of the knowledge they are referring to. Holders of indigenous knowledge, according to this view, may come from a diverse range of (indigenous and non-indigenous) populations and occupational groups, such as traditional farmers, pastoralists, fishermen and nomads, whose knowledge is linked to a specific place and is likely to be based on a long period of occupancy spanning several generations. Often this knowledge is differentiated from more generally held knowledge and from the knowledge of urbanised and western (or westernised) societies.

Still others would claim that such conceptual approaches are unnecessarily narrow, in the sense that traditional knowledge is not necessarily local and informal. To assume otherwise would exclude formalised traditional systems of knowledge that are well documented in ancient texts and are part of the cultural mainstream of some countries, such as the Ayurvedic, Siddha and Unani health systems of the South Asian countries. In some countries, these systems are formalised to such an extent that they are studied at universities and have just as high a status as western biomedicine. In India, some commentators differentiate these knowledge systems from local folk knowledge which still tends to be orally transmitted, even though they consider all these kinds of knowledge to be traditional.

TK-holding individuals, groups and communities, then, may be members of culturally distinct tribal peoples as well as traditional rural communities that are not necessarily removed from the cultural mainstream of a country. TK-holding societies may inhabit areas of both the developing and the developed world, although they are more likely to be found in culturally (and biologically) diverse developing countries where indigenous groups continue to – in the terminology of the Convention on Biological Diversity – embody traditional lifestyles.[6] But while TK holders tend to inhabit rural areas, including very remote ones, individual members of such peoples and communities may live in urban areas and still continue to hold TK. Indeed, TK may even be held and used by individuals in urbanised and westernised societies that have no other connection with the societies from which the TK may have originated.

---

[5] *Id.* art. 1.1(b).
[6] Preamble, Convention on Biological Diversity, 5 June 1992, 31 I.L.M. 818, *available at* http://www.biodiv.org/convention/articles.asp (last accessed 28 July 2004).

Evidently, we should avoid a fixed and dogmatic idea of what TK holders and their communities look like. At the same time, we should not conflate the differing concerns and interests of the various types of TK-holding societies. For indigenous and tribal groups facing cultural extinction, preserving their knowledge may take on a special importance, even if respect for their land rights could be more crucial still.

B. Negative definitions

Because TK is difficult to define, some experts have tried to clarify its meaning either by describing what it is not rather than what it is, or by identifying various features that totally distinguish it from scientific knowledge as the latter term is understood in urban, western, westernised or secular societies. Leaving aside the point made earlier that traditional knowledge also persists in the latter types of society, albeit to a limited extent, such a dichotomy seems at first to be quite plausible.

For example, Martha Johnson, a Canadian anthropologist, identified several ways that TK is generated, recorded, and transmitted, which the relevant academic literature uses to claim that TK is completely different from western scientific knowledge.[7] Thus, traditional knowledge:

i is recorded and transmitted orally;
ii is learned through observation and hands-on experience;
iii is based on the understanding that the elements of matter have a life force;
iv does not view human life as superior to other animate and inanimate elements but that all life-forms have kinship and are interdependent;
v is holistic rather than reductionist;
vi is intuitive rather than analytical, and mainly qualitative rather than quantitative;
vii is based on data generated by resource users themselves rather than specialised groups of researchers;
viii is based on diachronic rather than synchronic data;
ix is rooted in a social context that sees the world in terms of social and spiritual relations between all life-forms; and
x derives its explanations of environmental phenomena from cumulative, collective and often spiritual experiences. Such explanations are checked, validated, and revised daily and seasonally through the annual cycle of activities.[8]

Is this dichotomy simplistic or even false? While seemingly credible, based as it is on a thorough review of the literature, it needs at least to be qualified. Few, if any, populations are completely isolated or have been for a long time.

---

[7] Johnson, above n. 2, at 7–8.   [8] Id.

Cross-cultural transfers of knowledge and consequent hybridisation and cross-fertilisation between different systems of knowledge are thus likely to be the norm rather than the exception. One should therefore exercise caution in assuming that traditional knowledge systems are discrete, pristine and susceptible to generalisations of the kind made by Johnson. As another anthropologist has argued, the same story may be told about scientific knowledge, which "is indisputably anchored culturally in western society, where it largely originated, although with the contemporary communications revolution and cultural globalization, hybridization is occurring and blurring distinctions between scientific and other knowledge on socio-cultural grounds."[9]

Even if these differentiations were completely reliable, one should not conclude that TK is inherently unscientific. Johnson's findings confirm that a great deal of traditional environmental knowledge is empirical and systematic, and therefore scientific. Further support for the view that TK is scientific comes from anthropologists and other academics that use the ethnoscience approach to studying TK relating to nature,[10] and treat this knowledge as being divisible into western scientific fields. On this view, we find ethnobiology, ethnozoology, and ethnomedicine, for example.

Of course, not all TK would fall into these categories. After all, nowhere in the world is all knowledge associated with nature deemed scientific. But it seems reasonable to claim that some TK *is*, at least to some degree, scientific even if the form of expression may seem highly *un*scientific to most of us. For example, an indigenous person and a scientist may both know that quinine bark extract can cure malaria. They are likely to describe what they know in very different ways that may be mutually unintelligible (even when communicated in the same language).[11]

To some, traditional knowledge is by definition age-old knowledge, and creativity and innovation are generally lacking. Otherwise it would not be traditional. However, recent empirical studies of traditional communities have discredited this view. As Russel Barsh, a noted scholar and commentator on the rights of indigenous peoples argues,

> What is "traditional" about traditional knowledge is not its antiquity, but the way it is acquired and used. In other words, the social process of learning and sharing knowledge, which is unique to each indigenous culture, lies at the very heart of its "traditionality." Much of this knowledge

---

[9] P. Sillitoe, *What, Know Natives? Local Knowledge in Development*, 6 SOC. ANTHROPOLOGY 203, 207–09 (1998).

[10] *See id.* at 205.

[11] It might be countered that since the indigenous peoples of western Amazonia do not really understand why quinine works, their quinine-based treatment is a technology that is not science-based. However, one could equally infer that many western "scientific" applications ought likewise to be "downgraded" to technologies, since they are not based on a complete understanding of why they work.

is actually quite new, but it has a social meaning, and legal character, entirely unlike the knowledge indigenous peoples acquire from settlers and industrialized societies.[12]

In short, knowledge held and generated within "traditional" societies can be new as well as old. People who point this out are likely to emphasise that TK has always been adaptive because adaptation is the key to survival in precarious environments. Consequently, while TK is handed down from one generation to another, this does not mean that what each generation inherits is what it passes on. TK develops incrementally with each generation adding to the stock of knowledge.

Similarly, while the traditional classical health systems of China, India, Japan and Korea are based upon ancient texts, these systems continue to evolve and many present-day innovations take place. This is demonstrated by the existence of many Chinese patents on refinements of "traditional" medical formulations,[13] and also by the activities of the Chinese Academy of Traditional Medicine.

C. *The question of ownership*

Who owns knowledge in traditional societies? Is it the individual creator or holder? The leader or leaders of a community? The whole community? A group of people within a nation, tribe or community such as a clan or lineage group? Or alternatively, is traditional knowledge best viewed as something shared freely because traditional societies do not have concepts of property or at least do not apply them to knowledge?

Discussions of these questions are often characterised by tendentious and misleading generalisations. Even if we narrow the scope of our inquiry to indigenous peoples, such as those of the Amazon, Siberia or the Pacific, these questions defy easy answers. Many traditional communities have a strong sharing ethos, but this does not mean that every*thing* is shared with every*body*. This is confirmed by a wealth of anthropological literature, which reveals that such concepts as "ownership" and "property" – or at least close equivalents of them – also exist in most, if not all, traditional societies.[14] In fact, many traditional societies have their own custom-based "intellectual property" systems, which are

---

[12] R.L. Barsh, *Indigenous Knowledge and Biodiversity, in Indigenous Peoples, Their Environments and Territories, in* CULTURAL AND SPIRITUAL VALUES OF BIODIVERSITY 73 (D.A. Posey ed., IT Publications & UNEP 1999).

[13] Liu identifies five ways that traditional Chinese Medicine (TCM) inventions may fulfil the patentability requirements: (1) new techniques for preparation of TCM; (2) isolation of responsible component(s) of TCM; (3) new functions of TCM; (4) new prescriptions; and (5) new pathways of administration of TCM. Y. Liu, *IPR Protection for New Traditional Knowledge: With a Case Study of Traditional Chinese Medicine*, 25 EUR. INTELL. PROP. REV. 194 (2003).

[14] *See generally* D.A. Cleveland & S.C. Murray, *The World's Crop Genetic Resources and the Rights of Indigenous Farmers*, 38 CURRENT ANTHROPOLOGY 477 (1997) (discussing

sometimes quite complex. Customary rules governing access to and use of knowledge do not necessarily differ all that widely from western intellectual property formulations, but in the vast majority of cases they almost certainly do. They also differ widely from each other. Therefore, to assume either that there is a generic form of collective/community IPRs or some generic form of sharing would be misleading since it would ignore the tremendous diversity of traditional proprietary systems.

Despite this empirical reality, it is often assumed that traditional knowledge has been shared freely and that, where property rights do exist, they are always collective in nature rather than individual as in the West. This view may do a disservice to traditional societies concerned about the misappropriation of TK. Consider that once TK has been disclosed to non-members of a small community or group of people, it is usually considered to enter in the public domain unless its disclosure arose through illegal or deceptive behaviour by the recipient, such as a breach of confidence. If no property rights exist, then whose rights are being infringed by somebody's publishing this knowledge, commercially exploiting it, or otherwise appropriating it? Arguably nobody's.

Of course, one may view such behaviour as unjust, regardless of whether the knowledge in question was the property of the TK creator, holder or community. All the same, it becomes logically harder to justify this view if we overstate the case that TK is shared without restrictions.

Even this point, however, may elicit other arguments. One such argument derives from the problematic nature of the public domain concept, at least from the perspective of many traditional societies in which TK holders or others, such as tribal elders, have permanent responsibilities concerning the use of such knowledge, irrespective of whether it is secret, is known to just a few people, or is known to thousands of people throughout the world.[15] Custodianship responsibilities do not necessarily cease to exist just because

---

aspects of the debate over the protection of indigenous farmers' rights); T. Griffiths, *Indigenous Knowledge and Intellectual Property: A Preliminary Review of the Anthropological Literature* (1993) (unpublished paper commissioned by Working Group on Traditional Resource Rights, Oxford) (discussing the concept of exclusive rights as it is inherent in indigenous communities regarding magical knowledge). Shamans and other TK holder specialists may wish to restrict access to their knowledge for reasons other than because they consider it to be their property. For example, sacred knowledge – which may include knowledge of the therapeutic properties of plants – is often considered dangerous if it gets into the hands of the uninitiated. In other words, they may be concerned for the welfare of those who acquire the knowledge and try to use it. The author is grateful to the late Darrell Posey for this insight. *See also* J.W. Hendricks, *Power and Knowledge: Discourse and Ideological Transformation among the Shuar*, 15 AM. ETHNOLOGIST 216 (1988) (discussing the importance of the completion of an apprenticeship for shamans).

[15] *See* D.A. Posey, *Selling Grandma: Commodification of the Sacred through Intellectual Property Rights*, *in* CLAIMING THE STONES/NAMING THE BONES: CULTURAL PROPERTY AND THE NEGOTIATION OF NATIONAL AND ETHNIC IDENTITY 201 (Elazar Barkan & Ronald Bush eds., 2002).

the knowledge has been placed in the so-called public domain. There is no doubt that a tremendous amount of TK has been disclosed and disseminated over the years without the authorisation of the holders. In this context, the following observation about indigenous peoples by Barsh is revealing:

> Indigenous peoples generally think in terms of the freedom of individuals to be what they were created to be, rather than being free from certain kinds of state encroachments. Along with this highly individualized notion of "rights" is a sense of unique personal responsibilities to kin, clan and nation. Each individual's "rights," then, consists of freedom to *exercise responsibilities towards others*, as she or he understands them, without interference.[16]

In short, indigenous societies often consider each member as having *individual* rights and *collective* responsibilities that are linked inextricably. Indeed, the persistence of these responsibilities is probably more of a reason why the formal IPR system is inappropriate than the supposedly collective nature of customary rights over TK. Besides, individual property rights over knowledge are not necessarily absent from many traditional societies, but these will often be accompanied by certain duties.

Attribution is far from a simple matter in many traditional societies. Many commentators, especially those supporting the rights of traditional peoples and communities in the developing world, emphasise the collective nature of creative processes in traditional societies, which they contrast with the individualistic view of creativity (and of ownership in the end-product of that creativity) that prevails in western societies. Such generalisations have some truth to them, but we should not exaggerate the differences either. The sources of much TK are difficult to trace, either because two or more peoples or communities share the knowledge, or because the author is simply unknown.

What of the perceptions of indigenous peoples and other traditional communities? Again, views vary widely. Some indigenous groups actually consider it presumptuous to attribute authorship to a human being or a group of people. According to the late ethnoecologist Darrell Posey, who spent many years studying and working with the Kayapó people of the Amazon, "indigenous singers... may attribute songs to the creator spirit."[17] Australian lawyer Michael Blakeney states, "if the beliefs and practices of Australian indigenous peoples are any guide, authorship may reside in pre-human creator

---

[16] R.L. Barsh, *Indigenous Peoples and the Idea of Individual Human Rights*, 10 NATIVE STUD. REV. 35, 44–45(1995).

[17] D.A. Posey, Indigenous Peoples and Traditional Resource Rights: A Basis for Equitable Relationships?, Green College Centre for Environmental Policy and Understanding Conference Paper 17 (1995).

ancestors ... Authorship is replaced by a concept of interpretation through initiation."[18]

But for other groups, this may not be true at all. For example, many of the 10,000 "grassroots innovations" documented by the India-based Honeybee Network are attributed to *and claimed by* individuals.[19]

II. The economic value of traditional knowledge

The mainstreaming of this issue is undoubtedly linked to a better understanding of the wealth-generating potential of TK. Traditional peoples and communities are responsible for the discovery, development, and preservation of a broad range of medicinal plants, health-giving herbal formulations, and agricultural and forest products that are traded internationally and generate considerable economic value. TK is also used as an input into such modern industries as pharmaceuticals, botanical medicines, cosmetics and toiletries, agriculture, and biological pesticides.

Attempts have been made to estimate the contribution of TK to modern industry and agriculture. For pharmaceuticals, the estimated market value of plant-based medicines sold in OECD countries in 1990 was $61 billion.[20] Many pharmaceutical companies are likely to have used TK leads in their product development, as demonstrated by biochemist Norman Farnsworth's estimate that of the 119 plant-based compounds used in medicine worldwide, 74 percent had the same or related uses as the medicinal plants from which they were derived.[21]

A study of the use and value of traditional crop varieties (landraces) for rice breeding in India calculated that rice landraces acquired from India and overseas contributed 5.6 percent, or an annual present value of benefits worth $6.1 million, to India's rice yields.[22] There are no reliable estimates of the total contribution of landraces to the global economy. However, assuming that India's landraces contribute equally to other countries where rice is cultivated,

---

[18] M. Blakeney, *The Protection of Traditional Knowledge under Intellectual Property Law*, 22 EUR. INTELL. PROP. REV. 251, 251–52 (2000).

[19] For a discussion by the Director of the Honeybee Network regarding the origin of the knowledge leading to such "grass roots innovations," see A.K. Gupta, *Making Indian Agriculture More Knowledge Intensive and Competitive: The Case of Intellectual Property Rights*, 54 INDIAN J. AGRIC. ECON. 342, 346–52 (1999).

[20] Peter Principe, *Economics and Medicinal Plants, in* MEDICINAL PLANTS: THEIR ROLE IN HEALTH AND BIODIVERSITY 42, 44–45 (Timothy R. Tomlinson & Olayiwola Akerele eds., 1998). There do not appear to be any more recent estimates.

[21] Norman R. Farnsworth, *Screening Plants for New Medicines, in* BIODIVERSITY 83, 91 (E.O. Wilson ed., 1988).

[22] Robert E. Evenson, *Economic Valuation of Biodiversity for Agriculture, in* BIODIVERSITY, BIOTECHNOLOGY, AND SUSTAINABLE DEVELOPMENT IN HEALTH AND AGRICULTURE: EMERGING CONNECTIONS 153, 162 (1996).

the global value added to rice yields by use of landraces can be estimated at $400 million per year.

All this suggests that TK plays an important role in the global economy and that it has the potential to play an even greater one. However, the industrial demand for TK should not be overestimated either. While enhanced abilities to screen and analyse huge quantities of natural products might suggest that commercial ethnobiology will become more popular, it seems more likely that advances in biotechnology and new drug discovery approaches based, for example, on combinatorial chemistry, genomics, and proteomics will in the long term *reduce* industrial interest in natural products and their associated TK.[23]

One should note that TK is valuable first and foremost to indigenous and local communities who depend upon it for their livelihoods and well-being, as well as for enabling them to sustainably manage and exploit their local ecosystems such as through sustainable low-input agriculture. According to the World Health Organization, up to 80 percent of the world's population depends on traditional medicine for its primary health needs. For those comprising the poorest segments of developing country societies, traditional knowledge is indispensable for survival.[24]

Interest in TK, then, is largely driven by a perception that TK has the potential to make a tremendous contribution to developing country economies. The few studies conducted to investigate this indicate that possibilities exist, but suggest that one should be somewhat cautious and not exaggerate (as many are inclined to do).

III. Legal measures to protect traditional knowledge

As mentioned earlier, legal solutions to the protection of traditional knowledge may be sought in terms of "positive protection" and "defensive protection." To many countries and NGOs, defensive protection is necessary because the intellectual property system, and especially its patent component, is considered defective in certain ways and allows companies to unfairly exploit TK. Defensive protection may also be more achievable than positive protection, in part because some of the most commonly discussed defensive protection measures are basically enhancements to or modifications of existing IPRs. Effective positive protection is likely to require a completely new system

---

[23] The best-known company to adopt this screening approach in developing new drugs was Shaman Pharmaceuticals. Facing the threat of closure, however, the company left the pharmaceuticals sector and entered the market for botanical medicines. Consequently, the economic case for ethnobioprospecting has been notably weakened.

[24] UNCTAD Secretariat, Systems and National Experiences for Protecting Traditional Knowledge, Innovations and Practices, UNCTAD Background Note, Agenda Item 3, at 6, U.N. Doc. TD/B/COM.1/EM.13/2 (22 Aug. 2000), *available at* www.unctad.org/trade_env/index.htm.

whose development would require the active and committed participation of many governments.

A. Defensive protection measures

Two important proposals have emerged from international negotiations to provide defensive protection of TK through the patent system, and they are explained below. The first is to require patent applicants to disclose the origin of genetic resources and associated TK relevant to the invention and, according to one variant of the proposal, to provide proof that regulations governing the transfer of the resources and associated TK were complied with. The second is to compile databases of published information on TK to enable patent examiners to identify potentially novelty-destroying prior art. In addition, a promising alternative approach may be to develop a misappropriation regime.

1. Disclosure of origin proposals

The compulsory disclosure of genetic resources and associated TK in patent applications was originally mooted by civil society organisations. The proposal is intended to help realise fair and equitable benefit sharing as required by the CBD.[25] This aim is supposedly achieved by ensuring that the resources and TK were acquired in accordance with biodiversity access and benefit sharing regulations in the source countries.

Proposals relating to disclosure have weak, medium and strong forms. The weak form posits that disclosure should be encouraged or even expected but not required, and its omission would not prevent the patent from being granted. The medium form would make disclosure of origin mandatory.

The strong form goes beyond disclosure in the patent specification to require that patent applicants comply with the CBD's access and benefit sharing (ABS) provisions.[26] One way to implement this goal is to establish a certification of origin system, according to which applicants would have to submit official documentation from provider countries proving that genetic resources and – where appropriate – associated TK were acquired in accordance with the ABS regulations, including conformity with such obligations as prior informed consent and benefit sharing. Applications unaccompanied by such documentation would automatically be returned to the senders for re-submission with the relevant information.[27]

---

[25] *See* Convention on Biological Diversity, above n. 6, art. 1.
[26] *See id.*, especially arts. 1, 8(j), 15 and 16, but also arts. 17–21.
[27] The certification of origin idea was devised by Brendan Tobin. *See* B. Tobin, *Certificates of Origin: A Role for IPR Regimes in Securing Prior Informed Consent, in* ACCESS TO GENETIC RESOURCES: STRATEGIES FOR SHARING BENEFITS 329 (J. Mugabe et al. eds., ACTS Press 1997).

Two questions arise here. First, is compulsory disclosure of origin incompatible with TRIPS? Second, is it actually a good idea anyway? The answer to the first question depends upon whether we are talking about the weak, medium or strong versions. Clearly there is no problem whatsoever with the weak version. As for the medium version, it is difficult to accept the view that this establishes another substantive condition. One can easily argue that such disclosure of TK is essential for a full description of how the invention came about. In addition, by helping to describe the prior art against which the purported inventive step needs to be measured, its disclosure ought to be required anyway. As for the source of the genetic material, it is difficult to see why inventors should not be required to indicate where they obtained it, and this obligation would hardly be burdensome in most cases.

The medium and strong variants could conflict with TRIPS if failure to conform resulted in a rejection of the application. To one legal expert, the main issue is what the consequences of non-compliance with a disclosure requirement would be for the patent holder. If it results in a rejection of the application or a post-grant revocation, there would be a conflict. Consequently, to avoid a conflict with TRIPS, disclosure should not become a required condition for granting the patent, but it could be made a condition for its enforceability after a patent has been granted.[28] This expert suggests that framing the disclosure requirement as a condition for enforcement could be adopted multilaterally in the framework of WIPO and then, perhaps, incorporated into TRIPS.

However, a careful application of the strong variant may provide a more satisfactory resolution. There is no compelling reason why the compulsory submission of a document, such as a certificate of origin, would impermissibly impose another substantive condition as long as it is not linked to determining the patentability of the invention. After all, patent applicants and owners normally have to pay examination and renewal fees, and TRIPS does not prevent this merely because such duties are not mentioned in the Agreement. Similarly, the submission of documentation attesting to the fact that the applicant had complied with the relevant ABS regulations, such as a certificate of origin, could be viewed as just another administrative requirement.

In short, the following interpretation seems plausible: it would not be a violation of TRIPS for countries to require patent applicants (1) to describe the relevant genetic material and TK in the specification and (2) to submit documentary evidence that the ABS regulations were complied with. But it probably would violate TRIPS to require patent applicants also to disclose the geographical origin of the relevant genetic material and associated TK in the specification. If so, imposing such a requirement would entail a revision of TRIPS.

---

[28] N.P. de Carvalho, *Requiring Disclosure of the Origin of Genetic Resources and Prior Informed Consent in Patent Applications without Infringing the TRIPS Agreement: The Problem and the Solution*, 2 WASH. U. J.L. & POL'Y 371 (2000).

Alternatively, these requirements could be introduced outside of the search, examination and eligibility processes as ancillary administrative measures.

The problem is that a patent applicant may be tempted to omit disclosure of the relevant TK, and the examiner may have no particular reason to suppose that a given invention was based on TK unless the applicant discloses the fact. So, in most cases, his or her suspicions are unlikely to be aroused, and the patent will then be granted assuming it meets the normal requirements.

Turning to the second question, which requires us to evaluate these proposals, mandatory disclosure could probably operate quite well for TK resources pertaining to health applications, especially pharmaceuticals. The pharmaceutical industry generally bases its new drugs on single compounds. Tracing and declaring the sources of origin should not normally amount to a particularly onerous task. Proponents of this measure would still need to determine the extent to which the obligation would extend to synthetic compounds derived from or inspired by lead compounds discovered in nature.

In the case of plant varieties, however, which can be patented in some countries, genetic material may derive from numerous sources, some of which may no longer be identifiable because of the lack of documentation and the length of time between its acquisition and its use in breeding programmes. Since new varieties may be based on genetic material from many different sources, the value of individual resources is relatively low. In addition, the seed industry is much smaller than the pharmaceutical industry and will never generate as many benefits to share.

It follows that for plant varieties developed through conventional breeding methods, the system may prove unworkable and might not necessarily benefit developing countries even if it worked. The patent applicants may simply be unable to comply, and the examiners could not verify whether the identities of the countries and indigenous communities of origin have been fully and truly disclosed. The requirement could also reinforce the tendency of plant breeders to rely on material found in existing collections rather than to search for hitherto undiscovered resources from the countries of origin, which would increase the genetic uniformity of new plant varieties.

The United Nation's Food and Agricultural Organization (FAO) International Treaty on Plant Genetic Resources for Food and Agriculture may offer a solution.[29] This is because facilitated access to plant genetic resources for food and agriculture of those crop species covered under the multilateral system will become subject to a standard material transfer agreement (MTA). The MTA will require benefits to be shared from the use, including commercial use, of the resources acquired. Article 13(d) of the International Treaty thus requires that

---

[29] International Treaty on Plant Genetic Resources for Food and Agriculture, *opened for signature* 3 Nov. 2001, *official text available at* http://www.fao.org/ag/cgrfa/IU.htm.

a recipient who commercializes a product that is a plant genetic resource for food and agriculture and that incorporates material accessed from the Multilateral System, shall pay to [a financial mechanism to be established] an equitable share of the benefits arising from the commercialization of that product, except whenever such a product is available without restriction to others for further research and breeding, in which case the recipient who commercializes shall be encouraged to make such payment.[30]

In effect, this means that a recipient that sells a food or agricultural product incorporating material from the multilateral system *must* pay monetary or other benefits from commercialisation provided that he or she owns a patent on the product and – as is normally the case – there is no exemption in the domestic patent law that would freely allow others to use it for further research and breeding. If, instead, the product is a plant variety protected under domestic laws based on a version of the UPOV Convention, which do contain a research exemption,[31] the recipient selling the product would be *encouraged* to pay benefits.

As for the certification of origin system, one of the practical complications is that many countries still have not adopted ABS regulations in compliance with the CBD. If a patent must be accompanied by official documentation from the source country, no authority may exist to provide it. In this case, presumably, the requirement for a certification would have to be waived. But what then prevents a company from claiming that a resource was obtained from such a country when it was actually collected illegally from another country with ABS regulations in place?

In sum, mandatory disclosure and certification of origin rules are promising ideas that could help enhance compatibility between the CBD and the worldwide patent system. The practicalities still need to be thought out carefully, however.

2. Compiling databases of traditional knowledge to serve as prior art

India has been a particularly strong demander of TK databases, and it has already begun to develop a Traditional Knowledge Digital Library (TKDL), which is a searchable database of already documented information concerning traditional health knowledge spawned by the Ayurvedic system and medicinal plants used by practitioners. The government wants to make the TKDL available to patent examiners in India and elsewhere. Clearly, the question of TRIPS

---

[30] *Id.* art. 13(d). *See also* Michael Blakeney, *Stimulating Agricultural Innovation* [this volume]; Laurence Helfer, *Using Intellectual Property Rights to Preserve the Global Genetic Commons: The International Treaty on Plant Genetic Resources for Food and Agriculture* [this volume].

[31] *See* International Convention for the Protection of New Varieties of Plants, 2 Dec. 1961, 33 U.S.T. 2703, 815 U.N.T.S. 89, *as amended* 23 Oct. 1978, 33 U.S.T. 2703, 1861 U.N.T.S. 281 [hereinafter UPOV I], *as amended* 19 Mar. 1991, *available at* http://www.upov.int/en/publications/conventions/1991/pdf/act1991.pdf [hereinafter UPOV II]; *see also* Blakeney, above n. 30; Helfer, above n. 30.

incompatibility does not arise here because such databases would simply help to improve the efficiency of prior art searches.

Would TK databases actually prove useful? They could certainly stop patents like the one in the United States that was granted for the use of turmeric powder for wound healing, a remedy that was known to millions of people in India. That patent was subsequently revoked for lack of novelty following a re-examination request. It is by no means certain, however, that such compilations would have prevented other controversial patents from issuing. They might have narrowed their scope, but even this is by no means certain.

How would TK have to be described in order to constitute novelty-destroying prior art? Consider the example of a patented therapeutic compound isolated from a medicinal plant. Most likely, the examiner will treat the TK relating to the plant as being quite distinct from the chemical invention described in the specification.[32]

National and regional patent laws still vary with respect to how information or material in the public domain should be presented or described in order that they constitute novelty-defeating prior art. For example, the European Patent Convention considers an invention "to be new if it does not form part of the state of the art," which is "held to comprise everything made available to the public by means of a written or oral description, by use, or in any other way, before the date of filing of the European patent application."[33] This indicates that publicly available items may form the state of the art whether or not they have been described in writing or even orally.

In this context, it is noteworthy that the European Patent Office Technical Board of Appeal has ruled that "the concept of novelty must not be given such a narrow interpretation that only what has already been described in the same terms is prejudicial to it ... There are many ways of describing a substance."[34] Furthermore, the TBA subsequently found that it may not necessarily be the case that for novelty to be destroyed, "all the technical characteristics combined in the claimed invention need to have been communicated to the public or laid open for public inspection."[35] According to Bently and Sherman, "it has long been recognised that the information disclosed by a product is not limited to the information that is immediately apparent from looking at the product. Importantly, the information available to the public also includes information that a skilled person would be able to derive from the product if they analysed

---

[32] *See, e.g.*, Blakeney, above, n. 30.
[33] Convention on the Grant of European Patents, 5 Oct. 1973, 1065 U.N.T.S. 255; 13 I.L.M. 270 [hereinafter EPC], art. 54.
[34] Decision of EPO Technical Board of Appeal, Case No. T 12/81 – 3.3.1 (9 Feb. 1982). 2 DECISIONS OF THE BOARDS OF APPEAL OF THE EPO 35, 39–40 (Carl Heymanns Verlag 1982).
[35] Thomson/Electron tube – Decision of EPO Technical Board of Appeal, Case No. T 953/90 – 3.4.1 (12 May 1992). 13 EUROPEAN PATENT OFFICE REPORTS 415.

or examined it."[36] This might suggest that patents on isolated therapeutic compounds from medicinal plants were vulnerable to a challenge for lack of novelty. However, one should also be cautious about drawing this conclusion. To demonstrate lack of novelty, a person skilled in the art would have to be able to discover the composition or the internal structure of the product and reproduce it without undue burden. Isolating such compounds may well constitute an "undue burden."[37]

This analysis of how Europe defines and assesses novelty-defeating prior art suggests that many so-called biopiracy cases could not be legally challenged there. If so, the existence of TK databases will make little difference.

3. A misappropriation regime

Carlos Correa has proposed the development of a misappropriation regime. According to his proposal:

> National laws would be free to determine the means to prevent it, including criminal and civil remedies (such as an obligation to stop using the relevant knowledge or to pay compensation for such use)... as well as how to empower communities for the exercise and enforcement of their rights.[38]

He recommends that, in view of the lack of experiences to date in developing such a regime, a step-by-step approach may be necessary. In the first instance, such a regime should contain three elements: documentation of TK, proof of origin or materials, and prior informed consent.

Correa refers to two United Nations documents that implicitly support his proposal. The first of these is Decision V/16 of the CBD's Conference of the Parties, which states

> Request[ed] Parties to support the development of registers of traditional knowledge, innovations and practices of indigenous and local communities embodying traditional lifestyles relevant for the conservation and sustainable use of biological diversity through participatory programmes and consultations with indigenous and local communities, taking into account strengthening legislation, customary practices and traditional systems of resource management, such as the protection of traditional knowledge against unauthorized use.[39]

---

[36] L. Bently & B. Sherman, INTELLECTUAL PROPERTY LAW 420 (Oxford University Press 2001).
[37] Availability to the public – Decision of the Enlarged Board of Appeal, G01/92 (18 Dec. 1992), 8 EUROPEAN PATENT OFFICE REPORTS 241.
[38] C.M. Correa, Traditional Knowledge and Intellectual Property: Issues and Options Surrounding the Protection of Traditional Knowledge, Quaker United Nations Office Discussion Paper 18 (2001).
[39] Convention on Biological Diversity – Conference of the Parties, Decision V/16 (2000), *available at* http://www.biodiv.org/convention/cops.asp#.

The second is the "Principles and Guidelines for the Protection of the Heritage of Indigenous Peoples," which were elaborated in 1995 by Erica-Irene Daes, then Special Rapporteur of the UN Subcommission on Prevention of Discrimination and Protection of Minorities.[40] Paragraphs 26 and 27 state the following:

> National laws should deny to any person or corporation the right to obtain patent, copyright or other legal protection for any element of indigenous peoples' heritage without adequate documentation of the free and informed consent of the traditional owners to an arrangement for the sharing of ownership, control, use and benefits.
>
> National laws should ensure the labelling and correct attribution of indigenous peoples' artistic, literary and cultural works whenever they are offered for public display or sale. Attribution should be in the form of a trademark or an appellation of origin, authorized by the peoples or communities concerned.[41]

Arguably, such a misappropriation regime could and probably should incorporate: (1) the concept of unfair competition; (2) moral rights; and (3) cultural rights. Unfair competition would deal with situations in which TK holders engaged in commercial activities pertaining, for example, to know-how, medicinal plants, artworks or handicrafts, had their trade affected by certain unfair commercial practices committed by others. According to Article 10*bis* of the Paris Convention for the Protection of Intellectual Property, the following acts are prohibited on the grounds of constituting unfair competition:

1. all acts of such a nature as to create confusion by any means whatever with the establishment, the goods, or the industrial or commercial activities, of a competitor;
2. false allegations in the course of trade of such a nature as to discredit the establishment, the goods, or the industrial or commercial activities, of a competitor;
3. indications or allegations the use of which in the course of trade is liable to mislead the public as to the nature, the manufacturing process, the characteristics, the suitability for their purpose, or the quantity, of the goods.[42]

The TRIPS Agreement incorporates the substantive provisions of the Paris Convention by reference[43] and explicitly mentions Article 10*bis* in the sections

---

[40] United Nations Economic and Social Council, Commission on Human Rights, Sub-Commission on Prevention of Discrimination and Protection of Minorities, Principles and Guidelines for the Protection of the Heritage of Indigenous Peoples, U.N. Doc. No. E/CN.4/Sub.2/1995/26, annex 1 (21 June 1995).

[41] *Id.* ¶¶ 26–27.

[42] Paris Convention for the Protection of Industrial Property, 1883, 828 U.N.T.S. 305 [hereinafter Paris Convention], *as revised at* Stockholm, 1967, art. 10*bis*(3).

[43] Agreement on Trade-Related Aspects of Intellectual Property Rights, 15 Apr. 1994, Marrakesh Agreement Establishing the World Trade Organization, Annex 1C, LEGAL INSTRUMENTS – RESULTS OF THE URUGUAY ROUND vol. 31, 33 I.L.M. 81 (1994) [hereinafter TRIPS Agreement], art. 2.1.

dealing with geographical indications and undisclosed information.[44] Specifically, WTO members must provide legal means to prevent any use of geographical indications that would constitute unfair competition. Also, members must ensure effective protection against unfair competition with respect to undisclosed information.

Moral rights are provided in Article 6*bis* of the Berne Convention for the Protection of Literary and Artistic Works.[45] Moral rights usually consist of the right of authors to be identified as such (sometimes referred to as the right of paternity), and to object to having their works altered in ways that would prejudice their honour or reputation (the right of integrity).[46]

It could be argued that free-riding on the knowledge, cultural works, and expressions of traditional communities who are not themselves interested in commercialising them does no direct harm. Consequently, the doctrine of misappropriation does not apply to such acts. But is it really the case that there are no victims? One could reply that such behaviour infringes on certain cultural rights that these communities are entitled to enjoy. Lyndel Prott, formerly of the United Nations Education, Scientific and Cultural Organization (UNESCO), identified a set of individual and collective rights that could be described as "cultural rights," and which are supported to a greater or lesser extent by international law.[47] Of these, the following (of which only the first is an individual right) stand out in light of the present discussion:

- the right to protection of artistic, literary and scientific works
- the right to develop a culture
- the right to respect of cultural identity
- the right of minority peoples to respect for identity, traditions, language, and cultural heritage;
- the right of a people to its own artistic, historical, and cultural wealth
- the right of a people not to have an alien culture imposed on it.

To the extent that unauthorised or improper use of a cultural group's artifacts and expressions imbued with cultural, spiritual or aesthetic value

---

[44] *Id.* arts. 22.2(b), 39.1.
[45] Berne Convention for the Protection of Literary and Artistic Works, 1986, S. Treaty Doc. No. 99-27, 1161 U.N.T.S. 3 [hereinafter Berne Convention], *as revised at* Paris, 1971, art. 6*bis*.
[46] *Id.* art. 6*bis*(1) provides:

> Independently of the author's economic rights, and even after the transfer of the said rights, the author shall have the right to claim authorship of the work and to object to any distortion, mutilation or other modification of, or other derogatory action in relation to, the said work, which would be prejudicial to his honour or reputation.

[47] L.V. Prott, *Cultural Rights as Peoples' Rights in International Law, in* THE RIGHTS OF PEOPLES 102 (J. Crawford ed., Clarendon Press 1988).

erodes the integrity of the culture of origin, it is reasonable to treat such uses as manifestations of a form of misappropriation that the law should arguably provide remedies for.

B. Positive protection measures

Entitlement theory and experience to date both suggest that extant legal systems for protecting knowledge and intellectual works tend to operate as either property regimes, liability regimes, or as combined systems containing elements of both.[48] Perhaps a consideration of these is a good way to start.

1. *Sui generis* IP regimes

What is the difference between property and liability regimes? A property regime vests exclusive rights in owners, of which the right to refuse, authorise and determine conditions for access to the property in question are the most fundamental. For these rights to mean anything, it must of course be possible for holders to enforce them.

A liability regime is a "use now pay later" system according to which use is allowed without the authorisation of the right holders. But it is not free access because *ex post* compensation is still required.[49] A *sui generis* system based on such a principle has certain advantages in countries where much of the TK is already in wide circulation but may still be subject to the claims of the original holders. Asserting a property right over knowledge is insufficient to prevent abuses when so much traditional knowledge has fallen into the public domain and can no longer be controlled by the original TK holders. A pragmatic response is to allow the use of such knowledge but to require that its original producers or providers be compensated.[50]

There are different ways the compensation payments could be handled. The government could determine the rights by law. Alternatively, a private collective management institution could be established, which would monitor use of TK, issue licenses to users, and distribute fees to right holders in proportion to the extent to which their knowledge was used by others. They could also collect and distribute royalties where commercial applications are developed by users and

---

[48] *See most recently* Richard Epstein, *Steady the Course: Property Rights in Genetic Material*, in PERSPECTIVES ON PROPERTIES OF THE HUMAN GENOME PROJECT 153 (F. Scott Kief ed., 2003) [hereinafter PERSPECTIVES ON THE GENOME PROJECT] (advocating total reliance on exclusive IP rights); J.H. Reichman, *Saving the Patent Law from Itself*, in PERSPECTIVES ON THE GENOME PROJECT, above, at 289 (advocating expanded role for liability rules to alleviate tensions between exclusive IPRs and public domain).

[49] *See, e.g.*, J.H. Reichman, *Of Green Tulips and Legal Kudzu: Repackaging Rights in Subpatentable Innovation*, 53 VAND. L. REV. 1753 (2000). *See generally* J.H. Reichman, *Legal Hybrids Between the Patent and Copyright Paradigms*, 94 COLUM. L. REV. 2432 (1994).

[50] Jerome H. Reichman & Tracy Lewis, *Using Liability Rules to Stimulate Local Innovation in Developing Countries: Application to Traditional Knowledge* [this volume].

the licenses require such benefits to go back to the holders.[51] Such organisations exist in many countries for the benefit of musicians, performers and artists. Alternatively, in jurisdictions where TK holders are prepared to place their trust in a state or government-created competent authority to perform the same function, a public institution could be created instead.

While such organisations have the potential to reduce transaction and enforcement costs, considerations of economic efficiency should not be the only criteria for designing an effective and appropriate *sui generis* system. TK holders and communities will be its principal users and beneficiaries. They will not endorse a system that fails to accommodate their world views and customs but rather imposes other norms with which they feel uncomfortable and wish to avoid. Clearly, TK holders and communities must be partners in the development of a *sui generis* system lest it become an inappropriate and unworkable system.

Those who would oppose a liability regime may object on the ground that we should not have to pay for public domain knowledge. One may counter this view by observing that "the public domain" is an alien concept to many indigenous groups. Just because an ethnobiologist described a community's use of a medicinal plant in an academic journal without asking permission, this does not mean that the community has abandoned its property rights in that knowledge or its interest in ensuring that the knowledge be used in a culturally appropriate manner. Seen this way, a liability regime should not be considered an alternative to a property regime but as a means to ensure that TK holders and communities can exercise their property rights more effectively.[52]

Whichever approach is selected – and a combination of both is probably essential[53] – the question arises of whether rights must be claimed through registration, or whether the rights should exist in law irrespective of whether they are filed with a government agency. It seems only fair that the rights should exist regardless of whether they are declared to the government, and that these rights should not be exhausted by publication unless the holders have agreed to renounce their claims. Yet, protection and enforcement would probably become more effective with registration, and knowledge transactions would become much easier to conduct if claims over TK were registered.

---

[51] *See* above n. 50.
[52] Professor Reichman emphasizes that his compensatory liability regime would confer a clear entitlement (hence a property right), but the right would extend mainly to compensation for certain uses, especially value-adding uses, rather than a power to exclude. The end result would create an *ex ante* automatic license (not an *ex post* compulsory license) that would temporarily place the relevant TK in a semi-commons from which it could not be removed. *See* Reichman & Lewis, above n. 50.
[53] *See, e.g.*, Cottier & Panizzon, above n. 1.

Consequently, the *sui generis* system should encourage the registration of right claims but not make this a legal requirement for protection.[54]

Finally, it must be cautioned that devising the most sophisticated and elaborate system is useless if the potential users and beneficiaries remain unaware of its existence or have more immediate concerns, such as extreme poverty, deprivation and societal breakdown caused by the insufficient recognition of their basic rights. It will also fail if it does not take their world views and customary norms into account.

2. Database rights

Nuno Carvalho of WIPO has suggested that TK databases should be protected under a special database right.[55] Nowadays there is great interest in documenting TK and placing it in databases. However, as Carvalho points out, traditional communities and TK holders are rarely the ones responsible for compiling or holding the databases. One presumes that they would wish to control access to and use of the information held in the databases, which is not necessarily true under current practices. For these reasons, copyright law does not provide an adequate solution. As Carvalho explains: "it is necessary to establish a mechanism of industrial property protection that ensures the exclusivity as to the *use* of the contents of the databases, rather than to their reproduction (copyright),"[56] disregarding weighty questions about eligibility and scope of protection for factual matters under copyright law.[57]

The basis for his proposal may be found in Article 39.3 of TRIPS, which deals with test or other data that must be submitted to government authorities as a condition of approving the marketing of pharmaceutical or agrochemical products, where the origination of such data involves considerable effort.[58] The article requires governments to protect such data against unfair commercial use. It also requires them to protect data against disclosure except where necessary to protect the public. This provision allows for the possibility that certain information will have to be protected against unfair commercial use *even when that information has been disclosed to the public.*

To Carvalho, such additional protection could be extended to TK in the form of a legal framework for a TK database system. Such a system would retain the following three features derived from Article 39.3 of TRIPS: (a) the establishment of rights in data; (b) the enforceability of rights in the data against

---

[54] *See also id.* (discussing these issues).
[55] N.P. de Carvalho, *From the Shaman's Hut to the Patent Office: How Long and Winding is the Road?*, 41 REVISTA DA ASSOCIAÇÃO BRASILEIRA DE PROPRIEDADE INTELECTUAL 3 (July – Aug. 1999).
[56] *Id.*, at 28.
[57] *See* TRIPS Agreement, above n. 42, art. 10.2. [58] *See id.*, art. 39.3.

their use by unauthorized third parties; and (c) the absence of a predetermined term of protection.[59]

Carvalho suggests that such databases should be registered with national patent offices and that, to avoid the appropriation of public domain knowledge, enforcement rights should be confined to knowledge that complies with a certain definition of novelty. Novelty need not be defined in any absolute sense but as commercial novelty (as with the TRIPS provisions on layout-designs of integrated circuits[60] and the UPOV Convention).[61] In other words, knowledge disclosed in the past could be treated as "novel" if the innovation based upon it had not yet reached the market.

3. Global biocollecting society

Peter Drahos of Australian National University has suggested the creation of a Global Biocollecting Society (GBS).[62] This is a property rights-based institution that would reduce transaction costs while improving the international enforcement of rights over traditional knowledge associated with biodiversity. It would also generate trust in the market between holders and commercial users of TK.

The GBS would operate a kind of private collective management organisation, as is common in the area of domestic copyrights and related rights. One key difference is that the GBS would be an international institution. Another is that its mandate would be to implement the objectives of the CBD, particularly those relating to traditional knowledge. Membership of the GBS would be open to traditional groups and communities, and to companies anywhere in the world.

The GBS would constitute a repository of community knowledge registers voluntarily submitted by member groups and communities. These would be confidential except that the identities of the groups or communities submitting registers would be made known. In doing so, it would trigger a dialogue between a community known to have submitted a register and a company interested in gaining access to information in this register. The result would be an arrangement to access TK in exchange for certain benefits.

To improve the chances for successful transactions of benefit to traditional communities, the GBS could provide a range of services in addition to serving as a repository of TK registers. It could, for example, assist in contractual negotiations and maintain a register of independent legal advisors willing to assist traditional communities. It could monitor the commercial use of traditional knowledge, including the checking of patent applications.

---

[59] Carvalho, above n. 57, at 30. [60] TRIPS Agreement, above n. 42, art. 35.
[61] UPOV 1991, above n. 31.
[62] P. Drahos, *Indigenous Knowledge, Intellectual Property and Biopiracy: Is a Global Biocollecting Society the Answer?*, 6 EURO. INTELL. PROP. REV. 245 (2000).

The GBS could also have an impartial and independent dispute settlement function. Its recommendations would not be legally binding, but there would still be incentives to adhere to them. For example, failure to do so could result in expulsion from the GBS, in which case the excluded party, if a company, might face negative publicity that would be well worth avoiding.

4. Compensatory liability regime

The compensatory liability regime idea proposed by Professor Jerome Reichman of Duke University differs from the previous proposals in that it is – as its name indicates – a liability regime rather than a property-based system.[63] It adopts a conception of TK as know-how, or at least it aims to protect certain TK that may be characterised as know-how. Know-how is taken to refer to information that has practical applications but is insufficiently inventive to be patentable.

For such knowledge, a property regime is considered likely to afford excessively strong protection in the sense that it will create barriers for follow-on innovators. Such a regime will also intrude on the public domain. Reverse engineering ought to be permitted, but not improper means of discovering the know-how, such as bribery or industrial espionage. However, know-how holders face the problem of shortening lead time as reverse engineering becomes ever-more sophisticated.[64]

So what is to be done? In order to strike the right balance between the reasonable interests of creators of sub-patentable innovations and follow-on innovators, a liability regime could ensure that, for a specific period of time, users should be required to compensate the holders of know-how they wish to acquire. Compensation need not be paid directly but through a collecting society. The CLR would require know-how to be registered and in so doing would provide legal protection for a period of time during which most uses by second comers should be compensated. Royalty rates would be low and could be based on standard form agreements. The CLR would apply to new knowledge, particularly to new applications of old knowledge, while a misappropriation regime could apply to old knowledge that was not voluntarily made available to the public.[65]

IV. Strategic considerations

At least two important questions arise concerning the negotiation and implementation of legal solutions, which need to be considered carefully. First, should efforts be devoted to developing a national *sui generis* system first in order to gain experience that would make it easier to determine what a

---

[63] See above n. 50.
[64] See Reichman, *Saving the Patent Law from Itself*, above n. 48; Reichman, *Green Tulips*, above n. 49.
[65] For details and a specific model, see Reichman & Lewis, above n. 50.

workable international solution should look like; or is a multilateral settlement a pre-condition for the effective protection of the rights of TK holders in any country? Second, how might concerned countries overcome the limitation inherent in national *sui generis* systems to protect TK, which is that they will have no extra-territorial effect?

Each country will no doubt come up with good reasons to answer these questions differently. Nevertheless, there seems to be a consensus among countries supporting *sui generis* systems of positive protection and groups representing TK holding people and communities that the problem with any national system in a world where few such systems exist is that no matter how effective it may be at the domestic level, it would have no extra-territorial effect. Consequently, TK right holders could not secure similar protection abroad, and exploitative behaviour in other countries would go undeterred as before.

This problem requires us to consider what an international system should look like. As was pointed out by a Canadian indigenous peoples' organisation called the Four Directions Council in a paper submitted in 1996 to the Secretariat of the Convention on Biological Diversity,

> Indigenous peoples possess their own locally-specific systems of jurisprudence with respect to the classification of different types of knowledge, proper procedures for acquiring and sharing knowledge, and the rights and responsibilities which attach to possessing knowledge, all of which are embedded uniquely in each culture and its language.[66]

For this reason,

> Any attempt to devise uniform guidelines for the recognition and protection of indigenous peoples' knowledge runs the risk of collapsing this rich jurisprudential diversity into a single "model" that will not fit the values, conceptions or laws of *any* indigenous society.[67]

It therefore seems inappropriate for countries to come up with a one-size-fits-all international *sui generis* system. Any new international norms will have to be flexible enough to accommodate this jurisprudential diversity or risk failure. Close collaboration with TK holders and their communities becomes essential in the design of any *sui generis* system, a point that cannot be emphasised strongly enough.

Moreover, groups and individuals that retain control over their own destinies are far better placed to benefit from legal protection of their knowledge. For example, indigenous groups empowered with rights to control access to their lands and communities have a better chance of preventing misappropriation of their knowledge and negotiating favourable bioprospecting arrangements.

---

[66] Four Directions Council, Forests, Indigenous Peoples and Biodiversity: Contribution of the Four Directions Council (1996).
[67] *Id.*

But in all too many cases, indigenous groups and TK holders suffer from extreme poverty, ill health, unemployment, lack of access to land and essential resources, and human rights violations. Human cultural diversity is eroding at an accelerating rate as the world steadily becomes more biologically and culturally uniform. According to the IUCN Inter-Commission Task Force on Indigenous Peoples:

> [C]ultures are dying out faster than the peoples associated with them. It has been estimated that half the world's languages – the storehouses of peoples' intellectual heritages and the framework for their unique understandings of life – will disappear within a century.[68]

This suggests that measures to protect TK and the rights of the holders, custodians and communities need to be implemented with some urgency. As the late Darrell Posey so poignantly expressed it,

> With the extinction of each indigenous group, the world loses millennia of accumulated knowledge about life in and adaptation to tropical ecosystems. This priceless information is forfeited with hardly a blink of the eye: the march of development cannot wait long enough to even find out what it is about to destroy.[69]

Yet this tragedy is not inevitable. As Posey explained, "if technological civilization begins to realize the richness and complexity of indigenous knowledge, then Indians can be viewed as intelligent, valuable people, rather than just exotic footnotes to history."[70]

Finally, while it may reasonably be argued that protecting TK legally would further reduce the public domain and that to do so is therefore a bad thing, the first clarifying response is that not all traditional knowledge has entered the public domain. Second, unconsented placement of knowledge into the public domain does not in itself extinguish the legitimate entitlements of the holders and may in fact violate them. Third, the question of *how* traditional knowledge usually falls into the public domain cannot be overlooked.

It has never been common practice to place TK in the public domain and disseminate it with prior informed consent *and* with respect for the holders' customary laws and regulations concerning access, use, and distribution of knowledge. One could argue, then, that the right of other people to use this knowledge should not be treated as automatic or devoid of moral or even legal responsibilities.[71]

---

[68] IUCN INTER-COMMISSION TASK FORCE ON INDIGENOUS PEOPLES, INDIGENOUS PEOPLES AND SUSTAINABILITY: CASES AND ACTIONS 60 (IUCN & International Books 1997).
[69] D.A. Posey, *Indigenous Knowledge and Development: An Ideological Bridge to the Future*, in D.A. POSEY, KAYAPÓ ETHNOECOLOGY AND CULTURE 59 (K. Plenderleith ed., Routledge 2002).
[70] *Id.*   [71] *Accord* Cottier & Panizzon, above n. 1.

19

Saving the village: Conserving jurisprudential diversity in the international protection of traditional knowledge

ANTONY TAUBMAN*

I. Introduction: Protect the knowledge but betray the tradition?
II. The paradox: To globalise diversity holistically
    A. The point of access as the fulcrum of protection
    B. The international layer of TK protection: What practical choices?
    C. Recognizing customary laws and protocols beyond IP law
    D. Revisiting the public domain: Which public, and whose domain?
III. What is *sui generis* about TK?
    A. Further reflections on the definition of traditional knowledge
    B. Locating the normative centre of TK protection
    C. Revisiting the boundaries of intellectual property and the public domain
IV. TK protection as a global public good
V. Options for recognition of customary law in the IP system
    A. Implications for the international context
    B. What international mechanisms can do justice to customary law?
    C. Conclusion: What kind of international system?

---

* Antony Taubman is Senior Lecturer, Australian Centre for Intellectual Property in Agriculture (ACIPA), Faculty of Law, Australian National University, currently on secondment to WIPO as Head, Traditional Knowledge Division, (Global IP Issues). This chapter draws on private research, including research carried out under the auspices of the Australian Centre on Intellectual Property in Agriculture (ACIPA), School of Law, the Australian National University. The views expressed are those of the author only, do not represent the views of the World Intellectual Property Organization, nor of its Secretariat and Member States, and do not advocate any particular outcome from any international debate or negotiation.

I. Introduction: Protect the knowledge but betray the tradition?

In early ecclesiastical law, "tradition" was the crime of handing over sacred texts and information about the community to persecutors;[1] indeed the word "tradition" shares its roots with "traitor" and "betrayal,"[2] which invokes the concept that "handing over" or "passing on" of knowledge need not be benign, but may be injurious, even perfidious. "Tradition" does more positively connote customs, laws, practices and beliefs that are passed down within a community. However, the two-edged nature of the word recalls that some forms of transmitting traditional knowledge (TK) and making it available to the public can be seen as a betrayal or a violation of customary laws, which causes offence or gravely damages a community. Jefferson's characterization of knowledge, establishing it as the iconic non-rivalrous public good – "he who receives an idea from me ... as he who lights a taper at mine, receives light without darkening me"[3] – may not convince those communities who fear that careless acts by others to gain illumination from TK may in fact diminish, or extinguish, the original flame, and darken their communities' future.

Many local and indigenous communities are concerned that growing global interest in their TK and traditional cultural expressions is not matched by respect for the customs, laws and beliefs that identify and sustain their communities and that shape the very heritage that appeals to external consumers. Initiatives to safeguard TK, for instance through documenting and publishing it, may in fact amount to a betrayal of sacred or social duties to protect their heritage, to the detriment of customary means of preserving and passing on TK. It may amount to an unwanted transfer of treasured knowledge to the public domain, or to passing it on to external interests who are not bound by the traditions embedded in the knowledge that define its spiritual and ethical context.

Systems of indigenous or local knowledge in such areas as medicine[4] and ecological management[5] are increasingly recognized as having a rigorous

---

[1] "Bishops ... had collaborated during the Persecution of Diocletian beginning in 303 A.D., handing over copies of the Holy Scriptures to be burnt by the pagan magistrates. This craven act, the *traditio*, the 'handing-over' of the Holy Books, would have deprived the guilty bishop, the *traditor*, of all spiritual power." PETER BROWN, AUGUSTINE OF HIPPO 218 (Berkeley 1967).

[2] *See also* J.M. Balkin, *Tradition, Betrayal, and the Politics of Deconstruction*, 11 CARDOZO L. REV. 1613 (1990) (discussing the etymological implications of these terms and "tradition" in jurisprudence).

[3] Thomas Jefferson (letter to Isaac McPherson), *quoted in* THE FOUNDERS' CONSTITUTION, vol. 3, art. 1, § 8, cl. 8, Doc. 12 (Philip Kurland & William R. Kenan eds.), *at* http://press-pubs.uchicago.edu/founders/documents/a1_8_8s12.html.

[4] *See, e.g.*, World Health Organization, WHO Policy and Strategy on Traditional Medicine (2002).

[5] *See* Article 8(j), Convention on Biological Diversity, *entered into force* 29 Dec. 1993, 31 I.L.M. 818 [hereinafter CBD].

empirical basis and scientific and technological value. Documenting and publishing TK may serve a broader public good in making such useful or culturally enriching material available in the public domain – and it can yield commercial benefits for third parties. However, in the absence of effective intellectual property (IP) rights or other legal means of constraining unauthorized use of TK beyond the original community, entry of TK into the public domain can create a sense that commercial and cultural benefits are enjoyed at the expense of destroying the integrity of the cultural and spiritual framework that gave birth to the TK, while violating its custodians' rights and responsibilities.

This sense of loss or violation, in turn, fuels demands for distinct, *sui generis* forms of protection for TK, within or beyond the IP system, that respect and respond to the distinctive characteristics of TK and to the needs of holders of TK, on the assumption that existing IP rights are inadequate or inappropriate. These claims are based on broader public good arguments with a utilitarian flavour – the cultural survival and welfare of indigenous and local communities, and the promotion of their role in preserving biodiversity – but also on grounds of equity and natural rights. The demand for equity arises in the sense of procedural fairness – basing use of TK on prior informed consent[6] – and in a distributive sense – the principle of equitable sharing of benefits from the use of TK.[7]

Claims for TK protection thus raise searching questions about the prevailing policy basis and equitable assumptions of the current IP system. The solution may not be a parallel *sui generis* system in tension or contradiction with conventional IP systems. To the contrary, it may actually entail validating the principles that underpin the IP system and form the rationale for IP rights, while highlighting the need to apply these principles more effectively for the practical benefit of TK holders.[8] The debate should also clarify the proper and realistic limits of any policy approach based on IP rights, and consider how other legal and policy approaches may better address some concerns of traditional communities concerning erosion of customary laws and protocols, and the loss of TK and its social context.

In approaching this task, one must point out that knowledge is not "traditional" because of specific subject matter or content, nor its age or antiquity, nor for that matter its aesthetic qualities. What makes it traditional is the way it has been preserved and transmitted between generations within a community: "its nature relates to the manner it develops rather than to its antiquity."[9] This

---

[6] *E.g.*, ¶ 2(b)(iii), Draft Decision on Traditional Knowledge, *annexed to* WTO, Taking Forward the Review of Article 27.3(b) of the TRIPS Agreement, Joint Communication from the African Group, WTO Doc. IP/C/W/404 (26 June 2003).

[7] CBD, above n. 5, art. 8(j). *Cf.* Peter Gerhart, *Distributive Values and Institutional Design in the provision of Global Public Goods* [this volume].

[8] *See, e.g.*, Thomas Cottier & Marion Panizzon, *Legal Perspectives on Traditional Knowledge: The Case for Intellectual Property Protection* [this volume].

[9] Draft Decision on Traditional Knowledge, above n. 6.

definition gives TK a profoundly local quality. The social structures that create, use, preserve and pass down TK between generations, and the customary laws and protocols that govern these processes, are deeply rooted in their traditional location and community setting, and indeed may be conceived as integral to the land and environment itself.

Equitable considerations alone would then suggest that TK should be protected and treated with due consideration of the community's own values, and its ethical and legal systems.[10] The design of *sui generis* ways of protecting TK – protection that is tailored to fit its distinctive qualities – may also need to give effect to the original community's own approach to defining, protecting and managing the relevant knowledge. In many cases, these customary systems of custodianship and intergenerational transmission are under pressure, and more effective protection of TK could mean reinforcing these systems within the community. Clarification of customary systems may also be needed where the boundary is blurred between the traditional community itself and the general population, and there is consequent uncertainty about the scope and reach of customary law.

In practice, however, current initiatives for IP protection of TK aim above all to create enforceable rights that have effect beyond the original community, in the broader marketplace where inappropriate commercialization of TK is more likely to occur. While conceptually distinct, the *in situ* and *ex situ* objectives may overlap: for example, the Crucible Group points out that external legal recognition of TK "will make the learning and development of such knowledge a more attractive prospect for the younger members of such communities, thus perpetuating its existence."[11]

Another point worth clarifying at the outset is that traditional knowledge is not simply information: it has an inherent normative and social component. But the central problem in protecting TK is that, as information, it can be easily communicated beyond its original context, while the norms, social practices and values that define its "traditional" aspect, being intrinsically local and innate to a traditional community, are much less readily transmitted. The inherent qualities that distinguish TK from other forms of knowledge begin to break down once it leaves the community.

An idealized form of protection would bind the normative and knowledge components together in the external environment. It would effectively transplant a local, community-bound normative tradition, propagate it in foreign jurisdictions, and give it legal effect in an environment that is alien to its original social context. This may seem a quixotic endeavour in that either the

---

[10] *See also* Graham Dutfield, *Legal and Economic Aspects of Traditional Knowledge* [this volume].

[11] THE CRUCIBLE II GROUP, SEEDING SOLUTIONS vol. 2, at 10 (IDRC-IPGRI 2001) [hereinafter SEEDING SOLUTIONS].

normative context must be lost when the TK passes beyond the community, or the system might become hopelessly unworkable. The choice may not, however, be so stark. Customary law can, for instance, influence external legal systems without being formally recognized as a source of law. Specific elements of customary law may also be reflected in certain technical determinations under conventional IP law, for instance, in determining ownership, equitable interests and the assessment of remedies.

The increasing cultural, commercial and technological interest in TK, and in realizing its perceived value, is not neatly confined to specific jurisdictions. The concerns articulated about misappropriation and misuse of TK have regional and global contexts, and responses to these concerns have an inevitable international dimension. This realization fuels interest in the development of international law concerning TK, possibly built around the non-binding expression of common principles, a binding international treaty,[12] amendments to existing treaty provisions,[13] other international instruments, or concrete practical mechanisms for more effective protection of TK through conventional IP rights, through *sui generis* and non-IP protection, or some combination of the two.

This chapter seeks to clarify the nature and implications of international options for a *sui generis* form of protection, but it takes no view on whether this outcome is in itself desirable. Such policy choices can only coherently be made by states in dialogue with one another, and crucially in consultation with the intended beneficiaries of TK protection, TK holders especially.

II. The paradox: To globalise diversity holistically

International endeavours to protect TK as a distinct, *sui generis* form of IP confront a deep paradox: how to give broader, even global meaning and effect to norms and knowledge systems that are intrinsically and irreducibly local in character, and that rely on the original community context for their full significance, without eliminating the essential qualities of TK. Too strong and pre-emptive an international *sui generis* model for IP protection risks homogenizing the subject matter of protection.[14] The diversity of subject

---

[12] *E.g.*, the proposal for "a legally binding international instrument" made at the WIPO Intergovernmental Committee on Intellectual Property and Genetic Resources, Traditional Knowledge and Folklore, 5th Sess. Rep., Doc. WIPO/GRTKF/IC/5/15 ¶ 175 (4 Aug. 2003).

[13] *See, e.g.*, the range of proposals submitted for revision of the TRIPS Agreement (Agreement on Trade-Related Aspects of International Property Rights, 15 Apr. 1994, Marrakesh Agreement Establishing the World Trade Organization, Annex 1C, LEGAL INSTRUMENTS – RESULTS OF THE URUGUAY ROUND vol. 31, 33 I.L.M. 81 (1994) [hereinafter TRIPS Agreement]), such as the revision of Article 29 proposed in Draft Decision on Traditional Knowledge, above n. 6.

[14] *See, e.g.*, Four Directions Council, *Forests, Indigenous Peoples and Biodiversity*, Submission

matter and of its customary modes of protection may require, instead, a *suorum genorum* framework – an heterogeneous network of mutual recognition that does not confine TK to one distinct genus, but recognizes that divergent knowledge traditions, integrated with customary law, warrant recognition as distinct genera, under the *aegis* of a general set of core principles.

It may transpire that international processes need to focus more on the articulation of general principles and norms, and to forge operational linkages between divergent national systems, rather than codifying distinctive customary legal, social and cultural practices. Even so, the concept of globalising what is inherently local may not prove to be a true paradox, but may serve as an insightful critique of mainstream, ostensibly objective IP standards and constructions of the public domain.

Conventional IP law and TK protection could be reconciled by observing, first, that the interpretation and implementation of mainstream IP law naturally draws on custom or convention. Forms of knowledge that are validated by IP systems in general are recognized and protected partly because of their conformity with established modes of analysis and selection that have an implicit customary element ("all knowledge is traditional"). Second, in their actual operation, IP systems do in practice reflect distinctive local or cultural qualities that may not be apparent from objective international IP standards ("legal protection is customary").

Delivering equity is a practical task. An injudicious choice of mechanism to protect TK may turn out to provide Pyrrhic protection: a dubious in-principle benefit gained at too great a practical cost that undercuts the longer-term interests of the TK holder. As for IP more generally, protection of TK is not a beneficial end in itself, but should rather coherently promote both right holders' interests and public policy outcomes. This goal, in turn, requires careful reflection on what public goods are, or should be, promoted through TK protection.

The status of knowledge *per se* as an iconic public good has to be reconciled with customary knowledge management systems and IP rights that impose excludability on certain categories of knowledge.[15] This reconciliation will here be attempted by setting the debate in terms of advancing higher-level public goods, such as the survival of distinctive cultures and incentives to maintain and preserve TK, and more abstract public policy goals, such as a

to the Secretariat for the CBD (1996):

> Any attempt to devise uniform guidelines for the recognition and protection of indigenous peoples' knowledge runs the risk of collapsing this rich jurisprudential diversity into a single "model" that will not fit the values, conceptions or laws of any indigenous society.

[15] *Cf.* Keith E. Maskus & Jerome H. Reichman, *The Globalization of Private Knowledge Goods and the Privatization of Global Public Goods* [this volume], Part III. B ("Maintaining the Supply of Knowledge as a Global Public Good").

broader conception of equity and greater respect for indigenous and local communities.

A. The point of access as the fulcrum of protection

Ideally, perhaps, for many communities, the existing modes of preserving and passing on TK within the traditional circle would continue, without external involvement and without the dubious benefits of fresh policy or legal initiatives by outside players, least of all by international institutions. The elusive *sui generis* form of protection that is sought is often already present in the life of the community itself. It may be inherently contradictory and fruitless to seek global, holistic recognition for these diverse, community-level knowledge systems. Nevertheless, a strong practical need for distinct forms of TK protection – including, importantly, protection with an international or interjurisdictional element – arises when TK or the cultural expressions that embody it are removed or alienated (consensually or adversely) from their local context and used beyond the traditional circle by third parties who may or may not have a legal relationship with the original community.

Efforts to protect TK need to focus on this point of alienation. IP rights are often not clarified or enforced when TK is disclosed, documented or transmitted beyond the community. When this occurs, it is problematic in principle and in practice to recognize rights retrospectively.

It is also at this point, when the customary normative overlay is separated from knowledge, that it becomes necessary to consider how to preserve and extend the reach of this traditional normative context, for example, by ensuring that customary law constraints are recorded and agreed upon at the same time as the information content of TK is documented. Reinforcing *ex situ* protection (extending the effective reach of customary protocols) may also help to bolster customary law within the community, as TK systems and protocols come under external pressure and erode through social change.

Typically, the call for protection of TK has been a defensive and retrospective response to a sense of misappropriation, after TK has been taken beyond the community and is used in ways that affront the community's own values.[16] It may only be after the customary protocols or laws governing TK are felt to have been violated – when it is "too late" in terms of the usual construction of the public domain – that the need for strengthened respect for those laws becomes clear. Indeed, where the customary laws and protocols are deeply embedded in the way of life of a community, it may only be the sense of violation that arises when TK is alienated or misused that enables the truly normative character of these practices to crystallize and become fully recognized and articulated, in retrospect, as a binding norm. In this way, a general sense of misappropriation or

---

[16] *See* G. Dutfield, above n. 10.

of violation of cultural norms and customary law can spur demands for better legal recognition of the community's rights in its TK, and can encourage the codification or formal documentation of informal norms and values.

An analogous case arises when the use of a familiar geographical term by a foreign merchant triggers interest in stronger and better defined geographical indication (GI) protection. Despite a visceral sense that the term has been misappropriated or misused, there may actually be no legal basis for a claim against the foreign party. This is particularly so if the term is not explicitly protected as a geographical indication in the country of origin,[17] and there are no clear rules constraining its use.

It may be difficult retrospectively to translate a culturally rooted sense of misappropriation into a firm legal rule against misuse that one can sustain in foreign jurisdictions. Similarly, in seeking to protect TK, it may be difficult to define (and prove) the normative element of traditional cultures and knowledge management, and to provide an adequate basis for legal remedies that reach beyond the originating community, despite the general sense of misappropriation that communities often express. Hence, protection of TK will require more than an overall legal framework. Establishing an adequate basis (normative and evidentiary) for protection of specific elements of TK within that framework may become the greater challenge.

B. The international layer of TK protection: What practical choices?

An ideal foundational principle for *sui generis* TK protection would be to defer to its customary normative context, to apply globally what one commentator terms the principle of locality: "to resolve any disputes over the acquisition and use of indigenous people's heritage according to the customary laws of the indigenous peoples concerned,"[18] akin to the principle of *lex loci*. The focus would shift from codifying or specifying anew the relevant forms of legal protection towards giving effect more broadly to the rules or norms that already govern TK in its customary context.

This task has a legal/policy component and a practical component. If traditional conceptions of ownership, custodianship and responsibility over TK are in principle to be given wider legal expression, this normative development should be underpinned by the legal and practical tools that would make it a realistic possibility to defend TK-related interests through the full range of IP rights.

---

[17] *See* Article 24.9 of the TRIPS Agreement, above n. 13, which makes the obligation for protection abroad conditional on protection in the country of origin.
[18] Dr. E.A. Daes, Defending Indigenous Peoples' Heritage, Keynote Address at the Conference on Protecting Knowledge: Traditional Resource Rights in the New Millennium, Union of British Columbian Indian Chiefs (Feb. 2000).

The strictly international legal dimension of TK protection has two broad aspects: (1) the articulation of general norms or overarching principles to guide or bind States in protecting TK through national laws and policy measures; and (2) the creation of technical legal mechanisms that would trigger enforceable rights over TK in foreign jurisdictions.[19] The evolution of international IP law has typically started with the creation of mechanisms to make rights available in foreign jurisdictions (such as through the national treatment principle or right of assimilation, or reciprocity mechanisms), then has moved over time towards the establishment of harmonized minimum standards and overarching normative statements.

Minimum standards for substantive IP law were developed incrementally over many years, and the public policy objectives of IP protection were first explicitly articulated as a substantive provision of an international norm-setting instrument[20] over a century after the first multilateral IP treaties were concluded. The framing of extensive doctrinal standards that define the core of IP protection at the national level is typically a late stage in the development of international IP law.

The diverse, still exploratory nature of national approaches to *sui generis* TK protection suggests that the international dimension of TK protection may need to take the same trajectory, by initially creating mechanisms to trigger protection in foreign jurisdictions through national treatment or reciprocity. This approach would leave scope for the evolution of national systems in line with diverse domestic needs and for possible future convergence in the light of practical experience. Alternatively, the international process could proceed directly to articulate guiding principles and general normative recommendations, or could go still further and establish binding minimum standards for national protection of traditional knowledge.

What rights could and should be triggered by such a system, and what standards should apply? One practical yardstick for an international system is

---

[19] Inasmuch as established intellectual property rights can be used to protect TK, or aspects of it, national treatment obligations under existing treaties (Paris Convention for the Protection of Industrial Property, 20 Mar. 1883, 828 U.N.T.S. 305 [hereinafter Paris Convention], art 2; Berne Convention for the Protection of Literary and Artistic Works, *adopted* 1886, 1161 U.N.T.S. A [hereinafter Berne Convention], art. 3; TRIPS Agreement, above n. 13, art 3) would extend to TK protection (provided that the TK holding community has the necessary legal identity, a matter on which international law traditionally defers to the laws of the country of origin, which may in turn take account of customary law, as discussed below). In addition, and more speculatively, the broad definition of "industrial property" under the Paris Convention (Article 1 (3): "industrial property shall be understood in the broadest sense") raises the possibility that existing treaty obligations may extend to new *sui generis* forms of TK protection, provided that they are considered a form of industrial property, since the obligation to extend national treatment applies in very general terms "as regards industrial property," and is *prima facie* not confined to established forms of industrial property rights.

[20] Note in particular article 7 of the TRIPS Agreement, above n. 13.

to consider what actual outcomes TK right holders wish to secure in practice. What is it that a TK holder in a community, say, in South America or in the Pacific, would want to happen in an Asian, European, or North American court? What course of action and remedies should be available; what activities should be restrained, how, and by what legal means; what practical constraints have to be considered? This point alone could weigh against a strong customary law approach, which could make it highly burdensome for the plaintiff or prosecutor to establish a case based on infringement of customary law. It may entail establishing the nature of customary law obligations, comparable to the *lex loci* interpretation of contractual obligations. Evidentiary problems would arise, especially if the customary law is not codified and relies on oral tradition. A court would need to bridge wide legal and cultural gaps to interpret and apply customary law that is rooted in a traditional culture unfamiliar in the country where relief is sought.

TK holders have reported difficulties in securing effective outcomes in their own and in foreign jurisdictions even when using existing, conventional IP rights. If a *sui generis* TK right is to be effective internationally in addressing alleged misappropriation or misuse of TK, the choices made would need to be at least as workable in management and enforcement terms as the conventional IP system, and sensitive to the resources and capacities of TK holder communities.

C. Recognizing customary laws and protocols beyond IP law

Such practical considerations may even suggest that, in the short term, it could be more effective to concentrate not on creating new IP rights as such, but on establishing alternative dispute settlement resolution mechanisms tailored to deal with the specific aspects of disputes over TK and related genetic resources. *Sui generis* rules of procedure could respond to the interests involved, show flexibility in applying customary law considerations, and yet create certainty and such legally-binding outcomes as are required. Other approaches recognize customary law governing TK without creating an IP right or otherwise interacting directly with the IP system.

Some *sui generis* forms of TK protection pivot on the right to be consulted or to give prior informed consent in relation to access to TK, rather than by creating distinct property rights in TK as such. This occurs, for instance, when the TK associated with biological resources is protected through direct regulation of access to the resources and knowledge. This kind of protection arguably lacks the essential qualities of a distinct IP right, although it may well become an effective means of enforcing customary law protocols governing TK.

Practical experience has already been gained with a range of methods that protect TK outside the framework of IP law and that respect customary law. Examples include:

- obligations under contracts, such as knowledge transfer agreements, to respect and comply with customary law as a direct contractual obligation on the party gaining access to TK;
- access regimes for genetic resources and associated TK that require consultation with TK holders, or accord to indigenous and local communities a right of prior informed consent, with the prospect of consent being conditional on respect for customary law governing the knowledge that has been accessed;
- resort to the law of confidentiality to restrain use of TK material, including unauthorized publication contrary to customary law;[21]
- use of electronic databases storing TK that have access control mechanisms that mirror customary law, for instance, in restricting access to sacred knowledge to elders only;[22] and
- ethical guidelines or standards, under which an industry or researcher may be ethically bound to follow or respect the customary laws of the source community.

These approaches are more adaptable than formal property rights systems, and this very flexibility affords wide scope for TK holders to give effect to customary legal or cultural concerns when setting conditions on use of TK.

Their chief defect, from the TK holder's point of view, is not a practical matter but a policy issue: they leave the legal character of the public domain untouched. Indeed, the crux of TK protection is the call for rights over TK that is in fact available to the public and is considered under conventional IP law to fall in the public domain. *Sui generis* protection is invoked as a means of restraining use of such TK by third parties who are not bound by any contractual or fiduciary relations to the TK holders, and who do not infringe conventional IP rights. Hence, it is a call for true property rights that are "binding on the world."[23] However, this need can be partly addressed by *sui generis* regimes for equitable sharing of benefits without the creation of exclusive IP rights. For instance, *domain public payant* systems[24] and a proposed

---

[21] Foster v. Mountford & Rigby, 29 F.L.R. 233 (1976).
[22] E.g., the customary law element of the "digital repatriation" movement described in *Ancient Traditions Preserved*, AUSTRALIAN IT, 10 June 2003, *available at* www.news.com.au: "the entire intellectual system of Elcho Island's various clans is being reconceived in digital form, and shaped into an elaborate, multi-level database," with discrete levels for public, private and secret knowledge; *see also* the Tulalip Tribes *Cultural Stories* project, and the Indigenous Collections Management Project (Jane Hunter et al., Software Tools for Indigenous Knowledge Management (Sept. 2002) and Kathryn Wells, a Model and Pilot Options for Digital Image and Text Archive of Indigenous Arts and Knowledge; A Progress Report (1997)).
[23] *See, e.g.*, Cottier & Panizzon, above n. 8.
[24] E.g., Bangui Agreement Establishing the African Intellectual Property Organisation (OAPI), 2 Mar. 1977, 11 WIPO, INDUSTRIAL PROPERTY LAWS AND TREATIES, MULTILATERAL TREATIES, TEXT 1–018, art. 59.

hybrid compensatory liability regime[25] would appropriate to the TK holder some of the value of TK in use while permitting general access to TK. While stopping short of creating exclusive property rights in TK, such approaches may be considered part of the broader landscape of IP law (with rough analogies to public lending rights, mechanical licenses, and tape levies).[26] In practice, little may distinguish a compensatory liability regime from an exclusive IP right that is subject to mandatory licensing with a residual right to equitable remuneration.[27]

Some TK holders seek the validation and recognition that a strong IP right provides and do see exclusivity as a necessary goal. Customary law obligations may require more stringent protection than an entitlement to compensation. Where certain uses cause spiritual offence and threaten cultural integrity, for example, rather than commercial damage, monetary payment may not be viewed by TK holders as acceptable "benefit sharing" nor as an equitable form of compensation. A right to enjoin use altogether, or to restrain derogatory or offensive use, may be seen as vital.[28] What is at issue, therefore, is the presumption that TK falls into the public domain unless covered by conventional IP rights or contractual obligations.

---

[25] *See, e.g.*, J.H. Reichman & Tracy Lewis, *Using Liability Rules to Stimulate Local Innovation in Developing Countries: Application to Traditional Knowledge* [this volume]; J.H. Reichman, *Of Green Tulips and Legal Kudzu: Repackaging Rights in Subpatentable Innovation*, 53 VAND. L. REV. 1743, 1797 (2000) [hereinafter *Green Tulips*].

[26] Criminal law has also been used in place of "the grant of a property right in the nature of a copyright" to implement performers' rights by punishing those who make and/or use performances without consent. C. MASOUYÉ, GUIDE TO THE ROME CONVENTION AND TO THE PHONOGRAMS CONVENTION (World Intellectual Property Organization, Pub. No. 617E [1981]).

[27] Consider, for example, the various ways that States have implemented the compulsory licensing provisions of Berne Convention, above n. 19, art. 11bis (2), relating to various usage of broadcast copyright works, itself a form of compensatory liability regime; and hybrid regimes for test data protection (*see* TRIPS Agreement, above n. 13, art. 39.3) combining periods of data exclusivity with compensated cross-referencing.

However, many mandatory licensing schemes cut back upon an exclusive property right and typically intervene *ex post*, which can skew the investment calculus. Professor Reichman's compensatory liability regime is a clear *ex ante* entitlement – hence a property right – that can exclude wholesale duplication, but not value-adding follow-on uses, for which only reasonable compensation must be paid. He prefers the term "automatic licence" because it defines the right itself. *See* Reichman, *Green Tulips*, above n. 25. *See generally* J.H. Reichman, *Legal Hybrids Between the Patent and Copyright Paradigms*, 94 COLUM. L. REV. 2432 (1994).

[28] Ancillary unfair competition norms are not incompatible with compensatory liability, and become essential when the TK owners have not voluntarily consented to making their knowledge available. *See, e.g.*, Dutfield, above n. 10 (discussing interface between Carlos Correa's misappropriation proposal and the compensatory liability proposal).

The call for TK protection has parallels with the emergence of claims for performers' rights, in two key senses. First, technological change has accelerated the phenomenon of perceived misappropriation and created a utilitarian argument for protection. Second, changing social values attributed greater value to the performer as creative artist and enhanced the claim for an inherent "natural" right. Performers could once maintain control over their performances by contractual means and by restricting access to their performances; the technological developments that made bootlegging possible created a demand for distinct rights in the performance *per se*, including a right over fixation.[29] In the absence of performers' rights, third parties were technically free to exploit their fixations of performances. Recognition of rights in the performance entailed an in-principle transfer from the public domain into the scope of private rights. Similarly, the call for *sui generis* TK protection responds to changing external factors, both technological and social, and critically revisits the policy basis and equitable footing of the existing IP regimes and the very conception of the public domain.[30]

D. Revisiting the public domain: Which public, and whose domain?

TK holders' apprehension about the public domain flows through to unease about defensive protection strategies in general. To be sure, TK holders' interests can be defended by the deliberate use of the public domain to preempt or to overcome adverse IP rights illegitimately asserted by third parties over TK subject matter. For example, this may entail strengthened legal measures (improving the recognition of orally disclosed TK as prior art[31]) or practical measures (ensuring that TK is actually considered by examiners when assessing the validity of a patent claim).[32]

In some celebrated cases, it has been the assertion of IP rights by a third party (such as a patent application allegedly covering TK subject matter) that has triggered a community's interest in IP protection of TK. Hence, the initial impulse is to protect TK from IP rights rather than through IP rights. But

---

[29] TRIPS Agreement, above n. 13, at art. 14.1. The parallel can become more than an analogy, as rights over performances of expressions of folklore can operate as IP protection of a traditional way of expressing and transmitting TK.

[30] See also A.S. Taubman, *Nobility of Interpretation: Equity, Retrospectivity, and Collectivity in Implementing New Norms for Performers' Rights*, 12 J. INTELL. PROP. L. (forthcoming 2005).

[31] See the proposal for an extended scope for prior art to take account of TK in COMMISSION ON INTELLECTUAL PROPERTY RIGHTS, INTEGRATING INTELLECTUAL PROPERTY RIGHTS AND DEVELOPMENT POLICY 83 (2002) and the proposal for a universal standard for prior art in Article 8 of the Draft Substantive Patent Law Treaty, WIPO Doc. SCP/9/2 (3 Mar. 2003).

[32] See the extensive discussion of defensive mechanisms in Practical Mechanisms for the Defensive Protection of Traditional Knowledge and Genetic Resources within the Patent System, Doc. WIPO/GRTKF/IC/5/6 (14 May 2003).

defensive protection can be Pyrrhic in effect when it relies on the public domain status of TK that is not itself protected by IP rights. When a claimed invention either directly misappropriates TK or draws on TK that was placed in the public domain without a community's prior informed consent, the patent may not create the principal problem, but may be more a symptom of a failure positively to safeguard TK (physically or legally). A defensive strategy aimed at invalidating such a patent might have the perverse effect of placing the TK unambiguously in the public domain, so that instead of just the patent holder, anyone would be free to use the TK, to the still greater detriment of its custodians.[33]

Despite an initial defensive impulse and, indeed, because of the potential negative effects of a purely defensive response, TK holders have identified the need for clear positive protection – distinct rights in TK as such – to complement defensive protection.[34] Positive protection may be afforded through conventional IP (such as when TK is protected as a trade secret), through *sui generis* elements or adaptations of conventional IP law to deal with TK subject matter (such as provisions in trade mark law that recognize offence to indigenous communities), or through true *sui generis* systems that establish or recognize some distinct right in TK as such. In addition, many TK holders wish actively to exploit elements of their TK in the broader marketplace, either as the basis for community industries or through appropriate commercial partnerships.

The judicious use of conventional IP systems and *sui generis* adaptations or extensions of conventional IP systems is of much potential value for TK holders, as are non-IP forms of protecting and safeguarding TK. Any comprehensive and realistic approach to TK protection needs to weigh carefully the potential value of each of these mechanisms, not least because of the likely negotiation and transaction costs in constructing and administering newly-crafted *sui generis* rights. Where, however, a policy decision is made to create *sui generis* protection, the form of protection should follow its intended function and should be based on elucidation of the policy goal for protection.

This criterion, in turn, raises deep questions about the policy interests to be favoured through TK protection and about the reconciliation of overlapping and potentially conflicting public goods. A coherent approach to these

---

[33] For example, the topical benefit-sharing case involving a patent on technology associated with TK of the San people entails payment to San Hoodia Benefit Sharing Trust, which relies on the successful commercialisation of the patent. Press Release, The San and the CSIR announce a benefit-sharing agreement for potential anti-obesity drug (March 24, 2003), *available at* http://www.csir.co.za/plsql/ptl0002. A more systematic use of alternative dispute resolution tailored to TK holders' needs may facilitate more such benefit-sharing outcomes.

[34] "Development of new IP tools to protect TK not protected by existing TK tools" was identified as an objective in WIPO, INTELLECTUAL PROPERTY NEEDS AND EXPECTATIONS OF TRADITIONAL KNOWLEDGE HOLDERS 226 (2001).

questions requires a closer consideration of the distinctive qualities of TK, and accordingly, of the public good implications of its protection.

III. What is *sui generis* about TK?

The policy choices taken for TK protection vary according to divergent definitions or conceptions of TK, and a greater coordination internationally may be contingent on a clearer shared understanding of the distinctive qualities of TK as subject matter for IP protection. This premise does not mean, however, that a single, exhaustive definition of TK is a prerequisite for effective protection, particularly at the international level, any more than the successful development and elaboration of the Paris Convention over more than a century has needed a settled definition of "invention." Since existing national approaches for TK protection already display considerable diversity in how TK has been conceived, a flexible approach to conception and definition of TK is a likely prerequisite for the successful coordination of protection internationally.

A. *Further reflections on the definition of traditional knowledge*

In some cases, TK has been defined with reference to its content – it is *sui generis* because it is *about* "traditional" subject matter. It may be knowledge with a specifically local character, such as knowledge of traditional ecological practices linked with a local ecosystem. Or it may be knowledge with an inherent spiritual dimension associated with traditional belief systems or knowledge that construes "technical" information in a spiritual context.

TK subject matter may also be limited according to a particular policy goal, such as protection for traditional medical knowledge,[35] or, as in the CBD, to knowledge that is "relevant for the conservation and sustainable use of biological diversity"[36] (similarly in national TK laws that partly give effect to the CBD by focusing on TK relevant to the preservation of biodiversity[37]).

Another approach, analogous to the way *sui generis* IP rights have been established in other subject matter (e.g. integrated circuit layout designs or plant varieties), would be to recognize TK as a *sui generis* category of knowledge. It would thus be delineated deliberately to meet a specific policy goal, so that the category of knowledge was a construct of the policy process. In still

---

[35] See, e.g., Thailand's Act on Protection and Promotion of Traditional Thai Medicinal Intelligence, B.E. 2542, *summarized in* Comparative Summary of Existing National Sui Generis Measures and Laws for the Protection of Traditional Knowledge, WIPO Doc. WIPO/GRTKF/IC/5/INF/4 (20 June 2003) [hereinafter, WIPO Comparative Summary].
[36] CBD, above n. 5, Preamble.
[37] See, e.g., India's Biological Diversity Act of 2002, art. 36(5) (protecting "knowledge of local people relating to biological diversity"), *available at* http://www.forests.tn.nic.in/biodiversity_act.htm (last visited 15 Aug. 2004).

other cases, TK has been defined in part with reference to its actual or potential value.[38] This follows because IP protection will typically operate to ensure that value arising from the use of TK beyond the community is appropriated by the community, or that at least the benefits are shared equitably. Such approaches define TK by reference to the policy purpose of protection or respond to gaps in existing forms of protection. Limiting an international framework to these approaches may, however, attract criticism for excessively narrowing the scope of TK and for overlooking its diversity and local qualities.

Instead of a deterministic policy-led construction of TK, a more open-ended approach would be to consider it as a form of knowledge and to analyse *how* it is known. Is TK known in a *sui generis* way, or is there a distinct epistemological basis for TK? If it is intellectual property, is TK "intellectual" in a way that distinguishes it from other categories of IP ? For example, the collective and cumulative characteristics of TK are often stressed, which suggests the possibility of constructing a kind of group epistemology: TK as a kind of knowledge that is known in a collective sense over generations and through initiation to a group consciousness.[39] Yet, this would be unlikely to facilitate practical outcomes in the immediate term (it might be difficult even to find a consistent dichotomy between TK proper and supposedly atomistic individual knowledge).

The search for a distinct sense of knowledge proper to TK alone may also overlook knowledge that is generated and known by individuals within a traditional context. The collective characteristic of TK cannot be pushed too far, as it would neglect the role (and rights) of individuals. Indeed, this kind of analysis obscures the important practical distinction between the underlying knowledge and the specific aspects of knowledge that are accorded legal protection.

The legal mechanisms that currently regulate the "knowledge economy" do not pivot on a rigorous analysis of the nature of knowledge; indeed, IP protection does not protect knowledge as such. Rather, the IP system distinguishes expressions of knowledge from its content (as in copyright law) or constructs specific embodiments of knowledge for protection (such as the notion of invention in patent law, which abstracts protected subject matter from a broader substrate of knowledge). It is therefore probably a fruitless

---

[38] *See, e.g.*, Article 7(ii) of Brazilian Provisional Measure No. 2186–16 (2001) (regulating access to genetic heritage, protection of and access to associated TK); *cf.* "socio-economic value" in the African Model Legislation for the Protection of the Rights of Local Communities, Farmers and Breeders and for the Regulation of Access to Biological Resources, art. 1 (2000) [hereinafter African Model Legislation], *summarized in* WIPO Comparative Summary, above n. 35.

[39] *Cf.* Reichman & Lewis, above n. 25 (comparing slow accretion of cumulative traditional knowledge by trial and error to the faster process of acquiring cumulative and sequential know-how by routine engineers who resort to reverse-engineering by honest means).

category error to assume that the means of protection of TK can or should map all the essential characteristics of traditional epistemologies. This would be to conflate a mere legal tool for protection of readily misappropriated aspects of TK in the external environment with the vastly richer cultural, social and spiritual domain of the original context of TK.

Between the two extremes of a policy-driven approach and an analytical epistemology of TK lies an approach that would concentrate not on the content or way of knowing TK, but on the tradition that plainly sets TK apart from knowledge in general. TK is anchored in the community or social context in which it has been generated, transmitted, shared and preserved. The *sui generis* quality of TK may be situated in this relationship with a community. Examining whether TK has a distinctive community context has descriptive and normative aspects. What makes knowledge "traditional" may be the unadorned fact that it forms part of the community's intellectual heritage. In that case, it would be sufficient to observe objectively that traditions that surround and define TK are followed simply as a matter of practice. Or there may be a stronger requirement for a distinct normative quality, so that the community considers that the knowledge *should* be preserved, maintained and transmitted within a framework of binding obligations.

A rough analogy may be drawn with customary international law, where the enquiry moves from whether States do actually follow a practice to whether the practice is considered by States as a norm that binds behaviour. Thus, we find the requirement of *opinio juris:* "[n]ot only must the acts concerned amount to a settled practice, they must also be such, or be carried out in such a way, as to be evidence of a belief that this practice is rendered obligatory by the existence of a rule of law requiring it."[40] Hence, the enquiry may become factual. To the external observer, has the community actually dealt with the knowledge as a component of tradition? Alternatively, one may seek to establish whether there is a conscious normative element in the way the knowledge is traditionally maintained and transmitted.

Shifting from the external perspective to the subjective, the community itself may need to recognize the knowledge as an element of its traditional heritage, and indeed to define its own cultural identity in part through the TK. If a *sui generis* form of protection for TK – a new normative instrument – were to be based on the distinctive characteristics of TK, then it would be desirable to give weight to the traditional normative context. A subjective element, roughly akin to *opinio juris*, could be required as a necessary link between the source community and eligible TK.

However, seeking objective evidence of normative content may be problematic in the context of a traditional community. A practice may be so deeply

---

[40] Federal Republic of Germany v. Denmark and Federal Republic of German v. The Netherlands (North Sea Continental Shelf Cases), 1969 I.C.J. 3 (20 Feb.).

embedded in the community's way of life that an *opinio juris* is only clearly manifested or articulated after the norm has been broken or subjected to stress – after the time of external access or alienation of the knowledge. This factor again raises practical questions about proof of the existence of custom and of a normative element. On the face of it, the more subjective and responsive to local factors the system is, the more burdensome it would become to exercise the right in foreign jurisdictions.[41]

It may be useful to move beyond this uncertain distinction between actual practice and subjective normative component – which is difficult enough in international law, potentially contentious and counterproductive if it requires passing external judgement on community practices in a time of social flux and external pressures – and instead consider customary practice and law combined as the original community's integrated conception of *sui generis* knowledge management. The normative component does not operate in isolation as a stand-alone rule governing knowledge, but it is often integral to community life, and may indeed be subordinate to broader processes, such as environmental management and maintenance of a spiritual and cultural identity. Thus, the knowledge component of TK should be considered as integral with (i) practices that define custodianship or the nature of community ownership, (ii) the rights and responsibilities that determine custody, access rights, means of dissemination and preservation of knowledge, and (iii) the customary mode in which TK is passed on between generations. *Sui generis* knowledge management may also extend to such questions as dispute settlement (including competing claims over knowledge), the sharing of benefits within and between communities, and sanctioning infringement of customary laws governing the TK.

Some objective, culturally neutral conception of TK is still needed at the level of national law or an international framework if the system is to be at all workable and coherent, precisely because of the rich diversity of TK systems. At the same time, TK holders themselves, such as tribal elders, may be the source of authority on what knowledge conforms with the operative definition of TK, and the nature and scope of protection may take account of traditional constraints on the use of the protected TK. Their *opinio juris* should be influential.

Judicial decisions have already taken account of the customary normative framework and related subjective considerations relevant to TK, for instance in determining whether there is the necessary "substantial concern to the plaintiff" for information to be protected as confidential,[42] and in assessing the

---

[41] This is directly analogous to the "problem of considerable difficulty" discerned by J. Brennan in the practical establishment of a customary law basis for native land title in *Mabo v. Queensland* [No. 2] 175 C.L.R. 1 (1992).

[42] Gordon Coulthard v. South Australia, Austl. Torts Rep. 81 (1995) (applying customary law considerations to the test articulated by Deane, J. in Moorgate Tobacco Co. Ltd. v. hillip Morris Ltd., 156 C.L.R. 414, 437–8 (1984)).

extent of damages caused by copyright infringement.[43] Resolving the paradox of globalising inherently local customary law becomes a practical question of how the perspective of the holders of TK themselves can be taken into account in defining the TK that is eligible for protection and how it is to be protected.

B. Locating the normative centre of TK protection

Even the task of defining TK exposes a tension between an external, policy-driven approach, and an holistic conception of TK rooted in the traditional context, in the life, practices and values of the custodian community. Similarly, in setting the bounds of protection or the scope of rights, tension arises between an inclusive, descriptive approach that would capture all aspects of the customary management of TK, and a more reductionist approach limited to those practical forms of protection that are considered essential for defending TK holders against misappropriation of its value when it is alienated from its traditional setting. The choice seems to lie between the idealised aim of extending the effect of existing, customary law knowledge systems, and the more nuanced goal of creating more limited and neutral derivative rights, filtered by specific policy objectives, that would only allow for certain specific remedies.

This latter role is already performed, in part, by positive and defensive protection modalities available from conventional IP rights systems. A *sui generis* right could, therefore, be based on an appraisal of existing IP rights and be tailored to fill a perceived gap; or it could more ambitiously seek to recognize and extend the effect of TK management protocols, so that the normative context accompanied the knowledge when it left the originating community. Ideally, perhaps, it should do both. Yet, it seems unlikely that any regime could fulfil both roles and still remain coherent and workable. Broader recognition of customary law and knowledge management protocols is a consistent demand by holders of TK,[44] and it should arguably be maintained as a desideratum or guiding principle for any architecture for TK protection. But, as already argued, it would be self-defeatingly burdensome to require proof of customary law at the community level as a prerequisite for triggering legal protection of TK, and it would greatly limit the practical scope of protection to that TK only which is demonstrably defined and supported by customary law at the community level.

Much TK is no longer linked to a distinct customary law framework, for instance, when a broad knowledge tradition is shared between different

---

[43] M* v. Indofurn Pty. Ltd. 30 I.P.R. 209 (1995) [Australia].
[44] Articulated, for example, in the WIPO Intergovernmental Committee (most recently in its 5th Sess. Rep., above n. 12, at nn. 38, 53, 54, 55, 56, 76, 103, 129 & 172 (4 Aug. 2003)).

communities, including a diaspora, and an exclusive or determinate linkage between the TK and one specific community cannot be established. Practical choices already taken bear this out. Some national laws that formalize *sui generis* IP protection for TK do not recognize customary law, or confine it to particular functions. Indeed, customary law and practices may, tellingly, be recognized as *exceptions* to *sui generis* TK protection.[45]

The legitimacy of *sui generis* TK protection may yet require giving the originating community or TK holders some say over what subject matter counts as legitimate TK, and how it should be protected. The distinctive qualities of TK suggest that the TK holder should be set at the normative centre of gravity.[46] If so, this premise would appear to set TK protection apart from conventional forms of IP rights.

Under most IP laws, an essentially objective external standard is conventionally applied to determine whether subject matter complies with a specific definition and specific criteria for IP protection; and the nature and scope of protection is constrained by external standards (public policy exceptions, compulsory licensing, etc.) The right holder's own subjective perception as to whether subject matter is eligible for protection – for instance, whether a work is original or an invention not obvious – is not decisive, and is technically irrelevant. Similarly, the right holder is not entitled to define the legal scope of the right granted (such as in assessing the permissible scope of fair use by third parties). Equally, the subject matter of IP protection is discrete and is generally assessed for eligibility apart from the context of its origin. An invention is patentable whether it was invented by one or a collective of inventors, or developed in a traditional healer's hut or a medical laboratory.

By contrast, a TK protection system may require as a very condition of protection the sense on the part of a community that its knowledge is traditional, and the existence of a positive relationship between the content of knowledge and its traditional context. Moreover, the scope of the right (i.e. the kind of third party acts it constrains) may likewise be determined by the traditional context.

Most modern IP rights are created by the operation of an IP statute (this was not historically nor exclusively the case, but in general the common law roots of IP law are now supplanted by statute). By contrast, a *sui generis* system for IP protection of TK may be considered as giving broader recognition to a right that

---

[45] See, e.g., Panama, Executive Decree (2001) concerning the Special Intellectual Property Regime Governing the Collective Rights of Indigenous Peoples for the Protection and Defence of their Cultural Identity and their Traditional Knowledge, art. 11.

[46] See Michael R. Dove, *Center, Periphery, and Biodiversity: a Paradox of Governance and a Developmental Challenge*, in STEPHEN BRUSH & DOREEN STABINSKY, VALUING LOCAL KNOWLEDGE 41 (Island Press 1996). See also Rosemary Coombe, *Protecting Cultural Industries to Promote Cultural Diversity: Dilemmas for International Policymaking Posed by the Recognition of Traditional Knowledge* [this volume].

already exists under customary law, similar to the way early IP rights systems evolved as a formalization of underlying common law rights.[47] Ideally, at least, the policy function of a *sui generis* TK system may not be so much as to create the right – in the way the modern patent right is the artefact of a formal grant process under a statute – but to recognize and substantiate it so as to strengthen its application in a wider context. This approach would give formal, more objective recognition to TK rights that have roots already in a traditional community, and that are considered by that community as constituting a binding norm, while the knowledge protocols would carry with them the community's own *opinio juris*.

C. Revisiting the boundaries of intellectual property and the public domain

These conceptual difficulties in locating the normative centre for TK protection cause us to interrogate and reevaluate how general IP protection is conceived as an international system of common standards. There is, ostensibly, a critical difference between the subjective character of TK, and the objective standards of IP law. In reality, conventional IP systems also rely in practice on custom, on unstated cultural assumptions, indeed, on the concretion of traditional lore and the evolution of IP rights from the common law.[48]

The TK debate brings these subjective elements to light. For instance, strengthening the status of TK as prior art within patent law,[49] and practical adjustments to the prior art base,[50] amount to a modest shift in the epistemic centre of gravity of the patent system that implicitly acknowledges a past cultural subjectivity. Similarly, commentators have questioned the cultural assumptions that determine how the concept of the person skilled in the art is applied in

---

[47] Justine Pila, *The Common Law Invention in Its Original Form*, 2001 INTELL. PROP. Q. 209.
[48] Consider as examples the evolution of the notion of "invention" in the common law tradition, the role of distinctive patent office practice in applying patentability criteria, and the cultural assumptions that apply to establishing the person skilled in the art, as well as the more obvious culturally-rooted relativism that may apply to morality and *ordre public* exceptions to IP rights. This is not to suggest that there is anything inherently wrong with such customs and assumptions; to the contrary, they may be essential for the correct application of established principles and may form one important component of the national "flexibilities" within international standards that are invoked in policy debate. Yet, highlighting and illuminating these cultural factors from the TK vantage point may help in the adaptation and adjustment of broad international standards to specific national contexts.
[49] *See* above n. 31.
[50] For example, see the work of the WIPO Task Force on Classification of Traditional Knowledge, Doc. IPC/CE/32/12 ¶¶ 83–91 (16 Jan. 2003), and proposals for the amendment of PCT minimum documentation to enhance TK coverage considered in Doc. PCT/MIA/7/3 ¶ 11 (2 Dec. 2002).

patent law.[51] When inventive activity blends traditional and formal scientific knowledge, is it necessary, desirable or practical to build TK perspectives into the assessment of nonobviousness?

In a broader context, the movement in international IP law towards the articulation and implementation of minimum substantive standards, as against mutual recognition or reciprocity and the right of assimilation, may bring to the surface the distinctions and tensions between different cultural and legal assumptions and divergences between the subjective application of formally objective standards. Analysis of options for the protection of TK, therefore, offers an instructive critique of the conceptual basis for IP protection generally, and it may shed light on the subjective cultural or epistemological bases of other areas of IP law.

For instance, the call for TK protection obliges us to probe further the fault line between public policy interests and private property rights, already a closely contested issue in international debate. The TRIPS Agreement has been criticised as a decisive shift towards the privatisation of the public domain, with its implementation leading to the exercise of private property rights in ways that privilege private interests over public policy interests.[52] Whatever its direct effect may have been (one could argue, for instance, that the influence of TRIPS on contested trends in biotechnology patenting and the grant of TK-related patents in the major patent jurisdictions is negligible[53]), TRIPS often serves as a metonymy for a broader process of identifying and pursuing IP rights in areas previously considered to be in the public domain, either due to legal limitations (e.g. restrictions on patentable subject matter) or specific choices (the past tendency of public research institutions not to seek patent protection on research outcomes). Even the perception alone that TRIPS symbolises a general shift in values and in policy choices for the provision of public welfare may have influenced a reappraisal of the public

---

[51] "'[T]he person with ordinary skill in the art' with reference to whom the inventive step of TK-related inventions is determined may have to include a person with ordinary skill in the relevant TK system(s), in addition to a person with ordinary skill in the relevant discipline(s) of modern science. There is a need to develop practical means of integrating the relevant teachings of TK systems and modern science when determining inventive step during the substantive examination of patent applications which claim TK-related inventions." The Asian Group, Technical Proposals on Databases and Registries of Traditional Knowledge and Biological/Genetic Resources, Doc. WIPO/GRTKF/IC/4/14, Annex, at 3 (6 Dec. 2002).

[52] *See* TRIPS Agreement, above n. 13, Preamble ("*Recognizing* that intellectual property rights are private rights").

[53] Cases such as E.P.O. Patent No. 0436257 (1994) ("Method for controlling fungi on plants by the aid of a hydrophobic extracted neem oil") and U.S. Patent No. 5,663,484 (1997) ("Basmati rice lines and grains"), were granted under patent laws that had developed through domestic and regional legal evolution rather than under TRIPS-influenced revisions.

domain,⁵⁴ such as in the area of genetic resources, where the concept of a common heritage of humankind has progressively given way to a strengthened articulation of national sovereignty and community rights over such resources.⁵⁵

Yet, TRIPS, unlike the earlier international law of IP, sets the protection of IP and the international normative framework squarely in a broader public policy context by articulating the powerful equitable standards that protection and enforcement of IP should be "conducive to social and economic welfare, and to a balance of rights and obligations."⁵⁶ This principle could be extended to TK protection, informally through its broad normative status in international law (it is arguably an equitable principle for international IP law) or formally through proposals to extend TRIPS explicitly to protect TK.

If so, then the policy debate over TK protection exposes the questions begged by this general equitable standard. Whose social and economic welfare is to be considered – the public in general, or the community that "owns" the TK? What rights and obligations should be balanced, and how? Reconciling equitable considerations may constitute an avenue for the introduction of customary law considerations. Indeed, the concept of responsible custodianship over TK within customary law systems can itself be a model for a comprehensive blending of rights and obligations.

Often, in practice, the impulse towards strengthened protection of TK originates from a sense that IP rights have been used to misappropriate material that might otherwise have fallen into the public domain. This initially provokes a questioning of the role of the IP system and the development of defensive measures to safeguard against the assertion of illegitimate IP rights over TK subject matter. But the focus then moves to the idea of the public domain, and to the assumption that TK is in the public domain when not subject to third party rights. The concern provoked by IP rights can thus lead to a reassessment of the public domain; and the traditional community's interest may be undermined by the presumption that, whether through the limitations of applicable law or through the choices made by community members in the past, TK that has been disclosed in the absence of legal constraints is, and

---

⁵⁴ See, e.g., James Boyle, *The Second Enclosure Movement and the Construction of the Public Domain*, 66 LAW. & CONTEMP. PROBS. 33 (2003); Arti K. Rai & Rebecca S. Eisenberg, *Bayh-Dole Reform and the Progress of Biomedicine*, 66 LAW & CONTEMP. PROBS. 289 (2003). See generally THE PUBLIC DOMAIN, 66 LAW AND CONTEMP. PROBS. [Symposium Issue] 1–483 (2003).

⁵⁵ Described in A.S. Taubman, Cereal Offenders? Owning, Controlling and Exploiting Biological Resources, Paper delivered at Intellectual Property in Agriculture: The International Policy Agenda (23 Nov. 2001), *available at* www.anu.edu.au/acipa. See also Laurence Helfer, *Using Intellectual Property Rights to Preserve the Global Genetic Commons: The International Treaty on Plant Genetic Resources for Food and Agriculture* [this volume].

⁵⁶ TRIPS Agreement, above n. 13, art. 7.

should be, in the public domain.[57] A representative of the Indigenous Saami Council has pointed out that:

> indigenous peoples have rarely placed anything in the so called "public domain," a term without meaning to us ... the public domain is a construct of the IP system and does not take into account domains established by customary indigenous laws.[58]

The principle of "prior informed consent," conceived in the Convention on Biological Diversity as an exercise of state sovereignty over genetic resources,[59] is also widely viewed as applying to local and indigenous communities' entitlement to set the conditions for access to TK and related genetic resources,[60] even when municipal law fails to provide formal mechanisms to exercise this consent. Indeed, prior informed consent may, arguably, take its place among international equitable principles. Applied to TK, this principle may include consent to the commercial or research use of the TK; consent to third parties' steps to secure IP rights derived from TK; or consent to entry of the TK into the public domain.

The practical implementation of TK protection may hinge on the extent to which rights can or should be exercised retroactively over TK that has already entered the public domain without the prior informed consent of the traditional community or in the absence of any municipal law governing the TK. This entails revisiting the notion, or even the legitimacy, of the public domain as currently conceived.

Uncontested "public domain" status may only apply to material that enjoyed IP protection, which subsequently lapsed. However, knowledge is also put into the public domain in one sense when disclosed to the public in exchange for limited patent rights over how it may be used. Public domain status may also flow from a failure to seek IP rights at the appropriate time (but from the TK holder perspective, rights may already have existed in customary law, and no informed decision was made to waive other IP rights); or from a policy determination that certain materials are inherently ineligible for IP protection (again, from the TK perspective, simply raising questions about the validity of these policy assumptions[61]). It may also prove helpful to

---

[57] *See* the extended discussion in Van Caenegem, *The Public Domain: Scientia Nullius?*, 24 EUR. INTELL. PROP. J. 324 (2002).

[58] WIPO Intergovernmental Committee, above n. 12, ¶ 53 (7 July 2003).

[59] CBD, above n. 5, art. 15.1: "Access to genetic resources shall be subject to prior informed consent of the Contracting Party providing such resources."

[60] *See, e.g.*, Taking Forward the Review of Article 27.3(b) of the TRIPS Agreement, Joint Communication from the African Group, WTO Doc. IP/C/W/404, Annex, ¶ 2(c)(iii) (26 June 2003).

[61] *See, e.g.*, WIPO Performances and Phonograms Treaty, 36 I.L.M. 76 (1997), which has the effect of removing performances of expressions of folklore from the public domain by

distinguish between true public-domain status and a commons or "semi-commons," in which the covered subject matter is freely available for some purposes, such as non-profit scientific research, but not for others, such as value-adding commercial applications.[62]

In short, from the perspective of some TK holders at least, TK did not "fall" into the public domain: it was pushed there, unjustly, either by access and publication that overrode customary law or otherwise by the operation of an IP system that inadequately respects TK. What is seen from an IP policy point of view as an insupportable retrospective claim on the public domain could be seen from another vantage point as a lengthy grace period to preserve rights against self-disclosure with unintended consequences. There is, accordingly, a true policy dilemma when considering TK that is conventionally given public domain status, when this status results from disclosure without the prior informed consent of the source community, particularly when such disclosure violates customary law.

This dilemma imposes difficult policy choices. For instance, can public domain status be reversed on equitable grounds, and if so, what rules should apply? These "application in time" issues have been resolved in other contexts in IP law, for instance, in dealing with the impact of retrospective protection when copyright terms are extended, and this practical experience may facilitate equitable solutions for a TK right. The options include a right of equitable remuneration[63] subject to exceptions for the continuation of *bona fide* prior use, recognition of moral rights akin to the rights of integrity and attribution, and a right limited to remedies against culturally offensive use.[64]

Yet, these options should not obscure the fundamental policy and practical difficulty posed by retrospective exercise of newly recognized rights over TK subject matter, whatever the circumstances that led to the disputed "public domain" status of the protected material. Such difficult policy choices could ideally be guided by a broad and inclusive conception of equity, which would balance continuing customary law interests against *bona fide* third party

---

providing for economic and moral rights over them for performers of expressions of folklore.

[62] See, e.g., J.H. Reichman, *Saving the Patent Law from Itself*, in PERSPECTIVES ON PROPERTIES OF THE HUMAN GENOME PROJECT 289, 293–97 (F. Scott Kieff ed. Elsevier Academic Press 2003) (depicting subpatentable know-how generated by routine engineers under trade secret law as a semi-commons).

[63] Article 13 of Peruvian Law No. 27811 provides that "In cases where the collective knowledge has passed into the public domain within the previous 20 years, a percentage of the value, before tax, of the gross sales resulting from the marketing of the goods developed on the basis of that knowledge shall be set aside for the Fund for the Development of Indigenous Peoples...."

[64] See proposals noted in Consolidated Analysis of the Legal Protection of Traditional Cultural Expressions, Doc. WIPO/GRTKF/IC/5/3 ¶ 19 (2 May 2003).

interests and would provide a clearer framework for assessing what remuneration would be equitable.

IV. TK protection as a global public good

It follows that *sui generis* protection of TK could entail a major recalibration of the policy settings and normative basis of the public domain and the existing IP system. Indeed, one background reason for the reluctance to recognize TK as a distinct form of IP right is apprehension that it may be aimed at discrediting the IP system rather than consolidating it. Another constraint is the lack of clarity about the purpose and policy basis of *sui generis* protection. The approach taken may be guided by pragmatic policy objectives (TK protection as a factor in the cultural survival and economic well-being of indigenous and local communities, or as an element in the trading relations between nations), or by more abstract normative and equitable considerations (a "natural rights" argument, based on respect and protection of TK as a self-standing entitlement).[65]

The international policy debate has invoked both justice and utilitarian arguments; an actual policy choice would likely combine elements of both approaches. The conception of global public goods[66] could provide a workable framework for assessing and implementing policy options. Public good analysis is at core a tool for determining the optimal funding of public goods – "a pure theory of government expenditure on collective consumption goods"[67] – because they are by definition nonrivalrous and non-excludable. This is a technocratic assessment about the optimal deployment of public resources to furnish society with necessary facilities.

Yet, there is an ethical intentionality, potential cultural bias and privileging of certain policy objectives in the choice of public goods; even the identification of public goods is in effect to set them in a distinct category as of intrinsic worth to society, a judgement with utilitarian and normative aspects.[68] Malkin and Wildavsky conclude that a public good "becomes public by the social decision to treat it that way."[69] Hence, the debate about public goods shifts ground and instead considers how optimally to order collective priorities, rather than analysing how public goods should best be provided: "international debates

---

[65] *See, e.g.*, SEEDING SOLUTIONS, above n. 11, at 106 (stating that "rights are rights, and should not be undermined by utilitarian considerations").
[66] GLOBAL PUBLIC GOODS: INTERNATIONAL COOPERATION IN THE 21ST CENTURY (Inge Kaul et al. eds., Oxford University Press 1999).
[67] P. Samuelson, *The Pure Theory of Public Expenditure*, 36 REV. ECON. & STAT. 387, 388 (1954).
[68] *See, e.g.*, Peter Drahos, *The Regulation of Public Goods* [this volume].
[69] *Cited in* FRANCISCO SAGASTI & KEITH BEZANSON, FINANCING AND PROVIDING GLOBAL PUBLIC GOODS 5 (Ministry of Foreign Affairs, Sweden 2001).

on global public goods often address only the question of which goods to produce," not "how much of each to produce and at what net benefit to whom."[70]

Because of the positive ethical and utilitarian character accorded to both concepts, there is a temptation to conflate the public domain with a public good, or to identify the public domain as an inherent public good. The public domain of knowledge is, indeed, nonrivalrous and non-excludable. Yet, such a conflation would make a major assumption about the ordering of public goods; it would overlook the differing policy bases of the public domain and public good status; and it would reduce the scope for analysis of optimal provision of public goods. It is helpful to make two key distinctions among public goods: first, between basic public goods (the supply of roads or water as bulk public commodities) and higher-order public goods, which have a more abstract or ethical dimension (equity, good governance and efficiency in the provision of roads and water); and second, between innate public goods (clean air) and public goods that are an artifact of public policy (public libraries).

The IP system precisely defines the distinction between the public domain and the provision of public goods, as it constrains the public domain to secure higher-order, deliberately constructed public goods. The purposive construction of the interface between IP rights and the public domain is a model for the provision of certain public goods. By creating excludability and allowing the right holder to appropriate returns from knowledge,[71] the IP right generates incentives for certain public goods to be provided (notably technological innovation and the disclosure of enabling knowledge about inventions) when these would not otherwise come about. Through the law of trademarks, geographical indications, and the suppression of unfair competition, it also promotes other higher-order public goods, such as fairness, merchant responsibility and equitable protection of reputation in the marketplace. The challenge for IP policymakers, which applies to TK as to any other form of IP, is to make the judgement as to what form of exclusion of protectable material from the public domain is likely best to provide for public goods. But this also begs the question of what public goods are to be privileged over others. Hence, a public good framework may help in resolving the dilemma about reconstructing the public domain so as to respond to the concerns of TK holders.

If knowledge *per se* is "a global or international public good,"[72] because of its inherent nonrivalrous and non-excludable nature (and its obvious social utility), does this characterization apply directly to knowledge that is

---

[70] Inge Kaul et al., *How to Improve the Provision of Public Goods*, in PROVIDING GLOBAL PUBLIC GOODS 43 (UNDP 2002).
[71] Joseph E. Stiglitz, *Knowledge as a Global Public Good*, available at http://www.worldbank.org/knowledge/chiefecon/articles/undpk2/ (visited 21 June 2004).
[72] *Id.*

traditional? As noted, in broad terms, IP protection is invoked to create excludability when public policy interests (including, in some constructions, natural rights and equity considerations, not merely utilitarian objectives) require it. In other words, IPRs apply when a higher-order public good is served by ensuring that knowledge is not left in the public domain. Excludability in this context may include literal inaccessability, so that the knowledge itself does not enter the public domain at all (the basis of protection of confidentiality and trade secrets),[73] or exclusion from certain forms of use, when the knowledge becomes knowable to the public (as is the case of the patent system, under which formerly undisclosed knowledge is necessarily projected into the public knowledge domain, if not immediately into the public *use* domain).

A hard utilitarian approach would presumably argue for the benefit of as much TK as possible to reside in the public domain. No additional incentive is needed to create it, apparently, since it has been already created, so no more elaborate policy mechanism is needed to promote the provision of this public good. Yet, this approach would set aside higher order public goods in favour of a simple view of knowledge as a commodity. Here the TK debate serves a valuable broader purpose, in illuminating the ethical and cultural assumptions in the construction of the public domain and the IP system. Further, it illustrates that the simple conception of knowledge as a public good risks commodifying knowledge and stripping it of its public interest characteristics in the way that overzealous IP protection is claimed to do.

Where indigenous communities are concerned, such a conflation of the public domain as public good may set the notion of a global public interest in tension with the collective interests of a specific community. From the indigenous perspective, misuse of TK can

> cause severe physical or spiritual harm to the individual caretakers of the knowledge or their entire tribe from their failure to ensure that the Creator's gifts were properly used, even if misuse was used by others outside of the tribe, or by tribal members who were outside of the control of customary authority. For this reason ... misappropriation and misuse [are] not simply a violation of "moral rights" leading to a collective offense, but a matter of cultural survival for many indigenous peoples.[74]

Hence, the value of TK as a public good may lie not in its ready unencumbered accessibility; it may provide for a higher-order public good *in that* it is withheld from the public domain, even if it is a "collective consumption good"

---

[73] However, the excludability of trade secrets is only relative, not absolute, because third parties may obtain the secret know-how by honest or proper means, especially reverse-engineering. *See* above n. 62; Pamela Samuelson & Susan Scotchmer, *The Law and Economics of Reverse-Engineering*, 111 YALE L.J. 1575 (2002).

[74] Representative of the Tulalip Tribes of Washington, *see* WIPO Intergovernmental Committee, above n. 12, ¶ 56.

for the traditional community which identifies with it, but not for the public at large. Whether this result can be justified depends on whether, and how, a clear ordering of competing public goods can be established.

The recognition of *sui generis* rights in TK also probes the boundary between public and private, and the assumption that IP rights inherently operate to favour the individual's interest over that of the collective. Exclusive IP rights may be held and exercised on behalf of a community. TK that is held exclusively by the traditional community that develops, preserves and identifies with it is a good for *its* public – the traditional community – even when it is withheld from the global public domain, a tension that potentially sets the community's public good against the international public good. After all, global public good considerations may involve broadening access to TK:

> the skills, knowledge and institutions evolved by people on the margins, who have already been coping with [environmental] stresses for the last several millennia, will become a major source of survival. Is this the reason why global institutions are suddenly finding so much merit in local knowledge?[75]

An IP protection of TK may, therefore, need to use the kind of balancing mechanisms that lie at the core of the IP system, including a renegotiation of the boundary between community domain and the global public domain.

The CBD requirement for "equitable sharing of the benefits" from the use of TK, and the conception of equity behind this provision,[76] reflect the same need to find a fair and just way of balancing international public good interests with the interests of the community. It is in this expanded notion of equity, which accommodates customary law considerations and the values of the source community, that one may reconcile conservation of biological diversity with jurisprudential and cultural diversity, and one may mediate between the community public good and the international public good. Once again, the policy analysis that should precede the creation of *sui generis* TK protection has the helpful side effect of clarifying the tendentious character of some international public good analysis, just as the objectivity of the public domain and the IP system come under scrutiny. Is public good analysis an essentially practical and objective tool for most efficiently organizing the financing of public necessities, or is it an essentially ethical or normative privileging of some interests over others?

It is suggested that competing public good notions of TK can only be reconciled at the more abstract, or higher order, level of international public goods, and that this task requires us to consider how a more inclusive notion of international

---

[75] Anil K. Gupta, *Centres on the Periphery: Coping with Climatic and Institutional Change*, 13 HONEY BEE 1 (Sept. 2002).
[76] CBD, above, n. 5, art. 8(j).

public goods can accommodate specific interests of the communities who hold and identify with TK. Just as the nub of the problem of developing or applying IP protection for TK is how to respect its specifically traditional character, considering TK as a public good entails examining how its traditional characteristics set it apart from other forms of knowledge. If knowledge is viewed as a public good because it is nonrivalrous and non-excludable, how does this standard analysis apply to TK? Two immediate difficulties arise: first, the dynamic quality of the policy and legal environment (so that what has not been hitherto excludable may become so); and, second, the expression of a greater diversity of policy interests, including indigenous and local community concerns (which challenge the assumption that TK is nonrivalrous, by highlighting, for instance, that the knowledge itself is diminished by its alienation from the traditional community in violation of customary law, which also impairs the community's interests).

What, then, is the international public good basis for seeking to reverse or forestall the entry of TK into the public domain and to make it excludable, for instance, by deliberate legal intervention to extend the effective reach of customary law? For existing TK, the incentive argument normally used to justify state intervention to create limited excludability through the creation of IP rights may not apply: commentators have pointed out that no additional incentive appears to be necessary for a continuing knowledge tradition with deep customary roots.[77] However, the arguments for TK protection tend to depart from a limited public good, essentially utilitarian perspective, and to invoke more fundamental equity and human rights considerations.

Besides, a more searching incentive argument for TK protection can in fact be developed. The social, economic and environmental structures that have developed and sustained TK – in a reductionist sense, providing an incentive structure for traditional innovation – are themselves under pressure and in danger of dilution or loss, and this loss would be felt in time by the international community. For this reason, the CBD provides for measures to "respect, preserve and maintain knowledge, innovations and practices of indigenous and local communities embodying traditional lifestyles relevant for the conservation and sustainable use of biological diversity."[78] It recognizes, in effect, that strengthening incentives for the preservation of TK is a desirable means to promote the global public good of conservation of biodiversity. Similarly, TK protection can promote – as international public goods – the survival, well-being and distinctive identity of traditional cultures (the

---

[77] "[T]he purpose of intellectual property is to serve as an incentive for future creative endeavours, while, by definition, traditional knowledge needs no such incentive for development," Review of Existing Intellectual Property Protection of Traditional Knowledge, WIPO/GRTKF/IC/3/7, ¶ 32, p. 11 (6 May 2002).

[78] CBD, above n. 5, art. 8(j).

conservation of cultural diversity[79]) and the preservation of the ethical and normative structures of traditional societies (including the conservation of jurisprudential diversity as an end in itself).

Apart from equitable considerations, cultural and jurisprudential diversity have utilitarian aspects due to their role in promoting social well-being and the continuity of TK systems that valuably complement conventional technological knowledge. Hence, a broader incentive argument can be deployed to create a new means of legal excludability of TK, so as to promote not merely the development and preservation of the TK itself, but also the social, cultural and legal framework in which the TK has been developed and sustained.

The movement towards strengthened, or broader, protection of TK therefore provides new insights into the interplay between public interest and exclusive right, or between the public good and the policy basis of excludability. It challenges the conventional contours of the relationship between public domain and private right, by forcing us to question the legitimacy of the established conception of the public domain, and by making us recast the public – or *a* public, at least (i.e. the traditional community) – as the right holder, and as the collective beneficiary of a direct, rather than indirect, interest in TK protection.

V. Options for recognition of customary law in the IP system

These public good considerations would imply that a TK protection system will enhance welfare and serve a broader public interest inasmuch as it promotes respect for the traditional community and its knowledge management customs, both within and beyond the community, while balancing the broader public interest in securing equitable access to beneficial knowledge. This does not mean that an external legal structure need aim to replicate intramural customs and practices, but it should at least entail some form of supportive or validating function, or some positive correspondence between the traditional context and the external legal environment.

Sui generis legal systems may accordingly be classified according to their degree of displacement from customary law, within the range of the following options:

- the traditional or indigenous knowledge system itself, including any customary laws and practices that govern the holding, use and transmission of knowledge;
- a distinct legal system that recognizes and externally applies rights that already define a customary TK system within the community (i.e. giving legal effect to existing customary law beyond its traditional circle);[80]

---

[79] United Nations Educational, Scientific and Cultural Organization (UNESCO), Universal Declaration on Cultural Diversity, 36 COPYRIGHT BULL. 4 (2 Nov. 2001).
[80] E.g., the African Model Legislation, above n. 38, provides that "[t]he State recognizes and protects community rights ... as they are enshrined and protected under the norms,

- a distinct set of rights reflecting rights within the customary TK context, under which a right over TK is granted on the basis of rights enjoyed within a discrete legal system, so that the prior existence of a customary law right is established as a matter of fact with relevance to the existence of rights in the TK, rather than as a source of law in itself;[81] or
- a distinct set of rights recognized and granted according to distinct, objective criteria, that has no direct relationship to the customary law context (but which may provide for exceptions to allow customary practices to continue notwithstanding the distinctly recognized TK right).

This linear scale, while clarifying the options, may misleadingly suggest that such options are mutually exclusive or exhaustive. Policymakers can construct hybrid systems that amalgamate external legal structures with elements of customary law, drawn on variously as a source of law or of facts. In practice, a *sui generis* system is more likely to give discrete recognition to distinct aspects of customary law, rather than wholly integrating a customary law right or entirely setting it aside.

The existing or mainstream IP system has already shown an unexpectedly generous capacity for acknowledging customary law, as a specific point of reference rather than as a complete legal system. For instance, customary law has been drawn upon separately for the following purposes:

- to establish standing,[82] even on the part of an unincorporated entity,[83] or other relevant legal capacity;
- to apply customary dispute settlement mechanisms to resolve or reconcile competing claims of ownership, and to resolve disputes more generally between or within traditional communities;[84]

---

practice and customary law found in, and organized by the concerned local and indigenous communities, whether such law is written or not."

[81] "Native title has its origin in and is given its content by the traditional laws acknowledged by and the traditional customs observed by the indigenous inhabitants of a territory. The nature and incidents of native title must be ascertained as a matter of fact by reference to those laws and customs. The ascertainment may present a problem of considerable difficulty..." Mabo, above n. 41, at 58 (Brennan, J.); *cf.* in the recognition of equitable interests in copyright, Bulun Bulun, below n. 85, at 210–11 treats "the law and custom of the Ganalbingu people as part of the factual matrix which characterizes the relationship as one of mutual trust and confidence. It is that relationship which the Australian legal system recognizes as giving rise to the fiduciary relationship, and to the obligations which arise out of it..."

[82] Onus v. Alcoa of Australia Ltd., 149 C.L.R. 27 (1981) [Australia] (stating that "the members of the [Gournditichjmara] community are the guardians of the relics according to their laws and customs and they use the relics. I agree ... that in these circumstances the applicants have a special interest in the preservation of these relics, sufficient to support *locus standi*") (Mason, J.).

[83] Foster v. Mountford & Rigby, 29 F.L.R. 233 (1976) [Australia] (concerning the Pitjantjatjara Council).

[84] *See* Republic of the Philippines, Indigenous Peoples' Rights Act § 65 (1997).

- to assert an equitable interest (*in rem*) in IP nominally owned by another, or a more general fiduciary relationship (*in personam*) between traditional owners and an individual IP right holder;[85]
- to sustain a claim of breach of confidence relating to secret sacred material,[86] and to recognize customary law considerations as "substantial concerns" in sustaining a claim of confidentiality;[87]
- to confer legal identity on a community as the basis of collective ownership of an IP right;[88]
- as the basis of a general right over biological resources and TK,[89] including specific rights to grant access to biological resources[90] and the application of prior informed consent for access, as well as general rights to benefit from TK;
- to enshrine a distinct right for continuing customary use in spite of or in parallel with formally recognized rights in TK;
- as the basis for a claim against public order, cultural offence[91] or vilification, or more specifically to determine entitlement for damages based on "personal and cultural hurt,"[92] including establishing the basis for and quantum of damages; and
- to determine the status of a claimant as a member of an indigenous or other traditional community, to identify a community as being an eligible local or traditional community,[93] or to establish a specific indigenous or aboriginal right.[94]

---

[85] Bulun Bulun v. R&T Textiles Pty. Ltd., 41 I.P.R. 513 (1998) [Australia].
[86] *Foster*, above n. 83.
[87] Gordon Coulthard v. The State of South Australia, Austl. Torts Rep. 81 (1995).
[88] Note the latitude accorded to the definition of "association" in the Paris Convention, above n. 19, Article 7*bis*, for collective marks, which requires the protection of collective marks "belonging to associations the existence of which is not contrary to the law of the country of origin, even if such associations do not possess an industrial or commercial establishment" even where "such association is not established in the country where protection is sought or is not constituted according to the law of the latter country."
[89] African Model Legislation, above n. 38, art. 8.
[90] *Id.*, art. 8(1)(ix).
[91] For example, New Zealand's Trade Marks Act 2002, § 17(1)(b), establishes absolute grounds for refusal of a trade mark that would "offend a significant section of the community, including Māori."
[92] M* v. Indofurn Pty. Ltd., 30 I.P.R. 209 (1995) [Australia], *discussed in* Terri Janke, Minding Culture, WIPO/GRTKF/STUDY/1 (2002).
[93] See the definition of "local community" in the Brazilian law including reference to a group that traditionally organizes itself through successive generations and through its own customs and preserves its social and economic institutions. Art. 7(iii), Provisional Measure No. 2186–16 (2001), *summarized in* WIPO Comparative Summary, above n. 35.
[94] For example, the definition of "aboriginal right" in *R. A Van der Peet*, 2 S.C.R. 507 (1996), subsequently elaborated in *Delgammuukw v. British Columbia*, 2 S.C.R. 1010 (1997) [Canada], to incorporate both common law and aboriginal perspectives, including prior aboriginal law.

Each of these examples illustrates how subjective, customary considerations can be acknowledged in broader, ostensibly objective legal systems.

Some of the tests listed here explicitly give weight to the subjective perspective of the TK holder (for instance, the test of "substantial concern" necessary to sustain a claim of confidentiality,[95] and the concept of cultural harm or cultural offence). This perspective strengthens jurisprudential diversity and validates customary law, in turn promoting the recognition and potentially the survival of traditional communities and their legal and value systems. Even on seemingly "technical" legal questions in IP law – such as the question of legal identity, ownership of rights, or equitable or other interests in an IP right – the recognition of customary law considerations may become a powerful factor in promoting cultural recognition and survival, and it may have potentially more weight in this context than on substantive issues, such as the scope of IP rights and their exceptions.

Just as the IP system has accommodated customary law considerations in these more precise operational contexts, practical experience with *sui generis* systems established so far suggests a preference for limited, focused recognition of customary law. The Philippines Indigenous Peoples' Rights Act of 1997 does give broad recognition by establishing a right of restitution of cultural, intellectual, religious and spiritual property taken, *inter alia* "in violation of [indigenous] laws, traditions and customs."[96] This law stipulates that access to indigenous knowledge should be subject to prior informed consent obtained in accordance with customary laws,[97] and it requires the use of customary laws and practices in settling disputes.[98]

Especially when it is linked to regimes regulating biological and genetic resources, access to TK is often conditioned on prior informed consent of traditional communities,[99] which creates an avenue for the operation of customary law, even if this is not explicitly acknowledged in the laws. The Costa Rican Biodiversity Law[100] requires that *sui generis* community IP rights and the question of ownership should be determined by a participatory process with indigenous and small farmer communities; it also establishes custom as a source of law in determining the existence of a *sui generis* community intellectual property right, which "exists and is legally recognized by the mere existence of the cultural practice or knowledge"

---

[95] Note that such a test is broader than the test of "commercial value" stipulated in the TRIPS Agreement, above n. 13, art. 39.2(b).
[96] The Philippines Indigenous Peoples' Rights Act, Republic Act 8371, sec. 32 (29 Oct. 1997).
[97] *Id.*, sec. 35.   [98] *Id.*, sec. 65.
[99] E.g. the need for "prior informed consent of the representative organizations of the indigenous peoples possessing collective knowledge," Article 6 of Peru's Introducing a Protection Regime for the Collective Knowledge of Indigenous Peoples Derived from Biological Resources, Law No. 27,881 (2002).
[100] Law No. 7788, arts. 82–84 (1998) [Costa Rica].

and does not need "prior declaration, explicit recognition nor official registration."[101]

A number of TK and biodiversity-related laws provide exceptions to formally recognized rights so as to allow the continuation of customary practices. The recognition of custom as an exception to TK rights is a good measure of the normative gap, perhaps inevitable, between the traditional normative context and the formal articulation of rights in TK. Nonetheless, the acknowledgement of customary law for specific purposes, while still well short of a blanket extension of its legal effect, is clearly not inherently at odds with the existing IP system and is an element of several *sui generis* TK regimes.

A. Implications for the international context

This practical experience suggests at least that it is possible to take a selective, functional approach to the recognition of local customary law, by drawing on those aspects of customary knowledge management systems that are already analogous to conventional IP rights systems. The difficulty increases if customary law is to be used – whether as a true source of law or as part of the "factual matrix" – as the basis for the definition of protected subject matter and for determining the scope of rights.

Operational and pragmatic constraints on any *sui generis* TK system may need to be weighed against the need for legitimacy and acceptance by TK holders that would be provided by recognizing their customary law, perhaps even in application to the definition and identification of TK as such. Achieving this balance is primarily a task for national policymakers, legislators and judicial authorities, who would need to interpret, accommodate or otherwise apply local customary law[102] within national laws. Yet, calls for recognition of TK as a distinct form of IP right within international legal instruments pose the question at the international level as well, returning to the paradox of finding common standards for giving global recognition to the irreducibly diverse and local. Resolving this question may help to determine whether the goal of equitable, inclusive and effective protection of TK can be advanced through a workable international framework, without stripping the TK of its vital local qualities and its normative context.

---

[101] *Id.* The registration of collective IP and TK rights under Panamanian law requires the rules of use of the collective right to be determined in part with reference to the "history (tradition) of the collective right." Article 7(iiii), Executive Decree No.12 (2001) (regulating Law No. 20 of 26 June 2000, on the Special Intellectual Property Regime Governing the Collective Rights of Indigenous Peoples for the Protection and Defence of their Cultural Identity and their Traditional Knowledge) [Panama].

[102] "Local customary law" (law governing a traditional community) is the term used in this passage to avoid confusion with the distinct concept of international customary law (governing relations between States).

A particular challenge at the international level would be the consistent recognition of local customary laws and protocols where they span international borders, a potential dilemma for an international framework analogous to, and no less taxing than, the "regional folklore" question, which was one obstacle to an earlier endeavour to create an international framework.[103] The broader context of international law may also influence how indigenous legal personality,[104] and traditional or customary law perspectives, are recognized. For instance, giving due recognition to customary law and traditional cultural values is arguably one element of the conception of equity that underpins "equitable sharing of the benefits arising from the utilization" of TK under the CBD.[105] More generally, if TK protection should be based on a conception of "equity" as fairness and balance in relations between the source community and external players,[106] then the ethical basis of this conception should be interpreted with at least some reference to the values of the source community, as embodied in formal or informal customary laws and protocols.

The conventional legal architecture of the international IP system seems ill adapted to the direct recognition of customary law. It would be a reductionist contradiction in terms to attempt substantive harmonization of diverse communities' customary laws or the codification of customary protocols in the form of universally applicable minimum standards. Direct extraterritorial application of local customary law through the operation of international law would become legally complex and practically burdensome. It would be difficult enough to harmonize internationally the principles or rules that govern recognition of local customary law even in existing *sui generis* TK laws.

Another international mechanism, registration or notification, could be effective in giving notice of the existence of customary law considerations

---

[103] See, e.g., Mihaly Ficsor, *Attempts to Provide International Protection for Folklore by Intellectual Property Rights*, in UNESCO-WIPO WORLD FORUM ON THE PROTECTION OF FOLKLORE 223 (UNESCO/WIPO 1998).

[104] Recognition of indigenous communities' interests in sharing of benefits as an equitable principle in international law finds an interesting parallel in the Cayuga Indian arbitral case, *Great Britain v. United States*, 6 R.I.A.A. 173 (1926). The tribunal did not recognize the Cayuga as having distinct identity in international law ("so far as an Indian tribe exists as a legal unit, it is by virtue of the [applicable] domestic law and so far only as that law recognizes it"); but it held that the general principles of equity, fair dealing and justice recognized by international law entitled the Cayuga to an equitable share in the annuities that had been agreed in a treaty between the Cayuga Nation and the State of New York concluded in 1795, which had not been paid since 1810 to Cayuga who had migrated to Canada in the context of the war of 1810. The tribunal observed that its arbitral award would be justifiable on the basis of international equitable principles alone. *Id.* at 179–84.

[105] CBD, above n. 5, art. 8(j).

[106] Carlos Correa, Traditional Knowledge and Intellectual Property, Quaker United Nations Office Discussion Paper, at 5 (2002).

concerning TK and in reducing the costs of securing protection in many jurisdictions.[107] However, enforceable rights would still be contingent on creating an adequate legal basis for the application of these standards in national jurisdictions. The diversity and uncertain contours of national protection of TK suggest an initial approach closer to the early history of the Paris and Berne Conventions, which would concentrate on more flexible general principles for interaction between jurisdictions, such as national treatment or protection based on reciprocity or mutual recognition. It would leave the core areas of substantive law – scope of protected subject matter, scope of rights and exceptions – in the hands of national lawmaking processes.

Many of those aspects of customary law that can most readily be accommodated within the formal IP system, such as those affecting standing, legal identity, ownership, succession, equitable interests and the like, are mostly issues on which international IP legal systems already defer to municipal law. If an indigenous community, defined by customary law, is already recognized as having legal identity sufficient to hold IP rights as a national in one country, then this may constitute a sufficient basis for rights in foreign jurisdictions.[108] On this model, it may only be necessary for an international system to recognize these aspects of local customary law indirectly, through the vector of national treatment, reciprocity and mutual recognition mechanisms. In some instances, there may remain a role for private international law, such as when establishing ownership of IP rights or similar interests on the basis of access and benefit-sharing contracts that reflect customary law.

B. What international mechanisms can do justice to customary law?

No international mechanism can supplant the role of national laws in protecting TK. At best, an international instrument, whether a formal legal instrument or a form of policy guidance, can only influence or provide access to protection provided through the operation of national law. Any model of TK protection must accordingly be rooted in a practicable conception of how TK would be protected within a national legal system.

---

[107] A TK registration or notification system could draw on elements of such systems as the Madrid system for international trade mark registration established under the Madrid Agreement Concerning the International Registration of Marks (1891); the international system for registration of armorial bearings, flags, and other State emblems established under the Paris Convention, above n. 19, and the registration system established by the Lisbon Agreement for the Protection of Appellations of Origin and their International Registration (1958). The Geneva Treaty on the International Recording of Scientific Discoveries, 3 Mar. 1978, 11 WIPO INDUSTRIAL PROPERTY LAWS AND TREATIES, MULTILATERAL TREATIES, TEXT 1–003, also provides an interesting analogue.

[108] Cf. Paris Convention, above n. 19, art. 7bis.

In the absence of such workable models, an international approach is likely to be a more abstract gesture – a broad statement of principles and general guidelines. One should not dismiss such an approach as a second-best outcome, provided that it is understood that a general international normative statement does not substitute for more precise policy and administrative choices within domestic systems. Thoroughgoing international harmonization is rendered problematic, in any event, by the very diversity of the cultural traditions and customary law in which TK is embedded, and by the varied quality of existing domestic laws, including *sui generis* TK laws.

Given these constraints, what international architecture would do justice to TK subject matter? International IP instruments can set a framework of broad principles and harmonized minimum standards within which national laws operate, but they can also facilitate the recognition of individual IP rights in national laws, through the operation of national treatment or assimilation, through mutual recognition or reciprocity mechanisms, or through a combination of these. International systems may also provide ready conduits for the registration of specific subject matter, either through administrative facilitation or international registration.

An international mechanism is vital to achieve coordinated legal effect in multiple jurisdictions, but any *de jure* or *de facto* harmonization effect would elicit tension with the goal of fully respecting the customary normative content of TK. If locally-based customary practice is integral to TK and its epistemological, cultural and legal qualities, how can an international *sui generis* system recognize this distinctive characteristic? The very conception of TK as a form of IP suggests to some TK holders a form of alienation, reduction, or commodification of an holistic cultural and spiritual heritage, a trivialisation of cultural identity that is viewed with scepticism.[109]

Yet, the need is strongly articulated for a tailor-made legal mechanism, with international (or at least multi-jurisdictional) effect, that actually restrains unauthorized, illicit or offensive use of TK, and is realistic and workable from the point of view of TK holders. An holistic approach to TK protection that, when enforced, required foreign courts to take full account of the laws and customs of the source community, and privileged these over local laws, might be highly desirable in principle, but it seems unworkable in practice and could become a poor investment of political capital and legal resources. Conversely, to lose the customary context could rob the system of legitimacy: dismantling customary law to save the TK has unfortunate echoes of "we had to destroy the

---

[109] Many TK holders shrink from the very characterization of their collective heritage as a form of IP and view its enclosure within distinct IP rights with apprehension: "once you have done to indigenous and local knowledge whatever is necessary to make it fit into the IP mould, it would not be recognizable as indigenous and local knowledge anymore." CRUCIBLE GROUP, SEEDING SOLUTIONS, above n. 11, at 94.

village to save it."[110] Far from conserving jurisprudential diversity, an homogeneous approach to TK protection runs the risk of undermining it.

The question of whether it is legally coherent to protect TK internationally in a way that respects and, indeed, gives legal effect to customary law thus gives way to the underlying question of what mechanisms would be appropriate to the capacities and resources of TK holders and their representatives. An approach to protecting TK that is theoretically agreeable but in practice impossible effectively to monitor and enforce would be another empty form of protection, which would undermine the credibility of IP protection of TK among sceptics and proponents alike.

Clearly, an international architecture for TK protection cannot coherently aim at wide reach and influence while remaining fully congruent with the legal and cultural environment of the TK holders it seeks to serve. Here it is crucial to observe the distinction between underlying TK subject matter, and the scope of subject matter eligible for protection and the mode of its protection. An overarching architecture will not be able to replicate all aspects of customary law that determine how TK is to be managed and maintained by the original community.

If a pragmatic, piecemeal approach is deemed acceptable, the international IP system may already accommodate customary law to a surprising degree. International IP law generally defers to national legal systems on such questions as the legal personality of right holders,[111] the conditions for ownership[112] including succession of title, and on equitable interests in IP rights[113] and other interests, such as those arising from employment relations. Where recognized in national laws, customary law may already be applicable in these areas in the operational context of existing IP treaties.

Other aspects of customary law may be recognized in practice within existing broad principles in international IP law: for instance, a scandalous infringement of customary law that causes offence or violates *ordre public*, or an exception to IP rights based on secret prior use in a traditional context. Claims by merchants that certain products are of authentic indigenous origin may be construed as a claim that they have been developed in compliance with

---

[110] Widely attributed to an anonymous officer in the Vietnam War, but since challenged as apocryphal.
[111] Paris Convention, above n. 19, Article 7*bis* (*see* above n. 88 and accompanying text).
[112] "[WTO] Members have the right, subject to the national and most-favoured-nation treatment and other safeguards contained in the TRIPS Agreement, to require, as a condition for filing and registration, that the applicant be the owner of the trademark, unless there are specific provisions in the Paris Convention (1967) that are an exception to Article 6(1) and that regulate trademark registration so extensively as to restrict the ability of a Member to deny trademark registration for reasons related to ownership." United States – Section 211 Omnibus Appropriations Act of 1998 ("Havana Club" case), WT/DS176/R ¶ 8.56 (6 Aug, 2001).
[113] M* v. Indofurn Pty. Ltd., 30 I.P.R. 209 (1995) [Australia].

customary law: the suppression of unfair competition in accord with international norms should address such spurious claims.[114] Customary law constraints on knowledge have been found to be a sufficient basis for protection as undisclosed information,[115] in line with international standards in this area.[116] Even the notion of equity espoused in provisions for equitable sharing of benefits[117] or equitable remuneration[118] can be interpreted with reference to customary laws and values. Clarification and codification of some of these linkages would in itself contribute to the protection of TK through existing international instruments in a manner that is responsive to customary law.

Recognition of customary law is a greater conceptual challenge as one approaches the core issues of TK protection: the identification of eligible subject matter and the determination of the scope of rights and exceptions. Here the tension between a universal objective standard and a subjective standard rooted in local custom or practice becomes more evident, especially if an international mechanism is intended to set standards for specific IP rights in TK. The difficulties are not merely legal, but also tap into the core policy issues discussed above, *viz*, how the public domain can or should be reconstructed, and what public goods should be privileged and directly promoted by TK protection.

Yet, it is not beyond the reach of national and international legal mechanisms to give direct recognition to customary law governing how TK is to be defined and used, and to enable these rules to have effect beyond the traditional circle. Certification marks or geographical indications (GI) illustrate how this might work. The set of rules that define a GI or certification mark can serve as a self-contained capsule of customary law. They are a jurisprudential nugget that codifies and defines that portion of customary laws and practices that are embodied in the product to which the mark is applied. For instance, whether by virtue of GI protection[119] or certification mark protection,[120] cheese designated as "Roquefort" cannot be sold in many jurisdictions unless it has been produced according to traditional practices in the Roquefort district of France.

---

[114] E.g., the Australian Competition and Consumer Commission obtained consent orders against Australian Icon Products Pty. Ltd. concerning claims over "authentic" and "Aboriginal" artworks, 45 ACCC JOURNAL 39 (Mar.-Apr. 2003).

[115] Foster v. Mountford & Rigby, 29 F.L.R. 233 (1976) [Australia].

[116] TRIPS Agreement, above n. 13, art. 39.

[117] *E.g.*, CBD, above n. 5, art. 8(j) (establishing the objective of the "fair and equitable sharing of the benefits arising out of the utilization of genetic resources").

[118] *See* the requirement for "equitable remuneration" in articles 11*bis* and 13 of the Berne Convention, above n. 19.

[119] Granted to the Confédération Générale des Producteurs de Lait de Brebis et des Industriels de Roquefort under European Commission Regulation (EC) No. 2081/92.

[120] U.S. Certification Mark 0571798 of 10 March 1953, in the name of the Community of Roquefort.

If one considers these customary practices as a set of rules – and specific GIs and certification marks may have very detailed sets of rules governing their use[121] – this customary law reaches beyond the original community and has some degree of direct effect in foreign jurisdictions. A producer in the Roquefort region can produce cheese not in conformity with traditional practices, and an external producer can attempt to imitate – or for that matter improve upon – these practices, but cheese cannot be sold in protected markets as Roquefort unless it complies with the customary rules.[122] This results not from recognition of the customary rules as having direct legal effect, but from the original community seeking to appropriate the returns of its TK by placing their cheese on the market. Laws and customary practices with local effect regulate and define how Roquefort cheese is made. Then, in regulating the use of the term "Roquefort," laws with external effect (including those in foreign jurisdictions) apply the customary rules and practices, either explicitly through partial codification of traditional practices, or indirectly by requiring products so designated to be produced within the original geographical jurisdiction where those customary laws and practices apply.[123]

Hence, the extraterritorial or multijurisdictional recognition of customary laws and practices comes about through the GI or certification mark operating as a normative vector via the operation of the international legal framework, which conveys a precise set of customary rules and practices associated with a cheesemaking tradition. This has the effect of increasing the economic return to the source community of their TK when it is alienated from the community (consensually in this case, through the willing sale of the product embodying the knowledge).

This analogy is not intended to suggest that the certification mark or GI system is a solution, or even a model, for the protection of TK. What is being

---

[121] *See* Decree relating to the protected designation of origin Roquefort, Official Journal of the French Republic, No. 21, 25 Jan. 2001, p. 1283.

[122] The application for GI protection under EC Regulation 2081/92, above n. 119, provides that: "[i]n the manufacture of Roquefort unchanging methods are respected. The Penicillium roqueforti is introduced either in liquid form when the rennet is added or by sprinkling the curds when they are put into the moulds. After draining and salting, the cheeses are transported to the caves of Roquefort sur Soulzon, in fallen rock from the Combalou mountain, where it is specified that the ripening process must take place ... The special quality of Roquefort is a product of intimate collaboration between man and nature. It derives on the one hand from the characteristics of the traditional breeds of ewe that are fed in accordance with local custom and on the other hand from the unique atmosphere of the natural cellars in caves entirely hewn out of the rocks at the foot of the limestone cliffs of the Combalou, where a miracle of nature takes place to give Roquefort its incomparable flavour."

[123] The U.S. registration, above n. 120, provides that "the certification mark is used upon the goods to indicate that the same has been manufactured from sheep's milk only and has been cured in the natural caves of the Community of Roquefort, Department of Aveyron, France."

directly protected is the term – the mark or indication itself, not the knowledge. And there is a host of competing public goods issues and questions about the public domain status of descriptive and allusive terms in relation to geographical indications that is the subject of a complex ongoing debate.[124] But this analogy does show the simple possibility of a legal framework providing for vectors of customary law to be effectively transmitted through the operation of international law and enforced under foreign domestic law to the benefit of the original community.

It remains an open question whether such a mechanism can be developed to deal with TK more generally, for instance, when the TK is not embedded in or associated with a physical product and the aim of protection goes beyond the safeguarding of the reputation and economic interests of the community that are associated with a particular term or mark. Yet, it illustrates that an international framework can undoubtedly provide for limited, focused recognition of customary law in foreign jurisdictions on the two core matters identified above – the scope of protected material, and the rights that govern the use of that material.

It also points to the possibilities for practical protection of TK-related subject matter, for the benefit of TK holders, provided a distinction is drawn between the holistic character and context of the TK, and the specific aspects of it that are to be protected in multiple jurisdictions. In this instance, it is not necessary for foreign registration authorities or courts to investigate intensively the traditional local context; the rules governing the use of the geographical indication or certification mark, or indeed the simple fact of the physical location of production, may be sufficient to constrain illegitimate commercial use of the reputation associated with the TK.

C. Conclusion: What kind of international system?

This analysis does not suggest that *sui generis* protection of TK is a desirable policy objective in itself. This remains an important threshold question for national policymakers guided by the needs and expectations of TK holders, who should be the principal beneficiaries of any policy initiative in this area. It seeks only to clarify policy options and their implications, should policymakers seek to construct a *sui generis* framework, particularly one with an international dimension.

The choices seem to lie along a spectrum between a community-based, diverse, essentially subjective approach, fulfilling an holistic conception of TK and according fully with TK management systems; and a conventional

---

[124] *See* A.S. Taubman, The Way Ahead: Developing International Protection for Geographical Indications: Thinking Locally, Acting Globally, *in* WIPO/DNPI Symposium on the International Protection of Geographical Indications, Doc. WIPO/GEO/MVD/01/9 (15 Nov. 2001).

international mechanism that provides for objective, harmonized standards and gives right holders consistent formal recognition in foreign jurisdictions. Moving along this spectrum would entail a progressive loss of the traditional normative component and respect for customary knowledge management systems, but greater clarity, predictability and workability of the mechanism as a practical tool for objectively defining and enforcing rights in foreign jurisdictions. Yet, there is scope for a more nuanced approach, in which the distinction between the TK system and the legal means of protecting it is acknowledged, and components of customary law are recognized, through national law, as providing guidance on specific questions, such as ownership, interests, and the nature of remedies.

A medium point on this spectrum could entail two key elements: first, a clear articulation of general principles that should guide national policymakers in making more specific arrangements for protecting TK under national law; and second, a mechanism for recognition of significant components of TK and such matters as collective ownership, legal personality, standing and collective equitable interests, in such a way as can be given reciprocal recognition in foreign jurisdictions. This solution could be supplemented by a notification, registration or certification system that provides a legal or evidential platform for a community-based identification of those aspects of TK rights that need to be recognized for the enforcement of specific IP rights beyond the reach of customary law or practices, i.e., legal identity, ownership, distinctive qualities of TK susceptible of commercial misappropriation, or aspects of commercial application of TK that would contravene standards of fair trading.

It is a principle in patent law that "an invention may be based on the formulation of a problem to be solved,"[125] when the solution is obvious once the problem is clearly stated. The problem for TK protection may not be the definition of TK as such, nor indeed the definition of rights attached to TK, but rather greater clarity about the objectives of protection. TK holders know full well what their TK is and how it should be protected, and have no need to be told; equally, from the point of view of the original communities, the normative basis for protection generally already exists. There is, accordingly, a strong desire for a community-based, subjective standard of recognition of subject matter and rights.

Unsurprisingly, it is tradition that differentiates TK from knowledge in general, and gives it a *sui generis* quality that should, ideally, influence any attempt to craft distinct protection mechanisms tailor-made for TK. The policy dilemma over TK may be resolved by respecting the traditions that yield, sustain and define TK: "respect" here is used in the sense both of regarding with honour and esteem, and of complying with as a legal obligation.

---

[125] WIPO, PCT International Preliminary Examination Guidelines IV-8.4(i) (9 Oct. 1998).

Respect in the first sense could be shown through an overarching statement of principles and an acknowledgement of the value of the preservation of TK and its cultural context as an inherent international public good (by contrast, the CBD opens with a preambular acknowledgement of the "intrinsic value of biological diversity"). Respect in the second sense could entail providing practical means of ensuring that rights are effectively available in foreign jurisdictions, through conventional and tailored *sui generis* IP systems, through recognizing the customary law and practice in the definition of right holder, of enforceable interests in IP rights, of entitlement to seek remedies, and of the nature of remedies available.

What is needed is not an unworkable melange of homogenized customary law, but an effective framework that sets broad norms and standards in line with core IP principles, and that allows functional vectors of customary law, linked to the subject matter of protection, to pass from the original jurisdiction to foreign jurisdictions. To find the precise legal expression that such a system might take is an important and pressing task for the international community, so that the global interest in TK protection is duly rewarded by the effective protection of truly local interests. This may mean limiting protection to those aspects of TK that can be distinguished as susceptible to commercial misuse, or contrary to a community-based standard of *ordre public*, and extending the general and adaptable legal doctrines of unjust enrichment or unfair competition to suppress such use. The model discussed above suggests that it is not beyond the reach of international IP law for such normative content to be transmitted, through selective jurisprudential vectors, to jurisdictions beyond the scope of the original customary laws and practices, although conceiving and constructing such an architecture, and making it workable practically and politically, remains a daunting challenge.

20

Legal perspectives on traditional knowledge: The case for intellectual property protection

THOMAS COTTIER

MARION PANIZZON*

Abstract

Introduction

I. The strategic case for intellectual property protection
    A. Limits of existing law and pending initiatives
        1. The public domain as point of departure
        2. International instruments in brief
    B. Traditional knowledge as an appropriate subject of intellectual property protection
        1. Traditional knowledge as a knowledge good
        2. TK protection as a benefit to developing countries
        3. Need for an international system

II. A proposal for traditional IP rights in traditional knowledge
    A. Subject matter and beneficiaries of the rights
        1. Subject matter
        2. Rights holders
    B. The content and scope of rights
        1. Content
        2. Scope of protection
    C. The duration of rights
    D. The creation and registration of rights
        1. Registration requirements
        2. Opposition procedures and judicial review
    E. Relation to other laws
        1. The complementary function of geographical indications
        2. Relation to plant breeders' rights

Conclusions

---

* Thomas Cottier is Professor of Law and Director, World Trade Institute, University of Bern, Switzerland; Marion Panizzon (LL.M. Duke) is Doctor of Laws and Lecturer in Law at the University of Zurich. This chapter is based on a paper presented to the Conference on International Public Goods and Transfer of Technology under a Globalized Intellectual Property Regime, held at Duke University School of Law on 4–6 April 2003. It is an offshoot of a research project on the legal protection of traditional knowledge sponsored by the Swiss Agency for Development and Cooperation, Department of Foreign Affairs, Bern, Switzerland.

ABSTRACT

This chapter explores the feasibility of devising a new form of intellectual property (IP) protection that would recognize the social value of traditional knowledge (TK) and promote its integration into domestic and international trade regimes while respecting and preserving local autonomy and cultural values. Interest in the protection of TK is rooted in the goal of promoting social, economic, and ecological development of rural areas. It responds to concerns about fairness and equity in international economic relations affecting the livelihood of the bulk of the world's population. The topic is also of importance in the context of redefining the relationship between public goods, private rights, and the transfer of technology. Taken together, these concerns lead us to evaluate the policies and legal instruments pertaining to traditional knowledge that are best suited to achieving equity, validation, and sustainability while preserving open access to plant genetic materials for scientific research.

Introduction

The term "traditional knowledge" (TK) expresses the ways and means by which individuals or communities identify and improve genetic resources over time, including processes related to their extraction from nature and their preparation for human usage. Also implicated by the term are methods and techniques for preserving the communities' accumulated information about genetic resources for future generations.

On the surface, TK does not readily lend itself to present-day IP protection because it does not directly yield "innovation" in the conventional sense of the term. Rather, traditional knowledge arises through "circumstantial discoveries,"[1] which lay the groundwork for subsequent formal innovation, but too much resemble existing information to qualify for extant modes of IP protection.

Nevertheless, there are good reasons for adapting the worldwide IP system to accommodate a suitable form of protection for traditional knowledge. As matters stand, existing IPRs serve the short- and medium-term interests of industrialized and industrializing countries. Defenders of the current system are all countries depending on effective and worldwide protection of IPRs to protect investments in research and development. These countries should seek to broaden the system so as to enable rural populations to gear their lives to the

---

[1] *See* Christophe Germann, *The Protection of Plant Genetic Resources, in* Rights to Plant Genetic Resources and Traditional Knowledge: Basic Issues and Perspectives in Law and Policy, SDC/WTI First Expert Workshop, 24–26 Nov. 2002, Bern, Switzerland (on file with the authors).

world of modern technology – this time as providers, and not just receivers, of commercially valuable information.

In building their economies, many developing countries will depend, for decades to come, on promoting and advancing sustainable agriculture, while they leave subsistence farming behind. Strategic and ethical thinking in the field of IPRs needs, accordingly, to recognize that TK can become the trigger point for new product development, especially in sectors of specialty foods and beverages, horticulture, pharmaceuticals, personal care, and cosmetics. In an era of global trade, large-scale production is the most competitive format for generating revenue, as the spread of supermarkets replacing the "traditional supply and distribution systems for food" in Africa has shown.[2] We contend that carefully designed IPRs in traditional knowledge could help developing countries become full players in global agricultural markets while equitably rewarding indigenous peoples for their contributions to international well-being. It could thus constitute a significant step towards "improv[ing] confidence in the international IP system."[3]

An IPR would also protect TK from misappropriation by outsiders, who without offering either compensation or reward have often taken it from its custodians,[4] a practice that advances in biotechnology are likely to increase. Finally, a lack of adequate legal protection may tempt TK holders to maintain their nomadic traditions, which depend on generating revenues from the sheer volume of plant genetic resources for food and agriculture (PGRFA) and of plant genetic material collected in the wild. IPR protection could encourage custodians to undertake formal, stable, and sustainable agricultural cultivation of such material.[5]

In the rest of this chapter, we explore and elaborate on these premises. Part I focuses on the strategic case for IP protection of traditional knowledge. It reviews the current state of the law and pending initiatives to reconcile the protection of TK with the basic goals of the evolving international IP system. Part II of the article expounds our proposals for a tailor-made Traditional Intellectual

---

[2] *See* Rise of Supermarkets across Africa Threatens Small Farmers, FAO Release, 8 Oct. 2003, reprinted in Bridges Trade BioRes, vol. 3 Nr. 16, 16 Oct. 2003, *available at* http://www.ictsd.org.

[3] Review of the Provisions of Article 27.3(b) of the TRIPS Agreement, Communication from the European Communities and Their Member States, Council for Trade-Related Aspects of Intellectual Property Rights, WTO Document IP/C/W/254 5, para. 27 (13 June 2001) [hereinafter WTO Document IP/C/W/254].

[4] *See* David R. Downes, *How Intellectual Property Could Be a Tool to Protect Traditional Knowledge*, 25 COLUM. J. ENVTL L. 255 (2000) [hereinafter Downes, *Intellectual Property*].

[5] *See* Bio-Anbau mit Schweizer Hilfe, Foerderung der Good Governance, Neue Zuercher Zeitung, 18 Oct. 2003, *available at* http://www.nzz.ch (describing how a Swiss Government funded project assisted a Georgian village community to actually start an agricultural production of medicinal plants, instead of depleting their natural environment of such plants and risking the loss of their own biological resources).

Property Right ("TIP Right") that would apply to plant genetic resources for food and agriculture. Such a right would cover both the seed (as carrier of information about nature) and the information that humans develop in the form of traditional knowledge, but it would not protect genetic material as such. The proposed regime thus aims not only to reward the intellectual efforts of the community as embodied in knowledge about seed, it also ensures that the allocation of seed would remain under the sole proprietorship of that community.

I. The strategic case for intellectual property protection

Before discussing our proposals, we think it helpful to clarify the impact of conventional IPRs on this subject matter. We particularly seek to identify the lacunae in the current system, which remains primarily focused on activities undertaken at the national level, despite a growing number of international agreements that bear on the protection of traditional knowledge.

A. *Limits of existing law and pending initiatives*

In evaluating the current state of the law, we call readers' attention to the anger and resentment that has been triggered by several notorious patent cases where the rights were not granted to the TK holding communities, but to subsequent owners of innovations built upon traditional information and its use. When the United States Patent Office (USPTO) granted industrial "inventors" patents on the use of neem bark in pesticides and the treatment of skin conditions,[6] on the use of turmeric to heal wounds,[7] and on the use of the ayahuasca vine as an anti-depressant,[8] all without checking for prior invalidating art, it caused outcries of anger in India and Brazil, and demonstrated the

---

[6] See, e.g., U.S. Patent No. 6,623,766 (issued 23 Sept. 2003), *available at* http://patft.uspto.gov, assigned to the Council of Scientific and Industrial Research, New Delhi, India, concerning the insecticidal formulation of neem controlling malarial vector, mosquitoes; all other US patents involving neem *available at* www.uspto.org. *See also* Rheka Ramani, *Note and Comment: Market Realities v. Indigenous Equities*, 26 BROOK. J. INT'L L. 1148, fn 4 (2001) [hereinafter Ramani, *Indigenous Equities*]; Naomi Roht-Arriaza, *Of Seeds and Shamans: The Appropriation of the Scientific and Technical Knowledge of Indigenous and Local Communities*, 17 MICH. J. INT'L. L. 919, 921–22 (1996).

[7] See U.S. Patent No. 5,401,504 (issued 28 Mar. 1995), *available at* http://patft.uspto.gov, "use of turmeric in wound healing," assigned to the University of Mississippi Medical Center. *See also* Ramani, *Indigenous Equities*, above n. 6, at 1148, fn 5.

[8] See U.S. Patent No. 5,256,533 (issued 26 Oct. 1993), *available at* http://patft.uspto.gov, concerning betacarboline, which the literature refers to as found in ayahuasca plants. The patent's assignees are the Board of Regents, The University of Texas System. *See* http://www.biopark.org/peru/schultes-ayahuasca.html. Use of the ayahuasca plant by the indigenous people of Amazonian Peru, Ecuador, Bolivia, Colombia, and Western Brazil was described as early as the 1850s by British and German ethno-botanists.

extent to which existing law fails to resolve competing claims to commercially valuable information.[9] These cases of alleged "biopiracy" often fuel anti-IP sentiments and are invoked by those who oppose any intellectual property protection of traditional knowledge.

1. The public domain as point of departure

Under current international law, traditional crops bred and developed over generations by customary and informal farming practices, as well as landraces not systematically used, are subject to the principle of permanent sovereignty over natural resources. Governments are free to regulate their use and ownership within the bounds of international agreements in force for state parties. For example, under the Food and Agriculture Organization's (FAO) International Treaty on Plant Genetic Resources for Food and Agriculture ("ITPGR"),[10] which will enter into force on 29 June 2004, traditional crops are to be collected for, and donated to, the public domain.[11] Such crops are treated as public goods under the theory that their use is not exclusive but open to others in the community.[12] This baseline approach, which presumes that any form of private ownership is incompatible with practical, ideological, and systemic goals, is reinforced by an array of legal instruments and policies that all seek to place plant genetic resources in the public domain as global public goods.[13]

---

[9] *See* WTO Secretariat, The Protection of Traditional Knowledge and Folklore, Summary of the Issues Raised and Points Made, WTO Document IP/C/W/370, at 5 (8 Aug. 2002) [hereinafter WTO Document IP/C/W/370].

[10] *See* International Treaty on Plant Genetic Resources for Food and Agriculture, UN Food and Agriculture Organization, 31st Sess. (2001) [hereinafter ITPGR] (not yet registered with the UN), *available at* www.fao.org/Legal/treaties/033t-e.htm. *See also* Laurence R. Helfer, *Using Intellectual Property Rights to Preserve the Global Genetic Commons: The International Treaty on Plant Genetic Resourses for Food and Agriculture* [this volume].

[11] *See* G.C. Hawtin et al., *International Plant Germplasm Collections under the Convention on Biological Diversity – Options for a Continued Multilateral Exchange of Genetic Resources for Food and Agriculture*, *in* GLOBAL GENETIC RESOURCES – ACCESS, OWNERSHIP, AND INTELLECTUAL PROPERTY RIGHTS 247–62 (K.E. Hoagland & A.Y. Rossman eds., Natural Science Collection 1997). *See also* G.C. Hawtin & T. Reeves, *Intellectual Property Rights and Access to Genetic Resources in the Consultative Group on International Agricultural Research (CGIAR)*, *in* INTELLECTUAL PROPERTY RIGHTS III. GLOBAL GENETIC RESOURCES: ACCESS AND PROPERTY RIGHTS 41 (S. Eberhart et al. eds., Miscellaneous Publication, Crop Science Society of America 1998) (recalling that prior to the concept of a public domain, the concept of free availability for use to benefit present and future generations was assimilated to the ideal of a common heritage of mankind).

[12] *See* H.M. Spencer, *IP Skepticism*, *in* INTELLECTUAL PROPERTY 539 (P. Drahos ed., Ashgate Publishing 1999).

[13] *See, e.g.*, the FAO Leipzig Declaration's Global Plan of Action of 1996, and its 2000–2004 Global Conservation Trust, led on behalf of CGIAR by SGRP and IPGRI; SGRP stands for System-Wide Genetic Resources Program. *See also* the International Plant Genetic Resources Institute (IPGRI)/ Consultative Group on International Agricultural Research's

Once limited to the public domain, plant genetic resources for food and agriculture, as well as the TK underlying their uses, are freely accessible to public and private operators alike. The public good is deemed best served by making these resources freely available and by supporting their conservation and use with public funding.

All public goods approaches tend to restrict private rights as much as possible. Neither contractual limitations nor specific means of compensation for the guardians of traditional crops are envisaged. The most recent treaty affecting traditional knowledge, the ITPGR, respects existing intellectual property rights but does not elaborate on them. Rather, this treaty obliges breeders who are issued patent rights on genetic material they obtained from the commons to contribute their outputs to the public domain for research purposes.[14] The ITPGR thus seeks to reinforce an open international system of exchange of plant genetic resources for food and agriculture, with a view to optimizing access and use of the gene pool.

The literature describes well-known inequities that may impinge on rural communities when the private biotechnology sector can rely on this pure public domain approach.[15] There are different strategies to redress this imbalance, including proposals for taxpayer-funded public development programs to support conservation.

Private rights nonetheless coexist with this broad public-domain approach, in the sense that entrepreneurs may have recourse to existing forms of IP protection available under international law. So long as a product meets the eligibility criteria required by such different modalities of intellectual property protection as plant breeders' rights, patents, trademarks and geographical indications, copyrights for cultural heritage aspects of TK, and undisclosed information in exceptional cases, the commercialization of genetic resources remains partly protected under existing IP standards.[16] Established IPRs,

---

(CGIAR) SINGER network of 1994, the World Conservation Union's (IUCN) Global Biodiversity Forum of 1993, *available at* http://www.iucn.org/themes/ssc/; and the WTO's Doha Development Agenda Global Trust Fund (DDAGTF) of 2002, http://www.wto.org/english/news_e/spmm_e/spmm79_e.htm. The Doha Development Agenda Global Trust Fund (DDAGTF) was established by the WTO General Council on 20 December 2001. *See generally* STEPHEN A. HANSEN & JUSTIN W. VAN FLEET, A HANDBOOK ON ISSUES AND OPTIONS FOR TRADITIONAL KNOWLEDGE HOLDERS IN PROTECTING THEIR INTELLECTUAL PROPERTY AND MAINTAINING BIOLOGICAL DIVERSITY 31ff (American Association for the Advancement of Science 2003), *available at* http://shr.aaas.org/tek/handbook/ [hereinafter HANSEN & VAN FLEET].

[14] *See* ITPGR, above n. 10, art. 12.3 (a); *see also id.* art. 13.

[15] *See* Susette Biber-Klemm, *Incentives to Bring about Conservation and Sustainable Use of Genetic Resources in the Framework of the World Trade Order, in* THE WORLD TRADE FORUM, VOL. III: INTELLECTUAL PROPERTY: TRADE, COMPETITION AND SUSTAINABLE DEVELOPMENT 482 (Thomas Cottier & Petros C. Mavroidis eds., 2003).

[16] *See* Thomas Cottier, *The Protection of Genetic Resources and Traditional Knowledge: Towards More Specific Rights and Obligations in World Trade Law*, 4 JIEL 561, 569–73 (1998).

however, do not encompass the information that comprises traditional knowledge as such but only formal inventions or innovations based upon plant genetic resources. Established IPRs thus cannot function as a basis for controlling the redistribution of TK in a variety of different products.

2. International instruments in brief

a. Convention on Biological Diversity and Benefit Sharing. With the adoption of the Convention on Biological Diversity (CBD) in 1993[17] legal protection in the realm of plant genetic resources for food and agriculture (PGRFA) was introduced for a "product of nature."[18] The CBD responded to emerging inequities stemming from private industry's use of PGRFA by reasserting national sovereignty and jurisdiction over such resources. In order to keep international trade in PGRFA free of protectionism under national IP laws, the CBD imposed access and benefit-sharing (ABS) principles and devised the instruments of "mutually agreed terms" and "prior informed consent" (PIC).[19] However, these flanking policies proved too cumbersome to sustain continued investment by transnational corporations. They also proved ineffective in developing countries that lacked the means to install national registration systems, obtain patents, or oppose the patents of others on relevant TK.[20]

Despite its title, the "access and benefit sharing" principle does not liberalize market access (to the North) for goods, but only opens access to TK extant in the South. It does not guarantee that a TK-derived good can effectively enter an industrialized country market. The need to promote market access for TK-related products is thus an additional reason for allocating the legal protection of TK to the WTO.[21]

b. Plant Variety Protection (UPOV). In its 1978 and 1991 Acts, the International Union for the Protection of New Varieties of Plants

---

[17] *See* Convention on Biological Diversity, 5 June 1992, 31 I.L.M. 818 [hereinafter CBD].
[18] Geoffrey Hawtin, *Management of Plant Genetic Resources in the CGIAR: Problems, Prospects and the Quest for Equity* [hereinafter Hawtin, *Management*], *in* INTELLECTUAL PROPERTY: TRADE, COMPETITION AND SUSTAINABLE DEVELOPMENT, above n. 15, at 429–30.
[19] CBD, above n. 17, art. 17. *See also* Susan Bragdon, *Major Legal Regimes Affecting Plant Genetic Resource*, *in* INTELLECTUAL PROPERTY: TRADE, COMPETITION AND SUSTAINABLE DEVELOPMENT, above n. 15, at 442–43.
[20] *See especially* Anil K. Gupta, *Rewarding Creativity for Conserving Diversity in the Third World: Can IPR Regimes Serve the Needs of Contemporary and Traditional Knowledge Experts and Communities in the Third World?*, *in* STRATEGIC ISSUES OF IP MANAGEMENT IN A GLOBALIZING ECONOMY 119 (Thomas Cottier et al. eds., 1999) (discussing the question of costs relating to patent enforcement in developing countries).
[21] In a section of this article that has been omitted for reasons of space, the authors argue that the WTO is the most suitable forum for implementing decisions concerning the global protection of traditional knowledge.

(UPOV) established a *sui generis* system of plant-related IPRs for plant breeders.[22] This effort to invest breeders with private rights to their improved varieties obliged even the FAO to weaken the pure public domain approach that had been embodied in the International Undertaking (IU). Three interpretative resolutions pertaining to the IU confirm that plant breeders' rights are FAO-compatible.[23]

Developing countries, which were then still relying on national sovereignty and the principle of benefit sharing to protect their plant genetic resources from biopiracy, found themselves at an even greater disadvantage when confronted by assertions of plant breeders' rights. They responded by developing hybrid regimes that combined UPOV rights with CBD duties.[24]

c. FAO's International Undertaking (IU) and International Treaty, and the Consultative Group on International Agricultural Research (CGIAR). The United Nations' Food and Agricultural Organization (FAO) deserves credit for raising international awareness of genetic diversity as "one of humanity's most important resources."[25] The IU of 1983 recognized plant genetic resources as the "common heritage of humanity,"[26] and its official policies are hostile to the idea of protecting these resources by means of IPRs.[27] It was feared that private intellectual property rights could undermine the public domain status of plant genetic resources for food and agriculture. Consistent with this outlook, the International Treaty on Plant Genetic Resources for Food and Agriculture (ITPGR), adopted in 2001, reluctantly recognized that plant breeders (protected by UPOV) using plant genetic materials available from the gene banks of CGIAR Centres, may "take out

---

[22] *See* International Convention for the Protection of New Varieties of Plants, Paris, 2 Dec. 1961, as revised at Geneva on 19 Mar. 1991, UPOV Doc. 221(E), (1996) [hereinafter UPOV]. *Cf.* Bragdon, above n. 19, at 444.

[23] International Undertaking on Plant Genetic Resources, UN Food and Agriculture Organization, 22nd Sess., para. 285, Annex, U.N. Doc. C/83/REP (1983) [hereinafter IU]; FAO Conference Resolution 4/89 acknowledges that UPOV's plant breeders' rights are not at odds with the IU's objectives; FAO Conference Resolution 5/89 recognizes and defines Farmers' Rights; FAO Conference Resolution 3/91, finally, recognizes national sovereignty over genetic resources.

[24] *See* Tshimanga Kongolo, *New Options for African Countries Regarding Protection for New Varieties of Plants*, 4 J. WORLD INTELL. PROP. 355 (2001).

[25] *See* Hawtin, *Management*, above n. 18, at 430.

[26] *See* above n. 23.

[27] FAO's Global Plan of Action for the Conservation and Sustainable Utilization of Plant Genetic Resources for Food and Agriculture, *available at* http://www.fao.org/ag/cgrfa/PGR.htm, was introduced by the Leipzig Declaration in June 1996 and is monitored by the Commission on Genetic Resources for Food and Agriculture. It addresses foremost the *ex situ* and *in situ* preservation of plant genetic resources. It promotes "core collections" of germplasm through national governments in cooperation with IGOs and NGOs and warns against the seed industry's use of gene banks as an excuse to neglect collecting biodiversity-rich crops, under-utilized crops, and local varieties.

IPRs" on new products.[28] Article 12.3(f) and (g) of this treaty do not prevent private parties from claiming IPRs on modifications of plant genetic materials nor on materials for which access (under the CBD) had been legally obtained.[29] When the plant genetic material is already patent protected, the ITPGR provides that it is only the patent holder who can release control over it.

Otherwise, article 12.3 is opposed to introducing IPRs on traditional knowledge and on plant genetic resources for food and agriculture in general. The Treaty emulates the CBD's goals of "conservation and sustainable use of plant genetic resources for food and agriculture and the fair and equitable sharing of benefits derived from their use."[30] Nonetheless, the Treaty does not attenuate the competition between holders of traditional knowledge and plant breeders and farmers over the ownership and use of TK-related material. Any new intellectual property right in traditional knowledge must accordingly take account of the relationship between TK protection and existing rights of breeders and farmers.[31]

d. The WTO Agreement on Trade-Related Aspects of Intellectual Property Rights (TRIPS Agreement). With the adoption of the TRIPS Agreement in 1994,[32] the patenting of plant genetic resources for food and agriculture benefited from a major step towards global recognition and enforcement. Article 27.3(b) of the TRIPS Agreement specifically requires Members to provide either patents or a *sui generis* regime for novel and stable plant genetic resources. In addition, Art. 27.3(b) narrows the scope of exclusions from patentability.

In practice, the flexibility inherent in the *sui generis* option has reportedly created more problems than solutions, and it has also proven ineffective as an instrument for addressing the protection of traditional knowledge as such.[33] Indeed, the TRIPS Agreement makes no express reference to traditional

---

[28] *Compare* art. 12.3(d), *with* arts. 12.3(e), (f), ITPGR, above n. 10.
[29] *See* Nuno Pires de Carvalho, From the Shaman's Hut to the Patent Office: In Search of Effective Protection for Traditional Knowledge, paper presented to the Conference on Biodiversity and Biotechnology and the Protection of Traditional Knowledge, Washington University School of Law, St. Louis, Missouri, 4–6 Apr. 2003, at 97, *available at* http://law.wustl.edu/centeris/Confpapers (last visited 1 Aug. 2004).
[30] ITPGR, above n. 10, art. 1.1.31.
[31] FAO Conference Resolution C5/89 (1989), above n. 23; *see also* MARTIN A. GIRSBERGER, BIODIVERSITY AND THE CONCEPT OF FARMERS' RIGHTS IN INTERNATIONAL LAW: STUDIES IN GLOBAL ECONOMIC LAW, VOL. 1 (Peter Lang Publishing 1999).
[32] Agreement on Trade Related Aspects of Intellectual Property Rights, 15 Apr. 1994, Marrakesh Agreement Establishing the World Trade Organization, Annex 1C, LEGAL INSTRUMENTS – RESULTS OF THE URUGUAY ROUND vol. 31, 33 I.L.M. 81 (1994) [hereinafter TRIPS Agreement].
[33] *See id.* art. 27.3(b). *Cf.* Margaret Llewelyn, *Which Rules in World Trade Law – Patents or Plant Variety Protection?, in* INTELLECTUAL PROPERTY: TRADE, COMPETITION AND SUSTAINABLE DEVELOPMENT, above n. 15, at 305–08; Bragdon, above n. 19, at 446–48.

knowledge.[34] At the Council for TRIPS, efforts are currently underway to make the CBD and its Bonn Guidelines mutually compatible with TRIPS. If successful, this initiative would require IPRs under TRIPs to be given an interpretation consistent with the principle of "access and benefit sharing," and conversely, the CBD would have to be viewed as consistent with TRIPS-imposed IP obligations.[35]

e. Other international initiatives. The World Intellectual Property Organization (WIPO) and the United Nations Educational, Scientific and Cultural Organization (UNESCO) have jointly devised model provisions for national laws on the protection of folklore.[36] WIPO has also compiled databases to assist national legislative efforts to protect TK, and it has devoted considerable effort to seeking a consensual definition of TK. As a result, regional model laws based on the WIPO initiatives are full of definitions but rather devoid of operational language.[37]

To date, WIPO proposes a bottom-up approach under which developing countries would first assess how existing national mechanisms of intellectual property could be more effectively used to protect TK before introducing protection at the international level.[38] Midway between WIPO's emphasis on national legal protection for TK and the WTO's top-down approach lies the United Nations Conference on Trade and Development's (UNCTAD) proposal for agreed minimum standards to support an internationally recognized *sui generis* system.[39]

---

[34] *See* Graham Dutfield, Protecting Traditional Knowledge and Folklore: A Review of Progress in Diplomacy and Policy Formulation, UNCTAD/ICTSD Capacity Building Project on Intellectual Property Rights and Sustainable Development (6 Oct. 2002), *available at* http://www.iprsonline.org [hereinafter Dutfield, Capacity Building].

[35] *See* Graham Dutfield, *Sharing the Benefits of Biodiversity – Is there a Role for the Patent System?*, 5 J. WORLD INTELL. PROP. 918 (2002) [hereinafter Dutfield, *Benefits of Biodiversity*]. *See also* W. Bradnee Chambers, *Emerging International Rules on the Commercialization of Genetic Resources – The FAO International Plant Genetic Treaty and CBD Bonn Guidelines*, 6 J. WORLD INTEL. PROP. 311 (2003).

[36] *See* Dutfield, Capacity Building, above n. 34, at 32–34.

[37] *See, e.g.*, the Draft African Model Legislation for the Protection of the Rights of Local Communities, Farmers and Breeders, *cited in* Traditional Knowledge – Operational Terms and Definitions, Report of the Third Session of the Intergovernmental Committee on Intellectual Property and Genetic Resources, Traditional Knowledge and Folklore, WIPO Doc. WIPO/GRTKF/IC/3/9 § 37 (20 Mar. 2002) [hereinafter WIPO, Traditional Knowledge – Operational Terms], which defines traditional knowledge as "accumulated knowledge that is vital for conservation and sustainable use of biological resources and/or which is of socio-economic value, and which has been developed over the years in indigenous/local communities."

[38] *See* Elements of a Sui Generis System for the Protection of Traditional Knowledge, Report of the Third Session of the Intergovernmental Committee on Intellectual Property and Genetic Resources, Traditional Knowledge and Folklore, WIPO Doc. WIPO/GRTKF/IC/3/8 §§ 4, 5, 8, 17–57 (29 Mar. 2002) [hereinafter WIPO, Elements of a Sui Generis System, Third Session]. *But see id.* §§ 8, 42–43.

f. Selected domestic legislation. As of 1 January 2001, at least 22 countries and three regional integration organizations had made or were in the process of making available some specific legal protection for TK-related subject matter.[40] A number of developing countries had made particular efforts to move TK beyond existing IPRs and to develop *sui generis* regimes. With WIPO's support, for example, India adopted the Indian Biological Diversity Bill of 2000, which was the first legislation of its kind. This law established a National Biodiversity Authority (NBA), whose approval will be required when firms apply for IPRs to protect any invention based on a biological resource from India or on TK that originated in India. When granting its approval, the NBA can impose benefit-sharing conditions. These may include fees or royalties, joint ownership, transfer of technology or a venture capital fund for benefit claimers, or the payment of monetary or other forms of compensation.[41]

The Brazilian approach recognizes indigenous and local communities' rights to prevent unauthorized third parties from using, exploiting, experimenting with, disclosing, transmitting or re-transmitting data and information that integrate or constitute TK.[42] Protection is conferred by contracts of access (a bilateral approach), which provide for the sharing of benefits arising from the use of genetic resources and associated TK.[43] Peru's draft legislation similarly would protect traditional knowledge emanating from identifiable communities, but it would not confer rights on individual holders.[44] Nor does it protect

---

[39] *See* The Sustainable Use of Biological Resources: Systems and National Experience for the Protection of Traditional Knowledge, Innovations and Practices, Agreed Recommendations, UNCTAD Document TD/B/COM.1/L.16 (27 Mar. 2001) (stating that "The Commission makes the following recommendations at the international level: ... (d) Exchange information on national systems to protect TK and to explore minimum standards for an internationally recognized *sui generis* system for TK protection.").

[40] *See* WIPO, Elements of a Sui Generis System, Third Session, above n. 38, § 36.

[41] *See* Philippe Cullet, *Property Rights over Biological Resources, India's Proposed Legislative Framework*, 4 J. WORLD INTELL. PROP. 212 (2001) [hereinafter Cullet, *Biological Resources*].

[42] Provisional Measure No. 2.186–16 [Brazil], 23 Aug. 2001, art. 9 *cited in* Review of Existing Intellectual Property Protection for Traditional Knowledge, Report of the Third Session of the Intergovernmental Committee on Intellectual Property and Genetic Resources, Traditional Knowledge and Folklore, WIPO Doc. WIPO/GRTKF/IC/3/7 § 16 (6 May 2002) [hereinafter WIPO, Review, Third Session].

[43] *See* WIPO, Review, Third Session, above n. 42, § 16.

[44] *Compare* art. 9, Proposal of Regime of Protection of the Collective Knowledge of the Indigenous People (Peru), *cited in* WIPO, Traditional Knowledge – Operational Terms, Annex II, above n. 37, § 1.5 *and* art. 1, Law No. 27.811 of 10 Aug. 2001 [Peru], *cited in* Elements of a Sui Generis System for the Protection of Traditional Knowledge, Report of the Fourth Session of the Intergovernmental Committee on Intellectual Property and Genetic Resources, Traditional Knowledge and Folklore, WIPO Doc. WIPO/GRTKF/IC/4/8 § 61, fn 48 (30 Sept. 2002) [hereinafter WIPO, Elements of a Sui Generis System, Fourth Session], *with* art. 8, Brazilian Biodiversity Law, Provisional Measure No.

innovations and practices of given communities that are based upon TK.[45] An important feature of this system is that it requires the free exchange of knowledge between the different communities holding the same TK. Peru's system also affords some protection against unfair competition, in addition to IPRs, in order to avoid misappropriation of TK by third parties.

The IPR component of the Philippine system functions through licensing. These licenses are only granted upon the written consent of a knowledge-holding community.[46]

The Organization of African States' (OAU) Model Legislation for the Protection of the Rights of Local Communities, Farmers and Breeders of 1998 provides for a "hybrid system" focused primarily on the interests of farmers, while acknowledging breeders' rights and "community intellectual property rights." There are two innovative features. Part I(a) of the legislation recognizes and protects "the inalienable right of local communities including farming communities in their biological resources and crop varieties, knowledge and technologies." Article 23(1) recommends that states take steps to ensure that at least 50 percent of the benefits obtained through sharing resources are channeled to "the concerned local community or communities in a manner which treats men and women equitably."[47]

B. Traditional knowledge as an appropriate subject of intellectual property protection

The TRIPs Agreement in its present form and scope primarily responds to the needs of industrialized countries.[48] It does not offer much to farming communities. It was acceptable to developing countries mainly because it formed

---

2.186–15, of 26 July 2001, *cited in* WIPO, Elements of a Sui Generis System, Third Session, above n. 40, § 42 fn 43, with reference to § 16 fn. 21, which codifies Brazilian custom, whereby a community may hold the rights to the TK even though the knowledge belongs to a single individual. As WIPO explains, "Article 8 is not mandatory, however, which seems to indicate that the ultimate decision on attribution of rights lies on the community."

[45] Proposal of Regime of Protection of the Collective Knowledge of the Indigenous People (Peru), *cited in* WIPO, Traditional Knowledge – Operational Terms, Annex II, above n. 37, § 1.5 (discussing art.9).

[46] *See* Indigenous Peoples Rights Act (Republic Act No. 8371) of Oct. 1997 [The Philippines], and Rules and Regulations Implementing Republic Act No. 8371 [The Philippines], *cited in* Final Report on National Experiences with the Legal Protection of Expressions of Folklore, Report of the Third Session of the Intergovernmental Committee on Intellectual Property and Genetic Resources, Traditional Knowledge and Folklore, WIPO Doc. WIPO/GRTKF/IC/3/10 § 121 (25 Mar. 2002) [hereinafter WIPO, National Experiences]. The Philippines recognize the ownership of TK by identifiable communities, and empower these to manage it in accordance with their customary laws.

[47] Kongolo, above n. 24, at 364–66, 368.

[48] *See* Downes, *Intellectual Property*, above n 4, at 253, 255.

part of an overall package and single undertaking, which included a pledge to liberalize market access for agriculture and textiles. Progress toward these goals has materialized slowly and has not remedied a basic imbalance concerning the costs and benefits of that Agreement. For this reason, the introduction of new types of IPRs specifically aimed at developing countries could constitute a step towards a more balanced WTO.

While the protection of traditional knowledge as a form of intellectual property thus presents an opportunity, proposals to this end have proved extremely controversial. Opponents of this approach reflect quite heterogeneous philosophical perspectives. For example, those who normally support strong IPRs tend to view TK as an inappropriate subject matter because it fails to exhibit the defining eligibility criteria of novelty and innovative activity. Traditionalists also find it difficult to conceptualize intellectual ownership of these resources and their encapsulation in private rights.

In contrast, public-interest advocates view proposals for IPRs in traditional knowledge with skepticism because of their potentially adverse impact on the public domain. This camp sees IPRs as antithetical to the goals of developing an open system of crop exchange, of encouraging donations of genetic materials, and of ensuring accessibility to genetic resources for purposes of breeding and research.[49] A related concern of public-interest advocates stems from the emphasis on maintaining biodiversity in the CBD.[50] From this perspective, intellectual property standards set out in other treaties, such as the TRIPS Agreement, are to be respected only to the extent that the "exercise of those [other treaties'] rights and obligations do not cause a serious damage or threat to biological diversity."[51]

Finally, some argue that IPRs, as a system of private rights, are alien to the informal sector of human social organization and to the indigenous communities' customary laws that reflect it. On this view, IPRs would destroy traditions of free exchange and mutual communal support. While sympathizing with these public-interest concerns, we believe that a properly constructed IP regime for TK can take them into account while extending the benefits of IP systems generally to farming communities. We do not see the protection of traditional knowledge as intrinsically inconsistent with IPR systems that support private ownership of information,[52] even as it respects the concept of national sovereignty over natural resources.[53] In the rest of this section, we briefly summarize some of the reasons why we think traditional knowledge constitutes an appropriate subject matter for intellectual property protection.

---

[49] *See, e.g.*, ITPGR, above n. 10, Preamble, arts. 1.1, 12.3(d). The ITPGR codifies a public domain approach hostile to IPR protection of TK. *See, e.g.*, Helfer, above n. 10.
[50] CBD, above n. 17, art. 22; TRIPS Agreement, above n. 32, art 27.3(b).
[51] *See* Downes, *Intellectual Property*, above n. 4, at 253, 255.
[52] *See* HANSEN & VAN FLEET, above n. 13, at 4ff.
[53] Art. 3(b), Joint Statement of FAO and CGIAR, 1994, *cited in* Cary Fowler, *The Status of Public and Proprietary Germplasm and Information*, 7 IP STRAT. TODAY 6 (2003).

Then, in Part II, we will elaborate the elements of a protection regime that could reconcile the benefits of IP protection with the public-interest concerns that critics have expressed.

1. Traditional knowledge as a knowledge good

Traditional knowledge concerns information about how to achieve certain agriculture-related outcomes that is not appreciably different from other forms of information that intellectual property law traditionally deems worthy of protection. In general, intellectual property law assigns exclusive rights to the use of information for economic gain in order to solve problems of appropriability and to avoid market failure. The assignability of rights to information distinguishes IP protection from other forms of protection for intellectual creations, such as farmers' rights access legislation, and cultural heritage laws.[54] There is nothing to justify the exclusion of information about traditional knowledge from any of the classical utilitarian grounds for IP protection.[55]

On the contrary, further extending and adapting the social benefits of IPR regimes to the needs of agrarian communities is a worthwhile endeavor.[56] Historically, it is only to the extent that agriculture itself turned to and adopted the principles of industrialization that IPRs were established in that sector.

The protection of trademarks, geographical indications, appellations of origin, collections of data, and trade secrets all have some features in common with those of traditional knowledge.[57] The goal in all cases is to protect the fruits of human labor and of financial investment from undue appropriation by third parties. This is what lies at the core of the system, what justifies in the

---

[54] See Susette Biber-Klemm, *in* Rights to Plant Genetic Resources and Traditional Knowledge: Basic Issues and Perspectives on Law and Policy, SDC/WTI First Expert Workshop, 24–26 Nov. 2002, Bern, Switzerland (on file with the authors).

[55] See FREDERICK ABBOTT et al., THE INTERNATIONAL INTELLECTUAL PROPERTY SYSTEM: COMMENTARY AND MATERIALS, VOL. 1 6–7 (Kluwer Law International 1999).

[56] *Cf.* Ikechi Mgbeoji, *Patents and Traditional Knowledge of the Uses of Plants: Is a Communal Patent Regime Part of the Solution to the Scourge of Biopiracy*, 9 IND. J. GLOBAL LEG. STUD. 163 (2001) (noting that the system takes little note of distributional and ecological concerns and that the effect of globalized patents on TK has given rise to criticism).

[57] *See, e.g.,* Report on the Review of Existing Intellectual Property Protection of Traditional Knowledge, Report of the Fourth Session of the Intergovernmental Committee on Intellectual Property and Genetic Resources, Traditional Knowledge and Folklore, WIPO Doc. WIPO/GRTKF/IC/4/7, Annex II (5 Nov. 2002) [hereinafter WIPO, Review, Fourth Session], on "concrete examples how currently available standards of intellectual property have been used to protect traditional knowledge," whereby Canada, Italy, Mexico, Portugal, the Russian Federation, and Viet Nam have used existing IP-standards to protect TK. *See also* WIPO, Review, Third Session, above n. 42, § 40 (discussing TK in relation to trademarks, including collective marks); Felix Addor & Alexandra Grazioli, *Geographical Indications beyond Wines and Spirits: A Roadmap for a Better Protection for*

end the grant of exclusive rights, which makes it possible to deter free riding and to combat counterfeiting and piracy within a market economy.

2. TK protection as a benefit to developing countries

Under the TRIPs Agreement, developing countries have begun to introduce advanced standards of IP protection that affect the manufacturing and service industries. In agriculture there is no tradition of protecting crops by means of IPRs. Crops and seeds are thus left entirely to the public domain in what still amounts to an informal sector of a subsistence economy in many countries. Even where IPRs have been introduced, they mainly benefit foreign breeders, and do little to promote local agriculture. Braga and Fink show that only 10 percent of the total grants of such rights originated in developing countries, half of which were awarded to foreigners.[58] Thus, even when a developing country has installed a Plant Variety Protection (PVP) regime, it cannot be sure that its rewards will stay in the country where the knowledge that led to subsequent innovation had originated. Protection of TK by means of IPRs may be one step towards earning such rewards.

Ironically, those who most criticize the post-TRIPS IP system because it disfavors developing countries often refuse to cooperate in improving the system for such countries' benefit. Most NGOs – with the exception of the Center for International Environmental Law (CIEL)[59] – have been opposed to expanding the scope of international IP protection. Their inflexible position stems from their categorical opposition to the TRIPS Agreement.[60] Protection for TK is seen as merely a fig leaf, which leaves the basic inequality untouched.

Conversely, both the plant breeding industry and the research-based biotech industry – mostly operating in developed countries – also disdain IP protection for traditional knowledge because they believe such a regime would work against their interests. Specifically, these industries fear that IPRs in TK would limit open access to genetic resources, force them to operate within a narrow research exemption, and oblige them to pay for the added value TK brought to their products. However, within the boundaries of international

---

Geographical Indications in the WTO TRIPs Agreement, 5 J. WORLD INTELL. PROP. 118 (2002) (discussing geographical indications); *see also* UNCTAD, Trade and Development Board Commission on Trade in Goods and Services, and Commodities Expert Meeting on Systems and National Experiences for Protecting Traditional Knowledge, Innovations and Practices, Geneva, 30 Oct.–1 Nov. 2000, UNCTAD Document, TD/B/Com.1/EM.13/2, 22 Aug. 2000, at 11–13 (stressing that the protection of undisclosed information is unrelated to the novelty of the product, and it may well have emerged from the use of TK, which is kept to a small number of people).

[58] *See* Carlos A. Primo Braga & Carsten Fink, *Reforming Intellectual Property Rights Regimes: Challenges for Developing Countries*, 1 JIEL 545 (1998).

[59] *See* David Downes, Using Intellectual Property as a Tool to Protect Traditional Knowledge, CIEL Working Paper (1997).

[60] *See* above nn. 33–35 and accompanying text.

treaties, states already remain free to impose restrictions on the free flow of plant genetic materials for food and agriculture in the interest of protecting the traditional knowledge of their communities.

An important limitation on states' rights exists in the FAO's International Treaty, which sets out a limited number of specific crops that cannot be removed from the public domain. To what degree this list will be extended in a process of progressive liberalization depends on the willingness of governments to finance the international system by means of taxpayers' contributions. However, those who favor IP protection for traditional knowledge believe it is undesirable to lengthen the list of crops open to free use by researchers and farmers alike. Instead, in keeping with the proposals set out below, a properly constructed IP right would cover the seed in question as well as information about use of relevant technical knowledge.[61]

As regards the CBD, that treaty limits recourse to IPRs, especially patents, only insofar as existing rights are concerned, and it does not address new forms of IPR protection for TK that could otherwise be made consonant with its goals.[62] Whether such new rights would have detrimental effects on biodiversity depends on the incentive structures created and the scope of rights defined.

Further objections are made that IPRs in traditional knowledge would prove inoperable because communities, not individuals, possess the knowledge in question, or that such rights would destroy traditional ways of life. Yet, the protection of collective rights is already well established in the existing international IP system. For example, trademark law protects collective marks. Communitarian rights of particular regions define geographical indications (GIs) and appellations of origins. Even the enforcement of copyrights and related rights has a long tradition of operating on the basis of collection societies to which authors and artists belong. Formed under private law, these associations may easily cross national boundaries and comprise producers and owners unrelated in territorial terms.[63]

We concede that allocating private rights to TK depends on identifying "owners" in a specified territory. That this process can be problematic, is

---

[61] *See* below text accompanying nn. 81–106. One potential benefit to all countries from IP protection of TK would arise if it eased some of the pressures on the patent systems. It is no secret that even in industrialized countries with the resources to thoroughly investigate patent claims, the examination process has been wanting, and many bad patents are regularly issued. *Cf.* Dutfield, *Benefits of Biodiversity*, above n. 35, at 910–11.

[62] Countries that have taken major steps to implement the CBD's benefit sharing and mutual access initiatives may not view proposals to introduce IPRs on TK favorably; *cf.* International Cooperative Biodiversity Groups (ICBG), *available at* http://www.fic.nih.gov/programs/icbg.html.

[63] *See* Christophe Germann, *Flanking Policies, Institutional Design, Collecting Societies*, in Rights to Plant Genetic Resources and Traditional Knowledge: Basic Issues and Perspectives in Law and Policy, SDC/WTI Second Expert Workshop 27–29 Apr. 2003, Bern, Switzerland (on file with the authors).

demonstrated by a recent study showing that IP protection is not feasible for many crops and for some plant genetic resources for food and agriculture because one cannot properly trace their origins to a particular source.[64]

Nevertheless, the same study confirms that there are crops for which such determination is possible, especially if the time-span under consideration for granting such rights is limited and accounts only for recent decades. Pending further studies (and a testing of political will), we suggest at this stage that a time frame of 50 years should be envisaged.

Finally, one must evaluate concerns that private property rights are poorly suited for preserving the biodiversity of a region compared to traditional pastoral collectives operating with public ownership of the land.[65] While this is true for indigenous peoples and thus for a small minority of the global population, it does not hold true for settled farming in general. Farmers are perfectly accustomed to notions of property and ownership of land.

Unfortunately, many farmers cannot dispose of basic rights to mortgage property and thus to obtain access to investment. An IPR in TK constitutes another proprietary instrument for empowering farmers and agricultural communities. Moreover, nothing impedes a given farmer or community from declining to invoke particular rights in TK that might be granted to them.[66]

3. Need for an international system

The goals of social and intergenerational equity, as well as economic and environmental sustainability and biodiversity, cannot be achieved on a national level alone.[67] Protection of TK is only effective if it binds industrialized and developing countries alike. This is only possible with a global-scale protection. Only a paramount level of international law can safeguard indigenous communities against a violation of their rights by their own governments or by other states.[68]

---

[64] *See* THE CRUCIBLE II GROUP, SEEDING SOLUTIONS, 71, VOL. 1 (International Development Research Centre, International Plant Genetic Resources Institute, Dag Hammerskjöld Foundation (IPGRI) 2000).

[65] *See Nomadism in Mongolia,* THE ECONOMIST, 21 Dec. 2002, at 48–50 (citing the example of pastoral nomadism in Mongolia to show that the prevailing nomadic pastoral society structure has proven effective in ensuring the proper mobility and flexible access that are crucial for raising healthy herds while ensuring vegetation growth and preventing overgrazing).

[66] *See* Joel I. Cohen & Per Pinstrup-Andersen, *Biotechnology and the Public Good, available at* SciDevNet, http://www.scidev.net (posted 27 Aug. 2002).

[67] *See* WIPO Elements of a Sui Generis System, Fourth Session, above n. 44, §§ 9, 10, 26.

[68] *Cf.* Thomas Cottier & Maya Hertig, The Prospects of 21st Century Constitutionalism, World Trade Institute Working Paper 40–43 (2003), *available at* www.wti.org (arguing that only a multi-story legal system based on primacy can provide legal protection for the individual).

Another reason for a comprehensive international regime is that it could reconcile the different concepts currently used at the international level, which hinder the development of mutually compatible regimes.[69] Finally, an agreed set of global rules concerning traditional knowledge could significantly contribute to the further development of the TRIPS Agreement. A revision of Article 27.3(b) of TRIPs (concerning the scope of patenting life forms and genetically modified organisms) cannot be envisaged without taking traditional knowledge of plant genetic resources into account.

II. A proposal for traditional IP rights in traditional knowledge

Projects to protect information concerning the development, conservation, and use of plant genetic materials through IPRs can be pursued under different labels.[70] WIPO has explored, but delayed, the adoption of a working definition for TK.[71] The World Health Organization (WHO), in contrast, has already agreed on such a definition, but they have restricted it to medicinal TK. In general, international IP instruments tend to "leave specific determinations of the boundaries of protectable subject matter up to domestic authorities."[72]

With particular regard to traditional knowledge bearing on plant genetic materials for food and agriculture, it is tempting to use and further develop the concept of farmers' rights. Farmers' rights has remained a vague concept lacking the qualities of true legal rights. Another problem with farmers' rights is that the FAO's ITPGR reduces them to domestic concerns and seems to disregard any international dimension. Some scholars define TK protection in terms of broad human rights. However, we prefer to rely on the more

---

[69] See WIPO, National Experiences, above n. 48, at §§ 150–53, 155; see also Technical Cooperations on the Legal Protection of Expressions of Folklore, Intergovernmental Committee on Intellectual Property and Genetic Resources, Traditional Knowledge and Folklore, Fourth Session (Geneva, 9–17 Dec. 2002) WIPO Doc. WIPO/GRTKF/IC/4/4, § 4 (20 Oct. 2002); Note on the Proceedings, Tripartite Meeting on Moving to Sustainable Agricultural Development through the Modernization of Agriculture and Employment in a Globalized Economy, Geneva 18–22 Sept. 2002, International Labor Organization Document TMAD/2000/13, *available at* http://www.ilo.org.

[70] See Dutfield, Capacity Building, above n. 34, at 8–11; See also DARELL A. POSEY & GRAHAM DUTFIELD, BEYOND INTELLECTUAL PROPERTY: TOWARD TRADITIONAL RESOURCE RIGHTS FOR INDIGENOUS PEOPLES AND LOCAL COMMUNITIES 12–13 (International Development Research Center 1996).

[71] See Brief Summary of Working Documents, Intergovernmental Committee on Intellectual Property and Genetic Resources, Traditional Knowledge and Folklore, Fourth Session (Geneva, 9–17 Dec. 2002) WIPO Doc. WIPO/GRTKF/IC/4/INF/6 3 (6 Dec. 2002).

[72] WIPO, Traditional Knowledge – Operational Terms, above n. 37, §§ 4, 9 (citing the WTO TRIPS Agreement as an example in that it does not give a definition of "invention," and thus does not define how much innovation is necessary for protection by international IP laws).

operationally settled concept of IPRs, but acknowledge that TK protection fosters human dignity regardless of the terminology employed.[73]

We also reject any activity-specific approach that would differentiate among traditional medicinal knowledge, traditional ecological knowledge, traditional and local technology knowledge, and general know-how and practices. These terms artificially disaggregate components of a single reality and make it more difficult to enforce a viable system of legal protection.

A. Subject matter and beneficiaries of the rights

1. Subject matter

This study suggests a more general term – Traditional Intellectual Property Rights ("TIP Rights") – that is left deliberately open to encompass new and changing forms of traditional knowledge. TIP rights express the concept of a *sui generis*, private law entitlement vested in communities, which covers data and information about plant genetic resources for food and agriculture (PGRFA) and medicinal plants. The concept encompasses methods of use and includes the seed (but not the genetic resource) that embodies a given community's traditional knowledge.

One might object that the term "customary" IPRs is more accurate than "traditional," because it assimilates the "contemporary indigenous practices and beliefs which form an inherent part of any TK definition."[74] We use the term "traditional" only to signify the "conventional" nature of the process of gathering information, as distinct from bio-prospecting and other modern forms of collecting knowledge.

2. Rights holders

We believe that a TIP right should be inclusive, rather than exclusive, with respect to prospective beneficiaries of protection. It should encompass the spectrum of all relevant persons touched by such a law, ranging from individuals to communities, from associations to cooperatives. Given the strong intergenerational component of TK, it will be difficult to identify a single holder. Because TK is often held by families and even lineages, TIP rights should partake of a communitarian nature.[75]

In the event that individuals add value to traditional knowledge, they could qualify for conventional modes of IP protection, such as utility models or petty patents, copyrights or database rights in value-adding collections of

---

[73] *See* ITPGR, above n. 10; Helfer above n. 10. *Cf.* Cullet, *Biological Resources*, above n. 41, at 228 (arguing that IPRs recognize a human rights dimension by limiting the duration of the right and by requiring that the invention be disclosed; and specifically suggesting that article 7 of the TRIPS Agreement, which requires a balance of rights and obligations, could be interpreted to require such compatibility with human rights).
[74] WIPO, Traditional Knowledge – Operational Terms, above n. 37, at § 19.
[75] *See* Downes, *Intellectual Property*, above n. 4, at 255.

information. That the TIP right as such is reserved for a collective entity hardly presents a new phenomenon in IP law. Consider, for example, that even a modern patent law deals more with teams of inventors than single persons, and "most intellectual property assets are owned by collective entities, which in many cases represent large and diffuse groups of individuals."[76]

Moreover, different communities in different regions of the world may hold the same TK independently from each other. In this case, they are prohibited from applying for joint ownership, because – not knowing about each other's respective work – they do not fulfill the requirement of "aggregate efforts" and "collaboration."[77]

Given that different communities might assert parallel rights to the same traditional knowledge, cooperative efforts in assigning or transferring such knowledge to firms for industrial application would be in their mutual interests. Also beneficial might be agreements setting prices for such purposes, short of collusion running afoul of antitrust laws. In this regard, states participating in the proposed IP regime would need to adopt appropriate exceptions for collective administration of TIP rights, so as to avoid pitting different communities against one another in ways that would drive down the prices paid for their traditional knowledge. It would undermine a primary goal of establishing such rights if antitrust laws would deny traditional communities an exceptional use of monopolistic market power.[78]

B. *The content and scope of rights*

Defining the content and scope of TIP rights in traditional knowledge poses the most difficult issue before us. This topic above all others is particularly subject to negotiations and compromise. The scope of protection may range from fully

---

[76] Review of the Provisions of art. 27.3(b), Relationship between the TRIPS Agreement and the Convention on Biological Diversity and Protection of Traditional Knowledge, Information from Intergovernmental Organizations, Addendum, Convention on Biological Diversity (CBD), Council for Trade-Related Aspects of Intellectual Property Rights, Committee on Trade and Environment, WTO Doc. IP/C/W/347/Add.1, WT/CTE/W/210 § 34 (10 June 2002). The WTO cites the example of General Motors, which owns intellectual property rights on behalf of a community of shareholders that is much larger and more diffuse than most identified traditional communities.

[77] Philippe Cullet, *in* Rights to Plant Genetic Resources and Traditional Knowledge: Basic Issues and Perspectives in Law and Policy, SDC/WTI Second Expert Workshop 27–29 Apr. 2003, Bern, Switzerland (on file with the authors) viewing the concept of "joint inventorship," as recognized by 35 U.S.C. § 116 (2000), as a likely form for defining the right holder. Adopting that concept for TK, this author proposes that the determining test be that "the contribution of the joint inventor must be essential in distinguishing the invention from the prior art."

[78] Where necessary to avoid a loss of self-empowerment, the state itself can become the designated custodian of the interests and rights of TK holders. *See* WIPO, Elements of a Sui Generis System, Fourth Session, above n. 44, § 63.

developed property rights to a limited entitlement focusing on compensation without entailing powers to prevent others from using materials for commercial purposes. However, it should be clear that TIP rights only extend to commercial activities undertaken by public or private entities. The very rationale for such rights is to introduce a new level of economic benefits that alters the balance of power between those who possess traditional knowledge and commercial actors who seek to exploit and build upon such knowledge with a view to marketing new products.

In keeping with general principles of intellectual property law, activities partaking of private use should not be covered. Nothing therefore would bar individuals from using TK generated by others for private purposes short of engaging in commercial activities.

A difficult question arises from the need to compensate holders of rights in TK adequately when a TK component is claimed as part of a "combination patent" in jurisdictions that recognize such patents. Here the object is to prevent would-be patentees from avoiding the need to license the traditional knowledge or otherwise to compensate its holders simply because they filed for a combination patent.[79]

Where the TK is associated with a biological resource, as when it pertains to the effects of medicinal plants or the specific quality of a crop, the TIP right must necessarily encompass certain uses one can elicit of that plant. An open question is whether the genetic information encapsulated within the plant (or seed) should be eligible for any form of IP protection. The communities have usually neither identified the genetic sequences making up the seed nor have they matched the function of any given seed to a certain strand of the genetic code, and for contemporary international treaty law, genetic information falls under the research exemption.[80]

1. Content

It is important to emphasize that the IPRs in question are limited to knowledge that can be used for commercial purposes.[81] However, a tension arises from the need to distinguish such commercially valuable information from other components of TK that are interwoven with the processes of everyday life and merely reflect the community's values.[82] A properly designed TIP right would only protect commercially valuable information that was not interwoven with the processes of everyday life.[83]

---

[79] See HANSEN & VAN FLEET, above n. 13, at 11.
[80] Whether the identification of genetic information as such should ever qualify as a patentable invention or should be left in the public domain is a much-debated question that lies beyond the scope of this article.
[81] See HANSEN & VAN FLEET, above n. 13, at 9.
[82] See WIPO, Review, Third Session, above n. 42, § 33.
[83] Cf. WIPO, Traditional Knowledge – Operational Terms, above n. 37, §§ 33, 59, suggesting that one needs to be cautious when drawing the line. The *sui generis* system of Panama

While there is no need to require novelty as a prerequisite of protection, a certain level of intellectual activity should accordingly be required for IP protection. TK not eligible for IP protection thus encompasses "items not resulting from intellectual activity in the industrial, scientific, literary or artistic fields, such as human remains, languages in general, and other similar elements of 'heritage' in the broad sense."[84] TIP rights covering plant genetic resources in particular should protect TK relating to nutrition, health prevention, healing and other human activities. In order to identify TK protectable by IP rights, and to render it eligible for legal protection, the specific subject matter needs to be recognized or documented in some codified knowledge system.[85]

2. Scope of protection

The purpose of establishing TIP rights is to define ownership and the obligations that result from commercial use of information that takes the form of traditional knowledge. The normal scope of any IPR is to prevent a third party from using information for commercial purposes without the consent of the right holder. The restricted usage is further defined by specific operations, such as putting the protected item on the market. Beyond such typical concerns, policy makers must carefully delimit the extent to which TK rights should be subject to a research exception, under which use of the otherwise protected information would not require the right holders' consent. Similarly, policy makers must decide whether to allow potential licensees to test their products and obtain market approval prior to obtaining the consent of the right holders.

We reiterate that any TIP right pertaining to plant genetic resources for food and agriculture (PGRFA) should also encompass use of the seed but should not protect the genetic information contained in the seed. This would establish an equitable relationship between plant breeders and the TK holders. Whether the relevant TK is only associated with plant genetic material (e.g., pharmaceutical plants) or integrated into the PGRFA (e.g., seed, domesticated animal), the

---

(art. 1 Law No. 20, of 26 June 2000) distinguishes TK that has commercial utility from other TK. Such a distinction had, to a certain extent, the effect of disintegrating the holistic aspect of TK in which commercial use and spiritual components are intertwined. WIPO suggests allocating to customary law the function of managing the sacred sources of TK, leaving it to international and national laws to regulate the commercially relevant TK.

[84] WIPO, Traditional Knowledge – Operational Terms, above n. 37, § 25, notices that "human remains" are part of the "heritage of indigenous people." In a broad sense, heritage includes the result of any kind of "intellectual activity" protected by IPRs. But heritage also contains artistic creations, as well as human objects, sites, removed from intellectual activity, and which IPRs are not designed to protect. Both types of "heritage of indigenous people" fall under the UNESCO preservation regime pursuant to the "Principles and Guidelines for the Protection of the Heritage of Indigenous Peoples" developed under the Auspices of the United Nations (UN) Working Group on Indigenous Populations, UN Doc. E/CN.4/Sub.2/1994/31, *cited in id.* Annex II, at 9.

[85] See id. § 32.

right should protect both the traditional knowledge as such and the product derived from its use.[86]

As to the underlying genetic information, the desirable compromise with research goals should preserve the status quo of the public domain approach. Research parallel to or in combination with TK relies on genetic data from the public domain.

We concede that it may sometimes prove difficult to distinguish the product that TK identified and that the TIP right properly protects – such as a plant – from what counts as the underlying genetic information. We suggest a process-oriented rather than a product-oriented approach to making such distinctions. The key question is whether merely identifying the genetic code of a plant discovered by some indigenous communities should trigger a duty to license the use of the plant or whether identifying the genetic code is of such value to all human beings and research that it should be regarded as an activity falling within the public domain.

Another question is whether using the genetic code to create a new or improved product amounts to using the "plant" in a restricted sense that should be licensed by the TK holder. A research-friendly approach might subject only those products that were created without interfering with the genetic material to licensing (such as extracting or synthesizing substances), while piecing together strands of genetic information to develop a new product would remain unaffected by the TIP right's scope.

Beyond these threshold issues, the modalities of protection remain open to debate and negotiations. Logically, the poorest developing countries would prefer a strong exclusive property right in TK, unencumbered by research exceptions that required all users to be licensed. Users, especially those in developed countries, may prefer to limit the right to compensation or to adopt the compensatory liability regime (CLR) proposed by Professor Reichman.[87]

Between an exclusive right and a clear entitlement to compensatory liability lies the possibility of adopting a misappropriation regime.[88] Such a regime, as suggested by Professor Correa among others, seems consistent with a broader unfair competition approach, which others have proposed.[89] The African Group within the Council for TRIPS endorsed the misappropriation approach

---

[86] See Germann, above n. 1, at 24–26.
[87] J.H. Reichman & Tracy Lewis, *Using Liability Rules to Stimulate Local Innovation in Developing Countries: Applications to Traditional Knowledge* [this volume]. *See generally* J.H. Reichman, *Of Green Tulips and Legal Kudzu: Repackaging Rights in Subpatentable Innovation*, 53 VAND. L. REV. 1743 (2000).
[88] See Carlos Correa, Protection and Promotion of Traditional Medicine, Implications for Public Health in Developing Countries, Study (Aug. 2002) (unpublished manuscript, on file with the authors); *cf.* Dutfield, Capacity Building, above n. 34, at 29 (referring to Correa).
[89] *See* Correa, above n. 88, at 30.

in 2003.[90] An approach rooted in unfair competition can benefit from article 10*bis* of the Paris Convention for the Protection of Industrial Property. Just as undisclosed information has been protected on this basis by article 39 of the TRIPS Agreement, which established a new IPR category in international law,[91] so it can be argued that to use information and knowledge generated by others and expressed in a specific product is unfair to the extent that it serves to facilitate copies or a derived product without the consent of the creator.

All of these proposals need to be carefully evaluated in light of their potential impact on the free flow of genetic material envisaged by the FAO's International Treaty and their human rights implications.[92]

C. *The duration of rights*

IPRs that stimulate innovation and creation are generally limited in time. After a period in which innovators reap their rewards, innovation enters the public domain of human knowledge and becomes freely available. With TIP rights, the process is reversed. Traditional knowledge that resides in the public domain without being privatized by law becomes, as of a particular date, subject to an intellectual property right owned by an individual or a community.

Active use of TK should constitute the required limit of protection. Rights to TK should only arise so long as the process or information exists within, and is being used by, a particular community. Once it fades into the past, it is no longer of commercial interest to the community and should no longer be granted protection.

When the use of active TK is protected, however, the period of liability for specific uses will have to be determined by law. Regardless of whether an exclusive rights regime or a compensatory liability regime is adopted, the question arises as to how long the licensee must remain liable to the licensor.[93] The problem here is that a new product will often only be placed on the market after a

---

[90] Taking Forward the Review of Article 27.3(b) of the TRIPS Agreement – Joint Communication from the African Group, Council for Trade-Related Aspects of Intellectual Property Rights, WTO Doc. IP/C/W/404 (26 June 2003).

[91] *See* TRIPS Agreement, above n. 32, art. 39 (embodying the protection of confidential information within the framework of art. 10bis of the Paris Convention).

[92] *See* Cullet, *Biological Resources*, above n. 41, at 228 (citing Audrey R. Chapman, Approaching Intellectual Property as a Human Right, Obligations Related to Art. 15(1)(c), U.N. ESCOR, 24th Sess., U.N. Doc. E/C.12/2000/12 (2000)). *See also* Audrey R. Chapman, *The Human Rights Implications of Intellectual Property Protection*, 5 JIEL 861 (2002).

[93] *Cf.* Jerome H. Reichman *with* Catherine Hasenzahl, NON-VOLUNTARY LICENSING OF PATENTED INVENTIONS: HISTORICAL PERSPECTIVE, LEGAL FRAMEWORK UNDER TRIPS, AND AN OVERVIEW OF THE PRACTICE IN CANADA AND THE UNITED STATES, UNCTAD/ICTSD Capacity Building Project on Intellectual Property Rights and Sustainable Development, 9–13 (Sept. 2002), *available at* http://www.iprsonline.org (noting that TRIPS Agreement, art. 31, marks an important step for developing countries,

number of years of research and testing, and the amount of equitable sharing of benefits cannot be properly defined during the first years of licensing.

One solution would be to differentiate the licensing fees according to a menu of options, with one charge for a period of R&D, and additional compensation to become due once the product reaches the market. Such compensation would then be limited for a certain period of time sufficient to generate adequate profit sharing. At some point, e.g. after 10 years, the duty to compensate would cease and the use of TK by that licensee would no longer trigger a duty to remunerate the right holder.

We stress that the TIP rights in traditional knowledge as such should not lapse and would again become operational if the TK were used by another economic operator or for different purposes. At this point, the process of licensing or compensatory liability would revive and additional revenues would be generated. In effect, one could envisage that TK protection could last indefinitely, so long as active use is made of the relevant information, and this solution would be consonant with the intergenerational and incremental nature of traditional knowledge.[94]

D. The creation and registration of rights

1. Registration requirements

Costly registration procedures can be avoided by linking the registration process to existing and updated inventories of knowledge.[95] In addition to a registration requirement for TK holders, industries interested in using TK could be obliged to disclose the origin of the genetic resources in question.[96] This requirement, in turn, would help to foster the creation of TK inventories.

However, according to de Carvalho, a disclosure requirement must be reconciled with the TRIPS Agreement.[97] He argues that a disclosure

---

because it recognizes compulsory licensing on grounds other than abuse of rights and thus permits the use of such licensing to promote public policy goals).

[94] *But see* WIPO, Elements of a Sui Generis System, Fourth Session, above n. 44, § 78 seeming to say that once TK becomes commercially viable, it should be limited to a specified period of protection, beginning with the point in time of commercial exploitation.

[95] *See id.* § 49.

[96] *See* Review of the Provisions of Art. 27(3)(b), Relationship between the TRIPS Agreement and the Convention on Biological Diversity and Protection of Traditional Knowledge and Folklore, WTO Doc. IP/C/W/347/Add. 3 §§ 17–22 (11 June 2002) (noting that the CBD codifies, in decision VI/24C, para. 2 and VI/10, paras. 31, 46 of the Conference of the Parties, the disclosure of origin, albeit as a self-standing requirement). UPOV, by contrast, concerned about additional barriers to access to genetic resources, does not wish to see disclosure of origin become another condition for application for plant variety protection.

[97] *See* Nuno Pires de Carvalho, *Requiring Disclosure of the Origin of Genetic Resources and Prior Informed Consent in Patent Applications Without Infringing the TRIPS Agreement*, 2 WASH. U. J.L. & POL'Y. 371 (2000).

requirement that operates as a condition to patentability should only apply when the genetic resource concerned is preserved *in situ*. Where the active components are isolated from those resources or even synthesized, i.e., the genetic resource is preserved *ex situ*, the link between the invention, the know-how (including the TK), and the resources may become too weak to be of any significance for patent protection.[98]

Registration of the right itself can be either declaratory or constitutive. A declaratory registration might have the advantage that it could strengthen the claims of traditional communities against infringement prior to the vesting of a formal legal title.[99] An examination would presuppose the creation of a core of examiners specialized in the IP rights of indigenous people.[100]

The problem of finding the resources to apply for adequate protection and/or enforcement of a TIP right in TK is aggravated by the manner in which knowledge has often been unsystematically transmitted from one generation to another. Ideally, these rights should be registered at the international level by an international organization, in cooperation with national agencies and NGOs. Information technology facilitates linking different sources and building a coherent system. Registered information about TK and its uses should be made publicly available, as in patent law.

An optimal solution aimed at reducing registration costs must invest a TIP right with a built in "presumption of protection" in traditional knowledge. Any user of TK would labor under a burden to disclose the origin of biological or genetic resources and to establish that he had obtained prior informed consent to their use, unless these resources were otherwise demonstrably free of claims by indigenous people or in the public domain. Such disclosure and prior informed consent requirements have not yet been included in international patent treaties.[101] Yet, conditioning the grant of a patent on such a requirement would successfully link the objectives of the CBD access and benefit-sharing system to that of IPR protection.

2. Opposition procedures and judicial review

Registration should be subject to opposition and eventually to legal challenges. Once an application has been published, other claimants may object to the exclusive generation of TK-related information and argue that they are equally entitled. They may claim that there is a previous or simultaneous "like practice." They may demand exclusive ownership or joint ownership.

In certain jurisdictions, it is possible to grant patents on an inventive combination of two individually "known" substances. In the Maca and Velvet Deer Antler

---

[98] The Andean decision No. 391 of 16 August 1996 and the Biodiversity Law of Costa Rica have both required disclosure prior to use in their statutes. *See* de Carvalho, above n. 97.
[99] See WIPO, Elements of a Sui Generis System, Fourth Session, above n. 44, § 76.
[100] *See id.* § 73.   [101] *See* Cullet, above n. 77.

cases, for example, the USPTO had correctly refused patent protection of the fertility boosting plant, Maca, and of a modern producer using the similar Velvet Deer Antler, since prior art known to the Andean population had been shown.[102] However, the patent applicants succeeded in obtaining a patent on the combination of the two substances, since absent prior art relating to the combination, the recipe became eligible for patent protection.[103]

With a proper system to protect TK in place, the grant of combination patents should be screened under various good faith standards so as to avoid their being abused to circumvent compensation and/or the licensing of the individual components. Another option would be to adopt, pursuant to TRIPS Art. 8.2, a specific prohibition of abus de droit relating to combination patents.

The use of opposition procedures could lead to negotiations among applicants and objectors, with a view to sharing the property rights in question. This may lead to the formation of associations of shared ownership that might include communities and regions around the world. There is no need for contiguity, but the responsible international organization must be in a position to administer all these rights.

Finally, rights in traditional knowledge, like any IP right, must be subject to judicial review. Users may argue that the registration was unlawful because the information was no longer actively used or did not really exist in the first place. Right holders, on the other hand, may need court proceedings to stop unlawful use of TK-related information and to ban the commercialization of products due to lack of consent or due to lack of adequate compensation. Disputes may also arise in interpreting and applying licensing agreements. Ideally, claims of this kind should be adjudicated by centralized global authorities, as exemplified by the WIPO dispute settlement process for domain names.

E. Relation to other laws

1. The complementary function of geographical indications

As discussed at the outset, a fully effective regime to protect traditional knowledge will depend on a number of policies, some related and others unrelated to IPRs. Within the field of IPRs, a TIP right in traditional knowledge particularly needs to be supplemented by enhanced protection for geographical indications of origin, taking into account the special needs of developing countries. This important but highly technical subject lies beyond the scope of this article.[104]

---

[102] *See* U.S. Patent No. 6,093,421 (issued 25 July 2000), *available at* http://www.uspto.gov/patft.
[103] *See* HANSEN & VAN FLEET, above n. 13, at 11.
[104] *See* Addor & Grazioli, above n. 57, at 865–79. *See also* Dwijen Rangnekar, A Review of Proposals at the TRIPS Council: Extending Art. 23 to Products Other than Wine and Spirits, UNCTAD/ICTSD Capacity Building Project on Intellectual Property Rights and

2. Relation to plant breeders' rights

A system to provide TIP rights in traditional knowledge would have to be carefully aligned with the existing regime that protects plant breeders' rights under the UPOV treaties.[105] How to reconcile the conflicting interests of plant breeders and TK rights holders is crucial to determining how the benefits from TK will be shared and how rights to TK can be exchanged for technical support. In our view, the line of demarcation between the two regimes will require resort to the dispute resolution system of an intergovernmental organization, which would dispose of impartial scientists and experts who could allocate relevant TK to its legitimate assignees.[106]

As matters stand, well-funded plant breeders relying on their R&D capacities can locate plant genetic resources for food and agriculture and exploit them without any legal or compensatory obligations. Once a TIP right was established, it would oblige plant breeders to search for a potential right holder to whom some legal obligations had to be discharged. Developing countries lack the resources to systematically document TK surrounding the PGRFA relating to the foods they eat, the sicknesses they cure, the textiles they weave, and the like. One beneficial side effect from obliging plant breeders to seek, search and disclose TK associated with PGRFA could be that the TK at long last might become properly documented and safeguarded. Identifying and categorizing TK in PGRFA will help to separate the rights of the traditional knowledge holder from those of plant breeders, which in the end will facilitate the dealings between the two sets of rights holders.

A TIP right protects the communities' traditional knowledge and so conserves the PGRFA at an earlier stage than the protection that plant breeders' rights also gives to PGRFA. This follows because the TIP right would confer proprietary protection on the relevant traditional knowledge before the plant breeder had taken any innovative step to modify plant genetic resources. Once a TIP right was established at the international level, it would thus saddle future plant breeders with an international legal obligation to seek a license to use any such resources that were linked to protected traditional knowledge and to compensate the right holder.

The coexistence of these two regimes raises many other difficult questions that can only be hinted at here. For example, if the plant breeding industry isolates a genetic sequence from traditional material, does the genetic sequence also count as information emanating from TK or simply as genetic material

Sustainable Development, 12–15, 44–45 (May 2003), *available at* http://www.iprsonline.org.
[105] *Cf.* UPOV, art. 17, above, n. .22.
[106] Choosing the right forum for future negotiations is thus particularly important, and in our view, the WTO is the preferred forum for a number of reasons. For reasons of space, this topic lies beyond the scope of this article.

barred from qualifying for any IP protection? Does the process of extracting genetic information – absent any modification of that genetic material – amount to an innovation, which would confer an IP right on the plant breeder? Should the international system reward a process that required intellectual creativity, even if the material itself, the genetic sequence laid open, is not (yet) modified? The answer to this question is in turn linked to the ethical and political debates about the patentability of life forms, which we cannot go into here.

We recognize that critics may argue that opening the door to the protection of traditional knowledge by proprietary rights could elicit related claims that genetic research results should be similarly protected. Without staking out a position on these more abstract issues, we believe that a workable solution, allowing science sufficient leeway for research on PGRFA, would result from applying the TIP right to protect both the traditional knowledge and the seed that it produces, but not the underlying genetic information as such.

Conclusions

Many commentators have argued that the idea of creating a new *sui generis* system of IPRs is unsuitable for farming communities. They ask why methods employed to protect modern innovations are needed to protect traditional knowledge. They also challenge the principle of resorting to a property rights approach for resources that have traditionally been available for use in the public domain. While we take these issues seriously, we believe that there is a stronger case for adopting a properly crafted and balanced regime of IPRs to protect traditional knowledge.

Accommodating IPRs to this subject matter is primarily a learning process. As farmers adopt and familiarize themselves with the concepts of real and movable property rights, they may grow accustomed to the concept of property in intangible knowledge goods that underlies intellectual property systems. Because IPRs can potentially enhance farmers' standing, bargaining powers, respect and incomes, these proposals seem likely to attract attention and support from rural communities.

In practice, single farmers or small communities would not typically acquire these rights. Rather, the traditional IP entitlements we envision would normally vest in or be attributed to regional, national, or even international bodies, not unlike collection societies, which would administer rights, licensing, and the equitable distribution of proceeds. These functions may be absorbed by existing institutions that defend farmers' interests or by organizations yet to be created. There is a risk of generating additional and costly bureaucratic structures, but this risk in itself is not sufficient to negate the approach. Conditions of good governance will be needed to ensure that these institutions become workable.

We contend that IP protection for traditional knowledge must be shaped by an international agreement specifically designed for this purpose. Neither the national sovereignty approach of the CBD nor the public goods approach of the FAO's International Treaty is alone sufficient effectively to empower communities whose TK has enabled them to identify, collect, develop, and conserve plant genetic resources for food and agriculture.

We, therefore, propose the creation of a traditional intellectual property right (TIP right), the scope of which will need to be more fully defined, but which at least should entail a right to compensatory liability. We support the requirements of prior informed consent and disclosure of origin as a precondition to patent applications. At the same time, we stress that existing IPRs and TIP rights are not mutually exclusive. Quite the opposite, they all need to be made part of an overall package of measures to support viable agricultural structures in developing countries. In particular, stronger protection of geographical indications of origin would further enhance the potential to develop local and international niche markets for products based on traditional knowledge.

If action is taken at the international level to implement IPRs for traditional knowledge along the lines we envision, the end results should become part of the global trading system and, thus, of WTO law. We maintain that it is only the WTO, which combines global trade rules with worldwide IP protection, that can ensure better market access and conditions for commercially valuable assets resulting from a TK-related production process.

In an age of globalization, monetary value creates power, and trade transcends borders. Those whose traditional knowledge acquires value in identifiable plant genetic resources for food and agriculture and in the corresponding seed will not become "players" in the global market place unless these assets attract tradable IPRs. International disputes arising from the exercise of these rights should be resolved within the existing dispute settlement framework, and trade-related enforcement mechanisms should ensure that treaty rights are fully implemented. The Least-Developed Countries would particularly benefit from such an arrangement, and it would thus help to rebalance the social costs of the TRIPS Agreement.

COMMENTARY

Comment: Traditional knowledge, folklore and the case for benign neglect

DAVID L. LANGE[*]

Let us think about folklore a bit more closely.

At the very northeasternmost corner of Vietnam, hard by the China Sea, some sixty statute miles above Haiphong and Hanoi, just below the border where the Chinese mainland begins, lies a secluded bay, its waters clear and deep and emerald in color, a place of magic and surreal beauty, called Ha Long. The Vietnamese say this is the birth place of their country and their people. Their folklore abounds with stories about Ha Long Bay, none more beautiful than this story, which I shall share with you:

In the dawn of time, when magic creatures lived upon the earth, and some men were free and others not, a great dragon came down from the north, bearing a people and their destiny in its mouth, a people rescued by the dragon from enslavement, whom it now sheltered safely among its many sharp and fearsome teeth. But the day was hot, and the dragon was exhausted after its long journey. When at last it came to the place called Ha Long, it could go no farther. Slowly, as the sun was setting, the dragon allowed itself to sink into the brilliant green waters of the bay – so cool, so inviting – until at last nothing could be seen except the sharp scales along its back which jutted above the waters as if they were thousands of islets made of karst or extruded limestone, rather than, as in fact they were, evidence of the miracle of creation that marked this bay as a sacred place. There the dragon slumbered – and for that matter, slumbers still. In time the people the dragon had rescued made their way to the surface of the waters and then on southward into a land of green and fragrant beauty, where they lived, sometimes enslaved again and sometimes free. And so it has been, from that time until ours. But one day, these people know, the dragon will awaken and rouse itself from the sea bed in which it has been lying, and then the fortunes of its people, the Vietnamese, will be full and rich, and they will live in harmony and freedom forever.

Were I a film producer, I would think of producing an animated feature based on this story, but with the addition of some modest T & A and perhaps a score by Moby. Assuming a distribution agreement with Buena Vista, which I'm pretty

---

[*] David Lange is Professor of Law, Duke University School of Law, at Durham, North Carolina.

sure I could wangle if I didn't let the T & A get out of hand (so to speak), and given a wide domestic and foreign theatrical release, followed by suitable windows in pay per view, an eventual third-stage release in VHS and DVD, and of course by merchandising, I should make a killing. Or as an economist would put it, no doubt more felicitously, I should realize net rents at a rate of return sufficient to justify my investment, taking fully into account certain hypothesized opportunities otherwise foregone. These rents would have justified and induced this production of my latest contribution to the global information economy, which is to say, this cheesy and exploitative movie aimed at the cretinous subteen market and their parents, to whom I would propose to appeal through the now standard device of securing a PG rating for a soft R film.

But what of the Vietnamese and their niggling objections to this profanation of their sacred mythology, should they have any?

If I understand the regimes envisioned by the proponents of new rights for traditional knowledge and folklore, then so long as I am prepared to speak in suitably circuitous and solemn platitudes, and perhaps throw off a point or two on the backside of the deal, aimed more or less in the general direction of Hanoi or someone there, I'm golden.

I'm not underestimating the platitudes. It's a foreign language to a producer like myself: access and distributive justice and horizontal equity; a decent concern for the preservation and perpetuation of the culture of these indigenous peoples. And I do have a question here. Are the Vietnamese indigenous? I suppose so, but then I would have supposed that I am indigenous for that matter, and that can't be right. What exactly lies at the center of this exercise? Do we really mean aboriginal or something like it? And why should someone else's culture, aboriginal or otherwise, be an object of patronage by me? This is beginning to sound like a rewrite of Rousseau. I mean, unless I'm missing something here, we're remaking Lo! The Noble Savage all over again, right? (While I'm at it I probably ought to make a note to reread Edward Said on Orientalism, too. Not that I actually read these days. I'm a producer. But I can have one of my people do that and give me a page.)

So anyway, platitudes I can get someone to handle. It's money that concerns me, which is OK, because everything about traditional knowledge and folklore is really about money, am I right or am I right? The traditional knowledge people might say they're stepping in to bundle up some sixty billion dollars a year in revenues from something or other that's been hanging around unnoticed for the last 60 thousand years or so, and therefore might disappear any minute now if we don't act. I say, it's about time. And let's save folklore while we're at it. When you think about it, what's the percentage in not reaping where someone else has sown? Cut them in for a fair share, sure, maybe – say something on the order of ten percent, distributive justice and all that, and then let's get on with maximizing the wealth. If they haven't done it already themselves, it's time for someone else to step up to the plate. I say Ted Turner is right: lead, follow or get out of the way!

But what if Vietnam doesn't go along with the program? What exactly do we do with a country that has its own ideas about IP regimes? Invade?

If I were not a producer, I would take that question very seriously.

What if I were Vietnamese? Suppose I said I do not want the global community's assistance? What if I imagine I am capable of assisting myself? Suppose I think it insulting to propose solutions on my behalf? What if I conclude that the proposals are not in my interest? Suppose I find them (you should pardon the expression) foreign?

If I were Vietnamese, I imagine I might think all of these things and more. I would not welcome initiatives on my behalf, whether from WIPO or WTO or UNESCO or from Bellagio or from any other group of well-intentioned global planners, including economists and lawyers and academics, not to mention movie producers and other representatives of the IP industries (including in the latter categories today the Trade Representatives of the United States of America).

Now as it happens in fact I have some idea of what the Vietnamese think about these matters. More precisely, I have some idea of what they think publicly, and what they think privately. But I shall leave it to the Vietnamese to speak for themselves should they choose to do so.

For it is just here that my own personal thinking necessarily intervenes. I say necessarily, for I have four rules when it comes to traditional knowledge and folklore, and the first of them is this:

Speak for yourself. It is wildly inappropriate to presume to speak for others. This includes the Vietnamese, who are (as I have indicated) capable of speaking for themselves. They will let you know if they need your help. That isn't likely.

Second, do not presume to define others. This is no better than speaking for them. If you do not propose to speak for them, it will be unnnecessary to know who the "others" are, much less to try to define them. That is all to the good.

Third, do not confuse an impulse to do good with an unconscious wish to do well. As James Michener observed many years ago, the Congregationalist missionaries made this mistake when they came to Hawaii in the eighteen hundreds. Now look at the place. No more missionaries. No more Hawaiians. Nothing but tourists and pineapples all the way down.

Fourth, as Frederick Law Olmstead advised in other circumstances, make no little plans. Make no big ones either. In fact make none at all. What we want here is a failure to communicate. No smarmy platitudes. No slippery analysis. No patronizing intrusion into the sacred precincts of others. Nothing but a finger at our lips. No.

Let the Vietnamese be Vietnamese without our leave or say so. Let us respect borders where there are borders, and let us recognize them equivalently where they do not in fact exist, for the medicine we prescribe here is *sans frontieres*. The Kurds can eat their whey; the Kiowas dispose of whatever interests they may recognize in ancient signs. Respect for the autonomy of others does not oblige us to define them nor to establish them in law, but rather merely to stay our hand when they present themselves.

But I hear you grumbling. What will economists and lawyers and academics do if we are not to meddle? What of the alphabet agencies, the NGOs? What of the MPAA and the RIAA and Pharma, who stand waiting in the wings, with others like them, ready to lend their assistance in distributing equity horizontally or whatever? Above all, what about the revenues? As Senator Everett Dirksen once observed, a billion here, a billion there, and pretty soon you're talking real money. Are we just to leave it lying on the table?

Well not exactly. I propose a kind of horizontal equity of my own. We allow Vietnam to deal with the question of folklore on its own behalf. We remain free to do the same on ours. I can make my movie if I am crass enough to do so, without a license from Hanoi. But Hanoi can refuse to protect it under the IP regimes it is otherwise obliged to establish and enforce. And it can exclude the film from exhibition if it wants.

These are modest rights. Their reservation will not greatly impede the advance of our larger global commerce. Nor do they require ingenuity in their devising. The truth is, until bilateral and multilateral treaties began to intervene, and additional obligations still later came to be advanced as a condition of membership in the WTO, this was the state of the law in Vietnam, and for that matter in China and India and elsewhere throughout a very large portion of the world. Indeed I recognize the essential lack of originality in what I am endorsing here. It is, as my friend and sometime colleague, and onetime student Shakeel Bhatty (now of the WIPO Office of Traditional Knowledge and Folklore), assures me, the position more or less of those indigenous peoples who have opposed these initiatives for a very long while. I acknowledge the antecedents to my position here, and accept them altogether cheerfully. Indeed I revel in them. For this is the very outcome I would have wanted, the very point I mean to make. Who am I to improve upon the wishes in the matter of those who are most affected?

No less so, who are we? The late (and I have no doubt now sainted) Senator Daniel Patrick Moynihan once proposed the practice of benign neglect in a rather distant setting. Whether he was right on that occasion I need not consider here. It is enough to borrow the thought.

The case for benign neglect in the matter of traditional knowledge and folklore is simple and straightforward. Its essential power lies along the axis of respect for the autonomy of others that we profess in settings of this sort.

It is right and just to stay our hands when traditional knowledge and folklore are at issue. Against this course of action, all others seem naive, ill-considered, disingenuous or worse. There is no middle ground. We cannot act to save the interests that we value without intrusion. We cannot intrude without destroying the very essence of the things that make them valuable.

We would be well advised to act by not acting. We should let sleeping dragons lie.

21

Protecting cultural industries to promote cultural diversity: Dilemmas for international policymaking posed by the recognition of traditional knowledge

ROSEMARY J. COOMBE[*]

I. An anthropological view of traditional knowledge
II. The intellectual property conundrum
III. Cross-cultural relations and respect for religious diversity
IV. Respecting the holistic nature of traditional knowledge
V. Political dimensions
VI. Human rights, cultural diversity, and public goods

While the contributors to this section of the volume were invited to assess the suitability of intellectual property rights for traditional knowledge and cultural industries, none of the other contributors specifically examines the relationship between proposed rights and industries of a cultural nature.[1] I will suggest that it is precisely this relationship that needs to be considered and that the policy issues posed by considerations of cultural identity and cultural diversity are likely to be the most difficult ones to engage in ongoing international negotiations with respect to cultural forms, forms of property, norms of expression and the optimal range of public goods.

I. An anthropological view of traditional knowledge

The term "traditional knowledge" is most often used to refer to knowledge, innovations, and practices relevant to the preservation of biological diversity,

---

[*] Rosemary J. Coombe is Canada Research Chair in Law, Communication and Culture at York University.
[1] The Frankfurt School tradition of critical theory coined the term "The Cultural Industry" to refer to industries of mass culture. My use of the term cultural industries is not a pluralization of that term (now supplanted by the concept of the entertainment industry), but rather an acknowledgment of the cultural dimensions of human industry and the desire to create new opportunities for those who understand their efforts in cultural terms and seek acknowledgment for and benefit from the value of these efforts to human sustainable development.

pursuant to the Convention on Biological Diversity,[2] which may include knowledge concerning agricultural and medicinal techniques as well as forms of animal and landscape management. The terms indigenous knowledge, tribal knowledge, farmers' knowledge, rural knowledge and folk knowledge are also widely used. The coupling of traditional knowledge with folklore by the World Intellectual Property Organization (WIPO) in its Intergovernmental Committee on Intellectual Property and Genetic Resources, Traditional Knowledge, and Folklore has encouraged intellectual property scholars to use the term more loosely so as to include other forms of collectively held cultural goods. Most recently, the term "traditional cultural expressions" has been adopted by WIPO as a synonym for "expressions of folklore" because the latter was considered to have negative connotations by many communities for whom it implied antiquated knowledge. Nonetheless, the cultural dimensions of traditional knowledge are often avoided in legal and economic considerations of the issue, and the importance of cultural issues in emerging struggles for social justice is even more rarely appreciated.[3]

Traditional knowledge is clearly social, innovative, dynamic and often tacit in nature. It is often uncodified or codified in forms that may be culturally specific and difficult to access. Recognizing its value may require new forms of intellectual and political discourse. As the Assistant Director-General for Natural Sciences at the United Nations Educational, Scientific, and Cultural Organization (UNESCO) observed, there is a tendency in the Western world to reduce indigenous knowledge to those elements judged of most interest to science, which is regarded as a rational, objective and culture-free activity.[4] Western scientists believe that the rational and irrational are easily separated and that fact can be distinguished from fiction, or truth from superstition.

Philosophers, historians, and cultural studies theorists have shown us, however, that science has developed and continues to work through very specific cultural practices that are neither universal nor sufficient to meet the challenges we face in the twenty-first century. Because traditional knowledge may encode very sophisticated information about ecology, medicine, agriculture and animal care and behavior, judging it from the purely rationalistic

---

[2] Convention on Biological Diversity (CBD), 5 June 1992, 31 I.L.M. 818 (1993), *available at* http://www.biodiv.org/convention/articles.asp (last accessed 28 July 2004).

[3] For considerations of the role of traditional knowledge in new social movements that are difficult to classify using modern European rights categories (social, economic, cultural, political or civil), see Rosemary J. Coombe, *Protecting Traditional Environmental Knowledge and New Social Movements in the Americas: Intellectual Property, Human Right or Rights to an Alternative Form of Sustainable Development?*, 17 FLA. J. INTL. L. REV. (forthcoming 2005).

[4] Walter Erdelen, Linking Traditional and Scientific Knowledge for Sustainable Development, Opening Address at the World Summit on Sustainable Development (29 Aug. 2002), *available at* http://portal.unesco.org.

perspective of Western science alone is not only ethnocentric, it also fails to recognize its efficacy and import for human developmental objectives.

Anthropological scholarship provides ample evidence of the validity and value of such knowledge and suggests that the very Western definition of "science" creates narrow and inappropriately ethnocentric boundaries around the knowledge relevant to sustainable development. "Do Cree hunters practice science?" Colin Scott asks.[5] If by science we mean "a social activity that draws deductive inferences from first premises, that these inferences are deliberately and systematically verified in relation to experience, and that models of the world are reflexively adjusted to conform to observed regularities in the course of events, then yes, Cree hunters practice science – as surely all human societies do."[6] If however, we need to restrict science by recourse to Western metaphors that oppose nature to mind and eliminate any cultural or spiritual elements, then we narrow the field considerably. As Carlos Correa suggests with respect to traditional medicine, methods of diagnosis and treatment are strongly influenced by cultural values; they may not *translate* without an understanding of the social and spiritual context in which they are performed and may become ineffective when applied in radically different contexts.[7]

Some processes "work" only when ritually administered. In her excellent study of traditional medicine in Zimbabwe, anthropologist Chloe Frommer shows that it involves cultural practices central to a social and symbolic system that links individuals, families and communities in ongoing relationships.[8] Their "protection," she suggests, will involve the "protection" of ways of life. Although this knowledge can be and is used in non-customary ways, especially by those healers who have held themselves out as a trade union of experts, its abstraction from particularized experiences in local villages may disable its continuing evolution and growth as a dynamic system.

The growing international recognition of this knowledge may afford new opportunities for practitioners, but the growing global emphasis on empirical pharmacology may overemphasize technical expertise without providing any protection for the social and ritual matrix in which healers have the most power and in which the most effective innovations in traditional medicine emerge. This is one of the reasons that many customary healers object to the use of

---

[5] Colin Scott, *Science for the West, Myth for the Rest? The Case of James Bay Cree Knowledge Construction*, in NAKED SCIENCE: ANTHROPOLOGICAL INQUIRIES INTO BOUNDARIES, POWER, AND KNOWLEDGE 69, 69 (Laura Nader ed., 1996).

[6] *Id.*

[7] Carlos Correa, *Protection and Promotion of Traditional Medicine: Implications for Public Health in Developing Countries* (South Centre 2002), *at* http://www.southcentre.org/publications/traditionalmedicine/toc.htm (last visited 3 June 2003). *See also* Antony Taubman, *Saving the Village: Conserving Jurisprudential Diversity in the International Protection of Traditional Knowledge* [this volume].

[8] Chloe Frommer, *The Cultural Right to Practice Traditional Medicinal Knowledge in Zimbabwe*, *at* https://upload.mcgill.ca/cdas/frommer.pdf (last visited 3 Jun. 2003).

databases. Although more widely known practices and plant sources may be archived as public domain material that would ideally serve as prior art in patent searches, the most significant knowledge cannot be codified or made static and retain all its social, physical, and psychological effects.[9] Perhaps this is less true of local agricultural knowledge, which although held in culturally specific ways, is often, if not always, combined with more "scientific" forms of knowledge in hybrid forms.[10] In any case, there appear to be fewer objections to the creation of databases that accumulate agricultural knowledge.

II. The intellectual property conundrum

Intellectual property scholars might be tempted simply to ignore such knowledge as necessarily falling outside their purview. After all, most intellectual property regimes operate under the assumption that protected technologies and creative works may be known and available for use through standard forms of publication that do not require any particular channels of communication beyond those necessary to achieve an arms-length commercial licensing transaction or to support an appeal to an administrative licensing body. Acquiring traditional knowledge, however, may require rather different forms of social relationship that involve trust, collaboration, and possibly even apprenticeship. Indeed, one of the byproducts of the ongoing negotiations around the protection of traditional knowledge under the Convention of Biological Diversity has been the emergence of cross-cultural exchanges between traditional knowledge practitioners in different indigenous communities.

If Cree and Mayan healers visit each others' territories in Quebec and Mexico to share their practical knowledge and insight, it is because they know that this knowledge cannot be conveyed abstractly, but involves local interpretation and perception. These powers of healing may be locally understood as ancestral gifts, but traditional lore that is individually inherited by consecrated authorities may still be shared with those who show respect for the cultural context of their significance. This kind of sharing requires forms of respect that our intellectual property laws, with the possible exception of moral rights traditions, do little to encourage.

To the extent that trade secret protection relies upon relationships of confidentiality that are often akin to fiduciary obligations, it does hold some

---

[9] *Id.*

[10] For an extended discussion, see AKHIL GUPTA, POSTCOLONIAL DEVELOPMENTS: AGRICULTURE AND THE MAKING OF MODERN INDIA (Duke University Press 1998). Similar arguments about the necessary hybridization of traditional agricultural knowledge are made by Arun Agrawal in *Dismantling the Divide Between Indigenous and Scientific Knowledge*, 26 DEV. & CHANGE 413 (1995), and *Indigenous Knowledge and Scientific Knowledge: Some Critical Comments*, 3(3) INDIGENOUS KNOWLEDGE AND DEV. MONITOR (1995), *available at* http://www.nuffic.nl/ciran/ikdm/3-3/articles/agrawal.html.

promise for modeling rights to account for the value of traditional knowledge, provided that the value to be protected is recognized as more than simply commercial. The TRIPS Agreement also requires that, in the course of repressing unfair competition, members of the WTO must protect "undisclosed information" against unlawful acquisition,[11] which would reasonably include breaches of trust and confidentiality and arguably might provide a greater scope of protection than the common law doctrine of trade secrets. This form of protection is being modified for use by local communities with respect to the sharing of information registered in traditional knowledge databases.[12]

We should more generally consider how intellectual property rights could be shaped to promote the sharing of traditional knowledge and practices in a fashion that respects those who hold it. Indeed, the recent proliferation of aboriginal networks and international communities of shamans and healers communicating through new information technologies suggests that a cross-cultural commons is in fact developing. As I have argued extensively elsewhere, however, when it comes to traditional knowledge, the goal of providing and protecting public goods cannot be met by simply assuming their position in a singular public domain, particularly if that public domain is considered merely a source of resources free for general appropriation.[13] Multiple public domains that serve a number of distinct "publics" may be more appropriate.

Proposals for the protection of cultural forms have a tendency to annoy or provoke many American intellectual property scholars, who associate progressive positions on most copyright and trademark issues with the principle of fair use and the First Amendment. From an international perspective, however, freedom of expression is only one of a number of important human rights, and individual rights must be balanced with collective social and cultural rights. This appears to be recognized by many jurisdictions with significant indigenous populations. For example, in Australia, amendments scheduled to be introduced into Parliament in 2004 would enable indigenous communities to

---

[11] Agreement on Trade-Related Aspects of Intellectual Property Rights, 15 Apr. 1994, Marrakesh Agreement Establishing the World Trade Organization, Annex IC, LEGAL INSTRUMENTS – RESULTS OF THE URUGUAY ROUND vol. 31, 331 I.L.M. 81 (1994) [hereinafter TRIPS Agreement], art. 39.

[12] One recent endeavor involving indigenous peoples in Ecuador uses a trade secret model to protect traditional knowledge in closely held databases. It is discussed in Graham Dutfield, *TRIPS-Related Aspects of Traditional Knowledge*, 33 CASE W. RES. J. INT'L L. 233, 264–65 (2001). Similar initiatives are underway in Peru and in India (Personal communication from Alejandro Argumedo, and Anil Gupta at the World Intellectual Property Organization Intergovernmental Committee on Intellectual Property and Genetic Resources, Traditional Knowledge and Folklore, Fourth Session (Dec. 2002)).

[13] Rosemary J. Coombe, *Fear, Hope and Longing for the Future of Authorship and a Revitalized Public Domain in Global Regimes of Intellectual Property*, 52 DEPAUL L. REV. 1171 (2003).

take legal action to protect against inappropriate, derogatory or culturally insensitive use of copyright material.[14] As a collective moral right, this provision would provide communities with "legal standing to safeguard the integrity of creative works embodying traditional community knowledge and wisdom."[15] The legislation is designed to enable users of protected works to identify those works to which the new rights attach and to "facilitate cooperation and respect between artists, authors, film-makers and indigenous communities."[16] The latter objective is significant. These new rights are meant not simply to protect abstract works, but to forge cross-cultural understanding and relationships. Certainly, the proposed law will tend to limit activities in the public domain, if by these we mean totally unconstrained arts of appropriation. There is no way of knowing whether Australians will see fewer culturally hybrid works as a consequence of this need to consult with Aboriginal peoples, but those works that do derive from aboriginal cultural traditions are much less likely to misrepresent them or cause injury to those obliged to protect them.

Although WIPO's Intergovernmental Committee acknowledges that the propriety of relegating traditional knowledge to public domain status remains one of the most controversial areas in formulating policy, they also recognize that a wholly unregulated public domain will not meet the needs of indigenous and local communities.[17] The rights of states and communities to prevent uses that falsely suggest a connection with a cultural community, that are derogatory or offensive, or that make use of sacred or secret knowledge are affirmed.[18]

III. Cross-cultural relations and respect for religious diversity

With respect to environmental traditional knowledge, the benefits of consultation and engagement with indigenous peoples are also becoming evident. Recent research tracking seal migration in Alaska was successful precisely because it combined the traditional hunting knowledge of native peoples with new technologies of satellite tracking. The combination of these culturally distinct forms of knowledge led to the first success in tracking a ringed seal in

---

[14] Minister for Immigration and Multicultural and Indigenous Affairs, Government of Australia, *Indigenous Communities to Get New Protection for Creative Works* (19 May 2003) [hereinafter *New Protection for Creative Works*], *available at* http://www.atsia.gov.90/media/index.htm. The bill was intended for introduction to Parliament in the spring of 2004 but appears to have been postponed. A succinct history of the bill is provided by the Australian Copyright Council, *Article for Australian Intellectual Property Law Bulletin: Indigenous Communal Moral Rights, at* http://www.copyright.org.au/PDF/Articles/A03n24.pdf.

[15] *Id.* [16] *Id.*

[17] Consolidated Analysis of the Legal Protection of Traditional Cultural Expression, WIPO/GRTKF/IC/5/3, at 6 (2 May 2003).

[18] *Id.*

open sea ice. Not only was knowledge about the seal's life history and migration improved for both parties, but the project created "an enhanced trust and mutual respect between scientists and custodians of traditional ecological knowledge."[19] This newfound trust and respect bodes well for the cross-cultural relationships of mutual learning that will be crucial to the larger National Science Foundation (NSF) project of establishing an onshore environmental observatory in the Bering Strait that collects chemical, biological and physical data on the transport of nutrient-rich waters.

Freedom of religion and respect for religious diversity are also principles that must be taken into account when we consider the intersection of intellectual property and traditional knowledge. In many societies a people's religion or, more specifically, the cosmology of a given community encodes information and institutions basic to economy and ecology. Traditional ecological knowledge may involve beliefs that would appear "superstitious" or "primitive" to an outsider. Zapotec science, for instance, is heavily informed by spiritual beliefs but encodes insights that are empirically accurate, sophisticated and pragmatic. Athapaskans and Australian aboriginal traditional knowledge succeeds in enabling hunting and gathering in marginalized environments, and it has become legally obligatory in many jurisdictions to consult with holders of this knowledge in formulating environmental impact assessments. Although it might be more convenient for government decision makers simply to consult a database, in most cases it is recognized that proper regard for the environmental insight encoded by traditional knowledge requires consultation with, if not prior informed consent from and benefit-sharing arrangements with those who hold it. Moreover, demands that peoples with oral traditions publish their knowledge for it to be taken into account (as prior art or otherwise) are inherently discriminatory.

As anthropologist Colin Scott notes, the mere presence of aboriginal peoples on environmental co-management boards will not necessarily motivate a cultural hybridization of environmental knowledge and practice. What is required is support for the intensive involvement of aboriginal governments as research partners in all matters of resource extraction, with a view to developing activities that promote long term sustainability of resource bases and that create revenue and benefit-sharing opportunities to maintain economically viable communities within their traditional territories.[20] We need, in other words, to foster cultural industries. Successful instances of

---

[19] Gay Sheffield of the Alaska Department of Fish and Game (ADFG), *quoted in* Press Release, Natural Science Foundation, NSF-Funded Researchers Track Alaska Seal Migration for the First Time (29 Oct. 2001), *at* http://www.nsf.gov/od/lpa/news/press/01/pr0186.htm.

[20] Colin H. Scott, Institute of Intergovernmental Relations Conference, Co-management and the Politics of Aboriginal Consent to Resource Development (1 Nov. 2002), *at* http://www.iigr.ca/conferences/archive/pdfs3/Colin_Scott.pdf (1 Nov. 2002).

environmental management may also involve respect for and deference to customary legal norms. Recognition of customary legal norms regarding traditional knowledge is acknowledged by the WIPO Intergovernmental Committee and is, from my perspective, one of the most important aspects of the proposals made by Antony Taubman in this volume.[21]

IV. Respecting the holistic nature of traditional knowledge

To divorce "science" from "religion" and to tear away the "cosmological" or spiritual gloss from an allegedly "practical" core will undermine many forms of traditional knowledge, because these may be part of more integrated systems of understanding. The holistic nature of indigenous worldviews can certainly be exaggerated, but the wholesale dismissal of this possibility under the guise of rejecting "romanticism" represents more an anxiety on the part of Western scholars than the results of empirical inquiry (and shows a remarkable ignorance about Romanticism itself). If, for instance, certain Mexican plants, which Western science regards as belonging to the same species, turn out to possess very different biochemical properties that are indicated by indigenous categorical systems and local knowledge,[22] then dominant scientific paradigms obscure potentially important forms of variability that constitute the biological diversity we seek to protect. As various studies commissioned by the United Nations suggest, when we lose languages and the cultural categorical systems they encode, we also lose points of entry into new forms of diversity that no single language or terminology can encompass.[23]

These other, more holistic forms of "human ecology" are known by people living in particular environments. Instead of merely conceding that their knowledge is valuable, we should consider means to respect their lives and expertise and support their livelihoods. This is why *in situ* rather than *ex situ* forms of preserving biological diversity have been given priority in international negotiations with respect to implementing the CBD's provisions on protecting and maintaining traditional knowledge, and an "ecosystem approach" is favored.[24] One of the more compelling arguments made against any form of "protection" for traditional knowledge that abstracts it from the

---

[21] Taubman, above n. 7.
[22] *See* CORI HAYDEN, WHEN NATURE GOES PUBLIC: THE MAKING AND UNMAKING OF BIOPROSPECTING IN MEXICO (Princeton University Press 2003).
[23] *See* the studies collected in CULTURAL AND SPIRITUAL VALUES OF BIODIVERSITY: A COMPLEMENTARY CONTRIBUTION TO THE GLOBAL BIODIVERSITY ASSESSMENT (Darrell Addison Posey ed., Intermediate Technology Publications 1999) (Published for and on behalf of United National Environment Programme, Nairobi (1999)).
[24] CBD, above n. 2, art. 8. For a list of considerations, guidance to the Parties and related references see items collected *at* www.biodiv.org.convention/articles.asp?a=cbd-08&inf=1#inf.

lifeworlds of those who hold it was expressed by the agricultural economist, Arun Agrawal:

> If the primary motive for highlighting the knowledge of the marginalized poor is to find them a greater voice in development, then it would seem preferable to foreground this objective, rather than framing it in terms of the confounding rhetoric of indigenous vs. Western/scientific knowledge. If indigenous knowledge systems are disappearing, it is primarily because the pressures of modernization and cultural homogenization, under the auspices of the modern nation-state and the international trade system, threaten the lifestyles, practices and cultures of nomadic populations, small agricultural producers and indigenous peoples. The appropriate response from those who are interested in preserving the diversity of different knowledge systems, might then lie in attempting to reorient and reverse state policies to permit members of threatened populations to determine their own future, thus facilitating *in situ* preservation of indigenous knowledge. *In situ* preservation cannot succeed unless indigenous populations and local communities gain control over the use of the lands on which they dwell and the resources on which they rely. Those who are seen to possess knowledge must also possess the right to decide on how to conserve their knowledge, and how and by whom it will be used.[25]

Such an approach would undoubtedly be more costly for outsiders, and the political and ethical challenges we face in creating the mechanics for implementing it are daunting. Still, it is preferable to *ex situ* forms of protection, which are more likely to freeze knowledge in its current forms than promote ongoing innovation within and across traditions and are more likely to provide opportunities only to those who are socially connected to powerful external actors.

At the World Conference on Science, organized by UNESCO in cooperation with the International Council for Science in 1999, a set of recommendations was addressed to governments, non-governmental organizations (NGOs), and international organizations. It advised them to "sustain traditional knowledge systems through active support to the societies that are keepers and developers of this knowledge, their ways of life, their languages, their social organization and the environments in which they live, and fully recognize the contribution of women as repositories of a large part of traditional knowledge."[26]

Peter Drahos has suggested that "other-regarding preferences can only be taken up by unpredictable alliances amongst unknown actors."[27] The movement to protect traditional knowledge is not limited to indigenous peoples, nor is the identity of actors recognized as "indigenous" static in nature. On the contrary, the identities of actors deemed to be indigenous or of communities recognized as local and embodying traditional lifestyles are emergent. As

---

[25] Arun Agrawal, *Indigenous and Scientific Knowledge*, above n. 10.
[26] Erdelen, above n. 4.   [27] Peter Drahos, *The Regulation of Public Goods* [this volume].

Benedict Kingsbury has exhaustively documented, there is no singular definition of indigenous peoples under international law, and it is increasingly accepted as a norm of customary law that indigenous peoples identify themselves.[28]

V. Political dimensions

Increasingly, groups of healers, tribal peoples, and farmers, many of whom are women, are organizing to assert rights with respect to their knowledge, practices, and livelihoods. Political and legal anthropologists have long understood that people's and peoples' identities do not exist "before the law," but that identities are shaped in relation to legal regimes that accomplish new forms of interpellation. In the short term, this trend is likely to create conditions of uncertainty and potential for conflict. Any new forms of collective rights will undoubtedly produce political effects in situations where community identities are undefined. Anthropologist Shane Green's study of the local struggle over benefit-sharing provisions in the International Cooperative Biodiversity Group (ICBG) bioprospecting agreements with "the Aguaruna" in Peru is illustrative.[29] These approximately 240 communities "are at the forefront of Amazonian indigenous political organizing" and are affiliated with local organizations and panindigenous organizations advocating at national and international levels. Nevertheless, the formulation of a "know-how license" with universities and a pharmaceutical company to share benefits from a collection of plant genetic resources and related knowledge created a crisis in terms of the legitimate location of political authority and representation.[30]

Anthropologist Cori Hayden recounts similar struggles over bioprospecting in Mexico with respect to the role of "local communities" and the legitimacy of "community" consent to the collection of plant resources and traditional medicinal knowledge under two other ICBG agreements.[31] Ironically, whereas the Peruvian instance gave rise to unrealistic expectations of future wealth on the part of the indigenous groups involved, the Mexican crisis resulted in a situation where scientists involved in one project went out of their way to avoid dealing with local communities – picking up plants from the sides of roads or purchasing them dried in public markets so as to avoid any issues of distributional ethics. The Chiapas-based project, however, gave rise to an international

---

[28] Benedict Kingsbury, *Indigenous Peoples in International Law: A Constructivist Approach to the Asian Controversy*, 92 AM. J. INT'L L. 414 (1998).
[29] Shane Green, *Intellectual Property, Resources, or Territory? Reframing the Debate over Indigenous Rights, Traditional Knowledge, and Pharmeceutical Bioprospection*, in TRUTH CLAIMS AND HUMAN RIGHTS 229, 232 (M.P. Bradley & P. Petro eds., 2002). *See also* Shane Green, *Indigenous People Incorporated? Culture as Politics, Culture as Property in Pharmaceutical Bioprospecting*, 45 CURRENT ANTHROPOLOGY 211 (2004).
[30] *Id.*   [31] HAYDEN, above n. 22.

controversy about the ethics of "biopiracy" so widely-publicized and so rancorous that an expensive and time-consuming research project involving the collection of Mayan medicinal knowledge was eventually cancelled with great bitterness and recrimination.

Still, it is important to keep in mind that these controversies arose precisely because the peoples involved had no rights and were therefore contracting in a political and legal vacuum. Without state or international recognition of them as having juridical identities, contracts involving "local or indigenous communities" may well invite political opportunism from many quarters. We should not underestimate the role of international NGOs in these disputes, who may polemically politicize these issues for their own publicity purposes.

Anthropological work suggests that those villages enmeshed in social networks that link them to national and international NGOs may in fact be in the best position to represent themselves as "local" communities, to characterize their knowledge as "traditional," and to defend their identity as "indigenous" in parts of the world where peoples who rely upon subsistence economies are marginalized or under pressures to assimilate.[32] However, here again we need to understand that these pressures and accompanying inequities emerge in situations where states have recognized no rights and peoples are compelled to appeal to international NGOs for protection from incursions into their territories that threaten their traditional subsistence resources and practices.

However daunting the political challenges ahead of us, it is both rather late and rather patronizing to assume, as David Lange appears to do,[33] that indigenous, tribal, rural, or local "others" are indifferent to investments in, and benefits from, the new recognition afforded by emerging international legal regimes. The claim that "we" should just leave "them" alone is simply a recipe for the continuing loss of languages, livelihoods, and the resources and knowledge that the world's poor rely upon for more than eighty-five percent of their food, fuel, shelter and medicine.[34] It is also a recipe for undermining the continued survival of modern medicine and agriculture, which are crucially dependent on the genetic resources produced with the knowledge held by the world's poor.

The global project of compensating people for the contributions of their cultural industries to global agriculture, medicine, and environmental

---

[32] Tania Murray Li, *Articulating Indigenous Identity in Indonesia: Resource Politics and the "Tribal Slot"*, 42 COMP. STUD. SOC'Y & HIST. 149 (2000). *See also* the various studies collected in TANIA MURRAY LI, TRANSFORMING THE INDONESIAN UPLANDS: MARGINALITY, POWER AND PRODUCTION (Harwood Academic Publishers 1999).

[33] David Lange, Comment: *Traditional Knowledge, Folklore, and the Case for Benign Neglect* [this volume].

[34] For an extensive discussion of the importance of traditional knowledge relating to biological resources both to the world's most vulnerable peoples and to "modern" industries, *see* Rosemary J. Coombe, *The Recognition of Indigenous Peoples' and Community Traditional Knowledge in International Law*, 14 ST. THOMAS L. REV. 275 (2001).

sustainability is not just something externally imposed upon them, but a struggle in which they are centrally involved. Having had the privilege of sitting in on the Indigenous Working Group sessions during several CBD meetings, I can attest to the keen desire of many representatives of indigenous, forest-dwelling, rural, and farming peoples (as well as traditional medicinal practitioners and women's alliances) to forge new forms of economic opportunity and recognition for their peoples that would revitalize and enable them to maintain their traditional cultural identities.

Nonetheless, there remains great uncertainty about the appropriate means for accomplishing this goal and a continuing distrust of intellectual property protection (which many see primarily as a means for corporate expropriation and capital accumulation).[35] The WIPO secretariat is aware of these tensions and has recognized that it must reach out to new beneficiaries and provide them with some stake in the intellectual property system if they are to hold it in any esteem.

Many environmental, indigenous, farmers, and women's groups, as well as food activists and health practitioners, are committed to seeing intellectual property regimes change to prevent practices – described as "biopiracy" by some and irresponsible granting of patents by others – as well as the patenting of genetic resources, genetically modified organisms, and technologies that limit plant reproduction. Thousands of Indian villagers collectively organized more than a decade ago to oppose the patenting of seeds. Hundreds of thousands more are now engaged in the project of creating databases of their own knowledge and looking for means to use it to leverage themselves out of poverty. Such intellectual property issues motivated many grassroots political struggles long before they appeared on the scholarly agendas of intellectual property professors in the developed countries. Rather than imposing an agenda upon them, I would suggest that "we" are only beginning to learn from them what the salient issues are, and an ongoing dialogue with the participants in this struggle is in order before "we" leap to judgment about what "they" require.[36]

---

[35] Scholars are similarly divided. *Compare, e.g.,* Taubman, above n. 7 (expressing reservations about the application of IP regimes to TK) *with* Thomas Cottier & Marion Panizzon, *Legal Perspectives on Traditional Knowledge: The Case for Intellectual Property Protection* [this volume] (strongly advocating IP protection).

[36] The continuing exclusion of NGOs representing indigenous peoples and local communities embodying traditional lifestyles from academic conferences addressing traditional knowledge is indicative of this refusal to engage with, or to show respect for, those who hold this knowledge. Even when the rationale for limiting participation is that the conference is academic, the indigenous and Third World academic authorities who actually participate in these international legal deliberations are not invited to represent the participants in these global negotiations.

VI. Human rights, cultural diversity, and public goods

There appears to be some consensus that intellectual property and trade-related intellectual property regimes will need to be transformed to prevent expropriations of traditional knowledge and genetic resources and appropriations of cultural heritage. They will also need to operate more transparently within an expanded global institutional framework to which they are accountable. Similarly, the exercise of intellectual property rights by private actors should be monitored to ensure that other, more fundamental rights are not being violated. Peter Drahos rightly asserts that any new intellectual property "solutions" must be tied to global norms.[37] The only global normative framework that currently has sufficient legitimacy to command the allegiance of the diverse political actors engaged in this dispute is that provided by international human rights, although their consideration has been negligible in discussions of the issue in the United States.

Both the activities of the WTO and the interpretation of the TRIPS Agreement are subject to international human rights law. Intellectual property rights are cultural rights within the international human rights framework.[38] As such, they are integrally related to other recognized human needs bearing on cultural expression, the maintenance of cultural diversity, the protection of cultural heritage, and the right to participate in cultural life of the arts and sciences in culturally specific ways.[39]

New intellectual property rights are, as Thomas Cottier and Marion Panizzon point out, insufficient unless tied to public policy strategies,[40] and the desire to support cultural traditions and maintain cultural diversity is certainly emerging as an important issue of international public policy.

---

[37] Drahos, above n. 27.
[38] Rosemary J. Coombe, *Intellectual Property, Human Rights, and Sovereignty: New Dilemmas in International Law Posed by the Recognition of Indigenous Knowledge and the Conservation of Biodiversity*, 6 IND. J. GLOBAL LEGAL STUD. 59 (1998).
[39] There is now a large body of literature suggesting that cultural and religious rights in international human rights law conflict with women's rights. Although I cannot engage with these arguments in the space afforded to me here, I direct the reader to Modhavi Sunder, *Piercing the Veil*, 112 YALE L.J. 1399 (2003) for an overview of these debates. Like Sunder, I believe that cultural communities are evolving and that people have desires both to maintain cultural traditions and to strive for new forms of equality and justice within those traditions. Based on observation of negotiations at Convention on Biological Diversity and WIPO Intergovernmental Committee meetings, it would appear that the commitment to finding means of protecting traditional knowledge is widely understood to provide new forms of positive recognition and compensation for the work that women do and new forms of self-esteem and economic opportunity for youth. Unlike many critical legal scholars, I do not believe it is possible to adopt any single position on the evocation of culture in international law, given the range of contexts in which it figures and the number and complexity of the political issues thereby invoked.
[40] Cottier and Panizzon, above n. 35.

As I have argued elsewhere, the growing concern with "cultural" issues and the designation of issues as "cultural" in nature, is integrally linked with globalization and the growing hegemony of informational capital.[41] These concerns, however, are not limited to indigenous peoples, rural peoples, or isolated communities. An extensive civil society network of creators, artists, and cultural industries, together with government ministers from fifty-three states, is committed to the creation of a legally binding Instrument of Cultural Diversity that builds on prior work done by the Council of Europe.[42]

Insisting that monocultures are as dangerous to democracy as they are to agriculture, this movement recognizes cultural diversity as a public good that promotes social cohesion and economic development. The adoption by acclamation of the UNESCO Universal Declaration on Cultural Diversity in November 2001,[43] and the recent release of a Preliminary Draft of a Convention on the Protection of the Diversity of Cultural Contents and Artistic Expression,[44] following the adoption, signature and registration of the International Convention for the Safeguarding of Intangible Cultural Heritage[45] as a legal Convention in November 2003, indicates that there is strong international support for the proposition that states have a legitimate right to promote and maintain a favorable environment for the creation and expression of diverse forms of culture through the formulation of cultural policies. Culture itself is understood as an important resource for human development.

Cultural diversity presupposes the existence of a process of exchanges that is open to renewal and innovation but also committed to tradition, and does not aim at the preservation of a static set of behaviors, values and expressions. It is a concept premised on the belief that different forms of inspiration are generated from within distinctive cultural heritages and that their maintenance as sources for ongoing creativity constitutes a public good. Indigenous peoples are given special priority because their thousands of

---

[41] Rosemary J. Coombe, *Works in Progress: Traditional Knowledge, Biological Diversity and Intellectual Property in a Neoliberal Era*, in GLOBALIZATION UNDER CONSTRUCTION: GOVERNMENTALITY, LAW AND IDENTITY 273 (Richard W. Perry & William Maurer eds., 2003). *See also* Rosemary J. Coombe, *Legal Claims to Culture in and Against the Market: Neoliberalism and the Global Proliferation of Meaningful Difference*, 1 L. CULTURE & HUMAN. (forthcoming 2005).

[42] *See* Ivan Bernier, *A New International Instrument on Cultural Diversity: Questions and Answers*, at http://www.incd.net/html/english/conf/bernier.htm (22 Sept. 2001); The Honorable Sheila Copps, Minister of Canadian Heritage, Closing Remarks at the Second International Meetings of Professional Cultural Organizations (4 Feb. 2003).

[43] *At* http://www.unesco.org/culturelink/review.

[44] UNESCO, CLT/CPD/2004/CONF-201/2 *at* http://unesdoc.unesco.org/images/0013/001356/135649e.pdf.

[45] *Available at* http://portal.unesco.org/en.

languages are understood to represent most of the world's remaining linguistic diversity.[46]

These initiatives are motivated by the belief that globalization and trade liberalization are undermining cultural diversity and that the strategy of carving out cultural exemptions in trade agreements is less than effective.[47] Rather than continuing to assert rights to protect cultural traditions defensively, the states involved seek to positively affirm cultural diversity among and within nation-states as a valued social good. Cultural goods, as vectors of identity, value and meaning should not be understood merely as commodities or consumer goods. In a country such as Canada, for instance, where over fifty-five percent of the population come from national backgrounds that are neither British nor Quebecois (and where, by the year 2006, forty-three percent of the population will have origins that are not aboriginal, French or English[48]), it is essential that publicly available cultural forms represent the society's true diversity.

Given a small population size, markets alone will not provide this variety. A culturally pluralistic public sphere requires a range of cultural expression and a space for cultural choices and expressive opportunities beyond those inherent in the consumption of standardized goods sold by multinational corporations. Internationally, better relations between states and among communities will require the development of institutions to promote cross-cultural dialogue, exchange, and fertilization.

When we talk about protecting the cultural commons as a public good, we need to think about what content we wish to maintain there. In addition to requiring "sustainable access" to cultural goods, we also need to consider models for the sustainable production of culturally diverse content. Traditional cultures, although (and perhaps because) they do not exist in isolation and are inevitably hybridized with forms of modernity provide the basis for forms of creativity and innovation necessary for sustainable economic development for many of the world's peoples. Different forms of creativity are nurtured within different cultural traditions and nonmarket institutions will be necessary to promote and nurture culturally diverse innovations and creative works and to promote their dissemination. As the WIPO Intergovernmental Committee acknowledges:

---

[46] Anthropologists and linguists are divided about the validity of claiming linguistic "loss," and the equation of this with cultural "loss," which is itself a problematic concept. Nonetheless, these concepts appear to have been widely embraced by policy-makers for whom they sufficiently capture or describe processes of undesirable change that inflict great social and economic costs for communities and nation states. For a discussion, see Stuart Kirsch, *Lost Worlds: Environmental Disaster, "Culture Loss," and the Law*, 42 CURRENT ANTHROPOLOGY 167 (2001).

[47] For elaboration, see Bernier, above n. 42; Ivan Bernier, *Preserving and Promoting Cultural Diversity: Necessity and Prospects for Action*, at http://www.cdc-ccd.org/Anglais/Liensenanglais/events/meeting/text_bernier_eng.html (last visited 4 June 2003).

[48] Copps, above n. 42.

> Challenges of multiculturalism and cultural diversity, particularly in societies with both indigenous and immigrant communities, require cultural policies that maintain a balance between the protection and preservation of cultural expressions – traditional or otherwise – and the free exchange of cultural experiences. Mediating between the preservation of cultural heritage and cultural distinctiveness on the one hand, and nurturing and nourishing of "living" culture as a source of creativity and development on the other, is another challenge.[49]

There are many challenges before us. If, as Carol Rose suggests, "seeing property is an act of imagination,"[50] then the protection of traditional knowledge, and the inclusion of cultural industries reflecting a fuller range of the world's peoples will require cultural industry of another sort – the effort to transcend the cultural limitations through which we imagine intellectual property.

---

[49] Consolidated Analysis of the Legal Protection of Traditional Cultural Expression, above n. 17, at 2.

[50] CAROL ROSE, PROPERTY AND PERSUASION: ESSAYS ON THE HISTORY, THEORY AND RHETORIC OF OWNERSHIP 296 (Westview Press 1994).

PART IV

Reform and regulation issues

SECTION 1
Balancing public and private interests in the global intellectual property system

22

Issues posed by a world patent system

JOHN H. BARTON*

Abstract
Introduction
I. Substantive principles for an international patent
   A. International integration of the patent granting function
   B. Standards for granting a patent
II. Substantive issues for international patent enforcement
   A. Infringement and defenses
   B. Exhaustion and parallel trade
III. Institutional issues
   A. Language
   B. Patent granting institutions and appeal process
   C. Litigation and appeal
   D. Supervision
   E. Financial and international political issues

ABSTRACT

There is a strong drive toward a world patent system, but such a system may pose special problems for the developing world. After reviewing the existing steps toward a global system, this chapter describes the standards appropriate to a reasonable global patent, taking the perspective of the developing nations. It then describes a reasonable international enforcement procedure and the defenses appropriate in that process. It finally explores the institutional, financial, and political issues involved in creating such a global system. Movement to

---

* John H. Barton is George E. Osborne Professor of Law Emeritus, Stanford Law School. I want to thank the participants at the Duke Law School Conference on International Public Goods and Transfer of Technology Under a Globalized Intellectual Property Regime, 4–6 April 2003, especially Peter Gerhart and Samuel Kortum, as well as Paul Goldstein and Richard Wilder, who have read previous versions. Of course, the responsibility for the content is entirely mine. I also want to express my appreciation to Kathryn Judge, who provided highly capable research assistance in preparing this chapter. In particular, she suggested the review process discussed in the last part of the chapter.

an international patent would save money, both by reducing filing fees and by reducing the legal costs of preparing parallel filings.

It is possible to globalize the system in a way that raises the standards needed to obtain a patent. This would be better for the developing world, and industry (as opposed to the intellectual property bar) may actually be pleased with such a development. The alternate pattern, exemplified in the WIPO harmonization negotiations, is to create a system like that of the United States with relatively weak patentability standards and broad subject-matter standards and to harmonize those standards with those of generally like-minded nations and regions. The likely political next step is for the major developed countries to encourage developing nations to sign up to that system. This alternative would be a mistake for the developing nations, and possibly for the developed nations as well.

Introduction

National and international patent systems are coming under severe pressure. Practically every day there are new examples of questionable U.S. patents being granted,[1] patent litigation costs are enormous and have often made the litigation a game of extortion,[2] financial pressures are pushing toward integration of patent granting institutions,[3] and the impact of the patent system on the developing world has been criticized.[4]

This chapter explores a portion of the possible response – an international system using realistic standards. There is a drive toward such a system and it

---

[1] David Streitfeld, *Note: This Headline is Patented*, LOS ANGELES TIMES, 7 Feb. 2003, Part 1, at 1.

[2] *See, e.g.*, Robert Barr, Speech to Federal Trade Commission, Public Hearings on Competition and Intellectual Property Law and Policy in the Knowledge-Based Economy (28 Feb. 2002), *available at* www.ftc.gov/opp/intellect/barrrobert.doc (noting that parties trying to game the current patent system for profit without contributing innovation "benefit from the high cost of litigation by demanding license fees that are less than the cost of litigation, hoping that people will pay even if they don't infringe").

[3] The costs of searching the growing number of patent applications are among the primary reasons for the current substantive harmonization negotiations being conducted under the auspices of the World Intellectual Property Organization. Director General, Agenda For Development of the International Patent System, WIPO Doc. A/36/14WIPO (adopted subject to modification by the WIPO General Assembly, Sept. 2002, *see* A/36/15 §§ 192–219). With substantive harmonization, it would be possible for patent offices to rely on one another not only for searches but also in decisions whether or not to grant a patent. For general background, see James E. Rogan (Director, U.S. Patent and Trademark Office), Global Recognition of Patent Rights, Speech at WIPO Conference on the International Patent System (26 Mar. 2002), *available at* http://patentagenda.wipo.int/meetings/2002/program/index.html#2.

[4] Integrating Intellectual Property Rights and Development Policy (Commission on Intellectual Property Rights 2002) [United Kingdom] [hereinafter Commission Report]; *see also* John H. Barton, *The Economics of TRIPS: International Trade in Information-Intensive Products*, 33 GEO. WASH. INT'L L. REV. 473 (2001).

derives from the developed world – yet, the system may pose special problems for the developing world. The chapter explores ways that these emerging world concerns could be taken into account in world patent integration. After reviewing the existing steps toward such a system, it describes the standards appropriate to a reasonable global patent, taking, as in the rest of the analysis, the perspective of the developing nations. It then describes a reasonable international enforcement procedure and the defenses appropriate in that process. It finally explores the institutional, financial, and political issues involved in creating such a global system.[5]

There are already substantial international harmonization efforts underway. The Convention on the Grant of European Patents[6] (hereinafter EPC) provides for a patent effective in all European nations for which the patent applicant has paid the necessary fee, and there are other regional patent organizations that similarly streamline the issuance process.[7] Realistically, this European patent is not a regional patent but a bundle of national patents, bringing rights in each nation defined by the law of that nation.[8] There are long-standing discussions within Europe on a new system in which there would be a genuine European patent and the patent infringement litigation process would be internationalized.[9]

---

[5] Although they might not agree with all that is said in here, I want to give particularly strong credit to Gerald J. Mossinghof and Vivian S. Ku, who argue for the importance of an international patent in *World Patent System Circa 20XX, AD*, 38 IDEA 529 (1998). For a dissent, see John Duffy, *Patent System Reform: Harmony and Diversity in Global Patent Law*, 17 BERKELEY TECH. L.J. 685 (2002).

[6] 5 Oct. 1973, 13 I.L.M. 276.

[7] *See, e.g.*, Agreement Revising the Bangui Agreement of 2 March 1977 on the Creation of an African Intellectual Property Organization, 24 Feb. 1999 (granting the Organisation Africaine de la Propriété Intellectuelle (OAPI) the power to grant a single patent that is valid in all twelve member nations, which are African nations that had been French colonies); Lusaka Agreement, *adopted* 9 Dec. 1976 (creating the African Regional Industrial Property Organization (ARIPO), which coordinates pre-grant procedures for intellectual property applications in English-speaking African countries); Eurasian Patent Convention, adopted 9 Sept. 1994, *available at* 36 INDUS. PROP. & COPYRIGHT 30 (1997); Free Trade Area of Americas, Ministerial Declaration of Quito (1 Nov. 2002) (recognizing a negotiating group on intellectual property).

[8] Vicenzo Di Cataldo, *From the European Patent to a Community Patent*, 8 COLUM. J. EUR. L. 19, 20 (2002).

[9] There are two parallel negotiations, one within the E.U. and one in the European Patent Office (EPO) context. For the E.U., see Proposal for a Council Regulation on the Community Patent – Text revised by the Presidency, Doc. 8539/03 (16 Apr. 2003); Commission Proposal for a Council Regulation on the Community Patent, 2000 O.J. (C 337) E (COM(2000)412 final); E.U. Commission, Promoting Innovation through Patent: Green Paper on the Community Patent and the Patent System in Europe, COM(97)314. For the EPO, see the Draft European Patent Litigation Agreement (negotiated by a sub-group of the Working Party on Litigation of the Diplomatic Conference of the EPC Contracting States), *available at* http://www.ige.ch/E/jurinfo/j110201.htm. *See generally* Di Cataldo, above n. 8; Hanns Ullrich, *Patent Protection in Europe: Integrating Europe into the Community or the Community into Europe?*, 8 EUR. L.J. 433 (2002).

And there is an ongoing negotiation at the World Intellectual Property Organization (WIPO) to harmonize standards so that the world's leading patent offices (United States Patent and Trademark Office in Alexandria, Virginia, European Patent Office in Munich, Germany, and Japan Patent Office in Yokohama, Japan) can rely more on one another's decisions and thus save resources.[10] These negotiations are of particular significance to the developing nations, for such a treaty may not provide as much flexibility as is available under TRIPS.[11]

Moreover, there is a Patent Cooperation Treaty,[12] which simplifies the processes of filing and searching in a large number of national and regional patent offices, and there is, of course, an effective first step toward harmonization under TRIPS. It is not yet clear whether the WIPO negotiations or the European negotiations will ultimately provide either globally harmonized patent standards or a genuinely international enforcement mechanism (which is much more difficult) – but they are certainly serious efforts and seem more likely to succeed in the next few years than they have in the past.

---

[10] *See* above n. 3; *see also, e.g.,* Japan Patent Office, Examination Cooperation between the United States Patent and Trademark Office (USPTO) and the Japan Patent Office (JPO) §§ 1–2 (Nov. 2002), *available at* http://www.jpo.go.jp/infoe/j-us_sinsakyouryokue.htm (instituting an "experimental near-term bilateral project" between the United States and Japan that "concerns mutual exploitation of search results"). In addition to the numerous bilateral agreements, the U.S., the E.U., and Japan have been engaged in an attempt at trilateral coordination of such efforts since 1983; however, such efforts have yet to come to fruition. Thus, the next step of coordination may be more multilateral, as reflected in the Patent Cooperation Treaty. *See* below n. 12. For example, one of WIPO's current priorities is the creation of WIPONET, "a vehicle for strengthening the relationship between WIPO's constituencies and the Secretariat through [a] global information network that operationally unites the world's intellectual property offices." Vision and Strategic Direction of WIPO, WIPO Doc. A/34/3 (*adopted* 29 Sept. 1999).

[11] TRIPS is the Agreement on Trade-Related Aspects of Intellectual Property Rights, 15 Apr. 1994, Marrakesh Agreement Establishing the World Trade Organization, Annex 1C, LEGAL INSTRUMENTS – RESULT OF THE URUGUAY ROUND vol. 31, 33 I.L.M. 81 (1994). The immediate issues are only those of the standards of patentability, which pose such issues of interest to developing nations as the non-obviousness standard, the coverage or not of software and genomic information, and the possibility or not of requiring a patent applicant to provide information about the origin of biological materials. Future negotiations will consider the enforcement question, which raises such important issues as compulsory licenses.

[12] Patent Cooperation Treaty of 19 June 1970, 26 U.S.T. 7645, T.I.A.S. No. 8733 (put into force in U.S. on 24 Jan. 1978) [hereinafter PCT]. The PCT provides a single filing date, which is particularly valuable for filing in nations using a first-to-file system and it allows for an international search to be conducted that allows the applicant to gauge the likely success of the patent application. This eases part of the administrative burden an applicant who wants to file for protection in multiple jurisdictions must face. *See generally Administrative Instructions Under the Patent Cooperation Treaty,* PCT GAZETTE, 25 June 1998, Sect. IV (outlining the process of filing an international application under the PCT and the rights associated with such a filing).

I. Substantive principles for an international patent

A. *International integration of the patent granting function*

There is little excuse for maintaining parallel national patent systems in a world of international trade. To conduct parallel searches and make parallel patent granting decisions in a variety of jurisdictions is a waste of human resources (and of skills that are particularly scarce in much of the world). One source suggests that it costs between $750,000 and $1,000,000 to obtain worldwide coverage in 1998, and that this number was growing by 10 percent each year.[13]

In contrast, the USPTO charges $750 per application (with certain additional fees in some cases), and returns money to the U.S. Treasury,[14] while in Europe, an applicant filing with the EPO must pay a search fee of 690 Euros, a central filing fee of 125 Euros and an additional 75 Euros for each country designated on the application, in addition to other miscellaneous expenses.[15] The average overall cost of filing a European patent in 1999, including legal representation and translation expenses was 29,800 Euros.[16] And in Japan the basic filing fee for a patent is ¥ 21,000, ¥ 35,000 if the patent is filed in English.[17]

Considering that some 300,000 applications are filed each year in the United States, and conservatively half of those are filed in more than one jurisdiction,[18] the duplication represents an enormous waste, on the order of $150 million just for excess filing fees for filing in two jurisdictions.[19] If more than two jurisdictions are involved and translation and extra legal fees taken into account, the numbers seem likely to rise by at least an order of magnitude and perhaps much more. Such costs for business are an unnecessary tax on innovation. Hence there are strong reasons to move to a single global patent system.

---

[13] Mossinghof & Ku, above n. 5, at 530.
[14] USPTO Fee Schedule, *effective* Jan. 2003, 37 C.F.R. 1.16(a), fee code 1001/2001, *available at* http://www.uspto.gov/web/offices/ac/qs/ope/fee20030101.htm#patapp.
[15] Schedule of fees, costs and prices of the EPO effective as from 3 January 2002 *available at* http://www.european-patent-office.org/epo/fees1.htm.
[16] *See* European Patent Office, Cost of an Average European Patent (1 Jan. 1999). The translation expenditure was the single biggest expense. At 39 percent of the total, the average applicant spent more on translations than they did on legal representation, highlighting the importance of this issue when moving to a global scale.
[17] Japan Patent Office, Schedule of Fees (7 Oct. 2002), *available at* http://www.jpo.go.jp/tetuzuki_e/index.htm.
[18] According to the USPTO's U.S. Patent Statistics, Calendar Years 1963–2001, 326,508 applications were filed in 2001. The breakdown by national origin is not available for that year, but 44.3 percent of the filings were from abroad. Most of the foreign filings were probably paralleled abroad, and some of the U.S. filings were certainly paralleled abroad. Table *available at* http://www.uspto.gov/web/offices/ac/ido/oeip/taf/us_stat.pdf.
[19] These are technically only transfer payments, yet they are also a tax on innovation – probably the worst kind of tax.

The most important counterargument to this point is that the system is not as valuable to the developing world as it is to the developed world, and, in some situations, can positively harm developing nations.[20] The incentives provided by the patent system are much less useful when there are few scientists and engineers available to make inventions – the number of U.S. patent filings from the poorest nations is minuscule.[21] And to the extent that patents raise prices on products (which is how they are intended to create an incentive), the developing world has to pay a premium for its research-based products, just as does the developed world. Considering the lesser ability to pay of the developing world, this is an inequitable allocation of the cost of research.

There are several ways to maintain the transaction-cost benefits of a global patent system and, at the same time, to provide equity for developing nations. One essential step is to ensure that the system uses economically reasonable standards. Patents on non-inventions create a barrier to all, and the standards that are reasonable for the more advanced developing nations are also reasonable for developed nations.[22] A second essential step is to ensure that the developing nations can maintain and use appropriate defensive measures, such as compulsory licensing under proper circumstances.[23] A third is to provide preferential fee arrangements (and perhaps weakened language translation requirements) to those from developing nations and elsewhere who lack resources for filing.[24] Should these measures be thought inadequate, it is possible to make the patent term shorter in developing nations. In any case, it would be wise to exclude at least the least-developed countries[25] from patent coverage altogether. These approaches would give the world the benefit of unification, while limiting the costs of the system to developing nations.

---

[20] *See* Commission Report, above n. 4.
[21] *See* the numbers in USPTO, Number of Patent Applications Filed in the United States by Country of Origin, Calendar Year 1965 to present. For example, during the 1996–2000 period, there were 4 patent applications from Haiti, 1 from Liberia, and none from Malawi or Mali – these are fairly representative numbers. Data *available at* http://www.uspto.gov/web/offices/ac/ido/oeip/taf/appl_yr.pdf.
[22] *See* Commission Report, above n. 4, at 111–36.
[23] *See* TRIPS Agreement, above n. 11, art. 31.
[24] *See, e.g.*, Ullrich, above n. 9, at 471 (referring to applicants unable to pay a larger fee).
[25] The "least developed countries" are the poorest on a list regularly maintained by the United Nations General Assembly, with aid from UN Conference on Trade and Development (UNCTAD), which sets the official qualifications for whether a country is classified as a least developed country. As of 2002, 49 countries met these criteria. The list of which nations qualify is regularly updated by UNCTAD. *See* UNCTAD, The Least Developed Countries, 2002 – Escaping the Poverty Trap (2002).

B. Standards for granting a patent

A patent monopoly is justified only if the monopoly is likely to lead to genuine incentives for research and for bringing new products to market. This means that the traditional patent criteria should be applied,[26] and – in light of experience under the system – that they should be applied in a way much more restrictive of patent monopolies than occurs under the current U.S. system.[27] Thus, patents should be granted only for inventions that are really novel, that are really nonobvious or really have a substantial inventive step, that are really useful or really technological, and that are really enabled.[28]

The non obviousness/inventive step standard is particularly important – it has an extremely low threshold in the United States, and must be significantly higher to avoid harming innovation.[29] Similarly, enablement must be used in defining the scope of the claims of the patent (it is these claims that define the effective monopoly). Claims should not be issued that go beyond what is enabled. Standards for dealing with these various issues are already being discussed in the context of the current WIPO harmonization negotiations.[30]

The scope of patentable subject matter is also extremely important. In light of the growth of information and computer-oriented innovation, and of the

---

[26] Edmund Kitch, *Elementary and Persistent Errors in the Economic Analysis of Intellectual Property*, 53 VAND. L. REV. 1727, 1728 (2000) (noting that despite some real drawbacks, "the intellectual property regimes of the United States, in particular, and of the developed economies are, as a general matter, economically sensible").

[27] *See* Commission Report, above n. 4, at 116–17.

[28] *E.g.*, 35 U.S.C. § 101 (2000) ("Whoever invents or discovers any new and useful process, machine, manufacture, or composition of matter, or any new and useful improvement thereof, may obtain a patent therefor, subject to the conditions and requirements of this title"); 35 U.S.C. § 103(a) (2000) ("A patent may not be obtained though the invention is not identically disclosed or described as set forth in section 102 of this title, if the differences between the subject matter sought to be patented and the prior art are such that the subject matter as a whole would have been obvious at the time the invention was made to a person having ordinary skill in the art to which said subject matter pertains."); 35 U.S.C. § 112 (2000) ("The specification shall contain a written description of the invention, and of the manner and process of making and using it, in such full, clear, concise, and exact terms as to enable any person skilled in the art to which it pertains, or with which it is most nearly connected, to make and use the same, and shall set forth the best mode contemplated by the inventor of carrying out his invention.").

[29] *See* John H. Barton, *Non-Obviousness*, 43 IDEA 471 (2003); John H. Barton, *Reforming the Patent System*, 287 SCIENCE 1933 (2000); Robert Hunt, Nonobviousness and the Incentive to Innovate: An Economic Analysis of Intellectual Property Reform, Federal Reserve Bank of Philadelphia, Working Paper No. 99–3 (Mar. 1999), *at* http://www.ftc.gov/os/comments/intelpropertycomments/.

[30] *See, e.g.*, Requirements Concerning the Relationship of the Claims to the Disclosure, WIPO Standing Committee on the Law of Patents, 7th Sess. (Geneva, 6–10 May 2001), SCP/7/6 (2 Apr. 2002), *available at* http://www.wipo.org/activities/en/index.html?wipo_content_frame=/activities/en/development_iplaw.html.

close relationship between discovery and innovation in the biological sciences, patent offices (and their supervising courts), especially in the United States, have been expanding the scope of patentable subject matter.[31] This is partly out of a belief that patents will help facilitate innovation in these areas, and partly out of the difficulty of drawing lines between what should and should not be patentable in such areas.

There are good reasons for a global system to use a narrow definition of patentable subject matter and to exclude from patentability such areas as computer software, algorithms, business methods, and measured properties of nature, such as genomic sequences or protein coordinates (provided some mechanism remains to provide protection for therapeutics based on natural products). First, there are very serious doubts that patents in many of these areas serve the useful purpose of promoting innovation – their value in encouraging litigation may be greater than their value in encouraging research.[32] Second, it is patents in some of these areas that particularly complicate (and may even deter) subsequent research. And, third, it is in these areas that there is the greatest international conflict as to the appropriateness of patentability.[33]

It is certainly preferable to use a first-to-file system rather than a first-to-invent system. This is partly because most of the world is already on a first-to-file system.[34] It is also because priority disputes are resolved much more readily through the first-to-file approach, both within patent offices and in infringement litigation. Establishing priority by reconstructing the history of parallel research efforts is incredibly expensive and difficult. The cases in which

---

[31] *See, e.g.*, AT&T v. Excel Communications, Inc., 172 F.3d 1352 (Fed. Cir. 1999); State St. Bank & Trust Co. v. Signature Fin. Group, 149 F.3d 1368 (Fed. Cir. 1998); Nuffield Council on Bioethics, The Ethics of Patenting DNA: A Discussion Paper (July 2002) *available at* http://www.nuffieldbioethics.org; David Korn & Stephen J. Heinig (eds.), *Public v. Private Ownership of Scientific Discovery: Legal and Economic Analyses of the Implications of Human Gene Patents*, 77 ACAD. MED. 1301 ff (Dec. 2002) (special issue).

[32] *See* Barr, above n. 2; *see also* Julia Alpert Gladstone, *Why Patenting Information Technology and Business Methods Is Not Sound Policy: Lessons from History and Prophecies for the Future*, 25 HAMLINE L. REV. 217 (2002).

[33] Consider, for example, the language expressing ethical concerns about certain patents on genomic information in the European Union Directive 98/44/EC of the European Parliament and of the Council of 6 July 1998 on the legal protection of biotechnological inventions; *see also* Commission Proposal for a Directive of the European Parliament and of the Council on the patentability of computer-implemented inventions, 2002 O.J. C 151; *see also* Erwin J. Basinski, *An Open-and-Shut Case: The Diplomatic Conference to Revise the Articles of the European Patent Office Votes to Maintain the Status Quo Regarding Software Patents in Europe Pending Issuance of a New Software Patent Directive by the European Union*, 6 INT'L J. COMM. L. & POL'Y 1 (2001).

[34] For a discussion on the challenges this issue poses for a global patent system and the main rationales for both approaches, see Kevin Cuenot, *Perilous Potholes in the Path Toward Patent Law Harmonization*, 11 U. FLA. J.L. & PUB. POL'Y 101, 114–16 (1999).

a genuine first inventor is not first to file are so rare that the real cost they represent under a first-to-file system are outweighed by the costs of the first-to-invent system.[35] And, particularly with the laying open and opposition suggested later in this section, there is no need to combine the first-to-file system with the adoption of a grace period. The grace period is the provision in U.S. law under which publication does not bar patentability until a year has elapsed.[36] This is a provision that has been unique to U.S. law, but the current WIPO draft treaties include it also, perhaps as a balance for the United States adopting a first-to-file approach.[37]

It is not enough just to define standards; it is also important to define how well patents should be examined and what presumption of validity they should be given in litigation. A reasonable patent system could simply register applications and then give them no presumption of validity in litigation; or it could attempt an exhaustive investigation and then give the patents a relatively strong presumption of validity.[38] There are several reasons for an international system to work near the exhaustive investigation end of the spectrum. The first is that an issued patent – whether strong or weak – creates a barrier to research and economic activity in the area it covers. One must face at least a lawyer's fee and possibly much more in order to determine whether it should be taken seriously.[39]

Second, under a global system, the enormous resources of duplicate application evaluation are reduced, and it is possible to do a more careful search and make a better judgment. There is enough global revenue available to patent offices under integration to allow significant reduction of the total costs and increased expenditure per search. Such funding can help improve the quality of the patent granting process.

There are two further measures that can help. One is to include a solid opposition process under which the patent application is laid open for criticism and comment by potential opponents; otherwise the patent granting process

---

[35] *See* Mossinghof & Ku, above n. 5, at 549.   [36] 35 U.S.C. § 102(b) (2000).
[37] *See* Standing Committee on the Law of Patents, 7th Sess. (Geneva, 6–10 May 2002), SCP/7/73, art. 9, *available at* http://www.wipo.int/news/en/index.html?wipo_content_frame=/news/en/conferences.html.
[38] For consideration of the balance, see Mark A. Lemley, *Rational Ignorance at the Patent Office*, 95 Nw. U. L. Rev. 1495 (2001).
[39] In the U.S. federal legal system there is a constitutional requirement that one have standing to bring a case. In the patent realm, this has been interpreted to mean that a company cannot get a declaratory judgment that a patent held by another is invalid until the patent holder has actually threatened to sue for infringement. Cygnus Therapeutic Sys. v. ALZA Corp., 92 F.3d 1153 (1996). The result is that a company may be afraid to do research in a particular field if it believes the product it wants to create would infringe on a patent, even if it believes that the patent is not valid, because the R&D investment risk is simply too great without some certainty about the legal status of the patent rights of the potentially infringed patent holder.

becomes entirely *ex parte*. Such a process is already the law under the EPC and is included in the proposed Community Patent Convention regime.[40] A somewhat similar (but weaker) re-examination process is available under U.S. law.[41] Finally, the burden of proof with respect to patent requirements must, in general, fall upon the applicant. There is no reason that a monopoly right should be granted without the applicant bearing the burden of proof to demonstrate that the invention satisfies the requisite criteria. Note that this is not the case under today's U.S. law.[42]

II. Substantive issues for international patent enforcement

There has long been international harmonization of standards for granting patents, at least under the EPC. And the current WIPO negotiations are still concentrating on standards for granting patents. Save for the current negotiations in Europe, however, which have not yet led to a final procedure, there is no similar experience in the creation of international procedures for enforcing patents. This is a difficult problem and the analysis in this area must be much more speculative.

A. Infringement and defenses

The determination of patent infringement is, in the first instance, a matter of interpreting the patent claims and comparing them with the "accused" article.[43] The institutions best suited to this task will be discussed below. But there are also much broader questions that must be considered in the infringement context. A first is the scope of appropriate exemptions – and it is clear that a broad group of exemptions are essential if the global system is to be wise and economically appropriate for developing nations.

---

[40] Convention on the Grant of European Patents (European Patent Convention), 5 Oct. 1973, arts. 99–105 (creating right and procedure for opposition).
[41] 35 U.S.C. §§ 311–18 (2000).
[42] *See, e.g.*, USPTO, Manual of Patent Examining Procedure § 2142; *In re* Oetiker, 977 F.2d 1443 (Fed. Cir. 1992). I must admit that allocating the burden of proof against the applicant poses some difficulty with respect to enablement and the scope of the patent claims. The breadth of claims in a patent should reflect what is enabled in the disclosure of the invention – but, in some areas of technology, that may not really be known at the time of the application. In such a case, some kind of provisional claim seems appropriate.
[43] Infringement may reasonably be defined in terms of making, using, or selling a patented product or the direct product of a patented process. Under the global system, it is always possible to reach the infringer in another nation, so there is no need to add import of a patented product or of the direct product of a patented process to the list of infringing acts, save when the product is produced in a developing country that is authorized to use the invention as a result of a shorter patent lifetime or permitted the choice not to have a patent system.

Here one needs a research-tool exemption, designed to permit inventions to be used rather broadly for research purposes – otherwise the whole research-promotion role of the patent system is undercut. There are several possible versions of such exemptions and, although the precise approach is subject to reasonable debate, substantial breadth is wise.[44]

A very useful approach would be a dependency license, as is now found under French law, under which the inventor of a substantial improvement on a patented invention can gain a royalty-bearing license to use the underlying invention.[45] Further, it is unwise to have a procedure such as the U.S. treble damages procedure for "willful infringement,"[46] because of the risk that such a procedure will deter those within a firm from reading patents that may apply to their technologies.[47]

Since enforcement would become internationalized under the proposal set out in this article, it is essential to take into account the questions of public use and of compulsory licensing. Under U.S. law, the government holds a license to use any patented invention – it must pay royalties, which can be litigated in the Court of Claims, but is not subject to an injunction to bar infringement.[48] This pattern seems reasonable for global application, considering the possible global public sector needs for use of particular inventions.

The most politically contentious issue, of course, is compulsory licensing. Although such licensing is not authorized in U.S. law (save to the extent that the provision for government use effectively permits a form of compulsory licensing), authorization for such licensing is found in the law of many nations and is also included in TRIPS article 31. Considering the possible importance of such licensing in developing nations, it is essential to include compulsory licensing provisions if there is to be a global agreement. The TRIPS article is

---

[44] See generally Janice M. Mueller, No "Dilettante Affair": Rethinking the Experimental Use Exception to Patent Infringement for Biomedical Research Tools, 76 WASH. L. REV. 1 (2001); but see Madey v. Duke Univ., 307 F.3d 1351 (Fed. Cir. 2002).

[45] Code de la Propriété Intellectuelle, Loi 92–597, art. L. 613–15 (1 July 1992); John H. Barton, Patents and Antitrust: A Rethinking in Light of Patent Breadth and Sequential Innovation, 65 ANTITRUST L.J. 449, 457–58 (1997). The use of such a system is authorized by TRIPS Agreement, above n. 11, art. 31(l).

[46] 35 U.S.C. § 284 (2000).   [47] Barr, above n. 2.

[48] 28 U.S.C. § 1498(a) (2000) (declaring that when the United States uses a patent without a license, the owner can bring a claim against the United States in the Court of Federal Claims, but can sue only for "the recovery of his reasonable and entire compensation for such use and manufacture"); see also Irving Air Chute Co. v. United States, 93 F. Supp. 633, 635 (Ct. Cl. 1950) (Statute held, "in effect, an eminent domain statute, which entitles the Government to manufacture or use a patented article becoming liable to pay compensation to the owner of the patent."). Courts have also recognized that the rights granted to the government under this statute are effectually a compulsory license. Motorola, Inc. v. United States, 729 F.2d 765 (Fed. Cir. 1984) ("In this context, the United States is not in the position of an ordinary infringer ... but rather a compulsory, nonexclusive licensee.").

a reasonable starting place for a model, but it might be wise to add more substantive standards to that article, which, in its current form, relies more on procedural standards than on substantive standards.[49]

B. Exhaustion and parallel trade

One of the most important issues under an international patent is that of exhaustion.[50] The issue is whether rights are exhausted when a product is exported to a new national market after being put on the market in a different nation with the consent of the patent holder. Under a national exhaustion principle, the patent holder can prevent the import into a new market (by asserting the separate patent held in the nation of import); under a global exhaustion principle, the opposite result holds. Today's law permits flexibility on this issue, and TRIPS article 6 is effectively an agreement to disagree on the issue.

As a purely logical matter, exhaustion of a global patent should be at the global level. Yet, patent holders prefer national exhaustion because it permits the maintenance of different prices in different nations, and thus maximizes the economic rents from the patent (and may, in fact, allow lower prices in some jurisdictions). Such price discrimination is, moreover, economically sounder than other ways of increasing the patentee's return, such as extended term. Moreover, differential pricing of some products, and particularly of pharmaceuticals, is an obvious and important solution to some of the pharmaceutical access problems facing developing nations – and it can be facilitated by a national exhaustion system.

It is best therefore to permit pharmaceuticals and other products that have a substantial intellectual property component, and for which price discrimination between the developed and the developing world appears wise, to be subject to a national exhaustion principle when exported from a developing nation to a developed nation. There might be value in an exception to deal with situations in which products have relatively little intellectual property component, and the exclusion principles are being used to prevent otherwise beneficial trade – although it is difficult to visualize such a case.

---

[49] Of the two European enforcement proposals, one, the Draft European Patent Litigation, above n. 9, has no arrangement for such licensing, while the other, the European Union Commission Proposal for a Council Regulation on the Community Patent, above n. 9, has such an arrangement (in articles 21–22). The WIPO harmonization process has not yet reached this issue.

[50] See Frederick M. Abbott, *Political Economy of the U.S. Parallel Trade Experience: Toward a More Thoughtful Policy*, in INTELLECTUAL PROPERTY: TRADE, COMPETITION, AND SUSTAINABLE DEVELOPMENT 177 (Thomas Cottier & Petros C. Mavroidis eds., 2003); Barton, above n. 4, at 491–95.

III. Institutional issues

A. Language

One of the most contentious issues is likely to be the official language of patents – this has long been a serious issue in Europe and has contributed to delay in adoption of a more fully integrated system.[51] Almost certainly, the right approach is that which appears to be emerging from the European negotiations: to have the patent issued and published in a small number of widely used languages, and to have it translated into the local language should there be an infringement dispute. This process avoids unnecessary translation, leaves the patent accessible, and provides fairness to local litigants who may use a less common language.

B. Patent granting institutions and appeal process

The nub of the issue is, of course, the patent office – how can the patent offices of the 164 members of the Paris Convention,[52] many of whom have their own patent offices, be integrated into one office? There needs be no more than one office and the economic benefits of integration are lost if there is more than one.

There are three major barriers, all of which will be reflected in the politics of negotiating a new international system. One is the bureaucratic barrier – patent offices provide jobs and their examiners will object to their elimination (as will the local bar of patent agents which finds employment preparing the applications). A second is the economic barrier – patent offices are profit centers that take in fees far in excess of their costs and thus contribute to the support of their national governments. This is true in the developing world and in the developed world as well.[53] And a third is quality – some are much better than others.

The basic response necessarily involves integration of the different national patent offices into one decentralized office. Although it is not the only way of managing a decentralized process, it is certainly possible that the (former) offices of different nations can specialize in different subject matter areas or perhaps different original languages or different phases of the process, just as the Munich, Berlin, and The Hague offices of the EPO integrate their activities. Computerized connections (and potentially computer-based translation) can facilitate this process.[54] And it is possible to contribute to quality by providing various forms of examiner training and testing.

---

[51] *See* Di Cataldo, above n. 8, at 29.
[52] *See* Paris Convention for the Protection of Intellectual Property, Status on 4 Feb. 2003, *available at* http://www.wipo.int/treaties/ip/paris/index.html.
[53] *See* Commission Report, above n. 4, at 137–53.
[54] *See* discussion on creation of WIPONET, above n. 10.

To simplify the politics, it is also possible to make the international system optional, allowing parallel national systems to remain in place; this is what was done in the EPC, and there is a sense that at least some of the national systems may eventually wither in that region. In the global case, this is likely to have an especially strong effect as applicants and the best staff both move to the international system.

Two additional steps are essential to ensure quality. One is the opposition procedure described above. At an appropriate time (12 months after filing – why wait for the 18 months used in Europe?), the patent application should be made public, in all official languages, so that there can be public comments placed in the record. This procedure should contribute greatly to the strengthening of the patent.

The second is a solid appeal procedure, which will be essential to maintaining global uniformity among the various examiners and to resolving hard issues of interpreting the basic treaty that defines patent standards. Considering the scope of the system, it is likely to be necessary to have at least two levels of appeal, one corresponding to the U.S. Board of Patent Appeals and Interferences,[55] and one corresponding to the Court of Appeals for the Federal Circuit (CAFC). These would be judicial entities, comparable to the Board of Appeals of the European Patent Organization.

There is, of course, a serious risk of bias in a specialist court – one is unlikely to want to serve on a specialist patent court unless one is reasonably confident that a strong patent system is a good thing.[56] Yet, there is no general-purpose international court that would be available as an alternative. The best approach therefore is to use a specialist court and to devise a supervisory process to deal with overall adjustments of the directions taken by the specialist court.

C. *Litigation and appeal*

The same issues of specialist versus generalist courts apply to infringement litigation. Fundamental fairness requires that infringement litigation should normally take place at a forum convenient to the alleged infringer, but the

---

[55] 35 U.S.C. § 6 (2000) (establishing and setting up duties of the Board of Patent Appeals and Interferences); 28 U.S.C. § 1295 (2000) (establishing jurisdiction of the United States Court of Appeals for the Federal Circuit).

[56] Many argue that there is a strong pro-patent tendency in the CAFC. *See, e.g.*, Alan P. Klein, *A Funny Thing Happened to the Non-obvious Subject Matter Condition for Patentability on Its Way to the Federal Circuit*, 6 U. BALT. INTELL. PROP. J. 19, 21 (1997) (arguing that "the Federal Circuit's position is clearly more pro-patent than the position of the Supreme Court"); Arti Rai, *Addressing the Patent Gold Rush: The Role of Deference to PTO Patent Denials*, 2 WASH. U. J.L. & POL'Y 199, 205 fn. 14 (2000) ("The CAFC's decisions expanding the scope of patentability in biotechnology and computer software may be the result not only of institutional competence limitations but also of a systematic bias in favor of patent applicants.").

general purpose courts of few nations are capable of managing difficult patent litigation. Hence, it is essential to rely on special purpose courts, which will best be made up of experts (possibly of international experts).[57] These courts must have the power to declare the patent valid or not, infringed or not, and to issue an injunction or a monetary remedy that can be enforced in any national court of member nations.[58] In light of the careful procedures discussed above in connection with the issuance of patents, there should be a presumption of validity,[59] but certainly all issues involved in the validity of the patent should be open to consideration by the enforcing court.

There is a crucial political issue in letting a court strike down a patent in a different country from the inventor's. This is particularly problematic if, in spite of the best efforts of the designers of the international system, that court does not have solid analytic capability. This problem of giving effect to a single court's decision to strike down a patent has been a serious issue in the European discussion, where an initial expectation that the first decision would be made by a national court is changing to one of using international courts.[60]

There are two answers to this problem. One is, as already suggested, to use expert (and sometimes international) initial decision makers – there does not need to be a patent court in each nation, but there does need to be one in easy reach of each nation. That much expertise is certainly available. Second, there should also be a solid review process. Just as for patent issuance disputes, there should be the possibility of appeal to a global court, probably best the same court as that used for ultimate review of patent issuance decisions. The decision of that court should certainly be adequate to declare a patent invalid

---

[57] In Markman v. Westview Instruments, Inc., 517 U.S. 370, 377 (1996), the Supreme Court stated that "there is no dispute that [patent] infringement cases today must be tried by a jury," but went on to hold that claim construction should be determined by the judge rather than the jury. It is not resolved whether a substitute forum can constitutionally be created by treaty. *Compare* Reid v. Covert, 354 U.S. 1 (1957) *with* Missouri v. Holland, 252 U.S. 416 (1920).

[58] There is a precedent for such enforcement for monetary damages in The Convention on Recognition and Enforcement of Foreign Arbitral Awards, adopted into law in the United States by 9 U.S.C. § 201 (2000), "to encourage recognition and enforcement of commercial arbitration agreements in international contracts and to unify standards by which agreements to arbitrate are observed and arbitral awards are enforced in signatory countries." 9 U.S.C.S. § 201 fn. 1. The extension to enforcement of injunctions (which, in many cases, is essential for patents) may be difficult.

[59] The presumption of validity is not unique to the United States. *See, e.g.,* Compaq Computers Ltd. v. Hsi Kuang Ma, Transcript: Martin Walsh Cherer (Laddie, J., 1998) [U.K.] ("This patent having made its way through the Patent Office, it starts out with the presumption of being valid.").

[60] *See* Commission Proposal for a Council Regulation on the Community Patent, above n. 9, § 2.4.5 (laying out the proposed judicial system for determining the legal validity of a community patent and asserting that in making a final determination, "[o]nly a centralised Community court can guarantee without fail unity of law and consistent case law"); *see also* Di Cataldo, above n. 8, at 27.

with global effectiveness; perhaps an unappealed trial court decision to declare a patent invalid should be effective only in the territory of the trial court.

But there are other exceptional issues that are not best handled by the patent appellate court (and, in general, not by the local patent court either). The two most obvious are the grant, or not, of a compulsory license and the determination of antitrust/competition law issues that relate to intellectual property. Both involve issues very different from those typical of patent infringement litigation or patent application litigation, and the adjudicating body must be able to respond to policy concerns far beyond patent law. Experience with the U.S. CAFC in patent/antitrust cases is not encouraging; this court has not generally been sympathetic to antitrust-based arguments.[61] Hence, both types of determination seem reasonably made in national courts (or administrative tribunals), with a possibility of resorting to a certified-question type of inquiry of the patent court if a patent validity or interpretation issue is involved.

D. Supervision

In addition to the institutions to grant and enforce patents, there should be a supervisory body, based on a regular conference of the parties.[62] This is essential because there will be many issues on which regular discussions and changes are needed, such as regular updating of the fees and the appointment of key personnel. But, because of the great economic importance of patent systems, this will have to be more than a routine assembly. There must be regular studies of whether the patent system is working well, and there will need to be a legislative/amendment process to make it possible to modify the system and, if necessary, reverse important appellate court decisions should they prove to have been mistaken. The entity that provides this regular review should operate much as the Conferences of the Parties under international environmental agreements.[63]

The obvious risk is that this assembly will be captured by patent interests and will push the patent system too far. But, it should also be remembered that national patent offices will be going out of business (over time if not immediately). Hence, the national representatives who supervise this organization need not be from patent offices. Not only need they not represent patent offices, they should represent ministries of trade, development, and science. It is logical and parsimonious that the organization to supervise the

---

[61] *See, e.g.*, Rambus Inc. v. Infineon Techs. AG, 318 F.3d 1081 (2003) (fraud issue with substantial antitrust overtones); *see also* above n. 56.

[62] Such a group can be a response to some of the concerns raised by Professor Duffy, in Duffy, above n. 5.

[63] *See* Robin R. Churchill & Geir Ulfstein, *Autonomous Institutional Arrangements in Multilateral Environmental Agreements: A Little-Noticed Phenomenon in International Law*, 94 AM. J. INT'L L. 623 (2000).

international patent evolve from WIPO; it is essential, however, that the international control process for WIPO be significantly revised to change the place within national governments to which WIPO reports. What is crucial is to ensure that the objectives are to foster the advancement of technology – objectives which overlap with, but are not identical to – strengthening the intellectual property system.

E. Financial and international political issues

Movement to an international patent would save money, both by reducing filing fees and by reducing the legal costs of preparing parallel filings. Moreover, if a good expert process is designed, the costs of litigation might also be reduced. The likelihood, in fact, is that the administering institution would make money, and that one of the real political management problems would be to control how the institution uses that money.[64] (As an economic matter, it is not at all clear that the optimal cost of a patent is the same as the expense incurred in deciding whether the patent should be issued.) If there is extra money, some could be used for litigation expenses (and perhaps even patent filings) for developing country inventors who are otherwise unable to afford to use the patent system.

But the most significant question is whether an international system of the type envisioned in this paper is feasible. What is envisioned here, in an effort to be responsive to developing-nation concerns, is a pattern in which the system globalizes in a way that raises the standards needed to obtain a patent (as compared with the standards exemplified by today's U.S. patent law). This creates a cost to the patent bar and patent offices. Industry (as opposed to the intellectual property bar) may actually be pleased with such a development, although some will be unhappy with the exemptions, such as the compulsory license arrangement. But, in return, industry gains a major benefit in reducing transaction costs.

The alternative pattern, exemplified in the WIPO harmonization negotiations, is to create a system like that of the United States, with relatively weak patentability standards and broad subject-matter standards, and to harmonize those standards with those of generally like-minded nations and regions. The likely political next step is for the major developed countries to encourage developing nations to sign up to that system – consider, for example, the strong intellectual property provisions in U.S. bilateral trade agreements, such as the new one with Chile. Assuming Europe moves within the next several years to an

---

[64] This is already an issue for WIPO. "About 85% of the Organization's budget[ ] ... come[s] from the registration systems. The remaining 15% ... come[s] mainly from contributions from member States and sales of WIPO publications." WIPO, General Information: WIPO's Budget, *available at* http://www.wipo.org/about-wipo/en/index.html?wipo_content_frame=budget.html.

integrated patent enforcement system, that system will be used as a model and, if successful, could ultimately be extended to the rest of the world in a similar fashion.

The effective world system would then include U.S.-style harmonized patent standards and perhaps U.S.-style restrictions on compulsory licensing. Based on the analysis above and of the U.K. Commission,[65] such a result would be a mistake for the developing nations (and possibly for the developed nations as well).[66] And there is certainly a chance that the developed world negotiations will fail. But it is very likely that the wisest step for the developing nations is to put forward an alternative along the lines described here that provides the benefits of harmonization and includes both substantive and procedural safeguards for the very important needs of the developing world.

---

[65] *See* Commission Report, above n. 4.

[66] *See also* Keith E. Maskus & Jerome H. Reichman, *The Globalization of Private Knowledge Goods and the Privatization of Global Public Goods* [this volume], Pt. III.A. (calling for a "moratorium on stronger international intellectual property standards").

23

Intellectual property arbitrage: How foreign rules can affect domestic protections

PAMELA SAMUELSON[*]

Abstract
I. Differences in national rules enable IP arbitrage
II. Effects of differing rules on domestic and foreign markets
   A. Software license terms prohibiting reverse engineering
   B. Products of research tools
   C. Country codes
   D. Peer-to-peer file-sharing technologies
   E. Factors affecting IP arbitrage
III. Possible responses to IP arbitrage and attendant difficulties
   A. Enhancing domestic protections
   B. Putting pressure on the "rogue" nation
   C. Filing a complaint with the WTO
   D. Proposing more detailed harmonization
   E. Choosing isolation
   F. Accepting IP arbitrage
Conclusion

ABSTRACT

Differences in national intellectual property rules may cause economic activity to shift from one jurisdiction to another, so that a higher-protection rule will be undermined by lower-protection rules of other jurisdictions. This chapter illustrates this phenomenon with four examples: different rules on the enforceability of anti-reverse engineering clauses of software licenses, on the protectability of bio-engineered research tools, on peer-to-peer file sharing, and on exceptions to anti-circumvention rules. It considers several options nations may have to respond to such intellectual property arbitrage, none of which is likely to be very effective.

---

[*] Chancellor's Professor of Law and Information Management, Boalt Hall, University of California at Berkeley. This chapter began as a joint work with Suzanne Scotchmer. Thanks to Eddan Katz for prodigious research assistance. Research support for this chapter was supplied by National Science Foundation Grant No. SES 9979852. An earlier version of this chapter appeared in 71 U. CHI. L. REV. 223 (2004).

I. Differences in national rules enable IP arbitrage

The Agreement on Trade-Related Aspects of Intellectual Property Rights (TRIPS), concluded in 1994, has narrowed the range of issues on which nations can adopt differing IP rules. All World Trade Organization (WTO) Members, for example, must now protect computer programs by copyright law.[1] Yet, TRIPS plainly contemplates continued differences in national laws by signaling that nations are free to adopt higher-protection rules than the required minima[2] (which presumably means they need not do so). Members are also "free to determine the appropriate method of implementing the provisions of this Agreement within their own legal system and practice."[3] TRIPS restricts national autonomy by forbidding nations from treating foreigners less well than their own nationals,[4] but this implicitly "accepts the proposition that states may differ in their substantive laws."[5] Other TRIPS provisions recognize that Members can adopt IP rules "in a manner conducive to social and economic welfare" and "to promote the public interest in sectors of vital importance to their socio-economic and technological development."[6] That significant variations in national laws continue to exist a decade after TRIPS should not be surprising given the diversity of countries' social, economic, and legal traditions, stages of development, and cultures.[7]

Nations have incentives to adopt higher-protection rules when an already innovative domestic sector demonstrates a need for stronger rules to enable firms to recoup R&D investments, or when nations believe that doing so will spur investments and economic development in that field of innovation.[8]

---

[1] *See* Agreement on Trade-Related Aspects of Intellectual Property Rights (15 Apr. 1994), Marrakesh Agreement Establishing the World Trade Organization, Annex 1C, LEGAL INSTRUMENTS – RESULTS OF THE URUGUAY ROUND vol. 31, 33 I.L.M. 81 (1994) [hereinafter TRIPS Agreement], art 10.1.

[2] *See id.* art. 1.1 ("Members may, but shall not be obliged to, implement in their law more extensive protection than is required by this Agreement, provided that such protection does not contravene the provisions of this Agreement."); *see also* Jerome H. Reichman, *Securing Compliance with the TRIPS Agreement After U.S. v. India*, 1998 JIEL 585–601.

[3] TRIPS Agreement, above n. 1, art. 1.1.   [4] *See id.* art. 3.

[5] GRAEME B. DINWOODIE ET AL., INTERNATIONAL INTELLECTUAL PROPERTY LAW AND POLICY § 2.06 at 79 (LexisNexis 2001).

[6] TRIPS Agreement, above n. 1, arts. 7–8.

[7] *See, e.g.*, Pamela Samuelson, *Implications of the Agreement on Trade Related Aspects of Intellectual Property Rights for Cultural Dimensions of National Copyright Laws*, 23 J. CULTURAL ECON. 95 (1999).

[8] Higher-protection rules may also be manifestations of public choice problems with IP legislation insofar as innovative industries are well organized, well funded, and well situated to benefit significantly from higher-protection rules, making it reasonable to invest in legislation to increase protections to higher levels. Because of the distributed costs of higher-protection rules, collective action problems may prevent those who will bear those costs from organizing effectively to block higher-protection legislation.

Nations have incentives to adopt lower-protection rules if they are predominantly users or net importers of products of that kind, if they aspire to incentivize investments in follow-on innovation, or if they believe that a lower-protection rule will induce more investments than a higher-protection rule.[9]

National differences in IP rules may be unproblematic when the differing rules do not undermine domestic protections. If country A protects a certain innovation (say, patents for higher life forms) and country B does not, country A may be willing to accept that country B's rule is different as long as it can stop at the border any products from B that would infringe its nationals' IP rights. Firms can set up R&D facilities in country A and hope to recoup R&D expenses by exploiting the innovation in A's market. They have at least partial protection in the global market.[10]

One country's decision to provide more extensive protection than TRIPS requires can produce large externalities for the rest of the world. Innovators may be able to recoup investments by selling products in the market where the high-protection rule applies, but they cannot expect to have the same advantage in the world market. Protection in one or a small number of nations necessarily creates a voluntary outflow of profit from the country's own users to foreign innovators without a reciprocal inflow from foreign users to domestic innovators. What is remarkable is that some countries nevertheless do this.

But legal rules in foreign jurisdictions can sometimes limit the force of IP rights in the domestic country. That is, sometimes country B's decision not to protect an innovation, or to protect it less strongly than A, has spillover effects for country A. Country B's decision may, moreover, attract domestic and foreign investments. As Part III will show, country A may not always be able to prevent products developed in country B from entering its market. Unless country A can persuade all nations to harmonize around its higher-protection rule, a lower-protection rule in even one jurisdiction may undermine A's rule. Innovators may either have protection everywhere (because A persuaded all nations to adopt its rule) or effectively nowhere (because the lower-protection

---

[9] The E.U. was a net importer of software when it adopted the Council Directive 91/250 of 14 May 1991 on the Legal Protection of Computer Programs, 34 O.J. (L 122) 42 (17 May 1991) (E.U. Software Directive) (establishing uniform protections for software in the E.U.). The E.U. hoped its rules would enable E.U. firms to engage in follow-on innovation by developing software that would interoperate with U.S. software. *See* JONATHAN BAND & MASANOBU KATOH, INTERFACES ON TRIAL: INTELLECTUAL PROPERTY AND INTEROPERABILITY IN THE GLOBAL SOFTWARE INDUSTRY 229–44 (Westview 1995) (describing the legislative history of the E.U. Software Directive and the goal of the Directive to "demonstrate support for interoperability and competition, which copyright protection ... would frustrate").

[10] The U.S. decision to grant more extensive patent protection for biotechnological innovations than other nations has caused some German biotech firms to set up R&D facilities in the United States. *See* SUSAN K. SELL, PRIVATE POWER, PUBLIC LAW: THE GLOBALIZATION OF INTELLECTUAL PROPERTY RIGHTS 112 fn. 16 (Cambridge 2003).

rule undermines A's rule). This is the IP arbitrage issue on which this chapter principally focuses.

That differences in national IP rules can affect arbitrage is easily illustrated.[11] Australia currently facilitates arbitrage by permitting the importation of certain IP products (for example, CDs of recorded music) from countries where these products can be purchased at a lower price (say, Thailand) than the recording industry wishes to be the prevailing price in Australia; the arbitrageurs' competition reduces the local authorized sellers' rents. The U.S. has put pressure on Australia to ban such parallel imports.[12] Because no consensus exists about whether national exhaustion of rights[13] (the rule preferred by U.S. trade officials) or international exhaustion (the Australian-preferred rule) is the "best" rule,[14] the negotiations leading up to TRIPS did not resolve the international debate on this particular type of IP arbitrage.[15] If national approaches to the exhaustion of rights issue differ, arbitrage will occur.

The IP arbitrage that is the main focus of this chapter resembles classic arbitrage in that it impairs the ability to maintain a higher protection rule (or higher price) in one location because market participants can take advantage of a lower-protection rule (or lower price) elsewhere.[16]

---

[11] *See, e.g.*, Dan L. Burk, *Virtual Exit in the Global Information Economy*, 73 CHI.-KENT L. REV. 943, 945, 969–72 (1998) (discussing competition among nations as to IP rules).

[12] *See, e.g.*, Office of the United States Trade Representative, 2002 National Trade Estimate Report on Foreign Trade Barriers: Australia 10–11, *available at* http://www.ustr.gov/reports/nte/2002/australia.PDF (visited 4 Nov. 2003) (discussing the practice of parallel importation in Australia).

[13] For an explanation of exhaustion of rights, see World Intellectual Property Association, International Exhaustion and Parallel Importation, *available at* http://www.wipo.org/sme/en/ ipbusiness/export/internationalexhaustion.htm (visited Nov 4, 2003).

[14] Trade and IP perspectives on this issue pull in opposite directions. Trade experts would logically favor international exhaustion because this rule permits goods to flow more freely in the global market, while IP experts often favor national or regional exhaustion because these rules help IP owners recoup R&D expenses. *See, e.g.*, Rochelle Cooper Dreyfuss & Andreas F. Lowenfeld, *Two Achievements of the Uruguay Round: Putting TRIPS and Dispute Resolution Together*, 37 VA. J. INT'L L. 275, 280 fn. 12 (1997) (noting the tension at the TRIPS talks between the free-trade goals of the General Agreement on Tariffs and Trade (GATT) and the WTO, and TRIPS's goal of protecting intellectual property rights).

[15] *See id.*; TRIPS, above n. 1, art. 6 ("Nothing in this Agreement shall be used to address the issue of exhaustion of intellectual property rights.").

[16] *See, e.g.*, A. Michael Froomkin, *The Internet as a Source of Regulatory Arbitrage*, in BORDERS IN CYBERSPACE: INFORMATION POLICY AND THE GLOBAL INFORMATION INFRASTRUCTURE 129, 142–54 (Brian Kahin & Charles Nessen eds., MIT 1997) (describing examples of regulatory arbitrage, such as the E.U.'s practice of limiting transborder data flows to countries with comparable data protection laws).

II. Effects of differing rules on domestic and foreign markets

This Part discusses four examples of IP arbitrage. In each, high-protection domestic rules may be undermined by lower-protection foreign rules that can plausibly be justified as a legitimate national policy choice.

A. Software license terms prohibiting reverse engineering

Suppose that a country (say, the U.S.) decides to enforce terms of software licenses that prohibit reverse engineering.[17] A nation might do so to enable domestic developers of proprietary software to protect internal program interfaces as trade secrets, or simply to promote freedom of contract values.[18]

Other nations (say, the European Union) may allow software reverse engineering for interoperability purposes and refuse to enforce license restrictions on reverse engineering.[19] Such a rule may foster competition and follow-on innovation in its domestic software market.[20]

Foreign developers who obtain U.S. software can reverse engineer it in the E.U. to make compatible products. The resulting software may then be marketed in U.S. and European markets, as long as the compatible software does not infringe U.S. copyrights.[21] The lower-protection European rule would create incentives for U.S.-based software developers, as well as E.U. developers, to set up reverse engineering facilities in the E.U. for development of compatible products.

Thus, a foreign rule in favor of reverse engineering may foil a domestic strategy in favor of protecting platforms with proprietary interfaces. The domestic rule enforcing anti-reverse engineering license terms may just shift development offshore – disadvantaging certain domestic innovators but perhaps increasing competition and ongoing innovation.

---

[17] *Compare* Vault Corp. v. Quaid Software Ltd., 847 F.2d 255, 269–70 (5th Cir. 1988) (holding anti-reverse engineering clauses unenforceable) *with* Bowers v. Baystate Techs., Inc., 320 F.3d 1317, 1323 (Fed. Cir. 2003) (holding anti-reverse engineering clauses enforceable).

[18] *See* Pamela Samuelson & Suzanne Scotchmer, *The Law and Economics of Reverse Engineering*, 111 Yale L.J. 1575, 1607–30 (2002) (discussing reasons why firms adopt proprietary interfaces and assessing economic effects of reverse engineering and contractual restrictions on reverse engineering).

[19] *See* E.U. Software Directive, above n. 9, arts. 6(1), 9(1).

[20] *See, e.g.*, Thomas Vinje, *The Legislative History of the E.C. Software Directive*, in A Handbook of European Software Law 39, 61–63 (M. Lehmann & C.F. Tapper eds., Clarendon 1993) (discussing the competition policy rationale for the interoperability provisions of the E.U. Software Directive).

[21] *See, e.g.*, Computer Assocs. Int'l, Inc. v. Altai, Inc., 982 F.2d 693, 701–15 (2d Cir. 1992) (stating that interfaces are not protected by copyright law).

B. Products of research tools

If a bio-engineered research tool is patented in one nation (say, the U.S.), but not in other countries,[22] the patentee may find it difficult to control commercially valuable uses of the tools not only in the markets in which no patent has issued, but even in the market in which it was patented.

The main utility of bio-engineered research tools is in developing bio-engineered products, such as drugs or enzymes. If a foreign national obtains a U.S.-patented bio-engineered research tool and uses it outside of the U.S. to develop a commercial drug, the foreign firm can sell the drug developed with the research tool not only in foreign markets in which the tool is not patented, but also in the U.S. market. While the U.S. has forbidden importation of products made outside the U.S. with a U.S.-patented process since 1988,[23] it does not forbid importation of products made outside the U.S. with U.S.-patented products.[24]

Thus, the domestic protection of research tools may only shift their use to other countries. The tool's proprietor may effectively have no protection, as the tool is unlikely to be used where it is protected. The lack of protection in even one nation may be tantamount to a lack of protection everywhere in the world.[25]

---

[22] A bio-engineered research tool might be unpatentable for a number of reasons. *See, e.g.,* Integrating Intellectual Property Rights and Development Policy, Report of the Commission on Intellectual Property Rights 22–24 (2002) (urging developing countries to enact stringent rules as to the patenting of research tools); Rebecca S. Eisenberg & Robert P. Merges, Opinion Letter as to the Patentability of Certain Inventions Associated with the Identification of Partial cDNA Sequences, 23 A.I.P.L.A. Q.J. 1 (1996) (discussing various reasons to question the patentability of some research tools). *See also* Arti K. Rai, *Proprietary Rights and Collective Action: The Case of Biotechnology Research with Low Commercial Value* [this volume].

[23] *See* 35 U.S.C. § 271(g) (2000).

[24] *See, e.g.,* Bayer AG v. Housey Pharm., Inc., 340 F.3d 1367, 1377 (Fed. Cir. 2003) (holding that § 271(g) applies only to importation of physical goods, not importation of data); Amgen, Inc. v United States Int'l Trade Comm'n, 902 F.2d 1532, 1538–40 (Fed. Cir. 1990) (refusing to stop importation of an artificial hormone made abroad using U.S.-patented cells, because cells are a "product" rather than a "process").

[25] Another type of IP arbitrage arising out of differing patent rules may occur when some countries embrace, and others deny, research exceptions to patent infringement. Follow-on innovators may decide to establish R&D facilities in countries with such exceptions. Otherwise-infringing research may result in the development of noninfringing new products, which may then be imported to compete with the patentee and its licensees. Exempting research and experimental uses of inventions from the scope of the patent right has achieved considerable acceptance in the international community. *See, e.g.,* Janice M. Mueller, *No "Dilettante Affair": Rethinking the Experimental Use Exception to Patent Infringement for Biomedical Research Tools*, 76 Wash. L. Rev. 1, 37–40 (2001).

C. Country codes

Developers of computer games may try to enhance their profits by embedding country or region codes, so that their games will play only on platforms embedded with the same code. This allows game-makers to sell the same product at different prices in different countries.

Some countries (say, the U.S.) may outlaw circumvention of technical measures, such as country codes, on the theory that strict rules against circumvention will protect game developers from "piracy" (that is, widespread infringement).[26] Foreign jurisdictions (say, Finland) might adopt weaker anti-circumvention rules – for example, allowing purchasers of digital products to bypass country codes so they can play games on a platform of their choice[27] – on the ground that country coding (and concomitant price discrimination) is anticompetitive.[28]

A weaker anti-circumvention rule in Finland may mean that the price prevailing there will be the lowest price available anywhere, which would undermine the game-makers' price discrimination strategies. Moreover, insofar as global digital networks permit nationals of a lower-protection jurisdiction to disseminate the means to bypass country codes, the game-makers' price discrimination could be undermined worldwide.[29]

The welfare effects of IP arbitrage that undermines price discrimination are unclear. Price discrimination can, of course, enhance consumer welfare by increasing the total number of users; overall use of an IP product may fall

---

[26] See 17 U.S.C. § 1201(a)(1)(A) (2000) ("No person shall circumvent a technological measure that effectively controls access to a work protected under this title."); Sony Computer Ent'm't Am. Inc. v Gamemasters, 87 F. Supp. 2d 976, 987 (N.D. Cal. 1999) (deeming the bypass of a country code a § 1201(a)(1)(A) violation). But see R. Anthony Reese, Will Merging Access Controls and Rights Controls Undermine the Structure of Anticircumvention Law?, 18 BERKELEY TECH. L.J. 619 (2003) (criticizing the treatment of country codes as persistent access controls under § 1201(a)(1)(A)).

[27] Finland proposed to allow circumvention of technical measures for private purposes so long as the person had lawful access to the work. See email from Ville Oksanen, Researcher, Helsinki Institute for Information Technology (18 Nov. 2002) (on file with author).

[28] See, e.g., Michael Owen-Brown, Regulator Challenges DVD Zones, THE ADVERTISER (Australia), 24 May 2001, at 27 (reporting Australian investigation of DVD country coding spurred by market allocation and discriminatory pricing concerns). See also Joint Answer to Written Questions E-1509/00 and E-1510/00 given by Mr. Monti on Behalf of the Commission, 44 O.J. (C 53) 157–59 (20 Feb. 2001) (addressing E.U. competition concerns about country coding of DVD players).

[29] DeCSS, a computer program designed to bypass the Content Scramble System (CSS) used to enforce DVD region coding, is widely available on the Internet. See, e.g., David S. Touretzky, Gallery of CSS Descramblers, at http://www2.cs.cmu.edu/dst/DeCSS/Gallery/index.html (visited Nov 4, 2003) (cataloging more than thirty different versions of the DeCSS code, including graphical and musical versions).

if the producers' price discrimination regime collapses.[30] However, price discrimination in IP markets is not always benign,[31] and TRIPS contemplates that nations can prevent abuses of IP rights.[32] Country coding achieves technologically what national exhaustion of rights rules would otherwise achieve, and if nations under TRIPS are free to adopt international exhaustion rules, they should also have discretion to adopt anti-circumvention rules to achieve the same objective.

D. Peer-to-peer file-sharing technologies

Peer-to-peer (P2P) file-sharing technologies are widely used to exchange digital music in the MP3 file format.[33] Downloading digital music without paying for it, as P2P technology permits, may constitute copyright infringement.[34] While developers of P2P software are typically not directly liable, the recording industry has charged P2P developers with indirect copyright infringement on various theories.[35]

P2P technology creates another IP arbitrage opportunity. Suppose courts in country A (say, the U.S.) decide that makers of such technologies are indirect infringers,[36] but courts in country B (say, the Netherlands) decide that they are

---

[30] See, e.g., William T. Fisher III, *Property and Contract on the Internet*, 73 CHI.-KENT L. REV. 1203, 1238–40 (1998) (explaining the socially beneficial distributive effects of price discrimination).

[31] See, e.g., Michael J. Meurer, *Copyright Law and Price Discrimination*, 23 CARDOZO L. REV. 55, 67, 93 (2001) (noting as an example that price discrimination for entertainment products results in a net transfer from poorer consumers to wealthier shareholders).

[32] See TRIPS Agreement, above n. 1, art. 8.2 ("Appropriate measures, provided that they are consistent with the provisions of this Agreement, may be needed to prevent the abuse of intellectual property rights by right holders or the resort to practices which unreasonably restrain trade or adversely affect the international transfer of technology."). See also Hanns Ullrich, *Expansionist Intellectual Property Protection and Reductionist Competition Rules: A TRIPS Perspective* [this volume].

[33] See, e.g., Benny Evangelista, *Net Music Swappers Fear Wrath of Industry*, S.F. CHRON., 25 July 2003, at A1 (estimating 60 million people in the U.S. have used P2P software to download digital music).

[34] See *In re* Aimster Copyright Litig., 334 F.3d 643, 653 (7th Cir. 2003) (upholding a preliminary injunction on the ground that a P2P developer was unable to articulate noninfringing use of its product); A&M Records, Inc. v. Napster, Inc., 239 F.3d 1004, 1014–19 (9th Cir. 2001) (concluding that Napster users had engaged in copyright infringement).

[35] See, e.g., Napster, 239 F.3d at 1019–24 (affirming contributory infringement and vicarious liability findings against a P2P developer and granting a preliminary injunction).

[36] See, e.g., id. But see Metro-Goldwyn-Mayer Studios, Inc. v. Grokster, Ltd., 259 F. Supp. 2d 1029, 1043, 1046 (C.D. Cal. 2003), aff'd 380 F. 3d 1154 (9th Cir. 2004), cert. granted 125 S. Ct. 686 (2004) (granting P2P developers summary judgment on secondary copyright infringement claims against them because of substantial noninfringing uses).

not because of substantial noninfringing uses of these technologies.[37] Courts in country A cannot enforce a judgment against a foreign maker of P2P technologies in the absence of domestic assets; furthermore, enjoining the foreign P2P developer will fail to stop domestic users from accessing the technology from foreign sites via the Internet.[38]

The principal result of national differences on indirect copyright liability rules may be to shift development of P2P technologies offshore.[39] The development and distribution of P2P technologies will not stop unless they are banned in all countries.[40]

E. Factors affecting IP arbitrage

A foreign rule's undermining of domestic protection via IP arbitrage is not inevitable. A given form of IP arbitrage is less likely if it involves physical goods that must be transported in a traditional manner (for example, by ships, trucks, or airplanes) because infringements can readily be detected by examining the goods at the border. Information technologies are more susceptible to IP arbitrage owing to their more intangible nature, the relative invisibility of the

---

[37] *See, e.g.*, Brian Grow, *Netherlands Court Ruling Offers Haven to File-Sharing Services*, WALL ST. J., 18 Dec. 2002, at B7 (describing a Dutch appellate court ruling that developers of filesharing software were not liable for copyright infringement, even if their users might be). *See also* Timothy Wu, *When Code Isn't Law*, 89 VA. L. REV. 679, 734–37 (2003) (discussing the effect of legal rulings such as Napster on decisions about the architecture of subsequent P2P systems).

[38] *See, e.g.*, Burk, above n. 11, at 960 ("Because of the Internet, interdiction of infringing products may become nearly impossible.").

[39] This helps to explain why some P2P developers have moved their headquarters to remote locations. *See* Wu, above n. 37, at 736 (noting that KaZaA's parent company is incorporated in Vanuatu, while Grokster's servers are located in Nevis).

[40] Highly decentralized software systems may continue to be used even if developers have shut down their operations. *See* Grokster, 259 F. Supp. 2d at 1045:

> Defendants provide software that communicates across networks that are entirely outside Defendants [sic] control. In the case of Grokster, the network is the propriety [sic] FastTrack network, which is clearly not controlled by Defendant Grokster. In the case of StreamCast, the network is Gnutella, the open-source nature of which apparently places it outside the control of any single entity.

> Another example of IP arbitrage involving digital copyrights is the streaming of digital content that is unlawful in one jurisdiction (say, the U.S.) but lawful in another (say, Canada); streaming services could locate servers in Canada, but attract U.S. residents who access the streamed content online, thereby creating an opportunity for arbitrage. One effort to exploit differences in national rules about streaming digital content resulted in the higher-protection rule prevailing over the lower-protection rule. See Gerry Blackwell, iCrave Just a Hint of Things to Come, Toronto Star (Mar 9, 2000) (describing the shuttering of Canadian web rebroadcasting service iCrave in response to lawsuits filed by U.S. copyright owners alleging violations of U.S. copyright law).

key innovations they embody, and the ease of transmitting many of them via the Internet.[41] Derivative innovations that do not bear the imprint of infringement in the product being distributed (say, drugs made with the aid of research tools) are also more susceptible to IP arbitrage.

III. Possible responses to IP arbitrage and attendant difficulties

A nation that objects to a form of IP arbitrage that undermines its domestic policy has several options. First, it can change its domestic law to broaden import controls or expand the extraterritorial reach of domestic law. Second, it can pressure the "rogue" nation to synchronize rules. Third, it can initiate a complaint against the other nation under the Dispute Settlement Understanding (DSU) of the TRIPS Agreement. Fourth, it can propose amendments to the TRIPS Agreement to achieve a finer degree of harmonization of minimum standards. Fifth, it can close off trade or communication to protect its domestic rules. Sixth, it can accept that some IP arbitrage may be inevitable and adjust its expectations about the benefits it will be able to derive from TRIPS.

Various difficulties attend each option. None is likely to be a foolproof solution to IP arbitrage.

A. Enhancing domestic protections

An obvious step for a nation to take in response to IP arbitrage is to amend domestic laws to block that arbitrage. As to products made elsewhere from research tools patented domestically, for example, a nation could ban importation of products made with the aid of domestically patented research tools. As to interoperable software, a nation could change its copyright laws to prohibit importation of computer programs developed in violation of a mass market license outside that nation. Also possible is legislation authorizing an expansion of the extraterritorial reach of domestic law.

One precedent for expanding domestic law to stop IP arbitrage is Section 271(g) of the U.S. patent law, which forbids the importation and sale of products made from processes patented in the United States.[42] This provision's potential to disrupt domestic businesses sparked controversy when initially proposed. Retailers not only "feared [the abuse of] extended process patent protection ... to harass sellers of products legitimately produced by non-infringing processes" abroad, but also faced liability for selling imported products while unaware of the infringing process by which they were made – a liability that might have extended to "unwitting" downstream purchasers.[43]

---

[41] *Cf.* Burk, above n. 11, at 944–45. [42] 35 U.S.C. § 271(g).
[43] *See* Dan L. Burk, *Patents in Cyberspace: Territoriality and Infringement on Global Computer Networks*, 68 TULANE. L. REV. 1, 63 (1993).

To address these concerns, Congress limited the reach of Section 271(g) by shielding noncommercial uses and retail sales,[44] and exempted products materially changed by subsequent processes and products that are trivial components of other products.[45]

Similar resistance may arise if nations try to ban importation of products of research tools, unlicensed interoperable software, or the like – especially if domestic support for the stronger-protection rule is weak or equivocal. For example, even if some software developers, such as Microsoft, would support amendments to U.S. copyright law favoring enforcement of license restrictions on reverse engineering of software, these amendments would be opposed by other firms, such as Sun Microsystems, that support reverse engineering.[46] Thus, internal domestic politics may check a nation's efforts to avoid IP arbitrage by expanding the scope of domestic legal protections.

Nations can also extend the extraterritorial reach of domestic IP law.[47] U.S. courts regularly invoke a presumption that U.S. laws do not apply abroad unless Congress has expressly so provided.[48] That Congress has not yet done so is notable, given how much harm U.S. firms claim they suffer from foreign infringements.[49] Even assuming their enforceability against nonresidents, extending the reach of domestic IP laws extraterritorially may subvert foreign policy.[50]

In sum, domestic and foreign policy considerations are likely to constrain the ability of a nation to avoid IP arbitrage by amending domestic laws to broaden import controls or to extend the reach of its laws beyond its territorial boundaries. Moreover, banning the import of derivatives, such as products of research tools or products of patented processes, may be difficult to enforce,

---

[44] The shield applies "unless there is no adequate remedy under this title for infringement on account of the importation or other use, offer to sell, or sale of that product." 35 U.S.C. § 271(g) (2000).

[45] Id.

[46] See, e.g., BAND & KATOH, above n. 9, at 31–39, 332–34 (documenting the conflicting views toward IP regulation of Microsoft and Sun Microsystems).

[47] See, e.g., Curtis A. Bradley, Territorial Intellectual Property Rights in an Age of Globalism, 37 VA. J. INT'L L. 505, 506 (1997) ("Courts in the United States are increasingly being asked to apply the federal patent, copyright, and trademark statutes to conduct that takes place outside of the country's territorial boundaries.").

[48] See id. at 507. The Federal Circuit, however, has upheld injunctions against foreign activities. See, e.g., Spindelfabrik Suessen-Schurr v. Schubert & Salzer Maschinenfabrik Aktiengesellschaft, 903 F.2d 1568, 1577–78 (Fed. Cir. 1990) (enjoining foreign manufacture of infringing machines "for use in the United States").

[49] See, e.g., International Intellectual Property Alliance website, at http://www.iipa.com (visited 4 Nov. 2003) (estimating $12.3 billion in losses from copyright infringement in 49 nations in 2002).

[50] See Bradley, above n. 47, at 546 (noting a strong international reaction to congressional decisions to confer extraterritorial reach to U.S. law).

particularly when the products do not bear the imprint of the infringement and there is more than one way to make them.[51]

B. Putting pressure on the "rogue" nation

Nations affected by an IP arbitrage may also pressure the other nation to change its law. There is, of course, nothing new about unilateral pressure as a strategy for dealing with perceived inadequacies of other nations' IP laws or practices.[52] Many expected TRIPS to cause such pressure to subside,[53] and some have even argued that it is inconsistent with TRIPS obligations for member states to engage in unilateral retribution as to matters covered by the TRIPS Agreement.[54]

The U.S. has been the most active and aggressive user of unilateral pressure to induce changes in other nations' IP laws. Prior to the adoption of TRIPS, the U.S. implemented procedures for taking action against nations having IP policies it deemed deficient. The U.S. Trade Representative has authority to investigate whether particular nations adequately protect IP rights, and if not, to deny them trade benefits unless their policies change.[55] It publishes an annual report assigning a level of priority to the perceived inadequacies of other nations' laws, and takes prompt action against priority violators.[56] The U.S. has used these procedures to put considerable pressure on other nations to change their IP policies both before and after TRIPS.[57]

Yet, unilateral pressure may founder against some trading partners and as to some issues, depending on the clout of the beneficiaries of the foreign low-protection rule. For example, the E.U. has insisted on the U.S. adopting stricter rules about geographical origin designations for wine, while the U.S. has demanded that the E.U. broaden the availability of patents for biotechnology inventions.[58] Neither bilateral negotiations nor TRIPS has fully resolved these differences. If the U.S. objected to IP arbitrage involving interoperable software, the E.U. would almost certainly resist changes to its policy against enforcement of license restrictions on reverse engineering, given how deliberately the E.U.

---

[51] See, e.g., Rebecca S. Eisenberg, *Technology Transfer and the Genome Project: Problems with Patenting Research Tools*, 5 RISK 163, 169–70 (1994).

[52] See, e.g., Kim Newby, *The Effectiveness of Special 301 in Creating Long Term Copyright Protection for U.S. Companies Overseas*, 21 SYRACUSE J. INT'L L. & COMM. 29, 39–46 (1995) (describing U.S. tactics to encourage Taiwan, China, and Thailand to curb copyright and patent infringement).

[53] See SELL, above n. 10, at 165.

[54] See, e.g., J.H. Reichman, *The TRIPS Agreement Comes of Age: Conflict or Cooperation with the Developing Countries?*, 32 CASE. W. RES. J. INT'L L. 441, 454 (2000).

[55] See, e.g., Newby, above n. 52, at 35–39. [56] See SELL, above n. 10, at 92.

[57] See id. at 124–29. See also Newby, above n. 52, at 39–50 (providing examples).

[58] See SELL, above n. 10, at 111–12.

developed its Directive on the Legal Protection for Computer Programs to enable competition and innovation in the software industry.[59]

Less powerful nations have sometimes repulsed U.S. attempts to compel the shoring up of lower-protection rules, such as in the context of developing countries' access to essential medicines. The U.S. put considerable pressure on South Africa and Brazil to prevent them from adopting a compulsory licensing scheme for AIDS drugs to which the pharmaceutical industry objected.[60] Counter-pressures, however, arose from alliances among developing countries with similar concerns, non-governmental organizations concerned with health policy, and a global publicity campaign focusing on the effects of restricting access to essential medicines.[61] The U.S. eventually backed off, although access to essential medicines remains a hotly contested issue.[62]

Unilateral pressure also undermines incentives for voluntary compliance with TRIPS.[63] If nations experience equally relentless unilateral pressure after TRIPS as before it, they may believe they have been denied a key benefit of the bargain they thought they had struck when agreeing to TRIPS.[64]

C. *Filing a complaint with the WTO*

Nations aggrieved by a particular form of IP arbitrage may file a complaint alleging that another WTO member state's low-protection rule violates the TRIPS Agreement.[65] A WTO Member may file a "violation complaint" if another WTO Member has adopted a measure impairing or nullifying a TRIPS obligation, or a "non-violation complaint" if "a member ... asserts that any objective of the Agreement is being impeded as a result of any measure applied by another member ..., whether or not it conflicts with the TRIPS Agreement."[66] The complainant's burden is easier to meet in violation cases: breach of a TRIPS obligation is presumed harmful.[67] To win a non-violation

---

[59] *See* Vinje, above n. 20, at 61–63.
[60] *See* SELL, above n. 10, at 146–62 (describing efforts by public health groups and consumer activists to construe TRIPS as permitting compulsory licensing of pharmaceutical patents and the U.S. response); *see also* Frederick M. Abbott, *Managing the Hydra: The Herculean Task of Ensuring Access to Essential Medicines* [this volume].
[61] *See* SELL, above n. 10, at 148–50.   [62] *See id.* at 155–58; Abbott, above n. 60.
[63] *See, e.g.,* Reichman, above n. 54, at 458–59 (discussing developing countries' possible responses to maximalist interpretations of TRIPS).
[64] *See* Peter M. Gerhart, *Reflections: Beyond Compliance Theory – TRIPS as a Substantive Issue,* 32 CASE W. RES. J. INT'L L. 357, 368–72 (2000) (modeling TRIPS as an international contract for which developing nations lack an independent arbiter of substantive validity).
[65] *See, e.g.,* David Palmeter, *National Sovereignty and the World Trade Organization,* 2 J. WORLD INTELL. PROP. 77, 79–82 (1999) (discussing the dispute settlement process). A flow chart of the WTO dispute settlement process can be found at World Trade Organization, The Panel Process, *at* http://www.wto.org/english/thewtoe/whatise/tife/disp2e.htm (visited Nov 4, 2003).
[66] Dreyfuss & Lowenfeld, above n. 14, at 283.   [67] *See id.*

case, by contrast, "the complaining party must demonstrate not only that it suffered a trade injury ... but that it was justified in relying on the nonoccurrence of that measure or event."[68] Furthermore, there is presently a "working understanding" that non-violation complaints should not be filed.[69]

Challenging forms of IP arbitrage, such as those discussed in Part II, as direct violations of TRIPS will, however, be difficult because they do not involve TRIPS minima.[70] These forms of arbitrage also involve new technology issues as to which there may be no established international norm for the dispute panel to apply.[71] Even if the moratorium on non-violation complaints eventually lapses, winning a non-violation complaint would be difficult because of the need to prove both harm and reliance on the other's forbearance from adopting the low-protection rule. Thus, concerns posed by IP arbitrage may be difficult to resolve through the WTO dispute process.

D. *Proposing more detailed harmonization*

Nations affected by IP arbitrage may propose that the TRIPS Agreement should be amended to incorporate additional, more detailed minimum standards.[72] Amending TRIPS to increase the level of IP protection required of WTO members, however, will not be easy.[73] Article 71.2 provides that TRIPS may be amended to adjust Members' obligations to higher levels of protection when such norms have been "accepted under [other multilateral] agreements by all Members of the WTO," after which they can be referred "to the Ministerial Conference for action ... on the basis of a consensus proposal

---

[68] *Id.* at 284. [69] Gerhart, above n. 64, at 384.

[70] A WTO panel may deem an IP rule to be a TRIPS minimum standard even if not expressly required by TRIPS if the rule, by consensus, is a well-established international norm of IP law. *See, e.g.*, Dreyfuss & Lowenfeld, above n. 14, at 289–91. The WTO Appellate Body has rejected arguments premised on disappointment of competitive expectations as a basis for claiming a direct violation of TRIPS. *See* Reichman, above n. 2, at 595–97.

[71] TRIPS is silent on anticircumvention laws and regulation of technologies with substantial noninfringing uses. Nor does it directly address research tools or software reverse engineering. *But see* Charles McManis, *Taking TRIPS on the Information Superhighway: International Intellectual Property Protection and Emerging Computer Technology*, 41 VILL. L. REV. 207, 232–52 (1996) (setting forth possible arguments that TRIPS permits reverse engineering of software).

[72] *See* Frederick M. Abbott, *The Future of the Multilateral Trading System in the Context of TRIPS*, 20 HASTINGS INT'L & COMP. L. REV. 661, 667–69 (1997) (discussing the process of amending TRIPS).

[73] *See* Graeme B. Dinwoodie, *The Development and Incorporation of International Norms in the Formation of Copyright Law*, 62 OHIO ST. L.J. 733, 777–82 (2001) (arguing that national courts should develop substantive bodies of international copyright law to resolve disputes because neither amending TRIPS nor pursuing WTO disputes is likely to achieve international harmonization in light of strong underlying notions of national cultural diversity).

from the Council for TRIPS."[74] Negotiations leading up to new multilateral agreements may take many years.

There are several reasons to believe that proposing more detailed TRIPS minima to overcome IP arbitrage would encounter resistance. The lower-protection Member can be expected to oppose any proposal to override its domestic rule. Insofar as that Member could articulate a pro-competition, pro-innovation, or other policy-based rationale for its rule, it may well win support from other WTO Members. Even if the contested measure does not directly impact developing countries, they may ally with the lower-protection nation to fend off more fine-grained harmonization. Proposing new harmonized standards would, moreover, open up opportunities for bargaining and concessions that proponents of higher-protection rules might ultimately find very costly.[75]

Finally, the norms in TRIPS will almost inevitably be at a sufficiently high level of abstraction that more than one interpretation will be plausible. No matter how detailed TRIPS minima become, ambiguities and differing interpretations will almost certainly persist, especially given that the emergence of new technologies so frequently poses interpretive challenges for existing norms.

E. Choosing isolation

Nations affected by IP arbitrage may also isolate themselves from the global trading community or the Internet, so that IP arbitrage cannot occur.[76] Alternatively, nations can adopt much more restrictive border control measures or build an elaborate firewall to impede Internet communications deemed objectionable.[77]

However, isolationism entails considerable costs. An underlying premise of TRIPS and other WTO Agreements is that international trade is a net positive for Members, their nationals, and the world economy. Self-imposed embargos, virtual or real, prevent domestic firms from accessing goods and services that may be important to domestic industrial capabilities.[78] They also dampen

---

[74] TRIPS Agreement, above n. 1, art 71.2. *See also id.* art 71.1. (permitting the TRIPS Council to consider modifications or amendments to TRIPS in light of new developments).

[75] *See* Gerhart, above n. 64, at 360 (noting that new rounds of negotiations for higher levels of protection under TRIPS may create new opportunities and incentives for developing countries to exaggerate the costs of compliance and insist on new concessions). *See also* Keith E. Maskus & Jerome H. Reichman, *The Globalization of Private Knowledge Goods and the Privatization of Global Public Goods* [this volume], Part III. A (calling for a moratorium on stronger international IP standards).

[76] Only North Korea and Myanmar have chosen not to connect to the Internet. *See* Froomkin, above n. 16, at 144.

[77] *See id.* at 144–46 (describing Vietnamese, Singaporean, and Chinese efforts to control Internet access).

[78] *See id.* at 146:

> The tighter the filter, the greater the opportunity cost in lost ability to access the rest [of] the world's data.... In order for such a strategy to have any

prospects for foreign investment. Moreover, developing more extensive border controls or building firewalls will be expensive, with costs rising with restrictiveness.[79] The costs of isolationism are likely to be so substantial as to make this option infeasible for most nations.

F. Accepting IP arbitrage

It is, of course, possible for nations confronted with IP arbitrage simply to accept that the arbitrage has occurred and that their rule is infeasible to enforce. In some cases, nations can resort to other mechanisms for enabling domestic innovators to obtain resources necessary to support R&D in the particular field. For example, public funding for the development of research tools may provide adequate incentives for their development, which could obviate the need for patents to serve this function.[80]

Conclusion

The TRIPS Agreement has not eliminated economic incentives for nations to adopt, depending on their domestic circumstances, higher- or lower-protection rules. Innovators in nations with higher-protection rules will often, but not always, be able to enjoy at least partial protection in that nation's market. A lower-protection foreign rule will sometimes undermine a higher-protection domestic rule by creating incentives to shift the locus of economic activity to the less protective jurisdiction. Nations affected by IP arbitrage may encounter difficulties when responding either by adjustments to national rules or by actions in the international arena.

Whether IP arbitrage is consistent with TRIPS depends on one's viewpoint. Under a very broad interpretation of TRIPS,[81] IP arbitrage seems inconsistent with TRIPS because such arbitrage frustrates its objective

---

        hope of success, the government must be prepared to resist domestic pressure, pressure from abroad, and especially pressure from foreign firms with local offices that, like those established in Singapore, are likely to protest loudly at having their data and communications monitored.

[79] See id.
[80] See, e.g., Eisenberg, above n. 51, at 165–75 (discussing government policy with respect to publicly funded research since 1980).
[81] See, e.g., Jane C. Ginsburg, *International Copyright: From a "Bundle" of National Copyright Laws to a Supranational Code?*, 47 J. COPYRIGHT SOC'Y 265, 284 (2000) ("International uniformity of substantive norms favors the international dissemination of works of authorship. If the goal is to foster the world-widest possible audiences for authors in the digital age, then one might conclude that national copyright norms are vestiges of the soon-to-be bygone analog world.").

to enable innovators to recoup R&D investments on a global basis.[82] Yet, if one takes the broad view seriously, the most appropriate responses to IP arbitrage would be either to file a WTO complaint or propose amendments to TRIPS. A WTO complaint would be unlikely to succeed as long as the working moratorium on non-violation complaints persists. Unilateral pressure or expansion of the scope of domestic law or its territorial reach may be much more likely to succeed than a WTO complaint or a proposal to amend TRIPS, but these measures would be inconsistent with broadly conceived multilateral obligations.

Under a narrow view,[83] TRIPS allows broad national discretion to adopt locally appropriate rules to promote domestic development objectives. Because some nations will have incentives to adopt higher-protection rules and others lower-protection rules, IP arbitrage may be the inevitable result of economic forces playing themselves out in the global arena. But if TRIPS obligations are truly minimal, it may be fair game for nations with higher-protection rules to exert pressure on nations with low-protection rules or to extend the scope of domestic protection or territorial reach of domestic laws in an attempt to restore partial protection, given the futility of filing a WTO complaint or proposing more detailed harmonization.

If neither the broad nor narrow view of TRIPS is indisputable, it is perhaps understandable that nations with higher-protection rules would both interpret TRIPS very broadly and continue to pressure nations with less protective rules to change them, and that developing nations would both view TRIPS narrowly and yet also object to attempts to strong-arm them into adopting higher-protection rules.[84]

IP arbitrage may neither be inherently at odds with TRIPS nor inherently compatible with TRIPS, but perhaps sometimes at odds, and sometimes compatible, depending on its economic effects.[85] IP arbitrage is a manifestation of

---

[82] Although the WTO Appellate Body has rejected a "competitive expectations" test as a measure of TRIPS violations, *see* above n. 70, that may change if the moratorium on non-violation complaints lapses. *But see* Reichman, above n. 2 (arguing that WTO Appellate Body understood that "competitive expectations" test in the IP context would result in unbargained – for trade concessions).

[83] *See, e.g.*, Reichman, above n. 54, at 448 (concluding that "TRIPS law consists essentially of the negotiated rules and no more," and arguing for a "strict constructionist" interpretation of TRIPS obligations); *see also* Maskus & Reichman, above, n. 75 (arguing that optimal level of protection in incipient transnational system of innovation remains unknown and requires period of experimentation).

[84] *See* Dreyfuss & Lowenfeld, above n. 14, at 281 ("The architects of the TRIPS Agreement used words – and a concept of minimum standards – that allowed each state to read into the Agreement what it wished to see.").

[85] *See, e.g.*, Steven P. Croley & John H. Jackson, *WTO Dispute Procedures, Standard of Review, and Deference to National Governments*, 90 AM. J. INT'L L. 193, 208–09 (1996) (arguing that deference to national decision-making on IP rules is appropriate, except when "self-serving interpretations of the agreement that are *arguably* but not *persuasively* faithful to the text" would "erode the agreement through interpretation").

competition among higher- and lower-protection rules in the global economy; a higher-protection rule may sometimes be necessary to create adequate incentives for particular classes of innovation, and sometimes not. If lower-protection rules promoting research uses, interoperability, the public domain, and related values are economically sound, then as long as at least one nation adopts them, beneficiaries may include not only residents of the adopting nation, but those of other nations that can obtain access to products via the Internet or through the normal operation of international trade.[86] For those concerned that very strong IP rules are impeding innovation, competition, and other societal goals,[87] as well as for those who believe that "user rights" should become part of the TRIPS agenda,[88] IP arbitrage may provide some good news.

---

[86] IP arbitrage may also serve as some, albeit incomplete, check on the public choice problem with intellectual property rules in high-protection jurisdictions.

[87] *See, e.g.*, Reichman, above n. 54, at 450–51 (discussing developing countries' concerns about TRIPS's social costs); Maskus & Reichman, above n. 75 (questioning impact of high IP standards on the proper provision of global public goods).

[88] *See, e.g.*, Rochelle Cooper Dreyfuss, *TRIPS-Round II: Should Users Strike Back?*, 71 U. CHI. L. REV. 21 (2004); *see also* Peter Gerhart, *Distributive Values and Institutional Design in the Provision of Global Public Goods* [this volume].

24

An agenda for radical intellectual property reform

WILLIAM KINGSTON*

I. Capture of intellectual property law
II. Globalization of laws
III. Implications of the WTO
IV. A radical agenda for reform
V. Compulsory arbitration
VI. Improving the measurement of grants
VII. Conclusion

The topic of this volume is one aspect of a broader issue, which is the capture of the laws of property by interests that can benefit from them. Individual property rights have intrinsic social value because they can civilize self-interest by forcing it to serve the public good. This phenomenon provides escape from "the tragedy of the commons" by preserving natural resources, and it also makes innovation possible.[1] Because information constitutes a "natural commons," the production of valuable information goods could fail to attract investment without property rights. Since innovation is the turning of information into concrete reality, if copying could not be prevented, there would be little information worth copying and little innovation.

However, the fruitful harmony between private interest and public good that property rights can deliver is inherently unstable. Those who are forced to promote the public good with what they own readily learn how to escape such constraints. They do this by gaining control of the relevant property laws and reshaping them to advance their private interests. Indeed, because property laws are always under threat of corruption in this way, John Stuart Mill could rightly note that "the laws of property have never yet conformed to the principles on which the institution of private property rests."[2]

---

* William Kingston is Research Associate at the School of Business Studies, Trinity College, Dublin: wkngston@tcd.ie.
[1] See the most influential article on economics ever written by a biologist, Garrett Hardin's *The Tragedy of the Commons*, 162 SCIENCE 1243 (1968).
[2] JOHN STUART MILL, PRINCIPLES OF POLITICAL ECONOMY, bk. II, ch. I. (1862) (*reprinted in* Longman 1994).

The ability of property owners to influence legislation has accelerated greatly during the last century, a trend that was noted as early as 1962 by Buchanan and Tullock in their famous book "The Calculus of Consent:"

> We may observe a notable expansion in the range and extent of collective activity over the last half-century – especially in that category of activity appropriately classified as differential or discriminatory legislation. During the same period we have witnessed also a great increase in investment in organized interest-group efforts designed specifically to secure political advantage.[3]

An important element of this influence has been the growing cost of financing election campaigns. Since Buchanan and Tullock wrote, political campaign expenses have grown at what looks like an exponential rate in every democratic country. In particular, the advent of television has escalated the costs of becoming elected and has made politicians correspondingly vulnerable to those who bear these costs.[4] This accounts for the size and dynamism of the contemporary lobbying industry, and the new kinds of property that have been created by its efforts, as well as the strengthening of older kinds.

I. Capture of intellectual property law

So what we are discussing here is how other values that are necessary for holding a society together may or may not provide an environment for just one kind of property, within which self-interest is disciplined so as to serve the public good. Interest groups will invariably try anything to shape the laws to suit themselves, as was evident quite early in the history of modern intellectual property – long before the TRIPS Agreement provided such an egregious example of this same tendency. Werner Siemens, for example, went into politics to bring about the German 1877 Patent Law, which the emerging electrical and chemical industries needed.[5] The German chemical industry financed three successive referenda in Switzerland to ensure the passage of a patent law there. They also skillfully used the "national treatment" provision of the Paris Convention to dominate world chemical markets, until their patents in the U.S. and U.K. were expropriated at the outset of the first world war.[6]

---

[3] J.M. BUCHANAN & G. TULLOCK, THE CALCULUS OF CONSENT 289 (1962).
[4] BRUCE L. NEWMAN, THE MASS MARKETING OF POLITICS (Sage Publications 1999).
[5] ALFRED HEGGEN, ERFINDUNGSSCHUTZ UND INDUSTRIALISIERUNG IN PREUSSEN 1793–1877, 115–118 (Göttingen, Vandenhoeck & Ruprecht 1975).
[6] *See* JONATHAN LIEBENAU, THE CHALLENGE OF NEW TECHNOLOGY (Gower Publishing 1988). The German 1877 Patent Act only granted patents for chemical processes, not products. But under the national treatment provision of the Paris Convention for the Protection of Industrial Property (1863), as Revised at Stockholm 1967, art. 2(1), German chemical firms were able to get product patents in countries that offered such protection, including the U.S. and U.K. To enjoy the benefit of process patents, local manufacture is

It is also telling to consider the contrast between the ways in which the first and the present United States Patent Acts came into being. Behind the 1790 Act was a philosophical discussion between Jefferson and Madison on the dangers of monopoly. By contrast, the current Act was shaped by the pharmaceutical industry. In the words of a judge who, as a patent attorney, played an important part in the process,

> The [1952] Patent Act was written basically by patent lawyers... A good 95% of the members [of Congress] never knew that the legislation was under consideration, or that it had passed, let alone what it contained.[7]

Copyright law is no different. Professor Litman has shown how great the influence of private interests in shaping it has been for over a century.[8] And both Professors Susan Sell and Pamela Samuelson have monitored and described how this kind of lobbying actually operates.[9]

II. Globalization of laws

The capture of lawmaking by private interests is also reflected in the accelerating globalization of property laws and rights since the second World War. United States firms came out of the war with an ability to produce physical goods that surpassed anything ever seen before, and consequently, they wanted the widest possible markets to take advantage of this ability. Every country had tried to cope with the great depression of the 1930s by erecting trade barriers, so the U.S. took the initiative in setting up the General Agreement on Tariffs and Trade (GATT) in 1947 to prevent the revival of these barriers. Over a series of "Rounds" of tariff and quota reductions, the GATT was very successful in freeing up access to world markets for many kinds of manufactured goods.

It was easy for the United States to lead this process so long as its own dominance in manufacturing capability persisted. But with the astonishing and unforeseen emergence of similar and even greater capabilities in the Far East – first in Japan, then in countries such as South Korea, Taiwan, and now China – the American manufacturing industry became highly vulnerable, and even experienced rustbelts in its home market. At the same time, other U.S. industries, such as entertainment and information processing, became the

---

necessary, but that is not true for product patents. The German industry very quickly learned how to use this advantage.

[7] Judge Rich, *quoted in* P.J. Federico, *Origins of Section 103*, *in* Nonobviousness – The Ultimate Condition of Patentability 1:10, 1:11 (John F. Witherspoon ed., Bureau of National Affairs 1978).

[8] Jessica Litman, *Copyright, Compromise, and Legislative History*, 72 Cornell L. Rev. 857 (1987).

[9] Susan Sell, Private Power: Public Law (Cambridge University Press 2003). *See also* Pamela Samuelson, *The U.S. Digital Agenda at WIPO*, 37 Va. J. Int'l L. 360 (1997).

victims of wholesale copying, especially in countries such as China, Hong Kong and Singapore.

When the Uruguay Round of multilateral trade negotiations began in 1986, the United States was determined to use this forum to reverse these trends. The eventual result was the changing of the GATT into the World Trade Organization (WTO), whose emergence in 1994 can only be understood as a reflection of American despair about the growth of worldwide competition, most of which seemed to be unfair.

The most important difference between the two sets of international arrangements is the inclusion in the Agreement Establishing the WTO of intellectual property through the TRIPS Agreement,[10] and trade in services (primarily banking) through the General Agreement on Trade in Services (GATS).[11] The problem that the United States faced with the pre-existing intellectual property Conventions was that they were gentlemen's agreements and were cynically treated as such by those who were free-riding on American-originated ideas, information and innovations. There was no compulsion for countries to join – India, for example, built up a formidable pharmaceutical industry using discoveries made in the advanced countries by keeping out of the Paris Convention. Nor could anything be done about the failure of judicial systems to be even-handed in adjudicating intellectual property disputes between natives and foreigners. In particular, the way in which Japan enjoyed all the advantages of membership of the Conventions, such as being able to obtain strong trademark, patent and copyright protection in the United States by dint of national treatment clauses,[12] while giving minimal protection to U.S. firms in return, was particularly damaging and infuriating.[13]

One reason why the GATT had worked well was that it provided for sanctions against countries that broke its rules. The Great Conventions had no equally effective dispute-settlement provisions, so an obvious line of improvement to follow was to shift intellectual property into the GATT framework, where trade concessions could also be given as side payments for IP protection. The Uruguay Round negotiations began in this way, but the goal of

---

[10] Agreement on Trade-Related Aspects of Intellectual Property Rights, 15 Apr. 1994, Marrakesh Agreement Establishing the World Trade Organization, Annex 1C, LEGAL INSTRUMENTS – RESULTS OF THE URUGUAY ROUND vol. 31, 33 I.L.M. 81 (1994) [hereinafter TRIPS Agreement].

[11] General Agreement on Trade in Services, 15 Apr. 1994, Marrakesh Agreement Establishing the World Trade Organization, Annex 1B, LEGAL INSTRUMENTS – RESULTS OF THE URUGUAY ROUND, 33 I.L.M. 1167 (1994).

[12] See, e.g., Paris Convention for the Protection of Industrial Property, 20 Mar. 1883, as revised at Stockholm on 14 July 1967, 828 U.N.T.S. 305, art. 2(1); Berne Convention for the Protection of Literary and Artistic Works, 9 Sept. 1886, as revised at Paris on 24 July 1971, 1161 U.N.T.S. 3, art. 5(1).

[13] See, e.g., D.W. Spero, Patents or Piracy? A CEO Looks at Japan, 86 HARV. BUS. REV. 58 (1990).

the aggressive campaign of the U.S. Trade Representative quickly became instead "to impose a comprehensive set of intellectual property standards on the rest of the world."[14]

On the issue of the increasing ability of special interests to capture lawmaking, it is worth pointing out that it was the German chemical *industry*, not the government, which brought pressure to bear on Switzerland to create a Patent Act, whereas in the TRIPS case, the industrial interests were able to act through the U.S. Trade Representative.[15]

III. Implications of the WTO

The secondary group of OECD countries all joined the WTO, which involves accepting the TRIPS Agreement, as a necessary condition for getting inward foreign investment, especially from U.S. high-technology firms. Japan had to start abandoning its protectionist intellectual property policies and procedures. India has also joined and will now have to grant patents to Western pharmaceutical firms.

Third-world countries agreed to accept the obligations of the TRIPS Agreement, including dispute-settlement and enforcement provisions, in exchange for promises of better access to the markets of the rich countries for their textiles and agricultural produce and for some traditional manufactures. Even the poorest of the signatory countries are now being forced to adopt minimum standards of intellectual property law and to establish arrangements for its enforcement.

Disgracefully, some of the undertakings given to them in exchange have been reneged upon. E.U. barriers against third-world produce remain as high as ever, and U.S. support for its own agriculture has actually increased.

It is bad enough for countries to be pushed into accepting an intellectual property system that does not suit their needs, without this system being flawed to start with. But the international system is saddled with problems that have progressively arisen from its inflexibility in the face of new kinds of information products and new ways of generating them.[16] For example, patent laws have never properly come to grips with innovations brought about through large-scale investment in R&D, and copyright laws have similarly failed to match the shift from individual creative work to material produced

---

[14] J.H. Reichman, *Securing Compliance with the TRIPS Agreement After U.S. v. India*, 1 J. INT'L ECON. L. 585 (1998). *See also* Keith E. Maskus & Jerome H. Reichman, *The Globalization of Private Knowledge Goods and the Privatization of Global Public Goods* [this volume].

[15] PETER DRAHOS, & JOHN BRAITHWAITE, INFORMATION FEUDALISM: WHO OWNS THE KNOWLEDGE ECONOMY? 90 et seq. (The New Press 2003); SELL, above n. 9.

[16] *See* W. Kingston, *Intellectual Property's Problems: How Far is the U.S. Constitution to Blame?*, 4 INTELL. PROP. Q. 315 (2002).

"for hire." New ways of inventing and new kinds of information goods that really need *sui generis* protection have been forced into existing arrangements, as happened with copyright protection of computer programs and patents for biotechnology. There is no shortage of evidence that this process is becoming more and more difficult and that the results are correspondingly less satisfactory.[17]

The intent of the TRIPS Agreement is perfectly clear. From the start of the industrial revolution, every country that became economically great began by copying: the Germans copied the British, the Americans copied the British and the Germans, and the Japanese copied everybody. The thrust of the TRIPS Agreement is to ensure that this process of growth by copying and learning by doing will never happen again. As a vehicle for increasing worldwide market power, it can only result in intensifying and perpetuating inequality in technology and wealth between the rich and poor countries of the world. Its benefits will be enjoyed by the firms in the advanced countries that are either technologically innovative or owners of major brands. The extension of market power through the TRIPS Agreement will relegate the indigenous firms of all but the richest countries to secondary status in both economic areas.

IV. A radical agenda for reform

What can be done to improve matters? The flaws in the existing IP system are too deep-seated to be dealt with by tinkering, which is all that even diplomatic conferences can do (when they are not actually dominated by special interests). Root and branch reform is needed, but a start could be made with a proposal for alleviating some problems with the TRIPS Agreement itself that would not require legislation, and consequently, could well be achievable in the medium term. There seems to be a reasonable chance that it would not be opposed by the interests most concerned, and it might even be welcomed by them.

My proposal is to establish a formal link between intellectual property and Third-World aid. Policies for giving aid to poor countries have been almost completely insulated from policies for trading with them, such as those which the WTO exists to administer. But what if we were to use a significant portion of foreign aid funds to *buy out* the foreign intellectual property rights of Western firms and dedicate them to the local indigenous sector? A start could be made with patents, and if this were successful, copyrights might follow.

It is now widely accepted that there is little benefit to show from the aid policies the rich countries have been following. Everyone knows that apart from being prodigiously wasted, much of the money provided by government-to-government aid ended up in secret accounts in the tax havens of corrupt politicians in the receiving countries. The recent U.S. Millennium Challenge

---

[17] *See, e.g.*, D. Vaver, *Patently Absurd*, OXFORD TODAY (MICHAELMAS ISSUE), 2000, at 21.

Account and the British International Finance Facility proposals at the 2002 meeting of the G8 countries reflect a fundamental shift in emphasis away from the government-to-government model. It is now better understood that escape from poverty in poor countries will largely depend upon private enterprise, just as it did in the West. But directing human creative energy into economic channels depends upon individual property rights. Consequently, intellectual property has a big part to play in the economic development of today's poor countries, just as it has contributed to Western prosperity, but it must be of a kind that is appropriate to local needs.

It would be absolutely essential that buying out the foreign intellectual property of Western firms should not reduce the profits they need for continuing and expanding R&D investment. This should not be a problem, since the total aid budget of the contributing countries currently amounts to $50 billion a year, and this figure is intended to be doubled by 2015. Even by the most generous estimates of its value, the cost of buying out Western intellectual property in the poorest countries could easily be absorbed into this amount.

This scheme would also be one of the very best ways of spending aid funds. Firms in Third-world countries would become free to use and develop our technologies as far as their resources allowed, and they would learn essential lessons for economic development even from failed attempts to do so. At the same time, innovative firms in the West would probably get more net revenue from their intellectual property than they do under present arrangements, given that they would have no litigation costs to obtain it. In political terms, making such a gesture would free Western countries from a significant charge of economic imperialism, and it could generate considerable goodwill in parts of the world where it is in particularly short supply at present. In poor countries, the potential for indigenous innovation is probably greatly overestimated, and resentment of the TRIPS Agreement as the scapegoat for their failure to achieve it is correspondingly bitter.

Of course, any such measures would have to be accompanied by more precise controls on imports into Western countries, so that leakage from products made and sold abroad would not undermine the profits that are needed for high-risk investment in invention and innovation. It seems likely, however, that the measures necessary to deal with international terrorism (itself partly fuelled by perceptions of Western economic aggressiveness) could include these controls.

V. Compulsory arbitration

As Professor Barton has shown, returns on investment in innovation are being increasingly eroded by the litigation costs of attempting to protect the results or of resisting attempts by others to restrict the use of information that they claim to own.[18] It is particularly absurd to have an elaborate system for making grants of intellectual property that only has value to the extent that the grantees have the resources to protect it in court and are willing to bear the high risk of doing so. An invalid patent in the hands of a firm with large resources to litigate is, for all intents and purposes, a valid one. Intimidation of weaker owners of intellectual property by those with greater resources for litigation has been clearly documented in recent survey work and case studies for the European Commission.[19]

A practical solution would be compulsory, pre-litigation technical arbitration. Indeed, the viability of this solution is strongly supported by empirical data.[20] In particular, the United States Patent and Trademark Office's interference procedures provide a very good working model of arbitration of patent disputes by experts. Over the twelve year period studied, only five percent of decisions were even partially changed as a result of appeal to courts.

Outside the intellectual property arena, disputes arise all the time regarding technical contracts, yet very few of them reach the courts because such contracts normally have built-in provisions for arbitration by experts. But as far as intellectual property is concerned, financially strong firms will not voluntarily agree to arbitration, since this would end their ability to intimidate weaker firms by threatening to impose heavy litigation costs upon them. The fact that the arbitration system set up by the World Intellectual Property Organization (WIPO) has been so rarely used for settling patent disputes confirms this point. Legislation for compulsory arbitration of intellectual property disputes is clearly in the public interest, but private pressures have prevented it from being introduced and could be expected to be mobilized against any move in that direction.

VI. Improving the measurement of grants

By far the most promising potential reform of intellectual property would be to add a financial dimension to duration in the existing measure of intellectual property grants. The famous nineteenth-century English scientist, Lord Kelvin, claimed that "we advance according to the precision of our measures," and this surely does not apply only to science. The use of time alone to measure IP grants is an aspect of intellectual property's inflexibility, and is a hopelessly primitive yardstick for the complex arrangements for information protection that are needed today.

---

[18] J. Barton, *Reforming the Patent System*, 287 SCIENCE 1933 (2000). *See also* John H. Barton, *Issues Posed by a World Patent System* [this volume].
[19] Enforcing Small Firms' Patent Rights, European Commission Publication (2001), available at http://www.cordis.lu/innovation-policy/studies/2001/management03.htm.
[20] W. Kingston, *The Case for Compulsory Arbitration: Empirical Evidence*, 4 EUR. INTELL. PROP. REV. 154 (2000).

An E.U. Expert Committee has recommended investigation of a specific proposal for measuring grants of intellectual property in terms of money as well as time by means of compulsory licensing provisions that require *capital* payments for licenses.[21] These payments would be a prescribed, socially-acceptable multiple of the investment that brought about the innovation.[22] Empirical research has shown that the calculation of such "multiples" is feasible.[23]

Among the advantages claimed for this approach are that it would reduce the number of patents of doubtful validity granted in complex technologies, not for protection of genuine invention, but as bargaining counters to enable firms to gain access to their competitors' incremental improvements to their products. It would also improve diffusion of innovations and put an end to the growing and worrying tendency to grant exclusive rights "on what used to be considered as 'science' and introduced into the public domain."[24] And it would remove the need for worldwide concern about the grant of patents that deliver real monopolies on genetic material and on related research instruments, while still providing appropriate protection for computer software and databases.

VII. Conclusion

The TRIPS Agreement has been sold in the name of "harmonization," but this is the Trojan horse of intellectual property, and those of us who place a high value on human creativity must do all we can to keep it outside the walls of our City. Because diversity is characteristic of creativity, any intellectual property system should correspondingly reflect this diversity and fight shy of standardization.

In most cases, firms that have the resources to spend heavily on research and development also have large investments in production and marketing assets (which give them the valuable protection of lead time). Except in the pharmaceutical industry, these investments generally create enough market power to protect their inventions without the need for intellectual property protection as well. Because firms without such resources cannot do without intellectual property protection if they are to invent and innovate, it is to their needs that the system should be tailored.

---

[21] Strategic Dimensions of Intellectual Property Rights in the Context of Science & Technology Policy: An ETAN Report, EUR 18914 § 3.4 (Publications Office of the Commission of European Communities 1999).
[22] W. Kingston, *Intellectual Property Needs Help from Accounting*, 11 EUR. INTELL. PROP. REV. 508 (2002).
[23] William Kingston, *Compulsory Licencing with Capital Payments as an Alternative to Monopoly Grants for Intellectual Property*, 23(5) RES. POL'Y 661 (1994).
[24] R. Mazzoleni & R.R. Nelson, *Economic Theories about the Benefits and Costs of Patents*, 32 J. ECON. ISSUES 1031 (1998). *See also* Richard R. Nelson, *Linkages Between the Market Economy and the Scientific Commons* [this volume].

COMMENTARY

Comment: Whose rules, whose needs? Balancing public and private interests

GEOFF TANSEY*

This comment is a broad personal reflection on some major issues arising in the world of intellectual property (IP) today. It is based on my experiences over the past few years, especially with the Quaker United Nations Office (QUNO) in Geneva.

I. Background

Fundamentally, I came to see that IP rules matter because they increasingly affect the distribution of power and wealth and determine the roups that drive and control the direction and pace of change and the dimensions of the space within which we all work and exist. I have always remembered a Wizard of ID cartoon from years ago in which the King says "he who make the rules gets the gold." And that, in essence, is what today's IP rules are about.

The globalized rules on IP are part of a broader rewriting of the rules of the world, a development I first came to understand through my work on the global food system.[1] At the heart of this reformation lie issues of power and control, risks and benefits – who has what power to control their part of the system and thereby to minimize risks and maximize benefits. Two key trends are evident in the food system, for example. One is an increasing concentration of economic power within any sector. The other is use of various tools by the different actors in the system (input suppliers, farmers, traders, manufacturers, processors, distributors, retailers, caterers) to maximize control of the operations they perform as much as possible. To do this, they use science and technology and information and management tools within a framework of rules and regulations in which they try to influence the broader political process.

A blossoming scientific revolution in biology underpins technological developments that promise improved means of controlling plants and animals

---

* Geoff Tansey is an independent writer and consultant who works part time for the Quaker United Nations Office in Geneva, and has also worked with the U.K. Department for International Development. He is a member and a director of the Food Ethics Council and also an honorary visiting fellow in Peace Studies at the University of Bradford. The author wishes to thank Brewster Grace and Peter Drahos for helpful comments.

[1] See GEOFF TANSEY & TONY WORSLEY, THE FOOD SYSTEM – A GUIDE (Earthscan 1995).

for different actors in the food system.² These biological innovations also require alterations of the IP rules, among other things, if private innovators and corporate developers, rather than public research institutes, are to secure returns on their investments. This for me is the context underlying the revision of rules governing genetic resources and intellectual property rights (IPRs). But it is part of a bigger picture in which innovations in genetic information-based biology and digital-information technologies were powerful motivators for commercial investors to seek an extension of IPRs and a globalization of their effects.³ Both these goals were achieved in the TRIPS regime.⁴ It is also clear that IPRs are important tools used by firms in developing markets, who use them to seek market share, and to set competition and R&D strategies.⁵

Here are the key questions we as citizens must ask: are they the right rules, who helps shape and make them, in whose interests do they operate, and are they just and fair? How true are the justifications used to underpin them? How far are claims about rewarding creativity and providing an incentive for invention a mask for the protection of corporate investment? How can we as citizens balance the private interests of some with the public interest of humankind in the sharing of knowledge, a sound and healthy environment, food security, and equitable development? There are enormous philosophical and ideological differences in how different groups see the public and private sphere. There are often different perceptions between many in the United States and Europe and between those in developed countries and those in developing countries.

Apart from issues of food security, the other factor that drew me into the sometimes bizarre and odd mix of ingredients lumped together under the rubric of IPRs was some voluntary work in the mid-1990s with British Quakers. I was asked to join a small advisory committee supporting the Environmental Intermediaries Programme of Britain's Yearly Meeting. This work on the environment and development drew its inspiration from the Quakers' long-standing interest in peace and justice and a history of mediation in disputes. The program worked in two areas where there were, or were

---

² Robert E. Evenson, *Agricultural Research and Intellectual Property Rights* [this volume]; Timothy Swanson & Timo Goeschl, *Diffusion and Distribution: The Impacts on Poor Countries of Technological Enforcement within the Biotechnology Sector* [this volume].
³ See Keith E. Maskus & Jerome H. Reichman, *The Globalization of Private Knowledge Goods and the Privatization of Global Public Goods* [this volume]; Ruth L. Okediji, *Sustainable Access to Copyrighted Digital Information Works in Developing Countries* [this volume]. *See also* Laurence R. Helfer, Comment: *Using Intellectual Property Rights to Preserve the Global Genetic Commons: The International Treaty for Food and Agriculture* [this volume].
⁴ Agreement on Trade-Related Aspects of Intellectual Property Rights, 15 Apr. 1994, Marrakesh Agreement Establishing the World Trade Organization, Annex 1C, LEGAL INSTRUMENTS – RESULTS OF THE URUGUAY ROUND vol. 31, 33 I.L.M. 81 (1994) [hereinafter TRIPS Agreement].
⁵ *See, e.g.*, ASHISH ARORA ET AL., MARKETS FOR TECHNOLOGY: THE ECONOMICS OF INNOVATION AND CORPORATE STRATEGY (MIT Press 2001).

expected to be, conflicts of interest over environmental resources. In the area of genetic resources, its work initially focused on the little-known negotiations to revise the International Undertaking on Plant Genetic Resources at the UN's Food and Agriculture Organisation (FAO).[6] The aim was to help ensure that the countries of Southern Africa played an effective part in these negotiations, rather than offer them positions to take. This focus on process rather than promoting positions of substance has been at the heart of the QUNO approach.

This approach reflects the central concern of the Quakers that the processes bringing about new rules should be just and equitable. An important insight, based on the experience gathered over decades of Quaker involvement in conflict resolution, is that agreements reached by very unequal partners or in ways where one side feels considerably disadvantaged or dominated tend to sow the seeds of future disputes and conflict.[7]

By the mid-1990s, it was clear that new TRIPS rules coming into effect with the establishment of the World Trade Organization (WTO) would affect the future of genetic resources. Subsequently, the Quakers' genetic resources work was switched from London to the QUNO in Geneva and focused on the TRIPS Agreement.

A scoping exercise revealed that negotiation of the TRIPS Agreement – and Article 27.3(b) in particular[8] – had left a legacy of ill feeling and a range of concerns about its impact and validity.[9] Developing countries expected their concerns to be addressed in the mandated review of Article 27.3(b) in 1999. However, many developing-country missions felt unprepared for this review. They wanted an overview of the policy issues and an opportunity to develop greater analytical and negotiating capacity in this area. There was also a sense that while some of the larger developing countries had been involved in negotiating TRIPS and had secured some safeguards for their interests, many nations had little or no knowledge about its impact and felt unprepared to deal with the review. There was a feeling, moreover, that TRIPS as a whole was something they had acceded to only reluctantly or under pressure in order to gain benefits from other elements of the WTO agreements.[10]

II. Building more informed negotiators

A considerable gap in capacity to deal with these issues existed between developed and developing countries, both in the missions in Geneva and in national

---

[6] For details, see Michael Blakeney, *Stimulating Agricultural Innovation* [this volume].

[7] See Patents and Quaker Action, QUNO and the Quaker International Affairs Programme, *available at* www.geneva.quno.info *and* www.qiap.ca.

[8] Article 27.3(b) of the TRIPS Agreement, above n. 3, requires WTO Members to provide patent protection for micro-organisms and to establish a protection system for plant variety rights.

[9] This view is based on insights gained through various interviews with negotiators from developed and developing countries in 1998 prior to the QUNO work on TRIPS.

[10] See KEITH E. MASKUS, INTELLECTUAL PROPERTY RIGHTS IN THE GLOBAL ECONOMY (Institute for International Economics 2000).

capitals. As a contribution to redressing this imbalance, a policy discussion paper on Food, Trade, Intellectual Property and Biodiversity was produced in 1998, financed by the U.K.'s Department for International Development.[11] After publication, QUNO began a series of informal, off-the-record meetings in 1999 for members of developing-country missions to meet and improve their understanding of these issues. They provided an opportunity to hear from a range of perspectives and also to engage with officials from developed countries. These meetings provided a space for missions to debate issues and develop confidence to engage with developed countries, whose interests they saw as different from their own. Despite QUNO's expectation that the program would be short, it has continued to the present and now encompasses IPRs and health as well.

This experience has shown that the processes by which rule-making operates are deeply flawed and unfair. It also illustrates the great difficulties faced by developing countries, not just in the WTO but also through pressure in bilateral trade negotiations to go beyond what they had already accepted in the TRIPS Agreement. That a small non-governmental organization, with hardly any resources, should be important for developing countries in their ability to understand issues and gain advice on drafting text is, in any rational world, crazy. Sadly, we do not live in a rational negotiating world. Our challenge is, at least in part, to make the system sufficiently rational that all human interests are represented and accounted for.

III. Towards a new system of rule-making

Some of these problems can be partly addressed through capacity-building, as indeed is going on in the TRIPS and Development Capacity-Building Project undertaken by the United Nations Conference on Trade and Development (UNCTAD) and the International Center for Trade and Sustainable Development (ICTSD).[12] Many problems cannot be addressed this way and require a rethinking about how we make rules and the substantive effects they have. It is clear in many areas that the emerging IP regime is not meeting human needs but rather bolstering the protectionist status quo.[13]

---

[11] Geoff Tansey, Trade, Intellectual Property, Food and Biodiversity: Key Issues and Options for the 1999 Review of Article 27.3(b) of the TRIPS Agreement, QUNO Discussion Paper (Feb. 1999), *available at* www.geneva.quno.info.
[12] For details about this project, *see* the ICTSD website *at* www.ictsd.org.
[13] *See*, COMMISSION ON INTELLECTUAL PROPERTY RIGHTS, INTEGRATING INTELLECTUAL PROPERTY RIGHTS AND DEVELOPMENT POLICY (2002); Jenny Lanjouw & Iain Cockburn, *New Pills for Poor People? Empirical Evidence after GATT*, 29 WORLD DEV. 265 (2001); Macroeconomics and Health: Investing in Health for Economic Development, Commission on Macroeconomics and Health Report (World Health Organization 2001); Generic Competition, Price and Access to Medicines, Oxfam Briefing Paper No. 26 (2002); Médecins Sans Frontières & Health Action International, Improving Access to Essential Medicines in East Africa: Patents and Prices in a Global

If we look back to the nineteenth century, a powerful case can be made that it witnessed a rewriting of the rules on IP, on treating corporations as real persons, and on limited liability that helped shape the institutional economy we see today. In that century, technological innovation was already seen as a way of entering an industry, and patent-protected innovation was viewed as a means of gaining legal quasi-monopolistic control of certain products and sectors. Such inventors as George Eastman (Kodak) and Thomas Edison sought patents to enable them to capture monopoly profits. Even then, by institutionalising innovation in R&D labs, "large corporations sought to control technological change as a means of protecting and fortifying their positions in the industry."[14] They still do so today, and this broadly includes biotechnology.[15]

It often seems that innovation is assumed to be a good thing, automatically desirable for its own sake, which incorporates a protective bias into the IP system. Remarkably, we are less ready to look at innovation in our institutions and the rules that shape them. Much of the current pressure to expand and extend IP protection is a conservative force, likely to protect the structure of existing and narrow private interests rather than to expand and help institutional innovation in more public-interest structures.[16]

Why does it seem that there is a divine right for corporate institutions to survive and be protected behind more and more IP legislation, from copyright extensions for long-dead creators to patent rights given in lax regimes for dubious levels of inventiveness?[17] Should we not see the consequences of the IP regime as helping to bolster the creation and maintenance of unaccountable oligopolies and giving them power to impose a kind of private taxation built around their IP rights? Perhaps the software companies and pharmaceutical enterprises today are agencies of private taxation as much as innovation.

Here is where I think we need to change the language we use to talk about IP to reflect more closely the reality of what it is and what it allows. Then we would be better able to have a debate that sought to balance public and private interests and into which more people would feel able to enter. Creativity is a

---

Economy, Report on the East African Access to Essential Medicines Conference (Nairobi, 15–16 June 2000).

[14] R. JENKINS, IMAGES AND ENTERPRISE: TECHNOLOGY AND THE AMERICAN PHOTOGRAPHIC INDUSTRY 1839 TO 1925, at 6–7 (Johns Hopkins University Press 1975).

[15] R. Eisenberg & M. Heller, *Can Patents Deter Innovation? The Anticommons in Biomedical Research*, 280 SCIENCE 698 (1998).

[16] Paul A. David, *Koyaanisqatsi in Cyberspace: The Economics of an "Out-of-Balance" Regime of Private Property Rights in Data and Information* [this volume]; Richard R. Nelson, *Linkages Between the Market Economy and the Scientific Commons* [this volume]; Maskus & Reichman, above n. 3.

[17] Sonny Bono Copyright Term Extension Act, Pub. L. 105–298, 112 Stat. 2827 (1998). For a critical analysis of the operations of the United States Patent and Trademark Office (USPTO) in issuing low-quality patents, *see* TO PROMOTE INNOVATION: THE PROPER BALANCE OF COMPETITION AND PATENT LAW AND POLICY, Federal Trade Commission Report (Oct. 2003).

fundamental trait of human beings and it is fair and just that people should have the opportunity to be creative and to be rewarded for it. But IPRs are not necessarily the way to accomplish these ends. The languages of both property and rights pose problems, as we discussed in the Food Ethics Council report,[18] from which I quote and paraphrase below.

Human rights are inalienable and integral to people. They cannot be divorced from a personage, nor assigned by anyone to someone else. The various forms of IP may be a way of providing material rewards, but they should not be confused with human rights.[19]

Intellectual property rights can be assigned, licensed, bought and sold. However, for many people today, whether in universities or private companies, the IP arising from their creativity and invention belongs to their institutions. Companies themselves are a legal fiction, by which they are given the juridic equivalence of a real person. But they are not people. It is, rather, human beings who are creative, who enjoy the fruits of creativity and who also share knowledge and receive recognition. We have developed various institutional forms to harness and organize that creativity. In the process, we have produced a motor to drive the interests of institutions through their capacity to control and appropriate the skills of their employees.

The generic term "intellectual property rights" masks the different nature and origins of the various forms of IP, and conflates ideas and justifications that might be appropriate for one, such as copyright, with another, such as patents. If, as Peter Drahos, argues "The privilege that lies at the heart of all intellectual property is a state-based, rule-governed privilege to interfere in the negative liberties of others,"[20] then as a way of changing our understanding of IPRs we should use language that more accurately reflects what they are. It is time to take up his suggestion that "the language of property rights would be replaced by the language of monopoly privilege."[21]

Perhaps we should start talking about intellectually-based monopoly privileges (IMPs) to reflect more accurately that they are privileges granted by society to a few to exclude the rest. They can enrich the few, in the name of producing things society wants or as a means of rewarding creativity, but they may often be means of protecting investment and minimizing corporate risk. Such a change in language could help to restructure the debate about the kind of IP system and rules society wants, whom society wants to benefit, and the range of activities we want IMPs to cover. It would help regain sight of the social contract that lies

---

[18] TRIPS with Everything? Intellectual Property and the Farming World, Food Ethics Council Report (2002), *available at* www.foodethicscouncil.org.
[19] *See, e.g.*, Heinz Klug, Comment: *Access to Essential Medicines – Promoting Human Rights Over Free Trade and Intellectual Property Claims* [this volume].
[20] PETER DRAHOS, A PHILOSOPHY OF INTELLECTUAL PROPERTY 213 (Aldershot 1996). *See also* Peter Drahos, *The Regulation of Public Goods* [this volume].
[21] DRAHOS, above n. 20, at 223.

behind IP policy, which perspective is essential in food and farming. Another change needed to improve the process of making rules and to improve their substance is a much broader involvement of a wide range of people and interests, not simply those representing the vested interests that IPRs serve today.

Recent developments have shown that IPRs at heart are not just a legal and technical matter but an issue that affects relations between all human beings.[22] Intellectual property rights affect our access to, and ability to share, knowledge, medicines, food, art and literature, and many other critical public goods. The rules that societies invent help constrain or liberate the human spirit and affect human life. Therefore, they must be drawn up with wide public participation and in the recognition of both current and future public interests, and they must enhance the development capacity of the poor.

These imperatives mean that IP cannot be treated as a separate domain of its own, but rather as an element central to the development goals and objectives of society. The privileges they grant need to be matched not just by responsibilities, but also by liability regimes, by the prevention of restrictive practices, and so on.[23] They should not be used to promote the narrow sectoral or national interests of the currently powerful, but can be used, if appropriate, to empower the poor and weak. And these needs may mean changing the rules of the game internationally and resisting processes to seek ever-higher levels of IP protection.

For that to happen, IPRs need to become accessible as a topic of public interest and of political importance to societies at large. The challenge is to move the discussion and debate from scholarly fora to the general public and to engage people in ways that will help shape the rules for a new millennium. The challenge is also to make the rule-making processes more just within and between countries, and to do so in ways that prioritize the needs of the poor and empower them in their development efforts. Without this element, the dangerous prospect would remain of rules that bolster the growing divide in wealth and power around the world.[24] This division is not only immoral and unsustainable, but is also a threat to all our futures.

---

[22] For example, in the Doha Declaration of November 2001, Members of the WTO agreed that intellectual property rights policy could not take precedence over the needs of public health, and in August 2003, WTO members negotiated an explicit waiver to Article 31(f) of the TRIPS Agreement. WTO Doha Ministerial Declaration on the TRIPS Agreement and Public Health, WT/MIN(01)/DEC/2 (14 Nov. 2001) [hereinafter Declaration on TRIPS and Public Health]; Implementation of Paragraph 6 of the Doha Declaration on the TRIPS Agreement and Public Health, WTO General Council Decision No. WT/L/540 (30 Aug. 2003), *available at* http://www.wto.org/english/tratop_e/trips_e/implem_para6_e.htm#asterisk.

[23] *See, e.g.*, J. H. Reichman & Tracy Lewis, *Using Liability Rules to Stimulate Local Innovation in Developing Countries: Application to Traditional Knowledge* [this volume]; Hanns Ullrich, *Expansionist Intellectual Property Protection and Reductionist Competition Rules: A TRIPS Perspective* [this volume]; Josef Drexl, *The Critical Role of Competition Law in Preserving Public Goods in Conflict with Intellectual Property Rights* [this volume].

[24] See JOSEPH E. STIGLITZ, GLOBALIZATION AND ITS DISCONTENTS (Norton 2002).

25

Diffusion and distribution: The impacts on poor countries of technological enforcement within the biotechnology sector

TIMOTHY SWANSON
TIMO GOESCHL[*]

Abstract
I. Introduction
II. Biotechnology as regime change
    A. The need for plant variety protection
    B. International protection of plant breeders' rights
    C. Technological enforcement through genetic use restriction technologies (GURTs)
    D. Determination of the fair use of proprietary materials
    E. Policy interests in the use of plant varieties for further R&D
    F. Concluding evaluation of the movement to technological enforcement
III. The impacts of technological enforcement on benefit distribution
    A. Impacts of technological enforcement – Static and dynamic dimensions
    B. Impacts of GURTs on diffusion
    C. Benefits from technological enforceability
    D. The aggregate impact of GURTs: Assessing the full meaning of regime change
IV. Predicting industry's response by extrapolating from hybrid maize
    A. Comparative performance of crops with and without technological enforceability
    B. Forecasting the impacts of technological enforceability
    C. Aggregate impact of technological enforceability
V. Conclusion

---

[*] Timothy Swanson is Professor of Economics, University College London. Timo Goeschl is Lecturer in Environmental and Resource Economics, Cambridge University. The authors are grateful to Keith Maskus, Jim Symons, and participants in previous conferences and workshops for helpful suggestions.

ABSTRACT

Technological enforcement of proprietary rights in biotechnological innovations will result in uniformly and universally enforced rights in those innovations. These rights should generate enhanced returns to innovation, but at the cost of reduced rates of diffusion. The study estimates the impacts of technological enforcement on different states, depending on their initial conditions, and finds that those countries on the technological frontier will gain most, while those furthest from the frontier must wait many years to receive any benefits whatsoever. Technological enforcement will generate additional benefits but at the cost of a regressive impact on world benefit distribution.

I. Introduction

This chapter considers the impacts of biotechnological changes that are likely to eliminate the need for the domestic application of intellectual property rights (IPRs) laws within the agricultural sector. New technologies will soon render it feasible to sell biological organisms (such as seeds and plants) that are unable to be reproduced by the purchaser.[1] This innovation, once applied universally, will render unnecessary the domestic enforcement of seed patent legislation and plant variety protection. Then the restrictions on use inherent within those laws will be enforced technologically rather than legally, and these will have uniform impact on purchasers across the world. Technological enforcement will generate a globally uniform and universally enforceable system of proprietary rights.

What will be the impact of this movement away from a world of IPRs and toward a world of technologically enforced rights in innovations? At first blush, it might seem that this could only be bad for consumers, as their "own use" of the purchased products becomes carefully restricted by the producer. However, in the longer run, the movement toward inbuilt technological enforcement might redound to the consumer benefit. It would continue to be possible for producers to market both forms of products: plants with and plants without the capacity for reproduction. Those consumers who desired merely a "once only" use of the seed would pay a much lower price than those who wished to purchase the right to reproduce the plant indefinitely (akin to the difference in the price between a single copy of software and the price of a multiple use license).

In addition, inventors of new plant varieties would be able to capture the benefits of their innovations without the need for costly enforcement activities. This low-cost system of rent appropriation would then increase incentives to

---

[1] The technologies to which we refer are discussed in detail in the following section.

invest in innovation in the field of agriculture. It would, in effect, operate as a relatively costless and perfectly enforced system of IPRs.

Nevertheless, there is something disquieting about this movement away from legal regimes and toward IPRs perfectly enforced through technology. How can factors other than efficiency (such as fair use or equity) be taken into consideration under such a system? What will be the impact on the prevailing distribution of benefits under existing standards of use?

We address these issues in this chapter. We consider the impact of biotechnologies with the inbuilt capacity for enforcement, which we call "restriction technologies," and their inherent impacts on the diffusion and distribution of the benefits flowing from those technologies. This is a critical issue for consideration within the context of global negotiations on trade-related intellectual property rights. Such technologies allow innovators to move away from reliance upon negotiated outcomes and national IP systems and toward globally uniform protection systems. Future negotiations over the distribution of the benefits from innovation should take into consideration the impact of restriction technologies on that distribution.

We set out the major issues concerning technological enforcement, diffusion and distribution within a case study of the plant breeding industry. We explain why we expect these changes to occur in the agricultural industries in Section Two. Then we describe the anticipated impacts of such changes in Section Three. In Section Four, we discuss a study that examined how such changes affected developing and developed countries in the past, and we predict how diffusion and distribution will be influenced in the future.

We offer concluding remarks in Section Five. We find that technological enforcement should have substantial benefits for those countries nearest the technological frontier, but at the costs of slower diffusion and reduced benefits for those countries furthest from that frontier.

II. Biotechnology as regime change

Biotechnological advances in agriculture refer to two distinct forms of change: those directed to technological advances and those directed to industrial restructuring. The technological advances primarily involve improvements in genetic marking and transfer technologies, which enable new and sometimes dramatic changes in life forms to occur in short amounts of time.[2] The changes we investigate in this chapter concern the dramatic alterations to be expected within the *industry* of modern agriculture.[3] These changes concern primarily

---

[2] See ECONOMICS OF MANAGING BIOTECHNOLOGIES (Timothy Swanson ed., Kluwer 2003).
[3] For further analysis, see AGRICULTURE, BIOTECHNOLOGY AND THE DEVELOPING WORLD: THE DISTRIBUTIONAL ASPECTS OF TECHNOLOGICAL CHANGE (Timothy Swanson ed., Edward Elgar Publishing 2003).

the manner in which firms within the agricultural industry, including plant breeders and seed companies, make money, not how they make plants. The organizational trends that are underway will dramatically affect the manner in which these firms market their products in the future.

A. The need for plant variety protection

Why are industrial changes happening in the plant breeding industry? Consider the dilemma of the plant breeder who sells unprotected new plant varieties. Suppose the plant breeder recognizes that a widely used variety of, say, wheat is facing increasing problems of pest infestation. Suppose further that the breeder were to isolate the characteristic of a particular wheat variety that is resistant to the pest problems and to develop techniques that incorporate this characteristic into the widely used variety. After experimental trials, the firm would grow the new variety on sufficient land area to allow it to market its seed. Finally, the breeder would offer the new wheat variety to farmers. It would be offered on the market at a substantial premium over declining wheat varieties but with the promise of higher yields. Assume that a minority of farmers were to purchase the new variety the first year and found that it increased their yields substantially over the non-resistant variety. Then, at the end of the harvest year, these farmers could withhold some of their crop for re-planting the following year and could even sell seeds to neighboring farmers.

How much would such farmers charge for the seed? If there were enough of them, they would charge only the opportunity cost of the seed to them, or a little more than the price of a unit of wheat on the market. Thus, after just one year of a partial return on its investment, the plant breeder would find itself in competition with a multitude of sellers of its own product, all operating at the competitive price. In this way, the private market provides little prospect of a return from investments in the necessary research and development (R&D) on new plant varieties.

This is known in economics as the problem of the "durable goods monopolist."[4] The durable-goods monopolist is faced with the paradox that sales of its own product invite competitors into its market because the good's durability permits its purchasers to become re-sellers. Agricultural innovations fit this paradigm, but there is an additional problem contained within innovative plant varieties. These plant varieties not only may be re-sold, they also contain the *reproductive technology* that enables the plants to be re-produced identically and re-sold in large quantities. Furthermore, this activity may be undertaken with little investment other than the land required to plant the purchased seed. Therefore, the sale of an innovative plant variety introduces the prospect of

---

[4] *See, e.g.*, Lawrence M. Ausubel & Raymond J. Deneckere, *Durable Goods Monopoly with Incomplete Information*, 59 REV. ECON. STUD. 795 (1992).

competing producers, not just competing sellers. The innovator must consider the possibility that any sale of the new plant variety contains an implicit license to enter into its replication and production.

This problem implies that the innovator must either price its new product to include this implicit license or attempt to exclude purchasers from re-selling it. Either option is costly.[5] The sale of innovative plant varieties bundled with a license to reproduce or re-sell them would require a very high price and hence exclude those farmers who wished only to make a single-season's purchase. The innovator would need to recoup its investment in a single season's sales to a limited number of purchasers. In contrast, if the plant variety were sold without the license to reproduce, there must be a means of enforcing rights held privately. This solution would involve costly monitoring and enforcement activities by the country where the plant variety was sold.

Hence, the plant breeding industry in agriculture is faced with a serious variant of the durable-goods monopoly problem. But why should the world's agricultural consumers care about the resolution of this problem? The answer lies in the need to provide returns from the investments by the producers of new plant varieties, in order to induce them to continue working on solutions to recurring problems of pest resistance and yield decline.[6] Central to this need is that the widespread use of a small number of plant varieties – as often occurs in modern agriculture – implies that pest infestation and epidemics increase over the time of use.[7] Because of these dynamics, a widely-used plant variety tends to have a commercial life of only about five to seven years.[8] In turn, plant breeders must work continuously on producing new, innovative varieties in order to replace the old. If these new varieties did not come on-line at the same rate that the old ones declined, modern agriculture would become impracticable.

The plant breeding sector must make substantial investments in R&D before a new plant variety can be developed and released.[9] The only way in which this

---

[5] Timo Goeschl & Timothy Swanson, *Genetic Use Restriction Technologies and the Diffusion of Yield Gains to Developing Countries*, 12 J. INT'L DEV. 1159 (2000).

[6] Plant breeders' research and development efforts are increasingly addressed to the ongoing problems of pest adaptation and resistance. Pests and disease now account for average annual crop losses of 28.9 percent, increasing with each year of the use of a given plant variety. E.C. OERKE ET AL., CROP PRODUCTION AND CROP PROTECTION – ESTIMATED LOSSES IN MAJOR FOOD AND CASH CROPS (Elsevier 1994); L.T. EVANS, CROP EVOLUTION, ADAPTATION, AND YIELD (Cambridge University Press 1993).

[7] Well-established laws of evolution exist to describe this type of pathogen response, driven by the scale of application of a new technology within a biological environment. J. HOFBAUER & K. SIGMUND, THE THEORY OF EVOLUTION AND DYNAMICAL SYSTEMS (Cambridge University Press 1988).

[8] P.W. Heisey ed., Accelerating the Transfer of Wheat Breeding Gains to Farmers: A Study of the Dynamics of Varietal Replacement in Pakistan, CIMMYT Research Report No. 1 (1990).

[9] *See* R. Evenson & D. Gollin, Priority Setting for Genetic Improvement Research, paper presented at International Rice Research Institute Workshop on Rice Research Prioritization

sector can acquire compensation for these investments in the private marketplace is by means of some sort of exclusive marketing rights in the resulting innovative varieties. Simply selling the seed in competition with others would generate no return to the innovator. Rather, it would generate only a return from the land planted. The standard economic rationale for IPRs, that they provide a limited monopoly right in order to generate returns from investments in new innovations, holds precisely as regards the plant breeder's dilemma. Without a clear means for appropriating the value of its investments, the firm has little incentive to pursue R&D in this field. But without this activity, modern agriculture would have little capacity for continuing into the indefinite future.

B. *International protection of plant breeders' rights*

The plant breeding industry has lobbied for an enforceable method of appropriating the value of innovation for several decades. So-called "Plant Breeders' Rights" came into being originally in Europe and then in the United States more than a half-century ago.[10] These rights were made more uniform through the formation of L'Union pour la Protection des Obtentions Végétales (UPOV) in 1961.[11] These laws vested plant breeders with exclusive marketing rights in registered plant varieties. Analogous to patent systems, the plant breeder was required to register the plant lines used to generate the innovative variety and to demonstrate that the desirable characteristics of the variety were stable and replicable. Once these requirements were met, the plant breeder was recognized reciprocally across UPOV member states to hold the exclusive right to market that plant variety.

The existence of plant variety protection legislation is not sufficient to generate adequate returns to plant breeders. For this to occur, it is necessary for these laws to be implemented and enforced. However, the level of enforcement has varied across the globe in line with the perceived interests of individual states, which feel differently about the fair use or reproduction of protected materials. The reason that many countries have little incentive to enforce these rights is the asymmetry between the nationality of most rights holders and the

---

(Philippines, 13–15 Aug. 1991). *See generally* Robert E. Evenson, *Agricultural Research and Intellectual Property Rights* [this volume]; *see also* ECONOMIC AND SOCIAL ISSUES IN AGRICULTURAL BIOTECHNOLOGY (Robert E. Evenson et. al. eds., CABI 2002).

[10] Michael Blakeney, *Protection of Plant Varieties and Farmers' Rights*, 24 EUR. INTELL. PROP. REV. 9 (2002); Michael Blakeney, *Stimulating Agricultural Innovation* [this volume].

[11] L'Union pour la Protection des Obtentions Végétales (UPOV), 2 Dec. 1961, *as revised at* Geneva on 10 Nov. 1972, 23 Oct. 1978, and 19 Mar. 1991, S. Treaty Doc. No. 104–17. *See* M. BLAKENEY & P. DRAHOS, INTELLECTUAL PROPERTY IN BIODIVERSITY AND AGRICULTURE (2001).

nationality of most users.¹² For example, for many years the plant breeding industry has been concentrated in a few large multinationals based primarily in Europe and the United States.¹³ For this reason, only a few nations view the enforcement of these "producers' rights" against "users" as a governmental function that generates direct benefits for their own citizens. Since the line between producers' and users' rights is a policy decision determined by a balance of interests, the outcome of this balancing process will be different given the weight each state places on producer and consumer interests.¹⁴

This has been the case in practice as well as in theory. Various countries have enforced plant variety protection laws differently, depending on their interpretation of their own state's interests. Moreover, allocating scarce resources to the monitoring and enforcement of the legal rights of foreigners is generally not a high priority.¹⁵ In poor countries it is readily apparent why this object is given little weight. Hence, in many countries without a plant breeding industry, the enforcement of plant variety laws has been problematic.

The unwillingness of many states to make any effort in the enforcement of plant breeders' rights, even where they existed on the books, was at the heart of the long-running Uruguay Round of multilateral trade discussions, culminating in 1994 with the relevant provisions of the TRIPs Agreement.¹⁶ Article 27.3(b) of the TRIPs Agreement provides that . . . "Members shall provide for the protection of plant varieties either by patents or by an effective *sui generis* system or by any combination thereof."¹⁷ WTO membership now confers upon a state the responsibility to enact plant variety protection legislation (such as that consistent with UPOV standards), as well as the responsibility to enforce that legislation within its jurisdiction. Under the TRIPS Agreement, developed countries were to have their implementing legislation enacted in compliance with Article 27.3(b) by 1996. The developing countries were allowed until 1st January 2000 to implement the agreement, and the least-developed countries were set a target of 2006. However, many developing countries lagged behind schedule in

---

[12] *See, e.g.*, W. Jaffe & J. van Wijk, The Impact of Plant Breeders' Rights in Developing Countries, Technical Paper of the Special Programme on Biotechnology and Development Cooperation (Ministry of Foreign Affairs of the Netherlands 1995).
[13] C. JUMA, THE GENE HUNTERS (Zed Books 1988).
[14] KEITH E. MASKUS, INTELLECTUAL PROPERTY RIGHTS IN THE GLOBAL ECONOMY (Institute for International Economics 2000), discusses such tradeoffs.
[15] *Id.*
[16] Agreement on Trade-Related Aspects of Intellectual Property Rights, 15 Apr. 1994, Marrakesh Agreement Establishing the World Trade Organization, Annex 1C, LEGAL INSTRUMENTS – RESULTS OF THE URUGUAY ROUND vol. 31, 33 I.L.M. 81 (1994) [hereinafter TRIPS Agreement].
[17] *Id.*, art. 27.3(b).

implementing Article 27.3(b). In 2000, the World Bank claimed that 70 percent of developing countries had not fully implemented the new rules.[18]

C. Technological enforcement through genetic use restriction technologies (GURTs)

We have identified the fundamental problem of appropriation affecting the plant breeding industry. We also discussed why this problem was generated in part by the perceived self-interest of those countries without a plant breeding industry. This industry had made long-standing and expensive efforts at establishing enforcement efforts, but the fundamental asymmetry in interests kept them from coming to fruition.

This situation explains the need perceived by breeders for a technological, rather than legal, solution to the problem of local rights enforcement. The industry has achieved such a technological solution with respect to a few of its products. For certain plant varieties (including maize and sorghum), the norm is cross-breeding, which affords an in-built enforcement strategy.[19] When the second generation of two distinct lines (first generations) is produced through hybridization, it exhibits a mix of traits that is not identical to either of the parent plants. If the second, or hybrid, generation again reproduces via cross-breeding, it also mixes the gene pool and creates a new mix of characteristics dissimilar from itself or its parents. Thus, the marketing of hybrid varieties enables the sale of innovative characteristics without the bundled sale of the technology for reproducing these characteristics. Innovative hybrid crop varieties are, therefore, marketable by their breeders without the threat of reproduction and re-sale by the consuming public. Hybridization was the first technology used as a method for "use-restriction" in plant breeding.[20]

It would be a short-sighted industry indeed that did not appreciate the commercial importance of this difference, and did not consider the possibility of extending this characteristic to other crop varieties. The advent of new biotechnologies reduced the barriers between various species (including plant varieties). The possibilities for transferring desirable traits between species were expanded as never before. An obvious "next step" within the plant breeding industry was to investigate the translocation of these use restriction technologies through genetic transference.

The area of biotechnological R&D focused on the problem of appropriability is referred to as "genetic use restriction technologies" or GURTs. GURTs

---

[18] World Bank, Indigenous Knowledge and Intellectual Property Rights, IK Notes, No. 19 (Apr. 2000).
[19] See Goeschl & Swanson, above n. 5.
[20] A brief history of this and other technological changes in agriculture is provided in the chapter by Robert E. Evenson, above n. 9.

come in two distinct forms, at least theoretically.[21] Variety-based GURTs (V-GURTs or "Terminators") are plant varieties that are not reproducible in any way by the purchaser. The basic idea is to create a seed that will generate the desired plant variety that itself results in sterile seed.[22] Thus, with V-GURTs the purchaser acquires the innovative plant variety without acquiring the technology for reproducing any part of the plant. Trait-based GURTs (or T-GURTs) are plant varieties having the potential for innovative traits but requiring the application of a complementary product (an initiator) that brings the trait to fruition. With T-GURTs, the purchaser acquires the reproductive technology for the standard plant variety, but must purchase the complementary product to acquire the benefits of the innovation. It should be noted that neither technology is yet in commercial use, but both are feasible.

Agriculture has evolved into an enterprise heavily dependent on R&D, one that is characterized by the cycling of widely-planted varieties subjected to increasing pest and pathogen problems.[23] The international legal system has struggled to create an incentive system capable of rewarding investments in R&D. Technology has stepped in to fill this gap by evolving the means by which use restrictions might be built into most crop varieties.

Thus, an important part of the biotechnology revolution in agriculture concerns this fundamental change in industrial structure. Biotechnologies are pursued for profits by the private sector, and the solution of the appropriability problem in plant breeding becomes an important potential source of increased profitability. Much effort has gone into developing technologies for enhancing the appropriability of returns from innovation, rather than into innovation itself. Thus, the pursuit of GURTs in biotechnology was predictable, and probably unavoidable.

D. *Determination of the fair use of proprietary materials*

Technological enforcement of proprietary rights within agriculture will result in the replacement of legislated systems of rights with those that are technologically determined.[24] This implies that private producers will be able to override previously legislated standards regarding the use of proprietary materials. The division of use rights between producers and consumers is a

---

[21] *See* T. Goeschl & T. Swanson, *The Development Impact of Genetic Use Restriction: A Forecast Based on the Hybrid Crop Experience*, 8 ENV'T & DEV. ECON. 149 (2001); *see also* AGRICULTURE, BIOTECHNOLOGY AND THE DEVELOPING WORLD, above n. 3.

[22] *See* Martha L. Crouch, How the Terminator Terminates, Edmonds Institute Occasional Paper (1998), *available at* http://www.edmonds-institute.org/crouch.html (last visited 27 Aug. 2004).

[23] Goeschl & Swanson, above n. 5.

[24] *See* the discussion on this general topic by J. Reidenberg, *The Formation of Information Policy Rules Through Technology*, 76 TEX. L. REV. 553 (1998), and that specifically related to genetic programming by D. Burk, *Lex Genetica: The Law and Ethics of Programming Biological Code*, 4 ETHICS & INFO. TECH. 109 (2002).

fundamental policy decision, sometimes loosely referred to as "fair use."[25] The line between permissible private use and illegitimate infringement is difficult to draw and, especially, to enforce with regard to products where reproduction technology is prevalent. When the reproduction technology is inbuilt, the line between fair use and infringement becomes an even more critical decision.

The permissibility of the marketing of restrictive reproduction technologies has been the subject of legal analysis, especially in the context of information technologies. The recent court decision in *A&M Records v. Napster*[26] illustrates the difficulties involved in drawing the line between permissible and impermissible uses. In earlier cases, such as *Sony v Universal Studios*,[27] the courts had allowed the sale of reproduction technologies (viz. video cassette recorders) under the rationale that the technologies could be used to foster the legitimate private use (including limited copying) of copyrighted materials. The fair use doctrine required consideration of several factors in the determination of infringement, but the mere possession or transfer of a reproductive technology was not in itself sufficient to constitute infringement.[28] In *Napster*, the court held that the producer need not shut down its website, but had the obligation to remove copyrighted materials from it.

Thus, the sale of reproductive capacity (for reproducing files within computers) has not in itself been found to be an illegal infringement of copyright, and the sole issue is the extent to which fair use allows individuals to make copies and transfer them to others. Under the reasoning of *Sony*, individuals had the right to make at least a single copy for their own use in the interests of "shifting use in time." The line between legitimate and illegitimate private uses of reproduction technologies is never clear-cut, and always involves a policy determination concerning the fair division of the use of protected materials between consumers and producers.[29] In the following paragraphs we list a few important criteria for considering the validity of moving toward technological enforcement, which essentially would constitute a denial of fair use in biological agricultural technologies.

---

[25] Fair use is a classical concept of copyright law and increasingly, of industrial property law as well. *See, e.g.*, Ruth L. Okediji, *Sustainable Access to Copyrighted Digital Information Works in Developing Countries* [this volume]; Graeme Dinnoodie & Rochelle Cooper Dreyfuss, *WTO Dispute Resolution and the Preservation of the Public Domain of Science under International Law* [this volume].

[26] 239 F.3d 1004 (9th Cir. 2001).

[27] 464 US 417 (1984).

[28] The four factors determining fair use that are listed within the U.S. Copyright Act (17 U.S.C. § 107 (2000)) are: 1) the purpose or character of the use; 2) the nature of the copyrighted work; 3) the amount copied; and 4) the effect on the market or value of the work.

[29] *See* W. CORNISH & D. LLEWELYN, INTELLECTUAL PROPERTY: PATENTS, COPYRIGHTS, TRADEMARKS AND ALLIED RIGHTS (Sweet & Maxwell 2003).

E. Policy interests in the use of plant varieties for further R&D

There are several policy issues militating against the comprehensive withdrawal of the concept of fair use in agriculture. One complicating factor is the important role that consumers (i.e., farmers) play within the R&D process. Agricultural R&D is a system that makes use of many factors in producing its outputs. It is wrong to think of the plant breeding sector as a stand-alone entity relying only on modern science and base genetic resources. The production of a new plant variety involves, at a minimum, human inputs (scientists), capital inputs (land, laboratories), and natural inputs (diverse genetic resources).

Contributions to agricultural R&D come from all parts of the world. While scientists are located primarily in the developed world, land and natural inputs are often found in the developing countries. Indeed, farmers themselves may be the suppliers of genetic resources. Production-function studies have estimated that diverse genetic resources provide approximately *one-third* of the contribution required for the production of new plant varieties.[30] Therefore, it is inaccurate to believe that the final segment of the R&D industry – centered in the developed world – is capable of developing these innovative varieties by means of its efforts alone.

The plant breeder, as the entity at the end of the industry pipeline, is the only part of the industry able to claim an exclusive marketing right *vis-a-vis* consumers. In contrast, few attempts have been made to compensate farmers directly for their contributions to the plant breeding process. This legal capacity for appropriation should not be equated with the right to earn the full return from R&D.[31] It is important that the benefits from the R&D process are appropriable, but it is equally important that the contributions of the various factors of production are compensated.

This aspect of the problem is analogous to the circumstance in which one innovation builds upon the foundation of another, as in the case of use of parody in copyright law.[32] Uses that transform the prior creative work into a new use have been held to constitute fair use of the work. A justification for this doctrine is the need for a degree of reciprocity among agents that are both consumers and producers. Allowing transformative uses recognizes that such consumers are also producers who are themselves contributing to the set of societal innovations.[33]

---

[30] *See* Evenson & Gollin, above n. 9; *see generally* AGRICULTURAL VALUES OF GENETIC RESOURCES (Robert E. Evenson et al. eds., CABI 1998).

[31] *See* T. Swanson & T. Goeschl, *Ecology, Information, Externalities and Policies: The Optimal Management of Biodiversity for Agriculture*, *in* FOOD SECURITY, DIVERSIFICATION AND RESOURCE MANAGEMENT: REFOCUSING THE ROLE OF AGRICULTURE (G.H. Peters & J. von Braun eds., Brookfield 1999).

[32] Campbell v. Acuff-Rose Music, Inc., 510 US 569 (1994).

[33] This idea also provides the foundation for recasting certain types of intellectual property rights as elements of a liability regime among users and producers. *See* J.H. Reichman &

In global agriculture, fair use might be maintained because the consumers of end products (i.e. new plant varieties) are also contributors to their production. Farmers both supply the R&D process (with genetic resources), and then also purchase its ultimate outputs. In the past, these separate roles have been confounded, and farmers have come to expect to receive their share of modern agriculture's benefits in their consumption of new plant varieties. This is analogous to the fair use of innovative works for transformative purposes, and it is a reason for concern about restrictions on one's own use.[34]

Another related aspect of the problem of technological enforcement concerns its capacity to override negotiated agreements. The international debate concerning the rights to reuse seeds has continued for over 25 years. The so-called "seed wars" date back to the onset of the Green Revolution, and debates have continued since that time within the United Nations Food and Agricultural Organization (FAO).[35] In 1978, the UPOV convention initiated discussions on this point by conferring a limited "Farmers' Right" to the private reuse (re-planting) of registered seeds. This provision came under fire from the biotechnology industry almost immediately as a means of disguising improper use.[36] At about the same time, the FAO adopted the International Undertaking on Plant Genetic Resources (IUPGR), which provided for the reciprocal recognition of both plant breeders' rights and farmers' rights.[37] The concept of farmers' rights and the advocacy of rights in traditional knowledge are both movements for the recognition of the right to share in the benefits from agricultural R&D.[38]

Tracy Lewis, *Using Liability Rules to Stimulate Local Innovation in Developing Countries: Application to Traditional Knowledge* [this volume].

[34] In addition to the recognition of transformative uses of proprietary rights, there is also the public-goods argument in favour of keeping research within the public domain, especially when it clearly constitutes a joint production process. *Cf.* J.H. Reichman & J. Franklin, *Privately Legislated Intellectual Property Rights: Reconciling Freedom of Contract with Public Good Uses of Information*, 147 U. PA L. REV. 875 (1999).

[35] See JUMA, above n. 13.

[36] BLAKENEY & DRAHOS, above, n. 11.

[37] See D. Cooper, *The International Undertaking on Plant Genetic Resources*, 2 REV. EURO. COMMUNITY & INT'L ENVTL. L. 158 (1993). The international undertaking remains to be implemented, but its adoption clearly indicates that the line between legitimate and illegitimate uses of purchased plant varieties remains under discussion within international fora. There is now also a newly minted International Treaty on Plant Genetic Resources, developed within the FAO. These agreements are discussed by Blakeney, *Stimulating Agricultural Innovation*, above n. 10 and Laurence R. Helfer, *Using Intellectual Property Rights to Preserve the Global Genetic Commons: The International Treaty on Plant Genetic Resources for Food and Agriculture* [this volume].

[38] See Michael Blakeney, *Intellectual Property Aspects of Traditional Knowledge*, in ECONOMIC AND SOCIAL ISSUES IN AGRICULTURAL BIOTECHNOLOGY, above n. 9. Rights to traditional knowledge are recognized within the Convention on Biological Diversity, below n. 39, and various states have attempted to develop legislation vesting these rights in indigenous peoples or communities, as discussed by R.V. Anuradha, *IPRs:*

The existing benefit distribution has been negotiated and debated within many international arenas for decades. This process has culminated in the adoption of those parts of the Convention on Biological Diversity (CBD) that enshrine sovereignty in genetic resources and mandate benefit sharing with those supplying those resources.[39] The first article of the CBD stipulates that it is intended to ensure "the fair and equitable sharing of the benefits arising out of the utilisation of genetic resources." The treaty was opened for signature on 5 June 1992 at the Rio Earth Summit and entered into force in late 1994. Since 1992, the signatories have recognized the concept of national sovereignty over biological and genetic resources. The CBD guaranteed to member states sovereignty over their biological resources and ushered in a shift away from the application of the doctrine of "common heritage" to the use of those resources in agriculture.

It can be argued that these international agreements should take precedence over private, technologically generated outcomes, such as GURTs. An equivalent debate within some societies is that concerning whether private technologies should be allowed to exceed the constraints imposed by statutory or constitutional standards. That is, the coercive powers conferred by technology may not exceed the limitations imposed by or upon the state itself.[40] In this context, ratifying states are bound by international agreements to observe the standards established within them, and so these agreements should likewise delimit the extent to which privately employed technologies conflict with their provisions. The long-negotiated conclusions of international negotiations should not be subject to private technology veto.

The final criterion to consider concerning the adoption of technological enforcement is the impact of the new regime on the prevailing distribution of benefits. If the new regime had little or no impact on the distribution of benefits between producers and consumers, there would be little reason for concern about its adoption. Technological enforcement would merely enhance the rate of innovation without affecting the manner in which the resulting benefits were ultimately distributed. Debates concerning fair use and analogous concerns would then be more about the form of the change than its substance. In the final analysis, fair use concerns the division of benefits from use of an innovation between consumers and producers. Thus, any substantive change in that distribution is critical to the determination of impact on fair use.

Implications for Biodiversity and Local and Indigenous Communities, 10 Rev. Euro. Community & Int'l Envtl. L. 27 (2001).
[39] Convention on Biological Diversity, 5 June 1992, 31 I.L.M. 818, available at http://www.biodiv.org/convention/articles.asp (last accessed 28 July 2004).
[40] This is the so-called Cohen Theorem. *See* J. Cohen, *Copyright and the Jurisprudence of Self-Help*, 13 Berkeley Tech. L.J. 1089 (1998).

F. Concluding evaluation of the movement to technological enforcement

In agriculture, the prospect of biotechnologies that enable absolute technological enforcement is real and imminent.[41] Technological enforcement will enable private firms to override existing doctrinal exceptions and conventions regarding the fair use of biological materials (plant varieties and seeds) in agriculture. There are several bases on which it might be argued that such a change would be undesirable, including the impacts on future research and on existing laws. Chief among these reasons is that the change in regime might result in a fundamentally different distribution of benefits between the producers and consumers of agricultural innovations. In the remainder of this paper, we assess this substantive argument concerning the distributive impacts of technological enforcement systems in global agriculture.

III. The impacts of technological enforcement on benefit distribution

Assessing the effects of global technological change is a complicated enterprise. In this section, we develop a framework within which we may analyze such impacts. It is developed on a foundation that assumes countries benefit disproportionately from technological change on account of their institutional differences. It is possible to consider technological enforcement as the movement from this heterogeneous system towards one that is both universal and uniform.[42]

A. Impacts of technological enforcement – Static and dynamic dimensions

The change to technological enforcement has relatively straightforward static implications, but more complex dynamic ones. Statically, the shift to universal and uniform enforcement of property rights should enable producers to capture a more significant share of the rents from production. That is, the first implication is a shift of consumer surplus toward producers. In addition, it may be possible for producers to engage in more refined forms of price discrimination and thus to both shift consumer surplus toward producers and simultaneously avoid deadweight loss.[43]

---

[41] Patents in both the basic technology for V-GURTs and the enabling technologies for T-GURTs have been granted in the U.S. Control of Plant Gene Expression, U.S. Patent No. 5,723,765 (issued 3 Mar. 1998).

[42] This analysis is built on the work reported in Goeschl & Swanson, above n. 5.

[43] This would occur by reason of enabling producers to sell multiple-year licenses to those users who desired further use of the variety, and single-year licenses to those who desired only a single use. See Fisher, *The Legal Implications of Terminators*, in BIOTECHNOLOGY, AGRICULTURE, AND THE DEVLOPING WORLD: THE DISTRIBUTIONAL IMPLICATIONS OF TECHNOLOGICAL CHANGE, above n. 3.

In dynamic terms, the impact of technological enforcement is less straightforward but equally important. Many economists analyze the dynamic effects of technological change within the framework established by Hayami and Ruttan.[44] This approach argues that national differences or frictions result in differential time lags in the responsiveness of individual societies to changed technological conditions. These differences may be cultural, physical, economic or institutional. The greater are the differences among countries, the more uneven will be their responsiveness to the impacts of a given technological change. In short, some societies will be more able to take on board the changes than others, and these institutional and cultural differences will determine the rate at which technological change diffuses.

The importance of technological enforcement is that it provides the groundwork for a uniform and universal system of property rights. This system may enable these institutional differences or frictions to be avoided. Thus, the dynamic impact of technological enforcement might be positive for consumers. First, the shift of surplus toward producers should act as an incentive for them to diffuse innovative technologies more rapidly. This means that consumers might receive innovations, and hence earn their share of benefits, sooner than they would have in the absence of such incentives. Second, the dynamic impact of technological enforcement should result in an increased rate of arrival of new technologies because of higher rewards to R&D. In sum, the dynamic effects of technological enforcement could be to alter the pattern and rate of arrival of innovations across different countries.

The aggregate impact of technological enforcement must be gauged by its net effect on: (i) the distribution of surplus from any innovation; (ii) the rate of diffusion of any single innovation; and (iii) the general rate of arrival of innovations. It is equally necessary to consider these aggregate effects as they occur across time. Thus, the net effect will depend on both the static impact of benefit redistribution and, even more, on the dynamic impact on technological diffusion.

B. Impacts of GURTs on diffusion

General use restriction technologies enable the producer to sell its innovative product without the reproductive technology bundled along with it. This allows the price of the seed to be set at the single use price and permits purchasers individually to elect the number of years they will buy the product. Thus, some farmers may choose to purchase the innovation for use in a single year, while others may choose to use it each year for a number of years. Others may disdain the innovative feature and elect not to purchase the variety at all.

---

[44] *See* Yujiro Hayami & Vernon Ruttan, Agricultural Development: An International Perspective (Johns Hopkins University Press 1985).

In the abstract, this change in marketing technology can only benefit both producers and consumers. This is because it enables a finer segregation of the market and allows for the specific targeting of individual user's needs.

The problem with this approach is that it elides the issue of the available alternatives. In the first years of use, the GURTs consumer has a clearly welfare-enhancing choice. He makes use of either the freely-available standard plant variety or the standard plant variety with the innovative trait imbedded within it. The user makes the decision whether, given individual conditions, he is willing to pay the market price for the innovative trait. If the user is willing to purchase the use of the trait for that year, then the technology must be welfare-enhancing. In this regard, GURTs may be analogised to the sale of an annual license for the use of new software (the innovative trait), and the consumer is allowed to choose whether to acquire the license.

The problem is that, in the case of plant varieties, the software and the hardware become commingled over time. If the plant breeding industry introduces traits only within the context of GURT varieties, then over time the freely-available standard variety may become something very unlike the variety into which the innovative traits are imbedded. That is, the proprietary traits may be allowed to accumulate within the commercial sector, without allowing their diffusion into the public arena. Then the commercial breeders would be able to work with the commercial "hardware" (by paying for licenses for one another's innovations), while the public-sector breeders (individual farmers, universities, government researchers) might be left with antiquated varieties as their choices. Within five or ten years, there may be no real alternative to the use of the GURT varieties, because the hardware within the public sector would lack a decade's worth of developments. Then users would become wholly dependent on the plant breeding sector for their seed.[45]

GURTs provide even more substantial protection than would perfectly enforced intellectual property rights. Unlike IPRs, there are no time limitations on GURTs. Unless the state concerned has the biotechnological capability to reverse engineer the GURT variety, the trait would not be reproducible through conventional breeding techniques. This means that a GURT-protected innovation would remain protected indefinitely. Individuals and nations without biotechnology capabilities would have only two stark choices: purchase the technology or live without it. And this choice would become even more stark over time, as other traits and technologies become available that are dependent on purchase of the first.

Therefore, in addition to technological enforceability, GURTs are unlike IPRs in that they have the capacity to accumulate and do not erode over time.

---

[45] This outcome would be unlike the situation at present, wherein 80 percent of farmers in developing countries use retained seed. C. Thirtle & S. Srinivasan, *The Economics of Genetic Use Restriction*, in AGRICULTURE, BIOTECHNOLOGY AND THE DEVELOPING WORLD, above n. 3.

These two aspects of GURTs contribute to their tendency to inhibit diffusion. New innovations become bundled together within a single plant line, and the requirement to purchase them on an "all or nothing" basis means that individual innovations are not available to be diffused.[46] It also means that there is no fixed period after which the innovation becomes part of the basic capital stock for general R&D; it forever remains a purchasable innovation. In some respects, GURTs would do more than inhibit diffusion and would actually prevent it altogether.

C. Benefits from technological enforceability

Against this rather dark picture of GURT-based technological progress needs to be placed the potential benefits from the new system. The most important concerns the potential increase in R&D investments resulting from increased expected appropriability. In particular, there is an economic argument that there could be a disproportionate rate of investment in R&D benefiting innovation in, and diffusion to, precisely those countries where current institutional frictions are greatest, because this is where the greatest returns from such investments are available. Then the move to a universal and uniform system of enforcement would benefit disproportionately investments in precisely those states where enforcement is now most lax.

Studies of the plant breeding sector within the developing world find that the private investments occurring there at present are almost exclusively within the hybrid sector.[47] This makes sense, because claims in rights over these varieties are not dependent on the availability of governmental institutions or resources for their enforcement. And since these institutional deficiencies are less problematic in the case of hybrid varieties, the private sector would be willing to operate in these markets. The development of GURTs could not just enhance the overall level of R&D investments, but also could cause investments to occur in places where none had occurred before.

Thus, an alternative view on the future of plant breeding under GURTs would be that the private sector would expand its level and range of operations, including R&D investment, in order to incorporate all countries and all crops. Then the future of modern agriculture would consist of local-level plant breeding operations working within global networks, finely tuned to local environmental conditions and popular demands but receiving information and innovations from throughout the global network. The industry would become more diverse in its operations and offerings, as local investments respond to local demands and conditions. Most importantly, innovations would diffuse almost instantaneously across the globe, applied where sensible

---

[46] This is because individual innovations within GURT varieties cannot be crossed into other lines.
[47] See Jaffe and van Wijk, above n. 12.

under varying conditions, as multinational firms rendered national institutions and boundaries irrelevant.

D. The aggregate impact of GURTs: Assessing the full meaning of regime change

The fundamental difference between these two alternative views lies in the expected impact of enhanced appropriability on global investment patterns (and hence on institutional change). General use restriction technologies should have their greatest impacts on appropriability in those states where enforcement is now lax, and hence the greatest share of new investment and beneficial change could occur there as well. If those changes occurred, GURTs might have a substantial impact on the way in which plant breeding operations occur globally. However, if rent appropriation simply increased without a significant alteration in investment patterns, then GURTs primarily would have distributional impacts.

A globally uniform system of use restrictions and enforcement will disable the currently heterogeneous system of IPRs in agriculture and impose in its place a standardised system in a heterogeneous world. This change could be beneficial if the industry and the public sector responded in the appropriate fashion and encouraged diffusion where it is now restricted. It could be disastrous for poor countries if the uniform system were imposed without inducing other complementary changes in investment and diffusion. Therefore, the full impact of technological enforceability would depend on how the private sector – largely in the developed world – responds to the needs for enhanced diffusion to those states off the technological frontier in the developing world.

IV. Predicting industry's response by extrapolating from hybrid maize

Although GURTs are of recent origin, technologies with similar characteristics have existed for many decades, specifically the hybridization of cultivated varieties. This technique has been available for commercial seeds since the 1920s. Hybridization of cultivars has two implications. First, the replanting of seeds from a hybrid results in a rapid deterioration of yield potential.[48] Second, hybridization protects against unauthorised reproduction by farmers, and composition of the hybrid can be withheld from other breeders if the innovator does not disclose the inbred lines. GURT crops share these two characteristics with hybrid crops, albeit in more extreme forms. Replanting of GURT seeds results in an expected yield loss of close to 100 percent, and the reproduction of the crop's underlying genetic structure by a third party is currently not feasible since reproduction of the seed itself is impossible.

---

[48] The first-generation loss is normally in the order of 25 to 30 percent.

Widespread application of hybridization in the commercial seed sector also suggests that the availability of use restriction has been deployed by private companies when investing in R&D.[49] Thus, hybrid crops and GURTs share fundamental features of use restriction, although these features operate to different degrees of perfection in these two applications. Further, industry has made significant use of these features as a form of rent protection. In this section, we assess how the developed world has responded to the advent of the use restriction technologies implicit in hybrid crops (principally maize) and extrapolate from this to forecast the impacts of GURTs on developing countries.

A. *Comparative performance of crops with and without technological enforceability*

In a previous paper we estimated the rate of diffusion of innovations in hybrid and non-hybrid crops over the last 40 years.[50] These estimates are indicative of the likely impacts of the adoption of GURTs by crop innovators. Here we use these estimates as the basis for forecasting what probably constitutes the lower bound on the impact of GURTs in developing countries. These impacts are expected to arise out of the application of GURTs to non-hybridized crops, such as wheat and rice.

Table 1 presents some summary data about the eight crops examined. The crop with the highest global acreage in 1999 was wheat, with 214.2 million hectares, and the least significant crop was cotton, with 34.3 million hectares. The growth rates of yields in these crops have been lower in developing as opposed to developed countries[51] for five of eight crops, with the exception of rice, soybeans and wheat. Correspondingly, the relative yield gap between developed and developing countries has decreased only for these three crops, while it has widened for the five others. Yet, even for those crops for which the gap has narrowed, wide differences in global agricultural productivity persist. Across all eight crops, average yields in developing countries were about 57 percent lower than the crop yields in developed countries in 1999.[52]

---

[49] See L.J. Butler & B.W. Marion, The Impact of Patent Protection on the U.S. Seed Industry and Public Plant Breeding, Food Systems Research Group Monograph 16 (University of Wisconsin Madison 1985); L.J. Butler, *Plant Breeders' Rights in the U.S.: Update of a 1983 Study*, in THE IMPACT OF PLANT BREEDERS' RIGHTS IN DEVELOPING COUNTRIES 17 (J. van Wijk & Walter Jaffe eds., University of Amsterdam 1995).

[50] Goeschl & Swanson, above n. 5.

[51] The classification of countries into "developing" and "developed" follows P. PARDEY, AGRICULTURAL RESEARCH POLICY: INTERNATIONAL QUANTITATIVE PERSPECTIVES (Oxford University Press 1991), rather than the FAO classification.

[52] This estimate gives equal weight to each country and is based on the country classification adopted in PARDEY, above n. 51, and taken up by the wider literature on agricultural R&D. A comparison of yields on an area-weighted basis directly based on FAO data and its classification of developing and developed countries produces an even more dramatic

Table 1: *Acreage, global distribution, growth and relative yield gap in eight major crops*

Crop	Global Acreage in million ha in 1999	Average Growth Rate in Developed Countries, 1961–1999	Average Growth Rate in Developing Countries, 1961–99	Relative Yield Gap in 1961	Relative Yield Gap in 1999
Barley	58.6	1.53%	1.03% (40)	−57%	−59.9%
Cotton	34.3	2.45%	1.54% (60)	−24%	−47.4%
Maize	139.2	2.27%	1.42% (95)	−65%	−72.4%
Millet	37.2	0.93%	0.41% (46)	−49%	−57.4%
Rice	153.1	0.85%	1.24% (60)	−64%	−57.9%
Sorghum	44.8	2.08%	0.54% (64)	−48%	−67.2%
Soybeans	72.1	1.24%	1.58% (32)	−46%	−40.0%
Wheat	214.2	1.75%	1.89% (54)	−60%	−54.5%

Developing countries are therefore still far off the productivity frontier in agriculture. There are, however, significant differences in the relative yield gaps among the eight crops. In 1999, the smallest yield gap existed in soybeans at around 40 percent, while the greatest gap could be found in maize at around 72 percent.

The growth rates in developed countries reflect dramatic technological improvements in agricultural production across all crops. Yields have been expanding at different rates, ranging from 0.85 percent per annum in rice to 2.45 percent per annum in cotton. This translates into a total increase of yield of around 157 percent in cotton and of around 40 percent in rice over the 40 year period 1960–1999. In general, it is worth noting that the two hybrid varieties (maize and sorghum) experienced much higher rates of growth on average than did the vast majority of the non-hybrid varieties. We would argue that this was the result, at least in part, of the positive impact of use restriction in the case of these varieties.

However, a look at individual country experiences with the most widely-used hybrid crop (maize) is instructive about how widely results might vary. The "technological gap" between the frontier states and single developing countries can vary widely, in this case from a −2 percent yield gap in Egypt to a −96 percent yield gap in neighboring Sudan.[53] These gaps are representative

picture, while leaving the ranking of crops basically unaffected. *See* Goeschl & Swanson, above n. 5.

[53] That is, the high rate of innovation in maize resulted in generally high rates of growth, but there was a wide variation in the experience of different countries; thus, some countries fell

of the aggregate impacts of the combined set of institutional frictions that keep technological advances from diffusing into a particular country such as Sudan.

In sum, the past 40 years' experience with maize indicates both a relatively rapid rate of increase in yields at the "technological frontier" (those countries where innovations are occurring, primarily the United States and the European Union) and a relatively slow rate of diffusion as some poor countries fall farther from that frontier. This finding implies that the tradeoff inherent in genetic use restriction is the advantage of increased rates of innovation in the most developed economies, as against reduced rates of diffusion to the least-developed countries. Thus, as a country falls farther away from the "technological frontier" (e.g. Sudan as opposed to Egypt), it receives a diminishing share of the immediate benefits from the genetic use restriction.[54]

Our estimate is that the general impact of genetic use restriction is to reduce the rate of diffusion of yield enhancements from developed to developing countries by approximately *seven percent* of the gain per annum.[55] We estimate this by use of a growth model that provides for an estimation of how both current yields and the yield-gap (distance from the frontier) are affected by the plant variety in use. We then ran the estimation on a panel data set that included all countries using the above eight varieties in their agricultural sectors. The studies indicate that the hybrid varieties (with inbuilt use restriction) generated the increased rate of innovation indicated within Table 1 above, but with the attendant cost of the reduced rate of diffusion indicated above.[56]

B. *Forecasting the impacts of technological enforceability*

This study indicates that the impacts of use restriction technologies depend on the initial conditions of the country concerned. Figures 1 to 4 report these expected impacts in four representative nations over a 20-year time horizon.[57] The forecasts show that individual country experiences should vary quite

---

far off the technological frontier as the frontier moved more rapidly and they failed to keep up. The result was large yield gaps, as in the case of Sudan.

[54] All countries must benefit from enhanced rates of innovation ultimately, but the date at which this yield increase is experienced will occur farther into the future (as diffusion is restricted). Thus, as indicated in the next section's simulations, we measure the aggregate impact of GURTs by forecasting the date at which this change generates a net beneficial impact within any particular country.

[55] *See* Goeschl & Swanson, above nn. 5 and 21.

[56] All of these calculations are taken from the works of Goeschl and Swanson, above nn. 5 and 21. Please refer to these publications for the models used and the estimations of the diffusion effect.

[57] The study from which these simulations derive is reported in Goeschl and Swanson, above n. 21. The simulations depict the impact of the tradeoff from GURTs on countries starting from differing levels of development. GURTs heighten the overall rate of innovation, but reduce the rate of diffusion. Thus, those countries on or near the technological frontier will receive an immediate benefit from the introduction of GURTs (Figure 1),

Comparison of yields under the use restriction and baseline scenarios, developed countries, 2000–2020

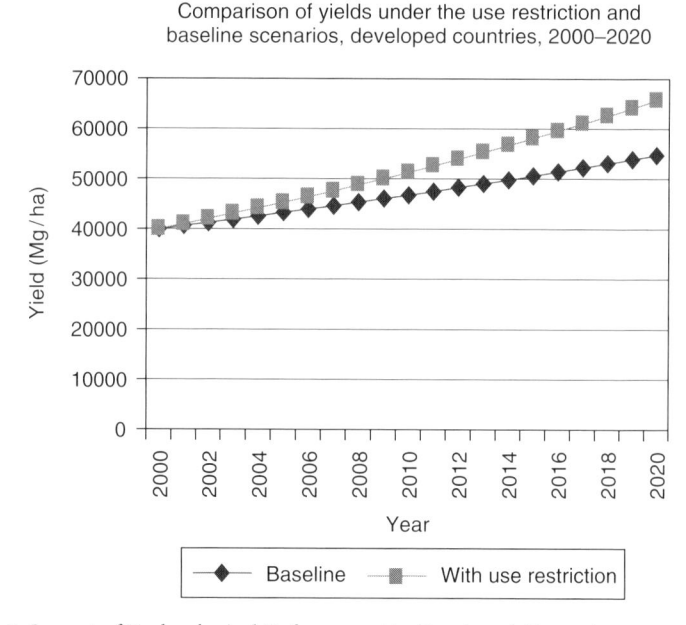

Figure 1: Impact of Technological Enforcement in Developed Countries

considerably. In developed countries (Figure 1), the adoption of use restriction would result in higher growth rates in yield and a more favorable yield development over the time period. This result is because the developed countries exist on the technological frontier, and enhanced appropriability involves no tradeoffs for these states.

There are developing countries where the experience would be quite similar to developed countries, but would arise in a slightly delayed fashion. In China (Figure 2), for instance, yields in the first ten years are expected to be similar under both scenarios. Then the impact of use restrictions on the yield frontier begins to push yields in China above the baseline. China is an example of a developing country that is close to the technological frontier in terms of agricultural production of maize, and so the delayed diffusion has little impact.

The case of Ethiopia (Figure 3) illustrates a country that, in the short run, would be better off under the current regime, as the flow of innovations would diffuse more rapidly. However, towards the end of the 20-year horizon, the more rapid expansion at the technological frontier would have compensated for the slower diffusion inherent in this regime. Ethiopia is an example of a

> while those farther from that frontier will benefit from the introduction of GURTs much later in the future (Figures 2–4). Figures 1–4 depict the year in which it would be anticipated that the forecasted yield from GURTs would "cross over" that from current agricultural production and represent a net benefit to the indicated country.

THE IMPACTS ON POOR COUNTRIES OF TECHNOLOGICAL ENFORCEMENT 691

Comparison of yields under the use restriction and baseline scenarios, China, 2000–2020

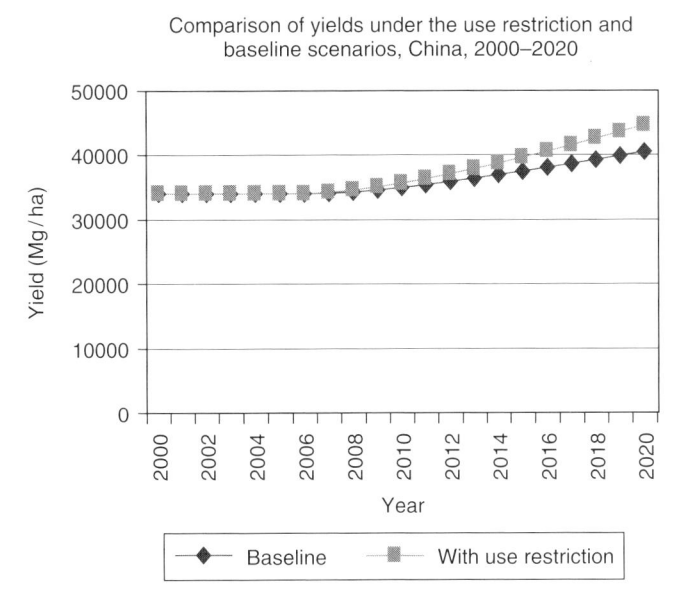

Figure 2: Impact of Technological Enforcement in Developing Countries (China)

Comparison of yields under the use restriction and baseline scenarios, Ethiopia, 2000–2020

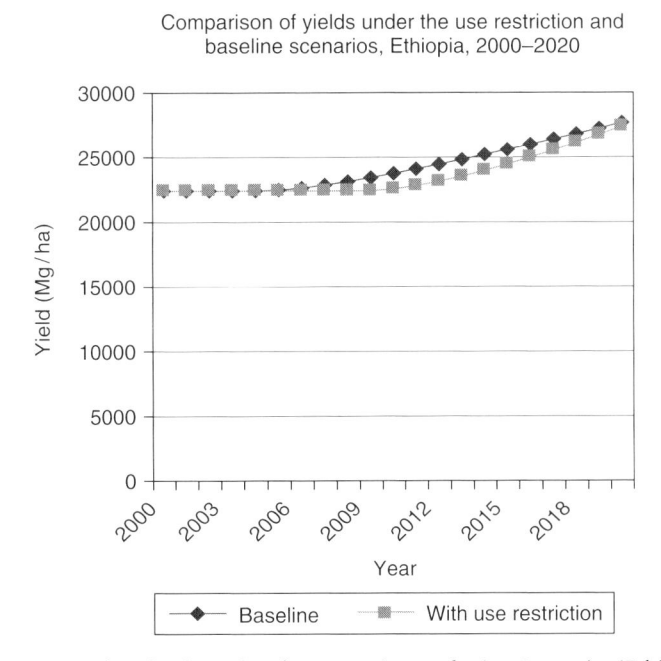

Figure 3: Impact of Technological Enforcement in Developing Countries (Ethiopia)

Comparison of yields under the use restriction
and baseline scenarios, Tanzania, 2000–2020

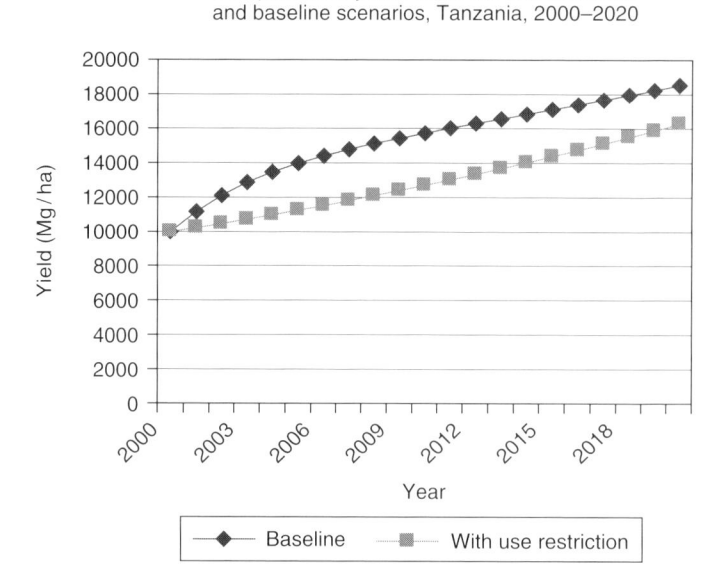

Figure 4: Impact of Technological Enforcement in Developing Countries (Tanzania)

mid-tier developing country in terms of agricultural development. It would tend to benefit from the advent of enhanced use restriction only in the medium term.

Lastly, the case of Tanzania (Figure 4) illustrates a case where, for the foreseeable future, the country would be worse off under a use restriction scenario than under a perpetuation of the current regime. Tanzania is a developing country that falls farthest from the technological frontier. Due to lack of investment and numerous institutional frictions, innovations diffuse very slowly to these states under existing policies. The advent of additional use restrictions would render a bad situation worse for these states.

These four cases illustrate the range of outcomes that can be expected from the potential adoption of genetic use restriction technologies and the shift away from IPR regimes as the primary means of enforcing intellectual property. This diversity implies that, over a policy-relevant time horizon, countries will not be indifferent as to the regime adopted. The charts demonstrate that the most advanced countries stand to benefit most from use restrictions while the least advanced stand to lose most.

When projected sufficiently far into the future, the productivity gains from the stimulation of private R&D through use restrictions result in the baseline scenario being overtaken in every country.[58] However, the present value of

---

[58] *See* above, n. 57.

these future gains may be perceived as insufficient for developing countries to outweigh the mid-term losses. It is interesting to note that, even if GURTs led to a doubling of the rate of innovation seen in hybrids at the same rate of diffusion, it would take more than 10 years in the case of Tanzania for yields under use restriction to outperform the baseline yields.

C. *Aggregate impact of technological enforceability*

The maize hybrid experience indicates that the shift in the growth trajectory from technological enforceability must lead in the long run to higher yields everywhere. However, most countries, and particularly the least-developed ones, will first have to pass through a phase of yield losses relative to the present regime. These losses are the consequence of a reduced rate of diffusion from the technological frontier to lagging states. If history repeats itself, the poorest countries would benefit least from the regime change to GURTs, while the developed countries would benefit most. For the least developed countries, it is unlikely that the net present value of this regime change would be positive.

V. Conclusion

In the agricultural sector, it is possible to foresee the imminent demise of the IPR system as the primary means for channelling returns from innovations to innovators. The advent of genetic use restriction technologies foretells of a future in which seed patents and plant variety legislation is a "thing of the past." Future biological innovations will be protected biologically.

This scenario means that the current system of domestically enforced IPRs will be displaced by a globally uniform system of property right enforcement. Innovators will no longer be dependent upon domestic regimes for protection. It also means that individual states will no longer have the discretion to select where they will lie on the innovation-diffusion tradeoff. Every country will exist within a "one size fits all" system that has perfectly enforceable innovation appropriation.

Our analysis indicates that the impact of such a regime change will depend on the initial situation of the nation concerned. Perfectly enforceable intellectual property rights make sense for those countries at the technological frontier, but would have radically different implications for those countries that innovate little but benefit from the diffusion of innovation. The impact of perfectly enforceable rights for these countries would be to restrict the free flow of innovations.

The restriction of the free flow of information need not be a bad thing, even for the poorest of countries. If firms and states at the technological frontier would make the effort to disseminate the information (once it no longer flows freely), then it would become possible for the poorest countries to benefit as well. However, our studies indicate that both public-sector and private-sector investment in the poorest countries would be required for this to occur.

Experience to date indicates that such investment is highly unlikely to emerge. The 40-year history of experience with hybrid (use restriction) technologies is one of enhanced rent appropriation but little change in investment patterns.[59] Developing countries have seen the diffusion benefits from new technologies arrive more slowly than those from non-hybrids. This means that enhanced rent appropriation is not increasing the international diffusion of innovation, but mainly the distribution of rents.

In short, the advent of technological enforceability within biotechnology threatens to have seriously negative implications for developing countries, especially the poorest among them. The intellectual property system at least has the capacity for countries to take into consideration their individual circumstances when determining the extent of implementation and enforcement. The shift to GURTs would remove the option to tailor the system to individual circumstances and would, therefore, raise problems for those countries that are far off the technological frontier.

---

[59] Goeschl & Swanson, above n. 5.

26

Equitable sharing of benefits from biodiversity-based innovation: Some reflections under the shadow of a neem tree

GUSTAVO GHIDINI*

I. Biodiversity-based innovation as a cooperative tradeoff between developed and developing countries
II. Equitable sharing of benefits upon mutually agreed terms – The legal framework
   A. Sharing of what?
   B. From "agreed dominance" to better balanced terms of trade
   C. Clarifying the uncertain status of a local working requirement
III. Towards a cooperative, not a confrontational approach

I. Biodiversity-based innovation as a cooperative tradeoff between developed and developing countries

As everybody knows, much advanced innovation in the pharmaceutical sector, as well as in the agricultural field (concerning seeds, in particular) is based on germplasm (the physical embodiment of so-called biodiversity). Much of this resource "wealth," which rarely survives in developed countries, has been preserved by farmers in developing countries "for cultural reasons which may escape those of us who equate wisdom to economic calculus."[1]

Such innovation is typically based on cooperation between developed countries and developing countries. The former possess the technology that enables them to develop new products for mass consumption (more advanced and efficient drugs, healthier and more resistant or abundant food) from the germplasm provided by plant and animal genetic resources that the latter have preserved, and made available. The end result can, of course, be patented: for

---

* Gustavo Ghidini is Professor of Intellectual Property and Competition Law, Luiss Guido Carli University, Rome, Italy.
[1] Marco Ricolfi, *Biotechnology, Patents and Epistemic Approaches*, 2002 J. BIOLAW AND BUSINESS 77, SPECIAL SUPPL. (2002).

example, the patenting of "an invention based on biological material of plant or animal origin" is expressly permitted by the European Directive on Biodiversity of 1998,[2] and it is commonly allowed in most non-EU countries, including the U.S. and Japan. Thanks to patent protection, biodiversity-related innovation – chiefly concerning the pharmaceutical and the agricultural industries – can yield potentially very high benefits, both in strictly economic terms (returns from sales and/or royalties) and in terms of technical and scientific progress (further impulse to R&D activities) and industrial and commercial advancement.

II. Equitable sharing of benefits upon mutually agreed terms – The legal framework

I want briefly to summarize the basic legal framework underpinning the concept of "equitable sharing" of benefits accruing from biodiversity-related innovation. This topic was specifically addressed by the Convention on Biodiversity (CBD) of 1992, in force from 1993,[3] which first of all acknowledged the contracting States' sovereign rights to exploit their biological and genetic resources.[4] It accordingly mandated that these States shall have the "authority to determine access to their genetic resources."[5]

The Convention requires, as a fundamental goal, "the fair and equitable sharing of the benefits arising from the utilization of genetic resources."[6] The justification for this principle seems obvious. Providing the germplasm cannot be assimilated to the simple "physical" supply of a raw material. That material, indeed, is the result of – and thus embodies – the developing countries' traditional knowledge and labor in maintaining the agricultural and environmental conditions for the preservation of germplasm and in identifying pharmaceutical and nutritional properties of local plants.

Germplasm embodies, in other words, a form of *know-how*,[7] which – although normally not qualifying *per se* as an "inventive contribution" in the meaning of patent law and thus not validly supporting a claim of "joint

---

[2] E.U. Directive No 98/44/EC of 6 July 1998 on the legal protection of biotechnology inventions (quotation from Recital 26 to be read in connection with arts. 2.1 (a), 3.1, 8, 13, 14).
[3] Convention on Biological Diversity, 5 June 1992, 31 I.L.M. 818, *available at* http://www.biodiv.org/convention/articles.asp (last accessed 28 July 2004) (emphasis supplied).
[4] *Id*. arts. 2, 3.   [5] *Id*. art. 15.
[6] *Id*. arts. 1, 8(j). The principle is also supported by the International Treaty on Plant Genetic Resources for Food and Agriculture, 3 Nov. 2001 [hereinafter ITPGR], *available at* http://www.fao.org/ag/cgrfa/itpgr.htm#text (last visited 14 July 2004), art. 10 – Farmers' Rights, para. 2b. *See* Michael Blakeney, *Protection of Plant Varieties and Farmers' Rights*, 2002 E.I.P.R. 9; *see also* EC Directive 98/44, above n. 2 (Preamble, recitals 56 & 11).
[7] *See, e.g.*, J.H. Reichman & Tracy Lewis, *Using Liability Rules to Stimulate Local Innovation in Developing Countries: Application to Traditional Knowledge* [this volume].

inventorship"[8] – represents the fundamental pre-condition of all subsequent R&D work carried out by the recipient industries. This realization also supports the view that new claims to "fair and equitable sharing of benefits" should not depend on either the validity of patents derived from genetic resources nor their duration. Indeed, they should not depend on the existence of patents at all because the industry's decision to patent or not is irrelevant. Such rights should simply follow from the *fact* of development and exploitation of biodiversity-based industrial products.

To achieve the goal of equitable sharing, the Convention provides as follows:

> Each Contracting Party shall take legislative, administrative or policy measures, as appropriate, and in accordance with Articles 16 and 19, [. . .] with the aim of sharing in a fair and equitable way the results of research and development and the benefits arising from the commercial and other utilization of genetic resources with the Contracting Party providing such resources. *Such sharing shall be upon mutually agreed terms.*[9]

Hence, there is a straightforward encouragement to implement the objective under a "cooperative," not a "confrontational" approach, with a view to benefiting (maybe most of all) the developing countries.[10]

A. Sharing of what?

While such an approach is typically pursued within a contractual perspective, that approach is the source of real problems in this context. It is usually based on a license to exploit biological material granted by a rural community (or an official entity) in a developing country to a firm located in a developed country. This license allows the recipient industries, which typically enjoy much greater bargaining power, to pay the biogenetic providing local communities *a just financial return*, either as a lump sum or a royalty (or both), from commercial exploitation of the new biogenetic based drug or food product.[11]

Of course, the contractual framework can provide, and sometimes actually does provide for more advanced schemes, whereby, for instance, a duty is placed on the "industrial party," licensee of the biological material and developer and owner of the patent on the new drug or seed, to "grant back" to the

---

[8] See Michael Blakeney, *Bioprospecting and the Protection of Traditional Medical Knowledge of Indigenous Peoples: An Australian Perspective*, 1997 E.I.P.R. 298, 299–300.

[9] CBD, above n. 3, art 15(7) (emphasis supplied).

[10] See J.H. Reichman, *The TRIPS Agreement Comes of Age: Conflict or Cooperation with the Developing Countries?*, 32 CASE WESTERN RES. J. INT'L L. 441 (2000).

[11] *See, e.g.*, such U.S. contractual models as the Diversa-Yellowstone CRADA–Cooperative Research and Development Agreement, and INBio-Merck, both involving mere profit-sharing, *in The Need and Possible Means of Implementing the Convention on Biodiversity into Patents Law*, AIPPI YEARBOOK 2001/II, XXXVIIIth Congress, Report of the U.S. Delegation on Question 159, 388.

providing licensor (the local community) a non-exclusive license "for research use."[12]

Even in this more advanced example, however, the license was "not for any commercial use,"[13] and thus it could not be invoked by, and shared with, a locally operating industry. Moreover, this contract expressly stated that, while the indigenous people remained free to continue to make and sell their traditional products, the new drugs developed and patented by the industrial licensee could not possibly be deemed an expression of "traditional knowledge" within the ambit of this provision.[14] Hence, there is no provision for any participation by the local communities in the industrial development of the new products. It clearly emerges, indeed, that the biogenetic-related innovation, whether patented or not, will not belong, even in part, to the indigenous people who provided the genetic resources.[15]

In my view, a purely financial reward – however equitable, and even generous – does not fulfill the terms requiring a "fair and equitable sharing" of "the results *of research and development* and the benefits arising from the commercial and other utilization of genetic resources," as the CBD mandates.[16] Those terms appear broad enough to embrace participation in that "spread" of applied technical and scientific know-how, and the development of new industrial and commercial activities, which embody the main socio-economic benefits pertaining to innovation. Also, such expectations are *not* substitutable by the provision of mere "abstract" knowledge, as by the grant of a sort of "fair use" right,[17] or by the information provided by patent specifications.[18] Thus, in Professor Reichman's words, "Governments in developing countries should ... regulate the manner in which foreign firms obtain access to local germplasm, with a view to sharing in both the technical knowledge that may result and the proceeds of commercial exploitation."[19]

This position was implicitly and expressly endorsed by a number of national (and Western) delegations at the 2001 Congress of the International Association for the Protection of Industrial Property (AIPPI).[20] It seems, indeed, to reflect the most appropriate balance of interests, the most

---

[12] *See, e.g.*, art. 6.03 of the Agreement between the Peruvian Communities representing the Aguaruna and Huambisa peoples, and a U.S. Company, G. D. Searle & Co., of Monsanto Group, *in* Charles McManis, *Recent Publications on Indigenous Knowledge Protection – New Directions in Indigenous Knowledge Protection*, ATRIP 1999 COLLECTED PAPERS, at 71.

[13] *See id.* [14] *Id.* art. 6.05. [15] *Id.* [16] CBD, above n. 3, art. 8(j) (emphasis supplied).

[17] As provided in the Searle-Aguarunas Agreement, above n. 12.

[18] *See* G. DUTFIELD, INTELLECTUAL PROPERTY RIGHTS, TRADE AND BIODIVERSITY 59–60 (IUCN 2000).

[19] J.H. Reichman, *From Free Riders to Fair Followers: Global Competition Under the TRIPS Agreement*, 29 N.Y.U. J. INT'L L. & POL. 11, 39 (1997).

[20] *See* AIPPI Summary Report, above n. 11, at 397 et seq. (on Question Q 159). For example, the position of the Italian delegation affirmed that "the conditions aiming at favouring and promoting a local exploitation of patents and the related technology would be more

geopolitically correct tradeoff: namely, that in exchange for the developing country releasing to the developed country their traditional knowledge as embodied in the germplasm, the latter should release to the former their technical and commercial knowledge as embodied in the newly developed products and processes based on the biological material.

It follows that the fulfillment of the goal under discussion implies that the provider country be granted the chance to participate in, and benefit from, the industrial and commercial exploitation of biogenetic-related innovation (and thus, particularly, from related patents and know-how), on its own national market. Such a result could technically be achieved either by relegating domestic production to local licensees under voluntary or compulsory licenses with the patent holder, or by requiring the patentee directly to work the patent in the local territory. Even direct production exclusively performed by the foreign firm would yield, in the developing country (and aside from employment-related benefits), a "spill over" of industrial know-how and capacity that could constitute a necessary, although not sufficient, condition for the subsequent development of a domestic industry.

In the next section, I will outline a tentative proposal for "cooperatively" achieving that "fair and equitable sharing" of benefits. This proposal tries to apply (and reconcile) the CBD's and TRIPS'[21] principles, and to reasonably balance the interests of developed and developing countries.

B. From "agreed dominance" to better balanced terms of trade

As previously hinted – and as several examples show – there is a serious risk that we might never attain the goal of equitable sharing within a purely private contractual framework characterized by the substantial disproportion of contractual and economic power between developed and developing countries. This imbalance is often aggravated by robust, not always transparent, diplomatic and political pressures by governments in developed countries on their developing country counterparts, a not-so-private third party intervention in a so-called private agreement.

To avoid such a risk, it is imperative to ensure the substantive compliance of any agreement between recipients and providers of biological resources with basic legal principles, internationally acknowledged, that support the broad goal of equitable sharing. To this end, the cooperative approach mentioned above should be implemented under procedural guarantees capable of ensuring

---

adequate and effective measures to compensate the owners of the genetic resources and to meet the objectives of the CBD, than royalties or lump sums payments." *Id.* at 331 et seq.

[21] Agreement on Trade-Related Aspects of Intellectual Property Rights, 15 Apr. 1994, Marrakesh Agreement Establishing the World Trade Organization, Annex 1C, LEGAL INSTRUMENTS – RESULTS OF THE URUGUAY ROUND vol. 31, 33 I.L.M. 81 (1994) [hereinafter TRIPS Agreement].

a mutually satisfactory equilibrium of interests, and not just a simple reflection of the existing imbalance of power between the parties.

As for the first point, reference should be made both to the CBD and to the TRIPS Agreement, and especially to their *interaction*, that is, the need to implement both instruments "in a mutually supportive way," as the European Commission recently suggested.[22] As noted, article 15.7 of the CBD empowers each Contracting Party to adopt legislative, administrative or policy measures aimed to achieve the requisite fair sharing with respect to both R&D results and the commercial benefits arising from the use of genetic resources.[23] The same article provides that such action must take place "in accordance" with articles 16 and 19 of the Convention. Article 16 enjoins the parties to the Convention – including both provider and recipient countries – to cooperate, subject to national legislation and international law, in order to ensure that patents and other IPRs "are supportive and do not run counter to its (i.e., the Convention's) objectives" in general and to the norm of "equitable sharing" in particular.[24] Article 19 provides that all parties to the Convention "shall take *all practical measures* to promote and advance priority access on a fair and equitable basis by Contracting Parties, *especially developing countries, to the results and benefits arising from biotechnologies based upon genetic resources provided by those Contracting Parties.*"[25]

For its part, the TRIPS Agreement allows WTO Members "in *formulating or amending* their laws and regulations, [to] adopt *measures necessary* to promote the public interest in sectors of vital importance to their *socio-economic and technological development.*"[26] The TRIPS Agreement also specifically allows Members to impose compulsory licenses on patent rights holders, a provision that should be read in the light of both articles 8.1. and 7.[27]

---

[22] *See, respectively*, Communication by the European Communities and their Member States on the Relationship Between the Convention on Biological Diversity and the TRIPS Agreement (3 Apr. 2000); *and* Communication by the European Communities and their Member States to the TRIPS Council on the Review of Article 27.3(b) of the TRIPS Agreement, and the Relationship between the TRIPS Agreement and the Convention on Biological Diversity (CBD) and the Protection of Traditional Knowledge and Folklore – "A Concept Paper" (12 Sept. 2002). *See also* WTO Doha Ministerial Conference, Declaration on the TRIPS Agreement and Public Health, WT/MIN(01)/DEC/W/2 (14 Nov. 2001) [hereinafter Doha Declaration], para. 19 (instructing the TRIPS Council to examine the relationship between the TRIPS Agreement and the CBD, particularly in light of articles 7 and 8 of the TRIPS Agreement). *See generally*, DUTFIELD, above n. 18, chs. 3–6.

[23] CBD, above n. 3, art. 15.7.   [24] *Id.* art. 16.   [25] *Id.* art 19 (emphasis supplied).

[26] TRIPS Agreement, above n. 21, art. 8.1 (emphasis supplied); *see also id.* art. 7.

[27] *Id.* art. 31. *See* CARLOS M. CORREA, INTELLECTUAL PROPERTY RIGHTS: THE WTO AND DEVELOPING COUNTRIES 241 et seq. (2000). *See also* B. Remiche & H. Desterbeq, *Brevet et GATT: Quel Interêt?*, 1996 REV. DROIT INTELLECTUEL-L'INGENIEUR-CONSEIL, 81, 94 et seq (1996); B. Remiche & W. Desterberq, *Les Brevets Pharmaceutiques dans les Accords du GATT: L'enjeu?*, 1996 REV. INT. DROIT. ECON. 7, 43–46.

In my view, the tensions in this legislative framework empower the providing country's government to adopt, upon the granting of a domestic patent, a set of ad hoc measures requiring patent holders either to establish local production of the biodiversity-based innovative products or processes or, failing that, to license to domestically located industries the production and sale of products covered by their patent. In other words, under this scheme, should the patent owner refuse to produce locally (even by appointing a local licensee or co-venture of its own choice), the country providing the biogenetic resource could grant a compulsory license to a local third party. This license, in compliance with article 31 of the TRIPS Agreement, should be non-exclusive, non-discriminatory, based on fair terms (fair, of course, also to the provider country in view of its essential contribution to the innovation in question).[28] Such a license should primarily focus on the supply of the local market and thus exclude, except perhaps marginally, any export activities of the licensee.[29]

This proposal does not express a one-sided view of the developing countries' interests. Rather, it represents a reasonable compromise solution, one that is respectful of both CBD's and TRIPS' principles. It safeguards the exploiting industries' competitive advantages as derived from their patents better than would be the case of a straightforward imposition of a compulsory license under articles 31 (and 8.1) of the TRIPS Agreement. Let us see why.

C. Clarifying the uncertain status of a local working requirement

A possible objection to the foregoing proposal is its inconsistency with the widely held, although still much debated, view that the TRIPS Agreement (as well as subsequently amended national patent laws) repealed the long established principle of local working of patented inventions at the national level.[30] This principle, embodied in article 5A of the Paris Convention,[31] requires a patentee to produce the patented goods in the country where protection is sought if the country issuing a patent so desires.

In discussing this objection, I will make the assumption least favorable to my position concerning the tension between article 5A of the Paris Convention and article 27.1 of the TRIPS Agreement. The former provision (incorporated bodily into the TRIPS Agreement by dint of article 2.1[32]) treats a failure to work

---

[28] See above n. 27.   [29] TRIPS Agreement, above n. 21, art. 31(f).
[30] See TRIPS Agreement, above n. 21, art. 27.1.
[31] Paris Convention for the Protection of Industrial Property of 20 Mar. 1883, 828 U.N.T.S. 305 [hereinafter Paris Convention], *as revised at* Stockholm 14 July 1967, *as amended* 28 Sept. 1979, art. 5A.
[32] TRIPS Agreement, above n. 21, art. 2.1; J.H. REICHMAN WITH CATHERINE HASENZAHL, NON-VOLUNTARY LICENSING OF PATENTED INVENTIONS: THE LAW AND PRACTICE OF THE UNITED STATES II.C.2 (UNCTAD/ICTSD, draft 2003).

the patent locally as an abuse of the patentee's exclusive rights.[33] The latter provision makes "patent rights enjoyable without discrimination as to the place of invention ... and whether products are imported or locally produced."[34] On the least favorable assumption, the need to reconcile these two provisions means that WTO Members can no longer consider a patentee's failure to work the patent locally as a *per se* abuse, notwithstanding the plain language to the contrary of article 5A of the Paris Convention.[35]

According to this not universally shared thesis,[36] patentees – while retaining the right to manufacture, hence actual capability to implement the relevant know-how in their own homeland or in any other country they deem convenient – would commit an "abuse" within the meaning of article 5A (and thus become subject to a compulsory license under the same article of the Paris Convention) *only* if they should not provide, even by mere exports, enough products to the country that granted the patent.[37] In other words, undersupplying the market would displace a failure to work the patent locally as grounds for abuse under this interpretation.[38]

If this interpretation holds, there would be no legal means for developing-country governments to require the foreign patentees of products derived from locally generated biogenetic resources to work their patents locally (in addition to paying compensation under private agreements) without resorting to compulsory licenses rooted in either a government use provision or the public interest rationale that article 31 of the TRIPS Agreement expressly permits.[39] The patentee would enjoy a TRIPS guaranteed right to supply the local territory by means of imports while discharging the duty to pay compensation. In so doing, however, we may note that an across-the-board application of article 27.1 of the TRIPS Agreement along these lines would in fact allow the foreign holders of the relevant patents to renew the typical colonial scheme of trade whereby the developing country exports its raw materials, and the industrialized country returns its finished goods.[40] This tradeoff, disregarding any other

---

[33] *See* above n. 31.   [34] *See* above n. 30.
[35] *See* Joseph Straus, *Implications of the TRIPS Agreement in the Field of Patent Law*, in FROM GATT TO TRIPS, ICC Studies vol. 18, at 204 (Beier-Schricker eds., 1996).
[36] For a skeptical view of this position, *see* REICHMAN WITH HASENZAHL, above n. 32, II.C.2.
[37] *See* above nn. 33, 34 and accompanying text; Straus, above n. 35.
[38] *Cf.* TRIPS Agreement, above n. 21, arts. 8.2, 40.2.
[39] *Id.* art. 31. *See generally* REICHMAN WITH HASENZAHL, above n. 32. One should note, that any residual flexibility left in the TRIPS Agreement, which requires technical mastery to exploit, "could be squeezed out by high protectionist standards incorporated into a new international agreement on patents." *Id.*
[40] The repeal of the local working requirement for patents functions as a truly anti-protectionist, pro-competitive legal instrument within a context of developed economies. However, in a North-South context, it basically sanctions, as hinted in the text, a colonial-type scheme of international trade, where developing countries act as mere importers of advanced finished goods from developed countries.

considerations,[41] would substantially delay the diffusion and acquisition of industrial know-how among developing countries and help to keep them in a long-term condition of economic and technical dependence.

Nevertheless, I do not think that the reference to article 27.1 of the TRIPS Agreement truly settles the question. My argument is rooted in legal logic and in a bit of armchair economic analysis, and it is articulated as follows.

If one compares the compulsory licenses that WTO Members may generally impose under article 31 of the TRIPS Agreement with the local working requirement rooted in the Paris Convention, it will readily appear that the latter inflicts a much smaller restriction on the patentee's freedom of action than the former. In terms of the adverse affects on the patentee's competitive advantage that could result from either option, it seems clear that working the patent locally (or through a partner or licensee of choice) would yield a considerably more diluted and slower spillover of industrial and commercial know-how than would be the case under general compulsory licenses that would directly breed competitors. Local working would less significantly reduce the patentee's lead-time advantage over competitors than would a compulsory license in favor of third parties. At the same time, the developing country that enforced a local working requirement would not necessarily experience a net loss of public benefits because one would logically expect the patentee's provision of technical know-how and financial resources to equal or exceed, in quality as well as in quantity, those of an unrelated compulsory licensee.

If these premises hold true, then the need to reconcile the obligations that the CBD imposes in articles 1, 8(j), 16, 15.7 and 19[42] with the reserved power of WTO Members under articles 7, 8.1, and 31 of the TRIPS Agreement[43] could be leveraged to support a derogation from the patentee's exclusive right to import (under article 27.1 of that Agreement), at least enough to justify imposition of a local working requirement in connection with a private agreement to transfer biogenetic resources to foreign entrepreneurs. While the developing countries that implement this option must continue to observe the conditions set out in article 31,[44] they would have chosen a relatively less intrusive instrument than a straightforward compulsory license in favor of third parties with which "to promote the public interest in sectors of vital importance to their socio-economic and technological development," within the plain language of article 8.1 of the TRIPS Agreement.[45]

---

[41] Such as those related to the traditionally strong price imbalance between the cost of raw materials in poor countries and the price of finished products, as well as the growth of employment in developing countries generally.
[42] CBD, above n. 3, arts. 1, 8(j), 15.7, 16, 19.
[43] TRIPS Agreement, above n. 21, arts. 7, 8.1, 31.
[44] *See* TRIPS Agreement, above n. 21, art. 31(a)-(k).
[45] *Id.* art. 8.1. *See also* Remiche & Desterbeq, *Brevet et GATT*, above n. 27, at 98.

Let me emphasize that the proposal outlined above would not violate any interpretation of article 27.1 of the TRIPS Agreement *as an expression of a general principle*. To the extent that the Agreement effectively repealed local working requirements in general, that repeal would continue to apply in all other countries, whereas the exception I advocate would concern only the biodiversity providing countries and only for this specific purpose.

III. Towards a cooperative, not a confrontational approach

Let me restate that, for all the reasons convincingly and extensively expressed by prominent scholars when addressing the subject of disputes between industrialized and developing countries in matters related to TRIPS rules, I strongly share the preference for a "cooperative" rather than a "confrontational" approach.[46] Under such an approach, possible conflicts arising between developed and developing countries about the means of implementing the goal of "equitable sharing" should first be aired, for consultation and mediation, before the Council for TRIPS.[47] Only then, if necessary, should they be settled under the rules and procedures set out in the Understanding on Rules and Procedures Governing the Settlement of Disputes (DSU), by ad hoc panels and, ultimately, by the Appellate Body.[48]

As far as my specific topic is concerned, such a strategy appears the most suitable to encourage each party to achieve, on the basis of the legal arguments put forth above, a settlement reasonably balanced and respectful of the aforementioned substantive principles of international law. On one side, the developing country would be guaranteed that the agreements between its indigenous providers and those firms in the developed country would effectively allow the biodiversity providing country to partake of a *really* fair share of the overall scientific, industrial and commercial benefits from the deal. In this way, the providing country will be enabled to progressively grow its own R&D capacity and to develop a domestic industry that can flourish after the patents expire as well as a domestic trade in new biogenetic-based products and processes.

---

[46] See esp. Reichman, above n. 10; *see also* Rochelle Cooper Dreyfuss & Andreas F. Lowenfeld, *Two Achievements of the Uruguay Round: Putting TRIPS and Dispute Settlement Together*, 37 VA. J. INT'L L. 275 (1997); Intellectual Property and Genetic Resources, WIPO Doc. WIPO/IP/GR/00/2 (17–18 Apr. 2000).

[47] *Cf.* TRIPS Agreement above n. 21, arts. 64, 68. For another dispute avoiding proposal, see G. Graff & D. Zilberman, *Towards an Intellectual Property Clearinghouse for Agricultural Biotechnology*, 2001 IP STRATEGY TODAY, 1, et seq (2001).

[48] *See* WTO Agreement, above n. 21 Annex 2, Understanding on the Rules and Procedures Governing the Settlement of Disputes (DSU). *See generally*, R. Cooper Dreyfuss & A. Lowenfeld, above n. 46.

On the other side, substantial economic benefits (disregarding an improved image) would accrue to the developed country's own firms.[49] First, in return for accepting the onus of local working, they would generally avoid the risk of a compulsory license being issued to third parties, since this option would now be implemented only if the patent owner failed to work the patent locally.[50] Second, within such a cooperative framework, the developed country's firms could be allowed the right to contractually impose on the local licensees or co-venturer of their choice strict restraints on their power to export outside the biodiversity providing country, without the patent holder's authorization. As a concession, these restraints might even be allowed to cut back upon the amount of foreign exports that article 31(f) of the TRIPS Agreement normally allows a compulsory licensee to make.[51]

---

[49] *See e.g.*, G. Van Overwalle, *Belgium Goes Its Own Way on Biodiversity and Patents*, 2002 EUR. INTELL. PROP. REV. 233, 235–236 (2002).

[50] In this regard, the compulsory license would express its most useful, and "virtual" role, that of a threat, a Damocles' sword facilitating fair and voluntary settlements. *See also* WILLIAM CORNISH, INTELLECTUAL PROPERTY: PATENTS, COPYRIGHT, TRADE MARKS AND ALLIED RIGHTS 205 (Sweet & Maxwell 1989).

[51] *See* TRIPS Agreement, above n. 21, art. 31(f) (allowing 49 percent of production to be exported).

PART IV

Reform and regulation issues

SECTION 2
The role of competition law

27

The critical role of competition law in preserving public goods in conflict with intellectual property rights

JOSEF DREXL[*]

I. Introduction
II. What is meant by public goods?
    A. Non-rivalry and non-excludability
    B. IP laws as a response to a public goods problem?
    C. The new concept of global public goods
III. The role of competition law
    A. IP law and competition law in general
    B. Competition law, social interests, and their international dimension
        1. The economics of local markets
        2. The case of international exhaustion
        3. Limiting IPRs for social reasons
IV. Conclusions

I. Introduction

Drawing the line between intellectual property protection and the application of competition laws poses one of the most difficult issues legislators and other public authorities have to face in the field of market regulation. Complicating this task is the distrust that experts in each of these fields have for the application of the others' legal principles to their respective specialties. Quite frequently, IP lawyers consider competition law an instrument of intervention, one that infringes the right holder's entitlements and, thereby, affects the very foundations of intellectual property law. Conversely, antitrust lawyers sometimes criticize IP protection for creating monopoly rights against the interests of consumers.[1]

---

[*] Josef Drexl is Professor of Law at the Institute for International Law of the University of Munich and Director at the Max Planck Institute for Intellectual Property, Competition and Tax Law (Munich).
[1] Awareness of this antagonism is rising on both sides of the Atlantic. See, e.g., Stéphane Lemarchand et al., *Bien informationnels: entre droit intellectuels et droit de la concurrence*, PROPRIETES INTELLECTUELLES 11(2003).

A similar conflict became apparent at the beginning of the Uruguay Round of Multilateral Trade Negotiations. The developed world, under the leadership of the U.S., successfully pursued implementation of substantive standards of protection as a trade-related aspect of intellectual property law in order to guarantee better protection of their national right holders abroad.[2] On the other side, developing countries supported a competition law perspective on the trade-related aspects of IP rights.[3] The TRIPS Agreement globalizes the standards of protection for patents, copyrights, trademarks, and other rights, whereas the need of controlling abusive behavior of right holders and restraints of competition in licensing contracts is only taken into account through a confirmation that the application of national competition laws remains lawful.[4]

In recent years, TRIPS has received considerable criticism and high public awareness. In particular, discussions held in the aftermath of the Seattle WTO Ministerial Meeting of 1999 and, as a consequence, the WTO Doha Declaration on TRIPS and Public Health of 2001, refer to the interests of the users of IP rights, such as public health needs, and rights to information, which are now thought to be incorporated into a revised TRIPS legal system.[5]

The Duke Conference on International Public Goods and Transfer of Technology under a Globalized Intellectual Property Regime[6] was a welcome initiative, at which predominantly IP experts reacted to this criticism with the objective of striving for new legal and economic approaches to the national and international regulation of IP systems. Of course, competition law is one of the legal instruments we have to consider when better defining the limits and boundaries of intellectual property protection.

---

[2] *See* Agreement on Trade-Related Aspects of Intellectual Property, 15 Apr. 1994, Marrakesh Agreement Establishing the World Trade Organization, Annex 1C, LEGAL INSTRUMENTS – RESULTS OF THE URUGUAY ROUND vol. 31, 33 I.L.M. 81 (1994) [hereinafter TRIPS Agreement].

[3] *Cf.* JOSEF DREXL, ENTWICKLUNGSMÖGLICHKEITEN DES URHEBERRECHTS IM RAHMEN DES GATT (C.H. Beck München), 308, 365 et seq. (1990).

[4] TRIPS Agreement, above n. 2, art. 40. *See* Andreas Heinemann, *Antitrust Law of Intellectual Property in the TRIPS Agreement of the World Trade Organization*, in FROM GATT TO TRIPS 239 (Friedrich-Karl Beier & Gerhard Schricker eds., VCH 1996). *See also* Hanns Ullrich, *Expansionist Intellectual Property Protection and Reductionist Competition Rules: A TRIPS Perspective* [this volume].

[5] *See, in particular*, Ministerial Declaration, Ministerial Conference, 4th sess., Doha, WTO-Doc. WT/MIN(01)/DEC/1 ¶ 17 (14 Nov. 2001), *available at* http://www.wto.org/english/thewto_e/minist_e/min01_e/mindecl_e.htm.

[6] Held at Duke University School of Law, Durham, NC, USA on 4–6 Apr. 2003. Oral presentations *available at* http://www.law.duke.edu/trips/webcast.html.

II. What is meant by public goods?

The contributors to this volume try to capture the conflicting interests of IP owners and users with the concept of "public goods." They also give some important examples of such goods, including sustainable development, accessible health care, technology transfer, and broad-based advances in science and education.[7]

A. *Non-rivalry and non-excludability*

In economic theory, public goods as distinguished from private goods are characterized by their non-rivalry in consumption and non-excludability of benefits.[8] Non-rivalry means that consumption of a given commodity by an additional person does not add any costs to its provision. The building and operation of a lighthouse entails fixed costs irrespective of how many vessels will benefit from its operation.[9] At the same time, public goods are non-exclusive: once provided, nobody can be excluded from their benefits. In this sense, everyone in a given community will profit from, say, measures taken against a particular epidemic. The most frequently cited example of a public good is national defense.

Neoclassical economics views public goods as a specific form of market failure. Individuals are not willing to pay so long as they can hope to benefit from the provision of public goods as free riders. Private markets do not directly provide public goods. Governments are in the best position to provide public goods. They are able to charge members of a given community on the basis of average benefits received or other criteria, including social criteria.

In the very strict economic sense, public goods require both non-rivalry *and* non-excludability. If only rivalry of consumption exists, as in the case of scarce environmental goods, such as water and air, the goods in question belong to the so-called *commons*. In cases in which consumers might be excluded from consumption of a good, but consumption by an additional consumer does not add any costs to its provision, the good in question is called a *club good*. Examples of club goods are pay-tv, public performances of films in movie theatres, and tolls introduced for congested traffic facilities.

---

[7] *See, e.g.*, Peter Drahos, *The Regulation of Public Goods* [this volume]; Richard Nelson, *Linkages Between the Market Economy and the Scientific Commons* [this volume]; Carlos Correa, *Can the TRIPS Agreement Foster Technology Transfer to Developing Countries?* [this volume]; Frederick Abbott, *Managing the Hydra: The Herculean Task of Ensuring Access to Essential Medicines* [this volume].

[8] This is the classical economic understanding; *see, e.g.*, Oliver Morrisey et al., *Defining International Public Goods: Conceptual Issues*, *in* INTERNATIONAL PUBLIC GOODS: INCENTIVES, MEASUREMENT, AND FINANCING 1, ch. 2, pt. 2 (Marco Ferroni & Ashoka Mody eds., Kluwer Law International 2002).

[9] *Cf.* Ronald H. Coase, *The Lighthouse of Economics*, 17 J.L. & ECON. 1 (1960).

However, the line of demarcation between public goods and club goods is not conceptually well drawn. In fact, technical or legal measures may be implemented with the objective of transforming public goods into club goods. For instance, television programs may be transmitted nowadays in encrypted form, which enables broadcasters to grant access only to persons willing to pay for the decryption code, whereas in the past, broadcasters were unable to exclude anybody with a television set from consumption. Transforming public goods into club goods solves the core problem of public goods, namely, that private markets will not provide public goods.

B. *IP laws as a response to a public goods problem?*

As the title of this volume suggests, the issue arises as to whether IP systems have the objective of providing public goods.[10] From the perspective of economic theory, the introduction of IPRs may be looked at as a conscious policy decision in favor of enhancing the production of technology and other knowledge goods. By granting exclusive rights, the legislator enables the right holder to charge prices for the use of such goods and to exclude persons from consumption who are unwilling or unable to pay. Consequently, the introduction of IPRs transforms the protected subject matter from a public good into a club good: its provision to additional consumers does not create additional costs of production, but the right holder can charge users and exclude additional consumers.

The public goods concept of IPRs can explain why persons and enterprises might have an incentive to invest in the production of knowledge and creativity, and, in particular, it offers a convincing depiction of IPR protection, especially in the U.S. This concept is overwhelmingly utilitarian and meets the goals of the U.S. Constitution, which grants power to the Congress "to promote the Progress of Science and useful Arts by securing for limited times to Authors and Inventors the exclusive Right to their respective Writings and Discoveries."[11]

Another approach to the economics of IPRs is offered by *property rights theory*. Property rights are thought to solve the problem of positive externalities, namely, the advantages of consumers who would benefit from the provision of knowledge without having to contribute to the necessary investment. In order to create an incentive for such investments, these benefits need to be internalized by the adoption of an IP system.

Both the public goods and the property rights approach are utilitarian and efficiency-oriented. In comparison, however, the property rights approach has

---

[10] *See generally* Keith E. Maskus & Jerome H. Reichman, *The Globalization of Private Knowledge Goods and the Privatization of Global Public Goods* [this volume].

[11] U.S. CONST. art. I, § 8, cl. 8.

certain advantages. It provides a theoretical explanation for where to draw the line between protection and the public domain. Internalization by property rights can only be justified so long as the benefits of internalization, i.e., of the incentive to create and to invent, outweigh its costs, especially the costs of excluding individuals from consumption. In practice, the problem remains of how these benefits and costs should be measured by a legislator who has to draft legal provisions with a general scope of application.[12]

One should add that the economic rationale is not the only possible justification for implementing IP systems. This is especially true for copyright law in Continental Europe, which adheres to the author's rights approach. Moreover, the expected financial return is not a necessarily decisive incentive for the creative activity of authors.

C. The new concept of global public goods

Although they cannot be equated with true public goods, the interests of concern to the contributors to this volume – sustainable development, transfer of technology, affordable public health, broad-based advances of science and education – demonstrate a particular closeness to them. With respect to classical public goods, such as internal and external security or the above-mentioned lighthouse, economists argue that government should provide them because private businesses cannot do so. Provision by the government has the positive side effect of satisfying the needs of all consumers, whereas private markets exclude consumers who are unable to pay the market price. Because public goods often meet basic human needs that are sometimes even crucial for the survival of individual or of whole societies, provision by the government – taking into account the social factor in spreading the costs – becomes a matter of social policy.

Private markets are not unsocial by nature. On the contrary, they contribute to society by maximizing economic output at the lowest costs in the interest of consumers. This may also apply to the market for intangible goods protected by IPRs. However, by internalizing positive externalities, IP systems increase the price of goods. Therefore, IP regimes exclude poorer consumers from access to indispensable goods and may give rise to serious social problems.

In contrast, public goods often demonstrate higher social value. Not only should consumers not be excluded from the consumption of public goods, we also want to guarantee equal access to public health, a clean environment and internal and foreign security as a matter of social justice – and in some countries, such as Germany, also as a matter of fundamental constitutional

---

[12] *Cf.* the criticism relating to the practical deficiencies of the property rights approach expressed by ANDREAS HEINEMANN, IMMATERIALGÜTERSCHUTZ IN DER WETTBEWERBSORDNUNG 21–23 (Mohr-Siebeck 2002).

rights – irrespective of the individual's ability to pay. While the provision of public goods by governments will achieve this end, poorer states usually lack the financial means adequately to finance the provision of such public goods.

The protection of intellectual property under the WTO/TRIPs Agreement conflicts with the interest of poorer states and societies in guaranteeing access of individuals to the protected subject matter, especially in the field of essential medicines and educational material.[13] Reacting to the anti-globalization movement, the new concept of "global public goods," especially promoted by officials of the United Nations Development Program (UNDP), has fostered understanding and analysis of the conflict between IP protection and the problem of access of poorer societies to indispensable technology and knowledge.[14]

According to this new concept, global public goods (GPG) are defined as "goods whose benefits extend to all countries, people, and generations."[15] The concept has to be understood in a dynamic sense. While some public goods are public by nature, others become public by dint of human action or by policy decisions. In a similar and larger sense, a public good will be considered global if "it benefits more than one group of countries and does not discriminate against any population group or generation."[16]

This dynamic concept has several advantages. Although lawyers have adopted the term private property, the dynamic character of the GPG concept highlights the fact that IPRs protect public goods that have been privatized by political decisions. In a time of globalization, its dynamic character explains the expansion of global public goods in comparison to mere national public goods. Consequently, the policy decisions about whether global public goods should be privatized, and to what extent, have to be made at the international level.[17]

The problem of global public goods is one that affects predominantly the developing countries. Whereas the public budget or a functioning public health system may be endowed with the financial means to provide patented essential medicines, such as HIV drugs, to all patients in rich countries, such medicines remain high-priced private goods in poorer countries. Whereas water can be

---

[13] *See, e.g.*, Abbott, above n. 7; Ruth Okediji, *Sustainable Access to Digital Information Works in Developing Countries* [this volume].

[14] *See* PROVIDING GLOBAL PUBLIC GOODS (Inge Kaul et al. eds., Oxford Univeristy Press 2003); *see also* the predecessor volume, GLOBAL PUBLIC GOODS: INTERNATIONAL COOPERATION IN THE 21ST CENTURY (Inge Kaul et al. eds., Oxford University Press 1999). Some authors prefer the notion of "international" public goods. For the work done in the framework of the World Bank, see Marco Ferroni & Ashoka Mody, *Global Incentives for International Public Goods: Introduction and Overview, in* INTERNATIONAL PUBLIC GOODS, above n. 8, pt. 1, at 5 et seq. (defining international public goods as goods which reduce poverty).

[15] Inge Kaul & Ronald U. Mendoza, *Advancing the Concept of Public Goods, in* PROVIDING GLOBAL PUBLIC GOODS, above n. 14, at 78, 95.

[16] *Id.* at 96   [17] *Id.*

sold as an affordable low-cost private good in rich countries, it largely remains in the commons – non-exclusionary, but rivalrous – in developing countries. These few examples demonstrate that poorer countries routinely lack the option of deciding whether to provide their citizens with indispensable goods in the form of public or private goods. Nor will their citizens be able to fall back on private goods if public goods are not provided in sufficient quantities.[18] As a result, inequality and social injustice among the citizens of different states emerge. The concept of global public goods seeks to activate stakeholders everywhere to participate in the political dialog concerning the need for an adequate global legal regime.

In a globalized economy, firms in national economies have to rely on intangible goods protected by IPRs in order to compete internationally. Similarly, the individual has to rely on a high standard of education in order to succeed in the labor market, which has come under increased pressure from international competition. Moreover, national economies will only start to produce knowledge goods qualifying for IP protection if their populations are sufficiently well educated. Hence, the problem of the TRIPS Agreement is not so much anchored in the question of whether it promotes or hampers transfer of technology to poorer countries. In any event, TRIPS decreases the chances of poorer countries and their populations to compete fairly in the ongoing process of economic globalization.

Sustainable development, affordable health care, technology transfer, and broad-based advances in science and education are not exclusively dependent on economic considerations, but also depend heavily on notions of social justice, human rights and public welfare. Nevertheless, all these interests have strong economic implications in a globalized world. In this context, it is not only important that the most efficient suppliers produce necessary goods. We also need to consider the distribution of efficiency gains[19] and how competitiveness will be spread globally among countries and their citizens.

The analysis so far argues in favor of restructuring IP systems, especially the TRIPS system, from a social and global perspective. This goal becomes especially difficult because social ends, i.e., distributive justice, lie outside what neoclassical economic theory can explain and describe. This difficulty, however, does not diminish the legitimacy of the social argument in law. In this sense, economic arguments have to be balanced against social arguments.

The concept of global public goods offers an economic, social and political approach to the problems that a globalized IP regime have raised. To what extent this concept may also provide solutions still remains to be seen. One legal instrument that could help to integrate the economic, the social and the

---

[18] *Cf. id.* at 99 et seq. (underlining the non-existence of "private exit options" for underprivileged people).
[19] See, e.g., Peter Gerhart, *Distributive Values and Institutional Design in the Provision of Global Public Goods* [this volume].

political arguments is competition law. The following analysis will look at the features of competition law and policy that make it a suitable means to solve the problem of global public goods.

III. The role of competition law

Competition law works against excessive protection of IPRs and, thereby, may promote the social interest in gaining access to otherwise protected subject matter as a global public good. The following analysis distinguishes between the role of competition law in relation to IP protection generally and its role in relation to social interests that may conflict with IPRs.

A. *IP law and competition law in general*

The objectives of national competition laws may differ widely. However, there is unanimity that competition laws pursue economic welfare that results from economic efficiency as at least one of its goals.[20] In this sense, competition law shares the objectives of IP law, contrary to what many experts in one or the other field of law may think.

From an economic perspective, IP rights usually consist of exclusive rights (property rights) designed to internalize positive externalities. Thereby, they enable an investor to include the costs of creative and inventive endeavors in the price of a given product. Consequently, IPRs raise prices without necessarily creating economic monopolies. Indeed, IPRs produce monopolistic outcomes only in specific situations, such as in the case of patents that give rise to new product markets. Goods not infringing the patent will compete with the patented good if the two products are substitutable from the consumer's perspective. Consumers can likewise choose between competing works of literature and movies, although a dominant position may exist when access to information stored in copyrighted form becomes indispensable to competition. Trademarks reward the right holder for investment in goodwill, but do not exclude competition with other similarly branded goods.

In principle, IPRs and competition laws thus are two complementary instruments for the establishment and preservation of competitive markets. Similarly, both IPRs and competition laws induce creativity and inventiveness. Conversely, a dominant firm will not have to invest in innovation as long as considerable barriers to entry protect it against competitors.[21] Both the IP

---

[20] *See, e.g.,* Eleanor M. Fox, *Can Antitrust Policy Protect the Global Commons from the Excesses of IPRs?* [this volume]. However, economic objectives may differ in detail. Some laws may pursue economic efficiency as an end in itself; others protect competition as such, as a wealth-producing institution.

[21] The Microsoft antitrust case, litigated in the U.S., provides a good example. A dominant firm may prefer to invest in keeping barriers to entry high rather than investing in

systems and competition laws contribute to efficient markets, not only in terms of allocative efficiency, but also of innovative efficiency.[22]

Despite these functional complementarities, IP rights remain a very sensitive issue from the perspective of competition law. At least four scenarios may be identified in which competition law and policy are called upon to control IP protection.

The first two scenarios evoke the classical applications of competition law to IPRs. In the first, transfer of IPRs under licensing agreements may be used to restrict competition between the licensor and the licensee or between a number of licensees. In the second situation, IPRs may give the right holder a market-dominant position, either by virtue of the exclusive right, without more, for example, when patents create new product markets,[23] or because the IPRs combine with other factors, such as network externalities.[24]

The other two scenarios do not pertain to the application of competition law as such, but rather to the design of IP laws. As previously observed, property rights theory offers a theoretical approach to defining the goals of IP protection.[25] However, it may be difficult in practice to determine the point at which the costs of restraining free use start to outweigh the benefits of incentives for creativity and inventiveness. Since competition law relies on a similar economic rationale, its analytical principles may be applied in order to evaluate the design of IP laws.

---

innovation. *See, e.g.*, Warren Grimes, *The Microsoft Litigation and Federalism in U.S. Antitrust Enforcement: Implications for International Competition Law*, in THE FUTURE OF TRANSNATIONAL ANTITRUST – FROM COMPARATIVE TO COMMON COMPETITION LAW 237 (Josef Drexl ed., Staempfli Publishers & Kluwer Law Int'l 2003).

[22] As to the latter concept, see Josef F. Brodley, *The Economic Goals of Antitrust: Efficiency, Consumer Welfare, and Technological Progress*, 62 N.Y.U. L. REV. 1020, 1025 et seq. (1987) (referring to the capacity of competition law to promote investment in innovation, a capacity which has to be considered most crucial for the creation of additional social wealth).

[23] Such a situation may also be found in regard to copyrighted works. For example, copyright protection of television programs may create a dominant position for the broadcasting company on the market for television program listings; *see* the *Magill* decision of ECJ, Cases C-241/91 P & C-242/91 P, RTE & IRP v. Comm'n, 1995 E.C.R. I-743 (6 Apr. 1995).

[24] This, along with a lock-in effect, might be the rationale behind the decision of the European Commission in the *IMS Health* case, which usually is discussed as an essential facilities case; *see* Thomas Eilmansberger, *Abschlusszwang und Essential Facility Doktrin nach Art. 82 EG*, 14 EUROPÄISCHES WIRTSCHAFTS- UND STEUERRECHT 12 (2003); Frank Fine, *NDC/IMS: A Logical Application of Essential Facilities Doctrine*, [2002] E.C.L.R. 457. *See also* the judgment of the ECJ on referral of the Frankfurt Court of Appeals (Oberlandesgericht) Case C-418/01, *IMS Health*, [2004] ECR (not yet officially reported), *available at* http://curia.eu.int/jurisp/cgi-bin/form.pl?lang=de&Submit=Suchen&docrequire=alldocs&numaff=&datefs=&datefe=&nomusuel=IMS+Health&domaine=&mots=&resmax=100 in which the Court did not discuss the underlying economic problems of the case.

[25] See above text accompanying nn. 11–12.

Under the third typical scenario, IP laws as such should not tend to produce market-dominant positions. National law granting design protection to spare parts most likely violates that rule.[26] Such laws, by nature, do not just allow investors to pass on the costs of innovation to consumers; they also allow them to charge monopoly prices as a matter of law and, therefore, to exploit consumers. Whether European *sui generis* protection of databases[27] and patent protection for software and business methods in the U.S. offer additional examples still needs to be analyzed.

The last scenario is the most difficult one from an analytical perspective. Whereas the preceding scenario pertained to the protected subject matter, this last scenario involves the scope of protection. One issue to be analyzed in this context is the principle of international exhaustion. Property rights theory explains why an exhaustion principle or a first-sale doctrine should be applied. Extending the right of distribution to subsequent sales could lead to overcompensation of the right holder.[28] In addition, subsequent sales do not affect the competitiveness of the right holder, because the buyer and subsequent seller had initially to pay the internalization price and had to consider these costs when calculating the resale price.

Competition law would argue in favor of a principle of international exhaustion. The right holder has been rewarded for the investment abroad by means of his first sale and there is no reason why intrabrand competition should be excluded to the disadvantage of domestic consumers, whereas a principle of national exhaustion allows discrimination between national markets against the logic of transnational markets of supply.

The foregoing analysis may be summed up as follows. Competition law plays a major role in defining the limits of IP laws in general or in controlling their exercise in individual cases. IP laws may only develop their own rationale within the framework of competition law analysis because both fields share the same economic goals, namely, the establishment of a functioning competitive and innovative market. In limiting IP protection, competition law also supports the protection of the above-mentioned global public goods concept by lowering the costs of access to indispensable goods.

---

[26] In such a case, the relevant market has to be defined as the market for the single-brand end product and not for all brands, since the consumer has to face considerable information problems relating to the likelihood of necessary repairs and their costs when buying the product. The consumer cannot revise his earlier decision so long as buying a totally new product does not yield the cheaper option (so-called lock-in effect). *See* the very instructive U.S. Supreme Court decision in Eastman Kodak Co. v. Image Technical Servs., Inc., 504 U.S. 451 (1992) (dealing with a tie-in of the provision of service for copiers and spare parts).

[27] *Cf.* J. H. Reichman, *Database Protection in a Global Economy*, REVUE INTERNATIONALE DE DROIT ECONOMIQUE 455–504 (2002).

[28] *Cf.* DAVID T. KEELING, INTELLECTUAL PROPERTY RIGHTS IN EU LAW: Volume I, at 76 (Oxford University Press 2003).

These considerations, in turn, give rise to two remarks concerning the TRIPS Agreement: First, current TRIPS rules need to be complemented by obligations to introduce competition laws controlling the exercise of IPRs. This proposal responds to the first two scenarios mentioned above. Second, the minimum rights approach set out in article 1.1 of the TRIPS Agreement[29] allows WTO Members to cross the borderline of a competitive design of IP laws, which then might induce right holders to market products only in those states that afford excessive protection. The minimum rights approach might consequently increase market prices for products and restrict access of consumers in poorer countries.

The analysis so far would also seem to argue for an obligation of WTO Members to accept a principle of international exhaustion, an option left open by article 6 of the TRIPS Agreement.[30] However, the interest in protecting global public goods may lead to a more cautious approach in the end.[31]

B. Competition law, social interests, and their international dimension

Competition law reasoning, as applied to the design and application of IP laws, contributes to social welfare by increasing the number of consumers who can afford to pay the market price. However, in the case of indispensable products, the problem remains that even competitive markets may not satisfy the most urgent needs of all consumers. In a second step, therefore, we have to look at the relationship between competition law and global public goods, as described above, with their specific social implications in mind.

Obviously, a concept of competition law entirely based on an efficiency rationale would not work in the direction of providing global public goods. It would rather argue for a completely integrated global market with a worldwide, highly harmonized IP system.

However, competition law may also be understood as a social institution. Competition law does not only guarantee efficient markets; it also furthers distributive justice by according a maximum share of the economic surplus to

---

[29] See TRIPS Agreement, above n. 2, art 1.1 (allowing domestic IP laws to exceed the minimum standards).

[30] A WTO rule on international exhaustion was proposed by Frederick M. Abbott to the International Law Association (ILA). See Frederick M. Abbott, *First Report (Final) to the Committee on International Trade Law of the International Law Association on the Subject of Parallel Importation (June 1997)*, 1 J. INT'L. ECON. L. 607(1998). At its London Conference of 2000, the ILA adopted a resolution, distinguishing different types of IPRs and clearly recommending a principle of international exhaustion for trademarks only. See ILA, Report of the Sixty-Ninth Conference. 19–21 (International Law Association 2000).

[31] See below text at B. 2.

consumers.[32] From a theoretical point of view, competition law reasoning may thus also serve as a tool for measuring and explaining the distributive advantages of a particular IP system.[33]

1. The economics of local markets

On the surface, it might seem that competition law could hardly contribute to improving access to knowledge goods protected by IPRs so long as both competition laws and IP laws shared the same economic rationale. Nevertheless, a counter-argument may be drawn from the fact that the relevant product markets usually have a limited geographical scope.

Whereas intangible goods protected by IPRs may be exploited worldwide, the geographical market for products based on such IPRs is not necessarily a global one. The relevant market has to be defined in light of the criterion of substitutability. Specific circumstances, such as high transport costs and low consumer ability to pay in local markets, may exclude imported products as a consumer option, in which case competition will be limited to the local or national market. For instance, in poorer countries that are net importers of agricultural goods, small farmers will not compete with farmers on foreign markets. In such a scenario, the lack of IPRs, such as plant breeders' rights, would not necessarily result in competitive disadvantages for foreign producers.

Ardent proponents of global IP protection will still argue that denial of IP protection in some countries might affect the incentive structure of IPRs elsewhere. However, since separate markets also produce separate prices and since, in the less-developed world in particular, the willingness and the capacity to pay are much reduced, the economic loss to the right holder may be minor and may hardly influence his or her decision to make the initial investment. Consequently, no economic rationale argues against the farmers' privilege and other exceptions to plant breeders' rights[34] in countries in which farmers only produce for local markets and in which consumers' ability to pay remains very

---

[32] This concept of a competition law with social effects is opposed to the "consumer welfare" paradigm of the Chicago School. According to that School, consumer welfare would also be increased by welfare gains made by producers exclusively. Those gains accruing from productive efficiency (economies of scale and scope) may outweigh a reduction of allocative efficiency to the disadvantage of consumers. See Charles F. Rule & David L. Meyer, *An Antitrust Enforcement Policy to Maximize the Economic Wealth of all Consumers*, in COLLABORATIONS AMONG COMPETITORS 77, at 79 et seq. (Eleanor M. Fox & James T. Halverson eds., 1991). But See Herbert Hovenkamp, *Antitrust Policy after Chicago*, 84 MICH. L. REV. 213, 231 (1985) (criticizing Chicago School positions).

[33] Cf. Peter M. Gerhart, *Distributive Values and Institutional Design in the Provision of Global Public Goods* [this volume] (stressing mix of efficiency and distributive goals in designing appropriate international IP system).

[34] See Michael Blakeney, *Stimulating Agricultural Innovation* [this volume] (discussing exceptions to plant breeders' rights in international law).

low. Of course, those foreign farmers who have to respect the IP right may eventually have problems when seeking to enter the local market. However, low willingness to pay and comparative high costs of transportation tend to exclude the foreign competitor from the local market anyway.

This example demonstrates that, in the case of local markets, national limitations on IP rights do not necessarily affect the incentive structure of the global IP system or restrain competition. On the contrary, such limitations could contribute to low consumer prices, improve supply in poorer countries and support the business opportunities of local producers, all of which promote sustainable development.

The example argues in favor of limitations to IP protection where markets in the less-developed world are mainly local in character. Indeed, Article 31(f) of the TRIPS Agreement refers to local markets as a criterion for issuing compulsory licenses.[35] However, the application of this provision is limited to patents alone and requires payment of adequate remuneration to the right holder.[36] In light of the analysis above, these requirements may be too strict and unnecessary.

Even in a period of globalization, the WTO legal system, in contrast to European Community law, is not able to eliminate all barriers to trade. Considerable customs tariffs, especially on so-called sensitive products, such as food and textiles, still exist. WTO Members still apply antidumping laws. The General Agreement on Trade in Services (GATS)[37] has only managed to liberalize some service sectors. Despite these obvious barriers to trade, which exclude or distort competition on transnational markets, the TRIPS Agreement pursues worldwide standards of IP protection. In a world of still separate national and regional markets, however, it is difficult to argue that the same substantive standards of protection are necessary in even the least important economies, whose low consumer prices do not contribute anything to the incentive structure of the global IP system.

From this perspective, the TRIPS Agreement deserves serious criticism.[38] In the framework of the WTO, Members decided to initiate the establishment of a global internal market with the upward harmonization of intellectual property rights, whereas they should have started with more advanced guarantees of fundamental economic freedoms and with attention to competition law. By proceeding in this way, WTO law has disregarded the previous experience of the European countries, where harmonization of IP laws among Member States of comparable economic strength only became an issue when differences

---

[35] TRIPS Agreement, above n. 2, art. 31(f).   [36] *Id.* art. 31(h).
[37] General Agreement on Trade in Services, 15 Apr. 1994, Marrakesh Agreement Establishing the World Trade Organization, Annex 1B.
[38] *Cf.* interview with Jagdish Baghwati, 76 SÜDDEUTSCHE ZEITUNG 26 (1 Apr. 2003) (equating TRIPS and its impact on world trade with a virus and its impact on the hard drive of a computer).

in the law led to distortions of competition after the establishment of the principles of economic freedom.

2. The case of international exhaustion

In particular, the inability of WTO Members to resolve the issue of exhaustion[39] merits severe criticism. In practice, rejection of the principle of international exhaustion by economically advanced states further hampers the emergence of cross-border markets.

From a competition law perspective, the argument that international exhaustion harms the legitimate interests of the right holder should not be accepted. Although one must concede that, where the doctrine of international exhaustion applies, both consumer prices and the revenues of IP holders are lower, this doctrine is consistent with the principle of competition and with IP doctrines generally. First, international exhaustion intensifies competition, and IP laws should not insulate the right holder from competition. Second, the relevant market expands in a world where international exhaustion applies. National markets become transnational in effect. In such markets, parallel imports will only take place so long as they remain profitable. Therefore, international exhaustion leads to more uniform prices in expanded markets, with rising prices in the exporting country and falling prices in the importing country. At least with regard to trademarks, efforts to exclude parallel imports can only be explained by the desire to protect a national distribution system by limiting competition.

The practice of national exhaustion in the developed world has a very ambiguous impact on local markets in poorer countries. While the rejection of international exhaustion in richer countries is detrimental to developing countries to the extent that it reduces the export opportunities of local firms, it also helps to maintain lower prices for local consumers.

Moreover, as seen above, keeping markets small can function as an economic justification for imposing limitations on IPRs in developing countries so long as the right holder can recover his or her investment by charging higher prices in the protected national markets of the developed world. Therefore, as long as rich countries stick to the idea of national exhaustion, developing countries have a good argument supporting more freedom to limit the IPRs of foreign right holders.[40]

---

[39] *See* TRIPS Agreement, above n. 2, art. 6 (taking no position on Members' right to adopt a doctrine of national or international exhaustion).

[40] Naturally, such limitations must normally be imposed without violating the principle of national treatment. *See* TRIPS Agreement, above n. 2, arts. 1.3 (national treatment), 2.1 (incorporating substantive provision of Paris Convention), 9.1 (incorporating substantive provisions of Berne Convention).

3. Limiting IPRs for social reasons

A different situation arises when a given country, mostly for social reasons, grants compulsory licenses in order to guarantee consumer access to specific technology.[41]

Traditional competition law in the European Union, with its prohibition of abuse of dominant positions, would only allow a compulsory license with an obligation to pay a reasonable license fee.[42] In such situations, the compulsory license guarantees that the right holder does not extract monopoly prices from consumers.

Beyond the competition-law-oriented approach to compulsory licenses, the question arises whether developing countries should be allowed to suspend IP protection in order to gain cheap access to essential medicines, even without having to pay reasonable remuneration.[43] If so, and in contrast to the previous situation, consumers in developing countries would obtain the economic advantage of not having to pay the price for the internalization of these public benefits. For the right holder, negative consequences will be negligible so long as the law guarantees that goods produced without authorization of the right holder may not be sold outside the national territory.

The argument that such limitations on protection in developing countries would result in higher consumer prices in richer countries is largely unfounded. If South Africa were authorized to confer the right of producing patented HIV drugs on local companies for local consumption, it would not change market conditions in the U.S. or Europe. While such a decision would cause the right holder to lose a national market, that market, given the limited capacity of consumers to pay, would not contribute substantially to the foreign producer's recovery of prior investment, even though the number of potential consumers in South Africa is extremely high.

---

[41] See Jerome H. Reichman with Catherine Hasenzahl, *Non-Voluntary Licensing of Patented Inventions: Historical Perspective, Legal Framwork under TRIPS, and an Overview of the Practice in Canada and the United States* (UNCTAD/ICTSD 2002); *see also* Jerome H. Reichman with Catherine Hasenzahl, *Non-Voluntary Licensing of Patented Inventions: The Canadian Experience* (UNCTAD/ICTSD 2002).

[42] Such payment is also required by the TRIPS Agreement, above n. 2, art. 31(h). However, United States law and practice does not necessarily require a "reasonable" royalty where antitrust violations are concerned, or even potential restraints on trade through mergers and acquisition; and nominal royalties (sometimes even zero royalties) have been imposed. See J. H. Reichman with Catharine Hasenzahl, *Non-Voluntary Licensing of Patented Inventions: The Law and Practice of the United States* (UNCTAD/ICTSD 2003). Article 31(k) of the TRIPS Agreement, above n. 2, accommodates U.S. law in this respect by stating that the "need to correct anti-competitive practices may be taken into account in determining the amount of remuneration in such cases."

[43] *See generally* Frederick Abbott, *Managing the Hydra: The Herculean Task of Ensuring Access to Essential Medicines* [this volume].

Only the aggregate effect of similar exceptions in a number of countries might negatively affect the incentive structure of the IP system globally. To avoid this result, additional criteria should limit the permissibility of such exceptions to situations in which vital social interests in any given country are seriously affected. Another criterion may be found in the extent to which the right holder has to rely on revenues from developing countries. For example, pharmaceuticals to combat tropical diseases might present such a case, whereas the incentive structure of the patent law system would remain unaffected in the case of exceptions for HIV drugs.

IV. Conclusions

The achievements of creativity and inventiveness may be defined as public goods in a very broad sense. IP laws transform them into private goods (club goods), which makes it possible to exclude users who are unwilling or unable to pay for their individual benefits. According to property rights theory, IP laws internalize positive externalities and, thereby, create incentives to invest in creative activity and innovation. However, the social costs of excluding users from access to knowledge goods covered by IP rights should not exceed the social benefits of innovation.

The concept of global public goods provides an economic, social and political approach to the problems of globalization. According to this concept, the citizens of the developing countries depend on access to public goods whereas WTO law is built on the idea of protecting private goods exclusively. Sustainable development, affordable health care, technology transfer, and broad-based advances in science and education cannot be classified as public goods in the strict neoclassical economic sense of this term. Nevertheless, the need to protect them as social interests, while at the same time expressing a principle of global distributive justice, may be encompassed by the concept of global public goods.

In line with the concept of global public goods, competition law promotes economic efficiency and distributive justice, and it serves political – freedom-oriented – ends. Competition law and policy should accordingly be analyzed as a possible instrument for promoting the provision of global public goods in conflict with IPRs. IP laws and competition law share the same economic rationale. They are both crucial for the establishment of competitive and innovative market conditions. These complementarities justify the application of competition law analysis with the objective of defining the limits of IP protection.

In order to guarantee the competitive function of IP systems, the TRIPS system would have to be complemented by an obligation of WTO Members to introduce competition laws prohibiting restraints of competition in licensing agreements and abuses of dominant positions based on IP laws. IP laws should not lead to market dominance by the right holder as the necessary consequence of their scope of application and protection. Such IP laws would create excessive protection and exploit the consumer.

Competition law argues against the minimum protection approach of the TRIPS Agreement. Its universal standards allow excessive protection in single countries and possibly restrain the competitive structure of IP laws to the disadvantage of other trading nations.

Whereas TRIPS protects IPRs worldwide, the relevant markets for products based on IPRs are not necessarily global. Local product markets, with low willingness and ability of consumers to pay, especially in the developing world, may well be irrelevant for the global incentive structure of IP rights. Limitations on, and exceptions to, IP rights in local markets will create only negligible income losses to the right holders and will not affect competition or prices in other markets.

National exhaustion of IP rights leads to smaller relevant markets and, thereby, has the potential of restraining competition. Rejection of the international exhaustion principle in richer countries harms the export interests of poorer nations. Because of the effect of separating local markets, less-developed WTO Members may leverage this rejection as an additional argument for limiting IP protection in their territories. An international obligation to introduce international exhaustion of IP rights worldwide could well have the negative impact of raising consumer prices in the markets of poorer countries.

The WTO system implemented a project of advanced harmonization of IP laws, although the guarantees of economic freedoms remain incomplete. This project was undertaken without sufficient economic justification, and the end result is a transferring of wealth from the less-developed world to right holders in the developed world.

When severe social problems mandate the cheapest possible access to goods, especially pharmaceuticals, exceptional free use arrangements should be accompanied by legal or organizational safeguards, such as an export prohibition, guaranteeing that such use does not affect competition on foreign markets. These exceptions should only be allowed in situations defined by international law.

28

Expansionist intellectual property protection and reductionist competition rules: A TRIPS perspective

HANNS ULLRICH[*]

Abstract
Introduction
I.   National competition rules and the TRIPS Agreement
     A.   Points of departure
     B.   Principles
          1.   National antitrust control over the exercise of domestic IPRs
               (a)   Regulatory standards
               (b)   Is there a duty to regulate?
          2.   The requirement that national competition policy should be TRIPS-consistent
          3.   The dissemination concern
II. International competition rules after the TRIPS Agreement
     A.   The new reality
          1.   Innovation and the unilateral exercise of exclusive rights in the information economy
               (a)   Defining abuses
               (b)   Technology as a product
          2.   Toward group innovation incentives: Pooling, cross-licensing, joint research and development
     B.   The global response: An internationally uniform and innovation-oriented competition law?
          1.   From competition policy to innovation policy
          2.   The European Union's example
          3.   Outlook for the TRIPS Agreement
Conclusion

---

[*] Hanns Ullrich is Professor of Law at the European University Institute, Florence, Italy. The author is deeply indebted to Jerome H. Reichman for all his advice and assistance. Of course, the usual disclaimer fully applies in that any mistakes are mine.

ABSTRACT

The chapter is divided into two parts. In the first, an examination of the competition rules in the TRIPS Agreement confirms the authority of WTO Members to develop their own antitrust policy regarding IP-related restrictive practices, provided this is done consistently with the TRIPS principles of IP protection. In the second part, the preceding analysis is confronted with the new reality of IP policies, the changed function and modes of exploitation and protection in the innovation-driven, globalized high-tech economy. I argue that the backward-looking focus of TRIPS competition rules on technology dissemination does not match the actual trend of cooperation-based innovation, since, there, a level playing field may only be established by early participation in the innovation process and by early access to enabling information. As industrialized countries have revised their competition policy with a view to supporting group innovation and additionally enhancing the incentives resulting from IP protection, reliance on TRIPS competition rules as a model for domestic antitrust law might contribute to deepening rather then overcoming the technology dependence of developing countries.

Introduction

While the "preservation of public goods" as such is not a typical role for competition law,[1] the application of this body of law to so-called knowledge goods presents particularly complex issues. Knowledge does not fit neatly into a framework of analysis that treats property as either private or public. Because knowledge is non-rivalrous in character, anyone may adopt it for his or her own individual purposes in the raw state of affairs.[2] The state may accordingly decide to stimulate the creation of knowledge by providing private parties with legal means of appropriating it, as for example, by laws protecting trade secrets and confidential information, by enforcing contractual agreements, or by

---

[1] As a rule, one cannot contractually exclude private competitors from access to public infrastructure facilities, although the status of radio and broadcast frequencies presents a borderline case. However, competition law may intervene in the reverse situation by insisting that certain private property must be made accessible to competitors under the "essential facilities" doctrine. This doctrine has lately attracted considerable attention because so many infrastructure facilities have become privatized. See German Act Against Restraints of Competition of 26 August 1998, BGBl. I S.2546 § 19(4) [hereinafter GWB]. The literature on the doctrine is abundant. See, e.g., W. Möschel, in GWB-KOMMENTAR ZUM KARTELLGESETZ § 19 annot. 178, 186 et seq. (U. Immenga et al. eds., 3d ed. 2001) (for Sect. 19(4)); Doherty, Just What Are Essential Facilities?, 38 COMMON MKT. L. REV. 397 (2001) (for European Community law).

[2] For the public good nature of knowledge and its economic consequences, see Paul David, Koyaanisqatsi in Cyberspace: The Economics of an "Out-of-Balance" Regime of Private Property Rights in Data and Information [this volume].

enacting the exclusive rights of intellectual property regimes. In that event, competition law intervenes to ensure that private parties do not either jointly or individually, by the exercise of market power, extend that appropriation beyond the limits allowed by law.

Competition law thus responds to fears that private ordering might otherwise unduly encroach on what ought to remain a free resource for independent innovation or that it might transform the process of appropriating knowledge into actual control of markets. In so doing, competition law performs a critical but rather traditional role, one that concerns the much discussed interface between the protection of intellectual property laws, whose exclusive rights seem to confer legal monopolies, and free intra-brand competition.[3] The major goal here is to safeguard the incentive and reward rationales of intellectual property protection while at the same time controlling the risks of an undue extension of legal exclusivity. Its doctrinal and jurisprudential approach has shifted over the years from immunizing IPR-based restraints on trade from antitrust challenges to subjecting the exercise of IPRs to the general rules of competition law as they apply to any property-related restraints of competition.[4]

In this chapter, the IPR-antitrust interface is considered only to the extent that it is reflected in the competition rules embodied in the Agreement on Trade Related Aspects of Intellectual Property Rights of 1994 ("TRIPS Agreement").[5] The TRIPS Agreement expressly addresses some of the better known methods by which IPRs may be abused in order to secure a private appropriation of public goods. For example, this sometimes occurs when rights holders impose "no challenge" clauses in licensing agreements.[6] Parts I and II of this chapter discuss this general topic from both the domestic and international perspectives.

---

[3] See Mark D. Janis, *"Minimal" Standards for the Patent-Related Antitrust Law under TRIPS* [this volume].

[4] For a general discussion of the development of the law, *see* N. Gallini & M. Trebilcock, *Intellectual Property Rights and Competition Policy: A Framework for the Analysis of Economic and Legal Issues*, in COMPETITION POLICY AND INTELLECTUAL PROPERTY RIGHTS IN THE KNOWLEDGE-BASED ECONOMY 17 et seq. (R. Anderson & N. Gallini eds., 1998); W. Tom & J. Newberg, *U.S. Enforcement Approaches to the Antitrust-Intellectual Property Interface*, in COMPETITION POLICY AND INTELLECTUAL PROPERTY RIGHTS IN THE KNOWLEDGE-BASED ECONOMY, above, at 43 et seq.; H. Ullrich, *Intellectual Property, Access to Information, and Antitrust: Harmony, Disharmony, and International Harmonization*, in EXPANDING THE BOUNDARIES OF INTELLECTUAL PROPERTY: INNOVATION POLICY FOR THE KNOWLEDGE SOCIETY 365 et seq. (Rochelle Dreyfuss et al. eds., 2001) [hereinafter EXPANDING THE BOUNDARIES OF IP]; A. HEINEMANN, IMMATERIALGÜTERSCHUTZ IN DER WETTBEWERBSORDNUNG 24 (2002).

[5] Agreement on Trade-Related Aspects of Intellectual Property Rights, 15 Apr. 1994, Marrakesh Agreement Establishing the World Trade Organization [hereinafter WTO Agreement], Annex 1C, LEGAL INSTRUMENTS – RESULT OF THE URUGUAY ROUND vol. 31, 33 I.L.M. 81 arts. 8.2, 40 (1994) [hereinafter TRIPS Agreement].

[6] TRIPS Agreement, above n. 5, art. 40.2.

We must also consider the extent to which the TRIPS provisions on competition law apply to phenomena typical of the "new economy," in which IPRs have led to an ever-broadening privatization of intangible public goods.[7] One question, for example, is what the TRIPS Agreement might say about the use of certain intellectual property as an "essential facility"[8] or as a "raw material" or interface[9] for access to various peripheral and after-markets. Because legislators often fail to properly define the limits of exclusive property rights,[10] the exercise of these rights in new situations, and especially with regard to new technologies, attracts scrutiny under competition law, with a view to preventing anticompetitive market foreclosure. This topic is discussed in Part III of this chapter.

Still other questions concerning the impact of the TRIPS Agreement merit attention. One is whether the competition rules in that Agreement cover the many roles that technological property[11] now plays with regard to innovation that affects both the new economy and the broader economy in general. Another question is whether the TRIPS Agreement's rules on competition adequately reflect modern policy approaches to innovation-related restrictions on competition, which tend to favor the creation rather than the diffusion of new technologies. These questions are also addressed in Part III of this chapter.

Because both old and new approaches to competition policy vary from country to country, there is a further question of how to deal with such diversity. To the extent that the TRIPS Agreement promotes a globally harmonized intellectual property regime while leaving competition policy to the sovereign determination of Members and their regional economic institutions, the key issue is not which competition policy is best or even adequate. Rather, it is how international public goods – more precisely, an inherent international public good such as knowledge – may be preserved under a patchwork transnational regime rooted in a multiplicity of national and regional competition

---

[7] *See, e.g.*, Case C-241/91P & Case C-242/91P, RTE, ITP v. Commission, 1995 E.C.R. 743 [hereinafter *Magill TV Guide*].

[8] *See* above n. 1; *see also* Helmuth Schröter, in KOMMENTAR ZUM EUROPÄISCHEN WETTBEWERBSRECHT, art. 82 annot. 263 et seq. (Helmuth Schröter et al. eds., 2003).

[9] *See Magill TV Guide*, above n. 7.

[10] For the controversies surrounding the decompilation rule of article 6, E.C. Directive of 14 May 1991 on the legal protection of computer programs, 1991 O.J. (L 122) 42, *see* J. SCHNEIDER, HANDBUCH DES EDV-RECHTS 254 et seq., 391 et seq., 568 et seq. (3d ed. 2002); X. Linant de Bellefonds, *Le Droit de Décompilation des Logiciels: Une Aubaine pour les Cloneurs?*, JCP 1998 I 118, 479 et seq. As regards database protection, the legislator was so worried about the anticompetitive potential of its own law that it provided for a specific monitoring rule. *See* article 16(3), E.C. Directive 96/9 of 11 March 1996 on the legal protection of databases, 1996 O.J. (L 77) 20 [hereinafter E.C. Directive on Databases].

[11] This chapter focuses on what I shall call "technological property," which includes patent (or utility model) protection for inventions, trade secret law, design protection for the non-technical features of technical products, and copyright protection for computer programs and databases, as well as *sui generis* database protection.

laws. This issue raises not only problems of conflict avoidance and conflict resolution, but ultimately it affects the international harmonization of IPR-related and/or innovation-related competition laws and the role that the TRIPS Agreement may play in this regard. These topics are discussed in Parts III and IV below.

I. National competition rules and the TRIPS Agreement

The TRIPS Agreement does not introduce its own rules of competition law, but instead authorizes Members to establish or maintain such rules. This reservation in favor of Members' sovereign competition policy represents a concession that the industrialized countries made in response to an earlier effort by developing countries to enact a Code of Conduct for the Transfer of Technology.[12]

A. Points of departure

Article 8.2 of the TRIPS Agreement states, as a "Basic Principle," that "Appropriate measures, provided that they are consistent with the provision of this Agreement, may be needed to prevent the abuse of intellectual property rights by right holders or the resort to practices which unreasonably restrain trade or adversely affect the international transfer of technology."[13] This principle is given greater specificity in Part II, entitled "Standards Concerning the Availability, Scope and Use of Intellectual Property Rights," in which Section 8 deals with "Control of Anti-Competitive Practices in Contractual Licenses." This section consists of a single article – article 40 – which covers both matters of substance[14] and of procedure.[15] There are no other rules pertaining to competition law in the TRIPS Agreement except for a provision allowing Members to impose compulsory licenses on intellectual property owners in order to remedy anticompetitive practices.[16]

---

[12] *See* D. GERVAIS, THE TRIPS AGREEMENT: DRAFTING HISTORY AND ANALYSIS, sub. 2.48, 2.182 et seq. (1998); Thomas Cottier, *The Prospects for Intellectual Property in GATT*, 28 COMMON MKT. L. REV. 383, 409 et seq. (1991); P. Roffe, *Control of Anticompetitive Practices in Contractual Licenses under the TRIPS Agreement*, in INTELLECTUAL PROPERTY AND INTERNATIONAL TRADE – THE TRIPS AGREEMENT 261, 278 et seq. (C. Correa & A. Yusuf eds., 1998) [hereinafter INTELLECTUAL PROPERTY AND INTERNATIONAL TRADE]. The developing countries had unsuccessfully proposed a Code of Conduct for the Transfer of Technology. *See e.g.*, Pedro Roffe, *The Unfinished Agenda*, in INTERNATIONAL TECHNOLOGY TRANSFER: THE ORIGINS AND AFTERMATH OF THE UNITED NATIONS NEGOTIATIONS ON A DRAFT CODE OF CONDUCT 381 (S. Patel et al. eds., 2001) [hereinafter INTERNATIONAL TECHNOLOGY TRANSFER].

[13] Part I of the Agreement is entitled "General Provisions and Basic Principles"; Section 8 is entitled "Principles." TRIPS Agreement, above n. 5, art. 8.2.

[14] *Id.* arts. 40.1–.2.   [15] *Id.* arts. 40.3–.4.

[16] *Id.* arts. 31(c), (k). Issues of procedure and remedies regarding antitrust violations are beyond the scope of this article.

Taken together, articles 8.2, 40.1, and 40.2 may be viewed as both broad and narrow in scope. The provisions seem broadly applicable to restrictive practices relating to all the different intellectual property rights that the TRIPS Agreement covers, although both the legislative history and the examples given in article 40.2 focus primarily on the licensing and transfer of technology rather than on trademark or copyright licensing.[17]

At the same time, these provisions are only concerned with the abusive exercise of intellectual property rights and with certain licensing practices and conditions. In this sense, both unilateral and bilateral IPR-related conduct of an anticompetitive nature is covered. A further distinction is then made between restrictive practices affecting licensing in general and those bearing on technology transfer in particular. However, other potentially anticompetitive arrangements, including mergers and acquisitions, which are more generally innovation-related, are left outside the reach of the TRIPS Agreement. The consequences of these distinctions, and of this self-imposed limitation, will be discussed later.

B. Principles

Three guiding principles emerge from the competition rules set out in the TRIPS Agreement. These are first, the reservation of IPR-related competition policy to sovereign national determination; secondly, a requirement of consistency between national IPR-related competition policy and the TRIPS Agreement's principles of IP protection; and thirdly, there is a concern to primarily target practices restricting the dissemination of protected technologies.[18]

1. National antitrust control over the exercise of domestic IPRs

The reservation of IPR-related competition policy to sovereign national determination directly results from the very wording of articles 8.2 and 40.2 of the Agreement. Reading them together, as consistency requires, these provisions tell us that the measures Members may take (under articles 8.1 and 8.2), in the form of domestic legislation (under article 40.2), are those that may be needed to prevent abuses and restrictive practices.[19] There is hardly any prescription made as to the nature or content of such measures, the procedural mechanisms for controlling

---

[17] A conceivably broader reading of "package licensing," as mentioned in the TRIPS Agreement, above n. 5, art. 40.2, could also cover copyright exploitation by way of block-booking; and "no challenge" clauses may likewise be read so as to cover delimitation agreements in trademark law. However, article 40.1 suggests the narrower understanding stated in the text.

[18] For a more technical analysis, see UNCTAD & ICTSD, TRIPS AND DEVELOPMENT – RESOURCE BOOK, PART THREE: INTELLECTUAL PROPERTY RIGHTS AND COMPETITION (2003), available at www.iprsonline.org/unctadictsd/docs/RB_3_Cometition.pdf [hereinafter UNCTAD & ICTSD, RESOURCE BOOK].

[19] TRIPS Agreement, above n. 5, arts. 8.1, 8.2, 40.2.

restrictive practices, or the eventual remedies. The only substantive condition of importance is a systemic one: articles 8.2 and 40 recognize the Members' "interventionist" powers to control certain practices only if they produce demonstrably negative effects on trade, competition, or the transfer of technology.[20]

(a) **Regulatory standards** The regulation of technology transfer is not limited to restrictive practices, nor is a member that takes steps to control such practices obliged to evaluate them under a "rule of reason" analysis.[21] When negotiating the TRIPS Agreement, leading Members (such as the European Union) still subjected some restrictive licensing practices to a type of per se rule, thus holding them a priori unreasonable. While these delegations were probably not keen about introducing such rules into the TRIPS Agreement, they could hardly ignore *per se* restrictions in their own domestic laws.[22] Likewise, article 40.2 expressly refers to certain pernicious practices only as illustrative examples; hence, it indicates no more than a threshold level of regulation. Members thus retain broad leeway to impose more sophisticated competition rules, provided that they are sufficiently specific.[23] Finally, by virtue of an *argumentum e contrario* from the consistency requirement, article 8.2

---

[20] *See, e.g.*, UNCTAD & ICTSD, RESOURCE BOOK, above n. 18, ¶¶ 3.1.1, 3.2.1 (stressing that, while these provisions employ different language, they must be read in a consistent manner); *see also* H. Ullrich, *Competition, Intellectual Property Rights and Transfer of Technology*, in INTERNATIONAL TECHNOLOGY TRANSFER, above n. 12, at 363, 365 et seq. In particular, it suffices that technology transfer is "affected" (art. 8.2), it need not be literally "impeded" (art. 40.1).

[21] Put differently, the restrictive nature of a technology transfer agreement is made a necessary connecting factor for its control, but not a factor determining the outcome of the control. *See* UNCTAD & ICTSD, RESOURCE BOOK, above n. 18, ¶¶ 3.1.1(d), 3.2.1(b, iii); Ullrich, above n. 20, at 366 et seq. Note that article 7 of the TRIPS Agreement elevates technology transfer to an objective of the Agreement. For the distinction between the "competition approach" and the "technology transfer" approach to technology transfer, *see* P.-T. STOLL, TECHNOLOGIETRANSFER – INTERNATIONALISIERUNGS- UND NATIONALISIERUNGSTENDENZEN 365 et seq (1994); G. CABANELLAS, ANTITRUST AND DIRECT REGULATION OF INTERNATIONAL TRANSFER OF TECHNOLOGY TRANSACTIONS 157 et seq. (1982).

[22] *See* E. Fox, *Trade, Competition, and Intellectual Property – TRIPS and its Antitrust Counterparts*, 29 VAND. J. TRANSNAT'L. L. 481, 492 et seq. (1996). Obvious examples are horizontal or vertical price fixing, quantity restrictions, and absolute territorial segregation of markets even under the reform proposals for IPR-related competition policy in the EU. *See* Commission Evaluation Report on the Transfer of Technology Block Exemption Regulation No. 240/96, 2001 O.J. (C 786), Nos. 186, 187, *available at* http://europa.eu.int/comm/competition/antitrust/technology_transfer [hereinafter Commission Evaluation Report on the Transfer of Technology].

[23] National competition law must specify either by statute or by administrative or judicial practice the types of licensing practices or conditions that may be subject to control; in view of the different legal traditions of Members, the provision may not be read to mean that IPR-antitrust control can be exercised only on a case-by-case basis. *See* UNCTAD & ICTSD, RESOURCE BOOK, above n. 18, ¶ 3.2.1(c)(i).

recognizes that Members have broad authority to define what may constitute an abusive unilateral exercise of intellectual property rights.[24] The power to regulate abusive licensing practices is then expressly conferred by article 40.2.

(b) Is there a duty to regulate? Articles 8.2 and 40.1 differ in that the former provision is limited to recognizing the need to prevent abuses and restrictive practices[25] while the latter declares the Members' unanimous and affirmative opinion that "some licensing practices or conditions ... which restrain competition may have adverse effects ...."[26] Article 40.2 then gives illustrative examples of such practices. In view of the generally recognized pernicious nature of the examples listed, one might conceivably argue that the difference of wording means that, under article 40.1, Members obliged themselves to actually control these practices.

These provisions could thus constitute some sort of a platform for the minimum harmonization of IPR-related competition rules.[27] This view appears more plausible in as much as article 40 applies to a narrower range of restrictive practices than those covered by article 8.2, namely, anticompetitive practices pertaining to contractual licenses, a topic about which developing countries have long sought an international agreement. Given the nature of the practices listed, it is hard to imagine that Members remain totally free to ignore them in their domestic competition regimes. This said, the nature and the scope of any such obligation would need to be defined more clearly before it could be taken seriously. On closer analysis, indeed, the view that article 40.1 represents a minimum step toward international harmonization of IPR-related competition rules for global markets seems strained. Article 40 establishes only a duty to protect national IPR systems against practices that undermine their proper operation on domestic markets.

This interpretation seems more persuasive for two reasons. First, according to the legislative history,[28] the overall purpose of the TRIPS Agreement was to safeguard adequate levels of national IP protection. Hence, the restrictive, exception-like language embodied in articles 40.1 and 40.2 reflects only a reservation, which Members made with regard to the possibly uncontrolled exercise of the broad intellectual property regime that the TRIPS Agreement established. Politically speaking, the rules on competition policy merely constituted a sort of a "concession" to Members, which in effect recognized their

---

[24] For example, abuse may exist in case the IPR holder has either absolute or only relative market power, and it may even be held to exist in the absence of any proof of market power. Dysfunctional use or misuse in general is covered by art. 8.2.
[25] TRIPS Agreement, above n. 5, art. 8.2 ("... may be needed to prevent ...").
[26] *Id*. art. 40.2.
[27] *See* UNCTAD & ICTSD, Resource Book, above n. 18, ¶ 3.2.1(b)(i); *but see* Heinemann, above n. 4, at 584 fn. 107, 592.
[28] *See* above n. 12 and accompanying text.

residual sovereignty as regards this public policy area. As such, these rules cannot, by way of interpretation, be transformed into affirmative obligations.

Second, because the TRIPS Agreement was negotiated and conceptualized as a trade agreement, it is based on the principles of territoriality, of the protection of home markets, and of substantive trade reciprocity,[29] rather than on principles of protecting intellectual property or competition as such, let alone on principles of protecting the intellectual property or competition regimes of other Members or in their markets.[30] The promise Members made is not to respect foreign intellectual property rights, but to expose the trade regulations governing domestic markets to claims by foreign intellectual property owners that either the level of protection or of competition afforded them is inadequate.

There is, of course, a harmonizing effect but its rationale is not one of coordination as such.[31] Rather, the TRIPS Agreement represents a system of exchange, whereby access to foreign markets is traded against a loss of political control over domestic markets, the yardstick of equivalence being the level of protection afforded by exclusive intellectual property rights. Since the price is a loss of sovereign control over the legal regulation of domestic markets, it may not be expanded beyond the bargain. And since the object of the bargain is the proper operation of the domestic intellectual property system, it is only to the extent that restrictive practices undermine such proper operation that Members may be held to a duty to actually control them. Irrespective of the controversies about whether intellectual property protection and antitrust law stand in a conflicting or in a complementary relationship,[32] clear cases of competition rules serving to enhance the operation of the intellectual property system are presented by some of the examples set out in article 40.2, namely, no challenge clauses,[33] exclusive grant back

---

[29] For a more detailed analysis, see H. Ullrich, *Technology Protection According to TRIPS: Principles and Problems*, in FROM GATT TO TRIPS – THE AGREEMENT ON TRADE-RELATED ASPECTS OF INTELLECTUAL PROPERTY RIGHTS 357, 361 et seq., 377 et passim (F.-K. Beier & G. Schricker eds., 1996) [hereinafter FROM GATT TO TRIPS]; H. Ullrich, *TRIPS: Adequate Protection, Inadequate Trade, Adequate Competition Policy*, 4 PAC. RIM. L. & POL'Y J. 153, 186 et seq. (1995). Predictably, intellectual property has become the subject of retaliatory action: in the infamous *Banana* case, Nicaragua obtained some satisfaction by being authorized to disregard intellectual property rights. See E. Vranes, *Principles and Emerging Problems of WTO Cross Retaliation*, 10 EUZTSCHRWIR (2001).

[30] But see Fox, above n. 22, at 493.

[31] TRIPS Agreement, above n. 5, art. 40.3 is not an exception, since it is only intended to procedurally facilitate enforcement of domestic competition law on domestic markets, not to protect foreign markets from anticompetitive practices by virtue of domestic antitrust laws.

[32] See above n. 4.

[33] See Lear v. Adkins, 395 U.S. 653 (1969) (invalidating such clauses on public policy grounds). For a critique, see R. Dreyfuss, *Dethroning* Lear: *Licensee Estoppel and the Incentive to Innovate*, 27 VA. L. REV. 677 (1986); see also Studiengesellschaft Kohle m.b.H. v. Shell Oil Co, 112 F.3d 1561 (Fed. Cir. 1997). Community law approaches the

conditions,[34] and coercive package licensing.[35] Still others may be conceived of,[36] but they ought to be equally well-defined and of an equally subversive nature to render the absence of at least some antitrust control over them tantamount to an "impairment"[37] of the bargained-for level of adequate intellectual property protection. Under the TRIPS provisions at least, such antitrust control need not necessarily result in a *per se* verdict, but it ought to be introduced and exercised as a matter of safeguarding adequate IPR protection.

---

question as a problem of competition policy, but still is in search of consistency. *See* Commission Regulation 240/96 on the Application of Article 85(3) (now 81(3)) of the Treaty to categories of technology transfer agreements, 1996 O.J. (L 31) 2, art. 4(2)(b) [hereinafter Commission Reg. 240/96]; Commission Evaluation Report on the Transfer of Technology, above n. 22, Nos. 169 et seq. (referring to inconsistent case law of the CJEC). *But see* Commission Regulation 2659/2000 on the Application of Article 81(3) of the Treaty to Categories of Research and Development Agreements, 2000 O.J. (L 304) 7, art. 5(1)(b) [hereinafter Commission Reg. 2659/2000].

[34] Exclusive grant-back requirements for improvements made by the licensee devaluate the licensee's IPR, stifle the innovation incentive of the IPR-system, or at the very least bias it unduly in favor of the licensor, and run afoul of the legislative policy underlying the compulsory licensing rules. *See* Proposal for a Council Regulation on the Community Patent, 2000 O.J. (C 337) 278, art. 21(2); French Code de la propriété intellectuelle, Comm. Reg. 240, arts. L 613–15; U.K. Patents Act of 1977 § 48(3)(d)(ii); Commission Reg. 240/96, above n. 33, arts. 2(4), 6; Commission Evaluation Report on the Transfer of Technology, above n. 22, Nos. 165 et seq.; U.S. DEPARTMENT OF JUSTICE & FEDERAL TRADE COMMISSION, ANTITRUST GUIDELINES FOR LICENSING OF INTELLECTUAL PROPERTY (6 Apr. 1995) (providing pertinent U.S. antitrust law), *available at* http://www.usdoj.gov/atr/public/guidelines/ipguide.htm [hereinafter U.S. ANTITRUST GUIDELINES].

[35] Coercive package licensing by virtue of the exercise of sufficient market power is a less clear case. However, as a matter of principle, it conflicts with the proper functioning of the IPR system to the extent that the licensee's free choice of licenses and of the licensor is the counterpart of the licensor's autonomy as regards the choice of licensees. *See* Case 19/84, Pharmon v. Hoechst AG, 1985 E.C.R. 2281, [1985] 3 C.M.L.R. 775 1985, 2281 (1985). Indeed, coercive licensing does not only foreclose alternative licensing opportunities of the licensee, but also undercuts its interest in innovation efforts of its own, and, therefore, the IPR-system's incentive to individually innovate. Moreover, market power is at odds with the IPR system as it undercuts its balanced operation by transforming legal exclusivity into an economic monopoly. *See* A. S. GUTTERMAN, INNOVATION AND COMPETITION POLICY 305 et seq. (1997) (providing a comparative view of antitrust treatment of package licensing).

[36] An example is "suppression of technology" by external acquisition and non-use. *See* J. Cohen & A. Burke, *An Overview of Antitrust Analysis of Suppression of Technology*, 66 ANTITRUST L.J. 421 (1998); Y. Wah Chin, *Unilateral Technology Suppression: Appropriate Antitrust and Patent Law Remedies*, 66 ANTITRUST L.J. 441 (1998); J. Flynn, *Antitrust Policy, Innovation Efficiencies, and the Suppression of Technology*, 66 ANTITRUST L.J. 487, 506 et seq. (1998).

[37] *See* TRIPS Agreement, above n. 5, art. 64 (applying article XXIII: 1(b) of GATT to dispute-settlement actions for nullification or impairment of benefits). *See also* M. Furse, *Competition Law and the WTO Report: "Japan-Measures Affecting Consumer Photographic Film and Paper,"* 20 EUR. COMPETITION L. REV. 9 (1999) (analyzing the Kodak/Fuji camera film distribution case and providing a discussion of the problems of an impairment claim under GATT art. XXIII: 1(b)).

2. The requirement that national competition policy should be TRIPS-consistent

Conversely, articles 8.2 and 40.2 limit the Members' sovereign power to prescribe national competition policy by requiring that measures adopted to control abusive or anticompetitive practices must be "consistent with the provisions of this Agreement."[38] This requirement of TRIPS-consistency represents more than a mere limitation on remedial action, which is always subject to a principle of proportionality.[39] Rather, the consistency requirement concerns the substantive scope of IPR-related competition rules. As such, it does not establish a standard of evaluation for restrictive practices that affect IPRs,[40] but only a safety zone for the core of intellectual property protection. In particular, there is no attempt here to reintroduce an "inherency" or a reasonable reward test for IPR-related anticompetitive conduct, which leading Members have abolished.[41] Rather, this provision must be read as a caveat against an excessive exercise of competition policy, which the TRIPS Agreement, by its purpose and express wording, otherwise leaves Members free to define. It means that they may not use antitrust regulation as a pretext to undermine the protection of IPRs as guaranteed by the TRIPS Agreement.

This constraint has at least two implications. First, competition policy must remain true to its purpose and keep within the bounds of safeguarding competition; it may not outlaw uses and forms of intellectual property that the TRIPS Agreement seeks to safeguard. It follows from this negative limitation that national competition rules must respect the constitutive elements of intellectual property protection, such as contracts that ensure confidentiality and the protection of trade secrets,[42] use restrictions necessary to defining the scope of a service rendered by the lease of software,[43] or licensing restrictions needed to control the dissemination of protected subject matter.[44] More

---

[38] See TRIPS Agreement, above n. 5, art. 8.2 (which presumably controls article 40.2 in this respect).

[39] See UNCTAD & ICTSD, RESOURCE BOOK, above n. 18, ¶ 3.1.2(b).

[40] In fact, the competition rules of the TRIPS Agreement have not been the object of detailed negotiations that would allow one to read them as establishing definite antitrust law standards. See Cottier, above n. 12, at 410.

[41] See, e.g., ANTITRUST GUIDELINES, above n. 34, ¶ 12.1; the EU officially abandoned the inherency/reasonable reward doctrine when it withdrew the so-called Christmas Notice subsequent to the issuance of the first group exemption regulation on patent license agreements in 1984. See Notice on Patent License Agreements 84/C220/35, 1984 O.J. (C 220) 14.

[42] See Commission Reg. 240/96, above n. 33, art. 2(1)(3); for details, see H. Ullrich, in EG-WETTBEWERBSRECHT 1241 et seq., No. 33 (U. Immenga & E.-J. Mestmäcker eds., 1997).

[43] See H. Ullrich, in H. ULLRICH AND E. KÖRNER, DER INTERNATIONALE SOFTWAREVERTRAG 272 et seq., 277 et seq. (1995).

[44] Case 27/87, Erauw-Jacquéry v. La Hesbignonne, [1988] E.C.R. 1919, recital 10.

generally, the power of licensors to impose limiting conditions may be regulated only with regard to potential anticompetitive effects, and modes of exploitation that the TRIPS Agreement expressly allows may not be prohibited as such.[45]

Second, the requirement of consistency serves to safeguard only TRIPS standards of intellectual property protection. The consistency requirement thus prevents competition law from encroaching on national intellectual property protection, but it says nothing about the extraterritorial impact of national competition policy on the exercise of intellectual property rights abroad. The TRIPS Agreement only obliges Members to afford adequate protection in their domestic territories. It is not an Agreement about the mutual respect of foreign property titles, but about protecting foreign technology in national markets when domestic law recognizes the entitlements. Therefore, spillovers of national competition policy enforcement on foreign markets and on intellectual property held there are matters to be dealt with on the basis of public international law or of antitrust cooperation and assistance agreements, but they are not a matter for TRIPS.[46]

Moreover, while the consistency requirement seeks to safeguard the TRIPS standards of protection, it does not apply to conflicts between domestic competition policy and modes of domestic intellectual property protection that fall outside the TRIPS Agreement. This constraint on the consistency requirement may prove particularly important with respect to modern forms of protecting innovation, such as the E.U.'s *sui generis* regime to protect investment in databases (i.e., for subcopyrightable subject matter).[47] It may also exonerate the treatment of subpatentable subject matter,[48] or signs and

---

[45] Thus, national competition laws may not make non-manufacturing on the domestic territory a *per se* violation, *see* TRIPS Agreement, above n. 5, art. 27; but, conversely, a licensor may require the licensee to exploit the license by domestic manufacturing. Likewise, competition laws may not impose stricter use requirements for trademarks than provided for by article 19, TRIPS Agreement, above n. 5, yet a licensor may impose a stricter obligation of use on the licensee.

[46] *But see* Fox, above n. 22; A. Odman, *Using TRIPS to Make the Innovation Process Work*, J. WORLD INTEL. PROP. 343, 364 et seq. (2000).

[47] *See* E.C. Directive on Databases, above n. 10, art. 16(3) (providing for a monitoring rule obliging the Commission to examine "in particular the application of the *sui generis* right including articles 8 and 9, and especially whether the application of this right has led to abuse of a dominant position or to other interference with free competition which would justify appropriate measures being taken, in particular the establishment of non-voluntary licensing arrangements"). This could lead to a compulsory licensing rule in the interest of competition, and it would virtually transform protection from a property to a liability regime. *See, e.g.*, J.H. Reichman, *Database Protection in a Global Economy*, 16 REVUE INTERNATIONALE DE DROIT ECONOMIQUE 455, 479–80 (2002).

[48] Such as utility model protection, which exists under many national laws, and which is under consideration by the European Community. *See* R. Krasser, *Harmonization of Utility Model Law in Europe*, 31 IIC 797 (2000); Consultations on the impact of the Community utility model in order to update the Green Paper on the Protection of Utility Models in the Single Market (COM(95)370 final), Commission Staff Working Paper: Doc.

indications which do not qualify as marks (such as domain names) or as geographical indications. Thus, with regard to such non-TRIPS intellectual property rights, Members may introduce more stringent rules on restrictive licensing or on technology transfer, just as they may control the exercise of these rights systematically and regardless of the existence of market power.

3. The dissemination concern

Reliance on exclusive intellectual property rights to stimulate investment in new technology poses a twofold economic dilemma. First, the exclusive rights, which provide incentives to innovate in order to reap market-induced rewards, may also block the development of improved, related or complementary technology. This is known as the vertical innovation dilemma. Second, exclusivity may impede optimal exploitation of protected technology, since by definition, optimal exploitation will occur only under conditions of full intra-brand competition, at least if inter-brand competition is not perfect. This is known as the horizontal diffusion dilemma. To some extent, both domestic laws and the TRIPS Agreement address the vertical innovation dilemma in a general fashion by imposing a disclosure requirement on patented technology,[49] although there is no similar requirement for copyrightable technology, notably computer programs.[50] The problem is further mitigated by allowing members to enact a limited range of exceptions to both patent and copyright protection in their domestic laws.[51]

In practice, both the vertical and horizontal dilemmas are primarily overcome by obliging follow-on innovators to take out licenses for their activities.[52] There are, of course, other ways of overcoming these dilemmas, such as through cooperation or concentration, but the TRIPS Agreement does not cover these other approaches, which have become so widespread and economically important.[53] It is only concerned with IPR-based restrictive practices, particularly "anticompetitive practices in contractual licenses."[54] Even then, it

---

SEC 1307, 1307 (2001), *available at* http://europa.eu.int/comm/internal_market/en/indprop/model/consultation_en.pdf (26 July 2001).

[49] *See* TRIPS Agreement, above n. 5, art. 29.

[50] *See generally* Pamela Samuelson et al., *A Manifesto Concerning the Legal Protection of Computer Programs*, 94 COLUM. L. REV. 2307, 2343–65 (1994).

[51] *See* TRIPS Agreement, above n. 5, art. 13 (exceptions to copyright protection); *id.* art. 30 (exceptions to patent protection).

[52] The term follow-on innovator is meant positively in the sense that technological progress is a multi-phased, helical, interactive process, which may involve both lead innovations and complex component innovation, and in both cases, the follow-on innovator makes its own, cumulative contribution either by improvement or by supplying a component. *See* B.A. Kemp, *The Follow-on Development Process v. the Conventional Patent Protection Concept*, 16 IDEA 31 (1974); Richard Nelson, *Intellectual Property Protection for Cumulative Systems Technology*, 94 COLUM. L. REV. 2674 (1994).

[53] *See* below text accompanying nn. 67–85.

[54] *See* TRIPS Agreement, above n. 5, Part. II, § 8.

focuses mainly on "the transfer and dissemination of technology."[55] i.e., on the propagation or diffusion of technology, rather than on reinforcing the innovation process by R&D-oriented or invention-enhancing licensing. Indeed, both the negotiating history of the TRIPS Agreement and its structure point to an underlying tension between the goal of promoting and protecting innovation by elevating universal intellectual property standards to the level that the industrialized nations deemed appropriate[56] and the goal of safeguarding the dissemination of technology on terms favorable to developing countries by some rather vaguely defined and reluctantly conceded bottom-line competition rules.[57]

Nevertheless, the weight of these concessions should not be underestimated, given that they were made in recognition of the Members' sovereign authority over competition policy. They were also apparently premised on the same donor–recipient relationship that characterized the preceding discussions and disputes concerning the proposed Code of Conduct for Technology Transfer,[58] which complicates the issues. The appendix-like character of article 40, as well as its defensive wording and embryonic rules, make it sufficiently clear that it was not devised as an invitation to counterbalance increased IP protection by a pro-active licensing and technology transfer strategy, but rather as a cautious form of containment. It does not directly seek to ensure realization of the technology transfer objective set out in article 7, it merely promotes the attainment of that goal by resort to the rules of competition law governing domestic markets. These rules constitute a sphere of national policymaking comparable to decisions to grant compulsory licenses[59] or to admit parallel imports,[60] two other areas of major concern for developing countries. While acknowledging that it cannot prevent Members from invoking such rules, the TRIPS Agreement nonetheless keeps them within certain limits.

---

[55] See id. art. 7.
[56] See J.H. Reichman, *Universal Minimum Standards of Intellectual Property Protection under the TRIPS Component of the WTO Agreement*, in INTELLECTUAL PROPERTY AND INTERNATIONAL TRADE, above n. 12, at 21–144.
[57] For the general polito-economic background, see G.E. Evans, *Intellectual Property as a Trade Issue – The Making of the Agreement on Trade-Related Aspects of Intellectual Property Rights*, 18 WORLD COMPETITION L. REV. 137 (1994); M. O'Reagan, *The Protection of Intellectual Property, International Trade and the European Community: The Impact of the TRIPs-Agreement of the Uruguay Round of Multilateral Trade Negotiations*, 1 LEGAL ISSUES EUR. INTEGRATION 1 (1995); H. Ullrich, *GATT: Industrial Property Protection, Fair Trade and Development*, in GATT OR WIPO, NEW WAYS IN THE PROTECTION OF INTELLECTUAL PROPERTY 127, 131 et seq. (F.-K. Beier & G. Schricker eds., 1989).
[58] The examples given in article 40.2 point to this relationship of unequal bargaining power, which overshadowed the topic of international technology transfer. See W. FIKENTSCHER, THE DRAFT INTERNATIONAL CODE OF CONDUCT ON THE TRANSFER OF TECHNOLOGY 5 et seq., 22 et seq. (1980); P. Jefferies, *Regulation of Transfer of Technology – An Evaluation of the UNCTAD Code of Conduct*, 18 HARV. INT'L L.J. 199 (1977).
[59] See TRIPS Agreement, above n. 5, art. 31.   [60] Id. art. 6.

II. International competition rules after the TRIPS Agreement

A. *The new reality*

The tension between innovation and dissemination in the TRIPS Agreement becomes pronounced with regard to the competition rules governing the unilateral exercise of exclusive intellectual property rights. It has been aggravated by a shift from an economy built around a multiplicity of independent innovators to an economy built on collaborative research and pooled incentives to innovate.

1. Innovation and the unilateral exercise of exclusive rights in the information economy

It is only in article 8.2 of the TRIPS Agreement that the risks of abusive conduct are at least mentioned.[61] There is, however, no indication as to the criteria that members should employ in determining either the existence of abuses or the limits on efforts to control them.

(a) Defining abuses Clearly, Members cannot invoke the need to regulate abuses every time that rights holders fail to comply with "adequate standards and principles concerning the ... use of trade-related intellectual property rights."[62] Such a strict standard would render any unlawful exercise of IPRs abusive, and it would thus deprive article 8.2 of any functional importance in its own right. Conversely, "abuses" may cover "misuses,"[63] and they need not be limited to cases of absolute or relative market power alone.[64]

As previously suggested, the open-ended wording of article 8.2 in this and other contexts suggests that it was intended as a rule of containment for national competition policy rather than as a norm informing the proper development of such policy. At bottom, the TRIPS Agreement is an international convention dealing with intellectual property rights and not competition law. Even so, this reticence amply confirms the "backwards looking" character of those competition rules that are set out in the TRIPS Agreement, as noted earlier.

The TRIPS negotiations got underway in the mid-1980s as an anti-piracy and anti-counterfeiting undertaking. It was transformed into trade negotiations concerning intellectual property in general under pressure from major

---

[61] *Id.* art. 8.2.
[62] *Id.* Preamble, Recital 2(b) (recognizing "the need for new rules and disciplines concerning ... the provision of adequate standards and principles concerning the availability, scope and use of trade-related intellectual property rights").
[63] For the misuse doctrine in U.S. law, see L. SULLIVAN & W. GRIMES, THE LAW OF ANTITRUST – AN INTEGRATED HANDBOOK 882 et seq. (2000). *See also* H. HOVENKAMP ET AL., IP AND ANTITRUST ch. 3 (2002).
[64] *See* UNCTAD & ICTSD, RESOURCE BOOK, above n. 18, ¶ 3.1.1(b).

industrial stakeholders, especially those engaged in the development and exploitation of new technologies, who faced heightened competition, particularly from firms in Newly Industrialized Countries.[65] Considerations of competition law were not, however, similarly elevated to the level of this new reality. On the contrary, international efforts to achieve a "Code of Conduct on Transfer of Technology" definitively broke down at this same period even though newly identified issues of technology-related competition law already merited attention.[66]

(b) Technology as a product The new reality posed some hard questions about the proper limits on the unilateral exercise of exclusive intellectual property rights. For starters, IPRs were extended to new subject-matter categories (for example, copyrights in computer programs and *sui generis* protection of databases); the protection of some new categories was tightened (for example, patents were granted ever more readily for computer programs in addition to copyright protection);[67] and pre-existing exceptions or limitations on the scope of protection were also weakened so as to render the protection of new subject matters ever more opaque and inaccessible.[68] Even more telling, rights holders tended to use their IPRs to maintain ever closer

---

[65] *See* Evans, above n. 57, 149 et seq., 158 et seq.; *see also* Basic Framework of GATT Provisions on Intellectual Property, Statement of Views of the European, Japanese and United States Business Communities (June 1988), *reprinted in* FROM GATT TO TRIPS, above n. 29, at 355 et seq. (which was very influential).

[66] *See* UNCTAD Secretariat, *Status of Negotiations*, *in* INTERNATIONAL TECHNOLOGY TRANSFER above n. 12, at 140, 142.

[67] It is at least questionable whether European efforts to keep the patentability of computer programs within the limits of technology-dependent inventions is theoretically meaningful and practically promising in view of the broader availability of patents in the US. *See* Commission Proposal for a Directive of the Parliament and the Council on the patentability of computer-implemented inventions, COM(2002)92 final (Feb. 2002); European Parliament, Committee on Legal Affairs and the Internal Market, Draft Report on the Proposal of 13 February 2003, 2002/0047 (COD); Council, Common Approach: Proposal for a Directive on the Patentability of Computer Implemented Inventions, Doc. 14017/02 (8 Nov. 2002); *see also* A. Howard, *Patentability of Computer-Implemented Inventions*, CRI 97 (2002); R. Bakels & P. Hugenholtz, The Patentability of Computer Programs – Discussion of European-Level Legislation in the Field of Patents for Software, Working Paper, European Parliament, Directorate-General for Research, Legal Affairs Series (2002).

[68] *See* the combined effect of the broad concept of reproduction and the limitations on reverse engineering in articles 4(1)(a) and 6 of E.U. Directive 91/260 on the legal protection of computer programs, 1991 O.J. (L 132) 42, together with the imposition of technical protection measures by article 6 of E.U. Directive 2001/29 of 22 May 2001 on the harmonization of certain aspects of copyright and related rights in the information society, 2001 O.J. (L 167) 10. Even then, the level of protection seems neither sufficient nor balanced. *See* I. Lloyd, *Intellectual Property in the Information Age*, EUR. INT. PROP. REV. (E.I.P.R.) 291 (2001); K. Retzer, *On the Technical Protection of Copyright*, CRI 134 (2002).

control over the modes of exploiting these new subject matters of protection in their disembodied states, and not just in tangible material embodiments as in the past.

The disembodied technological subject matter itself – rather than some particular embodiments of it – thus increasingly became the product that was directly sold on the market. This is true, for example, in biotechnology to the extent that inventions are not transformed into goods, but are exploited as research tools or directly applied as a technology. It is particularly true of computer software and databases when licensed (as they normally are) as services rather than distributed as physical products. In all these cases, use of the protected matter is subject to strict contractual limitations and direct quantitative control; and there is no possibility of freeing trade from these constraints and promoting intra-brand competition by resorting to the doctrine of exhaustion.[69] On the contrary, any potential network effects – though dependent in scope on the functional properties of the subject matter at issue – may become fully internalized, to the benefit of proprietors. The implications for competition and, consequently, for properly defining what constitutes undue restraints on trade of this shift from protecting a manufacturing process or the design of a machine[70] to the direct exploitation of disembodied technology as a product, and the corresponding transition away from distribution in the form of tangible embodiments, have yet to be worked out. There are at least two important economic consequences that merit attention here.

First, in the absence of tangible embodiments subject to the rules of appropriation and consumption that traditionally reflected the market value of any given technology, proprietors will seek to fully capture the value of the informational products by controlling the specific amounts and purposes of use, either directly by virtue of their exclusive rights or indirectly by virtue of

---

[69] Any gray market analogy fails, because, by definition, the "exhausted" embodiments are traded lawfully, whereas in cyberspace, "gray market" transactions still need to be qualified as lawful or unlawful. See S. Ghosh, *Gray Markets in Cyberspace*, 7 J. INT. PROP. L. 1 (1999); D. Rice, *Digital Information as Property and Product: U.C.C. Article 2B*, 22 U. DAYTON L. REV. 622, 630 et seq. (1997).

[70] Product patents normally protect a new technical configuration of an apparatus, a machine, a tool, a component, or the like. The point is that, at least as far as patents are concerned, the distinction between process and product invention becomes blurred when the protected subject matter (the technical teaching) becomes the product that is sold as such. In this state, the patentee's exclusivity becomes "perfect," because there is no competition any more on the downstream level of tangible products made according to different processes or designed differently, but meeting the same function (without being technical equivalents in the patent law sense), but only and directly on the level of the technical instructions as such, provided that alternative problem-solving methods are available at all. The risk, therefore, is that the scope of protection might become ever larger, since the issue will no longer be whether a given product configuration is equivalent to the teaching of the invention at stake, but whether the different teachings are functionally equivalent.

contract stipulations.[71] Second, when the protected subject matter is commercially exploited in this disembodied state, the rights holders may effectively capture all the returns from all uses on different market segments without spillovers or other uncontrolled social benefits. In other words, the rights holder may privatize all the multi-functional or multi-purpose qualities of knowledge that were previously available to the public when distributed in tangible embodiments.

It is this latter effect that has particularly attracted the attention of competition law. Quantitative or qualitative restrictions on use were usually recognized as an economically necessary means of defining the contractual quid pro quo.[72] Functional restrictions on use, by contrast, have raised problems precisely when they resulted from the unilateral exercise of exclusive rights, namely, from refusals to license or to deal. Such refusals were tolerated in conjunction with the conventional uses of protected subject matter as a manufacturing design for tangible products, for example, as spare parts.[73] However, when the transaction pertains to information as such, courts begin to worry and have declined to validate a refusal to license when it blocked additional uses of the protected subject matter. In such cases, the concern underlying the illegality ruling seems usually (though not always) to be the restraint on add-on or value-added innovation in adjacent markets,[74] with market power serving only as a connecting factor for the application of rules

---

[71] Which raises the issue as to whether and to what extent contract law may limit the use of information in connection with the exercise of exclusive intellectual property rights. See P. Samuelson, *Licensing Information in the Global Information Market: Freedom of Contract Meets Public Policy*, EUR. INTELL. PROP. REV. 386 (1999); T. Dreier & M. Senftleben, *Das Verhältnis des Urheberrechts zum Vertragsrecht – Grenzen des Vertragsrechts durch Intellectual Property Law*, in DER E-COMMERCE VERTRAG NACH AMERIKANISCHEM RECHT 81 (M. Lejeune ed., 2001). See also N. Elkin-Koren, *A Public-Regarding Approach to Contracting Over Copyrights*, in EXPANDING THE BOUNDARIES OF IP, above n. 4, at 191; J.H. Reichman & Jonathan Franklin, *Privately Legislated Intellectual Property Rights: Reconciling Freedom of Contract with Public Good Uses of Information*, 147 U. PA. L. REV. 875 (1999).

[72] See above n. 43.

[73] See Case 238/87, Volvo v. Veng, Ltd., [1988] E.C.R. 6211 (Oct. 1988). The outcome, however, remains controversial and legislation has failed to solve the problem. See EU-Directive 98/71 of 13 Oct. 1998 on the legal protection of designs, 1998 O.J. (L 289) 28, arts. 14, 18; Commission Regulation 6/2002 of 12 Dec. 2001 on Community Designs, 2002 O.J. (L 3) 1, 35, art. 19(1).

[74] The paradigmatic case is *Magill TV Guide*, above n. 7; it stands for similar issues of interface access and innovation pre-disclosure claimed by manufacturers of peripheral products. See also H. Ullrich, above n. 4, at 381 et seq.; D. Valentine, *Abuse of Dominance in Relation to Intellectual Property: U.S. Perspectives and the Intel Cases*, COMPUTER L. REV. INT'L 73 (2000) (discussing, *inter alia*, Intergraph Corp. v. Intel Corp., 195 F.3d 1346 (Fed. Cir. 1999)). Important claims for access to source code have also been raised to enable the supply of maintenance services. See OLG München of 17 Sept. 1998, WuW E DE-R 251.

rooted in competition law.⁷⁵ By contrast, market power will itself become an element of an illegal restraint when it is used to block alternative innovation on the same market segment.⁷⁶

2. Toward group innovation incentives: Pooling, cross-licensing, joint research and development

While the antitrust implications of this trend away from hardware-based exploitation of IPRs remain to be clarified,⁷⁷ the increasing ubiquity and technological or economic interdependencies of IPRs have led to a revival of interest in pooling and the cross licensing of such rights. In economic terms, this interest is not necessarily indicative of competitive creativity but rather of follower conduct in the technological mainstream and of decreased technological opportunities.⁷⁸ However, competition lawyers nowadays tend to downplay the risks of concerted behavior and to stress the reduction of transaction costs on the road to collective technological progress.⁷⁹ Risks of market foreclosure due to access limitations, and of enhanced market power

---

⁷⁵ At least in the absence of a misuse doctrine, such as may be applied in the U.S. See DSC Communications Corp. v DGI Techs., Inc., 81 F.3d 597 (5th Cir. 1996); A. Fellmeth, *Copyright Misuse and the Limits of the Intellectual Property Monopoly*, 6 J. INTELL. PROP. L. 1, 26 (1998); R. Hoerner, *The Decline (and Fall?) of the Patent Misuse Doctrine in the Federal Circuit*, 69 ANTITRUST L.J. 669 (2001). Note that in *Magill TV Guide*, above n. 7, exercise of the copyright simply protected existing market power, but did not serve to extend market power.

⁷⁶ *See* U.S. v. Microsoft, 253 F.3d 34 (D.C. Cir. 2001). Literature on the Microsoft case is abundant. *See* H. Hovenkamp, *IP Ties and Microsoft's Rule of Reason*, 47 ANTITRUST BULL. 369 (2002) (providing a discussion of the core issue); R. Picker, *Pursuing a Remedy in Microsoft: The Declining Need for Centralized Coordination in a Networked World*, 158 J. INSTITUTIONAL & THEORETICAL ECON. 113 (2000) (providing a broader account and analysis). In some cases, the copyright misuse doctrine may offer approaches independent of market power. *See* Lasercomb Am., Inc. v. Reynolds, 911 F.2d 970 (4th Cir. 1990); Practice Mgmt. Info. Corp. v. Am. Med. Ass'n, 121 F.3d 516 (9th Cir. 1997). However, both cases concerned licensing restrictions rather than refusals to license.

⁷⁷ For additional illustrations of the problems, see M. O'Rourke, *Property Rights and Competition on the Internet: In Search of an Appropriate Analogy*, 16 BERKELEY TECH. L.J. 561 (2001).

⁷⁸ Just as patent protection is needed more as a technology matures than at its origins, so pooling and exchanging of rights may become important as technological alternatives become scarce or are made scarce by standardization. *See* C. Shapiro, *Setting Compatibility Standards: Cooperation or Collusion, in* EXPANDING THE BOUNDARIES OF IP, above n. 4, at 81, 93 et seq.

⁷⁹ *See* U.S. Patent and Trademark Office, Patent Pools: A Solution to the Problems of Access in Biotechnology Patents? (5 Dec. 2000), *available at* http://www.uspto.gov/web/offices/pac/dapp/opla/patpoolcover.html; R. Merges, *Institutions for Intellectual Property Transactions: The Case of Patent Pools, in* EXPANDING THE BOUNDARIES OF IP, above n. 4, at 123, 156 et seq.; T. Beard & D. Kaserman, *Patent Thickets, Cross-licensing, and Antitrust*, 47 ANTITRUST BULL. 345 (2002); CHR. FOLZ, TECHNOLOGIEGEMEINSCHAFTEN UND GRUPPENFREISTELLUNGEN 239 et seq. (2002). For a critical view, see J. Barton, *Antitrust*

are, of course, recognized,[80] but they need not be dealt with here in detail. The point rather is that the supposed defects of the intellectual property system, or, more precisely, of its individualistic orientation and its emphasis on single proprietors is overcome by institutional arrangements, which may or may not be market-driven, and these are used to support innovation. Whether this approach also implies group innovation or not will depend on whether a given pool is built around convergent, component, or complementary technologies. At the very least it certainly means that the incentives are shifted away from exclusivity to group access, if not membership.

Moreover, the balance between stimulating innovation and promoting the dissemination of technology may tilt toward the former once pools and cross-licensing are tolerated as innovation-enabling arrangements, not as systems of technology propagation. They build upon the IP system, but, at least in part, they modify its primary incentive rationale, and to this extent they reach beyond the confines of the TRIPS Agreement.

Similar considerations apply to cooperative research and development agreements. As an increasingly common way of promoting and facilitating technological innovation,[81] this generalized form of inter-firm cooperation falls outside the ambit of the competition rules in the TRIPS Agreement.[82] However, it remains relevant here for two reasons. First, when countries ease antitrust control of joint R&D arrangements, they may provide an innovation incentive in its own right.[83]

Second, while cooperative R&D is driven by techno-economic necessity rather than by a desire to escape techno-legal dependencies (a motive for pools), it is directly related to intellectual property protection, both as regards the use and acquisition of rights. The intellectual contributions to, and results

---

Treatment of Oligopolies with Mutually Blocking Patent Portfolios, 69 ANTITRUST L.J. 851 (2001).

[80] See FOLZ, above n. 79, at 259 et seq.; SULLIVAN & GRIMES, above n. 63, at 873 et seq.

[81] See OECD, NEW PATTERNS OF INDUSTRIAL GLOBALISATION – CROSSBORDER MERGERS AND ACQUISITIONS AND STRATEGIC ALLIANCES 25 et seq., 49 et seq. (2001); R. Narula & J. Hagedoorn, *Innovating Through Strategic Alliances: Moving Towards International Partnerships and Contractual Agreements*, 19 TECHNOVATION 283 (1999); J. Hagedoorn et al., *Research Partnerships*, 29 RES. POL'Y 283 (1999); M. Sakakiba, *Cooperative Research and Development: Who Participates and in which Industries Do Projects Take Place?*, 30 RES. POL'Y 993 (2001). For a theoretical explanation, see T. Hämäläinen & G. Schienstock, *The Comparative Advantage of Networks in Economic Organisation: Efficiency and Innovation in Highly Specialised and Uncertain Environments*, in INNOVATION NETWORKS 17 et seq. (OECD ed., 2001).

[82] See UNCTAD & ICTSD, RESOURCE BOOK, above n. 18, ¶ 3.1.1(e).

[83] See art. 157(1), 163(2) E.U. Treaty; Commission Regulation 2659/2000, above n. 33, recital 2; A. Link et al., *An Analysis of Policy Initiatives to Promote Strategic Research Partnerships*, 31 RES. POL'Y 1459 (2002); H. ULLRICH, KOOPERATIVE FORSCHUNG UND KARTELLRECHT 83 et seq., 95 et seq., 165 et seq. (1988).

of, cooperation can only be defined, delimited, and attributed by virtue of the exclusive rights that protect them. This creates an additional incentive to acquire and enlarge protection individually by sophisticated patent strategies deployed prior to and during the various phases of cooperation. At the same time, the joint R&D effort itself constitutes a productive source of intellectual property, which is to be held in common or cross-licensed among partners, and possibly even to third parties.

Competition laws favor cooperation by means of safe-harbor provisions, low-key enforcement or outright exemptions.[84] They also generously permit intellectual property arrangements that enable partners to safeguard their relative competitive positions during and after the cooperative ventures, which may be enhanced by the jointly produced R&D results. Here again, and much more overtly, a layer of group competition policy is superimposed on the individualistic, exclusivity-based orientation of the intellectual property system. Yet, as competition rules evolve more into "coopetition" rules, the shift to problems of access and exposure to collective rivalry seems likely to result in tighter antitrust control only at the threshold to market dominance.[85]

B. The global response: An internationally uniform and innovation-oriented competition law?

The first observation that follows from this summary of current trends is that the principles of competition embodied in the TRIPS Agreement are obsolete. While concerns about technology transfer persist, the Agreement's emphasis on post-innovation transfers by means of bilateral licensing transactions, i.e., the diffusion of technologies into additional markets, corresponds to a marginal component of real world issues.

1. From competition policy to innovation policy

Insofar as present-day competition law affects licensing at all, it mainly deals with either problems stemming from the distribution of protected, relatively disembodied subject matter as a product or with the acquisition of technology at the top-end of the innovation chain. The real issue is early access to information, and

---

[84] See National Cooperative Research and Production Act, 15 U.S.C. §§ 4301–4305 (2000); for the EU, Commission Regulation 2659/2000, above n. 33; Commission Guidelines on the Applicability of Art. 81 of the EC Treaty to Horizontal Cooperation Agreements, 2001 O.J. (C 3), sub. 2, Nos. 39 et seq.
[85] For a U.S.–E.U. comparison, see A. FUCHS, KARTELLRECHTLICHE GRENZEN DER FORSCHUNGSKOOPERATION 447 et seq., 461 et seq., 472 et seq. (1989); H. Ullrich, *Competitor Cooperation*, in THE FUTURE OF TRANSNATIONAL ANTITRUST LAW 159 et seq. (J. Drexl ed., 2003).

it is raised mainly in the context of cooperation, concentration, and the control of market power.[86]

This state of affairs reflects a shift from independent technological competition by individuals to industrially coordinated innovation, and to competition for full market control,[87] which accompanies a change in the function of intellectual property law. Whatever its past role as a provider of individual incentives to innovate may have been, IP law's current role is mainly to provide ancillary support for incentives to innovate that are not just set by market forces,[88] but that are determined by coordinated group efforts and by the political acceptance of private control over the infrastructure governing certain information technologies.[89]

---

[86] See above text accompanying nn. 48 et seq. For IPR issues relating to innovation merger control, see R. Pitofsky, *Antitrust and Intellectual Property: Unresolved Issues at the Heart of the New Economy*, 16 BERKELEY TECH. L.J. 535, 552 et seq. (2001); L. Sullivan, *Is Competition Policy Possible in High Tech Markets?: An Inquiry into Antitrust, Intellectual Property, and Broadband Regulation as Applied to the "New Economy"*, 52 CASE W. RES. L. REV. 54 et seq. (2001); H. Ullrich, *Antitrust Law Relating to High Technology Industries – A Call For or Against International Rules?*, *in* TOWARDS WTO COMPETITION RULES 277 et seq. (R. Zäch ed., 1999); J. KAIRO & M. PAULWEBER, HIGH TECHNOLOGY INDUSTRIES, PRIVATE RESTRAINTS ON INNOVATION, AND EU ANTITRUST LAW: THE EUROPEAN APPROACH TO MARKET ANALYSES OF R AND D COMPETITION Part II 68, 73 et seq. (2001). On the one hand, IPR-licensing restraints may be considered ancillary to acquisition or to the establishment of joint ventures, *see* Notice on restrictions directly related and necessary to concentrations (ancillary restraints), 2001 O.J. (C 188) 5; on the other hand, IPR-licensing to third parties may be required as a condition for the authorization of a merger, *see* N. Ersboll, *Commitments under the Merger Regulation*, EUR. COMPETITION L. REV. 357, 363 (2001).

[87] *See* D. Encoua & A. Hollander, *Competition Policy and Innovation*, 18 OXFORD REV. ECON. POL'Y 63, 65 et seq. (2002); Charles River Associates, Innovation and Competition Policy, Report for the Office of Fair Trading, Part I, 16 et seq., 24 et seq., 118 et seq., 122 et seq. (Mar. 2002); MONOPOLKOMMISSION, HAUPTGUTACHTEN 2000/2001 – NETZWETTBEWERB DURCH REGULIERUNG 340, No. 665 (2003).

[88] The incentives are set by market opportunities, the profit potential of which may be more fully controlled in the information economy by intellectual property than in the hardware economy, but they are determined by the economic nature of the subject-matter sold on the market (e.g., its general qualities such as simplicity and reliability, or its information-specific qualities, such as network effects, compatibility etc.), that is, by the demand it may attract, and not so much by the legal terms of protection. *See* Ullrich, above n. 4, at 367 et seq., 381 et seq. (citing authorities). In this context efforts to define, for competition law purposes, the limits of intellectual property in accordance with the economic nature and effects of the subject matter, as is frequently advocated (*see* Encoua & Hollander, above n. 87, at 76 et seq. with references), would be a highly interventionist exercise. *See* P. Carstensen, *Remedying the Microsoft Monopoly: Monopoly Law, the Rights of Buyers, and the Enclosure Movement in Intellectual Property*, 44 ANTITRUST BULL. 577, 610 et seq. (1999).

[89] Such as basic science and its results (discoveries) or technologies showing large direct network effects (see with respect to the Microsoft case, P. Carstensen, above n. 88, at 592 et

This longstanding shift of competition law enforcement from safeguarding free and individual competition to merely controlling the relative efficiency of competitor transactions corroborates the innovation policy rationale, which underlies both the tolerance of coordinated group efforts by IPR-related antitrust law today, and its reluctance to regulate anything short of the excessive exercise of actual market power. Moreover, this efficiency-based innovation policy rationale increasingly governs the application of competition rules to the traditional area of bilateral licensing transactions, including so-called "anticompetitive" technology transfers.[90]

2. The European Union's example

The recent reform proposals regarding block exemptions for technology transfer agreements under article 81(3) of the E.C. Treaty may serve to briefly illustrate both the overall trend toward allowing, if not fostering, group-supported innovation, and the pro-innovation approach now taken in assessing licensing transactions.[91] This quite radical change of approach was outlined in an "Evaluation Report on the Transfer of Technology Block Exemption,"[92] which represents a complementary step in the Commission's overall reformulation of E.U. competition policy. This report, which interested parties have generally welcomed,[93] suggests abandoning the Community's typical focus on territorial exercises of exclusive IPRs. Instead, it proposes to follow a strict systematic division between vertical and horizontal licensing, with a narrow and flexible definition of potential competition between licensor and licensee.[94]

---

seq.). It is with regard to such infrastructure technologies that specific regulations may be envisaged, just as this is accepted with respect to traditional infrastructure facilities subsequent to their privatization. Regulation is not only a remedy to control former public monopolies, but a way to ensure the sufficient supply of at least basic infrastructure services, and, to this effect, it may even be extended to private enterprises beyond competition law control over essential facilities, albeit at the risk of stifling innovation. *See* for an illustrative example the German discussion on whether telecommunications may be sufficiently controlled by competition law, in particular its rules on abuse of market power, including refusals of access to essential facilities, or whether and how long they should be subject to direct regulation. MONOPOLKOMMISSION, above n. 87, at 49 et seq.

[90] For the link that the TRIPS Agreement establishes between the control of technology transfer and restrictive conduct, see above text accompanying nn. 21 et seq.

[91] A history of measures that have gradually liberalized E.U. competition policy in this regard from 1984 onward lies beyond the scope of this article. *See generally* Hanns Ullrich, *in* EG-WETTBEWERBSRECHT, above n. 42, at 1268; Hanns Ullrich, *IP-Antitrust in Context – Approaches to International Rules on Restrictive Uses of Intellectual Property Rights*, 48(4) ANTITRUST BULL. (2003).

[92] See above n. 22.

[93] All reactions are *available at* http://europa.eu.int/comm/competition/antitrust/technology_transfer.

[94] Commission Evaluation Report on the Transfer of Technology, above n. 22, Nos. 125, 127, 130(c).

The recent drafts of a new block exemption for technology transfer agreements and of new Guidelines for applying article 81 to such agreements[95] adopt this same distinction and most, though not all, of the detailed suggestions set out in the Evaluation Report. Vertical licenses will be treated under a regime that closely tracks the treatment of vertical restraints in general. With the exception of hardcore restrictions, such as minimum resale price fixing and excessive territorial protection, the block exemption applies to all the well-known forms of restrictive licensing terms up to a market-share threshold of 30 percent ("safe harbor" concept).[96] Likewise, horizontal agreements are dealt with by measures analogous to the general treatment of agreements between competitors.[97] Such agreements are "safe" from antitrust challenge up to a combined market share of 20 percent (the report proposed even 25 percent), unless they impose the typical unacceptable restrictions, namely, price-fixing, output and sales limitations, and allocations of markets or customers.[98]

It is mainly with respect to multiparty agreements that, given the complexity of the legislative process,[99] the draft block exemption does not follow the Evaluation Report's suggestion for a broader exemption. However, the Draft Guidelines, when addressing the issue of multiparty licensing,[100] seem to take it for granted that these arrangements may benefit from the same treatment as bilateral agreements. At least they submit this proposition without further explanation. It is only with respect to technology pools that the Draft Guidelines take some pains to explain the reasons why and when they should be dealt with liberally, a matter which, indeed, needs explanation, because pools do subject third parties seeking licenses to a collectively held bundle of exclusive rights.[101]

---

[95] *Available at* http://europa.eu.int/comm/competition/antitrust/legislation/entente3_en.httml#technology [hereinafter Draft Block Exemptions and Draft Guidelines].

[96] *See* Draft Block Exemption, above n. 95. As a result, quantitative and customer restrictions generally become permissible, *see* Draft Guidelines, above n. 95, Nos. 165 et seq., 173 et seq. The relevant market shares are those of either the licensor or the licensee, whichever is greater.

[97] *See* Draft Block Exemption, above n. 95, art. 3, No. 1. As to the treatment of horizontal agreements in general, see Commission Guidelines on the Applicability of Art. 81 of the Treaty to Horizontal Cooperation Agreements, above n. 84.

[98] In addition, Article 5 of the Draft Block Exemption, above n. 95, excludes certain stipulations from the block exemption (but does not invalidate the agreement as a whole from the exemption), that oblige the licensee to grant back to the licensor exclusive licenses for severable improvements or to assign to him such improvements, or oblige him to abstain from challenging the validity of the licensed property rights.

[99] Extension of the block exemption to multiparty agreements would require an amendment of Council Regulation 19/65 of 2 March 1995 on the application of art. 85(3) of the Treaty to categories of agreements and concerted practices, art. 1(1), 1965 J.O. (36) 553, which is the Regulation enabling the Commission to grant block exemptions by way of regulation.

[100] Draft Guidelines, above n. 95, No. 33.   [101] *Id.* Nos. 202 et seq.

Under the modernized procedural regime for the enforcement of the Treaty's competition rules, block exemption regulations no longer validate otherwise provisionally invalid restrictive agreements – these are valid or invalid by direct operation of article 81(3) of the Treaty – but only shield them against *ex post* declaratory invalidation.[102] The draft block exemption regulation and the all-encompassing Draft Guidelines, taken together, must accordingly be viewed as complementary and equally efficacious. They spell out a unitary and coherent policy, laid down in the Evaluation Report, which affirms an almost one-dimensional focus on realizing efficiency gains and on promoting innovation. Thus, in a concluding statement, the Report summarizes its "philosophy" as follows:

> In reviewing the current rules and devising a future regime, account has to be taken of the fact that innovation in new products and new technologies are the ultimate source of substantial and major competition over time. Undue emphasis on short-term allocative efficiency may therefore create a socially unfavorable tradeoff between static and dynamic efficiency.[103]

3. Outlook for the TRIPS Agreement

The European Union's approach follows a trend set by the United States, in particular by the Department of Justice's and the Federal Trade Commission's Antitrust Guidelines for the Licensing of Intellectual Property.[104] The aim of the competition analysis is to bolster the licensor's incentives to innovate. The tools are, first, a narrow definition of the licensee as an existing potential competitor; and, second, a broad definition of the efficiency gains to be expected from restrictive licensing in terms of profit potentials and improvement opportunities accruing mainly, albeit not exclusively, to the licensor.[105]

The perspective is that of competition as a dynamic process, with market power regarded as both ephemeral and necessary as a foundation for broad-ranging innovation. The surprising result is that we are back to the reasonable

---

[102] *See* Council Regulation 1/2003 of 16 December 2002 on the Implementation of the competition rules laid down in Arts. 81 and 82 of the Treaty, 2003 O.J. (L 1) 1. The regulation abolishes the Commission's exclusive jurisdiction to grant exemptions by individual decisions as well as the notification requirement, and it thus switches from an *ex ante* control of restrictive agreements, and from the principle of provisional invalidity, to an *ex post* control by declaratory decision.

[103] Commission Evaluation Report on the Transfer of Technology, above n. 22, No. 190.

[104] *See* above n. 34.

[105] This follows from the liberal treatment of grant-back clauses, of tie-ins (both in terms of determining technically necessary and economically reasonable tying clauses), of all IPR-related restrictions in "vertical" relationships, and of most of them in horizontal relationships. *See* Commission Evaluation Report on the Transfer of Technology, above n. 22, Nos. 142, 146 et seq. (vertical customer restrictions and quantitative restrictions), Nos. 161 et seq. (tie-ins), Nos. 165 et seq. (grant backs); U.S. ANTITRUST GUIDELINES, above n. 34, ¶ 5.3 (tie-ins), ¶ 5.6 (grant backs).

reward doctrine, both conceptually and practically, in that the innovation incentives or the reward constitutes a promise stemming as much from a goal-oriented application of the antitrust laws as from the protection of intellectual property law. Conduct that restrains competition has become part of the innovation process, over and above the well-known restraints on trade inherent in, and guaranteed by, the exclusive rights of intellectual property law. The right holder is viewed as the innovator, the licensee as a follower.[106] From this angle, antitrust law serves to promote innovation, rather than competition, even though one might otherwise have supposed that innovation should be deemed a part of, and the result of, competition.

This ostensibly forward-looking focus of competition policy on not hindering innovation thus overshadows the fact that, while all the restraints on the licensee's use of IPRs that are tolerated today operate as a reward, they are in reality a grant of additional incentives (or a price) for tomorrow's unrestricted innovation.[107] The licensor is viewed as master of the game, whether or not he has market power, and the licensee is seen as an adopter, or at best, as an adapter. However, this approach ignores the possibility that the licensee might transform the licensed technology to suit his own needs and those of the market segment on which he operates, or that he might otherwise diversify its application, develop its potential, and create added value by contributing complementary technology or service know-how of his own. So long as this approach implements only a broad concept of intra-brand competition, which, in effect, is left to the control of patentees, and ignores the propensity for development of inter-brand competition, the real potential for harm to competition is thus analytically and legally suppressed.

Whatever the merits of this policy orientation may be,[108] from a TRIPS perspective it implies much more than merely extending IPR-related competition policy beyond the licensing restrictions that the Agreement embraces. Here we are faced with a concerted effort in major markets to allow restrictive licensing agreements to reinforce the IPR-based protection of innovation

---

[106] *See, e.g., id.* ¶ 4.1.2; Commission Evaluation Report on the Transfer of Technology, above n. 22, Nos. 117 et seq.

[107] These effects should not be overlooked when comparing and contrasting the innovation-oriented and dissemination-oriented competition policies. *See, e.g.*, Gallini & Trebilcock, above n. 4, at 25 et seq. (stressing undue separation of *ex ante* innovation incentives and *ex post* licensing incentives).

[108] For the various objectives, orientations, and instrumentalizations of competition policy, *see, e.g.*, D. Hart, *Antitrust and Technological Innovation in the US: Ideas, Institutions, Decisions, and Impacts, 1890–2000*, 30 RES. POL'Y 923 (2001) (for technical innovation); EUROPEAN COMPETITION LAW ANNUAL 1997: THE OBJECTIVES OF COMPETITION POLICY (Cl. Ehlermann & L. Laudati eds., 1998); D. GERBER, LAW AND COMPETITION IN TWENTIETH CENTURY EUROPE: PROTECTING PROMETHEUS 346 et seq. (2001) (for a European perspective); SULLIVAN & GRIMES, above n. 40, at 9 et seq. (for a U.S. perspective).

opportunities and profits, with a view to enhancing the productive and innovative capacity of the IPR owner and to spurring the licensee to join in and cooperate with the former's projects.

The end result tends to undermine the political balance that was struck by the TRIPS negotiations. Competition law, rightly or wrongly,[109] had been looked upon as a counterweight, and as a means of enabling third parties to participate in the benefits of "adequate" intellectual property protection, in particular by safeguarding "the transfer and dissemination of technology," an objective set out in article 7 of the Agreement.[110] Suddenly, under the new dispensation, competition law turns out to support the exploitation of exclusive rights and innovation in general. The technological and competitive position of rights holders, the bulk of which reside in industrialized countries, is accordingly strengthened.

In principle, all countries remain free to formulate their own competition policies.[111] As a practical matter, however, full and successful enforcement of a conflicting national competition policy – for example, a policy that insists on refusing to validate tight grant-back clauses, broad tie-ins, or territorial or field-of-use restrictions with their potential for price discrimination – will become a difficult task so long as other countries allow such agreements, if only because licensors might choose their licensees accordingly. Striking down the exclusivity requirement in a grant-back clause or a limitation on the use of the licensed technology will concern only those intellectual property rights that have been granted under the laws of the enforcing State, not those granted elsewhere, even if covered by an "international" license. Therefore, while the domestic market may become liberalized, the overall competitive position of the licensee may not, and if domestic markets are too small for efficient exploitation, antitrust control may remain altogether ineffective.

At best, therefore, a technology-transfer oriented competition policy would be effective only at the local level. When assessed in the context of other adverse competition policies,[112] it would most likely fail to promote the larger goal of enhancing the licensee's international competitiveness. Compulsory licensing to remedy discriminatory international licensing practices, even if applied in

---

[109] Politically, the ill-fated Code of Conduct on Transfer of Technology, above n. 11, and the ineffective Set of Multilaterally Agreed Principles (*see* R. Dhanjee, *The Set of Multilaterally Agreed Equitable Principles and Rules for the Control of Restrictive Business Practices – An Instrument of International Law?*, 28 LEGAL ISSUES ECON. INTEGRATION 71 (2001)) should have cautioned against any reliance on competition policy.

[110] TRIPS Agreement, above n. 5, art. 7.

[111] *See* above text accompanying nn. 18 et seq.

[112] Put differently, it will lose in "regulatory competition," whether as a result of a "race to the bottom" or of a "race to the top" is a circular question in that it refers back to the issue of what is the right competition policy. *See* MONOPOLKOMMISSION, SYSTEMWETTBEWERB, SONDERGUTACHTEN, sub. 4.1 (1998) (pointing to the increased risks of "races to the bottom" precisely in case competition policy is instrumentalized for specific policy purposes).

cases of merely relative market power, and even if lawful and legitimate,[113] will not help except in a few really straightforward cases. Over time, moreover, the systemic operation and constraints of this innovation-efficiency approach to competition policy are likely to limit the scope of sovereign policy decisions by technologically less advanced countries.

For one thing, as evidenced by the example of the European Union's adopting the United States' approach, a pro-active competition policy with a focus on innovation itself constitutes a powerful means of regulating competition. It invites emulation by other countries that are already in, or wish to join, the innovation race, and it helps to disadvantage those countries that are technologically less advanced. This is true not only in economic terms, in the sense that such a competition policy might actually strengthen the innovation process, but also as a political fact of life. Because a pure dissemination rationale for competition policy can easily be criticized as rather parasitic and as hindering innovation, whereas a cooperative relationship between licensor and licensee might advance it, the dissemination approach to competition policy simply looks weaker than the innovation approach in political terms.

Given the overall framework of the GATT/WTO Agreements, of which the TRIPS Agreement is an integral part, the size of national markets becomes the basis for trade negotiations on market access and on ancillary considerations of market protection or regulation. In this context, countries possessing market power will have considerable leverage to push other countries to abandon dissemination-oriented competition rules as an impediment to investment, in exchange for access to markets.

This leverage is facilitated by the fact that, under the TRIPS Agreement, IPR-related competition policy is thought mainly to concern limiting domestic intellectual property protection, which, however, is deemed a necessary component of, rather than an impediment to trade. Because the countries holding strong intellectual property positions and adhering to innovation-oriented competition policies are precisely those that afford the most attractive markets for other countries, they would be in a position to extract onerous concessions from any Members that sought to persuade them to modify such a policy in favor of dissemination, in the unlikely event that this issue should ever reach the negotiating table. Powerful countries would counter-argue, indeed, that in addition to its principal role of safeguarding free competition in domestic markets, competition policy was intended to strengthen the international competitiveness of industry by ensuring highly innovative home markets.[114]

---

[113] *See* above n. 46. Little if any use has so far been made of rules against discriminatory conduct, which, under national law, apply to enterprises having relative market power. For German law, *see* K. Markert, *in* GWB-KOMMENTAR ZUM KARTELLGESETZ § 20 n. 170 (U. Immenga et al. eds., 3d ed. 2001).

[114] This applies both as a defense against inward competition by foreign rivals and as a tactic to foster outward competition on foreign markets; for a discussion of competition policy

Conversely, from the perspective of innovation-oriented countries, access to other markets by virtue of dissemination-based competition rules normally is not an issue. On the contrary, they would like to control these markets, too, so as to further protect and bolster their own innovation efforts. The very reasons that led them to require "adequate" intellectual property protection abroad by bringing the TRIPS Agreement into the GATT/WTO framework will induce them to support, and, if possible, to export an innovation-oriented competition policy.

Conclusion

Innovation-oriented competition policy extends largely beyond the narrow framework of the competition rules set out in the TRIPS Agreement. Unlike these rules, it follows an affirmative rather than a defensive strategy, and it does so on all fronts rather than only with respect to IPR-based restrictions. By its very objective, such a competition policy will supplement or expand – rather than counterbalance – the exclusivity effects of intellectual property protection. From the perspective of transnational globalized markets, which nonetheless remain territorially separable by virtue of national intellectual property laws,[115] and which are economically different, the system's logic as well as the trade logic of such a competition policy tends to produce both extraterritorial conflicts and pressures for an internationally applicable uniform approach.

Within the TRIPS framework, an innovation-oriented competition policy would only in exceptional cases allow authorities to limit excesses of IP protection, namely, when they attract regulatory attention precisely because they obstruct innovation. This abstentionist view does not seem to conflict with the principles of the TRIPS Agreement. Instead of relying on competition policy to control excessive intellectual property protection, Members may directly revise their IPR laws to provide adequate levels of protection consistent with the flexibility that the TRIPS Agreement affords.[116]

as "new trade policy," see R. S. Khemami & R. Schöner, *Competition Policy Objectives in the Context of a Multilateral Competition Code*, in EUROPEAN COMPETITION LAW ANNUAL 1997, above n. 108, at 187, 239 et seq.

[115] This potential for market separation explains the controversies surrounding exhaustion, as retained by article 6 of the TRIPS Agreement and the TRIPS-conformity of compulsory licenses for the exportation of patented pharmaceuticals. See N. Zürcher Fausch, *Die Problematik der Nutzung von Zwangslizenzen durch Staaten ohne eigene Pharmaindustrie: Zur instrumentellen Umsetzung von Art. 6 der Erklärung zum TRIPs und zum öffentlichen Gesundheitswesen*, 5 J. AUẞENWIRTSCHAFT 495 (2002); J. Bourgeois & Th. Burns, *Implementing Paragraph 6 of the Doha Declaration on TRIPS and Public Health*, 5 J. WORLD INTELL. PROP. 835 (2002).

[116] For the broad margin of discretion WTO Members enjoy under the TRIPS Agreement with regard to the legislative definition of the scope of intellectual property protection, see J.H. Reichman & D. Lange, *Bargaining around the TRIPS Agreement: The Case for Ongoing Public–Private Initiatives to Facilitate World Wide Intellectual Property*

Indirectly, however, a competition policy that views IPR-related restrictions through the lens of innovation and incentives raises problems for the balanced operation of the Agreement. The reason is that this bias tends to shift the political balance between intellectual property protection and the control of anticompetitive forms of exploiting IPRs, which tacitly underlies the Agreement, too much to the side of intellectual property stakeholders. After all, exclusive rights operate as an incentive because they allow beneficiaries to control markets. In the minds of the developing country negotiators of the TRIPS Agreement, it was precisely this danger of external control of domestic markets by virtue of private IP rights that the competition rules in the TRIPS Agreement ought to allow domestic authorities to contain within adequate limits. An innovation-biased competition policy also tends to undermine the dissemination-oriented technology transfer objective of the TRIPS Agreement, and, generally speaking, the goal of technology access that has become so crucial today.

The innovation/dissemination alternative regarding IPR-related competition policy faces, of course, a potential conflict of its own. Because the innovation approach becomes more promising the larger the markets are to which it applies, collision with the dissemination approach will bring with it problems of a territorial split: dissemination claims will most likely be asserted by Members that are specifically affected by foreign dominance of innovation. Thus, there might arise a typical globalization problem in that multinational industry's interest in operating on and benefiting from transnational markets conflicts with the nation states' interest in protecting and promoting industry in domestic markets.

Once again, the problem reaches beyond TRIPS in that the innovation approach is all-embracing whereas the dissemination approach mainly focuses on licensing restrictions, at least as conventionally conceptualized in *ex post* adoption of certain technologies rather than in terms of *ex ante* participation through early information access. One should not indulge in false hopes that the conflicts between, and the biased effects of, these two approaches may readily be overcome by "regulatory competition," or by the harmonization of rules. The problem with both approaches is not any inherent theoretical or practical weakness, but precisely their policy orientation.

However well and objectively reasoned each may be in terms of economic theory, these policy approaches are chosen in accordance with political-economic interests, either directly by rule-makers and governments, or indirectly by administrative or judicial authorities as they implement what they (tacitly) feel or (expressly) consider those interests to be. If economic globalization and the concomitant interdependency of global, regional, and national markets with respect to their regulatory needs make international harmonization of

---

Transactions, 9 Duke J. Comp. Int'l L. 11 (1998); *see also* UNCTAD, The TRIPS Agreement and Developing Countries, pp. 83 et seq., 123 et seq., 176 et seq. (1996).

competition law desirable,[117] it can hardly succeed if this endeavor is based on either the interest-biased trade rationale of the TRIPS Agreement[118] or on a policy approach to competition law, whatever its tint may be.

More precisely, if one were to extend the TRIPS Agreement, or to apply its trade mechanisms to IPR-related competition policy in general, the likely outcome would be that, instead of consensual competition rules limiting possible excesses of IP protection, the innovation-oriented approach would prevail. A better route to harmonization might accordingly be to return to old fashioned principles, and to place more reliance on legal norms that focus on the virtues of a free-enterprise market organization rather than on the likely outcome of an efficiency-enhancing arrangement of competition.[119]

Needless to say, a proposal to reorient competition policy towards a system of essentially legal values is not likely to engender a mass movement in the near future. At a lower level of abstraction, where one might focus on the restrictive licensing of technological property, for example, it might prove more beneficial to try to overcome the innovation/technology-transfer conflict by abandoning the implicit assumption of an innovator/follower relationship. Basically, a licensing agreement is a negotiated transaction, which poses a dilemma. However desirable licenses are both for licensor and licensee, they enable the licensee to eventually compete with the licensor. Hence, the licensor must be allowed to keep the licensee at a competitive distance or else the former might refuse to grant a license altogether.

Restrictive licensing is, therefore, often a precondition to licensing. All that antitrust control of the transaction must achieve is to ensure whether, and to what extent, these conditions appropriately occur, and to limit restrictive licensing accordingly. This is a free-market approach, which may be reconciled with a fairness approach to competition policy.[120] However, unlike the

---

[117] For this controversy, see COMPARATIVE COMPETITION LAW: APPROACHING AN INTERNATIONAL SYSTEM OF ANTITRUST LAW (H. Ullrich ed., 1998), in particular the contributions by H. First, *Theories of Harmonization: A Cautionary Tale* (7 et seq.) and H. Ullrich, *International Harmonization of Competition Law: Making Diversity a Workable Concept* (43 et seq.); TOWARDS WTO COMPETITION RULES (R. Zäch ed., 1999), in particular the contributions by F. Jenny, *Competition-Oriented Reforms of the WTO World Trade System – Proposals and Policy Options* (3 et seq.); E.U. Petersmann, *Antitrust, Market Conceptualization and the World Trade Organization – The Convention Approach* (43 et seq.), H. First, *Competition Culture and the Aims of Competition* (95 et seq.); see also THE FUTURE OF TRANSNATIONAL ANTITRUST LAW (J. Drexl ed., 2003), in particular H. First, *Evolving Toward What? The Development of International Antitrust* (23 et seq.).

[118] *But see* R. Marschall, *Patents, Antitrust, and the WTO/GATT: Using TRIPS as a Vehicle for Antitrust Harmonization*, 28 LAW & POL'Y. INT'L BUS. 1165 (1997).

[119] H. Ullrich, *Competitor Cooperation*, in THE FUTURE OF TRANSNATIONAL ANTITRUST LAW, above n. 117.

[120] For the distinction, see Fox, above n. 22, at 498 et seq. The approach advocated here is a competition approach, not one of equity or power compensation: it presupposes that only restrictions on competitive autonomy matter, not "unjust" prices or other "harsh" conditions.

innovation-oriented approach of IP-related competition policy, this approach directly addresses a problem of maintaining competition rather than masking the existence of such a problem and contributing to the persistence of a relationship of innovation dominance and technological dependence.

29

Can antitrust policy protect the global commons from the excesses of IPRs?

ELEANOR M. FOX*

I. Introduction
II. An American history
III. The European Union
IV. Shifting the balance: Shrinking immunity
V. The international mission

I. Introduction

Can antitrust protect the global commons from the excesses of intellectual property protection?

Antitrust law might be seen as a natural tool to limit excessive IP monopolies, for antitrust law protects competition and competition is the antithesis of monopoly. This chapter gives small comfort, however, to those who hope to restrike a balance in favor of more antitrust and less intellectual property protection. The most obvious channels through which antitrust *could* assert greater dominance over intellectual property protections (e.g., an antitrust duty to license)[1] are not available in many or most jurisdictions. The chapter ends by exploring one less obvious channel wherein antitrust law might modestly push back the boundaries of undue IP protection; namely, limiting the antitrust doctrine of immunity for petitioning the government for an anticompetitive measure or outcome. The cases drawn upon are from the

---

* Eleanor M. Fox is Walter J. Derenberg Professor of Trade Regulation at New York University School of Law. The author is grateful for the support of the Filomen D'Agostino and Max E. Greenberg Faculty Research Fund of the New York University School of Law.

[1] *Anticompetitive use* of intellectual property rights to gain or expand market power is normally illegal under antitrust law, unless protected by an immunity. *See, e.g.,* United States v. Microsoft Corp., 253 F.3d 34 (D.C. Cir. 2001), *cert. denied,* 122 S. Ct. 350 (2001). But a choice to refuse to license is not a "use"; it is not normally considered "conduct." Licensing is one of the available remedies for anticompetitive conduct. This essay does not concern such anticompetitive uses or affirmative conduct.

United States, but the doctrine of immunity is shared by most antitrust jurisdictions in the world.

The point is a small one and is raised not because it could give great relief to the problem of anticompetitive uses of IP-derived power. Rather, it is raised in the context of the essential limits to antitrust. I ask: if there is any point at which the antitrust/IP balance might reasonably be expected to shift in favor of antitrust, where is that point? The answer is: erosion of the petitioning immunity. This repositioning might strike a sympathetic chord with antitrust authorities around the world and might in the future, unlike a frontal assault on the exclusive right to practice patents and copyrights, provide a basis for world consensus.

Here is the problem. Patent grants, by their nature, convey rights of exclusivity. Exclusivity is deemed to enhance incentives to invent. But it is widely questioned today whether the monopoly[2] conferred by IP protection is much greater than necessary to promote incentives to invent.[3] Indeed, grants of broad exclusive rights can counteract such incentives. To the extent of its overbreadth, the IP monopoly may impair allocative efficiency and dynamic efficiency, including the intangible benefits that flow from access to information and products. Overprotection of intellectual property may also undermine distributive justice, including access of the least well off to needed medicines.

If intellectual property rights protect too much, can antitrust law police its borders? The chapter treats the issues in four parts. First, it gives a short history, concentrating on U.S. law. Second, it describes the somewhat more expansive law of the European Union. Third, having concluded that antitrust cannot do much to police the borders of excessive IP protection, it identifies what may be the only point of likely consensus in the antitrust community for more antitrust and less IP: shrinking of antitrust immunities.

II. An American history

Antitrust is anti-turf. Competition is enhanced when people have ideas, borrow (copy) ideas, and build on ideas. In the world of antitrust it is no defense to say – as Dr. Miles tried in 1911,[4] as IBM tried in the 1930s and the 1970–80s,[5] and as Microsoft tried in recent memory[6] – "I created this market; it's mine."

---

[2] I use "IP monopoly" to include the benefits of exclusivity, even when the intellectual property protection does not confer monopoly power.
[3] See, e.g., Thomas Dreier, *Balancing Proprietary and Public Domain Interests: Inside or Outside of Proprietary Rights?*, in EXPANDING THE BOUNDARIES OF INTELLECTUAL PROPERTY: INNOVATION POLICY FOR THE KNOWLEDGE SOCIETY 295 (R. Dreyfuss et al. eds., 2001).
[4] Dr. Miles Med. Co. v. John D. Park & Sons Co., 220 U.S. 373 (1911).
[5] Int'l Bus. Mach. Corp. v. United States, 298 U.S. 131 (1936); Transamerica Computer Co. v. Int'l Bus. Mach. Corp., 481 F. Supp. 965 (N.D. Cal. 1979), *aff'd*, 698 F.2d 1377 (9th Cir. 1983), *cert. denied*, 464 U.S. 955 (1983).
[6] United States v. Microsoft Corp., 253 F.3d 34 (D.C. Cir. 2001), *cert. denied*, 122 S. Ct. 350 (2001).

For many years, antitrust held the upper hand over claimed prerogatives of intellectual property. Two cases, among many others, make this point. In an early classic case, *Fashion Originators' Guild of America*,[7] designers, manufacturers and sellers of designer fabrics and dresses boycotted any enterprise that sold "pirated" styles and anyone who dealt with the copiers. The Supreme Court condemned the designer industry for its vigilante protectivism, which, it held, was a prohibited boycott. Much later, Telex brought an equally classic case against IBM for monopolization of peripheral attachments (disks, memories) to mainframe computers. IBM asserted an IP defense: it claimed as a justification that Telex had improperly reverse-engineered IBM's attachments, cashing in on the lucrative market that IBM pioneered. IBM lost its antitrust defense (although it won a parallel infringement action and it also won the antitrust war).[8] There was no IP infringement defense to IBM's exclusionary strategies.

For most of the first century of American antitrust law, dominant firms whose positions were entrenched by patents asserted unsuccessfully that antitrust must recede in the face of their exclusionary conduct, lest free riders appropriate their investments and chill incentives to invent. Also, for most of the first century of antitrust, a firm's use of intellectual property power to gain advantages beyond the strict bounds of the IP right was an antitrust violation. The courts and the agencies were quick to point out that IP rights were monopoly-protecting, and antitrust was monopoly-destroying.[9] Moreover, at least until the mid-1970s, the U.S. antitrust case law established strong presumptions of the pervasiveness of private power and the likelihood that power would be abused,[10] and IP was identified as one source of this dangerous power.

Even in this period of strong antitrust vis-à-vis IP, however, U.S. law did not prohibit excessive pricing,[11] including excessive pricing of a patented good, and it did not impose affirmative duties on IP holders to license their technology simply because they had a monopoly of something people wanted or needed.[12] There are costs to such uses of antitrust, and U.S. law has always been sensitive to these costs.

---

[7] Fashion Originators' Guild of Am., Inc. v. Fed. Trade Comm'n, 312 U.S. 457 (1941).
[8] Telex Corp. v. Int'l Bus. Mach. Corp., 367 F. Supp. 258 (N.D. Okla. 1973), *rev'd*, 510 F.2d 894 (10th Cir. 1975).
[9] *See* Bruce B. Wilson, Patent and Know-How License Agreements: Field of Use, Territorial, Price and Quantity Restrictions, Address before the Fourth New England Antitrust Conference (6 Nov. 1970).
[10] *See* E. Fox & L. Sullivan, *Antitrust – Retrospective and Prospective: Where Are We Coming From? Where Are We Going?*, 62 N.Y.U. L. Rev. 936 (1987).
[11] *See* Berkey Photo, Inc. v. Eastman Kodak Co., 603 F.2d 263 (2d Cir. 1979).
[12] *See* E. I. du Pont de Nemours & Co. (Titanium dioxide), 96 F.T.C. 650 (1980).
The philosophy of U.S. antitrust regarding single-firm monopoly is generally: Rely on the market, not government, to cure the imperfections. A government solution is likely to be worse than the disease; it may chill the incentive to be the best. *See* Paul D. Marquardt & Mark Leddy, *The Essential Facilities Doctrine and Intellectual Property*

The world of antitrust changed dramatically beginning in the early 1980s, for matters other than cartels.[13] The presumptions regarding the pervasiveness and dangerousness of private power and its ease of abuse were largely reversed, and the law shrank.[14] The presumption is, today, that a firm, even a monopoly firm, acts to serve consumers.[15] Moreover, free riders are seen as rampant, and the scourge of free riding presumptively justifies various restraints that had once been viewed with suspicion.[16] While strategies of monopolists to increase market power by acts against consumer interests are normally illegal under Section 2 of the Sherman Act, mere *uses* of market power that do not also aggrandize market power are normally not U.S. antitrust violations today.[17]

Accordingly "mere" misuse of intellectual property (gaining market advantages but not increased power), even by a monopolist, is probably not an antitrust violation.[18] *A fortiori*, a patent holder has no duty to license its patent when it has simply done nothing; e.g., it simply says "no" to a request for a license. The Court of Appeals for the Federal Circuit is quite clear on this point: there is no stand-alone duty to license technology. The right of exclusive use is the essence of the IP right; the antitrust laws have no purview to narrow the essential core.[19] While there is (or was) some room for argument that an exception applies when access to the technology is essential for competitors of the IP holder to compete in an adjacent market,[20] the Federal Circuit view appears to be the dominant view in the United States, and the sympathies of the U.S. Supreme Court lie with the freedom to choose not to deal.[21]

Rights: A Response to Pitofsky, Patterson and Hooks, 70 ANTITRUST L.J. 847 (2003). *See also* Verizon Communications Inc. v. Law Offices of Curtis V. Trinko, 124 S. Ct. 872 (2004).

[13] The rule against cartels was and remains strong. Cartels are both inefficient and abusive, and there are virtually no costs of error in prohibiting cartels.

[14] *See* E. Fox, *The Modernization of Antitrust: A New Equilibrium*, 66 CORNELL L. REV. 1140 (1981). *See also Trinko*, 124 S. Ct. 872.

[15] *See, e.g.*, Bus. Elec. Corp. v. Sharp Elec. Corp., 485 U.S. 717 (1988); Olympia Equip. Leasing Co. v. W. Union Tel. Co., 797 F.2d 370 (7th Cir. 1986).

[16] *See* Rothery Storage & Van Co. v. Atlas Van Lines, Inc., 792 F.2d 210 (D.C. Cir. 1986).

[17] *See Trinko*, 124 S. Ct. 872, 883 fn 4; United States v. Microsoft Corp., 1998–2 Trade Cas. ¶ 72,261 (D.D.C. 1998) (dismissing states' leveraging claims).

[18] *See* above n. 17. Antitrust case law protects freedom of contract and freedom to act even where defendant is a wrongdoer. *See* NYNEX Corp. v. Discon, Inc., 525 U.S. 128 (1998). NYNEX cut off its supplier as part of a strategy to engage in a fraudulent, price-raising transaction. The Supreme Court denied *per se* antitrust treatment and the district court, on remand, dismissed the case.

[19] *In re* Indep. Serv. Org. Antitrust Litig., CSU, L.L.C. v. Xerox Corp., 203 F.3d 1322 (2000), *cert. denied*, 531 U.S. 1143 (2001); Intergraph Corp. v. Intel Corp., 195 F.3d 1346 (1999).

[20] *E.g.*, Digidyne Corp. v. Data Gen. Corp., 734 F.2d 1336 (9th Cir. 1984); Robert Pitofsky et al., *The Essential Facilities Doctrine Under U.S. Antitrust Law*, 70 ANTITRUST L.J. 443 (2002); *but see* Marquardt & Leddy, above n. 12.

[21] *Trinko*, 124 S. Ct. 872; *NYNEX*, 525 U.S. 128.

Correspondingly, if consumers (e.g. of necessary drugs) were to make an antitrust claim of excessive pricing, the claim would not be viable under U.S. law. High price creating unavailability of a good is not a U.S. antitrust violation.[22] Solutions, if any, must come from the legislature.

III. The European Union

In the European Union, the Treaty of Rome gives its Member States the right to grant intellectual property protection and to define the bounds of the property right.[23] Also under the Treaty of Rome, while state restraint of internal market trade is prohibited, an exception is made for exercise of intellectual property rights, so long as the exercise is not a disguised restraint of trade.[24] While these two provisions might seem to point towards the primacy of IP over competition, this is not the case. Freedom from undistorted competition is a Treaty right of almost constitutional dimension. Article 82 of the Treaty prohibits abusively high prices, and excessive pricing of intellectual property may constitute an abuse (although it usually does not).[25] Moreover, when competition rights are in tension with IP rights, E.U. law protects only the essence of the IP right, and essence has been narrowly conceived.[26] Indeed, in exceptional circumstances, European competition law may trump even the essence of IP rights. In one famous case, the European Commission won a duty-to-license competition case.[27] More recently, the European Court of Justice gave guidance that expands the first precedent.[28]

The first of these cases is *Magill*.[29] Irish law (atypically) gave copyright protection to broadcasters' schedules. Each of the three large TV broadcasters

---

[22] *See* Berkey Photo, Inc. v. Eastman Kodak Co., 603 F.2d 263 (2d Cir. 1979).
[23] Treaty of Rome Establishing the European Community, 24 Dec. 2002 O.J. (C 325), art. 295.
[24] *Id*. arts. 28, 30.
[25] Case C-40/70, Sirena S.r.l. v. Eda S.r.l. and others, 1971 E.C.R. 69.
[26] *Compare* Case C-238/87, Volvo v. Veng, 1988 E.C.R. 6211 *with* Cases C-56/64 *and* 58/64, Consten & Grundig v. Comm'n, 1966 E.C.R. 299. *See also* Microsoft, Case Comp/C-3/37.792, Comm'n Decision of 24 Mar. 2004, Microsoft's application for interim stay of relief denied, Case T-201/04 R, Court of First Instance, 22 Dec. 2004 (pending appeal) (finding Microsoft's disruption of its supply of interface information to its work group server rivals constituted an abuse of dominance; the supply of interface information – so as to allow for seamless interoperability – entailed the licensing of intellectual property).
[27] Commission Decision in Magill T.V. Guide, O.J. (L 78) 43 (1989), *aff'd*, Cases T-69/89, RTE v. Comm'n, 1991 E.C.R. II-485, T-76/89, ITP v. Comm'n 1991 E.C.R. II-575, T-70/89, BBC v. Comm'n, 1991 E.C.R. II-535, *aff'd*, Case C-241 & 242/91, RTE & ITP v. Comm'n, 1995 E.C.R. I-743 (where necessary to bring to market a new product that consumers demanded).
[28] Case C-418/01, IMS Health GmbH & Co. OHG and NDC Health GmbH & Co. KG, 24 April 2004.
[29] *See* above n. 27.

published its own schedule, and sold it, lucratively, with advertising. Magill was an aspiring publisher of an integrated TV guide. Magill requested licenses from each of the three broadcasters, and each refused. Consumer demand existed for a TV guide that integrated the schedules of the broadcasters, but this demand was frustrated by each broadcaster's refusal to license. The Court of Justice held that each broadcasters' refusal to license constituted an abuse of a dominant position.

The second case is *IMS*.[30] IMS pioneered a format – a geographic grid – for data collection for the use of pharmaceutical companies in Germany. The format (called a brick structure) was thought to be protected by German copyright law, and was protected by an EC data directive. NDC, a competitor in data collection, sought and was denied a license from IMS, tried its own format, which the pharmaceutical companies resisted, then used the IMS format. The European Commission found, provisionally, that the refusal to license was an abuse of dominance, on grounds that the format had become a standard to which competitors needed access if there was to be any competition with IMS. The interest of competition was thought to outweigh the interest in protecting the intellectual property.[31] The provisional order to license was suspended by the Court, however, pending a full decision on the merits.

Meanwhile, IMS brought proceedings in a German court to prohibit NDC from using its brick structure. The German court granted the injunction but then stayed the proceedings, observing that IMS could not legally refuse to license NDC if the refusal constituted an abuse of dominance under article 82 of the E.C. Treaty. The national court asked the Court of Justice when such a refusal constitutes an abuse of dominance. The Court of Justice answered that the exercise of an exclusive IP right constitutes an abuse of dominance only in exceptional circumstances. First, access to the product or IP must be indispensable to enable the undertaking to carry on business. Second, where access is indispensable, "it is sufficient that three cumulative conditions be satisfied, namely, that that refusal is preventing the emergence of a new product for which there is a potential consumers demand, that it is unjustified and such as to exclude any competition on a secondary market." (para. 38)

The Court ruled that it was for the national court to decide whether access to the brick structure was indispensable in the supply of German regional sales data for pharmaceutical products, and whether IMS's refusal to license use of the structure was capable of excluding all competition on the market for the supply of the data. By so ruling, the Court indicated that the supply of the data

---

[30] Case T-184/01 (R), IMS v. Comm'n, Order of the President of the Court of First Instance of 26 Oct. 2001, *aff'd*, Case C-481/01 P(R), IMS v. Comm'n, Order of the President of the Court of Justice of 11 Apr. 2002, *available at* www.curia.eu.int/jurisp. *See* above n. 28.

[31] The Commission did not cast aspersions on the insubstantiality of the "creation," probably because it lies with the Member State to determine what qualifies for copyright protection.

was capable of being a secondary market, i.e., secondary to rights to use the brick structure; and that NDC's product, if differentiated, was capable of qualifying as a new product. Accordingly, the Court extended by some margin the doctrine of *Magill*.

Even so, even in Europe, an antitrust violation for refusal to license intellectual property is exceptional. The two dominant antitrust jurisdictions in the world are reluctant to push back the boundaries of IP by applications of antitrust, although the European Union is much better poised to do so than is the United States.[32] Thus, in this author's view, if one wants to contain excessive power derived from IP, one should not look to antitrust law as a significant tool.

IV. Shifting the balance: Shrinking immunity

Thus far we have spoken of the most obvious ways in which antitrust could in theory rein in intellectual property rights: namely, through excessive pricing prohibitions and compulsory licensing requirements. But many nations' antitrust laws, including those of the United States, do not prohibit excessive pricing; and many nations, including the United States, do not support the notion of refusal to license intellectual property as an antitrust offense. Does this leave any room for antitrust as police officer to discipline IP? In general, no. The negative answer is particularly clear at a time when U.S. antitrust philosophy strongly favors antitrust abstention in non-cartel situations and particularly favors a strong right of property holders to choose not to deal.

This section asks: is there *any* point of likely consensus that antitrust should be expanded at the expense of IP protections? The answer is yes; shrinking antitrust immunities. The libertarian right (deferent to markets and against government interference) and the liberal left (respectful of markets but worried about private power) tend to converge on the mission to shrink government-granted immunities from antitrust; the right because it believes that government interference in markets is the worst kind of market interference, and the left because it believes that both private power and the government action it procures usually harm the public.

This insight suggests the possibility of consensus to shrink both the state action immunity doctrine and the exemption from antitrust for petitioning government. Recent IP/antitrust cases have tended to involve petitioning, and therefore that is our focus.[33]

---

[32] It is not clear that the United States and the European Union will lead the way for the world. South Africa, for example, where millions of people in poverty have dire needs for certain life-saving drugs, and where the Constitution itself establishes social and economic rights to dignity and health, might choose a different path.
[33] For FTC efforts to tighten up the state action defense, see Matter of Alabama Trucking Assn., Inc., Dkt. 9307, 4 Dec. 2003, 5 CCH Trade Reg. Rep. ¶ 15,501 (consent order FTC);

Antitrust in most jurisdictions recognizes a petitioning-government exemption.[34] The exemption derives from the proposition that democracy requires the right and freedom to petition government. In the United States the doctrine is called the *Noerr-Pennington* doctrine, or the *Noerr* doctrine, after a famous case in which railroads carried on a fraudulent and deceitful campaign to cause the governor of a state to veto a bill that would have allowed heavy trucks on interstate roads.[35]

Timothy Muris, Chairman of the U.S. Federal Trade Commission from 2001 to 2004, developed an agenda to shrink immunities. In relation to intellectual property, the effort centered on *Noerr*. The Muris FTC identified cases, especially pharmaceutical and standard-setting cases, in which IP holders were extending their IP rights anticompetitively and deceptively. To this end, the FTC launched several significant challenges, which aimed to expand the sham exception to the petitioning immunity and to create an exception to the immunity doctrine for material misrepresentations at least in non-political fora.[36]

The Muris FTC attacked the petitioning immunity in "Orange Book" cases. The Orange Book is a volume issued by the Food and Drug Administration that describes government-approved drugs. A patentee's listing of a patent in the Orange Book automatically triggers a 30-month stay of a fast-track approval of new drugs (provided by the Hatch-Waxman Act) if the new drug would infringe a listed patent. Typically, when a patent expires, generics enter the field. The FTC identified several situations in which a pharmaceutical company with a successful original patent fraudulently listed follow-on patents in the Orange Book in order to delay the entry of generics and thereby maintain its patent monopoly.

Bristol-Meyers allegedly had listed in the Orange Book a follow-on patent for use of buspirone, an anxiety-reducing drug, just before its original patent expired. When the original patent expired and generic makers sought to enter the market, Bristol-Meyers sued them for infringement. In turn, generic makers and purchasers sued Bristol-Meyers for monopolizing the market. Bristol-Meyers moved to dismiss on grounds that its Orange Book listing constituted petitioning activity (petitioning the FDA) and was protected by *Noerr*. The FTC filed an important amicus brief in the case, opposing the

---

Movers Conf. of Mississippi, Inc., Dkt. 9308, 30 Oct. 2003, 5 CCH Trade Reg. Rep. ¶ 15,502 (consent order FTC).

[34] For European Union law, see Richard Wainwright & André Bouquet, *State Intervention and Action in EC Competition Law*, in INTERNATIONAL ANTITRUST LAW & POLICY 539 (B. Hawk ed., 2004).

[35] E. R. R. President's Conf. v. Noerr Motor Freight, 365 U.S. 127 (1961).

[36] T. Muris, Looking Forward: The Federal Trade Commission and The Future Development of U.S. Competition Policy, Speech Before Milton Handler Annual Antitrust Review (New York, 10 Dec. 2002), *available at* www.ftc.gov/speeches/muris/handler.htm.

motion to dismiss. The court upheld the Commission's arguments for containment if not cut-back of the *Noerr* doctrine. It held:

(1) Orange Book filings do not constitute "petitioning government." They are merely informational filings before a body exercising a ministerial task. The FDA merely publishes the listings; it does not vet and decide on the claims made in the listings.
(2) If the filings did constitute petitioning, they were sham petitioning. Bristol-Meyers engaged in fraud on the FDA by falsely claiming in its listing that the new patent covered approved uses of buspirone.[37]

In *Matter of Biovail*, Biovail was a manufacturer of pharmaceutical products, including Tiazac. Andrx developed a generic version of Tiazac, and submitted an application to the FDA certifying that its product would not infringe any patent claiming Tiazac (the '791 patent). Biovail then filed a patent infringement suit alleging that Andrx's generic patent would infringe the '791 patent. Biovail's suit triggered a 30-month stay of approval of Andrx's application. A district court found that Andrx's patent did not infringe the '791 patent. Biovail appealed. The FDA tentatively approved Andrx's application. A month before the circuit court affirmed the district court, Biovail contracted to acquire exclusive rights to the '463 patent and listed it in the Orange Book as claiming Tiazac (even before the acquisition was complete), allegedly for the purpose of again blocking Andrx's entry into the Tiazac market. The FTC brought proceedings for unfair methods of competition. Biovail signed a consent order with the FTC, agreeing to divest certain of the acquired rights. Thus, the FTC refused to allow Biovail to hide behind a petitioning-government defense.[38]

A third case involved standard-setting for low-emissions gasoline in California. The standards were set by the California Air Resources Board (CARB). The FTC brought proceedings against Union Oil Company of California (UNOCAL), alleging that UNOCAL induced CARB to adopt standards that substantially overlapped with its patent rights, while misrepresenting that it had no proprietary rights in the proposed standard. The fraud and the adoption of the standard, the FTC alleged, cost consumers hundreds of millions of dollars a year. The administrative law judge dismissed the case on the basis of a traditional interpretation of *Noerr* – that it protected even false petitioning, in order not to undermine rights of speech and petitioning. The FTC reversed. False petitioning does not disqualify from *Noerr* protection in the political arena, the FTC said; but when such petitioning occurs outside of the political arena, it loses *Noerr* protection when "the misrepresentation is deliberate, factually verifiable, and central to the outcome of the proceeding or case; and it is possible to demonstrate and remedy this effect without

---

[37] In re Buspirone Patent Litig., 185 F.Supp. 2d 363 (S.D.N.Y. 2002).
[38] Biovail Corp., Dkt. No. C-4060, 2 Oct. 2002, 5 CCH Reg. Rep. ¶ 15,246 (consent order FTC).

undermining the integrity of the deceived governmental entity."[39] Thus, again, the FTC shaved away a petitioning immunity that was unnecessarily broad to achieve the goals of this doctrine.

In dealing with antitrust state-related immunities, there are two approaches: one, a generous view of immunities, on theories of state sovereignty and autonomy and a prophylactic view of facilitating the freedoms to petition the state; the other, a narrow approach to immunities based on a perspective that favors the market. The Muris FTC chose the second. This choice has the effect of freeing knowledge for the global commons, and promises to have resonance with antitrust authorities around the world.[40]

In the next section, we propose that the mission to narrow immunities could find its way to a world antitrust agenda, even while excessive pricing and compulsory licensing proposals will not.

V. The international mission

In a world of global markets and world ramifications of local action, both antitrust and intellectual property law cry out for global conceptions.

On the IP side, we have TRIPS,[41] a trade agreement that lays down minimum rules for the protection of intellectual property rights. It prohibits compulsory licensing except in specified circumstances, particularly, cases in which the proposed user has made unsuccessful efforts to obtain authorization from the right holder on reasonable terms, cases of extreme urgency, government use, and cases in which compulsory licensing is an appropriate remedy to correct anticompetitive practices (articles 31, 40). It recognizes that some IP licensing practices or conditions may restrain trade and "impede the transfer and dissemination of technology," and it acknowledges that members may adopt legislation regulating "abuse[s] of intellectual property rights having an adverse effect on competition in the relevant market" (article 40).[42]

---

[39] Matter of Union Oil Co. of California, Dkt. No. 9305, 6 July 2004, 5 CCH Trade Reg. Rep. ¶ 15, 618 (FTC).

[40] *See* T. Muris, Creating a Culture of Competition: The Essential Role of Competition Advocacy, Remarks before the International Competition Network (Naples, 28 Sept. 2002), *available at* www.internationalcompetitionnetwork.org/muris_naples.pdf.

[41] Agreement on Trade-Related Aspects of Intellectual Property Rights, 15 Apr. 1994, Marrakesh Agreement Establishing the World Trade Organization, Annex 1C, LEGAL INSTRUMENTS – RESULTS OF THE URUGUAY Round vol. 31, 33 I.L.M. 81 (1994) [hereinafter TRIPS Agreement].

[42] *See* E. Fox, *Trade, Competition, and Intellectual Property – TRIPS and its Antitrust Counterparts*, 29 VAND. J. TRANSNAT'L L. 481 (1996). Article 31 of the TRIPS Agreement does not cut back upon the power of states to issue compulsory licenses of patented inventions in the public interest when its other conditions are met. *See, e.g.,* Jerome H. Reichman with Catherine Hasenzahl, *Non-Voluntary Licensing of Patented Inventions: Historical Perspective, Legal Framework under TRIPS, and an Overview of the Practice in Canada and the United States* (UNCTAD/ICTSD 2002).

On the antitrust side, there is much informal networking but no multilateral agreement. The Declaration at the WTO Ministerial Meeting at Doha, Qatar, November 2001,[43] anticipated possible negotiations of antitrust principles. Those possible negotiations were to concern: clarification of core principles including transparency, non-discrimination and procedural fairness; provisions against hardcore cartels; modalities for voluntary cooperation; and assistance in capacity building for developing countries; all taking special account of the needs of least-developed countries.[44]

Moreover, the Doha Declaration states: "We are committed to addressing the marginalization of least-developed countries in international trade and to improving their effective participation in the multilateral trading system."[45] It stresses the importance of access to medicines and research, and it instructs the Council for TRIPS to review certain issues of implementation.[46]

The Doha Declaration seemed to hold the promise of a world agreement that would give special regard to the most needy populations of the world. It seemed willing to limit excessive exploitations of intellectual property, and it reflected values of fairer distribution and access to necessities of life.[47]

An antitrust initiative in the Doha round was not to be. To bring the nations back to the table on the most prominent issue of the day, i.e. ratcheting down agricultural subsidies, the competition agenda was jettisoned.[48] That, however, is not the only reason why we will not get a WTO antitrust agreement that limits IP rights in favor of the less and least-developed world. No such agreement can be expected to materialize for the very reasons suggested in part II above. The United States would be a critical player in the consideration of possible antitrust rules for the world, and the U.S. antitrust philosophy is not sympathetic with the philosophy signaled by the Doha Declaration.

The U.S. antitrust laws are guided by allocative efficiency and aggregate wealth or aggregate consumer wealth. They are not informed by distributive (fairness) principles. This contemporary interpretation of U.S. antitrust is staunchly defended by the government agencies and the influential antitrust bar; and it is borne out by the most recent antitrust jurisprudence of the Supreme Court. If antitrust principles should be bent to effectuate a fairer distribution of wealth, opportunity or access, this (it is said) would degrade antitrust and impose costs on the world.[49]

---

[43] WTO Ministerial Conference held in Doha (Qatar), Fourth Session, Ministerial Declaration, *adopted* 14 Nov. 2001, WTO Document WT/MIN(01)/DEC/1 (20 Nov. 2001), *available at* http://www.wto.org/english/thewto_e/minist_e/mindecl_e.htm.

[44] *Id.*, Doha Declaration, paras. 23.-25.   [45] *Id.* para. 3.   [46] *Id.* paras. 17–19.

[47] *See* E. Fox, *Globalization and Human Rights: Looking Out for the Welfare of the Worst Off,* 35 J. INT'L L. & POLITICS 201 (2003).

[48] *See* WTO General Council Decision WT/L/579, at 1(g) (1 Aug. 2004).

[49] *See* ABA Antitrust Section and Section of International Law and Practice, Comments and Recommendations on the Competition Elements of the Doha Declaration before the USTR (2003), *available at* http://www.abanet.org/antitrust/comments/doha.doc.

It is notable that the only substantive antitrust principle on the inchoate Doha agenda is a principle against cartels. Cartels are inefficient; they distort the allocation of resources to their highest-value uses in view of what people want *and can pay for*. Monopolization or abuse of dominance (the law applicable to unilateral exploitations of intellectual property) was not on the provisional (and jettisoned) Doha antitrust agenda. One cannot expect it to be on a world agenda for the foreseeable future, precisely because U.S. monopolization law is not an abuse of dominance law,[50] and the American authorities will not support a world abuse-of-dominance principle that aims to protect powerless players and people.

In the area of antitrust with IP relevance, we will not get an antitrust rule for the world that prohibits excessive pricing. We will not get an antitrust rule that requires compulsory licensing of even desperately needed overpriced drugs. Yet, we might move toward consensus on limiting immunities – a point at which allocative and distributive goals (efficiency and fairness goals) coincide. A future world rule or principle narrowing the scope of antitrust immunity in the context of abuse of process involving intellectual property is feasible. It has the potential to command wide support. It could evolve into a second consensus principle after agreement against hard core cartels. The WTO is not now an available forum, in view of the failure of the Doha antitrust agenda. But less formal venues may be accessible. The informal network of antitrust agencies – the International Competition Network – may provide antitrust officials and their non-governmental advisors the best opportunity to find common ground in formulating immunity-limiting principles that make legal, economic, and practical sense. Immunity-limiting principles would be no small advance for the world.

---

[50] *See* P. Areeda & H. Hovenkamp, Antitrust Law, ¶ 652, at 89 (2d ed. 2002), cited for the proposition in Brief of Amici Curiae United States and the Federal Trade Commission, Verizon Communications, Inc. v. Law Offices of Curtis V. Trinko, LLP, 124 S. Ct. 872 (2004).

COMMENTARY I

Comment: Competition law as a means of containing intellectual property rights

CARSTEN FINK*

The past decades have seen an expansion in the reach of intellectual property rights (IPRs). This has occurred both over time, as IPRs are adapted to new areas of technology and to new ways of using technology, and across countries, as international intellectual property (IP) treaties, such as the WTO's Agreement on Trade Related Intellectual Property Rights (TRIPS), are extended to developing countries.[1] There is a virtual consensus among lawyers and economists that competition law plays an important role in regulating markets characterized by strong IPRs ownership.[2] Yet, how precisely is this role defined?

The most ambitious view is that competition law may be able to contain "excessive" protection of IPRs, or levels of protection that go beyond those which would optimally balance incentives for innovation and competitive access to goods and services. A corollary to this view is the notion that the expansion of IPRs has occurred, not because policymakers, after careful analysis, have concluded that societies as a whole would benefit from stronger IPRs, but because of political economy influences – notably the weight of narrow interest groups that stand to gain from strengthened protection.[3]

From the perspective of public policy, assigning such a containment role to competition law does not appear to be first best. If IP standards do not optimally serve the needs of societies, it seems best to adjust those standards to more appropriate levels. But if this is not possible – for example, due to political economy influences – can competition law become a second-best

---

* Carsten Fink is Economist in the Geneva office of The World Bank. The views expressed here are those of the author and should not be attributed to the World Bank or its Executive Directors.
[1] Agreement on Trade-Related Aspects of Intellectual Property Rights, 15 Apr. 1994, Marrakesh Agreement Establishing the World Trade Organization, Annex 1C, LEGAL INSTRUMENTS – RESULTS OF THE URUGUAY ROUND vol. 31, 33 I.L.M. 81 (1994) [hereinafter TRIPS Agreement].
[2] See ROBERT ANDERSON & NANCY T. GALLINI, COMPETITION POLICY AND INTELLECTUAL PROPERTY RIGHTS IN THE KNOWLEDGE-BASED ECONOMY (University of Calgary Press 1998).
[3] See Keith E. Maskus & Jerome H. Reichman *The Globalization of Private Knowledge Goods and the Privatization of Global Public Goods* [this volume].

instrument to correct a non-optimal policy? Three of the excellent contributions to this section provide a pessimistic outlook in this regard.

The chapter by Professor Fox offers a perspective on U.S. antitrust law and E.U. competition law and suggests that, in these jurisdictions, such legal regimes have not been successful in limiting excessive exploitation of IPRs.[4] The chapter by Professor Ullrich warns that competition law is increasingly regarded as subordinate to intellectual property policies, which may dilute its independent role as a guardian of the competition mechanism.[5] The contribution by Professor Janis, among other things, points to the institutional weaknesses of competition regimes in developing countries and argues for minimal standards as a first-stage approach in formulating patent-related competition law.[6]

Yet, even if competition law is unlikely to shift the balance implied by IP policies in a major way towards improved competitive access to public goods, it would be wrong to conclude that competition law does not serve a useful purpose in relation to IPRs, as Professor Drexl's chapter also contends.[7] There are numerous ways in which the application of competition law to private IPRs-related practices can lead to better economic outcomes.[8] Let me point to one specific example here.

Policymakers around the world are confronted with the question of whether or not to permit the parallel importation of goods protected by IPRs domestically.[9] From a legal perspective, the question is to what extent the right of IPRs holders to prevent further distribution of a good exhausts once the good has been first sold on the market. Under national exhaustion, the IPRs holder has a statutory right to prevent parallel importation. By contrast, under international exhaustion, no such statutory right exists. Economic studies of parallel importation have demonstrated that it is generally ambiguous whether a regime of national exhaustion is welfare-enhancing or welfare-reducing. The desirability of restraints on parallel trade depends critically on what motivates such trade, the structure of demand and supply, and the level of development of the country from which parallel imports originate.[10]

---

[4] See Eleanor M. Fox, *Can Antitrust Policy Protect the Global Commons from the Excesses of IPRs?* [this volume].
[5] See Hanns Ullrich, *Expansionist Intellectual Property Protection and Reductionist Competition Rules: A TRIPS Perspective* [this volume].
[6] See Mark D. Janis, *Minimal Standards for the Patent - Related Antitrust Law under TRIPS* [this volume].
[7] See Josef Drexl, *The Critical Role of Competition Law in Preserving Public Goods in Conflict with Intellectual Property Rights* [this volume].
[8] For additional analysis, see Keith E. Maskus & Mohamed Lahouel, *Competition Policy and Intellectual Property Rights in Developing Countries*, 23 WORLD ECON. 595 (2000).
[9] Global policy issues regarding parallel imports are discussed in Keith E. Maskus, *Parallel Imports*, 23 WORLD ECON. GLOBAL TRADE POL'Y 2000, at 1269 (2000).
[10] For further perspective and a review, see Carsten Fink, *Entering the Jungle of Intellectual Property Rights: Exhaustion and Parallel Imports*, in COMPETITIVE STRATEGIES FOR INTELLECTUAL PROPERTY PROTECTION (O. Lippert ed., The Fraser Institute 2000).

From an economic perspective, a case-by-case approach to the permissibility of parallel trade seems warranted. However, such an approach may not be feasible if exhaustion rules apply uniformly across one particular type of IPR (trademarks, patents, copyright, etc.). One possible way forward would be to opt for a regime of international exhaustion, but to allow IPRs holders to establish private territorial restraints in license and purchase agreements.[11] These international territorial restraints could be scrutinized by competition law on economic welfare grounds, in the same way as domestic territorial restraints are regularly subject to scrutiny by competition authorities.[12]

One may also ask whether there is any role for the World Trade Organization (WTO) with regard to IPRs-oriented competition law? This seems a propitious question, as competition policy is one of the so-called "Singapore issues," about which Members of the WTO are struggling to decide whether or not to negotiate a dedicated agreement.[13] Could such an agreement be a useful complement to TRIPS? The answer is "probably not." Even the most ambitious proposals for such an agreement are confined to rules in favor of transparency and voluntary cooperation and against hard-core cartels.[14] While such rules are not irrelevant to IPRs-related competition concerns, the proposals leave out the private practices that are most centrally linked to IPRs ownership – notably, abusive unilateral conduct and vertical restraints in licensing agreements.

In addition, developing countries have legitimate concerns about adding a new agreement to an already complex web of WTO law, given their lack of negotiating capacity and substantial implementation challenges. The case for collective action in the form of harmonized competition law standards also seems muddled and has little to do with the traditional *raison d'être* of the WTO. Building up an IPRs-related competition policy is primarily the domain of domestic policy, and much can and should be achieved unilaterally by developing countries.

---

[11] *See* Nancy T. Gallini & A. Hollis, A Contractual Approach to the Gray Market, Working Paper No. UT-ECIPA-GALLINI-96–01, Department of Economics, University of Toronto (1996).

[12] Of course, this approach presupposes the existence of adequate competition laws and the capacity to implement them – both may not exist in a large number of developing countries – as well as a certain level of international cooperation on competition policy.

[13] Disagreement among WTO members over the treatment of the "Singapore issues" was a chief contributor to the failure of the Cancun WTO Ministerial Meeting of 2003. Since this Ministerial Meeting, an emerging working hypothesis has been to remove competition policy from the Single Undertaking of the Doha Development Agenda. However, it is unclear to what extent competition policy will remain a subject of WTO discussions outside the Single Undertaking.

[14] For a review of the various proposals submitted to the WTO Working Group on Competition Policy, see Julian Clarke & Simon J. Evenett, *A Multilateral Framework for Competition?, in* THE ROAD TO CANCUN 77 (Simon J. Evenett ed., SECO 2003).

Having said this, one proposal for action under the WTO deserves careful consideration. The effects of private business practices easily transcend national boundaries, yet in most jurisdictions competition law does not take into account the harm incurred by foreign consumers and producers.[15] Moreover, individuals and firms residing in foreign countries often do not have a legal standing in domestic courts. A WTO obligation could be created that would require Member countries to take into account foreign damages in domestic competition law (provided such a law exists and whatever its level of sophistication) and to give a legal standing to foreign residents.[16]

Creating such an obligation would not involve subjecting competition law standards to harmonization, which may be neither feasible nor desirable. Nor would it entail prolonged negotiations and large implementation costs. Yet, developing countries would likely benefit from such an arrangement. Most IPRs-holders have their headquarters in developed nations, which could allow poor countries to make use of the competition law infrastructure that is well-developed in rich country jurisdictions.

In conclusion, correcting non-optimal IPRs policies is unlikely to be achieved by competition law, but will need to rely on changing the policies themselves. But there is still an important, if limited, role for IPRs-oriented competition law, and there is scope for promoting better economic outcomes through competition law reforms, both at the national and international level.

---

[15] This type of policy externality is discussed by Keith E. Maskus, *Regulatory Standards in the WTO: Comparing Intellectual Property Rights with Competition Policy, Environmental Protection, and Core Labor Standards*, 1 WORLD TRADE REV. 135 (2002).

[16] Further discussion is provided by Aaditya Mattoo & Arvind Subramanian, *Multilateral Rules on Competition Policy: A Possible Way Forward*, 31 J. WORLD TRADE 95 (1997).

30

"Minimal" standards for patent-related antitrust law under TRIPS

MARK D. JANIS*

I. Introduction
II. TRIPS freedom to operate in the competition realm
    A. Article 8.2
    B. Article 40
III. Minimal standards for a developing country's patent-related competition law
    A. Why minimal standards?
    B. Institutional considerations
    C. Substantive minima
        1. Anticompetitive license restrictions
        2. Unilateral anticompetitive conduct
        3. Patent misuse
IV. Conclusion

I. Introduction

In this chapter, I take up the following question: in formulating patent-related competition law and policy, what lessons might developing countries learn from the United States experience? This is a perilous exercise in at least two respects. First, it may seem to treat developing countries as a monolith, when in fact they are likely to vary widely, for example, with respect to their economic development potential and their legal traditions. My analysis takes heed of this probable variance; but, for purposes of discussion, I nevertheless posit a hypothetical, model developing country. Specifically, I consider the case of a developing country that is a WTO Member; that has committed to formulating a TRIPS-compliant intellectual property (IP) regime[1] but has no substantial legal

---

* Mark D. Janis is Professor of Law and H. Blair & Joan V. White Intellectual Property Law Scholar, University of Iowa College of Law.
[1] Agreement on Trade-Related Aspects of Intellectual Property rights, 15 Apr. 1994, Marrakesh Agreement Establishing the World Trade Organization, Annex 1C, LEGAL INSTRUMENTS – RESULTS OF THE URUGUAY ROUND vol. 31, 33 I.L.M. 81 (1994) [hereinafter TRIPS Agreement].

tradition in the area of intellectual property; that is interested in formulating a patent-related competition policy but has little or no experience with such laws; and that lacks any firm institutional foundation for either IP or competition regimes, and cannot devote substantial resources to establishing such institutions immediately. Although it is approximate, this model fairly accurately portrays the state of affairs in many countries routinely designated as "Least-Developed Countries" (LDCs), and most "developing" countries experience at least some of these conditions, if not all of them.

Second, to suggest that developing countries look for guidance from the patent/competition laws of developed countries may seem to reflect characteristic Western hubris. My analysis is sensitive to this problem. I do not propose that U.S. law has revealed the ultimate truths about the patent/antitrust interface and now stands ready to enlighten the world. Quite to the contrary, one of the major themes of this essay is that U.S. patent/antitrust law affords only a modest handful of grand lessons to offer. Indeed, developing countries should look critically at U.S. patent/antitrust law, should consider it in historical context, and should select cautiously from modern doctrines rather than attempting any wholesale transplant of U.S. law.[2]

Part II of this chapter takes up a necessary antecedent question: what freedom does the TRIPS Agreement allow for the development of patent-oriented competition legislation? Part III then asks to what extent developing countries should adopt U.S. patent/antitrust law in the course of exercising that freedom.

II. TRIPS freedom to operate in the competition realm

In its approach to substantive intellectual property standards, the TRIPS Agreement was largely coercive, especially from the perspective of developing countries that lacked Western-style intellectual property systems. In its approach to the intellectual property/competition law interface, by contrast, the TRIPS Agreement makes reference to competition-oriented standards,[3] but allows member countries surprisingly broad freedom to operate.[4] In this section, I briefly describe the scope of that freedom to operate and synthesize the relevant literature.

---

[2] On the obstacles to wholesale legal transplants, see Paul E. Geller, *Legal Transplants in International Copyright: Some Problems of Method*, 13 U.C.L.A. PAC. BASIN L.J. 199 (1994).

[3] Developing countries appear to have been responsible for formulating proposals that led to the inclusion of some competition law concepts in TRIPS. Pedro Roffe, *Control of Anti-Competitive Practices in Contractual Licenses under the TRIPS Agreement*, in INTELLECTUAL PROPERTY AND INTERNATIONAL TRADE: THE TRIPS AGREEMENT 280 (Carlos M. Correa & Abdulqawi A. Yusuf eds., 1998).

[4] One commentator predicts that the non-coercive approach to patent-related competition policy is likely to be more productive for both developed and developing countries than the coercive approach that characterizes TRIPS intellectual property policy. SUSAN K. SELL, POWER AND IDEAS: NORTH-SOUTH POLITICS OF INTELLECTUAL PROPERTY AND

A. Article 8.2

Articles 8.2 and 40 of the TRIPS Agreement primarily define the scope of Members' freedom to craft competition-oriented restrictions on patent rights.[5] Article 8.2 provides that

> Appropriate measures, provided that they are consistent with the provisions of this Agreement, may be needed to prevent the abuse of intellectual property rights by right holders or the resort to practices which unreasonably restrain trade or adversely affect the international transfer of technology.[6]

Article 8.2 is a structural oddity, both in the conflicted nature of its internal structure and in the ambiguities of its relationship to other TRIPS articles. As for its internal structure, article 8.2 seems to invite Members to create competition-oriented exceptions to the TRIPS Agreement's substantive minimum standards by referring to "[a]ppropriate measures" to "prevent the abuse of intellectual property rights."[7] Yet, article 8.2 tolerates only measures that are "consistent" with other TRIPS minimum substantive "provisions," which suggests that any competition-oriented exceptions might be out of compliance merely by virtue of being exceptions.[8] Some observers have suggested interpretations that ease this internal tension. For example, the United Nations Conference on Trade and Development (UNCTAD) asserts that the consistency clause means "that national control of anti-competitive and related practices must meet some sort of *proportionality test* in order to be acceptable under the TRIPS agreement."[9] Notwithstanding this construction, it seems likely that arguments

---

ANTITRUST 175 et seq. (1998) (criticizing as ineffective the coercive approach to imposing minimum intellectual property standards on developing countries; contrasting the approach of "choice within constraints" that has characterized the adoption of antitrust policy in developing countries).

[5] See TRIPS Agreement, above n. 1, arts. 8.2, 40; Hanns Ullrich, *Expansionist Intellectual Property Protection and Reductionist Competition Rules: A TRIPS Perspective* [this volume]. See also TRIPS Agreement, above n. 1, arts. 6 (exhaustion of rights), 7 and 8.1 (general statements of objectives and principles), 30 (exceptions to patent rights) and 31 (compulsory licenses). While these provisions may also play a role, they are only peripherally relevant to my topic.

[6] TRIPS Agreement, above n. 1, art. 8.2.

[7] Article 8(2) merely observes that such measures "may be needed," allowing room for argument that the article does not independently authorize any such measures.

[8] See Andreas Heinemann, *Antitrust Law of Intellectual Property in the TRIPS Agreement of the World Trade Organization*, in FROM GATT TO TRIPS – THE AGREEMENT ON TRADE-RELATED ASPECTS OF INTELLECTUAL PROPERTY RIGHTS 239, 241–42 (Friedrich Karl-Beier & Gerhard Schricker eds., 1996) (observing that it is "unexpected" to find a "compatibility" requirement in a provision that otherwise seems to be designed to allow for exceptions).

[9] UNCTAD, THE TRIPS AGREEMENT AND DEVELOPING COUNTRIES 54 ¶ 264, U.N. Doc. UNCTAD/ITE/1, U.N. Sales No. E.96.II.D.10 (1997) [hereinafter UNCTAD, DEVELOPING COUNTRIES].

over the scope of article 8.2's authority to serve as a vehicle for patent-related competition policy will persist.

It is also difficult to discern the contours of article 8.2's relationship to other TRIPS articles. Some commentators have read this article to establish an overarching principle[10] that confers on Members minimally constrained authority to enact competition rules under the rubric of intellectual property misuse, which encompasses both unilateral anticompetitive behavior and anticompetitive licensing practices.[11] A set of doctrines formulated under the model of "misuse" might be particularly potent to the extent that they swept more broadly than affirmative antitrust causes of action – for example, to the extent that such doctrines did not entail a showing of market power or other elements ordinarily required of an affirmative antitrust cause of action.[12]

Other observers have questioned whether article 8.2 can be read so freely when understood against the backdrop of other TRIPS articles. There is some force to the proposition that article 8.2 "is essentially a policy statement that explains the rationales for measures taken under arts. 30, 31, and 40," rather than a grant of independent authority to craft intellectual property "abuse" legislation.[13] This interpretation draws from the fact that article 8 is entitled "Principles," and resides in the part of the TRIPS Agreement devoted to "Basic Principles," alongside other provisions that should also arguably be treated as pronouncements of general policy.[14]

---

[10] *Id.* at 53 ¶ 261 (1996) (asserting that article 8.2 must be "construed broadly" because it forms part of the Part I basic principles of the TRIPS agreement).

[11] *Id.* at 54 ¶ 263 (asserting that article 8.2 seems to allow technology transfer control as such). Thus, unilateral practices adversely affecting technology transfers by enterprises not enjoying market power or intra-enterprise transactions between parent and affiliate companies may be controlled, as the TRIPS Agreement clearly distinguishes between those practices that restrict competition and those that affect technology transfer. *See further* Ullrich, above n. 5.

[12] *See* Heinemann, above n. 8, at 243 (discussing the possibility that article 8.2-compliant concepts of misuse might not require a showing of market power). United States law on patent misuse currently requires a showing of market power for almost every variety of misuse allegation. *See* below, nn. 70–76, and accompanying text (describing the Federal Circuit's tripartite scheme for adjudicating patent misuse; only post-expiration royalty provisions are treated as *per se* misuse irrespective of market power).

[13] DANIEL GERVAIS, THE TRIPS AGREEMENT: DRAFTING HISTORY AND ANALYSIS 68 (1998).

[14] *See, e.g.*, TRIPS Agreement, above n. 1, art. 8.1 ("Members may, in formulating or amending their national laws and regulations, adopt measures necessary to protect public health and nutrition, and to promote the public interest in sectors of vital importance to their socio-economic and technological development, provided that such measures are consistent with the provisions of this Agreement."); *id.* art. 7 ("The protection and enforcement of intellectual property rights should contribute to the promotion of technological innovation and to the transfer and dissemination of technology, to the mutual advantage of producers and users of technological knowledge and in a manner conducive to social and economic welfare, and to a balance of rights and obligations.").

In sum, plausible arguments exist for both broad and narrow conceptions of article 8.2.[15] A developing country desiring to formulate patent-related competition policy that complies with the TRIPS Agreement could plausibly look to article 8.2 for authority, although other considerations may counsel against testing the outer limits of this provision.[16]

B. Article 40

Article 40 of the TRIPS Agreement, which is limited to the area of anti-competitive licensing practices, provides a mixture of broad pronouncements and slightly more concrete provisions marking out Members' freedom to operate in the competition area.[17] Article 40.1, like article 8.2, arguably does little more than announce a general principle:

> Members agree that some licensing practices or conditions pertaining to intellectual property rights which restrain competition may have adverse effects on trade and may impede the transfer and dissemination of technology:[18]

Similarly, the opening section of article 40.2 seems to reiterate broad goals:

---

[15] The same may be said for other components of article 8.2; there are plausible interpretations, both broad and narrow, of the "unreasonable restraint of trade" and "international" transfer of technology clauses. See, e.g., Heinemann, above n. 8, at 243 (asserting that neither the "unreasonable restraint of trade" nor the "international" transfer of technology clauses in article 8.2 have substantive significance; "[t]hey amount to nothing more than references to the legal matter that shall be introduced into the balance vis-a-vis the requirements of intellectual property protection"); but cf. UNCTAD, DEVELOPING COUNTRIES, above n. 9, at 53–54 ¶ 262 (urging that article 8.2 be interpreted to cover three distinct kinds of anticompetitive practices: (1) "abuse of intellectual property rights by the right holder independently of any market power he may enjoy"; (2) "practices which unreasonably restrain trade"; (3) "practices which adversely affect the international transfer of technology." The UNCTAD document argues that categories (2) and (3) could involve either unilateral or bilateral conduct. Id.

[16] See below, Section III.

[17] TRIPS Agreement, above n. 1. article 40 is the sole article in the TRIPS section entitled "Control of Anti-Competitive Practices in Contractual Licenses." Id. § 8.

[18] TRIPS Agreement, above n. 1, art. 40.1. See Heinemann, above n. 8, at 245 (arguing that article 40.1 operates as a preamble or "declaration of the Members' common opinion on the detrimental consequences of certain conditions of license"). One commentator argues that the reference to "adverse effects" signals the adoption of the developed world's approach to patent/competition law: a "competition" approach holding that practices should be condemned as restrictive only when they have anticompetitive "effects." A contrary "development" approach, articulated by developing countries in negotiations over the UNCTAD transfer of technology code, held that practices which are not anti-competitive in effect might still be deemed violative of competition law when they have an adverse impact on domestic economic development ambitions. Roffe, above n. 3, at 267–68, 283–84.

> Nothing in this Agreement shall prevent Members from specifying in their legislation licensing practices or conditions that may in particular cases constitute an abuse of intellectual property rights having an adverse effect on competition in the relevant market.[19]

The remainder of article 40.2, however, is more definitive:

> As provided above, a Member may adopt, consistently with the other provisions of this Agreement, appropriate measures to prevent or control such practices, which may include for example exclusive grantback conditions, conditions preventing challenges to validity and coercive package licensing, in the light of the relevant laws and regulations of that Member.[20]

Although article 40.2 demarcates a clear, core area in which members may formulate competition-oriented regulations, it also leaves a great deal to interpretation. First, article 40 does not contain clear language establishing the relationship between its specific provisions and the general pronouncements of article 8.2.[21] Second, article 40.2 refers to "particular cases," suggesting application of a case-based rule of reason approach, but it cannot plausibly be read to preclude altogether legislation that would identify some licensing practices as *per se* competition law violations; such a reading would run counter to practice in some developed countries.[22] Third, article 40.2 seems to make clear that its list of target licensing practices is non-exhaustive, yet the Brussels draft of the TRIPS Agreement included a much longer list of exemplary proscribed practices, most of which were omitted from the final draft of

---

[19] TRIPS Agreement, above n.1, art. 40.2.
[20] *Id.* Article 40 also details a consultation procedure whereby WTO Member X may request consultations with WTO Member Y when a domiciliary of Member Y may be exploiting intellectual property rights in violation of Member X's domestic competition laws. *Id.* arts. 40.3–40.4.
[21] Article 40.2's first sentence does include language reminiscent of article 8.2 (specifying that a Member may adopt "appropriate measures," "consistently with the other provisions" of TRIPS), and ties that language to some previous provision (via the opening clause "[a]s provided above"). However, it is not clear whether "[a]s provided above" refers to article 8. *See, e.g.,* Heinemann, above n. 8, at 245 (asserting that "[a]s provided above" refers either to prior sentences of 40.2 or to 40.1).
[22] UNCTAD, Developing Countries, above n. 9, at 55 ¶ 268 (noting that article 40.2 does refer to "particular cases," which might be argued to preclude legislation that renders certain licensing clauses per se unlawful; this construction, however, would be so restrictive that even developed countries' patent/antitrust law would be in violation); Roffe, above n. 3, at 284 fn. 74 (suggesting that the article 40.2 "particular cases" language may be a reaction to calls from developing countries to include presumptions of *per se* unlawful practices, and that the language therefore may be construed to call for a rule of reason approach). A related problem is article 40.2's silence on any methodology for defining the relevant market in the course of any rule-of-reason analysis of "particular cases." Roffe, above n. 3, at 286.

article 40.2.²³ This presents a curious question about whether the "omitted" practices can be read back into the final draft of article 40.2.²⁴ The same question might be raised about slight variations between the listed practices of article 40.2 and their previous incarnations in the Brussels draft.²⁵

III. Minimal standards for a developing country's patent-related competition law

What should WTO Members – especially developing countries – do with the freedom to operate that the TRIPS Agreement affords in the IP/competition realm? In this section, I first briefly explain why a developing country might choose to embrace a model of "minimal" standards for patent-related competition law, even though the TRIPS Agreement arguably allows a much more aggressive approach. I then survey more specific concerns about relevant institutions and relevant substantive standards, and seek to extract lessons from the U.S. patent/antitrust experience.²⁶

A. Why minimal standards?

Formulating patent-related competition policy is sufficiently complex and resource-intensive that developing countries may well find that they must pursue an incremental approach to legislation in this area. Purely practical considerations may point developing countries towards minimal standards in patent/competition law as a short-run strategy, followed in due course by more elaborate, potentially more aggressive sets of standards.²⁷

---

[23] The Brussels draft of the TRIPS Agreement, which authorized legislative measures against licensing practices deemed to be "abusive or anti-competitive," offered a lengthy list of example practices that might be subject to regulation: (i) grant-back conditions (ii) challenges to validity (iii) exclusive dealing (iv) restrictions on research (v) restrictions on use of personnel (vi) price fixing (vii) restrictions on adaptation (viii) exclusive sales or representation agreements (ix) tying arrangements (x) export restrictions (xi) patent pooling or cross-licensing agreements and other arrangements (xii) restrictions on publicity (xiii) payments and other obligations after expiration of industrial property rights (xiv) restrictions after expiration of an arrangement. *See* GERVAIS, above n. 13, at 189.

[24] For a discussion, see HERBERT HOVENKAMP ET AL., IP AND ANTITRUST § 40.2 (2001) [hereinafter IP AND ANTITRUST].

[25] For example, the Brussels draft would have allowed restrictions on anticompetitive grant-back conditions, while the final draft of article 40.2 specifically calls out "exclusive" grantback conditions, leaving a potential ambiguity about the regulation of non-exclusive grantbacks.

[26] I do not mean to exclude other sources of learning on patent/antitrust law from other jurisdictions. Those topics might be explored fruitfully in a longer article.

[27] J.H. Reichman, *From Free Riders to Fair Followers: Global Competition under the TRIPS Agreement*, 29 N.Y.U. J. INT'L L. & POL. 11, 56 (1997) (asserting that developing

A minimal standards approach may also serve other strategic objectives. As Professors Reichman and Lange pointed out, aggressive assertions of competition law restrictions on intellectual property rights by developing nations may destabilize the foreign investment climate.[28] Uncertainties about whether such restrictions comply with the TRIPS Agreement may compound the problem. Moreover, truly aggressive use of patent-related competition law by developing countries could backfire because developed countries might react by demanding that international standards be created for patent-related competition law under WTO auspices – standards that developing countries may perceive as contrary to their interests.[29] Thus, both practical and strategic considerations counsel in favor of a cautious approach to patent-oriented competition policy in the short term.[30] In the following sections, I describe some of the components of this cautious approach.

B. Institutional considerations

The problems of designing an appropriate institutional foundation for patent-related competition law are far-ranging and serious.[31] U.S. patent/antitrust law provides some guidance here, but only at a very fundamental level.

countries should not attempt to impose centralized control over technology transfer; instead, a government should intervene only when private licensing conditions constitute a clear abuse of market power – with the caveat that distinguishing between clear abuses of market power and reasonable licensing protections "will require considerable expertise").

[28] J.H. Reichman & David Lange, *Bargaining Around the TRIPS Agreement: The Case for Ongoing Public-Private Initiatives to Facilitate Worldwide Intellectual Property Transactions*, 9 DUKE J. COMP. & INT'L L. 11, 31 (1998) ("In this permissive environment, the challenge for developing countries is not that of justifying their right to apply competition law to limit abuses of intellectual property rights, but rather that of avoiding self-defeating applications of such laws that could undermine transfers of up-to-date technology and the acquisition of needed foreign investment."); UNCTAD, DEVELOPING COUNTRIES, above n. 9, at 53 ¶ 260 (stating "overzealous use of competition law can increase uncertainty and limit incentives for investment").

[29] J.H. Reichman, *The TRIPS Agreement Comes of Age: Conflict or Cooperation with the Developing Countries*, 32 CASE W. RES. J. INT'L L. 441, 459 (2000) (noting that the TRIPS Agreement leaves "room for states to use competition law to limit the social costs of higher standards of intellectual property protection" and suggesting that this risk "seems likely to trigger serious initiatives to bring competition law within the WTO disciplines, despite the lack of consensus surrounding all but the most basic norms even in the developed countries").

[30] MICHAL S. GAL, COMPETITION POLICY FOR SMALL MARKET ECONOMIES 7–8 (2003) (urging competition authorities in small market settings to "choose their cases cautiously so as to ensure that the benefits – both to the specific industry at hand and from setting guiding principles for other market participants – justify the costs").

[31] *See, e.g.*, William E. Kovacic, *Getting Started: Creating New Competition Policy Institutions in Transition Economies*, 23 BROOKLYN J. INT'L L. 403, 408–09 (1997) (listing a variety of institutional foundations for a Western-style competition system, including a sophisticated judiciary experienced in deciding business issues; a tradition of safeguards for legal

The U.S. experience amply demonstrates that a mixture of both government and private enforcement mechanisms should be provided for in even a first-stage developing country's patent/competition law. On the government enforcement side, even when resources are adequate, U.S. experience shows that government competition authorities take time to build up expertise and credibility within the bureaucracy and within the patent/competition community more generally.[32] Even then, if U.S. experience is any guide, competition authorities may need to learn how to adapt to the shifting politics of competition law enforcement[33] and periodically to reinvent themselves.[34]

Policymakers in developing countries may find that historical studies are at least as useful as studies of modern U.S. patent/antitrust institutional machinery. The state of United States patent/antitrust institutions in the early twentieth century may be particularly instructive for many developing countries.[35] At that time, the Sherman Antitrust Act was relatively new, the Federal Trade Commission had just been created, and judicial experience with patent/antitrust matters was minimal.[36] These conditions may well mirror the conditions in present-day developing countries.[37]

U.S. experience also shows that much of patent/antitrust law will be case-driven. In the U.S., it has always been largely shaped by common law extrapolations from very generalized statutory provisions.[38] This trend shows no sign of reversal; indeed, the infusion of fact-sensitive economic analysis

---

process; resources for government enforcement agencies; and a robust academic and professional infrastructure).

[32] *Id.*

[33] For example, U.S. antitrust law on patent licensing restraints has been characterized by several cycles of high and low enforcement across the past century. For an overview, see Steven P. Reynolds, *Antitrust and Patent Licensing: Cycles of Enforcement and Current Policies*, 37 JURIMETRICS J. 129 (1997); *see also* Laurence I. Wood, *Patents, Antitrust, and Prima Facie Attitudes*, 50 VA. L. REV. 571 (1964).

[34] For example, consider the current effort at the U.S. Federal Trade Commission (FTC) to reformulate a role for itself in patent-related competition law in the current political climate. *See, e.g.*, To Promote Innovation: The Proper Balance of Competition and Patent Law and Policy, FTC Report (Oct. 2003).

[35] The post-World War II reconstruction of Japan might also provide an interesting setting for a similar historical study. *See* JOHN O. HALEY, ANTITRUST IN GERMANY AND JAPAN: THE FIRST FIFTY YEARS 1947–1998 (2000).

[36] Perhaps one could even draw parallels between developing country economies of the present day and the heavy manufacturing economy of the United States in the early twentieth century. Here I must defer to experts in economic history for evaluation of that suggestion.

[37] *Cf.* Eleanor M. Fox, *Trade, Competition, and Intellectual Property – TRIPS and its Antitrust Counterparts*, 29 VAND. J. TRANSNAT'L L. 481, 490 (1996) ("When the United States was less industrialized, less challenged by foreign competitors, and not a net exporter, it preferred more competition to more protection of intellectual property rights.").

[38] Sherman Act, 15 U.S.C. §§ 1–2 (2000), as well as patent provisions concerning patent misuse, 35 U.S.C. § 271(d) (2000), all are highly generalized.

would seem to ensure that patent/antitrust in the U.S. remains a highly complex, case-driven area of law. The TRIPS Agreement, particularly in article 40, may acknowledge the prevalence of the case-based approach,[39] and developments in Europe point in a similar direction.[40]

Developing countries that lack the tradition of a sophisticated judiciary (or administrative apparatus) vested with significant decisionmaking authority may find it very difficult to implement U.S.-style patent/antitrust principles. A developing country's judicial/administrative infrastructure may be taxed by even a small volume of patent-related competition law matters.[41] As a long-term solution to this problem, developing countries might consider creating specialized tribunals to hear all patent and patent-related competition cases. Here, U.S. experience is only partly helpful – the Court of Appeals for the Federal Circuit has jurisdiction over cases arising under the patent laws, but not over patent-related competition cases; a better design would bring both types of cases before the same specialized tribunal.[42] In addition to its possible conceptual advantages, such a court may also be more politically palatable in developing countries where policymakers view TRIPS mandates concerning intellectual property as onerous and in need of counterweight from competition law.

Developing countries are likely to face serious challenges when attempting to develop a proper institutional foundation for a robust patent-oriented competition law. For some countries, the obstacles enumerated in this section may simply be insurmountable. Developing countries that anticipate this outcome may be forced to create regional coalitions that could coordinate substantive standards, and, perhaps, create supranational institutions for patent

---

[39] Fox, above n. 37, at 491 (characterizing TRIPS as "leaning in the direction of case-by-case development of the interface").

[40] For example, Commission Regulation 2790/1999 (1999 O.J. (L 336)), the Block Exemption on Vertical Restraints, supersedes several narrower block exemptions and appears to leave far more room for case-by-case application. *See generally* IP AND ANTITRUST, above n. 24, ch. 45 (discussing the regulations).

[41] The problem would be especially severe at the administrative level if a developing country sought to rely on the *ex ante* evaluation of licensing restrictions by way of a notification scheme (until recently a dominant feature of EU competition law). Experience suggests that *ex post* evaluation, the approach used in the U.S., is more likely to be a viable option for developing countries. UNCTAD, DEVELOPING COUNTRIES, above n. 9, at 56–57 ¶ 280 (noting the divergence between U.S. law, which operates on an *ex post* approach, and EU law, which traditionally assumed heavy reliance on an *ex ante* approach). For a summary of EU competition law as it relates to intellectual property, *see, e.g.*, IP AND ANTITRUST, above n. 24, ch. 45.

[42] For relevant arguments focusing on U.S. patent/antitrust law, see Mark D. Janis, The Federal Circuit's Benevolent Imperialism (working paper under preparation); Rochelle Cooper Dreyfuss, *The Federal Circuit: A Case Study in Specialized Courts*, 64 N.Y.U. L. REV. 1 (1989). *See also* UNCTAD, DEVELOPING COUNTRIES, above n. 9, at 57 ¶ 282 (noting the need for specialized administrative agencies and courts, and observing that "[a]s regards specialized courts, it is important that they have experience in both competition matters and intellectual property law").

and competition matters.⁴³ A regional exercise in patent/competition lawmaking on a relatively modest scale seems far more likely to succeed, and far more likely to represent developing countries' interests, than another effort to fashion international standards for the patent/competition interface.⁴⁴

C. *Substantive minima*

If a developing country decides to adopt minimal standards of patent/competition law as a first-stage exercise in lawmaking, which substantive standards should it select? More specifically, what relevant lessons here can be extracted from U.S. patent/antitrust experience? United States substantive patent/antitrust law may be divided into three general areas: (1) regulation of anticompetitive licensing practices; (2) regulation of anticompetitive unilateral conduct; and (3) regulation of patent misuse.⁴⁵ Developing countries pursuing

---

[43] UNCTAD, DEVELOPING COUNTRIES, above n. 9, at 4 ¶ 21 (asserting that developing countries "may have an interest in coordinating their efforts to develop coherent and internationally acceptable antitrust standards in the area of IPRs," and that "coordination may help to make sure that future harmonization is effected with due regard to developing countries' interests"); GAL, above n. 30, at 8 (referring to potential benefits of establishing a regional competition regime, perhaps even including a regional competition authority); Roffe, above n. 3, at 294. *See also* UNCTAD, DEVELOPING COUNTRIES, above n. 9, at 56 ¶ 275 (observing that developing countries may wish to form regional organizations that would facilitate harmonization of national standards on IP-related competition law). *See also* S.K. Verma, *The TRIPS Agreement and Development*, in INTERNATIONAL TECHNOLOGY TRANSFER: THE ORIGINS AND AFTERMATH OF THE UNITED NATIONS NEGOTIATIONS ON A DRAFT CODE OF CONDUCT 321, 345–50 (S.J. Patel et al. eds., 2001) (proposing national, regional, and international measures).

[44] Hanns Ullrich, *Intellectual Property, Access to Information, and Antitrust: Harmony, Disharmony, and International Harmonization*, in EXPANDING THE BOUNDARIES OF INTELLECTUAL PROPERTY: INNOVATION POLICY FOR THE KNOWLEDGE SOCIETY 398–402 (Rochelle Dreyfuss et al. eds., 2001) (expressing doubts about the feasibility of international harmonization of IP-related competition law); Fox, above n. 37, at 505 (concluding that "separate world principles of IP-antitrust would be inadvisable," but encouraging "dialogue" to "develop principles linking antitrust to trade"). *Cf.* Carlos Correa, *Reviewing the TRIPS Agreement*, in UNCTAD, A POSITIVE AGENDA FOR DEVELOPING COUNTRIES: ISSUES FOR FUTURE TRADE NEGOTIATIONS 221, 231, U.N. Doc. UNCTAD/ITCD/TSB/10 (2000) (suggesting consideration of revisions to the TRIPS Agreement, including "vertical restraints, such as tying arrangements and restrictive practices in license agreements, as well as on horizontal restraints, such as pooling and cross-licensing and industry standardization").

[45] *Accord* UNCTAD, DEVELOPING COUNTRIES, above n. 9, at 53 ¶ 259 (identifying the following three types of conflicts that might arise between the competition system and the IP system: (1) "intellectual property may be used contrary to the objectives and conditions of its protection – a situation called misuse;" (2) "existing market power or market power resulting from intellectual property may be used to extend the protection beyond its purpose or, conversely, the exclusive right may be exercised to enhance or to extend or abuse monopoly power"; and (3) "agreements on the use or the exploitation of intellectual property may be concluded in restraint of trade or limiting the transfer or the dissemination of technology ... ").

a first-stage patent/competition strategy are likely to find that the components of U.S. law pertaining to licensing restraints will be instructive for formulating competition policy. However, they are also likely to find that U.S. law on the regulation of unilateral conduct and on patent misuse is either unlikely to emerge as a centerpiece of developing country patent/competition policy, or simply gives too few clear guidelines for informing sound competition policy. I discuss each of these areas briefly below.

One overarching lesson from substantive patent/antitrust law in the U.S. will sound trite to many, but is nonetheless worth repeating. The law of the patent/antitrust interface, from both descriptive and normative standpoints, is exceedingly complex, and still not well understood, despite relatively extensive experience with it in the United States. While it is now a commonplace that the patent and antitrust regimes are complementary components of a well-balanced competition policy,[46] the history of U.S. patent/antitrust law suggests that this rapprochement may not endure. Developing countries must always approach patent/competition policy with the understanding that the relationship between the regimes in the U.S. is highly nuanced,[47] still unstable, and still in need of many refinements. There is abundant evidence that the same holds true elsewhere.[48]

1. Anticompetitive license restrictions

The most important step for a developing country seeking to create first-stage patent/competition substantive law is to focus on creating a "jurisprudence of licensing" that draws selectively from practice in developed countries.[49]

---

[46] See, e.g., Mark D. Janis, *Transitions in IP and Antitrust*, 47 ANTITRUST BULL. 253, 254 fn. 3 (2002) (collecting relevant commentary). See also Willard K. Tom & Joshua A. Newberg, *Antitrust and Intellectual Property: From Separate Spheres to Unified Field*, 66 ANTITRUST L.J. 167 (1997). The relevant TRIPS provisions may be understood as being consistent with this approach. E.g., UNCTAD, DEVELOPING COUNTRIES, above n. 9, at 3 ¶ 19 (arguing that because TRIPS negotiations focused on establishment of minimum intellectual property standards, "Articles 8.2 and 40 therefore constitute an appeal to Members to set up a competition policy, at least at the national level, that complements TRIPS standards rather than acting merely as a limit on the use of IPRs.").

[47] Ullrich, above n. 44, at 373 (pointing out that patent rights would not be valuable in the absence of any threat of competition; "[c]onsequently, competition is a prerequisite to the well functioning of the intellectual property system which, in its absence, has no purpose").

[48] Roffe, above n. 3, at 288 (observing that implementation of article 40 will be a complex, very difficult challenge for developing countries with little or no experience in either IP or antitrust); UNCTAD, DEVELOPING COUNTRIES, above n. 9, at 56 ¶ 277 (incorporating substantive competition rules into a TRIPS-compliant intellectual property system in a developing country "is a complex and time-consuming endeavour" which is "one of the great challenges posed by the TRIPS Agreement to developing countries").

[49] Reichman, above n. 27, at 57 ("As regards legal limits on the power of technology transferors to impose harsh or oppressive conditions on their local transferees, state practice in developed

U.S. practice can be of considerable value here. First, as I have previously mentioned, U.S. patent/antitrust law in its earliest stages developed law around patent licensing restraints; that formative period may be instructive for developing countries.

More importantly, modern U.S. law and policy should offer appropriate guidance to developing countries on substantive standards and principles. The DOJ/FTC licensing guidelines[50] can be quite helpful in this task. Specifically, a developing country's set of "minimal" patent/competition standards could incorporate general principles such as the refusal to presume market power from the existence of a patent right,[51] the notion of an antitrust "safety zone" based on market power,[52] and the predominance of a rule of reason approach for most types of licensing restraints under most conditions.

The U.S. guidelines, and U.S. experience more generally, would also counsel against the development of an extensive laundry list of licensing restraints that are deemed per se anticompetitive, at least in the context of a first-stage patent/competition law. Instead, a sound "minimal" standards approach would borrow from U.S. law to identify those restraints that have demonstrably hurt competition the most, and devote their scarce resources to policing such restraints. Specifically, licensing conditions that facilitate hard core cartel behavior through price-fixing or market division should be accorded *per se* treatment,[53] while most other types of restraints should be accorded rule of reason treatment, or even left unregulated in the first-stage competition policy and pursued when the country's competition law infrastructure matures and second stage competition law becomes more feasible.

Perhaps paradoxically, article 40.2 of the TRIPS Agreement may actually set many developing countries on the right path towards manageable first-stage

---

countries affords an array of legal doctrines that governments in developing countries can invoke under the proper circumstances."). Professor Reichman has suggested that such a jurisprudence could operate on a "fairness norm" that is cautiously applied to egregious cases, so as to preserve competition incentives without creating such uncertainty in the investment climate that technology producers decline to invest. *Id.* at 58.

[50] Department of Justice (DOJ) & FTC, Antitrust Guidelines for the Licensing of Intellectual Property (1995), *reprinted in* IP AND ANTITRUST, above n. 24, app. B [hereinafter Antitrust Guidelines].

[51] *Id.* at B-5 2.2 ("The Agencies will not presume that a patent, copyright, or trade secret necessarily confers market power upon its owner.").

[52] *Id.* at B-26 (4.3) (proposing an antitrust "safety zone" for licensing restraints; under this concept, "[a]bsent extraordinary circumstances, the Agencies will not challenge a restraint in an intellectual property licensing arrangement if (1) the restraint is not facially anticompetitive and (2) the licensor and its licensees collectively account for no more than twenty percent of each relevant market significantly affected by the restraint").

[53] Under the U.S. guidelines, *per se* treatment is generally limited to such conduct. *Id.* at B-19 (3.4) (noting that "[a]mong the restraints that have been held per se unlawful are naked price-fixing, output restraints, and market division among horizontal competitors, as well as certain group boycotts and resale price maintenance").

patent/competition law. Its modest, exemplary list of targeted licensing practices may provide a minimalist starting point for competition regulation of patents,[54] even if one might quibble over the choices made in article 40.2 to explicitly list some practices while omitting others.[55]

The approach that I am suggesting – "cherry-picking" from existing U.S. precedent on licensing restraints – may be correctly characterized as short on coherence and conceptual purity. Certainly, one might prefer to articulate an overall vision for patent/competition policy and then proceed to craft rules that implement that vision. My approach effectively works in the reverse direction by encouraging developing nations to pick and choose rules, motivated by pragmatic considerations, and gradually to build up an overall vision of patent/competition policy over the long term in the course of the picking and choosing.

This approach is preferable, in my view, even if untidy, because it may sidestep what has been described as a wide divergence in perspectives between the developed and developing world on the overarching vision for regulating technology licensing restraints.[56] As commentators have pointed out, that divergence stymied efforts to create an international code of conduct on technology transfer.[57] A resolution of this conflict of perspectives internationally appears no closer today than it was two decades ago. Developing countries may find it in their

---

[54] Regarding the article 40.2 list of prohibited practices, Professor Fox has argued that this "first-cut positive list, while helpful in setting the stage, is not a robust step in the direction of answering the interface question, because it is enabling rather than limiting" and "the enabling of antitrust is not the issue; the issue is the limits to antitrust." Fox, above n. 37, at 491. While it is true that article 40 is not a robust step towards a long-term answer to the question of standards development at the patent/antitrust interface, it does set the stage, and for purposes of developing country lawmaking, the modest step of stage-setting may actually be productive.

[55] For example, from a U.S. law perspective, article 40.2's express mention of exclusive grantback conditions may overstate the potential threat to competition posed by such conditions. *See, e.g.,* Antitrust Guidelines, above n. 50, at B-34 5.6 (explaining that grantbacks may be pro-competitive and will be evaluated under the rule of reason).

[56] *See, e.g.,* Fox, above n. 37, at 499, who emphasizes that what the United States calls "antitrust" is not necessarily what developing countries call "antitrust." To some extent, the two bodies of doctrine are opposites. United States antitrust law today is largely based on efficiency policy (often called Chicago School economics), which aims to increase aggregate wealth, not redistribute wealth. For better or worse, efficiency policy advocates have succeeded in nearly abolishing antitrust as applied to conduct and transactions other than cartels and mergers that produce monopoly or cartel-like behavior. Developing countries' perspective on antitrust – which tends to be in accord with certain U.S. policies of the 1960s – is against power, exploitation, and exclusion of the weak by the powerful (a fairness rationale), and it is also especially concerned with *de facto* barriers to entry.

[57] Professor Fox proceeds to argue that "[t]he United States sharp disassociation from this perspective in the 1970s led to the death of the UNCTAD project on the Transfer of Technology (TOT). The clear commitment of the United States to the aggregate welfare path in the 1980s and 1990s seems to assure that a TOT will never be resurrected." *Id.* at 499.

interests to move ahead with first-stage patent/competition law, untidy as it may be, and postpone deeper policy debates for future, second stage lawmaking efforts.

2. Unilateral anticompetitive conduct[58]

U.S. patent/antitrust law has also condemned certain types of unilateral anticompetitive conduct on the part of patentees. The most commonly alleged type is anticompetitive patent enforcement.[59] In a prototypical case, a patentee sues to enforce a patent against the alleged infringer, and the alleged infringer asserts that the act of bringing the infringement suit was designed to stifle competition. For example, the alleged infringer might assert that the patent owner pursued the infringement action despite knowing that the patent-in-suit was unenforceable due to the patent owner's inequitable conduct during patent prosecution. An anticompetitive patent enforcement regulation patterned after U.S. law would presumably draw no challenge under the TRIPS Agreement. A Member facing any such challenge would presumably argue that a U.S.-style anticompetitive patent enforcement regulation falls within the scope of appropriate measures under article 8.2.[60]

Experience with U.S. doctrine on anticompetitive patent enforcement suggests that developing countries should not expect the doctrine to play a major role in an overall patent/competition policy. It is difficult to make the case that anticompetitive patent enforcement law in the U.S. has fulfilled expectations. The definitive case, *Walker Process*,[61] generated high expectations in some quarters about the ability of anticompetitive enforcement doctrine generally to achieve substantial competition policy goals.[62] Yet, modern U.S. standards

---

[58] This section focuses on anticompetitive patent enforcement, which is only one example of unilateral anticompetitive behavior involving patent rights. Allegations of unilateral refusals to license are also important, though less prevalent than anticompetitive enforcement claims. However, no consensus has been achieved among U.S. courts on the antitrust significance of a patentee's unilateral refusal to license. See IP AND ANTITRUST, above n. 24, ch. 13 (describing the split jurisprudence). Developing countries wishing to incorporate core components of U.S. patent/antitrust law into their competition regimes would do well to focus elsewhere than on U.S. law on refusal to license, at least at present, in the absence of recent definitive Supreme Court precedent.

[59] See generally IP AND ANTITRUST, above n. 24, ch. 11.

[60] See above, nn. 5–16, and accompanying text (discussing article 8.2. generally, as well as whether it confers independent authorization for competition law measures, and whether it encompasses unilateral anticompetitive conduct).

[61] Walker Process Eqpt. Co. Inc. v. Food Mach. & Chem. Corp., 382 U.S. 172 (1965) (holding that fraudulent patent procurement can serve as a basis for the conduct element of a Sherman Act § 2 violation). For a brief synopsis of the case against the context of then-existing patent law standards of inequitable conduct, see Janis, above n. 46, at 268; see also IP AND ANTITRUST, above n. 24, §11.2.

[62] For example, Robert Bork argued for a broad reading of *Walker Process* as a major statement against abusive litigation rather than as a "mere patent decision." ROBERT H. BORK, THE ANTITRUST PARADOX: A POLICY AT WAR WITH ITSELF 348–49 (1978).

for prevailing on a *Walker Process* claim are very stringent,[63] and even though such claims are not uncommon, litigants who file *Walker Process* claims rarely prevail, at least in the Federal Circuit era.[64] Accordingly, *Walker Process* doctrine as currently formulated captures only an extremely narrow band of behavior.[65] Although the Federal Circuit could loosen the standards, it seems an unlikely and perhaps unwise decision. The stringent standard may be a natural point of equilibrium for *Walker Process* doctrine, given the manifest uncertainties of pursuing patent litigation (which make it difficult to distinguish between good faith and bad faith litigation). At bottom, it is difficult to tell whether *Walker Process* doctrine is currently serving any substantial deterrent function, or would ever be likely to emerge as a major instrument of competition policy.[66]

The regulation of anticompetitive patent enforcement was a relative latecomer to the U.S. patent/antitrust jurisprudence: *Walker Process* did not arrive until the 1960s.[67] Monographs on U.S. patent/antitrust through the 1960s and early 1970s commonly omitted any mention of anticompetitive enforcement.[68] Instead, early twentieth century U.S. patent/antitrust law focused almost exclusively on licensing restrictions.[69]

Any effort to import U.S. law on anticompetitive patent enforcement doctrine should also take account of probable differences between U.S. civil litigation and litigation elsewhere. Bad faith patent enforcement poses a plausible threat in the U.S., in part because patentees can take advantage of

[63] *See* Nobelpharma AB v. Implant Innovations, 141 F.3d 1059, 1067–68 (Fed. Cir. 1998), *cert. denied*, 525 U.S. 876 (1998). Compared to inequitable conduct rules, *Walker Process* rules call for a higher level of intent, a more stringent showing of materiality (under a "but-for" standard), reliance, higher threshold showings of proof, and no opportunity to balance materiality and intent. *See* Janis, above n. 46, at 274–75 (comparing the standards).

[64] *See* Janis, above n. 42 (discussing statistics on patent/antitrust cases in the Federal Circuit).

[65] On the other hand, if the *Walker Process* claim succeeds, the patentee may face treble damages, so the threat of a *Walker Process* claim may still have some deterrent effect even though the scope of the doctrine is limited.

[66] Although I focus on *Walker Process* claims in this discussion, the same general points can be made about other varieties of sham patent litigation claims, even if they are not technically *Walker Process* fraud claims.

[67] Some references to anticompetitive patent enforcement do appear in prior cases, including Supreme Court cases, *e.g.*, Precision Instrument Mfg. v. Auto. Maint. Mach., 324 U.S. 806, 816 (1945); but no definitive enunciation of the doctrine appears at the Supreme Court level before *Walker Process*.

[68] *E.g.*, WARD S. BOWMAN, JR., PATENT AND ANTITRUST LAW: A LEGAL AND ECONOMIC APPRAISAL (1973) (post-*Walker Process* work focusing on licensing practices); LAURENCE I. WOOD, PATENTS AND ANTITRUST LAW (1941) (pre-*Walker Process* work focusing on licensing practices, with heavy emphasis on patent pooling arrangements).

[69] This may reinforce a point made earlier, that developing countries may do well to consider the points of emphasis in U.S. patent/antitrust law of the early twentieth century, rather than the early twenty-first.

relatively liberal (and expensive) discovery practices and face a very low risk of liability for the opponent's attorney's fees. Bad faith patent enforcement may be a less robust threat in other jurisdictions where civil litigation proceeds differently.

For these reasons, I am ambivalent about the benefits to developing countries of incorporating U.S. doctrine on *Walker Process* fraud or sham litigation more generally. Adopting the standards may be harmless enough, but developing countries should resist any expectations that such law will blossom into a vigorous instrument of patent/competition policy.

3. Patent misuse

Patent misuse[70] is an equitable defense to patent infringement, built on the principle that equity should intervene against a patentee who has illegitimately sought to extend a patent's enforceable scope.[71] Over the past several decades, the doctrine has been marked by cycles of ascendancy and decline roughly corresponding to similar cycles in antitrust enforcement generally.[72]

---

[70] Unlike the antitrust doctrines discussed in the previous sections, patent misuse is one of a few select doctrines that are expressly competition-oriented while being internal to patent law. Other examples include compulsory licensing and exhaustion doctrine. *See, e.g.,* Manisha M. Sheth, Note, *Formulating Antitrust Policy in Emerging Economies*, 86 Geo. L.J. 451, 475 (1997) (arguing against broad use of compulsory licensing on the ground that "[i]n developing countries where a large percentage of the technology is imported from abroad in the form of licensing agreements, antitrust laws that limit the market power of the patent holder will result in less imported technology"); Commission on Intellectual Property Rights, Integrating Intellectual Property Rights and Development Policy 120 (2002) (predicting that "[a]n extensive use of compulsory licensing in developing countries is unlikely given the procedural complexities of the system," but proceeding to recommend "an effective and credible compulsory license system" as "an essential part of any patent policy," especially "for countries lacking a coherent or effective general competition policy").

[71] Specifically, Federal Circuit patent misuse case law currently recognizes (1) acts that qualify as *per se* misuse, such as license provisions extracting post-expiration royalties; (2) acts that qualify as *per se* permissible, such as those acts expressly excluded in 35 U.S.C. § 271(d) (2000); (3) all other acts. Virginia Panel Corp. v. MAC Panel Co., 133 F.3d 860 (Fed. Cir. 1997). As to the last category, a court must determine if that act is "reasonably within the patent grant, *i.e.*, that it relates to subject matter within the scope of the patent claims," and if the practice does extend the patent scope, and does so with anticompetitive effect, the practice must be evaluated under the rule of reason. *Id.* at 860 (*quoting* Mallinckrodt, Inc. v. Medipart, Inc., 976 F.2d 700, 708 (Fed. Cir. 1992)). In many patent misuse cases, the patentee's illegitimate extension of patent scope is by way of restrictive licensing practices, such as tying. *See, e.g.,* Mercoid Corp. v. Mid-Continent Inv. Co., 320 U.S. 661 (1944); Morton Salt Co. v. G.S. Suppiger Co., 314 U.S. 488, 491 (1942); Carbice Corp. v. American Patents Dev. Corp., 283 U.S. 27 (1931).

[72] IP and Antitrust., above n. 24, § 3.2a (noting that patent misuse enjoyed a resurgence in the 1960s and 1970s, but contracted from the 1980s to the present). *See also* James B. Kobak, Jr., *The Misuse Defense and Intellectual Property Litigation*, 1 B.U. J. Sci. & Tech. L. 2, 2–7 (1995) (briefly summarizing the history of patent misuse in the U.S.).

Most commentators agree that the doctrine has recently been on the wane, with some raising questions about whether the doctrine has become obsolete.[73]

Developing countries should approach U.S. misuse law guardedly, given cool U.S. attitudes toward the doctrine. Other, more potent, rationales also support this skeptical approach. First, the relationship between misuse standards and antitrust standards in U.S. law has never quite congealed. Patent misuse doctrine would be of interest to developing countries if it showed how policymakers might step outside the traditional contours of antitrust law and create effective and balanced competition-oriented standards for patent exploitation. U.S. patent misuse doctrine, however, has not reached this level of sophistication. Indeed, U.S. law is still grappling with the question of whether misuse standards are distinct from antitrust standards in the first place.[74] This debate is not likely to end soon, and may simply mirror the debate surrounding the larger project of understanding the relationship between intellectual property systems and competition regimes.

Second, Federal Circuit era debates about the proper scope of patent misuse law as distinct from antitrust law may actually be more about procedure than substance. The Federal Circuit has plenary power over the patent misuse doctrine, but only limited power over patent-related antitrust doctrine.[75] Accordingly, continuing debates over the reach of the patent misuse doctrine, and its substantive role in general competition policy may actually have a lot to do with the peculiarities of U.S. decisions about the scope of the Federal Circuit's appellate jurisdiction and choice of law. These matters are only indirectly relevant, if relevant at all, to developing country competition policy. Indeed, to the extent that the misuse versus antitrust debate does respond in part to institutional power issues, the U.S. experience may conceivably overstate the need for a misuse law separate from competition

---

[73] Note, *Is the Patent Misuse Doctrine Obsolete?*, 110 HARV. L. REV. 1922 (1997) (concluding that the doctrine is verging on obsolescence, though it may retain some future role).

[74] *See, e.g.,* C.R. Bard, Inc. v. M3 Sys., 157 F.3d 1340 (Fed. Cir. 1998) (noting that misuse may be a broader concept than antitrust); *Mallinckrodt*, 976 F.2d at 704 (observing that patent misuse "arose to restrain practices that did not in themselves violate any law, but that drew anticompetitive strength from the patent right, and thus were deemed to be contrary to public policy"). *See also* Assessment Techs. of Wisconsin, LLC v. Wiredata, Inc., 350 F.3d 640, 647 (7th Cir. 2003) (Posner, J.) (expressing sympathy for the position that copyright misuse may extend more broadly than antitrust); *but cf.* USM Corp. v. SPS Tech., Inc., 694 F.2d 505, 512 (7th Cir. 1982) (arguing that the reach of patent misuse should be congruent with the reach of antitrust).

[75] By this I mean that most cases raising patent misuse defenses will fall within the scope of the Federal Circuit's appellate jurisdiction, and most (if not all) elements of a patent misuse defense are likely to be decided as a matter of Federal Circuit law. For a discussion of appellate jurisdiction and choice of law in patent/antitrust matters, see Janis, above n. 42; IP AND ANTITRUST, above n. 24, ch. 5.

law.[76] Nevertheless, where U.S. patent misuse law may advocate a more encompassing standard than would U.S. antitrust law, a developing country could certainly adopt the patent misuse standard, but it should incorporate misuse into the country's competition law regime rather than articulating it as a "patent misuse" doctrine.

IV. Conclusion

I have urged developing countries to choose "minimal" standards as a first-stage approach to lawmaking at the patent/competition interface. These standards could draw upon U.S. experience to identify and regulate the most egregious forms of anticompetitive patent exploitation. Adoption of a minimal standards approach is not intended to prejudice developing countries against further, more aggressive regulation in the long term, when national or regional competition institutions have matured and more challenging questions of patent/competition policy can be confronted.

---

[76] *See also* J.H. REICHMAN WITH CATHERINE HASENZAHL, NON-VOLUNTARY LICENSING OF PATENTED INVENTIONS: THE LAW AND PRACTICE OF THE UNITED STATES (ICTSD/UNCTAD Draft 2003) (discussing lessons of U.S. misuse doctrine for developing countries).

COMMENTARY II

Comment: Competitive baselines for intellectual property systems

SHUBHA GHOSH[*]

I. Introduction

My thesis is that competitive markets, appropriately structured and regulated, are instrumental in preserving and expanding the global commons and that intellectual property systems and competition policy should work in tandem to protect the global commons.[1] Unfortunately, the example of the developed countries, particularly the United States,[2] is one of the failures of creating adequate and appropriate competitive baselines for intellectual property systems. Mahatma Gandhi famously quipped about Western Civilization: "It's a good idea. We should try it sometime." Developing a more rigorous relationship between competition and intellectual property law is a good idea, worth trying. The advent of TRIPS[3] makes this idea especially necessary.

There are two principal reasons why intellectual property law and competition law have passed each other by. The first has to do with the ambiguity in defining competition law. Under United States legal doctrine, competition law is often seen as overlapping with antitrust law, a body of legislation consisting of the Sherman Act, the Clayton Act, and the Federal Trade Commission Act. However, limiting competition policy to these bodies of law alone severely limits our understanding of the relationship between intellectual property law and competition policy and the possibilities for jurisdictions that are now developing their own legal schemes.

---

[*] Shubha Ghosh is Professor of Law, University of Buffalo Law School, State University of New York.
[1] For excellent background articles on global public goods, intellectual property, and competition, see Carlos M. Correa, *Managing the Provision of Knowledge: The Design of Intellectual Property Laws*, in PROVIDING GLOBAL PUBLIC GOODS: MANAGING GLOBALIZATION 410 (Inge Kaul et. al. eds., 2003); Joseph E. Stiglitz, *Knowledge as a Global Public Good*, in GLOBAL PUBLIC GOODS: INTERNATIONAL COOPERATION IN THE 21ST CENTURY 308 (Inge Kaul et. al. eds., 1999).
[2] Space considerations limited my ability to discuss European Union Law here. For a discussion, see KAREN V. KOLE & ANTHONY D'AMATO, EUROPEAN UNION LAW ANTHOLOGY 207–284 (1998).
[3] Marrakesh Agreement Establishing the World Trade Organization, Annex 1C, Agreement on Trade-Related Aspects of Intellectual Property Rights, 15 April 1994, 33 I.L.M. 81 (1994) ("TRIPS Agreement").

For example, limiting our focus to antitrust law would ignore the important role that constitutional doctrine, particularly the law of preemption, has played in balancing competition policy and intellectual property law. Preemption has historically limited the ability of intellectual property owners to extend their rights through contract.[4] For example, the Supreme Court has invalidated attempts to extend the duration of patents through contract[5] and to grant protection to unpatentable subject matter through state statutes.[6] Lower courts have followed suit.[7] While the state of preemption doctrine is currently in flux, the historical role of preemption as a form of competition policy should not be ignored. Consequently, to limit competition law solely to antitrust law would overlook the intricate way in which competitive limits on intellectual property rights have been structured in the United States.

Secondly, the United States experience has been built on the misconception that intellectual property law can be separated from competition law. This misconception has appeared in many recent judicial opinions on the scope of antitrust liability for intellectual property management.[8] Although the roots of the separation principle cannot fully be explored here, one source is certainly the perspective of certain theorists in law and economics on the role of property rights in resolving the externality problem.[9] Externalities arise when one person's use of a resource affects another's use. In other words, there are interdependencies among people that may not be properly valued through market decisions. A solution to the externality problem, associated with Ronald Coase, is to define property rights in order to establish entitlements over the resource.[10] Once these entitlements are established, the externality can be properly valued and internalized through market transactions.

One example of the externality problem is the revelation problem in intellectual property.[11] If I have a new invention, my telling someone the elements of my invention without clear property rights over the invention allows anyone who learns of my disclosure to potentially use the invention. Intellectual property law,

---

[4] *See, e.g.*, Mark Lemley, *Beyond Preemption: The Law and Policy of Intellectual Property Licensing*, 87 CAL. L. REV. 111, 136–150 (1999) (describing the preemption doctrine and analyzing its limits).

[5] Brulotte v. Thys Co., 379 U.S. 29 (1964).

[6] Sears, Roebuck & Co. v. Stiffel, Co., 376 U.S. 225 (1964); Compco Corp. v. Day-Brite Lighting, Inc., 376 U.S. 234 (1964); Bonito Boats, Inc. v. Thunder Craft Boats, Inc., 489 U.S. 141 (1989).

[7] The most recent, and perhaps most controversial, example of how lower courts analyze preemption is Bowers v. Baystate Techs., Inc., 320 F.3d 116 (Fed. Cir. 2003) (holding that a contractual provision that limited reverse engineering was not preempted).

[8] *In re* Indep. Serv. Org. Antitrust Litig., 203 F.3d 1322 (Fed. Cir. 2000).

[9] For an overview of these issues, see ROBERT COOTER & THOMAS ULEN, LAW AND ECONOMICS 40–42 (2000).

[10] *See* Ronald H. Coase, *The Problem of Social Cost*, 3 J.L. & ECON. 1 (1960).

[11] See Kenneth J. Arrow, *Economic Welfare and the Allocation of Resources for Inventions*, in THE RATE AND DIRECTION OF INVENTIVE ACTIVITY 625 (R. R. Nelson ed., 1962).

through trade secret and patent laws, permit resolution of this revelation problem. If I have exclusive rights to use the invention, then I can feel comfortable in disclosing it to third parties without fear that it can be appropriated by someone else. Defining the rights allows me to capture the returns from the invention and therefore aids in the creation of a market for the invention.

An unexamined assumption of the property rights theory is that once property rights are defined, markets will work to allocate resources efficiently. However, the determination of property rights may shape the structure of the market. For example, property rights weakened through compulsory licensing will produce a different market structure from a strong property rights system with no compulsory licensing. To take a more subtle example, Coase in an important, but often ignored, 1972 article pointed out that a monopolist supplying a durable good, that is, a product that is consumed over time rather than immediately, will have incentives to charge a price very close to the competitive level.[12] As I explain in this comment, this "Coase Conjecture" implies that the way in which intellectual property rights are defined can affect how markets are structured. In other words, the separability assumption is at best misleading and at worst incorrect.

In this comment, I discuss the ways in which intellectual property and competition law can be better aligned in order to promote dynamic, growing, and competitive markets. Clarifying the relationship between intellectual property and competition law is not simply a good idea, it is also a necessity in regulating and structuring the global commons. Fleshing out this good idea requires an examination of developed countries' experiences with intellectual property and competition law. From these experiences we can determine appropriate competitive baselines for intellectual property systems.

I structure my analysis as follows. In the next section, I examine the fallacy of separability and demonstrate the need for establishing competitive baselines for intellectual property systems. In section three, I illustrate these possible baselines from the experience of the United States. In section four, I discuss the recently enacted Indian Competition Bill as an example of how one developing country has addressed competition policy post-TRIPS. Section five summarizes and concludes.

II. The inseparability of intellectual property rights and competition policy

This section addresses the separability assumption that often appears in the discussion of the relationship between intellectual property and competition law. I do not present a detailed analysis of the roots of this assumption nor its pervasiveness. It suffices for my argument that the assumption does exist and arises in important legal contexts.

---

[12] *See* Ronald H. Coase, *Durability and Monopoly*, 15 J.L. & ECON. 143 (1972).

The most salient example of the separability assumption is provided by the Federal Circuit, which stated in the *Xerox* case:

> [A] patent owner who brings suit to enforce the statutory right to exclude others from making, using, or selling the claimed invention is exempt from the antitrust laws, even though such a suit may have an anticompetitive effect, unless the infringement defendant proves one of two conditions.[13]

The two conditions are a showing either of fraud in gaining protection from the patent office or of sham litigation. The court quoted similar language about copyrights:

> [T]he limited copyright monopoly is based on Congress' empirical assumption that the right to "exclude others from using their works creates a system of incentives that promotes consumer welfare in the long term by encouraging investment in the creation of desirable artistic and functional works of expression .... We cannot require antitrust defendants to prove and reprove the merits of this legislative assumption in every case where a refusal to license a copyrighted work comes under attack."[14]

The two quotations together present a clear picture of the relationship between intellectual property and antitrust in United States jurisprudence. The systems of property rights created by the patent and copyright laws are antecedent to antitrust and represent a balance of incentives designed to increase consumer welfare from innovation. Antitrust law should rarely upset this balance, and the use of antitrust, and presumptively competition law more broadly, should occur with caution.

The separability assumption can be grounded in the theory of externalities, with deep and rich roots both in economic theory and jurisprudence. Inventive activities create externalities. New inventions and new expressions provide benefits to society that are arguably greater than the benefits to the creator. These external benefits are often described as a difference between the social rate of return from innovation and the private rate of return. In a significant study in the 1970s, Professor Edwin Mansfield, in joint work with several other economists, estimated the social and private rates of return from innovation in several sectors and found a significant difference between the two.[15] The study presented an estimated average social rate of return of 56 percent and an estimated average private rate of return of 25 percent.[16] The authors are cautious in drawing policy implications from this study, but their estimates

---

[13] 203 F.3d at 1326.
[14] *Id.* at 1328–1329 (citing *Data General Corp. v. Grumann System Support Corp.*, 36. F.2d 1147 (1994)).
[15] *See* Edwin Mansfield et al., *Social and Private Rates of Return from Industrial Innovations*, 91 Q.J. ECON. 221 (1977).
[16] *Id.* at 234.

are consistent with the theoretical prediction that externalities arise in the process of innovation.

Economists and legal policymakers respond to the existence of externalities through some form of regulation. The regulation may take the form of a subsidy that permits the private investor to obtain a greater rate of return on his investment in innovation. We see examples of this type of regulation in government grants and tax breaks for research and development. Another approach is to allocate property rights so that the externality is internalized, a goal facilitated by intellectual property laws. By granting to the inventor or author an exclusive right to use the invention or work of authorship, intellectual property law allows the inventor or author to appropriate the social rate of return. Ideally, this appropriation will equalize private and social rates of return, internalizing the externality by allowing the intellectual property owner to capture the social return as private return.

When the Federal Circuit refers to Congress' empirical assumption, it is referring to the problem of externalities and specifically to the property-rights solution. The externality theory provides a justification for intellectual property rights. Notice that this discussion did not refer to competition law at all. The implicit assumption is that once intellectual property law internalizes the externalities associated with innovation, the market will work to allocate properly the fruits of innovation. While this market might be contaminated by anticompetitive practices, antitrust law can combat those practices without upsetting the balance provided by intellectual property law. Antitrust law should intervene to upset the balance only when the intellectual property right was obtained fraudulently or is being used in an illegitimate manner not related to the protection of property rights.

While I did not make reference to competition law in the summary of the externality argument, implicit in the discussion was an understanding of how markets are structured. The property-rights solution to the innovation externality problem rests on the assumption that the property-right owner can capture all the social returns to innovation, which equalizes private and social return. Whether this equalization will occur either in theory or in fact rests on the market structure. If the market in which the fruit of innovation is exchanged remains competitive, the owner may capture very little of the social return. The market may be one in which there are several available substitutes for the innovation or it may be easy to invent around the innovation, which conditions make the costs of entry into the market relatively low.[17] With such ease of entry, competitive rents will be dissipated, the innovation may disseminate into the market place, and the owner may capture very little of the social return.

---

[17] *Id.* at 233.

Professor Mansfield and his co-authors described the problem as follows:

> If the innovator is faced with a highly competitive environment, it is less likely that it will be able to appropriate a large proportion of the social benefits than if it has a secure monopoly position or it is part of a tight oligopoly. Of course, the extent to which an innovator is subjected to competition, and how rapidly, may depend upon whether the innovation is patented.[18]

The authors also refer to the ease of inventing around the patent as a factor in determining the differential between social and private rates of return.

The broader point is that the solution to the externality problem is not solely a question of property rights, but also one of market structure. The two must be considered together if the goal is to equalize private and social rates of return from innovation.

Professor Mansfield's analysis, however, seemingly implies that competition law, by promoting competition, may in fact undermine the goals of intellectual property law. In other words, limits on competition are needed for intellectual property to be effective, which supports a claim for an exemption for intellectual property from competition law, including antitrust. Such a conclusion would also be supported by the Schumpeterian hypothesis, which predicts that innovation will be the greatest in highly concentrated, monopolized industries.[19] The support for creating an exception, however, is far from clear for two reasons.

First, if intellectual property is exempted from competition law, the question still remains as to how social and private rates of return are to be equalized. The property-based solution is implemented by the definition of rights, through a combination of legislative and judicial processes, which serve to define the scope of intellectual property rights. If property rights are designed without consideration of competition policy, there is the risk that we may overshoot and define rights in ways that make private rates of return greater than social rates of return.

Further, excessive concentration in the marketplace can serve as the basis for excessive concentration in the legislative process. Jessica Litman and other scholars have pointed to the capture of copyright legislation and intellectual property legislation more broadly by industry interests that support strong intellectual property protection.[20] Protection would exceed the social optimum if it led to private rates of return being greater than social rates. In other words, there may be too much innovation.

---

[18] *Id.* at 235.
[19] For a discussion of Schumpeter's theory of innovation, see MORTON I. KAMIEN & NANCY L. SCHWARTZ, MARKET STRUCTURE AND INNOVATION 8 (1982) ("The main theme of Schumpeter's theory is that in the conflict between entrepreneurial activity and perfect competition, the latter should be sacrificed.").
[20] *See* JESSICA LITMAN, DIGITAL COPYRIGHT (2001).

While the connection between economic power and political power is a complex one, the argument exists that economic concentration can support the type of capture described by Professor Litman. Revisions to copyright law in the twentieth century were undertaken largely through the influence of the recording and motion picture industries, both of which relied on copyrighted content as a major input.[21] The influence of copyright industries is also apparent in the recent expansion of digital copyright and the use of access and copy controls to supplement existing property rights under traditional copyright.[22] The potentially anti-competitive effects of copyright law are made apparent by the exemptions that were created from copyright protection for the first-sale doctrine and new technologies, such as the player piano at the turn of the twentieth century. Each exemption from copyright protection has created new markets and industries, whether it is video cassette rentals or photocopying services.[23] The history of copyright legislation supports the proposition that legal property rights do not simply promote the growth of industry, but may often result from industry pressures.[24] Competition policy, by limiting the degree of concentration, can serve to cure the problem of overshooting and excessive innovation.

Second, even if there is no industry capture, we need to be careful about how our definition of property rights affects market structure. For example, an intellectual property law that limits infringement to literal infringement with no basis for a doctrine of equivalents in patent law, or for a derivative works right in copyright law, would have a readily predictable effect on the structure of the market. Holding all else constant, such a regime would lower barriers to entry and support a more competitive environment for the development and dissemination of the fruits of innovation. Obviously, broader definitions of infringement will create a different market structure. At this point, I am not advocating one regime over the other. I am simply pointing out the difficulty in separating property-rights definitions from determinations of market structure.

There is, however, a richer theory underlying my discussion. Part of this theory has its pedigree in the important, and controversial, piece by Stephen Breyer questioning the need for copyright law.[25] The theory I am advocating also has its foundation in the work of Ronald Coase on durable-goods monopoly.[26] Although the work of Breyer is well known in intellectual property

---

[21] *Id.* at 51–53.   [22] *Id.* at 122–154.   [23] *Id.* at 106–107.

[24] For an insightful theoretical discussion of the implications of property rights created by rent seeking for a Coasean analysis of law, see Chul Ho Jung, et al., "The Coase Theorem in a Rent-Seeking Society", *International Review of Law and Economics*, vol. 15, No. 4 (September 1995), pp. 259–68.

[25] *See* Stephen Breyer, *The Uneasy Case for Copyright: A Study of Copyright in Books, Photocopies, and Computer Programs*, 84 HARV. L. REV. 281 (1970).

[26] *See* Coase, above n. 12.

circles, Coase's theory of durable-goods monopoly is less well known. There are, however, connections with Breyer's ideas.

Justice Breyer's famous case against copyright law rested on the first-mover advantage of the creator. Since the creator, by definition, will be the first to market a new product, the lead time will allow her to capture market rents that will compensate her efforts. The equally famous criticism of this argument demonstrated that, in many industries, this lead-time advantage would be rather small given the competitive pressures to imitate and otherwise enter the market.[27] As one scholar described the current understanding of the role of lead-time advantage:

> Laws of intellectual property, including trade secret and unfair competition law, may not have evolved sufficiently to reward innovators whose inventions have short market lives. Whether head-starts in bringing such products to market provide adequate profits is a significant question, especially when existing intellectual property protections for innovations slow in developing but long-lasting in economic impact, the sort the patent system best protects, have proven inadequate.[28]

The effectiveness of intellectual property protection depends upon the structure of the market for the fruits of intellectual property. Justice Breyer's argument rested on imperfections in the market that made it difficult for competitors and new entrants to imitate the innovator. Intellectual property law rests on the premises of creating a lead time by giving the property owner an exclusive right to use the innovation.

The Coase Conjecture on durable-goods monopoly suggests that even the exclusive rights conferred by intellectual property law may not be enough to ensure an advantage. If a seller has exclusive rights in a market for a durable good, price competition will lead to a perfectly competitive result. In other words, according to Coase, a monopolized market for a durable good will result in all rents being dissipated. This counterintuitive result rests on one simple observation: whenever a seller of a durable good manufactures and sells his product, he is creating a substitute that will compete with his own product in the resale market. The competitive pressure from the resale market will force the price of a durable product to be driven down to competitive levels. In other words, a monopolist will provide a durable good efficiently without the usual deadweight loss in a monopolized market for a non-durable good.

---

[27] See Barry Terman, *The Economic Rationale for Copyright Protection for Published Books: A Reply to Professor Breyer*, 18 U.C.L.A. L. REV. 1100 (1971).

[28] See Mark Kelman, *Could Lawyers Stop Recessions? Reflections on Law and Macroeconomics*, 45 STAN. L. REV. 1215, 1283 (1993).

The Coase Conjecture, however, holds true, if at all, only when the monopolist controls the allocation of the good through price.[29] If the monopolist can price discriminate or product differentiate, then the allocation will not be efficient. In fact, the Coase Conjecture supports the prediction that in the case of a durable good, a monopolist will market the product in ways that reduce its durability and through mechanisms that facilitate price discrimination.[30]

The implication of this result is that the exclusive seller of a durable product will not compete solely on price. Instead, he will try to differentiate his product, work to lessen the life of a product, and distribute the product through leases that restrict resale rather than direct sales. The relevance of the Coase Conjecture to intellectual property and competition law becomes apparent when one recognizes that many of the products protected through intellectual property, such as movies, books, machines, and production processes, are durable and that intellectual property rights can create at least localized monopolies over them. The Coase Conjecture also implies that an intellectual property owner will use his property right to market products in ways that limit potential competition.[31]

The Coase theory highlights the heart of Justice Breyer's critique of copyright law. According to Justice Breyer, copyright law is unnecessary because the barriers to entry through imitation are high. The high barriers to entry limit competition and allow the innovator to obtain rents. In short, limits on competition aid the intellectual property owner. The Coase Conjecture demonstrates that the intellectual property owner himself has incentives to compete not solely on price, but on other dimensions that limit competition. While intellectual property law does aid in resolving the externality problems associated with innovation, the structure of intellectual property rights also affects the organization of markets and competition. In short, the separability

---

[29] For analyses of the Coase Conjecture and implications for the structure of markets, *see* Michael Waldman, *Durable Goods Pricing When Quality Matters*, 69 J. BUS. 489 (1996) (demonstrating the effects of price and quality competition); Mark Bagnoli et al., *Durable-Goods Monopoly with Discrete Demand*, 97 J. POL. ECON. 1459 (1989) (demonstrating that the Coase Conjecture depends on assumption that there are an infinite number of consumers and that the conjecture is false if there are a discrete number of consumers); Nils-Henrik Morch von der Fehr & Kai-Uwe Kuhn, *Coase versus Pacman: Who Eats Whom in the Durable-Goods Monopoly?*, 103 J. POL. ECON. 785 (1995) (expanding the work of Bagnoli et al.); Marc Dudley, *On the Foundations of Dynamic Monopoly Theory*, 103 J. POL. ECON. 893 (1995) (showing the results of Bagnoli et al. to be a special case of a general model in which the conjecture holds true).

[30] *See* Michael J. Meurer, *Copyright Law and Price Discrimination*, 23 Cardozo L. REV. 55 (2001).

[31] *See* Jeremy Bulow, *An Economic Theory of Planned Obsolescence*, 101 Q.J. ECON. 729 (1986) (demonstrating how the Coase Conjecture highlights the incentives a firm may have to limit the durability of a product). *Cf.* Arthur Fishman et al., *Planned Obsolescence as an Engine of Technological Progress*, 41 J. INDUS. ECON. 361 (1993) (demonstrating how planned obsolescence may be necessary for technological progress).

assumption that the Federal Circuit exhibited in the *Xerox* decision should be seriously questioned.

Once the separability assumption is relaxed, the problem arises of how to reconcile intellectual property and competition law. I frame this problem in terms of establishing appropriate competitive baselines for intellectual property systems. The next section focuses squarely on how to conceptualize these baselines.

III. Baselines for intellectual property systems

Many countries are rethinking their intellectual property and competition laws in light of TRIPS. In Section IV, I focus on the specific case of India. In this section, I present the problem of how to address the relationship between intellectual property and competition law once the separability assumption is relaxed. Two issues are discussed: the choice between rules and standards, and the choice of the appropriate baseline for intellectual property systems.

Rules versus standards. The choice between *per se* rules and rule of reason has been central to the debate over the application of Section One and Section Two claims in United States antitrust law.[32] While the early terms of this debate were framed around choices between a common-law standard and literal interpretation of the language of the Sherman Act, the contemporary debate is about institutional competence and expectations of actors in the marketplace.[33] The adoption of competition law in developing countries should take its cue from the modern institutional and economic debates.

The case for *per se* rules may seem strong for developing countries. The strength of the case may rest on the scarcity of judicial competence in handling the mass of economic and other data needed for the application of the rule of reason. However, an emphasis on weak institutional competence is misplaced. The real questions are what rules are appropriate and how they are to be devised and implemented.

In some ways, the demarcation between *per se* rules and rule of reason is far from clear. The case law on characterization of agreements in the United States is an example. While one bright-line rule in antitrust law is the *per se* illegality of price fixing and horizontal territorial divisions, it is far from clear when an agreement is about price or territory.[34] Similarly, while the merger guidelines offer a rule-like approach to ascertain when excessive market power warrants scrutiny, the determination of market definition and the calculation of

---

[32] Section One of the Sherman Act prohibits agreements among competitors in an industry that restrict trade. Section Two of the Sherman Act prohibits acts by a large firm in a given industry that monopolize or have a tendency to monopolize a market.

[33] *See, e.g.*, Thomas C. Arthur, *A Workable Rule of Reason: A Less Ambitious Role for the Federal Courts*, 68 ANTITRUST L.J. 337 (2000).

[34] *See, e.g.*, Broad. Music, Inc. v. Columbia Broad. Sys., Inc., 441 U.S. 1 (1979) (a famous case raising the issue of characterization).

numerical market-concentration indexes require fact-intensive and statistical inquiry, arguably as extensive and as demanding as that required for a rule of reason analysis.[35] Competition law itself is a fact-intensive, contextual inquiry, and the designers of the law must think in terms of the nature of the industry and the marketplace to which the law will be applied.

The real question is one of the architecture of competition law. *Per se* rules may be appropriate if enough thought and analysis has taken place in the creation of the rules. Similarly, contextual standards may be equally appropriate if institutional actors, namely, agencies, judges, and lawyers, are competent in the articulation of the standards.

The tradeoff is among political, legal, and economic processes. In the absence of law and politics, economic processes will determine the structure of competition as established firms rise to dominance in the market and expectations become settled. The creation of law will upset and rearrange existing expectations and market structures. The shift in expectations will in turn translate into political reshaping of the law through legal reform. The choice of rules versus standards rests on which of these three institutional arrangements are most trustworthy and competent in supporting the goals of competition and intellectual property law.

The U.S. experience offers some guidance concerning how these institutional players have shifted over time. Early U.S. antitrust law was judge-made law. In fact, some scholars refer to a constitutional antitrust law to suggest that the dynamic of legal development rested on judges interpreting text, provided by the Sherman Act in the case of antitrust law.[36] Some of the problems with the early common law of antitrust were fixed by judges themselves through the development of the rule of reason and notions of market power.[37]

The problems were also addressed legislatively through the passage of the Clayton Act, which established more structure and rule-like precision to the open-ended Sherman Act, and through the creation of agencies, such as the Federal Trade Commission (FTC). During the Great Depression, attention shifted from the courts to the legislature, particularly state legislatures, with the passage of fair-pricing statutes, the development of the state-action doctrine, and the expansion of the regulatory state that often bumped up against antitrust law.

During the New Deal, the United States also saw the development of an administrative antitrust law with the recognition of the enforcement powers of

---

[35] U.S. Dept. of Justice and FTC Joint Horizontal Merger Guidelines (1992).
[36] *See, e.g.*, Thomas C. Arthur, *Farewell to the Sea of Doubt: Jettisoning the Constitutional Sherman Act*, 74 CAL. L. REV. 263–375 (1986); William F. Baxter, *Separation of Powers, Prosecutorial Discretion, and the "Common Law" Nature of Antitrust Law*, 60 TEX. L. REV. 661–703 (1982).
[37] *See, e.g.*, United States v. Addyston Pipe & Steel Co., 85 F. 271 (6th Cir. 1898); Standard Oil Co. of New Jersey. v. United States, 221 U.S. 1 (1911).

the FTC in the important case of *Fashion Originators' Guild*.[38] After the Second World War, there was a return to the importance of the courts in fashioning the demarcation between *per se* rules and the rule of reason and in attempting to identify problems of market power. The 1980s and 1990s witnessed the development of a strong and important administrative antitrust law, with the implementation of the merger guidelines and other guidelines jointly drafted by the Department of Justice (DOJ) and the FTC. The development of the quick-look rule of reason also facilitated the expansion of the role of administrative agencies, an expansion that arguably has been capped by the Supreme Court's recent decision in *California Dental*.[39] In short, the debate between rules and standards is largely one of institutional competence and balance that has shifted over time.

The real lesson for implementing competition law in developing countries is the importance of care in designing the political, legal, and market institutions that enliven the choice among types of legal regimes. It is simplistic to say that *per se* rules are the only option for a developing country's initial attempts at competition law. The focus should be on creating the necessary institutional infrastructure that allows competition law to function. That is the lesson to be gathered from the developed country experience.

Which competitive baselines? The architecture of competition law may have many foundations, and the difficulty is choosing basic premises that reflect the goals of the developing country and allow for flexibility as those goals and needs change. Based upon the United States experience, there are three possible baselines: a populist approach, a structural approach, and a conduct-based approach. Countries should think through which of these approaches, either alone or in combination, is most suitable.

The populist baseline dovetails with the early history of U.S. antitrust law and with the early checks on monarchical power under the Statute of Monopolies.[40] A populist baseline is largely a political one, emphasizing competition law's role in preserving democratic institutions through checking the concentration of wealth. In developing countries, such a baseline would be appropriate particularly as a potential check on multinational corporations and dominance among domestic industries.[41] The dangers are that an implicitly political approach to antitrust may undermine the institutional legitimacy

---

[38] Fashion Originators' Guild of Am. v. Fed. Trade Comm'n, 312 U.S. 457 (1941).
[39] Cal. Dental Ass'n v. Fed. Trade Comm'n, 526 U.S. 756 (1999).
[40] *See* William L. Letwin, *The English Common Law Concerning Monopolies*, 21 U. CHI. L. REV. 355 (1954).
[41] For a discussion of the uses of competition law in South Africa and Indonesia to combat discrimination and aid small businesses, see Eleanor M. Fox, *Equality, Discrimination, and Competition Law: Lessons from and for South Africa and Indonesia*, 41 HARV. INT'L L.J. 579 (2000).

of courts and may be antithetical to the objectives of economic growth and competitiveness.[42]

The structuralist baseline, like the populist baseline, challenges bigness of business organizations but rests on economic rather than political grounds. Having its greatest influence on merger analysis, the structuralist approach, rooted in the structure-conduct-performance paradigm from the industrial organization literature, turns on the normative ideal of either a perfectly competitive market or an oligopolistic market structure.[43] Legal rules are designed to correct departures from these ideal market structures. With its economic emphasis, this approach supports growth-oriented policies, if appropriately applied.

The problem is identifying: (i) the ideal market structure to employ as a competitive baseline; (ii) realities of the marketplace that may not be fully captured by the models, such as problems of information or market formation; and (iii) the connections between market structure and growth. In many instances, departures from the competitive or oligopolistic model may be necessary for innovation and growth.[44]

Finally, the conduct baseline, while also premised on economic theory, cures many of the problems with the structuralist baseline. Rooted in institutional and transaction costs economics and enriched by game theory, the conduct baseline is used to identify and remedy anticompetitive conduct rather than to cure defects in market structure.

Two problems arise from applying a pure conduct baseline to the developing world. First, such a baseline has had the greatest application in more mature economies, particularly those involving services or intangible assets.[45] To the extent that antitrust law is being designed for a largely manufacturing based economy, the pure conduct approach may not prove as effective as a structuralist approach. Second, a pure conduct baseline implies a tort-like approach to antitrust law, with the sundry problems that a fact-intensive, context-specific tort approach may entail for a court or administrative system.

The experience of the developed countries with these various baselines offers three lessons and several implications for the implementation of competition law in the developing world. The first lesson is the distinction between monopoly and market power. The exclusivity provided by intellectual property rights does not translate necessarily into the kind of market power that is suspect under competition law. While intellectual property law creates certain status-based relationships, competition law is pitched to regulate conduct. The challenge lies in identifying the conduct to be condemned and in reconciling

---

[42] See Robert Pitofsky, *The Political Content of Antitrust*, 127 U. PA. L. REV. 1051 (1979).
[43] See F. M. SCHERER & DAVID ROSS, INDUSTRIAL MARKET STRUCTURE AND ECONOMIC PERFORMANCE 18–19 (1990).
[44] See KAMIEN & SCHWARTZ, above n. 19.
[45] See, e.g., Eastman Kodak Co. v. Image Technical Servs., Inc., 504 U.S. 451 (1992) (for an example of the conduct approach).

the rights granted to the intellectual property holder with the norms and regulations of competition law.

The second lesson requires local authorities to recognize the role that intellectual property and competition law together play in shaping and defining the contours of markets and other institutions. Although the textbook model of perfect competition posits an ideal type of market relations, actual market institutions vary, which reflects differences in culture, the nature of the product or service being distributed, and the institutional arrangements of consumption, production, and distribution. Consequently, intellectual property law and competition law need to reflect these actual institutions.

Finally, both intellectual property and competition policy are informed by democratic theory. Access and progress are at the heart of intellectual property law, and competition policy has developed as responses to concentration in wealth and political power. The democratic values of the two areas of law should also help to shape both intellectual property law and competition policy as they are developed together.

Several implications flow from these three lessons. First, intellectual property doctrine should be designed to limit the possibility of creating anti-competitive bottlenecks.[46] The scope of protected subject matter, fair use (and other limitations on exclusive rights), and use of compulsory licensing should reflect these concerns. Second, competition law should focus on licensing and other practices that entail the abuse of a dominant position or the possibility of overreaching absent the existence of actual market power.[47] Third, market definition should be at the forefront of intellectual property law as much as it has been at the forefront of competition law. Market definition, while based on technical analyses of supply and demand functions, should also reflect institutional realities, such as local custom and usage. Finally, the development of joint ventures, research consortia, and standard-setting organizations should be encouraged, while careful scrutiny should be applied to them under competition laws.[48]

IV. The Architecture of TRIPS and the Indian Competition Bill

The rights of TRIPS signatories to enact competition law in accord with the protection of intellectual property rights holders were at issue in the Doha

---

[46] *See, e.g.*, Arti K. Rai, *Fostering Cumulative Innovation in the Biopharmaceutical Industry: The Role of Patents and Antitrust*, 16 BERKELEY TECH. L. J. 813 (2001). *See also* Arti K. Rai, *Proprietary Rights and Collective Action: The Case of Biotechnology Research with Low Commercial Value* [this volume].

[47] *See, e.g.*, Mark R. Patterson, *The Market Power Requirement in Antitrust Rule of Reason Cases: A Rhetorical History*, 37 SAN DIEGO L. REV. 1 (2000).

[48] *See, e.g.*, Mark A. Lemley, *Intellectual Property Rights and Standard-Setting Organizations*, 90 CAL. L. REV. 1889 (2002).

Ministerial Declaration adopted on 14 November 2001.[49] The then-pending South African lawsuit against Glaxo, challenging the company's pricing policies for AIDS drugs as an abuse of a dominant position, and the recent enactment of a new competition bill in India, are just two salient examples of the ongoing legal debate. In this section, I briefly note the balance between intellectual property and competition law under TRIPS and discuss features of the new Indian bill in light of this balance.

A. The TRIPS balance

While the TRIPS Agreement provides the substantive minimum level of protection that each WTO member must grant to intellectual property holders, it also allows members to limit intellectual property rights through competition law and policy, directly under articles 8.2 and 40, and indirectly under articles 6, 31, 13 and 30.[50] The opportunities available to developing countries under articles 8.2 and 40, which directly apply to competition law as such, have been amply explained by other contributors to this section.[51] I will concentrate on the possibilities inherent in other provisions that implicate aspects of competition policy.

Articles 6 and 31: Exhaustion and compulsory licensing

Parallel importation and compulsory licensing are two other areas – besides abuse and limits on licensing – that implicate limitations on intellectual property rooted in competition policy. Parallel importation creates competition for domestic intellectual property owners from foreign sales of patented or copyrighted products. The legality of parallel importation rests on the scope of the principle of exhaustion. If the first-sale doctrine applies to foreign as well as domestic sales, then parallel importation will be permitted.

Article 6 states that, in the context of dispute settlement and limited by the principles of national treatment and most-favored nation treatment, "nothing in [TRIPS] shall be used to address the issue of the exhaustion of intellectual property rights."[52] While the meaning of this provision is far from clear, a liberal interpretation that would provide a broad grant of authority to

---

[49] TRIPS Agreement, above n. 3, arts. 8.2, 40; WTO Fourth Ministerial Conference (Doha), Ministerial Declaration, WT/MIN(01)/Dec/1 (14 Nov. 2001) *available at* http://www.wto.org.
[50] *See id.*, arts. 6, 8, 13, 30, 31, 40.
[51] *Id.*, arts. 8.2, 40. *See, e.g.*, Joseph Drexl, *The Critical Role of Competition Law in Preserving Public Goods in Conflict with Intellectual Property Rights* [this volume]; Hanns Ullrich, *Expansionist Intellectual Property Protection and Reductionist Competition Rules: A TRIPS Perspective* [this volume]; Mark D. Janis, *"Minimal" Standards for the Patent-Related Antitrust Law under TRIPS* [this volume].
[52] TRIPS Agreement, above n. 3, art. 6.

WTO Members in applying the doctrine of exhaustion was confirmed by the Doha Declaration on TRIPS and Public Health.[53]

Compulsory licensing is a controversial remedy under United States antitrust law,[54] and it has been a source of debate about the manner in which member states may fashion their patent and copyright laws.[55] Article 31 sets out the procedural and substantive limitations on compulsory licensing.[56] The provision describes procedural protections that must be granted to the intellectual property holder and certain substantive prerequisites for the use of compulsory licensing. As is well documented, the scope of compulsory licensing lies at the heart of the debate over patent protection for pharmaceuticals in developing countries.[57]

Articles 13 and 30: Limitations on rights.

Any limitations imposed by Members on intellectual property rights must meet the requirements of articles 13 and 30.[58] For limitations on copyrights, article 13 states that they must be confined "to certain special cases which do not conflict with a normal exploitation of the work and do not unreasonably prejudice the legitimate interests of the right holder."[59] In the context of patents, article 30 also confines limitations to those that do not conflict with normal exploitation and do not unreasonably prejudice the legitimate interests of the right holder, "taking into account the legitimate interests of third parties."[60]

---

[53] WTO Ministerial Conference, Declaration on the TRIPS Agreement and Public Health, WT/MIN(01)/DEC/W/2(14), (Nov. 2001); *see also* Keith E. Maskus, *Parallel Imports*, 23 WORLD ECON. GLOBAL TRADE POL'Y 2000, 1269–84 (finding the provision in Article 6 to be broad in scope and commenting on the economics of parallel imports).

[54] *See, e.g.*, J. H. Reichman with Catherine Hasenzahl, Non-Voluntary Licensing of Patented Inventions, Part I, Historical Perspective, Legal Framework under TRIPS and an Overview of the Practice in Canada and the United States (UNCTAD/ITCSD 2002); *id.*, Part III, The Law and Practice of the United States (Draft, UNCTAD/ITCSD 2003).

[55] *See, e.g.*, Thomas A. Haag, *TRIPS Since Doha: How Far Will the WTO Go Toward Modifying the Term for Compulsory Licenses?*, 84 J. PAT. & TRADEMARK OFF. SOC'Y 944 (2002); John M. Taladay & James N. Carlin, Jr., *Compulsory Licensing of Intellectual Property Under the Competition Laws of the United States and the European Community*, 10 GEO. MASON L. REV. 443 (2002).

[56] TRIPS Agreement, above n. 3, art 31.

[57] *See, e.g.*, Frederick M. Abbott, *Managing the Hydra: The Herculean Task of Ensuring Access to Essential Medicines* [this volume].

[58] TRIPS Agreement, above n. 3, arts. 13, 30.

[59] *Id.* art. 13; *see* Ruth L. Okediji, *Sustainable Access to Copyrighted Digital Information Works in Developing Countries* [this volume].

[60] TRIPS Agreement, above n. 3, art. 30; *see* Graeme Dinwoodie & Rochelle Cooper Dreyfuss, *WTO Dispute Resolution and the Preservation of the Public Domain of Science under International Law* [this volume].

Actions sounding in competition policy that interfere with intellectual property rights must meet the standards of articles 13 and 30. Arguably, limitations on patents are more liberal than limitations on copyrights. Article 13 does not allow consideration of third party interests except to the extent they help to determine "normal exploitation" and "legitimate interests." Furthermore, article 13 speaks of "certain special cases," suggesting that the ambit of limitations on copyright is smaller than those on patents.

The potentially different treatment accorded copyrights and patents is exemplified by the two major WTO Dispute Settlement Panels interpreting articles 13 and 30, respectively. In the action brought against the United States for its copyright exemptions for use of publicly performed recorded music under Section 110(5) of its Copyright Act, the panel struck down a portion of the statute mainly because its copyright exemptions were not clearly defined and were not narrow in scope.[61] The panel in addition found a conflict with the normal exploitation of musical works and the legitimate interests of the copyright owners.

In contrast, the panel adopted a somewhat more liberal approach in the action brought against Canada for its limitations on the rights of patent holders of pharmaceuticals.[62] While the panel did strike down the portion of the Canadian law permitting stockpiling of generic drugs before expiration of the relevant patents, it carefully considered the interests of third parties in allowing reverse-engineering prior to expiry for purposes of regulatory approval. The following language from the opinion illustrates this concern:

> It was significant that Articles 8.2 and 40 acknowledged that Members could invoke measures to control the abuse of patent rights by curtailing ... the patent right for some or all of the remainder of its term of protection.... [A] *fortiori* similar measures, which did not conflict with a normal exploitation of the patent, could also be taken consistently with the Agreement to prevent the anti-competitive effects of the patent after its term of protection has expired.[63]

The language may support a broad grant of power to Members to limit patent rights and their anti-competitive effects to protect third party interests.

Two preliminary lessons can be drawn from this discussion of the architecture of TRIPS. First, competition law limits on patents may be more likely to survive a challenge than similar limits on copyrights.[64] Second, in the case of

---

[61] United States – Section 110(5) of the U.S. Copyright Act, WTO DSB Report, WT/DS160/R (15 June 2000).
[62] Canada – Patent Protection of Pharmaceutical Products, WTO Dispute Settlement Panel, WT/DS114/R (17 Mar. 2000).
[63] *Id.*
[64] But this may depend on the nature of the subject matter and the purpose of use. As regards educational uses, for example, see Okediji, above n. 59 (finding space for competition policy limits on exclusive rights of copyright law).

copyright law, the requirement that limitations be confined to "certain special cases" requires that Members develop competition law limits on copyrights on a case-by-case basis, which implies the use of rule of reason rather than a *per se* approach.

B. A look at the Indian Competition Bill

In December, 2002, the Indian Parliament enacted the Competition Bill of 2001.[65] The Bill repealed the Monopolies and Restrictive Trade Practices Act, India's first comprehensive competition law enacted in 1969. The goals of the Bill are to ensure fair competition and to permit competition in the global marketplace.

One of the hallmarks of the Bill is the dissolution of the Monopolies and Restrictive Trade Practices Commission, an independent prosecutorial agency, and its replacement with the Competition Commission of India, a quasi-judicial entity. The Bill also introduces a new statutory scheme based on conduct baselines rather than structuralist baselines. For example, the new scheme regulates abuses of dominant positions rather than dominant positions themselves. Furthermore, several *per se* categories are created, including price fixing, geographical divisions, and market divisions. More standards-like treatment is accorded to tying arrangements, refusals to deal, resale price maintenance, and exclusivity agreements, each of which becomes a basis for liability if "they cause an appreciable adverse effect on competition."

The Indian Competition Bill is nonetheless a disappointment for many reasons. First, Section 3(5) expressly removes intellectual property from the section prohibiting anti-competitive agreements. This express exemption means that challenges to the anti-competitive use of intellectual property rights would have to be brought under Section 4, which prohibits abuse of a dominant position. Section 4 defines abuse of a dominant position broadly to include: (i) unfair or discriminatory prices; (ii) restrictions on production or on technical and scientific development; (iii) practices that result in denial of market access; and (iv) tying and market leverage. While these limitations are potentially quite broad, the express exemption for intellectual property under Section 3(5) is troubling.

Finally, there is no discussion of exhaustion, parallel importation, or compulsory licensing.[66] The main conclusion to draw from these omissions is that the Indian Competition Bill illustrates an extremely cautious approach to

---

[65] Information about the Competition Bill can be obtained at the following website: http://dca.nic.in/comp_bill2k1.htm (last visited 1 Aug. 2004).

[66] For extensive comments on the Bill, particularly the failure to address parallel importation and compulsory licensing, see the articles from *Financial Express* by Pradeep S. Mehta & Ujjwal Kumar *available at* http://www.financialexpress.com (last visited 1 Aug. 2004).

drafting competition law post-TRIPS, and it is not a good model for a developing country that wants to test the limits of Articles 6, 8, 13, 30, 31, and 40.

Unfortunately, the new competition law regime in India mimics many aspects of the current U.S. antitrust regime. This demonstrates that the separability assumption remains influential.

V. Looking ahead

The TRIPS Agreement provides room for creative uses of competition law to check the potential imbalances that may arise in intellectual property systems. Competitive baselines for intellectual property systems can be developed in many ways: through competition law, through administrative agencies, through limits within intellectual property law itself (such as through a doctrine of misuse or fair use), or a combination of these and other means. Theoretical work on the interface between competition law and intellectual property law, as well as doctrinal and institutional experience from the developed world, should aid in the construction of these baselines. Nevertheless, the principal aim of this comment is to show that the developing world should avoid making the error of adopting the assumption of separability between intellectual property rights and competition law.

Several specific initiatives can help to achieve this broadly described goal. These initiatives are not intended to be exhaustive, and they are based upon the experience of the developed economies with systems of intellectual property and competition law. I divide the proposed initiatives into two categories: those that are internal to intellectual property law and those that are external.

Many aspects of intellectual property law regulate competition. Definitions of protectible subject matter, post-sale restrictions, and permitted uses of intellectual property all limit the rights owners' ability to control access to knowledge and entry into new markets. The design of intellectual property systems should be undertaken with conscious considerations of how limits internal to intellectual property law affect competition.[67]

Within copyright law, for example, the idea/expression distinction, judiciously applied, can better define the public domain and exclude critical information inputs, such as data, facts, and standards, from proprietary ownership. Within patent law, similar restrictions on ownership exist with respect to laws of nature, abstract ideas, and natural phenomena. Furthermore, patent administration and review of inventions for novelty and nonobviousness can help to prevent bottlenecks in industries by placing critical knowledge in the public domain.

---

[67] *Cf.* Peter Gerhart, *Distributive Values and Institutional Design in the Provision of Global Public Goods* [this volume].

Within both patent and copyright laws, limitations on post-sale restrictions, as implemented through the first-sale and exhaustion doctrines, can help to ensure competitive entry into markets without undermining incentives to innovate. These limitations can also help to further follow-on innovations. Doctrines such as fair use for reverse engineering in copyright law and experimental use in patent law are examples of how cumulative innovation can be fostered. Each of these initiatives internal to intellectual property law underscores the practical ways in which the pitfalls of the separability hypothesis can be avoided.

These internal initiatives should be supplemented by policies that are external to intellectual property law. The simple lesson is that competition policy, such as antitrust or unfair competition laws, should be designed with intellectual property in mind. Nevertheless, the problems of the separability hypothesis apply to other regulations that have a direct or indirect effect on competition. For example, drug regulation, while ostensibly directed to assuring drug safety and efficacy, affects the structure of pharmaceutical markets through the creation of entry barriers for generics. Consequently, drug regulation should be designed with intellectual property law and competitive effects in mind.

Similar lessons apply to international trade regulation, particularly rules pertaining to transfer of technology and to parallel importation.[68] Implementation of these external initiatives, in combination with the internal standards, is an important step in avoiding the fallacy of separability identified in this comment.

In thinking about these issues, we should not lose sight of the broader jurisprudential and historical problems. Designing the global commons in the information age is the most recent phase of a process, starting in the Enlightenment, of designing social, political, economic, and legal institutions that permit the channeling of private interests into public virtue.[69] The current state of the project is informed by developments in economic, social, and political theory that demonstrate the difficulties with purely laissez-faire or purely statist arrangements.

The challenge is to recognize the need for a mix of market, state, and other public and private institutions that facilitate the development and growth of an equitable and successful commons.[70] The developed countries' experiences

---

[68] *Cf.* Carlos M. Correa, *Can the TRIPS Agreement Foster Technology Transfer to Developing Countries?* [this volume].

[69] See ALBERT O. HIRSCHMAN, THE PASSIONS AND THE INTERESTS: POLITICAL ARGUMENTS FOR CAPITALISM BEFORE ITS TRIUMPH (1997).

[70] *Cf.* Peter Drahos, *The Regulation of Public Goods* [this volume]; Keith E. Maskus & Jerome H. Reichman, *The Globalization of Private Knowledge Goods and the Privatization of Global Public Goods* [this volume].

with competition law and intellectual property rights offer important insights to advance this understanding. But developing countries should not be restricted by this history, they should avoid its conceptual errors, and they should recognize the latitude given by the TRIPS Agreement to create intellectual property systems with responsive competitive baselines.

PART IV

Reform and regulation issues

SECTION 3
Dispute settlement at the WTO and intellectual property rights

31

WTO dispute settlement: Of sovereign interests, private rights and public goods

JOOST PAUWELYN*

I. The problem spelled out
II. The WTO is about private (mainly export) interests defended by governments
III. The nature of WTO obligations: Bundles of bilateral relations or collective obligations – contract or crime?
IV. Notes on the defense of public goods in the practice of WTO dispute settlement
V. Enhancing the role of public goods in the WTO dispute settlement process
VI. Conclusion

I. The problem spelled out

The focus of this section on intellectual property rights begs the larger question of whether the WTO mechanism to settle trade disputes between states[1] takes *sufficient* account of so-called "public goods" in general. It obliges us immediately to ask what public goods could be relevant in WTO disputes as a whole.

The very objective of trade liberalization, the *leitmotif* of the WTO, as well as its ancillary aim of protecting intellectual property (IP), as enshrined in the TRIPS Agreement,[2] could in their own right be seen as public goods. Their achievement is said to make everyone better off. Fewer trade restrictions result in a more efficient allocation of world resources and *more* IP protection spurs

---

* Joost Pauwelyn is Associate Professor of Law, Duke University School of Law. He formerly served with the Legal Affairs Division and Appellate Body Secretariat of the World Trade Organization (WTO), Geneva, Switzerland.
[1] *See* Understanding on Rules and Procedures Governing the Settlement of Disputes, Marrakesh Agreement Establishing the World Trade Organization, Annex 2, LEGAL INSTRUMENTS – RESULTS OF THE URUGUAY ROUND, 33 I.L.M. 1226 (1994) [hereinafter DSU].
[2] *See* Agreement on Trade-Related Aspects of Intellectual Property Rights, 15 Apr. 1994, Marrakesh Agreement Establishing the World Trade Organization, Annex 1C, LEGAL INSTRUMENTS – RESULTS OF THE URUGUAY ROUND vol. 31, 33 I.L.M. 81 (1994) [hereinafter TRIPS Agreement].

innovation and economic growth. Market forces – when it comes to freer trade, in particular domestic *political* markets – do not sufficiently provide these goods, hence the need for regulatory intervention (in the field of trade, intervention of a *negative* nature, prohibiting restrictions; in the IP field, intervention of a *positive* nature, prescribing minimum levels of protection) and the *public* nature of these goods.

WTO disputes may also touch upon other public goods, often portrayed as goods or objectives that clash with the primary WTO aims of trade liberalization and IP protection. Examples of such public goods are the protection of the environment, respect for human rights, sustainable development, and the transfer of technology and resources from developed to developing countries. Those objectives as well are of a public goods nature in that market forces alone may not supply them sufficiently.[3]

The two types of public goods just described are, of course, often in conflict, especially in the WTO dispute settlement process. One country challenges restrictions on its exports to another country in pursuit of the public good of freer trade. The other country explains that it imposed the trade restriction to protect dolphins[4] or endangered sea-turtles,[5] in pursuit of the public good of environmental protection.

Besides the question of whether *public goods* are sufficiently recognized in the WTO, another contrasting problem, which is raised increasingly, is whether WTO dispute settlement pays due respect to *private rights* or the individual interests of private economic operators or right holders who are, after all, the engine and main actors in the world trading system.[6] Are WTO rights sufficiently predictable and enforceable so that *private* economic operators can rely on them, or do WTO rights and obligations remain in the realm of international diplomacy guided as much by the sovereign interests of the day as by the rule of law?

The rest of this chapter will further assess this triangle of sovereign interests, private rights and public goods. Section II reminds us that, although trade is

---

[3] *See, e.g.*, Peter Drahos, *The Regulation of Public Goods* [this volume]; Carlos Correa, *Can the TRIPS Agreement Foster Technology Transfer to Developing Countries?* [this volume]; Gregory Shaffer, *Recognizing Public Goods in WTO Dispute Settlement: Who Participates? Who Decides?* [this volume]; Keith E. Maskus & Jerome H. Reichman, *The Globalization of Private Knowledge Goods and the Privatization of Global Public Goods* [this volume].

[4] *See* the so-called Tuna/Dolphin Dispute: United States – Restrictions on Imports of Tuna, DS 29/R, *circulated on* 10 June 1994 (not adopted), *available at* http://www.wto.org.

[5] *See* the so-called Shrimp/Turtle Dispute: United States – Import Prohibition of Certain Shrimp and Shrimp Products, WT/DS58/R and Appellate Body report, WT/DS58/AB/R, *adopted* 6 Nov. 1998, *available at* http://www.wto.org; *see also* the related Recourse to Article 21.5 of the DSU, above n. 1, by Malaysia, WT/DS58/RW and Panel and Appellate Body reports, WT/DS58/AB/RW, *adopted* 21 Nov. 2001.

[6] For a discussion, see the Panel Report on United States – Sections 301–310 of the Trade Act of 1974, complaint by the European Communities, WT/DS152/R, *adopted* 27 Jan. 2000 (no appeal).

largely a private enterprise, the WTO is run by governmental interests. Section III examines the nature, not of the WTO as an institution, but of WTO *obligations*. It posits that WTO obligations remain essentially of a bilateral/contract nature and are – unlike, for example, human rights obligations – not collective or of the *erga omnes partes* type. Against this background, Section IV offers some notes on how the above-mentioned public goods have fared in the WTO dispute settlement process. Section V offers some suggestions on how the system could be improved to give more prominence to these public goods. Section VI concludes.

II. The WTO is about private (mainly export) interests defended by governments

With a steadily declining public sector economy in most countries of the world, the lion share of trade activities are nowadays conducted by *private* economic operators. Yet, as an inter-governmental organization, the WTO is a gathering of *governments* promising each other, to varying degrees, not to intervene in the process of free trade. Although governments normally represent all sectors and interest groups of the country in question, it is fair to say that around the WTO table, governments have traditionally represented mainly *producer* interests, more particularly those of *exporters*. WTO negotiations are normally about obtaining market access for one's exports to other countries; market openings in one's own economy are referred to as "concessions."

When it comes to WTO disputes, this private operators/government representation dichotomy is translated as follows. In most cases, it will be private operators/exporters who see their trade restricted and who will want to remove certain trade impediments. However, since these private operators do not have direct standing before WTO bodies, they will have to lobby their national government to take their case to the international, state-to-state WTO level (with all the governmental discretion that comes with it).

It follows that, at the outset of a WTO complaint, one invariably finds an objection voiced by export interests in pursuit of the public good of trade liberalization or IP protection. Exporters are, in other words, the *demandeurs*, claimants or right holders in the WTO system. The other public goods, say, environmental protection, are never originating grounds of a WTO complaint (no WTO member can challenge another member for insufficient protection of the environment). Rather, these other public goods always take second stage[7] and enter into play only as part of a possible *defense* that a WTO member can invoke to *justify* its trade restriction.

---

[7] *Cf.* Laurence R. Helfer, *Regime Shifting: The TRIPS Agreement and New Dynamics of International Intellectual Property Lawmaking*, 29 YALE J. INT'L L. 1 (2004).

III. The nature of WTO obligations: Bundles of bilateral relations or collective obligations – contract or crime?[8]

In discussing the public goods nature of the WTO, it becomes crucial to ask whether WTO obligations can be reduced to bundles of bilateral obligations, comparable to the domestic law analogue of a contract, or whether we should construe WTO obligations as "collective" in nature, which would make them comparable to a domestic criminal law statute or even domestic constitutions.[9] The WTO Agreement is, obviously, a multilateral agreement. It will soon have 150 signatories. But what is the nature of WTO obligations? Are they of the bilateral (or reciprocal) type, in that WTO obligations can be reduced to a compilation of bilateral treaty relations, each of them detachable one from the other? Or are they of the multilateral (*erga omnes partes* or integral) type, in the sense that their binding effect is collective and the different relationships between WTO members cannot be separated into bilateral components?

This ambiguity concerning the nature of WTO obligations harbors major consequences for how we construe the WTO legal matrix. Classifying WTO obligations as bilateral/contractual in nature offers more scope for two WTO members to settle trade disputes between themselves, or to re-negotiate or modify their WTO contract (so long as they do not thereby change the rights or obligations of third parties). It highlights the "private" nature of the WTO in the sense of a compilation of bilateral contracts between two states (multi-lateralized subsequently under the WTO umbrella).

In contrast, treating WTO obligations as collective obligations – much like human rights obligations or national criminal or constitutional norms – would transform the WTO into a one-form-fits-all construct where all WTO members could complain about any breach of WTO law, no matter whether they were individually affected, and all WTO relations could only be altered by a consensus of all WTO members. This interpretation makes WTO law the world's trade "constitution,"[10] and increases the "public" nature of the

---

[8] This section is based on, and further elaborated in, Joost Pauwelyn, *A Typology of Multilateral Treaty Obligations: Are WTO Obligations Bilateral or Collective in Nature?*, 14 EUR. J. INT'L L. 907 (2003).

[9] The contract *versus* crime analogy is referred to in ROBERT Z. LAWRENCE, CRIMES AND PUNISHMENTS?; RETALIATION UNDER THE WTO (Institute for International Economics 2003). The contract versus statute paradigm is not new. *See, e.g.,* Paul Reuter, *Solidarité et divisibilité des engagements conventionnels, in* INTERNATIONAL LAW AT A TIME OF PERPLEXITY – ESSAYS IN HONOUR OF SHABTAI ROSENNE 623 (Yoram Dinstein & Mala Tabory eds., Dordrecht 1998).

[10] *See* the Petersmann–Alston debate: Philip Alston, *Resisting the Merger and Acquisition of Human Rights by Trade Law: A Reply to Petersmann*, 13 EUR. J. INT'L L. 815 (2002) and Ernst-Ulrich Petersmann, *Taking Human Rights, Poverty and Empowerment of Individuals More Seriously: Rejoinder to Alston*, 13 EUR. J. INT'L L. 845 (2002). *See also* the cautionary notes in Robert Howse & K. Nicolaides, *Legitimacy and Global Governance: Why*

WTO. Just as perpetrator and victim cannot settle a criminal charge (on the ground that crimes affect society at large), so two WTO members would be precluded from settling an alleged WTO violation, which – as a breach of collective obligations – would then affect the rights of all other WTO members.

In more precise legal terms, the above distinction has the following consequences. A first set of consequences relates to the potential response to breach of WTO obligations. When a WTO obligation is breached, does this breach occur as against one or more other WTO members in a series of bilateral relationships or as against the collectivity of WTO members as a whole? As a matter of general international law (subject, of course, to *lex specialis* in the WTO treaty itself), if the former is true, only the WTO member(s) at the other end of the bilateral relationship(s) have standing to invoke state responsibility,[11] and only those WTO members may be permitted to suspend their own WTO obligations in response to the breach.[12] If the latter interpretation prevails, all WTO members have standing[13] and all of them may have a right to suspend their own WTO obligations vis-à-vis the wrongdoer.[14]

A second set of consequences pertains to the contractual freedom of WTO members to change or modify WTO obligations as between a sub-set of WTO members only, or to suspend WTO obligations as a countermeasure in response to breach of other, non-WTO obligations. Unlike the first set of consequences concerning the potential response to breach of WTO obligations *within the WTO* (who has standing; what can be done in response to breach?), this second set of consequences bears on the freedom of WTO members acting *outside the WTO* (to what extent can WTO members change/suspend their WTO obligations for reasons unrelated to WTO breach?). As a matter of general international law (subject, again, to *lex specialis* in the WTO treaty itself), if WTO obligations are bilateral obligations, subsequent treaties as between a sub-set of WTO members may validly *prevail* over the WTO treaty[15] and countermeasures under the WTO treaty to induce compliance with other, non-WTO obligations, *can* be tolerated.[16] In that event, the later treaty or the countermeasure could be tailored in such a way that it affects only the bilateral relation(s) of the specific WTO members involved, leaving untouched the rights and obligations of other WTO members.

Constitutionalizing the WTO is a Step Too Far, in Efficiency, Equity, and Legitimacy: The Multilateral Trading System at the Millennium (R. Porter et al. eds., 2001).

[11] Article 42(a) of the 2001 Articles on State Responsibility of the International Law Commission, ILC Report on the 53d Session, U.N. Doc. A/56/10, at 43 et seq. [hereinafter ILC Articles].

[12] Article 60.2(b) of the Vienna Convention on the Law of Treaties, *adopted* 22 May 1969, 1155 U.N.T.S. 331 [hereinafter Vienna Convention].

[13] Article 48.1(a) of the ILC Articles, above n. 11.

[14] Vienna Convention, above n. 12, art. 60.2(b) and (c) (subject to *id.* art. 60.5).

[15] *Id.* arts. 30, 41.   [16] Articles 49.2 and 50 of the ILC Articles, above n. 11.

If, in contrast, WTO obligations are collective obligations, any subsequent treaty modifying rights or obligations as between some WTO members only, and any countermeasure under the WTO treaty for breach of other, non-WTO obligations, *cannot* be tolerated.[17] In that event, the later treaty or the countermeasure will necessarily affect all other WTO members and can, therefore, not be permitted pursuant to the principle that treaties cannot affect the rights or obligations of third parties without their consent (*pacta tertiis nec nocent nec prosunt*).[18]

In terms of potential response to breach, characterizing WTO obligations as collective obligations is, therefore, seriously "empowering" for WTO members, all of which could then challenge and respond to *all* breaches of WTO law. By the same token, with regard to the permissibility of *inter se* changes or suspension of WTO rights and obligations, classifying WTO obligations as collective in nature greatly "inhibits" WTO members' freedom of action. Because all *inter se* changes or suspensions would then also affect *all other* WTO members, no such changes or suspensions can be tolerated. WTO rights and obligations would thus be transformed into constitutional-type rules, written in stone, to be altered or affected only by the consensus of all WTO members, without regard to *the bilateral relationship between any two WTO members*. In contrast, if WTO obligations were of a bilateral nature, such *inter se* modifications or suspensions – much needed, in my view, to accommodate the wide diversity of WTO members – would be permitted so long as the specific rights of third parties were left untouched.

For reasons explained elsewhere, I contend that most WTO obligations remain essentially bilateral in nature.[19] This argument is supported by a number of features that characterize WTO obligations. These include:

- their subject matter (country-to-country trade);
- their origins (reciprocal trade concessions negotiated bilaterally and multilateralized subsequently under the most-favored nation doctrine);
- the objective of WTO obligations (trade liberalization as a common interest, though not a genuine collective interest, like the one at stake when protecting human rights, which transcends the sum total of individual state interests (trade as an instrument, not a value);
- the treatment of breach and the enforcement of WTO obligations (through an almost exclusively bilateral, state-to-state mechanism, explicitly permitting bilateral suspensions of obligations in response to continuing breach).[20]

All of these elements illustrate the bilateral/contract nature of WTO obligations with the legal consequences, described earlier, that attend it.

---

[17] Respectively, article 41.1(b)(i) of the Vienna Convention, above n. 12, and articles 49.2 and 50 of the ILC Articles, above n. 11.
[18] Vienna Convention, above n. 13, art. 34.   [19] *See* Pauwelyn, above n. 8.
[20] For details, see *id*.

For present purposes, portraying WTO obligations as bilateral in nature further highlights the importance of sovereign or government interests at stake in WTO dispute settlement. Given the contractual nature of WTO obligations, two governments can legitimately settle a particular dispute, even if this means altering WTO rights and obligations between them (so long as they keep third party rights untouched). Put differently, classifying WTO obligations as bilateral in nature would open the door to what economists call "efficient breaches" of WTO law, that is, for the WTO dispute settlement mechanism to *tolerate* "a situation where the benefit to the promisor of the breach exceeds the harm to the promisee resulting from the breach."[21] Such efficient breaches of WTO law could take the form of a bilateral settlement, of compensation (paid by the wrongdoer to the victim(s)) or of a suspension of concessions (by the victim(s) as against the wrongdoer), on condition in each case that the victims of the breach were fully compensated and third party rights were left unaffected.

To be candid, this efficient breach methodology is effectively what already occurs in cases such as *EC – Hormones*, where non-compliance has continued for years in combination with a suspension of equivalent concessions by the members that won the dispute.[22] Under the current system, however, "equivalent" suspension or compensation may yield so little that the victim(s) of the breach are never fully compensated, especially if the remedy operates prospectively only, in which case the breach is not truly "efficient."

Granted, permitting efficient breach in the WTO context would not enhance predictability for private economic operators, in particular traders (although, if correctly compensated, in economic terms they might be equally well off). But this may be the price to be paid for securing legally enforceable WTO obligations in the first place, as well as a welcome democratic safety-valve that may actually make WTO obligations more, rather than less, legitimate in the eyes of some private operators, in particular consumers and citizens at large. Indeed, to permit the suspension of equivalent obligations in response to, for example, a WTO illegal ban on hormone treated beef – a ban that seems democratically supported among consumers mainly for reasons other than trade protectionism – could provide an important safeguard that may, in the long run, serve to legitimize WTO obligations, rather than to undermine them.[23]

---

[21] For a view of the WTO treaty as already permitting such "efficient breaches," see W. Schwartz & A. Sykes, *The Economic Structure of Renegotiation and Dispute Resolution in the WTO*, 31 J. LEGAL STUD. 179 (2002); *see also* LAWRENCE, above n. 9.

[22] *See* Decision by the Arbitrators, European Communities – Measures Concerning Meat and Meat Products (Hormones) – Original Complaint by the United States – Recourse to Arbitration by the European Communities under Article 22.6 of the DSU, WT/DS26/ARB (12 July 1999), DSR 1999: III, 1105.

[23] As Joseph Nye pointed out, "the procedure is like having a fuse in the electrical system of a house – better the fuse blows, than the house burns down" (JOSEPH NYE, THE PARADOX OF AMERICAN POWER (2002) quoted with approval by the former Director-General of

Upon reflection, therefore, construing WTO obligations as bilateral/contractual in nature does not risk undermining the rule of law. Rather, it seems likely to strengthen and further legitimize the WTO as a system with an increasing number of common rules, but that nonetheless remains flexible enough to allow for the diverse interests, aspirations and priorities that exist among the peoples of some 150 WTO members.

IV. Notes on the defense of public goods in the practice of WTO dispute settlement

Turning to the specific rules and practice of WTO dispute settlement, one can identify some elements that make it easier for public goods to be taken into account, while other elements may make this exercise more difficult. On the plus side, recall that only governments, not private operators, can activate the WTO dispute settlement mechanism. Normally, before a case is initiated, the complainant will consider not only the private interests of the particular exporter(s) involved, but also the wider, public interest of all constituencies that the government in question is supposed to represent.

One explicit hurdle that must be surmounted is that "[b]efore bringing a case, a Member shall exercise its judgement as to whether action under these procedures would be fruitful."[24] Another feature that can facilitate public interest representation is the Appellate Body's willingness to allow NGOs, be they public interest groups or business associations, to submit so-called *amicus curiae* briefs.[25] In these "friend of the court" briefs, evidence can be introduced and arguments raised that the interested private parties to the dispute might otherwise seek to exclude. A more standard procedure is for WTO members that are neither complainant nor defendant to intervene as third parties.[26] This procedure broadens the proceedings from a discussion between two governments to one in which the interests of other countries are also heard.

On the negative side, one can point to elements of the dispute-settlement process that may inhibit decision-makers from taking public goods or interests into account. Most prominent is the fact that all WTO dispute settlement procedures are held behind closed doors and all documents submitted by the parties remain confidential in principle.[27] This constraint obviously

---

the WTO, *in* MICHAEL MOORE, A WORLD WITHOUT WALLS – FREEDOM, DEVELOPMENT, FREE TRADE AND GLOBAL GOVERNANCE 109 (2003)).

[24] DSU, above n. 1, art. 3.7. On how this could limit standing and interest to sue in the WTO, see Rutsel Martha, *The Duty to Exercise Judgment on the Fruitfulness of Actions in World Trade Law*, 35 J. WORLD TRADE 1035 (2001).

[25] *See, in particular,* the Appellate Body Report on United States – Import Prohibition of Certain Shrimp and Shrimp Products, above n. 5, at VII, 2755.

[26] *See* DSU, above n. 1, arts 4.11 & 11.   [27] *Id.* arts 14, 18.

highlights the inter-governmental/diplomatic nature of the mechanism. It may make – or at least *appear* to make – the injection of public interest considerations into the system more difficult because government representatives can make statements and adopt positions in defense of limited private interests in the knowledge that these actions may escape scrutiny and, therefore, not be criticized afterwards by other segments of the wider society that is supposedly represented. One of the main U.S. demands in the ongoing review of the WTO dispute settlement mechanism is to make the system more accessible and transparent.[28]

Another feature that may make it more difficult to represent public goods is the divergence in decision-making procedures between the state-to-state dispute settlement mechanism or judicial branch of the WTO, on the one hand, and the political or legislative branch of the WTO, on the other.[29] WTO dispute settlement reports still need to be adopted by the WTO's Dispute Settlement Body where all WTO members have a seat and a vote. Nonetheless, for such reports to become legally binding a reverse or negative consensus rule now applies: the report will be adopted unless all WTO members (including the member who won the case!) vote against it.[30] This rule means that dispute settlement reports are almost automatically adopted.

In contrast, before the other branches of the WTO can take decisions (be it the Ministerial Conference, General Council or any other WTO organ), for all practical purposes, a *positive* consensus of all WTO members is needed. This means, crucially, that in the event a dispute settlement report which, after all, is the end-product of a disagreement between only a limited number of WTO members, is not to the liking of the WTO membership more generally, this report can only be corrected if all WTO members, without exception, support such action. This rule makes legislative action to correct outcomes of the bilateral dispute settlement mechanism to take account of the public interest of all WTO members extremely difficult.

V. Enhancing the role of public goods in the WTO dispute settlement process

Let us next consider a number of ways in which public goods could be better represented in the WTO dispute settlement process. To start with the concepts of trade liberalization and IP protection as public goods in themselves (the first type

---

[28] *See, e.g.*, the U.S. proposal for review, Contribution of the United States to the Improvement of the Dispute Settlement Understanding of the WTO, TN/DS/W/13 (22 Aug. 2002).

[29] On this contrast, see further Frieder Roessler, The Institutional Balance between the Judicial and the Political Organs of the WTO, paper presented at the Center for Business and Government (Harvard University, June 2000) (on file with author). *See also* GAIL E. EVANS, LAWMAKING UNDER THE TRADE CONSTITUTION – A STUDY IN LEGISLATING BY THE WORLD TRADE ORGANIZATION 35–50 (2000).

[30] DSU, above n. 1, arts 16.4, 17.14.

of public goods pointed out in Section I), thought could be given to making the enforcement of WTO obligations more *multilateral* in character, rather than a purely bilateral, state-to-state exercise. One could consider, for example, making WTO remedies more collective in nature. This could entitle not only the complainant, but also all other WTO members affected by a breach, to suspend concessions in response to a continuing violation. It could also allow so-called membership sanctions, such as the suspension of voting or dispute settlement privileges in case of continuing violations, instead of state-to-state suspensions of tariff concessions, as a means to induce compliance.[31]

Another suggestion could be to increase the role of the WTO Dispute Settlement Body (where all WTO members are represented) and make it more of a compliance or monitoring body, comparable to the monitoring bodies enforcing compliance with multilateral environmental agreements. In that context, the operating principle is not so much that of one country suing another to obtain redress, but rather one in which the collective membership, examining and monitoring compliance with obligations by particular members, offers both sticks and carrots to obtain eventual compliance.[32] Along these lines, thought could be given to grant standing not only to individual members, but also to a form of "public prosecutor," either an individual or a commission, who could then act in the broader WTO interest at its own initiative or at the demand of governments or of private parties, albeit with the necessary political filters to avoid abuse or opening the flood-gates to dubious claims.

As noted in Section I above, WTO dispute settlement proceedings may also affect public goods other than those of trade liberalization and IP protection – such as environmental protection, human rights or the transfer of technology – that can be invoked to justify trade restrictions or limitations on IP protection. How could the representation of this second category of public goods be improved?

One previous suggestion was to make the dispute settlement *process* more open and transparent. Another procedural devise that might increase public interest representation is to make the system more inquisitorial in nature, with a greater role for the panels and Appellate Body (or even the WTO Secretariat) to raise matters (other than new legal claims of violation) at their own initiative, rather than having them depend on a purely adversarial system where the disputing parties alone control the process. The adage that the judge knows the law (*iura novit curia*) is well accepted. It means that, when examining a claim

---

[31] For further elaboration, see Joost Pauwelyn, *Enforcement and Countermeasures in the WTO: Rules are Rules – Towards a More Collective Approach*, 94 AM. J. INT'L L. 335 (2000).

[32] For further elaboration, *see* Joost Pauwelyn, *Proposals for Reform of Article 21 of the DSU*, in IMPROVEMENTS AND CLARIFICATIONS OF THE WTO DISPUTE SETTLEMENT UNDERSTANDING: WTO NEGOTIATORS MEET ACADEMICS (European University Institute 2003).

made by either party, a panel or the Appellate Body may come up with its own legal arguments or reasoning that might better reflect public goods or interests than the often narrowly focused presentations of the parties themselves. Some precedent for such inquisitorial practice can be found in the case law regarding panel jurisdiction and the right of panels to examine *at their own initiative* whether they have jurisdiction to assess a particular claim (irrespective of whether the parties themselves made objections in this respect).[33]

When it comes to more substantive features of the WTO dispute settlement system, the following proposals could enhance the stature of non-trade public goods. In the *interpretation* of WTO rights and obligations, sufficient account should be taken of other, non-WTO rules of international law, in particular those concluded in pursuit of non-trade public goods, such as multilateral environmental agreements or conventions to protect human rights or the transfer of technology.[34] Rules governing the interpretation of public international law – explicitly incorporated into the WTO dispute settlement mechanism – call for judicial reference to non-WTO rules when giving meaning to WTO provisions.[35] Pursuant to those rules, treaty terms must be interpreted, not only according to their strict textual meaning, but also "in good faith," "in context" and "in the light of object and purpose."[36]

Moreover, terms must be interpreted taking account of "any relevant rules of international law applicable in the relations between the parties."[37] In the *U.S.–Shrimp/Turtle* case, for example, the Appellate Body interpreted the WTO term "exhaustible natural resources" as set out in article XX(g) of the General Agreement on Tariffs and Trade (GATT),[38] with reference to, *inter alia*, the UN Law of the Sea Convention,[39] the Convention on Biological Diversity[40] and the

---

[33] *See* the Appellate Body Report on United States – Anti-Dumping Act of 1916, WT/DS136/AB/R, WT/DS162/AB/R, ¶ 54 and fn. 30, *adopted* 26 Sept. 2000: "some issues of jurisdiction may be of such a nature that they have to be addressed by the Panel at any time" since "it is a widely accepted rule that an international tribunal is entitled to consider the issue of its own jurisdiction on its own initiative."

[34] *See* Gabrielle Marceau, *A Call for Coherence in International Law – Praises for the Prohibition Against "Clinical Isolation" in WTO Dispute Settlement*, 33 J. WORLD TRADE 87 (1999); Joost Pauwelyn, *The Role of Public International Law in the WTO: How Far Can We Go?*, 95 AM. J. INT'L L. 535 (2001).

[35] Article 3.2 of the DSU, above n. 1, in effect, incorporates articles 31 and 32 of the Vienna Convention, above n. 12. *See* Report of the Appellate Body, United States – Standards for Reformulated and Conventional Gasoline, AB–1996–1, WT/DS2/AB/R, at 17, *adopted* 20 Mar. 1996.

[36] Vienna Convention, above n. 12, art 31.1.   [37] *Id.* art. 31.3(c).

[38] Multilateral Agreements on Trade in Goods, 15 Apr. 1994, WTO Agreement, Annex 1A, 33 I.L.M. 1154 (1994) [hereinafter GATT 1994].

[39] United Nations Law of the Sea Convention, *opened for signature* 10 Dec. 1982, U.N. Doc. A/CONF.62/122 (1982), 21 I.L.M. 1261 (1982).

[40] Convention on Biological Diversity, 5 June 1992, 31 I.L.M. 818, *available at* http://www.biodiv.org/convention/articles.asp (last accessed 28 July 2004).

Convention on International Trade in Endangered Species ("CITES")[41] so as to include not only mineral or non-living resources, but also living resources, such as sea-turtles.[42]

Nonetheless, the process of *interpretation*, or giving meaning to terms that WTO members have agreed to, has obvious limits. Because one cannot disregard or overrule unambiguous language in WTO provisions in the process of *interpreting* WTO norms, other, non-WTO treaties can never prevail over explicit WTO terms. In addition, only other non-WTO rules or concepts of international law that represent the "common intentions" or that may be deemed agreed to by all WTO members can be used to give meaning to WTO terms (pursuant to the adage *ejus est interpretare legem cujus condere*).[43] Under this principle, for example, a bilateral agreement between two WTO members cannot be relied on to give meaning to WTO terms as they apply to all WTO members.

That said, however, besides the process of treaty interpretation, there is, in my view, a second role for non-WTO treaties expressing non-trade public goods, namely, as a full-fledged part of the law *directly applicable* as between the two disputing parties. In this case, we are not dealing with rules to be relied on to give meaning to WTO terms, but rather with rules that can be invoked as a self-standing defense by the defendant to justify a trade restriction or limitation on IP protection that is otherwise not consistent with WTO law (including, for example, the exceptions set out in article XX of GATT).[44] Indeed, if two countries first agree, for example, in a human rights treaty that trade sanctions can be imposed in case of human rights violations, should one of these countries then not be allowed to invoke that treaty to justify such trade sanction as against another country that violated human rights when the latter challenges the trade sanction before a WTO panel? The unpalatable alternative would allow the human rights violator faced with a trade sanction – after it had itself agreed to such sanctioning mechanism – to circumvent its international obligations before a WTO panel because such panel would, in the examination of WTO claims, take account only of WTO rules, not of any other rules equally binding as between the parties.[45]

---

[41] Convention on International Trade in Endangered Species, *opened for signature* 3 Mar. 1973, 27 U.S.T. 1087, 12 I.L.M. 1085.
[42] U.S.–Shrimp/Turtle Dispute, above n. 5, ¶¶ 128–32.
[43] *See* Appellate Body Report on European Communities – Customs Classification of Certain Computer Equipment, WT/DS62/AB/R ¶ 84, *adopted* 26 June 1998. As the Permanent Court of International Justice stated in its Advisory Opinion on the Question of Jaworzina: "[I]t is an established principle that the right of giving an authoritative interpretation of a legal rule belongs solely to the person or body who has the power to modify or suppress it." Delimitation of the Polish-Czechoslovakian Frontier (Question of Jaworzina), 1923 P.C.I.J. (ser. B) No. 8 (Dec. 6) (advisory opinion).
[44] *See* GATT 1994, above n. 38, art. XX.
[45] For further elaboration on a real example, see Joost Pauwelyn, *What to Make of the WTO Waiver for "Conflict Diamonds": WTO Compassion or Superiority Complex?*, 24 MICH. J. INT'L L. 1177 (2003).

VI. Conclusion

The foregoing discussion has examined the question of "recognition of public goods in WTO dispute settlement" in light of a triangular relationship of some prominence in WTO affairs, namely the tension between sovereign/government interests, private rights, and public goods. It was noted that at least two types of public goods may be at stake in WTO dispute settlement proceedings: trade-related public goods (trade liberalization and IP protection) and non-trade related public goods (such as environmental protection or the transfer of technology). At its origin, the WTO is about how governments (sovereign interests) can or cannot regulate private activities, namely trade (thereby impacting private rights). Traditionally, however, governments operating in the GATT/WTO framework have often over-represented producer and, in particular, export interests. In WTO dispute settlement proceedings, moreover, complaints are limited to matters pertaining to the pursuit of trade-related public goods; non-trade public goods only come into play as defenses that may justify trade restrictions or limitations on IP protection.

When looking at the nature of WTO obligations, I argued that these are essentially bilateral/contractual, and not collective/statute-like obligations. This classification, if correct, has important legal consequences and highlights the somewhat private/contractual nature of WTO affairs, where government/sovereign interests remain in control of bilateral trade matters (so long as the rights of other WTO members are left untouched). Characterizing the WTO Agreement as a contract rather than a criminal code or constitution limits the public goods content of the undertaking. However, it also strengthens the collective WTO enterprise by affording sufficient flexibility to reflect the diversity of opinions and preferences of some 150 member countries.

I then considered how some specific rules and practices of the WTO dispute settlement process take account of public goods. On the positive side, reference was made to the fact that standing in the WTO is limited to governments and that the public interest may also be represented by third parties and by so-called "friends of the court" who have been authorized to participate in WTO dispute settlement actions. On the negative side, we find the closed and confidential nature of the WTO mechanism and the imbalance between the WTO's judicial and political branches, which renders political correction, in the public interest, of dispute settlement reports extremely difficult.

Finally, I offered some suggestions for improving the public goods content of WTO dispute settlement decisions. First, in terms of process, we could make dispute settlement actions more collective/multilateral in nature, rather than purely state-to-state; we could open up the process to the public and make it more transparent; we could augment its inquisitorial features instead of relying on a purely adversarial system. Second, in terms of substance, we could highlight the role of non-WTO norms and treaties in pursuit of non-trade public goods both in the *interpretation* of WTO provisions and as rules to be *directly applied* by the WTO judiciary as self-standing defenses.

Returning then to the triangular relationship between sovereign/government interests, private rights and public goods, it is clear that all three elements must be represented and subjected to carefully calibrated checks and balances for the WTO to be a successful and legitimate organization, one that is supported by, and promotes the interests of governments, private operators, and the public at large.

32

The economics of international trade agreements and dispute settlement with intellectual property rights

ERIC W. BOND[*]

1. Introduction
2. The dispute settlement mechanism of the WTO
    2a. The WTO dispute settlement process and the TRIPS Agreement
    2b. Economics of the dispute settlement process.
3. A model of intellectual property rights
    3a. Non-cooperative equilibrium
    3b. Efficient patent policies with lump-sum transfers
    3c. International agreements to reduce discrimination
    3d. Minimum standards for IPRs
4. Conclusions

1. Introduction

Economists usually think of international trade agreements as attempts to solve the prisoner's dilemma that is inherent in trade policy.[1] Each country would like to protect its own market, either because of powerful political interests in the import-competing sector or the desire to exercise its market power in trade. However, each country's protection has a negative impact on the welfare of its trading partners by denying market access to their exporters and worsening

---

[*] Eric W. Bond is Professor of Economics, Vanderbilt University. He is grateful to Wilfred Ethier and other participants at the Duke Conference on International Public Goods and Transfer of Technology under a Globalized Intellectual Property Regime (24–26 April 2003) for helpful comments on an earlier draft.

[1] The prisoner's dilemma is a standard game used in economics and political science to demonstrate that individual actors, behaving rationally, can make themselves jointly worse off than they would be had they coordinated their strategies. *See* ROGER B. MYERSON, GAME THEORY: ANALYSIS OF CONFLICT 97–98 (Harvard University Press 1991).

their terms of trade. Unilateral actions of countries in setting trade policy will thus result in an inefficiently high level of protection. The role of international trade agreements, such as the Agreement Establishing the World Trade Organization (WTO), is to provide a forum in which countries may negotiate mutually beneficial reductions in those trade barriers.[2]

As a result of the Uruguay Round of trade negotiations, the scope of the WTO was expanded to include the Agreement on Trade-Related Aspects of Intellectual Property Rights (TRIPS).[3] The TRIPS Agreement represents a substantial departure from previous international conventions on intellectual property rights (IPRs). First, it covers a broad range of IPRs under a single accord. Previously, there were separate agreements covering copyrights (Berne Convention)[4] and industrial property (Paris Convention)[5] that had widespread membership, but other aspects of intellectual property, such as computer software and trade secrets, were not covered by significant treaties. A second departure of TRIPS is its utilization of the WTO process of dispute settlement to handle intellectual property disputes between member countries that arise under its rules. Prior treaties had generally suffered from the lack of dispute settlement procedures.[6]

This chapter addresses two questions that are raised by the approach to IPRs protection embodied in TRIPS. The first is whether it is appropriate to extend WTO negotiating principles and institutions to international agreements on IPRs.[7]

---

[2] Marrakesh Agreement Establishing the World Trade Organization, 15 Apr. 1994, LEGAL INSTRUMENTS – RESULTS OF THE URUGUAY ROUND vol. 1, 33 I.L.M. 1144 (1994) [hereinafter WTO Agreement]. The classic reference is H.G. Johnson, *Optimum Tariffs and Retaliation*, 21 REV. ECON. STUD. 142 (1953–54). *See also* BERNARD M. HOEKMAN & MICHEL M. KOSTECKI, THE POLITICAL ECONOMY OF THE WORLD TRADING SYSTEM: THE WTO AND BEYOND 25–36 (Oxford University Press 2d ed. 2001); KYLE BAGWELL & ROBERT W. STAIGER, THE ECONOMICS OF THE WORLD TRADING SYSTEM (MIT Press 2003).

[3] The WTO succeeded the General Agreement on Tariffs and Trade (GATT). Along with GATT, TRIPS became one of the foundation agreements of the WTO itself. Agreement on Trade-Related Aspects of Intellectual Property Rights, 15 Apr. 1994, Marrakesh Agreement Establishing the World Trade Organization, Annex 1C, LEGAL INSTRUMENTS – RESULTS OF THE URUGUAY ROUND vol. 31, 33 I.L.M. 81 (1994) [hereinafter TRIPS Agreement].

[4] Berne Convention for the Protection of Literary and Artistic Works, 1161 U.N.T.S. 3 (1886), Paris Act of 24 July 1971, *as amended* 28 Sept. 1979.

[5] Paris Convention for the Protection of Industrial Property, *as amended* 28 Sept. 1979, 828 U.N.T.S. 305 (1883).

[6] *See* KEITH E. MASKUS, INTELLECTUAL PROPERTY RIGHTS IN THE GLOBAL ECONOMY 15–16 (Institute for International Economics 2000).

[7] Various considerations on this subject are provided by Arvind Panagariya, *TRIPS and the WTO: An Uneasy Marriage*, *in* THE NEXT NEGOTIATING ROUND: EXAMINING THE AGENDA FOR SEATTLE (J. Bhagwati ed., Columbia University Press 1999); Keith E. Maskus, *Regulatory Standards in the WTO: Comparing Intellectual Property Rights with Competition Policy, Environmental Protection, and Core Labor Standards*, 1 WORLD TRADE REV. 135 (2002); Gene M. Grossman & Edwin Lai, International Protection of Intellectual Property (manuscript, Princeton University 2004).

I address this question using a model in which IPRs generate two types of spillovers that create a prisoner's dilemma. One spillover results from the fact that the national cost of offering IPRs to foreigners is higher than that of providing them to domestic residents, leading to an incentive to discriminate against the former in granting protection. A second spillover arises because the benefits from the innovation generated by protection of IPRs are an international public good.[8] Both of these spillovers will lead to a level of IPRs protection that is below that which would maximize world welfare.

The history of national policies on IPRs provides evidence of the prisoner's dilemma associated with national policies, as highlighted in the model. Goldstein described the discriminatory nature of early laws on copyright, noting that "... if they did not altogether exclude protection of foreign nationals, they generally conditioned protection on compliance with one or more formal requirements."[9] In the case of patent laws, Lerner performed an empirical analysis of patent protection in 60 countries and reported that the average law in the mid-nineteenth century contained one of four different types of restrictions against foreign applicants.[10] In response to this discrimination, a major focus of early international accords on IPRs was the extension of national treatment to the parties signing them. Furthermore, these agreements typically dealt with the tendency toward under-provision of protection by setting minimum IPRs standards.[11]

The model developed here suggests that the appropriate application of the tools of international trade agreements to IPRs requires some modifications to those tools because of the nature of the spillovers between countries generated by innovations. If the home country were to extend its IPRs protection to foreign firms, it would suffer an adverse terms of trade effect because the policy would raise the prices at which foreign firms can sell there. This impact is similar to the adverse terms of trade effect that a large country would

---

[8] See Peter Drahos, *The Regulation of Public Goods* [this volume]; Keith E. Maskus & Jerome H. Reichman, *The Globalization of Private Knowledge Goods and the Privatization of Global Public Goods* [this volume]. Further analysis is provided in GLOBAL PUBLIC GOODS: INTERNATIONAL COOPERATION IN THE 21ST CENTURY (Inge Kaul et al. eds., Oxford University Press 1999).

[9] PAUL A. GOLDSTEIN, INTERNATIONAL COPYRIGHT: PRINCIPLES, LAW, AND PRACTICE 16 (Oxford University Press 2001).

[10] Josh Lerner, *150 Years of Patent Protection*, AMERICAN ECONOMIC REVIEW: PAPERS AND PROCEEDINGS vol. 92, at 221–225 (2002). The four types of restrictions identified were awarding patents of shorter duration, charging higher fees, terminating the local patent coverage if the foreign patent expired first, and granting shorter extensions to foreigners. EDITH PENROSE, THE ECONOMICS OF THE INTERNATIONAL PATENT SYSTEM (Johns Hopkins University Press 1951) also noted that many national patent laws required foreign patent holders to produce the good locally within a specified period of time. The frequency of these discriminatory policies had been reduced by two-thirds by the early part of the twentieth century, presumably as a result of international agreements.

[11] See Berne Convention, above n. 4, and Paris Convention, above n. 5.

experience when it reduced tariffs on imported goods, because the resulting increase in demand would raise the relative price of imported goods. Bagwell and Staiger argued that WTO principles and institutions can be understood as a means of dealing with this price externality.[12] Thus, these institutions should also be useful in addressing the profit transfers created by the extension of IPRs to foreigners.

However, the second, and dynamic, spillover created by IPRs has the nature of an international public good that has no analog in multilateral trade liberalization. Measures of the benefits of reciprocal increases in IPRs need to be adjusted to take into account the public-good effects of innovations, as do the calculations of equivalent concessions that might be made for purposes of dispute settlement. In addition, it can be shown that the principles of national treatment and the use of minimum standards are not necessarily consistent with an efficient international agreement on IPRs.

The second issue examined in this chapter is the desirability of incorporating agreements on IPRs into multilateral trade agreements. The main point is that since a relatively small number of countries account for the vast majority of technology exports, the expansion of patent protection under TRIPS is likely to cause a large income transfer from technology importing nations to technology exporting nations. McCalman estimated the net transfers from the revaluation of patent stocks under TRIPS for 29 (primarily developed) economies and found that only six of them would be net gainers.[13] He found that the United States would be the primary beneficiary, with a gain almost six times that of the next largest recipient. In order for such an agreement to be in the interest of technology importing countries, it would need to be tied to trade concessions that compensate for their loss on IPRs.[14] Similarly, the dispute settlement process must trade concessions across functional areas in order to make TRIPS enforceable against technology importing nations.

The potential difficulties in international intellectual property (IP) agreements are illustrated by the case of Switzerland's participation in the Paris Convention of 1883, one of the first international agreements on patents.[15] Swiss inventors held a number of patents in foreign countries but Switzerland had no patent law of its own. The model developed in this paper suggests that such a policy may have been rational from the point of view of a small country,

---

[12] BAGWELL & STAIGER, above n. 2.
[13] Phillip McCalman, *Reaping What You Sow: An Empirical Analysis of International Patent Harmonization*, 55 J. INT'L ECON. 161 (2001).
[14] Bond and Park examined trade agreements between a large country and a small country when the large one is better off in Nash equilibrium (that is, with unilaterally set tariffs) than in free trade. A similar problem arises in that case, for trade liberalization must be bundled with side payments or agreements on other issues in order to achieve a mutually beneficial free trade pact. *See* Eric W. Bond & Jee Hyeong Park, *Gradualism in Trade Agreements with Asymmetric Countries*, 69 REV. ECON. STUD. 379 (2002).
[15] *See* Paris Convention, above n. 5.

because the adoption of a patent law would have had no impact on aggregate international innovation but would have required substantial payments to foreign innovators in the form of monopoly markups on patented products. Since the Paris Convention called mainly for national treatment, Switzerland was a free rider by receiving concessions in foreign markets without giving anything of value to other members.

Switzerland eventually adopted a patent law, with the implicit threat by other countries of withdrawal of national treatment playing a significant role.[16] The pressure prevailed in this case because Switzerland was a significant innovator, and compensatory transfers could be made within the context of a patent agreement. In general, however, countries that were not technology exporters could not be forced to adopt a patent law, because other members of any IP agreement would have no credible threats within the bounds of the pact.

Section 2 of this chapter provides a summary of the WTO dispute settlement procedures, and it discusses how the agreement bundles trade and IP instruments together by allowing for the withdrawal of trade concessions as compensation for the failure of a country to fulfill a TRIPS obligation. That section also provides a review of the existing literature on the economics of the dispute settlement process as applied to conflicts involving trade in goods. Section 3 sets out a simple model of patent protection that highlights the basic tradeoff between allowing profits to encourage innovation and reducing the deadweight loss due to monopoly created by IPRs. This model is used to identify both the international spillovers resulting from national choice of IPRs and the potential for mutually welfare-improving agreements. It is shown that when countries set policies unilaterally, they have an incentive to offer a lower degree of patent protection to foreign firms. Section 4 offers concluding remarks.

2. The dispute settlement mechanism of the WTO

The dispute settlement procedures of the WTO represent a significant strengthening of the system that operated under the General Agreement on Tariffs and Trade of 1947 (GATT 1947). The GATT system required unanimity among all the Contracting Parties in order to impose a punishment, so that in many cases defendants simply ignored findings against them. Under the WTO process, a majority decision against a defendant results in the imposition of penalties unless a satisfactory adjustment is made in the defendant's offending policy or there is a unanimous decision to reject the panel's report.[17] The WTO procedures have been more successful at achieving compliance with rulings.[18] The purposes of

---

[16] See PENROSE, above n. 10, at 120–124.
[17] See HOEKMAN & KOSTECKI, above n. 2, at 74–91; Joost Pauwelyn, *WTO Dispute Settlement: Of Sovereign Interests, Private Rights and Public Goods* [this volume].
[18] See Joost Pauwelyn, *Enforcement and Countermeasures in the WTO: Rules are Rules – Towards a More Collective Approach*, 94 AM. J. INT'L L. 335 (2000).

this section are to highlight some of the main features of the dispute settlement process as they have applied to trade disputes and to discuss how this process has been applied in recent cases involving TRIPS. The literature on the role of the process in the enforcement of trade agreements is also briefly reviewed.

2a. The WTO dispute settlement process and the TRIPS Agreement

A key feature of the WTO dispute settlement procedure is that it is primarily a rules-based system that has the flavor of a judicial proceeding.[19] Article XXIII of the GATT 1994 gives members the right to initiate a complaint against another member that has taken actions that "nullified or impaired" the benefits resulting from the agreement. These complaints could arise when a member has taken actions that are either directly in conflict with its obligations (a "violation case") or have the effect of undermining benefits due another member (a "non-violation case").[20] Under the Dispute Settlement Understanding (DSU),[21] these complaints are evaluated by a three-member panel of experts.[22] Members of the panel are chosen for their expertise in international trade policy and law, and they evaluate the submissions of parties to a dispute for their consistency with the WTO agreements. The DSU also established a process by which parties could appeal a panel decision to a permanent Appellate Body.

A second feature is that the punishments involve the suspension of concessions or obligations of the complaining party that are of equivalent magnitude to the nullification or impairment it suffers as a result of the violation. The DSU evinces a strong preference for the implementation of panel findings or, if they are not implemented, for the negotiation of mutually agreed compensation between the parties. The DSU also provides guidelines on the imposition of punishments, which indicate that a complainant should first seek to impose the punishments on the same sector in which the violation occurred. The DSU states that for violations of obligations on trade in goods, suspension of concessions in any other category of trade in goods is considered to be in the same sector. In

---

[19] *See* Pauwelyn, *WTO Dispute Settlement*, above n. 17.
[20] HOEKMAN & KOSTECKI, above n. 2, at 74–78.
[21] Understanding on Rules and Procedures Governing the Settlement of Disputes, Marrakesh Agreement Establishing the World Trade Organization, Annex 2, 33 I.L.M. 1226 (1994).
[22] The original GATT 1947 did not clearly specify the process by which complaints were to be handled, and initially disputes were referred to a working party of members. The working party procedures were more of a bargaining framework, where disagreements could be resolved through multilateral negotiations. However, the process evolved in 1955 to the use of a panel of experts to evaluate disputes. JOHN H. JACKSON, THE JURISPRUDENCE OF GATT AND THE WTO, ch. 4 (Cambridge University Press 2000) interprets this as a shift from a "bargaining" process to a "judicial" or "arbitrational" process. The system continued to evolve over subsequent GATT negotiating rounds in the direction of making the process more legally precise and judicial.

contrast, with respect to TRIPS, a "sector" is defined as a particular category of intellectual property as identified under the agreement. Thus, a violation of obligations on patent protection should be met with withdrawal of equivalent concessions on patent protection by the complaining nation where feasible.

If punishments of comparable magnitude to the violation are not available in the same sector, the DSU permits the withdrawal of concessions in other sectors under the same Agreement. The second choice for a violation of patent protection obligations would thus be the suspension of concessions on a different category of IPRs. Finally, the DSU specifies that if neither of these options yields appropriate punishment and if " ... the circumstances are serious enough," the complainant can seek to withdraw concessions under another covered Agreement.[23] This process allows for the punishment to take place across agreements when trade in intellectual property is not balanced between countries.

As of July 2003, TRIPS-related disputes had accounted for 23 of 282 WTO dispute settlement cases.[24] Consultations between the parties resulted in a mutually agreed solution in 13 of these cases and consultations were pending in four more. In the remaining six cases, the panel decisions found at least some violations by the defendant and requested that laws or practices be altered to make them compliant with TRIPS obligations. Compliance with the panel's report was accomplished in three of these cases and the defendants agreed to comply within a reasonable period of time in two others. In the only TRIPS case by that time where punishments were proposed for a violation, in this instance of copyright rules by the United States, the derogation was to be punished by a withdrawal of concessions on European Union copyright measures.[25] This punishment was consistent with the principle that the preference for sanctions under TRIPS should be for withdrawal of concessions within the same section of the agreement. There has also been one case where withdrawal of a TRIPS concession was approved for a violation of an obligation on goods trade because withdrawal of concessions on goods and services could not be sufficient to reach the level of the violation.[26]

---

[23] Dispute Settlement Understanding, above n. 21, art. 3(c).
[24] Information on disputes is available at http://www.wto.int/english/tratop_e/dispu_e/dispu_e.htm.
[25] The copyright case involved section 110(5) of the U.S. Copyright Act (WTO Doc. WT/DS160). These punishments had not been imposed as of July 2003, and the parties have reportedly negotiated a resolution that entails payment by the United States authorities to designated beneficiaries in the E.U., but not a change in the offending U.S. law.
[26] In the case against the European Union's regime for importing bananas, the arbitrators found that Ecuador had suffered nullification and impairment of benefits on over $200 million of trade per year. Ecuador was allowed to request suspension of concessions on obligations under GATT and the General Agreement on Trade in Services (GATS) (with regard to wholesale trade services). If these suspensions proved unable to achieve the required level of compensation, Ecuador was allowed to request suspensions of the TRIPS Agreement under the sections covering copyrights, geographical indications, and industrial designs. See WTO Case WT/DS27/18 (18 Aug. 1998).

2b. Economics of the dispute settlement process.

One interpretation of the economic role of the WTO dispute settlement procedure is that it serves as a punishment mechanism to prevent countries from deviating from their obligations. As has been emphasized by Professor John Jackson, international trade agreements do not have the force of domestic law in many countries (such as the United States), which can imply that policymakers are not bound to follow the commitments made in them.[27] This means that agreements must be structured for self-enforcement in the sense that it is in the interest of the countries involved to follow their WTO obligations. The lack of international mechanisms to enforce contracts between sovereign states under GATT 1947 prompted economists to model trade agreements as a repeated prisoner's dilemma.[28] The theory of repeated games suggests that trade liberalization can be sustained when countries interact repeatedly because any country that deviates can be punished by a trade war. The agreement is sustainable if each country is better off by carrying out its promised tariff cuts than by deviating from the agreement and suffering the resulting punishment.

While the theory provides important insights about the value of having future market access in sustaining current trade liberalization, some predictions of the simplest versions of the theory seem inconsistent with the way the dispute settlement process actually operates. The theory suggests that, in order to sustain the greatest amount of cooperation among countries, the punishments meted out by the dispute settlement procedure must be credible and as severe as possible. For example, the most effective punishment that could be imposed is the use of arbitrarily high tariffs that eliminate all international trade, because this would result in the lowest payoff for any country that deviates from the underlying agreement. It is clear that the punishments specified in the WTO dispute settlement process even after 1994 are not intended to be this severe, for they prescribe compensatory tariffs rather than punitive tariffs to be imposed on a country that fails to fulfill its obligations. Furthermore, disputes – but not formal actions under the DSU – can carry on for years, which substantially would reduce the severity of punishments.[29]

---

[27] JOHN H. JACKSON, THE WORLD TRADE ORGANIZATION: CONSTITUTION AND JURISPRUDENCE (Royal Institute of International Affairs 1998).

[28] The application of the theory of repeated games to trade agreements was first proposed by Avinash Dixit, *Strategic Aspects of Trade Policy*, in ADVANCES IN ECONOMIC THEORY (Truman Bewley ed., Cambridge University Press 1987).

[29] Punishments should be carried out as quickly as possible, because rapid sanctions reduce the gain from deviation. In the limiting case, instantaneous observation of deviations would make it possible to support the efficient agreement fully. This insight argues for delegating retaliation decisions to the executive branch of the complaining country, which could retaliate in a short time under executive order. This situation stands in stark contrast to the GATT 1947 process, which often took years to handle disputes, and even to the

These features of the dispute settlement process are not well explained by the repeated-game approach. One explanation is that extremely severe punishments are not renegotiation-proof. If the punishments were to eliminate trade, all countries could be made better off by renegotiating tariffs to a level that permitted positive trade. In consequence, extremely harsh punishments would not be carried out, and, therefore, could not be used to deter deviations. It has been shown that this problem is particularly acute if the countries are involved in recurrent trade negotiations because then no trade liberalization can be supported in principle.[30] Any attempt to impose punishment on a country that did not fulfill its obligation in one period would be renegotiated away in the subsequent period. Thus, the only way to achieve cooperation is to have punishments imposed by an external enforcement body in a way that does not involve negotiations between the parties. This approach would explain the value of having the dispute settlement process become judicially adjudicated rather than treating it as a negotiation between disputants.

Wilfred Ethier proposed an alternative explanation for the weakness of punishments, which is that trade agreements are incomplete contracts.[31] Since contracts are not complete there would be some states of nature where a country would face domestic political pressure to violate its obligations.[32] Countries would be unwilling to accept an agreement that specifies quite severe punishments for violations because all know that there is a positive probability that they will need to deviate from the agreement. Ethier showed that this framework generates punishments that are commensurate with the deviation when a country violates the ruling of a dispute panel. He also proposed that the deviating country might prefer either to abide by the ruling or to violate it, depending on the weight put on the adjudication phase in its welfare calculation.

WTO DSU process, which can reach an adjudicative decision expeditiously, but may still take years to fully implement that decision by the parties. At the same time, the WTO process discourages unilateral actions by countries in favor of a judicial process. One explanation could be that third parties to trade disputes might have more trouble determining whether a deviation had occurred and might not be able to distinguish between a deviation and a punishment.

[30] This point is made by Mikhail Klimenko et al., Recurrent Trade Agreements and the Value of External Enforcement (2001) (manuscript, on file with The University of California at San Diego).

[31] This concept refers to contracts that cannot anticipate all potential situations that may arise after negotiations have been made. See Wilfred Ethier, Punishments and Dispute Settlement in Trade Agreements (2001) (manuscript, on file with The University of Pennsylvania). *See also* Wilfred Ethier, *Intellectual Property Rights and Dispute Settlement in the World Trade Organization* [this volume].

[32] The GATT Agreement provided in article 23 an escape clause provision that could be used by nations that felt that fulfilling a particular commitment would cause undue injury on a domestic industry.

Although there are questions about the severity of punishments provided by the WTO dispute settlement procedure, the members themselves seem to think that this process contributes to the enforcement of agreements. Professor Jackson notes that one of the selling points of incorporating TRIPS into the WTO was the potential to use the WTO dispute settlement process.[33] The effectiveness of this process is a critical feature establishing the credibility of the WTO itself. Indeed, the activity level of disputes under TRIPS may be contrasted with that under the Berne Convention, wherein disputes over copyright law could be taken to the International Court of Justice, but that mechanism was never used.[34] This suggests that the WTO process is perceived as more credible for resolving disputes.

3. A model of intellectual property rights

This section sets out a simple two-country model in which the government chooses the extent of patent protection afforded inventors that develop new consumer products. The model captures the basic tradeoff between an increased level of innovations and a greater deadweight loss from monopoly that arises when the government strengthens its patent protection. It also allows for the hypothetical possibility that governments could offer differential degrees of protection to home and foreign innovators, although the national treatment clauses of existing conventions normally impede this solution in practice. The purpose of the model is to identify the international spillovers associated with patents and the gains that can be obtained from international agreements on such protection. The theory also indicates how the withdrawal of equivalent concessions might be defined for the patent regime.

The model follows two earlier authors in considering a two-period model of innovation.[35] Firms choose the amount of innovation to undertake in developing a differentiated product in the first period, which determines the number of varieties of the product available in the second period. The latter period may be interpreted as a representation of the useful life of a new product. At the beginning of the first period, governments commit to the strictness of patent protection that is provided to successful innovations. This decision determines the fraction of potential profits that can be obtained from a successful

---

[33] JOHN H. JACKSON, above n. 22, at 120. Indeed, this process was of particular interest to developing countries.

[34] The 1971 Paris Act of the Berne Convention provides for the use of the International Court of Justice to settle disputes. GOLDSTEIN, above n. 9, at 29, notes that this method of resolving disputes was "an unused procedural route that has in any event been eclipsed by the more effective dispute settlement procedures" of the WTO.

[35] Alan V. Deardorff, *Welfare Effects of Global Patent Protection*, 59 ECONOMICA 35 (1992); Suzanne Scotchmer, *The Political Economy of Intellectual Property Treaties*, 20 J.L. ECON. & ORG. 415 (2004).

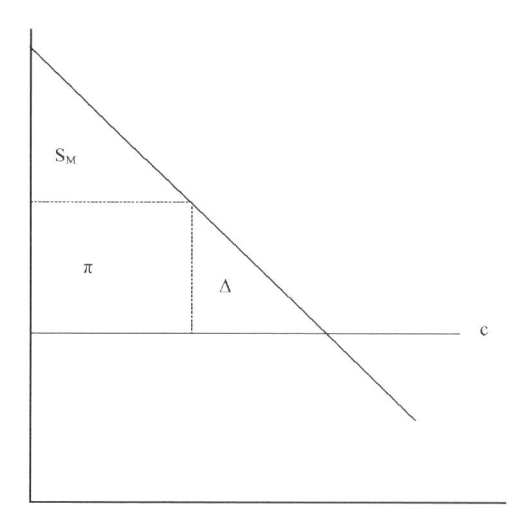

Figure 1: Static cost of patent protection

innovation in the later period. The model can be considered to represent the steady state of an infinite-horizon general equilibrium theory, in which firms innovate in every period and products have an exogenously given useful life.[36]

The static efficiency loss from extending patent protection is illustrated in Figure 1, which shows the demand curve in the home market for a representative new product. This good may be produced with a constant marginal cost of c. If a patent on the product were fully enforced, the owner could generate a monopoly profit of π per period, and consumers would enjoy a surplus benefit of S_M per period. If the patent were not in force and the technology could be copied by any firm, the market price would be driven to the marginal cost, and consumers would earn a surplus benefit of $S_C = S_M + \pi + \Delta$. The social cost per period to the home country of providing patent protection is Δ when a home firm owns the patent, and $\Delta+\pi$ when it is owned by a foreign firm. There are similar per-period surpluses (S_M^*, S_C^*) and profit levels (π^*) associated with the sale of the product in the foreign market.

Let β denote the present value of $1 per period over the life of the product. Then the expected profit that a home-country patent owner receives in that market is $\beta\theta\pi$, where θ is a parameter between zero and one indicating the strictness of the home-country patent system on behalf of home-country firms. Similarly, consumer surplus in the home market is $\beta[\theta S_M + (1 - \theta)S_C]$. The parameter θ may be interpreted to reflect the duration of the patent and the probability that the patent holder can prevent infringement through legal action during the patent life. For a foreign firm, the strictness of the home patent system is denoted by μ. The foreign patent system may similarly be

---

[36] This interpretation was shown in a similar context by Grossman & Lai, above n. 7.

characterized by the strictness with which patents held by foreign firms are enforced, θ^*, and the strictness applied to home firms, μ^*.[37] The principle of national treatment would require that $\theta = \mu$ and $\theta^* = \mu^*$.

The dynamic gains from a patent system result from the incentive to innovate, which is assumed here to increase with the strictness of the patent system. Suppose that there is a continuum of potential goods (each with demand curves identical to the one in Figure 1) that could be introduced. Let $C(N)$ represent the cost of research and development (R&D) required to generate a measure N of new products in the home country. Firms would invest in R&D up to the point where the cost of introducing an additional product equals the expected return from the product over the life of the patent,

$$C'(N) = \beta(\theta\pi + \mu^*\pi^*). \quad (1)$$

Inverting this equation yields the equilibrium level of home-country innovation, $\widetilde{N}(\theta, \mu^*)$, which is increasing with the strictness of patent protection received in each country. Similarly, the measure of foreign products is determined by $C^{*\prime}(N^*) = \beta(\mu\pi + \theta^*\pi^*)$, which yields an equilibrium level of foreign innovation, $\widetilde{N}^*(\theta^*, \mu)$. Letting $\varepsilon = \frac{C'(N)}{NC''(N)}$ and (correspondingly, ε^*) express the elasticities of supply of innovations with respect to the profit from introducing a new product, the comparative static effect of patent protection on innovations will be

$$\frac{dN}{N} = \varepsilon\left(\frac{\pi d\theta + \pi^* d\mu^*}{\theta\pi + \mu^*\pi^*}\right) \quad \frac{dN^*}{N^*} = \varepsilon^*\left(\frac{\pi^* d\theta^* + \pi d\mu}{\theta^*\pi^* + \mu\pi}\right). \quad (2)$$

Letting $\lambda = \pi/\pi^*$ denote the relative profitability of the home-country market, equation (2) indicates that the extension of patent protection by the home country will have a bigger impact on innovation the greater is λ. The level of patent protection in the larger market will be relatively more important in determining the level of innovation. The difference in the levels of innovation across countries is determined by comparative advantage in product development, as reflected in variations of the marginal cost of innovation, and the degree of discrimination among patent laws.

To formalize the magnitude of the static and dynamic effects of patent protection, we can write the discounted welfare from innovations of the home country introduced in the current period as

$$W = \beta[(\theta S_M + (1-\theta)S_C)N + (\mu S_M + (1-\mu)S_C)N^* + (\theta\pi + \mu^*\pi^*)N] - C(N) \quad (3)$$

---

[37] Note that this specification implies that the fact that a patent has expired or has been infringed in one market does not necessarily affect the probability of infringement in the other market. This would be the case if there were border measures in place that prevented the import of goods for which a patent had not expired. *See* TRIPS Agreement, above n. 3, arts. 51–60.

Totally differentiating equation (3), and using equation (1), yields

$$\frac{dW}{\beta} = -\Delta N d\theta - (\Delta + \pi)N^* d\mu + [\theta S_M + (1-\theta)S_C]dN \\ + [\mu S_M + (1-\mu)S_C]dN^* + N\pi^* d\mu^* \qquad (4)$$

The first two terms in equation (4) capture the per-period cost of changes in the strictness of patent protection for home and foreign firms, respectively. The third and fourth terms indicate that an increase with the number of home or foreign innovations provides a dynamic gain resulting from the consumer surplus associated with the new products. The final term demonstrates that increases in the strictness of foreign patents provide a static gain to the home country by increasing the profits earned on home innovations. There would be a corresponding welfare expression for the foreign country, which is not shown here.

The decomposition in equation (4) illustrates two channels through which foreign patent policies have spillover impacts on the home country. The first is through the effect of foreign patent regimes on the profits of home firms. This is analogous to a terms of trade spillover, since the denial of patent protection would result in a reduction of the price received by home entrepreneurs from p_M^* to c^* on each unit sold in the foreign market. Note, however, that the magnitude of this price effect is not necessarily proportional to the volume of home exports, because home firms may be serving the foreign market by licensing the product to foreign producers or by direct foreign investment. The fact that patent denial will not necessarily be reflected in changes in trade flows means that the GATT structure prior to TRIPS was inadequate for handling the international spillovers created by changes in IP protection.[38]

The second externality from foreign patent policy is through its impact on the rate of innovation. The extension of patent protection by the foreign government, whether through increases in θ^* or μ^*, would, by assumption, raise the amount of R&D. All countries would benefit from the increased consumer gains generated by more new products, with the benefit being greatest in countries where the surplus levels are largest because of high demand. This situation illustrates the international public-goods feature of innovation, since the introduction of new products increases consumer benefits in all markets where the product becomes available.

---

[38] BAGWELL & STAIGER, above n. 2, argue that the WTO process can prevent countries from using changes in domestic standards (for example, competition policy or labor rights) to undermine commitments made on tariffs. If the effect of such changes in standards were to reduce the volume of trade, the trading partner could make a "nonviolation" complaint under GATT article XXIII, as discussed above. This mechanism would be inadequate in the case of IPRs, however, because of the other channels through which intellectual property may be transacted across borders, apart from the moratorium on nonviolation complaints under the TRIPS Agreement, which may or may not be allowed to expire once again.

3a. Non-cooperative equilibrium

By substituting from equation (2) into equation (4), we can characterize the optimal home-country policy toward protecting innovations by home and foreign firms,[39] respectively, as

$$\Delta = \left(\frac{\theta S_M + (1-\theta) S_C}{\theta + \left(\frac{\mu^*}{\lambda}\right)} \right) \varepsilon \quad (5a)$$

$$\Delta + \pi = \left(\frac{\mu S_M + (1-\mu) S_C}{\mu + \left(\frac{\theta^*}{\lambda}\right)} \right) \varepsilon^* \quad (5b)$$

The left-hand side of each expression is the increased static deadweight cost of extending the life of the patent. The right-hand side is the marginal benefit of extending patent protection, which is the increased consumer surplus generated by more innovations. Since the right-hand side decreases with the strength of the respective types of patent rights, equations (5) generate unique solutions for θ and μ, given foreign policies.

These equations may be used to derive predictions about unilateral IP policies. One prediction is that small countries would provide less protection. Very small countries (i.e., with λ approaching zero) would have no incentive to protect intellectual property, whether it is produced by foreigners or domestic residents, because the local market contributes too little to firm profits to affect the rate of innovation. This is consistent with the examples cited by an early author, who noted that some small countries adopted patent legislation only as a result of pressure from abroad.[40]

Equations (5) also indicate that there would be a bias toward providing less protection to foreign patent holders. The static cost of extending patent protection to foreign firms is higher than is its extension to domestic firms, since the profits would go abroad. The home country would, therefore, wish to discriminate against foreign innovators as long as they are not too much more responsive to patent policy than are home innovators and as long as the foreign country does not discriminate too much against home firms. A similar welfare decomposition may be derived for the foreign country, with optimal patent policies given by expressions similar to those in equations (5).

---

[39] This model assumes that government policy is chosen to maximize national welfare. Political economy considerations could be introduced by assuming that policymakers maximize a weighted social welfare function, with greater weight put on the welfare of politically powerful groups. Such an extension would not change the prisoner's dilemma flavor of the analysis, but would affect the characterization below of efficient policies.

[40] See PENROSE, above n. 10.

3b. Efficient patent policies with lump-sum transfers

Before turning to the potential effects of IP agreements among countries, it is useful to characterize the patent policies that would maximize world welfare. These policies would be chosen if it were possible to make lump-sum transfers between countries, because they generate the largest surplus to be divided between nations. While in practice lump-sum transfers are not typically made in trade agreements, the previous discussion noted that implicit transfers may be made by the simultaneous negotiation of a trade agreement and its side agreements. A country that loses from the TRIPS Agreement might nonetheless accept the WTO Agreement if the losses on TRIPS are offset by gains of equal or greater magnitude from other parts of the Agreement. Thus, these efficient agreements serve as a useful benchmark by characterizing the patent lives that lead to the least deadweight losses from an IP agreement.

The first result identifies conditions under which innovations by firms from a given country should receive longer patent lives in the home market.[41]

> *Proposition 1: Choose the identity of countries such that $\Delta/\pi \geq \Delta^*/\pi^*$.*
>
> a) *If $\Delta/\pi = \Delta^*/\pi^*$, then world welfare will be the same for any combination of patent lives for foreign innovations that holds constant the profits of home entrepreneurs, $\pi\theta + \pi^*\mu^*$. Similarly, world welfare is the same for any combination that holds constant the profits of foreign entrepreneurs.*
>
> b) *If $\Delta/\pi > \Delta^*/\pi^*$, then world welfare can be increased by a rise in μ^* and a reduction in θ that holds profits of home entrepreneurs constant.*

The ratio Δ/π is the deadweight loss in consumption generated per dollar of profit in the home market. In case a) of Proposition 1, this cost is the same across markets, so it is equally efficient to extend patent life in the home and foreign markets. As a result, world welfare depends only on the level of profits of home firms, and not on the country in which those profits are earned. Adjustments in the home and foreign patent lengths can be used to redistribute income across countries. In case b), however, the deadweight loss per dollar of profits is higher in the home country, so it will always be more efficient to extend the patent life in the foreign country. The optimal policy would involve no patents in the home country unless $\theta^* = 1$ or $\mu^* = 1$.

Proposition 1 establishes conditions under which it is desirable to discriminate in favor of consumers in one country. The next result establishes

---

[41] Proposition 1 is derived by considering the effect on $W + W^*$, using equation (4), of a change in patent policy such that $\pi d\theta + \pi^* d\mu^* = 0$.

conditions under which the efficient policy should discriminate in favor of firms from one of the countries.[42]

> Proposition 2: Suppose $\Delta/\pi = \Delta^*/\pi^*$. Then efficient patent laws will give higher profits to foreign (home) firms if $\varepsilon^* > (<) \varepsilon$.

If $\varepsilon^* > \varepsilon$, then a given increase in patent life (and hence deadweight loss) would generate more innovations from foreign firms than from home firms. Therefore, foreign entrepreneurs should be favored at the margin because they are a more efficient source of new innovations. Non-discrimination would be efficient only when $\varepsilon^* = \varepsilon$.

Turn now to an examination of the gains from cooperative agreements on IPRs and how mechanisms could be used to punish countries that deviate from the agreed terms. We concentrate on two features of the TRIPS Agreement, which are the requirement of national treatment and the setting of minimum standards for eligibility, duration and enforcement of patents.

3c. International agreements to reduce discrimination

Figure 2 illustrates the prisoner's dilemma that arises in the setting of μ and μ^*, the patent lengths each country offers firms located in the other nation. The value $\mu^N(\mu^{N^*})$ in the figure denotes the Nash equilibrium values of patent lives for non-residents in the home (foreign) country, and the $V^N(V^{N^*})$ contour illustrates the values of μ and μ^* that yield the same home (foreign) country welfare as in the Nash equilibrium (holding constant the patent lengths each country offers its own innovators, θ and θ^*).[43] It follows from equation (3) that each country benefits from a strengthening of property rights protection for its firms in the other country's market. An increase in μ^* would raise the profits earned by home firms in the foreign market and raise the rate of home innovation, both of which would raise home welfare. Therefore, points to the right of V^N yield higher home-country welfare than is attained in the Nash equilibrium, and points above V^{N^*} yield higher foreign welfare than in the Nash equilibrium. Note that contour V^N is vertical at the Nash equilibrium, which results from the fact that μ maximizes home welfare at the given value of μ^*. A similar argument establishes that V^{N^*} is horizontal at the Nash equilibrium point.

---

[42] Proposition 2 is proved by assuming national treatment at home ($\theta = \mu$), and abroad ($\theta^* = \mu^*$), and examining discriminatory adjustments in patent protection such that $d\theta = -C''(N)d\mu/C^{*''}(N^*) > 0$. A similar result can be derived for the case where $\Delta/\pi > \Delta^*/\pi^*$.

[43] Such contours are called "iso-welfare" lines in economics.

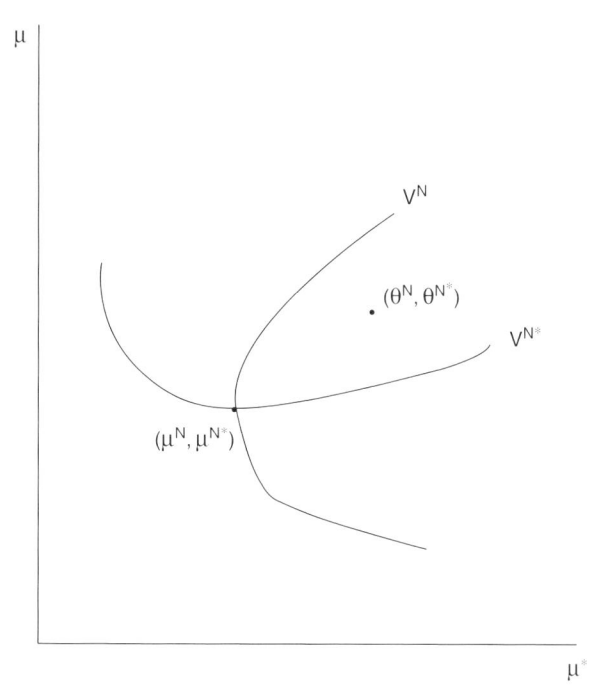

Figure 2: Nash equilibrium protection of nonresidents

A simultaneous increase in both μ and μ^* (holding θ and θ^* constant) in the neighborhood of the Nash point must raise the welfare of both countries, because it moves patent protection into of the lens-shaped area of mutually welfare-increasing agreements to the northeast of the equilibrium in Figure 2. Since the failure to do this (only the Nash point is a sustainable equilibrium under unilateral policy making) represents a prisoner's dilemma, as in the case of trade liberalization, the threat of reversion to the Nash equilibrium plays a role similar to that in the case of trade disputes. A cooperative agreement to raise μ and μ^* in this case could be supported by the threat to revert to the levels of policy discrimination if the countries placed enough weight on future payoffs.[44]

One factor that may make IPRs agreements more difficult to sustain than trade agreements is the difficulty of observing deviations from the coordinated solution. The longer it takes either country to observe deviation by the other, the more attractive it would be for either to deviate and, therefore, the more difficult it would be to sustain the pact supporting national treatment. Since the protection of IPRs requires firms to be able to pursue damages against

---

[44] This argument relies on application of standard "folk theorem" arguments in game theory. See MYERSON, above n. 1.

infringers, deviations from national treatment that involved discrimination against foreigners in their ability to enforce IPRs through the court system might take longer to be detected. The minimum discount factor required to support a given level of cooperation would be higher when the delay in observing a deviation is greater.

The discussion above established a case for a mutual reduction in the degree of discrimination between countries. Note, however, that TRIPS imposed a stronger requirement, which involves national treatment to non-resident patent holders (that is, $\theta = \mu$ and $\theta^* = \mu^*$). Such an agreement would be acceptable to both countries if it is contained in the lens of mutually welfare-improving agreements. Unfortunately, this is not necessarily the case, as illustrated in Figure 2. In the situation depicted, the home country is a significant net importer of patented products. In order for the home country to be willing to accept an agreement with national treatment, the agreement would need to be bundled with another accord giving that country sufficiently large gains to make up the welfare loss from the IPRs pact.[45]

It should also be noted that even if national treatment policies were constrained to lie in the lens of mutually welfare-increasing agreements, they might not constitute an efficient accord in the global sense, for such efficiency requires a tangency between iso-welfare contours of the two countries. Consider the case in which $\Delta/\pi = \Delta^*/\pi^*$ and $\varepsilon^* = \varepsilon$. It follows from Propositions 1 and 2 that, in this case, there would be a level of profits $\widetilde{\Pi}$ such that any combination of patent lengths for which $\pi\theta + \mu^*\pi^* = \widetilde{\Pi}$ and $\pi^*\theta^* + \mu\pi = \widetilde{\Pi}$ would yield a world welfare-maximizing level of innovations. If national treatment were imposed, efficiency could be achieved with any combinations of home and foreign patent lives such that $\pi\theta + \theta^*\pi^* = \widetilde{\Pi}$.

This result shows that an efficient agreement with national treatment can always be found if countries negotiate all of the patent parameters. On the other hand, suppose that countries treat $\{\theta, \theta^*\}$ as given and negotiate over $\{\mu, \mu^*\}$. An efficient agreement would be attainable so long as $\widetilde{\Pi}$ can be achieved with both μ and μ^* lying between zero and one, but the agreement would be unlikely to involve national treatment.

In order to characterize the reciprocal increases in patent protection that would raise home welfare, combine equations (2) and (4) to obtain

$$\frac{dV}{\beta} = N\left[\pi^* + \frac{(\theta S_M + (1-\theta)S_C)\varepsilon\pi^*}{(\theta\pi + \mu^*\pi^*)}\right]d\mu^*$$
$$+ N^*\left[-(\pi+\theta) + \frac{(\mu S_M + (1-\mu)S_C)\varepsilon^*\pi}{(\theta^*\pi^* + \mu\pi)}\right]d\mu \qquad (6)$$

Expression (6) can be used to obtain a definition of reciprocity for IRPs agreements and also to identify what might be considered the equivalent

---

[45] This point was made by Suzanne Scotchmer, above n. 35.

concessions to be withdrawn by the dispute process if a country deviated from its obligations. The second bracketed term in equation (6) would be negative for concessions that exceeded the unilateral optimal patent treatment of patent lives. The reciprocal lengthening of patent durations would provide home firms increased profits of $N\pi^* d\mu^*$, but would have a consumer cost of $N^* \pi d\mu$ through higher profits to foreign firms.

One strategy for defining a reciprocal increase in patent lives would be to choose the extension such that the net profit transfers between countries were zero. This would leave two effects of reciprocal extension: the deadweight loss from the extension of patent life in the home market and the increased consumer surplus from the rise in home and foreign product varieties through induced innovation.

3d. Minimum standards for IPRs

A similar argument to that above can be used to demonstrate that the welfare of both countries can be improved by a mutual increase in θ and θ^*, in the neighborhood of the Nash equilibrium. This case is illustrated in Figure 3, which shows iso-welfare contours for the home and foreign countries associated with the Nash-point choices of θ and θ^*. The home welfare decomposition in equation (3) shows that that country's well-being would be increasing in θ^* because an increase in that parameter would raise N^*. Thus, domestic innovations would be under-protected in the Nash equilibrium because some of the benefits of increased product development in one country accrue to consumers in the other country.[46] There exist mutually welfare-improving agreements that would result in the extension of patent life in both countries.

In contrast, the setting of a minimum standard on patents would not necessarily raise the welfare of both countries. Suppose that $\theta^N > \theta^{N^*}$. Then a minimum standard that requires the foreign country to set a patent length exceeding θ^{N^*} would reduce its welfare, as illustrated in Figure 3. In order for the foreign nation to be willing to participate in an agreement on minimum patent standards, it would need to be compensated by the home country with concessions on some other aspects of the overall agreement.

This model is capable of showing that an accord with minimum IPRs standards can be supported by concessions in tariff rates (market access) by countries already above the minimum requirement. However, such an agreement does nothing to deal with the potential spillovers associated with

---

[46] This argument is based on the assumption that μ and μ^* are held constant. A similar argument can be used in the case where national treatment has been imposed, so that $d\mu = d\theta$ and $d\mu^* = d\theta^*$. In this case an extension of patent life by the foreign country would increase home profits, the number of home brands (products), and the number of foreign brands. All three of these effects would provide favorable spillovers to the home nation, so its iso-welfare contours would be similar to those in Figure 3 in this case also.

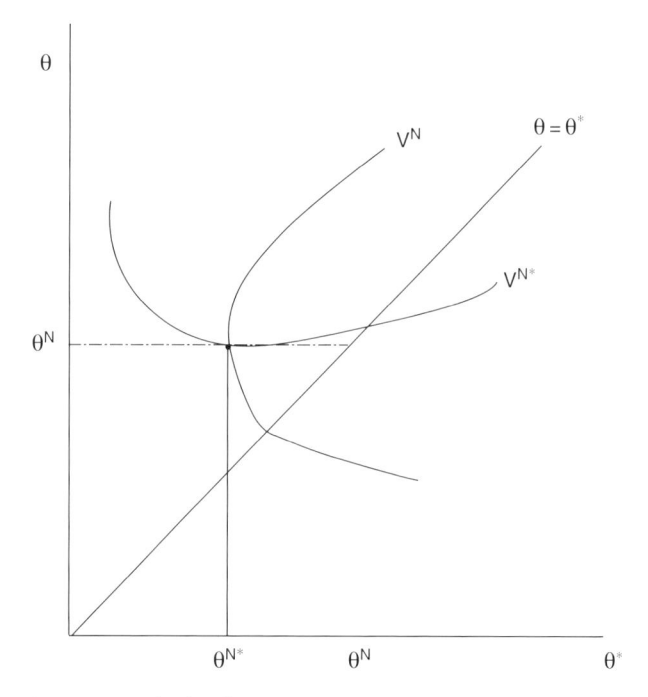

Figure 3: Minimum standards of patent protection at the home country level

innovations by countries whose IPRs are above the minimum. This raises the question of why TRIPS took the form it did, rather than calling for a reciprocal expansion of patent lengths in all countries.[47]

An agreement with reciprocal expansion would not need to be tied to a trade agreement to be self-enforcing, because violations of the patent agreement could be punished by a withdrawal of equivalent patent extensions. The fact that the impetus for TRIPS came from developed economies suggests that the developing nations placed relatively little value on expansions of patent duration by the former group. The welfare decomposition in equation (4) above shows that the home country would receive a small benefit when the extension in foreign patent life had a small impact on the total number of innovations. Thus, the form TRIPS took could be explained if developed-country patent regimes had already internalized the beneficial spillovers created by increases in the number of innovated products. The minimum standard would then be a way of transferring income from developing to developed countries.

The theoretical model utilized here assumes that the expiration of patent rights in one location has no effect on the security of patents in another

---

[47] TRIPS set a global minimum patent length of 20 years from the date of filing, which had already been the policy in place in many developed economies. See TRIPS Agreement, above n. 3, art. 33; MASKUS, above n. 6.

country. If border enforcement were not perfect, the expiration of patent rights in one location might make it more costly to enforce remaining rights elsewhere. This type of spillover might strengthen the argument for an agreement specifying a minimum standard for IPRs, since short patent lengths would provide a negative spillover to other countries. However, this would still not change the basic observation that the setting of minimum standards would involve a transfer from low-standard nations to high-standard nations.

4. Conclusions

This chapter has examined the role of the dispute settlement process in the TRIPS Agreement and has identified several ways in which disputes involving IPRs may differ from those involving trade in goods. One difference is the greater difficulty of identifying a deviation from obligations concerning IPRs. The presence of laws satisfying TRIPS requirements would not be satisfactory to protect intellectual property if the laws were not enforced, and the intensity of enforcement may be more difficult to observe and prove in the dispute process. This would reduce the level of cooperation on IPRs that can be supported because the cost of deviating from the Agreement would be lower.

A second difference arises from the fact that the costs of deviations from an IPRs agreement would be more difficult to quantify because of international spillovers created by innovation in open economies. While the costs of TRIPS violations in terms of foregone profits could be calculated by a dispute-resolution panel, the impact on the rate of innovation may be much more difficult to quantify.

Finally, the fact that TRIPS involves the setting of minimum standards means that the Agreement reflects a transfer from countries with lax IPRs to countries with strict IPRs. This situation implies that deviations from TRIPS standards cannot in many cases be punished by withdrawal of equivalent concessions within the context of the Agreement itself. For such cases, it is necessary to permit withdrawal of concessions made under other parts of the WTO Agreement. This fact suggests that a major gain from incorporation of TRIPS into the WTO Agreement, rather than having it as a separate agreement, is the ability to punish deviators by using tariffs on trade in goods.

33

Intellectual property rights and dispute settlement in the World Trade Organization

WILFRED J. ETHIER*

Abstract
I.   The economist's conventional view of trade agreements
II. The meaning of dispute settlement
III. Dispute settlement and TRIPS
Conclusion: Trade and TRIPS externalities

ABSTRACT

With the advent of the TRIPS Agreement, international disputes about governmental regulation of intellectual property rights (IPRs) are now subject to adjudication within the WTO dispute resolution mechanism. The standard model used by economists to explain dispute settlement procedures is misleading, for the process is not about preventing countries from exercising market power. Rather, the system is designed to resolve political market failures arising within countries that would be harmful to market access for foreign firms. These issues arise particularly in the context of intellectual property rights (IPRs), which may be used as cross-market bargaining chips. This possibility is illustrated by the petition of Ecuador to suspend concessions in this area for European firms in the context of the *EU – Banana* case. The scope of such an approach remains unclear, and there are many fundamental questions deserving close analysis. In this chapter, I make several basic points relating to the economics of IPRs and to the World Trade Organization's (WTO) dispute settlement process. These comments underscore the fact that the injection of IPRs into the global trading system raises a new dimension for settling disputes.

I. The economist's conventional view of trade agreements

The prevalent view among international trade theorists is that trade agreements exist to deal with terms-of-trade externalities between countries. Specifically,

---

* Wilfred J. Ethier is Professor of Economics, University of Pennsylvania. He wishes to acknowledge helpful comments by Keith Maskus and Petros Mavroidis.

when such large nations or aggregations as the United States and the European Union implement business standards or undertake regulatory actions, they may have the secondary effect of restricting trade and worsening market-access opportunities for exporting countries.[1] Or, more directly, a country large enough to have monopoly power in international trade could gain welfare at its trading partner's expense by imposing a tax on its exports. As Eric Bond points out in his chapter,[2] the basic features of the General Agreement on Tariffs and Trade (GATT) and the WTO[3] are widely thought – by trade theorists but by almost no one else – to reflect this function.

This view, prevalent though it might be among trade theorists, is a fantasy. The GATT articles, incorporated into the WTO Agreements, and the associated schedules of national concessions do not, with very rare exceptions, constrain a country from exploiting monopoly power in world markets by taxing its exports. Article XI explicitly exempts "duties, taxes or other charges," and, therefore, export taxes, from its elimination of quantitative restrictions "or other measures."[4] The GATT does require most-favored-nation (MFN) treatment for export taxes, and it does allow countries to bind export taxes in their schedules of concessions. But, with very rare exceptions, they have just not done so. In contrast, even sophisticated economic theories employ a two-commodity model, in which export taxes are completely equivalent to import tariffs for everything the government is assumed to care about. They therefore analyze WTO trade rules in an environment in which the actual WTO rules would be completely meaningless.[5]

It is not sensible, therefore, to base a theory of the WTO's Agreement on Trade-Related Aspects of Intellectual Property Rights (TRIPS Agreement)[6] on an entirely imaginary theory of multilateral agreements about trade in goods. However, the received economic model does bear relevance, for its true value lies in its insistence that trade agreements should be viewed as responses to international externalities. Identifying this externality exclusively with the

---

[1] *See, e.g.,* JAGDISH BHAGWATI ET AL., LECTURES ON INTERNATIONAL TRADE (MIT Press 2d ed. 1998). The approach is developed beautifully in KYLE BAGWELL & ROBERT M. STAIGER, THE ECONOMICS OF THE WORLD TRADING SYSTEM (MIT Press 2002).
[2] Eric W. Bond, *The Economics of International Trade Agreements and Dispute Settlement with Intellectual Property Rights* [this volume].
[3] Marrakesh Agreement Establishing the World Trade Organization, Annex 1A, Multilateral Agreements on Trade in Goods, 15 Apr. 1994, 33 I.L.M. 1154, (1994) [hereinafter GATT 1994].
[4] *See* GATT 1994, above n. 3, art. XI.
[5] See BAGWELL & STAIGER, above n. 1, for the leading exposition. I do not mean to single out Bagwell and Staiger for blame. They are doing what most other trade theorists have been doing for half a century, but they do it better.
[6] Agreement on Trade-Related Aspects of Intellectual Property Rights, 15 Apr. 1994, Marrakesh Agreement Establishing the World Trade Organization, Annex 1C, LEGAL INSTRUMENTS – RESULT OF THE URUGUAY ROUND vol. 31, 33 I.L.M. 81 (1994) [hereinafter TRIPS Agreement].

terms of trade, though understandable in light of the existing trade theory literature that recent authors followed and further developed,[7] was most unfortunate. It has condemned the work to apparent irrelevance.

Fortunately many of the ideas in this literature, such as the role of reciprocity, can still be applied when the externality is more relevant than the terms of trade: various types of international political externalities, for example.[8] By and large, these theories deliver trade agreements consistent with the actual WTO rules only if political externalities dominate terms-of-trade externalities.

II. The meaning of dispute settlement

It is widely believed that the WTO's Understanding on Rules and Procedures Governing the Settlement of Disputes (DSU)[9] has something to do with punishment. It does, after all, authorize a retaliatory withdrawal of concessions when a country fails to comply with an obligation it has accepted. The common view among economists, as Bond explains, is that at least one of the purposes of the DSU (viewed as a process) is to facilitate punishments that can deter violations of trade agreements.[10] From this viewpoint, the interesting question is why the punishments are so weak. These punishments are sometimes characterized by economists as tit-for-tat, meaning that the country believing its trade benefits to have been nullified or impaired is permitted to implement retaliatory sanctions on volumes of trade that are only roughly equivalent to the reduced trade it has suffered.[11]

I believe this view reflects a fundamental misunderstanding of the punishment role of the WTO dispute settlement process. That role is not to facilitate punishment; rather, it is to constrain it. The actual source of punishment potential is not to be found in the formal activities of the Dispute Settlement Body (DSB), but in the bilateral essence of the bargains embodied in the multilateral trade agreements. If one country's trade partner does not supply the access that was bargained for, it will not deliver the access it had promised. The bilateral nature of the WTO and its DSU in a legal sense was argued persuasively by Pauwelyn.[12] I argue here that there is an important economic aspect to this bilateralism as well.

---

[7] BAGWELL & STAIGER, above n. 1.
[8] See Wilfred J. Ethier, Trade Policies and Trade Agreements Based on Political Externalities: An Examination, University of Pennsylvania PIER Working Paper 04–006 (2004); Wilfred J. Ethier, *Political Externalities, Nondiscrimination and a Multilateral World*, 12 REV. INT'L ECON. 303–320 (2004).
[9] Marrakesh Agreement Establishing the World Trade Organization, Annex 2, Understanding on Rules and Procedures Governing the Settlement of Disputes, 15 Apr. 1994, 33 I.L.M. 1226 [hereinafter DSU].
[10] Bond, above n. 2. [11] On the tit-for-tat game, see BAGWELL & STAIGER, above n. 1.
[12] See Joost Pauwelyn, *WTO Dispute Settlement: Of Sovereign Interests, Private Rights and Public Goods* [this volume].

The DSU constrains this punishment potential in three crucial ways. First, it accords the peaceful resolution of trade disputes primacy over punishment for past violations. Article 22, paragraph 1 of the WTO Dispute Settlement Understanding (DSU) states:

> Compensation and the suspension of concessions or other obligations are temporary measures available in the event that the recommendations and rulings are not implemented within a reasonable period of time. However, neither compensation nor the suspension of concessions or other obligations is preferred to full implementation of a recommendation to bring a measure into conformity with the covered agreements. Compensation is voluntary, and, if granted, shall be consistent with the covered agreements.[13]

Second, the DSU seeks to maintain reciprocity by restricting the punishments to a substantially equivalent withdrawal of concessions. As stated in article 22, paragraph 4 of the DSU: "The level of the suspension of concessions or other obligations authorized by the DSB shall be equivalent to the level of the nullification or impairment." Further, DSU itself calculates what is substantially equivalent. That is, the purpose is not to punish; it is to maintain reciprocity in the face of violations.

Of course, there is still some element of punishment because a complainant country can choose to withdraw those concessions that are the most damaging politically to the government of its non-compliant partner. But this reflects inherent bilateralism rather than an underlying intent of the DSU. A government that feels it needs to back out of a trade commitment can do so legally, by negotiating with the foreign countries principally affected over appropriate reciprocal suspensions, or illegally, by simply refusing to honor its commitment.[14] The latter route allows the government to accommodate domestic interest groups and to postpone the implementation of reciprocal retaliation. But, in the end, it must either negotiate or forsake playing a role in determining what those reciprocal suspension actions will be.

Third, the DSU attempts to constrain disputes in order that they remain bilateral and not develop into multilateral issues. All the details of the DSU reflect the aim of keeping disputes bilateral. Most notable is the fact that, although collective punishment would greatly enhance deterrence, the DSU has no provision for any kind of collective punishment. Only complainants themselves may punish noncompliance under a finding by the DSB. The purpose is not to limit the ability of other countries to become involved. They can either become co-complainants or declare themselves to be interested parties, thereby reserving the right to contribute input to the process. Rather, the purpose is to prevent an individual dispute from escalating into a conflict that could threaten or split the WTO.

In summary, the WTO dispute settlement process has nothing really to do with facilitating punishment. Its purpose is to prevent retaliation from

---

[13] DSU, above n. 9, art. 22. [14] *See* Pauwelyn, above n. 12.

undermining the nature of trade agreements as a collection of bilateral, reciprocal, non-discriminatory deals between sovereign states.[15] The underlying philosophy of the GATT/WTO is that no country should be forced, *ex post*, to implement policies that it does not want to implement, typically due to domestic political opposition. Presumably no country would be willing to sign on, *ex ante*, without such assurance. However, this effective possibility of renegotiation must preserve reciprocity in order to maintain the integrity of the original agreement. Thus, the purpose of the DSU is simply to preserve reciprocity even when renegotiation does not succeed.[16]

III. Dispute settlement and TRIPS

I turn next to the protection of intellectual property rights in this environment. The significance of the TRIPS Agreement is not that it addresses IPRs in an international context, for international patent and copyright conventions have done this for over a century.[17] The TRIPS Agreement moves beyond this situation in two ways. First, the earlier conventions were essentially concerned with national treatment (a U.K. inventor should be able to apply for a patent in Japan on the same terms as a Japanese inventor), whereas TRIPS addresses harmonization (all countries should implement a common minimum standard of intellectual property protection).[18]

Second, TRIPS promotes harmonization in a comprehensive global context with a formal dispute settlement mechanism, the dispute settlement process at the WTO. Note that the DSU is not an international enforcement mechanism that can be utilized by, or for the necessary benefit of, private parties with grievances, for the WTO is a contract between members (who are states or international entities, such as the E.U.).[19] This fact may be what is most important from a legal perspective[20] and presumably will have fundamental economic implications.

---

[15] *See* BERNARD HOEKMAN & MICHEL KOSTECKI, THE POLITICAL ECONOMY OF THE WORLD TRADING SYSTEM: THE WTO AND BEYOND (Oxford University Press 2d ed. 2001).

[16] Wilfred J. Ethier, Punishments and Dispute Settlement in Trade Agreements, University of Pennsylvania PIER Working Paper 01–021 (2001).

[17] Thus, the Paris Convention for the Protection of Industrial Property was signed in 1883 and the Berne Convention for the Protection of Literary and Artistic Works in 1886. *See* WORLD INTELLECTUAL PROPERTY ORGANIZATION, WIPO INTELLECTUAL PROPERTY HANDBOOK: POLICY, LAW AND USE, *at* http://www.wipo.int.

[18] For an analysis of harmonization, see KEITH E. MASKUS, INTELLECTUAL PROPERTY RIGHTS IN THE GLOBAL ECONOMY (Institute for International Economics 2000); Suzanne Scotchmer, *The Political Economy of Intellectual Property Treaties*, 20 J.L. ECON. ORG. 415/2004).

[19] HOEKMAN & KOSTECKI, above n. 15.

[20] *See* Graeme B. Dinwoodie & Rochelle Cooper Dreyfus, *WTO Dispute Resolution and the Preservation of the Public Domain of Science under International Law* [this volume] (analysing the significance of the TRIPS Agreement for future development of U.S. patent law).

From the perspective of economics, however, I think the most interesting and significant aspect of TRIPS could eventually lie elsewhere. Previous international agreements and conventions regarding IPRs were concluded among countries regarding the protection of such rights to be in their mutual self-interest. Countries believing that such protection would not, on balance, promote their self-interest, because they were net importers of intellectual property, simply did not participate.[21] Thus, in the nineteenth century, the United States declined to conclude a copyright agreement with Britain when the U.S. was a heavy consumer of British literature, but experienced a change in values as the literary balance of trade changed.[22]

The TRIPS Agreement has changed these tradeoffs. The Uruguay Round can be seen, on one interpretation, as including a Great Bargain (the so-called "Single Undertaking"), in which many developing countries believed – rightly or wrongly – that the protection of intellectual property was not in their self-interest, but agreed to it in exchange for trade concessions on goods, such as textiles and apparel, that were important to them as exports or as potential exports.[23] Newer WTO Members have accepted it to gain accession.[24] This was the first really significant example of such an inter-bloc bargain in all the GATT rounds.

The Great Bargain featured an asymmetry of implementation reflecting an asymmetry of power. The TRIPS Agreement was to be implemented reasonably promptly, but the developed-country trade concessions were to be delayed.[25] For example, abolition of the Multi-Fiber Agreement (MFA), the main developed-country concession, was to be gradually adopted over a ten-year period, with most of the trade-barrier elimination scheduled for the final year. At this point it is far from clear that the Great Bargain will in fact be consummated.

In view of the Great Bargain, it is likely that disputes will emerge in which the suspension of trade concessions becomes the threatened response, or the action necessary to maintain reciprocity, in response to an asserted failure in the protection of IPRs. Thus, I welcome Bond's emphasis on the possibility of such suspensions.[26]

---

[21] MASKUS, above n. 18; see also Zorina Khan, Intellectual Property and Economic Development: Lessons from American and European History, Commission on Intellectual Property Rights, study paper 1a, at http://www.iprcommission.org/graphic/documents/study_papers.htm.

[22] Khan, above n. 21.

[23] This should not be interpreted as a bargain between monolithic blocs of developed and developing countries, respectively. For example, some developing countries value highly the rents that accrue to them from export quotas on textiles and apparel. See MASKUS, above n. 18; see also SUSAN K. SELL, PRIVATE POWER, PUBLIC LAW: THE GLOBALIZATION OF INTELLECTUAL PROPERTY RIGHTS (Cambridge University Press 2003).

[24] HOEKMAN & KOSTECKI, above n. 15.

[25] See J. Michael Finger & Philip Schuler, Implementation of Uruguay Round Commitments: The Development Challenge (World Bank 1999) (manuscript).

[26] Bond, above n. 2.

The opposite possibility, of a country suspending its TRIPS commitments in response to a goods trade violation, is probably even more interesting. For example, when the E.U. declined to abide by a negative DSB finding in its banana dispute with the U.S., Ecuador, a co-complainant (and the country with the world's largest banana exports), was authorized to suspend concessions in response. When a country is authorized to suspend concessions to a trading partner that has refused to abide by a negative DSB ruling, the concessions ordinarily should be in sectors reasonably close to that in which the original violations are taking place.[27] If this is not practical, either because withdrawals in such sectors would be unduly damaging to the aggrieved country or because they would not be politically painful enough to the government in violation, the suspensions may take place in more distant sectors. If necessary, they may even involve suspension under related agreements, such as the General Agreement on Trade in Services (GATS) or TRIPS.

Ecuador did not think that suspending market-access concessions in merchandise trade would be useful in this regard. It imports small quantities (relative to world markets) of a wide variety of consumer goods, and so could not inflict political pain on the E.U. with such restrictions. Moreover, Ecuador's imports of producer goods were intermediate products vital to Ecuadorian industry. Thus, the country sought, and was awarded, approval to suspend some of its TRIPS obligations in favor of the E.U.[28]

This threat got the attention of the E.U., which complained to the DSB and asked for arbitration under article 22, paragraph 6 of the DSU. The final result was largely in Ecuador's favor. Thus, the policy advocated by Bond[29] is indeed currently available. The main question is how strictly the "practicality" test is to be applied. The fact that in the *E.U. – Banana* case the WTO permitted Ecuador to suspend concessions in IPRs suggests that the test will not be applied strictly enough to prevent such cross-agreement suspensions. I think, however, that the reason the possibility of such cross-agreement suspensions is desirable is not that without them the set of retaliatory responses is too small, though that no doubt often is true. It is that this situation is necessary for the DSU to fulfill its function of maintaining the reciprocity of relevant bilateral bargains across agreements within the Great Bargain.

Indeed, this situation should give pause to critics of TRIPS, who often assert that it amounts to a massive transfer from poor countries to rich countries, with the former having little prospect of developing significant intellectual property of their own and the latter little incentive to invest in innovations

---

[27] *See* DSU, above n. 9, art. 22, para. 3.
[28] *See* European Communities: Regime for the Importation, Sale and Distribution of Bananas, WTO Doc. WT/DS27/18 (1998).
[29] Bond, above n. 2.

especially useful for the poor countries.[30] There may be considerable validity to these points. There is, however, another significant consideration that could turn out to be of greater long-term importance. Since the late 1980s, numerous developing countries have dramatically reoriented their trade policies from import substitution to open participation in the multilateral trading system.[31]

Most of these countries, like Ecuador, are unable to exert much negotiating leverage through an ability to withdraw trade concessions. The TRIPS Agreement, along with the possibility of cross-agreement suspensions, could help to change that situation. It may well give at least some developing countries meaningful hostages in their relations with developed countries. For this to be possible, the former countries must adopt TRIPS-consistent policies with sufficiently strong standards to be thought significant by the developed countries.[32]

It is sometimes claimed that the developing countries have been slow to utilize the WTO dispute settlement process and that the lack of significant punishment ability in the event of noncompliance could be part of the reason.[33] The TRIPS Agreement conceivably could turn out to be just what is required for developing countries to make full use of their DSU rights. In any event, it cannot but help aid those countries in trying to make sure that the Great Bargain is indeed consummated and that the MFA is actually eliminated.

Conclusion: Trade and TRIPS externalities

There is still much to think about. A combination of a TRIPS violation and the threatened withdrawal of a trade concession (or the opposite) could involve other closely related concessions in still other ways, despite their asymmetric natures. For example, the implementation of IP protection by a developing country could stimulate more inward technology transfer, inducing the production of goods that can, because of a developed-country trade concession, be exported.[34]

---

[30] *See* Commission for Intellectual Property Rights, Integrating Intellectual Property Rights with Economic Development (2002).

[31] HOEKMAN & KOSTECKI, above n. 15; GLOBALIZATION, GROWTH AND POVERTY: BUILDING AN INCLUSIVE WORLD ECONOMY (The World Bank 2002).

[32] For a relevant discussion, see Gene M. Grossman & Petros Mavroidis, *Section 110(5) of the Copyright Act, Recourse to Arbitration under Article 25 of the DSU: Would've or Should've: Impaired Benefits Due to Copyright Infringement*, in THE WTO CASE LAW OF 2001 (H. Horn & P. Mavroidis eds., Cambridge University Press 2004).

[33] The evidence on this point is mixed. *See* Henrik Horn et al., Is the Use of the WTO Dispute Settlement System Biased?, Center for Economic Policy Research Discussion Paper 2340 (1999); Chad Bown, *Developing Countries as Plaintiffs and Defendants in GATT/WTO Trade Disputes*, 27 WORLD ECON. 59 (2004).

[34] *See* Kamal Saggi, Encouraging Technology Transfer to Developing Countries: Role of the WTO, Report to the Commonwealth Secretariat (2003).

Thus, noncompliance by either side in a dispute could undermine the efficiency of both markets.

More generally, I would like to see an analysis of a model of trade agreements based on an exchange of market access in goods or services trade for concessions regarding the protection of IPRs. What are the relevant political and economic externalities?[35] Should such agreements possess the same features as agreements based solely on goods trade, including MFN, national treatment, and reciprocity? What should be the role of a DSU in such agreements, and what features should it possess?

---

[35] *See* Keith E. Maskus, *Regulatory Standards in the WTO: Comparing Intellectual Property Rights with Competition Policy, Environmental Protection, and Core Labor Standards*, 1 WORLD TRADE REV. 135 (2002).

34

WTO dispute resolution and the preservation of the public domain of science under international law

GRAEME B. DINWOODIE
ROCHELLE COOPER DREYFUSS*

Abstract
I. Introduction
II. Upstream patenting and its relationship to technological progress
III. Hypothetical solutions and their international implications
  A. Subject matter exclusions
  B. Exemptions
    1. Article 30's "three-part test"
      (a) Scope of uses: "Limited" exceptions
      (b) Economic impact: Conflict with normal exploitation
        (i) National practices
        (ii) Typical means of exploiting the patent
        (iii) Source of commercial capacity
      (c) Types of uses: Unreasonable prejudice to legitimate interests
    2. Article 27's technological neutrality
  C. Remedies
IV. Concluding observations

ABSTRACT

The TRIPS Agreement can be read to reflect a static view of the structure of intellectual property law. In this chapter, we address whether – and how – the TRIPS Agreement can be interpreted to give it more fluidity, and thus to allow adjustments in national intellectual property regimes designed to reflect the

---

* Graeme Dinwoodie is Professor of Law and Norman & Edna Freehling Scholar, Director, Program in Intellectual Property Law, Chicago-Kent College of Law; Rochelle Cooper Dreyfuss is Pauline Newman Professor of Law, New York University School of Law. The authors wish to thank Brian Havel, Tim Holbrook, and Carlos Correa for comments on an earlier draft of this paper. Thanks also to participants in Rebecca Eisenberg and Molly Van Houweling's patent law workshop at the University of Michigan, and to the Filomen D'Agostino and Max E. Greenberg Research Fund at NYU for financial support. Copyright 2004, Graeme B. Dinwoodie and Rochelle Cooper Dreyfuss.

dynamic nature of information production. To focus that inquiry, we concentrate on efforts to ensure a broader public domain for "upstream" inventions by modifying various elements of U.S. patent law. The paper considers three stylized examples and asks whether each approach could be adopted by the United States without falling afoul of the TRIPS Agreement, as it is currently understood. Our purpose is to identify interpretive approaches that allow Members to keep their laws attuned to the developments and needs of science. In so doing, we also raise broader questions regarding the level of formalism generated by the WTO dispute settlement system, and the extent to which the TRIPS Agreement allocates power between supranational and national institutions, and between international and national laws.

I. Introduction

The size and content of a rich public domain are affected by a constellation of national intellectual property rules: provisions that define protectable subject matter, establish threshold requirements for protection, delineate the scope of the rights awarded, create defenses and exemptions from liability, and set remedies for infringement.[1] Since 1995, the Agreement on Trade Related Aspects of Intellectual Property (the TRIPS Agreement)[2] has imposed specific limitations on the contours of these rules, and it thus serves to regulate on an international level the ways in which members of the WTO can shape the contents of the private and public domains.

At the time the TRIPS Agreement was negotiated, the main focus of attention was on codifying then agreed-upon norms of protection. As a result, the Agreement can be read to reflect a static view of the structure of intellectual property law. Information production is, however, a dynamic enterprise. Additions to the domain of knowledge can change the intellectual landscape and thereby alter the creative opportunities – and challenges – facing artists and inventors. New industries emerge, others mature; nations have traditionally administered, interpreted, and modified their rules to achieve the balance between public and private rights that is appropriate, at any given time, for each field. The question we address in this chapter is whether – and how – the TRIPS Agreement can be read with equivalent fluidity, in order to allow adjustments in national regimes that reflect the dynamic nature of information production. In a sense, this

---

[1] Public access to intellectual products can also turn on who owns the rights and how the owner exploits the work. *See, e.g.*, Arti K. Rai & Rebecca S. Eisenberg, *Bayh-Dole Reform and the Progress of Biomedicine*, 66 LAW & CONTEMP. PROBS. 289 (2003) (arguing that funding agencies should have greater authority to demand patent rights in fundamental research results produced by universities in government-funded projects).

[2] Agreement on Trade-Related Aspects of Intellectual Property Rights, 15 Apr. 1994, Marrakesh Agreement Establishing the World Trade Organization, Annex 1C, Legal Instruments – Results of the Uruguay Round vol. 31, 33 I.L.M. 81 (1994) [hereinafter TRIPS Agreement].

problem is not new, as many of the WTO nations have operated under the constraints of international obligations for over a century. Nonetheless, the TRIPS Agreement raises unique concerns because it addresses a broader range of issues than prior instruments and, as the first global intellectual property agreement to include a compliance mechanism, it has unprecedented bite.

To focus the inquiry, we concentrate on efforts in United States patent law to ensure a broader public domain for "upstream" inventions, that is, for discoveries so directly related to fundamental principles that they dominate broad swaths of inventive opportunities.[3] The expansion of patentable subject matter to include upstream inventions has led concerned observers to suggest that other elements of patent law must also be modified in order to re-create public-domain space in which work can be undertaken in accordance with traditional scientific norms.[4] To be sure, *expanding* the categories or the scope of protectable subject matter in domestic law comports with a basic premise of the TRIPS Agreement, which leaves considerable discretion to WTO members to provide protection in excess of mandated minimum levels.[5] But these proposed modifications, by *contracting* protection, would arguably raise TRIPS-compliance concerns and thus bring into question the resilience of the Agreement.

The public domain could be reconstituted in a variety of ways: by modifying the definition of statutory subject matter, elevating the threshold for protection, adjusting the scope of rights, creating new exemptions, or imposing new types of relief. Its contours could also be changed by revising non-intellectual property regimes (including administrative and procedural law) and by altering the mechanisms and institutions that facilitate private ordering. Evaluating a broad range of approaches would allow us to fully probe the provisions of the TRIPS Agreement to see which are most hospitable to protecting the public domain of science. At this point, however, we look at only three stylized examples. These are: (1) excluding certain discoveries from the subject matter of eligible patent protection; (2) creating a statutory exemption that gives courts discretion to permit unauthorized uses of sufficient social significance; and (3) varying the right to relief. This chapter asks whether each approach could be adopted by the United States without falling afoul of the TRIPS Agreement as it is currently construed.

---

[3] We concentrate on patent law rather than on other intellectual property regimes because it confers a greater level of exclusivity and is concerned with cutting-edge developments that are most likely to undermine core assumptions of intellectual property law; we deal with U.S. law because the problem appears to us more acute there. For example, because the European Patent Convention (EPC) and the Japanese Patent Act require that inventions be susceptible to "industrial application," these statutes may not so easily cover upstream inventions. *See* John R. Thomas, *The Patenting of The Liberal Professions*, 40 B.C. L. REV. 1139, 1178 (1999).

[4] *See* below text accompanying nn. 6–11.

[5] *See* Pamela Samuelson, *Intellectual Property Arbitrage: How Foreign Rules Can Affect Domestic Protection* [this volume].

Our purpose is not to predict the outcome of future disputes – there are far too few WTO precedents for that. Rather, our goal is to identify interpretive approaches that allow Members to keep their laws attuned to the developments and needs of science. We also raise broader questions regarding the level of formalism generated by the WTO dispute settlement system, and the extent to which the TRIPS Agreement allocates power between supranational and national institutions, between international and national laws.

II. Upstream patenting and its relationship to technological progress

As suggested earlier, there is growing concern that prospects for innovation are jeopardized by trends in U.S. patent law that increasingly recognize private claims to core principles of knowledge, of special significance to basic research. At one time, science was considered distinct from technology, and intellectual property law was predicated on the existence of an analogous doctrinal boundary between basic and applied research.[6] Increasingly, however, United States patent law recognizes private claims that cross the border between fundamental knowledge and commercial application. This development may reflect the science-intensive nature of modern technology, which makes recent advances inherently dual in character;[7] it may also be caused by changes in the organization of science, including the reliance of small, highly networked knowledge-intensive firms on patents to signal technical and business competence,[8] or by the emergence of research organizations (such as universities) that look to patent rights to support fundamental research.[9] Whatever the cause, patent protection has moved upstream.

---

[6] *See, e.g.*, Brenner v. Manson, 383 U.S. 519 (1966) (defining the utility required for patent protection as end-use rather than research-use utility). *See also* Funk Bros. Seed Co. v. Kalo Inoculant Co., 333 U.S. 127, 131 (1948) (holding that packets containing mixtures of bacteria were "no more than the discovery of some of the handiwork of nature" and hence unpatentable); O'Reilly v. Morse, 56 U.S. (15 How.) 62 (1853) (holding that abstract principles are not statutory subject matter).

[7] *See, e.g.*, Diamond v. Chakrabarty, 447 U.S. 303 (1980); State St. Bank & Trust Co. v. Signature Fin. Group, Inc., 149 F.3d 1368 (Fed. Cir. 1998), *cert. denied*, 119 S. Ct. 851 (1999). *See also* Francis Narin & Dominic Olivastro, *Status Report: Linkage Between Technology and Science*, 21 RES. POL'Y 237 (1992) (using citation measures to demonstrate that the tie between science and technology is becoming closer over time and is more pronounced in drugs, medicine, chemistry, and computing than in fields such as machinery and transportation).

[8] *See, e.g.*, Clarisa Long, *Patent Signals*, 69 U. CHI. L. REV. 625 (2002); Walter M. Powell, *Networks of Learning in Biotechnology: Opportunities and Constraints Associated with Relational Contracting in Knowledge-Intensive Fields*, *in* EXPANDING THE BOUNDARIES OF INTELLECTUAL PROPERTY: INNOVATION POLICY FOR THE KNOWLEDGE SOCIETY 251 (Rochelle Dreyfuss et al. eds., 2001).

[9] *See, e.g.*, Bayh Dole Act, 35 U.S.C. §§ 200–212 (2000).

The net result is troublesome. Patents may now confer power not only in *product* markets, but also in *innovation* markets.[10] As such, these patents can have broad significance. Because second comers can often invent around end-use inventions, patents rarely monopolized product markets. In contrast, a patent on, say, the structural information of a protein, or on a metabolic pathway, or a computer operating system, could give the patentee control over all work involving that protein or pathway, or all opportunities to create application programs for that system. As a result, there is growing evidence suggesting that – at least in the United States – patent rights over research opportunities have begun to hinder progress by chilling innovation and impeding the production of new knowledge.[11]

III. Hypothetical solutions and their international implications

There is considerable debate among policymakers on such matters as whether the benefits of these developments outweigh their costs and whether private parties will find their own ways to contract around potential bottlenecks. In this chapter, however, we ask a different question: what can national legislators who perceive a problem do to fix it, consistent with their countries' international obligations under the TRIPS Agreement?

A. Subject matter exclusions

The most direct way to deal with the problem of upstream patenting might be to define patentable subject matter in a way that excludes inventions with significant upstream applications from eligibility for protection. This approach could be implemented across the board, or limited to areas where evidence suggests that the chill to research is potentially great. Although drawing such lines would be difficult, advocates of this approach claim it is superior to alternative means of protecting the public domain because it creates bright-line rules on which investors can rely.

For example, Richard Epstein has suggested that the "use value" of patents – their value in product markets – should be compared to their "blocking" value – their upstream significance in innovation markets. When the blocking value exceeds the use value in a particular field, inventions within that field should not

---

[10] In this context, product market means the market for products, processes, and the products of processes. *See also* Ashish Arora *et al.*, *Markets for Technology, Intellectual Property Rights and Development* [this volume].

[11] *See, e.g.*, Rebecca S. Eisenberg, *Bargaining Over the Transfer of Proprietary Research Tools: Is This Market Failing or Emerging?*, *in* EXPANDING THE BOUNDARIES, above n. 8. *See generally*, NATIONAL RESEARCH COUNCIL, A PATENT SYSTEM FOR THE 21ST CENTURY 59–64 (Stephen A. Merrill et al. eds., 2004).

be considered patentable.[12] He gives the example of expressed sequence tags (ESTs), short sequences of coding DNA, noting that while the useful applications of ESTs barely meet the utility standard of current patent law, "[e]ach EST is a gateway to some gene on which useful work could be done." Since the primary use of a patent on an EST would thus be to block others from entering that gateway, Epstein argues that such patents should not issue.

John Barton takes a different approach. He would exclude specific subject areas whenever the blockage problem becomes acute. He gives, as an example, proteomics – information about the shape of the body's protein molecules that is crucial to understanding and predicting how the body will respond to pharmaceutical interventions.[13]

Would such carve-outs meet the requirements of article 27.1 of the TRIPS Agreement, which provides that, subject to defined exceptions, "patents shall be available and patent rights enjoyable without discrimination as to the ... field of technology"?[14] To analyze that question, one can usefully distinguish between *de iure* and *de facto* forms of discrimination. In the former situation, specific fields of technology are carved out for special treatment; in the latter, rules that are facially neutral have disparate effects on particular subject areas.

The language of article 27 is clearly aimed at prohibiting *de iure* discrimination with respect to the availability and enjoyment of patent rights. The legislative history of the Agreement is replete with indications that a primary concern of the negotiators was to eliminate blanket exclusions of certain types of patentable subject matter (most notably drugs, agrochemicals, and foodstuffs).[15] Thus, a subject matter exclusion directed at biotechnology generally, or at specific areas within biotechnology, such as proteomics, would almost certainly run afoul of the Agreement.

An approach that comes conceptually closer to Richard Epstein's suggestion is, however, more difficult to analyze. Facially, the approach is neutral – it would bar patents on discoveries of predominantly upstream significance in every field of technology. Nonetheless, it would more profoundly affect fields that are science-intensive and fields where the targets of protection have high informational content. For example, it would have greater impact on biotechnology and computer science than on chemistry or mechanical engineering. Thus, while the proposal would not directly implicate the motivating *rationale* for article 27.1, its potentially disparate effect on different fields could conceivably fall afoul of *the literal text* of article 27.

---

[12] Richard A. Epstein, *Steady the Course: Property Rights in Genetic Material*, in PERSPECTIVES ON PROPERTIES OF THE HUMAN GENOME PROJECT 153, 168–88 (F. Scott Kieff ed., 2003).
[13] John H. Barton, *United States Law of Genomic and Post-Genomic Patents*, 33 INT'L REV. INDUS. PROP. & COPYRIGHT L. 779–910 (2002).
[14] TRIPS Agreement, above n. 2, art. 27.1.
[15] *See* Canada – Patent Protection of Pharmaceutical Products, WT/DS114/R ¶ 4.6 fn.27 (WTO Dispute Settlement Panel 2000) (hereinafter "Canada – Pharmaceutical Products").

Thus far, there have been no decisions directly addressing subject matter exclusions under article 27, but we inform our analysis with the observation that WTO panels tend to hew closely to text when resolving disputes.[16] For example, the panel in *Canada – Pharmaceutical Products* considered article 27 in the course of reviewing the TRIPS consistency of two exemptions that Canada had enacted in its patent law. One of these, the so-called regulatory review exemption, permitted use or manufacture of a patented invention solely for purposes of obtaining regulatory approval. The intent was apparently aimed at promoting competition between generic and proprietary pharmaceutical companies by facilitating market entry by generics at the moment of patent expiration. While the exemption was expressed in technologically neutral language, the European Union argued that its impact on the pharmaceutical industry violated article 27.1 under, essentially, a disparate impact theory.

The WTO panel rejected the E.U.'s specific contention, but only after Canada assured it that the exemption was indeed neutral in the sense that it was legally available to every product subject to marketing approval requirements. In fact, the panel agreed with the E.U.'s larger point, that the Agreement barred both *de iure* and *de facto* discrimination. In other words, it appears that under this decision, the mere lack of a textual limitation to particular fields will not immunize a provision from challenge.

Still, it may be possible to salvage Epstein's approach. Patent laws tend to apply differently across industrial sectors, depending on such factors as the level of skill in particular fields.[17] It is difficult to believe that Members of the WTO would have so readily committed themselves to altering this approach to their domestic lawmaking. Indeed, the panel acknowledged as much, stating, "article 27 does not prohibit bona fide exemptions to deal with problems that may exist only in certain product areas."[18]

In fact, the panel's report can be read as prohibiting *de facto* discrimination only when the claim includes some additional element, such as an allegation of an intent to discriminate. Thus, the panel stated, "it was not proved ... that the objective indications of purpose demonstrated *a purpose to impose disadvantages* on pharmaceutical patents in particular, as is often required to raise a claim of de facto discrimination."[19] While panels, both in the TRIPS[20] and

---

[16] *See* Graeme B. Dinwoodie, *The Architecture of the International Intellectual Property System*, 77 CHI.-KENT L. REV. 993, 1005–06 (2002) ("Webster's has become an essential research tool in WTO TRIPS litigation.").

[17] *See* Dan L. Burk & Mark A. Lemley, *Policy Levers in Patent Law*, 89 VA. L. REV. 1575 (2003); Dan L. Burk & Mark A. Lemley, *Is Patent Law Technology-Specific?*, 17 BERK. TECH. L.J. 1155 (2002).

[18] Canada – Pharmaceutical Products, above n. 15, ¶ 7.92.

[19] *Id.*, at ¶ 7.105 (emphasis added).

[20] *See* United States – Section 110(5) of the US Copyright Act, WTR/DS/160/R (WTO Dispute Settlement Panel 2000) [hereinafter United States – Section 110(5)].

broader WTO contexts,[21] have acknowledged the difficulty of identifying (and scrutinizing) the purposes behind particular national laws, we find it entirely appropriate that those claiming *de facto* discrimination should be required to demonstrate some element – such as intent – over and above those required to establish *de iure* cases of discrimination. At the very least, those defending an exclusion should be permitted to rebut a showing of disparate treatment by demonstrating a legitimate purpose. What these demonstrations might entail, we leave to another day, but they might be satisfied by, for example, demonstrating a close linkage between the exclusion and the particular organizational or institutional structure (such as a bifurcated generic and proprietary drug industry, or a decision to rely on patents to selectively support fundamental research) in the country in question.

The foregoing suggests that variations in result must be evaluated carefully when determining whether national law violates the technological-neutrality principle. Discrimination is not the same as differential treatment. This is not to foreclose the possibility that a claim for *de facto* discrimination under article 27.1 could succeed; but this reading does suggest that nations retain power to modify their notions of statutory subject matter along the lines of the Epstein proposal in order to deal with changes in the relationship between basic science and end-use technologies.

In fact, even more targeted carve-outs of the sort proposed by Barton may be permissible. Although we recognize that such a conclusion runs headlong into the literalism that panels have exhibited in interpreting TRIPS, if a legitimate policy objective can be effectuated by a narrow, technology-specific exclusion, we fail to see why article 27.1's commitment to formal neutrality should force WTO members to adopt exclusions that are broader than necessary. Such an approach would appear to run counter to the underlying thrust of the TRIPS Agreement toward enhanced protection. We address this paradox below in connection with our discussion of article 30.[22]

B. Exemptions

To the extent that the problem with upstream patents is their capacity to block pure research, another solution would permit certain activities to be undertaken without a patentee's authorization, in return for payment of a nonmarket-based rent (or for free). For example, Maureen O'Rourke proposed a patent law exception, analogous to the fair use defense of copyright law, tailored to the unique concerns of the patent industries. Her analysis would consider (i) the nature of the advance represented by the infringing work;

---

[21] *See generally* Robert E. Hudec, *GATT/WTO Constraints on National Regulation: Requiem for an "Aim and Effects" Test*, 32 INT'L LAW. 619, 626–633 (1998).

[22] *See* text below at n. 54.

(ii) the purpose of the infringing use; (iii) the nature and strength of the market failure that prevents a license from being concluded; (iv) the impact of the use on the patentee's incentives and overall social welfare; and (v) the nature of the patented invention.[23] A court would use these factors to determine whether a patented invention could be used without authorization, and also to assess royalties.

Professor O'Rourke's proposal, if enacted into domestic law, could indeed solve the upstream patent problem by freeing patented inventions for use in fundamental research. However, articles 27 and 30 of the TRIPS Agreement each present problems for this approach.

1. Article 30's "three-part test"

Article 30 provides that exceptions from liability for patent infringement are permissible if they (a) are limited, (b) do not unreasonably conflict with a normal exploitation of a patent, and (c) do not unreasonably prejudice the legitimate interests of the patent owner, taking account of the legitimate interests of third parties. O'Rourke's proposal appears to accommodate these criteria by requiring courts to consider similar parameters. This conclusion, however, is not without doubt because there is a question whether WTO adjudicators will tolerate the amount of discretion that this approach gives to domestic courts. Certainly, the factors that courts consider when exercising that discretion would become critical to a finding of TRIPS-compatibility.

Our analysis of the relevant issues is informed by two panel reports, *Canada – Pharmaceutical Products* discussed above, and *United States – Section 110(5)*.[24] In the former, two exemptions were challenged: the regulatory review exemption described earlier, and a stockpiling exemption that enabled the generic industry to manufacture patented products within the last six months of a patent term (for sale upon expiry of the term). Two exemptions were also at issue in the *Section 110(5)* case, both of which permitted the playing of recorded copyrighted music in commercial establishments. In each case, it was claimed that the exemptions at issue satisfied each of the cumulative three steps of the applicable test for permissible exceptions (article 30 for patents, article 13 for copyright).[25]

(a) Scope of uses: "Limited" exceptions. The *Canada – Pharmaceutical Products* panel stated that the term "limited," which is found only in

---

[23] See Maureen A. O'Rourke, *Toward a Doctrine of Fair Use in Patent Law*, 100 COL. L. REV. 1177, 1205 (2000).
[24] See Canada – Pharmaceutical Products, above n. 15; United States – Section 110(5), above n. 20.
[25] See TRIPS Agreement, above n. 2, arts. 13, 30.

article 30,[26] required that the exemption be a narrow one, which the panel measured by reference to the extent to which the rights of the patentee were curtailed.[27] The stockpiling exemption was found not to be "limited" because, during the last six months of the statutory term, it negated all protection under three of the patentee's five guaranteed rights (make, use, or sell) with no limitations on the quantities produced or the market destination of the products.[28] In contrast, the regulatory review exemption was considered "limited" because it narrowly curtailed the patentee's exclusive rights. The extent of the acts permitted (i.e., those that were necessary to comply with the regulatory approval process) was small and narrowly bounded.[29]

On its face, O'Rourke's proposed exemption resembles the invalid stockpiling exemption in that it would appear to curtail potentially all of a patentee's exclusive rights. One could certainly argue that if a provision was facially unlimited, then it should be doomed. However, the Appellate Body has cautioned that panels should not assume that a member would act inconsistently with its international obligations.[30] If, in fact, courts develop principles that limit the broad language of O'Rourke's proposal to bring it closer to the approved regulatory review exception, then it should satisfy the first step of the three-step test in article 30.

(b) Economic impact: Conflict with normal exploitation. The *Canada – Pharmaceutical Products* panel concluded that the normal practice of exploitation was "to exclude all forms of competition that could detract significantly from the economic returns anticipated from a patent's grant of market exclusivity."[31] Courts could ensure compliance with this standard most directly by considering whether a challenged domestic provision compromised significant economic

---

[26] The first step of the copyright test confines copyright exceptions to "certain special cases," which requires, among other things, that the exception be clearly defined. United States – Section 110(5), above n. 20, ¶¶ 6.107–6.110.

[27] The panel concluded that the first step in the three-step test does not require consideration of the economic impact of the exemption because that concern was taken up by the second and third step of the test. *See* Canada – Pharmaceutical Products, above n. 15, ¶ 7.49. Thus, even if the adoption of the proposed fair use or experimental use exemption did give rise to substantial economic impact (because, for example, protecting research opportunities represents a large part of the patentee's return at present), that would not of itself prevent the exemption from being regarded as limited.

[28] In certain respects, the panel appeared to be incorporating some of the considerations relevant to analysis under article 31, which governs the grant of compulsory licenses, into the article 30 analysis.

[29] Canada – Pharmaceutical Products, above n. 15, at ¶ 7.45.

[30] United States – Section 211 of the Omnibus Appropriations Act of 1998, WT/DS176/AB/R ¶ 259 (WTO Appellate Body 2001) (citing Chile – Taxes on Alcoholic Beverages, WT/DS87/AB/R, WT/DS110/AB/R, ¶ 74 (WTO Appellate Body 2000).

[31] Canada – Pharmaceutical Products, above n. 15, ¶ 7.55.

opportunities.[32] Yet, the defense might survive challenge even if it were to render non-infringing certain uses or acts for which patentees currently extracted payment. The notion of normalcy should not be static but should evolve through successive interpretations of article 30 by panels, the Appellate Body, the TRIPS Council, and future ministerial negotiations.[33] As the two panels acknowledged, while this understanding should take account of national practices, especially with regard to typical means of exploiting the patent and the source of that commercial capacity, normalcy is ultimately a normative question – it depends on a vision of the just balance between proprietary rights and public access interests, and not purely on past practices. We suggest that the factors mentioned by the panels and the Appellate Body should be considered, but that the normative question should permeate the entire analysis.[34]

(i) National practices. In part, the *Canada – Pharmaceutical Products* panel treated the ability to exploit the invention exclusively even after patent expiration as normal because it was typical. Here the panel may have meant that several WTO members had established premarket clearance procedures that effectively prolonged the period of exclusivity beyond the time of patent expiration.[35]

---

[32] Such an approach might appear unduly internationalist in the current political climate. Thus, we would rest on the canon of statutory construction that instructs judges to interpret domestic law, where possible, in accordance with international obligations.

[33] *Cf.*, Declaration on the TRIPS Agreement and Public Health, WT/MIN(01)/DEC/2, ¶ 5 (WTO Ministerial Conference, 14 Nov. 2001) ("while maintaining our commitments in the TRIPS Agreement, we recognize ... flexibilities"). The traditional sources of customary international law (including the Members' local institutions) might also supply meaning to the concept.

[34] These factors are not meant to be exclusive; in other cases, additional considerations may be relevant.

[35] Canada – Pharmaceutical Products, above n. 15, at ¶ 7.56. It is possible that the panel was referring to the fact that some post-exploitation was typical of patents generally or that it was employed by "most patent owners." Thus, in rejecting Canada's categorical assertion that post-expiration market exclusivity could not be normal, the panel obliquely referred to the fact that "some of the basic rights granted to *all* patent owners, and routinely exercised by *all* patent owners, will typically produce" such exclusivity. Id. at ¶ 7.56 (emphasis added). Likewise, the panel rejected the E.U.'s argument that patent expiration should be irrelevant to normalcy because it did not address itself to the panel's view of normal, namely, it did not offer a "demonstration that *most* patent owners extract the value of their patents in the manner barred by the [challenged exemption]." Id. at ¶ 7.58 (emphasis supplied). Thus, although the panel sought to examine what was "common within a relevant community," Canada – Pharmaceutical Products, above n. 15, at ¶ 7.54, it did not carefully define the "relevant community." Moreover, in United States – Section 110(5), the panel declined to address the E.U.'s contention that "comparative references to other countries with a similar level of socio-economic development could be relevant to corroborate or contradict data from the country primarily concerned." *See* United States – Section 110(5), above n. 20, ¶ 6.189.

In one sense, O'Rourke's proposal does well under this subtest. Exemptions to support research are, in fact, typical of member states' intellectual property laws. For example, the United States has long had an experimental use defense for work that is solely for the "purpose of gratifying a philosophical taste."[36] So, too, do other industrial nations, such as Japan and Germany.[37] Moreover, the E.U. is currently proposing exemptions for "acts done privately for non-commercial purposes," and for "acts done for experimental purposes relating to the subject-matter of the patented invention."[38] In another sense, however, O'Rourke's proposed approach could be in trouble. The "typical" defense is extremely narrow;[39] because O'Rourke's proposal is multi-factored and heavily based on judicial discretion, it will be difficult to predict its applicability to any given situation. The resulting uncertainty could act as a drag on patent value.

Nonetheless, we think the proposal can be salvaged. Although state practice is clearly relevant to the creation of customary international law, existing national laws should not of themselves be permitted to entrench an international norm. Such an approach exalts national laws inappropriately. The norms of international law are cautiously and appropriately driven by concerns of consensus and permitting variations in national laws. National laws represent a more ambitious attempt to articulate an ideal norm suited to a more focused and homogenous context.

Furthermore, because states are generally free to exceed internationally mandated minima, there is a baseline issue: a denial of exclusivity may be from a level of protection that exceeds the internationally mandated standard. Privileging a particular national standard would, in fact, be somewhat perverse. States would have a hard time experimenting with higher levels of protection if international intellectual property law prevented them from later re-assessing and restoring the level of protection to one that hews closer to the minimum standard.

Moreover, barring reforms of this type would prevent WTO Members from adjusting their national laws to accommodate changing economic and social

---

[36] See, e.g., Peppenhausen v. Falke, 19 Fed. Cas. 1048, 1049 (C.C.S.D.N.Y. 1861) ("experiment with a patented article for the sole purpose of gratifying a philosophical taste, or curiosity"); W. ROBINSON, THE LAW OF PATENTS FOR USEFUL INVENTIONS, § 898 (1890).

[37] See German Patent Act of 1981, § 11, No. 2 ("[T]he effects of the patent shall not extend to acts performed for experimental purposes relating to the subject matter of the patented invention."); Japanese Patent Law of 1959, as amended through 6 May 1998, effective 1 June 1998, § 69(1) ("working of the patent right for the purposes of experiment or research"); see also APS van der Merwe, *Experimental Use and the Submission of Data for Regulatory Approval*, INT'L REV. INDUS. PROP. & COPYRIGHT 380 (2000).

[38] See Commission of the European Communities, Proposal for a Council Regulation on the Community Patent, arts. 9(a) & (b) (1 Aug. 2000), *available at* http://europa.eu.int/eur-lex/pri/en. *See generally*, The Royal Society, Keeping Science Open: The Effects of Intellectual Property on the Conduct of Science (2003), *at* http://www.royalsoc.ac.uk.

[39] See, e.g., Madey v. Duke Univ., 307 F.3d 1351 (Fed. Cir. 2002).

circumstances. It would thus validate the refrain of many critics of recent international intellectual property developments that the system operates as a one-way ratchet. Indeed, the *Canada – Pharmaceutical Products* panel suggested as much, noting that "the specific forms of patent exploitation are not static ... for to be effective exploitation must adapt to changing forms of competition due to technological development and the evolution of marketing practices."[40] Because it is the complexity of modern technology that gives rise to the complications in O'Rourke's proposal, an argument could be made that the proposal would be consistent with typical national practice.

(ii) Typical means of exploiting the patent. In determining normalcy for purposes of article 30, the *Canada – Pharmaceutical Products* panel may alternatively have been considering what right holders regard as typical *exploitation practices*. However, it was clearly unwilling to rely on that ground alone. Likewise, the *United States – Section 110(5)* panel held that the extent to which rights holders actually exercised their rights could not be "fully indicative of normal exploitation."[41] Indeed, both panels offered a definition of "normal" that explicitly encompassed a normative assessment as well as an empirical analysis of what was "regular, usual, typical or ordinary."[42]

The application of this subpart to O'Rourke's approach is difficult to reckon. In part, there is another baseline issue. As noted earlier, it was not typical for rights holders to assert control over innovation markets in the past; now it has become more common. Neither panel provided a time frame in which typical exploitation should be judged, yet it is difficult to see how practices in 2004 have any greater claim to determine normalcy than practices in 1994. Thus, restoring the level of protection to that which existed before the line between basic and applied research was blurred could pass muster.[43]

We are especially concerned that despite the panels' language, neither set of adjudicators took the normative dimension seriously; neither went so far as to articulate a normative vision of exploitation. Instead, as Jane Ginsburg has

---

[40] Canada – Pharmaceutical Products, above n. 15, ¶ 7.55. Admittedly, this language appears largely directed at efforts to expand forms of exploitation, but the general proposition holds true.

[41] United States – Section 110(5), above n. 20, ¶ 6.196. The patent standard in article 30 (but not the copyright equivalent in art. 13) allows such conflicts provided they are reasonable. It would thus appear to afford member states greater latitude on the second leg of the patent exemptions test. But in both provisions, the permissible conflict is measured against the same norm, that is, "normal exploitation."

[42] *See id.* ¶ 6.166 ("dynamic ... approach, i.e., conforming to a type or standard"); Canada – Pharmaceutical Products, above n. 15, ¶ 7.54 ("The term ['normal'] can be understood to refer to an empirical conclusion about what is common within a relevant community, or to a normative standard of entitlement." The panel concluded that the word 'normal' was being used in article 30 in a sense that combined the two meanings.).

[43] *See* above text accompanying n. 7.

commented, the analysis in the *Section 110(5)* case sought only to "anticipate what the empirical situation [would] be, [rather] than [provide] an explanation of what the right holder's markets *should* cover."[44] The literature includes a rich body of intellectual property theory, and the opening for normative assessment provides a vehicle for panels to use this scholarship to develop international law. Of course, a commitment to a broader approach would inevitably draw panels into more intrusive assessments of national legislative values. But, as the Appellate Body recognized in its first TRIPS report,[45] and as the *United States – Section 110(5)* panel hints in its discussion of "normal," it is the responsibility of panels to make critical assessments of national law.[46] Presumably, a WTO Member defending an exemption of this type could aid the adjudicators by elaborating on the normative underpinnings of its approach (as O'Rourke did in her article).[47]

(iii) Source of commercial capacity. The *Canada – Pharmaceutical Products* panel declined to treat as normal the "additional period of de facto market exclusivity created by using patent rights to preclude submissions for regulatory authorization" because it was "not a natural or normal consequence of enforcing patent rights."[48] Instead, it was the product of a combination of patent laws and the regulatory approval scheme – a commercial rather than a legal effect.

Clearly, a rigorous inquiry into the nature and source of control should inform the analysis. Enhanced commercial exploitation may arise from the availability of technological protection measures that reinforce statutory rights; from contracts that parties enter on account of industry structure or because the costs of challenging an exclusive right outweigh the benefits of cooperation; or more darkly, from market power and undue commercial leverage. Absent

---

[44] Jane C. Ginsburg, *Toward Supranational Copyright Law? The WTO Panel Decision and the "Three Step Test" for Copyright Exemptions*, 187 REVUE INTERNATIONALE DU DROIT D'AUTEUR 3, 17 (2001).
[45] India-Patent Protection for Pharmaceutical and Agricultural Chemical Products, WT/D550/AB/R (WTO Appellate Body 1997).
[46] Determining the contexts in which international norms should trump national determinations will obviously depend on both the substantive intellectual property values and systemic values underlying the international system. The Appellate Body seems to have left room for deference to national welfare considerations if not in direct conflict with the literal text. *See* TRIPS Agreement, above n. 2, Preamble; J. H. Reichman, *Securing Compliance with the TRIPS Agreement After U.S. v. India*, 1 J. INT'L ECON. L. 585, 597 (1998).
[47] Indeed, an interpretative approach that encourages articulation of the rationales behind national legislation may greatly enhance the transparency of national law, to the benefit of intellectual property lawmaking. *See* Graeme B. Dinwoodie & Rochelle C. Dreyfuss, *TRIPS and the Dynamics of Intellectual Property Lawmaking*, 36 CASE WEST. RES. J. INT'L L. 95 (2004).
[48] Canada – Pharmaceutical Products, above n. 15, ¶ 7.57.

such inquiry, invalid assertions of rights and the flexing of market muscle may be elevated to international law.

This analysis is not, however, helpful to O'Rourke's proposal, which is clearly aimed at curbing a control created by force of law. Nevertheless, it is important to remember that the conclusion on normalcy depends on an interaction of relevant factors, not a cumulative satisfaction of each. The entire analysis must also be infused with normative content. To the extent that O' Rourke is preserving a competitive research (as opposed to end-use) market, her proposal furthers the goals of intellectual property law.

(c) *Types of uses: Unreasonable prejudice to legitimate interests*. As the *Canada – Pharmaceutical Products* panel acknowledged,[49] the third step of article 30 clearly involves a normative assessment. Thus, much of what we said above is relevant here. However, because upstream patenting is new, there is no international norm that deals with its impact on the research environment.

When the *Canada – Pharmaceutical Products* panel found that there was no controlling international norm in that case, it suggested deference to local autonomy,[50] and that approach may well support the O'Rourke proposal, were it adopted by the United States. As noted earlier, the traditional market for patented inventions is a *product* market; the right to control research is, in most fields, slim. Hence, removing rights over *innovation* markets in sectors where they become suddenly available should not be regarded as prejudicing a legitimate interest (especially if all of the other forms of exploitation continue to be recognized). Members of the WTO should be free to realign the components in their constellation of patent law rules and to restore the stable universe that once existed.[51]

The validity of the exemption is bolstered by the last clause of the third step in article 30, which (unlike its copyright counterpart in article 13) explicitly calls for a panel to "take account of the legitimate interests of third parties." The panel hinted that considerations such as society's interest in promoting progress, and scientists' interest in free inquiry, might be considered "legitimate" within the meaning of article 30.[52] Further, although the panel cautioned that articles 7 and 8, which speak of promoting technological innovation to the mutual advantage of producers and users, and of protecting public health and promoting the public interest, cannot be used to reargue the balance struck in article 30 of the TRIPS Agreement, they can shed light on the meaning of

---

[49] *Id*. at ¶ 7.73.
[50] *Id*., at ¶ 7.82. *Cf*. India – Patent Protection for Pharmaceuticals, above n. 45, ¶¶ 46, 59. This approach illustrates that pro-public goods arguments might flow either from substantive intellectual property preferences embedded in the TRIPS Agreement, or from neo-federalist principles found in the international intellectual property system.
[51] *See* above text accompanying nn. 42–43.
[52] Canada – Pharmaceutical Products, above n. 15, ¶ 7.69.

"legitimate interests."[53] Thus, if the availability of the exemption depends, as O'Rourke contemplates, on market failures that preclude contracts that would advance overall social welfare, a panel might accept the argument that the exemption was TRIPS-consistent.

2. Article 27's technological neutrality

Another possible challenge to O'Rourke's approach is rooted in the technological neutrality principle of article 27, which the *Canada – Pharmaceutical Products* panel read as imposing an additional hurdle for WTO members seeking to invoke article 30 to justify domestic exemptions to the exclusive rights required by international patent law. The panel appeared to regard article 27.1 as a structural provision, part of the fabric of the Agreement as a whole, which can be transposed to the analysis of other provisions.

If article 27 does apply to exemptions within article 30, the O'Rourke proposal appears vulnerable to challenge. Although this "fair use" exemption would not be aimed at specific subject matters of invention, it is likely that it would play out differently in different fields. Indeed, the fifth factor in the O'Rourke analysis – the nature of the patented invention – makes this possibility explicit.

We believe, however, that the O'Rourke approach is appropriate because the policy concerns that underlie her analysis are more acute in some fields than in others. To put this another way, we think the panel was wrong in applying article 27.1 to exemptions. As noted earlier, there are good reasons why different technologies or different uses may require different judicial or legislative treatment. It seems counterproductive to require socially desirable exemptive solutions to extend to all technologies when technology-specific problems require technology-specific solutions.[54]

Indeed, requiring exemptions to be technologically neutral appears particularly anomalous in that it tends to make a broader than necessary exemption more sustainable under international law than a narrow exemption. This outcome conflicts with the norm contained in article 30 that expressly requires the availability of exemptions to be evaluated in terms of whether any given exemption is "limited." A targeted exemption that differentiated between different types of invention would limit a patentee's rights only in areas where there was a perceived imbalance between public and private interests. Regardless of whether a panel might be more sympathetic to an exemption that is cast in general terms, the policies underlying the TRIPS Agreement favor exemptions that are either targeted or, though framed broadly, evolve

---

[53] *Id.* ¶ 7.26.
[54] If the approach of the Canada – Pharmaceutical Products panel prevails, we could present this argument under the rubric that, as explained above, a mere difference in treatment of different technologies might not amount to discrimination in violation of art. 27. *See* above text accompanying nn. 14–21.

to permit particular limited uses. A formalist commitment to technology neutrality is inconsistent with a purposive reading of the TRIPS Agreement.

To sum up, an analysis of O'Rourke's proposal produces a mixed picture. On the one hand, strong arguments could be made that the scope of the exempted uses should be regarded as *limited*; as having an acceptable *economic impact*; and as not interfering with *legitimate interests*. But these arguments will be accepted only if panels assess article 30 issues through a normative filter. A panel would also have to agree with us that the structural use of article 27 is a mistake. If a more literalist view is taken, the proposal may not be regarded as acceptable. It requires faith in the discretion of domestic courts, it produces uncertainty and therefore potentially reduces patent value. Moreover, it permits unprecedented intrusions into important innovation markets that are protected by the force of patent law, and it is specifically crafted to have a differential impact on upstream technologies.

C. Remedies

A third way to protect the public domain of science is to vary the terms of relief so as to immunize upstream researchers from liability for patent infringement. One idea, proposed by one of us and modified by Richard Nelson, would benefit non-commercial research organizations, especially universities and their employees, if 1) the patented materials they wished to utilize were not made available on reasonable terms; 2) the investigators agreed to publish their research results; and 3) the investigators agreed either to refrain from patenting the research results or to patent and then license the result on a nonexclusive basis and on reasonable terms.[55]

The compatibility of this solution with TRIPS obligations is difficult to gauge in light of the disputes resolved so far because none of them has involved remedial issues.[56] Immunizing certain users from liability could be

---

[55] See Rochelle Dreyfuss, *Varying the Course in Patenting Genetic Material: A Counter-Proposal to Richard Epstein's Steady Course*, in PERSPECTIVES ON THE HUMAN GENOME PROJECT, above n. 12, 195, 204–208; Richard Nelson, *Linkages Between the Market Economy and the Scientific Commons* [this volume]. See also Rochelle Dreyfuss, *Protecting the Public Domain of Science: Has the Time for an Experimental Use Defense Arrived?*, 46 Ariz. L. Rev. 457 (2004). An analogue to this approach has been adopted in US law to limit liability for certain uses of patented surgical and medical processes, where there was also a fear (albeit on different grounds) that important developments would be inadequately licensed and used. *See* 35 U.S.C. § 287(c)(2) (2000). *See generally* Gerald J. Mossinghoff, *Remedies Under Patents on Medical and Surgical Procedures*, 78 J. PAT. & TRADE. OFF. SOC'Y 789 (1996).

[56] United States – Section 211, above n. 30, discusses remedies, but not in ways that would substantially influence our analysis here.

categorized as an exemption to the right conferred and analyzed under article 30.[57] If so, then the argument would be similar to the one set out above, with the added observations that this approach curbs the judicial discretion that engendered some ambivalence in our analysis of the open-ended exemption. It also seems unlikely to intrude seriously on the patentee's own interests. While it could reduce markets for research tools, only those markets that the patentee refused to supply would be affected. Some opportunities may also be lost in the innovation market, but because these opportunities would likely be non-commercial fundamental research opportunities, they are likely to be rather low on a profit-minded patentee's own priority list.

We are not, however, convinced that article 30, standing alone, should provide the appropriate framework of analysis. While article 30 imposes well-established strictures of international law on what WTO members can do, the TRIPS Agreement as a whole appears to envision far more latitude at the remedial phase. The flexibility that the TRIPS Agreement preserves is most evident in article 41, which sets out WTO Members' enforcement obligations.[58] Subsection 5 explicitly provides that members are not required to enforce intellectual property law in a manner different from how they enforce their laws in general. This deference makes considerable sense. Members need discretion to choose the means by which they satisfy effective enforcement obligations because enforcement implicates questions of resources and institutional priorities that go to the heart of national political ordering in ways that far transcend intellectual property law.

Other more specific remedies provisions also create substantial flexibility. Article 45 requires WTO Members to give judicial authorities power "to order the infringer to pay the right holder damages adequate to compensate."[59] However, when a court exercises that authority, adequacy is measured entirely by local conditions. In markets where demand for the product – or ability to pay – is low and in markets that have price controls in place, the compensatory award will be low.[60] The award will, in other words, reflect local conditions, desires, and needs. This is as it should be: a patent is a right to exclude, not a right to exploit.

Even the provisions that protect the right to exclude can be read as creating substantial space for sovereign interests. Although article 44.1 requires member states to give judicial authorities *power* to order injunctive relief, nothing in the provision expressly *requires* courts to enter such orders. United States law reads

---

[57] *Cf.* Mossinghoff, above n. 55, at 796 (examining the surgical immunity provision under art. 30).
[58] TRIPS Agreement, above n. 2, art. 41.   [59] *Id.* art. 45.
[60] TRIPS does not apparently proscribe price controls, although some effort to do so has reportedly been made in bilateral negotiations.

the same way in that it is interpreted to give courts considerable discretion to tailor injunctions to specific (local) conditions.[61]

Given this degree of flexibility, an approach based on remedial immunity should be considered consistent with the TRIPS Agreement. Monetary rewards could be reduced to zero for the same reasons that monetary relief is traditionally low in some situations: the relevant user groups – in this case, non-commercial research institutions – lack resources to pay for the inputs they need. Moreover, the economic value of the use – in this case, basic research – is highly speculative, and courts do not generally award speculative damages.[62]

Injunctive relief is also denied for familiar reasons, sounding in the need to deal with important social problems. In this case, that might include an organizational structure for science in which fundamental and applied scientific research are conducted in different institutions or in networked environments. It could also be considered an effort to deal with cultural aversions to entering into binding transactions with strangers in the face of scientific and business uncertainty.

Admittedly, relief under this proposal is withheld across the board, rather than on the typical case-by-case basis. Yet, efficiency or other values often require the articulation of a rule that constrains equitable discretion and reduces reliance on case-by-case analysis.[63] An approach to the enforcement provisions of TRIPS that prevented a WTO Member from choosing between a case-by-case or a rule-based approach might be thought to impose on such a Member the obligation to enforce intellectual property law in a manner different from the enforcement of laws generally. Indeed, where TRIPS negotiators thought that Members had to be constrained in permitting a broad rule-based approach to adjudication, they included a provision to that effect.[64] Finally, the requirement of "effective remedies" in article 41.1 is preserved in that the patent remains valuable for many purposes. For example, it can be used to extract remuneration in other markets, and it retains its value as a signal to potential collaborators and investors.

---

[61] 35 U.S.C. § 283 (2000); Burk & Lemley, *Policy Levers*, above n. 17. *See, e.g.*, Foster v. Am. Mach. & Foundry Co., 492 F.2d 1317 (2d Cir. 1974) (preserving the market for an invention the patentee was not practicing). The provisions on government uses take a similar case-by-case approach. *See* TRIPS Agreement, above n. 2, arts. 44.2, 31(h).

[62] In United States contract law, speculative damages are not available. *See, e.g.*, RESTATEMENT (SECOND) OF CONTRACTS § 352 (1981) ("damages are not recoverable for loss beyond the amount that the evidence permits to be established with reasonable certainty.").

[63] For example, in intellectual property cases it is presumed that irreparable harm will ensue if the plaintiff with a likelihood of success on the merits could not obtain preliminary injunctive relief.

[64] *See* TRIPS Agreement, above n. 2, art. 31(a); *see also* DANIEL GERVAIS, THE TRIPS AGREEMENT: DRAFTING HISTORY AND ANALYSIS 165 (Sweet & Maxwell 1998).

As a matter of policy, it makes sense that the net result should be that WTO Members retain authority to control the terms on which basic research is conducted. Given that Members appear free to hold down the profits that innovators can earn by such actions as permitting parallel imports, or imposing compulsory licenses or price controls,[65] it is important that they remain equally free to control the costs that innovators face. Otherwise, price could, in theory, fall to the worldwide demand price (or to the price set by the government with the most stringent price controls), while the costs of research and development would be entrenched by the Agreement.[66]

IV. Concluding observations

Our case studies demonstrate that a country that perceives a problem with the patenting of upstream research has a variety of ameliorative approaches at its disposal, each with different pay-offs as a matter of domestic policy. Subject matter carve-outs are easy to administer, but hard to legislate; exemptions may be easier to legislate, but difficult to administer; and changing remedies has limited application. These approaches are also likely to provoke different responses at the international level. Unless article 27 of the TRIPS Agreement is read narrowly, subject matter exclusions may be impermissible; while an open-ended exemption could be heavily dependent upon a domestic interpretation that tracks international standards. Although the immunity approach may have the best chance of being approved by the WTO, it may be thought to violate remedies obligations, especially for patented technologies that are principally utilized in basic research.

Should the TRIPS Agreement be read to constrain national choices in this formalistic way? Consider, for example, the provision of current United States law on which the immunity defense outlined above was based. It immunizes a "medical practitioner's performance of a medical activity" that would otherwise constitute infringement. If the analyses of articles 30 and 44 that we put forward are rejected, then this provision could also be found to violate the TRIPS Agreement. Yet, a subject matter approach to surgical method patents would clearly be upheld under article 27.3(a), which permits members to exclude surgical methods from patentability.[67] It is difficult to see why WTO panels should adhere strictly to this formalistic approach, which requires these choices to be analyzed separately.

---

[65] TRIPS Agreement, above n. 2, arts. 6, 31.
[66] Arguably, the immunity approach could be viewed as a government subsidy that violates other provisions of the General Agreement on Tariffs and Trade. However, subsidization of basic (as opposed to applied) work has long been regarded as permissible. *See, e.g.*, Mary Lowe Good, *Technology and Trade*, 27 LAW & POL'Y INT'L BUS. 853, 857–58 (1996).
[67] *See* TRIPS Agreement, above n. 2, art. 27.3(a).

Of course, formalism may have a role to play. Our analysis also raises the question whether any provisions of the TRIPS Agreement are what we have called structural or horizontal in nature, part of the fabric of the Agreement as a whole, which should be transposed to the analysis of other provisions. The *Canada – Pharmaceutical Products* panel appeared to regard article 27.1 as one such provision and superimposed its technological neutrality principle on article 30. Although the Agreement no doubt contains some provisions (such as national treatment) that possess this structural character, panels should be cautious before elevating any particular provisions to this status, especially when these are ostensibly directed at specific issues rather than delineated in that part of the Agreement that addresses General Provisions and Basic Principles.[68]

In its latest TRIPS report, *United States – Section 211*, the Appellate Body attached great weight to the characterization of the law being challenged.[69] Such formalism may be necessary in the early stages of a lawmaking enterprise. However, characterization must be performed with attention to substantive goals. In multistate private litigation where choice of law is an issue, courts have long used a similar process. In those cases, the forum does not regard itself as bound by the characterization of the state that enacted the rule, but instead it makes its own assessment based on the state interests that underlie the law.[70] In our present context, WTO panels should do likewise, especially in the early years when they are considering local laws that were not formulated with TRIPS categories in mind. The appearance of arbitrariness will best be avoided by a process of characterization that is alert to the substantive purposes of intellectual property law.

It is also important for panels to keep what might be called the "neo-federalist" underpinnings of the TRIPS Agreement in mind. The Agreement, as an instrument of intellectual property law, must strike a balance between sufficient levels of protection to stimulate the desired social and commercial activity undertaken by first-comers, and sufficient limits on those rights to ensure the maximum socially useful exploitation of that activity. It partly achieves this balance substantively by allocating rights as between private and public interests, that is, between producers and users of intellectual property. But the Agreement does not articulate an international code authoritatively fixing that balance. It could not because the precise balance is still heavily contested within individual countries. Furthermore, where a particular

---

[68] *See* TRIPS Agreement, above n. 2, arts. 1–8.
[69] United States – Section 211, above n. 30, ¶ 105.
[70] *See* Restatement (Second) of Conflict of Laws § 7 (1971). *Cf.* Dicey & Morris, The Conflict of Laws ¶ 2.034–035 (Lawrence Collins et al. eds., 13th ed. 2000) (noting that it is "pointless" to look for the true or inherent meaning of legal categories and suggesting that courts avoid such "mere conceptualism" by examining the purposes of the substantive rule at issue).

country has settled on a specific balance, there is no guarantee that that balance would optimize the supply of innovation in a country of different competitive structure or economic status.

TRIPS, like any international agreement, must also deal with issues such as sovereignty, diversity, and legitimacy that pervade international relations. It must accordingly allocate power between supranational and national institutions, between national and international laws. Even when prescriptive power resides at the international level, that power is typically the authority to set boundaries within which a WTO Member can act, rather than to impose a specific rule of law. But when power remains vested in the Members, their governments have substantial legislative discretion, subject only to structural principles of the international intellectual property and trade regimes. In the TRIPS context, these allocations have the additional effect of giving WTO Members an important role in striking the producer/user balance of intellectual property law.[71]

In the discussion above, much of our argument rested on recognizing the importance of this neo-federalist structure. Thus, a decision to allow WTO Members to create a larger public domain by one method or another may be a product not of an intellectual property balance that the TRIPS Agreement mandated, but rather a consequence of the conferral of autonomy on national governments. For our case study, it seems to follow that the United States can enact a particular regime not because it embodies a balance between public and private interests that was struck in the TRIPS Agreement, but rather because that Agreement allows its Members to make a range of determinations, of which the one adopted by the United States is a permissible option.

To put it another way, because the TRIPS Agreement was negotiated with the goal of promoting international trade, the goals of substantive balance common to domestic intellectual property systems are barely discernable in its provisions. Nevertheless, panels must take seriously the autonomy interests implicit in the structure of the international intellectual property system, and they must allow sovereigns to respond to changes in science, to the structure of their patent industries, or to other social needs. Otherwise, a series of worldwide disutilities will result. These include costs stemming from the imposition of a uniform balance of producer and user interests which is in fact suitable for only one or a few countries, and inefficiencies caused by the long-term entrenchment of a balance appropriate for one point in time.[72] The goals of

---

[71] Characterization will also be a tool for implementing the principles of neo-federalism that we discuss above. *Cf.* DICEY & MORRIS, above n. 70, at 2–039 (noting that in private multinational litigation, characterization by a forum is simply the refinement or redefinition of the forum's conflicts rule).

[72] *Cf.* Keith E. Maskus & Jerome H. Reichman, *The Globalization of Private Knowledge Goods and the Privatization of Global Public Goods* [this volume] (arguing that the proper balance of interests for an emerging transnational system of innovation needs to be determined gradually, by regional experimentation, over time).

intellectual property law will thus be subverted, not furthered, by the international regime. The costs of disregard for the autonomy interest of states will also be borne by the international intellectual property system, whose long-term legitimacy and credibility rests in part upon participating states being best able to achieve the international welfare goals that purportedly underlie the system.

In passing, we have suggested various systemic values that are crucial to this approach to analyzing TRIPS obligations: the incentives likely to optimize social utility may vary widely from country to country. Permitting some diversity of approach allows nation states to act as laboratories in the development of international rules; affording space for the self-determination of sovereign states encourages voluntary and ultimately more effective compliance with international norms. Besides, universality may have costs, whether measured in economic or non-economic terms. We plan to develop these systemic values at greater length in another article. Fully articulating the latitude afforded WTO Members under international intellectual property law will provide scholars and national policymakers with a sense of the boundaries within which these domestic debates can then occur.

35

Recognizing public goods in WTO dispute settlement: Who participates? Who decides? The case of TRIPS and pharmaceutical patent protection

GREGORY SHAFFER[*]

Abstract
Introduction
I. Making choices between the production of competing public goods
II. Interpreting the TRIPS Agreement to advance public goods concerns: The institutional choices
III. Participation in WTO dispute settlement: Who participates? Who decides?
IV. Strategies for developing countries to overcome structural biases and advance their public goods concerns in WTO dispute settlement
Concluding Remarks

ABSTRACT

The question of how to produce "global public goods" in a world of sovereign states with divergent norms and preferences, reflecting differences in economic development levels, increasingly confronts the international policy agenda. It raises issues not only for political decision-making but also for judicial interpretation of existing international agreements. This chapter analyzes this fundamental question in the context of the Agreement on Trade-Related Aspects of Intellectual Property Rights (TRIPS) of the World Trade Organization (WTO), with particular emphasis on patent protection for pharmaceutical products. The TRIPS Agreement's provisions raise concerns over at least three public (or quasi-public) goods in this area: the generation of new knowledge, the provision of public health, and the maintenance of rules fostering open trade and competition. WTO judicial panels charged with

---

[*] Gregory Shaffer is Professor of Law, University of Wisconsin Law School. He is also Director, UN European Union Center and Co-Director, UN Center on World Affairs and the Global Economy. Thanks go to Benjamin Rickert and Zrinka Rukavina for their research assistance and to my colleagues, Neil Komesar and Pilar Ossorio, for their invaluable comments.

resolving disputes regarding patents on medicines must determine, in interpreting ambiguous or conflicting legal texts, the extent to which they defer to national sovereignty, various multilateral processes, or their own interpretations of the appropriate balance among these objectives. Questions of "who participates" and "who decides" will be critical in this determination. The chapter notes structural weaknesses in the ability of developing countries to participate meaningfully in the WTO judicial process and offers suggestions for making their participation more meaningful so as to protect their interests.

Introduction

Policy analysts increasingly pose the question of how to produce "global public goods" in a world of sovereign states governing constituencies with divergent norms, preferences, and priorities that reflect gaping differences in levels of economic development.[1] They pose this challenge in the context of increasing world population, complexity, and interdependence, and limited (if not decreasing) social solidarity.[2] The question raises issues of not only political decision-making, but also judicial interpretation of existing international agreements.[3] This chapter examines the choices that judicial panels face in recognizing public goods, in juxtaposition to private rights, when they address the issue of pharmaceutical patent protection under the Agreement on Trade-Related Aspects of Intellectual Property Rights (the "TRIPS Agreement").

The TRIPS Agreement addresses concerns over at least three public (or quasi-public) goods: the generation of knowledge, the facilitation of "undistorted" trade, and the protection of public health. This chapter addresses how a judicial panel of the World Trade Organization ("WTO"), when hearing a dispute over pharmaceutical patent protection, implicitly must allocate and thereby shape decision-making responsibilities that affect the appropriate balancing of these public goods concerns among national and international political, judicial, and market processes.

---

[1] *See, e.g.*, PROVIDING GLOBAL PUBLIC GOODS: MANAGING GLOBALIZATION (Inge Kaul et al. eds., UNDP 2003); GLOBAL PUBLIC GOODS: INTERNATIONAL COOPERATION IN THE 21ST CENTURY (Inge Kaul et al. eds., 1999) [hereinafter GLOBAL PUBLIC GOODS]; *The Health of Nations*, THE ECONOMIST, 22 Dec. 2001 (citing a report by the Commission on Macroeconomics and Health, set up by the World Health Organization).

[2] With global tensions rising in light of the U.S. government's "war on terrorism," global social solidarity may well be in decline. As regards declining civic engagement within the United States, see ROBERT PUTNAM, BOWLING ALONE: THE COLLAPSE AND REVIVAL OF AMERICAN COMMUNITY (2000).

[3] *See, e.g.*, Joost Pauwelyn, *WTO Dispute Settlement: Of Sovereign Interests, Private Rights, and Public Goods* [this volume]; Eric W. Bond, *The Economics of International Trade Agreements and Dispute Settlement with Intellectual Property Rights* [this volume]; Wilfred J. Ethier, *Intellectual Property Rights and Dispute Settlement in the World Trade Organization* [this volume]; Graeme Dinwoodie and Rochelle Cooper Dreyfuss, *WTO Dispute Resolution and the Preservation of the Public Domain of Science under International Law* [this volume].

After defining the concept of "public goods," Part I raises three challenges that WTO judicial panels face if they are to recognize public goods under the TRIPS Agreement. Most importantly, it raises the dilemma of conflicts among public goods, and, in consequence, the central importance of participation in the framing of the issues. Part II, after providing an overview of the relevant provisions of the TRIPS Agreement, shows how WTO dispute settlement panels effectively allocate decision-making responsibilities about the appropriate balance among competing public goods to national or international political processes, the marketplace, or themselves. Part III examines the structural biases that most developing countries face in advancing their concerns under the WTO's dispute settlement system, which potentially skews the framing of the issues. Part IV sets forth strategies that developing countries could deploy to enhance their ability to participate in the shaping of understandings and priorities concerning the public goods at stake, and, in the process, ensure a space for implementing intellectual property regimes in a manner appropriate to their needs.

I. Making choices between the production of competing public goods

Under the classic definition, public goods are distinguished from private goods in two respects. First, public goods are non-excludable in their benefits, so that they cannot be withheld practicably from one individual without withholding them from others. Second, they are non-rivalrous in their consumption, so that their consumption by one individual does not diminish their availability.[4] National defense is a classic public good that requires government funding because of collective action and free rider problems when production is left to the private market. This two-fold "publicness" of a good, however, typically lies along a continuum, so that goods may combine public and private attributes, complicating the assessment of how to generate them. Economists often refer to goods that do not fully meet the two criteria, but have significant public attributes, as "impure" public goods.

This section makes three central points concerning the production of public goods in the context of the debate over pharmaceutical patent protection under the TRIPS Agreement. First, the key problem with public goods is how to produce them, particularly in light of free rider problems. If public goods are non-excludable, then why would a private party ever invest in their production? The simple solution is to rely on the state for their production. For example, public

---

[4] *See* RICHARD CORNES & TODD SANDLER, THE THEORY OF EXTERNALITIES, PUBLIC GOODS AND CLUB GOODS (Cambridge University Press 1986); Paul Samuelson, *Pure Theory of Public Expenditure and Taxation*, in PUBLIC ECONOMICS (J. Margolis & G. Guitton eds., Macmillan 1969); Peter Drahos, *The Regulation of Public Goods* [this volume].

grants, such as through the National Science Foundation and the National Institute for Health, can finance basic research that otherwise would not be funded sufficiently through the private market. However, production by the state is beset by tradeoffs, ranging from bureaucratic inefficiencies (shirking) to political corruption (stealing, pork barrel projects, logrolling, and disinformation).

An alternative for the production of public goods is to tie their production to private goods, as through the recognition of private rights that generate positive externalities. For example, knowledge and technological development can be viewed as public goods generated through the recognition and enforcement of private patent rights, provided that the invention is published in a public registry and the rights are limited in scope and time. However, the granting of private rights also gives rise to strategic behavior, as when private actors threaten litigation to chill research and productive activity of competitors.[5] There are numerous options for tying public goods to private rights beside patents, including through liability, as opposed to property rights, regimes.[6] Yet all of these alternatives involve tradeoffs.

Second, more than one public good is at stake in the TRIPS context, and these public goods can conflict. Choices over the generation of at least three public goods arise in the pharmaceutical patent context: knowledge-generation, liberalized trade, and public health. To start with knowledge, it has public good attributes since once knowledge enters the public domain, it is no longer excludable and our consumption does not diminish its availability. However, knowledge can be subject to some excludability, as through trade secrets and patents, so that it is not a pure public good.[7]

The central issue is how to most effectively and equitably generate knowledge that facilitates new inventions and understandings. The choice must be made in light of the tradeoffs between the inefficiencies and inequities of granting private monopoly rights that take knowledge out of the public domain, the inefficiencies and inequities of markets that fail to recognize intellectual property rights and reduce incentives to invent, and the inefficiencies and inequities of government funding decisions. Any meaningful analysis must be comparative.

Free trade similarly has significant public good attributes, since the benefits of free trade policies, once adopted, are non-excludable and non-rivalrous.[8]

---

[5] *See, e.g.*, Stuart Macdonald, *Exploring the Hidden Costs of Patents*, in GLOBAL INTELLECTUAL PROPERTY RIGHTS: KNOWLEDGE, ACCESS AND DEVELOPMENT 13 (Peter Drahos & Ruth Mayne eds., 2002)

[6] *See* J.H. Reichman, *Of Green Tulips and Legal Kudzu: Repackaging Rights in Subpatentable Innovation*, 53 VAND. L. REV. 1743 (2001); J.H. Reichman, & Tracy Lewis, *Using Liability Rules to Stimulate Local Innovation in Developing Countries: Application to Traditional Knowledge* [this volume].

[7] *See, e.g.*, Joseph Stiglitz, *Knowledge as a Global Public Good*, in GLOBAL PUBLIC GOODS, above n. 1, at 308 (labeling knowledge an "impure public good").

[8] *See, e.g.*, Nancy Birdsall & Robert Lawrence, *Deep Integration and Trade Agreements: Good for Developing Countries*, in GLOBAL PUBLIC GOODS, above n. 1, at 128, 133. Hegemonic

We all benefit from the wider variety of products available at lower prices that trade liberalization facilitates. The creation of a global system of trade rules coupled with legalized dispute settlement likewise has public good attributes. A rule-based international legal system facilitates a more secure and stable international trading system from which all nations benefit. It helps avoid the beggar-thy-neighbor policies that undermined the global economy of the 1930s.

Yet, liberalized trade is an impure public good as well, since it can be subject to some excludability, whether through restricting membership to the WTO or through use of "unfair trade laws" to exclude exports from targeted countries. Moreover, the delineation of the boundaries of liberalized trade policies inevitably raises conflicts over values, as when trade rules interfere with domestic regulatory policies having trade effects. How free trade policies are defined affects rival public welfare concerns, including environmental and social protection, health care policies, and cultural diversity.

Public health constitutes a third public good.[9] We all benefit from the global eradication of diseases, and we do not diminish that good when we benefit from it. Like the ripple effects from financial shocks and beggar-thy-neighbor trade policies, diseases do not respect borders, as the AIDS and SARS epidemics have made terribly clear. The central issue, once again, is comparative, regarding how, among the alternative choices, do we produce the public good of public health in a relatively efficient and equitable manner.

The fact that these public goods may conflict further complicates national and global decision-making. The recognition and enforcement of "strong" patent rights interferes with competitive market forces and diminishes the benefits of liberalized trade. Firms can lobby to rig intellectual property systems and to lock in private monopoly rights over products and processes involving minimal scientific advances. The extent to which patent rules need to be harmonized globally is subject to serious question.[10]

---

stability theory, which contends that global free trade policies require a hegemon to secure a liberal economic order, posits that free trade is a public good. *See, e.g.*, Charles Kindelberger, *Dominance and Leadership in the International Economy: Exploitation, Public Goods, and Free Riders*, 25 INT'L STUD. Q. 242 (1981); ROBERT GILPIN, THE POLITICAL ECONOMY OF INTERNATIONAL RELATIONS (1987). The theory's critics counter that free trade is not a public good, but rather a club good whose benefits can be excluded to non-members of the club. *See, e.g.*, John Conybeare, *Public Goods, Prisoner's Dilemma, and the International Political Economy*, 28 INT'L STUD. Q. 5 (1984) (maintaining that free trade is better conceived as a prisoner's dilemma than a public goods problem); Joanne Gowa, *Rational Hegemons, Excludable Goods, and Small Groups: An Epitaph for Hegemonic Stability Theory?*, 41 WORLD POL. 307 (1989); Duncan Snidal, *The Limitations of Hegemonic Stability Theory*, 39 INT'L ORG. 579 (1985).

[9] *See, e.g.*, Todd Sandler & Daniel Arce, *A Conceptual Framework for Understanding Global and Transnational Goods for Health*, 23 FISCAL STUD. 195 (2002).

[10] *See, e.g.*, Alan Deardorff, *Should Patent Protection Be Extended to All Developing Countries?*, 13 WORLD ECON. 497, 507 (1990) (suggesting that if patent protection were limited

Strong patent rights also interfere with the provision of public health policies, as the global AIDS epidemic demonstrates. UNAIDS estimates that approximately 30 million people are infected with AIDS in Sub-Saharan Africa, resulting in 2.4 million deaths from AIDS and 3.5 million new AIDS infections in 2002 alone.[11] As you read these paragraphs, hundreds of people have died of AIDS because of their lack of access to medication. Balancing enforcement of developed country patents against millions of avoidable Sub-Saharan African deaths is indefensible. Yet, advocates of patent protection point out that if free trade and public health policies always override patent protection, then the private sector will invest less in the development of new medications, which potentially affects public health and technology transfer over the long run.[12]

As must any other court, a WTO judicial panel asked to "recognize" public goods when it hears a case involving pharmaceutical patent protection faces a major dilemma. It cannot simply recognize a public good in interpreting the TRIPS Agreement. It must rather take account of concerns about competing public goods as reflected in the Agreement's provisions.

Because public-goods concerns conflict, the third (and central) issue is institutional. That is, who decides who decides how the competing concerns should be balanced? Decisions as to how to produce public goods ultimately depend on decisions by national, regional, and international political and legal bodies that, in turn, affect market processes. Where institutions create, recognize, and enforce private intellectual property rights, such as patents, key issues arise concerning their duration, scope, and exceptions. While the choice among alternatives may be complicated at the national level, the choice becomes much more so at the international level where problems of numbers and complexity multiply. Balancing concerns about competing public goods and defining the means for the production of these goods involve tradeoffs over preferences and priorities that vary in a world of divergent levels of development and limited public finances. The dynamics of participation in national, regional, and international decision-making about the production of public goods thus becomes decisive.

>to developed countries, then world welfare would increase). *See also* CARLOS CORREA, INTELLECTUAL PROPERTY RIGHTS, THE WTO AND DEVELOPING COUNTRIES: THE TRIPS AGREEMENT AND POLICY OPTIONS 35 (2000) (citing World Bank and IMF studies on detrimental impacts of TRIPS on developing countries); Frederick Abbott, *The WTO TRIPS Agreement and Global Economic Development, in* PUBLIC POLICY AND GLOBAL TECHNOLOGICAL INTEGRATION 39 (Frederick Abbott & David Gerber eds., 1997).

[11] UNAIDS estimates that the virus will have infected 5 million people and killed 3 million worldwide in 2003. *See* UNAIDS, AIDS Epidemic Update, Dec. 2002, *available at* http://www.unaids.org/.

[12] *See, e.g.*, Alan Sykes, *TRIPS, Pharmaceuticals, Developing Countries, and the Doha "Solution"*, 21, *available at* http://www.law.uchicago.edu/Lawecon/index.html (suggesting that the lack of research on diseases present in developing countries "is attributable in significant part to heretofore weak intellectual property protection for pharmaceuticals in developing countries").

The ultimate issue in choosing among the production of public goods becomes institutional because different institutions offer different opportunities for actors to participate, and this affects which perspectives on the appropriate balancing are advanced. Problems of biased participation beset each institutional alternative on account of informational and resource asymmetries and divergent incentives to participate due to varying per capita stakes in outcomes.

The key issue from a public policy perspective is the assessment of the relative merits of institutional processes in terms of the relatively unbiased participation of affected parties compared to the (non-idealized) institutional alternatives.[13] That is, who decides who decides? Or put differently, which institutional process, among alternative political, judicial, and market processes at the local, national, regional, and international levels, should decide about the appropriate balancing? This institutional choice, in turn, affects how different interests, directly and indirectly, are taken into account, and thus ultimately determines who decides.

A WTO dispute settlement panel inevitably faces these institutional choices when hearing a dispute about pharmaceutical patent protection. As examined in Part II, a WTO judicial process itself can determine the appropriate balancing of the conflicting public goods concerns, or it can effectively allocate decision-making to an alternative institutional process at the national or international level. Who participates in the institutional process affects which arguments will be presented, and this outcome, in turn, affects how the competing concerns about patent protection, public health, and market competition will be weighed.

II. Interpreting the TRIPS Agreement to advance public goods concerns: The institutional choices

Provisions of the WTO agreements address each of the three public goods of knowledge-generation, liberalized trade, and public health. First and foremost, the central goal of the WTO is the promotion of liberalized trade. The preamble of the Agreement Establishing the WTO, to which the TRIPS Agreement is an annex, calls for "the substantial reduction of tariffs and other barriers to trade." This language mirrors the preamble of the WTO's predecessor, the General Agreement on Tariffs and Trade (GATT) of 1947. The first and third declared goals of the TRIPS Agreement in the first paragraph of its preamble are "to reduce distortions and impediments to international trade" and "to ensure that measures and procedures to enforce intellectual property rights do not themselves become barriers to legitimate trade." The GATT 1994, which is now

---

[13] See the work of Neil Komesar, including IMPERFECT ALTERNATIVES: CHOOSING INSTITUTIONS IN LAW, ECONOMICS AND PUBLIC POLICY (1995); LAW'S LIMITS: THE RULE OF LAW AND THE SUPPLY AND DEMAND OF RIGHTS (2002).

the first annex to the Agreement Establishing the WTO, explicitly recognizes national intellectual property laws as a potential barrier to trade.

The GATT creates certain exceptions to its requirements in article XX, which lists intellectual property protection as a legitimate ground for trade restrictions. These trade restrictions, however, are subject to the condition that they must not be more trade restrictive than "necessary to secure compliance with laws or regulations which are not inconsistent with the provisions of this Agreement [the GATT], including those relating to ... the protection of patents, trademarks and copyrights."[14] The first part of article XX, known in trade circles as the "chapeau," further provides that these trade restrictions must not constitute "unjustifiable discrimination" or "a disguised restriction on international trade." In 1989, a GATT panel held that Section 337 of the U.S. Trade Act of 1930, which provides for the exclusion of goods that infringe a U.S. patent, violated GATT's non-discrimination provisions and was not protected by the article XX(d) exception because foreign products accused of infringing a U.S. patent were treated less favorably than domestic products.[15]

Knowledge generation is arguably the primary public good addressed by the TRIPS Agreement. Article 7, which sets forth the agreement's "Objectives," states:

> The protection of intellectual property rights should contribute to the promotion of technological innovation and to the transfer and dissemination of technology, to the mutual advantage of producers and users of technological knowledge and in a manner conducive to social and economic welfare, and to a balance of rights and obligations.[16]

In other words, the Agreement aims to spur "innovation" and "dissemination of technology" (i.e. knowledge) through the protection of intellectual property, subject to "social and economic welfare" considerations. The TRIPS Agreement's preamble notes the Members' desire "to promote effective and adequate protection of intellectual property rights," including through "effective and appropriate means for the enforcement of trade-related intellectual property rights." The preamble further recognizes these rights as "private" rights.[17]

Articles 27–34 of the TRIPS Agreement set forth the required provisions for patent protection, including the scope of patentable subject matter, the

---

[14] Marrakesh Agreement Establishing the World Trade Organization, Annex 1A, Multilateral Agreement on Trade in Goods, 15 Apr. 1994, General Agreement on Tariffs and Trade, Article XX(d), 33 I.L.M. 1154 (1994) [hereinafter GATT].

[15] See United States – Section 337 of the Tariff Act of 1930, 1989 WL 587604 (GATT 16 Jan. 1989).

[16] Agreement on Trade Related Aspects of Intellectual Property Rights, 15 Apr. 1994, Marrakesh Agreement Establishing the World Trade Organization, Annex 1C, LEGAL INSTRUMENTS – RESULTS OF THE URUGUAY ROUND vol. 1, 33 I.L.M. 81 (1994) [hereinafter TRIPS Agreement], art. 7.

[17] Id. ¶¶ 1, 2, 4 of the preamble.

exclusive rights conferred on the patent owner, the patent term (20 years from filing), the conditions imposed on patent applicants, the "limited exceptions" to these exclusive rights, and the conditions of compulsory patent licenses.[18] As regards the issue of patented medicines, the 2001 Doha Declaration on the TRIPS Agreement and Public Health (the "Doha Declaration"), while "reaffirming" the "flexibility" of the TRIPS Agreement for Members to "protect public health," also confirms Members' recognition "that intellectual property protection is important for the development of new medicines."[19]

Finally, the TRIPS Agreement expressly recognizes the third public good at issue – the promotion of public health. Article 8 of the TRIPS Agreement sets forth the agreement's "Principles," confirming that Members "may, in formulating or amending their laws and regulations, adopt measures necessary to protect public health and nutrition." As regards patents specifically, article 27.2 provides for the exclusion of patentability where "necessary to protect *ordre public* or morality, including to protect human, animal or plant life or health or to avoid serious prejudice to the environment." Article 30 declares that "Members may provide for limited exceptions to the exclusive rights conferred," such as in recognition of the Agreement's objectives and principles. Article 31 sets forth exceptions to the requirement of obtaining authorization from a right holder to use the patent, including "in the case of a national emergency or other circumstances of extreme urgency."[20]

When concerns arose that the provisions of the TRIPS Agreement could nonetheless impede developing countries' public health policies, most immediately in light of the AIDS epidemic, the United States and other developed countries were pressed into signing the Doha Declaration, which declared that the TRIPS Agreement provides "flexibility" for Members to take measures to protect public health. Paragraph 5 of the declaration sets forth a list of what these flexibilities included, and in particular that "each provision of the TRIPS Agreement [i.e. including the patent provisions in articles 27–34] shall be read in light of the object and purpose of the agreement as expressed, in particular, in its objectives and principles" (i.e. articles 7–8 that include the protection of public health and social welfare). Just before the Cancún Ministerial meeting in September 2003, the WTO General Council issued a decision implementing paragraph 6 of the Doha Declaration (the "Paragraph 6 Decision").[21] This decision waived obligations set forth in paragraphs (f) and (h) of article 31 of

---

[18] *Id.* arts. 27–34.
[19] Paragraph 3 of the Declaration on the TRIPS Agreement and Public Health, WT/MIN(01)/DEC/2 (20 Nov. 2001) (adopted at the fourth WTO Ministerial Conference in Doha, Qatar).
[20] TRIPS Agreement, above n. 16, arts. 8, 27.2, 30, 31(b).
[21] *See* Doha Declaration, above n. 19; Council for TRIPS, Decision of 30 Aug. 2003, Implementation of Paragraph 6 of the Doha Declaration on the TRIPS Agreement and Public Health, WT/L/540 (2 Sept. 2003).

the TRIPS Agreement so as to facilitate the grant of "compulsory licenses" for the supply of medicines from any third country to countries with insufficient manufacturing capacities in the pharmaceutical sector. The decision, which "is without prejudice to the rights, obligations and flexibilities that Members have" under the TRIPS Agreement, is to continue until such time as "an amendment to the TRIPS Agreement replacing its provisions takes effect."[22]

The inclusion of the terms "flexibilities" and "without prejudice" suggests that other provisions of the TRIPS Agreement, such as the article 30 exceptions clause, could shield developing countries from challenge if a complaint involving pharmaceutical patent protection were brought against them before a WTO panel. Already under the Vienna Convention on the Law of Treaties, WTO panels are to interpret and apply the provisions of WTO agreements in light of their object and purpose.[23] Through the Doha Declaration and Paragraph 6 Decision, WTO Members simply confirmed the importance of a "flexible" interpretation of intellectual property requirements in line with the TRIPS Agreement's general "objectives" and "principles." The challenges facing a future WTO panel are thus considerable.

A WTO panel's choice involves not only competing policy goals, but also at least three institutional alternatives for balancing these goals. First, the WTO panel could interpret the TRIPS Agreement "flexibly" to show deference to national determinations of the appropriate balancing of public goods concerns (as reflected in the Agreement's statement of "Objectives" and "Principles" and confirmed in the Doha Declaration and Paragraph 6 Decision). The panel would essentially allocate the balancing decision to the national level.

Second, the panel could stringently apply the specific provisions of the TRIPS Agreement on patent protection (paragraphs 27–34) as setting a "floor" for international intellectual property protection that all Members must meet, so as to limit national determinations of the appropriate balancing.[24] Any diminutions of the intellectual property rights set forth in these paragraphs would then have to be determined by the TRIPS Council or through a future round of WTO intergovernmental negotiations, perhaps informed by negotiations concerning other international regimes.[25]

Third, the panel could itself engage in what it deems to be the most appropriate balancing of liberalized trade, patent rights protection, and public

---

[22] *Id.* para. 11.
[23] *See* art. 31, Vienna Convention on the Law of Treaties, 23 May 1969, 1155 U.N.T.S. 331, 8 I.L.M. 679.
[24] Article 1.1 of the TRIPS Agreement, above n. 16, provides, "Members shall give effect to the provisions of this Agreement. Members may, but shall not be obliged to, implement in their law more extensive protection than is required by this Agreement, provided that such protection does not contravene the provisions of this Agreement."
[25] *Cf.* Richard Steinberg, *In the Shadow of Law or Power? Consensus-Based Bargaining and Outcomes in the GATT/WTO*, 56 INT'L ORG. 339 (2002).

health goals on a case-by-case basis. In this latter instance, the judicial panel would allocate the balancing to itself (an international judicial process) and take a more activist role in flexibly applying open-ended provisions of the TRIPS Agreement to assess the costs and benefits of competing public goods concerns in a specific factual context. In doing so, the panel could take account of not only the Doha Declaration and Paragraph 6 Decision, but also the wider national and international context, including the programs of the World Health Organization (WHO), UNAIDS, and the United Nations Conference on Trade and Development (UNCTAD).[26]

These implicit institutional decisions affect who participates in the weighing of the competing public goods since participation will vary depending on whether the assessment is made through a national political or judicial process or alternative international political and judicial processes. The WTO judicial panel's decision shapes political bargaining in these alternative fora and, ultimately, market processes. As regards market processes, a stringent application of patent rights will keep market prices high in developing countries because of the lack of competition. Similarly, a judicial decision that is factually-contextualized and case-specific can give rise to considerable legal uncertainty. This legal uncertainty would reduce the incentive for producers of generic medicines to invest in the production of the desired drugs, since the producers may fear costly legal challenges that would undermine their investments.[27]

Were the WTO judicial process to interpret the TRIPS Agreement "flexibly" and show broad deference to national decision-making over pharmaceutical patent protection to meet public health goals, the United States and European Community (E.C.), as demanders of strict enforcement of pharmaceutical patent rights, could still bargain with the regulating country, but the bargaining context would change. As a result, developing countries would no longer have to offer something to the United States and E.C. in return to obtain an "exception" to the TRIPS requirements.

---

[26] *See* above nn. 19 & 21. Concerning the WHO's work, see DAVID FIDLER, INTERNATIONAL LAW AND PUBLIC HEALTH: MATERIALS ON AND ANALYSIS OF GLOBAL HEALTH JURISPRUDENCE (2000); DAVID FIDLER, INTERNATIONAL LAW AND INFECTIOUS DISEASES (1999). Concerning UNCTAD's work, see UNCTAD-ICTSD Project on Intellectual Property Rights and Sustainable Development, *available at* http://www.iprsonline.org/unctadictsd/projectoutputs.htm (visited 3 Nov. 2003).

[27] For a study of how commercial actors use the uncertainty created by the factually-contextualized rulings of a supranational court to challenge national rules, see Richard Rawlings, *The Eurolaw Game: Some Deductions from a Saga*, 20 J.L. & SOC'Y. 309 (1993) (examining how lawyers for large retail chains used decisions of the European Court of Justice to challenge British rules limiting Sunday business hours). The European Court of Justice eventually issued a bright line ruling that the British laws were valid under E.C. law (*see* Cases C-418 to 421/93, Semeraro Casa Uno Srl v. Sindaco del Commune di Erbusco, 1996 ECR I–2975), but only after much of the domestic battle was lost.

Moreover, the normative framework of the bargaining would change. An international panel would have held that the developing countries' actions were lawful. In addition, U.S. and European multinational firms could still participate in national bargaining within developing countries over the appropriate interface of pharmaceutical patent protection and health care policies, even if a WTO panel deferred to those countries' policy decisions. U.S. and European firms would still retain significant leverage in light of the investment and other financial resources that they offer.

Yet, the institutional setting would be quite different on account of the effective allocation of authority to national institutional processes made by the WTO panel. Such a decision would not only intensify price competition for the sale of pharmaceutical products in developing countries. It could also spur the development of markets that might not exist because monopoly right holders lack the incentive to tailor production for developing country purchases because of right holders' focus on rich-country markets.[28]

In short, in disputes over pharmaceutical patent protection under the TRIPS Agreement, WTO panels necessarily confront concerns over competing public goods, on the one hand, and institutional choices, on the other. In evaluating how WTO dispute settlement panels should recognize public goods or how they should allocate decision-making to other institutional processes, we first need to assess who currently participates in the WTO judicial process, and then address mechanisms to ensure relatively less biased participation in framing the analysis and assessing the impact of alternative choices. It is to these issues that we now turn.

III. Participation in WTO dispute settlement: Who participates? Who decides?

While others have written cogent accounts of biases in the negotiation of the TRIPS Agreement,[29] as well as in WTO Agreements as a whole, this section addresses biases affecting participation before the WTO dispute settlement system.[30]

---

[28] *Cf.* Sykes, above n. 12 (maintaining that patent enforcement in developing countries combined with a ban on parallel imports should increase the incentive for pharmaceutical companies to create and market new drugs for the needs of developing country constituencies). Sykes, however, while calling this an empirical question, fails to mention the empirical work that has been done. *See, e.g.*, sources cited above n. 10.

[29] *See* Susan Sell, Private Power, Public Law: The Globalization of Intellectual Property Rights (2003) *and* Power and Ideas: North-South Politics of Intellectual Property and Antitrust (1998); Peter Drahos, Information Feudalism: Who Owns the Knowledge Economy? (2002); Michael Ryan, Knowledge Diplomacy: Global Competition and the Politics of Intellectual Property (Brookings Institution Press 1998).

[30] *See generally* Gregory Shaffer, *Power, Global Governance and the WTO*, *in* Power and Global Governance (Michael Barnett & Raymond Duvall, eds., Cambridge

Participation in WTO judicial processes is arguably more important than is participation in analogous judicial processes for shaping law in national systems. The difficulty of amending or interpreting WTO law through the WTO political process enhances the impact of WTO jurisprudence. WTO law requires consensus to modify, resulting in a rigid legislative system, with rule modifications occurring through infrequent negotiating rounds. Because of the complex bargaining process, rules often are drafted in a vague manner, thereby delegating de facto power to the WTO dispute settlement system to effectively make WTO law through interpretation.

As a result of the increased importance of WTO jurisprudence and the rigidity of the WTO political process, those governments that are able to participate most actively in the WTO dispute settlement system are best positioned to effectively shape the law's interpretation and application over time. Not surprisingly, the United States and European Community remain by far the predominant users of the system, and thereby are most likely to advance their interests through the judicial process. As repeat players, the United States and E.C. strive not only to win individual cases. They also play for rules, and attempt to shape judicial interpretation of WTO rules over time.

From 1948 through the end of June 2000, the United States was either a complainant or defendant in 340 GATT/WTO disputes, which amounted to 52 percent of the total number of 654 disputes, while the European Community was a party in 238 disputes, or 36 percent of that total.[31] Moreover, the United States and E.C. are typically third parties in cases where they are not complainants or defendants. As parties and third parties, the United States and E.C. attempt to defend their systemic interests in shaping the interpretation of WTO rules over time.

As of February 2003, the United States had participated as a complainant, defendant, or third party in every proceeding that resulted in an adopted panel or Appellate Body report but one, constituting a 97 percent participation rate. The E.C. had participated as a party or third party in 81 percent of such fully litigated WTO cases. The U.S. and E.C. participation rates, in particular, are much higher than the United States' and E.C.'s percentages of global trade, which in 1999 were 16.8 percent and 20.1 percent of world exports, respectively.[32] In contrast, the

---

University Press 2004). This section's arguments are further developed in GREGORY SHAFFER, HOW TO MAKE THE WTO DISPUTE SETTLEMENT SYSTEM WORK FOR DEVELOPING COUNTRIES: SOME PROACTIVE DEVELOPING COUNTRY STRATEGIES (ICTSD 2003).

[31] *See* Marc Busch & Eric Reinhardt, *Testing International Trade Law: Empirical Studies of GATT/WTO Dispute Settlement, in* THE POLITICAL ECONOMY OF INTERNATIONAL TRADE LAW: ESSAYS IN HONOR OF ROBERT E. HUDEC 457, 462 (Daniel Kennedy & James Southwick eds., 2002) [hereinafter Busch & Reinhardt, *Testing International Trade Law*].

[32] *See* BERNARD HOEKMAN & MICHEL KOSTECKI, THE POLITICAL ECONOMY OF THE WORLD TRADING SYSTEM: THE WTO AND BEYOND 59 (2d ed. 2002).

vast majority of developing countries have participation rates of zero percent or in the single digits in respect of WTO cases that resulted in an adopted report.[33] As of 1 December 2004, no Sub-Saharan African country had initiated a WTO complaint.

As for complaints under the TRIPS Agreement, either the United States or E.C. initiated 21 of the 23 TRIPS complaints brought through January 2003 (15 by the United States and 6 by the E.C.). Brazil and Canada each initiated one TRIPS complaint, but these were merely symbolic claims that they filed in response to WTO complaints brought by the United States and E.C. against them. Brazil and Canada never seriously pursued their claims to advance commercial interests, but rather searched for bargaining chips for a potential settlement of the U.S. and E.C. complaints. As regards TRIPS complaints that resulted in an adopted panel or Appellate Body report, the United States was a party or third party in all seven, and the E.C. in six of the seven cases.

Law matters not only for the litigation of specific disputes, but, even more importantly, for settlements negotiated in the law's shadow.[34] There are two primary shadow effects of law: the law's substance and the costs of invoking the law's procedures. First, WTO law's substance, as defined through WTO jurisprudence, provides bargaining chips, informing and constraining settlement negotiations. Second, as Herbert Kritzer writes, "the ability to impose costs on the opponent and the capability of absorbing costs" affect how the law operates in practice.[35]

When large developed countries, such as the United States and E.C., can absorb high litigation costs by dragging out a WTO case, while imposing them on developing country parties, they can enhance developing countries' incentives to settle a dispute unfavorably. Developing countries' relative participation in the international trade dispute settlement system in complaints against developed countries has declined since the advent of the WTO compared to their relative participation under the less-legalized GATT. As Reinhardt has documented, developing countries were "one-third less likely to file complaints against developed states under the WTO than they were under the post-1989

---

[33] See chart in GREGORY SHAFFER, DEFENDING INTERESTS: PUBLIC–PRIVATE PARTNERSHIPS IN WTO LITIGATION 157–58 (2003).

[34] See, e.g., Marc Galanter, Contract in Court; or Almost Everything You May or May Not Want to Know about Contract Litigation, WIS. L. REV. 577, 579 (2001) (Contracts Symposium 2001) (referring to "litigotiation" to remind us "that the career of most cases does not lead to full-blown trial and adjudication but consists of negotiation and maneuver in the strategic pursuit of settlement through mobilization of the court process").

[35] HERBERT KRITZER, LET'S MAKE A DEAL: UNDERSTANDING THE NEGOTIATION PROCESS IN ORDINARY LITIGATION 73–75, 103–04, 132–33 (1991). See also Herbert Jacob, The Elusive Shadow of the Law, 26 LAW & SOC'Y REV. 565, 586 (1992) (noting "the language in which a claim is initially framed combined with the manner in which attorneys are used and the success of consultation with personal networks are perhaps the key variables in determining the strength of the shadow of the law").

GATT regime." In contrast, Busch and Reinhardt show that "the fraction of cases targeting [developing countries] has risen dramatically, from 19 to 33 percent," suggesting that a developing country "is up to five times more likely to be subject to a complaint under the WTO."[36]

Bernard Hoekman and Michel Kostecki confirm that, under the WTO, "the developing country share in terms of being a defendant rose to 37 percent" compared to "only 8 percent of all cases brought during the GATT years."[37] Constantine Michalopoulos has documented how developing countries' use of the WTO dispute settlement process against developed countries is considerably less than their share of developed country trade. "By mid 2000, 46 percent of the developed countries' complaints had been lodged against developing country WTO Members, while the latter accounted for only about 25 percent of developed-country trade. Just over 50 percent of the developing countries' complaints, on the other hand, were lodged against developed countries, considerably less than the latter's share of trade with developing countries."[38] In many cases, developing countries' participation is overstated by reference to numerical charts, since the developing country is piggy-backing on a U.S. or E.C. complaint in what U.S. officials dub "me too" cases.

Developing countries, other than the largest ones, such as Brazil and India, are less likely to participate actively in WTO litigation because of two central structural factors respectively affecting the benefits and costs of their participation: (i) individual developing countries' relatively smaller value, volume and variety of exports, resulting in lower absolute benefits from participation in the WTO dispute settlement system, and (ii) the relatively high cost of access to the system and developing countries' reduced economies of scale for mobilizing legal resources.

First, developing countries often have high per capita stakes in individual cases, so that WTO law could be of potential benefit to them. In fact, a developing country may have much higher relative stakes in the determination of a given trade measure than the United States and E.C. in relation to their respective economies, but the developing country's case is likely to be of smaller aggregate value. To give an example, in their study of U.S.–E.C. trade disputes, Busch and Reinhardt rank a dispute that affects over U.S. $150 million in annual trade as a "high stakes" dispute.[39] However, a $150 million claim only represents about .0015 percent of U.S. gross domestic product.

---

[36] See Busch & Reinhardt, *Testing International Trade Law*, above n. 31, at 466–67 (citing a table as well as other work by Reinhardt).
[37] See HOEKMAN & KOSTECKI, above n. 32, at 394–95.
[38] See CONSTANTINE MICHALOPOULOS, DEVELOPING COUNTRIES IN THE WTO 167 (2001).
[39] Marc Busch & Eric Reinhardt, *Transatlantic Trade Conflicts and GATT/WTO Dispute Settlement*, in DISPUTE PREVENTION AND DISPUTE SETTLEMENT IN THE TRANSATLANTIC PARTNERSHIP (Ernst-Ulrich Petersmann ed., Oxford University Press 2003).

A claim of comparable importance for Honduras would equal around U.S. $255,000.⁴⁰ Since an average WTO claim costs in the range of U.S. $300,000–400,000 in attorneys' fees (although they possibly can be much more),⁴¹ such a developing country could not even cover its attorneys' fees were it to prevail in a "high stakes" claim before the WTO Dispute Settlement Body, and Honduras is not even a "least-developed country." Even for larger developing countries, such as Peru and Malaysia, although a comparable "high stakes" claim would be valued at around US $2–3 million, the risk of loss or noncompliance would significantly discount the case's value.⁴²

Second, the cost of bringing an individual WTO case has risen, which also reduces developing countries' incentives to participate. The WTO Appellate Body and WTO panels employ a highly contextualized, case-based approach, based on jurisprudence where individual case opinions average in the hundreds of pages. As a consequence, the demand on lawyers' time, and thus the cost of specialized legal expertise, has skyrocketed.

Litigation at the international level involves a distant forum in which legal expertise is U.S. and Euro-centric, highly specialized, and quite expensive. Developing countries can face fees ranging from $200–$600 (or more) an hour when they hire private law firms to advise and represent them in WTO cases.⁴³ Developing countries not only must weigh these costs against the uncertain, but smaller, benefits of litigating a WTO case. They must also consider the opportunity costs of expending money on outside trade counsel instead of otherwise addressing development and social concerns in countries where the population makes less than $2 a day.

The factors of developing country stakes and WTO litigation costs are interrelated. The costs of participation in WTO dispute settlement are absolute, regardless of the relative benefits. As Lawrence Friedman and Robert Percival write regarding domestic litigation, "[a]s costs rise, so does the threshold at which litigation becomes worthwhile."⁴⁴ Since developing countries export a vastly narrower array and limited value and volume of exports than

---

⁴⁰ In 2001, the United States gross domestic product (GDP) equaled approximately U.S. $10.1 trillion. In 2000, Haiti's GDP was about $12 billion, Senegal's about $16.2 billion, and Honduras' approximately $17 billion, in terms of purchasing power parity. A "high-value" claim under Busch and Reinhardt's criteria respectively would equal from around $180,000 to $255,000 for these three countries. See CIA World Factbook, *available at* http://cia.gov/cia/publications/factbook (visited 3 Nov. 2003).
⁴¹ Discussion with lawyers in Geneva, 7 Feb. 2003.
⁴² Peru's GDP was around $123 billion and Malaysia's around $212 billion, based on purchasing power parity. *See* CIA World Factbook, above n. 40.
⁴³ Confirmed in e-mail messages from two Washington DC trade lawyers, 15 and 18 Jan. 2003. In 2001, Michalopoulos cited a figure of "$250–1000 an hour." MICHALOPOULOS, above n. 38, at 94.
⁴⁴ Lawrence Friedman & Robert Percival, *A Tale of Two Courts: Litigation in Alameda and San Benito Counties*, 10 LAW & SOC'Y REV. 276 (1976).

do the United States and E.C., they are less likely to be repeat players in WTO litigation.[45] Because of their less frequent use of the WTO system, they benefit from fewer economies of scale in deploying legal resources. As a result, the benefits for a developing country from bringing a WTO case are less likely to exceed the threshold of litigation costs that make the suit worthwhile, especially in light of the uncertainty of WTO remedies.[46]

Because of developing countries' lack of resources, low aggregate stakes in WTO dispute settlement, and inability to benefit from economies of scale, these countries are not developing human capital and know-how in WTO law that can be tapped, when needed, for WTO disputes. Most developing countries have few law schools and no professors that teach WTO law. In consequence, private lawyers are not available within developing countries to advise local firms, trade associations, and government officials on WTO rights and to work with them and developing country governments to defend those rights in WTO litigation and settlement negotiations. The small supply of lawyers educated in WTO law within developing countries thus increases the cost for developing country firms and governments to become aware of WTO rights.

In contrast, well over 100 law professors teach aspects of WTO law each year in the United States to over 3,000 law students.[47] Large and well organized U.S. and European interests hire lawyers, economists, and other consultants on WTO matters, and then coordinate with U.S. and E.C. public authorities.[48] The dozens of lawyers working for U.S. and E.C. trade authorities are thus supplemented by legal assistance financed by the U.S. and European private sectors.

Because of developing countries' less frequent use of the WTO system and their lack of local legal capital, the alternative for a developing country to train internal lawyers with WTO expertise is typically worse than hiring expensive U.S. or European outside legal counsel. Training internal counsel entails a significant long-term allocation of resources, which is not cost-effective if a country is not an active player in the litigation system. Start-up costs are high and potential economies of scale low. Moreover, where a developing country's internal lawyers develop expertise and exhibit talent, they can be snatched up by private law firms that pay salaries against which governments in developing countries cannot compete.

---

[45] The term "repeat players" is taken from Marc Galanter's classic piece, *Why the "Haves" Come Out Ahead: Speculations on the Limits of Legal Change*, 9 LAW & SOC'Y REV. 95 (1974).
[46] See Shaffer, above n. 30.
[47] In 2002, the American Association of Law Schools listed 598 law professors teaching "International Transactions" in U.S. law schools, and 123 who noted international trade or the WTO as a specific subject area for teaching. See THE AALS DIRECTORY OF LAW TEACHERS 2002–2003 (AALS West Group and Foundation Press 2002). I have estimated conservatively that around 30 students enroll per class. This calculation may be on the low side, since some professors teach more than one international trade-related class per year to many more students per class.
[48] See SHAFFER, above n. 33.

Although lawyers regularly leave government in the United States for the private sector, the fact that they largely remain in Washington and often subsequently return to government as part of Washington's "revolving door" bureaucratic culture means that U.S. trade authorities are much more likely to take advantage of their acquired expertise. In the language of economics, a revolving door bureaucratic culture can have positive externalities for the United States in international litigation, since the developed expertise is available locally to be used predominantly by U.S. firms and government officials. The spillover effects for developing countries, in contrast, are largely negative, since, once a developing country trade official leaves to work for the private sector in the United States or Europe, that individual is not available locally within the developing country and almost never returns to government service.

Developing countries' perceptions of the WTO system also feed back on their awareness of whether they have legal defenses and claims available. Where developing countries and their commercial constituents have little faith in the WTO system, they are less likely to develop mechanisms to detect manipulations and violations of WTO law that affect their interests. Even when they become aware of measures against which they could invoke their legal rights, developing countries are less likely to develop pro-active strategies to defend these rights and interests if they believe that the system is structured in a way that they cannot do so in a cost-effective manner.

As is the case in domestic legal systems, those with greater wealth and education (in this case, U.S. and European governments and commercial constituents) are more likely to recognize situations where they can deploy legal rights (in this case, WTO rights).[49] When they do so, they are well placed to "bargain" in the law's shadow and realize their objectives. The following section addresses strategies that developing countries could pursue to overcome some of the challenges that they face.

IV. Strategies for developing countries to overcome structural biases and advance their public goods concerns in WTO dispute settlement

Much of the struggle over the interpretation of the TRIPS Agreement will be discursive. It will be a struggle over competing principles that involve competing conceptions and priorities concerning the public goods at stake. These principles and conceptions will be advanced by competing coalitions of public and private actors. In light of the severe disadvantages that most developing countries face before the WTO dispute settlement system (Part III), developing countries will need to devise strategies to mobilize resources to advance their conceptions and priorities, on the one hand, and to undermine

---

[49] See, e.g., Charles Cortese, *A Study in Knowledge and Attitudes Toward the Law: The Legal Knowledge Inventory*, 3 ROCKY MTN. SOC. SCI. J. 192 (1966).

the extra-legal coercion that the United States and (to a lesser extent) the E.C. deploy, on the other. They need to find ways to make such coercive acts politically unpalatable for U.S. and E.C. government and corporate elites.

The United States, the E.C., and their multinational pharmaceutical companies know how to play the knowledge game.[50] As Susan Sell writes, "it was not merely [U.S. corporate actors'] relative economic power that led to their economic success [with the TRIPS Agreement], but their command of IP expertise, their ideas, their information, and their skills in translating complex issues into political discourse."[51] Following the conclusion of the TRIPS Agreement, U.S. industry continued to work with U.S. public officials to "educate" foreign governments. The United States regularly sent lawyers for its pharmaceutical and copyright industries to Geneva as "faculty" of the World Intellectual Property Organization (WIPO) to teach developing country representatives about intellectual property matters and to draft "model" laws for their consideration.[52] Industry successfully lobbied Congress to allocate funds for these "educational" efforts.[53] Industry similarly wishes to shape WTO panelists' conceptions of the appropriate interpretation of the TRIPS Agreement.

This section addresses WTO dispute settlement strategies from a broad perspective. Developing countries' legal strategies necessarily have relevance beyond dispute settlement, since participation in WTO political and judicial processes are complementary. The shadow of WTO judicial processes shape bilateral negotiations, just as political processes and contexts inform judicial decisions. If developing countries can clarify their public goods priorities and coordinate their strategies, then they will more effectively advance their interests in bargaining conducted in WTO law's shadow, and in WTO legal complaints heard in the shadow of bargaining.[54] They, in turn, will be better prepared to exploit the "flexibilities" of the TRIPS Agreement, tailoring their intellectual property laws accordingly, and will gain confidence in their ability to ward off U.S. and E.C. threats against their policy choices. In other words, developing countries' international legal strategies have implications for their

---

[50] DRAHOS, above n. 29.
[51] *See* Susan Sell, *Multinational Corporations as Agents of Change: The Globalization of Intellectual Property Rights*, in PRIVATE AUTHORITY AND INTERNATIONAL AFFAIRS 169, 192 (Claire Cutler et al. eds., 1999). *See also id.* at 190.
[52] Telephone interviews with members of the Pharmaceutical Research and Manufacturers of America (PhRMA) and International Intellectual Property Association (IIPA) (17 & 20 May 1999).
[53] Telephone interviews with members of PhRMA and IIPA (17 May 1999).
[54] WTO panels are not courts, but "dispute settlement" panels formed pursuant to the Marrakesh Agreement Establishing the World Trade Organization, Annex 2, Understanding on Rules and Procedures Governing the Settlement of Disputes, 15 Apr. 1994. WTO panel decisions are perhaps best viewed in the shadow of bargaining, since the WTO Appellate Body shapes its decisions to facilitate compliance or settlement.

leverage in international political negotiations and for the policy space in which they implement domestic intellectual property and public health regimes.

This section examines the following three strategies: pooling government resources at the national, regional, and international levels; coordinating with private parties in the United States and Europe to undercut industry pressure in the formation of U.S. and E.C. negotiating positions and litigation strategies; and working with generic producers of pharmaceuticals in political negotiations and judicial disputes, so that the TRIPS Agreement's provisions are interpreted in a clear manner that induces the generic sector to invest the necessary resources to produce the desired drugs. These three strategies complement those proposed by others for the implementation of intellectual property regimes within developing countries to promote their economic growth and social welfare.[55]

First, developing countries could pool their resources through national, regional, and international centers specializing in trade-related intellectual property issues.[56] Developing countries currently are forced to work with *ad hoc* assistance in WTO dispute settlement on a case-by-case basis. The development of national, regional, and international centers to advance their priorities can have mutually reinforcing effects.

To participate effectively in regional and international centers, developing countries would need to better coordinate interagency policy-making at the national level. Interagency coordination would address the linkages between intellectual property protection, economic development, public health, and social welfare. Regional centers could create benchmarks for policy, provide a forum for the sharing of experiences, and identify best practices. Regional centers could also better coordinate training of developing country officials and non-governmental representatives.[57]

These centers could work with academics, or be tied to an academic institution and benefit from student interns, like the Center for International and Environmental Law (CIEL) based at American University in Washington, DC (for trade-environment matters) and the Trade Law Centre for Southern Africa

---

[55] *See, e.g.*, CORREA, above n. 10; KEITH MASKUS, INTELLECTUAL PROPERTY RIGHTS IN THE GLOBAL ECONOMY 199–234 (2000); J.H. Reichman, Managing the Challenge of a Globalized Intellectual Property Regime (draft for the second Bellagio meeting on Intellectual Property and Development 2003) (on file); Frederick Abbott, *The TRIPS-Legality of Measures Taken to Address Public Health Crises: Responding to USTR-State-Industry Positions that Undermine the WTO*, in THE POLITICAL ECONOMY OF INTERNATIONAL TRADE LAW, above n. 31.

[56] *See also* Peter Drahos, *When the Weak Bargain with the Strong: Negotiations in the World Trade Organization*, 8 INT'L NEGOTIATION 79 (2003).

[57] Reichman, above n. 55. *See generally* Keith E. Maskus & Jerome H. Reichman, *The Globalization of Private Knowledge Goods and the Privatization of Global Public Goods* [this volume], at III.A (2) (discussing institutional infrastructure for reconciling international IP standards with needs of national and regional systems of innovation).

(TRALAC) based at Stellenbosch University.[58] These centers could, in turn, work with a cross-national "Academic Resource Group" on trade and intellectual property matters, as discussed by Peter Drahos and Michael Blakeney.[59]

Developing countries now have the opportunity to obtain legal assistance on WTO law in a more cost-effective manner through an international legal services organization – the Advisory Center on WTO Law in Geneva.[60] There are two problems, however, with the Advisory Center from the standpoint of intellectual property negotiations and disputes. The Center has only eight lawyers who must be prepared to litigate over 19 WTO agreements. It thus lacks specific expertise in trade-related intellectual property matters. In addition, the Advisory Center's sole focus is on WTO dispute settlement, while developing countries need to coordinate political and judicial strategies, since intellectual property matters are advanced in a strategic fashion before multiple fora.

Developing countries need to defend their legal interests not only before the WTO Dispute Settlement Body, the TRIPS Council, and at WTO ministerial meetings, but also before the WIPO, the WHO, UNAIDS, in regional negotiations, such as over a Free Trade Agreement of the Americas, and in bilateral negotiations, such as the trade agreements that the United States recently negotiated with Jordan, Singapore, and Chile, and is now pressing on numerous fronts.[61] The United States attempts to leverage stronger intellectual property protection from these bilateral trade negotiations, using the TRIPS Agreement as a foundation.

Developing countries could form a complementary international public interest law and policy center to assist them on intellectual property matters. National interagency committees and regional centers could act as focal points for coordinating international strategies. Such an international center could be funded through an endowment and user fees, as is the Advisory Center on WTO Law.[62] The intellectual property center would combine a longer-term strategic outlook with intervention in specific cases. Because it would be a repeat player, it would develop a reservoir of expertise into which developing countries could tap, as needed.

---

[58] See Victor Mosoti, *Does Africa Need the WTO Dispute Settlement System?*, in TOWARDS A DEVELOPMENT-SUPPORTIVE DISPUTE SETTLEMENT SYSTEM IN THE WTO (ICTSD 2003); Interview with member of TRALAC, Berne, Switzerland (17 June 2003).

[59] Peter Drahos & Michael Blakeney, Rockefeller Report for Bellagio Conference (2002), *cited in* Reichman, above n. 55 (proposing the formation of an "Academic Resource Group").

[60] *See* Advisory Ctr. WTO Law, Welcome to the Advisory Center on WTO Law, *at* www.acwl.ch (visited 13 Dec. 2002). The Center is funded through an endowment and user fees, the fees being imposed on a sliding scale in relation to the country's pro rata share of global trade and its per capita GNP, based on World Bank criteria.

[61] *See* Philippe Legrain, *Last Resort*, THE NEW REPUBLIC, 3 Nov. 2003, at 21 (noting U.S.T.R. Robert Zoellick's "push for free trade through bilateral regional agreements" with what Zoellick terms "can do countries").

[62] *See* above nn. 57, 60.

By coordinating strategies at the national, regional, and international levels, developing countries could more effectively offset the relentless U.S. and E.C. bilateral pressure to ratchet up global patent rights over the longer term through constant forum-shifting.[63] They could continue to raise these issues through international organizations where they wield greater clout and where their public health concerns have greater resonance, such as the WHO's World Health Assembly, the UN Committee on Economic, Social and Cultural Rights, and the UN High Commissioner for Human Rights. They could strategically use these fora not only to shape global debates, but also perceptions within the WTO of the way that TRIPS itself should be read.[64] A global public interest law center for intellectual property matters could also collaborate with the Advisory Center on TRIPS cases brought before WTO panels, just as public interest law firms coordinate in domestic litigation.

Second, developing countries need to work consistently with U.S. and European political allies to alter the U.S. and European domestic political contexts. International negotiations involve a two-level game in which national constituencies compete in the formation of national positions, and those national positions then are advanced in international negotiations.[65] If developing countries cannot neutralize the clout of large pharmaceutical firms in the formation of U.S. and European positions, then they will face the full brunt of U.S. and European coercion in the negotiation and enforcement of pharmaceutical patent rights.

In a world of asymmetric power, developing countries enhance the prospects of their success if other U.S. and European constituencies offset the pharmaceutical industry's pressure on U.S. and European trade authorities to aggressively advance industry interests. Domestic and international non-governmental advocates, such as ACT UP, Doctors Without Borders, and Oxfam, have been natural allies. They raise fundamental moral issues to hold U.S. and E.C. political leaders accountable. They also harness the public's

---

[63] See JOHN BRAITHWAITE & PETER DRAHOS, GLOBAL BUSINESS REGULATION (2000); see generally LLOYD GRUBER, RULING THE WORLD: POWER POLITICS AND THE RISE OF SUPRANATIONAL INSTITUTIONS (2000).

[64] See, e.g., World Health Assembly, Resolution 52.19, Revised Drug Strategy (24 May 1999), available at http://www.who.int/governance/en; United Nations High Commissioner for Human Rights, The Impact of the Agreement on Trade-Related Aspects of Intellectual Property Rights on Human Rights, E/CN.4/Sub.2/2001/13 (27 June 2003); United Nations Development Program, Making Trade Work for People (2003).

[65] See, e.g., Robert Putnam, *Diplomacy and Domestic Politics: The Logic of Two-level Games*, 42 INT'L ORG. 427 (1988); DOUBLE EDGED DIPLOMACY: INTERNATIONAL BARGAINING AND DOMESTIC POLITICS (Peter B. Evans et al. eds., 1993). For an application to the U.S. and E.C. contexts, see Mark Pollack & Gregory Shaffer, *Transatlantic Governance in Historical and Theoretical Perspective*, in TRANSATLANTIC GOVERNANCE IN THE GLOBAL ECONOMY (Mark Pollack & Gregory Shaffer eds., 2001); SHAFFER, above n. 33.

self-interest over the cost of prescription drugs and public officials' struggles to finance health care commitments within the United States and Europe themselves. As Braithwaite and Drahos write, "Had TRIPS been framed as a public health issue, the anxiety of mass publics in the U.S. and other Western states might have become a factor in destabilizing the consensus that U.S. business elites had built around TRIPS."[66]

This strategy has worked in a number of cases. The United States backed off from challenging South Africa's and Brazil's pharmaceutical patent laws primarily in the context of U.S. domestic political pressures. The United States withdrew its threat of initiating a WTO claim against South Africa in response to pressures from AIDS activists who gathered at Vice President Gore's presidential campaign stops holding placards for the nightly news and chanting "Gore's greed kills!"[67]

In June 2001, the Bush administration withdrew the United States' claim against Brazil's compulsory licensing provisions under Brazil's patent law following widespread protest against the U.S. action from advocacy groups who maintained that the U.S. government was placing corporate interests above life-and-death medical concerns.[68] Support from international health and human rights organizations complemented this NGO pressure.[69] USTR Robert Zoellick similarly abandoned the U.S. pharmaceutical industry with little consultation in agreeing to the Declaration on the TRIPS Agreement and Public Health at Doha.[70] The Bush administration did so in the context of post-September 11 domestic politics, where the administration was undercut on compulsory licensing issues following the anthrax scare, and felt an intensified need to compromise on intellectual property matters in order to launch a new trade round. In short, when TRIPS issues become politicized domestically within the United States and Europe, developing countries retain greater leeway to formulate intellectual property policies to fit their own needs.

Third, developing country governments and their legal advocates should work with the generic pharmaceutical sector, including companies from

---

[66] BRAITHWAITE & DRAHOS, above n. 63, at 576.
[67] *See* Steven Meyers, *South Africa and U.S. End Dispute over Drugs*, N.Y. TIMES, 18 Sept. 1999, at A8; Doug Ireland, *AIDS Drugs for Africa*, NATION, 4 Oct. 1999, at 5. Vice-President Gore was co-chairman of the U.S.-South Africa Bi-national Commission on pharmaceutical issues.
[68] *See, e.g., U.S., Brazil End WTO Case on Patents, Split on Bilateral Process*, 19 INSIDE U.S. TRADE, 29 June 2001, at 1, 2. Doctors Without Borders and Oxfam launched campaigns in the United States and Europe against U.S. policies. *See, e.g., Drug Companies vs. Brazil: The Threat to Public Health, at* http://www.oxfam.org.uk/what-we-do/issues/health/drugcomp_brazil.html (visited 1 Aug. 2004).
[69] *See, e.g., UN Rights Body Backs Brazil on AIDS Drugs*, News24.com (24 Apr. 2001), *available at* http://www.news24.com/ (visited 1 Aug. 2004).
[70] E-mail from Washington insider (27 June 2002) (concerning the lack of consultation). *See also* Gary Yerkey & Daniel Pruzin, *Agreement on TRIPS/Public Health Reached at WTO Ministerial in Doha*, 18 INT'L TRADE REP. (BNA) 1817 (15 Nov. 2001).

Third-World countries, if they are to develop an effective strategy. The generic pharmaceutical sector in countries such as Brazil and India knows what it requires if it is to supply developing countries with the drugs they need. The Doha Declaration on the TRIPS Agreement and Public Health confirms that "each Member has the right to grant compulsory licenses and the freedom to determine the grounds on which such licenses are granted."[71] The Paragraph 6 Decision creates a means for the grant of licenses from any third country to developing countries that lack the capacity and know-how to produce high-quality pharmaceuticals, as they lack the market size to justify the investment.[72]

Yet, if the interpretation of the conditions for granting compulsory licenses under the Paragraph 6 Decision creates legal uncertainty, then generic companies will not invest in the needed production because of the threat of legal challenge. The United States Trade Representative has worked closely with the pharmaceutical industry and its trade association, PhRMA, to develop U.S. negotiating positions and litigation strategies.[73] To ensure the effective supply of low-cost pharmaceuticals, public authorities in developing countries will need to coordinate similar strategies with the private generic pharmaceutical sector in third countries.

Concluding Remarks

Knowledge is not simply a private right and source of profits, though that is the way corporate stakeholders wish us to see it. Nor is knowledge only a public good, though that is the conception advocated by some promoters of a knowledge commons. Knowledge is a form of power, shaping how we perceive the world and the alternative choices available to us, including options for the production of knowledge itself. How will the WTO agreements be read to promote public goods in juxtaposition to private rights? How will the various goals of patent protection, liberalized trade, and public health be weighed?

Although WTO dispute settlement panels should recognize public goods, doing so is not a simple task. This chapter has shown how the TRIPS Agreement raises issues of competing public goods, and, in particular, now it fosters conflicts among policies promoting liberalized trade, knowledge-generation, and public health (Part I). Since the object and purpose of the TRIPS Agreement includes the promotion of competing public goods, there is no single way that this Agreement can be read (Part II).[74] WTO panels must thus confront the tradeoffs among these concerns.

---

[71] *See* above n. 19. [72] *See* above n. 21.
[73] *See* SHAFFER, above n. 33. *See also* Tom Hamburger, *U.S. Flip on Patents Shows Drug Makers' Growing Clout*, WALL ST. J., 6 Feb. 2003.
[74] The United States has been the first to argue that WTO agreements are subject to multiple readings in other contexts, such as regards WTO Members' obligations under WTO antidumping rules.

In doing so, a WTO panel faces institutional choices as to who should decide the appropriate balancing. In rendering a decision, a WTO panel can interpret the TRIPS Agreement to provide significant "flexibility" for national decision-making processes. It can apply intellectual property rules strictly and public health concerns as narrow "exceptions" and leave the determination of broader exceptions to a subsequent international political process. It can itself assess the costs and benefits of competing public goods in a fact-specific context.

In each institutional setting, deliberation and bargaining will occur over the competing goals. In each setting, participation will be biased in one way or another, since institutions provide different opportunities for affected parties to participate. A WTO judicial panel's choice, in itself, will be shaped by who participates before it. As Part III demonstrated, most developing countries are at a significant disadvantage in WTO dispute settlement proceedings and negotiations conducted in their shadow.

In order for developing countries to use the WTO dispute system effectively and thereby enhance their leverage in bilateral bargaining and their policy discretion domestically, they need to coordinate through multi-level, public-private networks. As the U.S. and European pharmaceutical industry has long understood, it's a long-term, multi-level, high-stakes game. Developing countries need to work with strategic partners to frame perceptions about intellectual property matters and the particular provisions of the TRIPS Agreement in light of developing country objectives. They can thereby increase the chances that WTO panels will interpret public good concerns from their perspectives. As a consequence, they could enlarge the policy space in which they might implement domestic regulatory regimes to suit their needs, and gain confidence in their ability to ward off U.S. and E.C. legal threats to these choices. If U.S. and European legal challenges are constrained, generic pharmaceutical producers will more likely invest in the production of the needed life-saving drugs.

INDEX

A&M Records v. Napster case 678
Abbott, Frederick M. 393–424
accountability 183, 446, 447
Advisory Centre on WTO Law 904, 905
Africa 389, 399, 486, 576, 690, 692
  South Africa 410, 486, 723, 903
African Group 382
Agrawall, A. 128, 607
Agricultural Experiment Station programs 192, 194, 212
Agricultural Plant Health Inspection Service 204
agriculture 686, 189, 605, 607
  and biotechnology 290, 304, 670, 671–82
  chemical revolution 191–2
  crop genetic improvement 192–3
  fair use doctrine 678–80
  future of research 211–14
  Gene Revolution 194, 203–7, 211, 212, 213–14
  genetic use restriction technologies 693
  Green Revolution 192–3, 194–203, 207, 211, 215, 680
  hybrid maize 686–93
  innovation in 366–90, 672
  livestock industrialization revolution 193–4
  mechanization revolution 191
  modern high-yielding varieties 194–203
  Public-Sector Intellectual Property Resource for Agriculture 300–1
  research 188–216, 677, 678–9
  rice landraces 504, 569
  technological revolutions 188–90
AIDS 447, 453, 473, 486
  antiretroviral drugs 409–10, 418, 421, 465, 486
  in developing countries 397, 399–400, 418, 449
  public health challenge of 395, 396, 481–3, 491
  treatments for 409–10, 424, 465, 647, 723
  and TRIPS patent rights 31
  vaccine for 303, 478, 479
Alma-Ata Declaration 488–91
antitrust law 71, 632, 759–62, 803
  enforcement of 20, 22
  immunity for petitioning 758–9, 764–7, 769
  and IP law 246, 731–5, 744, 797
  and IP rights 323, 728, 736, 758–69
  minimal standards for 774–92
appropriation 9, 70, 87, 231, 511–14, 517, 686

arbitrage and IP protection 635–52
  factors affecting 643–4
  responses to 644–50
Arora, Ashish 316, 321–36
artifacts, regulation of 55–6

Bagwell, K. 834
Bar-Shalom, A. 138
bargaining 73–4, 144, 364
Barsh, Russel 500
Barton, John 77, 99, 617–34, 659–60, 866, 868
Bayh-Dole Act 42, 92, 130, 131, 136–8
Beachy, Roger N. 300
Bently, L. 510–11
Bernal, J.D. 129
Berne Act 153–5
Berne Convention 61, 155, 156, 158–60, 161, 175–8, 183–4
  administrative apparatus 159–60
  Appendix to 147, 151, 162–8, 185
  authorial protection 156–7, 159
biodiversity 384, 495, 581, 606, 608
  laws 554–5
  sharing of benefits from 695–705
biopiracy 569, 590–1, 609, 610
biotechnology 136, 203, 579, 742, 866
  and agriculture 215, 290, 295–6, 304
  Cartagena Biosafety Protocol 206–7
  Chakrabarty-Diamond case 204
  diffusion of 683–5, 689
  Hibberd case 204
  impact of 670, 671–82
  life science companies 204
  and patents 203, 291, 640, 646, 658, 669–94
  R&D 676
Biovail case 766
BIRPI 158, 160
Blakeney, Michael 366–90, 503, 904
Blizzard Entertainment 58–9
Boldrin, Michael 109, 110
Bond, Eric W. 831–51, 853, 854, 857, 858
Boyle, James 22
Braga, Primo 579
Braithwaite, J. 906
Bransetter, Lee G. 309–20
Brazil 575, 906–7
Breyer, S. 799–800, 801

Budapest Treaty on the International Recognition of the Deposit of Microorganisms for the Purposes of Patent Procedure 56
Busch, M. 897, 898
Bush, Vannevar 122, 129

California Air Resources Board 766
Cameron, Edwin 486
Campbell, Eric 294, 299
Canada 519, 613
Canada – Patent Protection for Pharmaceutical Products case 234–5, 242, 867, 869–76, 881
capacity building 76, 258
capture 632
  of copyright law 798–9
  of IP law 653, 654–5
  of IP standard setting 28
  pharmaceutical industry 402, 405
cartel 19, 29, 768, 772
Carvalho, Nuno P. de 516–17, 589–90
Cassis de Dijon case 67
Cell-Pro case 138
Center for International Environmental Law 579, 903
Center for the Application of Molecular Biology to International Agriculture 301
Centre for the Management of Intellectual Property in Health Research and Development 302
chemical industry 331–4, 654, 657
China 422, 423, 690–1
Cho, Mildred 295
Ciba/Geigy determination 378
civil society, international 61, 612
club goods 711–12, 724
Coase, Ronald 794, 795, 799, 800–1
Codex Alimentarius 206
collective action 41, 43, 44, 50, 60, 61, 288–306, 297–300
  barriers to 298, 305
  in the public sector 300–3, 301–2, 304–5
  and universities 299, 301
collective obligations 820–4, 826
collective responsibility 503
collective rights 603–4
commercial capacity 874–5
Commission on Genetic Resources for Food and Agriculture 217–18
Commission on Intellectual Property Rights 347
commons 653, 711, 758–69, 793, 907
  dilemma 51, 59
  genetic 217–24, 385
  intellectual 51, 58
  knowledge 113–18
  research 12, 28, 42, 51, 357

scientific 121–38
  community of users 58
  compensatory liability 342–8, 348–64, 587
    Green Tulip Model 349, 351, 354
    rights under 349–51
    and traditional knowledge 354, 594
  competition 44, 109, 342, 351, 417, 651, 744, 770
    and copyright 167
    and developing countries 35–41
    institutions 781–4
    and IP regimes 22
    and knowledge goods 86
    and regulation 435–6
    social benefits of 15, 16
    and technology transfer 15, 330
    unfair 89, 90, 343, 512–13, 547, 588, 756
  competition law 8, 185, 731–9, 748, 803, 804
    harmonization of standards 733, 773
    international 746–54
    IP system and 716–24, 770–3, 774–92, 793–805
    national 730–9, 779
    and public goods 709–25
    separability assumption 795–802
  competition policy 729, 737, 746, 752–7, 775, 780–1, 795–802
    national 740, 752
  compulsory licenses 162–4, 166, 176, 178, 240–7, 752, 764, 795
    measurement of 660–1
    and medicines 452–5, 456, 490, 491, 492, 723
    non-exclusive 248–9
    obligation to work a patent 240–3
    and public goods 182
    refusal to deal 243–7, 743, 763–4
    royalties and 249
    and the TRIPS Agreement 700, 721
  computer software 21, 96, 639, 657, 741
    open source 297, 644–5, 646
  concentration 798–9
  constitutional law 52, 67, 794
  constitutions 52
  Consultative Group on International Agricultural Research 214, 572–3
    Special Project on Impact Assessment 194–203
  consumers 720, 721, 725
    demand for pharmaceuticals 432, 434, 445, 446
  contract law 697, 699
  Convention on Biodiversity 205, 214–15, 511, 517, 544, 564, 610
    access and benefit sharing provisions 389, 506, 507, 509, 549, 556, 571, 697–704
    and national sovereignty 220, 593, 680–1, 696
    obligations of 355, 703

INDEX   911

and traditional knowledge 358, 495, 577, 580,
    600, 602, 606
and the TRIPS Agreement 574, 700
Cook-Degan, R. 138
Coombe, Rosemary J. 599–614
Cooper Dreyfuss, Rochelle 135, 138, 861–83
cooperation 51, 704–5, 745, 753, 772, 846
Copyleft principle 117
copyright law 88, 161, 179, 187, 666, 713, 798–9,
    801
    access to information 147–52, 184–5
    access to protected works 148–9, 149–52, 153,
        168–78, 179, 182, 184
    agreements 154–5
    capture of 798–9
    and computer software 21, 96, 657, 741
    and databases 104, 516
    and digital information 142–87
    and digital telecommunications 26
    disclosure 93
    and economics 90–91, 107–13
    exemptions 98, 134, 164, 182
    exhaustion doctrine 71
    international mechanisms 557–62
    legitimacy 160–2
    misuse 185
    national differences in 642–3
    national exceptions and limitations 150,
        169–71, 172–3
    need for 801
    and the New Economy 152–62
    policy 185
    and public welfare 107, 145, 152, 181
    and science 85
    scope of 173–5, 344
    standards 61, 101
Correa, Carlos M. 261, 601
    misappropriation 355, 511, 587
    technology transfer 227–56, 282
    the TRIPS Agreement 262, 263
Costa Rica, Biodiversity Law 554
Cottier, Thomas 565–94, 611
country codes 641–2
creativity 147–52, 663, 666–7, 716, 724, 744
crops, performance of major 687–9
cultural diversity 599–614
customary law 234, 525, 527–8, 530–3, 539, 549,
    872
    in the international context 555–7
    opinio juris 537–8
    and protection of traditional knowledge 560
    recognition in the IP system 551–64
    and traditional knowledge 564
Cutler, David 457

Daes, Erica-Irene 511
Danzon, Patricia M. 425–56

databases 42, 100, 110
    commercialization of public 95–6, 101–2, 106
    E.C. Directive on Databases 43, 103–7
    licensing 102, 116, 117
    in the new economy 99–103
    protection of 100, 101, 741, 742
David, Paul 66, 81–120, 139, 140
democratic deficit 18
developing countries 4, 5, 18, 184–5, 255, 268–9,
    658–9
    access to digital information 142–87
    and access to essential medicines 393–424,
        426, 443, 448, 452–5, 491–2, 647, 723
    access to information and technology 34, 176,
        177, 266, 733
    agriculture 194–203, 207, 214, 301, 567
    aid to 658–9
    and antitrust law 774, 782, 783–4
    and the Berne Convention 160, 161, 162, 164,
        168
    and biotechnology patents 669–94
    bulk access to copyright material 149, 166,
        168, 177, 180, 182
    capacities of 2, 19, 28, 174, 215, 258, 269, 802
    capacity for imitation and innovation 189,
        207–11, 212–13, 269
    and the CBD 205, 703
    chemical industry 331–3
    compensatory liability regime 346, 348,
        362–3, 365
    and competition 35–41, 772, 773, 780–92, 804
    and compulsory licenses 247, 627, 700–1, 702
    contribution to pharmaceutical R&D 420
    diversity of 10, 214, 215
    and enforcement of IP laws 116
    and global public goods 28, 724
    industrial growth 207, 211, 212, 213, 214
    and innovation 36, 38, 40–41, 44, 229, 337–65
    and IP policy 335
    and IP regimes 6, 8, 24, 27, 338, 669–94
    and IP standards 26, 36, 61, 62, 283–6, 310, 362
    labor skills 268–9
    and markets for technology 333–6
    negotiations with developed countries 664–5,
        704
    openness to trade and investment 268, 859–60
    and patent law 13, 352, 353, 702, 783–4, 791, 792
    and patents 622, 633–4
    and plant variety protection 194–203, 376,
        382, 389
    pooling of resources 904–5
    and public goods 901–8
    R&D 119, 305, 420, 472
    and technology transfer 261, 262, 265, 281
    and traditional knowledge 579–81, 587–8
    and the TRIPS Agreement 232, 234–5, 364,
        382–5, 664, 675, 859, 892

developing countries (cont.)
 and the WTO dispute settlement mechanism 859, 895–6, 899–901, 901–8,
Development Capacity-Building Project 665
development strategies, "laboratory effects" 37, 45
Diamond v. Chakrabarty case 377
differential pricing 416–18, 425–56
 and medicines 433–5, 436, 438, 441–4, 444–52, 455
digital divide 180–1
digital information 169–70, 180
 access to in developing countries 142–87, 185
 and the Berne Convention 176
 and copyright 178–81
Digital Millennium Copyright Act 97, 115, 172, 175, 179
Dinwoodie, Graeme B. 861–83
discrimination 866, 867–8
diseases: *see also* AIDS; leprosy; malaria; tuberculosis
 of developing countries 302, 304–5, 395, 427, 471, 472, 724
 neglected 422–3, 457–80, 472–4, 474–9
dispute settlement mechanisms 530, 656, 817–30, 826–7, 835–51
Dispute Settlement Understanding 183, 644, 836, 856, 858, 860
DNA, research into 203
Doctors Without Borders 423, 449
Doha Declaration on TRIPS and Public Health 29, 253, 414, 489–90, 710, 767–8, 892–3, 906
 and compulsory licensing 164–5, 452–5
 and flexibility 892–3, 894–5
 and technology transfer 235, 251
Drahos, Peter 46–64, 66, 140, 517, 607, 611, 667, 904, 906
Drexl, Josef 709–25
Drugs for Neglected Diseases Initiative 422
Dutfield, Graham 495–520
Dyson, Esther 111

e-commerce 110, 112
Eaton, Jonathan 284
E.C. – Hormones case 823
economic growth 99, 143, 144, 184, 187
economic theory 278, 281, 429, 711, 715
economics, information 85–8
education 184, 711, 713, 715, 724
 access to copyright material 149, 173, 177, 187
efficiency 68, 71–2, 716, 724, 769, 841
 and compulsory licenses 250
 and digital technology 97
 and markets 50, 719
 and price discrimination 437, 455
encryption technologies 97–8, 102, 114, 115
Environmental Intermediaries Programme 663
Environmental Protection Agency 204

environmental regulation 63, 215, 259, 818, 826
Epstein, Richard 865, 866, 867
Equitable Access Licence 302–3
equity 432, 581, 622, 790
 and traditional knowledge 556, 560, 563
Ethier, Wilfred 839, 852–60
Ethiopia 690–1
E.U. – Banana case 858
European Bioinformatics Institute 107
European Union 43, 94, 510, 905
 antitrust law 771
 competition law 723, 762–4
 competition policy 748–50
 E.C. Directive on Biodiversity 696
 E.C. Directive on Databases 43, 103–7, 114, 116, 179, 718, 737
 E.C. Directive on the Legal Protection for Computer Programs 647
 E.C. Directive on the Legal Protection of Biotechnological Inventions 377, 378
 E.C. Regulation on Community Plant Variety Rights 379
 information and communications technologies 101–2
 patent system 26, 349, 510, 619, 621, 625–6, 646–7, 718, 721
 pharmaceutical industry 399, 402, 448, 450
 plant variety protection laws 370, 378–9
 and the WTO dispute settlement mechanism 895–6, 898
Evenson, Robert E. 188–216
excludability 9, 50, 52
exhaustion doctrine
 international 444, 638, 718, 719, 725, 722, 771
 national 628, 771
external referencing 438–44, 443, 445, 448
externalities 10, 794, 796–8, 834
 and patent policy 637, 843
 and science 129–30
 and trade agreements 852–4
 TRIPS Agreement and 859–60

fair use doctrine 169, 182, 678, 876
farmers' rights 205, 375, 379, 387–9, 582
Farnsworth, Norman 504
Fashion Originators' Guild case 760, 803–4
Feist Publications v. Rural Telephone Service Co. 100, 101
Fink, Carsten 579, 770–3
flexibility 76
folklore 595–8
Food and Drug Agency 204, 464, 465–6
 fast-track program 467–8, 475, 765–6
 review program 477, 479
Food Ethics Council 667
foreign direct investment 6, 11, 215, 657

and technology transfer 262, 268–9, 271, 273–8, 281
forum shifting 29, 30, 398, 905
Fosfuri, Andrea 321–36
Fox, Eleanor M. 758–69, 771
France, patents system 627
free riding 39, 55, 75, 102, 109, 350, 352, 711
  and pricing 435–6, 760–1
  and traditional knowledge 357, 513
  and the TRIPS Agreement 656, 886
Friedman, Lawrence 899
Frommer, Chloe 601
FTC 750, 765–7, 782, 803
FTC v. Xerox Corporation 248

Gambardella, Alfonso 321–36
game theory 830–1
Ganslandt, M. 429
GATS 656, 721
GATT 15, 19, 655, 656, 845, 890
gene revolution in agriculture 194, 203–7, 211–14
  Golden Rice 206, 304
  regulatory and IP issues 203–7
genetic use restriction technologies 676–7, 681, 683–5, 687, 689
  impact of 685–6, 689, 693
genetically modified organisms 204
geographical indication protection 528, 547, 560–1, 580, 591, 594
Gerhart, Peter M. 69–77
germ plasm 695, 696, 699
Germany, patent system 654
Ghosh, Shubha 793–813
Ginsburg, Jane 873
Glass, Amy 271
Glaxo SmithKline 473
Global Alliance for TB Development 473
Global Biocollecting Society 517–18
Global Fund 7, 580, 600, 602, 606
  provision of 7, 11, 140
  and the TRIPS Agreement 574, 700
GNU General Public License 118
Goeschl, Timo 669–94
Goldstein, Paul A. 833
Gollin, D. 195
governance, global 18, 31, 66, 483
Grabowski, Henry G. 433, 457–80
Graff, Geoffrey 291
Green, Shane 608
Green Revolution in agriculture 194–203, 212–13, 215, 680
Griliches, Zvi 192
Group of Countries of Latin America and the Caribbean 384
GURTs 676–7, 681, 683–5, 687
  impact of 685–6, 689, 693

Hayami, Y. 683
Hayden, Cori 608
health care systems 395–404, 487–91, 711, 713, 715, 724, 895
  indigenous 498, 501
Helfer, Laurence 29–30, 217–24
Helpman, Elhanan 270–1
Henderson, R. 128
Hibberd case 380
Hoekman, Bernard 898
Howse, Robert 32
Human Genome Project 298, 299
human rights 30, 481–92, 611–14, 667, 819, 826, 827

Image Technical Services, Inc. v. Eastman Kodak Co. 246–7
imitation 275, 278, 282
  capacity for 189, 207–11, 212–13, 268–9
  cost of 281, 463
IMS case 763
incentives 65, 67, 68, 90
India
  Biological Diversity Bill 575
  customary law 577
  indigenous people 355, 358, 383, 388, 497, 511–12, 519, 520
  pharmaceutical industry 62, 422, 423, 430, 656
  rights of 554
  traditional knowledge 498, 501, 509, 522, 548, 549, 557, 580, 598, 608
industry associations 370
information 53–4, 56–9, 85, 86–7
  access to 87, 168–72, 186
  codified and uncodified 53–4, 85
information and communications technologies 26, 42, 97, 99–103, 114
information goods 83, 653
information space 106–7, 113
  low cost of reproduction 86, 107–8, 117
  non-rivalrous character 54, 86, 119
  private property rights in 81–120
  as a public good 86, 87
  upstream 22, 290–2, 305
innovation 16, 184, 692, 891
  in agriculture 366–90, 693
  and the balance of public and private interests 33–4
  and competition law 755
  costs of 462–3
  evolutionary theory of 229, 250
  group 744–6
  incentives 34, 253, 624, 747, 751
  and IP arbitrage 650
  market-driven 121
  nature of 139–40, 311–12, 317, 343, 356

innovation (cont.)
  and patents 309–20, 637, 840, 844
  in the pharmaceutical industry 462–3
  policy 746–8
  promotion of 8, 139, 186, 234
  and public goods 833
  subpatentable 346, 350, 353, 518
  and technology transfer 274, 278
  and traditional knowledge 566, 586
  transnational system 44–5
  and the TRIPS Agreement 740–4
institutions 58, 65, 68, 147, 158, 183, 889
  choice of 890, 890–5, 908
  design of 69–77, 781–4
  private collective management 514–15, 517
Instrument of Cultural Diversity 612
Intellectual Capitalism 84
intellectual commons 51, 58
intellectual property law 37
Intergovernmental Committee on Intellectual Property and Genetic Resources, Traditional Knowledge and Folklore 222, 364, 384–5, 389, 496, 600
Intergovernmental Copyright Committee 161
interest groups 50, 179–80, 654
international agreements 75, 140–1, 259, 489, 598, 846–9
International Agricultural Research Centres 195, 199, 203, 213, 215
International AIDS Vaccine Initiative 303, 304, 305, 473
International Association for the Protection of Industrial Property 368, 371, 372, 698
International Association of Plant Breeders for the Protection of Plant Varieties 371
International Breeders' Congress 371
International Center for Sustainable Development 665
International Center for Wheat and Maize Improvement 195, 203
International Chamber of Commerce 368
International Code of Conduct on Transfer of Technology 237, 257, 259
International Convention for the Protection of New Varieties of Plants 368
International Convention for the Safeguarding of Intangible Cultural Heritage 612
International Cooperative Biodiversity Group 608
International Depository Authorities 56
International Federation of Breeders of Staple Crops 370
International Finance Facility 658–9
International Monetary Fund 401, 402
International Rice Research Institute 195, 203
International Task Force on Global Public Goods 27–8
international trade law 41

International Treaty on Plant Genetic Resources for Food and Agriculture 219–24, 386–8, 389–90
  and traditional knowledge 508, 569, 572–3, 580, 582, 592
International Undertaking on Plant Genetic Resources 218–19, 572–3, 664, 680
International Union for the Protection of New Varieties of Plants 218
invention 121, 666, 716, 759
investment 265–81
IP law 37, 69, 70, 338, 540, 631–61, 666, 747, 802–5
  and aid to Third World countries 658–9
  capture of 653, 654–5
  and competition law 774–92, 793
  and customary law 551–64
  enforcement of 211, 657
  globalization of 655–7, 662
  inventions and discoveries 377, 563, 623
  limits of 568–76, 718
  measurement of grants 660–1
  and public goods 712–13
  revelation problem 794–5
  separability assumption 795–802
  standards of 17–20, 27–33, 61, 344, 529
  and traditional knowledge 523, 526, 530, 564, 565–94
  utility model 338–40, 362
IP policy 90, 179, 649–50, 667, 833
IP protection 14, 88–93, 114, 481–92, 491, 800, 889
  arbitrage in 635–52
  bilateralism 176
  classical system 21, 26, 357
  and competition law 709–25, 726–57
  complaints process 647–8
  costs of 98, 280, 345
  differences in national rules 635–52
  excludability 548
  exemptions for research and educational purposes 97, 106, 116, 117
  expansion of 114
  harmonization of standards 24–7, 335, 523, 619, 648–9, 661, 733, 773
  impact on costs 280
  incentives 636, 728
  and international trade 151
  legal perspectives on 565–94
  minimum standards of 4, 153, 154, 542, 648–9
  plant genetic resources for food and agriculture 217–24
  and the public domain 541–6
  reasonableness criterion 32, 33
  strengthening 23, 36–9, 43, 74, 93–9, 139, 144, 183
  and technology transfer 261

and traditional knowledge 565–94, 599–614,
    602–4
IP regimes 20–3, 24–7, 340–1, 578, 710
  sui generis 340–2, 514–16, 518–19
  and technology transfer 273, 328
IP rights 73, 87–8, 88–93, 281, 495, 667, 674, 819
  and agricultural research 190–4
  antitrust law and 758–69
  commercial application of 585
  and competition law 717, 770–3
  and competition policy 795–802
  and digital telecommunications 42
  dispute settlement mechanisms and 835–51
  enforcement of 115, 231, 270, 272, 529, 670–1,
    677–8, 686
  exclusive 5, 547
  expansion of 770, 863
  on genetic inventions 212
  and incentives 70, 94, 95, 721
  and innovation 39–41, 319
  international system 581–2
  and investment 260–1
  limiting 723–4
  and markets for technology 322
  and medicines 484
  minimum standards of 846, 849–51
  model of 842–51
  and multilateral trade agreements 834
  and ownership 580–1
  politics of 66
  and public goods 8–11, 47
  strengthening 6, 13, 36–9, 227, 254, 266, 310
  technological enforcement of 669–94, 681–2,
    682–6, 687, 689–93
  and technology transfer 227–8, 229–32, 257,
    260–1, 270–3
  Traditional Intellectual Property Rights 583–93
  and traditional knowledge 532, 582–93
  and the TRIPS Agreement 484, 832
  upstream 290–8, 305, 863
  and the WTO dispute settlement mechanism
    854–60
isolationism 649–50

Jackson, J.H. 838, 840
Janis, Mark D. 771, 774–92
Japan 315, 334, 339
  patent system 312–17, 621, 656, 657
  R&D 313, 314–15, 317
Jefferson, Thomas 85–6, 522, 655
Johnson, Martha 499
Judson, H. 131
jurisprudence and customary law 554
justice 715, 724; *see also* equity

Keohane, Robert O. 65–8, 75
Kettler, Hannah E. 475

Kingsbury, Benedict 608
Kingston, William 653–61
Klug, Heinz 481–92
knowledge 41, 42, 85–8, 94, 98, 259, 267
  codified and uncodified 85, 267
  efficiency of knowledge flows 327
  embodiment of 55, 56–9
  generation of 122, 884, 890–5
knowledge commons 113–18
knowledge economy 536
  nature of 55, 87, 123, 522, 547
  as a private good 15–33, 112
  as a public good 41–5, 86, 526, 548, 550, 907
  sharing of 111–12
knowledge goods 83, 258, 350, 593, 668, 715, 720
  and competition law 727
  globalization of 3–45
  impediments to the creation and diffusion of
    7, 16–27
  and international externalities 10
  nature of 49, 62
  regulation for the protection of 15–33
Kortum, Samuel 282–7
Kostecki, Michel 898
Koyaanisqatsi 81, 82
Kremer, Michael 429, 478
Kritzer, Herbert 897

labour, regulation of 56–9
Ladas, Stephen P. 37, 357
Lai, Edwin 271
Land-Remote Sensing Commercialization Act
  96
Landsat imagery 96, 106
Lange, David L. 595–8, 609, 781
Lanjouw, J.O. 430
Lasswell, Harold 66
leadership 396, 403, 424
learning economy 259
Least-Developed Countries (LDCs) 260, 263, 693
  and access to essential medicines 415–16
  and antitrust law 775
  and technology transfer 250–3
legal system, *sui generis* 551–2
Lemley, M.A. 350
leprosy 458, 473
Lerner, Joshua 311–12, 317, 833
Levine, David K. 109, 110
Lewis, Tracy 337–65
Li, Richard 111
liability rules 74, 337–65, 514, 515
Librizol (Hybrid Plants) case 379
licensing fees 289, 292, 294, 296, 319
licensing of technology 11, 13, 300, 324–5, 327,
    697–8, 746
  anti-competitive practices 236–8, 784, 785–8
  and antitrust law 751, 779

licensing of technology (cont.)
  cross-licensing 744–6
  and investment 273–8
  multiparty 749
  restrictive 732, 733, 743, 756
  and technology transfer 230, 265–81
  vertical 749
  voluntary 243, 248
life science companies 211, 215
Litman, Jessica 655, 798–9
lobbying 60

Magill case 244–5, 762–3
maize, hybrid 686–93
malaria 395, 447, 449, 453, 458
  vaccine 295, 473, 478, 479
Malaria Vaccine Institute 295
Mansfield, Edwin 796, 797–8
March, James 66
market failure 12, 422, 711
market power 750, 761
market separation 438–44, 444–52
markets 58, 64, 396, 734, 767, 865
  domination of 717–18
  effects of IP rules on 639–44
  and information 5, 17
  in intellectual property 88, 89
  local 720–2, 725
  structure of 797, 798–9
markets for technology 316, 322
  definition of 323–4
  and patents 325–31
  and the scientific commons 121–38
  specialized firms in 329–30, 331–3
  and technology transfer 331–3
Maskin, Eric 139–41
Maskus, Keith E. 3–45, 74, 183, 261, 262, 263, 265–81, 282
material transfer agreements 292–4, 299
Mattoo, A. 773
Maurer, Stephen 102
McCalman, P. 834
McClellan, Mark 457
Médecins Sans Frontières 423, 449
Medicare Prescription Drug Improvement and Modernization Act 476
medicine, preventive 484–5
medicines 404–5, 418, 419–20, 444–52, 488
  access to regulatory data 406–7
  bulk procurement 418–19, 454
  compulsory licenses 411–15, 456
  differential pricing 416–18, 425–56, 433–5, 444–52, 455
  external referencing 438–44, 443, 445, 448
  government use 411–15
  parallel importation 416–18, 438–45, 448
  and patents 405–6, 409, 412, 428–31, 444–5, 475–6
  pharmacy benefit managers 442
  prices of 303, 416–17, 418–19, 423, 427, 428, 430, 431–8, 441–4, 448–52, 486
  and the public sector 419–20
  purchase fund policy 478, 479
  R&D 420–3
  subsidies 442
  and technology transfer 419–20
  trademarks and 418
medicines, access to essential 30, 302, 393–424, 426, 481–92, 628, 768
  differential pricing and 426, 443
  factors in regulatory framework for 395
  IP obstacles to 408–18
  public finance and 395–404
  regulation 404–7
  socio-cultural factors 403–4
medicines, generic 413, 418–19, 423, 486, 765–6, 867, 903, 907
  and compulsory licensing 426, 452–5
  U.S. market 405–6
Merck 473
Merton, Robert 122
Merz, Jon 295
MFN principles 19
Michalopoulos, Constantine 898
Mill, John Stuart 653
misappropriation and traditional knowledge 511–14, 525, 527–8, 587, 588
modern high-yielding varieties of crops 194–203
  adoption of 197–8
  contribution of developed countries 199
  production of 196, 200–2
molecular biology 203, 301
monoclonal antibodies 133, 138
monopoly 20, 110, 437, 667, 760, 768–9
  durable-goods monopoly 672–3, 799, 800–1
most-favored nation treatment 19, 853
Mowery, David S. 20
MP3 file format 642
multinational firms 35, 272, 275, 454
Muris, Timothy 765–7

Nakamura, Yoshiaki 313, 314, 315
National Agricultural Research Services 199, 213, 215
National Institutes of Health 298, 299, 397, 421, 422
national treatment 654
  and traditional knowledge 529, 557, 558
  and the WTO 353, 363, 846, 846–7, 856
negotiations, multilateral 44, 664–5
Nelsen, Lita 302
Nelson, Richard 121–38, 877
New Economy 84, 85, 112, 114, 729

NGOs 18–19, 29, 30, 63, 483, 579, 609, 906
 amicus curiae briefs 824, 829
Noerr-Pennington doctrine 765–6
Nordhaus,William 423
norms 65–8, 75, 147, 519, 529, 829
 and public goods 59–61, 611
Novartis 473
Novartis/Transgenic Plant case 379

obligations, bilateral 819, 820, 826
OECD 402
Okediji, Ruth L. 142–87
Olsen, Johan 66
Olson, Mancur 50, 60, 61
Organization of African States 576
O'Rourke, Maureen 868, 869, 870, 872–5, 876–7
Orphan Drug Act 463–74, 480
orphan drugs 457–80
 costs of 467–9
 health benefits 470–2
 numbers of patients involved 468
 R&D cost structure 469–70
 revenues from 469–70
over-protection 340–1, 345
ownership of traditional knowledge 501–4

Panizzon, Marion 565–94, 611
parallel importation 182, 628, 722, 771
 and medicines 416–18, 438–5, 448
Paris Convention 364, 367, 372–4, 512, 701–2, 703, 832
partnerships, public–private 473–4
Patent Cooperation Treaty 285, 620
patent law 20, 239, 510, 632, 774–92, 833, 834–5
 anticompetitive conduct 784, 788–90
 institutions 781–4
 litigation costs 618, 633, 659–60
 remedies 877–80
 role in science 132–5
patent policy 132, 134, 844, 845–6, 865–80
patent system 30, 77, 617–34, 842
patents 88, 89–90, 93, 591, 627, 629, 660–1, 759
 and access to essential medicines 408–15, 427, 428–31, 475
 and access to information 91–2
 and agriculture 368
 appeal procedures 625, 629–30
 and competition law 780–1
 and computer software 741
 disclosure requirements 506–9, 738–9
 enforcement of 271, 619, 626–8, 632–3, 670, 784, 789–90
 exemptions for research and educational purposes 892
 expressions vs. ideas 104, 173–5
 extension of terms 405–6, 410, 475–6, 666

first-to-file system 624–5
government use 411–15, 627
harmonization of standards 24–7
incentives 721
and industrial sectors 866
informative effects of 240
and innovation 309–20
institutions for granting 629–30
international 621–5, 632–3
and IP rights in developing countries 283–6
judicial review 625, 630–2
litigation and appeal of 630–2
and markets for technology 325–31
means of exploiting 873–4
and medicines 412, 427, 428–31
misuse 20, 167, 740, 777, 784, 790–2
and natural phenomena 134
obligation to work 240–3, 701–4, 705
 in the pharmaceutical industry 462–3
principles for international 621–5
quality of 629–30
on research tools 118
scope of 134, 623–4, 651, 840
specialist courts 630–2
specifications 239, 247
standards for granting 24–7, 623–6, 780–92
strengthening 14, 312–17, 329
subject matter exclusion 865–8
and technology transfer 12, 265–81, 317–19
and traditional knowledge 568
and upstream innovation 864–5, 869, 880
utility criterion 134
value of 865
patronage 87–8
Pauwelyn, Joost 817–30
peer to peer (P2P) services 110–12, 642–3
Percival, Robert 899
performers' rights 533
Peru 575–6
Pfizer 473
pharmaceutical industry 330, 398, 408, 489, 661, 902, 908
 accountability 446, 447
 antiretroviral drugs 410
 competition 423, 459–63
 compulsory licenses 452–5, 647
 confidential rebates 445–8, 450, 451, 455
 and developing countries 406, 419–31
 innovation 458, 695
 market exclusivity for orphan drugs 463–4, 464–5, 476–6
 and patents 428–31, 462–3, 884–908
 philanthropic programs 473, 474
 pricing structure 431–8, 448–52, 454, 486
 public–private partnerships 473–4
 purchase guarantees 477–9
 R&D 56, 420–3, 451, 458, 459–63, 477–8

pharmaceutical industry (cont.)
  regulation 435–6, 451
  and traditional knowledge 508
pharmacy benefit managers 442, 446
Philippines 554, 575–6
piracy 108, 110, 569, 641–2; see also biopiracy
plant breeders' rights 373, 375–6, 381, 674–5, 679, 684
  international protection of 206, 215, 674–5
  legislation relating to 193, 572
  and traditional knowledge 579, 592–3
plant breeding industry 686–93
plant genetic resources for food and agriculture 217–24, 567, 582, 583, 587
  exchange of seeds and plant materials 219–20, 570, 586
  international agreements 571–6
  regulation and ownership of 219, 592–3, 663
Plant Patent Act 368, 380
plant varieties, novel 354, 368
Plant Variety Protection Act 192, 380
plant variety protection laws 366, 368, 369–76, 508, 672–4, 674–5
  differential from patentable inventions 377–85
  domestic 575–6
  policy interests in 678–81
  sui generis protection 381–5
  and the TRIPS Agreement 380–1
policy
  and access to essential medicines 415–16
  and antitrust law 775
    Least-Developed Countries (LDCs) 260, 263 693
  legal system, sui generis 551–64
policy-making 71–3, 903
political economy, problems of 65–8
Popper, K. 127
Porter, R. 131
Posey, Darrell 503, 520
Potrykus, Ingo 304
poverty 4, 76, 181, 458, 472, 473, 479
Powell, Colin 398
power 61–3, 65, 68, 750, 761
preferences 61–3, 607
President's Advisory Committee on Trade Negotiations 60
price: see also differential pricing
  competitive equilibrium 109
  discrimination 437, 628, 641–2, 682
  excessive 761–2, 764, 769
  fixing 802
prisoner's dilemma 831–3
privatization 121, 122
procurement, government 87–8
property rights 501–4, 517, 531, 683
  exclusive 344–5

history of 367–77
theory of 16, 712–13, 717–18, 724, 795, 799
and welfare gains 144
Prott, Lyndel 513
public and private interests, balancing 17, 81–120, 146, 653, 662–8, 817–30, 893
and innovation 33–4, 44
public domain 12, 22, 38, 81, 173–5, 515, 547, 593
for scientific and technical information
and traditional knowledge 502–3, 533–5, 569–71
public goods 7, 52–4, 663, 711–16, 724, 817–30
and access to essential medicines 395–404
choice of 546
classification of 52, 54
club goods 711–12, 724
and competition law 709–25
conflict among 886, 888
defense as 55–6
and developing countries 901–8
disclosure requirements 92
distribution 48, 66, 68, 71–3, 73–6
information as 86–7
and institutional design 69–77
international 729, 834
investment in 76
and IP law 712–13
knowledge as 41–5
and medicines 487
non-excludability 8, 9, 47, 50, 52, 711–12, 886
non-rivalrous character 8, 46–7, 130, 711–12, 886
and preferences 49–51
and private interests 59–61, 819
production of 884–7
provision of 8, 9, 17, 47, 63, 74–5, 85–8
and the public domain 547
and public welfare 145, 181, 714–15
regulation of 46–64
and science 129–30, 139–41
trade rules as a public good 886
and traditional knowledge 549, 561, 570, 593–4, 611–14
and WTO dispute settlement 824–25, 825–30
public health 29, 395–7, 482–3, 885–6, 887
and access to essential medicines 484–7
and the law 487–91
Public Sector Intellectual Property Resource for Agriculture 290, 300–2
punishment 835–6, 836–8, 838–40
Puttitanun, Thitima 261, 262, 265–81, 282

Quah, Danny 109, 110
Quaker United Nations Office 662, 664, 665

R&D 184, 260, 288, 319, 322, 324–5, 679
  in biotechnology 673, 676

costs and risks 459–60, 479, 487
economics of 459–63
expenditure on 232–3, 334, 461–2
incentives 429, 455, 456, 457–80, 463–4, 475, 477–9, 623
joint 744–6, 745–6
payment for 431–8
in the plant breeding sector 673
returns from 460–2, 477, 659–60
and traditional knowledge 589
Rai, Arti K. 261, 262, 282, 288–306
Ramsey pricing rule 116–17, 426, 431–8, 455
reciprocity 529, 557, 558, 734, 854
redistribution of wealth 76–7
regime shifting 29, 30
regulation 15, 23, 48–9, 51, 118
environmental 63, 215, 259, 818, 826
of public goods 46–64
of technology transfer 732–5
Reichert, Janice 468
Reichman, Jerome H. 3–45, 74, 183, 337–65, 518, 587, 698, 781
Reinhardt, E. 897, 898
religion 604–6
rents, capture of 60
research 22, 38, 83, 92, 95–6, 123
allocation of resources 83, 123
basic 124, 129, 130, 135, 136, 474, 879, 880
commons 12, 28, 42, 51, 357
consequences of IP protection for 95–6
funding of 30
impediments to 290, 292–6
institutions 871, 874; *see also* universities
on neglected diseases 474
overprotection of results 38
private funding 190–4
privatization 123
public funding of 21, 30, 70, 106, 262, 358, 650, 663
role of the private sector 190–4, 304–5
research tools 132, 292, 299, 742, 872
patents on 118, 133, 293, 626–7, 640, 644–5, 661, 873
reverse engineering 12, 330, 639, 645
rice 504, 569
rights
collective 262, 603–4
cultural 513
exclusive 743
private 818, 829
Roffe, Pedro 257–64
Rose, Carol 614
Rosenberg, Nathan 20
Ruttan, V.W. 203, 683

Saggi, Kamal 261, 262, 265–81, 282
Sakakibara, M. 313

Samuelson, Pamela 635–52
Samuelson, P.A. 52
Sandler, Todd 52
Sanitary and Phytosanitary Agreement 205, 206
Scholtz, Michael 485
Schumpeter, J. 125, 798
science 21, 122–3, 126, 711, 713, 715, 724, 864
and agriculture 190–4, 211–14
applied 127
areas in Pasteur's quadrant 123, 124, 127, 129, 133
basic 124, 129, 130, 135, 136, 474, 877, 882
commons 121–38
and IP monopoly rights 84, 85–8
life science companies 215
links with technology 124–8, 133–4, 136
molecular biology 136
on-line databases 100
openness 83–4, 88, 95, 98, 110, 112, 119, 136
privatization 131
and the public domain 38, 122–3, 124, 128–32, 135, 861–83
public funding of research 42–3, 87, 98, 190–4
and public goods 139–41
Republic of Science 122, 129, 131
sharing of knowledge 23, 42, 116
and traditional knowledge 600–1
Scott, Colin 601, 605
Searle, John 67
Securities Data Company database 324–5
self-interest 61, 66, 403–4, 653, 654
Sell, Susan 655, 902
Shaffer, Gregory 884–908
Sherman, B. 510–11
Sherman Antitrust Act 782, 803
Siemens, Werner 654
Smith, Adam 47
social welfare 178–86, 431, 543, 719, 881, 888
Sony v. Universal Studios case 678
South Africa 399, 410, 486, 723, 903
sovereignty, national 27, 154, 169, 172–3, 184, 681, 696, 817–30
and biological and genetic resources 681, 696
and competition law 730, 731, 739, 753
and copyright 146, 154, 166, 169, 172–3, 184
and IP standards 27–33
and the WTO 817–30
spillovers 833–4, 835, 849–50, 851
Staiger, R.W. 834
standing 821, 829
Stern, Nicholas 4
Stokes, Donald 123
Subramanian, A. 773
subsidies 86, 87, 253, 442, 463, 768
sustainable development 711, 713, 715, 724, 818
Swanson, Timothy 669–94
Switzerland 834–5

Tansey, Geoff 662–8
Tanzania 690, 692
Taubman, Antony 521–64, 606
Technical Barriers to Trade 205
technologies, restriction 671, 676–7
technology 126, 230, 254, 258, 335, 741–4; *see also* licensing of technology
    diffusion of 738–9, 752
    dissemination of 738–9, 745
    markets for 316, 322, 323–5
    pooling of 749–50
technology transfer 57, 257–64, 710, 711, 713, 724, 818, 891
    characteristics of countries and firms 268–70
    choice between investment and licensing 273–8, 282
    code of conduct for 739, 741, 787
    and competition law 5, 730–1, 752
    and compulsory licenses 247–50
    E.C. policy 748–50
    economics of 267–73
    and foreign direct investment 262, 270–2
    incentives for 230–1, 255, 263
    informal channels 267
    and IP rights 229–32, 270–3, 328
    and market failure 12
    and medicines 419–20
    and patents 265–81, 317–19
    regulation of 732–5
    and royalties 236
    transfer costs 327
    and the TRIPS Agreement 11–15, 227–56, 755
Towse, Adrian 425–56
trade, free 4, 481–92, 885
trade agreements 852–4
    bilateral 181, 184
    bilateral and regional 398, 402
    economics of 831–51
    and externalities 852–4
    multilateral 829
trade barriers 6, 655, 657, 742
trade law 484
trade policy 829
trade secret law 57, 341, 342, 343, 602
trademarks 547
Traditional Intellectual Property Rights 583–4
traditional knowledge 383–5, 388, 499–500, 549, 595–8, 601–2
    access to 554, 527–8
    active use of 588
    anthropological view of 599–602
    attribution of 503
    collective management of rights in 584
    commercial application of 358–61
    and compensatory liability 354–61
    and cultural diversity 599–614
    and databases of 509–11, 516–17
    defensive protection 496, 505, 506–14, 527–8, 533–4, 539, 613
    definitions 496–501, 535–9, 566, 599–602
    economic value of 504–5
    environmental 604–5
    holistic knowledge of 606–8
    incentive argument for protection 550–1
    international mechanisms for protecting 559, 562–4
    international protection of 521–64, 528–30
    and IP protection 565–94, 576–82
    IP rights in 549, 583–4
    as know-how 356–61, 365, 518
    legal and economic aspects 495–520
    and legal systems 357–8
    and liability rules 337–65
    misappropriation 511–14, 530, 543
    misuse of 525
    nature of 496–504, 524, 535–9, 558, 562, 563, 603
    and ownership 501–4, 528
    and patents 698
    political dimensions of 608–10
    positive protection 496, 505, 514–18, 519, 534, 539, 613
    protection of 31, 347, 354–61, 505–18, 523–35, 539–41, 563, 557
    and the public domain 520, 523, 531, 532, 544–5, 548, 550, 562, 604
    as a public good 546–51, 578–9, 613
    and research 586, 587
    and royalties 360–1, 363
    as social practice 53
    sui generis 534, 535–46
Traditional Knowledge Digital Library 509
transaction costs 289, 292, 293, 294, 296, 297–8
translation rights 163–4, 165, 166
transparency 446, 450, 772, 826, 829
treaties, interpretation of 828
TRIMS Agreement 255
TRIPS Agreement 60, 73, 656, 702, 734, 750–4, 878
    and access to essential medicines 415–16, 452–5
    and antitrust law 767, 774–92
    and the Berne Convention 168, 183–4
    and the CBD 389, 700
    and competition law 719, 724, 726–57, 730–9, 740–54, 775–80, 786–7
    compulsory licenses 165–6, 240–7, 247–50, 703, 767
    consistency clause 776–8
    and databases 114
    and developing countries 24, 363
    disclosure requirements 238–40, 589–90
    Dispute Settlement Understanding 644
    economic impact 870–2

exceptions and limitations to copyright provisions 169–71, 172–3
exceptions from liability for patent infringement 859–60
exemptions from patent rights 869–70, 875
flexibility in implementation 10, 27, 36, 167–8, 169, 181, 256, 420, 620, 636, 878–9, 890–1, 902
harmonization of standards 661
and human rights 611
impact of 37
and international copyright rules 153–6
international exhaustion 444
interpretation of 650–1, 704, 888–95
and IP rights 484, 490
jurisprudence 171–2
and knowledge goods 63–4
licensing practices 751, 778–80
and medicines 406–7, 420, 488, 491
members' obligations 250–1, 646
minimum standards 5, 39, 648–9, 710, 737, 849
misuse 740
and national competition law 730–9, 736–8
and national sovereignty 32–3, 776–8, 817–30, 882
non-discrimination clause 243
objectives of 10, 232–6, 252, 259, 658, 733, 882, 890
and patent law 353, 481, 786–7, 866–8, 879–80, 893
and patenting of plant genetic resources 380–2, 573–4, 675
and pharmaceutical patent protection 884–908
and restrictive practices 236–8
Single Undertaking 857
and stronger IP protection 726–57
technological neutrality 876–7
and technology transfer 11–15, 227–56, 263, 282–7
and trade externalities 860
and traditional knowledge 507, 512, 516, 576–7, 603
and WIPO 146
and the WTO dispute settlement mechanism 835–40, 850–1, 856–60, 868–9, 895–6
tuberculosis 395, 447, 449, 453, 458, 473–4, 479

Ullrich, Hanns 726–57, 771
UN 72
  FAO 205, 219, 368, 508, 569, 572, 664, 680
  High Commissioner for Human Rights 401
  human rights bodies 29
UNAIDS 401, 894
UNCTAD 401, 574, 665, 776, 894
UNDP 401, 714
UNESCO 513, 574, 607, 612

UNICEF 447
Universal Copyright Convention 158, 161
Universal Declaration of Human Rights 482
Universal Declaration on Cultural Diversity 612
Uniform Biological Material Transfer Agreement 299
universities 135–8, 137, 203–4, 289, 293–4
  collective action 299, 301
  and patents 112, 130, 137, 138, 291
Universities Allied for Essential Medicine 302
UPOV Act 193, 368, 369–76, 381, 388, 571–2, 592, 674–5
  definition of plant variety 378, 379
  list of plants 373, 374
upstream rights 22, 290–2, 305, 864, 865–6, 869, 880
U.S.
  access to medicines 442–4
  antitrust law 323, 750, 759–62, 771, 782, 784–5, 793, 803–4
  Bayh-Dole Act 42, 92, 130, 131, 136–8
  bureaucratic culture 901
  competition law 794
  Coordinating Committee (CoCom) 56
  copyright law 170
  defense technologies 55–6
  Environmental Protection Agency 204
  Food and Drug Agency 204, 464, 465–8, 475, 477, 479, 765–6
  FTC 750, 765–7, 782, 803
  government use of patents 412–13
  health care systems 472, 476
  IP law 655, 904
  medicines 409
  Millennium Challenge Account 658–9
  Orphan Drug Act 458, 463–74, 479, 480
  patent law 131, 246, 380, 644, 655, 775, 784–5, 864
  patent system 21, 24–7, 42, 94, 368, 646, 718
  plant variety protection laws 380
  property rights in databases 104, 114
  protection of expression and protection of ideas 174
  public funding of research 42, 129, 397
  public health 397–9, 443
  science-based R&D 316
  trade agreements 407, 633
  and the TRIPS Agreement 646
  TRIPS-plus agenda 74, 403
U.S. Patents Office 568, 590, 621, 660
U.S. Trade Representative 398, 402, 646, 656, 907
  and the WTO dispute settlement mechanism 895–6
  U.S.–Section 110(5) case 170, 869, 873
  U.S.–Section 211 case 881

U.S. Trade Representative (cont.)
  U.S.–Section 337 of the Tariff Act of 1930 case 243
  U.S.–Shrimp/Turtle case 827

values, distributive 70–1, 72
Vernon, J.M. 433, 461
Vincenti, W. 127

Walker Process case 788–90
WHO 401, 403, 405, 481, 491, 894
  essential medicines list 394, 485, 486, 487
  and traditional knowledge 505, 582
WIPO 5–6, 18, 37, 152, 158, 159, 401
  arbitration system 660
  data on patent applications and grants 284–7
  and developing countries 24
  and distribution issues 72
  draft convention on databases 103
  harmonization of standards 619, 633
  Intergovernmental Committee on Intellectual Property and Genetic Resources, Traditional Knowledge and Folklore 222, 364, 384–5, 389, 496, 600
  Patent Cooperation Treaty 285
  protection of folklore 574
  protection of traditional knowledge 347
  and traditional knowledge 516, 582, 610
  and the TRIPS Agreement 146
WIPO Copyright Treaty 152, 168, 171, 175–8
WIPO Internet treaties 180
WIPO Performances and Phonograms Treaty 152
World Bank 72, 401, 403, 489
WTO 15, 65, 401–2, 429, 488, 656, 657–8
  and antitrust law 768
  and competition law 772
  compliance with rulings 835–6
  Dispute Settlement Understanding 183, 644, 836, 854, 855, 856
  and distribution issues 72, 73
  legal system 721, 893, 902, 904
  Members' obligations 820–4, 824–5, 826, 875
  objectives of 817, 818, 890
  and private interests 818
  rule-making process 665, 668
  scope of 829–30
  suspension of concessions or obligations 835–6, 837, 854, 859–60
  Working Group on Trade and Technology Transfer 280
WTO dispute settlement mechanism 647–8, 651, 704, 817–30, 835–40
  costs of 899–900
  economics of the dispute settlement process 835–6
  IP rights and the 852–60
  participation in 884–908
  and public goods 861–908
  punishment role of 861–83
  TRIPS Agreement and the 832, 856–60
WTO panels 14, 33, 169, 170, 233, 242, 648, 828, 867, 874, 880, 881, 893, 895, 899, 902, 905, 907, 908
Wuesthoff, Franz and Freda 372

Xerox case 796, 802

Yang, Guifang 271

Zimbabwe 399
Zoellick, Robert 906